Human Development

SIXTH EDITION

Grace J. Craig

University of Massachusetts

  PRENTICE HALL, Englewood Cliffs, New Jersey 07632

Library of Congress Cataloging-in-Publication Data

CRAIG, GRACE J.
    Human development/Grace J. Craig.— 6th ed.
      p. cm.
    Includes bibliographical references and indexes.
    ISBN 0-13-437104-6
    1. Developmental psychology.   I. Title.
  BF713.C7   1992
  155—dc20   91-28677
                          CIP

Editorial/production supervision: Kari Callaghan
Development editor: Roy Dickinson
Acquisitions editor: Carol Wada
Editor-in-chief: Charlyce Jones Owen
Interior design: Lee Cohen
Cover design: Meryl Poweski
Cover photos: Robert Brenner, Myrleen Ferguson,
    Tony Freeman, and Alan Oddie, from PhotoEdit
Page layout: Natasha Sylvester
Photo research: Anita Dickhuth
Prepress buyer: Debbie Kesar/Kelly Behr
Manufacturing buyer: Mary Ann Gloriande

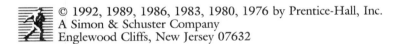

© 1992, 1989, 1986, 1983, 1980, 1976 by Prentice-Hall, Inc.
A Simon & Schuster Company
Englewood Cliffs, New Jersey 07632

Printed in the United States of America

10 9 8 7 6 5 4 3 2

ISBN 0-13-437104-6

PRENTICE-HALL INTERNATIONAL (UK) LIMITED, *London*
PRENTICE-HALL OF AUSTRALIA PTY. LIMITED, *Sydney*
PRENTICE-HALL CANADA INC., *Toronto*
PRENTICE-HALL HISPANOAMERICANA, S.A., *Mexico*
PRENTICE-HALL OF INDIA PRIVATE LIMITED, *New Delhi*
PRENTICE-HALL OF JAPAN, INC., *Tokyo*
SIMON & SCHUSTER ASIA PTE. LTD., *Singapore*
EDITORA PRENTICE-HALL DO BRASIL, LTDA., *Rio de Janeiro*

Contents

PART TWO

THE BEGINNINGS OF HUMAN LIFE

PART THREE

INFANCY: THE FIRST TWO YEARS OF LIFE

6 INFANCY: DEVELOPING COMPETENCIES 152

7 INFANCY: DEVELOPING RELATIONSHIPS 186

PART FOUR

AGES TWO TO SIX: THE PRESCHOOL CHILD

8 LANGUAGE: THE BRIDGE FROM INFANCY   222

9 DEVELOPING THOUGHT AND ACTION   252

PART FIVE

MIDDLE CHILDHOOD

PART SIX

ADOLESCENCE

13 ADOLESCENCE: A PERIOD OF TRANSITION   384

14 ADOLESCENCE: THEMES, CONFLICTS, AND EMERGING PATTERNS   410

PART SEVEN

ADULTHOOD

15 EARLY ADULTHOOD: ROLES AND ISSUES   434

PART EIGHT

LATER ADULTHOOD

Preface

The primary purpose of the earlier editions of *Human Development* was to introduce a wide range of college-level students to the study of life-span developmental psychology. The enthusiasm and loyalty of the text's many users have proved that it has succeeded in this task. This sixth edition is similarly aimed at a large cross section of students varying in academic background, career interest, and past experience with the social sciences. It is addressed not only to psychology students, but also to students interested in nursing, education, social work, and home economics. As with the previous editions, this text may be used in a student's introduction to human development or even in the only course a student takes in this discipline.

As before, this text views the periods of the life span as segments of the rich, complex drama that is human development. Its concepts, viewpoint, and data are drawn from many disciplines, such as education, psychology, biology, sociology, and anthropology. Because the field of human development is so challenging, open-ended, and controversial, we have given the student plenty of opportunity to consider a variety of perspectives and sources of evidence, weigh these against personal experience, and develop a point of view. The book presents facts, dominant theories, recent research, and cross-cultural perspectives in a clear, informal, and readable manner.

As in previous editions, the text provides a balanced look at every period in the life span. All chapters have been thoroughly revised to reflect the research of the early 1990s. There are separate chapters on the developmental milestones of early, middle, and late adulthood as well as topical chapters on the family, the world of work, and death and dying. In all periods, we have included new research and expanded topics of interest, such as modern reproductive technology, parent–infant bonding, the changing role of fathers, early cognitive and language development, the day-care dilemma, the effects of divorce on children, developing social knowledge, child abuse, computers and learning, learning disabilities, culture and learning, children and stress, adolescent identity, family systems, alternative lifestyles, the effect of AIDS on sexuality and intimacy, divorce, single parenting, stepparenting, dual-worker families, mentoring, fitness, stress, midlife transition, personality continuity and change, retirement, and controversial theories and issues related to the aging process.

Throughout the book, contemporary issues in the field of human development have been presented in boxes. The boxes include *research* ("Personality over the Life Course," "Identical Twins Reared Apart," and "Nicknames"), *issues* ("Reproductive Technology: What Are the Options?" "Caesarean Childbirth,"

"Trends in Breast-Feeding and Bottle-Feeding," "Early Infant Day Care: A Cause for Concern?" "Sudden Infant Death Syndrome," "Play Tutoring: The Role of Adults in Children's Play," "Adolescent Depression," "Timing of Parenthood," "Unemployment and Health," "Sleep Patterns and the Elderly," and "Alzheimer's Disease"), and *applications* ("Hothouse Babies," "Choosing an Infant Day-Care Center," "Children's Concepts of Their Bodies," "The New College Student," and "Reactions of Medical Staff to Death and Dying").

IN-TEXT STUDY AIDS   The sixth edition has a number of features that will help both students and instructors. All 21 chapters open with broad outlines of contents and objectives that help students to focus on what they need to learn from a particular chapter. Each chapter closes with a study outline (new in the sixth edition), a list of key terms, self-test questions, and annotated suggested readings. Within each chapter, numerous photographs, diagrams, tables, and figures enhance the text discussions and present material in visual form. The back of the book contains a glossary (new in this edition), a carefully updated bibliography, and name and subject indexes.

SUPPLEMENTS   This text would not be complete without a supplements package to help you teach even more effectively. With this new edition, we have kept those supplements that professors have said are most helpful to them and updated these items to reflect the new material. These include an Instructor's Manual, Study Guide, Test Item File, Computerized Testing for IBM, and acetate transparencies. The *Instructor's Manual* contains lecture and activity suggestions along with a variety of written and video references. This manual was again written by Marilyn Colemen at the University of Missouri–Columbia. The *Study Guide,* written by Lisa Reboy of the University of Kansas and based on her background in experiential teaching, gives you and your students test questions, thought-provoking essays, and activities that will teach the concepts in the text and apply the information to novel situations. The *Test Item File* contains approximately 2,600 questions, consisting of multiple choice, short answer, and essay questions. This was written by Jeff Parsons, who has experience in writing test files and in teaching. You can access this test item file in two ways to help you prepare exams. The *Prentice Hall DataManager* is an electronic classroom management system containing a test generating system *(Test manager)* and a grading program that includes scanning features *(Grade manager)*. All test items are included in DataManager, which is available for IBM and IBM compatible computers. The Prentice Hall Telephone Testing Service allows you to phone Prentice Hall to type your test.

With this new edition, we have provided many new supplements that will allow you to do even more in your class. In addition to the Series 1 set of 26 four-color acetate transparencies, a new Series 2 gives you over 30 new transparencies from this text and other sources. These include illustrations, photos, and data charts that will help your students understand important concepts.

Especially exciting is the custom reader that we are doing in conjunction with Ginn Press. From a list of articles provided, you may choose as many as you want to be published into a customized supplemental reader for your class. You will be able to provide the special emphasis you want, without having to research, pull, and get permission for all of the articles yourself. In special circumstances, articles provided by the professor may be included. This reader will be sold to the students at minimal cost.

Also, a variety of new videos is being offered free with this text. The ABC News/Prentice Hall Video Library for Human Development is comprised of professionally produced videos designed to coordinate and enhance the sixth edition of *Human Development* and your course. These videos explore a variety of issues in human development today that correspond to topics found in this book. Based on ABC News award-winning programs—Nightline, 20/20, This Week with David Brinkley, World News Tonight, and The Health Show—ABC and Prentice Hall have combined to select the most current videos that will provide especially good support for your lectures. The *Instructor's Manual* contains information about how to integrate these videos with the book and the content of your course. Other videos that Prentice Hall offers free upon adoption include Seasons of Life, from the Annenberg Foundation, and Catch 'Em Being Good.

Acknowledgments

As with previous editions, the sixth edition of *Human Development* incorporates the contributions of many individuals: people of all ages whom I have met or studied in classrooms, clinical encounters, and interviews; students and research assistants; colleagues, teachers, and mentors; family members and friends. Their experience, ideas, and insights are reflected in the text.

I would like to thank all the reviewers from all editions of the text. Their consistently insightful and thoughtful comments have helped improve the book. In particular, I'd like to thank the following reviewers who helped shape the sixth edition: Patrick Williams, *University of Houston–Downtown;* Barbara L. Watters, *SUNY–Oswego;* Anthony Fowler, *Florence Darlington Technical College;* Sharon Stiefel, *University of Alabama;* Sue Sommers, *Butler County Community College;* Nolan Embry, *Lexington Community College;* Henry Patterson, *Pennsylvania State University–Berks Campus;* Jane Krump, *North Dakota State College of Science;* Kathleen Hoyt, *Boise State University;* Karen Hancock Gier, *University of Alaska–Anchorage;* Patrick T. DeBoli, *Nassau Community College;* Janet Johnson, *University of Maryland;* and Cosby Steele Rogers, *Virginia Polytechnical Institute.*

I am most grateful for the writing assistance and editorial contributions of Lauren Meyer, Judy Harris, and Linda Smolak. Special thanks go to my researchers, Debra Ross, Feching Chen, and Yu-min Meng, whose welcome suggestions and conscientious search for new material helped renew and enrich this edition.

At Prentice Hall, I would like to thank my acquisitions editors, Charlyce Jones Owen and Carol Wada, who helped with the general planning and scheduling of the book. My production editor, Kari Callaghan, has spent long hours in coordinating and managing manuscript and proofs. I owe thanks as well to Anita Dickhuth, whose sensitive and thorough photo research has resulted in superb selections to complement the text. A special word of thanks is due my secretary, Eileen Besse, who willingly coped with sudden changes, missed deadlines, and the numerous loose ends that invariably accompany the final stages of book completion. And, finally, many thanks to my development editor, Roy Dickinson, whose ideas, suggestions, and careful editing made this edition special.

G.J.C.

Chapter 1

The more things change, the more they remain the same.

ALPHONSE KARR
LES GUÊPES, 1849

Development: Perspectives, Processes, and Research Methods

M illions of sperm—fragile and microscopic—swim against great odds to reach the egg cell. Only one unites with it to begin a new human being. A newborn gasps to fill its lungs and then cries out its own arrival.

Infants form bonds with those close to them and, as their physical, intellectual, and emotional needs are met, learn to trust the world.

Toddlers touch, taste, pull, push, climb over, under, and through to discover the nature of the world and their powers within it.

Kindergartners use the intricacies of words in sequence to command, to inquire, to persuade, to tease, and to attack—all to engage others in their quest.

Schoolchildren, through ritual chants, repeatedly trap one another in the "rules of the game."

Adolescents struggle with choice and decision, with the reexamination and reassertion of what is important and meaningful in life.

Adults rediscover beauty in music or nature and feel a childlike wonder at a new experience.

Older people review their lives and accomplishments, wondering if they've done what they set out to do.

Youths, adults, and the aged discover and rediscover the meaning of relationships. Whether sensitive and fragile, sturdy and supportive, stormy and anxious, or quietly comfortable and comforting, these relationships are a necessary and continuing part of human development.

Complex and rich, full of quest and challenge, the process of human development is the product of many strands—the blending of the biological and the cultural, the intertwining of thought and feeling. The process begins with conception and continues through old age.

In this book, our aim will be to examine developmental trends, principles, and processes throughout the human life span and across several disciplines. We shall investigate the human organism at all ages and stages with attention to biology, anthropology, sociology, and psychology.

CHAPTER OBJECTIVES

By the time you have finished this chapter, you should be able to do the following:

■ Discuss the goals of those who study human development.

■ Explain how historical, socioeconomic, and cultural factors influence our understanding of human development.

■ Define biological and environmental processes of development and explain how these two types of developmental processes interact.

■ Describe the research methodology that is used in the study of human development.

■ Describe the major categories of developmental research and explain their similarities and differences.

■ Discuss the ethical principles that researchers should follow when conducting research.

AN OBJECTIVE STUDY OF THE LIFE SPAN

What is the goal of studying human development? We seek to discover, amid all the complexities, some consistent common processes and major influences throughout the life span. We begin with careful observations and descriptions of human growth and behavior. Then we generate hypotheses, test these hypotheses, and progress to clear explanations and greater understanding.

Difficulties in understanding human behavior are often caused by those who try to explain and predict it. Whenever we evaluate what people can or cannot do, whenever we try to predict what they should do—in short, any time we pass judgment on the behavior of other human beings—we bring to our conclusions an accumulation of values and standards that are based on our own experiences and environments. It is difficult for us to set aside our subjective judgments and look at others objectively, or on their own terms.

In the development of value systems, for example, we find that an American child from one family quickly learns that fighting with one's peers is unacceptable behavior and is taught to use words to express anger. A child from another family, however, learns to use physical force to demonstrate the same emotions. Whole cultures can, in the same way, encourage either aggressive or cooperative behavior. One culture or socioeconomic group may forbid—or at least strongly disapprove of—the very behavior that another culture encourages. Cultural values thus form the basis for the behavior and the judgment of its members. Children gradually learn what is "right" and "normal," and they usually try to behave accordingly.

The same considerations apply to the development of sexual behavior. For instance, much of American culture generally discourages sex play and nudity among young children, frowns on homosexuality at any stage of development, and disapproves strongly of incest and open extramarital sex. In contrast, the Marind Anim tribe of New Guinea encourages sexual activity among young children and expects homosexual relations between adolescent boys and older relatives. A bride has public intercourse with male members of the husband's family before the husband is permitted access. This culture also encourages tribal women to engage in extramarital sex, as long as they do it with their husband's knowledge and approval (Van Baal, 1966). If we try to understand human behavior and development without knowing about such cultural variations, we shall be badly misled and our conclusions will be unsound.

In the study of human development, it is important to be aware of the full life span. Just as the explanation of adult behavior depends upon an understanding of child development, the study of child development is enriched by an awareness of the potential of adulthood (Neugarten, 1969). In this book, we will examine the periods of development—ranging from infancy to adulthood—individually, and we will study the various aspects of development (for example, physical development, cognitive development, and social development) as they apply to each age period. But it is very important to remember that all age periods and aspects of development are interrelated.

HISTORICAL, SOCIOECONOMIC, AND CROSS-CULTURAL PERSPECTIVES

Historically, attitudes toward both childhood and aging have varied widely. In the Middle Ages, European adults largely ignored the period of childhood. They viewed children as infants until age 6 or 7. Older children were considered small adults and treated to adult conversation, jokes, music, food, and other entertainment (Aries, 1962; Plumb, 1971). Painters of the period made no distinction between children and their elders except in size. Clothing, hair styles, and activities were the same for all ages.

By 1600, childhood was beginning to be considered a period of innocence, and an effort was made to protect children from the excesses and sins of the adult world. Children were less often considered an anonymous part of the clan, or community, and more as individuals within an individual family. By the 18th century, this attitude was broadly supported in the upper-middle classes, and children were treated as persons, with a status of their own (Aries, 1989; Gelis, 1989).

Adolescence as a separate period of childhood is of much more recent origin, and to a large degree is limited to developed countries. In the 18th, 19th, and early 20th centuries, when unskilled labor was in demand, youths capable of working blended into adult society and were accepted as adults. After World War I, however, advancing technology and rapid social change made it desirable for young people to stay in school longer, thus remaining dependent financially and psychologically on their parents. Clark (1957) has called this extended period of waiting for adult roles "vestibule adolescence." Because adolescents are excluded from active, productive participation in the economy, Clark feels that they stand to lose certain creative abilities that are often at a peak at this time.

Europeans in the Middle Ages ignored the period of childhood to a great extent. Children older than 6 or 7 were considered small adults, as illustrated in Copley's painting *Boy with Bow and Arrow*.

Changing Child-Rearing Practices

Methods of disciplining children have varied through the years. Harsh physical punishment was the rule in parts of ancient Greece just as it was in 19th-century Europe and America, and terrorizing children with stories of ghosts and monsters has long been a popular form of control (DeMause, 1974). In the United States, this century has brought not only a change toward more humane child-rearing practices, often with legal protection for children's rights, but also an increased questioning of all our preconceptions about children and their development. Practices that once seemed dangerous, such as thumb-sucking and masturbation, have generally been accepted as part of a child's normal activity. Rigid schedules for feeding, toilet training, and play have given way to a concern for self-demand, readiness, and self-expression (Wolfenstein, 1955). Parents are encouraged to relax and enjoy their children and to trust the "dialogue" between parent and child.

Attitudes toward children vary across cultures as well as across centuries. For example, Russians traditionally swaddle newborns tightly because they view infants as strong creatures who need to be restrained from injuring themselves. Other cultures, however, regard babies as fragile, vulnerable creatures who need to be protected (Mead, 1972).

Attitudes about family size, structure, and function have changed over the years. With these changes, the advice given by "the experts" to parents has changed accordingly (Young, 1990). Until the 1920s in the United States, families were large and were usually composed of members from three or more generations. Grandparents, parents, and children often lived under the same roof and shared the same kind of work. Children were expected to stay close to home because their parents needed help in running the farm, store, or home. Furthermore, parents produced many children because birth control was not widely practiced and

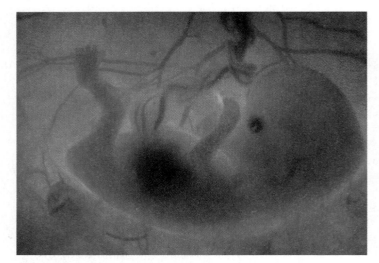

(a)

(b)

(c)

(d)

(f)

(g)

(h)

(i)

Life-span stages: (a) prenatal development, (b) infancy, (c) early childhood, (d) middle childhood, (e) adolescence, (f and g) young adulthood, (h) middle age, and (i) later adulthood.

because infectious disease carried off so many children necessary to the maintenance of the family.

Since World War II, parents have had general access to birth control, more often have planned the sizes of their families, and have shepherded their children through a long period of dependency. Children are now usually in their late teens to mid-20s before they find work and become financially independent. The high cost of raising children to maturity, the general use of contraception, and the growing number of working women have resulted in smaller families. (Whereas 35% of American families in the late 18th century had seven or more members, today only 3.5% of them do.) Children get a great deal of individual attention in small families, and parents, in turn, are making greater psychological investments in them.

However, both parents now work in the typical U.S. family, and the parenting roles of both mothers and fathers are shifting (Young, 1990). It is important to consider the social circumstances of families in a particular time or place, as well as their contemporary beliefs and values, in order to begin to understand their child-rearing practices (Jordanova, 1989).

In families where there are several children, where the mother has to work outside the home, or where there is a low level of income, older children often take care of their younger siblings. In these cases, children learn their social roles, values, and competencies from other children. The older children often learn nurturant, responsible behavior, while the younger ones often develop strong ties to their siblings and a sense of competence among their peers. Family bonds and affiliation tend to become stronger (Werner, 1979). In contrast, some children of the wealthy, who are often cared for by nonfamily staff members, may not develop strong family bonds and may have less contact with their parents and siblings (Coles, 1980). The attitudes, values, and expectations of children in these two groups will often be quite different.

Attitudes toward the Aged

Attitudes toward the aged, like attitudes toward children, are products of history and culture. For example, in our own country our view of the elderly has changed dramatically since colonial days. In the 17th and 18th centuries, most old men and old women were honored for their age. Long life, thought to be a special gift from God, was associated with wisdom and righteousness. The elderly were treated not just with respect and dignity, but also with a measure of awe. Few aged people came to the colonies, however, and infant mortality was high, so the bulk of the population was composed of young adults. By 1790, 1 out of 50 (2%) reached the age of 65, and the median age of the population was 16 (Fischer, 1978).

Our current national demography is quite different, and so are our attitudes toward the aged. Today, about one out of eight citizens (12.4%) is 65 or older, and the median age is 32.3. Slightly more than 5% of our population is over 75 (U.S. Bureau of the Census, 1990). Most people expect to reach age 75 and thus spend a significant portion of their lives in retirement. Our technology-based, consumer economy, however, treats the aged as obsolete, and our youth culture sometimes mocks them as pitiful and helpless (Fischer, 1978).

In Uganda, the Ik culture presents an even starker example of a society fragmented into age groups (Turnbull, 1972). The Iks turn their children out of the house when they are about 3 years of age. Parents make their children sleep in the open, and they are forced to provide their own shelter. The younger children of the tribe band together for protection against both the elements and older children. Even when the children fight viciously among themselves, the adults do not interfere. As a result, only the strongest children survive to adulthood. This harsh treatment has a purpose because the Iks consider children to be useless, expendable burdens, just as they do the aged. Adults are as cruel and neglectful of their elders as they are of their young children. Ik elders who become sick and infirm are not fed or nurtured, but are simply allowed to fend for themselves or die. Although their practices may seem extreme, they serve to illustrate that the "normal" American attitudes toward the old and young are, by no means, found in all cultures.

Historical and cultural differences in attitudes toward children and the aged are sometimes the result of social and economic conditions. The Iks, for example, are a dying tribe for whom mere survival is a difficult, daily problem (Turnbull, 1972). That children and the aged would seem a terrible burden to the adults is, therefore, not surprising. Although medieval European society relied on the physical labor of children and the aged, 20th-century America now needs only a small, educated labor force. Affluent social classes anywhere may consider having children and child rearing a desirable experience because they can afford to do so. But even within those groups where finding enough to eat and a place to live are not overwhelming problems, habits, customs, myths, and misconceptions continue to have an impact on the treatment of the generations closest to birth and death.

development The changes over time in structure, thought, or behavior of a person as a result of both biological and environmental influences.

DEVELOPMENTAL PROCESSES

Central to the concerns of developmental psychologists are the processes by which change takes place. No clear agreement exists on precisely how children acquire a nearly complete grammar of their language by age 5; or why reminiscing seems to be an essential part of aging; or how children learn to read or to assume a sex role or to express love, grief, or hostility. Nevertheless, some common terms and concepts are used by developmental psychologists—and by sociologists, anthropologists, and educators—to investigate and debate the issues.

Development refers to the changes over time in the structure, thought, or behavior of a person as a result of both biological and environmental influences. Usually these changes are progressive and cumulative, and they result in increasing body size, increasing complexity of activity, and the increasing integration of organization and function. For example, motor development seemingly progresses from an infant's random waving of arms and legs to purposeful reaching, grasping, creeping, and walking. Developing the ability to use symbols, especially words, is an important step that paves the way for reading, manipulating number concepts, and complex thinking. The development of thinking proceeds from the recognition of concrete objects in infancy to the forming of higher concepts and abstract thought in adolescence.

Some developmental processes, such as prenatal growth, are primarily biological, whereas other types of development depend mainly on the environment. Learning a new language while living in a foreign country or acquiring the

maturation The physical development of an organism as it fulfills its genetic potential.

growth The increase in size, function, or complexity toward the point of optimal maturity.

aging Biological changes that occur beyond the point of optimal maturity.

learning The basic developmental process of change in the individual as a result of experience or practice.

From the larval stage (top) to the time of full development (bottom), a moth develops according to a genetic code that is precise, allowing for little physical or behavioral alteration.

speech patterns and accent of one's family are examples of development strongly influenced by the environment. Most development, however, cannot be so neatly categorized as either biological or environmental, because it involves an interaction of both elements.

Biological Processes of Development

All living organisms develop according to a genetic code or plan. In some, like moths and butterflies, the plan is precise and allows for little physical or behavioral alteration. When psychologists refer to the process of growing according to a genetic plan, they use the term **maturation.** This consists of a series of preprogrammed changes not only in the organism's form but also in its complexity, integration, organization, and function. Faulty nutrition or illness may delay the process of maturation, but proper nutrition, good health, or even encouragement and teaching will not necessarily speed it dramatically. This seems to be true for the human life span and for such processes as an infant's motor development and an adolescent's development of secondary sex characteristics.

Physical structures and motor capabilities mature at different rates. Any single structure or capability usually has its point of optimal maturity. **Growth** usually refers to the increase in size, function, or complexity to that point of maturity. **Aging** refers to the kind of biological changes that occur beyond the point of optimal maturity. This does not necessarily imply decline or deterioration. Just as aging often improves the qualities of some cheeses and wines, it may also improve human judgment and insight. Furthermore, some tissues begin "aging" in adolescence or even childhood.

Environmental Influences on Development

The environment influences us every minute of the day. Light, sound, heat, food, drugs, anger, gentleness, severity—these and millions of other influences may fulfill basic biological and psychological needs, cause severe harm, attract our attention, or provide the components for learning. Some environmental influences are temporary and limited to just one situation; others may be permanent or appear often. Environmental influences can stunt an organism's growth or promote it, can create long-lasting anxieties or help to form complex skills.

The basic process by which the environment causes lasting changes in behavior is called **learning.**

LEARNING Learning is the basic developmental process of change in the individual, and it results from experience or practice. Learning occurs over an enormous range of activities—avoiding hot toasters, factoring algebra equations, running interference in football, falling in love, or losing one's temper. We learn skills and obtain knowledge while forming attitudes, feelings, prejudices, values, and patterns of thought.

Psychologists do not agree on the fine points of learning theories, but most agree that conditioning is one basic learning process. Some important learning theories—including the two major forms of conditioning—are presented in

Through the process of socialization, children learn the attitudes, beliefs, customs, values, and expectations of their society.

Chapter 2, and throughout the book we shall discuss other aspects of learning, such as modeling and imitation, verbal mediation, and hypothesis testing. We shall also consider the role of insight, discovery, and understanding in human development.

SOCIALIZATION Socialization is the general process by which the individual becomes a member of a social group—a family, a community, a tribe, or the like. This includes learning all the attitudes, beliefs, customs, values, roles, and expectations of the social group. It is a lifelong process that helps individuals live comfortably and participate fully in their society (Goslin, 1969).

During childhood, we are socialized into some roles immediately and into others later. A young girl might perform a multitude of roles every day: pupil, neighbor, big sister, daughter, Catholic, team member, best friend, and many others. When she reaches her teens, she will acquire several more roles. Each new role will require her to adjust to the behavior, attitudes, expectations, and values of the surrounding social groups.

Children and parents influence each other's behavior in infancy as well as in later stages of development.

Socialization is generally recognized as a two-way process. In the past, researchers saw children's behavior as almost entirely the result of how parents and teachers behaved. More recently, a great many studies have focused on how parents and children mutually influence each other's behavior (Hetherington & Baltes, 1988). Infants are socialized by their experience within the family, but their very presence, in turn, forces family members to learn new roles. Similarly, when an aged parent moves in with the family of a son or daughter, all the other family members must become socialized to new roles.

In summary, the socialization process occurs in all stages of life. Adults seek to learn new roles to prepare for expected life changes. A person wanting to change jobs will take a course to expand vocational skills. A recently divorced woman may

critical period The only point in time when a particular environmental factor can have an effect.

readiness A point in time when an individual has matured enough to benefit from a particular learning experience.

have to change her attitudes and seek training to support herself. A man about to retire may begin a hobby or prepare for the many leisure hours to come. The death of a spouse or friend may force a person to learn to live alone.

Interaction of Developmental Processes

Some psychologists continue to debate how much of our behavior is due to maturation and how much to learning. An infant first sits up, then stands, and finally walks—primarily because of maturational processes. Even this behavior, however, can be obstructed by drugs, poor diet, fatigue, disease, restriction, or emotional stress. Some skills, such as musical or athletic abilities, can be enhanced by extensive practice. Certain other behaviors are more difficult to categorize. In contrast to dogs, for example, children are born with the capacity for speech, but they must *learn* a language. Infants spontaneously show emotions such as anger or distress, but they must *learn* how to handle such feelings (Hebb, 1966).

Behavior, then, is a product of the interaction of maturation and learning. Certain behavioral limitations or characteristics are inherited in the genetic code, but all behavior develops within a specific environment. Robert Plomin (1990) points out, for example, that an inherited susceptibility to a disease, such as asthma or diabetes, can be triggered by environmental factors. The disease may also affect socialization or intellectual development if it prevents participation in social or athletic events and interferes with school attendance. The same type of interaction can be seen in the relationship between inherited physical characteristics (such as body type, skin color, or height) and a person's self-concept and social acceptance. Behavior may be based on stereotyped expectancies (fat people are jolly, adolescents are awkward) held by the individual as well as by others.

TIMING   The interaction of learning and maturation may depend on exactly when an environmental effect occurs. An example of the crucial nature of such timing is called a **critical period,** a time span when—and only when—a particular environmental factor can have an effect. Several such periods occur during prenatal development, when certain chemicals, drugs, or disease can adversely affect the development of specific body organs. (See Chapter 4.)

Other periods exist during which the individual is more or less sensitive to environmental influences. An *optimal period* is similar to a critical period; it is the particular time span when a specific behavior develops most successfully as a result of the interaction of maturation and learning. But an optimal period does not have the all-or-nothing quality of a critical period. Although there is an optimal time for a behavior to develop, the behavior can be learned at an earlier or later date. **Readiness** refers to a point in time when individuals have matured sufficiently to learn a particular behavior. They may not be able to learn the behavior before this maturational point, but it is not crucial that they learn it at the moment of readiness. For example, some children's cognitive development may be such that they are able to learn subtraction at about 6 years of age. If, for some reason, they are not taught to subtract until age 8 or 10, however, the opportunity will not have been lost forever, as would be true of a process for which a critical period exists.

The precise nature of timing in human development is not yet known. Are there critical periods for learning certain behaviors? Are there optimal periods for learning to read, to be a gymnast, or to speak a foreign language? These are some of the questions we shall examine in our study of development.

THE SYSTEMATIC STUDY OF HUMAN DEVELOPMENT

The search for reliable, verifiable facts about human development is a complex one. What are the differences between the evidence of our own personal experience and the researcher's data? At what point does the researcher stop looking for more evidence? Both the casual observer and the researcher must decide what constitutes "reliable evidence" and when enough has been gathered to support a theory. Personal experience can be useful and important, but it must be tested in a more systematic way before others are likely to believe it. We rarely prove anything with absolute certainty. Nevertheless, if we can gather enough convincing evidence, it is very possible that other people will come to similar conclusions.

Asking Good Questions

Most breakthroughs in the natural and social sciences have been stimulated by thoughtful questions and astute observation. Someone noticed something intriguing and different, asked probing questions, continued to observe it, and then systematically tested the phenomenon before he or she arrived at some basis for generalization and prediction. Suppose, for example, that we look at the pictures of a house and some human beings as drawn by a 5½-year-old (see Figure 1–1). On closer observation, we notice that the house sits directly on the ground

FIGURE 1-1

Piaget believed that drawings reveal the way young children think and understand reality. In these two drawings by a 5½-year-old, the chimney sits perpendicular to the roof and the heads and bodies of people are combined.

but the chimney leans at a strange angle. Looking at the small figures at the bottom, we notice that the bodies and the heads are combined, and that their limbs are out of proportion (these kinds of human figures are often called "tadpole people"). Are these just common "errors" caused by a child's poor motor coordination? Are they the idiosyncrasies of one particular child?

Jean Piaget, an astute observer of children, suggested that children's drawings are not just awkward reproductions of what they see; instead, they are representations of the way children think and construct "reality." After collecting pictures from many children, he proposed that pictures reveal children's understanding and lack of understanding about relationships between objects and the world. Young children have cognitive limitations; they may see things only from their own point of view, or they may focus on only one relationship at a time. In the child's experience, things "on" something else are usually related in a particular way. Therefore, their houses sit flat on the ground and their chimneys rise perpendicular to the angle of the roof—not to the walls of the houses or to the ground.

What about the "tadpole people"? Do children really think that people's faces are on their abdomens? "No," say Piaget and some others. This is a representation of the *important* things about people (Freeman, 1980). The child's drawing is not like a photograph; rather, it is the child's symbolic representation of her thinking and understanding of the world. Not all researchers agree with Piaget's interpretation of children's drawings. But Piaget was able to demonstrate certain common features often found in the drawings of children at different age levels, and he was able to stimulate others to do systematic research on children's thinking as expressed in their art (Winner, 1986).

The Scientific Method

Research in human development follows the same general plan as research in almost any other branch of the social and behavioral sciences. Researchers may differ on what to observe and how best to measure it, but most follow four general steps:

1. *Define a research problem.* The study of human development is full of interesting questions. What does the newborn infant see? How soon does the infant see the garden the way *we* see it? Is adolescence necessarily a period of storm and stress, or can it be a period of smooth transition to adulthood? Does memory necessarily decline with age? Such broad concerns as these are interesting but are not research questions. Before we can conduct a study, we need to narrow the problem to something testable. "How do children learn language?" is too broad. "How does the child begin to understand metaphor, sarcasm, or other forms of nonliteral language?" is a smaller question, but it is not yet testable.

In a recent series of studies, the researchers were interested in how children learn to understand sarcasm. Sarcasm is, after all, a very complicated language form. When the airline loses your luggage and your best friend says, "Well, this must be your lucky day!" he is using sarcasm. The speaker did not literally intend what he said. There is subtlety, irony, and nuance to the meaning of the literal words. There may be humor or cruelty in sarcasm.

Adults detect sarcasm using two cues: (1) the context contradicts what the speaker has said, and (2) the speaker often uses tone of voice to signal the meaning. But young children tend to miss these cues, and they understand things literally. Researchers can ask, "Which of these cues does the child first understand, and at what age, and in what context?" The researchers have now formulated a testable question (Capelli, Nakagawa, & Madden, 1990).

2. *Develop a hypothesis.* In most studies, the researcher specifies his or her expectations in the form of a hypothesis. He or she makes a prediction about what will happen in the study. In the study on children's understanding of sarcasm, the researchers predicted that children would be able to use intonation or tone of voice much sooner than they would understand the contextual cues. Even very young children listen to vocal expressions as a clue to emotions. However, understanding the contrast between the context and the literal meaning of the speaker is a much more difficult task.

3. *Test the hypothesis.* To test whether or not the hypothesis is correct, the researcher selects a particular procedure, decides on a setting, determines a measurement, and selects certain aspects of the situation to be controlled. The researcher must be careful to design the observations so that they are measuring the behavior systematically and without bias. In our study on understanding sarcasm, the researchers invented several stories. Each story had two versions: a sarcastic one and a serious one. They tape-recorded these stories in two fashions: Sometimes the punch line was said in a mocking, sarcastic way, sometimes it was said in a neutral tone of voice. Then they played these stories, some serious and some sarcastic, to third graders, sixth graders, and adults, and compared their reactions on a systematic questionnaire (Capelli, Nakagawa, & Madden, 1990).

4. *Draw conclusions.* Based on the evidence collected, the researchers must draw conclusions that neither overstate nor understate what has been found. In our study of sarcasm, the adults clearly identified all sarcastic responses whenever there were context cues (lost luggage) or intonation cues (a mocking tone of voice) or both types of cues available. Sixth graders had considerable difficulty when there was no change in intonation, and third graders almost never understood the sarcasm unless there was a sarcastic tone of voice. The authors simply concluded that children initially depend much more heavily on intonation than on context to recognize sarcasm (Capelli, Nakagawa, & Madden, 1990).

Types of Measurements

Research studies produce widely different findings depending on the measurements used and the individuals selected for study. Subjects may be observed in real-life situations, or they may be tested in controlled, contrived situations. They may take written tests to determine their level of achievement, their ability to solve problems, or their creativity. The researcher may observe their behavior directly, or he may ask the participants to report on it. Let's examine some of the specific types of measurement.

DIRECT OBSERVATION   Perhaps the most common type of measurement used

reliability The extent to which a measuring technique will produce the same results each time it is used.

validity The accuracy with which a procedure measures what it is supposed to measure.

with infants and young children is to observe the child's behavior directly in a particular situation. The researcher may look at how the child plays with a particular kind of toy or how the child reacts to a stranger. Children may be observed in school settings to see how they work together to solve a problem. The researcher often uses recording aids like videotapes to increase the accuracy of the observation. As one begins to study older children, adolescents, and adults, it becomes more and more difficult to design studies of direct behavior. Teenagers and adults are less willing to be "on stage" for observation, and they are more willing to report their thoughts and feelings to researchers.

ACHIEVEMENT AND ABILITY TESTS Written tests of achievement or ability are a common form of measurement. Yet, it is not always easy to construct a good test. To be effective, a good test (or any measurement) must be **reliable** and **valid.** A reliable measure is dependable, consistent, and repeatable. A test of artistic ability must be able to evaluate people in the same way each time. An unreliable test of artistic ability, for example, might be easily influenced by the mood of the participant taking the test or by the judge assigned to look at the product. Tests also must be valid—that is, they should measure what they intend to measure. In the *Peabody picture vocabulary test,* the child is shown a booklet containing pictures. For each item, the child hears a word and is asked to point to one of four pictures on a page. This is simply a test of comprehension of English vocabulary, presented orally. Yet, researchers sometimes mistakenly use this test as a measure of "intelligence."

SELF-REPORT TECHNIQUES Self-report techniques consist of interviews, surveys or questionnaires in which the researcher asks questions designed to reveal the subjects' feelings and behavior patterns. Sometimes, subjects are asked for information about themselves—as they are in the present, or were in the past. At other times, they may be asked to reflect on, or react to, statements or thoughts about themselves or to rate themselves on some personality traits. In each case, they are expected to try to be as honest and objective as possible.

Although interviews and questionnaires are commonly used with adolescents and adults, these techniques need considerable adaptation when they are used with children. In one such study, the researchers wanted to know about children's understanding of themselves and their family. They used a self-report technique called *interactive dialogues.* One of these dialogues was called "What I'm like and what others in my family are like." The interviewer brought a series of cards with pictures to the interview. Along with answering the questions, the children sorted the cards, indicating which pictures were more like their family and which were less like their family (Reid et al., 1990).

PROJECTIVE TECHNIQUES Sometimes, the researcher does not ask the question directly. In a projective technique, subjects are given an ambiguous picture, or task, or situation. Then, they must tell a story, interpret a picture, or guess the outcome of the situation. Because the task is ambiguous and there are no right or wrong answers, it is assumed that individuals will *project* their own feelings, attitudes, anxieties, and needs into the situation. Rorschach inkblots are probably the most famous projective technique. Word-association exercises and sentence-completion tests are also used. Subjects might be asked to finish a thought, such as "My father always. . ." Subjects might be shown a series of pictures, and asked to interpret, react to, analyze, or arrange them to construct a story. In one study, 4-year-olds participated in a game called *the bears' picnic*. The experimenter told a series of stories involving a family of teddy bears. The child was then handed one of the bears as "your bear" and was invited to complete the story (Mueller & Tingley, 1990).

CASE STUDIES   In the 19th century, Charles Darwin, the noted naturalist, kept a detailed account of his eldest son's activities in infancy and early childhood, in search of some understanding of human nature. Recently, John Bowlby (1990), an eminent psychologist, prepared a detailed retrospective biography of Charles Darwin to analyze the impact of parental loss in childhood. Case studies are rarely used in research because they involve problems of subjectivity and uncontrolled variables, and they relate to one specific individual. Cause-and-effect relationships cannot be established, nor can generalizations be made to others. But, occasionally, a good case study can stimulate additional research. In practical settings, such as medicine, education, social work, and clinical psychology, case studies are an important tool for diagnosis and prescription. Short-term case studies, such as the detailed analysis of a child's reaction to war or trauma, can be helpful in creating further understanding. Although they must be used with caution as a research tool, case studies provide a rich, clinical, descriptive picture of the changing, integrated individual in context.

RESEARCH DESIGNS

The design of any social science study structures and defines the type of information that can be collected as well as the manner in which it is analyzed. The growing, changing human organism develops within a changing environmental context. The researcher never captures the whole story. Instead, the researcher must select a particular setting, particular participants and particular methods of measurement and analysis to highlight the research question posed. This research plan constitutes the **experimental design.**

Natural versus Experimental Settings

Research settings may range from highly controlled, standardized laboratories to homes, supermarkets, schools, playgrounds, or hospitals. Some landmark developmental studies have been conducted in natural locations like waiting rooms, athletic events, preschools, and nursing homes. Studies in naturalistic settings have a certain *ecological validity*. They seem true to life. They involve real events and everyday settings. They may seem to be less artificial or contrived. The ongoing interactions between friends or family members can be examined as they really happen. Nevertheless, natural locations permit little control of individuals, events, or conditions, and they may cause some imprecision in measurement. Let's look further at the strengths and weaknesses of each approach.

EXPERIMENTAL SETTINGS   In a laboratory setting, the researcher can systematically change some of the conditions **(independent variables)** and observe the

experimental design The setting, subjects, and methods of measurement of a behavioral research study that serve to structure the type of information collected.

independent variable The variable that experimenters manipulate in order to observe its effects on the dependent variable.

dependent variable The variable in an experiment that changes as a result of manipulating the independent variable.

resultant behavior (**dependent variables**). For example, children learning vocabulary in the laboratory can do it in a very systematic way. The amount of noise and distraction is limited. The difficulty of the word list is controlled. The expectations and instructions of the experimenter, the reward or punishment, the pace of the presentation, can all be carefully monitored or controlled. Similarly, the behavior that is being observed can be measured precisely—be it the rate of learning, or forgetting, symptoms of anxiety, or anger. This is the ideal setting for testing a hypothesis and concluding a cause-and-effect relationship between the variables. Many studies of learning and memory have been conducted in just such settings, with children, adults, and the aged.

NATURALISTIC SETTINGS   Studies conducted in natural settings are much less easily controlled. The independent variables are usually controlled by selection only, not by manipulation. The researcher selects a particular classroom in a particular school, or compares teachers in Japan, Taiwan and the United States (Stevenson et al., 1989). Of course, teachers can be trained to use a particular approach, or instructional videotapes can be prepared. But rarely do the events in the classroom follow the script precisely. For some studies in a natural setting, the researcher must wait for the event to occur. For a study in class discipline, for example, the researcher may need to wait until the child misbehaves, and then be there with the camera at the right time. Sometimes in naturalistic studies, the researchers must rely on their notes or films and hope that they have selected the right details from an ongoing stream of potentially important events. In some cases, this method has resulted in imprecise observations and unsound conclusions.

Research sometimes takes place in natural settings like the classroom. These settings have been criticized for permitting little control of individuals, events, and conditions, as well as causing some imprecise measurements of behavior.

FOCUS ON RESEARCH

A NATURALISTIC STUDY OF CHILDREN'S SOCIAL BEHAVIOR

David E. Day, director of Early Childhood Education at the University of Massachusetts, has used a naturalistic study of children's social behavior to evaluate the effects of the integration of special-needs children and "normal" children in preschool classes. The naturalistic approach is used so that the experiment will not interfere with what the children are doing. Throughout the observation period, the teacher, the teacher's aides, and the children interact the way they normally would in the different activities and areas of the classroom—the block room, the art area, at story time, and so forth.

The evaluation procedure used in the study is a simple one. It begins with the completion of a profile on each child in the classroom. The profile includes such information as a history of the child's socializing experience, including the number of siblings, birth order, and prior preschool experiences; the child's medical history; the child's family structure, including the parents' reasons for enrolling the child in the program; the child's special needs, such as physical or intellectual handicap, recorded or threatened abuse, and emotional stress; and various developmental indices, such as the results of developmental tests and psychologists' assessments.

Once the profiles are completed, the central activity of the study—the observation of the children—begins. Each child is observed several times during a 5- to 10-day observation period. Each observation lasts for just 30 seconds, after which the behavior is coded on a Behavior Checklist Data Sheet. The data sheet is divided into several behavior categories: Task Involvement, Cooperation, Autonomy, Verbal Interaction, Use of Materials, Maintenance of Activity, and Consideration. The same data sheet is used to study several different kinds of questions, such as: Do the "normal" children pay attention to their task, or are they distracted by the special-needs children? Are they task-involved? Do they finish the task? Do they show consideration for other children, both special-needs and "normal"? What is their verbal interaction like? Do "normal" children talk only with "normal" children? Do physically handicapped children talk only with physically handicapped children? Which handicaps interfere most with normal interactions?

The behaviors coded onto the data sheet by the evaluators are derived from several observations made over the entire program day to ensure that the behavioral profile is a valid reflection of what has happened. The observation data are then summarized on a matrix, which provides a vivid picture of the frequency and location of each behavior. Information regarding the activity or area, number of children present, and the role of the staff in the activity is also recorded during each 30-second observation. This information reveals the range and type of interaction among the children and the adult role in each activity or area.

An analysis of the data from some of the preliminary studies using this procedure has produced some interesting findings. Some children with severe physical handicaps had fairly normal communication patterns with other children; however, children with minor speech problems often had considerable difficulty in communicating. "Normal" children with severely handicapped classmates often showed increased consideration for others, with no reductions in verbal interaction and learning (Day et al., 1979). Much more remains to be discovered. Yet, based on these positive results, integrated preschools with special needs and "typical" children in the same class are becoming a more common practice. The special needs children benefit from the example and help of their more common peers. The "typical" children benefit from improved social skills and positive attitudes with no loss of language and learning achievements (Turnbull & Turnbull, 1990).

Just as some naturalistic studies may be considered uncontrollable and imprecise, some experimental studies may be considered artificial and narrow. This may be due to the unfamiliar setting and isolated circumstances of the laboratory or to the absence of a realistic context in which the behavior makes sense. More and

longitudinal design A study in which the same subjects are observed continuously over a period of time.

more, researchers are attempting to combine the precision of the laboratory with the ecological validity of the naturalistic setting. They create or change particular conditions within an ongoing real-life setting. For example, in a nursing home it had been common to use physical restraints and tranquilizers to keep the patients quiet. New laws in 1990 required that nursing homes eliminate such physical restraints and the excessive use of tranquilizers simply to restrain patients. Researchers who studied the behavior of the patients both prior to the change in practices and afterward are able to do an ecologically valid study with some control over a key variable.

Longitudinal and Cross-Sectional Designs

Developmental studies, in contrast to other types of research, focus on change over time. In a **longitudinal design,** the scientists study the same individuals at different points in their lives. They are measured repeatedly over an extended period of time, and compared with themselves. Researchers can plot growth curves, or learning curves, in such areas as language development or cognitive development or physical skills. Children can be followed through adulthood to see which personality characteristics persist and which disappear.

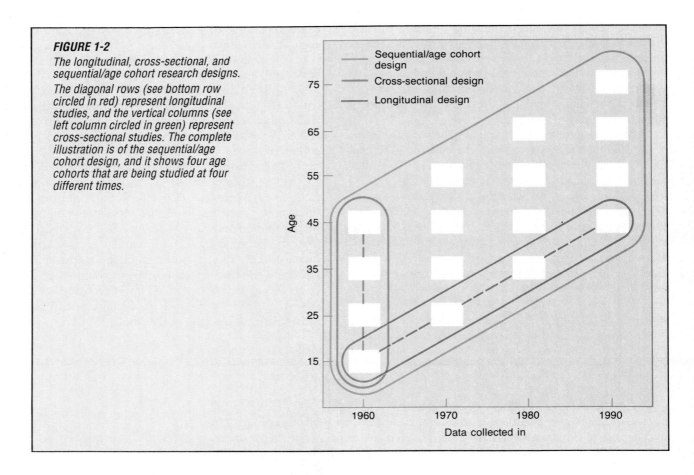

FIGURE 1-2

The longitudinal, cross-sectional, and sequential/age cohort research designs.

The diagonal rows (see bottom row circled in red) represent longitudinal studies, and the vertical columns (see left column circled in green) represent cross-sectional studies. The complete illustration is of the sequential/age cohort design, and it shows four age cohorts that are being studied at four different times.

They can follow the impact of key life events on the later life course or trajectory (see Focus on Research: Personality over the Life Course). In contrast, a cross-sectional study compares different groups of individuals at different ages at one point in time. In the study of sarcasm, for example, the researchers studied third graders, sixth graders, and adults on their understanding of the story dialogues. Both research designs have advantages and disadvantages, and both are necessary to the study of human development.

Longitudinal designs are particularly appealing to the developmental psychologist. Because individuals are compared with themselves at different points in time, test subjects do not have to be sorted out and carefully matched. Some developmental processes can be looked at very closely by studying these individuals every week, or even every day. In the study of language development in the second or third year of life, for example, a small group of children can be studied every week for a detailed picture of the emerging language. Or, in a study of adults, repeated measures can be taken each decade to note changing interests, attitudes, and values as the individuals age. But longitudinal studies also have several drawbacks. They require a great deal of time from both researchers and subjects. Subjects may become ill, go on vacation, move away, or simply stop participating in the research project. Some subjects get used to taking the tests and tend to do better than those being examined for the first time. Those subjects who stay in your sample tend to be those who are the most cooperative and stable. The researchers, too, may move away or lose interest. Often, longitudinal studies require extensive funding and the original purposes of the study may no longer be considered relevant to today's research needs. Longitudinal studies tend to be long-term affairs. As theories and techniques change, it is difficult to incorporate new techniques and ideas into the ongoing design.

Cross-sectional designs have the advantage of being quicker, cheaper and more manageable than longitudinal studies. Cross-sectional designs require careful sampling of participants to be sure that the groups at different age levels are reasonably comparable. In studies of adults of widely ranging ages, for example, it is often difficult to find a sample that is matched on variables such as health, education, or cultural and socioeconomic background. Studies of adult intelligence have been particularly plagued by problems of comparable samples. Is the sample of 60-year-olds, for example, as healthy or as well-educated or from the same cultural or socioeconomic background as the sample of those aged forty? Finally, in either longitudinal or cross-sectional designs, it is difficult to separate the effects of chronological age from those of the historical period.

Some researchers combine both approaches in a **sequential/age cohort design.** Whitbourne (1991) used such a design in a study of personality in young and middle adulthood. In 1968 and again in 1976, she surveyed college seniors on aspects of their self-image, social relationships, and values. She repeated this study in 1984 and 1990, with new groups of college seniors; she also re-surveyed those subjects studied earlier. Each of these age groups was considered an age cohort. The earliest age cohort has now been studied four times. That group can be analyzed for age differences in the same fashion as in a longitudinal design. How did these individuals change as they moved from college students in the late 1960s to starting their careers or marriages in the mid-1970s to parenting in the early 1980s and to re-examining their lives as 40-year-olds in 1990? But this group can also be compared to the other three age cohorts at each age level. In many ways, this group differs from the other three cohorts in their attitudes and values as

cross-sectional design A method of studying development in which a sample of individuals of one age are observed and compared with one or more samples of individuals of other ages.

sequential/age cohort design A combination of cross-sectional and longitudinal research designs in which individuals of several different ages are observed repeatedly over an extended period of time.

FOCUS ON RESEARCH

PERSONALITY OVER THE LIFE COURSE

"The child is father of the man," wrote the poet William Wordsworth in 1802. Nearly everyone has heard a grandparent comment on the continuity of some relative's temper, stubbornness, or other personality trait. But a social scientist looks for proof of the validity and extent of such statements. Is there essential stability of personality traits over the life course for most people? If so, what are the circumstances, processes, and influences that make this statement more or less true?

The obstacles to systematic research on the life course are formidable. Suppose some researchers simply want to know whether or not shy children are likely to be shy as adolescents and as young adults. They might try to design a test of shyness that is appropriate for each age level, give it to some children, and wait to test these same individuals again later on. This is a standard longitudinal design. But what if the researchers also want to know why shyness persists or what the life-course consequences of this behavioral style are? A more complicated and extensive longitudinal study, conducted over several decades, would be required in this case.

Fortunately for some current researchers, a few extensive and complex longitudinal studies that were started many years ago have amassed a body of information for the examination of some life-course questions. One such study—the Berkeley Guidance Study—tracked the development of every third child born in Berkeley, California, in 1928. In childhood, these children and their parents were monitored on an annual basis. From adolescence on, they were interviewed extensively every 10 years. Remarkably, researchers were able to stay in touch with 139 of the almost 200 initial subjects over a period of 40 years. The individuals in this age cohort were children during the Great Depression, teens during World War II, and young adults in the postwar boom. Yet, as individuals, they experienced these world events very differently. Why? What were some of the important factors in determining their development over the life course? There have been many studies using these data to examine economic factors, parental attitudes, personality factors, educational opportunities, and family crises. Let's look at one of these studies.

Caspi and Elder (1988) wondered if "ill-tempered" children became "ill-tempered" adults, and if inhibited children became inhibited adults. What were the adult consequences of these behavioral styles? What were the life-course patterns for the explosive children and for the withdrawn children, as compared to their peers?

To study these questions, Caspi and Elder selected the individuals in the sample who at ages 8 to 10 were reported by teachers and parents as either the most explosive or the most inhibited. These were the "under-controlled" children, who had frequent outbursts of temper, or the "over-controlled" children, who were anxiously inhibited in their ability to initiate activity. Did these explosive or inhibited behavior patterns persist into adulthood, even though the behavior was often maladap-

college students. Perhaps this can be attributed to the politically turbulent college campuses of the late 1960s. All of these cohorts showed a strong interest in achievement and productivity the second time they were surveyed, in their late twenties. This is perhaps an age-appropriate role, both for men and women, as they build their careers.

Such a combined design is almost essential in the study of adulthood in order to separate the effects of chronological age from the effects of the particular historical period. The psychological reality of college students, or of the parents of college students, may differ, depending on whether that person is living in the midst of conflict over Civil Rights and the Vietnam War in the late 1960s, or amidst renewed Civil Rights issues and the strong patriotism of the Persian Gulf War of 1991.

tive? For the most part they did, although there were several exceptions. More importantly, however, the researchers focused on the *life trajectory,* or the pattern of events over the life course, for individuals with these two different childhood behavior styles.

Children who exhibit problem behavior like an explosive temper or severe withdrawal at age 10 do not experience the same environment as their agemates. Teachers, parents, and peers react to them differently, both when they are children and when they are adults. Explosive behavior—whether it is expressed in school, in military service, in the workplace, or in dating and marriage—engenders predictable and usually unfavorable reactions in others. Consequently, the "explosive" children in the Berkeley Guidance Study, particularly the males, fared less well than did other children in many settings. As a group, they attended school for fewer years and earned fewer degrees than did their peers. They were less able to adapt to the educational system's demand for suppression of emotional expression. As adults, the men held lower-level jobs in the workplace and lower ranks in the military than did their peers. They changed jobs more frequently and were more likely to divorce. The women married men with lower job status, were more likely to divorce, and became ill-tempered mothers (Caspi et al., 1987).

Those individuals who were shy or withdrawn children had a quite different life-course pattern. Shy boys were likely to avoid or delay decisions about education, dating, marriage, or a career. Consequently, the adult roles of marriage and parenthood and the establishment of a stable career were delayed. Shy girls, who were young adults in the 1950s, were more likely than their peers to accept and follow a conventional pattern of marriage, child rearing, and homemaking (Caspi et al., 1988).

In both the explosive and the withdrawn patterns, the typical life course shows a progressive accumulation of the consequences of the early behavioral style. The life-course trajectories across 30 or more years are a result of both the continuing interpersonal behavior in numerous situations and the cumulative consequences of these events and of particular adult decisions made in work, marriage, and parenting (Caspi & Elder, 1988).

Although Caspi and Elder's findings are impressive, it is important to remember that these are general findings. As Professor J. W. Macfarlane and her team at Berkeley found in 1958, "A number [of individuals] who were hostile . . . in childhood have grown up to become friendly and nurturant parents." Some explosive children also triumphed over their emotional natures to succeed in the educational, military, and work arenas. It remains for future researchers to find the roots of this success and to determine whether these individuals found socially acceptable outlets for their emotional reactions or learned at some stage to "temper" their emotions.

INTERPRETING THE EVIDENCE

Three witnesses to a crime, or to the same research study, may submit three different reports. We do not all interpret evidence in the same fashion. In the scientific study of human development, it is important to establish procedures that are dependable, repeatable, and consistent and lead to similar conclusions.

Blocks to Good Observation

OBSERVER BIAS   Many of us see what we expect to see or what we want to see; this is called *subjectivity*. We either do not notice or refuse to believe whatever conflicts with our preconditions. Whether it results from cultural assumptions, prejudice, stereotyping or inexperience, a bias will invalidate the conclusions of an observation. Observing without a bias is called *objectivity*. An observer of female athletic skills, for instance, may not be completely objective if convinced that women either cannot or should not be skilled in this area.

INSENSITIVITY   When we observe the same thing every day, we often become so accustomed to it that we fail to recognize its significance. For example, the seat locations that students choose in a classroom may tell us something about their popularity, leadership, feelings of isolation, and the social groups to which they belong. But if we see these students in the classroom several times a week, we may overlook this readily available information.

LIMITS OF THE HYPOTHESIS   Another obstacle to good observation is the tendency to look at too large or too small or too arbitrary a piece of behavior. If, for example, we want to know something about memory in people over age 65, we could choose a number of different approaches. We might observe some people in this age group following the routine of a typical day, noting how many times they forget things. But this method is too arbitrary to measure memory functions precisely. Such observations would not reveal, for example, how well the subjects had learned the things they had forgotten, or what they did know. A laboratory setting might provide more accurate results.

In some early memory studies, researchers had individuals of different ages (for example, ages 20, 40, 60, and 80) learn lists of nonsense syllables. Then they measured how many of these nonsense syllables the individuals could recall 10 minutes later, 30 minutes later, and 24 hours later. In most cases, the older individuals had a much more difficult time both learning and remembering the nonsense syllables than did the younger subjects. In more recent studies, researchers have asked young adults and older adults to listen to and remember the important facts from selected material. In this kind of study, the performance of older subjects is much closer to that of younger ones. It seems that older people generally learn to use their memory abilities more selectively. They can learn and remember a good deal of information, provided it is meaningful and useful. In contrast, they seem to screen out apparently useless information (Botwinick, 1984).

Limiting Conclusions

It is easy to go beyond the data in an attempt to conclude more than was actually found in the study. This can happen in a number of ways, but we might be particularly on the alert for three of them.

PROBLEMS OF DEFINITION   In research, we normally have two different kinds of definitions: a *theoretical definition* and an *operational definition*. A theoretical definition of intelligence might be "the ability to adapt to one's environment." In contrast, an operational definition of intelligence might be: "those behaviors that the Stanford-Binet intelligence test measures." Researchers with different ideas of what intelligence means get different results when interpreting the same material. If they want to be sure they are talking about the same thing, they need to agree upon a definition that describes the techniques of observation and measurement that they employ in their study. That is an operational definition. But their work is more meaningful if they also provide a theoretical definition.

To illustrate this point, let us consider the problem of studying aggression. We might be able to agree on a theoretical definition of aggression as "behavior that is intended to injure or destroy." But how do we measure intent? What do we observe? To answer these questions, we need an operational definition of our research topic. One researcher might measure hitting, kicking, punching, and other physical acts against another person. A second researcher might measure verbal insults. A third might measure a teacher's rating of the child's aggressiveness on a five-point scale from high to low. A fourth might measure the aggressive content in a child's storytelling. But the child who scores high in fantasy aggression may be quite low in actual physical aggression as measured by the first researcher. These researchers are measuring different things.

GENERALIZING BEYOND THE SAMPLE   Research is conducted in a particular setting and under particular conditions, with particular individuals from a particular sociocultural context. The results of any study, therefore, must be limited to similar individuals in similar situations. For example, children who experience a great deal of sarcasm in their daily life may learn the cues much more quickly than those who grow up in families where sarcasm is a rare event.

CORRELATION OR CAUSALITY   It is very difficult to establish with any degree of certainty the **cause** of particular behaviors. For example, 8-year-old boys who watch a lot of television engage in more aggressive play with their peers (Liebert & Spraken, 1988). Did the television watching cause the aggression? Perhaps aggressive children watch more television because they like aggression. Several studies indicate that aggressive behavior and watching acts of aggression on television are related, but we are not sure which causes which or whether the two things are, in fact, influenced by a third factor. For instance, height and weight are related to each other. Does height cause weight, does weight cause height, or are they both the result of the genetic plan that interacts with the environmental context provided for growth?

Researchers use a statistical technique called **correlation** to measure the relationship between two variables. In the case of television watching and aggression, one might first measure the number of hours spent watching violent television shows and then measure the child's aggressive behavior. Children who watch more violent television shows tend to be higher in aggression, and children who watch very few violent shows tend to be very low in aggression. When both of these factors are true, there will be a strong, positive correlation between watching many hours of violent programming and acting aggressively. If children who watch many violent shows are less aggressive, the correlation would be negative.

When two variables are correlated, it is tempting to conclude that one causes the other. For example, parental spanking is positively correlated with children's aggressive behavior; that is, children who are spanked a lot tend to be more aggressive than those who are not. It is logical to conclude that the child's unruly behavior *causes* the frequent spanking. Conversely, if one believes that parental behavior usually causes a child's behavior, then perhaps physically aggressive behavior like spanking *causes* the child to imitate such aggression. Both conclusions are logical but are not necessarily correct. Correlation does *not* mean causation.

causality A relationship between two variables where change in one brings about an effect or result in the other.

correlation A mathematical statement of the relationship between two variables.

RESEARCH ETHICS

It hardly needs to be said that researchers should follow ethical principles when conducting research with human beings. They should never knowingly harm anyone, nor violate basic human rights. This is particularly true when conducting research on dependent groups such as children, the aged, or prisoners. Nevertheless, the issues of individual rights and what may be harmful to research participants are more complex than they may appear.

INFORMED CONSENT   Most major professional organizations have set guidelines for the conduct of research (American Psychological Association, 1982; Society for Research in Child Development, 1973). All such organizations hold that people should participate voluntarily, should be fully informed of the nature and possible consequences of the experiment, and should not be offered excessive inducements such as large amounts of money. Infants and young children do not offer their consent—their parents do. It is hoped that parents have the best interests of their children in mind. Children over the age of eight and adults should give their own consent. Researchers should be sensitive to other forms of inducement. How easily, for example, can a 9-year-old in school, or a 70-year-old in a nursing home, say "No" to someone who looks like a teacher or an administrator (Thompson, 1990)?

CONFIDENTIALITY   We all have a right to privacy; we therefore have a right to expect researchers to hold in confidence information about our private lives, thoughts, and fantasies. Also, test scores must be protected from inappropriate use by those outside the research project. Unfortunately, sometimes researchers forget to respect confidentiality with children and hospital patients. They may share the fears and strange misperceptions of a child with the child's teachers, despite the fact that the child offered those thoughts in confidence. Test scores may be categorized using phrases like "dull-normal intelligence" or "predelinquent" or "weak ego control" or "impulsive." Such labels shared with parents, teachers, or employers can easily be misinterpreted. Labels can become self-fulfilling; if teachers are told that a child is of limited intelligence, they may treat the child in a way that makes that description come true.

PROTECTION FROM PSYCHOLOGICAL HARM   Everyone agrees that researchers should never knowingly harm their subjects. While physical injury is easily avoided, often it is difficult to determine what is psychologically harmful. For example, in studies of obedience, is it reasonable to give children orders just to see if they will follow them? In the numerous studies of infants' responses to novelty, is it reasonable to expose children for long periods to increasingly novel items?

Another example concerns test failure. Sometimes a researcher wants to demonstrate that a 7-year-old can understand a particular concept but a 5-year-old cannot. All the 5-year-old children, knowingly or unknowingly, experience repeated failure. Should children have to experience the needless confusion involved in trying to solve what, for them, are unsolvable problems? How does one debrief such children or make them feel that they did well no matter what the outcome?

Most research organizations currently have screening committees to be sure that their studies are not harmful to the participants. Federal guidelines for social and psychological research with children specify that the study should have only

ETHICAL PROBLEMS IN RESEARCH

Stanley Milgram (1963) created an experiment that tested the obedience of subjects to an authority figure. Subjects in the experiment were told that the purpose of the experiment was to study the role of punishment in learning. Each subject was then assigned the role of the "teacher"; another subject (actually a confederate of the experimenter) was assigned the role of the "learner." The learner—seated in a chair with an electrode attached to his wrist—was told to learn a list of word pairs. The teacher was seated in another room in front of a shock generator with a range of switches labeled with the number of volts—from 15 volts (labeled "slight shock") to 450 volts (labeled "danger—extreme shock"). The teacher was instructed to administer a test, moving to the next item when the learner answered a question correctly and giving a shock when the answer was wrong. Each time an error was made, the level of the shock was to be increased.

Although the learner, in reality, received no shock at all, he pretended that he did. At 75 volts, he grunted; at 150 volts, he demanded to be released; at 285 volts, he gave an agonized scream; and so on. Even though many teachers wanted to stop the experiment, the experimenter commanded them to continue. Despite serious reservations, 65% of the teachers obeyed and continued to give presumably painful shocks, up to 450 volts, to the learners.

Milgram's experiment met with a great deal of criticism from other psychologists. Dr. Diana Baumrind, of the Institute of Human Development at the University of California at Berkeley, felt that Milgram's lack of regard for the subjects in his study was reprehensible and damaging both to the subjects and to the public image of psychology as a profession. It was Baumrind's (1964) belief that an experimenter must balance his or her career and scientific interests against the interests of prospective subjects. Subjects in the Milgram study were placed under tremendous stress. They were horrified and confused by their actions in the experiment, and they were unable to justify their behavior.

Although Milgram stated that "procedures were undertaken to assure that the subject would leave the laboratory in a state of well-being," Baumrind seriously questioned what sort of procedures could dissipate the type of emotional disturbance that these subjects experienced. Such upsetting procedures, according to Baumrind, are potentially harmful because they could easily effect an alteration in the subject's self-image or ability to trust adult authorities in the future.

"From the subject's point of view," continues Baumrind, "procedures which involve loss of dignity, self-esteem and trust in rational authority are probably most harmful in the long run." Baumrind felt that Milgram was indifferent to the effects of the experiment on his subjects, as well as to the reasons for which subjects volunteer for experiments and the value they derive from their participation.

Independent of the reactions to the Milgram experiment, the American Psychological Association (1973) adopted a document outlining ethical principles to be followed when conducting research with human participants. Among the provisions in the document were the following: Psychologists must carry out their research with respect for the participants and with concern for their dignity and welfare; they must inform participants of all features of the research that might influence their willingness to participate; they must respect the individual's freedom to decline to participate or to discontinue at any time; after the study, they must explain the nature of the study to the participant and remove any misconceptions that may have arisen; and they must make certain that there are no damaging consequences for the participant, including physical or mental harm or danger (should there be consequences, the researcher must detect and remove or correct these consequences). Finally, information obtained about the participants must remain confidential.

minimal risk: that is, risk of harm no greater than that experienced in daily life or in the performance of routine psychological tests (DHS, 1983). These screening committees are becoming more stringent in their protection of the participants. Many committees, for example, feel that they have a responsibility to protect people's rights to self-esteem, and to expose them only to test situations that will enhance their self-concept (Thompson, 1990).

BENEFITS TO THE PARTICIPANT   It may not be enough for researchers to seek the voluntary informed consent of their participants, respect their confidentiality and protect them from physical and psychological harm. Perhaps researchers should supply some positive benefits to individuals in return for their participation. At the very least, perhaps researchers should try to make participation in the experiments fun, interesting or informative, or to create a positive situation in which the person can be heard, supported, understood and respected. The rights of participants in research are still being explored and defined. Indeed, many studies considered permissible even two decades ago are no longer considered ethical.

STUDY OUTLINE

An Objective Study of the Life Span

The goal of studying human development is the discovery and understanding of common processes and major influences throughout the life span.

A focus on infancy and childhood can help explain adult behavior. Similarly, consideration of the complexities of adult behavior draws attention to the experiences of childhood.

Historical, Socioeconomic, and Cross-Cultural Perspectives

The student of human behavior considers historical change, socioeconomic factors, and cross-cultural variation. For example, attitudes toward children and the aged have varied dramatically over the centuries and have been shaped by powerful social and economic forces.

Developmental Processes

Development refers to the changes over time in the structure, thought, or behavior of a person, and is due to both biological and environmental influences. Some development is primarily biological, whereas other development depends on the environment. Most, however, involves an interaction between the two.

Biological Processes of Development. Biological processes include **maturation, growth,** and **aging.** Maturation refers to structural, functional, and organizational changes due to heredity. Growth usually refers to increases in size, function, or complexity up to maturity. Aging refers to changes that occur after maturity.

Environmental Influences on Development. The environment surrounds and influences us continually. It may fulfill basic needs, cause harm, or provide the components for learning. **Learning** is the process of change in behavior resulting from experience or practice. Socialization is the broad learning process by which we acquire the attitudes and values of our culture.

Interaction of Developmental Processes. Most behavior is a product of the interaction between maturation and learning. Physical development and long-term behavior patterns often depend on exactly when an environmental effect occurs, such as prenatal **critical periods** and the optimal periods in early childhood. Some behaviors will not develop until the individual has reached a point of **readiness,** a time when sufficient maturation has occurred.

The Systematic Study of Human Development

The systematic study of human development begins with asking good questions and making astute observations.

The Scientific Method. The four steps of the scientific method are: define the research problem, develop a hypothesis, test the hypothesis, and draw conclusions.

Types of Measurements. Research results depend on the types of measurements that are used. Direct observation of behavior is effective with infants and young children in real-life or laboratory situations. With older subjects, achievement and ability tests may be used. A **reliable** measure is dependable, consistent, and repeatable. **Validity** is the extent to which a test measures what it purports to measure.

Self-report techniques consist of interviews and questionnaires designed to reveal the individual's feelings, thoughts, and self-perception. Projective techniques reveal needs, feelings, and attitudes by asking the individual to respond to situations, pictures, or tasks. Case studies provide a rich integrated picture of development in context but have limited value as research because they are subjective, lack control of variables, and are limited to one individual.

Research Designs

The research design structures the type of information collected. Natural settings permit little control of individuals and conditions, but the events studied may be truer to life than those studied in laboratories. In experimental settings, the researcher can control conditions precisely and measure behavior, but the behavior measured may not be representative of behavior outside the laboratory.

Longitudinal and Cross-Sectional Designs. **Longitudinal studies** involve repeated observation of the same individuals over time. These studies have built-in controls but are difficult to conduct. **Cross-sectional studies** compare individuals of different ages at the same point in time. Although these studies are more manageable than longitudinal studies, they may yield invalid results if the individuals studied differ on important variables. A further difficulty exists in separating the effects of chronological age from those of the historical period. **Sequential/age cohort studies** are a combination of these two approaches.

Interpreting the Evidence

Blocks to Good Observation. The accurate interpretation of evidence depends on the researcher's objectivity, sensitivity to detail, and the selection of an appropriate level of analysis.

Limiting Conclusions. Conclusions will depend on how the events or behavior are *operationally defined*. Conclusions must be limited to individuals and conditions that are similar to those measured.

Causality is difficult to prove. **Correlation** is a statistical technique that measures the relationship between two variables, but it does not measure whether one variable causes another.

Research Ethics

In ethical research, participants should give their informed voluntary consent to the study and should have their thoughts, feelings, and actions held in confidence. Participants should be protected from psychological and physical harm.

KEY TERMS AND CONCEPTS

aging	development	maturation
causality	experimental design	optimal period
correlation	growth	readiness
critical period	independent variable	reliability
cross-sectional design	learning	sequential/age cohort design
dependent variable	longitudinal design	validity

SELF-TEST QUESTIONS

1. What is meant by the statement, "difficulties in understanding human behavior are often caused by those who try to explain and predict it"?

2. Compare historical, socioeconomic, and cross-cultural perspectives in terms of their respective contributions to the understanding of human development.

3. What is meant by the term *development* and what roles do biological processes and environmental influences play in bringing development about?

4. What is the relationship between learning and socialization?

5. How would you explain the relationship between biological and environmental development processes? What roles do timing and readiness play in this relationship?

6. List four basic steps involved in the scientific method.

7. Describe the major categories of developmental research and list their strengths and limitations.

8. List and describe the factors that must be considered in order to interpret evidence.

9. Describe the ethical considerations that researchers must consider when conducting research with human beings.

SUGGESTED READINGS

BOWLBY, J. *Charles Darwin: A new life*. New York: Norton, 1990. A powerful psychological analysis of Darwin's internal struggles and family life as well as his achievements as a naturalist.

COLES, R. *The spiritual life of children*. Boston, MA: Houghton Mifflin, 1990. Through the words and pictures of children, this noted teacher and child psychiatrist shares with the reader some surprisingly profound child understandings of the meaning of life and of human experience.

GIES, F., & GIES, J. *Life in a medieval village*. New York: Harper & Row, 1990. Two skilled historians reconstruct the customs, practices, and social conditions in rural medieval England.

HEWETT, S. *When the bough breaks: The cost of neglecting our children*. New York: Basic Books, 1991. A compelling social commentary on the plight of children in today's United States.

KAGAN, J. *The nature of the child*. New York: Basic Books, 1984. A noted developmental psychologist highlights the research of the last few decades. He editorializes on the effects of early experiences, yet suggests that there are also numerous opportunities for transformations in later childhood and adolescence.

Chapter 2

*Putting on the spectacles of science
in expectation of finding
the answer to everything looked at
signifies inner blindness.*

J. FRANK DOBIE
THE VOICE OF THE COYOTE, 1949

CHAPTER OUTLINE

Theories of Human Development: An Introduction

What is the essence of human nature? Are we primarily rational and goal oriented? Or are we driven by passions? How do we learn—by discovery, by insight, or by small sequential steps of increasing complexity? How are we motivated—by reward, pain, curiosity, or inner drives? What is a "conscience," and how does it develop? Do we have control over it? Or is it shaped by external and internal forces that we cannot control? Sometimes we study developmental psychology to seek answers to such basic questions. Any answer that we find will be based on a particular theory of human development—a set of assumptions or principles about human behavior.

Theories give shape to otherwise large and unmanageable collections of data. Social scientists use theories to help formulate significant questions, to select and organize their data, and to understand the data within a larger framework. The resulting body of information, together with the broader theory, allows the social scientist to make new predictions about future human behavior.

If you think about the questions raised above, you will probably realize that you have your own "theories" about the answers to them. You lean toward one explanation or another of a specific problem, and the assumptions implicit in your explanation probably have a lot to do with your thoughts about other people. For example, you may view juvenile delinquents either as responsible for their actions or as victims of their environment or early training. You may believe that 6-year-old children are able to decide for themselves what they should study in school, or you may think that children cannot be expected to know what they want. You probably have assumptions about the degree to which each individual is responsible for his or her behavior and the degree to which human rationality can be relied upon to direct our actions wisely.

Why is it important to understand the theories of human behavior? A broad understanding of various theories creates the detachment that lets us evaluate our own views, actions, and reactions. It is important for us to reexamine the assumptions behind our beliefs to see whether they make sense, whether they fit the evidence, and what follows from them. A familiarity with the major theories, then, allows us to examine, evaluate, and discipline our intuitions and our own "theories" on human behavior.

Besides helping us understand our own ways of thinking, a knowledge of the major theories makes us more eclectic. By acquainting ourselves with several different theories, we can examine behavior from more than one frame of reference and can see the value of other explanations.

Many psychologists, too, are eclectic. They select from numerous theories

CHAPTER OBJECTIVES

By the time you have finished this chapter, you should be able to do the following:

- Describe and compare the major theories of human development.
- Become familiar with major terms and concepts employed by each theory of human development.

How do you react when you see members of street gangs? Do you see them as delinquents or as victims of society? Are they to be feared, respected, or despised? Why do people join street gangs—for friendship? Because of peer pressure? To fight with other street gangs? How you answer these questions, what information you look for when considering them, and your solutions to the problem (if there is a problem) all depend on your personal theories about what causes and motivates human behavior.

those particular aspects that will help them in their work. Almost all psychologists have been influenced by the theories of others. Therefore, in describing the various theories given in this chapter, we do not intend to label or pigeonhole psychologists, but simply to present the basic outlines of some of the most popular beliefs.

LEARNING THEORIES

Learning theories find the key to a person's nature in the way that he or she is shaped by the environment. According to these theories most behavior is acquired, and it is acquired by learning. *Learning* is a pervasive process. It is not confined just to formal schooling or instruction; it also includes the acquisition of morality, biases, and mannerisms such as gestures or even stuttering. It covers a broad spectrum of behavior. The learning theorist sees development over the life span as a gradual, step-by-step accumulation of knowledge, skills, memories, and competencies. The child becomes an adolescent and then an adult primarily by the gradual, continuous addition of more experiences and more learning, which lead in turn to more skills and knowledge.

Behaviorism

In the early part of the 20th century, American psychologists set out to create a "science of human behavior." They were not interested in human thoughts, dreams, or feelings. Instead, they wanted to collect "the facts" by observing what people do. They studied human behavior in much the same way that other scientists studied biology or physics. These researchers carefully defined and controlled the stimuli present in the experimental setting and then observed and recorded their subject's behavioral responses to these stimuli. They did not start from a "grand design" but instead objectively constructed their theory, piece by piece, first by conducting simple experiments and later by designing more complex ones. In this fashion, they inductively built a theory of behavior. Because of their interest in overt, measurable behavior, these researchers were called **behaviorists.**

REACTIVE BEINGS   Behaviorists assume that human nature is neither bad nor good; people are reactive—they simply respond to their environment. Every individual is shaped by the process of associating stimuli and their responses or associating behaviors and their consequences. Thus the learning process occurs rather automatically. Some say this explanation is **mechanistic.** It views people as machines that are set in motion by input (a stimulus) and then produce output (a response). Behaviorists are not concerned with analyzing what happens between the stimulus and the response. The mind itself, particularly its internal stages, cannot be easily observed and described from the outside. Behaviorists do not trust people to give accurate reports of their subjective thoughts and feelings. Consequently, they have not given much attention to the mind.

The behaviorist's model has also been described as **deterministic.** Everything in the individual's behavior, including values, attitudes, and emotional responses, is believed to be determined by either the past or present environment. Therefore such concepts as blame, respect, and dignity are considered irrelevant. According to behaviorism, because people are products of their past learning history, they deserve neither credit nor blame for their actions. The title of a book by a modern learning theorist expresses this idea: B. F. Skinner's *Beyond Freedom and Dignity* (1971) implies that human behavior is programmed and therefore beyond the individual's control.

CLASSICAL CONDITIONING   Behaviorists were especially interested in describing and defining the processes of learning. Perhaps the most basic form of learning is called *conditioning.* There are several famous experiments that demonstrate different types of conditioning.

The experiments of the Russian psychologist Ivan Pavlov (1928) are among the most famous examples of **classical conditioning** (see Figure 2–1). Pavlov noted that dogs salivated when food was offered to them. He began to strike a tuning fork at the same time that he offered food to a dog, and he repeated the pairing of the neutral stimulus (the tuning fork) with the food several times. Before long, the sound of the fork alone was enough to make the dog salivate. He did *not* conclude that the dog "anticipated food when he heard the fork." That would imply thinking. Instead, he and the American learning theorists simply concluded that the dog was now *conditioned* to salivate at the sound of the tuning fork.

Emotional reactions are also thought to be easily conditioned. A famous experiment on the conditioning of fear was performed by John B. Watson, an important early behaviorist. An 11-month-old infant named Albert was the subject of Watson and Rayner's experiment (1920). Albert was confronted with a white rat. At first, he showed no fear of the animal, but then Watson made a loud clanging noise every time he showed the rat to Albert, causing the baby to cry and crawl away. It did not take many pairings of the previously neutral stimulus of the rat with the unpleasant loud noise for Albert to respond with anxiety and fear to the rat alone. Reportedly, Albert was soon frightened by other white or furry

behaviorists Early 20th-century psychologists who focused their research on overt, measurable, observable behavior rather than on internal medical processes.

mechanistic model In learning theory, the view of human beings as machines that are set in motion by input (stimuli) and that produce output (responses).

deterministic model The view that a person's values, attitudes, behaviors, and emotional responses are determined by past or present environmental factors.

classical conditioning A type of learning in which a neutral stimulus, such as a bell, comes to elicit a response—salivation—by repeated pairings with an unconditioned stimulus, such as food.

Behaviorists assume that people are reactive beings who simply respond to others and to the environment.

stimulus generalization The spread of a response from one specific stimulus to other similar stimuli.

counterconditioning A procedure to eliminate a previously conditioned negative response by replacing it with a new conditioned response in the same stimulus situation.

desensitization In behavior therapy, a technique that gradually reduces an individual's anxiety about a specific object or situation.

objects, even a Santa Claus beard. This spread of a response to other similar stimuli is called **stimulus generalization.**

Albert's case was a dramatic example of conditioning with stimulus generalization—although the experiment was a rather cruel and unethical one and was not very precise (Harris, 1979). We can see clear parallels in children's everyday lives. Doctors' white uniforms or medicinal smells may arouse fear in children because they associate these things with unpleasant experiences, such as painful injections. Positive emotional reactions can be conditioned just like negative ones. Reactions of relaxation or pleasure are easily associated with previously neutral stimuli, like an old song that brings back all the memories of a sunny day at the beach or the excitement of a high school dance.

If a person comes to associate a previously neutral stimulus, such as Albert's rat, with an unpleasant emotional state, what can be done to reverse this conditioned response? In **counterconditioning,** the subject is gradually introduced to the once neutral stimulus in the presence of a strong and opposite conditioning stimulus (like the caged rat introduced at a distance). This soon reverses the conditioned negative response pattern.

Wolpe, Salter, and Reyna (1964) have used counterconditioning to treat common phobias, such as fear of flying or driving, fear of authority figures, and fear of hospitals, where the conditioned stimuli are things like height, uniforms, hospital smells, and "the boss." The most common counterconditioning technique is relaxation training, or **desensitization.** Clients are taught to relax deeply, and in this state, they are told to imagine themselves approaching the feared situation. Each time clients report tension, they are immediately instructed to stop the image and return to a relaxed state. With repeated pairing, the new relaxation response replaces the old anxiety response, first to the image and finally to the real event or object. Two processes work together in counterconditioning. The old response

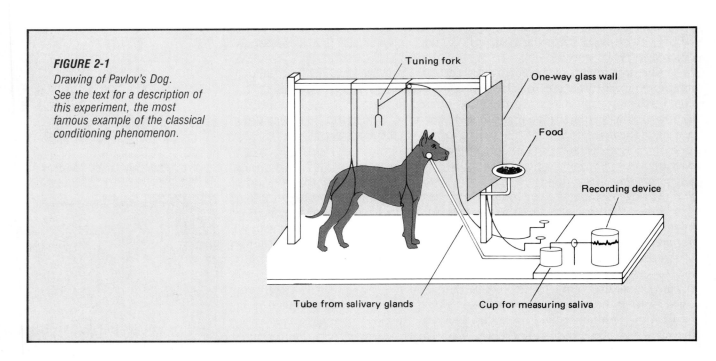

FIGURE 2-1

Drawing of Pavlov's Dog.

See the text for a description of this experiment, the most famous example of the classical conditioning phenomenon.

Tuning fork

One-way glass wall

Food

Recording device

Tube from salivary glands

Cup for measuring saliva

disappears gradually because it is not actively reinforced. And in the meantime, the clients learn a new, competing response through the process of classical conditioning.

OPERANT CONDITIONING The foregoing examples have illustrated classical conditioning. But these procedures do not apply as well to more complex behavior, such as learning to drive a car, playing baseball, or reciting poetry. These are all examples of predominantly voluntary, or **operant behavior.** The key difference between operant and classical conditioning is that in **operant conditioning,** behavior cannot be elicited automatically. The behavior must occur before it can be strengthened by conditioning, that is, before it can be associated with a reward. In operant conditioning, behaviors that are rewarded or reinforced are likely to occur again.

Edward Thorndike (1911) conducted experiments on voluntary behavior with cats. Cats placed in a puzzle box learned by themselves to escape from the box or to get food by manipulating a latch that opened the door. Thorndike saw in this learning phenomenon what he called the **law of effect:** The consequences of a behavior determine the probability of its being repeated. When first placed in the box, the cats typically explored the inside and pressed the latch only by chance. But reinforcement in the form of food strengthened the act until the cats were opening the door immediately after they were placed in the box. Years later, B.F. Skinner picked up the work of Thorndike and Watson, and, together with other learning theorists, he systematically expanded the laws of behavior.

B.F. SKINNER Skinner was a tinkerer who liked to invent research equipment that could more carefully measure behavior and could automatically deliver reinforcement. One invention of this type was called a *Skinner box,* which was essentially an animal cage built for a rat or pigeon, though larger animals were sometimes placed in it. The Skinner box contained a movable metal bar, and when the animal pushed this bar, a pellet of food dropped into its feeding tray. With this very simple device, he was able to measure the animal's behavior systematically under different conditions of reinforcement. Rats, pigeons, and sometimes humans were found to be quite predictable as they followed consistent laws of behavior, at least in this kind of situation. In Skinner's experiments (as in Thorndike's), the reinforcement was usually food. But in everyday situations, positive reinforcement may be a nod of approval, a smile, an interesting sight to see, or success in a video game.

Operant behavior can also be learned by **avoidance conditioning,** in which the reinforcement consists of the termination of an unpleasant stimulus. For example, a bright light can be turned off, a loud noise can be stopped, or an angry parent can be quieted. In operant conditioning, then, one learns a response to a particular stimulus (or set of stimuli) by repeatedly having that response paired with a positive reinforcement.

How can operant conditioning be used to teach a complex act? Very often, the final behavior must be built bit by bit, or **shaped.** In shaping, *successive approximations* of the final task are rewarded. For example, suppose a child is learning to put on socks. At first, the parent puts on one sock nearly all the way, lets the child pull it up, and then praises the child. The next day, the parent may put the sock on halfway and let the child finish a bit more of the task. It is not long before the child is putting on socks with no help.

operant behavior A behavior in which the individual operates on the environment or emits an action.

operant conditioning A type of conditioning that occurs when an organism is reinforced for voluntarily emitting a response. What is reinforced is then learned.

law of effect A principle of learning theory stating that a behavior's consequences determine the probability of its being repeated.

avoidance conditioning A form of operant conditioning in which the reinforcement consists of the termination of an unpleasant stimulus.

shaping Systematically reinforcing successive approximations to a desired act.

In order to avoid the unpleasant stimulus of a parent's scolding, this boy may behave differently in the future.

behavior modification A method that uses conditioning procedures, such as reinforcement, reward, and shaping, to change behavior.

response consequences The observed results of one's actions that individuals use to adjust their behavior.

Teaching machines introduced by Skinner applied many principles of operant conditioning (Skinner, 1968). With these machines, students learned in small incremental steps, starting with simple problem solving and building up to more complex tasks. The desired behavior, or answer, was reinforced at each step with feedback (some form of reward or acknowledgment) from the machine and by the appearance of a new problem to solve. Eventually, the student succeeded in mastering fairly complex problems. Now, some computer programs that are called "user-friendly" apply many of the same principles of learning.

Contemporary Behavioral Analysis

In the 1990s, the systematic study and application of classical and operant conditioning principles is called *behavioral analysis*. Numerous educational and therapeutic programs have been set up to train or retrain individuals to behave in a more appropriate or desirable way. Programs that shape human behavior for therapeutic goals are called **behavior modification.** One effective way to modify behavior is through the use of a token economy. Imagine a residential facility for delinquent adolescents. The rewards in this controlled world—like tasty food, time in the gym, a semiprivate or private bedroom, current magazines to read, and, eventually, a weekend pass—can all be bought with tokens. However, these tokens are earned for very precise, carefully defined behaviors in the classroom and in the work setting. The tokens now become effective reinforcement for paying attention and making progress in school, following the rules, and being productive in the workplace. They are effective, however, only when the trainer remembers operant conditioning principles, such as rewarding small incremental steps toward the achievement of the final goal.

Extensive research has shown that token economies can be used successfully with retarded and autistic people, with children in classrooms and at home, and with delinquents and psychiatric inpatients (Baker & Brightman, 1989). The aim of training with tokens is to improve a trainee's skills to the point where they are so useful to the trainee that tokens are no longer required. To this end, any token economy must have a plan for weaning the trainees off the tokens as early as possible. Otherwise, the trainees may become so dependent on the token economy that the effectiveness of the behavior modification program is lost.

Social Learning Theory

Social learning theorists have tried to enlarge the scope of learning theory to explain complex social patterns. To do so, they have gone well beyond a seemingly "automatic" conditioning process. Albert Bandura (1977), a leading social learning theorist, points out that in daily life people notice the consequences of their own actions—that is, they notice which actions succeed and which fail or produce no result—and adjust their behavior accordingly. Through such observed **response consequences** they gain information, incentive, and conscious reinforcement. They are able to hypothesize about what is appropriate in which circumstances and to anticipate what may happen as a result of certain actions. Unlike the more mechanistic learning theorists, social learning theorists give conscious thought a larger role in guiding behavior.

IMITATION AND MODELING   Just as people learn directly from experiencing the consequences of their own behavior, they also learn by watching another person's behavior and its consequences (Bandura, 1977; Bandura & Walters, 1963). And just as before, they derive basic principles from their observations and formulate rules of action and behavior. All of us (not just children) learn a wide variety of behaviors from observing and imitating (or avoiding) the actions of others around us. In their early years, children learn the many aspects of a sex-appropriate role and the moral expectations of their community. They also learn how to express aggression and dependency along with prosocial behaviors like sharing. As they grow to adulthood, they will learn career-appropriate attitudes and values, social-class and ethnic attitudes, and moral values.

In a well-known example of modeling, Bandura (1977) conducted a series of experiments in which children watched various levels of aggressive behavior in short films. One group of children saw the aggressive behavior rewarded; another saw it punished; a third group saw a film of nonaggressive behavior play; and a fourth group saw no film at all. The children who saw aggression rewarded were significantly more aggressive in their own play, whereas those who saw the model punished were less aggressive. There is no question that children may learn to express aggression in a particular way from the behavior they see on television programs. (Imitation and modeling are discussed at length in Chapter 10.)

SOCIAL LEARNING AND SOCIAL COGNITION   Bandura (1986) has compiled an updated summary of social learning theories, which he now calls *social cognitive theory*. Cognition means thinking, and this name change reflects a new emphasis on thinking as part of learning. Social learning theorists still talk about rewards and punishments, but they recognize that children observe their own behavior, the behavior of others, and the consequences of these behaviors. Children can also anticipate consequences based on past events. They form opinions about themselves and others and then behave in a fashion that is consistent with these opinions (Miller, 1989). This shift in emphasis by the social learning theorists has moved them away from their study of only observable behavior and has made them similar to the cognitive theorists, whom we will also discuss.

An Evaluation of Learning Theories

Learning theories, including behaviorism, contemporary behavioral analysis, and social learning theory, have made major contributions to our understanding of human development. These theories focus very closely on the situational factors that affect behavior. They specify the situation carefully and make predictions based on past research. In fact, their principles are probably more easily tested than those of any other theory. Some of their predictions have been demonstrated repeatedly. For instance, Skinner and his followers have shown that many types of behavior are indeed affected by reinforcement. Several techniques, such as modeling and various types of behavior modification, have been quite effective in changing behavior when skillfully applied in schools, weight control programs, and homes for disturbed children.

In spite of this precision, learning theorists may be attempting to explain too large an area of human development. For the most part, they have not paid enough attention to thought, emotions, personality, or the understanding of the self. They tend to seek universal processes and to ignore individual differences.

structuralism A branch of psychology concerned with the structure of thought and the ways in which the mind processes information.

Finally, despite their efforts, learning theorists have been baffled by one major human learning achievement. The laws of learning do not adequately account for the complex way in which young children learn a *language*. The development of language is more than simple imitation and reward. It depends on a complex interaction of the individual child's emerging language-learning abilities and a multifaceted language environment. In language development and in the learning of other aspects of one's culture, learning theorists seem unable to describe and account for the complexity of the naturalistic setting. Their behavioral predictions work best in the laboratory, where it is possible to control the stimulus environment closely (Miller, 1989).

COGNITIVE THEORIES

The empirical approach of the learning theorists is considered by some psychologists to be a "typically American" practice. In contrast to it is the comprehensive approach of the eminent Jean Piaget (1896–1980), a Swiss, who dared to weave a complex integrative theory and later test its parts.

Unlike learning theorists, who see human beings as types of passive machines that are acted upon by the environment, cognitive theorists see human beings as rational, active, alert, and competent. For them, human beings do not merely receive information—they also process it. Thus, each person is a thinker and a creator of his or her reality. People do not simply respond to stimuli—they also give them structure and meaning.

Cognitive theorists have appeared relatively recently on the American psychological scene, but their roots in European tradition are very old. The European rationalist tradition manifests a respect for the mind and for mental organizing principles. Learning theorists such as Watson advised psychologists to ignore such mental concepts because they could not be scientifically observed. Although by no means ignoring behavior, the cognitive theorists have sparked a renewed interest in the mind. They have encouraged research to determine what is in the mind and how the mind develops.

Piaget was trained to be a biologist, and he restored the use of a biological model to psychology. To Piaget, the mind, like any other living structure, does not simply respond to stimuli—it grows, changes, and adapts to the world. Piaget and other cognitive psychologists have been called **structuralists** because they are concerned with the structure of thought (Gardner, 1973b). The major cognitive theorists are Piaget, Jerome Bruner, and Heinz Werner; here we shall focus on Piaget.

Piaget

Piaget was one of the most influential and prolific 20th-century psychologists. As a young man, his two main interests were biology and epistemology, a branch of philosophy that seeks to define human knowledge. In his lifelong effort to understand human knowledge, Piaget used psychology to attempt to bridge the gap between biology and philosophy.

Jean Piaget

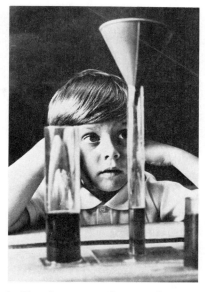

In Piaget's conservation experiment, a child is shown liquid from two identical glasses poured into a short, wide glass and a tall, narrow glass. When asked which has more or less, children under 6 say that the tall glass holds more.

According to Piaget, children learn by exploring their environment. If information fits children's existing concepts, the information is assimilated.

In his early years, Piaget worked with the Binet intelligence (IQ) test. While testing children, he became less interested in their right answers than in patterns he found in their wrong answers. These patterns seemed to provide a clue to the way thought processes develop in children. He theorized that the differences between children and adults were not confined to how much they knew, but the *way* they knew. Qualitative as well as quantitative differences appeared between the thinking of children and that of adults.

To illustrate his theory, Piaget devised one of his most famous problems. He showed a child two identical glasses, each containing the same amount of liquid. After the child agreed that the amount of liquid in each glass was the same, Piaget poured the liquid from one of the glasses into a tall, narrow glass. He then asked the child how much liquid was in the tall glass—was it more or less than in the original glass, or was it the same amount? Most children aged 6, 7, or older answered that the amount was the same. But children under 6 said that the tall glass held more. Even when young children watched the same liquid being poured back and forth between the original glass and the tall glass, they said that the tall glass held more. This experiment has been tried with children of many cultures and nationalities, and the results are always the same.

Piaget reasoned that until they reach a certain stage, children form judgments based more upon perceptual than upon logical processes. In other words, they believe what their eyes tell them. To the younger children, the liquid rose up higher in the tall glass, so there was more of it. Children 6 years or older, on the other hand, barely glanced at the glasses. They knew that the amount of liquid remained the same, regardless of the size or shape of the glass it was in. (Piaget called this the

conservation A cognitive ability described by Piaget as central to the concrete operational period. The child is able to judge changes in amounts based on logical thought instead of mere appearances; thus, an amount of water will remain the same even when it is poured into a glass of a different shape and size.

assimilation In Piaget's theory, the process of making new information part of one's existing schemes.

accommodation Piaget's term for the act of changing our thought processes when a new object or idea does not fit our concepts.

schema Piaget's term for mental structures that process information, perceptions, and experiences; individuals' schemes change as they grow.

equilibration Piaget's term for the basic process in human adaptation. In it, individuals seek a balance, or fit, between the environment and their own structures of thought.

principle of **conservation.**) They did not base their judgments solely on perception; they also used logic. Their knowledge came from within themselves, just as much as from outside sources.

THE ACTIVE MIND   According to Piaget, the mind is not a blank slate on which knowledge can be written nor a mirror that reflects what it perceives. If the information, perception, or experience presented to a person fits with a structure in his or her mind, then that information, perception, or experience is "understood"—it is assimilated. If it does not fit, the mind rejects it (or if the mind is ready to change, it changes itself to **accommodate** the information or experience). Piaget used the word **schema** to designate what we call structure here. Schemes are ways of processing information, and they change as we grow. Infants use a mouthing scheme to explore any objects that can be grasped and brought to the mouth. As infants grow and discover more and more objects that do not fit this scheme, they change to another scheme; they learn to explore with their hands.

Piaget proposed a biological model to describe the process by which we adapt to the world. An animal that is eating does two things. It accommodates to the food with a change in the digestive system that produces enzymes and begins the necessary muscular activity. It also assimilates the food, making it part of itself. Human beings gain intelligence, said Piaget, in the same way. We adjust our schemes to accommodate new information, but at the same time, we assimilate this learning into the mind's structure. On seeing a new object for the first time, we try to fit it into what we know. Is it a weapon? A grooming tool? A cooking implement? If it does not fit our existing concepts (if we cannot assimilate it), we may have to change our concepts or form a new concept (accommodation).

The mind always tries to find a "balance" between assimilation and accommodation, to eliminate inconsistencies or gaps between reality and its picture of reality. This process, called **equilibration,** is basic to human adaptation and, indeed, to all biological adaptation.

STAGES OF MENTAL DEVELOPMENT   As human beings develop, they use more complex schemes to organize information to understand the outside world. Piaget saw this development in four discrete and qualitatively different stages.

TABLE 2-1
Piaget's Stages of Mental Development

STAGE	AGE	ILLUSTRATIVE BEHAVIOR
Sensorimotor	birth to 18 months or 2 years	Infants know the world only by looking, grasping, mouthing, and other actions.
Preoperational	approximately 2 to 7 years	Young children form concepts and have symbols such as language to help them communicate. These images are limited to their personal (egocentric), immediate experience. Preoperational children have very limited, sometimes "magical" notions of cause and effect and have difficulty classifying objects or events.
Concrete operations	approximately 7 to 11 years	Children begin to think logically, classify on several dimensions, and understand mathematical concepts, provided they can apply these operations to concrete objects or events. Concrete operational children achieve conservation.
Formal operations	beginning at 12 years and beyond	Individuals can explore logical solutions to both concrete and abstract concepts: They can systematically think about all possibilities, project into the future or recall the past, and reason by analogy and metaphor.

Infants use comparatively few schemes, many of which involve actions such as looking, grasping, and mouthing. The first period of development is therefore called **sensorimotor** because infant intelligence relies on the senses and on bodily motion for equilibration.

A second stage begins about the time that children start to talk. The

sensorimotor period Piaget's first stage of cognitive development, lasting from birth to about 2 years. Infants use action schemes—looking, grasping, and so on—to learn about their world.

APPLICATION

PIAGET IN THE PRESCHOOL

The theories of Piaget have been widely used in planning the education of children. George Forman and Fleet Hill (1980) have used his theories to design toys for use in the preschool. The Silhouette Sorter is one of these toys. It is a sorting box designed to improve upon commercially made sorting boxes. A commercially made sorting box consists of a box with various shaped holes cut in it and various shaped blocks to be put through the appropriate holes. These sorting boxes do not encourage children to think about how shapes can change.

The Silhouette Sorter consists of a box with three holes and one block. Each hole shows a different perspective of the same block. In the photo, the child is placing an animal-shaped block through a hole shaped at the side silhouette of the block. The top of the box shows a top silhouette of the same animal-shaped block, and the rear of the box has a rear silhouette of the same block. While playing with the Silhouette Sorter, the child learns that the identity of the animal-shaped block stays the

same, whereas the shape or perspective of that block can change.

Some of the points that educators stress when applying the theories of Piaget include the following:

1. Children need to learn through experience.

2. Children need cognitive conflict as part of the process of equilibration.

3. Children need an open environment in which they can pose and test their questions.

4. Children should be helped to construct relationships between objects and the forms the objects can take (Forman & Fosnot, 1982).

The use of the Silhouette Sorter and similar toys helps meet these points by providing children with the learning experiences they need to think about objects and their environment.

Left: The child is placing the animal-shaped block through the side silhouette hole in the Silhouette Sorter.
Right: The animal-shaped block is ready to be placed through the rear silhouette hole.

preoperational period Piaget's second stage of cognitive development (about 2 to 7 years) begins when children are able to use symbols such as language. Their thinking tends to be overly concrete, irreversible, and egocentric, and classification is difficult.

concrete operations Piaget's third stage of cognitive development (7 to 11 years). Children begin to think logically. At this stage they are able to classify things and deal with a hierarchy of classifications.

formal operations The fourth and final stage of Piaget's cognitive theory; begins at about 12 years and is characterized by the ability to handle abstract concepts.

preoperational period (from about 2 to 7 years of age) is the time when children know about the world primarily through their own actions. They do not hold broad, general theories about block buildings, grandmothers, or dogs, but they build up specific knowledge about *their* blocks, *their* grandmothers, or *their* dogs. Preoperational children do not make generalizations about a whole class of objects (for example, all grandmothers), and they cannot think through the consequences of a particular chain of events. At the beginning of this stage especially, children will take names so seriously that they cannot separate their literal meanings from the things they represent. If a child decides that a wad of paper is the cake to be served at a party, and the mother unwarily throws the paper "cake" into the garbage, it may be just as upsetting to the child as it would be to a bride if someone threw away her wedding cake. At that age the child cannot tell the difference between the symbol and the object for which it stands. By the end of this period, however, the child has learned that language is arbitrary and that a word can just as easily represent one object as another.

In the next stage of **concrete operations** (about ages 7 to 11), children begin to think with some logic. They can classify things and deal with a hierarchy of classifications, they understand mathematical concepts, and they understand the principle of conservation. Preoperational children, for example, have difficulty understanding that a particular animal can be both a "dog" and a "terrier." They can only deal with one classification at a time. But 7-year-olds understand that terriers are a smaller group within the larger group dogs. They can also see other subgroups, such as terriers and poodles as "small dogs" and golden retrievers and St. Bernards as "large dogs." This kind of thinking shows an understanding of a hierarchy of classification. During the concrete operational period, children master several such logical operations before their thinking is qualitatively like that of adults.

The final stage in Piaget's theory is called **formal operations;** it usually begins sometime after age 12. At this point, adolescents can explore all the logical solutions to a problem, imagine things contrary to fact, think realistically about the future, form ideals, and grasp metaphors that younger children cannot comprehend. Formal operational thinking no longer needs to be tied to actual physical objects or events.

PIAGET'S NOTION OF DEVELOPMENT Piaget believed that intelligence is a biological adaptation. It evolves gradually in qualitatively different steps, as the result of countless assimilations and accommodations, while the individual attempts to reach new balances. The mind is active, not passive. Piaget's theory stresses interaction between the biological capacities of each person and the materials encountered in the environment. We all develop as a result of this interaction.

Can the stages of development be speeded up so that, for example, a bright 5-year-old can be taught concrete operations? Piaget called this the "American question" because someone asked it every time he visited the United States. His answer was that even if this were possible, its long-run value was doubtful. Instead, he stressed the importance of giving each child enough learning materials appropriate to each stage of growth, so that no areas of the mind are left undeveloped.

Information-Processing Theory

Piaget has many critics; among them are the *information-processing theorists*. Like Piaget, they are cognitive psychologists because they study thought and the mind. Unlike Piaget, they are skeptical of a theory that is based on qualitatively different stages. They believe human development, including human cognitive development, is a continuous, incremental progression, not a discontinuous one. These theorists resemble learning theorists because they, too, are trying to develop a science of human behavior. They want to identify basic processes like perception, attention, or memory and to describe precisely how these processes function.

Humans constantly process information. We selectively attend to some-thing—perhaps the words on this page. We translate the letters into words and the words into ideas. We then store these ideas for later reference.

Many information-processing theorists have used the computer as a model of the human brain. The computer has "hardware"—the machine itself—and "software"—the programs that instruct its operation. The mind also has hardware—the cells and organs of the brain—and software—the learned strategies for processing information. The computer must process "input," perform certain operations on the information, store it, and generate "output." The mind, too, must selectively attend and perceive, then associate, compute, or otherwise "operate" on the information. Routinely, information must be stored in the memory and later retrieved. Finally, output in the form of responses—words and actions—must be generated.

Some information-processing theorists have turned their attention to children and the aged as a way of studying how these processes develop and decline. Some have been particularly interested in a cognitive activity that they call *encoding*. This is the process of identifying key aspects of an object or event in order to form an internal representation of the event (Siegler, 1986). This internal representation is something like Piaget's "mental image." One developmental question might be, Do children of different ages select different aspects or fewer aspects of an event or object to store in a mental image? Do they select different strategies for encoding or retrieving information?

There are numerous studies on the information-processing capabilities of infants, children, and the aged. We will be looking at several of these studies throughout the book. Only in recent years have information theorists designed these studies to examine the question of how information processing develops or, in the words of some, how the "computer" reprograms itself to work with new material (Klahr, Langley, & Necher, 1987).

Cognitive Development in Social Context

For Piaget, the image of the child is one of an "active scientist" who interacts with his or her physical environment and forms increasingly complex thought strategies. This active, constructing child seems to be working alone at problem solving. Increasingly, however, psychologists are recognizing that the child is a social being who plays and talks with others and learns from this interaction (Bruner & Haste, 1987). In the psychologist's lab, children may work alone at solving the problem that is given to them by the researcher. Yet, outside of the lab, children will experience real events in the company of adults and older, more experienced peers who will translate or make sense of these events for them. Thus, children's cognitive development is an apprenticeship in which they are guided in their understanding and skill by more knowledgeable companions (Rogoff, 1990).

VYGOTSKY   The roots of this branch of cognitive psychology come from a noted Russian scholar, Lev Vygotsky (1896–1934). Americans have rediscovered his work during the past two decades, both revising and expanding it. Vygotsky was interested not only in the development of the individual mind in social context but also in the historical development of the community's knowledge and understanding. The central question for Vygotsky was: How do we, collectively, make sense of our world? He tried to incorporate aspects of sociology, anthropology, and even history to improve his understanding of individual development. Vygotsky concluded that we make sense of our world only by learning the shared meanings of others around us. Together, people construct shared meanings, and these shared meanings are passed down from generation to generation. This is true of simple things like learning how to cook or play sports in the particular style of one's culture. This is also true of more complicated things like the systematic learning of history, mathematics, literature, and social customs. We develop understanding and expertise primarily in an apprenticeship with more knowledgeable learners. We are allowed to participate and are guided in this participation, which enables us to understand more and more about our world and to develop an increasing number of skills.

For Vygotsky, one of the truly interesting questions was: How does the child become what he is not yet? To look at this problem, he defined two levels of cognitive development. The first was the child's *actual* developmental level as determined by his or her independent problem solving. The second was the level of *potential* development determined by the kind of problem solving the child could do under adult guidance or in collaboration with a more capable peer (Vygotsky, 1978). Vygotsky called the distance between these two points the *zone of proximal development* (Rogoff & Wertsch, 1984). He illustrated this concept by studying two children who, on an intelligence test, both had a mental age of 7 years. One child, with the help of leading questions and demonstrations, could easily solve the test items 2 years above his actual level of development. However, the other child, even with guidance and demonstration, could only solve problems a half-year ahead of his actual development. Vygotsky emphasized that we need to know both the actual and the potential levels of development in these children to understand fully their cognitive development and to design instruction for them (Vygotsky, 1956).

For Vygotsky and his followers, cognitive development is embedded in life's social and cultural context. The child's best performance demonstrates that what he or she knows comes from a collaboration with more competent peers or with adults. Barbara Rogoff (1990) describes this process as an "apprenticeship in thinking." Children and other inexperienced learners are allowed *guided participation* in culturally valued activities. The care-givers and companions in these activities structure the child's participation while providing support and a challenge. They build bridges from the child's present understanding to new understanding and skills—thus gradually increasing the child's participation and responsibility. In short, to understand the child's cognitive development, we must examine the processes that exist in the *social construction of knowledge*.

An Evaluation of Cognitive Theories

Cognitive theorists criticize learning theory. They find that the emphasis on "repeated practice" and positive reinforcement is too simplistic to explain much of human thought and understanding. They feel that when people solve problems, they are motivated by their own basic competence, not by a mere stimulus-response reinforcement (Bruner & Haste, 1987).

Cognitive theories respect human rationality and project an optimism not found in learning theories. They consider the human being of any age to be an integrated person who can plan and think through a problem. In addition, they allow us to account for the role that understanding, beliefs, attitudes, and values seem to play in so much of behavior. Many psychologists feel that cognitive theories, in dealing with language and thought, begin where learning theories end.

Cognitive theories have been widely applied to education. They have been especially useful in helping educators plan instruction to fit children's stages of development. The theories suggest ways to determine when a child is ready for a certain subject and which approaches to that subject are most appropriate for a particular age. Donaldson (1979), however, suggests that Piaget may have been too distinct in his stages of development, which may make educators too rigid in their ideas of what children can understand.

Cognitive theories are concerned mainly with intellectual development, and thus far they have been unable to explain all of human behavior. Some important areas still to be investigated include social, emotional, and personality development. Although cognitive theorists look chiefly at the development of perceptual abilities, language, and complex thought, they have not yet explored the individual's potentialities for dependence, nurturance, aggression, and sexuality. Psychoanalytic theory has traditionally been concerned with these areas, studying emotions and their relation to personality development.

psychoanalytic tradition Based on the theories of Freud, whose view of human nature was deterministic. He believed that personality is motivated by innate, biological drives.

THE PSYCHOANALYTIC TRADITION

The theories of Sigmund Freud, the neo-Freudians, and the ego psychologists form what we call the **psychoanalytic tradition.** The source of data for these theories has been primarily clinical case-study material. Freud's notion of human nature is a deterministic one, resembling the view of the learning theorists, but it emphasizes the determinism of innate drives instead of the determinism of the environment. According to psychoanalytic theory, human beings are driven creatures, constantly trying to redirect or channel potent inner forces. These forces, which are evident from childhood, are transformed as individuals develop various forms of behavior. Modern psychologists of the psychoanalytic tradition, such as Erik Erikson, no longer see animal drives as the sole basis for human behavior, but they still draw heavily from the traditions of Freud and the neo-Freudians.

Freud

Sigmund Freud (1856–1939) lived during the Victorian era, and in many ways, his theory was a reaction against his time. Freud's concern was human emotional life, as this was kept well hidden in the society in which he lived. Freud

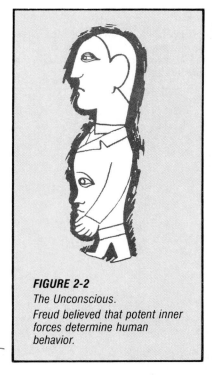

FIGURE 2-2
The Unconscious.
Freud believed that potent inner forces determine human behavior.

psychosexual stages Freud's stages of personality development.

erogenous zones Body areas that serve as the focus of pleasure and that, in Freud's view, change as one moves through the psychosexual stages.

oral stage Freud's first psychosexual stage during which the infant's sensual pleasure focuses around the mouth.

anal stage Freud's second psychosexual stage during which the child's sensual pleasure is related to the bodily processes of elimination. The child is concerned with issues of control, such as "holding on" and "letting go."

phallic stage Freud's third stage of psychosexual development (ages 3 to 5) during which the child's sensual pleasure focuses on the genitals.

Oedipal complex A strong but unconscious attraction of boys in the phallic stage to their mothers.

Electra complex A strong but unconscious attraction of girls in the phallic stage to their fathers.

identification Taking on the behaviors and qualities of a person whom one respects and would like to emulate.

pregenital period The immature psychosexual development of childhood; encompasses the oral, anal, and phallic stages.

Sigmund Freud

emphasized the unconscious as a determinant of behavior. He believed that the biological, or animal, drives, such as sex and aggression, were the primary forces behind human behavior. Freud's assertion that humans are biologically directed, along with his systematic study of the animal components of human nature, were important historically in opening the way for a scientific study of human behavior. Much of Freud's theory looked to childhood for clues about the underlying nature of the personality.

According to Freud, the personality develops in several **psychosexual stages.** The first three stages occur well before puberty: In them, children focus their pleasure in different body areas, called **erogenous zones.** The **oral stage** is the first, and it occurs in early infancy. Here, the child's mouth becomes the center of sensual stimulation and pleasure; infants love to suck things and mouth toys. Later, during the **anal** (ages 1 to 3) and the **phallic stages** (ages 3 to 5), the focus of pleasure moves from the mouth to the genital area.

If children experience too much frustration or too much gratification at any psychosexual stage, they may become fixated on the needs of that stage. Furthermore, the parents' reactions to any of these stages may profoundly affect the child's personality development. For example, if parents are too harsh in treating mistakes in toilet training during the anal stage, the child may develop into a compulsively neat and overcontrolled adult. Parents' reactions at the phallic stage are also critical. At this stage, children generally feel a strong but unconscious sexual attraction to the parent of the opposite sex. This is called the **Oedipal complex** in boys and the **Electra complex** in girls. (The term Electra complex was actually coined by Carl Jung.) Because such desires are clearly inappropriate, they result in anxiety. The child learns to suppress such feelings and reduce the anxiety by trying to become more like the parent of the same sex. This is known as **identification.**

The oral, anal, and phallic stages are part of the **pregenital period,** in which the child's sexual or sensual instincts are not yet directed toward reproduction. The **latency period,** lasting from about ages 6 to 12, is a time of relative calm. Girls play primarily with girls, boys play primarily with boys, and the focus is on acquiring knowledge and skills.

Freud's final stage of personality development is the **genital stage,** which begins during adolescence. Due to biological maturation, the old submerged sexual feelings—together with stronger physical drives—emerge. The goal of this stage is the establishment of a mature adult sexuality that will eventually be accompanied by biological reproduction. If things go well, the individual becomes capable of creating a mature balance between love and work. But this stage, like the others, is profoundly shaped by the resolution or lack of resolution of earlier stages. Unresolved earlier conflicts may reemerge periodically as adult neurotic behavior.

Freud's theory is far more complex than this short summary suggests. But instead of considering it in any more detail, we shall move on to the neo-Freudians, who have had a far greater influence on modern psychology. One of the most interesting and important of the neo-Freudians is Erik Erikson.

latency period The fourth of Freud's psychosexual stages of development characterized by a temporary dormancy in the interest in sexual gratification.

genital stage In psychoanalytic theory, the period of normal adult sexual behavior that begins with the onset of puberty.

psychosocial stages In Erikson's theory, the phases of development during which the individual's capacities for experience dictate major adjustments to the social environment and the self.

Erikson

Erik Erikson's theory of personality development has much in common with Freud's, but it is marked by some important differences. Erikson sees the development of the individual as occurring in several stages, many of which correspond to those of Freud. His model, however, is **psychosocial,** not psychosexual.

Erikson's stages expand upon the drives within the individual and the way in which these forces are treated by parents. In addition, Erikson sees the stages as periods of life during which the individual's capacities for experience dictate that he or she must make a major adjustment to the social environment and the self. Although parental attitudes do affect the way the individual handles these conflicts, the social milieu is extremely important, too (a good example is the "identity crisis" of many modern American Indians who are confused about the society to which they belong). Erikson's model expands upon Freud's in another important way. Erikson's eight stages of development encompass all ages of human life. He sees personality formation as a continuing process throughout childhood, adolescence, and adulthood.

Erikson's book *Childhood and Society* (1963) presents his model of the eight stages of human development. In Erikson's view, everyone experiences eight crises or conflicts in development. The adjustments a person makes at each stage can be altered or reversed later on. For example, children who are denied affection in infancy can grow to normal adulthood if they are given extra attention at later stages of development. But adjustments to conflicts do play an important part in the development of personality. The resolution of these conflicts is cumulative— that is, a person's matter of adjustment at each stage of development affects the way he or she handles the next conflict.

According to Erikson, specific developmental conflicts become critical at certain points in the life cycle. During each of the eight stages of personality development, a particular developmental task or conflict will be more significant than any other. Yet, although each conflict is critical at only one stage, it is present throughout life. For instance, autonomy needs are especially important to toddlers,

Erik Erikson

but throughout life people must continually test the degree of autonomy they can express in each new relationship. As presented, these stages are extremes. No one will actually become entirely trusting or mistrustful; rather, people will develop varying degrees of trust or mistrust throughout life.

1. *Trust versus mistrust.* From early care giving, infants learn about the basic trustworthiness of the environment. If their needs are met, if they receive attention and affection and are handled in a reasonably consistent manner, they form a global impression of a trustworthy and secure world. If, on the other hand, their world is inconsistent, painful, stressful, and threatening, they learn to expect more of the same and believe life is unpredictable and untrustworthy.

2. *Autonomy versus shame and doubt.* Toddlers discover their own bodies and how to control them. They explore feeding and dressing, toileting, and many new ways of moving about. When they succeed in doing things for themselves, they gain a sense of self-confidence and self-control. But if they fail continually and are punished or labeled messy, sloppy, inadequate, or bad, they learn to feel shame and self-doubt.

3. *Initiative versus guilt.* Children at age 4 or 5 explore beyond themselves. They discover how the world works and how they can affect it. For them, the world consists of both real and imaginary people and things. If their explorations, projects, and activities are generally effective, they learn to deal with things and people in a constructive way and gain a strong sense of initiative. Again, if they are criticized severely or punished, they learn to feel guilty for many of their own actions.

4. *Industry versus inferiority.* During the years from 6 to 11, children develop numerous skills and competencies in school, at home, and in the outside world of their peers. According to Erikson, one's sense of self is enriched by the realistic development of such competencies. Comparison with peers is increasingly important. A negative evaluation of one's self compared to others is particularly damaging at this time.

5. *Ego identity versus ego diffusion.* Before adolescence, the child learns a number of quite different roles—the role of student or friend, older brother, Christian, Italian, athlete, or the like. During adolescence, it is important to sort out and integrate these various roles into one consistent identity. The adolescent seeks basic values and attitudes that cut across these various roles. If the child fails to integrate a central identity or cannot resolve a major

TABLE 2–2

Comparison of Freud's and Erikson's Stages of Development

AGE	ERIKSON	FREUD
Birth to 1 year	Trust vs. mistrust	Oral stage
1 to 3 years	Autonomy vs. shame and doubt	Anal stage
4 to 5 years	Initiative vs. guilt	Phallic stage
6 to 11 years	Industry vs. inferiority	Latency stage
Early adolescence	Ego identity vs. ego diffusion	Genital stage
Late adolescence, early adulthood	Intimacy vs. isolation	
Adulthood	Generativity vs. self-absorption	
Late adulthood	Integrity vs. despair	

conflict between two major roles with opposing value systems, the result is what Erikson calls *ego diffusion*.

6. *Intimacy versus isolation.* In late adolescence and young adulthood, the central developmental conflict is that of intimacy versus isolation. The intimacy that Erikson talks about concerns more than sexual intimacy. It is an ability to share one's self with another person of either sex without fear of losing one's own identity. A person's success in establishing this intimacy will be affected by his or her resolution of the five earlier conflicts.

7. *Generativity versus self-absorption.* In adulthood, after the earlier conflicts have, in part, been resolved, men and women are free to direct their attention more fully to the assistance of others. Parents sometimes find themselves by helping their children. Individuals can direct their energies without conflict to the solution of social issues. However, failure to resolve earlier conflicts often results in a preoccupation with one's self—with one's own health, psychological needs, comfort, and the like.

8. *Integrity versus despair.* In the last stages of life, it is normal for individuals to look back over their lives and judge them. If one looks back over one's life and is satisfied that it has had meaning and involvement, then one has a sense of integrity. But if one's life seems to have been a series of misdirected energies and lost chances, one has a sense of despair. Clearly, this final resolution is a cumulative product of all the previous conflict resolutions.

An Evaluation of the Psychoanalytic Tradition

Although the psychoanalytic tradition is often thought of in historical terms, it continues to make important contributions to the study of human behavior. Its basic strength lies in the richness of its holistic approach: its willingness to look at the whole individual—including both conscious and unconscious mental activities—and to deal quite specifically with emotions. Its emphasis on unconscious processes allows it to explore important areas of human behavior that many other traditions barely touch. It is also a rich theory for dealing with interpersonal relationships, particularly the relationships of childhood and those in the primary family unit.

The basic weakness of psychoanalytic theory is inseparable from its strength. Although the theory explores the depths of personality, it is precisely this area that is almost impossible to define or to validate by experiment. The theory draws much of its data from case studies of adults who must subjectively reconstruct their childhoods. As a result, psychoanalytic theory is often vague, unscientific, and difficult to test.

HUMANISTIC PSYCHOLOGY AND THE SELF THEORIES

Humanistic psychology developed in the mid-20th century as a more optimistic "third force" in the study of personality (Maslow, 1968). It reacted against both the environmental determinism of learning theory and the Freudian determinism

humanistic psychology According to this theory, humans are spontaneous, self-determining, and creative; it has close ties with existentialism.

existentialism A 20th-century branch of philosophy that focuses on an individual's struggle to find meaning in his or her existence and to exercise freedom and responsibility in the pursuit of an ethical life.

self-actualization   Realizing one's full potential.

of the instincts. Humanistic psychology and the related "self" theories (which center on the individual's self-concept, the perception of personal identity) challenge deterministic learning and psychoanalytic theories. They point out that even those theorists like B.F. Skinner who deny human freedom continue to make choices and feel responsible for their actions in everyday life. The stated aim of these theories is to form a picture of human nature that is as close as possible to human experience: people who are more than the sum of the parts and more than a bundle of stimulus–response patterns or animal drives.

Humanistic psychology provides a holistic theory of personality and has close ties to existential philosophy. **Existentialism** is the branch of contemporary philosophy that focuses on an individual's struggle to find meaning in his or her existence and to exercise freedom and responsibility in the pursuit of an ethical life. Humanists, therefore, reject the determinism of drives, instincts, or environmental programming. They maintain that people can make choices about their own lives. They seek to maximize human potential.

Humans are set apart from other animals by their superior ability to use symbols and think in abstract terms. Although some of the higher primates, such as chimpanzees, are able to learn to use symbols, their abilities in no way approximate the richness and flexibility of human language and abstract thought. For this reason, humanistic psychologists say that many experiments with lower animals do not tell us much about people. A rat in a maze cannot conceptualize its problem as a human would.

Humanistic psychologists emphasize consciousness, as much as unconsciousness, as a basic human process. They reject the sharp division between the subjective and the objective in psychology. In their view, psychologists must realize that they, too, are subjects and objects of study. People experience themselves, as well as others, as spontaneously self-determining and creatively striving toward goals (May, 1983). This optimism of the humanistic psychologists is in marked contrast to most other theoretical approaches. Let's take a closer look at the humanistic views of Maslow and Rogers.

Maslow

An important psychologist of the humanist school is Abraham Maslow. His theory of self, proposed in 1954, stresses each person's innate need for **self-actualization** — the full development of potentialities. According to Maslow, self-actualization needs can be expressed or satisfied only after "lower" needs, such as safety, love, food, and shelter, have been met. For example, a child who is hungry most of the day will not attend to reading or drawing in school until properly fed.

Maslow arranged human needs in a pyramid, as shown in Figure 2–3. At the bottom are the most basic physiological survival needs; human beings, just as other animals, must have food, warmth, and rest to survive. The next highest are safety needs; individuals need to avoid danger and feel secure in their daily lives. They cannot reach higher levels if they live in constant fear and anxiety. When reasonable safety and survival needs are assured, the next most pressing need is to belong. Human beings need to love and to feel loved, to be in physical contact with one another, to associate with others, and to participate in groups or organizations (May, 1983). Beyond this, they also need to feel self-esteem; they need positive responses from others that range from simple confirmation of basic abilities to

Abraham Maslow

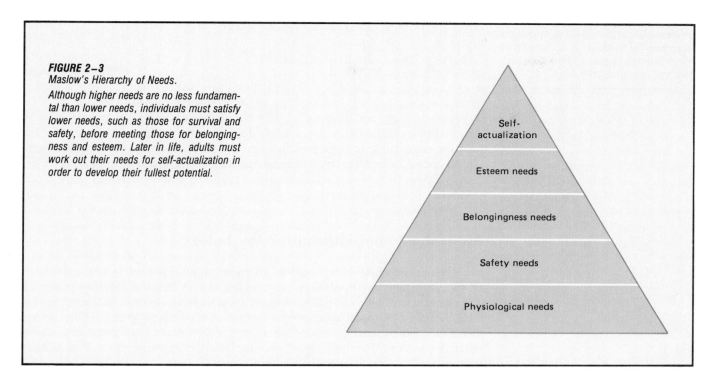

FIGURE 2–3
Maslow's Hierarchy of Needs.

Although higher needs are no less fundamental than lower needs, individuals must satisfy lower needs, such as those for survival and safety, before meeting those for belongingness and esteem. Later in life, adults must work out their needs for self-actualization in order to develop their fullest potential.

Self-actualization

Esteem needs

Belongingness needs

Safety needs

Physiological needs

acclamation and fame. All these provide a sense of well-being and self-satisfaction.

When people are fed, clothed, sheltered, established in a group, and reasonably confident in their abilities, they are ready to attempt the full development of their potential, or self-actualization. Maslow (1954, 1979) believed that the need for self-actualization was no less important to human nature than these other needs. "What a man *can* be, he *must* be." In a sense, the need for self-actualization can never be entirely satisfied. It involves a "search for truth and understanding, the attempt to secure equality and justice, and the creation and love of beauty" (Shaffer, 1978).

Maslow found that self-actualized people tended to be older (most of the fully self-actualized people that Maslow studied were over age 60). They had satisfied their lower-level needs and now were motivated by values that went beyond their own personal needs. They tended to be more spontaneous, creative, self-sufficient, and free of cultural stereotypes and limitations than others. Most had formed close relationships with a few friends and were open to others, but they frequently needed privacy and solitude (Maslow, 1968, 1979). Maslow also found that many self-actualized people have "peak experiences"—moments, or even extended periods, of joy from fulfillment and feelings of oneness with the universe.

Rogers

Another humanistic psychologist, Carl Rogers, has had great influence among educators and psychotherapists. Unlike the Freudians, who believe that human nature is controlled by inner drives, many of them harmful, Rogers (1980)

Maslow's theory of self-actualization stresses the importance of achieving the full development of potentialities in life. Maslow found that self-actualized people tend to be older, and, having satisfied their lower-level needs, they are motivated by values that go beyond their personal needs.

positive regard A "warm, positive, acceptant" attitude toward clients that Rogers found most effective in promoting personal growth.

held that the core of human nature consists of positive, healthy, and constructive impulses that come into play from birth onward. Like Maslow, Rogers is primarily concerned with helping people realize their inner potential. However, unlike Maslow, Rogers did not first develop a theory of personality with definite stages and then apply it to his clients. He was more interested in whatever ideas arose first from his practice. He found that the greatest personal growth would occur if he was genuinely and totally involved with his clients, and if his clients knew that he accepted them just as they were. He called this "warm, positive, acceptant" attitude **positive regard.** He felt that positive regard from the therapist would foster more self-accepting attitudes in the client and a greater tolerance and acceptance of others (May, 1983).

An Evaluation of Humanistic Psychology

Humanistic psychology has had an impact in several ways. It acts as a spur to other developmental psychology approaches, for it stresses the importance of keeping in touch with real life in all its richness. It has had considerable impact on the counseling of adults and on a generation of self-help programs. It has helped promote child-rearing approaches that respect the child's uniqueness and educational approaches that "humanize" the interpersonal relationships within schools (Weinstein & Alschuler, 1985).

As a scientific or developmental psychology, though, the humanistic perspective is limited. Concepts like self-actualization are loosely defined and are not easily used in standard research designs. Furthermore, humanists have been incomplete in their description of these concepts as they apply to different points in the life span. Humanists can define developmental changes over the course of

TABLE 2-3
A Brief Summary of the Theories of Human Development

	ASSUMPTIONS ABOUT HUMAN NATURE	PROCESSES	DOMAINS
Learning theories (Skinner, Pavlov, Watson, Thorndike)	Human nature is neither good nor bad; people simply react and respond to their environment.	Respondent conditioning Operant conditioning Shaping	Behavior modification Conditioned emotional reactions
Cognitive theories (Piaget, Bruner)	Human beings are rational, alert, active, and competent. They do not merely receive information; they also process it.	Assimilation/accommodation Equilibration	Education Moral reasoning
The psychoanalytic tradition (Freud, Erikson)	Human beings are driven creatures, constantly trying to redirect or channel potent inner forces	Psychosexual development Identification Accomplishment of developmental tasks	Study of human behavior, personality, and interpersonal relationships
Humanistic psychology and the self theories (Maslow, Rogers)	Human beings are more than the sum of the parts and more than a bundle of stimulus–response patterns or animal drives.	Self-actualization Positive regard	Counseling of adults

psychotherapy, but they have difficulty explaining normal human development over the course of a life span. The fact remains, however, that humanistic psychology has been an active influence in counseling and psychotherapy and has provided an alternative holistic perspective that is critical of overly simplistic explanations of human thought and behavior.

ethology The study of animal behavior, often observed in natural settings and interpreted in an evolutionary framework.

sociobiology A branch of ethology that holds the view that social behavior is largely determined by an organism's biological inheritance.

ETHOLOGY

Ethology is a branch of biology that studies patterns of animal behavior. Among psychologists, it has stimulated a renewed interest in the biological characteristics that humans have in common with animals. Ethologists stress the importance of studying both people and animals in their natural settings. Just as ethologists choose to study the social relationships of baboons in the wild, not in a wired cage, they also insist upon observing children at play during a school recess, not in a contrived laboratory setting.

Ethologists study patterns of human behavior in natural settings like this playground.

FOCUS ON RESEARCH

MEASURING ATTACHMENT

An important pattern of behaviors studied by ethologists is attachment. Attachment has been defined as a strong bond of affection between one person and another that connects them in space and time (Karen, 1990). Or we might say that attachment is a long-lasting love between two individuals who want to be together. The quality of an attachment indicates the character of a parent–child relationship and is a good predictor of a child's future behavior. For these reasons, researchers are very interested in measuring infant–care-giver attachment.

Attachment can be measured in a number of ways. The classic ethological studies of attachment were conducted by Mary Ainsworth in natural settings. While living in a village in Uganda, Ainsworth observed the way 28 pairs of mothers and infants related to each other. She noted when the babies cried, climbed on their mothers, clung to them, and wandered off on their own. In turn, she also observed how the mothers reacted when their infants made demands.

Ainsworth studied the infant behaviors that "triggered" responses in the mothers and looked at how patterns of nurturance changed over the weeks and months (Ainsworth, 1973). But naturalistic observation has certain drawbacks. Because natural settings are generally uncontrolled from a scientific point of view, it is difficult to draw firm conclusions from observations. Observed behavior may be open to several interpreta-

tions, and causal connections are virtually impossible to establish. For example, is a child's pattern of constant clinging to the mother the result of feelings of love or anxiety about the strange observer?

Laboratory experimentation, which provides a controlled environment for observation, usually offers firmer grounds for making inferences about cause and effect. When Ainsworth returned from Africa, she set up a laboratory experiment, combining aspects of both naturalistic and experimental methodology, known as the *strange situation test*. Her test functions much as a minidrama and is intended to measure the quality of mother–child attachment. The cast of characters in the test is a mother, her 1-year-old baby, and a stranger. The setting is an unfamiliar playroom that contains toys and the test extends through eight scenes.

1. Mother and child enter the room.

2. The pair settle comfortably, and the infant is allowed to roam, explore, and play with the toys.

3. Next, an adult who is unknown to the child enters.

4. The mother leaves unobtrusively, and the adult and infant are now alone in the room.

5. After a few minutes, the mother returns and the stranger leaves.

Ethologists use the same theoretical principles in studying the behavior of humans and animals. They see many similarities between animal and human behavior, and they believe that a similar evolutionary experience has preserved certain behavior traits in humans that are common to animals, too. Ethologists also propose that, like other animals, all human beings demonstrate *species-specific patterns of behavior* that are similar despite cultural differences. Even blind, deaf children smile and babble at the appropriate age, and they demonstrate pouting and laughing throughout their lifetime despite the absence of models to imitate (Eibl-Eibesfelt, 1989).

The idea that social behavior is largely determined by an organism's biological inheritance is the major feature of **sociobiology**, a branch of ethology. Like ethologists, sociobiologists see similarities between animal and human behavior, but they go further and claim that complex patterns of social behavior are genetically determined in both animals and humans (MacDonald, 1988; Wilson, 1975). To support this claim, sociobiologists cite examples of birds' nest-

6. Several minutes later the mother again leaves—this time the baby is alone in the room.

7. The stranger then returns to substitute for the mother.

8. As the mother returns, the stranger leaves.

The entire test runs for about 20 minutes and the interactions, especially the reactions of the infant, are observed through a one-way mirror (Ainsworth et al., 1979; Bretherton & Waters, 1985; Sroufe, 1985).

Prior to the strange situation test, researchers observe the mother and child in the home environment for an extended period. In this way, naturalistic home observations are coupled with more structured laboratory observations to reinforce or complement one another. Even though observation in a natural setting does not yield certainty or hard and fast conclusions, it does provide a realistic frame and often the initial hypothesis that can lead to further and more exacting study. Frequently, initial hypotheses based on naturalistic observations are refined in the structured and controlled settings of laboratory experiments. However, some laboratory settings may be too contrived or artificial; hence, precision may be gained at the expense of naturalness or reality. By joining field research with laboratory study, investigators hope to obtain the best of both worlds.

In her study, Ainsworth found three basic types of attachment. Between 60% and 70% of middle-class babies are securely attached. They can separate themselves fairly easily from their mothers, go exploring, and when their mothers are away from them, readily seek and find comfort with others if they need it. Most of the securely attached infants had warm, affectionate, and responsive interactions with their mothers in the 12 months prior to the tests. Follow-up studies indicate that securely attached children are more curious, sociable, independent, and competent than their peers at ages 2, 3, 4, and 5 (Matas et al., 1978; Sroufe et al., 1983; Waters et al., 1979).

Ainsworth found that about 32% of the infants were insecurely attached and that this insecure attachment took two forms. In one instance, a child avoided his or her mother upon her return during the strange situation test. This child was generally very angry. In another case during the test, a child responded ambivalently toward his or her mother by simultaneously seeking and rejecting affection. The insecurely attached children tended to be heavily dependent on authority figures as they got older (Sroufe et al., 1983). (See Chapter 7 for further discussion of attachment behavior.)

Adapted from Ainsworth et al., 1979; Bretherton & Waters, 1985; Sroufe, 1985.

building—a complex pattern of behavior that birds play out at the right time without the benefit of learning. Sociobiologists generalize from this and other complex unlearned social patterns of insects, birds, and lower mammals to suggest a similar basis for human behavior patterns. They believe that many human behavior patterns that are used to express dominance, territoriality, nurturance, mating, and aggression show a thin veneer of learned culture on top of a genetically inherited biological pattern of behavior. This has caused vigorous debate among psychologists, most of whom say that human social behavior is learned.

The ethologist's interest in inherited behavior patterns resembles that of the psychoanalyst in drive theory, but there is an important difference. The psychoanalyst sees human drives as remnants of archaic, biological drives that must be restrained if civilization is not to be destroyed. Ethologists and sociobiologists say that such drives and their resulting behavior patterns may be an integral part of civilization itself. Perhaps the successful civilization is the one that does not attempt to restrict human biological heritage (Hess, 1970).

Ethology adds another important dimension of analysis. Most developmental psychologists look at the situational and historical causes of behavior. The ethologist sees these but considers an adaptive function as well—the function of the behavior for the preservation of the individual or the species. For example, a baby cries. The situational cause may be that the baby is in pain. The historical cause may be that the baby has been rewarded by care after crying in the past. The immediate function is to alert the mother and to "trigger" her nurturance. Crying is an innate behavior pattern directed toward the specific target of nurturance. Finally, the evolutionary function is survival of the infant despite its immobility, which makes crying, rather than running to the mother, a dominant response (Hess, 1970). Ethologists emphasize the evolutionary function of many behavior patterns, including things like adult responsiveness to creatures that look babyish, flirting behavior as part of a courtship pattern, or aggressive posturing as part of territorial defense (Bowlby, 1982; Eibl-Eibesfelt, 1989). The seemingly universal as well as the culture-specific aspects of this behavior are analyzed.

Ethology's way of looking at human nature is making its mark on psychology. The process of infant–caretaker attachment has been extensively examined through this perspective (see the "Measuring Attachment" box in this chapter and the further discussion in Chapter 7). Numerous studies have been conducted on peer interaction, with a focus on dominance patterns in human groups. Ethologists suggest that a dominance hierarchy among children may cut down on aggressive conflicts in the playground or in the ghetto, much as ethologists have found in other primate groups (Eibl-Eibestelt, 1989). Even cognitive development is examined by ethologists, but here they also pay considerable attention to the biological, species-specific component of learning and thinking. Ethologists suggest that the human brain is prepared for certain kinds of learning but not for others. Complex learning, like that of language, may be done more easily in certain "sensitive periods" of development than it is in others (Bornstein, 1987). Even problem solving is influenced by the human brain's innate sensitivity to only certain aspects of a problem. Studies suggest that 4-year-olds solve problems in a trial-and-error fashion similar to the one used by chimpanzees. Yet, 8-year-old children in all cultures have distinctly human strategies for problem solving (Charlesworth, 1988).

In the 1990s, the research activities of ethologists, both in naturalistic settings and in the laboratory, are active and sometimes controversial.

STUDY OUTLINE

Learning Theories

Everyone has a theory about human nature, but not everyone has the detachment necessary to judge whether the theory fits reality. For this reason, we study many contrasting theories to adjust our own and enlarge our perspective.

Behaviorism. Learning theories take a **mechanistic** and **deterministic** view of human nature. They are based on the belief that the environment shapes and molds human behavior in accordance with the basic principles of learning. In **classical conditioning,** for example, a neutral stimulus (a bell) is paired with an unconditioned stimulus (an air puff) that elicits a response (an eyeblink). After repeated pairings, the response will be *conditioned* to the new stimulus (the bell). Some emotional responses may be learned according to classical conditioning principles.

In **operant conditioning,** the behavior must occur first before it can be strengthened by reinforcement. Skinner systematically extended the principles of operant conditioning and applied them to education. Practitioners in behavioral analysis now design behavior management programs for special populations.

Social Learning Theory. Social learning theory extends learning principles to social behavior. People observe their own and others' behavior and formulate rules on which to base future actions. In this way, children and adults learn sex roles, social attitudes, and moral judgments.

Learning theorists also believe that the learning process is the same for every age level. Human development consists of a gradual accumulation of knowledge and skills during the life span.

An Evaluation of Learning Theories. While learning theory has many practical and useful applications, it does not explain some complex behaviors, such as language learning, which seem to depend on innate mental structures.

Cognitive Theories

Piaget. Cognitive theorists see the mind as active, alert, and equipped with innate structures that process and organize information. Piaget's theory of cognitive development is based on a biological model and describes qualitative differences in the thinking of infants, children, and adults. He believed that development is a result of the process of equilibration, in which the mind tries to fit its structures to the environment. Basic to equilibration are **assimilation** and **accommodation,** in which mental structures, called **schema,** either incorporate new information that fits them or change to fit the information.

These schema develop in four periods and become more complex at each one. The first period occurs in infancy and is called the sensorimotor period because infants use the senses and bodily motion in dealing with the environment. The second is the preoperational period and lasts from ages 2 to 7. During this time, children begin to use symbols for actions, objects, and events. The third is the concrete operations period (ages 7 to 11), during which children begin to think with some logic and use hierarchies of classification. Nevertheless, their thinking is tied to physical events and objects. Finally, the fourth period, formal operations, is reached sometime after the age of 12. At this time a young person's thinking becomes fully logical, symbolic, and abstract.

Information-Processing Theory. Critical of Piaget's stage theory, **information-processing theorists** are cognitive psychologists who study lifelong mental processes, such as attention, perception, and memory, by using a computer model for the brain.

Cognitive Development in Social Context. For Vygotsky and his followers, cognitive development was embedded in the social and cultural context. Complex knowledge is acquired by guided participation in culturally meaningful activities.

An Evaluation of Cognitive Theories. Cognitive theories are concerned mainly with intellectual growth and, so far, do not explain many facets of emotional and personality growth.

The Psychoanalytic Tradition

Freud. The **psychoanalytic tradition** is based on the theories of Sigmund Freud. Freud's theory of human nature is deterministic; behavior and personality are controlled by innate sexual and aggressive drives. Personality develops in several **psychosexual stages.** The first three—the **oral, anal,** and **phallic** —occur well before puberty and are focused on the body's erogenous zones. During each stage the child must resolve certain conflicts and reach a balance between frustration and gratification of needs. The resolution of each stage will determine much of the child's future personality.

Erikson. Erikson's theory of development is similar to Freud's. In his theory, however, personality develops over a series of **psychosocial,** rather than psychosexual, stages. Eight critical periods of adjustment to society and the self take place during a person's life span. The needs of each period are critical at different ages; nevertheless, the needs are present throughout life.

Humanistic Psychology and the Self Theories

Humanistic psychologists like Maslow and Rogers reject the determinism of both learning theorists and Freudians. Because of its close ties to existentialism, **humanistic psychology** views human beings as spontaneous, self-determining, and creative.

Maslow. Maslow proposed the concept of **self-actualization** as an inner drive that comes into play only when more basic needs have been satisfied. Self-actualization is the development of inner, expressive needs by which humans strive toward greater understanding of themselves and the world.

Rogers. Rogers's humanistic theory is also concerned with the full development of human potential. Rogers sees human nature as basically positive, healthy, and constructive.

An Evaluation of Humanistic Psychology. Humanistic theory has been criticized for a lack of scientific evidence to support its claims. It is, however, an active and growing force in developmental psychology.

Ethology

Ethology is a branch of biology that studies patterns of behavior in animals. Ethologists study social behavior in natural settings and consider its adaptive function for the individual, group, and species. Sociobiologists have been criticized for assuming that complex human social behavior is as genetically determined as is some animal behavior.

KEY TERMS AND CONCEPTS

accommodation	behaviorists	concrete operations
anal stage	behavior modification	conservation
assimilation	classical conditioning	counterconditioning
avoidance conditioning	cognitive theory	desensitization

deterministic model
Electra complex
equilibration
erogenous zones
ethology
formal operations
genital stage
humanistic psychology
identification
information-processing theory
latency period
law of effect

learning theory
mechanistic model
modeling
Oedipal complex
operant conditioning
oral stage
phallic stage
positive reward
pregenital period
preoperational period
psychoanalytic tradition
psychosexual stages

psychosocial stages
response consequences
schema
self-actualization
sensorimotor period
shaping
sociobiology
stimulus generalization
structuralism
token economy
zone of proximal development

SELF-TEST QUESTIONS

1. When studying human development, why is it important to have a broad understanding of the various theories on the subject?

2. What are some of the basic assumptions about human behavior made by learning theorists?

3. Describe the process by which behaviorists attempt to build a "science of human behavior."

4. How would you compare classical and operant conditioning? Be sure to use key terms in formulating your answer.

5. How does behavior modification employ operant conditioning?

6. Explain how social learning theorists have expanded the scope of learning theory.

7. How are the concepts of imitation and modeling employed in social learning theory?

8. Explain information-processing theory. How is it similar to other learning theories?

9. What are some criticisms of learning theories?

10. How do cognitive theories differ from learning theories?

11. Describe Piaget's conservation experiment. What is the significance of its results?

12. What does Piaget mean by the "active mind"?

13. Describe Piaget's stages of cognitive development, including his use of schemes, assimilation, accommodation, and equilibration.

14. Compare Vygotsky's contributions to cognitive theory with those of Piaget.

15. What are some limitations of cognitive theories?

16. List some of Freud's assumptions about personality development.

17. Describe Freud's theory of psychosexual stages.

18. How is Erikson's theory of personality development distinguished from Freud's?

19. Name the developmental conflicts which, according to Erikson, become critical at certain points in the life cycle. Discuss the outcomes of these conflicts.

20. What are the strengths and weaknesses of the psychoanalytic tradition?

21. How are humanistic psychology and the related "self" theories distinguished from the theories previously discussed?

22. Explain Maslow's hierarchy of needs.

23. What are some criticisms of humanistic psychology?

24. What contributions has the field of ethology made to the study of human development?

SUGGESTED READINGS

BAKER, B.L., & BRIGHTMAN A.J. *Steps to independence: A skills training guide for parents and teachers of children with special needs,* 2nd ed. Baltimore: Paul H. Brookes Publishing Company, 1989. The basic principles of behavioral analysis are presented in a humane and engaging fashion and in lay terms for use by parents and teachers.

BRUNER, J., & HASTE, H. *Making sense: The child's construction of the world.* London: Methuen, 1987. A slim volume packed full of children's language, problem solving, and social interaction from the perspective of cognitive theorists concerned about the social context of learning.

EIBL-EIBESFELDT, I. *Human ethology.* New York: Aldine De-Gruyter, 1989. This compendium of research and related ethological interpretation of human behavior is well worth a few hours of exploration.

KEGAN, R. *The evolving self: Problem and process in human development.* Cambridge, MA: Harvard University Press,

1982. Kegan integrates aspects of several theories—Piaget, Kohlberg, Maslow, Erikson, and others—to define more fully the continued personality development that extends well into adulthood. Although somewhat difficult for the novice, this is probably a landmark theoretical piece for understanding adolescence and adulthood.

LORENZ, K. *King Solomon's ring*. New York: Crowell, 1952. Lorenz, a popular ethologist, provides fascinating descriptions of the ways and habits of various animals and birds. His accounts are humorous, affectionate, and provocative.

MILLER, P. *Theories of developmental psychology*, 2nd ed. New York: W.H. Freeman, 1989. Miller provides an excellent overview of the major developmental theories as well as a useful discussion of the role of theories in developmental psychology.

ROGERS, C.R. *On becoming a person*. Cambridge, MA: Riverside Press, 1961. In very readable style, Rogers presents a perceptive and hopeful model for personal growth throughout the life span.

ROGOFF, B. *Apprenticeship in thinking: Cognitive development in social context*. New York: Oxford University Press, 1990. An engaging yet scholarly integration of cross-cultural theory and research on the social construction of children's thinking as they participate in cultural activities.

Chapter 3

With him for a sire and her for a dam,
What should I be but just what I am?

EDNA ST. VINCENT MILLAY
"THE SINGING-WOMAN FROM THE WOOD'S EDGE,"
A FEW FIGS FROM THISTLES

CHAPTER OUTLINE

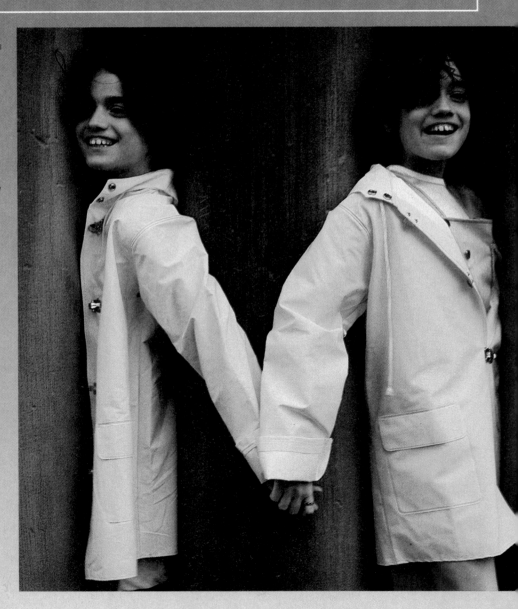

Heredity and Environment

Shortly after Leonardo da Vinci died in 1519 at the age of 67, his younger half-brother Bartolommeo set out to reproduce a living duplicate of the great painter, sculptor, engineer, and author. Since he and Leonardo were related, the father that Bartolommeo chose was himself. He chose as his wife a woman whose background was similar to that of Leonardo's mother: She was young and came of peasant stock, and had also grown up in the village of Vinci. The couple produced a son Piero, who was then carefully reared in the same region of the Tuscan countryside, between Florence and Pisa, that had nurtured Leonardo. Little Piero soon displayed an artistic talent, and at the age of twelve he was taken to Florence, where he served as an apprentice to several leading artists, at least one of whom had worked with Leonardo. According to Giorgio Vasari, the leading art historian of the period, the young Piero "made everyone marvel . . . and had made in five years of study that proficiency in art which others do not achieve save after length of life and great experience of many things." In fact Piero was often referred to as the second Leonardo.

At the age of 23, however, Piero died of a fever and so it is impossible to predict with certainty what he might have gone on to achieve—though there is some indication in that Piero's works have often been attributed to the great Michelangelo. Nor is it possible to say positively how much of Piero's genius was due to heredity and how much to environment. Full brothers share, on the average, fifty per cent of their genes, but Bartolommeo and Leonardo were half-brothers and so would have had only about a quarter of their genes in common. Piero's mother and Leonardo's mother do not appear to have been related, but in the closely knit peasant village of Vinci it is quite possible that they had ancestors in common and thus shared genes. On the other hand, a strong environmental influence cannot be ruled out. The young Piero was undoubtedly aware of his acclaimed uncle; and certainly his father, Bartolommeo, provided every opportunity that money could buy for the boy to emulate him. But Bartolommeo's efforts to give the world a second Leonardo by providing a particular heredity and environment might, after all, have had little influence. Piero possibly was just another of the numerous talented Florentines of his time. (From Peter Farb, *Humankind* [Boston: Houghton Mifflin, 1978], pp. 251–252. Reprinted by permission of Houghton Mifflin Co. and Jonathan Cape, Ltd.)

CHAPTER OBJECTIVES

By the time you have finished this chapter, you should be able to do the following:

- Explain the principles and processes of genetic reproduction.
- Describe the causes and characteristics of genetic abnormalities, and discuss the application of genetic research and counseling.
- Describe contributions and controversies in the field of behavioral genetics.
- Discuss various cultural and socialization processes that influence human development.
- Describe the relationship between heredity and environment in human development.
- Explain the development of gender-role identity and the factors that influence gender-role behavior.

*T*his example illustrates the age-old question of heredity versus environment, which has long fascinated historians and novelists—not to mention developmental psychologists and the relatives of geniuses. Only rarely can we ascribe a personality or behavioral trait, or even a physical characteristic, to a specific hereditary factor; and it is just as rare that we can be sure that a certain environmental influence is solely responsible for any physical or behavioral trait. Almost any behavior requires *both* inherited capacity and

DNA (deoxyribonucleic acid) A large, complex molecule composed of carbon, hydrogen, oxygen, nitrogen, and phosphorus; it contains the genetic code that regulates the functioning and development of an organism.

environmental experience. The important issue is not whether nature or nurture has the greater impact on human development; it is how genetics and culture interact in the shaping of an individual.

The genetic code, or genetic plan, present at birth is one starting point. From this plan we inherit certain physical and behavioral traits from our parents and ancestors. The unfolding, or maturation, of the genetic plan requires a supportive (or at least not harmful) environment, as we will see in the discussion of the prenatal period in Chapter 4. The environment, or the culture, is the other starting point. Our socialization, or what we learn about our culture and how this learning affects us and every other individual, depends on many cultural factors and on how, when, and by whom we are exposed to these factors. In this chapter we will begin to look at some of the processes by which heredity and environment interact.

PRINCIPLES AND PROCESSES OF GENETICS

Cells, chromosomes, genes, DNA, and RNA are all familiar terms. Nevertheless, a brief review of their significance should be helpful before we discuss the processes of inheritance.

DNA contains the genetic code that regulates the functioning and development of the organism. It is a large molecule that is composed of carbon, hydrogen, oxygen, nitrogen, and phosphorous atoms.

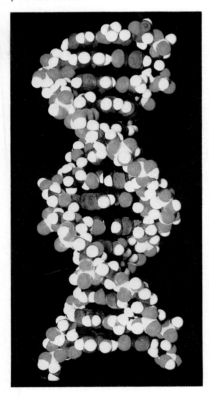

Genes and Chromosomes

Human life begins with a single fertilized cell. Within hours after the sperm penetrates the ovum, the pronucleus of the ovum, containing 23 chromosomes (literally, "colored bodies"), moves slowly toward the center of the ovum; there it joins the pronucleus of the sperm, which also contains 23 chromosomes. The resulting fertilized cell, the zygote, has 23 *pairs* of chromosomes (a total of 46 chromosomes), the number required to develop a normal human baby.

Once the zygote is formed, the process of cell division begins. The first cleavage, or cell division, produces two cells identical in makeup to the original zygote. As further cell division and cell differentiation take place, each subsequent cell that is formed contains exactly the same number of chromosomes as every other—46. Thousands of genes are strung out in chainlike fashion on a single chromosome. Estimates are that there are tens of thousands of genes on each chromosome and close to 1 million on all 46 chromosomes (Kelly, 1986).

Genes are made up of **DNA (deoxyribonucleic acid),** a large molecule composed of carbon, hydrogen, oxygen, nitrogen, and phosphorus atoms. It has been said that "the human body contains enough DNA to reach the moon and return 20,000 times if all of it were laid out in a line" (Rugh & Shettles, 1971, p. 199). The structure of DNA, as shown in the illustration, resembles a long spiral staircase; two long chains are made up of alternating phosphates and sugars, with cross-links of four different nitrogen bases that pair together. The order in which these paired nitrogen bases appear varies, and it is this variation in order that makes one gene different from another. A single gene might be a chunk of this DNA stairway, perhaps 2000 steps long (Kelly, 1986).

Watson and Crick (1953) suggested that when a cell is ready to divide, the DNA staircase unwinds and the two long chains separate by unzipping themselves down the middle of the paired bases. Each chain then attracts new material from the cell to synthesize a second chain and form a new DNA molecule. Occasionally, there is a **mutation,** or an alteration, in these long strips of nucleic acid. In most cases, this alteration is maladaptive and the cell dies, but a small number of mutations survive and affect the organism.

DNA, then, contains the genetic code, or "blueprint," to regulate the functioning and the development of the organism. DNA is the "what and when" of development, but it is locked in the nucleus of the cell. **RNA (ribonucleic acid)** is a substance formed from, and similar to, DNA and acts as a messenger to the rest of the cell. RNA is the "how" of development. Shorter chains of RNA, patterned from the DNA-like mirror images of the chain, move freely within the cell and serve as catalysts for the formation of new tissue.

Because the genes carry the hereditary potential and operating instructions for all cells, scientists have been eager to discover when, why, and how genes give orders to particular cells. Genes are very specific. The gene that produces insulin is present in every cell in the body, but it functions only within the pancreas. What turns it on or off? What will happen if it produces too little or too much insulin? What triggers cells to divide? In the embryo, genetic programming produces rapid cell division. What will happen, however, if cells begin to multiply uncontrollably in the adult, as in a cancer? Understandably, cancer researchers are carefully studying the intricate details of how genetic instructions are turned on and off. Genetic discoveries are being made at a tremendous pace. Within a single bacterium, geneticists have constructed synthetic DNA molecules, and they have explored the triggering mechanisms that initiate the sending of a message to a cell. They have even succeeded in the repair or replacement of malfunctioning genes in individual cells (Verna, 1990).

The chromosomes of an individual can be examined with a chart called a **karyotype.** A karyotype is prepared from a photograph of the chromosomes of a single cell (see Figure 3–1). The chromosomes are cut out of the photograph and are arranged in matched pairs according to length. These matched chromosomes are then numbered. The first 22 pairs, called **autosomes,** contain genes that determine a variety of physical and mental traits. The 23rd pair contains the sex chromosomes; there are two X chromosomes in a normal female (XX) and an X and a Y chromosome in a normal male (XY). These sex chromosomes contain genes that control the development of the primary and secondary sex characteristics and the various other sex-linked traits.

mutation An alteration in the strips of DNA and consequently in the genetic code.

RNA (ribonucleic acid) A substance formed from, and similar to, DNA. It acts as a messenger in a cell and serves as a catalyst for the formation of new tissue.

karyotype A photograph of a cell's chromosomes arranged in pairs according to length.

autosomes The chromosomes of a cell, excluding those that determine sex.

mitosis The process of ordinary cell division that results in two cells identical to the parent.

meiosis The process of cell division in reproductive cells that results in an infinite number of different chromosomal arrangements.

Cell Division and Reproduction

In the process of **mitosis,** or ordinary cell division, cells divide and duplicate themselves exactly. There are a number of steps in this process. First, the DNA of each gene unzips and replicates itself. Each chromosome then splits and reproduces the former chromosomal arrangement of the first cell. Thus, two new cells are formed, each containing 23 pairs of chromosomes exactly like those in the original cell.

The process of cell division that creates reproductive cells (ova or sperm) is called **meiosis.** The reproductive cells formed during meiosis have only one-half the genetic material of the parent cell—23 chromosomes. The rearrangement of genes and chromosomes resulting from meiosis is like the shuffling and dealing of

crossover A process during meiosis in which individual genes on a chromosome cross over to the opposite chromosome. This process increases the random assortment of genes in offspring.

alleles A pair of genes, found on corresponding chromosomes, that affect the same trait.

cards; the chance that any two siblings may receive the same assortment of chromosomes is about 1 in 281 trillion. This figure does not even allow for the fact that the individual genes on a chromosome often make a **crossover** to the opposite chromosome during cell division. It is, therefore, virtually impossible for the same combination of genes to occur twice.

When the fertilization of an ovum takes place, the sex of the resulting organism is determined by the sperm. All ova carry an X chromosome, whereas sperm have an equal probability of carrying either an X or a Y chromosome. It is the pairing of two X chromosomes that determines the female sex and the union of an X and a Y chromosome that determines the male sex.

Combinations of Genes

Nearly all of the tens of thousands of genes in an individual occur in pairs. Alternate forms of the same gene pair are called **alleles.** One gene in the pair is inherited from the mother, the other from the father. Some hereditary traits, such

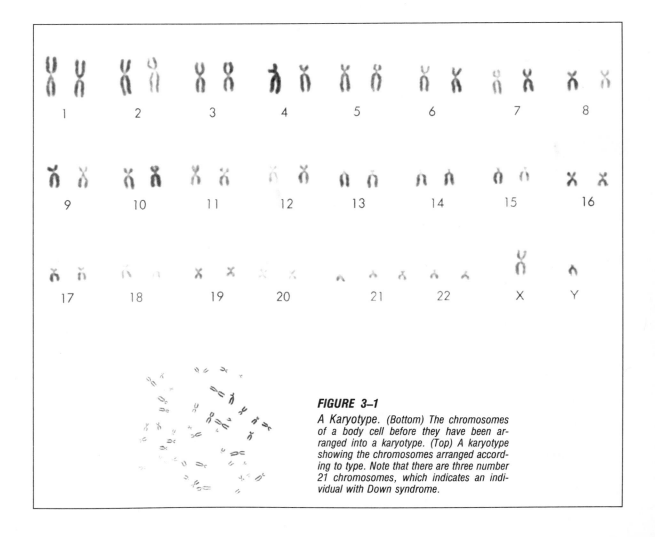

FIGURE 3–1

A Karyotype. (Bottom) The chromosomes of a body cell before they have been arranged into a karyotype. (Top) A karyotype showing the chromosomes arranged according to type. Note that there are three number 21 chromosomes, which indicates an individual with Down syndrome.

as eye color, are carried by a single gene pair. Other traits are carried by a pattern of several interacting gene pairs. For eye color, a child might inherit an allele for brown eyes (B) from the father and an allele for blue eyes (b) from the mother. The child's **genotype,** or gene pattern, for eye color would therefore be *Bb*. But how do these genes combine? What color will the child's eyes be? In eye color, the allele for brown eyes (B) is **dominant** and that for blue eyes (b) is **recessive.** When a gene is dominant, its presence in a gene pair will cause that particular trait to be expressed. Thus, an individual with either the genotype *Bb* or *BB* has brown eyes. The expressed trait, brown eyes, is called the **phenotype.**

In another example, let us assume that the father's genotype is *Bb* (brown eyes) and the mother had blue eyes (which must be the genotype *bb*). All the children of these parents will inherit a recessive gene for blue eyes from the mother. From the father, however, they may inherit either the dominant gene for brown eyes (B) or the recessive gene for blue eyes (b). Therefore, the children will be either blue-eyed *(bb)* or brown-eyed *(Bb)*. If we know the genotypes of the parents, we can determine all the possibilities of genotypes and phenotypes—and the probabilities of each—for their children.

Most traits, including eye color, do not usually result from a single gene pair, but from a combination of many gene pairs—with and without dominance—that interact in a number of ways. For the characteristic of height, for instance, several genes or gene pairs seem to combine with others in an additive fashion to create larger or smaller people, with larger or smaller limbs and other parts. Gene pairs may also interact in such a way that one gene pair either allows or inhibits the expression of another gene pair. A system of various types of interaction among genes and gene pairs is called a **polygenic system of inheritance.** Such systems frequently give rise to phenotypes that differ markedly from those of either parent.

genotype The genetic makeup of a given individual or group.

dominant In genetics, one gene of a gene pair that will cause a particular trait to be expressed.

recessive In genetics, one gene of a gene pair that determines a trait in an individual only if the other member of that pair is also recessive.

phenotype In genetics, those traits that are expressed in the individual.

polygenic inheritance A trait caused by an interaction of several genes or gene pairs.

GENETIC ABNORMALITIES

The normal human organism needs all 46 chromosomes with their usual complement of gene pairs. Usually, a gross chromosomal abnormality, such as a missing or an extra chromosome, is lethal to the fetus.

Chromosomal Defects

A few gross chromosomal abnormalities do occur, however, where individuals survive and exhibit certain characteristic patterns. The most common is *Down syndrome*. These individuals have an extra chromosome, 21, which either floats freely in the cell nucleus or is situated on top of another chromosome in piggy-back fashion. It causes improper physical and mental development.

A variation of Down syndrome is known as "mosaic" Down syndrome. It occurs in the following manner: At some point in mitosis, one cell divides improperly, allocating 47 chromosomes to one new cell and only 45 to the other. Cells with only 45 chromosomes cannot survive, but those with 47 do develop alongside normal cells with 46 chromosomes (Koch & Koch, 1974). Children with this genotype have both normal cells and cells with a Down syndrome pattern. Their impaired learning ability and the extent of their other Down syndrome traits, depend on the number of abnormal cells that are produced; these in turn depend

A boy with Down syndrome. Although mental development is impaired, learning is possible, and some people with such chromosomal abnormalities may have nearly normal intelligence.

on how early the developmental error occurred. Some of these people may have nearly normal intelligence. Even those children with more classic Down syndrome vary in the amount of mental retardation or physical symptoms that they display (Turkington, 1987).

Several abnormalities may occur in the arrangement of the sex chromosomes. One is *Klinefelter's syndrome,* in which individuals have an extra X chromosome, yielding an XXY arrangement. This phenotype usually includes sterility, small external male sex organs, and mental retardation.

Another abnormality in the arrangement of the sex chromosomes results in *Turner's syndrome.* In this condition, one X chromosome is either absent or inactive, making an XO arrangement. Individuals with Turner's syndrome usually have an immature female appearance (because they do not develop secondary sex characteristics), and they lack internal reproductive organs. They may be abnormally short and are sometimes mentally retarded.

A decade ago, popular attention was focused on the XYY pattern. This pattern appears in about 1 in 1000 men in the general population, but it is found in about 4 in 1000 men in prison populations. Physically, men with this pattern tend to be taller than average, and they have a greater incidence of acne and minor skeletal abnormalities. In most studies, the average XYY subject has slightly lower intelligence than the XY control group does. It was hypothesized that men in this genotype have a more aggressive personality and develop differently from males with the normal genotype. However, more extensive examination has indicated that this hypothesis was exaggerated. Although on average these men have a little less impulse control and some are more aggressive with their wives or sexual partners, there is little or no difference between the XYY males and the XY males in a broad range of aggression measurements (Theilgaard, 1983).

Sometimes, a chromosome may break, and the broken portion may be lost in later cell divisions. At other times, the broken portion may become attached to another chromosome. Environmental effects, such as viral diseases or radiation, may trigger such breaks. Chromosome breakage early in the development of an organism sometimes has a very marked effect on the organism's later growth. Certain parts of the body may fail to develop.

The most serious form of chromosomal breakage occurs in an inherited syndrome called *fragile X*. It is so named because a small portion of the tip of the X chromosome seems to be susceptible to breakage under certain conditions. Individuals with this syndrome may have growth abnormalities. Babies may have large heads, higher-than-normal birth weights, large protruding ears, and long faces. Some have unusual behavioral systems that may include hand clapping, hand biting, hyperactivity, or poor eye contact. This syndrome is also associated with mental retardation and various forms of learning disorders. It is estimated that fragile X is the second most common chromosomal defect associated with mental retardation. It is second only to Down syndrome.

Because the fragile X disorder is on the X chromosome, it affects males and females differently. As males have only one X chromosome, far more of them are affected. They also suffer much more seriously than do females who have a second X chromosome that is normal. This particular disability is very curious and is under considerable study by geneticists. It is interesting to note that almost 20% of the males who carry the fragile X chromosome do not experience the syndrome. This is very unusual for an X-linked defect (Barnes, 1989).

Sex-Linked Inheritance

The combining of the X and Y chromosomes provides opportunities for some unusual genetic events to occur. Most of the genes on the X chromosome are not able to pair with a corresponding gene on the much shorter Y chromosome. Males therefore express all traits, dominant and recessive alike, that appear on the X chromosome for which there are no mates, or alleles, on the Y chromosome. These single genes are known as sex-linked genes, and the traits that are related to them are called **sex-linked traits.**

Hemophilia, or bleeder's disease, is probably the most dramatic example of a sex-linked genetic abnormality. It is carried as a recessive gene on the X chromosome. Hemophiliacs are deficient in an element of the blood plasma needed for normal blood clotting. They may bleed for hours from a small wound that would normally clot within 5 minutes; internal bleeding is particularly dangerous, as it may go unnoticed and cause death.

Hemophilia was common among the royal families of Europe, and it has been traced to the mother of Queen Victoria (1819–1901) of England. Victoria, herself, was not a bleeder, but she transmitted the defect. (Women suffer from the disease only in the very rare instance when they inherit the recessive trait from both parents; otherwise, the gene for normal clotting is dominant.) Victoria had four sons and five daughters; the recessive gene was passed to her youngest son, a mild bleeder, and to three of her daughters. As transmitters, the daughters spread the disease through the royal families of Europe.

sex-linked traits Traits carried by genes on either of the sex-determining chromosomes.

nonsex-linked autosomal trait Trait caused by genes on the nonsex-determining chromosomes (autosomes).

Another example of sex-linked inheritance is *color blindness*. A girl will be color blind only if she receives the same gene from both parents. This means that her father must be color blind and her mother must carry the gene for the defect. A boy will be color blind if he inherits the recessive gene on the X chromosome from his mother. He cannot inherit the trait from his father, because he inherits only the Y chromosome from his father, and none of the traits of color blindness are expressed on it. There are three or four different types of color blindness, some of which have different patterns of inheritance.

Other kinds of sex-related traits occur as a result of genes on other chromosomes. A beard is an example of a sex-related trait. Women do not normally have beards, yet they carry the genes necessary to produce them. Thus, a son inherits traits that determine the type of beard he will grow from both his mother and his father. In fact, the dominant traits may be inherited through the mother, so that the beards of father and son may be completely different.

Nonsex-Linked Traits

The vast majority of inherited traits are carried not on the sex chromosomes but on the other 22 pairs, the autosomes. Many disorders are carried as single recessive genes. These include *sickle cell anemia* (a disorder that affects red blood cells and keeps them from transporting oxygen), *cystic fibrosis* (a metabolic disorder that causes an overproduction of mucus throughout the body), and *Tay-Sachs disease* (a disorder of fat metabolism that causes mental and physical retardation and early death). For such disorders to be expressed, a child must inherit the recessive gene from both parents—that is, both parents must be carriers of the **nonsex-linked autosomal trait.** When both parents are carriers of such a disease, approximately 25% of the children will inherit the disorder, 50% will be carriers, and another 25% will not inherit the recessive genes at all. See the example of the inheritability of Tay-Sachs disease shown in Table 3–1.

TABLE 3–1

Inheritability of Tay-Sachs Disease When Both Parents Are Carriers

		MOTHER CARRYING TAY-SACHS GENE		
		T	t	
FATHER CARRYING TAY-SACHS GENE	T	TT normal child noncarrier	Tt normal child but carrier	Note: If both parents carry the recessive gene, the possible genotypes are: TT = 1 chance in 4 (25%) of a normal child who does not inherit the Tay-Sachs gene
	t	Tt normal child but carrier	tt Tay-Sachs diseased child	Tt = 2 chances in 4 (50%) of a normal child but one who carries the Tay-Sachs gene tt = 1 chance in 4 (25%) of a child actually inheriting Tay-Sachs disease

T = normal gene
t = recessive gene for Tay-Sachs disease

An interesting characteristic of these particular disorders is that they occur almost solely within a specific nationality, race, or ethnic group. For example, Tay-Sachs disease occurs primarily among Eastern European Jews. Cystic fibrosis is most common among Caucasians. Sickle cell anemia is found among Africans, African Americans, and some Mediterranean populations. A disorder called *thalassemia* (or *Cooley's anemia,* a deficiency of hemoglobin in the blood) is prevalent among Italians and other eastern Mediterranean groups.

Some abnormalities are carried by dominant genes instead of by the pairing of recessives. In other words, some abnormalities may be caused by only one gene inherited from one parent. One such abnormality is *Huntington's chorea,* which is characterized by progressive dementia, random jerking movements, and a lopsided, staggering walk. This disorder does not appear until the victims reach middle age or later, after the childbearing years. Those who eventually develop this disease, unaware that they are carrying the defective gene, may produce children who also inherit the dominant gene.

The discovery that one is carrying a so-called bad gene is a rather frightening experience. The possibility of transmitting the disease to future generations should be acknowledged when a carrier is considering marriage or deciding whether or not to have children. Most people never know what kind of bad genes they carry, although we all probably harbor from five to eight potentially lethal ones at the very least. Most recessive and nonsex-linked genes will probably never be expressed. Still, should the need arise, we can obtain a great deal of information about our genetic inheritance, and about that of a potential partner, to make intelligent and responsible decisions.

Genetic Counseling

Once we know the dangers inherent in certain types of gene pairings and the tragic consequences of various chromosomal abnormalities, what can be done to avoid them? Genetic counseling is now a widely available resource that can help people evaluate such risk factors in childbearing and thus enable them to make intelligent decisions (Garver & Marchese, 1986).

Predicting a baby's vulnerability to any of the nearly 2000 genetic disorders that have been identified so far is often a complicated process. The potential parents' complete medical records are examined to uncover diseases that can be traced to a genetic abnormality. Each parent is given a complete physical examination, including biochemical and blood tests. A family pedigree is prepared to show which members of the family have been afflicted by any disorder and whether the inheritance pattern is dominant, recessive, or X-linked. If an inheritable genetic abnormality is found, a genetic counselor evaluates a couple's risk of having a baby with the genetic disorder, puts the risk in perspective, and suggests reproductive alternatives (such as adoption) if the couple sees the risk as too great.

PRENATAL SCREENING   During pregnancy, there are a number of relatively safe screening techniques to detect genetic defects in the fetus. Three types of tests deserve particular notice. In *amniocentesis,* about half an ounce of the amniotic fluid is withdrawn through the mother's abdomen wall with a syringe. The fluid contains fetal cells that can be analyzed for major chromosomal and some genetic

gene therapy The manipulation of individual genes to correct certain defects.

abnormalities. This procedure is usually not done until the 15th week of pregnancy, and it takes at least 2 weeks for all of the tests to be completed. The use of *ultrasound* in prenatal screening provides further information about the growth and health of the fetus. Here, high-frequency sound waves are used to outline the shape of the fetus and to form a picture called a *sonogram*. Sonograms can detect structural problems like a small head or body malformations. This procedure, too, is normally conducted around the 15th week of pregnancy and is offered to about half of the pregnant mothers in the United States. A newer procedure called *chorionic villus sampling* (CVS) can be conducted much earlier than amniocentesis, at around 8 to 12 weeks. In this procedure, cells are drawn from the membranes surrounding the fetal tissue and are analyzed in a fashion similar to that in amniocentesis. Because more cells are collected in this procedure, the tests can be completed within a few days. If there is a serious likelihood of a genetic defect, it is clearly an advantage to have test results 10 weeks into a pregnancy instead of 18. Early abortions (before 12 weeks) are much safer and are psychologically easier for the woman. But this technique poses some risks. A small proportion of fetuses abort spontaneously after this procedure (Wyatt, 1985). When this information is given to mothers who are at high risk for a genetic defect, about half choose to wait and use amniocentesis together with ultrasound as a screening technique (Reid, 1990).

PARENTAL DECISION MAKING   The genetic counselor's ultimate responsibility is to help prospective parents digest the information about genetic disorders and make the right decisions for themselves. The type of advice the genetic counselor gives often depends on the specific disease involved. When a genetic diagnosis shows the possibility of Tay-Sachs disease, the counselor explains that there is a 25% chance in each pregnancy that the child will have the disease. For couples who want to have children of their own, the only way to avoid the problem is to test for it with amniocentesis.

The counselor's role in advising sickle cell anemia carriers is less straightforward. In its worst form, the disease causes a general weakening of the body, increased susceptibility to infection, severe pain in the abdomen and joints, the deterioration of the heart, kidneys, and bones, and ultimately death. However, many sufferers lead relatively normal lives—and it is impossible to determine through prenatal testing which form of the disease an unborn child will have.

Advances in Genetic Research

Both the technology of genetics and our understanding of genetic determinants are advancing rapidly. Nearly 2000 types of genetic defects have been identified and carefully catalogued (McKusick, 1986). Some of the most common are cystic fibrosis, cleft palate, clubbed feet, juvenile diabetes, hemophilia, Alzheimer's disease, and sickle cell anemia. Over half of the mothers in the United States are given some option for prenatal screening. Furthermore, all 50 states have at least limited genetic screening programs for newborns.

Although several hundred individual genes for specific traits have been located on their respective chromosomes, corrective **gene therapy**—the repair or substitution of individual genes to correct certain defects—is proceeding at a careful pace. Geneticists have made amazing advances in genetic engineering with respect to plants, bacteria, and even lower animals. Scientists can transplant genetic materials from one species into the cell of another species. The result is a hybrid with characteristics of both donors. This *gene-splicing* technique has been used to create new plants. It is also possible to create a strain of bacteria that will produce a human growth hormone (Garber & Marchese, 1986). Through a process called *cloning,* scientists have been able to duplicate some laboratory animals from just one of the *somatic,* or body, cells. But the use of such genetic-engineering techniques on humans would involve a number of risks and challenges—physical, psychological, social, and ethical. It is appropriate that most professionals are proceeding with extreme caution.

In at least a few cases, however, gene therapy is progressing well and with little public outcry. In the 1970s, a boy named David became famous because he lived in a sterile bubble. He had a severe inherited disorder in his immune system that meant he was liable to die from the slightest infection. This rare condition, called severe combined immunodeficiency (SCID), has now become the target of the first federally approved clinical trials for human gene therapy. In September 1990, a 4-year-old girl with SCID began receiving a billion or so gene-altered immune system cells intravenously in a saline solution. The results have been good—so far. Many other diseases are under study for effective techniques in gene therapy. The most promising candidates are those diseases caused by a single gene that can be isolated, cloned, and transplanted. For cystic fibrosis, the gene treatment may be by an aerosol spray that is applied directly to the lungs. For sickle cell anemia, the cure would be a little more complicated. There must be a delivery of the healthy gene to the blood cells along with another gene that is capable of deactivating the damaged version. Ideally, scientists aim to remove the patient's damaged cells and then alter and return them to the patient. In each case, the genes must reach the right target—for example, the bone marrow, the liver, or cells in the skin. The process is extremely complex (Verma, 1990).

BEHAVIORAL GENETICS

It is one thing to consider the impact of genetics on the shape of one's nose or the color of one's eyes, but it is quite another to wonder if our short-tempered aggressiveness is, in part, genetically determined. Human behavior seems nowhere near as prescribed or preprogrammed as animal behavior, and what patterns do exist seem highly modifiable, depending on the culture and the circumstance. Nevertheless, the study of the genetic components of behavior has been a highly controversial field for decades. Researchers first look at genetic influences on the development of behavior for the whole human species. These influences include the typical patterns of growth along with perceptual and motor skill patterns. The genetic influence is evident beyond the prenatal period. In fact, genetic programming is involved throughout development. Pubescence, for example, occurs in adolescence as the organism becomes capable of sexual reproduction. There are physical aspects of this change that are genetically programmed, as well as some behavioral tendencies that are part of this sequence. Although certain tendencies can be altered slightly with health care and nutrition, the underlying pattern remains (Scarr & Kidd, 1983).

A second approach to the study of behavioral genetics concentrates on

IDENTICAL TWINS REARED APART

Oskar Stöhr was raised as a Catholic in Hitler's Germany and became a Nazi youth. Jack Yufe grew up in the Caribbean as a Jew and spent many years on an Israeli kibbutz. Identical twins who were separated at birth, Stöhr and Yufe did not meet until they became adults. Their lives, although markedly different in some superficial ways, show some startling similarities. Both men doze off while watching television; love spicy foods, liqueurs, and buttered toast dipped in coffee; have overbearing, domineering relationships with women whom they yell at when they are angry; and think it is funny to sneeze in a crowd of strangers. They also have amazingly similar mannerisms, temperaments, and tempos, and, when tested, showed very similar personality profiles (Holden, 1980).

Striking similarities have shown up in other pairs of identical twins separated at birth. Kathleen and Jenny sat in the same positions and laughed and wept over the same things. Both Olga and Ingrid stopped menstruating at the age of 18, when each assumed she was pregnant, arranged to marry the man responsible, found out she wasn't pregnant, and started menstruating again around the time of the wedding (Farber, 1981). When Bridget and Dorothy, both housewives, met for the first time at age 38, each wore seven rings on carefully manicured hands, two bracelets on one wrist, and a watch and bracelet on the other wrist (Holden, 1980).

How many of these similarities are pure coincidence? How many are the product of similar backgrounds? And how many are linked in some unknown way to the hereditary code locked in the genes?

In order to find where the truth lies, Thomas Bouchard and his colleagues at the University of Minnesota have been conducting a study of 48 pairs of identical twins who were separated at birth.

The researchers have compared the 48 sets of identical twins reared apart to a small group of fraternal twins reared apart and to a large sample of identical and fraternal twins reared together (Tellegen et al., 1988). In most cases, the IQ scores of the identical twins were remarkably similar, and even their brain wave tracings were almost the same (Bouchard, 1987). By comparing these twins with fraternal twins, researchers have concluded that perhaps 50% of measured intelligence in adulthood is due to heredity (Plomin, 1990).

Several personality traits were also quite similar in the identical twins who were reared apart. All of the twins in the study answered extensive self-report personality questionnaires. The correlation of traits for the identical twins reared apart was surprisingly high. Traits that were quite similar included sense of well-being, social potency, stress reactions, alienation, aggression, control/caution, harm avoidance, and absorption/imagination. Some traits had lower correlations, including achievement (works hard) and social closeness (intimacy). Whether they had been reared together or apart, the fraternal twins showed far less similarity in all of these traits.

Many of the twins also had similar neuroses. Even when they were brought up in totally different emotional environments, they shared mild depressions, phobias, and hypochondriacal traits. These similarities sparked the researchers into thinking about the role that heredity plays in common neurotic illnesses—a role that has already been established for psychoses.

The researchers themselves are the first to warn against drawing too many conclusions from these findings. They point to the problems—the size of their sample and the fact that most of the twins grew up in similar environments, so their similarities may not be traceable to their genes alone. Moreover, they warn, there is a tendency among researchers and laypeople alike to look for and find similarities in the twins' behavior even when differences are more informative. Bouchard and his colleagues also say these differences show that there is no one answer and that human behavior is a result of both our genetic inheritance and the environment that shapes us (Bouchard, 1987).

individual differences. Over the years, for instance, researchers have examined individual differences in intelligence: What proportion of variation in intelligence is due to genetic programming? It is clear that intelligence is a measure of both heredity and environment—inherited capacities must be exercised in an environmental context. But the study of intelligence has generated heated debate.

Consequently, researchers have shifted recently to the study of personality, where having more of a trait—sensitivity or impulsivity, for example—is not necessarily better. It simply makes a person different. They hope to be able to analyze inherited differences in personality, interests, or even learning style more objectively (Plomin, 1983; Scarr & Kidd, 1983).

ADOPTION STUDIES   One common strategy for attempting to identify genetic influences on behavior is to study adopted children. In the Minnesota Adoption Studies, for instance, adopted children were compared on a number of dimensions with their biological parents, their adoptive parents, and the biological children of their adoptive parents (Scarr & Weinberg, 1983). In addition, the adoptive parents were compared with their biological children. Findings showed that adoptive families were influential when test scores of adopted children were compared to scores of peers *not* adopted—as a group, the adopted children had higher IQs and achieved more in school. When individual differences within the group were analyzed, however, test scores were more closely related to the intellectual abilities of biological parents than to the abilities of adoptive parents. Several other studies have reported similar results (Horn, 1983).

Adoption studies have begun to focus on differences in attitudes, interests, personality, and behavior patterns like alcoholism (Fuller & Simmel, 1986). It might be assumed that such characteristics would be predominantly generated and nurtured within the child-rearing environment—that is, in the adoptive home. Nevertheless, according to several studies, some attitudes, vocational interests, and personality traits seem quite resistant to the adoptive family environment (Scarr & Weinberg, 1983). The reasons for this, however, are complex and may relate more to the subjects' level of social maturity and moral reasoning ability at the time of testing.

TWINS AND PERSONALITY   One of the more popular ways of studying genetic influences on personality is to compare differences among identical and fraternal twins. When identical twins are much more similar than are fraternal twins, it is usually assumed that the similarity is due to genetic influence. Repeatedly, studies of twins find that a wide range of personality traits are at least partly inherited. Three frequently inherited characteristics are *emotionality, activity level,* and *sociability*—sometimes called the *EAS traits* (Goldsmith, 1983; Plomin, 1990). Emotionality is the tendency to become aroused easily to fear or anger. Sociability is the extent to which individuals prefer to do things with others rather than on their own. Traits like emotionality and sociability are usually measured in lengthy questionnaires that are given to the twins during adulthood or to the parents or teachers of twin children. Activity level is observed and rated by the researcher or by the parents and teachers. Similarity in emotionality seems to last a lifetime, but the similarity in activity level and sociability diminishes somewhat in later adulthood, probably due to the many different life events the twins experience when they are apart (McCartney, Harris, & Bernieri, 1990).

Although these studies offer considerable evidence for a genetic influence on different temperaments and personality styles, they are unable to tell us how the genetic components interact with the environment. A quiet, easygoing child experiences a different environment from what an impulsive, angry, assertive child does. The child helps shape or trigger the environment that in turn limits and molds how the child expresses his or her feelings.

Some studies indicate that identical twins are more similar than fraternal twins are in personality traits like sociability, emotionality, and activity level. But how much of this similarity can be attributed to a genetic influence and how much to the environmental influence?

ethnocentrism The tendency to assume that one's own beliefs, perceptions, customs, and values are correct or normal and that those of others are inferior or abnormal.

CULTURE AND SOCIALIZATION

Although we speak of *a* culture and *a* social environment, we must keep in mind that these are not single, fixed entities. An individual's social environment, already complex at the moment of birth, changes constantly. Infants are born into many social groups—a family, perhaps a tribe, a social class, a racial or ethnic unit, a religious group, and a community. Each of these social entities has some shared ideas, beliefs, assumptions, values, expectations, and "appropriate" patterns of behavior. These shared expectations form the culture of the group.

Although some cultural characteristics are universal—food taboos and funeral rites, for example (Farb, 1978)—we shall focus here on cultural diversity and the rich variety of cultural patterns. In examining differences between cultures, however, many people find it difficult not to be a bit ethnocentric. **Ethnocentrism** is the tendency to assume that one's own beliefs, perceptions, and values are true, correct, and factual and that other people's beliefs are false, unusual, or downright bizarre. For instance, members of "primitive" tribes may be regarded by some as simple and unintelligent, exotic, perhaps, but quite "uncivilized"; others may see them as "noble savages," untainted by the evils of civilization and industrialized society. These oversimplifications miss both the complexity and the richness of unfamiliar cultures. But if it is difficult to be objective about distant cultures, it is even harder to suspend judgment on the cultural diversity close at hand. A visitor from abroad who speaks English with a pronounced accent may be accepted with fascination, but a neighbor who speaks with a regional or ethnic accent may be treated with indifference or even hostility.

Alternate Family Styles

The type of family into which a child is born can dramatically affect the expectations, roles, beliefs, and interrelationships that he or she will experience throughout life (Hartup, 1989). Here we shall examine three basic family styles and the cultural patterns that underlie them.

EXTENDED FAMILIES   In an extended family (one having many relatives and several generations close by), children may be cared for by a variety of people—uncles, aunts, cousins, grandparents, or older siblings, as well as by parents. Until fairly recently, many American and Western European children were raised in extended families, and people tended to live out their lives in the areas where they were born. As our society became increasingly industrialized, people became economically and physically mobile, often moving away from their family's base to raise their children alone. The extended family, however, is still a common pattern in many cultures, as it was throughout history—from the peoples of India to the Indians of the Americas.

COMMUNAL FAMILIES   Communal social systems are found in various forms in Israel, the Soviet Union, China, and, to a lesser degree, in Europe and the United States. Here the social relationships take a different form from those of the extended family. The peer group is often an intensely powerful force in the socialization of young children. Communal societies reinforce conformity and

The extended family can offer children many more people to interact with and learn from.

cooperation while discouraging individualism and significant deviance from group standards.

The Israeli *kibbutz* represents one of the most sustained and studied efforts to institutionalize communal child care in any modern progressive society. The kibbutzim were founded by self-declared idealists in open rebellion against their own families. They sought, among other things, to dismantle traditional family structures, to liberate women from sex-stereotyped roles, and to raise children in a collective, unpossessive way. The early kibbutzim were designed to prevent children from identifying strongly with their individual family units. To foster this collective spirit, the kibbutzim relied on a system involving many adults who supervised all of the children's activities. In these houses, four to eight children of the same age were cared for according to group-approved child-rearing methods. Boys and girls were treated alike. The children were taught to share, to think of group interests before individual desires, and to value their roles in the kibbutz society. Children benefited from the attention of the child-care specialists and from their relationships with their own parents, whom they saw daily during extended visiting periods.

Although the traditional kibbutz system deemphasized the concepts of private property and private enterprise, it recognized differences in individual potential and need. The peer group, whose members grew up in daily, intimate contact with one another, developed into a closely knit and supportive social unit. Rather than being isolated from the rest of the community, the children who grew up in children's houses were in fact central to the functioning of the kibbutz (Spiro, 1954). Extensive analysis and testing of kibbutz-raised children revealed very strong peer links and positive, but more diffuse, bonds with parents and adult care-givers (Beit-Hallahmi & Rabin, 1977).

Some communal groups in the United States have attempted a modified version of this child-care method; they have considered their children to be coherent segments of society, not the property of individual parents. Needless to say, a successful communal arrangement depends on a very high degree of consensus among parents on social values, ideals, and lifestyles.

NUCLEAR FAMILIES   The traditional nuclear family consists of a husband, a wife, and their unmarried children, all of whom live as a unit apart from relatives, neighbors, and friends. The husband and father is head of the household, and he spends much of the day away from home, working for the financial support of the other family members. Virtually all family members depend on the father for their material needs. The wife and mother is responsible for housekeeping, cooking, and most of the care and training of the children. Many people in the Western world assume that this pattern is the "natural" and customary family form. In fact, many Western countries have constructed legal safeguards to protect it. In the United States, husbands (but not wives) are obligated by law to support their families. As we have seen, however, the nuclear-family pattern is not the norm even in the United States. In the 1990s, nuclear families account for less than half of all American families. Unmarried women now bear a substantial number of children—over 25% of the infants born in 1988 were to unmarried women (National Center for Health Statistics, 1990). Many children grow up in single-parent families as a result of the continuing high divorce rate. Even in two-parent families, both parents normally work. In 1988, over 50% of the mothers of newborns returned to the labor force within the first year after giving birth (U.S. Bureau of the Census, 1990).

Parents in a nuclear family are responsible for their children's health care, moral training, and economic and emotional stability. Today, spouses/parents often share family responsibilities that once belonged to either one or the other.

The traditional nuclear family has carried a heavy responsibility for child care: health care, moral training, economic and emotional stability. Parents have been expected to meet all these demands with a minimum of outside assistance. The children, primarily influenced by family training, were expected to do as their parents told them. Parents were considered responsible for regulating the influence of the outside world on their children (Keniston, 1977). Now, however, they are influenced by a vast network of social institutions that includes television and the public school system. Parents encounter pressure from stressful jobs, the high economic cost of rearing children, and the advice of doctors, teachers, and other professionals. They delegate a tremendous amount of responsibility for child care to these professionals, but most parents lack real authority over these surrogate care-givers.

THE FAMILY AS TRANSMITTER OF CULTURE   Besides integrating the individual child into the family unit, parents or care-givers in all of the family styles discussed also interpret for the child the outside society and its culture. Religion, ethnic traditions, and moral values are conveyed to children at an early age. In a cohesive, homogeneous society like the Israeli kibbutz, people outside the family reinforce and expand parental teachings. There is little contradiction between the family's way of doing things and the customs of the community at large. In a more complex, multiethnic society, however, many cultural traditions often oppose one another. Some parents struggle to instill their own values so that their children will not become assimilated into the culture of the majority. Parents express many cultural values to their children in their attitudes toward such daily choices as food, clothing, friends, education, and play.

FAMILY SYSTEMS   Families are more than the sum of the individuals within them. They have structure and a hierarchy of authority and responsibility. They have rules for behavior, both formal and informal. They have customs, rituals, and patterns of relationships that persist over time (Kreppner & Lerner, 1989). Each family member may have a particular role in interactions with other family members. An older sibling may be responsible for younger siblings. Each family member may have alliances with some family members but not with others. Two sisters, for example, may frequently take the same side against their brother. The network of interrelationships and ongoing expectations is a major influence on the child's social, emotional, and cognitive development.

Patterns of mutual influence within the family are extremely complex. This is true even in small families. Siblings in the same family may share many similar experiences, such as an overly strict mother or middle-class suburban family values. Yet there is also a set of *nonshared experiences* and relationships. In one series of studies, the relationships between parents and their firstborn and parents and their second-born were compared over a period of time (Dunn, 1986). As one might expect, the relationships between mother and firstborn were often quite close and intense, at least until the birth of the second child. Things then became more complicated. If the firstborn child had an affectionate relationship with the father, this affection tended to increase, as did the conflict and confrontation between the mother and this firstborn. If the mother gave a good deal of attention to the second child, the conflict between the mother and the first child escalated. In fact, the more the mother played with the second baby at age 1, the more the siblings quarreled with each other a year later (Dunn, 1986).

socialization The lifelong process by which an individual acquires the beliefs, attitudes, customs, values, roles, and expectations of a culture or a social group.

Clearly, members of the same family do not necessarily experience the same environment. When adolescents are asked to compare their experiences with those of their siblings, they often note more differences than similarities. Although they may see some similarity in family rules and expectations, there are many differences concerning the timing and impact of the events—a divorce, for instance. Even larger differences occur in how each sibling is treated by the other siblings (Plomin, 1990). In a recent study, parents and adolescents were asked to rate their family environment. There was some agreement on whether or not the family was well organized, had a strong religious orientation, or was often in conflict. But there was considerable disagreement between parents and their adolescent children on how cohesive the family was, how much expressiveness or independence was allowed, and whether or not there was an "intellectual" family orientation (Carlson, Cooper, & Stradling, 1991).

The family may be an important microcosm in which the child learns about the broader cultural community, but the transmission of this culture is not simple. This is due in part to the complex nature of the family system itself.

Socialization Processes

These parental influences are just one element in the larger process of socialization. **Socialization** is the lifelong process by which individuals learn to become members of a social group, whether a family, a community, or a tribe. Becoming a member of a group involves recognizing and dealing with the social expectations of others—family members, peers, teachers, and bosses, to name only a few. Whether tense and anxiety-producing or smooth and secure, our relationships with these *socialization agents* determine what we learn and how well we learn it. Socialization also forces individuals to deal with new situations. Infants are born into families; children go to school; families move to new neighborhoods; adolescents begin to date; people marry and raise families; older people retire from jobs; friends and relatives get sick or die. Adapting to the major changes, or milestones, throughout life is an important part of socialization.

Children can take an active part in their own socialization. They have their own personalities and ways of interacting with their families and environments. As children learn, they can modify the behavior of their parents and other socializing agents. Even very young infants are capable of making socialization a two-way process.

Sometimes socialization is almost automatic, and sometimes it takes a great deal of effort. But how does it happen in the first place? How do people learn to adapt to new and different situations? To understand the process, we must consider the various social factors that influence behavior, particularly those that influence the development and control of the emotions.

LEARNING PROCESSES   Depending on the culture, a child can develop a wide range of human behaviors—passive or aggressive, dependent or independent, liberal or conservative, vegetarian or meat-eating. Much of the behavior that children adopt is the behavior that their social, ethnic, or religious group considers appropriate; that is, behavior that will help the child to become an individual who fits into the culture. Let us consider processes by which children will become fully participating members of society.

Receiving a reward reinforces behavior. Here, a teacher is using this method to encourage her students to do well in school.

Reward and Punishment.   It is no secret that most people learn to behave according to what "pays." Reward patterns commonly produce or reinforce behavior patterns. Thus, children who receive attention when they whine are very likely to become chronic whiners. The effects of punishment, on the other hand, are not so easily interpreted. Clearly, punishment is a problematic child-rearing method. Although it seems to be fairly effective in suppressing certain types of behavior, it may cause various far-reaching side effects, some of which may be even less desirable than the original offense. For example, care-givers who use physical punishment to discipline their children actually serve as aggressive models. Their children may learn to imitate the aggression in addition to—or rather than—learning to stop the behavior that provoked the punishment (Parke & Slahy, 1983).

Another effect of punishment involves anxiety—the feeling of fear without an awareness of the cause. If children are punished for aggressive behavior (or for dependent behavior), they often learn to feel anxious not only about those "bad" or "babyish" behaviors, but also about the angry feelings that went with them. They may learn these associations so well that as adults they regularly experience anxiety whenever they feel angry (or dependent), whether their feelings are justified or not. Still another potential effect of punishment is suppression of the wrong response or avoidance of the wrong part of the situation. For instance, if the father is always the one who does the spanking, the child may learn to avoid the father instead of the behavior that brought about the punishment. If this happens, the father will probably have less influence on the child's behavior than the mother.

Of course, punishment may be useful in certain situations. It can be a fairly effective means of suppressing behavior, especially when appropriately combined with rewards for correct behavior. But it must be closely related to the behavior that is being punished and should be carefully and consistently administered. In any event, the dangers of using punishment should always be weighed against the possible benefits.

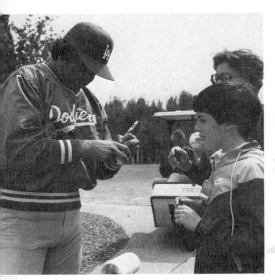

Many children choose famous athletes as models for behavior.

Modeling.   From early childhood on, we observe the actions of those around us and copy whole behavior patterns, often down to the most minute detail. Modeling (imitation) is also practiced by adults. We see it in the customs and conventions that shape many of our thoughts and actions and in the fads, fashions, and trends that regularly sweep whole countries.

The influence of modeling on learning has been the subject of a number of studies. Research has shown that certain models are more influential than others because they possess certain characteristics that invite imitation. The three most important are power, nurturance, and perceived similarity (Bandura, 1977). *Power* is the ability to control desirable resources and to exert influence over others. Studies involving a relatively powerful adult, a relatively powerless adult, and a child reveal that the child is more likely to imitate the powerful adult (Bandura, 1977). *Nurturance,* or affectionate care and attention, also plays a part. Children imitate the warm, rewarding, affectionate model rather than the cold, punitive, distant one. *Perceived similarity* with the model is a significant factor in the effectiveness of modeling. Boys tend to model other boys or men; blacks tend to model other blacks; muscular, athletic children tend to imitate athletes.

Modeling continues through the entire life span. At any level, imitation is a process that constantly shapes and augments our lives. Although training and modeling are responsible for a large portion of social learning, certain complex behavioral phenomena, which develop over time, may not be fully explainable in these terms. Many theorists find the concept of identification useful in explaining complex developmental patterns.

SOCIAL CONCEPTS   We learn more than just isolated patterns of behavior. With the help of older or more competent peers, we also learn to make sense of social events and social relationships. The preschooler is not able to understand the full meaning of "friendship" or "justice" or a wedding ceremony. But adults and older peers provide a framework, or structure, for interpreting social events as they happen. Every day, children and adults must engage in social problem solving. They define social goals (making a friend), get relevant information, select the social strategies (asking, bribing, grabbing), and make some judgment about these strategies (Is it socially acceptable?). Clearly, the success and sophistication of social problem solving depend on the sets of social concepts and social knowledge that a person has (Rose-Krasnor, 1988).

Two kinds of social concepts are essential to social problem solving. First, the child or adult must be able to make accurate *social inferences* about others' motives, emotions, or anticipated actions. Second, the individual needs basic *social knowledge* of things like norms, roles, or relationships. When adults visit foreign countries, they often lack many aspects of both kinds of social concepts. Often, they can overcome their lack of knowledge with the tutoring of a more experienced peer. The development of social concepts for children, however, involves the interaction of the child's developing cognitive abilities and the availability of more experienced adults to provide structure for the child's growing understanding (Hartup, 1989; Rogoff, 1990).

AN INTEGRATIVE SELF-CONCEPT   Most people spend a good deal of time thinking about themselves. They tend to interpret things subjectively, to see the world as it affects them personally. They may also worry about the way they affect others, about their appearance, their health, and their happiness. On another level, people may wonder about "who they are" and "where they are going." Such terms as ego, identity, and self-fulfillment have become part of the popular vocabulary, and the concepts they represent indicate important personal attitudes toward the self. How do these attitudes develop? How are they maintained? Theories of the self-concept are far too numerous and complex to study here, but we can trace the evolution of *self-awareness* through various life stages.

Infants are initially unable to differentiate between the self and the world around them. Gradually, however, they develop a body awareness; they realize that their bodies are separate and uniquely their own. Much of infancy is devoted to making this distinction. Later, young children compare themselves with their parents, peers, and relatives. They know that they are smaller than their older brothers and sisters, darker or fairer, fatter or thinner.

They can demonstrate their capabilities. Also, they can identify their preferences and their possessions (Harter, 1988). By middle childhood, self-knowledge expands to include a range of trait labels. A fifth grader may describe herself as popular, nice, helpful, smart in school, and good at sports. These self-attributes are logical, organized, and generally consistent. In adolescence, self-knowledge becomes more abstract, and there is considerable concern about how others regard us. For example, an adolescent is able to analyze the fact that she is usually a sensitive and understanding person who can sometimes be selfish. She is also aware that her selfishness may annoy her family and friends (Harter, 1988). Adolescents and adults formulate a very real, integrated idea of who they are within the social world. As we learned in Chapter 2, a major task for the adolescent is putting together an identity. It is during adolescence that the intellect becomes capable of formulating philosophies and theories about the way things are and the way they ought to be. With this new mental ability, adolescents begin to develop a sense of "ego identity"—a coherent, unified idea of the self.

The self-concept is crucial in the development of an integrated personality. An individual's self-concept, even as a child (and certainly by adulthood), must be fairly consistent, or the personality will be fragmented and the individual will suffer from "role confusion." The self-concept includes both a real and an ideal self—that is, the self we believe we are and the self we think we ought to be (Mead, 1934). The individual who perceives these selves as similar will be better prepared to mature and adapt than the one who sees the real self as much inferior to the ideal one.

As the social context helps to form the individual's self-concept, the self-concept is, in turn, influencing socialization. We tend to study our own behavior and attitudes and to monitor them according to our ideas about ourselves. If an attitude or value seems to fit in, we are likely to adopt it. If it is inconsistent with our idea of the self, we will filter it out no matter how much these inconsistent attitudes are rewarded or how powerful our role models are. In filtering out cultural behavior that is inconsistent with the self-image, a process of *integration* takes place. In other words, when the self-concept becomes strong enough to help dictate our behavior, it becomes an agent of socialization as well as a product of it.

The self-concept may be self-rewarding or self-punishing. When individuals behave in a way that is consistent with their self-image, they do not necessarily need a pat on the back from society; they feel pleased with themselves and are thus rewarded. For example, a boy who considers himself a good athlete will enjoy praise from his peers after playing a good game, but he will also gain satisfaction from performing in a way that is consistent with his self-image, even if he is just practicing alone. Self-concepts can also be self-punishing. People who perceive themselves as failures may unconsciously sabotage their own endeavors in order to maintain that image. Drastic change in an image—even for the better—can be very upsetting. A child with buck teeth may emerge from braces in acute psychological distress despite a radically improved appearance. The reflection in the mirror may no longer be consistent with the homely self-image, and the result may be a new struggle for identity.

THE INTERACTION OF GENETICS AND CULTURE

As mentioned in the introduction to this chapter, the ancient argument of heredity versus environment is still raging and is likely to continue. The important issue is not which influence on the personality is more powerful, but how heredity and environment interact in the development of human behavior. Studies of adoption and of twins show that to some extent our genes influence social traits like sociability, emotionality, and activity level. These inherited traits, in turn, influence the environments that we seek, the things that we attend to, and how much we learn. But children also help tailor their environment in other ways. For example, psychologists Sandra Scarr and Kathleen McCartney believe that children interact with their environment in three different ways, depending on their individual genetic predispositions. In the *passive* interaction pattern, the parents give and the child accepts both the genes and the environment, either favorable or unfavorable, for the development of particular abilities. A musical child in a musical family, for instance, receives an enriched musical environment in which to develop his skills. In an *evocative* interaction pattern, the child evokes particular responses from his parents and others based on his genetically influenced behavior. An active, sociable, extroverted child will demand responses from parents and teachers. A quiet, passive, shy child may be ignored. Finally, Scarr and McCartney (1983) suggest that an *active* relationship may exist between the child and his environment; that is, the child may actively seek particular environments (peers, opportunities) that are compatible with his temperament, talents, or predispositions.

Our physical appearance—whether we are tall or short, dark or light, plain or beautiful—is genetically determined, but the way in which our culture views these physical attributes can have a profound effect on personality development. In our culture, for example, people who are tall are often given more power and authority, not necessarily because they are worthy of it, but because they literally "stand head and shoulders" above the rest of us. For the same sort of cultural reasons, a beautiful, rugged child with learning disabilities who appears to have no disabling characteristics may be treated as if no handicap exists at all. In other words, inherited traits may be admired or not, depending on current cultural attitudes toward physical appearance. This makes it even more difficult to separate the effects of genetics and culture. For instance, the muscular, handsome boy who is not particularly intelligent may develop more self-confidence and become a more capable person because everyone around him believes that muscular, handsome males must be capable.

The interaction of heredity and environment may begin immediately with the newborn infant. T. Berry Brazelton and his students have spent several years

FOCUS ON RESEARCH

CHILDREN WHO SURVIVE

Throughout history children have been forced to grow up in seemingly brutalizing environments. Perhaps the major care-giver is mentally ill, or alcoholic, or abusive. Children may be exposed to oppressive poverty, overcrowding, or criminality. Some children experience repeated losses through war and disasters, whereas others are physically abused or seriously neglected. Usually, these unfortunate children develop lifelong personality scars. They may feel insecure, lonely, and helpless. As adults, these individuals are more likely to become child abusers, criminals, or drug addicts. Some may suffer with mental illness, whereas others may be unable to sustain meaningful relationships. But even the casual observer will note that some children survive such devastating childhood experiences without serious scars—they succeed despite their environments. Why is it that these children seem *invulnerable* to their oppressive experiences? What factors help to make children resilient? How do they learn strategies for coping with enormous stress? Perhaps if we understood these children better we could help other children in less extreme environments to develop more adequate coping strategies.

Norman Garmezy tells of a preadolescent boy growing up in the slums of Minneapolis (Pines, 1979). He lives in a run-down apartment building with his father, an ex-convict who is dying of cancer; an illiterate mother; and seven brothers and sisters, two of whom are retarded. Despite this environment, the boy's teachers report that he is unusually competent, performs well academically, and is liked by most of his classmates. How does he manage?

After studying hundreds of such children, researchers have identified certain characteristics that these resilient or seemingly invulnerable children share. First, they are *socially competent*. They seem to be at ease with both peers and adults. Adults often describe them as appealing or charming, and willing to learn from adults. Second, these children are self-confident. They see themselves as effective. They look at problems as challenges, and they believe that they have the ability to master new situations. Garmezy provides an example. A young girl wanted to bring her lunch to school like other children did, but there was nothing at home to put between the slices of bread. Not discouraged, she made bread sandwiches. After this, whenever she was forced to "make do," or she encountered a difficult situation, she would tell herself to "make bread sandwiches." Third, these children often are very independent. They think for themselves, and they listen to adults, but they are not necessarily dominated by them. Fourth, Michael Rutter (1984) emphasizes that these children usually have a few good relationships that provide security (Pines, 1984). These relationships may be with peers, or with a teacher, an aunt, or a neighbor. Finally, these children are achievers. Some children do well scholastically, whereas others become good athletes, artists, or musicians. They enjoy positive experiences of achievement—they learn that they can succeed and that they can affect their environment.

There is still a great deal that we don't know about resilient children. Clearly the interplay between these children's temperament and talents and their life circumstances is far more complex than can easily be discovered in one or two studies. Nevertheless, perhaps the research on resilient children will help us understand children in more normal situations as they learn coping strategies for the stress of everyday life (Anthony & Cohler, 1987).

---

studying individual differences in newborn infants all over the world. They've studied African, Asian, Latin American, European, and American infants. In one study, Brazelton compared Zambian infants and caucasian American infants (Lester & Brazelton, 1982). Many of the newborn Zambian infants were undernourished and dehydrated at birth. Their behavior reflected this physical state. They exhibited poor visual following and less motor activity, and they had poor head control. The Zambian culture, however, expected newborns to be vigorous, and so the parents ignored the limp behavior of the infants and handled them as if they were more responsive than they actually were. The infants were breast-fed frequently and on demand, and they showed rapid weight gain. Within a couple of weeks, the infants had become highly responsive, sturdy neonates. The American infants, on the other hand, were considerably stronger at birth. Most stayed in the hospital for 3 days (as compared to the Zambian infants, who went home the day after they were born), and they were handled gently at home. They were fed every 3 or 4 hours and were involved in little play activity. These infants changed very little in their general responsiveness or activity over the first 2 weeks.

It seems clear, then, that genetic endowment by itself does not determine neonatal behavior. The genetic endowment, the prenatal environment, the mother's reproductive and obstetric history, and the care-giving system all play a role in determining behavior.

The interaction of genetics and culture can perhaps be most clearly seen in the matter of gender. We inherit our gender, but from the point of conception, it is affected by our social environment. A crucial balance of masculinizing hormones at a critical period in prenatal development determines whether a male fetus will develop male or female genitals. If for some reason these hormones are not present at the right time, the fetus will develop female genitals, even if it is a genetic (XY) male. In short, the genetic code is not always followed exactly.

GENDER-ROLE IDENTITY

Orthodox Jewish boys thank God daily that they were not born female. Many of the world's other religions also believe women to be inferior in many ways. But what does being born female imply? Gender is genetically determined, and some suggest that men and women are inherently and dramatically different in intellect, personality, adult adjustment, and style—primarily because of genetic programming. The opposite point of view contends that men and women are different because of the way they are treated by their parents, their teachers, their friends, and their culture throughout life. When we argue about whether genetics or culture is more important in determining gender-role identity, we are probably addressing the wrong issue. Genetics and culture may set the outer limits of gender-role identity, but they interact like two strands of a rope in forming personality or psychosexual identity. We need to look more closely at this interplay throughout the life span.

Although gender-role identity is established in early childhood, it remains a developmental issue well into adulthood. Gender-role identity is perhaps our most fundamental self-concept, but it is not a permanent, rigid personality trait. Before we consider how gender role identity can change as a result of life situations, let us examine some of the clear differences between the genders and how these genetic "givens" may determine some aspects of behavior.

Male–Female Differences

Studies have shown that male babies, on average, are born slightly longer and heavier than are female babies. Newborn girls have slightly more mature skeletons, and they seem to be a bit more responsive to touch. As toddlers, boys are a bit more aggressive, and girls have a slight edge in verbal abilities. By age 8 or 10, boys are beginning to outperform girls in spatial skills and in mathematics. By age 12, the average girl is well into the adolescent growth spurt and maturation, while the average boy is still considered a preadolescent, physically. By mid-adolescence, the girl's superiority in verbal skills increases, and the boy's edge in spatial skills and mathematics increases. By age 18, the average female has roughly 50% less muscular strength than the average male. In adulthood, the male body carries more muscle and bone. The average female body carries more fat as insulation. There are built-in health advantages for women, including more pliable blood vessels and the ability to process fat more efficiently. By middle age, males are succumbing much faster to health hazards, such as emphysema, arteriosclerosis, heart attacks, liver disease, homicide, suicide, or drug addiction. By age 65, there are only 68 men alive for every 100 women; at age 85, women outnumber men almost two to one. At the age of 100, there are five times as many women as there are men (McLoughlin et al, 1988).

Many of these differences between males and females appear to be genetically caused. For example, Maccoby and Jacklin (1980) suggest that the greater aggressiveness in males may be due to their prenatal exposure to higher levels of some sex hormones. Tieger (1980) disagrees and states that there is no biological predisposition toward aggressiveness in males; rather, the difference in aggressiveness between males and females is due to sex-role socialization. A more recent review (Hyde, 1984) suggests that even these "well-established" differences between males and females in aggression—as well as in mathematical skills and verbal abilities—should be looked at with caution. After examining hundreds of studies, Hyde concluded that the differences noted between the average male and the average female were not found consistently.

Equally important are the findings in areas where males and females do *not* differ. Ruble (1988) reviewed many studies on sex-role differences and noted areas in which differences were not established. There appeared to be no consistent differences due to gender, for example, in sociability, self-esteem, motivation to achieve, or even in rote learning and certain types of analytical skills.

Furthermore, the differences that actually exist between males and females are small, often less than 5% of the full range. In many studies conducted in the mid-1980s, these tendencies were not as strong as previously believed (Halpern, 1986; Ruble, 1988). Men average only slightly higher in activity level, aggression, or mathematical reasoning, and women score only slightly higher in empathy. What is more, many of the personality differences that do exist are modifiable with training, with the situation, or with changes in cultural expectations.

Gender and Socialization

There are at least two interrelated components of what the child learns about his or her gender: *gender-related behaviors* and *gender concepts*. Social learning theorists have focused on how gender-appropriate behaviors are learned and combined into a sex role, or gender role. (Because the term "sex" has many meanings, there is some preference for the use of the word "gender" when we talk about maleness or femaleness. Some major authors, though, continue to use the terms "sex" and "gender" interchangeably [Ruble, 1988].) Cognitive theorists, in contrast, focus on how the child comes to understand gender-related concepts and

Males appear to excel in visual-spatial abilities, whereas females are believed to be superior in verbal abilities. Recent studies, however, suggest that the differences between the average male and the average female are small.

how he or she develops a gender identity. Let's begin by looking at the acquisition of the culturally defined behaviors that make up a sex (gender) role.

SEX-TYPED BEHAVIOR   In most cultures, children display clear sex-typed behavior by 5 years of age. Indeed, by age 3 many children have learned some sex-specific behaviors (Weinraub et al., 1984). In nursery schools, for example, girls are often observed playing with dolls, helping with snacks, showing greater interest than boys in art and music. Boys in nursery schools can be found building bridges, roughhousing, and playing with cars and trucks. Pitcher and Schultz (1983) found this clear differentiation among 2- and 3-year-olds, noting that sex-specific behaviors became stronger by the time children reached age 4 or 5.

Sometimes, these sex-typed behaviors are exaggerated or stereotypical. **Gender-role stereotypes** are rigid, fixed ideas of what is appropriate masculine and feminine behavior. They imply a belief that "masculine" and "feminine" are two distinct and mutually exclusive categories and that an individual's behavior must be one or the other. These ideas pervade nearly every culture. In the United States, for instance, parents expect their male children to be "real boys"—reserved, forceful, self-confident, tough, realistic, and assertive—and their female children to be "real girls"—gentle, dependent, high-strung, talkative, frivolous, and imprac- tical (Bem, 1975; Williams, Bennett, & Best, 1975). Some children are put under strong social pressure to conform to these gender-role stereotypes, regardless of their natural dispositions.

The learning of gender roles begins in infancy. Kagan (1971) reports that mothers respond more physically to their boys but more verbally to their girls when their infants babble. These differences in how the two sexes are treated are clearly detectable by the time a child is 6 months old, at least in Kagan's Boston-area study. A similar study conducted 20 years later in Montreal finds that the rooms and toys provided for infants of each sex are quite stereotyped. Parents still expect active, vigorous play with objects from their boys, and quieter play with dolls from their girls (Pomerleau et al., 1990). In many cases, however, studies are not necessary. Many care-givers recognize that their responses toward a 1-year-old boy differ from those used with a 1-year-old girl. It is not simply a matter of pink and blue blankets; often, it is hundreds of little things every day—the way children are held, how often they are picked up, how they are talked to, the kinds of things that are said to them, the amount of help they are given, how care-givers respond to crying. All of these behaviors are often subtly influenced by the child's sex.

How are gender roles learned? The processes of reward and punishment and modeling for appropriate or inappropriate behavior begin early in infancy. Society's baby boys are socialized toward a masculine stereotype of physical activity and prowess. Smith and Lloyd (1978) studied the behavior of mothers with 6-month-old infants who were not their own. The babies were "actors": Girls were sometimes presented as boys or boys as girls, as well as being presented as their true sex. Invariably, mothers encouraged the perceived boys more than the perceived girls in walking, crawling, and other physical play. Girls were handled more gently and were encouraged to speak. As children get older, parents consistently react more favorably when their children engage in behavior that is appropriate to their sex.

Fathers may be particularly important in the development of the child's gender role (Honig, 1980; Parke, 1981). While fathers teach children of both sexes to become more independent and autonomous, they also, more than mothers,

gender-role stereotypes Rigid, fixed ideas of what is appropriate masculine or feminine behavior.

Children begin learning roles during infancy. By the time they are 6 years old, they have very definite ideas about proper behavior for boys and girls.

teach specific gender roles by reinforcing femininity in daughters and masculinity in sons. It was once thought that fathers were important only in teaching their sons masculine behavior, and this seems to be somewhat true in the preschool period. Boys whose fathers have left before they reach age 5 are often more dependent on their peers and less assertive (Parke, 1981). For girls, the effect of father absence is more evident during adolescence. Effective fathers help their daughters learn to interact with men in appropriate ways (Lamb, 1979; Parke, 1981).

GENDER CONCEPTS   From the time they are toddlers, children are learning concepts like "boy," "girl," "man," or "woman," and then more specific concepts like "tomboy" and "sissy." Sometimes, these gender-based cultural standards, or stereotypes, are called *gender schema* (Levy & Carter, 1989). It is generally believed that the development of such gender schema is partly a result of the child's cognitive developmental level and is partly due to the particular aspects of the culture that the child is able to observe. Among the many concepts learned is the child's own gender identity. This gender identity develops in a particular sequence over the first 7 or 8 years of life. Children learn to label themselves "boy" or "girl" at an early age. They do not understand that they will be male or female forever or that gender is constant despite the clothes, activities, or hairstyles they may adopt. Children will gradually understand these factors of gender identification. However, it is not unusual for a preschooler to ask his father whether he was a boy or a girl when he was little. By age 6 or 7, most children no longer make mistakes like this. They have achieved what is called *gender constancy* (Stangor & Ruble, 1987).

There is more to learning gender concepts than simply achieving gender constancy, however. Our understanding of gender includes a web of interrelated concepts, attitudes, and expectations about traditional and nontraditional gender roles. Carol Martin studied people's attitudes toward "tomboys" and "sissies." She asked college sophomores whether they approved of certain behaviors of typical girls, typical boys, "tomboys," and "sissies." She asked the students what they would expect of these children when they grew up, and she questioned the students as to whether or not they would mind if their own child was a "tomboy" or a "sissy." It turns out that women in the study were more accepting of the cross-sex children than were men, and "sissies" were much more negatively evaluated than were "tomboys." It was assumed that "tomboys" would grow out of their cross-gender behavior. "Sissies," in contrast, were thought to be less well adjusted and more likely to grow up still showing inappropriate behavior (Martin, 1990). In another study, Martin wondered how these attitudes and expectations were developed. In a study of 4- to 10-year-olds, she found that the younger children could not use the label of "tomboy" or "sissy" to predict interests and behavior of another child. By age 8, however, children had well-developed concepts and possessed the culture's related attitudes toward "tomboys" and "sissies" (Martin, 1989).

Children develop gender concepts directly from what they are taught and from the models around them. They also develop them more indirectly from stories, movies, and television. Recent studies of the nature of stereotyped models in television indicate that the sex-role images presented on television over the past 10 to 15 years have been quite stable, traditional, conventional, and supportive of stereotypical roles (Signorelli, 1989). Even studies of children's elementary school reading books in 1972 and again in 1989 indicated that there was a preponderance of sex-stereotyped roles presented to young children in their school books (Purcell & Stewart, 1990). It is not surprising, therefore, that children's concepts about gender are sometimes stereotypical and strongly sex typed.

> **androgynous personality** A sex-role identity that incorporates some positive aspects of both traditional male and traditional female behavior.

The Androgynous Personality

Is it a good thing for children to learn a strong, clear pattern of behavior and set of concepts to define masculine and feminine behavior? Does it contribute to better mental health? Is it more "normal"? Two decades ago, parents and teachers were urged to help children establish clear, sex-typed behavior by the time they entered elementary school. Failure to do so might predispose individuals to psychological maladjustment. Now, however, much of the literature suggests that exaggerated sex-typed behavior restricts and limits the emotional and intellectual development of both men and women (Bem, 1985). In fact, several recent studies have provided little support for the traditional view that deviation from sex-role standards—either in personality or in interests—leads to psychological maladjustment (Orlofsky & O'Heron, 1987).

Many psychologists realize that a number of beneficial male and female traits can easily exist in the same person. Both men and women are capable of being ambitious, affectionate, self-reliant, gentle, assertive, and sensitive. This blend of personality traits goes into the makeup of what is called an **androgynous personality.** An androgynous personality, on the other hand, is not limited by such deficiencies and narrow abilities. Depending on the circumstances, men with

The androgynous personality is formed by specific child-rearing practices and parental attitudes that encourage cross-sex behavior.

androgynous personalities can be independent and assertive, yet able to cuddle an infant or offer a sensitive ear to another person's troubles. Likewise, women who have androgynous personalities are able to be effective and competent in the material world and still be fully expressive and nurturant when necessary.

Contemporary popular literature suggests that rigid sex-role stereotypes tend to restrict emotional and intellectual growth. Women who show a high degree of feminine behavior actually tend to be anxious and insecure. They are less creative and score lower on tests of intelligence and spatial perception than do women with fewer stereotypical feminine traits. Highly masculine men also score lower on tests of intelligence and creativity than do men with more androgynous personalities. Although rigidly masculine personalities assert themselves easily enough, they find it difficult to be playful and spontaneous (Ruble, 1988). Not all researchers agree, however, on the advantages of androgynous personalities for psychological adjustment. In a recent study, there seemed to be little difference in psychological development for men who were high in masculinity as compared to men who were androgynous (that is, men who were high in both masculine and feminine characteristics). Neither group was particularly prone to depression, anxiety, or social maladjustment. In contrast, low-masculinity men seemed to have problems of social maladjustment. For women, the results were more telling. Even women who showed strong masculinity and low femininity were no less well adjusted than were their strongly feminine or their androgynous peers (O'Heron & Orlofsky, 1990). It appears that sex-typing, or androgyny by itself, is not necessarily a ticket to positive psychological adjustment or maladjustment.

The androgynous personality is formed by specific child-rearing practices and parental attitudes that encourage cross-sex behavior. Traditionally, parents have accepted more cross-sex behavior in girls than in boys, as illustrated in the studies of "tomboys" (Martin, 1990). Lifelong androgynous gender identities that combine aspects of both masculinity and femininity are established most often in children where such behavior is modeled and accepted. It helps for the same-sex parent to provide a model of the cross-sex behavior and for the opposite-sex parent to reward this pattern (Ruble, 1988).

Gender Roles over the Life Span

Gender labels and gender identity affect behavior throughout the life span. In adolescence, pressures often intensify for individuals to assume fairly traditional sex-typed behavior. In adulthood, gender-role behavior varies depending on life circumstances and situations. Barbara Abrahams and her colleagues (1978) studied the permanence of sex-role behavior through four major life situations: cohabitation, marriage, anticipation of a first child, and parenthood. The researchers believed that men and women would modify their sex-role behavior in response to the demands of these situations, and they predicted a change toward an androgynous personality style as men and women moved toward parenthood. Quite the opposite occurred, however.

In cohabiting situations, where unmarried partners live together but are not necessarily committed to a long-term relationship, feminine characteristics (loyalty, compassion, sensitivity) were rated low in self-descriptions by both men and women. In marriage, where a greater commitment may exist for the needs of the partner, feminine characteristics were rated higher by both men and women. Couples expecting their first child were in an ambivalent life situation. Women felt more self-sufficient while simultaneously experiencing a greater need to be cared for. Men often felt a bit "left out"; at the same time, they were increasingly concerned with providing security for their wife and the expected child. Both men and women in this situation said that they felt stronger masculine *and* feminine impulses than did their married counterparts who were not expecting children.

In the parenting situation, both men and women reported more traditional sex-role characteristics. Shortly after the birth of their first child, men became preoccupied with business and finances. Women were now less independent and more home- and child-centered. The balance swung back to a traditional husband-dominated relationship. In other words, sex-role differences became increasingly traditional across the four situations. Men reported less role change across the situations than did women, probably because the behavioral changes required for women were greater.

STUDY OUTLINE

Principles and Processes of Genetics

Genes and Chromosomes. Every human being is the product of a delicate interaction between inherited genetic material and cultural behavior patterns. Children inherit their genetic identity from their parents through the pairing of 46 chromosomes (23 from the sperm, 23 from the ovum) that occurs during cell fertilization.

Each chromosome consists of many thousands of genes, which carry the hereditary potential for the new child. Genes are composed of long, complex, spiral molecules of **DNA.** Variations in the structure of genetic DNA determine the various cell characteristics and control the course of development of the new organism. **RNA,** a substance similar to DNA, determines how the development will proceed.

Some aspects of genetic inheritance can be examined by constructing a karyotype, which isolates the 46 chromosomes in a single body cell and groups them into 23 pairs. Twenty-two pairs of chromosomes (autosomes) carry physical and mental traits; the 23rd pair (XX for females, XY for males) carries the sexual characteristics and sex-linked traits.

Cell Division and Reproduction. A normal body cell divides by the process of **mitosis,** in which all 46 chromosomes duplicate themselves exactly. Reproductive cells—ova or sperm—contain only 23 chromosomes and reproduce themselves through **meiosis,** a process that greatly alters the arrangement of genes each time and is responsible for the wide range of individual variation.

The sex of a newborn infant is determined by the male's sperm cell, which carries either an X or a Y chromosome; the ovum carries only an X chromosome.

Combinations of Genes. Almost all genes occur in pairs, and hereditary traits are formed by single or multiple interactive gene pairs. One gene of a given pair (the genotype) can be dominant for a specific trait and can determine how that trait will be expressed (the phenotype). The complex combining and interacting of gene pairs give rise to a **polygenic inheritance system** in which children may differ greatly from their parents.

Genetic Abnormalities

Chromosomal Defects. Some genetic abnormalities are the result of too many or too few chromosomes and are responsible for such birth defects as *Down syndrome, Klinefelter's syndrome,* and *Turner's syndrome,* among others. Certain environmental influences can also cause abnormalities through chromosomal breakage.

Sex-Linked Inheritance. Unpaired single genes on the X chromosome are the source of sex-linked traits, such as *hemophilia* and *color blindness.*

Non-Sex-Linked Traits. Dominant and recessive genes, either singly or in pairs, on one or the other chromosome pairs may cause autosomal traits, such as *Tay-Sachs disease, cystic fibrosis, sickle cell anemia,* and *Huntington's chorea.*

Genetic Counseling. Genetic counselors help prospective parents evaluate the possible risks in certain gene pairings. The genetic counselor's task often involves highly volatile moral and emotional issues, and the counselor must weigh the parents' present sensitivities against the well-being of generations to come.

Advances in Genetic Research. Recent advances in genetics include gene therapy (which is still being developed), cloning (in which an entire organism is duplicated from only one of its body cells), and recombinant DNA (in which genes are split and recombined to create hybrid organisms).

Behavioral Genetics

Behavioral geneticists examine genetic influences on the

human species and on individuals within the species. Research on adopted children and on twins are two common methods of evaluating genetic influences on behavior.

Culture and Socialization

Alternate Family Styles Genes establish the codes for human development, but culture dictates how and if the genetic potential will be realized. Different family structures and child-rearing practices produce distinct personalities, values, and social behaviors. Three alternative family styles are the extended family, the communal family, and the nuclear family. These different styles not only integrate the child into the family unit, but also interpret the values of the larger outside culture to the child.

Socialization Processes. Along with other influential figures throughout life, care-givers and parents act as socialization agents. **Socialization** is a lifelong process during which individuals develop attitudes, values, beliefs, knowledge, awareness of social expectations, and appropriate behaviors. This is accomplished through learning processes—reward and punishment, modeling, and identification.

A crucial result of the socialization process is the individual's development of a self-concept, an idea of the self.

This self-concept must be integrated if one's role identity is not to be confused—that is, people must feel that their behavior is consistent with their ideal self.

The Interaction of Genetics and Culture

The ancient argument of heredity versus environment continues today. Psychologists Scarr and McCartney believe that children interact with their environment in three ways: *passively, evocatively,* and *actively.*

Gender-Role Identity

One of the most dramatic interactions of heredity and culture takes place in gender-role socialization. Although our sexual identities are being formed even before birth, gender roles develop well into adulthood. Gender identity is perhaps our most basic self-concept, but it is not permanent or fixed. Gender identity fluctuates throughout life as a result of our life situations. Societies assign particular behaviors to their male and female offspring. Children are quick to assimilate these complex, often rigid, role prescriptions (gender stereotypes), perhaps leading to emotional and intellectual damage in both sexes.

KEY TERMS AND CONCEPTS

alleles	gender schema	nonsex-linked autosomal trait
androgynous personality	genes	nuclear family
autosomes	gene splicing	phenotype
behavioral genetics	gene therapy	polygenic inheritance
chromosomes	genetic counseling	recessive
cloning	genetic engineering	reward and punishment
communal families	genotype	RNA
crossover	hemophilia	self-concept
cystic fibrosis	Huntington's chorea	sex-linked traits
DNA	integration	sex-typed behavior
dominant	karyotype	sickle cell anemia
Down syndrome	kibbutz	socialization
ethnocentrism	Klinefelter's syndrome	socialization agents
extended family	meiosis	somatic cell
fragile X	mitosis	Tay-Sachs disease
gender-role identity	modeling	thalassemia
gender-role stereotypes	mutation	Turner's syndrome

SELF-TEST QUESTIONS

1. Describe the process involved in the transmission of an individual's genetic code.

2. What is the difference between mitosis and meiosis?

3. How do genes combine to determine a person's traits?

4. What are some abnormalities caused by chromosomal defects? What is known about the causes and symptoms of these defects?

5. How are sex-linked disorders transmitted? What are some examples of sex-linked disorders, and who is most likely to manifest these disorders?

6. What are some diseases caused by non-sex-linked autosomal traits? Describe the characteristics of these disorders.

7. Explain genetic counseling.

8. What are the latest advances in genetic research? What are the advances we can look forward to in the near future? Are there limitations to this type of research? Explain.

9. Describe the types of studies common to behavioral genetics and the conclusions often reached by these studies. Why are these studies controversial?

10. Compare and contrast three basic family styles and the cultural patterns that underlie them. Are the values of the family and the values of society always consistent with each other? Please explain.

11. What are the various socialization processes that influence behavior? How do these processes operate?

12. Describe the relationship between heredity and environment in human development. Give an example.

13. What are the genetic differences, if any, between male and female behavior patterns?

14. Describe the process by which gender-role behaviors are established.

15. How might gender-role stereotypes inhibit the development of a well-rounded personality? How can this be avoided?

16. In what way do major life situations evoke changes in gender-role behavior?

SUGGESTED READINGS

ANTHONY, E. J., & COHLER, B. J. (EDS). *The invulnerable child.* New York: Guilford Press, 1987. A collection of well-researched articles about the resilient children who seem to do well despite oppressive childhood circumstances.

BROOKS-GUNN, E., & MATTHEWS, W. S. *He & she: Children's sex-role development.* Englewood Cliffs, N.J.: Prentice Hall, 1979. A readable explanation of the development of separate sex roles.

FEATHERSTONE, H. *A difference in the family: Living with a disabled child.* New York: Penguin, 1981. Featherstone, herself the parent of a severely disabled child, presents a well-researched, highly readable, and sensitive view of the family's struggle to cope with the worries, fears, doubts, and day-to-day demands and eventual meanings of life with a handicapped child. An excellent source book for social service personnel as well as parents and grandparents.

HALPERN, D. F. *Sex differences and cognitive abilities.* Hillsdale, NJ: Lawrence Erlbaum, 1986. A detailed, research-oriented summary of sex differences in cognitive abilities. It carefully summarizes the biological as well as the psychosocial hypotheses about such sex differences.

KELLY, T. E. *Clinical genetics and genetic counseling* (2nd ed). Chicago and London: Yearbook Medical Publishers, 1986. A carefully researched yet readable introductory textbook on genetics and its clinical applications.

PLOMIN, R. *Nature and nurture: An introduction to human behavioral genetics.* Pacific Grove, CA: Brooks/Cole, 1990. This brief, easily accessible paperback book translates the technical genetic research for the lay reader without losing the intriguing challenges of the field.

TOBIN, J. J., WU, D. Y. H., & DAVIDSON, D. H. *Preschool in three cultures: Japan, China, and the United States.* New Haven: Yale University Press, 1989. In detailed, case-study fashion, these authors present a vivid and persuasive picture of cultural variation in the way three preschools chose to nurture, educate, and socialize their students.

Chapter 4

The history of man for the nine months preceding his birth would, probably, be far more interesting and contain events of greater moment than for all the three score and ten years that follow it.

SAMUEL TAYLOR COLERIDGE

The Prenatal Period

Prenatal development—the unfolding of inherited potential—is one of the most dramatic examples of maturation. The prenatal maturation of human infants occurs within a highly controlled environment—the uterus—and it follows an orderly, predictable sequence. But even in the uterus there are environmental influences that affect development. Almost from the moment of conception, children are part of an environmental context. They do not begin life with a "clean slate." The expectations and anxieties, riches and deprivations, stability and disruptions, health and illnesses of the families into which they are born affect not only their life after birth but also their prenatal development. In this chapter, we will examine the biological and maturational processes during the prenatal period as well as the environmental influences on these processes.

CHAPTER OBJECTIVES

By the time you have finished this chapter, you should be able to do the following:

- Describe three prenatal developmental periods.
- Discuss the reproductive alternatives provided by modern technology, including the emotional, legal, and moral issues they raise.
- Describe the general trends that occur in prenatal growth and development.
- Explain the importance of critical periods in prenatal development.
- Discuss the factors that influence prenatal development.
- Discuss physical and emotional adjustments that the family faces during pregnancy.

PRENATAL DEVELOPMENT

The development of the unique human individual begins at the moment of conception. A one-celled, fertilized egg that can hardly be seen carries all of the genetic information needed to create a new organism. But the journey of the next 9 months is complex and, at times, perilous. It is estimated that over 50% of all fertilized eggs are lost within the first 2 weeks (Grobstein et al., 1983). Another 25% may be lost through miscarriage after the mother knows that she is pregnant. We will now look at the process of fertilization and the intricate sequence of development over the next 9 months.

Conception

About the 10th day after the beginning of the average woman's regular menstrual period, an **ovum,** or egg cell, that has developed in one of her two ovaries is stimulated by hormones and enters a sudden period of growth that continues for 3 or 4 days. By the end of the 13th or 14th day of growth, the follicle surrounding the ovum breaks, and the ovum is released to begin its journey down one of two **Fallopian tubes.** This release of the ovum from the ovary is called **ovulation.**

ovum The female reproductive cell (the egg or gamete).

Fallopian tubes Two passages that open out of the upper part of the uterus and carry the ova from the ovary to the uterus.

ovulation The release of the ovum into one of the two Fallopian tubes; occurs approximately 14 days after menstruation.

sperm The male reproductive cell (or gamete).

fertilization The union of an ovum and a sperm.

zygote A fertilized ovum.

germinal period After conception, the period of very rapid cell division and initial cell differentiation lasting approximately 2 weeks.

embryonic period The second pre-natal period, which lasts from the end of the second week to the end of the second month after conception. All the major structures and organs of the individual are formed during this time.

fetal period The final period of pre-natal development, lasting from the beginning of the third month after conception until birth. During this period, all organs, limbs, muscles, and systems become functional.

A living human ovum at the moment of conception. Although some sperm cells have begun to penetrate the outer covering of the ovum, only one will actually fertilize it.

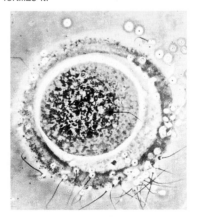

FERTILIZATION In most women, then, ovulation occurs about the 14th day after the onset of menstruation. The mature ovum survives for only 2 or 3 days. A man's **sperm,** deposited in a woman's vagina during sexual intercourse, also survives for as long as 3 days. A viable sperm, moving from the vagina through the uterus and up the Fallopian tube and reaching the ovum during the critical 48- to 72-hour period, can **fertilize** the ovum. Otherwise, the ovum continues down the Fallopian tube to the uterus, where it disintegrates.

The sperm and ovum are single cells, each containing half of the hereditary potential of the individual. The union of the two cells to produce a human being is quite a remarkable achievement. Some 300 million sperm are deposited in the vagina during intercourse, yet only one of these may fertilize an ovum. The sex and inherited traits of the child depend upon which of these millions of sperm cells survives to penetrate the ovum. For the sperm cells, the trip to the ovum is long and difficult. The microscopic sperm cells must work their way upward through a foot-long passage, through acidic fluids that can be lethal to them, through mucus and other obstacles—and finally one arrives at the proper place at the proper time.

INFERTILITY For 1 in 12 couples, conceiving a child in the manner described is not possible, but alternatives are now available (Mosher & Pratt, 1990). Fertilization that occurs outside of the womb is called *in vitro fertilization*. Ovum and sperm are united in a petri dish (not in a test tube, which is implied by the now common phrase "test tube babies"). This new ovum, which has been fertilized "in solution," grows for the first few days with rapid cell division, and then must be promptly implanted in a human uterus to survive. These procedures are no longer experimental, but are clinically approved, with established guidelines (*OB/GYN News,* June 1984). The guidelines insure the safety of the procedure and aid in the selection of couples who can appropriately be helped to achieve fertilization in this fashion. There are now dozens of fertility clinics in the United States and Canada.

We can describe much of what happens in fertilization, and in the development of the fetus that follows, but there are still many things we do not fully understand about the outcome of fertilization. Researchers are working on some rather interesting questions. For instance, for every 100 girls conceived, approximately 160 boys are conceived. Why are more male sperm successful at penetrating the ovum than female sperm? We know, for example, that compared to the female, the male sperm has a smaller, rounder head and a longer tail; it swims faster, is more affected by an acid environment, and tends to live for a shorter period of time (Rosenfeld, 1974). While many more boys are conceived, however, only 105 boys are born for every 100 girls. Why do more boys than girls die during the prenatal period? These are just some of the many challenging questions that are being investigated.

Periods of Development

After the ovum is united with the sperm, it is called the **zygote.** It then enters the **germinal period,** a time of very rapid cell division and initial organization of cells that lasts for about 10 to 12 days. This is followed by the **embryonic period,** during which structural development of the embryo takes place. This structural development stage lasts for about 7 weeks. From the beginning of the third month until birth—a time known as the **fetal period**—the organs, muscles, and systems

REPRODUCTIVE TECHNOLOGY: WHAT ARE THE OPTIONS?

In early 1985, William and Elizabeth Stern went to the Infertility Center of New York. They wanted to find a woman willing to carry their child implanted by artificial insemination. Both Sterns were in their late thirties, and a pregnancy was potentially dangerous for Elizabeth. They are among 2 million people who visit fertility centers each year in an effort to have children.

About 10 million people of childbearing age have difficulty conceiving (Lord et al., 1987). Most want children and have tried unsuccessfully for years to have them. Many turn to adoption agencies, only to find that it may be years before they have a chance to adopt a baby. For those on a tight budget, the cost, which can be over $10,000, may make adopting a child prohibitive. Because an increasing number of couples postpone trying for a child until they are in their late twenties or early thirties, many feel a rising sense of desperation as the years go by without having a child.

As couples get older, the rate of infertility increases. In 1988, the last year for which there are figures, about 5 million or 8.4% of women between the ages of 15 and 44 had fertility problems. In women ages 15 to 24, this figure drops to 4%, but for women 35 to 44 years of age, the figures rises dramatically to 21% (Mosher & Pratt, 1990). In many instances, female infertility is caused by a blockage or abnormality in the Fallopian tubes. For 70% of women with this problem, microsurgery can restore fertility. Among women with a complete blockage, only 20% can successfully conceive (Wallis, 1984).

There are several options available to would-be parents. The first that comes to mind, of course, is adoption. Most infertile couples try this route first, but they find it so time-consuming, costly, and frustrating that they soon look for other possibilities.

Modern advances in reproductive technology have given infertile couples several new alternatives. The oldest and still very widely used technique is artificial insemination. Simply stated, artificial insemination is the impregnation of a woman by the artificial introduction of semen. This can take several forms. A woman can be artificially injected with the sperm of her husband, or if the sperm is diseased or weak, with sperm donated by a stranger and kept frozen until used.

Another technique that infertile couples try is *in vitro* fertilization, a technique of fertilizing a woman's egg with a man's sperm in a laboratory dish, then placing the fertilized egg in the woman's uterus (Wallis, 1984). *In vitro* fertilization, more commonly known as the process of making test-tube babies, is an increasingly popular method of dealing with the infertility problem. However, clinics have long waiting lists for treatment that, at most, offers approximately a 20% chance of success (Wallis, 1984). A recent development of *in vitro* fertilization, known as "donated eggs," involves having the egg donated by a stranger, fertilized by the sperm of the mother-to-be's husband, and then placed in the mother-to-be's uterus. The technique of "donated eggs" makes it possible for an otherwise barren woman to have the experience of bearing a child. It is an alternative for couples who cannot conceive but can carry children. In contrast, an option available to couples who might be able to conceive but cannot carry children is to enter into a contract with a surrogate mother who will carry a child to term for them. This was the alternative chosen by the Sterns when they signed a contract with Mary Beth Whitehead to have her bear a child for them.

The unraveling of the arrangements between Whitehead and the Sterns, known as "the Baby M case," brought to prominence the emotional, ethical, and legal issues raised by solutions to the infertility problem. These issues have by no means been resolved. Federal and state legislatures are just beginning to examine the legal dimensions of the problem. Because the technology involved is so new, there is little hard data on the psychological aftereffects of carrying someone else's child or of rearing a child someone else bore at the legal parents' request. Nor does anyone yet know the eventual effects on the child. Most difficult of all are the moral questions raised by reproductive technology and its relation to traditional values. Is it right to hire a woman's uterus or a man's sperm so that some other couple can have a chance to raise a child? What are the implications of raising children for whom only one of the parents is a biological parent? On the other side of the equation: Is it right to deny a childless couple the opportunity to raise children and have a full family life that modern technology makes possible? Finally, we cannot ignore the trauma that infertile couples experience as they deal with miscarriage and innumerable visits to infertility specialists to achieve their goal—a healthy baby (Beck, 1988). As a society, we have not yet resolved these issues, just as we have not yet resolved other issues connected with reproductive rights.

identical (monozygotic) twins
Twins that result from the division of a single fertilized ovum.

fraternal (dizygotic) twins Twins resulting from the fertilization of two separate ova by two separate sperm.

blastula   The hollow, fluid-filled sphere of cells that forms several days after conception.

implantation The embedding of the prenatal organism in the uterine wall after its descent through the Fallopian tube.

begin to function. Many of the processes that the organism will need to survive at birth are developing during this period.

GERMINAL PERIOD   The process of cell division (cleavage) begins just a few hours after fertilization and produces two cells. The second cleavage, which takes place after about 2 days, produces four cells. A third cleavage then produces eight cells. The rate of cell division increases, and by the end of 4 days as many as 60 to 70 cells may have been produced.

In some cases, the first division of the zygote produces two identical cells, which then separate and develop into two individuals. The result will be **identical,** or **monozygotic, twins.** Because they develop from the same cell, identical twins always are the same sex, and they share the same physical traits. In other cases, two ova are released and each unites with a sperm; this produces **fraternal,** or **dizygotic, twins.** The genetic traits inherited by fraternal twins can be as different or as similar as those of any siblings conceived at different times. Fraternal twins may be of the same or opposite sex because the ova are fertilized by two separate sperm.

Beyond the early stages of cleavage, the cells continue to divide and begin to form a ball that moves through the Fallopian tube toward the uterus. At this point, the solid ball of cells forms a hollow sphere, or **blastula,** around an accumulation of fluid. During the formation of the blastula, the cells begin the process of differentiation—that is, they separate into groups according to their future function. Some of the cells move to one side of the hollow sphere and begin to develop into the embryo, while others develop into a protective covering for the embryo.

At the beginning of the second week, the blastula completes its journey down the Fallopian tube and arrives in the uterus, where it will develop during the coming months. Within a few days, it becomes embedded in the uterine wall, in a process called **implantation.** After a successful implantation, the developing organism enters the embryonic period.

Identical twins (left) share physical traits and are always the same sex; fraternal twins (right) can be as different or as similar as siblings born at different times.

EMBRYONIC PERIOD   Generally, the embryonic period is considered to extend from near the end of the second week to the end of the second month after conception. It is a crucial time when much that is essential to the baby's further prenatal development and future lifetime development occurs. During the embryonic period, all the tissues and structures that will house, nurture, and protect the embryo (and later the fetus) for the remainder of the 9 months are formed. In addition, the development begins, in form at least, of all organs and features of the embryo itself. During the embryonic period, this very tiny being develops arms, legs, fingers, toes, a face, a heart that beats, a brain, lungs, and all the other major organs. By the end of the embryonic period, the embryo is a recognizable human being.

The embryo develops within an **amniotic sac** filled with amniotic fluid; it is then nourished by means of an organ called the **placenta,** which develops specifically to assist the growth of the new organism. The placenta is a disk-shaped mass of tissue growing from the wall of the uterus; it is formed partly from the tissue of the uterine wall and partly by the **chorion,** the outer layer of tissue that surrounds the embryo and the amniotic sac.

The placenta begins to develop at the moment of implantation and continues to grow until about the seventh month of pregnancy. It is connected to the embryo by the **umbilical cord,** which is a "rope" of tissue containing two fetal arteries and one fetal vein. The placenta provides for an exchange of materials between mother and embryo, keeping out large particles of foreign matter but passing on nutrients. Thus, enzymes, vitamins, and even immunities to disease pass from the mother to

amniotic sac A fluid-filled membrane that encloses the developing embryo or fetus.

placenta A disk-shaped mass of tissue that forms along the wall of the uterus through which the embryo receives nutrients and discharges wastes.

chorion The protective outer sac that develops from tissue surrounding the embryo.

umbilical cord The "rope" of tissue connecting the placenta to the embryo; this rope contains two fetal arteries and one fetal vein.

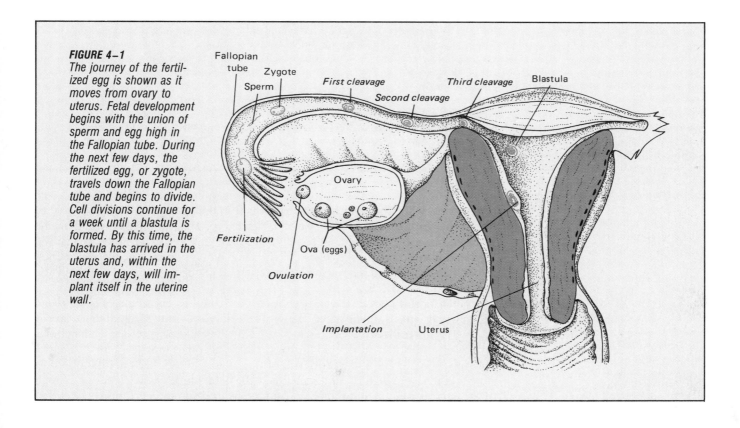

FIGURE 4–1
The journey of the fertilized egg is shown as it moves from ovary to uterus. Fetal development begins with the union of sperm and egg high in the Fallopian tube. During the next few days, the fertilized egg, or zygote, travels down the Fallopian tube and begins to divide. Cell divisions continue for a week until a blastula is formed. By this time, the blastula has arrived in the uterus and, within the next few days, will implant itself in the uterine wall.

Fallopian tube
Zygote
Sperm
First cleavage
Second cleavage
Third cleavage
Blastula
Ovary
Fertilization
Ova (eggs)
Ovulation
Implantation
Uterus

ectoderm In embryonic development, the outer layer of cells, which becomes the skin, sense organs, and nervous system.

mesoderm In embryonic development, the middle layer of cells that becomes the muscles, blood, and excretory system.

endoderm In embryonic development, the inner layer of cells that becomes the digestive system, lungs, thyroid, thymus, and other organs.

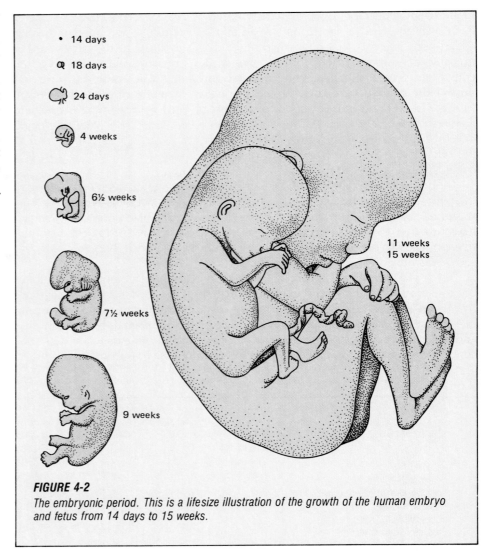

- 14 days

18 days

24 days

4 weeks

6½ weeks

7½ weeks

9 weeks

11 weeks
15 weeks

FIGURE 4-2

The embryonic period. This is a lifesize illustration of the growth of the human embryo and fetus from 14 days to 15 weeks.

the embryo, while the resulting waste products in the embryo's blood are passed to the mother for final elimination. Sugars, fats, and proteins also pass through to the embryo, but some bacteria and some salts do not. It is important to note that the mother and child do not actually share the same blood system. The placenta allows the exchange of nutritive and waste materials across cell membranes without the exchange of blood cells.

During this period, the embryo itself grows rapidly and changes occur daily. Immediately after implantation, the embryo develops into three distinct layers. They are the **ectoderm,** or outer layer, which becomes skin and the nervous system; the **mesoderm,** or middle layer, which becomes muscles, blood, and the excretory system; and the **endoderm,** or inner layer, which becomes the digestive system, lungs, and glands. Simultaneously, the neural tube (which is the beginning of the nervous system and the brain) and the heart begin to develop. At the end of the fourth week of pregnancy and only 2 weeks into the embryonic period, the heart is beating; the nervous system, in its somewhat primitive form, is functioning; and both are contributing to the development of the entire embryo. All of this often occurs before the mother is even aware that she is pregnant.

During the second month, all of the structures that we recognize as human develop rapidly. The arms and legs unfold from small buds on the sides of the trunk. The eyes become visible, seemingly on the sides of the head, at about a month, and the full face changes almost daily during the second month. The internal organs—the lungs, digestive system, and excretory system— are being formed, although they are not yet functional.

Many **miscarriages,** or **spontaneous abortions,** occur during the embryonic period. They are usually caused by inadequate development of the placenta, the umbilical cord, and/or the embryo (Beck, 1988). Because the embryo receives its nutrients from the mother through the placenta, it is obvious that an inadequate diet or the poor health of the mother may adversely affect the developing child. Later in this chapter, the many factors that influence prenatal development will be discussed.

FETAL PERIOD   The fetal period lasts from the beginning of the third month until birth—or for about 7 months—versus an average total **gestation period** of 266 days. It is during the fetal period that the organs, limbs, muscles, and systems become functional. The fetus begins to kick, squirm, turn its head and, eventually, its body. Even with its eyes sealed shut, the fetus begins to squint, frown, move its lips, open its mouth, swallow a little amniotic fluid, and make sucking motions.

During the third month, the first external signs of sex differentiation become apparent. The penis and scrotum in the male or the beginning of the labia in the female can be detected, although the male organs develop sooner than do those of the female. At the same time, the male fetus develops a prostate gland, vas deferens, and epididymis, and the female develops Fallopian tubes and ovaries.

The eyes, still set toward the sides of the head, develop their irises, and all of the nerves needed to connect the eye to the brain are now in place. Teeth form under the gums; ears begin to appear on the sides of the head; fingernails and toenails form. The fetus develops a thyroid gland, a thymus gland, a pancreas, and kidneys. The liver begins to function, and the lungs and stomach begin to respond. By the 12th week, the vocal cords have developed, the taste buds have formed, and ribs and vertebrae have begun to ossify (turn from cartilage to bone). The fetus, although unable to survive on its own, has acquired almost all of the systems and functions necessary for a human being. And at this point, it is only about 3 inches long and weighs around half an ounce.

During the fourth to sixth months (the second trimester), all of the processes begun in the first trimester continue. (The 9 months before birth are divided into three equal segments of 3 months each, called **trimesters.)** The body becomes longer, so the head does not look as out of proportion as it did during the preceding month. The face develops lips, and the heart muscle strengthens, beating from 120 to 160 times a minute. In the fifth month, the fetus acquires a strong hand grip and increases the amount and force of its movements. The mother will be able to feel an elbow, a knee, or the head, as the fetus moves around during its waking periods.

During this time, the fetus is also undergoing a process of skin-cell

miscarriage (spontaneous abortion) Expulsion of the prenatal organism before it is viable.

gestation period The total period of time from conception to birth; in humans, this averages about 266 days.

trimesters The three equal time segments that comprise the 9-month gestation period.

Stages of prenatal development: (a) A two-celled organism showing the first cleavage a few hours after fertilization. (b) The germinal period at 2 days—no cell differentiation exists yet. (c) An embryo at 21 days. Note the primitive spinal cord. The embryo grows rapidly at this time. (d) A 4-week-old embryo. One can now distinguish the head, trunk, and tail. The heart and nervous system have begun to function by this time. (e) A 5-week-old embryo. The arms and legs are beginning to unfold from the sides of the trunk. (f) A 9-week-old fetus showing the umbilical cord connection with the placenta. (g) A 16-week-old fetus. All internal organs have been formed but are not yet functional. (h) A 20-week-old fetus. At this stage, most internal organs have begun to function, and the fetus is able to kick, turn its head, and make facial expressions.

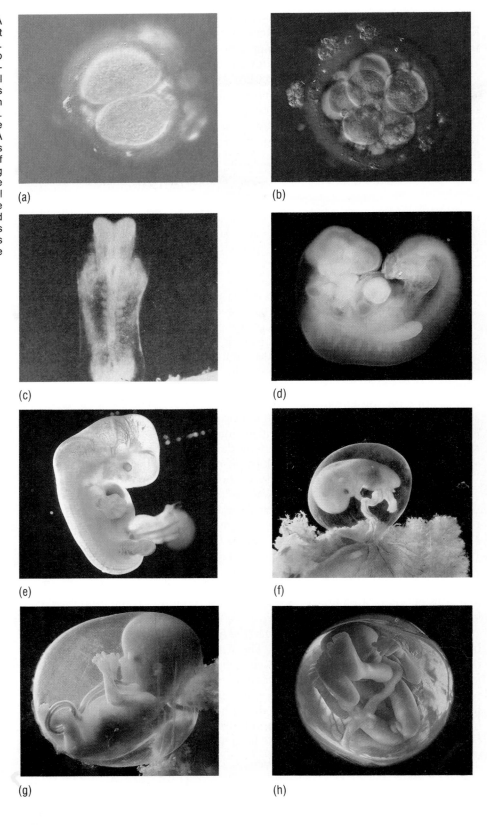

(a)

(b)

(c)

(d)

(e)

(f)

(g)

(h)

replacement. Oil glands form and secrete a cheesy coating, called the *vernix caseosa*, that protects the skin from the amniotic fluid. The fetus also develops a hairy covering on its body and begins to grow eyebrows and eyelashes.

In the sixth month, the fetus grows to about 12 inches in length and weighs approximately 1½ pounds. The eyes are completely formed, and the eyelids can open. Bone formation progresses, hair on the head continues to grow, and the fetus begins to straighten out its posture so that the internal organs can shift to their proper positions.

By the beginning of the third trimester (that is, after 24 weeks of development in the uterus), a healthy fetus is considered **viable**—it might survive

viable After 24 weeks of development, the ability of the fetus to live outside the mother's body, provided it receives special care.

TABLE 4–1

Three Stages of Prenatal Development

	TIME	DEVELOPMENT
Germinal Period	**0–2 weeks**	
Fertilization	0	Ovum impregnated by sperm
Cell division	2 hrs–12th day	Ball of 70+ cells forms
Implantation	12th–14th days	Blastula embedded in wall of uterus
Embryonic Period	**2 weeks–2 months**	
Nourishing structures	1st–4th weeks	Amniotic sac, placenta, chorion, and umbilical cord form
Cellular structures	1st–4th weeks	Ectoderm, mesoderm, and endoderm evolve
Heart and nervous system	3rd–4th weeks	Start to form and function
Head	3rd–4th weeks	Forms and grows rapidly
Organs and limbs	4th–8th weeks	Arms, legs unfold; lungs and digestive, excretory systems form
Facial features	4th–8th weeks	Eyes move to side of head; mouth, ears form
Fetal Period	**2 months–9 months**	
Eyes	8th–12th weeks	Irises and nerves are in place
Teeth	8th–12th weeks	Form under the gums
Ears	8th–12th weeks	Develop
Fingernails and toenails	8th–12th weeks	Appear on limbs
Sex organs	8th–12th weeks	Penis and scrotum in male, labia in female appear
Glands	8th–12th weeks	Thyroid and thymus form
Internal organs	8th–12th weeks	Pancreas, kidneys develop; liver, lungs, stomach start to work
Bone structure	12th week	Ribs and spine begin to change from cartilage
Vocal cords and taste buds	12th week	Are formed
Body	4th–6th months	Lengthens, is covered by hairy fuzz, replaces skin cells, starts moving so mother feels it
Face	4th–6th months	Grows lips, eyebrows, and eyelashes
Heart muscle	4th–6th months	Beats 120–160 times per minute
Hands	5th month	Acquire strong grip
Eyes	6th month	Completely formed, eyelids can open
Head	6th month	Hair grows
Fetus	24th–26th weeks	Viable, may survive outside mother's body if in incubator
Body	7th month	Weighs 3 pounds, nervous system can control breathing and swallowing
Brain	7th month	Forms tissues for sensory, motor activities; can experience pain, touch, and sound
Body	8th month	Increases in length to 17 or 18 inches, weighs 4 to 6 pounds, forms fatty layers under skin for use after birth
Baby	9th month	Continues to grow, turns in head-down position for birth, loses fuzzy body covering, weight gain slows, "drops"
Mother	Last week or two before birth	Uterus settles lower in pelvic area, muscles begin painless contractions, placenta starts to break down

outside the mother's body if it were placed in an incubator and given special, intensive care. With modern medical advances, however, some special care units for premature infants have been able to sustain babies who are born even earlier than this. Perhaps as many as 20% of fetuses born at 24 weeks survive, provided they are in the best-equipped neonatal intensive care units in the nation. At 29 weeks, fully 90% survive in such units (Kantrowitz, 1988).

At 7 months, the fetus weighs about 3 pounds, and its nervous system is mature enough to control breathing and swallowing. During this seventh month, the brain develops rapidly, forming the tissues that localize the centers for all of the senses and motor activities. The fetus is sensitive to touch and can feel pain; it may even have a sense of balance.

A frequently raised question is whether or not a fetus hears. It has long been known that a fetus is startled at a very loud sound occurring close to the mother, but hardly at all at a moderate sound. The reason for this is that the fetus is surrounded by a variety of sounds. There are digestive sounds from the mother's drinking, eating, and swallowing. There are breathing sounds. Also, there are circulatory system sounds that correspond to the rhythm of the mother's heartbeat. Loud conversational speech from outside the body can be heard, but it is muffled. In fact, the internal noise level in the uterus is thought to be as loud as that of a small factory (Aslin et al., 1983; Armitage et al., 1980).

Researchers have determined that the human organism does much more than just develop physically during the prenatal period. As early as 15 weeks, the fetus can grasp, frown, squint, and grimace. Reflex movements result from the touching of the soles of the feet or the eyelids. By 20 weeks, the senses of taste and smell are formed. By 24 weeks, the sense of touch is more fully developed, and there is response to sound. By 25 weeks, the response to sound grows more consistent. At 27 weeks, a light shown on the mother's abdomen sometimes causes the fetus to turn its head. In any case, a brain scan will show that the fetus has reacted to the light. All of these behaviors—facial expressions, turning, kicking, ducking actions—that occur late in the seventh month take place in the womb and may be purposeful movements that make the fetus more comfortable (Fedor-Freybergh & Vogel, 1988).

In the eighth month, the fetus may gain as much as a half-pound a week and begins to ready itself for the outside world. Fat layers now form under the skin in order to protect the fetus from the temperature changes that it may encounter at birth. Although the survival rate for infants born after 8 months is better than 90% in well-equipped hospitals, these babies do face risks. Breathing may still be difficult; initial weight loss may be greater than for full-term babies; and, because their fat layers have not fully formed, temperature control could be a problem. For these reasons, babies born at this developmental stage are usually placed in incubators and are given the same type of care as babies born in the seventh month.

Fetal sensitivity and behavior also develop rapidly in the eighth month. At the middle of the month, it is thought that the eyes open in the uterus, and the fetus may be able to see its hands and environment, although it is quite dark. Some doctors think that awareness starts at about 32 weeks, when many of the neural circuits are quite advanced. Brain scans show periods of dream sleep. As the fetus moves into the ninth month, it develops daily cycles of activity and sleep, and hearing is thought to be quite mature.

During the ninth month, the fetus continues to grow and begins to turn to a head-down position in preparation for the trip through the birth canal. The

DOES THE FETUS LEARN?

Is the fetus capable of learning? Can we train the unborn child and can this training give the child a head start on its later learning? What has the fetus already learned about its mother? For centuries, people have wondered about how experiences in the womb may affect the unborn child. The Greek philosopher Aristotle thought the fetus could acquire "sensation" (Hepper, 1989). In medieval Europe, some even believed that the fetus might possess "ideas." If Aristotle and these others are correct, how are these sensations or ideas acquired? Is there evidence that either supports or debunks these beliefs?

First, let us review what we already know about fetal capabilities. Researchers generally agree that the fetus is sensitive to touch and vibration and can hear in the final 2 months before birth (Hepper, 1989; Poole, 1987). It must be noted, however, that sounds coming from outside of the mother must compete with sounds inside the mother's body in order to be heard. Researchers who placed microphones in the wombs of sheep were shocked to discover the rather high volume of noise inside the sheep (Armitage et al., 1980). With the rhythmic noises of the circulatory system, the steady beat of the mother's heart, and the various rumblings of the mother's digestive system, the fetal environment seems to be as loud as a small factory. Researchers speculate that sounds coming from outside the mother's body must be quite muffled.

The fetus adapts to its noisy environment through a simple form of learning called *habituation*. Quite simply, the fetus learns to respond to certain sounds. Repetitive sounds, such as a steady heartbeat, are soothing. The fetus is startled by sudden new sounds or vibrations but seems to calm down as the sounds continue. Researchers have discovered that after birth, the sound of a metronome set to the pace of the mother's heartbeat is soothing to the newborn.

What does the fetus learn from the outside world? Peter Hepper (1988) created an interesting experiment with a group of expectant mothers in London. Hepper asked these mothers how often they watched Britain's most popular television soap opera, "Neighbours" (BBC1). He selected one group who watched the program nearly every day and another group who virtually never watched it. Within hours of the babies' birth, Hepper played the theme music from the show to the newborns while they were crying. As soon as they heard the music, the babies in the first group stopped crying and became alert. Newborn babies of the mothers who had not watched the program showed no reaction (Hepper, 1988). There seemed to be little doubt that the newborns who had been habituated to the music of the television program had learned something.

If the fetus can learn in the womb, is it possible for us to give the baby an academic head start before birth? Rene Van de Carr, founder and president of Prenatal University in Hayward, California, believes he can do just that. With a curriculum that includes the "kick game" and other exercises, Van de Carr's goal is to stimulate the fetal brain. Parents are instructed to tap the abdomen where the baby kicks and to speak loud encouraging words while teaching vocabulary to the fetus. Dr. Van de Carr claims that the newborn graduates of Prenatal University are more alert, quicker to develop, and are emotionally closer to their parents than are newborns who do not have these prenatal experiences. Other proponents of fetal training make even more expansive claims (Poole, 1987).

Most child development experts, however, view these claims with skepticism, caution, and even outright hostility. They believe that, at most, these programs may help to strengthen the bond between parent and child. Even this, they claim, is not due to the details of the programs, rather, it is due to the fact that the parents are more involved with their anticipated child. These experts also view the sale of expensive program kits and tapes as more of a commercial venture than as scientific research. In short, the search continues for a few compelling studies that capture the imagination and help to identify just what the fetus is capable of learning (Poole, 1987).

vernix caseosa begins to fall away, and the hairy coating dissolves. Immunities to disease pass from the mother to the fetus and supplement the fetus's own developing immune reactions. Approximately 1 to 2 weeks before birth, the baby "drops" as the uterus settles lower into the pelvic area. The weight gain of the fetus slows, the mother's muscles and uterus begin sporadic, painless contractions, and the cells of the placenta begin to degenerate—all is ready for birth.

cephalocaudal developmental trend
The sequence of growth in which development occurs first in the head and progresses toward the feet.

proximodistal developmental trend
The directional sequence of development that occurs from the midline of the body outward.

gross-to-specific developmental trend The tendency to react to stimuli with generalized, whole-body movements at first, while these responses become more local and specific later on.

differentiation In embryology, the process in which undifferentiated cells become increasingly specialized.

integration The organization of differentiated cells into organs or systems.

Developmental Trends

The whole process of prenatal development that we just described seems quite orderly and predictable. Nevertheless, each fetus develops with its own differences—in size and shape, in skin tone, in strength and proportions, in developmental pace, and so on. For example, the gestation period (the time for a full-term pregnancy as measured from the mother's last menstrual flow to the day of childbirth) is usually 40 weeks. But normal full-term infants are born as early as 37 weeks or as late as 43 weeks.

What general trends do we see in this process of prenatal development? Usually—although with some exceptions—development proceeds from the top of the body downward. This "head-to-tail" development is called the **cephalocaudal developmental trend.** (It is not a rule, or a law, or even a principle, but just a trend.) Similarly, development usually proceeds from the middle of the body outward. This "near-to-far" development is the **proximodistal trend.** These trends will be seen again, with a few exceptions, in the development of physical coordination and skill in infants and preschool children. Infants control eye and head movements first, then arms and hands, and finally legs and feet. They reach and grab with the full hand long before they can pick up something like peas with a finger and thumb.

A fetus reacts to a poke on the skin with gross, generalized, whole-body movements at first. At birth and later, the movements become more localized and specific. This is the **gross-to-specific trend.** (Children learning to write often move their whole bodies, including the tongue. Only later can they confine the action to the fingers, the hand, and slight arm motion.)

Finally, there are the developmental processes of **differentiation** and **integration.** In the biology of prenatal development, cells become *differentiated* into distinct and specialized layers. But these layers soon become *integrated* into organs or systems. Later, during the child's psychological development, the processes of differentiation and integration often work together. Watching a child learn how to skip shows that the individual actions must be mastered and combined as well. Most adult thought is, in fact, a result of many discrete or differentiated concepts combined into integrated systems.

PRENATAL INFLUENCES

At this point in our study of prenatal development, we have described only normal developmental processes. The predictable and predetermined sequence outlined would presumably take place under ideal environmental conditions. These ideal conditions include a well-developed amniotic sac with a cushioning of amniotic fluid; a fully functional placenta and umbilical cord; an adequate supply of oxygen and nutrients; and freedom from disease organisms and toxic chemicals. What we have not considered is the effect on the fetus of any alteration in these conditions.

Most pregnancies in the United States (92% to 95%) result in full-term, healthy, well-developed babies. In most cases, the protective system of shielding in the uterus and filtering through the placenta works efficiently. However, every year in the United States, some 150,000 or more babies (from 5% to 8%) are born with birth defects. These defects range from gross anomalies that spell certain and almost immediate death for the newborn to minimal physical or mental defects that may have little impact upon the future development of the child. Although we might like to assume that birth defects only happen to other people's babies and are probably caused by some inherited traits, the truth is that they can happen to anyone and that only a small proportion are the result of inherited factors. The majority of birth defects are caused by environmental influences during the prenatal period, or during childbirth, or by the interaction of heredity and environmental influences.

The study of developmental abnormalities is called **teratology** (derived from the Greek word *tera,* which means "monster"). A teratogenic agent, or **teratogen,** is the specific agent that disturbs the development of the fetus—a virus or chemical, for example. In revealing the causes of abnormalities in infants, teratology also helps us to understand the normal process of development and to prevent defects and abnormalities whenever possible.

teratology The study of developmental abnormalities or birth defects.

teratogens The toxic agents that cause these disturbances.

Critical Periods

During prenatal development, the effects of many environmental conditions depend upon the relative stage of development, that is, the point in the developmental sequence when the change in the prenatal environment occurs. Unfortunately, many environmental effects on prenatal development have maximal impact during the first trimester of pregnancy, the time when the internal organs, the limbs, and the various structures such as eyes and ears are forming. Often, a woman is not even aware of her condition. She may not be particularly concerned about her nutritional needs, not especially worried about minor diseases like rubella (German measles) or influenza, not thinking about the potential harmful effects of any drugs that she may be taking. In short, the damage is often done before a woman knows that there is an unborn child to worry about.

A critical period is the time when an organ, structure, or system is most sensitive to a particular influence. Figure 4–3 illustrates the critical periods in prenatal development, highlighting when specific organs and systems can be most seriously harmed.

The timing and nature of critical periods can be seen in the range of effects of the drug thalidomide. Thalidomide was prescribed as a mild tranquilizer for pregnant women, mostly in Great Britain and Germany in 1959 and 1960. It relieved insomnia and nausea and other symptoms of morning sickness. Within the next 2 years, as many as 10,000 deformed babies were born, and the deformities were attributed to the mothers' intake of thalidomide. A careful study of the history of these pregnancies showed that the nature of the deformity was determined by the timing of the mothers' use of the drug. If the mother took the drug between the 34th and 38th days after her last menstrual period, the child had no ears. If she took the drug between the 38th and 47th days the child had missing or deformed arms. If she took the drug between the 40th and 45th days, the child had defects in the intestines or gall bladder. If she took the drug between the 42nd and 47th days, the child had missing or deformed legs (Schardein, 1976).

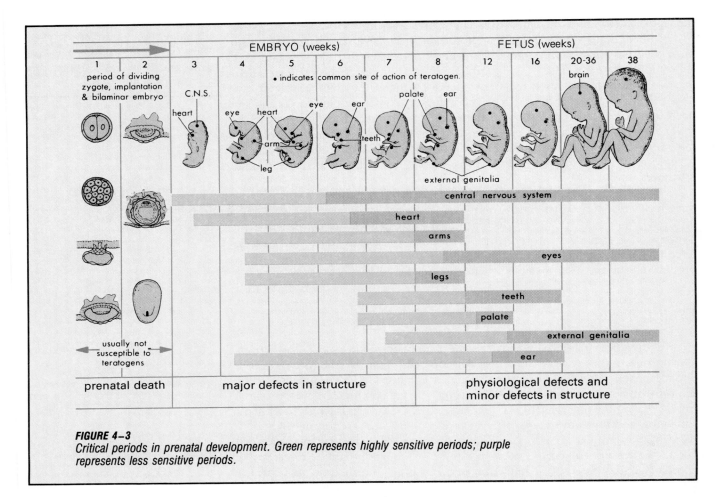

FIGURE 4–3
Critical periods in prenatal development. Green represents highly sensitive periods; purple represents less sensitive periods.

Types of Prenatal Influences

The variety of factors that have been found to influence prenatal development is impressive—even frightening. Nutrition, drugs, diseases, hormones, blood factors, radiation, maternal age at the time of conception, stress, and type of prenatal care all play a part in the development of the child. There is some concern that even though we know about the effects of many environmental factors, there are still drugs and other agents whose influences on the fetus have not yet been determined. It is relatively easy to study the direct effects of a drug like thalidomide on the infant's physical structure. It is much more difficult to discover the subtle neurological changes that lead to a learning disability at age 7 as a result of heavy air pollution (Needleman, 1986).

NUTRITION   One of the most important elements of the prenatal environment is nutrition. As the following excerpt points out, the effects of a lack of proper prenatal nutrition can extend throughout an individual's life span:

A fetus, malnourished in the womb, may never make up for the brain cells and structures that never came properly into being. Malnutrition both before *and* after birth virtually dooms a child to stunted brain development and therefore to considerably diminished mental capacity *for the rest* of his life. (Rosenfeld, 1974b, p. 59)

Fetal malnutrition may be caused by a mother's imbalanced diet, a vitamin deficiency, or deficiencies in the metabolism of the mother. In some cases, however, the fetus is unable to use the nutrients supplied by the mother. This may happen because of metabolic disorders, genetic abnormalities, or problems in the placenta. The most notable symptoms of fetal malnutrition are low birth weight, smaller head size, and smaller size overall, as compared to newborns who have been in utero for the same amount of time (Metcoff et al., 1981; Simopoulos, 1983). Malnourished pregnant women also often have spontaneous abortions, give birth prematurely, or lose their babies shortly after birth; even less severe nutritional deficiencies can cause problems that last a lifetime.

In countries ravaged by famine or war, the effects of malnutrition on child development are clear. There are high rates of miscarriages and stillbirths, and children born to malnourished mothers quickly develop diseases and fail to thrive unless immediate dietary adjustments are made. Even in developed societies such as ours, it is estimated that from 3% to 10% of all live births show indications of fetal malnutrition (Simopoulos, 1983). According to Zeskind and Ramey (1981), most cases of fetal malnutrition occur in low-income families. The truly unfortunate

The effects of malnutrition on child development are painfully clear in countries ravaged by famine or war.

outcome is that reduced brain development in the late fetal–early infant period probably does not get made up later.

If the period of malnourishment has been relatively short, however, it can sometimes be compensated for with infant nutrition programs, or with combined health, nutrition, and child-care programs. H. G. Birch and J. D. Gussow (1970) have cited a range of studies where carefully controlled "nourishment programs" for expectant mothers resulted in full-term, healthy babies. Research indicates that short-term malnutrition of the mother during pregnancy might have relatively minor effects on the fetus. Evidence of this is based on a study of pregnant women who, during the blockade in Holland in World War II, were on fairly limited rations for as much as 3 months during their pregnancies. Although these women were not starving, they were seriously undernourished. Except for a slight rise in the rate of stillborns and spontaneous abortions, those infants who survived were remarkably healthy once food was readily available, and they made up their initial low weight. Follow-up tests of these individuals at age 19 indicated no apparent reduction in intelligence and no marked behavioral abnormalities (Stechler & Shelton, 1982). Research with animals also demonstrates that the mother can buffer the fetus from the effects of malnutrition by drawing on her own stored resources, and she can also protect her own tissues from serious long-term drain. Both mother and fetus, therefore, appear capable of recovery from limited malnutrition (Jones & Crnic, 1986).

DRUGS AND CHEMICAL AGENTS Developing structures are usually more vulnerable to drugs than are structures that are already developed. Furthermore, some drugs may cross the placental barrier only to be trapped in the primitive system of the embryo or fetus. For example, fetal systems may not be able to handle a drug as efficiently as the maternal system can. Instead of being passed as a waste, the drug may accumulate in an organ or system of the fetus. Although a drug has been found "safe" for use by adults, it does not necessarily follow that it will be safe for the tiny developing organism that depends on and shares the environment provided by that adult. It may be true, in fact, that almost no drug is safe for the fetus.

Narcotics.   In general, narcotics like morphine, heroin, and even methadone depress fetal respiration and can cause behavioral disturbances in the infant. Babies born to women who use such drugs regularly are smaller than the norm and less responsive as newborns. More importantly, these babies experience withdrawal symptoms—extreme irritability, shrill crying, vomiting, shaking, and poor temperature control. They have disturbed sleep and have difficulty sucking. After the first few weeks, many continue to suffer from disturbed sleep, poor appetites, and lack of weight gain. At 4 months, they are more tense and rigid, more active, and less well coordinated than normal babies. Up to 12 months, they have difficulty maintaining attention. Some researchers suspect that these attention deficits may persist well into childhood (Vorhees & Mollnow, 1987). The severity of the symptoms depends on the extent of the mother's addiction, the size of the doses, and how close the last dose was to the time of delivery.

Barbiturates.   Additional research is needed on the effects of barbiturates on the developing fetus. Early studies suggested that even though barbiturates seemed to cross the placenta, the most serious effect was that such drugs appeared to cause minor depression in the growing child. Newer findings, however, show a clearly significant rise in the risk of learning disabilities among children whose mothers used barbiturates during pregnancy (Briggs et al., 1986; Gray & Yaffe, 1986, 1983; Nichols & Chen, 1981).

Alcohol. Until recently, it was believed that light drinking during pregnancy would not adversely affect fetal development. How much is too much is no longer clear, however, and the critical periods regarding alcohol consumption have not been defined. We are certain of the damage that heavy drinking leads to—as many as 32% of infants born to heavy drinkers showed congenital abnormalities (Ouellette et al., 1977). These abnormalities have been identified as part of the **fetal alcohol syndrome,** which is more closely examined in the box "Smoking and Alcohol: The Effects on the Fetus."

Children with the full range of symptoms of fetal alcohol syndrome are usually the offspring of mothers who drank heavily during pregnancy. More moderate drinkers place their infant at risk for less-severe effects commonly called *fetal alcohol effects* (FAE). These children show somewhat milder growth retardation and central nervous system dysfunction (Vorhees & Mollnow, 1987; Streissguth et al., 1989).

Smoking: Tobacco and Marijuana. The inhaled products of tobacco or marijuana smoke cross the placenta. Each time the mother smokes a cigarette, the heart of the fetus beats more quickly (Simpson, 1957). Among heavy smokers of either product, there is an increased risk of prematurity, low birth weight, spontaneous abortion, and infant mortality. Cigarette smoking has been thoroughly studied over the past two decades, with the results summarized in the box "Smoking and Alcohol: The Effects on the Fetus." The effects of marijuana use have been less thoroughly studied. However, researchers recently completed a series of studies in Jamaica, where marijuana is used in somewhat higher doses.

fetal alcohol syndrome Congenital abnormalities, including small size, low birth weight, certain facial characteristics, and possible mental retardation, resulting from maternal alcohol consumption during pregnancy.

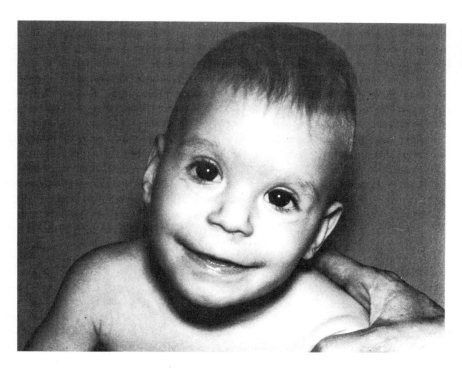

A child with fetal alcohol syndrome. Notice the characteristic thin upper lip, the lack of philtrum (vertical indentation between the upper lip and nose), the eyes set wide-apart, and the flat bones.

FOCUS ON AN ISSUE

SMOKING AND ALCOHOL: THE EFFECTS ON THE FETUS

Few people these days encourage pregnant women to smoke or drink. Since 1957, when the first reports appeared on the effects of cigarette smoking on fetal development, the link between smoking and fetal abnormalities has become increasingly clear. But as recently as the mid-1970s, many doctors advised their patients that moderate drinking was harmless or even good for their mental health. We are now learning that this is not so.

Smoking Each time the mother smokes a cigarette, the heart of the fetus beats more quickly. Among heavy smokers, a rate much higher than the norm is found for spontaneous abortions, stillbirths, and prematurity. Babies born to heavy smokers tend to weigh less at birth than those born to nonsmokers (Streissguth et al., 1989; Vorhees & Mollnow, 1987). Richard Naeye (1979, 1980, 1981) has examined the extensive research studies on smoking conducted over the past 25 years, and he has made the following points:

1. Newborns whose mothers smoke during pregnancy weigh approximately 200 grams less than newborns whose mothers do not smoke.

2. The more cigarettes a mother smokes per day, the smaller the newborn.

3. This growth disadvantage may continue for several years after birth.

4. Mothers who stop smoking during pregnancy often have normal-sized babies.

5. Smoking during pregnancy can also lead to congenital malformations, neonatal pneumonia, and a higher rate of newborn mortality.

Richard Naeye continues to examine the effects of maternal smoking during pregnancy. In a large follow-up study conducted on thousands of children, he has found that 7-year-olds whose mothers smoked 20 or more cigarettes per day scored lower on tests of spelling and reading and had a shorter attention span than did children of light smokers or nonsmokers (Naeye & Peters, 1984; Vorhees & Mollnow, 1987).

How does smoking damage fetuses? Research points to the placenta. The placenta is the site of an exchange between the blood of the mother and of the fetus. The mother's blood provides nutrients and oxygen to the fetus, along with many other substances. The fetus, in turn, passes waste materials out of its system to the mother's, where they can be dissipated. Some forms of damage to the placenta occur only among women who smoke, and other forms of damage occur often among women who smoke (Naeye, 1981). Researchers also suggest that smoking can constrict blood vessels in the uterus, reducing the flow of nutrients to the placenta (Fried & Oxorn, 1980). Both effects can reduce the amount of oxygen and nutrients supplied to the fetus, leading to reduced birth weight and possible fetal damage.

In light of the potential for harm, many doctors urge women who are trying to become pregnant not to smoke and those who are already pregnant to stop for the duration of the pregnancy.

Alcohol Consumption The consumption of alcoholic beverages by pregnant women is also being examined

---

Here, the newborn infants with prenatal marijuana exposure have somewhat high-pitched cries and behave in a fashion somewhat similar to that of infants experiencing mild narcotic withdrawal. It appears that high doses of marijuana affect the central nervous system and, hence, the neurological control of the infant (Lester & Dreher, 1989).

Cocaine. The decade of the 1980s saw a dramatic increase in the use of cocaine for "recreational purposes," sometimes sniffed in small amounts and other times smoked in the potent form called "crack." Some of the first studies that were more closely. Since 1968, a growing body of research has indicated a relationship between drinking during pregnancy and problems with spontaneous abortion, birth defects, and learning disabilities. By the mid-1970s, it was clear that as many as a third of the infants born to heavy drinkers (alcoholics) showed marked congenital abnormalities (Ouellette et al., 1977). These abnormalities have been identified as part of the *fetal alcohol syndrome* (FAS) and include small size and low birth weight, possible mental retardation, and neurological abnormalities. Certain distinct facial characteristics also are common, such as a small head, thin upper lip, a poorly developed indentation above the upper lip, a wide space between the margins of the eyelids, and flat cheekbones (Rosett et al., 1981).

FAS may be fairly common, perhaps occurring as often as one in every thousand births. This would make it the third largest cause of mental retardation in this country (Streissguth, 1983; Streissguth et al., 1983). It almost always occurs among mothers who drink heavily. Heavy drinkers consume *4 or more ounces of alcohol daily*. What, then, is the effect of light to moderate drinking on the developing embryo or fetus? (Moderate drinking may be defined as consuming from *1 to 4 ounces* per day.)

Many researchers believe that FAS is simply the worst of many insults and abnormalities that can result from drinking during pregnancy. Similar, yet milder, abnormalities are usually called *fetal alcohol effects,* or FAE (Vorhees & Mollnow, 1987). Since the mid-1970s, Dr. A. P. Streissguth and her colleagues have followed a group of over 1500 children who were born in the Seattle area. They have conducted a longitudinal study to determine the effects of the pregnant mother's drinking and smoking on the child's later behavior. Even in moderate amounts, alcohol seems to be related to the increased occurrence of heart rate and respiratory abnormalities in the newborn, to the newborn's difficulty in adapting to normal sounds and lights, and to lower mental development scores at 8 months. These findings cannot be attributed to nicotine or caffeine because both were carefully controlled in this project. At 4 years of age, the children of moderate alcohol users were less attentive and less compliant with their parents and performed less well on a laboratory test of visual attention than did children of nondrinking mothers (Streissguth et al., 1984). While the subjects were in elementary school, Streissguth and others found evidence suggesting that learning disabilities, attention problems, and hyperactivity may be more common among children born to mothers who were defined as moderate drinkers (Briggs, Freeman, & Yaffe, 1986; Streissguth et al., 1989).

Reviewing all of this evidence, the experts come to different conclusions. The Surgeon General advises abstinence for pregnant women. In contrast, many doctors still advise that drinking up to one glass of wine or beer each day is safe and is even advisable in some cases as a way of reducing anxiety. Yet, in a carefully conducted study of drug-free, light-drinking women in Dublin, Ireland, some effects on the newborn were found for women who drank as little as three glasses of beer per week (Nugent, Greene, & Mazor, 1990). Many experts now advise that no more than one small glass of beer or wine should be consumed in any single day during pregnancy.

done on the effects of prenatal exposure to cocaine uncovered very few negative symptoms (Madden et al., 1986). Unfortunately, some pregnant mothers, lulled into a false sense of security, consciously used cocaine prior to childbirth, believing the myth that it would produce easier labor. Recent, more extensive research, carefully monitoring the level of use, has demonstrated that not only is this myth false, but also that the risk of severe damage to the newborn infant is considerable. Mothers using cocaine experience more complications of labor. Their infants suffer from greater risk of growth retardation, prematurity, mental retardation, and even death by cerebral hemorrhage. Newborn infants have difficulty establishing motor control, orienting to visual objects or sounds, and achieving the normal regulation over waking and sleeping. The majority of cocaine-exposed infants can be classified as "fragile" infants, overloaded by normal environmental stimulation. They have few protective mechanisms to avoid overstimulation, and they have great difficulty controlling their overly excited nervous system. These infants cry frantically and seem unable to sleep. Even after a month, with the help of swaddling and pacifiers, they still have difficulty attending to normal stimulation without losing control and lapsing into frantic, high-pitched cries (Chasnoff, 1989). These infants pay an enormously high price, which may last for months or even years, for their mothers' "recreational" drug use.

Other Drugs.   Several studies have indicated that many women consume a wide range of drugs during pregnancy. In a Michigan study of nearly 19,000 women, it was found that these women averaged three prescription drugs during their pregnancies (Piper et al., 1987). Some of these drugs prescribed by physicians were clearly hazardous to the fetus. For example, tetracycline, an antibiotic, has been demonstrated to have adverse effects on teeth and bones, and contributes to other congenital defects. Heart medications, tranquilizers, and vaccines also appear to have a toxic effect on the fetus and cause behavioral difficulties in newborn children. Some anticonvulsant medications given to mothers who have epilepsy can cause structural malformations, growth delays, heart defects, or even mild mental retardation or speech irregularities (Vorhees & Mollnow, 1987). In addition to prescription drugs, pregnant women often use over-the-counter drugs such as aspirin, Tylenol, cough medicine, laxatives, and allergy pills. Yet, many of these substances are also not particularly safe. Aspirin in large doses can lead to excessive bleeding and other problems (Briggs et al., 1986). Even large doses of antacid tablets or cough syrups, particularly those containing codeine, may not be entirely safe (Brackbill et al., 1985). Stimulants like amphetamines, or even caffeine, readily cross the placenta and stimulate the fetus. Furthermore, these substances do not clear as easily from the fetus's system as they do from the mother's. The research on some of these substances is rather difficult to conduct. Yet, because many of these agents affect the central nervous system, they are being studied fairly extensively now for long-term behavioral effects and learning disabilities (Buelke-Sam, 1986).

Hormones.   Some hormones ingested by the mother, including oral contra-ceptives, may cause malformation of the fetal sexual organs. Mothers who took the hormone diethylstilbestrol (DES) to help prevent miscarriages have had daughters who have a higher risk of getting vaginal cancer or cervical abnormalities and sons who may be sterile. Hormones produced by both fetus and mother may alter the course of sexual development; in extreme cases, it may result in the development of a body type opposite to the baby's genetic sex (Briggs et al., 1986).

Chemical Agents.   Many chemical substances in the mother's environment may be harmful to the fetus. Yet pregnant women have little or no control over some of them. For example, in the late 1950s, an industrial plant in Japan discharged waste containing mercury into the ocean. People living in the surrounding community had children born with profound retardation and neurological impairment. It was found that the mercury had worked its way up the food chain in the ocean's system and had become deposited in the larger fish. Fish was the principal food source for many of these people (Reuhl & Chang, 1979).

There are similar stories concerning lead poisoning of mothers and infants. The exposure to moderate levels of lead, either prenatally or as infants, impairs cognitive development of the infant. Children have slower reaction time, have difficulty maintaining attention, and are more distractible, disorganized, and restless. Even in the 1980s, when we had reduced the levels of lead in car emissions, infants born in our cities had high enough levels of lead in their blood to produce lifelong behavioral deficits (Vorhees & Mollnow, 1987).

The damaging effects of mercury and lead are well established. Several other chemicals found in the environment are suspected to have negative effects. One study compared newborns whose mothers consumed fish contaminated with PCBs (a common set of compounds found in electrical transformers and paint) during pregnancy with a control group of normal infants (Jacobson et al., 1984). The infants exposed to this toxic substance showed weak reflexes and motor immaturity, and they startled more. Also, more than would be expected were born prematurely or were small for their gestation ages. Research continues on a wide range of other potential environmental toxins, including food preservatives, insecticides, and even some cosmetics.

DISEASES   Many diseases do not appear to affect the embryo or fetus at all. For example, most kinds of bacteria do not cross the placental barrier, so even a severe bacterial infection of the mother may have little or no effect on the fetus. On the other hand, many viruses—particularly rubella, syphilis, herpes, poliomyelitis, and many varieties of viral colds—do cross the placental barrier. The example of rubella (or German measles) has been carefully studied. This disease may cause blindness, heart defects, deafness, brain damage, or limb deformity, depending upon the particular time in the developmental sequence when the mother contracts it.

Perhaps the most devastating virus transmitted to the fetus is the human immunodeficiency virus (HIV). This transmits acquired immune deficiency syndrome (AIDS) to the newborn. Although the number of AIDS babies in the United States is small (547 infants died of AIDS in 1989), this is the fastest-growing group of AIDS sufferers in the country. Pregnant mothers diagnosed as HIV positive often need multiple services for their own physical and mental health, sometimes for drug dependence, and certainly for counseling in anticipation of a very ill and dying baby (Stuver, 1989).

STRESS   Regardless of what folklore may say, a mother's momentary thoughts will not affect the fetus. If a woman "thinks bad thoughts," her baby will not be born with some sort of psychic burden; if she is frightened by a snake, a spider, a bat, or some other creature, the child will not begin life with a personality defect or a birthmark. In other words, a mother's grief, worry, surprise, or other short-term emotional problems will not have an effect on her unborn child.

Prolonged and intense emotional stress during pregnancy, however, can have an effect on the developing child. During the prenatal period, the family makes adjustments for the impending birth. Sometimes this stress and change affect the emotional or nutritional state of the mother. Indeed, a family struggling with unemployment, illness, marital discord, or difficult relationships with in-laws may find a new child—especially an unplanned or unwanted one—too much of a burden. Similarly, a newly married couple who are still adjusting to each other's needs may not be ready to take on the additional responsibilities of parenthood. Single mothers face particularly difficult problems concerning financial and living arrangements, and social support is important at this time, when they feel most alone. Teenage mothers may also face these problems, as well as the equally difficult ones involving interrupted school and social lives, parental disapproval, and having to assume responsibilities they are not ready for. Prolonged stress during pregnancy may cause an expectant mother to neglect her diet, become frail or physically ill, ignore medical advice, or take harmful drugs. Furthermore, prolonged and intense emotional stress during pregnancy may cause either chemical changes—secretions of hormones from the endocrine system—or muscular tensions that can affect the environment of the developing child (Montagu, 1950).

RH FACTOR   Sometimes, there is incompatibility between the mother's blood and that of the developing fetus. The most well-known and well-studied component of blood is the Rh factor. The Rh factor is a component of the blood found in almost 85% of whites and nearly 100% of blacks; its presence makes a person's blood "Rh positive," its absence "Rh negative." The two Rh types are genetically inherited and are incompatible under certain conditions. If a mother's blood is Rh negative and her baby's is Rh positive, the trouble begins. Some of the baby's blood "leaks" into the mother's system; the mother's body builds up antibodies that then leak back into the baby's system and attack its blood cells. No danger exists for the mother, only for the unborn child. Furthermore, the antibody buildup does not usually happen quickly enough to affect a first child, only those born later. Today, with modern obstetrical care, an Rh-negative mother can be treated after her first Rh-positive pregnancy to prevent future Rh incompatibility problems (Freda, Gorman, & Pollack, 1966; Kiester, 1977; Queenan, 1975).

RADIATION   Excessive doses of radiation in early pregnancy, through the use of repeated X-rays, radium treatment administered to cancer patients, or through high levels of radiation in the atmosphere (resulting from nuclear explosions, for example), have produced marked effects on prenatal development (Sternglass, 1963). Careful review of the evidence in animals as well as humans indicates that moderate levels of radiation cause structural damage during the embryonic period (from 2 to 8 weeks), and tend to cause mental retardation or mild central nervous system damage in the period from 8 to 15 weeks of pregnancy. The effects of lower levels of radiation are not well established (Jensh, 1986).

MATERNAL AGE   The age of the mother can have an effect upon the prenatal development of the child. The incidence of prenatal defects or abnormalities is higher for first-time mothers over 35 years of age and for teenage mothers than for mothers between these ages. Although the precise reason for this is unclear, it is suspected that the hormonal balance and tissue development in the mother may play a role. For instance, Down syndrome occurs most often in children of mothers over age 35. Although we understand the cause of the abnormality (an incorrect number and pairing of chromosomes), we do not yet know why it occurs more frequently to mothers in this age group.

PERINATOLOGY A new branch of medicine, **perinatology,** considers childbirth not as a single point in time but as a span of time that begins with conception and goes on through the prenatal period, delivery, and the first few months of life. In order to deal with the multifaceted health problems of this period, many specialists—including obstetricians, pediatricians, geneticists, endocrinologists, biochemists, surgeons, social workers, and psychiatrists—work in teams.

Certain techniques allow for the early diagnosis and prompt medical treatment of potential problems. These techniques include **amniocentesis,** the use of **fetoscopes,** and **ultrasound** pictures. Amniocentesis involves the withdrawal of a small amount of amniotic fluid by means of a long, thin needle with syringe attachment. Fetal cells in the fluid can then be examined for various genetic defects. A fetoscope is a long, hollow needle with a small lens and a light source at its end. The needle is inserted in the amniotic sac so that a doctor may observe the developing fetus for major structural defects.

Pictures produced by ultrasound mapping show the location, position, size, and movement of the fetus. They can assist in amniocentesis by finding a safe place to insert the needle. As early as 7 weeks after conception, ultrasound pictures can diagnose pregnancy, and they can monitor the heartbeat, breathing, and movements made by the fetus throughout the rest of the pregnancy. Ultrasound images are used to judge the maturity of the fetus by helping to determine whether its size is proper for the number of weeks into the gestation period. They can also be used to identify a number of prenatal conditions, including defects of the fetus's neural tube, abnormal growth or development, and multiple pregnancies (Knox, 1980). As ultrasound pictures are a reliable and safe way to inspect fetuses, physicians and hospitals are using them with increasing frequency.

perinatology A branch of medicine that deals with childbirth from conception, the prenatal period, and delivery through the first few months of life.

amniocentesis A test for chromosomal abnormalities that is performed during the second trimester of pregnancy; it involves the withdrawal and analysis of amniotic fluid.

fetoscope A long, hollow needle with a small lens and light source at its end that is inserted into the amniotic sac for observation of the fetus.

ultrasound A technique that uses sound waves to produce a picture of the fetus while it is still in the mother's uterus.

MATERNAL AND FAMILY ADJUSTMENT

Adjustment to parenthood is a major developmental task for adults, particularly so with a first child. The new parents must make economic and social adjustments; often, they must reevaluate and modify existing relationships. Among the factors involved in this adjustment are the cultural attitudes of the family toward pregnancy, childbearing, and child rearing.

Motivations for childbearing vary considerably from culture to culture. In some societies, children are valued as financial assets or as providers for the parents in their old age. Sometimes children represent those who will maintain the family traditions, or they symbolize fulfillment of the parents' personal needs. At other times, children may be regarded as a duty or a necessary burden. Certain cultures accept children as inevitable, a natural part of life about which one does not make conscious decisions. In India, for example, Hindu women want to have children to guarantee them a good afterlife. Sons are needed to carry on the family name, to assist the father and follow in his footsteps, and finally to care for aged and ill parents. Although a daughter is a financial liability because her family must provide a dowry, custom still requires that an Indian man have at least one daughter to give away in marriage (Whiting, 1963).

Motivations for having children vary from culture to culture.

In all cultures, the pregnant woman must adjust to the physical, psychological, and social changes that come with motherhood. Profound bodily changes occur that can hardly be ignored. Even before the fetus is large enough to create a change in a woman's appearance, she may feel nauseous or experience a fullness or tingling sensation in her breasts. Often she may suffer fatigue and emotional hypersensitivity during the early weeks of pregnancy, but in the middle stage of pregnancy, she frequently experiences a sense of heightened well-being. In fact, increased capacity and functioning of some of the bodily systems occur, such as in the circulatory system. In the last stages of pregnancy, some physical discomfort is usual along with, at times, a feeling of emotional burden. Increased weight, reduced mobility, an altered sense of balance, and a pressure on internal organs from the growing fetus are changes experienced by all pregnant women. In addition, other symptoms such as varicose veins, heartburn, frequent urination, or shortness of breath may contribute to the discomfort that some women feel. Wide individual variation exists in the amount of discomfort, fatigue, or burden experienced during the last few weeks. Some women find this last period of pregnancy much easier than others do.

These physical changes have an impact upon the psychological state of the pregnant woman. She must come to terms with a new body image and an altered self-concept, and she must deal with the reactions of those around her. Some women experience a feeling of uniqueness or distance from old friends, or a desire for protection. Pregnancy may also be regarded with uncertainty by some women—they may be unsure about career plans following childbirth, anxious about their ability to handle a child, fearful of the possibility of birth defects, concerned about the financial burden, or simply uncomfortable with a markedly changed self-image. They may be eager to have the child, yet disappointed that they will have to share their time, energy, and husband with someone else (Jessner, Weigert, & Foy, 1970).

Compared to the major physical and emotional changes that the mother undergoes, the father's role seems minor. Fathers may seem to stay in the background, quietly providing for the mother and baby, but a closer look reveals that fathers also experience a major transition to parenthood. In many ways, pregnancy is a "family affair" (Parke, 1981). Both father and mother experience the problems and pleasures of expecting a child. During the first trimester, fathers not only need to cope with the morning sickness, fatigue, and "edginess" of their spouse, but perhaps as many as 65% of first time fathers experience some of the same symptoms themselves (Liebenberg, 1967). In addition, fathers worry about the future as much as mothers do; they are concerned about their ability to support an enlarged family and about what kind of parent they will be. They tend to be just as concerned as mothers over whether the child will like and respect them and whether they will be able to meet the child's emotional demands (Ditzion & Wolf, 1978; Parke, 1981). Some take this opportunity to learn more about children and parenting. Others make new financial arrangements. Many fathers provide increased emotional support for their wives. When there are other children in the family, fathers often spend more time with them and help them to prepare for the new arrival (Parke, 1981).

Both parents' attitudes toward pregnancy are shaped, to a significant degree, by those of the surrounding society. At times in our history—and some remnants of the attitude still remain today—pregnancy was considered to be an abnormal condition or an illness, something neither to be looked at nor discussed. A pregnant woman was confined and protected. She was not out in public, or in school, or in an office carrying on a career. Today, in our culture and in many others, pregnancy is considered a normal condition. In some cultures, it is even revered and accorded a special status as signifying the highest state of feminine fulfillment.

Western cultures have begun to accept pregnancy as "nothing out of the ordinary." Employers often encourage women to work and perform all normal tasks until the time of delivery. Some women experience little or no discomfort, fatigue, or excessive conflict with their other roles. Others take the discomfort and fatigue in stride and go on with their lives, minimizing the dramatic physical changes. Still others feel cheated because they are not given special treatment.

All of these conflicting feelings and social attitudes, when coupled with the parents' personal needs and mixed emotions, result in a major period of stress, change, and adjustment. None of these feelings will harm the unborn child, however, unless the mother suffers severe or prolonged emotional stress. Nevertheless, parental attitudes do help to create the atmosphere of the environment that the child enters at birth.

STUDY OUTLINE

Prenatal Development

Conception. Human development begins when the **sperm** fertilizes the **ovum.** In the process of **ovulation,** an ovum, or egg cell, is released from the ovary into the **Fallopian tube.** There, the genetic material of the egg unites with the genetic material of a single sperm cell.

Periods of Development. The fertilized ovum, or **zygote,** begins to divide, and at the same time, it descends the Fallopian tube toward the uterus. Rapid cell division continues for about 10 to 12 days until a hollow sphere of cells, the **blastula,** forms and becomes embedded in the uterine wall in a process called **implantation.**

The **germinal period** is now over and the **embryonic period** has begun. During the next 7 weeks, the structures and tissues of the embryo are formed. The embryo develops within the **amniotic sac** and receives oxygen and nourishment through the **placenta.**

The embryo develops from three layers of cells: the **ectoderm,** which becomes skin and the nervous system; the **mesoderm,** which becomes muscles, blood, and the excretory system; and the **endoderm,** which becomes the digestive system, lungs, and glands. The limbs unfold from the trunk, and the eyes and facial features begin to form.

The **fetal period** lasts from the beginning of the third month until birth. During this time, all organs, limbs, muscles, and systems become functional. The fetus steadily grows in size and gains weight; it also begins to move and kick within the mother's body. (By the seventh month, a healthy fetus could survive outside the mother's body, provided that intensive medical care is available at a well-equipped facility.)

By the last 3 months, the fetus can react to touch and sound, and fat layers form to protect it from changes in temperature after birth. In the last month, the fetus usually shifts to a head-down position, and then the mother's body prepares for birth.

Developmental Trends. Fetal growth follows several developmental trends. Among them are the **cephalocaudal trend,** which applies to physical and motor development from the top of the body downward; **proximodistal development,** which takes place from the middle of the body outward; and the **gross-to-specific trend,** which refers to the increasing specialization of motor responses.

The dual processes of **differentiation** and **integration** often occur together. For example, motor activities that were originally identical become separate and distinct; almost immediately, however, they are combined into a larger integrated system.

Prenatal Influences

The majority of birth defects are caused by environmental influences during the prenatal period, or during childbirth, or by the interaction of heredity and environmental influences. The study of birth defects is called **teratology.** Various environmental influences cause most of the harmful disturbances in fetal development.

Critical Periods. Environmental influences have their greatest effect at critical periods, times when the organism is acutely receptive to particular influences. For most fetal organ systems, these periods occur during the first **trimester** of pregnancy.

Types of Prenatal Influences. A variety of environmental factors may influence prenatal development. Malnutrition, drugs, certain chemicals, viruses, and prolonged emotional stress can have quite serious effects. The mother's nutrition is of primary importance to the normal development of the fetus's brain. Diseases such as rubella and syphilis in the mother can cause mental deficiency, blindness, and deafness in the infant. A mother with an Rh-negative blood type can produce antibodies that may damage her Rh-positive fetus's blood cells. The mother's smoking and alcohol consumption can cause numerous fetal abnormalities. Radiation can also damage the developing fetus. Finally, the older the mother is, the higher the probability of birth defects is in her infant.

Perinatology, a branch of medicine that studies the process of childbirth from conception to the first months of life, uses **ultrasound** pictures, **amniocentesis,** and **fetoscopes** to diagnose potential problems.

Maternal and Family Adjustment

The prenatal period has psychological and social, as well as biological significance for both the developing child and the family. According to the culture, individual and societal attitudes toward pregnancy and childbearing vary considerably. No matter how it is viewed, the prenatal period is a time of major adjustment that may influence the child before birth and does, most certainly, after birth.

KEY TERMS AND CONCEPTS

amniocentesis	fertilization	ovulation
amniotic sac	fetal alcohol syndrome	ovum
blastula	fetal period	perinatology
cephalocaudal development	fetoscope	placenta
chorion	germinal period	proximodistal development
cleavage	gestation period	sperm
conception	gross-to-specific development	teratology
critical period	implantation	trimester
differentiation	integration	ultrasound
dizygotic twins	in vitro fertilization	umbilical cord
ectoderm	maturation	vernix caseosa
embryonic period	mesoderm	viable
endoderm	miscarriage	zygote
Fallopian tubes	monozygotic twins	

SELF-TEST QUESTIONS

1. After a woman ovulates, what is the period of time during which she can become pregnant? Describe the process that occurs if the ovum is fertilized, and contrast it to the fate of an unfertilized ovum.

2. What is in vitro fertilization?

3. What is the germinal period, and what important processes do cells begin at this time?

4. What is the embryonic period? How long does it last?

5. What is the fetal period? List and describe the developmental processes of this period.

6. What are some of the advances in reproductive technology? What are the dilemmas they raise?

7. What is the purpose of the vernix caseosa?

8. List and describe the general prenatal developmental trends of a fetus.

9. What is a teratogen or a teratogenic agent?

10. How do environmental effects impact fetal development?

11. What is the relationship between thalidomide and the timing and nature of critical periods?

12. List the factors that have been found to influence prenatal development.

13. What is fetal alcohol syndrome?

14. What is the effect of cigarette smoking on a fetus?

15. How does prolonged and intense stress affect the environment of a fetus?

16. Name some physical and emotional adjustments a mother and father make during pregnancy.

SUGGESTED READINGS

BORG, S., AND LASKER, J. *When pregnancy fails: Families coping with miscarriage, stillbirth and infant death*. Boston: Beacon Press, 1981. These two authors have themselves lost an infant. Hence, they speak from personal experience as well as from the professional literature about the experience of loss and family adjustment.

COREA, G. *The mother machine*. New York: Harper & Row, 1986. A powerful and controversial examination of the social and ethical implications of the new reproductive technologies.

DORRIS, M. *The broken cord*. New York: Harper & Row, 1989. A sensitive and compelling account of a single father's struggle with raising a child who has fetal alcohol syndrome. Expanded discussion of the complex problem of FAS among the Native American population.

EISENBERG, A., MURKOFF, H. E. & HATHAWAY, S. E. *What to expect when you're expecting*. New York: Workman Pub-lishing, 1988. A popular, practical guide that addresses concerns of mothers- and fathers-to-be from the planning stage through postpartum.

KITZINGER, S. *Birth over thirty*. New York: Penguin Books, 1985. Kitzinger presents a thorough, sensitive discussion of physical, emotional, and social changes during and after pregnancy for the woman over 30.

NILSSON, L. *A child is born*. New York: Delacorte Press, 1990. Vivid full-color photography of the course of prenatal development with up-to-date text on the psychological as well as the medical facts of prenatal development and childbirth. An excellent gift for an expectant couple.

SHAPIRO, H. J. *The pregnancy book for today's woman*. New York: Harper & Row, 1983. This book addresses many current issues of pregnancy, including drug use, herpes, jogging, caesarean sections, and pregnancies in women over age 30.

Chapter 5

Hold a baby to your ear
As you would a shell:
Sounds of centuries you hear
New centuries foretell
Who can break a baby's code?
And which is the older—
The listener or his small load?
The held or the holder?

E. B. WHITE
"CONCH"

CHAPTER OUTLINE

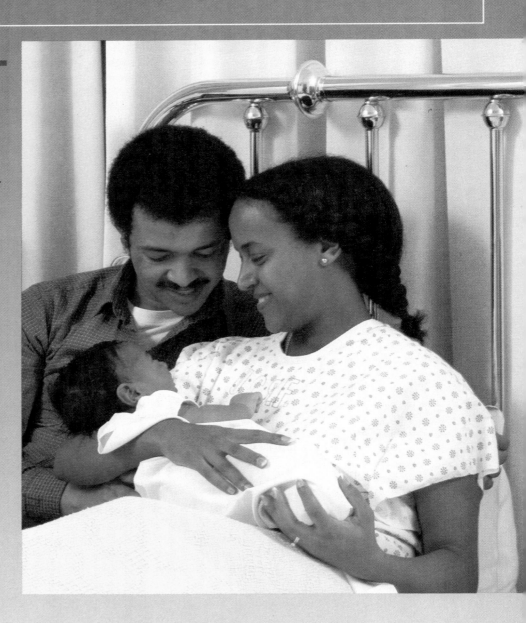

Childbirth and the Neonate

*A*ttitudes toward childbirth differ widely from one culture to another. Among the Jarara of South America, for example, women traditionally gave birth in public with everyone in attendance (Gutierrez de Pineda, 1948). In traditional Laotian culture, relatives and friends dropped by and visited a woman in labor. They played musical instruments, told jokes, and even made licentious comments to divert her attention (Reinach, 1901). In contrast to this public participation in childbirth, some cultures keep childbirth hidden. The Cuna of Panama tell their children that babies are found in the forest between deer horns, and children never witness even the preparations for childbirth (Jelliffe et al., 1961). The cultural ideal among the !Kung-San, a tribal society in northwestern Botswana, is that women tell no one about their initial labor pains and go out into the bush alone to give birth. They deliver the baby, cut the cord, and stabilize the newborn—all without assistance (Komner & Shostak, 1987).

What is the attitude toward childbirth in our own culture? In the United States and in most Western countries, babies are usually born in hospitals, out of view of society. The reason for this is not because our society dictates extreme modesty, such as we see among the Cuna; rather, it is dictated by the knowledge that hospital conditions have greatly reduced the hazards of childbirth for both infant and mother. The last three decades have witnessed dramatic progress in saving premature and high-risk infants through new medical technology and procedures.

The greater safety of the hospital, however, has had some important social side effects. The removal of childbirth from the family and the community has resulted in the loss of rich social support. The new mother, in many cases separated even from her husband except during hospital visiting hours, is apt to feel alone, exposed, and unsupported in one of her life's major events. Segregating the mother also means that children grow up knowing little about the birth process except what they learn from secondhand reports. Consequently, new parents are sometimes surprised at the appearance of their newborn infants—small, often wrinkled creatures whose soft-boned heads may be misshapen after the passage through the birth canal. In the past two decades, much has been written and said about childbirth as a medical and surgical event, rather than as a natural and family-centered event. As a result, customs are changing. Research indicates that early contact helps promote a deep bond between parents and the new child. Informed parents can make better decisions that balance the need for medical safety with the need for strong family bonds.

CHAPTER OBJECTIVES

By the time you have finished this chapter, you should be able to do the following:
- List and describe the three stages of childbirth.
- Discuss the benefits and liabilities of medical advances in childbirth.
- Explain "natural" childbirth.
- Describe parent–infant bonding.
- Discuss the neonate, including the following: neonatal adjustment, neonatal assessment, infant states, infant capacities, and temperamental differences.
- List the special needs of premature infants.

labor The first stage of childbirth, typically lasting 12 to 18 hours and characterized by uterine contractions during which the cervix dilates to allow for passage of the baby.

birth The second stage of childbirth, which is the time between full cervix dilation and the time when the baby is free of the mother's body.

afterbirth The placenta and related tissues, following their expulsion from the uterus during the third stage of childbirth.

false labor Painful contractions of the uterus without dilation of the cervix.

perineum The region between the vagina and the rectum.

episiotomy An incision made to enlarge the vaginal opening during childbirth.

In this chapter, we will examine the process of birth, the capabilities of the newborn, and the psychological effects of birth on both the infant and the family.

CHILDBIRTH

Although the attitudes toward pregnancy and childbirth vary from culture to culture, the birth of a child follows the same biological timetable in every society.

The Sequence of Childbirth

We usually describe the process of childbirth as occurring in three stages: **labor, birth,** and **afterbirth.**

Labor, the first stage, is the period during which the cervix of the uterus dilates to allow for the passage of the baby. Although labor can last from a few minutes to over 30 hours, it typically lasts 12 to 18 hours for the first child and somewhat less for later children. It begins with mild uterine contractions, generally spaced 15 to 20 minutes apart. As labor progresses, the contractions increase both in frequency and in intensity until they occur only 3 to 5 minutes apart. The muscular contractions of labor are involuntary, and the mother can best help herself by trying to relax during this period.

Some mothers experience **false labor,** especially with the first child. It is often difficult to distinguish false labor from real labor, but one test that often works is to have the expectant mother walk about. Real labor usually becomes more uncomfortable with simple exercise, but the pains of false labor tend to diminish.

During labor, two other events must occur. First, a mucous plug that covers the cervix is released. This process is called "showing" and may cause some bleeding. Second, the amniotic sac, or "bag of waters," which has enclosed the fetus, may break and some amniotic fluid may rush forth.

The second stage of childbirth is the birth of the baby. Birth is usually distinguished as the period between the time that the cervix is fully dilated and the time when the baby is free of the mother's body. This stage may last from 15 minutes to 2 hours, and, like labor, it tends to last longest for a first birth.

Generally, between 10 and 20 contractions occur during birth. These contractions are regular, with one every 2 to 3 minutes, and they are of greater intensity and longer duration than those occurring during labor. Each birth contraction lasts about 1 minute, and the mother can actively assist in the birth by bearing down with her abdominal muscles during each contraction.

Normally, the first part of the baby to emerge from the birth canal is the head. It "crowns," or becomes visible, and emerges more and more with each contraction until it can be grasped. The tissue of the mother's **perineum** (the region between the vagina and the rectum) must stretch considerably to allow the baby's head to emerge. In Western cultures, and especially in U.S. hospitals, the attending doctor often makes an incision, called an **episiotomy,** to enlarge the vaginal opening. It is believed that this can heal more neatly than the jagged tear that might occur if the incision is not made. Episiotomies are much less common in Western Europe. Obstetricians occasionally use a steel tool, called *forceps,* to grasp the head and hasten the birth, should complications arise.

In most normal births, the baby is born head first in a face-down position. After the head is clear, the baby's face turns to one side so that its body emerges with the least resistance. More difficult births occur when the baby is positioned in a **breech presentation** (buttocks first) or a **posterior presentation** (facing toward the mother's abdomen instead of toward her back). In each of these cases, the baby is usually assisted to prevent unnecessary injury to the mother or the infant.

The expulsion of the placenta and related tissues marks the third stage of childbirth. This stage is virtually painless and generally occurs within 20 minutes after the delivery. Again, the mother can help the process by bearing down. The placenta and umbilical cord (together known as the afterbirth once they have been expelled from the uterus) are then checked for imperfections that might signal damage to the newborn.

breech presentation The baby's position in the uterus is such that the buttocks will emerge first; assistance is usually needed in such cases to prevent injury to the mother or the infant.

posterior presentation A baby is positioned in the uterus facing the mother's abdomen rather than her back.

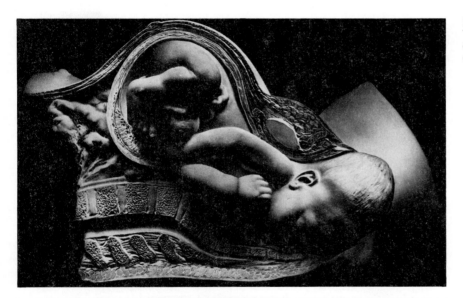

Labor: The Moment of "Crowning." The baby's head emerges from the birth canal. The baby is in the correct face-down position for a normal delivery.

Labor: A Breech Presentation. Delivery in this position is difficult for both mother and baby.

The Medical Technology of Childbirth

In most cases, birth is a safe, natural process. Mother and infant work tremendously hard, and at the very end, a doctor or midwife serves as babycatcher. Some deliveries, however, require major medical intervention due to problems like improper fetal position and prematurity. In the past 20 years, obstetrical medicine has made dramatic progress in dealing with difficult deliveries. Infants that would not have survived in 1960 are now thriving in record numbers. For example, today over 80% of premature infants weighing 750 to 1000 gms. (1.6 to 2.2 lbs.) will survive in a well-equipped intensive care unit for newborns (Ohlsson et al., 1987). In 1972, only one out of five such tiny newborns survived (*Newsweek*, 1976). (Premature infants are further discussed later in this chapter in the box "The 'Kilogram Kids.' ")

The new medical advances include drugs, microsurgery, diagnostic tools, and preventive measures. For instance, a vaccine given to an Rh-negative woman immediately after her first delivery can completely prevent blood incompatibility problems in future pregnancies. As we saw in Chapters 3 and 4, procedures like amniocentesis, ultrasound mapping, and the use of fetoscopes can help diagnose conditions prenatally, and steps can be taken to treat the fetus or the newborn.

The new technology of childbirth is a blessing to many families, especially those facing premature or high-risk deliveries. But some critics argue that it is too frequently applied to deliveries that should be routine. Some consumer advocates point to the increasing rate of Caesarean births as the inevitable result of increased technology in the delivery room. One device they frequently single out as unnecessary is the fetal monitor.

FETAL MONITORING Many hospitals have routinely measured the fetal heart rate during labor using devices called fetal monitors. These can be applied either externally or internally. The external type of monitor records the intensity of uterine contractions and the baby's heartbeat by means of two belts placed around the mother's abdomen. The internal monitor consists of a plastic tube containing electrodes; it is inserted into the vagina and attached to the baby's head. It also measures the fetal heartbeat, uterine pressure, fetal breathing, and head compression (Goodlin, 1979). Proper interpretation of the data yielded by the monitor can alert the obstetrician to compression of the umbilical cord, poor fetal oxygen intake, and fetal distress (*Pediatrics*, 1979).

Although fetal monitors can be quite effective in high-risk pregnancies, the routine or continuous use of them with low-risk or healthy mothers is now discouraged. The American College of Obstetrics and Gynecology has changed its standards and no longer considers fetal monitors part of standard care for maternity patients (BIRTH, 1988). These monitors can be easily misread, leading to unnecessary surgical procedures. Also, the monitors restrict movement, requiring the mother to remain in bed, on her back, rather than letting her get up and walk around. But, most importantly, research has not indicated that the routine use of such monitors produces healthier babies and fewer complications (BIRTH, 1988; Marieskind, 1989).

MEDICATION As discussed in Chapter 4, drug use during pregnancy can harm the developing fetus. For this reason, physicians avoid giving medication to the expectant mother, especially during the early months of pregnancy (Brackbill,

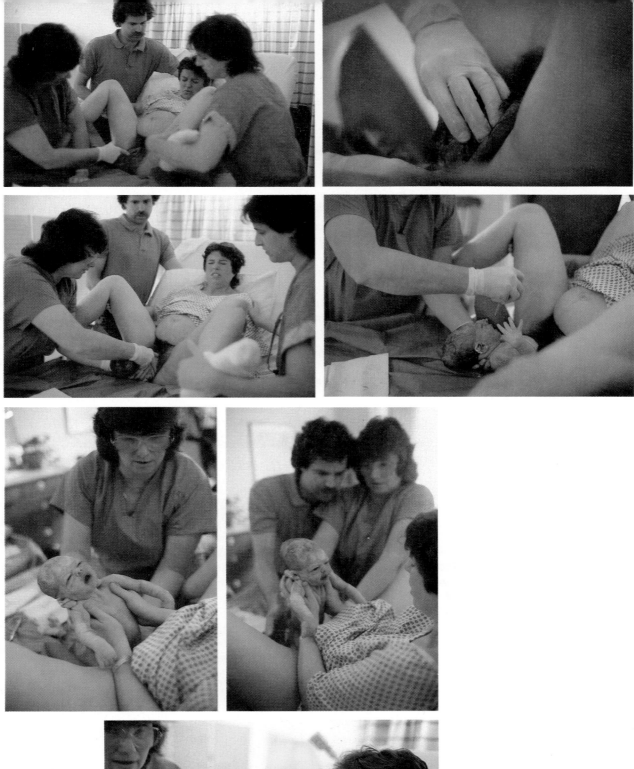

The birth process

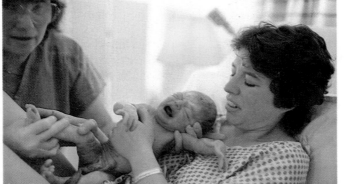

anoxia In prenatal development and childbirth, a lack of sufficient oxygen reaching the brain, which can cause irreversible brain damage.

1979). Parents and physicians try to weigh the use of anesthetics and painkillers for the mother during childbirth against the risk of possible damage to the baby. Recent evidence suggests that the routine use of general anesthetics at birth increases the incidence of brain damage and may delay the development of memory and coordination abilities in the child. Even regional anesthesia designed to block pain in the pelvic area may depress the newborn's early functioning (Murray et al., 1981). Physicians and medical researchers have long known that drugs that reduce the mother's level of awareness and sensitivity affect the infant's alertness and responsiveness at birth. Also, drug residues may remain in the infant's blood and urine for weeks after delivery (Broman, 1986). Are the effects of these drugs only temporary?

There is conflicting evidence about the long-term effects that may result from exposure at birth to powerful anesthetics given to the mother (Brackbill, 1979; *Pediatrics,* 1978). Researchers have discovered that a significant number of children whose mothers were given routine anesthetics during childbirth have been delayed in learning to sit up, stand, walk, and talk (Brackbill & Broman, 1979). Clearly, drugs that slow the birth process increase the danger of **anoxia,** a condition where an insufficient amount of oxygen reaches the baby's brain. Any lack of oxygen at this time can have serious, long-lasting effects on the child's later mental and motor

FOCUS ON AN ISSUE

CAESAREAN CHILDBIRTH

Despite the best preparations and expectations for a normal prepared childbirth, many mothers find themselves scheduled for delivery by Caesarean section. Medical procedures have improved sufficiently, making this a remarkably safe operation. Often it is done under regional anesthesia, so the mother is awake and aware. Also, because the procedure is done quickly, very little of the anesthesia reaches the infant. Doctors assure expectant mothers that they can expect an excellent outcome for both themselves and their infants if a Caesarean delivery is advised, given the new procedures.

Nevertheless, many consumer advocates wonder if we have gone too far in increasing our rate of Caesarean births. The rate of Caesarean sections performed in the United States in 1970 was 5.5%. The rate increased to 18% in 1980, and to 24.4% in 1987 (Cohen & Estner, 1983; Marieskind, 1989). Caesarean section is now the most frequently performed major surgery, with nearly a million performed each year and with some hospitals performing over 40% of childbirths by this method. But, if this is a relatively safe operation, why is this increase a problem?

First, the procedure is major abdominal surgery.

Any major surgery requires a period of recovery that is much longer than recovery from childbirth. Second, not all doctors performing Caesarean sections are sensitive enough to the special problems of these mothers, including the need to arrange early contact with their infants. Third, some consumer advocates argue that the sharp rise in the rate of Caesarean sections is a result of the increased use of certain medical procedures that seem to interrupt the natural process of labor. They argue that the use of fetal monitors and the regular administration of four or five different kinds of drugs, such as painkillers and drugs used to induce labor, create situations that lead eventually to the need for surgical childbirth. Perhaps the rapid rise in the rate of Caesarean sections is a signal that we ought to examine some other practices introduced in the past 2 decades.

The psychological reactions of mothers to Caesarean childbirth can be quite negative. Many mothers report feeling disappointed, disillusioned, or a sense of failure, particularly those who had general anesthesia and "missed the event." Repeated studies report that some mothers who have had a Caesarean section are disappointed or even angry at being cheated, are slow to development—it can result in learning disabilities or even more severe brain damage later in childhood. A few studies suggest, however, that mild anesthetics actually facilitate certain high-risk deliveries, as well as ease pain (Myers & Myers, 1978). Although no one disputes the importance of easing the mother's pain, it is clear that during pregnancy or childbirth any medication should be used with caution (Broman, 1986).

CAESAREAN SECTION   Most births, with or without anesthesia, occur through the birth canal as described earlier. In some cases, however, delivery through the birth canal may be dangerous or difficult. A fetus may be too large to pass between the mother's pelvic bones; the mother may have **toxemia** (a poisoning of the body caused by a metabolic disturbance); she may be in danger of excessive bleeding; she may have a disorder such as diabetes or some other illness that will put too much stress on the fetus. Occasionally, despite a lengthy labor, the uterine cervix does not dilate. A prolonged labor places a great strain upon the mother and also increases the danger that the fetus may suffer the serious effects of oxygen deprivation. Multiple births and breech presentations also commonly make vaginal delivery dangerous or impossible. In our culture, **Caesarean section** is usually advised for all of these conditions. This is a surgical procedure used to remove the baby and the

toxemia Poisoning of a mother's body during pregnancy due to a metabolic disturbance.

Caesarean section A surgical procedure used to remove the baby and the placenta from the uterus by cutting through the abdominal wall.

choose a name for the baby, test lower on self-esteem shortly after giving birth, and have more difficulty feeding their infants (Oakley & Richards, 1990).

And, finally, there appears to be a higher rate of grieving, or mourning, or actual depression following Caesarean sections than following vaginal deliveries (Cohen & Estner, 1983; Kitzinger, 1981). It is common for some mothers to experience mild depression after childbirth. Many factors may contribute to this, including major hormonal changes, the letdown following a long-anticipated event, the fatigue of late pregnancy and childbirth, and the rather insistent day-and-night demands of a new infant. It is not clear why mothers who have given birth surgically often experience more depression than others. Some mothers report that the loss of control, loss of involvement, and loss of participation in a critical life event contribute to a somewhat long, partially unexplained, sense of sadness (Cohen & Estner, 1983).

Physicians, too, have been concerned about the radical increase in the rate of Caesarean births since 1970. At first, they noted the continued drop in infant mortality and maternal mortality rates during this period

and the improved health of premature infants. The leading reasons, after all, for conducting Caesarean sections are failure to progress in labor, fetal distress, previous Caesarean delivery, and breech position of the fetus. But the increased use of surgical delivery in the 1980s was not accompanied by a major increase in the health of infants or by any related decrease in infant mortality. Alternative ways of coping with these situations are being investigated. For example, it is estimated that perhaps 60% of women who have delivered one child via Caesarean section could safely give birth vaginally in subsequent pregnancies if encouraged to do so (Donovan, 1986). Despite the pressure of malpractice suits, the American College of Obstetrics and Gynecology now regularly recommends more complete parent education about the risks and benefits of vaginal versus Caesarean delivery. This organization urges its members to recognize the imprecision of electronic fetal monitors, the safety of vaginal births after a previous Caesarean birth, and the benefits of "natural" childbirth for healthy mothers (Marieskind, 1989; DeMott & Sandmire, 1990).

"natural" childbirth A childbirth method that involves the mother's preparation (including education and exercises), limited medication during pregnancy and birth, and the mother's (and perhaps father's) participation during the birth.

placenta from the uterus by cutting through the abdominal wall. After a woman has had one Caesarean delivery, it is often recommended (but not always necessary) that future deliveries also be by this method. Because the procedure involves anesthesia and a long recovery period, it is not recommended for the sake of convenience. Nevertheless, it is no longer uncommon for a mother to have four or more babies by Caesarean section. (See the box "Caesarean Childbirth.")

THE EXPERIENCE OF CHILDBIRTH

Prepared Childbirth

The dangers of drugs given during pregnancy and childbirth are one of the reasons that **"natural" childbirth** was first suggested by doctors such as Grantly Dick-Read (1953) and Fernand Lamaze (1970). This method has increased in popularity in recent years. Basically, "natural" childbirth (we put the word *natural* in quotes because here it means a good deal more than having babies naturally) involves three things: preparation, limited medication, and participation. To Dick-Read, the key was preparation. In Western society, women often approach childbirth with limited knowledge and exaggerated fear. This fear produces tension, which causes tightening of the muscles and makes labor more difficult and painful than necessary. Dick-Read proposed that if the mother knew about the birth process—and knew how to help herself at each stage—she would be more relaxed during labor, the pain would be less intense, and she would probably not need medication. Drawing on Dick-Read's philosophy, Lamaze developed a childbirth preparation program that is taught to both mothers and fathers in classes throughout much of the Western world.

"Natural" childbirth classes prepare the mother and father as much as possible for the actual course of childbirth.

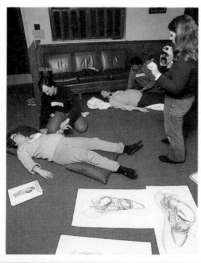

How does prepared childbirth work? The mother, and often the father too, attend from six to eight classes where they learn about pregnancy and the stages of labor. The expectant mother is taught exercises for relaxation, breathing, and muscle strengthening. When the time comes for birth, the mother knows which breathing procedures will minimize the pain. She even knows the most effective way to push so as to help deliver her baby. Often, her husband is encouraged to be with her during labor and delivery to coach her through the process and lend emotional support. During the actual birth, the mother is a full participant—awake, alert, working, and in control.

Is prepared childbirth as successful as it sounds? Often, it is. The infant has a quick and safe delivery because the mother is able to help, and drugs are not used. The birth experience is also rewarding for the parents. Although most participating couples admit that "natural" childbirth is hard work, the overwhelming majority report that it is one of life's most satisfying experiences.

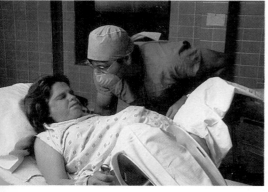

Changing Practices

The experience of childbirth varies widely, even in Western cultures, depending on where the baby is born, who is present, what medical practices the mother elects, and what practices the doctor requires. In many hospitals, the full-term mother is treated as if she were entering the hospital for some type of surgical procedure. She signs in, her pubic hair is shaved, she is given an enema, and she is allowed nothing to eat or drink. She lies in a hospital bed through much of her labor with a fetal monitor attached to her abdomen, and often an intravenous needle attached to her arm. She is prepared for a Caesarean section, should one be necessary. A husband or coach is with her; they talk quietly, and he or she may offer considerable encouragement and perhaps occasional back rubs, but there is not much activity. If the frequency and duration of contractions decrease, labor may be induced by an injection of a drug like pitocin, or by the artificial rupture of the amniotic membranes. These procedures often result in active, vigorous labor, which may occur quickly and sometimes almost violently. Finally, when the cervix is almost fully dilated, the mother is moved to the delivery room. Her legs are elevated and placed in stirrups. Medication is administered if needed, and the actual birth takes place.

Contrast this experience with that of another woman who enters the birthing center adjacent to the local hospital. A pleasant bedroom and lounge are available to her, and there are no standard orders for medical procedures. She and her partner are free to walk, talk, eat a bit, and sip some juice. She may try several positions, crouching down on all fours if it seems more comfortable. The mother is encouraged to walk frequently or to stand so that gravity can help the infant's progress through the birth canal. She is attended through much of the labor and the actual childbirth by a licensed nurse-midwife, who also may have provided childbirth education classes and exercises for the parents during the woman's pregnancy. When the time comes for the actual birth, the mother has a choice of positions—she may lie on her back, sit partly elevated, or sit in a birthing chair (Young, 1982).

Clearly, there are a number of options besides whether or not one has prepared childbirth, whether or not one uses medication, or whether or not one takes advantage of such technologies as fetal monitors.

MIDWIVES   Childbirth assistants who remain with a mother throughout her labor are known as **midwives;** they are increasingly relieving obstetricians in supervising births where no complications are expected. *Nurse-midwives* are usually trained in hospital nursing programs, where they study obstetrics and related subjects, such as nutrition and community health, for a year or more. Some states also permit *lay midwives* to deliver babies. Nurse-midwives are more common than lay midwives in the United States. Although the practice of midwifery has had a controversial history in the United States, midwives deliver 80% of the world's babies. In Sweden, Denmark, Finland, Holland, and Japan, where deliveries by midwives have been common, the infant mortality rate is consistently lower than that in the United States (Smith, 1987; National Center for Health Statistics, 1990). In the last decade, licensed nurse-midwives have participated in a greater number of hospital births as members of birthing teams and also in birthing centers (Eakins, 1986).

BIRTHING CENTERS   Birthing centers are a popular alternative to traditional hospital maternity care. The philosophy behind birthing centers is that childbirth is a natural, nonpathological event and that technological intervention should be kept to a minimum. They seek to combine the privacy, serenity, and intimacy of a home birth with the safety and medical backup of a nearby hospital, and they consider the parents' social, psychological, and aesthetic needs as equally important as medical requirements (Allgaier, 1978).

midwife A childbirth assistant who remains with a mother throughout labor and who can supervise births where no complications are expected; nurse-midwives have had training in hospital nursing programs, where they have studied obstetrics; lay midwives have had no formal medical or obstetrics training.

Birthing rooms at these centers are designed to accommodate the entire process from labor through delivery and recovery (Parker, 1980). The delivery itself is most often performed by a midwife rather than by a physician. Most birthing centers encourage prepared childbirth and an early return home. They also encourage mothers to keep their infants in their rooms to help promote early bonding (Allgaier, 1978; Parker, 1980).

Birthing centers are not equipped to handle everybody. They screen out women with high-risk factors or complications. Typical guidelines exclude women over 35 having their first baby, women having twins, women suffering from diseases like diabetes or cardiac problems, and women who have previously had Caesarean deliveries (Lubic & Ernst, 1978).

Most parents find birthing centers deeply satisfying. The centers keep birth focused on the family and give the parents the maximum amount of independence and control (Eakins, 1986). Physicians, too, find that as childbirth becomes more family centered, there is a different role and responsibility for them (Willson, 1990).

HOME BIRTHS   In the United States, some women are taking the idea of prepared childbirth one step further: They are choosing to have their children at home. There, in familiar surroundings, a woman can share the event with her husband, older children, and close friends. After the birth, she can spend as much time as she wants with her infant, instead of being regulated by a hospital's schedule. Some research indicates that the closeness of family members made possible with home births may greatly enhance early parent–infant attachment.

Although 85% to 90% of all childbirths are routine and uncomplicated, a prospective mother should consider a home birth only after taking two precautions. First, she should undergo a careful prenatal screening to detect the possibility of any high-risk conditions such as prematurity, toxemia, multiple birth, or maternal illness. If the woman is in a high-risk condition, she should plan to give birth where facilities exist to handle possible complications. Second, a prospective mother should be sure she has a physician or midwife on hand during birth; she should also have a backup emergency plan in case hospitalization is required.

Even though a great deal of attention has been focused on home births, the rate of such births is low—in fact, it has remained about 1% since 1975 (National Center for Health Statistics, 1989).

The Infant's Experience

In this discussion on the experience of childbirth, we have almost ignored the infant's experience. If the mother has been heavily anesthetized, the infant, too, will be groggy and may need to be revived. Often, mucus is removed from the nose and mouth with a syringe. Also, it is common for the infant to cry at birth, indicating its vigorous responsiveness. Sometimes, however, things are calmer than this.

Frederick Leboyer (1976), a French obstetrician, has developed a method of childbirth intended to make the birth process less stressful for the infant. He strongly objected to the bright lights, the noise, and the practice of holding the infant upside down and slapping it. He recommended that childbirth take place in a quiet, dimly lit room, that the cord remain connected for several minutes so that breathing would not be rushed, and that the baby be placed on the mother's abdomen, where it could be gently fondled and caressed. After a short time, the baby was given a warm bath to relax.

Most hospitals still use bright lights and don't use the warm bath. Most place the newborn on the mother's abdomen or chest. The cord is cut more leisurely than in the past, and many infants nurse at the breast within minutes of birth (Young, 1982; Nilsson, 1990).

Even with new hospital procedures, childbirth is a remarkably stressful event for the newborn. Despite this stress, the full-term baby is well equipped to handle the event (Gunnar, 1989). In the last few moments of birth, the infant produces a major surge of adrenalin and noradrenalin, the stress hormones. The adrenalin shock counteracts any oxygen deficiency and prepares the baby for breathing through the lungs. Almost immediately, as the infant experiences the bright, noisy delivery room and the cold air, there is a first cry. The first breaths may be difficult because the fluid that was in the lungs must be expelled, and millions of little air sacs in the lungs must be filled. Yet, within minutes, most infants have established fairly regular breathing, often with a lusty cry.

What about pain? The newborn has relatively high levels of a natural painkiller called beta-endorphins circulating in its blood system. Perhaps as a result of this, most infants experience a period of unusual alertness and receptivity shortly after birth. Many experts have suggested that this period of extended alertness, which may last an hour or more, is an ideal time for parents and infant to get acquainted (Nilsson, 1990).

Parent–Infant Bonding

Within minutes after birth, infant, mother, and father—if he is present—begin the process of **bonding,** or of forming an attachment. After the initial birth cry and filling of the lungs, a newborn calms down with time to relax on the mother's chest. After a little rest, she may struggle to focus her eyes on a face. She seemingly pauses to listen. The parents watch in fascination and begin talking to this new creature. They examine all of the parts—the fingers and the toes, the funny little ears. There is close physical contact, cradling, stroking. Many infants find the breast and almost immediately begin to nurse, with pauses to look about. Infants who have had little or no anesthesia may enjoy a half-hour or more of heightened alertness and exploration, as their mother or father holds them close, establishes eye contact, and talks to them. They seemingly want to respond. It has now been clearly established in at least eight different independent laboratories and in five different countries that babies are capable of doing some limited imitation of a parent. They move their heads, open and close their mouths, and even stick out their tongues in response to the facial gestures of their parents (Meltzoff & Moore, 1989).

It is now known that the baby's physical responses trigger important physical processes within the mother's body. When the baby licks or sucks on a breast nipple, it causes increased secretion of prolactin, a hormone important in nursing, and oxytocin, another hormone that contracts the uterus and decreases bleeding. The infant also benefits from early breast-feeding. Although milk is not yet available, the mother produces a substance called *colostrum*. This substance appears to help clear the infant's digestive system.

Some psychologists believe that these early parent–infant interactions are

bonding Forming an attachment; refers particularly to the developing relationship between parents and infant that begins immediately after birth.

Within minutes after birth, bonding can begin between parents and newborn.

EMERGING FATHERHOOD: CHANGING ROLES

George Russell awoke again feeling queasy. Ever since his wife, Kate, became pregnant and has had morning sickness, he too has felt ill in the morning. This morning was no different. George is experiencing what many other men with pregnant wives have experienced. Studies have indicated that between 10% and 15% of first-time fathers-to-be mimic some of the symptoms of their pregnant wives. They too occasionally experience nausea, abdominal discomfort, and strange cravings (Parke, 1981).

Some first-time fathers-to-be undergo a fair amount of stress as their wives go through pregnancy. It seems that mild depression, anxiety, and feelings of inadequacy are common. Among the natives of the Yucatan in Mexico, for example, pregnancy is confirmed when the woman's mate has nausea, diarrhea, vomiting, or cramps (Pruett, 1987). Not only do expectant fathers crave dill pickles with ice cream, they also have deeply troubling dreams and disturbing changes in sexual activity. It is obvious that in the cases that have just been described, husbands have identified with their wives (Pruett, 1987).

Certainly, not all fathers experience these symptoms. Yet, many fathers find the period of their wife's first pregnancy a time of anticipation, uncertainty, changing attitudes, and changing roles. The definition of an appropriate role for fatherhood in our society has expanded in recent years.

Many fathers are now urged and encouraged by their wives and even their friends to participate directly in their child's birth. In childbirth classes, they have learned techniques of physical and emotional support for their wives. They can coach the mother through childbirth and then immediately start getting to know the newborn infant. Fathers who have participated in their child's birth report an almost immediate attraction to the infant with feelings of elation, pride, and increased self-esteem (Greenberg & Morris, 1974). These fathers often continue to have frequent direct contact with their infants. Some studies report that these fathers are more deeply involved with and attached to their infants than those who do not take part in birth and early care (Pruett, 1987). They also feel a closer relationship to their wives because of this shared experience. New fathers who do not participate in childbirth and early infant play often report feeling more distant from their wives, and somewhat ignored when the baby arrives. Often, the companionship between husband and wife is sharply reduced while the mother's focus is on the infant (Galinsky, 1980).

Many studies report that fathers who have begun a relationship with their newborns continue to provide psychologically significant in helping to establish a strong parent–infant bond. In one study (Klaus & Kennell, 1976) of 28 first-time, low-income, high-risk mothers, the hospital staff provided half of the mothers with 16 extra hours of infant contact in the first 3 days after birth. The two groups of mothers and infants were later examined at 1 month, 1 year, and 2 years. Over the 2-year period, the extra-contact mothers consistently showed significantly greater attachments to their babies. They were more affectionate and attentive. Early extra contact may be particularly important for teenage mothers or those who have had little or no experience with newborns, and for mothers of premature and high-risk infants who are more likely to experience slow bonding patterns at birth due to the difficulties of accepting their babies' shortcomings. Some researchers feel that early bonding is not quite so essential, however. They have found that, except for high-risk mothers and infants, the increased contact following birth made little or no difference (Field, 1979).

In any case, mothers and fathers who spend the early period with their babies report more self-confidence in their ability as parents and greater self-esteem. Goldberg (1983) notes the importance of these feelings. She points out that because parenthood is a major transition, it is particularly important for parents to

more direct care and more play to their developing infants. This somewhat newer role of the nurturing father has many benefits for family development. In one study, infants whose fathers were actively involved in care giving scored higher on motor and mental development tests (Pederson et al., 1979). In another, such infants were found to be more socially responsive than average (Parke, 1979). Couples report less tension, more joint goals, and shared decision making when both of them actively parent the infant. But, in evaluating these studies, we must remember that fathers who choose to

have early contact with their infants may differ in many other ways from those who do not choose such contact (Palkovitz, 1985).

Actively involved fathers generally relate to their infants differently from the way mothers do. More often than not, these fathers play with their babies, while mothers wash them, diaper them, and feed them. Even when these fathers are involved in caretaking activities, they generally play while tending to their infants. Furthermore, the father's style of play is also much different from the mother's. They tend to play vigorously—tossing their babies in the air, moving their arms and legs to-and-fro, and bouncing them on papa's knee. Mothers, on the other hand, tend to coo at their babies, babble baby talk, and usually play more gently. At a very early age infants look to their fathers with great expectations. "At only six weeks of age, babies will hunch their shoulders and lift their eyebrows, as though in anticipation that 'playtime has arrived' when their fathers appear" (Brazelton & Yogman, 1984).

Fathers who develop a strong bond with their infants are usually more sensitive to the child's changing needs and interests in later years. These fathers also tend to have more influence over the child. They are more likely to be looked up to and listened to because of the close complex relationship established.

be encouraged in their new roles. She also suggests that as parents often have an idealized image of what their baby will be like, parent–infant contact during the first few hours and days following birth may help parents to adjust their expectations concerning the appearance and behavior of their infant. Furthermore, if parents are to become attached to their baby, they need to become acquainted. Why should they delay in getting to know each other? Goldberg concludes, however, that if things do not go well in those first few days, or if the infant is premature or handicapped, or the mother is ill or sedated, the relationship is not doomed—attachments can form later.

THE NEONATE

Until this point, we have been discussing the biological and psychological aspects of childbirth. We will now look at the condition of the new baby at birth and afterward.

neonate A baby in the first month of life.

A neonate's first cry symbolizes the beginning of its life as a separate individual.

During the first month of life, a baby is known as a **neonate.** The first month is a very special period in a baby's life. It is distinguished from the rest of infancy because during this time, the baby must adjust to leaving the closed, protected environment of the mother's womb to live in the outside world. The first month is a period of both recovery from the birth process and adjustment of vital functions, such as respiration, circulation, digestion, and body-heat temperature regulation.

At birth, the average full-term baby weighs between 5½ and 9½ pounds (2.5 and 4.3 kilograms) and is between 19 and 22 inches (48 and 56 centimeters) long. The baby's skin may be covered with the *vernix caseosa,* a smooth and cheeselike coating that developed during the fetal period. This coating is present especially in a Caesarean delivery because it has not been wiped off during the tight passage through the birth canal. The baby's skin may be covered with fine facial and body hairs that drop off during the first month. Temporarily, the newborn's head may look misshapen and elongated as a result of the process called *molding.* In molding, the soft bony plates of the skull, connected only by cartilage, are squeezed together in the birth canal. Also, the external breasts and the genitals of both boys and girls may look enlarged. This enlargement is temporary, too. It is caused by the mother's female hormones that passed to the baby before birth. The general appearance of the newborn, then, may be a bit of a shock to new parents, who expect to see the plump, smooth, 3- to 4-month-old infant shown in advertisements.

The Period of Adjustment

Despite their appearance, full-term neonates are sturdy little beings who are already making the profound adjustment to their new lives—from having their mothers do everything for them to functioning on their own as separate individuals. Four critical areas of adjustment are respiration, circulation of blood, digestion, and temperature regulation.

The birth cry traditionally symbolizes the beginning of the neonate's life. It also signals a major step in the child's development, for with the first breaths of air, the lungs are inflated for the first time, and they begin to work as the basic organ of the child's own respiratory system. During the first few days after birth, the neonate experiences periods of coughing and sneezing that often alarm the new mother, but they serve the important function of clearing mucus and amniotic fluid from the infant's air passages.

The onset of breathing marks a significant change in the neonate's circulatory system, too. The baby's heart no longer needs to pump blood to the placenta for aeration. Instead, the blood now circulates to the lungs to receive oxygen and to eliminate carbon dioxide (Pratt, 1954; Vulliamy, 1973). To achieve this, a valve in the baby's heart closes to redirect the flow of blood along the changed route. The circulatory system is no longer fetal; rather, it becomes entirely self-contained. The shift from fetal to independent circulatory and respiratory systems begins immediately after birth but is not completed for several days. Lack of oxygen for more than a few minutes at birth or during the first few days of adjustment may result in permanent brain damage.

Before birth, the placenta provided nourishment as well as oxygen for the infant. But, once free of the womb, the infant's own digestive system must begin

TABLE 5–1
Apgar Scoring System for Infants

	SCORES		
	0	**1**	**2**
Pulse	Absent	Less than 100	More than 100
Breathing	Absent	Slow, irregular	Strong cry
Muscle tone	Limp	Some flexion of extremities	Active motion
Reflex response	No response	Grimace	Vigorous cry
Color[1]	Blue, pale	Body pink, extremities blue	Completely pink

[1]For nonwhites, alternative tests of mucous membranes, palms, and soles are used.

Source: From "Proposal for a New Method of Evaluating the Newborn Infant" by V. Apgar, *Anesthesia and Analgesia,* 1953, 32, 260. Used by permission of the International Anesthesia Research Society.

to function. This change is a longer, more adaptive process than are the immediate and dramatic changes in respiration and circulation.

Another gradual adjustment involves the neonate's temperature regulation system. Within the uterus, the baby's skin was maintained at a constant temperature. After birth, however, the baby's skin must constantly work to give insulation from even minor changes in external temperature. During the first few days of life, babies must be carefully covered. Soon, they become better able to maintain their own body-heat temperatures, aided by a healthy layer of fat that accumulates during the first weeks of life.

All neonates are not equally equipped to adjust to the abrupt changes brought about by birth, and it is important to detect any problems at the earliest possible moment. Great advances have been made in this area in recent years. At one time, babies were considered healthy if they merely "looked" healthy. Then, in 1953, Virginia Apgar devised a standard scoring system, and hospitals were able to evaluate an infant's condition quickly (see Table 5–1). The Apgar score is taken at 1 minute and again at 5 minutes after the baby's birth. The attendant observes the pulse, breathing, muscle tone, general reflex response, and color of the skin (or the mucous membranes, palms, and soles for nonwhite babies). A perfect Apgar score is 10 points, with a score of 7 or more considered normal. Scores below 7 generally show that some bodily processes are not functioning fully and require at least watching and perhaps special attention. A score of 4 or less requires immediate emergency measures.

Competence of the Newborn

What can newborns do? What can they hear? How much do they see? What can they learn? We are still discovering some of the fascinating capabilities and skills that newborns possess.

Until the 1960s, psychologists thought that neonates were incapable of organized, self-directed behavior. It was common to read in psychological literature that infants did not use the higher centers of the brain until they were almost a year old, or that newborns saw light and shadow but not objects or patterns. Behavior in the first weeks of life was considered to be almost entirely reflexive. Later experiments have shown that we had underestimated newborns. We now know that neonates are capable of organized, predictable responses and mental activity that is more complex than was expected of them. They have definite preferences and show a striking ability to learn.

The key to this new understanding of infants lies in the development of more precise and creative ways of observing them. Early studies were poorly designed. They employed inadequate measurements and often put the infant at a disadvantage. Even adults who are placed flat on their back to stare at a white ceiling while being covered up to their necks with blankets are not their most perceptive or responsive selves. When infants are placed tummy down on the mother's skin in a warm room, however, they will display an engaging repertoire of behaviors (Prechtl & Beintema, 1965). This and other new study techniques allow infants to respond fully to testing.

INFANT STATES   When we watch sleeping newborns, we notice that at some times they lie calmly and quietly, and at other times they twitch and grimace, although their eyes remain closed. Similarly, when awake, babies may be calm but are still capable of thrashing about wildly and crying.

By observing infants' activity over a considerable time, P. H. Wolff (1966) was able to separate and identify six newborn behavioral states: *regular sleep, irregular sleep, drowsiness, alert inactivity, waking activity,* and *crying.* These states have a regular duration and seem to follow predictable daily cycles of waking and sleeping. The level of responsiveness in newborns depends largely on their particular behavioral state. For example, Wolff found that babies in a state of alert inactivity reacted to stimulation by becoming more active. Babies who were already in an active state had a different response: They seemed to calm down when stimulated. It is very important, therefore, to consider the state of newborns when trying to assess their reactions to outside events.

Ability to Be Soothed.   Crying is the infant state that causes parents and

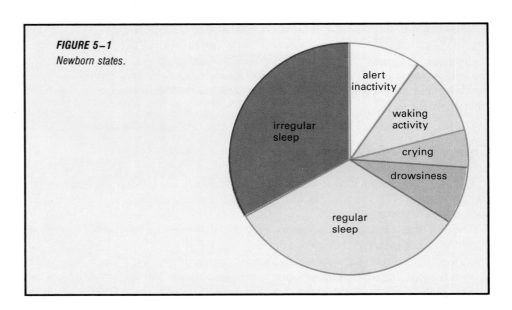

FIGURE 5–1
Newborn states.

care-givers the most worry; it challenges them to find the cause and then invent ways to stop it. Of the many techniques used to soothe babies, three stand out in their effectiveness: picking them up, providing constant rhythmic movement, and, for some, reducing the amount of stimulation that they get from their own bodies by swaddling them in blankets. (This is probably why some infants sleep so well when wrapped up and taken for a ride in a car.)

Newborns differ greatly in how easily they can be soothed and by which methods. Many infants quiet quite easily, either with their own self-comforting methods or to the sounds of an adult voice; other infants require more active soothing (Brazelton, Nugent, & Lester, 1987). Most important, some match must exist between the parents' technique for soothing the baby and the baby's ability to be soothed. When the match is wrong, awkward, or nonexistent, both mother and child may get themselves into behavioral patterns that later are hard to change (Brazelton, Nugent, & Lester, 1987).

REFLEXES Full-term infants confront the world with a number of complex **reflexes** and combinations of reflexes. Most disappear after 3 or 4 months. A few of them deserve special mention.

The *Moro reflex* is the newborn's startle reaction. When newborns are startled, as by a loud sound, they react first by extending both arms to the side, with fingers outstretched as if to catch onto someone or something. The arms are then gradually brought back to the midline. Some have thought the Moro reflex to be a remnant of our ape ancestry—in the event of a fall, infant apes who grasped their mothers' hair were the most likely to survive. Another body reflex is the *tonic neck reflex*. It

reflex An unlearned, automatic response to a stimulus. Many reflexes disappear after 3 or 4 months.

TABLE 5–2

Reflexes of the Newborn

REFLEX	DESCRIPTION
Moro (startle)	When infants are startled by loud sounds or by being suddenly dropped a few inches, they will first spread their arms and stretch out their fingers, then bring their arms back to their body and clench their fingers. Disappears after about 4 months.
Tonic neck	When infants' heads are turned to one side, they will extend the arm and leg on that side, and flex their arm and leg on the opposite side, as in a fencing position. Disappears after 4 months.
Stepping (walking)	When infants are held upright with their feet against a flat surface and are moved forward, they will appear to walk in a coordinated way. Disappears after 2 or 3 months.
Placing	Similar to the stepping reflex. When infants' feet are put against a table edge, they will attempt to step up onto it. Disappears after 2 months.
Grasping (palmar)	When a pencil or a finger is placed in infants' palms, they will grasp it tightly and increase the strength of the grasp if the object is pulled away. Disappears after about 5 months.
Babkin	If objects are placed against both palms, infants will react by opening their mouths, closing their eyes, and turning their heads to one side. Disappears after 4 months.
Plantar	Similar to the grasping reflex. When an object or a finger is placed on the soles of infants' feet near the toes, they will respond by trying to flex their feet. Disappears sometime after 9 months.
Babinski	If the soles of infants' feet are stroked from heel to toes, infants will spread their small toes and raise the large one. Disappears after 6 months.
Rooting	If infants' cheeks are touched, they will turn their heads toward the stimulus and open their mouths, as if to find a nipple. Disappears after 3 or 4 months.
Sucking	If a finger is put in infants' mouths, they will respond by sucking and making rhythmic movements with the mouth and tongue.
Swimming	Infants will attempt to swim in a coordinated way if placed in water in a prone position. Disappears after 6 months.
Ocular neck	Infants will tilt their heads back and away from a light shining directly into their eyes.
Pupillary	The pupils of infants' eyes will narrow in bright light and when going to sleep, and will widen in dim light and when waking up. Reflex is permanent.

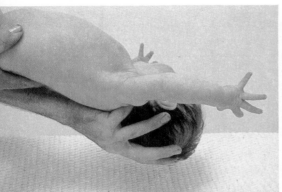
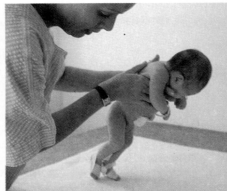
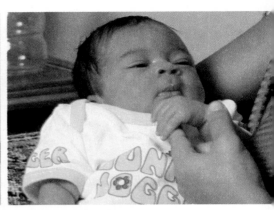

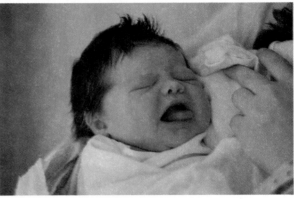

Some reflexes of the newborn: top left, Moro reflex; top middle, stepping reflex; top right, grasping reflex; bottom left, sucking reflex; and bottom right, rooting reflex.

occurs when babies' heads are turned sharply to one side. They react by extending the arm and leg on the same side while flexing the arm and leg on the other side, in a kind of fencing position. The *stepping reflex* occurs when newborn babies are held vertically with their feet against a hard surface. They lift one leg away from the surface, and, if tilted slightly from one side to the other, they appear to be walking. The *grasping reflex* applies to newborns' toes as well as to their fingers. Babies will close their fingers over any object, such as a pencil or finger, when it is placed on their palm. Some neonates can grasp with such strength that they support their full weight for up to a minute (Taft & Cohen, 1967).

A very useful reflex of the mouth is the *rooting reflex*. When one cheek is touched, babies "root," or move the mouth toward the stimulus. This aids them in finding the nipple. A mother who is unfamiliar with this response may try to push the infant's head toward the nipple. Because the reflex is toward, not away from, the stimulation, the baby will move toward the hand that pushes, thus seeming to reject the breast. The rooting reflex disappears by the third or fourth month (Taft & Cohen, 1967). The *sucking reflex*, like the rooting reflex, is clearly necessary for infant survival. Like some other reflexes, sucking begins in the uterus. Cases have been reported of babies born with thumbs already swollen from sucking.

Newborns' eyes are also capable of several reflex movements and motor patterns. The lids open and close in response to stimuli. The pupils widen in dim light and narrow in bright light; they also narrow when infants are going to sleep and widen when they wake up. Even an infant who is only a few hours old is capable of following a slow-moving object, like a bright red ball, with its eyes (Brazelton, 1969).

Many other reflexes govern the behavior of the newborn. Some, like sneezing or coughing, are necessary for survival. Others seem to be related to the behavior patterns of our ancient ancestors. Still others are not yet understood.

SENSORY AND PERCEPTUAL CAPACITIES   Can newborn babies see the details of an object directly in front of them? Can they see patterns? Can they see color and depth? Can they hear a low whisper? Are they sensitive to touch, or are they rather numb? Research indicates that all of the senses are operating at birth, but perception is limited and selective. **Perception** is the active process of interpreting sensory information. Visual perception is not just seeing; for example, it involves giving meaning to what we see. When infants turn their heads to selectively look at one thing and not another, or position themselves to get a better view of something in particular, they are exhibiting some perceptual competence. In Chapter 6, we will discuss the perceptual competencies of infants in greater detail. At this point, let us look briefly at the sensory and perceptual capacities of the newborn.

Vision.   From anatomical research, we know that infants are born with a full, intact set of visual structures. Most—but not all—of these structures are immature and need to develop over the next few months before they reach full capacity. However, neonates do have some visual skills. From the first moments, newborns' eyes are sensitive to brightness. Their pupils contract in bright light and dilate in darkness. They have some control over eye movements, and they can visually track an object that moves within their field of vision, such as a face or a doctor's penlight. The eye movements are initially short and jerky and are limited to a short span. Newborns are able to focus optimally within a narrow range of 7 to 10 inches (17.8 to 25.4 centimeters), and objects beyond this appear blurred. Their visual acuity for distance is estimated to be about 20/600, as compared to a normal adult with 20/20 vision. This means they are nearly blind to details across the room (Banks & Salapatek, 1983). Furthermore, newborns sometimes lack **convergence** of the eyes—they are not able to focus both eyes on the same point. They will not be able to do so consistently until the end of the second month (Fantz, 1961). Lack of convergence probably limits depth perception.

We know that newborns are able to perceive their environment by the fact that they are selective about what they watch. Newborns clearly prefer to look at complex patterns. They look particularly at the edges and contours of objects, especially curves (Roskinski, 1977). Newborn babies are also exceptionally responsive to the human face (Fantz, 1958). It is not surprising, then, that they develop an early recognition of their mothers' faces. An experiment by Carpenter (1974) showed a newborn's preference for his or her mother's face at 2 weeks. Carpenter presented each infant with pictures of its mother and another woman. At 2 weeks, the infants preferred to look at the familiar face. In some cases, they turned their heads completely away from the strange pictures, perhaps because the stimulus was too strong or too unfamiliar (MacFarlane, 1978).

One of the more startling examples of visual perception in neonates is their seeming ability to imitate facial expressions. A team of psychologists has run a series of experiments with infants, who are sometimes no more than 2 or 3 days old, to demonstrate imitation. First, the researchers find a time when the neonate is in a calm, alert state (a condition that is not always easy to find). The infant and

perception The complex process by which the mind interprets and gives meaning to sensory information.

convergence The ability to focus both eyes on one point.

adult look at each other, and the adult goes through a series of expressions in random order. He purses his lips; he sticks out his tongue; he opens his mouth wide; he opens and closes his hand. In between, the adult pauses and wears a neutral expression. Both infant and adult are videotaped. Later, observers view the videotape of both the adult and the baby, and they try to match what the baby was imitating. Meltzoff and Moore (1989) find remarkable consistency. It appears that many of these babies seem to match their expressions and hand movements to those of the adults. However, some researchers find slightly different results or argue that infants open their mouths wide to a variety of stimuli. In any case, the neonate seems to see the stimuli and to respond to them in a somewhat selective fashion.

The visual sensitivity and preferences of newborns depend not only on the objects they are shown but also on their own state of arousal. Most visual preference studies must be done when the infant is awake, alert, and not too hungry. Newborns who have been fed will watch stimulating displays, such as rapidly flashing lights, nearly twice as long as awake, alert newborns who are being tested before their feeding (Gardner & Karmel, 1984).

Hearing. We are certain that newborns can hear. They are startled by loud sounds, and they often turn toward a voice. Newborns are soothed by low-pitched sounds, such as lullabies, and they fuss after hearing high-pitched squeaks and whistles. Clearly, babies are responsive to the sounds in their environment. But how well developed is this hearing?

The anatomical structures for hearing are rather well developed in the newborn (Morse & Cowan, 1982). The brain structures for transmitting and interpreting hearing, however, are not fully developed. In fact, brain structures will continue to develop until the child is about 2 years old (Morse & Cowan, 1982; Aslin, 1987). Despite these limitations, newborns are capable of responding to a wide range of sounds. Even in the first month of life, they are particularly sensitive to speech sounds (Eimas, 1975). They also seem to show preference for the human voice. For instance, they will listen to a song sung by a woman rather than the same song performed on a musical instrument (Glen, Cummingham, & Joyce, 1981). Infants also seem to be able to localize sound. Even in their first few days, they will turn their heads toward a sound or a voice. One researcher has found that infants who turn toward a sound in the first few weeks of life seem to lose this ability during the second month and then pick it up again in the third month (Muir & Field, 1979).

Other Senses. We know less about newborns' senses of taste, smell, and touch than we do about seeing and hearing. Some studies suggest that these three senses are finely sensitive. Although evidence indicates that newborns may have reduced sensitivity to pain for the first few days, the senses of taste and smell are operating fully. Newborns discriminate between sweet, salty, sour, and bitter through clearly differentiated facial responses to the four taste groups (Rosenstein & Oster, 1988). Also, newborns react negatively to strong odors, whereas they are selectively attracted to positive odors, such as a lactating female (Makin & Porter, 1989). As early as 6 days, the infant can distinguish the smell of its mother from the odor of another woman. This reaction is based on body odor, not just milk or breast odor, and naturally, the infant shows a preference for the familiar scent (MacFarlane, 1978; Makin & Porter, 1989).

The sense of touch is especially important to the comfort of newborns. Often, the simple act of holding the arms or legs or pressing the abdomen will be enough to quiet infants. Swaddling, as already mentioned, has a similar effect (Brazelton, 1969).

LEARNING AND HABITUATION   We have already seen considerable evidence of infant learning. The neonate quiets to a familiar sound, song, or lullaby, even to a familiar soap opera theme song (see box in Chapter 4). The neonate's ability to imitate facial expressions demonstrates some learning. Improved methods of observation have yielded useful information about the capacities of infants to learn some fairly complex responses. The newborns' ability to turn their heads has been used in many learning experiments. Some pioneering conditioning studies were conducted by Papoušek (1961). In these experiments, newborns were taught to turn their heads to the left to obtain milk whenever they heard a bell. For the same reward, they also learned to turn their heads to the right at the sound of a buzzer. Then, to complicate the situation, the bell and the buzzer were reversed. The infants quickly learned to turn their heads according to the rules of the new game.

Because sucking is well developed in the neonate, this ability has also been used in studies of neonatal learning and visual preferences. Kalnins and Bruner (1973), in an expansion of an earlier study by Siqueland and DeLucia (1969), wanted to determine whether infants could control sucking when it was linked to rewards other than feeding. Pacifiers were wired to a laboratory slide projector. If the infants sucked, the slide came into focus; if they did not suck, the picture blurred. Bruner noted that the infants learned quickly to focus the picture and also adapted quickly if conditions were reversed—that is, they learned to stop sucking to get the picture into focus. In other words, the infants—some as young as 3 weeks old (Alexander, 1970)—not only coordinated sucking and looking but also effectively controlled the focus of the slide show. Their own reward was clear, rather than blurred, visual stimulation. Bruner concluded that infants had been greatly underestimated in both their perceptual capabilities and their ability to solve problems voluntarily.

Papoušek's (1961) experiments involved more than the buzzers and bells discussed earlier. He also used light to reveal a very important facet of newborn behavior. Infants were taught to turn on a light by turning their heads to the left. Infants would turn their heads several times during a short period in order to turn on the light. But then an interesting thing happened—the infants seemed to lose interest in the game. Papoušek found that he could revive the infants' interest by reversing the problem, but they soon became bored again. Papoušek's findings were important for two reasons. They supported Bruner's (1971) belief that competence, instead of immediate reward, motivates much of human learning, and they demonstrated a second learning phenomenon: **habituation.**

Infants habituate—they become accustomed to certain kinds of stimuli and then no longer respond to them. The process of habituation serves an important adaptive function. Infants need to be able to adapt to or ignore nonmeaningful stimuli, like the hissing of a radiator or the light touch of their clothing. Researchers use this process of habituation to find out a number of things about the perceptual capacities of infants. For example, a newborn's response at the onset of a moderately loud sound is a faster heartbeat, a change in breathing, and sometimes crying or general increased activity. As the sound continues, however, the infant soon habituates, or stops responding. When we change the sound

habituation The process of becoming accustomed to certain kinds of stimuli and no longer responding to them.

TABLE 5-3

Clusters in the Neonatal Behavioral Assessment Scale

Habituation	How quickly does the infant habituate to a light, bell, rattle, or pin prick?
Orientation	How readily does the child quiet him-/herself and turn toward a light, bell, voice, or face?
Motor tone and activity	How strong and steady is the motor activity?
Range of state	How quickly and easily does the infant change from sleeping to alertness? To crying?
Regulation of state	How does the infant calm or quiet him-/herself? How easily is he/she soothed?
Autonomic stability	Does the infant react with tremors or unusual startles?
Reflexes	Is there a regular and strong response to each of the 17 different reflexes?

Source: Adapted from Lester, Als, & Brazelton, 1982.

stimulus, even by a small degree, and the response begins anew, clearly the infant perceives the change and reacts to the small difference. This habituating ability has been the basis of many experiments that have provided information about the sensory capacities and perceptual skills of newborns.

ASSESSMENT During the first few days of a baby's life, most hospitals provide an extensive evaluation of the newborn. They may include a neurological examination and a behavioral assessment. Brazelton's (1973) Neonatal Behavioral Assessment Scale has been used increasingly by many hospitals. The scale includes the usual neurological tests, but it is designed primarily to assess the newborn's behavioral capabilities.

The 44 separate measures on this test can be grouped into seven behavioral clusters similar to the competencies discussed in this chapter. The seven clusters are presented in Table 5-3.

Newborns differ in their responses to new, prolonged, or slightly annoying stimuli. Some can easily detect, attend to, and habituate (grow accustomed) to changes in their environment. Others may be less responsive, or they may be overly responsive and too easily irritated—behaviors that decrease their attention spans and adaptability to changes. By assessing the newborn's competencies and ways of responding, the Brazelton scale may supply early information about a child's future personality and social development. Parents who observe a physician administer the Brazelton scale become much more sensitive to the capabilities and individuality of their own neonate (Parke & Tinsley, 1987).

The Individuality of Newborns

From the moment of birth, infants demonstrate their uniqueness and their variability. Parents with more than one child are quite aware of differences in their children's personalities, although all of the children were "brought up" more or less the same way. Many times these differences can be noted even before a child is born. One fetus may kick actively, whereas another will shift position gently or cautiously.

How profound are these differences in the temperament styles of neonates? What does the newborn's behavior tell us about his or her future personality? What are the dynamics between the baby's personality and the parents', and what are their effects? The individuality of the newborn has been the subject of many studies.

Most researchers agree that there are strong constitutional differences in temperament that appear early, are probably inherited, and are quite stable through much of the life span. There is little agreement, however, on which of these aspects of temperament can be reliably identified in the neonate (Bates, 1987). One of the simpler models of individuality lists just three characteristics that are present at birth—*emotionality, activity level,* and *sociability* (Buss & Plomin, 1984; Plomin, 1990). Emotionality refers to the ease and strength with which an infant is aroused by a stimulus to a behavior and to emotional expression. Activity level is the amount of energy that the infant expends as a normal part of his waking day and the speed at which this energy is spent. Sociability refers to the infant's preference for being with others and to his ability to be rewarded by this interaction. An extremely high or low level of any of these temperament characteristics is not necessarily an advantage or a disadvantage. These are just ways in which infants differ.

Researchers agree that different personality styles are evident at birth.

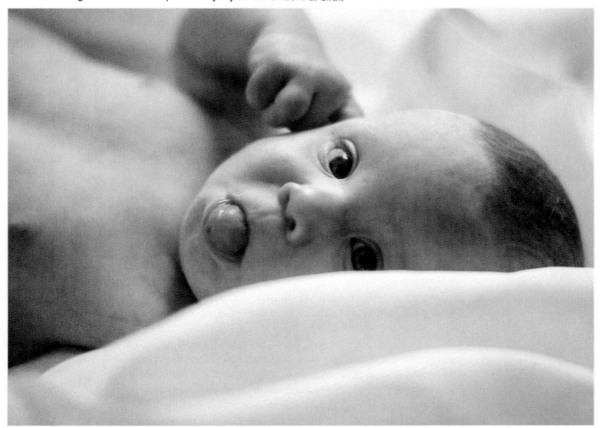

In contrast, Chess (1967) identified nine criteria to differentiate neonatal behavior: activity level, biological regularity, positive–negative responses to new stimuli, adaptability, intensity of reaction, threshold of responsiveness, quality of mood (overall amount of pleasure versus displeasure displayed), attention span and persistence, and distractibility.

Chess used these criteria to study 136 children. She found that children could be divided into three basic types. She also determined that qualities seen as early as 2 or 3 months of age could be traced throughout childhood. The largest of Chess's three groups consisted of the "easy children"—babies (and later, children) who were biologically regular and rhythmical. The easy child has regular sleeping and eating schedules, accepts new food and new people, and is not easily frustrated. The "difficult children" form a smaller group. They withdraw from new stimuli and adapt slowly to change; their mood is often negative. A third type is the "slow-to-warm-up child." Children in this group withdraw from activities quietly, whereas the difficult child does so actively and noisily. Slow-to-warm-up children will show interest in new situations only if they are allowed to do so gradually, without pressure. Chess found no evidence that these temperament types were influenced by parental behavior. On the contrary, children's temperaments seemed to be as much a part of them as the inherited color of their eyes.

One of the major developmental tasks for the newborn infant is self-regulation. As we have seen, the full-term neonate is well equipped with a variety of ways to respond and adjust to outside stimulation. For instance, infants are capable of habituating to repeated stimuli and of comforting themselves in response to stress. But these self-regulating mechanisms vary with individual temperaments. Some infants are easily overstimulated, others are more difficult to arouse. Some respond best to auditory stimulation, others to touch. Some are hypersensitive to particular types of stimulation. Sensitive caretakers can help the baby focus his or her reactions to sensory experiences, overcome overexcitement or underarousal, or make use of a particular sense (Greenspan & Greenspan, 1985).

Although the basis of newborn individuality is not entirely understood, researchers agree generally that widely different personality styles are apparent at birth and that these differences increase over the first few months of life. During this same early period, infants and parents will establish a relationship based on their own unique personalities (Lewis & Rosenblum, 1974). Many studies suggest that infants' temperaments and behavioral styles influence parental behavior and partially determine the quality of early interactions (Bates, 1987).

Researchers regularly find that babies differ greatly in the amount of attention they evoke from their parents, with irritable infants receiving more parental stimulation than overly placid ones. Such attentiveness, however, may be accompanied by feelings of anger, bewilderment, or self-pity in the care-giver when numerous efforts to soothe or amuse the baby have failed. Babies who are easily quieted and amused may cause their parents to feel competent and satisfied in their care giving (Segal & Yahraes, 1978). Thus, the predictability of an infant's behavior affects the care-giver as well. Mild personality differences between parent and infant are fairly common, and even the most willing and enthusiastic parent needs time and patience to become acquainted with the infant's unique personality. The development of mutuality, reciprocity, and a "symbiotic relationship" between parent and infant is certainly not automatic or instinctive, as we shall see in Chapter 7.

premature Having a short gestation period (less than 37 weeks) and/or low birth weight (less than 5½ pounds).

THE PREMATURE INFANT

So far, we have discussed only the development of healthy, full-term babies. A substantial number of newborns, however, are considered to be **premature**—a condition that can pose serious problems for infants and care-givers alike.

Two indicators of prematurity are frequently confused. The first is *gestation time*. The infant born before a gestation period of 37 weeks is considered premature. The second indicator is *low birth weight*. Because the average birth weight is 7½ pounds (3.4 kilograms), an infant who weighs less than 5½ pounds (2.5 kilograms) is usually classified as premature, or in need of special attention, although only half of such infants have a gestation period of less than 37 weeks. Low-birth-weight babies, even when full term, often have problems resulting from fetal malnutrition, for example. Therefore, both cutoff points—5½ pounds (2.5 kilograms) and 37 weeks—are used in classifying babies as premature (Babson & Benson, 1966). The World Health Organization defines a premature infant as one weighing less than 2.5 kilograms at birth.

Prematurity can occur for a number of reasons. The most common is a multiple birth, when two or more infants are born at the same time. Other causes include diseases or disabilities of the fetus, the mother's smoking and/or drug taking, and malnutrition. Some diseases of the mother, such as diabetes or polio, may lead the doctor to deliver the baby before full term.

Immediately after birth, premature infants usually have greater difficulty making adjustments than do full-term babies. Their adaptation to the basic processes of circulation, respiration, and temperature control is more complicated (see box). Among these, temperature control is a common problem. Premature infants have very few fat cells and thus poorly maintain body heat. Therefore, in industrialized nations, newborns weighing less than 5½ pounds are usually put into incubators immediately after birth. Another common problem is the feeding of premature infants. In their first few months, they seem unable to catch up in weight and height with full-term infants. It seems almost impossible to match the nutritional conditions of the late fetal period to produce a growth rate outside the uterus comparable to that inside.

It is often believed that the effects of prematurity may last long after infancy. Several studies have indicated that premature infants suffer more illnesses in their first 3 years of life, score lower on IQ tests, and are slightly more prone to behavioral problems than are full-term babies (Knobloch et al., 1959). More recent research seems to indicate that this is true only for a small proportion—less than one-quarter—of premature infants (Bennett et al., 1983; Klein et al., 1985). Researchers have found a high rate of prematurity among children later diagnosed as being learning disabled, having reading problems, or being distractible or hyperactive.

All such reports, however, must be very carefully interpreted. It cannot be concluded, for example, that prematurity causes any of these defects. Although the immature birth condition of babies may make them less able to adjust to the shock of birth, prematurity has a more complex association with problems in later life. For instance, conditions like malnutrition, faulty development of the placenta, or crowding in the uterus may result in a number of symptoms—only one of which is premature birth. In such cases, the prematurity is merely a symptom of a disability or malfunction; it is not a cause of the defect.

Parent–Infant Bonding with a Premature Infant

Some of the later problems of premature infants may also arise from the way that they are treated during the first few weeks of life. Because they are kept in incubators under conditions that are free of harmful microorganisms, they have little of the normal physical contact that most newborns experience. There is no opportunity to enjoy the early contact after delivery that Klaus and Kennell found to be so important in promoting bonding. Few premature infants are breast-fed; few are held even while being bottle-fed; and some are unable to suck at all for the first few weeks. These infants miss the social experiences of normal feeding, which establish an early mutuality between the care-giver and the full-term infant. The care-giver may become less responsive because the infant appears unattractive or sickly or has a high-pitched, grating cry. These are great obstacles to effective parent–infant bonding in the early weeks of life.

The consequences of faulty bonding due to prematurity are apparent throughout infancy (Goldberg, 1979). Preterm infants are held farther from the parent's body, touched less, and cooed at less. Later, these infants tend to play less actively than babies born full term and have difficulty absorbing as much external stimuli. Many of the differences between premature infants and full-term babies disappear by the end of the first year. This may be due to the efforts of parents who compensate for the infant's lack of responsiveness with more active parenting and intervention (Goldberg, 1979).

In many hospitals, parents are encouraged to become more involved with the care of premature infants. They can put on masks and gowns and enter the intensive care unit to help with feeding, diaper changes, and other care. They can stimulate the baby by gently stroking and talking to it. This promotes better bonding and care taking when the baby is sent home.

There have been several follow-up studies of premature infants whose parents became actively involved in their care while these infants were in the hospital. The parents learned early to be responsive to the very subtle behavior of their premature infants. As these children grew up, they improved at each stage. Infants developed more appropriately at social and intellectual tasks, and, at age 12, the children who had such responsive maternal care showed higher intellectual and social competence than those who missed it in the neonatal intensive care unit (Beckwith & Cohen, 1989; Goldberg et al., 1988).

Some of the potentially detrimental effects of prematurity may be offset by an enriched environment during the first year of life. Zeskind and Ramey (1978) ran a pilot program for infants born premature because of fetal malnourishment. These infants were provided with full-service day care in addition to the necessary medical and nutritional services. Most of them reached normal performance levels by 18 months. Another matched group of fetally malnourished infants received the same medical and nutritional services, but were cared for at home, not in the day-care program. These infants were slower to reach normal levels, and deficits in their performance were still apparent at 2 years. Zeskind and Ramey's study shows that with proper medical care, nutrition, and care giving during their early development, premature infants need not be seriously disadvantaged by the conditions of their birth.

High-risk infants present similar problems in early bonding. They are likely to be segregated from their mothers' room for medical reasons and often have developmental problems that interfere with their ability to signal and reward parents for successful care giving. The result is often a fussy, unresponsive baby and an overattentive mother. Sometimes, bonding patterns and mutual responses improve if the mother imitates her baby's behavior instead of providing completely new stimuli that overwhelm and confuse the infant (Field, 1979).

Bonding between parents and a handicapped infant is extremely difficult. While facing problems similar to those encountered with premature infants, such as early separation of infant and parents, there are other obstacles that must be overcome. The nature of the handicap may severely impair the baby's ability to

THE "KILOGRAM KIDS"

There is an "elite club" of perhaps 10,000 infants born each year who spend their first few months following birth fighting for their lives. These infants are born 2½ to 3 months ahead of schedule, and they weigh less than 1000 grams (2.3 pounds).

Three decades ago, virtually all of these infants would have died. But, according to a recent government survey, approximately 17,000 infants weighing less than 2 pounds are admitted annually to over 400 neonatal intensive care units around the country. Currently, they have about a 70% chance of survival, with the larger ones in this group doing much better than the tiny ones. Slightly larger infants, weighing between 2 and 3 pounds, have a 90% survival rate in these special facilities (Kantrowitz, 1988).

But what is the experience of these tiny creatures and their families over the first several months of life? The infant may lie in a waterbed in an incubator, connected by wires and tubes to banks of blinking lights and digital displays. The several electronic and computerized devices monitor or adjust temperature, respiration and heart rates, blood gases, and brain waves. Parents are encouraged to visit their infants often, and they are usually allowed to stroke and caress their children through the gloved portholes in the incubator. In many of these intensive care units, an effort is made to provide a "homelike," personal atmosphere (Fincher, 1982).

Daily life-threatening crises are not unusual—these tiny beings need nutrients and struggle to function in their alien environment. Excess fluid strains the heart and lungs, yet too little may lead to dehydration and disruption of the sodium and potassium balance. The tiny bones need calcium for bone development, but too much calcium clogs tubes and tiny blood vessels.

For parents, the premature birth of a child is traumatic. According to neonatologist Ron Cohen, the parents are "in shock. Mourning, grieving, going through denial, anger" (Fincher, 1982, p. 72). They are forced to deal with one crisis after another and hope that relatively little permanent damage will occur during this period. The staff in the special care units are very much aware of the parents' state and will try to help them cope.

Is there any way to avoid the struggle of premature birth and the enormous emotional and financial costs of saving the lives of these tiny newborns? Several studies have demonstrated that over 50% of very early births could have been prevented with regular prenatal medical care, beginning at 12 weeks (Knobloch et al., 1982; Monmaney, 1988). Dozens of studies have demonstrated that providing free care to low-income pregnant women dramatically cuts the need for high-tech rescues, and at half the cost (Monmaney, 1988). Even in those cases where very early birth cannot be prevented, the

respond. Moreover, parents often need to go through a period of mourning for the perfect child that did not arrive before they can accept, nurture, and become emotionally attached to the one that did.

Let us remember that almost 90% of all births go smoothly, without complications in either pregnancy or delivery. Many women consider giving birth as one of the most important and psychologically significant experiences in their lives. They are more likely to have this sense of deep satisfaction if they are involved in choosing various birthing procedures and can be surrounded by loved ones. They appreciate prepared childbirth for the opportunity it provides to be alert and actively engaged with the infant in the first few hours of life. Parents who share the childbirth experience often report a deepening of their marriage and a strong sense of elation. Childbirth is indeed a peak experience for many, a time for reaffirming ideals and basic values.

chances of survival are dramatically higher if the mother has had regular medical care.

In one study, 72.7% of the mothers of premature survivors had regular medical care, compared to only 25.2% of the mothers of nonsurvivors. It is much easier to treat a mother's ill health or poor nutrition early in pregnancy and thus reduce the risk of complex medical problems encountered by the neonate (Rahbar et al., 1985).

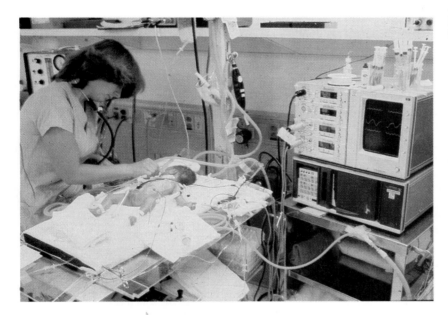

Infants born 2½ to 3 months ahead of schedule are closely monitored in neonatal intensive care units.

STUDY OUTLINE

Childbirth

The Sequence of Childbirth. Childbirth occurs in three stages: **labor,** lasting from 2 to 18 or more hours; **birth,** lasting from about 15 minutes to 2 hours; and **afterbirth,** lasting about 20 minutes, when the placenta and related tissues are expelled from the uterus.

The Medical Technology of Childbirth. Parts of obstetrical medicine have become dramatically technologized. New discoveries enable doctors to save unprecedented numbers of high-risk and premature infants. Some critics charge that the new technology is not just confined to high-risk cases, that it is inappropriately applied to what ought to be routine deliveries.

The Experience of Childbirth

Prepared Childbirth. Prepared childbirth has become increasingly popular in the United States because it allows the mother to participate in the experience of birth and enables her to deliver an undrugged, alert baby.

Changing Practices. An extension of the interest in prepared childbirth is the trend toward home births and out-of-hospital births in special childbearing facilities. As a result, **midwifery** has become a recently revived and popular profession.

The Infant's Experience. Childbirth is a very stressful experience for the infant. Frederick Leboyer, a French obstetrician, has developed a method of childbirth intended to make the birth process less stressful for the infant.

Parent–Infant Bonding. In the period immediately after birth, parents and child begin the process known as **bonding,** of developing deep feelings and learning patterns of mutual response. Bonding can be promoted by continual physical contact in the first hours and days of life, particularly for high-risk infants and parents.

The Neonate

The Period of Adjustment. Infants are called **neonates** during the first month after birth. During this period, they recover from the birth experience and adjust the basic life processes of respiration, temperature regulation, circulation, and digestion. The Apgar scoring system measures infants' health shortly after birth.

Competence of the Newborn. The behavioral state *(regular sleep, irregular sleep, drowsiness, alert inactivity, waking activity, or crying)* determines how the infant will respond to stimuli. Although rocking, swaddling, and sucking are soothing to distressed infants, marked individual differences exist in the ability of infants to be soothed or to soothe themselves.

The neonate has a large repertoire of **reflexes,** including the *Moro reflex* (startle reflex), the *tonic neck reflex,* and *stepping, sucking, rooting,* and *grasping reflexes.* Recent studies have shown that the belief that infants are capable only of reflex actions is unfounded; a great deal of learning takes place during infancy, beginning at birth.

Observations of newborns' sensory and perceptual capacities have revealed that they are born with a full set of visual structures. Newborns are sensitive to brightness; they see whole objects fairly clearly when nearby; they do not perceive colors until about the third week; and they have limited depth perception. During the first few days, newborns seem less sensitive to pain, but their senses of taste and smell are operating fully. Brazelton's Neonatal Behavioral Assessment Scale examines infants' individual responsiveness and receptivity to stimuli from the environment.

The Individuality of Newborns. Individual differences in infants' temperaments are being recognized increasingly. Differing temperament styles include easy, difficult, and slow-to-warm-up, with these styles remaining somewhat consistent throughout childhood. Only recently have investigators begun to question the effect of infant behavior on the care-giver, and they have found that infants differ greatly in the amount and kind of attention they evoke.

The Premature Infant

Premature babies make special adaptations after birth, and the effects of prematurity may last beyond infancy. Premature babies and their parents may have difficulty bonding properly because they are separated for long periods of time in the hospital and because the infant may be physically unable to signal distress and show satisfaction. High-risk and handicapped infants present a similar problem. In the case of a handicapped infant, parental shock and anger are additional obstacles to establishing early, deep attachments.

KEY TERMS AND CONCEPTS

afterbirth	habituation	posterior presentation
anoxia	infant states	premature
birth	labor	reflex
birthing center	midwife	rooting reflex
breech presentation	natural childbirth	sensation
convergence	neonate	stepping reflex
episiotomy	parent–infant bonding	sucking reflex
false labor	perception	tonic neck reflex
fetal monitor	perineum	toxemia
grasping reflex		

SELF-TEST QUESTIONS

1. Compare and contrast the attitudes toward childbirth among Western, !Kung-San, and Laotian cultures.

2. Describe the three stages of childbirth.

3. What is the purpose of the fetal monitor? Why is there a debate in the medical community concerning its use?

4. What are some side effects of giving medication during the birthing process? What causes anoxia?

5. Give several reasons why a Caesarean section may be performed during childbirth.

6. List the three fundamental keys to "natural" childbirth.

7. List and describe the available options that a pregnant woman has when delivering her baby.

8. Describe Leboyer's method of childbirth.

9. What is bonding and what do studies find significant concerning this interaction between parent and child?

10. What are the major physical developments that occur in the neonate immediately following birth?

11. Describe the Apgar score and explain what it measures.

12. List the six newborn behavioral states that were identified by Wolff in 1966.

13. What is the Moro reflex? List and describe other infant reflexes.

14. What is infant habituation? How does this ability provide information about the sensory capacities of the newborn?

15. What are two indicators of premature birth? What are the effects of prematurity on the development of the child?

SUGGESTED READINGS

BEAN, C. A. *Methods of childbirth*. New York: William Morrow, 1990. A wealth of practical information covering all aspects of childbirth from late pregnancy and delivery to postnatal treatment.

BRAZELTON, T. B. *Infants and mothers: Differences in development* (rev. ed.). New York: Delta/Seymour Lawrence, 1983. Three infant-mother pairs, all having different personalities and temperamental styles, are described just after childbirth and at selected periods during the children's first 2 years. Written in a highly readable fashion.

EISENBERG, A., MURKOFF, H. E., & HATHAWAY, S. E. *What to expect the first year*. New York: Workman Publishing, 1989. A comprehensive, month-by-month guide which clearly explains everything parents need to know about the first year with a new baby.

GOLDBERG, S., & DEVITTO, B. A. *Born too soon: Preterm birth and early development*. San Francisco: W. H. Freeman, 1983. These infancy specialists examine the many aspects of preterm infants, including carefully developed advice for their care and for aiding their development.

JONES, C. *Sharing birth: A father's guide to giving support during labor*. New York: Quill, 1985. A step-by-step guide, with photographs, to help fathers prepare for their role in childbirth.

KITZENGER, S. *Your baby, your way: Making pregnancy decisions and birth plans*. New York: Pantheon Books, 1987. A positive, helpful guide for expectant mothers and fathers written by a well-known childbirth educator. The physical and psychological facts are clearly presented together with options for decision making.

LEBOYER, F. *Birth without violence*. New York: Knopf, 1976. Portrays a classic set of birth procedures that are different from those once used in hospitals. Contains many compelling photographs.

Chapter 6

The child is a little inspector when it crawls
It touches and tastes the earth
Rolls and stumbles toward the object
Zigzags like a sail
And outmanuevers the room.
I am learning the child's way
I pick up wood pieces from the ground
And see shapes into them
I notice a purple velvet bee resting on a flower
And stop to listen to its buzz
They have included me
And though I will not be put away to rock alone
And don't roll down the plush hills
Nor spit for lunch
I am learning their way
They have given me back the bliss of my senses.

HY SOBILOFF
"THE CHILD'S SIGHT"

CHAPTER OUTLINE

Infancy: Developing Competencies

As we saw in Chapter 5, neonates come into the world able to sense and respond to their environment. They can see and hear, taste and smell, feel pressure and pain. They are selective in what they like to look at, and they are able to learn. They are still physically immature and dependent, however, and have limited cognitive ability. In the next 2 years, infants change more rapidly and more dramatically than during any other 2-year period. Some of these changes are obvious: Infants crawl, sit, walk, and talk. Other changes are more difficult to detect: It is difficult to see the brain grow and become more specialized; and it is difficult to tell just what the infant sees, hears, and thinks. In this chapter, we will highlight what we know about physical, motor, perceptual, and cognitive development in infancy. Although norms and averages of growth and behavior have been established for children at various stages of development, children essentially develop in their own style, at their own pace, and in response to the tasks of their particular social context:

> At 12 months of age, Joe was very active and independent. He had been walking for a month, but he often crawled when he wanted to get somewhere in a hurry. He cried whenever his mother tried to restrain him. From birth on, he was fussy. He slept irregularly and was given to long crying spells. At 8 months, Joe frequently howled when things did not go as he expected. He knew at an early age which toys, food, and people he preferred, and he did not like changes in his environment.
>
> His brother, Alex, born a year later, had developed in a different way. By the end of 12 months, he was quiet and placid, and he was content to sit in his playpen or crib for long periods of time. He had been able to pull himself upright at 7 months. He showed no signs of temper, frustration, or anxiety other than crying when someone unknown to him came near.

From the outset, these brothers differed on the three basic dimensions of temperament that we described in Chapter 5. Joe is more emotional and intense than is Alex, and he has a higher activity level than his brother does. However, Joe is also less sociable than Alex is. These individual differences become clearer as the children grow older.

> At 18 months, Joe's active, sensitive, and intense nature became even more distinct. He usually played alone. He enjoyed lining up small trucks and cars and endlessly rearranging them. He continued to disturb his parents' sleep occasionally, by his sudden waking and howling. His fussiness and unpredictability began to show in his eating habits; he would sometimes refuse to eat food that he had always enjoyed. He was often upset when he was taken out of

CHAPTER OBJECTIVES

By the time you have finished this chapter, you should be able to do the following:

- Describe the developing competencies of the infant during the first 2 years.
- Contrast breast-feeding and bottle-feeding.
- Describe the nutritional needs of the infant.
- Describe the infant's perceptual development during the first year.
- Explain and critique Piaget's theory of cognitive development in the infant.
- Discuss the effect of environmental stimulation on infant competency.

his home, sometimes crying uncontrollably when his parents took him for a visit to friends. His expressions of surprise, joy, and anger were always intense, which puzzled his parents, who themselves were quiet, calm people. Joe firmly resisted all attempts at toilet training.

Alex, at 18 months, continued to be an easygoing, gentle child, but he had become more outgoing and friendly. He laughed and smiled whenever he was picked up and played with, especially by those who came to visit. He knew the names of some objects in the room and the parts of the body. He got hungry at regular intervals and would sleep peacefully most nights. He kept his even temper, but he was afraid of loud music or sudden noises. He was easily distracted from whatever he was doing. At 24 months, he had almost toilet trained himself by imitating his older brother.

This brief description of Joe and Alex at 12 and at 18 months indicates that although common developmental changes occur during the first 2 years of life, great variations exist in temperament, interests, personality, and even in the social context that infants experience. Parent–child relationships will differ based on reactions to numerous events and on each infant's birth order and temperament. The older brother must take the lead in learning new skills. The younger brother has either the advantage of following a more competent model or the disadvantage of losing in competition with his more competent brother. Even in the same family, the social context of development is not identical.

INFANT COMPETENCIES: AN OVERVIEW

Infancy is a time of perceptual and motor discovery. Infants learn to recognize faces, food, and familiar routines. They explore flowers, insects, toys, and their own bodies. Every day is a discovery of the people, objects, and events that make up their environment. Such discovery is not only exciting but also is helpful in learning how to adapt to one's environment.

About half of all 8-month-olds can pull themselves into a standing position.

For decades, developmental psychologists have carefully studied the characteristics of infants and children. Arnold Gesell, a pioneer in the field, observed hundreds of infants and children over a period of time. He recorded the details of when and how certain behaviors emerged, such as crawling, walking, running, picking up a small pellet, cutting with scissors, managing a pencil, or drawing the human figure. From the resulting data, he reported the capabilities of "average" children at varying ages. By 15 months, for example, his "average" children were able to walk; by 18 months, they could walk fast and run stiffly; at 21 months, they were able to kick a large ball (Gesell, 1940).

In the healthy, well-nourished children that Gesell observed, these behaviors emerged in an orderly and predictable sequence. By knowing the age of a particular child, he could predict not only the child's approximate height and weight but also what the child knew or was able to do. He concluded that development does not primarily depend on the environment. Instead, Gesell believed that, given a normal environment, most achievements result from an internal biological timetable. Behavior emerges as a function of maturation.

There are weaknesses in Gesell's theory and method. The children studied by Gesell came from one socioeconomic class and one community setting; their similar environments may have influenced their similar behaviors. We now know that children raised in widely different social or historical contexts develop quite differently from those described in Gesell's developmental schedules. Gesell's infants of the 1930s normally walked at 15 months. Contemporary American infants normally walk at around 12 months. Also, infants raised in a small Guatemalan village—where they spent their first year confined to a small, dark hut, were not played with, were rarely spoken to, and were poorly nourished—were late on all major developmental milestones. Indeed, they did not begin to speak until the middle or end of their third year (Kagan, 1978). Nevertheless, Gesell's contribution remains a substantial one. If we use his developmental sequences carefully and do not overinterpret them, we have a useful baseline of common developmental milestones.

Developmental psychologists have gone well beyond the pioneering studies of Gesell and have undertaken a closer analysis of the structure and function of the infant's developing competencies. Perceptual, motor, cognitive, and emotional development go hand in hand in a particular social context. The infant reaches out for an attractive object that he sees and pulls it in for closer inspection. The baby who has just begun to walk steps precariously toward the outstretched arms of an eager, encouraging parent. If we are to understand fully the infant's developing competencies, we need to look at the rich complexity of these achievements within their social context (Thelen, 1987, 1989). Before we discuss this analysis, let's take an overview of the infant's accomplishments during the first 2 years.

The First 4 Months

At the end of 4 months, most infants resemble the chubby, appealing babies seen in magazine advertisements. Since birth, they have nearly doubled in weight, from 6 to 8 pounds (2.7 to 3.6 kilograms) to somewhere between 12 and 15 pounds (5.4 to 6.8 kilograms), and they have probably grown 4 or more inches (10 or more centimeters) in length. Their skin has lost the newborn look, and their fine birth hair is being replaced by new hair.

SUDDEN INFANT DEATH SYNDROME (SIDS)

One of the most shattering events a parent may experience is the sudden and unexplained death of his or her baby. Yet this is the most common cause of death among infants between 1 week and 1 year in age. There are approximately 10,000 deaths annually in what is known as the sudden infant death syndrome, or SIDS. SIDS is defined as the sudden death of an apparently healthy infant or child in whom no medical cause can be found in a postmortem examination. SIDS, sometimes called "crib death," tends to happen without warning, while the child is asleep. The high incidence of SIDS has produced a great deal of concern within the medical profession.

Researchers have been unsuccessful in finding the precise cause but have found circumstances where SIDS is common. Unmarried mothers under 20 years of age who have delayed or not sought prenatal care run a higher than normal risk of having a child with SIDS. This risk is also increased if the mother has been ill during her pregnancy, has a short interval between pregnancies, or has earlier experienced the loss of her fetus. Smoking and the abuse of narcotics by the mother are often connected with sudden infant death syndrome. Smoking mothers who are also anemic run a particularly high risk of having a child with SIDS (Bulterys et al., 1990).

Sociological factors connected with the father also increase the risk of SIDS. If he is under 20 and in a low socioeconomic group, the chances of his child having SIDS are increased. The father's ethnicity is also an important factor. In the United States, where the average risk of SIDS is about 2 deaths in 1000, Asians have the lowest incidence with about 1 death in 2000. American Indians run the highest risk, with about 6 deaths per 1000. Blacks are next, with about 5 deaths in 1000, and Alaskan natives have between 4 and 5 deaths per 1000.

Babies who have been born prematurely or were underweight at birth run a higher than average risk of SIDS. They generally have greater than average difficulty breathing and often need support from respiratory devices. Frequently, in the week prior to the occurrence of SIDS, infants have severe breathing and digestive problems. Second and third children also run more risks of SIDS than the average first born. Babies who are part of multiple births also run above average risks, particularly triplets and the second child of twin births. "Several twin pairs, both [fraternal and identical], have died on the same day. Among 32 twin pairs recorded, 3 were found dead together" (Shannon & Kelly, 1982).

Infants with SIDS have been described as less active and less responsive than their siblings. Some have also been described as having a strange cry. Deaths frequently occur at night when the infant is asleep and lying in any position. Winter seems to be the time when it occurs most often. Although medical researchers have not yet found a physiological cause, they suspect irregularities in the autonomic nervous system, particularly as relates to breathing and heart functions.*

Nurses who tend infants at risk for SIDS need skills in two main areas: educating the family with a child at risk and counseling the family in case of the infant's death. In tending the at-risk infant, nurses must be able to assess the needs of the baby and the family (Chan, 1987). If the infant needs constant monitoring, it may be best to do this in a hospital where trained personnel and necessary equipment are present. But most at-risk infants are healthy enough to be at home. There, a home monitoring device can alert the parents if the child stops breathing during sleep.

Parents should understand that home monitoring places added stress on the family. At-risk infants often make extra demands on financial resources, on parental time, and on family lifestyles (Dean, 1986; Rowland et al., 1987). Some of the stress may be relieved by having parents meet with others also undergoing home monitoring of an at-risk child (Lang, 1987).

The occurrence of an infant's seemingly unexplained death has a devastating effect on the family and everyone else connected with the child. All those associated with keeping the infant alive experience guilt, loss, and powerlessness (Mandell et al., 1987). The family's grief and loss are often mixed with anger and frustration. "Who is to blame?" "Why did this happen?" The family needs as much information as possible as well as support in their sorrow, and reassurance that there is a 98% certainty that later infants will not have SIDS (Chan, 1987). Until we understand the causes of SIDS, we will still fail to identify many infants at risk and fail to monitor them effectively.

*Adapted from Daniel C. Shannon and Dorothy H. Kelly, "SIDS and near-SIDS," *New England Journal of Medicine* 306 (April 1982): 961–962.

At birth, the size of an infant's head represents about one-quarter of the total body length. Around the age of 4 months, however, the body begins to grow and lengthen much more rapidly than the head, and these proportions change markedly (see Figure 6–1). By 12 years, a child's head is only one-eighth the length of the body, and by 25 years, only one-tenth of the total body length.

The infant's teeth and bones are also beginning to change. In some children, the first tooth erupts at 4 or 5 months, although the average age for this event is closer to 6 or 7 months. Many bones are not yet hard and heavily calcified but are still soft cartilage. They tend to be pliable under stress and rarely break. Muscles, however, may pull easily and be injured. Occasionally, well-meaning adults have discovered this when hoisting infants up by the arms and swinging them in play (Stone, Smith, & Murphy, 1973).

Much to the delight of parents and care-givers, by 4 months the average baby is usually sleeping through the night. This sleep pattern sometimes begins as early as the second month. Gradually, the baby settles down into the family routine, daytime as well as nighttime.

When 4-month-olds are placed in a stomach-down position, they can generally hold up their chests as well as their heads. In a sitting position, they hold the head steady and observe very carefully everything that is going on. Average infants of this age can roll over from stomach to back and from back to stomach (Dargassies, 1986; Stone et al., 1973). Most of the reflexes that are found in the newborn seem to dissolve in the second and third months, and they are gradually replaced by voluntary actions. The well-coordinated stepping reflex, for example, is replaced by seemingly more random, less-coordinated kicking (Thelen, 1989). This is also the time when sudden infant death syndrome is most common (see box).

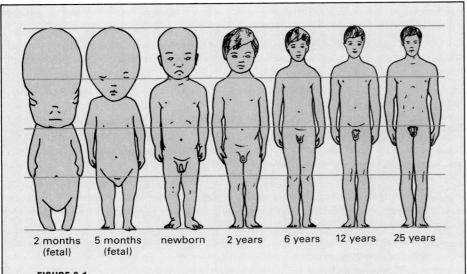

| 2 months (fetal) | 5 months (fetal) | newborn | 2 years | 6 years | 12 years | 25 years |

FIGURE 6-1
The cephalocaudal (head-downward) and proximodistal (center-outward) development that we saw in prenatal growth continues after birth, and the proportions of the baby's body change dramatically during infancy.

Self-discovery usually begins about this time. Infants discover their own hands and fingers and spend several minutes at a time watching them, studying their movements, bringing them together, grasping one hand with the other. Some 4-month-old infants also discover their feet and manipulate them in much the same way. It is quite normal, however, for some infants to be 5 or 6 months old before becoming aware of their feet, especially if they reach this age during the winter, when heavily bundled.

At 4 months, nearly all babies smile, laugh, and coo quite selectively. They will react with a wide range of emotional responses to persons or events. Many babies also begin to engage in elementary social games at this age. Imitative sound play—mimicking infant vocalizations so that they continue to babble—is one such game that will probably amuse both infants and others. At this age, adults will have to imitate the baby's sounds, not the other way around. Of course, the infant's state will influence the behavior response (see Chapter 5).

From 5 to 8 Months

By 8 months, babies have gained another 4 or 5 pounds (1.8 to 2.3 kilograms) and have grown about 3 more inches (7.6 centimeters), but their general appearance does not differ dramatically from that of 4-month-olds. They probably have at least two teeth, and perhaps a few more. Their hair is thicker and longer. By this time, too, their legs are oriented so that the soles of their feet no longer face each other.

At about 5 months, most infants achieve something called a *visually guided reach*. Before this age, they have possessed many of the component skills, such as a reflex grasp and then a more voluntary grasp, that are needed to perform this visually guided reach. They have been able to reach out toward an attractive object and have visually examined a variety of objects. It is a difficult task, however, to put all of these components together—to look, reach out, and successfully grasp an attractive object. Yet, in some ways, this one achievement transforms the world of the infant. Now begins a period of more systematic exploration of objects—with the hands, the eyes, and the mouth used individually or in combination (Rochat, 1989).

Most 8-month-old babies are able to pass objects from hand to hand, and some are able to use the thumb and finger to grasp. They may delight in filling both hands, and they are usually able to bang two objects together—a feat often demonstrated joyfully and endlessly.

Most 8-month-olds can get themselves into a sitting position, and nearly all babies of this age can sit without support once they are placed in position. If they are put on their feet, well over half of the 8-month-olds can stand while holding on to some support, and about half can pull themselves into a standing position. A few may even begin to sidestep around the crib or playpen while holding on, and some babies may be walking, using furniture for support.

During the period from 5 to 8 months, most babies develop some form of locomotion. They may learn to crawl (with body on the ground) or creep (on hands and knees). Other infants develop a method called "bear walking," which employs both hands and feet; still others "scoot" in a sitting position. The

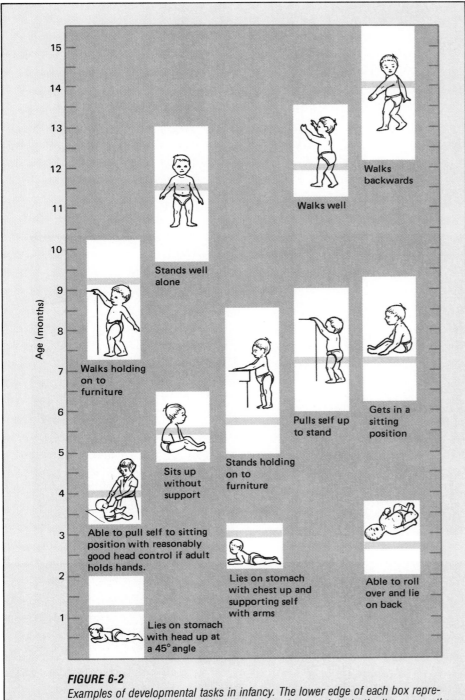

FIGURE 6-2

Examples of developmental tasks in infancy. The lower edge of each box represents the age at which 25% of all children perform each task; the line across the box, 50%; the upper edge of the box, 75%.

At 4 months, infants can lift their chests as well as their heads and can carefully observe what is happening around them.

(Left) Most 8-month-olds are able to grasp with both hands, and they delight in banging two objects together.

(Right) By 12 months, many infants are actively exploring their environment.

(Left) At 18 months, most toddlers are able to walk alone, and they like to carry or pull toys with them.

(Right) Two-year-olds walk, run, and can usually pedal a tricycle.

components of crawling are developing for several months beforehand. The infant is looking at more distant attractive objects and is reaching for them. There is a change in the pattern and flexibility of kicking and in other types of leg activity. Also, just before crawling, many infants have periods during which they rhythmically rock forward and backward. All these pieces of behavior need to be integrated into the task of crawling across the floor toward an attractive distant object (Goldfield, 1989).

Many babies of 8 months begin to play social games, such as peekaboo, bye-bye and patty-cake, and most enjoy handing an item back and forth to an adult. Another quickly learned routine is that of dropping an object and watching someone pick it up and hand it back. This "game" is usually learned accidentally by both baby and adult, but the baby is often the first to catch on to the possibilities for fun.

At 7 or 8 months, most babies experience *stranger distress*. They become quite cautious with strangers and will stare suspiciously at an unfamiliar face. If a stranger persists in attentions or attempts to handle the baby, the infant may burst into tears or seek comfort from someone familiar. As we shall see in the next chapter, this reaction is an important step in the baby's social and cognitive development.

Infants at 8 months pay more attention to speech than before. They will turn toward a voice and even imitate some speech sounds. Many infants of this age will utter repeated sounds, such as *baba,* or *nana,* or words like *mama, dada,* or *bye-bye,* although they will usually not know what the words mean. The sounds in infant babbling are much more complex and varied at 8 months than at 4 months.

From 9 to 12 Months

At 12 months, most infants are about three times heavier than they were at birth, and they have grown about 9 or 10 inches (22.9 to 25.4 centimeters) in length. Throughout this first year, girls tend to weigh slightly less than boys do.

By 9 months, most infants have some form of locomotion; most have pulled themselves to a stand, and half of them are beginning to take steps while holding on to furniture. By 12 months, about half are standing alone and are beginning to take their first few steps. The age at which free-walking begins varies widely, depending on both individual development and cultural factors. Over 50 years ago, Shirley (1931) and Gesell (1940) found that 15 months was the average age for free-walking to begin. Since 1967, however, researchers have observed that the period between 11 and 13 months is the average for this behavior to begin in healthy, well-fed infants who are given the opportunity and the encouragement to exercise (Frankenburg & Dodds, 1967).

The ability to stand and walk gives the infant a new visual perspective. Locomotion allows for more active exploration. Infants can get into, over, and under things. They can clean out a bureau drawer and can follow their mother into the kitchen. Their world is broadened once again. The infant's motor development is spurred on by the new and exciting things that he can see and hear. His ability to explore at new levels and with new abilities spurs on his cognitive and perceptual development (Thelen, 1989).

Twelve-month-olds actively manipulate the environment. They are able to undo latches, open cabinets, pull toys, and twist lamp cords. Their newly developed

pincer grasp The method of holding objects, developed around the age of 12 months, in which the thumb opposes the forefinger.

toddler The infant in his or her second year of life who has begun to walk—the child has a somewhat top-heavy, wide stance and walks with a gait that is not solidly balanced or smoothly coordinated.

---

pincer grasp—where the thumb opposes the forefinger—allows them to pick up grass, hairs, matches, and dead insects. They can turn on the television set and the stove, and they can explore kitchen cupboards, open windows, and poke things into electrical outlets. Because children are so busy exploring the environment, care-givers must set limits on their explorations. They have to strike a balance between too much restriction and sufficient control in order to keep the baby safe. "No" becomes an important word in the vocabulary of both the child and care-givers.

At 12 months, babies are often able to play games and can "hide" by covering their eyes. They can roll a ball back and forth with an adult and can throw small objects, making up in persistence what they lack in skill. Many children of this age begin to feed themselves, using a spoon and holding their own cup for drinking.

The 12-month-old is on the verge of language. Most infants of this age are struggling either to walk or to utter their first words—but generally not both. Most infants achieve control of walking first, then they start talking. Some 12-month-old children, however, can manage "mama," "dada," and two to eight other words, such as "no," "baby," "bye-bye," "hi," and "bow-wow." In Chapter 8, we will discuss in detail the infant's acquisition of language.

As they enter the second year, children become aware of themselves as individuals separate from their mothers (or care-givers); they increasingly exercise choice and preference. They may suddenly and vehemently refuse a food that they have always liked. They may protest loudly at bedtime, or they may engage in a "battle of the wills" with someone over a formerly trouble-free event, such as getting into a snowsuit or being placed in a highchair. Infants in their second year of life, once they have begun to walk, are usually referred to as **toddlers.**

Age 18 Months

The 18-month-old usually weighs between 22 and 27 pounds (9.9 and 12.2 kilograms), an indication that the rate of weight increase has slowed. The average height at this age is about 31 to 33 inches (78 to 83 centimeters). Almost all children at this age are walking alone. When walking, they generally like to push or pull something with them or carry something in their hands. They seldom drop down on all fours now, although walking may actually take more of their time and effort. Some are not yet able to climb stairs, and most have considerable difficulty kicking a ball, because their unsteadiness does not permit them to free one foot for kicking. Children of this age also find pedaling tricycles or jumping nearly impossible.

At 18 months, children may be stacking from two to four cubes or blocks to build a tower, and they can often manage to scribble with crayon or pencil. They have improved their ability to feed themselves and may be able to undress themselves partly. (The ability to put clothes on generally comes later.) Many of their actions are imitative of those around them—"reading" a magazine, sweeping the floor, or chatting on a toy telephone.

Most 18-month-olds have made great strides in language and may have a vocabulary of several words and phrases. They usually combine two words to make a single sentence, and they can point to and name body parts and a few very familiar pictures. They may now begin to use words effectively.

Age 24 Months

By their second birthdays, toddlers have added approximately another 2 inches and pounds. Again, the rate of gain is tapering.

Because, until recently, 2-year-olds were usually considered too young for most nursery schools, and yet too old for regular monthly visits to a doctor, relatively few studies had been made on this age group. Toddlers stayed with their families and their care-givers and were seen around the neighborhood, but they were generally out of the range of most research psychologists. Several studies show the 2-year-old as a fascinating active learner, just beginning to break through into new areas of skill, social understanding, and accomplishment (Bronson, 1981).

Two-year-olds not only walk and run, but they can usually pedal a tricycle, jump in place on both feet, balance briefly on one foot, and accomplish a fairly good overhand throw. They climb up steps and, sometimes, come down again with assistance. They crawl into, under, around, and over objects and furniture; they manipulate, carry, handle, push, or pull anything they see. They put things into and take things out of large containers. They pour water, mold clay, stretch the stretchable, and bend the bendable. They transport items in carts, wagons, carriages, or trucks. They explore, test, and probe. All of this exploration provides a vital learning experience about the nature and possibilities of their physical world.

The language development of most 2-year-olds shows some marked gains.

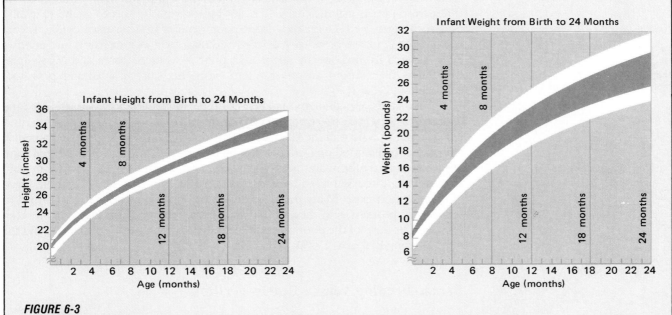

FIGURE 6-3

The weight and height of about 50% of the infants at a given age will fall in the gray regions; about 15% will fall in each of the white regions. Thus, on the average, 80% of all infants will have weights and heights somewhere in the gray and white regions of the graphs. Note that as the infants age, greater differences occur in weight and height within the normal range of growth.

They are able to follow simple directions, name more pictures, and use three or more words in combination; some even use plurals. Given a crayon or pencil, 2-year-olds may create "scribbles" and be fascinated briefly with the magical marks. They may stack from six to eight blocks or cubes to build towers, and they can construct a three-block "bridge." Their spontaneous block play shows matching of shapes and symmetry. If they are willing, 2-year-olds can take off most of their own clothing, and they can put on some items.

Physical, motor, and cognitive development during the first 2 years is a complex, dynamic process. For infants to thrive, they must have their basic needs met by their environment. They must get enough sleep, feel safe, receive consistent care, and have appropriate stimulating experiences. Each developing system—perceptual or motor skills, for example—supports the other. A blind child does not crawl or walk as soon as the seeing child does. There is no lure of a distant toy or of a parent's face. There is no visual feedback to guide this child's motor action. Cognitive development, too, depends on the information that the child receives from his actions and his sensory explorations. What is more, these interacting systems are helped or hindered by the social context in which the infant develops (Hazen & Lockman, 1989; Thelen & Fogel, 1989). In the next few sections, we will look at some of these components of infant development.

NUTRITION AND MALNUTRITION

Ours may be considered the best-fed nation in the world, but many Americans still suffer from nutritional deficiencies. R. H. Hutcheson, Jr. (1968) found that 20% of a study group of 1-year-olds from poor families in Tennessee suffered from severe anemia (a red blood cell deficiency caused by a lack of iron), and another 30% suffered from moderate anemia. In poor areas of Alabama and Mississippi, researchers have found anemia rates to be as high as 80% among preschool children.

Two kinds of malnutrition generally occur. One is due to an insufficient total quantity of food, the other to an insufficiency of certain kinds of food. The latter type is more prevalent in the United States than is the former. A great many people who can afford a good diet often consume too many "empty calories" in the form of foods high in carbohydrates but low in proteins, vitamins, and minerals. In poor areas of the United States, and in the less developed countries, however, both kinds of malnutrition exist. Many people who receive too few calories cannot afford to buy animal proteins, and they receive inadequate amounts of proteins from other sources. The diets of the poor most often lack vitamins A and C, riboflavin, and the mineral iron (Eichorn, 1979).

Breast-Feeding versus Bottle-Feeding

Milk is the major source of nutrients for infants. It is used almost exclusively in the diet for the first 6 months and together with solid foods for the next 6 to 12 months. Many women throughout the world choose to breast-feed their infants. The breast milk of a reasonably well fed mother contains a remarkably well-balanced combination of nutrients, as well as antibodies that protect the infant

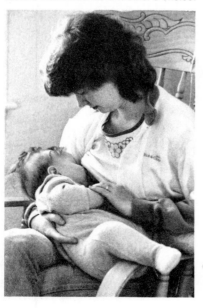

Breast-feeding or bottle-feeding? Although breast-feeding is more nutritious than bottle-feeding is, there are many factors that influence a mother's choice.

TRENDS IN BREAST-FEEDING AND BOTTLE-FEEDING

Despite the fact that breast-feeding is better for infants than bottle-feeding is, studies have shown that mid-20th-century mothers both in the developed and less developed countries of the world shifted from breast-feeding to bottle-feeding in record numbers. Mothers in the United States led this decline in breast-feeding as infant formulas became more available in the 1940s, 1950s, and 1960s. By 1971, less than 10% of babies born in the United States were breast-fed after the first 3 months of life. Although this practice has generally caused no hardship or nutritional problems for the great majority of infants in developed countries, the shift to commercial infant formula has resulted in widespread malnutrition and high infant mortality in poorer countries. Some recent statistics illustrate this shift: Over 90% of the infants in Chile were breast-fed in 1960; and in 1968, less than 10% were breast-fed. In Mexico, 95% of 6-month-old infants were breast-fed in 1960; in 1966, only 40% were breast-fed. In Singapore, 80% of 3-month-old infants were breast-fed in 1951; in 1971, only 5% were breast-fed. In the poorer countries, bottle-fed babies had a much higher mortality rate than those who were breast-fed (Latham, 1977). Malnutrition occurs when people lack the money to buy expensive milk substitutes; in addition, many babies die when the commercial formula is diluted with contaminated water, thereby transmitting intestinal diseases to the infants.

Recently, in response to the efforts of major national and world health organizations, many women have returned to breast-feeding their infants. In the United States, over 50% of mothers breast-feed their infants for at least a few weeks, and 35% continue this practice for at least 3 months (U.S. Department of Health and Human Services, 1989). Yet, even in the 1990s, the levels and trends of breast-feeding vary widely across socioeconomic, cultural, and religious groups. Breast-feeding is highest in women who are older, better-educated, and relatively affluent. It is more popular in the western United States and is less popular in the Southeast. Breast-feeding practices are also influenced by family and cultural ideas about how mothers should care for their children, by the amounts of time and money that are available, and by the advice mothers receive from health-care professionals. Curiously, the increase in the number of working mothers was not a major cause in the decrease, and then increase, in the trend toward breast-

The shift from breast- to bottle-feeding occurred in less developed countries as well as in Europe and the United States.

feeding. Breast-feeding declined among women who did not work between births as well as among those who did.

In developing countries, where there are high infant mortality rates, the high rate of bottle-fed babies is still a major public health concern. Here, too, despite extensive educational campaigns by the World Health Organization and other groups, the decision of whether or not to breast-feed and for how long is personal and is embedded in the sociocultural context. In Korea, boys are much more likely to be breast-fed than girls are (Nemeth & Bowling, 1985). In Nigeria, mothers with more education breast-feed less often, and Christian mothers breast-feed for a much shorter period of time than do Moslem mothers (Oni, 1987). In Zaire and many other countries, rural women use breast-feeding as a form of birth control, and, hence, they may continue it for several years (Mock et al., 1986).

Why do some mothers choose to breast-feed, whereas others prefer to bottle-feed? It appears that good nutrition is only one of the many factors that influence this choice.

from some diseases. The content of breast milk suits most babies, and breast-fed babies often have fewer digestive disturbances. Additionally, breast milk is always fresh and ready at the right temperature, doesn't need refrigeration, and is absolutely sterile. Unless the mother is very ill, has an inadequate diet, or takes a lot of drugs or alcohol, breast milk is better for a baby's health. In spite of these findings, many mothers in the United States and throughout the world have switched from breast-feeding to bottle-feeding. (See "Trends in Breast-Feeding and Bottle-Feeding.")

Weaning and the Introduction of Solid Foods

Some mothers in developed countries begin weaning babies from the breast at 3 or 4 months, or even earlier; others continue breast-feeding for as long as 2 or 3 years. Although such extended breast-feeding is rare among middle- to upper-class mothers in the United States, 2 or 3 years is not rare for certain American subcultures or for other cultures. (Occasionally, it even continues into middle childhood for a family's youngest child—it was reported that a girl in Baiga, India, was not weaned until her marriage at age 12 [Stephens, 1963].)

Normally, at about 3 months of age, infants gradually begin to accept some strained foods. Usually, they begin with the simple cereals such as rice, and expand to a variety of cereals and pureed fruits, followed somewhat later by strained vegetables and meats. It is possible that an infant may be allergic to one or a variety of foods, and it is therefore advised that foods be introduced slowly. Others seem to take to almost everything that is offered. By 8 months, most infants are eating a broad range of specially prepared foods, and milk consumption is usually reduced. As they acquire teeth, finger foods are introduced.

Weaning is a crucial time for the onset of malnutrition. Particularly vulnerable are the 1-year-olds, who have already been weaned from the breast and whose families have not money for milk or other nutritious foods. These children may survive on diets composed of potato chips, dry cereals, and cookies—foods that provide calories for energy but few nutrients. Even with enough milk or a variety of nutritious foods available, 1-year-olds may be unwilling to drink a sufficient amount of milk from a cup; they may also prefer crackers to more wholesome snacks of cheese and meat.

Public health programs in the United States have played an important role in efforts to improve the nutritional status of pregnant women, infants, and young children. In the early 1980s, the WIC program (a special supplemental food program for women, infants, and children) provided food supplements and education for over 3 million individuals monthly. The supplements of milk, cheese, iron-fortified cereals, eggs, and fruit juices have been recognized to improve the health of infants both during and after participation in the program (Ryan et al., 1985). Decreased funding of these programs by 1991 resulted in parallel increases in infant malnutrition (Children's Defense Fund, 1991).

Young children need large amounts of protein and other nutrients because they are experiencing a critical period in the growth cycle. Malnutrition at any time before birth and for 5 years afterward can permanently retard growth, particularly of the brain and nervous system (Perkins, 1977). Although some physical retardation from malnutrition can be reversed later, retardation in brain development is permanent (Winick & Brasel, 1977; Wyden, 1971). According to Wyden (1971):

> The rate of brain cell division decreases when a fetus is not given enough nourishment. A seriously malnourished fetus may have 20 percent fewer brain cells than normal fetuses. If a newborn baby is seriously undernourished during his first 6 months of life, cell division is also slowed down—also by as much as 20 percent. If an infant is malnourished both before and after birth, the brain may be 60 percent smaller.

Despite the dire consequences that can stem from severe malnutrition during infancy, serious remedial programs of food supplementation and education can produce dramatic results, even in the poorest developing countries. A study that was done in Bogota, Colombia, provided food supplements to children for the first 3 years of their lives. The food supplements were accompanied by periodic home visits. These children showed much less growth retardation and all-around better functioning than the control groups—even 3 years after the supplements were discontinued (Super, Herrera, & Mora, 1990).

We have examined the typical development patterns and nutritional needs of infants during their first 2 years. We will now analyze the process of perceptual and cognitive development.

PERCEPTUAL COMPETENCE

As explained in Chapter 5, perception is a complex process of interpreting our sensory environment. This process takes time to develop (Gibson & Spelke, 1983).

Through hard work and the use of imaginative research techniques, psychologists have discovered that the human infant is far more complex and has many more competencies than had once been supposed. New technology has helped researchers in their studies. Today, it is possible to measure certain basic physiological reactions of a baby to the environment and to specific stimulation. Heart activity, brain wave activity, and the electrical response of the skin can provide useful information about what infants perceive and how much they understand. Researchers can also gather information from highly refined pictures of an infant's movements—for example, eye movement or hand manipulation. But new technology is only part of the answer. A good research plan, or paradigm, is more important.

One such strategy is the **novelty paradigm.** It is well known that babies quickly tire of looking at the same image or playing with the same toy. Infants habituate to repeated sights or sounds (see Chapter 5). Also, very young infants often show their disinterest by looking away. If given a choice between a familiar toy and a new one, most infants will choose the new one. Even if there is only a very small difference in the new toy, the infant will choose it. Researchers have been able to use this information in setting up experiments to determine how small a difference in sound, pattern, or color the infant is capable of detecting.

Another important strategy for studying the infant's understanding of the world is the **surprise paradigm.** Human beings tend to register surprise—through facial expression, physical reaction, or vocal response—when something happens that they did not expect or, conversely, when something does not happen

novelty paradigm A research plan that uses infants' preferences for new stimuli over familiar ones in order to investigate their ability to detect small differences in sounds, patterns, or colors.

surprise paradigm A research technique used to test infants' memory and expectations. Infants cannot report what they remember or expect, but if their expectations are violated, they respond with surprise. For example, if the doll is not under the cloth where the infants saw it hidden, they are surprised.

that they did expect. Researchers are able to determine infants' surprise reactions by measuring changes in their breathing, heartbeat, or galvanic skin response or simply by observing their expressions or bodily movements. Researchers can design experiments to test very precisely what infants expect and what events violate their expectations (Bower, 1974). Because of research techniques like these, we know that even though newborns have limited sensory and perceptual competence, these abilities improve dramatically during the first 6 months.

Vision

During the first 4 to 6 months, infants' visual abilities develop rapidly. As we saw in Chapter 5, newborns can visually track a moving penlight and can discriminate between different shapes; however, they prefer to focus on complex patterns and human faces (Fantz, Ordy, & Udelf, 1962). Focusing ability itself improves rapidly during the first few months. Although newborns focus best on objects only 10 inches (25.4 centimeters) away, 3- to 4-month-olds focus almost as well as do adults (Aslin, 1987). Infants' visual acuity increasingly sharpens. Where newborns discriminate stripes $\frac{1}{8}$ of an inch (3.2 millimeters) apart and 10 inches (25.4 centimeters) away, 6-month-olds discriminate stripes $\frac{1}{32}$ of an inch (.8 millimeters) apart from that same distance (Banks & Dannemiller, 1987; Fantz et al., 1962).

Even newborns can see bright colors like yellow, orange, red, green, and turquoise. For the first 1 to 2 months, they actually prefer black-and-white patterns over color ones, probably due to the greater contrast. The color images may appear a bit blurry or washed-out. By 2 months, the infant picks up more subtle colors like blue, purple, or chartreuse, when compared with gray. Infants' color vision and preference for color improve rapidly. By 4 months, they discriminate between most colors, and, by 6 months, their color perception nearly equals that of adults (Bornstein, 1978; Maurer & Maurer, 1988; Teller & Bornstein, 1987).

Infants are selective in what they look at from the beginning. They look at novel and moderately complex patterns and at human faces. Some changes take place during the first year, however, in exactly what attracts their attention. Newborns look only at the edges of a face. A few months later, they will look at the eyes, and even later, at the mouth of a person who is talking. Researchers wonder what causes these changes in selective attention. Are they caused partly by the ways in which the neural system matures? Bornstein (1978), for example, discovered that 4-month-old infants prefer "pure" colors to other shades and look for a longer time at perpendicular lines than at slanted lines. He suggests that infants select these colors and lines because they trigger more "neural firing" in the brain. In other words, infants look at the things available that excite the most neural activity.

A number of other improvements in vision occur during the first 6 months. Compared to newborns, older infants are better able to control their eye movements; they can track moving objects more consistently and for longer periods of time (Aslin, 1987). They also spend more time scanning the environment. During the first month of life, only 5% to 10% of their time is spent scanning, whereas nearly 35% is spent scanning at $2\frac{1}{2}$ months (White, 1971). Although newborn infants are attracted to bright lights and objects, provided the objects are not too bright, 4-month-olds are able to see and respond to dimmer objects.

SEEING OBJECTS   Does the infant see objects the way adults see objects? It was once thought that infants had difficulty separating the object from the background. But, in reality, this problem is rare. Infants may not "see" that a cup is separate from a saucer without picking up the cup, but they can "see" that the cup and saucer are separate from the background. By 3 or 4 months, infants have had many visual experiences in which their head moves or the object moves. They will notice, for example, that a milk bottle, from another angle, is still a milk bottle. Infants can use motion as well as space to help define the objects in their world (Mandler, 1990; Spelke, 1988).

DEPTH PERCEPTION   Humans see things in three dimensions. We see that some things are closer and that others are farther away. Even with one eye closed, we can tell the approximate distance of objects. The objects that are close to us appear larger, and they block our view of more distant objects. If we close one eye and hold our heads still, the view resembles a two-dimensional photograph. But, if we move our head, the world comes to life with its three-dimensional aspect. If we use both eyes (binocular vision), we really don't have to move our heads. The left-eye view and the right-eye view are slightly different. The brain integrates these two images, giving us information on distance and relative size.

Do infants have depth perception? Are their brains preprogrammed to integrate the images from two eyes in order to gain information about distance or relative size? Can they use the information that is gathered by moving their heads to see the world in three dimensions?

It appears that the infant's brain can integrate two images in rudimentary form. Because the newborn's eyes are not well coordinated and because the infant has not learned how to interpret the information transmitted by the eyes, depth perception is probably not very sophisticated. It seems to take about 4 months for binocular vision to emerge (Aslin & Smith, 1988).

What is the evidence of developing depth perception? Even as young as 6 weeks, infants seem to dodge, blink, or show some form of avoidance reaction when an object appears to be coming directly at them (Dodwell, Humphrey, & Muir, 1987). At 4 months, infants are able to swipe with reasonable accuracy at a toy that is dangled in front of them. By 5 months, they have a well-controlled, visually guided reach for objects that are close to them. However, infants at 5 months who are wearing a patch over one eye are slightly less accurate at reaching for objects. Similarly, when given the choice of two objects, one slightly closer than the other, they don't always pick the closer object (Granrud, Yonas, & Pettersen, 1984).

One of the best-known experiments to test infants' depth perception is the **visual cliff.** Gibson and Walk (1960) created a special box to simulate depth. On one side, a heavy piece of glass covered a solid surface. On the other side, the heavy glass was 2 to 3 feet (60 to 90 centimeters) above a floor, simulating a cliff effect. Infants 8 months or older refused to crawl across the surface that appeared to be a cliff. Younger infants who were not yet able to crawl showed interest but not distress, as indicated by heart rate changes, when they were placed on the cliff side of the box (Campos, Langer, & Krowitz, 1970).

Further studies by Joseph Campos and his colleagues have focused on how children learn *not* to cross the cliff side. A baby who has just barely learned how to crawl can sometimes be coaxed across the cliff, provided it is not too deep.

visual cliff An experimental apparatus that tests depth perception of infants by simulating an abrupt dropoff.

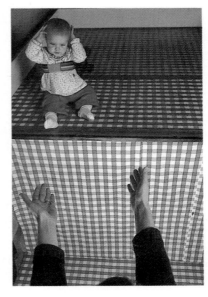

Even when coaxed by their mothers, infants will not crawl over the edge of the visual cliff.

The same baby will later refuse to cross if his mother has signaled to him that it is dangerous. She may tell him in an anxious voice not to cross, or, much more simply, she may express a look of fear, anxiety, or even horror (Kermoian & Campos, 1988). It appears that the visual cues for depth perception are developed within the first 4 to 6 months (Yonas & Awsley, 1987). The particular meaning of the information about distance or depth is learned more gradually, especially as the child begins to move about his or her environment.

Hearing

Within the first few months, infants' hearing acuity improves considerably. At birth, the middle ear is filled with fluid and tissue, most of which disappears after the first few weeks. Despite this blockage, newborns show changes in heart rate and respiration in response to moderate sounds (for example, 60 decibels—a normal telephone conversation). At 3 months, they respond to much softer sounds (43 decibels) and to even softer tones at 8 months (34 decibels) (Hoversten & Moncur, 1969). We also know by changes in their heart rates that infants detect fairly large changes in loudness, pitch, and duration of sound. Infants may even detect much smaller changes or hear much softer tones, although it is difficult to measure this, except under hospital experimentation conditions. This measurement is done by a study of the electrical activity of the brain (Hecox, 1975).

Infants do respond in other ways to sounds. They can be soothed, alerted, or distressed by them. Low-frequency or rhythmic sounds generally soothe infants. Loud, sudden, and high-frequency tones cause them distress. Infants also show—by turning their heads—that they can locate the source of the sound. These and other studies indicate that infants have fairly well developed auditory perception within their first 6 months of life.

An important aspect of infants' hearing during the first year is their seemingly inborn ability to differentiate between speech and nonspeech sounds. As early as 1 month, infants can detect subtle differences between speech sounds, such as "pah" and "bah" (Eimas, 1975). In fact, one researcher was amazed to find that infants in the first year could pick up differences in language that even she could not pick up. She had borrowed a tape containing sounds that are used in the Czechoslo-vakian language. After listening to it over and over, she could find no differences. When she called the language lab to complain, they told her that she was mistaken. She then played this tape to her Canadian babies, who detected the differences immediately (Maurer & Maurer, 1988). It is clear that infants' sensitivity to speech sounds helps them learn how to speak. This sensitivity and the infants' ability to recognize familiar voices help strengthen their attachment bond to parents and care-givers.

Integration

Researchers have generally agreed that at birth an infant's vision, hearing, and senses of touch, taste, and smell are nearly complete and that they improve rapidly over the next 6 months. In contrast, there has been great disagreement as to whether or not there is integration of these senses during early infancy. How do we ask infants whether they know that a particular sound comes from a particular object? How do infants acknowledge that the bumpy thing they just felt is now the same thing they are looking at? It is difficult to design experiments for the first 6 months of life. Recent, imaginative work, however, suggests that either the senses are interrelated at birth or the necessary learning is extremely rapid.

As you recall from Chapter 5, newborns will turn their heads to look at the source of a sound. They don't necessarily know what they will see, but there is a mechanism in place that will help them learn this. Some imaginative experiments have been done on integration. In one study, infants were allowed to suck on one of two different kinds of pacifiers: One was covered with bumps, and the other was smooth. When the pacifier was removed and the infants were shown both kinds of pacifiers, they *looked longer* at the nipple that they had just *felt* in their mouth (Meltzoff & Borton, 1979). In another experiment, infants at 4 months were shown two films of complex events that they had not seen before and that had only *one* soundtrack. The infants turned to look at the film that matched the sound. Next, the film was simplified so that only two speakers' faces were shown, and it looked as if both speakers were talking at exactly the same time. The infants were still able to pick the speaker's face that matched the soundtrack (Kuhl & Meltzoff, 1988).

Much of this sensory integration must, of course, be learned. Infants must learn which sounds go with which sights, what the soft fur feels and looks like, what the noisy puppy looks like, and so forth. Nevertheless, it appears that infants have a built-in tendency to seek these links. Integration advances rapidly over the first year. In another study, Rose, Gottfried, and Bridger (1981) found that even though 6-month-olds could sometimes visually identify an object that they had touched or were touching, this cross-modal transference (tactual–visual) was not as strong in these young infants as it was in older infants. Some of the research on the visual cliff makes this same point. Although young infants did recognize the depth in the visual cliff, and they noticed that one side was different from the other, they did not necessarily recognize that this was something unsafe or something not to be crawled across. They were interested more than afraid. The older infants who had a higher level of integration were more wary of the visual cliff.

Integration, then, is a process that becomes increasingly efficient and effective over the first year of the infant's life. One of the first steps in this process is the coordination of vision with reaching; this seemingly simple accomplishment takes several months.

The coordination of vision with reaching—the visually guided reach—is one of the first steps in the process of integration.

THE VISUALLY GUIDED REACH If 1-month-old infants are shown a very attractive object, they will do a number of things. Often, they will open and close their hands and wave their arms in a seemingly random way. Sometimes, they will open their mouths as if they are about to suck. They may even look intently at the object. But they cannot coordinate any of these reflexes—reaching out, grasping the object, and bringing it to their mouths. It takes at least 5 months to develop this skill.

Successful reaching requires a number of different abilities: accurate depth perception, voluntary control of grasping, voluntary control of arm movements, and the ability to organize these behaviors in a sequence (Bruner, 1973). Throughout the first 5 months, infants are learning about objects with their mouth and hands, then linking visual information to direct the exploration of the fingers (Rochat, 1989). Finally, in the visually guided reach, infants combine many bits and pieces of behavior; they *functionally integrate* and *subordinate* them to the total

cognition The process by which we know and understand our world.

pattern. When they are first learning the guided reach, children must attempt individually the acts of reaching, grasping, and mouthing. Later, the reach itself becomes a means to an end, and children can then turn to a larger task—like stacking blocks. Their reaching is then functionally integrated and subordinated to block building.

Brain Development and Experience

Recently, neuroscientists and developmental psychologists have been studying the relationship between sensory, perceptual, and motor experience and the development of certain areas of the brain. It is clear that the human brain grows considerably in size and complexity during the first 2 years. At birth, it is about 25% of the size and weight of the adult brain. By the infant's first birthday, it is double that size. At 2 years, it is at about 75% of adult size. In the first few months, there is rapid development in the primary sensory and motor areas of the brain. This corresponds to the time when we know there is rapid development of the perceptual systems. From numerous animal studies, we know that there are links between sensory and motor experience and actual brain growth. For instance, kittens who are raised in an environment where there are vertical lines but no horizontal lines actually lose the ability to make accurate perceptual judgments about horizontal lines. The kitten who lives in a deprived visual environment actually has fewer brain cells that respond to that kind of visual input after the period of deprivation. Many theorists believe that the brain is "prewired" for certain basic sensory and motor functions. However, this "prewiring" must be used in order to be "fine tuned" and even, in some cases, to continue to exist. This "wiring" is somewhat redundant, with many connections lost through disuse and others strengthened by use (Bertenthal & Campos, 1987; Greenough, Black & Wallace, 1987). This research on brain development gives further support to the view that development is neither purely genetic nor purely environmental, but depends on a combination of both factors.

COGNITIVE DEVELOPMENT

Cognition is the process by which we gain knowledge of our world. Cognition encompasses the processes of thinking, learning, perceiving, remembering, and understanding. Cognitive development refers to the growth and refinement of this intellectual capacity. Many theorists believe that infants take an active role in their own cognitive development. The problem is in finding out what infants do know and think about. When subjects cannot talk to you and tell you what they are thinking, how can you study their developing intellects?

The individual most influential in the study of emerging infant intelligence has probably been Jean Piaget. As was discussed in Chapter 2, Piaget was one of the few psychologists who had woven a design large enough to encompass all human intellectual development. Piaget had a personal fascination with the human mind, a passion that fueled his natural talents as an observer of behavior. Part of his work focused on the interaction between heredity and the environment, and part on the ways in which children manipulate the environment to exercise and develop their cognitive abilities.

As detailed in Chapter 2, Piaget saw humans as active, alert, and creative beings who possess mental structures, called *schemes,* that process and organize information. Over time, these schemes develop into more complex cognitive structures. Intellectual development occurs in four qualitatively different sequential periods that begin in early infancy and go on for the next 12 to 15 years into adolescence and beyond. His first period of intellectual development is called the sensorimotor period.

The Sensorimotor Period

Infants come into the world prepared to respond to the environment with the perceptual capacities just discussed and with a few ready-made sensorimotor patterns—sucking, crying, kicking, and making a fist. These sensorimotor patterns form the infant's schemes—the infant's only way of processing information from the environment.

But what about thoughts and concepts? How do infants develop an understanding of objects, people, or relationships? How do they code and store things in their memory without any words? What, after all, is infant intelligence? According to Piaget, these ready-made schemes—looking, visually following, sucking, grasping, and crying—are the building blocks for cognitive development. They are transformed over the next 18 months into some early concepts of objects, people, and the self.

ADAPTATION   Piaget viewed the sensorimotor period as six fairly discrete stages. Because other researchers have found some variations in the course of events, we will not discuss this period by these discrete stages but rather by some of the processes of development that occur during this period.

Infant schemes are elaborated, modified, and developed by a process that Piaget (1962) called **adaptation.** He described how his 7-month-old daughter, Lucienne, played with a pack of cigarettes. Unlike a 2-year-old, who might take out a cigarette and pretend to smoke it, Lucienne had no such behaviors in her repertoire. She treated the pack of cigarettes as if it were any other toy or object that she had been used to handling. Looking, mouthing, grasping, and banging were her only ways of interacting with the world: These were her toy-manipulating schemes. In other words, she *assimilated* the pack of cigarettes into her existing schemes. With each new object, children make minor changes in their action patterns, or schemes. The grasp and the mouth must *accommodate* the new object. Gradually, through assimilation and accommodation, these action patterns become modified and the infant's basic sensorimotor schemes develop into more complex cognitive capacities.

Piaget noted a particular form of adaptation in infancy that he called a **circular response.** Much of what infants learn begins quite by accident. An action occurs, and then infants see, hear, or feel it. For example, some babies may notice their hands in front of their faces. By moving the hands, they discover that they can change what is seen. They can prolong the event, repeat it, stop it, or start it again. Infants' early circular responses involve the discovery of their own bodies. Later circular responses concern how they use their bodies or themselves to change the environment, as in making a toy move.

adaptation In Piaget's theory, the process by which infant schemata are elaborated, modified, and developed.

circular response A particular form of adaptation in Piaget's theory, in which the infant accidentally performs some action, perceives it, then repeats the action.

According to Piaget, at the end of the sensorimotor period, most infants will have achieved a number of simple but fundamental intellectual abilities. These include concepts about the uses of familiar objects, an understanding of object permanence, memory development, and some beginning ways to symbolically represent things, people, and events. Each of the following sections examines a part of this development.

Play with Objects

Although they are often unnoticed by parents or care-givers, accomplishments in object play are important to children's cognitive development. By 4 or 5 months, infants generally reach out, grasp, and hold objects. These seemingly simple skills—together with their advanced perceptual skills—equip them for more varied play with objects. In their play with objects, children demonstrate a memory for repeated events, match their actions appropriately with various objects, and develop their understanding of the social world through pretending and imitation. Play, in other words, lays the groundwork for further complex thinking and language.

Object play goes through definite stages, starting with simple explorations by about 5 months and ending with complex imitative and pretending behavior by the end of 3 years (Garvey, 1977). By 9 months, most infants explore objects; they wave them around, turn them over, and test them by hitting them against something nearby. But they are not aware of the use or function of the things that they are handling. By 12 months, they stop first and examine objects closely before putting them in their mouths. By 15 to 18 months, they try to use objects as they were intended—for example, they might pretend to drink from a cup, brush their hair with a toy brush, or make a doll sit up. By 21 months, they generally use objects appropriately. They try to feed a doll with a spoon, put a doll in the driver's seat of a toy truck, or use keys to unlock an imaginary door. The play becomes still more realistic by 24 months. Toddlers take dolls out for walks and line up trucks and trailers in the right order. By 3 years, preschool children may make dolls into imaginary people with independent wills. They might have a doll go outdoors, chop wood, bring it back inside, and put it in an imaginary fireplace (Fein, 1981).

IMITATION The object play of 2-year-olds is rich with imitations of their world. Infants' imitations—of actions, gestures, and words—are not as simple as they might appear to adults.

Within the first 3 months, infants do some sporadic imitation in the context of play with the care-giver. For example, an infant may imitate facial expressions, or stick out his or her tongue and match the sound or pitch of the mother's voice. Normally, mothers begin this game by imitating the infant. In fact, it is sometimes hard to tell who is imitating—mother or child (Uzgiris, 1984). By 6 or 7 months, however, infants are much better at imitating gestures and actions. The first hand gestures to be imitated are those for which they already have action schemes: grasping, reaching, and so on. By 9 months, they can imitate novel gestures, such as banging two objects together. During the second year, infants begin to imitate a series of actions or gestures, even some that they have seen sometime previously. At first, children imitate only those actions they choose themselves. Later, they imitate those who show them how to brush their teeth or how to use a fork or

Adults and infants can mutually imitate the sounds that the infant produces.

spoon. Some toddlers even train themselves to use the toilet with relatively little struggle by imitating an older child.

Does imitation require a mental representation of the action? Is it thinking? Piaget believed that even simple imitation was a complex match of action patterns. He predicted that infants would not imitate novel action until they were at least 9 months old. *Deferred imitation*—imitating something that happened hours or days before—requires memory of an image or some use of symbolic representation. Piaget predicted that this would not occur until the age of 18 months. But infants seem to be able to imitate novel action somewhat earlier than Piaget predicted. For instance, children of deaf parents begin to learn and use sign language as early as 6 or 7 months (Mandler, 1988). Imaginative researchers, using novel toys, have demonstrated deferred imitation well before 18 months. One such study used a box with a hidden button. If you found the button, you heard a beep. There was another box with an orange light panel on top. If you leaned forward and touched the light panel with your head, a light went on. There was also a bear that danced when jiggled with a string. Infants were shown these actions but were not given an opportunity to play with the toys immediately. Infants at 11 months could imitate these actions 24 hours later and infants at 14 months could imitate them a week later. Infants who had not seen the demonstration did not spontaneously perform these actions (Meltzoff, 1988a; Meltzoff, 1988b). It seems that infants have more ability to remember and imitate an action sequence then we had previously thought.

Object Permanence

According to Piaget, **object permanence** is the primary accomplishment of the sensorimotor period. This is an awareness that an object exists in time and space regardless of one's own perception of it. Infants do not fully develop object permanence until they are about 18 months old. During the first year, "out of sight, out of mind" seems literally true for them. If they do not see something, it does not exist. Thus, a covered toy holds no interest, even if an infant continues to hold on to it under the cover.

To understand how infants develop the idea of object permanence, Piaget (1952) and other researchers investigated infant search behavior. They found that most infants do not sustain a successful search for an object that they have just seen until 18 months of age. They do, however, form an idea of their mothers' (or care-givers') permanence somewhat before this, but they do not generalize this insight to all other external objects.

The development of object permanence involves a series of accomplishments. First, infants must develop a recognition of familiar objects. They do this as early as 2 months; for example, they become excited at the sight of a bottle or their care-givers. Second, infants about 2 months old may watch a moving object disappear behind one edge of a screen and then shift their eyes to the other edge to see if it reappears. Their visual tracking is excellent and well timed, and they are surprised if something does not reappear. They do not seem to mind, however, when a completely different object appears from behind the screen. In fact, infants up to 5 months will accept a wide variety of objects with no distress (Bower, 1971).

Infants older than 5 months are more discriminating "trackers." They will be

object permanence According to Piaget, the realization in infants at about 18 months that objects continue to exist when they are out of sight, touch, or some other perceptual context.

In Bower's multiple mothers experiment, infants younger than 20 weeks are not disturbed by seeing more than one mother. Older infants, however, become upset at the sight of the multiple images.

definitely

disturbed if a different object appears or if the same object reappears but moves faster or slower than before. Even these older infants, however, can be fooled in this experiment: Imagine two screens side by side with a gap in the middle. An object disappears behind one screen; it does not appear in the gap, but it does reappear from behind the outer edge of the second screen. Not until infants are 9 months old will they expect the object to appear in the intervening gap. In fact, they are then surprised if it does not (Moore, Borton, & Darby, 1978).

As stated earlier, infants do form the complete idea of person permanence somewhat before object permanence, but the first developmental stages remain almost the same as for objects. T. G. R. Bower (1971) arranged mirrors so that infants would see multiple images of their mothers. He found that most infants less than 5 months old were not disturbed at seeing more than one mother; in fact, they were delighted. Infants older than 5 months or so, however, had learned that they had only one mother, and they were very disturbed at seeing more than one.

Infants learn more about objects when they begin to search for *hidden* objects. Searching behavior proceeds through a predictable sequence of development, and it begins at about 5 months. Infants younger than 5 months do not search or hunt; they seem to forget about an object once it is hidden. Hunting behavior begins somewhere between 5 and 8 months. Infants of this age enjoy hiding and finding games; they like being hidden under a blanket or covering their eyes with their hands and having the world reappear when they take their hands away. As we have seen, they are surprised if one object vanishes behind a screen and another emerges on the other side. If a toy disappears through a trapdoor and another reappears when the door is opened again, they are also surprised, but they accept the new toy. Older infants, between 12 and 18 months, are puzzled; they search for the first toy.

Some irregularities occur in 1-year-olds' hunting behavior, however. If a toy is hidden in place A and they are used to finding it there, 1-year-olds will continue looking for it at place A, *even when they have seen it hidden in place B*. Piaget (1952) suggests that infants of this age seem to have two memories—one of seeing the object hidden (the seeing memory) and another of finding it (the action memory). Not everyone agrees with Piaget's interpretation of this "hiding" experiment, however. Mandler (1990) has suggested that there are other explanations for the irregularities in 1-year-olds hunting behavior.

The final attainment of object permanence occurs at about 18 months and seems to depend on infants' locomotive ability. When infants crawl and walk, they can pursue their guesses and hypotheses more actively. If a ball rolls away, they may follow it and find it. If mother is out of sight, they may go and find her. In this way, they test the properties of the world around them through their own actions.

symbolic representation The use of a word, picture, gesture, or other sign to represent past and present events, experiences, and concepts.

Memory

Most of the sensorimotor abilities discussed so far require some form of memory. We have seen how 4-month-old infants prefer to look at new objects, which shows that they have already established some memory for the familiar (Cohen & Gelber, 1975). An infant who imitates must be able to remember the sounds and actions of another person. Infants who search for a toy where they have seen it hidden are remembering the location of that toy. Although sensorimotor abilities have been studied thoroughly, the role that memory plays in them has not.

Very young infants seem to have powerful visual memories (Cohen & Gelber, 1975; McCall, Eichorn, & Hogarty, 1977). Habituation studies have shown that infants as young as 2 months store visual patterns (Cohen & Gelber, 1975). Fagan (1977) found that 5-month-olds recognize patterns 48 hours after the first presentation and photographs of faces after 2 weeks. He discovered, too, that 5- to 6-month-olds, who had previously recognized facial photographs after a delay of 2 weeks, had trouble recognizing the photos if they had been shown similar photos in the meantime (Fagan, 1977). This could be reversed, however, by briefly presenting the original image.

A few studies have indicated rather long term memory in infants, at least for dramatic events. For instance, children who participated in an unusual experiment at a very young age remember the actions that took place when reintroduced to that setting several months later (Rovee-Collier, 1987). Indeed, in one study, children remembered aspects of their experiment 2 years later (Myers, Clifton, & Clarkson, 1987). These children were able to repeat their actions, although four out of five children could not verbally report them. These studies indicate that memory for sights, for actions, and even for events develops early and is relatively robust.

Symbolic Representation

During infancy, some of the earliest forms of representation are actions. Infants smack their lips before their food or bottle reaches their mouths. They may continue to make eating motions after feeding time is over. They may drop a rattle, yet continue to shake the hand that held it. They may wave bye-bye before they are able to say the words. These actions are the simplest forerunners of **symbolic representation**—the ability to represent something not physically present.

Imitating, finding hidden objects, and pretending—all point to an underly-

Children generally begin pretending between 6 and 12 months.

ing process of symbolic representation (Mandler, 1983). Between 6 and 12 months, children begin *pretending,* that is, using actions to represent objects, events, or ideas. They may represent the idea of sleeping by putting their heads down on their hands. As we have seen in object play, toward the end of the second year children use objects appropriately; they may, for example, have a doll drive a truck, which is represented by a shoe box. Such pretending behavior shows that children of this age create symbols independent of the immediate surroundings—a forward step in cognitive growth.

Pretending behavior, too, develops in a predictable sequence (Fein, 1981; Rubin, Fein, & Vandenberg, 1983). The first stage occurs by about 11 or 12 months; most children of this age pretend to eat, drink, or sleep—all familiar actions. In the next few months, there is a dramatic increase in the range and amount of pretend activities. At first, infants do not need objects to pretend, as when a child pretends to sleep, curled up on a rug. But as they get older, toys and other objects are used, too. By 15 to 18 months, they feed brothers and sisters, dolls, and adults with real cups and toy cups, spoons, and forks. At this point, children need realistic objects to support their pretend games. By 20 to 26 months, they may pretend that an object is something other than what it is; a broom may become a horse, a paper sack a hat, a wood floor a pool of water. Such forms of pretending represent a further step in cognitive development. By noting the rough similarities between a horse and a broom, children combine a distant concept with a familiar one and thus establish a symbolic relationship between the two. (Language, of course, is the ultimate system of symbolic relationships, as we shall see in Chapter 8.)

Critique of Piaget's Theory

Piaget's theory of infant cognitive development has fueled 30 years of research and debate. His careful, naturalistic observations of infants have challenged others to look more closely. His emphasis on the interaction of maturation and experience and on the infant's active, adaptive, constructive role in his own learning brought a new respect to infant research. For Piaget, the toddler is a "little scientist" who tests and discovers the nature of physical objects and of the social world. The younger infant wiggles and kicks and varies his motions to "make interesting sights last." Or he repeats and extends and varies his voice just to enjoy the sound of his own babbling. For some observers, Piaget made the infant more human—more like us—and definitely worthy of our study.

But Piaget was not correct in everything he found. Many critics feel he emphasized motor development far too much and ignored perceptual development. Some of his stages are probably wrong. It appears, for instance, that infants can imitate much earlier than Piaget would have imagined. Indeed, some newborns appear to imitate an adult sticking out his tongue. Even the development of object permanence may not occur precisely in the fashion that Piaget describes. In fact, some critics suggest that infants may have more sophisticated knowledge of objects based on their perceptual development, but that their motor development may lag behind. Hence, young infants might be able to show evidence of object permanence if they are given tests that do not require coordinated actions (Baillargeon, 1987; Gratch & Schatz, 1987; Mandler, 1990).

ENVIRONMENTAL STIMULATION AND INFANT COMPETENCIES

The environment has a powerful influence on the development of infant competencies. The presence or absence of stimulation can speed up or slow down the acquisition of certain behaviors. In addition, motivation, timing of stimulation, and the quality of care-giving also affect infant development.

Deprivation

Being deprived of normal experiences can have a marked and sometimes prolonged effect upon infant development. Wayne Dennis (1960, 1973; Dennis & Najarian, 1957) found that institutionalized children were severely retarded in even such basic competencies as sitting, standing, and walking when they had no opportunities to practice these skills. And because of the almost total lack of stimulation in their environment, these children were also retarded in language, social skills, and emotional expression:

> As babies they lay on their backs in their cribs throughout the first year and often for much of the second year. . . . Many objects available to most children did not exist. . . . There were no building blocks, no sandboxes, no scooters, no tricycles, no climbing apparatus, no wagons, no teeter-totters, no swings, no chutes. There were no pets or other animals of any sort. . . . They had no opportunities to learn what these objects were. They never saw persons who lived in the outside world, except for rather rare visitors. (Dennis, 1973, pp. 22–23)

In a 15- and 20-year-lag follow-up study, Dennis (1973) found that even those children who were adopted showed some developmental retardation in maturity. Those who remained in barren institutions showed marked retardation throughout life.

Normal versus Optimal Environments

MOTIVATION   The vast majority of infants seem motivated to develop their skills with self-rewarding experiences. For example, children show considerable persistence in learning to walk, for the sheer satisfaction of walking. Infants learn skills not only because they are intrinsically motivated, but also because the environment responds. They learn to push a toy simply to see it move. They practice motor skills to experience and gain mastery in a task.

The responsiveness of the environment is crucial. In one study, three groups of infants were presented with three different types of crib decorations (Watson & Ramey, 1972). Infants in the first group were given a mobile that they could control. The second group was given a stabile, which did not move. The third group was given a mobile, but the wind, not the infants, made it move. Infants in the third group were then allowed to control the mobile; they performed poorly both immediately and 6 weeks later. They had already learned that their behavior had no effect—the environment did not respond.

TABLE 6–1

A Summary of Infant Competencies

AGE (IN MONTHS)	PERCEPTION	MOTOR BEHAVIOR	LANGUAGE	COGNITION
4 Active looking	Visually tracks objects; perceives colors, discriminates between shapes, and focuses almost as well as an adult; responds to sounds as low as 43 db; turns toward sounds (bells, voices).	Holds up head, chest; grasps objects; rolls from stomach to back.	Babbles; coos; imitates own sounds.	Remembers objects, sounds; discovers, examines own hands, fingers; begins to play social interaction games (mimics care-givers' imitation of his or her own sounds).
8 On the move	Responds to sounds at 34 db; has integrated vision and hearing; has mastered visually guided reach.	Sits up without support; stands with support; crawls, creeps, "bear walks," or "scoots"; passes objects from hand to hand.	Imitates some repeated speech sounds ("mama," "dada"); babbles more complex sounds.	Discriminates between familiar and unfamiliar faces; exhibits stranger anxiety; hunts for hidden objects; plays more advanced social games; imitates some adult gestures and actions.
12 First words, first steps		Walks with support; masters pincer grasp; starts to feed himself or herself.	Understands and uses a few words, including "no."	Looks for a hidden object in its usual hiding place, but not in the place he or she last saw it; is aware of separation between self and care-giver and exercises choice; begins to pretend by symbolically representing familiar activities (eating, drinking, sleeping).
18 Pretend play		Walks without support; attains a better mastery of feeding himself or herself; can stack two or more blocks; can scribble.	Combines two words to form a sentence; names body parts, familiar pictures.	Understands the concept of object permanence; attempts to use objects for their intended purposes; includes a second person in pretend play; pretending includes imitative games ("reading").
24 End of infancy		Walks, runs, climbs stairs; can pedal a tricycle; can throw overhand.	Follows simple verbal directions; uses three or more words in combination.	Uses objects to represent other objects (a broom for a horse, a sack for a hat).

VARIETY AND TIMING OF STIMULATION   On the other hand, and contrary to the belief of some parents, grandparents, and other care-givers (and most toy manufacturers), infants do not require a vast assortment of toys or a massively enriched environment to develop cognitive skills (Yarrow et al., 1972). Instead, a moderately enriched environment, in which infants are given stimulating objects slightly ahead of the time that they would normally use them, seems to promote optimum growth (White & Held, 1966). The goal is to match the task with the child's development. Slightly accelerated stimulation, therefore, encourages growth and development; greatly accelerated stimulation confuses children. They will ignore or reject a task that is too difficult.

THE CARE-GIVER A stimulating environment is created by a concerned adult care-giver. As we shall see in Chapter 7, the interpersonal relationship with the care-giver is a major influence on a child's mental development. In the course of feeding, diapering, bathing, and dressing their infants, parents and other care-givers provide a constant source of stimulation; by talking with infants and playing games, they demonstrate relationships between objects as well as between people. Even simple behaviors like imitation occur most often in a rich dialogue of social play between adult care-giver and infant (Uzgiris, 1984).

Early Intervention

Some of the most hopeful and exciting applications of our knowledge of infant development have been the success stories from a number of *early intervention* programs. It is possible now to identify at birth (or even before) infants who fall into certain high-risk groups. Perhaps they are premature, malnourished, or developmentally delayed. Their mothers may be alcoholics or emotionally disturbed. Also, poverty restricts the diets, health care, and the quality of care some infants are likely to receive. Without help, many of these infants will have persistent learning disabilities or emotional scars. Over the past two decades, several programs have offered a variety of supportive services to parents and infants in these high-risk groups. Because adequate funding is limited, however, many of these programs serviced less than half of the children who needed them. Thus, it is possible to compare the progress of infants and their families within the programs with others who are not enrolled. By and large, these programs have demonstrated a real difference. They show that an optimal environment is critical for the high-risk child to flourish and thrive (Horowitz, 1982; Korner, 1987).

One of the first major home-based, parent-oriented intervention programs for infants was developed by Ira Gordon in the late 1960s (Gordon, 1969). He worked with poverty families in rural Florida, with the goal of enhancing the intellectual and personality development of the infants and the self-esteem of the parents. He trained women from the immediate community in child development, and they served as weekly home visitors. The women learned about the particular curriculum or activities to be offered at the appropriate developmental time for the infants they visited, and they learned interviewing skills. Those infants who participated in the weekly program on a regular basis for 2 or 3 years demonstrated significantly more advanced development over matched controls, at least as based on intelligence tests. Also, in follow-up measures, fewer children who had participated for at least 2 years were placed in special classes in public schools than children from the control group.

The second, somewhat similar, home-visitors' program was done in the mid-1970s at Peabody Teachers' College in Tennessee. This set of programs, the Darcee Infant Programs, focused more on assisting the parent, particularly the

This care-giver is attempting to teach the infant to read, using specially prepared flashcards.

"Don't let them know you're a prodigy. If they find out, they'll take away your teddy bear."

mother, than on the infant directly. Visitors were trained to participate as partners rather than as trainers. The goals of the program were to help the parents with general coping skills for daily living, to increase awareness of the child's development, and to encourage certain behaviors in the child. Children in this program, too, performed well on intelligence tests, and the mothers showed improved teaching styles. On the whole, the mothers became less directive and more supportive (Gray, 1976).

Early intervention programs also have been set up for children with more severe handicaps (Broussard, 1989; Sasserath, 1983). These programs offer a number of supports to both infant and family. Certainly, they help by demonstrating developmentally appropriate activities to capture the child's attention and to enhance learning. Also, they help parents to be aware of the milestones of development and sometimes the very small milestones of the severely delayed or retarded child. Beyond that, they help parents to be responsive to the child's needs and to the child's discoveries. But such programs must also meet the parents' needs. Parents should be supported in their adjustment to and parenting of a difficult or disabled child. Most experts on infant development would recommend a balanced program—even for the potentially gifted child. The National Association for the Education of Young Children (1988) recommends to parents and infant day-care workers that infants need:

1. A secure, predictable environment so that they can learn to anticipate events and to make choices.

2. An intimate, stable relationship with a warm, responsive care-giver who is sensitive to the child's interests, needs, and rhythms.

3. Respect for the infant as an active participant in the dialogue of living rather than a passive recipient of training.

4. Ample space to explore, objects to handle, and other children to observe, imitate, and with whom to socialize.

"HOTHOUSE" BABIES

We now know quite a bit about the infant's emerging competence. We know it is important to have a responsive environment, and to match the environmental stimulation to the infant's current abilities. We know that infants are learning and making associations from the day they are born, and perhaps even before. Knowing these things, why not create the best possible environment, one that maximizes the opportunity for learning? Why not create a "hothouse" environment that provides early training in academics and other skills with the aim of developing a "superbaby"? Several researchers, in fact, tried. Perhaps the most well-known is Glenn Doman, in his *Better Baby Program* (Moore, 1984). Doman has written several books, such as *How to Teach a Baby to Read* (1963), and he provides a week-long course for parents on how to stimulate advanced mental development. He believes that regular and systematic stimulation and early training actually accelerate brain growth. His program urges brief training sessions in reading and mathematics, beginning at 1 year. These training sessions, with flashcards, are to last 5 or 10 minutes at first and then are to be extended as the child gets older. Later, toddlers and 2-year-olds study Japanese or modern art, or learn to play the violin.

Other programs of infant stimulation are much less intense, but instruct parents on how to maximize the learning opportunities in daily routines. You might be surprised, for example, to find out how much a toddler can learn from kicking, banging toys, or from making a peanut butter sandwich (Lehane, 1976).

What are the results of these training programs? Certainly, there have been some rather remarkable case studies. There are many 3- or 4-year-old children who have been taught to read at a second- or third-grade level. There are children who play the violin at 4 years. But the results are not consistent, and there are some dangers. Sometimes an overeager parent teaches a child by the age of 2 to avoid anything that looks remotely like a flashcard. Children who spend a great deal of time in rote learning have less time to explore the world around them, and to initiate activities with other children, as well as with adults. There are less opportunities for simply discovering. Finally, an overemphasis on cognitive development can have negative effects on social and personality development. Children can become insecure, or overly dependent on their parents. Some children may become quite anxious because of the high expectations placed on them at an early age.

Several child development experts have gathered

Children as young as 4 and 5 years have become proficient at playing the violin.

together in a symposium to discuss the challenges and problems of the trend toward "hothousing" infants and young children. One of them defines "hothousing" as "inducing infants to acquire knowledge that is typically acquired at a later developmental level" (Sigel, 1987, p. 212). Most of these experts agreed that structured training of infants and young children too early in academic tasks tended to have serious negative side effects on children's social and emotional development. They not only lost play time, but they suffered achievement anxiety and limited informal social skills. Some had limited cognitive development as well, with gaps in their understanding of the physical world despite their rote memory for complex definitions or their advanced skills in reading. Professor Sigel suggested that "hothousing" was a wonderful metaphor. It reminded one of the tomato plant in the greenhouse, in an artificial climate, protected and sterile, and with chemicals and alien forces that force growth "out of season." Yet he suggested, "Who really likes hothouse tomatoes?" (Sigel, 1987, p. 218). Professor Sigel suggests that, just as tomatoes grown out of season taste flat, perhaps a "hothouse" child will be a flat, unexciting individual. Similarly, early harvesting of hothouse children may stunt full development, depress their emotional range, and limit their ability to explore, create, and even problem solve in new environments. He suggests that parents provide a rich and varied growth environment for children, complete with social supports, and that they make ample room for the child to self-select and self-pace cognitive development, together with social awareness, a strong self-concept, and positive ways of socially interacting (Sigel, 1987).

STUDY OUTLINE

Infant Competencies: An Overview

Although predictable changes occur in physical and cognitive development during the first 2 years of life, infants vary greatly in their growth and development rates. Arnold Gesell attempted to determine the physical, cognitive, and personality development of children at various ages. He emphasized that development depended on maturation.

The First 4 Months. Generally, most 4-month-olds are sleeping through the night and are being introduced to solid foods. Their motor behavior is limited, but they are beginning to explore with their hands and feet and to imitate their own sounds.

From 5 to 8 Months. By 8 months, most can sit up unsupported, stand, take a step with support, and grasp and pass objects. Most infants of this age imitate a few speech sounds.

From 9 to 12 Months. By 12 months, most infants walk unsupported, manipulate objects with a **pincer grasp,** and play simple games. They are becoming aware of themselves as individuals.

Age 18 Months. By 18 months—"toddlerhood"—infants are usually walking alone. They feed themselves, imitate some adult actions, and say a few words.

Age 24 Months. By 2 years, most **toddlers** walk, run, ride tricycles, and are physically active; their play becomes complex.

Nutrition and Malnutrition

Weaning and the Introduction of Solid Foods. The first 2 years is a critical period of growth. An infant's diet during this time determines the course of future physical and mental development. Infants in developed countries are usually weaned from the breast at 3 or 4 months and shifted to bottle formulas and solid foods. Infants require a diet that is high in both protein and calories. Malnutrition during the first 2 years can permanently retard growth, particularly in the brain and nervous system.

Perceptual Competence

Vision. Given optimum conditions, an infant's perceptual abilities mature rapidly during the first year. Focusing, acuity, color discrimination, and depth perception improve dramatically within the first 6 months. Infants begin to spend more time tracking and scanning the environment.

Hearing. Hearing also improves quickly during the first year. Generally, infants are soothed by low, rhythmic sounds and seem to have an innate ability to discriminate between speech and nonspeech sounds.

Integration. The senses of infants are preprogrammed to work together. Immediately, infants begin to link sights with sounds. Eye-hand integration accelerates after 5 months, with the achievement of the *visually guided reach.*

Cognitive Development

The Sensorimotor Period. Intellectual development first occurs during what Piaget calls the sensorimotor period. Infants process information from the environment by means of ready-made action patterns called schemes. They "build" their intelligence by elaborating and modifying these schemes in the process of **adaptation.** One particular form of adaptation is the **circular response** by which infants discover their bodies and use them to change the environment.

Infants acquire a number of fundamental intellectual abilities during the first 2 years. These include concepts about the uses of familiar objects, imitation, the understanding of object permanence, memory, and symbolic representation.

Play with Objects. Infants proceed through several stages in their play with objects, from simple exploration to complex imitating and pretending behavior. In the final stages of object play, infants demonstrate memory ability and show an understanding of social relationships and the appropriate use of objects.

Object Permanence. **Object permanence**—the realization that an object exists independently of one's own perception of it—begins to form by about 5 months and is fully attained by about 18 months.

Memory. Memory abilities develop in the course of object play, imitation, and symbolic representation. Infants, however, are able to remember visual patterns as early as 2 months.

Symbolic Representation. **Symbolic representation**—the ability to represent something not physically present—appears first in infants' actions and then in their *pretending* behavior. At 12 months, infants can pretend to perform familiar actions. During the second year, the pretended actions and concepts become more and more distant from the immediate surroundings and, therefore, more symbolic.

Environmental Stimulation and Infant Competencies

The environment has a powerful effect on the development of infant competencies. An environment responsive to the child's skills and stimulation, timed slightly ahead of the child's developmental level, will accelerate a normal child's progress. Lack of stimulation and an unresponsive environment retard the child's sensorimotor and cognitive development.

KEY TERMS AND CONCEPTS

adaptation
anemia
antibodies
breast-feeding
circular response
cognition
depth perception
functionally integrate
imitation

integration
"normative" behavior
novelty paradigm
object permanence
object play
Piaget
pincer grasp
pretending
protein

schemes
sensorimotor period
surprise paradigm
symbolic representation
toddler
visual cliff
visually guided reach
weaning

SELF-TEST QUESTIONS

1. Describe the developing competencies of the infant during the first 2 years.

2. List two types of malnutrition.

3. List the advantages of breast-feeding.

4. What are the nutritional needs of the infant during the first 2 years?

5. Discuss and compare the novelty paradigm and the surprise paradigm.

6. Discuss the relationship between brain development and sensory and motor experience during the first 2 years.

7. Describe Piaget's theory of cognitive development. What have been some of the major criticisms of Piaget's theory?

8. What do studies reveal about the long-term memory of the infant?

9. What is symbolic representation and what is its significance for infant development?

10. Explain the effect of deprivation on infant development.

11. Describe two intervention programs that provide optimal stimulation for the infant.

SUGGESTED READINGS

CAPLAN, F. *The first 12 months of life*. New York: Grosset & Dunlop, 1973. Written in a style appropriate for parents, this book supplies much practical information drawn from the Princeton Center for Infancy and Early Childhood. Contains monthly growth charts and many photographs.

CAPLAN, F. *The second 12 months of life*. New York: Grosset & Dunlop, 1979. A continuation of the above.

DITTMANN, L. L. (Ed.). *The infants we care for* (rev. ed.). Washington, DC: National Association for the Education of Young Children, 1984. This book is particularly addressed to infant day-care providers. It sensitively surveys the needs and capabilities of infants.

FIELD, T. *Infancy*. Cambridge, MA: Harvard University Press, 1990. Another title in the popular and highly readable Developing Child series. This book surveys the latest infant research and highlights the infant's surprising abilities. It also makes applications to current practical concerns, including day care, maternal drug use, and infants at risk.

HAZEL, R., BARBER, P. A., ROBERTS, S., BEHR, S. K., HELMSTET- TER, E., & GUESS, D. *A community approach to an integrated service system for children with special needs*. Baltimore: Paul A. Brookes, 1990. Early intervention services for special needs children from birth to age 3 are now federally mandated. This manual serves as a helpful guide to community service agencies.

OLDS, S., & EIGER, M. S. *The complete book of breast-feeding* (rev. ed.). New York: Bantam, 1987. A well-written, helpful guide for parents and others who work with young infants.

SIEGLER, R. *Children's thinking*. 2nd ed. Englewood Cliffs, NJ: Prentice Hall, 1991. An excellent text that integrates the latest research with central themes from several theoretical perspectives. It presents a coherent picture of cognitive development from infancy to adolescence.

ZIGLER, E. F. & FRANK, M. (eds.). *The parental leave crisis: Toward a national policy*. New Haven, CT: Yale University Press, 1988. A source book for analyzing the problems of those who care for our children in the face of changing family patterns.

Chapter 7

The two-month-old baby has hardly roused himself from the long night of his first weeks in this world when he is confronted with some of the most profound problems of the race.

We invite him to study the nature of reality, to differentiate between inner and outer experience, to discriminate self and not-self and to establish useful criteria for each of these categories . . .

SELMA H. FRAIBERG
THE MAGIC YEARS

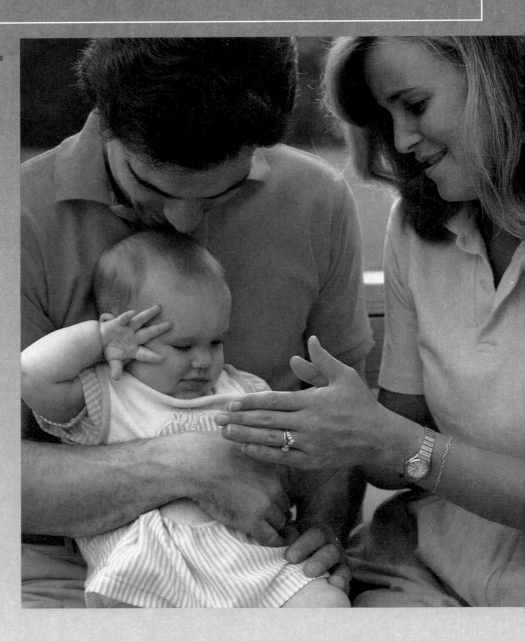

Infancy: Developing Relationships

Human infants are born into an environment rich with expectations, norms, attitudes, beliefs, values, traditions, and ways of doing things. A cultural heritage, complete with value systems and standards for social behavior, awaits them. Family members, of course, are already aware of their relationships to the infant, but newborns do not realize their relationships to those around them. An infant girl, for example, has no awareness of herself either as an individual or as an organism that can interact with the environment. She cannot recognize herself in a mirror. She does not know that her hands are part of her body or that she is actually the agent responsible for her own movement. She has not developed trust or mistrust and has no expectations concerning those who care for her. She is not conscious of being female.

A dramatic series of changes takes place during the first 2 years of human life, as was mentioned in Chapter 6. Within that period, the unaware newborns become toddlers. They become aware of their environment and of the ways in which they can act upon it; aware of whether the world around them is responsive or unresponsive to their needs; aware that they can do some things for themselves or seek help when necessary. They become aware of various family relationships and of what is good and what is bad. They become conscious of being a girl or a boy and learn how a sex designation imposes a certain style of behavior.

Babies come into the world with certain response styles. Some are more sensitive to light or to sudden loud sounds than others. Some react more quickly to discomfort than others. Some infants are fussy; some are placid; some are active, assertive, and vigorous. By age 2, the child has elaborated or restricted these basic response styles within a cultural context to produce what is called a *personality*.

In this chapter, we shall look at how the infant personality develops *within relationships*. We shall focus on primary, or first, relationships—those that establish patterns for the development of future relationships and for the acquisition of basic attitudes, expectations, and behavior.

ATTACHMENT AND SEPARATION

In the course of a lifetime, most individuals are involved in a number of significant interpersonal relationships. The first, and undoubtedly most influential, bond is the one that immediately begins to grow between the infant and the mother or care-giver. The bond becomes firmly established by the time the child reaches 8 or

CHAPTER OBJECTIVES

By the time you have finished this chapter, you should be able to do the following:

- Discuss attachment and separation behaviors.
- List six milestones in the emotional development of the infant within the first relationship.
- Discuss stranger anxiety and the theory that attempts to explain this behavior.
- Describe the effect on emotional development when a child does not form an attachment relationship, or when a child's progress toward attachment is interrupted.
- Describe the factors that affect the quality of the relationship between the infant and the care-giver.
- Discuss adjustments that must be made by a family for a handicapped infant.
- List different bonding disorders.
- Discuss the differences and similarities between father–child interaction and mother–child interaction.
- Describe infant emotional development in the context of a family system.
- List the problems of mothers who work outside the home.
- Compare the effect of different child-rearing patterns on the development of the infant.

attachment The bond that develops between a child and another individual as a result of a long-term relationship. The infant's first bond is usually characterized by strong interdependence, intense mutual feelings, and vital emotional ties.

imprinting The instinctual learning process by which newly hatched birds form a relatively permanent bond with the parent in a few hours or days.

9 months of age. Since the mid-1960s, many psychologists have applied the term **attachment** to the process of development of this first relationship. It is characterized by strong interdependence, intense mutual feelings, and vital emotional ties.

Attachments, as well as losses or separations, actually occur and affect us throughout life. The infant's first attachment, however, goes through several phases that lay the groundwork for future development. The process involves a characteristic series of events as the infant progresses from earliest awareness to the development of trust and confidence in the care-giver. Later, an equally characteristic sequence of events takes place in reaction to the loss of the relationship. These first responses to attachment and loss lay the foundation for later relationships, whether with peers, relatives, other adults, spouses, or lovers.

Imprinting and Attachment Behaviors

The psychologist Mary Ainsworth (1983) defines "attachment behaviors" as those that primarily promote nearness to a specific person to whom the infant is attached. These include signaling behavior (crying, smiling, vocalizing), orienting behavior (looking), movements relating to another person (following, approaching), and active physical contact behavior (clambering up, embracing, clinging). These behaviors indicate attachment only when they are specifically directed toward one or two care-givers, rather than toward human beings in general.

The important point is that the infant must *act* in order for attachment to take place. The infant's initial behavior seems to invite nurturant responses from the care-giver. She (or he) not only feeds, diapers, and generally cares for the infant's physical needs, but also communicates with the baby by talking, smiling, touching, and nuzzling. The attachment process, then, is a mutual system. The baby's behavior prompts the care-giver to act in certain ways, and the care-giver's actions set off responses in the baby.

Why does attachment occur? Is it a conditioned response, or is there an innate need to establish a relationship? For a long while, developmental psychologists thought that babies formed attachments to their care-givers only because they fulfilled the babies' primary needs. It was thought that children *learned* to associate the care-giver's nearness with the reduction of primary drives, such as hunger (Sears, 1963). Research—conducted primarily with animals—now indicates that this is only a small part of the situation.

We can probably better understand infants' first relationships with their care-givers if we look at some of the relationships that other animals have with their mothers. This relationship has been studied most extensively in ducks and geese.

Orphaned goslings, nurtured by Konrad Lorenz during the critical imprinting period, follow him as though he were their real mother.

IMPRINTING **Imprinting** refers to the process by which newly hatched birds form a relatively permanent bond with the parent in the period immediately following birth. More than 40 years ago, Konrad Lorenz, an Austrian zoologist, observed that goslings began to follow their mother almost immediately after hatching. This bond between goslings and parent was important in helping the mother protect and train her offspring. Interestingly enough, Dr. Lorenz also found that orphaned greylag goslings nurtured by him during their first 24 hours after hatching—the *critical period* for imprinting—developed a pattern of following *him*, not another goose. This pattern was relatively permanent—and sometimes annoyingly persistent. Some of Lorenz's greylag geese much preferred to spend the night in his bedroom than on the banks of the Danube (Lorenz, 1952).

The critical period for imprinting occurs after hatching, when the gosling is strong enough to get up and move around, but before it has developed a strong fear of large moving objects. If imprinting is delayed, the gosling will either fear the model parent or simply give up and grow limp, tired, and listless.

Baby birds may be imprinted to objects that differ greatly from the mother. In a laboratory setting, for example, ducks have been imprinted to duck decoys, flashing lights, windup toys, milk bottles, and even to a checkerboard wall (Hess, 1972). The strength of this bond varies, however, and seems to depend on the activity of the duckling and the type of stimulus. The object should move enough to require some, but not too much, exercise by the baby bird, and, if possible, the stimulus should respond with some kind of sound—like clucking, peeping, or humming.

Ethologists who study imprinting are concerned with distinguishing the types of stimuli necessary to *trigger* or *release* imprinting behaviors. A large moving object may be all that is necessary to release the behaviors of following and vocalizing and, thereby, to begin the process of imprinting. In a natural setting, this triggering or releasing process is mutual. The mother's clucking releases peeping, visual scanning, and following behaviors in the duckling. Similarly, the duckling's peeping triggers the mother's vocalizations (Hess, 1972).

Researchers disagree about the similarities and differences between imprinting on birds and bonding behavior in humans. There is no clear evidence that a "critical period" exists for human bonding. As we saw in Chapter 4, parents and infants may be particularly receptive to bonding in the first few days after birth, but this is hardly a critical period. On the other hand, it is clearly necessary for human infants to establish some kind of relationship with one or more major care-givers within the first 6 months or so in order for adequate personality development to occur. What we know about imprinting in birds provides promising parallels to human development, but they are not identical.

In Harlow's studies of attachment, young monkeys showed distinct preference for the cloth-covered surrogate mother over the wire mother, regardless of which one supplied food.

ATTACHMENT IN MONKEYS An important series of studies was done by Harry Harlow (1959) on social deprivation in monkeys. Because monkeys have closer biological ties to humans than birds have, studies of their social development are more relevant to humans than studies of goslings. An important series of observations began somewhat accidentally when Harlow was studying learning and conceptual development in monkeys. When he was setting up his laboratory conditions, he decided that it would be best to rear each young monkey without its mother in order to control the total learning environment. The mother was an uncontrolled variable. She taught the baby certain skills, and she rewarded and punished certain behaviors. She also served as a model for the baby to imitate. Harlow wanted to get at the basic process of learning, and to do this, he felt it necessary to remove the mother from the cage. In doing so, however, he stumbled upon a new and more exciting area of study.

Separation from the mother had a disastrous effect on the young monkeys. Some died. Others were frightened, irritable, and reluctant to eat or play. Obviously, the monkeys required something more than regular feeding to thrive and develop. Harlow experimented with surrogate monkey mothers, wire forms designed to hold a bottle (Harlow & Harlow, 1962). Some of the surrogates were covered with soft cloth while others were bare wire. Regardless of which surrogate supplied the food, all the young monkeys showed a distinct preference for the cloth form, clinging and vocalizing to it, especially when frightened. The infant monkeys developed bonds with their cloth surrogates and would not accept substitutes. The object they looked at and clung to was the focus of their psychological attachment, regardless of the food source.

Monkeys with cloth surrogates did not exhibit the extremely fearful, neurotic behavior of the completely orphaned monkeys, but they failed to develop normally nonetheless. As adults, they had difficulty establishing peer relationships and engaging in normal sexual activity. They were poor parents to their own offspring as well, despite Harlow's attempt at "psychotherapy"—he put them with "normal" monkeys.

Further studies in this series have indicated that peer contact among infant monkeys at least partially makes up for the deprivation of the infant–adult attachment bond (Coster, 1972). Infant monkeys who are raised with surrogate mothers and who have adequate opportunity to play with other such infant monkeys develop reasonably normal social behavior. Thus, mutually responsive social interaction is crucial for normal monkey development. One would suspect that it is true for humans, too, because they are also a social species!

Emotional Development in the First Relationship

In human infants, attachment occurs very gradually. Children go through stages of emotional and social growth that result in the firm establishment of this first relationship. Stanley and Nancy Greenspan (1985), drawing on the observations and research of many others, describe six milestones in the emotional development of the infant within the first relationship.

1. *Self-Regulation and Interest in the World—Birth to 3 Months.* In the early weeks, the infant seeks to feel regulated and calm, but at the same time, to use all of his senses and experience the world. The infant seeks a balance between over- and understimulation. Gradually, infants become increasingly socially responsive. Ainsworth (1973) noted particular similarity to monkey attachment behaviors in these first few months. Human infants use signaling and orienting behavior—crying, vocalizing, visual following—to establish contact. Infants at this stage, however, do not discriminate between primary care-givers and other people, and they react to everyone in much the same way.

2. *Falling in Love—2 to 7 Months.* At 2 months, self-regulated infants become more alert to the world around them. They recognize familiar figures and direct their attention more and more toward the significant care-givers rather than strangers. Infants at this time find the human world enticing, pleasurable, and exciting—and show it. They smile in eagerness and respond with their whole body.

3. *Developing Intentional Communication—3 to 10 Months.* This milestone overlaps considerably with the last. Infants now, however, begin to develop a dialogue. The mother and the baby develop their own playful sequences of

In the early stages of emotional development, infants do not discriminate between primary care-giver and other people, and they react to everyone in much the same way.

Between 9 and 18 months, infants make the startling discovery of an independent self.

Following the development of a separate sense of self, infants develop ambivalent needs of autonomy and dependency.

communication, of looking at each other, of playing short games, and taking rests. Fathers and babies, and siblings and babies, do this as well.

4. *The Emergence of an Organized Sense of Self—9 to 18 Months.* One year-old infants can do more things for themselves and can take a more active role in the emotional partnership with their mother and father. Infants at this time can signal their needs much more effectively and precisely. They begin to communicate with words. Sometime around 16 to 18 months, they make the startling discovery that they are the baby in the mirror! If there is a red spot on the nose of the baby in the mirror, the infant points to his own nose and looks coy or embarrassed. Before this time, there has emerged a number of emotions, such as anger, sadness, and happiness. But now, when infants can distinguish between themselves and the rest of the social world, they begin to develop the social emotions of pride, guilt, and embarrassment, for example. The infant now recognizes an independent self.

5. *Creating Emotional Ideas—18 to 36 Months.* During this period, the infant is able to symbolize, pretend, and form images in his head of people and things. He can learn about the social world through make-believe and pretend play. Now that he has a separate sense of self, he can feel the ambivalent needs of autonomy yet dependency.

6. *Emotional Thinking: The Basis for Fantasy, Reality, and Self-Esteem—30 to 48 Months.* Often, the give-and-take of close relationships with important people now settles into more of a partnership. The young child can discern what the care-giver expects of him, and then tries to modify his behavior to meet those expectations and thus achieve his own goals.

191

stranger, or separation, anxiety An infant's fear of strangers or of being separated from the care-giver. Both occur in the second half of the first year and indicate, in part, a new cognitive ability to detect and respond to differences in the environment.

discrepancy hypothesis A cognition theory according to which infants acquire, at around 7 months, schemata for familiar objects. When a new image or object is presented that differs from the old, the child experiences uncertainty and anxiety.

Stranger Anxiety

One of the developmental landmarks of the attachment relationship is the appearance of both **stranger anxiety** and **separation anxiety.** Pediatricians and psychologists often make no distinction between the two and refer to both as "7-months anxiety," because they often appear rather suddenly at just about 7 months. Babies who have been smiling, welcoming, friendly, and accepting suddenly become more shy and fearful in the presence of strangers. They become extremely upset at the prospect of being left alone in a strange place, even for a minute. No traumatic event, sudden separation, or frightening encounter is necessary. Children at this stage of attachment cry and cling to their mothers; they only cautiously turn around to explore a stranger. Stranger anxiety continues through the rest of the first year and much of the second year, with varying degrees of intensity.

THE DISCREPANCY HYPOTHESIS   If no event is needed to bring on such anxiety, why does it first occur, almost without fail, in most children at about the same age? Most psychologists see stranger and separation anxieties as a sign of intellectual development in infants. As infant cognitive processes mature, they develop schemes for the familiar and notice anything that is new and strange. They can distinguish care-givers from strangers, and they become keenly aware of the absence of the primary care-giver. When they detect a departure from the known or the expected, they experience anxiety (Ainsworth et al., 1978); this is known as the **discrepancy hypothesis.**

At about 7 months, infants become shy and fearful in the presence of strangers. This stranger anxiety is a landmark in the infant's social development.

The anxiety is based on the infant's new awareness that the care-giver's presence coincides with safety. Things seem secure with familiar care-givers around, but uncertain when they are not. Thus, anxiety at 7 months can be viewed as a demonstration of the baby's more complex and sophisticated expectations. The infant's anxiety and distress vary a bit based on a number of factors. Most infants are more distressed if the stranger is a male or if he towers over them. They are less distressed if the mother is close by or if the stranger is a child or a midget (Boccia & Campos, 1989).

Some psychologists believe that, at least by 9 months, the anxiety reaction is complicated by the learning that has already occurred. Bronson (1978) found that 9-month-old babies sometimes cry when they first notice a stranger, and even before the stranger has gotten close. This implies that children may have learned from negative experiences with strangers, and may be anticipating another disturbing encounter. But the learning may be more subtle than that. Perhaps the mother signals her baby by her facial expression or tone of voice. In one study, mothers of 8- to 9-month-old babies were carefully trained to knit their eyebrows, widen their eyes, pull down their lips, and demonstrate worry on their faces while greeting the stranger with a worried "Hello." The control group was trained to demonstrate a pleased, smiling face, and a cheery "Hello" to the stranger. As predicted, these 8- to 9-month-old infants picked up their mothers' signals quite accurately. Infants whose mothers posed joy were more positive toward the stranger, smiled more, and cried less when they were picked up by the stranger than did those infants whose mothers displayed worry (Boccia & Campos, 1989). This kind of emotional signaling by the mother is called *social referencing*.

It is likely, then, that by the time infants are 1 year old, stranger and separation anxiety are influenced both by the babies' ability to differentiate between the familiar and the strange, and by their past experiences with strangers and with their mother's reactions to strangers. Parents can assist their infants and toddlers in adjusting to strangers by their own emotional reaction and by giving the children time to get to know the strangers (Feiring, Lewis, & Starr, 1984).

Stranger anxiety is a milestone in the attachment process and in social development (Bretherton & Waters, 1985). Once children learn to identify the care-giver as a source of comfort and security, they feel free to explore new objects in the care-giver's reassuring presence. Children who fail to explore, preferring to hover near their mothers, may not feel a secure attachment and thus miss out on new learning. On the other hand, some infants are too readily comforted by strangers or show wariness when returned to their mothers. This is a second kind of social maladjustment; it indicates uncertainty about the care-giver's ability to support the infant (Sroufe & Fleeson, 1986). These children are likely to suffer a more pervasive and unresolved anxiety that interferes with further development.

Separation and Loss

If, as was discussed, the attachment relationship is an essential part of normal development—and if that relationship progresses through a series of predictable, nearly universal stages—what happens to the child who does not have such a relationship, or whose progress toward attachment is interrupted? What happens to the child who is brought up in an orphanage and is handled by numerous, changing care-givers during the first few years? What happens to the infant who must spend a prolonged period in a hospital? And what about the child who has begun to establish a relationship and is suddenly separated from the care-giver?

In Chapter 6, we saw that prolonged institutionalization retards the development of cognitive and sensorimotor competencies in infants. Social deprivation has an even more devastating effect on the young child's emotional development. Infants who are cared for by continuously changing care-givers who meet only their most basic physical needs are unable to develop an attachment relationship. The mutual responses between child and primary care-giver do not occur consistently; the social interaction that permits expression of emotion is missing (Bowlby, 1973, 1980, 1988). The result is profound apathy, withdrawal, and generally depressed functioning, which in time lead to inadequate personality development.

The child who has formed a full attachment relationship responds quite differently to separation from the primary care-giver than does the child who has never established such a relationship. The "attached" child goes through a series of rather dramatic reactions to both brief and prolonged separation.

John Bowlby (1973) divides the separation reaction of hospitalized fully attached toddlers into three stages: protest, despair, and detachment. During the protest stage, children refuse to accept separation from the attachment figure. They may cry, scream, kick, bang their heads against their beds, and refuse to respond at all to anyone else who tries to care for them.

During the second stage, which may come a few hours or even several days after the initial reaction, the children appear to lose all hope. They withdraw and become very quiet. If they cry, they do so in a monotonous and despairing tone, rather than with the anger they exhibited earlier.

Eventually, separated children begin to accept attention from the people around them and appear recovered from their misery. If they are visited by the primary care-giver, they react with detachment or even disinterest.

> A child living in an institution or hospital who has reached this state will no longer be upset when nurses change or leave. He will cease to show feelings when his parents come and go on visiting day; and it may cause them pain when they realize that, although he has an avid interest in the presents they bring, he has little interest in them as social people. He will appear cheerful and adapted to his unusual situation and apparently easy and unafraid of anyone. But this sociability is superficial: he appears no longer to care for anyone. (Bowlby, 1960, p. 143)

When faced with the first two stages of a child's separation reaction, well-meaning adults often try to subdue what they see as inappropriate behavior. But such adults underestimate the complexity of young children's reactions. These children need patient understanding and warm nurturance to help weather the stress. In fact, the child's response to separation is a prototype of behavior later in life. It foreshadows the turmoil that adolescents go through over the loss of a first love and the grief that adults experience upon the death of a spouse or a child. Both young children and adults need to "work through" these emotional reactions in order to come to terms with the inevitable separations that occur throughout life. Only if they are allowed to express these feelings can children reach a level of detachment that will permit them to survive emotionally in their new situation and eventually form new attachments.

PATTERNS OF EARLY RELATIONSHIPS

Most children, in most cultures, form a basic attachment within the first year of life. Infants all over the world show similar responses to their social environments; gradually, they establish an attachment relationship with the specific care-giver. Although the sequence of development of this first relationship occurs fairly consistently across cultures, the details of it vary dramatically depending upon the personality of the parents, their child-rearing practices, and the unique contribution of the child.

The Quality of the Relationship

THE SECURELY ATTACHED INFANT How do we judge the quality of the relationship that develops between the infant and the primary caretaker? Look back at the box on "Measuring Attachment" in Chapter 2 for the details of one of the most popular techniques, called the Strange Situation Test. There are, of course, other ways to measure the quality of the infant–caretaker relationship. There are rating scales and other types of observation. Yet, the Strange Situation Test is used more often than any other. Sroufe and his colleagues measured one group of babies at 12 and 18 months, carefully dividing them into the three categories: securely attached, avoidant, and ambivalent (Sroufe, 1977). Over the years, they followed

In most cultures, children form a basic attachment within the first year of life, but the intensity of bonding and anxiety varies according to specific child-rearing practices. Children reared in a kibbutz (left) are less attached to their care-givers than are children in other cultures who spend much of their infancy strapped to their mother's back.

these babies as they grew to elementary school children. Even at age 2, the differences between the securely attached infants and the others were dramatic. Those children with strong attachment relationships at 18 months had become more enthusiastic, persistent, and cooperative. By age 2, they were also more effective in coping with tools and in peer interactions than were the children in the other two categories. They spontaneously invented more imaginative and symbolic play than the others. These differences still existed when the children were 5 years old (Arend, Gore, & Sroufe, 1979). Later, in elementary school, children who were securely attached as toddlers persisted in their work longer, were more eager to learn new skills, and had more highly developed social skills both with adults and peers (Bretherton & Waters, 1985).

Numerous other studies, some with different methodologies, have quite similar findings (Belsky & Rovine, 1990). It seems that the quality of the relationship between care-giver and infant between 6 and 18 months provides the foundation for most aspects of child development. Securely attached toddlers and preschoolers do simple things, like explore playrooms, better than those children who are not securely attached. They maneuver around the furniture, find their way to interesting toys, and position themselves comfortably for appropriate play with greater ease than those children who have attachment problems (Cassidy, 1986). Also, securely attached 3-year-olds are better-liked by their peers in the nursery school (Jacobson & Wille, 1986).

A warm, supportive relationship between care-giver and infant, with ample verbal interaction, leads to higher levels of cognitive competence and greater social skills (Olson et al., 1984). It supports active exploration and an early mastery of object play and the social environment. The care-giver/infant attachment, therefore, lays the foundation for future development.

RESPONSIVENESS In her studies of children in Uganda, Ainsworth (1967) found that children who showed the strongest attachment behavior had a highly

A warm, supportive relationship established in infancy between care-giver and child gives the child a firm base from which to learn other competencies.

responsive relationship with their mothers. Back in the United States, she reported that securely attached 1-year-olds had mothers who were more responsive to their cries, more affectionate, more tender, less inept in close bodily contact, and were more likely than mothers of insecure 1-year-olds to synchronize their rate of feeding and their play behavior with the baby's own pace (Ainsworth et al., 1978). Since that time, researchers consistently found that infants who were securely attached at age 1 had mothers who were more responsive to their physical needs, their signals of distress, and their attempts to communicate with facial expressions or vocalization (Bornstein, 1989).

Does this mean that a mother must respond to every little thing her infant does? Of course not. Even highly responsive mothers do not respond 100% of the time. Bornstein and Tamis-Lemonda (1989) find that mothers' responsiveness is somewhat different depending on whether the infant is in distress or not. When infants are in distress, the average mother responds about 75% of the time quite quickly. The majority of mothers are quite consistent in responding to their infants' cries. A small minority, however, are quite unresponsive. In contrast, mothers respond quite differently to bids for attention, vocalization, and smiling. Some mothers respond as rarely as 5% of the time to such cues, whereas others respond as often as 50% of the time. What is more, mothers respond in a different way—some with physical play, others with vocal imitation, and still others with touching, playing, patting, and feeding. These researchers and others find that those mothers who are more highly responsive to their infants' cues, both in the first 6 months and later, tend not only to have more securely attached infants but also to have more cognitively advanced infants.

Clarke-Stewart and Nevey (1981) also studied the interactions of mothers and their children who were either securely or insecurely attached. They noticed that mothers who were more verbally responsive and attentive to their children tended to have children who were more autonomous and communicative. Interactions between the securely attached infant and mother were gentler and warmer, and these interactions drew more compliant and cooperative behavior from the infant (Londerville & Main, 1981). Source and Emde (1981) compared the interactions of mothers who were in a room with their infants and reading with those mothers who were not reading. They reported that the infants whose mothers were reading received less attention and exhibited less pleasure and less exploration of the room; the nonreading mothers gave their infants more sensitive responses as they explored the room. They concluded that the mothers' presence is not enough—the mothers must also be emotionally open to the children.

A MUTUAL DIALOGUE   In studying attachment, it is not enough to look at just the mother's behavior. Infants, too, contribute to the interaction. The behaviors of both evolve gradually, one responding to the other. This emphasis on mutual influence between mother and infant represents a new conceptual approach. Yet, clearly, an infant who is sociable and derives pleasure in close proximal contact can encourage even the most tentative new mother. In contrast, a fussy and irritable baby interrupts a caretaker's best efforts at soothing or verbal give-and-take (Belsky et al., 1984; Lewis & Feiring, 1989).

Schaffer (1977) has investigated the way in which **mutuality,** or **synchrony,** between infant and care-giver is achieved. He observed that most infant behavior followed an alternating on-off pattern—for instance, while visually exploring new objects, babies stared and then looked away. Some care-givers responded to these

mutuality (synchrony) The pattern of interchange between care-giver and infant in which each responds to and influences the other's movements and rhythms.

Early mutuality and signaling lay the foundation for long-standing patterns of interaction.

patterns with more skill than others did. Films of mothers face to face with their 3-month-old infants revealed a pattern of mutual approach and withdrawal; they took turns looking and turning, touching and responding, vocalizing and answering.

It is this rare kind of synchrony between infant and care-giver during the first few months that predicts a secure relationship at age 1 and also more sophisticated patterns of mutual communication at that time (Isabella, Belsky, & Von Eye, 1989).

Care-givers do not merely respond to the behavioral rhythms of the child. They also change the pace and nature of the dialogue with a variety of techniques: introducing a new object, imitating and elaborating on the infant's sounds or actions, or making it easier for the child to reach something of interest. By monitoring the baby's responses, care-givers gradually learn when the child is most receptive to new cues from them. No matter which technique is used, the mutual process takes many months to develop fully.

Some techniques seem to be particularly effective in developing synchrony (Field, 1977; Paulby, 1977). Field compared infant reactions to three different maternal behaviors: the mother's spontaneous behavior, her deliberate attempts to catch and hold the child's attention, and her imitation of the child. The infants responded most to the imitations, perhaps because of the slowed-down, exaggerated nature of imitative action. The closer the similarity between maternal and infant behavior, the less discrepancy babies have to deal with, and the more attentive they will be. Furthermore, each mother carefully observed her infant's cutoff, or gaze-away, point. Field suggested that respecting the child's need for a pause is one of the earliest rules of "conversation" that a care-giver must learn.

Some parents frequently overstimulate their infant despite signals from the baby that should indicate this. Babies turn away, hide their heads, close their eyes, and in general try to get a few minutes of pause. Some parents fail to stop the overstimulation until the child actually cries. Other parents frequently understimulate their infant. They ignore their baby's smiles and babbling, or other bids for attention. An infant whose cues for attention are ignored will soon give up trying unless he or she really needs it, and then the child is liable to cry. Often, parents have mixed patterns of sensitivity. Sometimes they overstimulate, sometimes they understimulate, and sometimes they misidentify the cues or signals from the infant. This tends to be particularly true of abusive mothers (Kropp & Haynes, 1987), of depressed mothers (Field, 1986), of some adolescent mothers (Lamb, 1987), and of mothers whose temperament is considerably different from that of the infant's (Weber, Levitt, & Clark, 1986).

The behavior of a very sensitive and responsive mother changes as the infant grows older (Crockenberg & McCluskey, 1986). Indeed, some have used the word "scaffolding" to describe the mother's or father's role in progressively structuring the parent–child interaction (Ratner & Bruner, 1978; Vandel & Wilson, 1987). That is, the parents provide the framework around which they and their infant interact. They pick particular games like imitation or peek-a-boo. As the child becomes older, the game becomes more sophisticated. Thus, early turn-taking, games, and free play gradually become structured by the parent. The child learns increasingly complex rules of social interaction—rules of pacing and give-and-take, rules of observing and imitating, how to maintain the game, and so forth.

Early mutuality and signaling lay the foundation for long-standing patterns of interaction. This has been illustrated in studies of maternal responses to crying. Mothers who respond promptly and consistently to infant crying in the first few months are most likely to have infants who cry less by the end of the first year. A quick response gives babies confidence in the effectiveness of their communications and encourages them to develop other ways of signaling their mothers (Bell & Ainsworth, 1972). When maternal care is inconsistent, infants fail to develop confidence and become either insistent or less responsive. Mutuality blossoms into a variety of behaviors in the second year of life. Some toddlers exhibit spontaneous sharing behavior, both with parents and with other children—showing a new toy, placing it in someone's lap, or using it to invite another child to play. Such behavior indicates toddlers' interests in the properties of toys, their delight in sharing, and their realization that others can see the same things that they see. Children apply skills acquired in the mother–child dialogue to a wider social context. This represents an important developmental stage and suggests that some toddlers are not as egocentric as Piaget believed (Eisenberg, 1989).

EXCLUSIVITY Infants who have a relatively exclusive relationship with a parent or care-giver tend to exhibit intense stranger and separation anxieties. They also show these anxieties at an earlier age than do infants whose relationship with the care-giver has not been that exclusive (Ainsworth, 1967). A child who is constantly with the parent, sleeps in the same room at night, and is carried in a sling on the parent's back during the day experiences a dramatic and intense separation reaction. On the other hand, the child who has had a number of different care-givers from birth tends to accept strangers or separation with far less anxiety (Maccoby & Feldman, 1972).

When toddlers first attend a day-care program, they often experience considerable separation distress. This seems to be particularly true when they are between 15 and 18 months old. But, even at this vulnerable age, some toddlers adjust more readily than others. Toddlers who have had an exclusive relationship with only one person have an especially difficult time. Conversely, those who have had too many separations and too many care-givers also experience a good deal of separation distress. Adjustment is easiest for toddlers who have had some experience with other care-givers and who have had a moderate degree of separation experience with several opportunities for reuniting (Jacobson & Wille, 1984).

The Handicapped Infant

Infants' handicaps often cause severe stresses in mutuality. Blind infants cannot search care-givers' faces or smile back. Deaf babies may appear to be disobedient. Infants with other severe handicaps cannot respond to signals as normal babies do. Obvious handicaps that are evident from birth, such as Down syndrome and cerebral palsy, are certain to create serious adjustment problems for all family members. Until recently, we too often ignored the way that an infant affects a care-giver and concentrated instead on the impact of the care-giver's behavior on the child. In the past decade, researchers have begun to devote more attention to the former situation. When we study how infants' behaviors influence the adults around them, we begin to notice all the subtle means by which these small people help in maintaining the fundamental links that seem so essential to their later socialization.

BLIND INFANTS   Visual communication between care-giver and child is usually a prominent element in the establishment of attachment relationships. Care-givers depend heavily on subtle responses from their infants—looking back, smiling, and visually following—to maintain and support their own behavior. Care-givers often feel, unconsciously, that a blind infant is unresponsive. It is essential for both that they establish a mutually intelligible communication system that overcomes this handicap.

In early life, one of the normal infant's best developed resources for learning is the visual-perceptual system. Babies look at and visually follow everything new and have distinct preferences. They particularly like to look at human faces. Blind infants, however, cannot observe the subtle changes in their care-givers' facial expressions or follow their movements. Thus, blind infants fail to receive information that sighted babies use in formulating their own responses.

Care-givers of sighted infants rely on visual signals of discrimination, recognition, and preference. Otherwise competent blind infants do not develop signals for "I want that" or "Pick me up" until near the end of the first year. Thus, the first few months of life are extremely difficult for both care-giver and infant. The child's seeming lack of responsiveness can be emotionally devastating for the care-givers unless they are wisely counseled by experienced people. The great danger is that communication and mutuality will break down and that the care-giver will start to avoid the child (Fraiberg, 1974).

Blind babies do not develop a selective, responsive smile language as early as

The diagnosis of deafness may come as a shock to parents who have been talking to their children all along. These parents need special training and counseling to help their handicapped children develop fully.

sighted children; they do not smile as often or as ecstatically. They have very few facial expressions. Yet they rapidly develop a large, expressive vocabulary of hand signals for their care-givers. Eventually, they are able to direct and relate these signals to unseen people and objects. Training parents and care-givers of blind infants to watch for and interpret hand signals greatly enhances the parent–child dialogue, attachment formation, and all subsequent socialization (Fraiberg, 1974).

DEAF INFANTS   The developmental difficulties of deaf infants follow a pattern that differs from those of blind infants. In the first few months of life, their well-developed visual sense generally makes up for the problems imposed by deafness. The children are visually responsive. After the first 6 months, however, communication between parents and infants begins to break down. The children's responses are not full enough to meet the parents' expectations. Often, the discovery of the child's deafness does not occur until the second year. By this time, the child has already missed a good deal of communication. One of the first indications of deafness in 1-year-olds is seeming disobedience, as well as frequent startling when people approach. (The child does not hear them coming.) In 2-year-olds, there may be temper tantrums, frequent disobedience (or, conversely, severe withdrawal), together with widespread failure to develop normal expectations about the world around them. The diagnosis of deafness may come as a shock to parents who have been "talking to my child all along." Like parents of blind children, they need special training and counseling to help the child develop fully. Without careful attention during infancy, deafness can result in poor communication during the preschool years and in severe social, intellectual, and psychological deficits later (Meadow, 1975).

SEVERE HANDICAPS   When an infant is born with a severe handicap, such as cerebral palsy, there is a high risk of maternal rejection, withdrawal, and depression. A severely handicapped infant strains marital ties and may trigger a variety of disturbances in other children in the family. Child-care workers can help almost immediately with a family's early adjustment problems, and they should be consulted at once. Early success or failure in coping with initial traumas will greatly affect parents' abilities to make wise decisions about life choices—such as whether or not to place their child in an institution.

Bonding Disorders

Occasionally, care-givers and infants encounter serious problems when they try to establish their relationship. Such problems are known as bonding disorders. The failure-to-thrive infant and the abused or neglected infant are products of such relationships. Failure-to-thrive infants are usually small and emaciated. They appear to be quite ill and unable to digest food properly. Sometimes, they begin eating very soon after arriving at a hospital; at other times, they are listless and withdrawn, almost immobile. These infants often avoid eye contact by staring with a wide-eyed gaze, actively turning away, or covering their face or eyes. By definition, failure-to-thrive infants weigh in the lower 3% for their age group and show no evidence of any disease or abnormality that would explain their failure to grow. Often, disruption in the home and social environment of these infants is indicated. In addition, there is some evidence of developmental retardation among these infants, but it can generally be reversed with appropriate feeding (Barbero, 1983; Drotar, 1985).

In many cases, the mother of failure-to-thrive and abused or neglected infants is mentally or physically ill, depressed, alcoholic, or using drugs. She may have experienced some recent crisis that has had a prolonged emotional impact. An important finding is that the parents of these children have experienced similar deprivations when they were infants. Some studies show that as many as 85% of abusive or neglectful parents have had very negative early childhood experiences themselves; that is, they, too, were abused or neglected. Certainly, not all people who were abused as children grow up to abuse their children. But, too often, the cycle repeats itself (Helfer, 1982).

In recent years, programs have been set up to assist parents in establishing healthy relationships with their infants. The most successful programs seem to involve parents and infants with relatively mild problems. Such programs include those designed to help parents learn to cope with premature, sickly, or irritable infants (Crawford, 1982; Crockenberg, 1981). Programs designed to improve the parenting skills of mothers and fathers who seriously abuse their children focus on a number of difficulties. Sometimes, these parents lack sensitivity to the feelings of others and are, therefore, unable to respond to their baby's emotional signals. In one study, mothers were shown photos of babies' faces and asked, "What is the baby feeling?" The abusive mothers often made mistakes. They might say "angry" or "sad" when the photo was of a frightened baby. They might even say "joy" when the baby was clearly distressed. Nonabusing mothers never made such mistakes (Kropp & Haynes, 1987). Clearly, if the parent cannot read the baby's signals, it is difficult to learn to respond appropriately.

As many as 85% of abusive or neglectful parents have been abused or neglected when they were children.

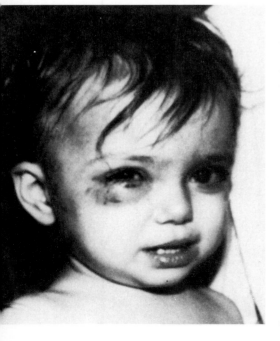

FATHERS, SIBLINGS, AND THE FAMILY SYSTEM

Most research in child development has focused on the relationship between mother and child and has neglected the rest of the family. Evidence shows that infants form strong early attachments to fathers as well as mothers, particularly when they have regular, close contact from birth. The stronger the early attachment, the more influence the father will have on later socialization. Siblings, too, form strong long-term bonds that often last a lifetime. The popular literature frequently highlights the competitive rivalry between siblings. The positive, supportive, mutual-caring roles have often been downplayed. But throughout life, siblings frequently protect and help one another. Many families also have a variety of other family members who play a strong role in the infant's development— including grandparents, aunts, uncles, and cousins. Indeed, most children develop in a social context that allows several early attachments. The strength of certain relationships can make up for some of the inadequacies of others. The infant has an opportunity to choose and discriminate between these relationships. His evolving emotional development is not attendant on the strengths and weaknesses of any one attachment bond.

Although the popular literature tends to highlight the rivalry between siblings, siblings form strong, long-term bonds and mutual-caring roles that often last a lifetime.

Fathers and Fathering

During the 1980s, much was learned about fathers and fathering in the American family system. There is some evidence that fathers are spending more time with their infants than they did in the past (Pleck, 1985; Ricks, 1985). Aside from breast-feeding, fathers are quite capable of routine child care. They can bathe, diaper, feed, and rock—sometimes as skillfully as the mother performs these tasks. They can be as responsive to the infant's cues as mothers are (Parke, 1981), and infants can become as attached to them as they are to their mothers. Fathers who spend more time taking care of young children form strong attachments to them, and the children benefit from this extended time (Ricks, 1985). Despite these similarities, however, fathers are not, by and large, taking over the major responsibility for infant care, and the nature of the father's relationship with the infant is different from that of the mother's.

The style of interaction between father and infant differs from the mother-infant relationship in that fathers are generally more physical and spontaneous.

FATHERING The style of interaction between the father and infant differs from interaction between the mother and infant. Whereas mothers are likely to hold infants for care-taking purposes, fathers are more likely to hold infants just to play with them (Parke, 1981). Fathers are also more often physical and spontaneous. Play between fathers and infants occurs in cycles that have peaks of high excitement and attention followed by periods of minimal activity. Mothers engage their infants in subtle, shifting, gradual play, or they initiate such conventional games as pat-a-cake. Fathers, however, tend toward unusual, vigorous, and unpredictable games, which infants find most exciting (Lamb & Lamb, 1976). The exception to this pattern occurs when the father is the primary care-giver—he then tends to act more as mothers do (Field, 1978).

As infants get older and require less direct care-taking, father–infant interaction is likely to increase. Fathers may engage in more rough-and-tumble play and interact more frequently with the young child in public places, such as zoos or parks (Lewis, 1987).

Fathers who frequently interact with their infants, who are responsive to their signals, and who become important individuals in their children's world are likely to develop into forceful agents of socialization later on. As the child grows older, the father becomes an important role model. He may also become an admirer and advocate of the child's achievements. An important link seems to exist between paternal interaction in infancy and interaction in later childhood. Fathers who are inaccessible to their infants may have difficulty establishing strong emotional ties later on. It is even possible that they will have a negative influence as the child grows older (Ricks, 1985).

Fathers who are the most influential in their young children's lives not only spend time with them, but are also sensitive to their wants, cries, and developmental needs (Esterbrook & Goldberg, 1984; Parke, 1981). Yet, in many families, mothers seem to be more "naturally" responsive to their children than are the fathers. Several reasons for this are possible. One may be that women have inherited nurturant traits from our mammalian ancestors. Another may be the strong emotions aroused by breast-feeding. A third may be the way in which women are socialized. In any case, some fathers have to learn to be responsive to

FOCUS ON RESEARCH

THE FORMATION OF FAMILY SYSTEMS

We know that the birth of a baby creates a lot of changes for a couple. Each parent has to balance the needs of this new family member with the need to maintain a reasonable relationship with one's spouse. But what happens with the introduction of a second child? Kreppner and his colleagues (1982) examined the formation of the family system when it changes from three members to four members after the birth of a second child. They also investigated how family interactions change over a 2-year period as this new infant grows. Are there some developmental events that pressure family members to interact with one another in new ways?

The researchers selected 16 families for observation. Each family, comprised of a mother, father, and one child who was 4 years of age or less, was expecting a baby. The first observations were recorded late in the pregnancies; both parents were interviewed concerning their individual and family histories and their parental attitudes. Following the birth of the second child, all families were videotaped periodically over a 2-year period, accumulating about 26 videotapes per family that each ran 30 or more minutes in length. The observers also visited with the families for at least 2 to 4 hours at

the time of each taping, acting in many ways like normal houseguests. These observations were supplemented by

The quality of the marital relationship determines the environment in which children are reared and influences their development.

their infants (Rossi, 1977). Increasingly, fathers are taking the time to broaden their parenting role, even when their children are infants (Parke, 1981).

FATHERS AND THE FAMILY SYSTEM There are social and psychological reasons why fathers are usually not equal partners in infant care. In one study, mothers and fathers were recruited from a childbirth class where, at least initially, the fathers were active participants and were expected to continue sharing infant care with their wives. But it did not work out that way (Grossman, Pollack, & Golding, 1988). Very soon after the birth of the child, both mothers and fathers rated the fathers as less competent in most infant-care skills. Fathers were then relegated to the role of "helping" the mother. No father in this study ever talked about the mother "helping" the father take care of the infant. The more competent one—the mother—generally took over the chief responsibility for the infant and, therefore, got more practice at performing infant care and interpreting the baby's signals. If someone feels incompetent, they do not enjoy doing a job (Entwhisle & Doering, 1988). Most families work this out by selecting complementary roles for father and mother. Less successful couples tend to become impatient with each other. In these cases, it is common for the father to play with the infant but to serve as a reluctant and occasional helper.

extensive interviews when the second child was 8 months, and at the end of the 2-year period.

What did the researchers conclude from their observations? Although there were many differences in family interaction patterns, the researchers were able to identify three phases in the process of family formation.

Phase One: Initial Integration of the Infant into the Family (Birth to 8 Months). Immediately after the arrival of the second child, there is a kind of doubling of parental tasks. Parents must care for the new infant and yet not neglect the older child. In addition, the first child may be confused about his or her position in the family, and may feel the need to compete for attention. This child often needs to reassert her- or himself as "already big," as superior, while still wanting and needing all the attention the baby is getting. Parents develop different ways to channel, limit, or satisfy this older child's needs.

Often, parents must experiment with different ways of dealing with their various jobs—they divide and delegate child-care and housekeeping tasks in their own fashion, forming a "working team." The researchers observed several different family solutions to these problems.

Phase Two: The Second Child Learns to Crawl and Walk (9 to 16 Months). When the second child begins to crawl and to move about, there are new tasks for the family. The second child can now interact directly with all members of the family—he or she can interrupt the play of the older child, for example. Parents must begin to cope with sibling problems, and hence, be mediators and teachers. Parents often state and enforce "the rules." The older child usually tries to maintain his or her leading position in the family. One solution for the child is to take on a parenting role for that second child. Another possibility is to join forces with the father while ignoring the baby.

Phase Three: Differentiation Within the Family (17 to 24 Months). When the second child begins to use words somewhat effectively, at 16 to 18 months, a new phase of family interaction begins. The second child seems more fully human now and, hence, a real partner in the family. New alliances form, including one between the siblings. There is often a clear and distinct boundary between the parents—the adults—and the children. The parents find that verbal rules can now apply to both children. At this stage, new patterns of interaction begin to develop.

The father's indirect influence on the infant and, indeed, on the whole family is considerable. Numerous studies have indicated that a father's emotional support of the mother during pregnancy and early infancy is important to the establishment of positive beginning relationships. The absence of a father during infancy creates considerable stress on the whole family system (Lewis, 1987).

Although in our culture the father is often a secondary care-giver, he plays an important part in a complex system of interactions. It is not enough just to study the ways in which a mother and baby or a father and baby interact. We must look at the way the three of them affect one another's behavior. Clarke-Stewart (1978), in her study of the three-way pattern in many families, finds that the mother's influence on the child is usually direct, whereas the father's is often indirect, through the mother. The child usually influences both parents quite directly.

The addition of an infant, especially a firstborn child, to a family affects the marriage itself. Studies have shown that the birth of the first child can create considerable stress on the marital relationship. A newborn makes heavy demands on the time and energy of both mother and father. Complementary roles need to be established. Decisions must be made about child-care arrangements, the mother's return to work, and so forth (Baruch & Barnett, 1986). The stress on the marriage may be greater if the infant is demanding, frequently sick, or handicapped. It is possible for stress to bring the couple closer together (Turnbull & Turnbull, 1990). Yet, if the marriage was vulnerable to begin with, the stress may cause increased dissatisfaction and turmoil.

Siblings

Siblings form important and long-lasting attachments to one another, beginning in infancy, although younger siblings are often more attached to the older siblings than the reverse (Lewis, 1987). Infants often form very strong attachments to a somewhat older sibling, and are upset with the loss of that sibling even when the separation is only overnight (Dunn & Kendrick, 1979). Older siblings provide important social models. Children learn how to share, cooperate, help, and empathize by watching their older siblings. They learn appropriate sex roles and family customs and values. In some cultures, the older siblings perform a major caretaking role, sometimes being the principal caretaker of the younger child (Whiting & Whiting, 1975). In many families, the positive aspects of sibling roles—helping, protecting, and providing an ally—last a lifetime. It is surprising, therefore, that the negative aspects of sibling relationships have received more attention (Lewis, 1987).

Two negative aspects of sibling relationships are sibling rivalry and the dethroning of the older sibling with the birth of the new infant. It is clear that the birth of the second child makes a profound impact on the first or older sibling. Parents pay less attention, time, and energy to the first child. The role of the older child must shift. Parents' attitudes in handling this change influence the amount of sibling strife, competition, and rivalry (Dunn & Kendrick, 1980; Lewis, 1987; Lewis, Feiring, & Kotsonis, 1984).

Grandparents and Others

In many cultures, including our own, grandparents have considerable contact with their adult children and their grandchildren—often on a weekly basis. In families where both parents work, grandparents are frequently the primary care-givers for much of the time. The grandparent's role is usually somewhat different from that of the parent, and a different attachment relationship takes place. Grandparents often offer more approval and support, or empathy and sympathy, and less discipline. Sometimes, the relationship is more playful and relaxed (Lewis, 1987).

MATERNAL EMPLOYMENT

The Social Ecology of Child Care

In modern societies, child care for young children is a complex issue. In the United States, more than half of mothers with children under age 2 work outside of the home (*Statistical Abstract of the United States,* 1990). In Sweden, 85% of mothers with children under school age work part time or full time outside of the home. But there is a difference. In Sweden, public child care is provided for every family that requests it. There are day-care centers, or day nurseries, and there are also family day-care providers (so-called day mothers). Both the day-care centers and the day mothers are hired and licensed by the municipalities. There is also a system of open preschools, where mothers or day mothers may take their children to meet and play with other children, and get advice and support in their caring roles. In other words, there is a publicly funded child-care system that provides support to families with infants and young children (Andersson, 1989).

In the United States, there is a quite different *social ecology* in most communities for the raising of infants and young children. Parents are often expected to make their own decisions about what type of child care they want and how much of it they will receive. They are financially responsible for providing supplemental child care and are assisted in this responsibility only if they have a low income. Because over 50% of mothers of infants and toddlers work outside of the home, many families face the difficult decisions of finding suitable alternative child care at affordable prices. Many working mothers are ambivalent about their dual role as worker and mother. Some receive criticism from other family members or from friends in the community. Yet most women work because they need the money, either as single mothers or as part of a dual-income family. After work, they must somehow find the time and energy to care for their children and handle the countless household responsibilities of family management. The stress for both mothers and fathers of juggling parenting and work responsibilities in a social ecology that offers very few supports can be quite considerable.

Infant Day Care

In Sweden, employers must provide *9 months* of parental leave (Welles-Nystrom, 1988). In the United States, however, *6 weeks* of leave is quite common. Mothers who must or who choose to return to work soon after birth face a number of difficult decisions. They must arrange for safe and reliable supervision of their children while they are at work. Some may hire a relative or friend, others seek licensed family day-care centers, and still others look for a reliable, high-quality day-care center.

Both family day-care homes and well-run day-care centers seem perfectly capable of fostering normal development in infants and toddlers. Several studies,

In families where both parents work, grandparents are often the primary care-givers for much of the time.

Day-care centers that are well run appear to be capable of fostering normal development in children.

conducted under ideal conditions, show that children ranging in age from 3 months to 30 months developed at least as well in a group care situation as did children with similar backgrounds who were reared at home (Kagan, 1978; Keister, 1970; Clarke-Stewart, 1982). In Sweden, where high-quality day care is the norm, children with early day care (beginning before age 1) were generally rated more favorably and performed better in elementary school than did the average child reared at home by his or her own mother. They were more competent in cognitive tests like reasoning and vocabulary, were rated better by teachers in school subjects such as reading and arithmetic, and were rated as more socially competent than their home-reared peers (Andersson, 1989). Some authors in the United States find similar small positive effects on cognitive or social development for children in group care (Clarke-Stewart & Fine, 1983).

The day-care services available to many families are not ideal, however. Staffs may be poorly trained, poorly paid, and have high turnover. These facilities rarely admit researchers. One study (Vandell & Corasaniti, 1990) looked at 349 third graders in an area of Texas where, it turns out, day care and family day care were of relatively poor quality and there were few enforced public standards. When these researchers compared children who had extensive day care beginning in infancy with groups who had less day care, they found highly significant, pervasive, negative effects. Those with extensive day care scored lower on peer relations, work habits, emotional health, cognitive skills, and standardized tests. They also earned lower grades in school. Some had serious behavior problems, including excessive aggressiveness. The authors agree that there are other factors—social factors and family dynamic factors—that lead some parents to need full-time infant care, whereas others do not need it. It is difficult to say whether the infant care interrupted attachment and, hence, caused the problematic behavior of the children in this study. Perhaps the problems may have been due to poor preschools, family dynamics, or an interaction of these factors.

What is the process that leads to trouble for some infants who have nonparental care for more than 20 hours per week beginning at age 1? (See the box entitled "Early Infant Day Care: A Cause for Concern?") Jaeger & Weinraub (1990) suggest two models. One is *the maternal separation model*. In this model, it is argued that daily, repeated separations from the mother are experienced by the

FOCUS ON AN ISSUE

EARLY INFANT DAY CARE: A CAUSE FOR CONCERN?

In the fall of 1986, a noted, responsible expert on infant development published a startling warning to infant-care professionals. He had reviewed several studies of infant and preschool development comparing children who had begun day care or other forms of nonparental care in their first year with children who had not begun so early. Although the studies varied widely in the quality of care received, the types of families served, and the consistency of care given, he reached one cautiously stated conclusion: that "entry into care in the first year of life is a 'risk factor' for the development of insecure-avoidant attachments in infancy and heightened aggressiveness, noncompliance, and withdrawal in the preschool and early school years" (Belsky, 1986, p. 7). This one statement produced an immediate and intense reaction from many researchers, day-care professionals, and parents.

The reason for the intense reaction was clear. Was it true that infants were "at risk" when both parents worked and placed their infants in some alternative care arrangement? If so, there were implications for the role and rights of women, implications for the profession of infant day care, and implications for the personal decision making of parents. Clearly, a whole lifestyle of dual-working parents was being challenged. Some day-care workers felt personally insulted, but a few others suggested that the possibility of harm due to very early care in less than ideal day care arrangements deserved close scrutiny (Fitzcharles, 1987; Miringoff, 1987). Other experts warned of a hasty conclusion drawn from diverse studies conducted in complex environmental circumstances (Chess, 1987).

What are the details of this complex warning, and what is the evidence that supports it? Jay Belsky presents his arguments carefully. He is well aware of the past research on the effects of infant day care on development. Prior to 1980, virtually all of this research was done in high-quality, often university-based, research-oriented centers. There was little, if any, evidence to suggest that such nonmaternal care was problematic. In fact, in some instances infants in these high-quality centers did better on social, cognitive, and emotional aspects of development than did similar home-reared infants. But since 1980, researchers have studied infants in a wide range of nonmaternal care arrangements. The families studied include some single-parent families, some families at risk for abuse or neglect, and a full range of dual-parent families at all economic levels. When Jay Belsky looked closely at these diverse studies as well as his own, he found disturbing commonalities. Among those children who have had nonmaternal care starting in the first year and for more than 20 hours per week, he found more children with anxious avoidant attachments to their mother. This is the case even when the nonmaternal care-giver is a neighbor or relative at home with her own child. It certainly does not happen to all children, or even the majority of children in these circumstances. But the proportion of infants who are not "securely attached," according to the standard Strange Situation Test, is nearly double (Belsky, 1986; Belsky & Rovine, 1988, 1990).

Other researchers reach quite different conclusions, even looking at much of the same data. It is clear that the quality of alternative infant care is an even more important factor. Infants who have low-quality care or who experience several changes in their primary caretaker are particularly vulnerable. Also, families who have many stresses in their life and place their infant in a low-quality caretaking arrangement have added risk (Phillips, McCartney, Scarr, & Howes, 1987).

It is clear that age alone is not the only, or even the primary, cause for concern. Yet, because a safe, secure attachment is so basic to later social and personality development, the debate over which factors or combination of factors put infants "at risk" will continue for some time.

infant as either maternal absence or as maternal rejection. The infant comes to doubt maternal availability or responsiveness. It is the psychological unavailability, or unresponsiveness, that leads to insecurity. Studies based on this model tend to focus on the infant's behavior at home or in day care. Then, there is another model called *the quality of mothering model*. In this perspective, it is not maternal employment or separation, per se, that determines the infant outcome, but how that maternal employment affects the maternal behavior. The employed mother is not able to be as sensitive and responsive a care-giver as she might be if she had more time and practice or if she did not have regular interruptions. It is this change in the maternal behavior that produces insecurity in the infant. Current research based on the quality of mothering model focuses on the competing demands of the mother's work and family, the quality of the child care (and whether or not she has

APPLICATION

CHOOSING AN INFANT DAY-CARE CENTER

During the first 2 years, infants need constant attention from a care-giver to encourage the development of their social and cognitive competencies. When both parents work, the role of care-giver is often taken over by a day-care center. How do parents know they have chosen a good day-care center for their children?

One important element to look for is the competence of the care-giver. Jacobson (1978) suggests considering the following questions:

1. Does the care-giver have the qualities one would want in a parent, such as child-centeredness, self-confidence, flexibility, and sensitivity?

2. Is the care-giver attentive and loving toward the infants?

3. Is the care-giver skilled in the physical care of infants?

4. Does the care-giver use different styles of care to meet the individual needs of the infants?

5. Does the care-giver display positive attitudes and values, or does he or she appear angry, unhappy, or depressed?

6. Is the care-giver culturally compatible with the infants?

7. Does the care-giver touch and smile at the infants? Look at them and hold them?

8. Does the care-giver speak in a positive tone, showing acceptance and affection?

9. Does the care-giver play with the infants, provide stimulation with toys, and let the infants explore their environment?

10. Does the care-giver teach and try to aid in learning and development?

There are other factors to consider when choosing an infant center. Good infant day-care centers include one care-giver for every three or four infants, with the same care-giver consistently working with the same infants. Parents should inquire about training and health requirements for care-givers. Centers often include a playroom and curriculum room, as well as a kitchen area, a teacher work area, and a separate sleeping room with a crib for each child. The equipment may include enough high chairs, playpens, walkers, and a variety of appropriate toys and books. In addition, provisions should be made for ill children. The daily program takes into consideration the needs of the individual infants, allowing them to sleep when tired, eat every 3 to 4 hours, participate in organized activities, and play for the rest of the day (Ramey, 1981).

In an excellent day-care center with enough space, a competent staff, and a well-planned program, infants develop as well as (and sometimes even better than) infants raised at home. A skillful, responsive caregiver can actually boost the social and language development of infants and toddlers who have otherwise had insufficient attention from their parents (Honig, 1989).

"Do you think she likes the babysitter better than she likes me?"

to worry about it), the characteristics of the infant, and whether or not the mother thinks that her infant is sturdy, can adjust, and is capable of coping with the situation. What is the general quality of the mother's life? Does she find satisfaction in her varying roles, employment status, and maternal satisfaction? How much role conflict is there, or marital strain or fatigue? If the mother feels strong separation anxiety when she leaves her child each day, the child tends not to do well (McBride, 1990).

The potential risks of early day care involve many factors, including the quality of day care, family dynamics, the infant's temperament, and the broader social ecology of child rearing in a community.

CHILD REARING AND PERSONALITY DEVELOPMENT

Commonly asked questions about child rearing by both parents and researchers include whether to breast-feed or bottle-feed, when or how to wean, whether to pick up babies immediately when they cry or to let them cry for a while, whether to allow thumb-sucking or blanket carrying, what to do about temper tantrums, when to toilet train and how. If we look at these specific practices separately, we tend to get answers that are contradictory. It is hard to put them together to form a clear theory of good child rearing. We often conclude, for example, that it does not matter much whether children suck their thumbs or carry a blanket.

Yet, such practices, when viewed in the context of the *total pattern* of child-rearing practices, clearly do matter. These *patterns* have a strong influence on later personality development. The way that we convey our culture to our children, beginning in infancy, is not at all subtle. From birth we try to instill in our children attitudes and values about the nature of their bodies—the acceptability of self-stimulation, the degree of physical closeness that is desirable, the amount of dependency allowed, and the goodness or badness of both their behavior and their basic nature as human beings. These attitudes and values, communicated through many child-rearing practices, have a very wide-ranging effect on personality development.

It is in the context of broad, cross-cultural child-rearing patterns that we shall examine specific child-rearing practices. We will concentrate on three particular aspects of child-rearing practices during the infancy period. First, we shall study the development of trust and nurturance in infants. As you recall from Chapter 2, this refers to the initial stage of Erikson's theory, and such questions as: What do infants learn about the basic trustworthiness of their social environment? Is the environment consistent and predictable? Is it responsive to the child's needs? Second, we will examine how children's attempts at autonomy are met. When toddlers begin to get up and move around, to do things for themselves, to control their bodies, to try to control their environment, how are their needs satisfied? Third, we will look at child-rearing practices during infancy in terms of their effect on growing self-awareness in childhood. Children who are heavily swaddled during the first year or who are bound to a cradleboard, for example, cannot explore their bodies as can children who are relatively free to move about. Children who have no access to a mirror do not discover their own images. But there are pervasive attitudes toward the body and the self that children learn each day.

Trust and Nurturance

If we look at infant care in other societies, we see quite dramatic differences both in approach and results. One study, for example, suggested a difference between the attitudes of American mothers and Japanese mothers toward their infants (Caudill & Weinstein, 1969). In general, the American mother viewed the infant as passive and dependent. Her goal was to make her child independent. The average Japanese mother held the opposite opinion of her infant. She saw her child as an independent organism who needed to learn about the dependent relationships within the family.

Such differences in attitude have resulted in two different child-rearing practices. American infants are ideally put in cribs in their own rooms, whereas Japanese infants traditionally share a bedroom with their parents. In the study, the Japanese mother tried to respond quickly when the baby cried, and she fed her child on demand. The American mother tended to let her child cry for a short while in the hope of establishing a regular, mature feeding schedule. The Japanese mother felt the need to soothe and quiet her baby often, whereas the American mother wanted to stimulate her baby to smile and vocalize. As a result of these different approaches, the Japanese baby quickly became less vocal and active than the American baby. But some of these differences may be due in part to the infant's initial temperament, as was mentioned in Chapter 4.

FEEDING, WEANING, AND COMFORT   Whether or not a mother breast-feeds or bottle-feeds her infant, the important question for psychological development is how the feeding method fits into the total pattern of nurturant care that the infant receives. Feeding time allows for the closeness between mother and child, and it expresses sensitivity and responsiveness between care-giver and child.

In some cultures, the transition period between the infant's birth and separation from the mother lasts for 3 years or more. Feeding is an integral part of this prolonged relationship (Mead & Newton, 1967). Children may sleep close to their mothers, be carried around in a sling during most of the first year, and be breast-fed until the age of 3 (Richman et al., 1988). In other cultures—particularly in America—some infants may be separated from their mothers almost immediately—separate bed, separate room, early weaning. Somewhat in jest, Mead and Newton described the transition period for some American babies as lasting less than a minute—until the umbilical cord is cut!

In Sweden, maternal leave has been extended to 9 months at 90% salary, with an additional 9 months at reduced salary, mandated by law. There is a public campaign that urges mothers to stay home with their children for at least 9 months in order to provide continuity of care and nurturance. Despite the fact that Sweden has perhaps the lowest infant mortality rate in the world, mothers are concerned about the vulnerability of their infants, and both mothers and fathers pay close attention to the diet and health of the infant (Welles-Nystrom, 1988).

In Italy, the nurturance of the infant is a social affair. Mothers and infants are rarely alone. Mothers do most of the feeding, dressing, and cleaning of their infants in an indulgent and caring fashion. The family, friends, and neighbors all contribute to the social interaction with the infant. In one study, 70% of the time, although the mother was present, other people were tending to the baby— hugging, talking, teaching, and even teasing the infants. The American observer was quite surprised at the amount of teasing that occurred, sometimes to the point of tears on the part of the infant. Infants were spanked; pacifiers were held just out of reach; candy was offered and then taken away. Adults said, "Here comes Daddy!" only to laugh and declare "He isn't here anymore!" and then swoop the tearful infant up to hug and kiss him or her amidst the laughter of onlookers. Even naptime was not sacred, as infants were jiggled and pinched to wake up when adults wanted to play with them. Despite this large amount of attention and stimulation, the infants seemed to learn to cope remarkably well (New, 1988).

Considerable research has been devoted to thumb-sucking and other comfort devices, but remarkably few definitive conclusions have been reached about them. For the most part, sucking experience seems to be a natural need. Yet, parents have responded to this need in a variety of ways (Goldberg, 1972; Richman et al., 1988). In much of early 20th-century Europe, thumb-sucking was considered a dirty habit, harmful to a child's general personality development. Elaborate devices, vile-tasting applications, or even simple sleeves were used to cover a child's hand to prevent thumb-sucking. This era, with its strong fear of pleasure and of sense exploration, seems to be over. Today, some children are given a pacifier to suck—on the assumption that they can more easily give up the pacifier than they can give up the thumb. Most children who use either thumbs or pacifiers, however, give them up as regular comfort devices by the end of the preschool years; those who remain avid thumb-suckers or avid comfort seekers generally have other needs that are not being met. Evidence that thumb-sucking causes major damage to the dental arch is not conclusive. Most of this damage seems to occur in children who are still sucking at age 5, 6, or 7, when they are getting their second teeth.

Children use a wide variety of comfort devices and comfort-seeking

Most children who use either thumbs or pacifiers as comforting devices give them up by the end of the preschool years.

behaviors. Favorite blankets, toys, and other objects, and twisting and rubbing their hair or skin all provide familiar sensations. Parents and care-givers convey their values and attitudes by their reactions to comfort seeking—attitudes toward the child's body, self-stimulation, and what they feel is an acceptable level of closeness and dependency. From such reactions, children learn whether they are considered good or bad, whether they should feel anxious or guilty, and when to feel comfortable and secure. They learn a great deal more than merely whether or not they should suck their thumbs or carry a blanket.

Social Referencing and Cultural Meaning

One important avenue of parental influence on the infant is a process called *social referencing*. In situations of uncertainty, infants look to the parent's face to detect an emotional signal as to whether or not this situation is safe or unsafe, good or bad. We have seen the effectiveness of social referencing in encouraging an infant to cross a visual cliff, or in deciding whether to become somewhat sociable to a stranger, for instance. But infants seem to look for an emotional signal under a wide range of circumstances, including how much to wander away from mother, or whether or not to explore a strange toy. Infants look at fathers as well as mothers for emotional signals, and, although they look more at mothers than at fathers when both are present, the father's signals seem to be equally effective in regulating the infant's behavior (Hirshberg & Svejda, 1990).

What happens if mother and father give conflicting emotional signals to their infant? What are the consequences of one parent encouraging the child to explore an unusual toy and the other frowning and displaying worry? In a study conducted with 1-year-olds, parents were coached to give consistent or conflicting emotional signals. The infants adapted much more easily to consistent signals, either both parents happy or both parents fearful, than they did to conflicting emotional signals. In fact, when they were given conflicting facial responses—happy from mother and fear from father, for example—the infants expressed their confusion in a wide range of anxious behaviors. Some did agitated sucking or rocking, or avoided the situation altogether. Others wandered aimlessly, or seemed disoriented. It seems that 1-year-olds are remarkably sensitive to the emotional signals from their parents. Some infants were much more able to handle the conflict than were others (Hirshberg, 1990).

What are some of the messages that parents are already teaching their children at age 1? In a series of studies, anthropologists have intensely observed the !Kung San, a group of hunters and gatherers in Botswana. In this culture, the sharing of objects is an important value. When the anthropologists looked at mothers and their 10- to 12-month-old infants, they were surprised to find that, in contrast to many American parents, these parents seemed to pay no attention to the infant's exploration of objects. They did not talk about the objects and did not smile—but they neither punished nor frowned as children picked up twigs, grass, parts of food, nutshells, bones, and the like. They used an expression that meant "He's teaching himself." However, there was one activity with objects to which they did pay attention. The adults focused on the sharing and the giving and taking of objects. In fact, grandmothers began symbolic training by guiding the giving of special beads to relatives. When adults paid attention to objects at all, they did it by encouraging sharing with words like "Give it to me" or "Here, take this" (Bakeman & Adamson, 1990). It appears that, through social referencing, games, and selective attention, parents are already teaching their 1-year-olds the values of their culture.

Autonomy, Cooperation, and Discipline

By the time infants are 1 year old, their parents or care-givers have taught them some guidelines for acceptable behavior, especially for their dependency needs and their needs for physical closeness. But, in the second year, care-givers cope with a whole new set of issues. Again, their personalities, as well as their cultural backgrounds, will affect their attitudes and methods of dealing with the toddler. To appreciate the diversity of problems facing those who care for toddlers, let us consider some typical 2-year-olds.

He explores the qualities and possibilities of almost everything in his environment. She discovers the delights of pulling the toilet paper roll—endlessly. He uses pencil and crayon on walls, floors, and furniture. She enjoys picking up small things, from cigarette butts to crumbs to pebbles; many of these things will be given a taste test. He wedges his body into, under, or over any space that looks interesting. She picks up and carries around glass figurines as well as toys. He alternates between clinging dependence and daring exploration, often within the space of a few minutes. She walks and runs and climbs for the sheer feel of walking and running and climbing. He tries to cheer up another child by sharing his bottle, or he willfully refuses to share. She is docile and eager to please one minute, and she challenges authority and routine the next. He wants to feed and dress himself on one occasion, and wants everything done for him on the next. She may rebel at bedtime, protest at bath time, refuse to have her shoes or snowsuit put on, or reject a food that she has always enjoyed. He learns to say "No!"

Toward the end of the second year, toddlers experience increased emotional conflict between their greater needs for autonomy and their obvious dependence and limited skills. The changes that occur in children around this age were observed at length by Margaret Mahler and her colleagues (1975). They noted an extraordinary ambivalence in 18-month-old children. The toddlers were torn between a desire to stay close to their mothers and a wish to be independent. Their new sense of being separate beings seemed to frighten them. They tried to deny it by acting as if their mothers were extensions of themselves. For instance, a child might pull the mother's hand in an effort to have her pick up an object that the child desired. In addition, the toddlers appeared to experience a wider range of emotions and were developing new ways of dealing with their feelings, such as suppressing the need to cry.

A new emotional experience—empathy—begins to develop. From 18 to 24 months, toddlers begin to engage in prosocial behavior, including cooperation, sharing, helping, and responding empathically to emotional distress in others. This new ability to interact with peers does not emerge smoothly. Often, when a toddler sees the distress of others, he is confused. He may laugh or not seem to know how to react. In one series of studies, mothers were asked to make believe that they had just hurt themselves. The toddler at 21 months was confused and anxious about the mother's distress. But mothers who regularly responded with empathy to their own child's distress soon promoted an empathy in their own children so that, 3 months later, some of these toddlers had learned soothing, comforting behaviors (Radke-Yarrow et al., 1983). In studies of cooperation in simple tasks, almost no 12-month-old infants can cooperate with each other. At 18 months, cooperation is infrequent and almost accidental. At 24 months, with a little coaching from adults, nearly all the toddlers were able to cooperate (Brownell & Carriger, 1990).

HARVARD PRESCHOOL PROJECT   Probably no ideal method of child rearing can be used by every family everywhere. For over two decades, however, Burton White and his colleagues have produced a profile of what they consider one pattern of effective parenting: Effective mothers are not necessarily full-time care-givers (White, 1975). Many have part-time jobs, and the rest are far too busy to spend long stretches of time closely directing their children's activities. They generally allow, and even encourage, a great deal of childhood exploration, provide a safe environment, set clear limits, and do not always drop whatever they are doing to answer a child's request. Yet they provide a rich educational environment and many bits and pieces of information.

Primarily, the effective care-giver acts as a consultant for the child concerning behavior and as an architect of the child's environment. She (or he) is available to explain a new phenomenon, to provide language for a new experience or object, to reinforce exploration and discovery, to set limits designed to protect the child from physical harm, and to help the child adjust to social requirements. At the same time, the care-giver provides an environment that stimulates and promotes both cognitive growth and physical development. Indeed, some researchers have found that a care-giver's reaction to, and interaction with, the child between the ages of 10 months and 2 years has a dramatic and lasting effect upon the child's cognitive and emotional development throughout childhood (White, 1988).

White's profile presents only one pattern of middle-class American child rearing. It applies some broad American cultural values to the actual behaviors of parents interacting with their children. It is certainly not the only effective style. Nevertheless, this child-rearing pattern has some clear advantages. Children raised this way acquire an active, exploratory learning style. They develop confidence in approaching problems, an understanding of limits, self-reliance, and a feeling of competence in learning about the world around them. These feelings, attitudes, and approaches may affect their learning throughout their lives.

TOILET TRAINING   Although much early research, suggested by Freudian theory, focused upon the methods and effects of toilet training, recent studies view it as a part of a cluster of child-rearing issues. Toilet training is just one aspect of behavior affected by adult attitudes toward both children's explorations and the handling of their own bodies and toward their need for autonomy.

Those who are severe and harsh in toilet training are usually just as strict about other behaviors requiring self-mastery and independence, such as feeding, dressing, and general exploration. Some adults demand that a child have early and total control of bowel and bladder; they regard "accidents" as intolerable and dirty. Such people are likely to be severe when children break a plate, play in the dirt, explore new places and objects, and attempt to feed themselves.

DISCIPLINE   How does a parent or care-giver set limits on a child's behavior? Some, afraid that any kind of control over their children's behavior will prevent creative exploration and independence, helplessly stand by while their 2-year-olds do whatever they please. Discipline, when it comes, is often harsh, reflecting the adults' own feelings of frustration. Others determined not to "spoil" their children, and convinced that 2-year-olds should act like responsible little citizens, set so many limits on behavior that their children, literally, cannot do anything right.

Although it is easy to see the errors in these extremes, it is not quite so simple to provide a set of guidelines that will be effective for every occasion. For example, adults who encourage exploration and manipulation may have to cope, sooner or later, with a child who wants to stick pins into electrical outlets. Obviously, guidelines must be tempered with common sense and must consider children's needs for safety as well as for independence and creative experience. Children permitted to run, jump, and climb can also be taught to walk quietly, to hold someone's hand, or to allow themselves to be carried in public places.

Children who have developed a strong attachment relationship, and whose needs are met through loving interaction with an adult, are neither spoiled by lots of attention nor frightened or threatened by reasonable limits. They are stronger and more confident because they have a trustworthy relationship from which to venture forth into independence.

Development of the Self

At first infants cannot differentiate between themselves and the world around them. Gradually, however, they begin to realize that they are separate and unique beings. Much of infancy is devoted to making this distinction. From 3 to 8 months there is active learning about the infant's body. First, the child discovers his hands, his feet, and some of the things he can do with them. Later, the child acts on the world and sees what happens. At 7 or 8 months, the infant makes a couple of important advancements. He becomes particularly wary of strangers. That means he is quite discriminating of those he knows well and of those he doesn't. He also becomes able to delay his actions, even for just a short time. This allows him the beginnings of a self/other schema. Infants now become more deliberate in their testing and exploring of their own responses and results. Also, by observing the behavior of those around them, infants learn the beginnings of how they should behave. They can imitate. They begin to know what's expected. In the period from 12 to 18 months, the infant is hard at work learning these social expectations and learning what happens when he tests or explores the social world. By the end of this period, he clearly recognizes himself in pictures and in the mirror. Now he is capable of some of the social emotions, like pride or embarrassment. He is ready for more detailed socialization (Lewis & Feinman, 1991). Finally, from 18 to 30 months, the child is developing considerable knowledge about himself with respect

Infants gradually learn that their bodies are separate and uniquely their own—the discovery of a foot gives great pleasure.

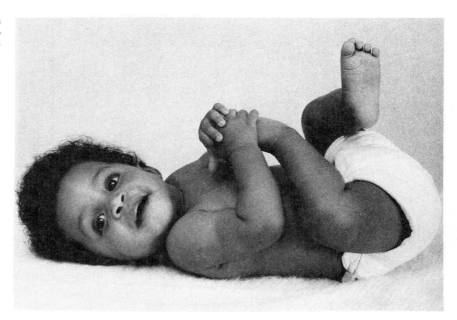

to the social world, about his gender, about his physical features and characteristics, about his goodness and badness, about what he can and cannot do.

At around the age of 21 months an awareness of sex roles has begun to develop (Goldberg & Lewis, 1969). Girls and boys begin to exhibit different behavior. Boys are likely to disengage themselves more dramatically from their mothers, whereas girls demand greater closeness to them and have more ambivalent feelings about being separate. This seems to be linked to the children's awareness of their sexual differences.

By the end of the second year, the child's language has considerable self-reference. Children know their names and use them, often describing their needs and feelings in the third person: "Terri wants water." The words "me" and "mine" assume new importance in the vocabulary. And the concept of ownership is clearly and strongly acted out. Even in families in which sharing is emphasized and ownership is minimized, and in spite of many spontaneous demonstrations of sharing, toddlers show fairly extensive evidence of possessiveness. It may be that they need to establish a concept of ownership in order to round out their definition of self. Sharing and cooperation come more easily once toddlers are confident about what is theirs.

Self-awareness is a result of self-exploration, cognitive maturity, and reflections about self. Toddlers can often be heard talking to and admonishing themselves ("No, Lee, don't touch") and rewarding themselves ("Me good girl!"). They incorporate cultural and social expectations into their reflections, as well as into their behavior, and begin to judge themselves and others in light of these expectations. If they enjoy consistent, loving interaction with the care-giver in an environment that they are free to explore and can begin to control, they learn to make valid predictions about the world around them. Gradually, they establish a perception of themselves—perhaps as acceptable, competent individuals.

STUDY OUTLINE

Attachment and Separation

The first relationship between infant and care-giver lays the foundation for personality development. Psychologists are not sure exactly how this happens, but they find parallels in animal behavior in the form of imprinting or the formation of the attachment bond.

Imprinting and Attachment Behaviors. Researchers disagree about how closely the animal model applies to human attachment. The process seems similar, but the timing may be less critical. Although the first few days of life are important in establishing basic components of the mother-child dialogue, none of these are immune to later influences and changes.

Emotional Development in the First Relationship. The developmental process of human **attachment** begins with an infant's response to a care-giver and matures into active partnership with others. Stanley and Nancy Greenspan describe six milestones in the development of the infant within the first relationship: *self-regulation and interest in the world, falling in love, developing intentional communication, the emergence of an organized sense of self, creating emotional ideas,* and *emotional thinking.*

Stranger Anxiety. A major phase in the process of emotional development is **stranger anxiety,** which generally occurs at about 7 months; it indicates the cognitive ability to detect discrepancies between the familiar care-giver and all others. By the age of 9 months, it may also reflect a learning process based on negative past experience.

Separation and Loss. A secure attachment provides a base that allows a child to explore new people and things. Separation from the care-giver or the presence of a stranger threatens that security. The degree of both separation and stranger anxiety in normal children varies according to the exclusivity and intimacy of the early relationship. When the attachment process has been interrupted, children suffer from impaired personality development, which often results in emotional difficulties.

Patterns of Early Relationships

The Quality of the Relationship. **Mutuality** and **synchrony** are terms describing communication that develops between care-giver and infant. Imitation, in particular, is highly effective in maintaining the infant's interest and attention. Skills that originate in the dialogue between infant and care-giver are later transferred to broader social settings, as illustrated by the spontaneous sharing often observed in toddlers.

The Handicapped Infant. Mutuality can be severely disrupted when a child is handicapped. In infancy, blindness is particularly devastating because of the care-giver's and child's reliance on visual cues. Special counseling is essential to compensate for and overcome such developmental problems.

Bonding Disorders. Care-givers and infants sometimes have trouble establishing a relationship; they experience bonding disorders. Failure-to-thrive infants and abused or neglected infants are products of such relationships.

Fathers, Siblings, and the Family System

Although much of the research in infant development focuses on the relationship between mother and child, most children develop within a social context that allows several early strong attachments, including siblings, grandparents, and others.

Fathers and Fathering. Fathers play an important role in the child's socialization, even during infancy. Infants become as attached to fathers as they do to mothers. The closer the early attachment between father and infant, the more influence the father will have on later socialization. As secondary care-givers, fathers initiate rough, vigorous play. As primary care-givers, they tend to behave more as mothers do, smiling, imitating, and vocalizing with the infant.

The entire family is affected by the birth of an infant. Stress is placed on the marital bond itself, either bringing the couple closer together or disturbing the marriage. The dynamics within the family system will change, with the relationship between parents and between parents and child determined by the quality of the marriage. The introduction of a second child causes further realignment.

Maternal Employment

About one out of every two mothers in the United States today is employed either part or full time. Parents are faced with a severe shortage of adequate day-care facilities. Although early research indicated that good day care could be a strongly positive experience, enhancing both cognitive and social growth, there is a growing concern that entry into day care in the first year of life is a risk factor for child development.

Child Rearing and Personality Development

Child-rearing practices vary greatly from one culture to another and result in distinctly different personality types. Parental attitudes toward feeding, weaning, comfort devices, and toilet training convey fundamental messages to children about their goodness, their ability to depend on themselves, and the nature of their bodies.

Development of the Self. Patterns of handling dependency and autonomy needs have particularly pervasive effects. Basic attitudes about the acceptability of physical closeness, self-stimulation, and dependency are learned very early, and they are followed quickly by beginning attitudes on authority and willfulness. From the sum total of their social experiences and growing cognitive skills, children develop attitudes about themselves.

KEY TERMS AND CONCEPTS

ambivalent	exclusivity	securely attached
attachment	imprinting	self-awareness
autonomy	mutuality	social ecology
avoidant	orienting behavior	stranger anxiety
bonding	protest, despair, and detachment	synchrony
discrepancy hypothesis	responsivity	target stimuli

SELF-TEST QUESTIONS

1. What are attachment behaviors and what is the significance for the relationship between the infant and the care-giver?

2. What is imprinting and when does it take place?

3. List six milestones in the emotional development of the infant within the first relationship.

4. What is stranger anxiety? When and why does it occur?

5. Compare what happens to a child who does not form an attachment relationship, or one whose progress toward attachment is interrupted, with a child who has formed an attachment relationship.

6. How does an exclusive relationship affect the adjustment of the infant?

7. Describe how a responsive environment can affect the development of attachment behavior and emotional development.

8. How did Schaffer define mutuality, or synchrony, and what effect does it have on infant development?

9. Compare and contrast the securely attached infant, the avoidant infant, and the ambivalent infant.

10. How does the handicapped infant influence the attitude of the care-giver?

11. List several bonding disorders.

12. Describe the differences and similarities between father–child interaction and mother–child interaction.

13. What are the negative and positive effects of sibling relationships?

14. What is the grandparent's role in the development of the infant?

15. List some problems faced by mothers who work outside the home.

16. Describe the controversy over early infant day care.

17. List several factors to consider when evaluating a day-care center.

18. Describe some of the child-rearing practices that vary from culture to culture and explain how these different patterns influence later personality development.

SUGGESTED READINGS

ALSTON, F. *Caring for other people's children: A complete guide to family daycare.* Baltimore: University Park Press, 1984. As the title suggests, this handy compendium covers numerous aspects of infant and young child development, activity planning, parent relations, laws and regulations, and more.

BOWLBY, J. *A secure base: Parent–child attachment and healthy human development.* New York: Basic Books, 1988. Bowlby's latest integration of his influential theory presented in a very readable style.

BRAZELTON, T. B. *Toddlers and parents: A declaration of independence.* New York: Delacorte, 1974. A colorful description of the phases of development during the second year. Contains suggestions to parents on how to manage their children's behavior.

LAMB, M. E. *The father's role: Cross-cultural perspectives.* Hillsdale, NJ: Erlbaum, 1987. Descriptions of the role of fathers in diverse cultures. English fathers, Chinese fathers, pygmy fathers, and many others are covered.

PARKE, R. *Fathers.* Cambridge, MA: Harvard University Press, 1981. Based on solid research, Parke presents the many roles of fathers and their importance with respect to childbirth, infant development, and several aspects of child development.

SPOCK, B., & ROTHENBERG, M. B. *Baby and child care.* New York: Simon & Schuster Pocket Books, 1985. Spock, now in his mid-80s, has thoroughly revised (with the aid of a coauthor) his classic guide to reflect the changing medical practices and cultural shifts of the 1980s.

ZIGLER, E. F., & LANG, M. E. *Child-care choices: Balancing the needs of children, families, and society.* New York: Free Press, 1991. A thorough overview of children's needs and a comprehensive look at current available child-care options, in light of today's economic and social realities.

Chapter 8

*Every vital development
in language
is a development
of feeling as well.*

T. S. ELIOT
"PHILIP MASSINGER"

Language:
The Bridge from Infancy

JASON: Maria broke the toy, didn't she?

MOTHER: Yes, dear. She did.

JASON: I don't break toys. I'm a good boy, amn't I?

MOTHER: I'm a good boy, *aren't* I?

JASON: Nah, You're a *girl!*

E ven newborn infants can communicate. It doesn't take long for them to discover how to let their parents know that they are hungry, wet, or bored. By about 1 year of age, most children begin to talk; by 4½, most have developed amazing verbal competence. Their vocabulary may be limited and their grammar far from perfect, but their implicit grasp of language structure is remarkable. They not only know the words with which to designate things and communicate thoughts, but they also exhibit a very sophisticated understanding of the rules that govern the combinations and uses of these words. They speak in full sentences with phrases, clauses, and appropriate grammatical constructions, such as proper tenses and plural forms. This is a startling cognitive achievement when we think of the enormous complexity of the underlying rules of syntax and semantics. Language is an elaborate system of symbols. To manipulate the symbols properly, a child must first master basic cognitive concepts.

The complexity and originality of the 4½-year-old's speech are perhaps best illustrated by the *tag question,* which is a direct statement followed by a tag, or request to confirm the statement: "Maria broke the toy, didn't she?" This apparently simple question actually involves a number of grammatical processes. In order to form the tag "didn't she," Jason had to understand several different rules. He had to know how to copy, or supply, the correct subject pronoun for "Maria," how to supply the auxiliary verb (the proper form of "do"), how to negate the auxiliary verb, and how to invert the word order of the auxiliary verb and pronoun. Somewhat younger children may have the general idea of the tag question but may not yet be able to master all of the grammatical processes. Thus, they might say, "Maria broke the toy, unh?"

Language development is more than a purely cognitive achievement, however. It also involves social growth. Children must learn a specific language, with all of its cultural ramifications. While they learn syntax and vocabulary, children also absorb social values, such as politeness, obedience, and gender roles. Therefore, language acquisition involves both cognitive and social development; it

CHAPTER OBJECTIVES

By the time you have finished this chapter, you should be able to do the following:

■ List three major dimensions of language.

■ Describe four components of language learning.

■ Discuss the sequence of language development in a young child.

■ Discuss the influence that care-givers have on their children's language development.

■ Discuss the cultural and social values that children assimilate in language development.

■ Discuss the problems raised by ethnic differences in language.

content The meaning of any written or spoken message.

form The particular symbol used to represent content.

use The way in which a speaker employs language to give it one meaning as opposed to another.

is a bridge between infancy and childhood. When children can understand and communicate their wants, needs, and observations, the world deals with them in quite a different fashion.

LANGUAGE DEVELOPMENT

The acquisition of language is a complex yet natural process. Perhaps better than any other single accomplishment, it illustrates the range and potential of the human organism. For this reason, it is a particularly fascinating area of psychological development. To understand this phenomenon fully, we should first be aware of some of its most basic elements.

Aspects of Language

We often think of language as having three major dimensions: content, form, and use (Bloom & Lahey, 1978). **Content** refers to the meaning of any written or spoken message. **Form** is the particular symbol used to represent that content—the sounds, the words, the grammar. **Use** refers to the social interchange, or exchange, between two people: the speaker and the person spoken to. The details of that social exchange depend on the situation, the relationship between the speaker and the listener, and on the intentions and attitudes of the two participants. In the example at the beginning of this chapter, Jason is talking about who broke the toy (content). He is using a particularly sophisticated grammatical form—a tag question. Jason is concerned about getting reassurance from his mother that he is

Expressing feelings and establishing and maintaining contact with others are just some of the uses of speech.

a good boy, whereas his mother is interested in correcting his grammar. In this simple exchange, a great deal has been communicated. The information is conveyed in a particular form, in a fashion that reflects the relationship and intention of both participants. The form and the use, therefore, also contribute to the meaning of the message.

Form can be examined on three levels. **Phonemes** are the basic sounds—the vowels and the consonants—that combine to form words. **Morphemes** are the meaning units—the basic words, prefixes, and suffixes. The sentence "Mommy warmed the bottles" can be divided into six morphemes: *Mommy, warm, ed, the, bottle,* and *s.* Finally, every language has a grammar—a complicated set of rules for building words **(morphology),** as well as rules for combining words to form phrases and sentences **(syntax).** In English, however, grammar is primarily concerned with syntax, and the two terms are often used interchangeably. It should be noted that aspects of form also convey meaning. "The dog bit the baby" is different from "The baby bit the dog," simply because of word order. Such distinctions are learned at a very early age.

The social use of language is complex. Children learn to be polite and deferential to their elders, to simplify their language for babies, to take turns when they are involved in a conversation, and to understand indirect as well as direct speech. They learn to determine the speaker's intention as well as to understand the actual words. For example, a sentence such as "What is this?" can have different meanings, depending on the situation. It can serve as a simple request for information, but it also can be an expression of horror.

We use speech for a number of purposes. We use it to satisfy wants and needs; to control others; to maintain contact with other people; to express feelings; to imagine, pretend, or create; and to inquire and describe (Halliday, 1973). Young children are exposed to and implicitly learn these functions of language, as well as specific words and forms.

phonemes The smallest units of sound—vowels and consonants—that combine to form morphemes and words.

morphemes The minimal units of meaning in language that form basic words, prefixes, and suffixes.

morphology The set of rules for building words that is present in all languages.

syntax The rules for combining words to form phrases and sentences.

The Processes of Language Learning

Just how do humans progress from crying to babbling to speaking the infinite forms of adult language? In recent years, a great deal of research has been devoted to this question, both for its own sake and for the insight an answer might give into other areas of learning. There has been much controversy as to precisely how the process works, but it is possible to highlight four components: imitation, reinforcement, innate language structure, and cognitive development. All four components are probably part of the process.

IMITATION   Imitation plays a large part in language learning. Children's first words—usually simple labels—are obviously learned by hearing and imitating. In fact, most early vocabulary must be learned in this way; children cannot invent words and make themselves understood. But the development of syntax is not so easily explained. No doubt some phrases result from imitation, but a form such as "amn't I" is clearly original. It is unlikely that children have heard anyone speak this way. Even when people use baby talk or attempt to correct children's errors, the children tend to adhere to their own consistent speech patterns, for which there are no immediate models.

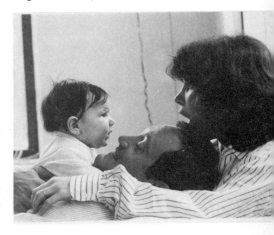

Imitation plays an important part in language learning, particularly in the early stages of development.

REINFORCEMENT   As we have seen in previous chapters, reinforcement is a powerful learning device, and this probably holds true for certain aspects of language acquisition. Certainly, children are influenced by reactions to their speech. Smiles, hugs, and increased attention will encourage learning to some extent. Also, when words produce favorable results, children are likely to repeat them. If an infant calls "Mommy" and she comes or if he says "Cookie" and gets one, he will use these words again. But reinforcement does not seem sufficient to explain the acquisition of syntax. As we know, much of children's speech is original and has never been reinforced. Even if some forms are encouraged and others discouraged, it simply would not be possible to reinforce all correct forms and extinguish all incorrect ones. Also, especially when children first begin to talk, adults tend to reinforce any speech at all, however unintelligible or incorrect. Even when they are more discriminating, they are likely to respond to content instead of form. If a child says, "I eated my peas," her parents will probably praise her—unless the statement is not true, in which case they will no doubt call her attention to the vegetables remaining on her plate.

INNATE LANGUAGE STRUCTURE   Linguist Noam Chomsky (1959) drew attention to the limitations of reinforcement theory. He believes that every human being is born with a mental structure for acquiring language. This language acquisition device (LAD) enables children to process linguistic data selectively

"What's the big surprise? All the latest theories of linguistics say we're born with the innate capacity for generating sentences."

from their environment and to formulate a generative grammar, from which they create language. Thus, when children hear people talk, they unconsciously induce rules and form their own language according to these rules. This process follows a developmental sequence; children can assimilate certain data before others. But according to Chomsky, at least some of the basics of language are preprogrammed into the human organism.

In order to show that innate language abilities exist, researchers have examined deaf children's ability to develop spontaneous systems of languagelike gestures (Goldin-Meadow & Mylander, 1984). They have also studied children's abilities to link specific ideas with specific words (Gleitman & Wanner, 1982). The theory of innate language structure helps to explain the ability of all peoples to create and transmit language and the natural responsiveness of infants to learn to speak. It takes into account the incredible complexity of human language and points out the inadequacy of simple imitation and reinforcement theories.

COGNITIVE DEVELOPMENT   The fourth major approach to language acquisition emphasizes the link between language learning and a child's developing concepts and relationships. This view is supported by the fact that basic grammatical structures are not present in earliest speech but develop progressively, leading theorists to conclude that they depend on prior cognitive development (Bloom, 1970). Thus, a particular speech pattern will not emerge before the child has grasped the concept behind it. Between the ages of 1 and 4½, children are actively constructing their own grammar, gradually approaching the full grammar of the adults around them. At any given time, however, children are capable of expressing only those concepts that they have mastered.

There are many parallels between cognitive development and language development. About the time that the child is acquiring object permanence and is interested in games of hiding and finding objects, his beginning language reflects these cognitive processes with words like "see," "all gone," or "more?" and "bye-bye." Comings and goings and hidings and findings become the focus of language and of vocabulary. A little later, when children are fascinated with possession and with what is theirs and what is someone else's, this, too, is reflected in their language development. They are, at about this time, learning aspects of syntax that reflect the possessive case—"Daddy sock," "baby bed," and later, "mine," and "Mommy's cup."

Which comes first, the understanding of concepts or the language to express them? Piaget (1962) theorized that the ability to conceptualize an idea precedes the ability to express it in words. Others have observed that very soon after a child begins to understand relationships such as "bigger" or "more than," words help shape and sharpen and transform conceptual thinking (Vygotsky, 1962; Bruner, 1983). Recent research indicates that the development of language and cognition may go hand in hand. For instance, words expressing concepts may be used productively and symbolically before children solve conceptual problems about how to compare and relate objects. These words are used mainly to categorize objects. Along with the development of the cognitive abilities to comprehend relationships between things, more relational words emerge (Gopnik, 1988). Generally, by the time children begin elementary school, their language and problem-solving skills have been integrated, enabling them to understand and interact with other people in many situations.

receptive language The repertoire of words and commands that a child understands, although he or she may not be able to say them.

productive language The spoken or written communication of preschool children.

LANGUAGE BEGINNINGS

During the preschool years, there are two key processes involved in language development. **Receptive language** is a child's understanding of the spoken or the written word. **Productive language** is what the child says or, later, what the child writes. These interrelated processes evolve simultaneously. Often, receptive language, or language comprehension, develops a little bit ahead of language production.

FOCUS ON AN ISSUE

WHY DO CHILDREN TALK TO THEMSELVES?

Josh is alone in his room playing a game in which he tries to fit pieces into a puzzleboard. If we look in on him, we might overhear Josh say to himself, "This piece doesn't fit. Where's a round one? No, it doesn't. It's too big. This one is small. . . ." Children between the ages of 4 and 8 have been observed directing their talk to themselves about 20% of the time in school environments that permit it (Berk, 1985). This is a high percentage. Why do they do so?

Psychologists call talking aloud to oneself *private speech*. All people, young and old, talk to themselves. But, unlike adults, young children do so in public situations, such as at school or in a playground. They also talk to themselves far more often than adults do. Some of the early observations of private speech among preschool children were made by Jean Piaget. He suggested that the private speech of young children indicated their immaturity. Social speech was more difficult because it required consideration of the listener's perspective. He called this talking to oneself *egocentric speech* (Piaget, 1926).

Piaget's observation stimulated other researchers to record the way children use social language and private speech. Early findings tended to raise questions about Piaget's explanation. Observers found that the amount of private speech varied a great deal depending on the situation, but even the youngest children used far more social speech to communicate and exchange ideas with others than they used private speech. Perhaps, private speech served a distinct and separate purpose.

A Russian observer suggested that private speech often mirrored adult social speech and served to help in the development of inner thought and self-direction. When observing children engaged in private activity, researchers have found three stages in the development of the children's private speech. In its earliest stage, private speech occurs after an action—"I made a big one." At the second stage, talking to oneself accompanies an action—"It's getting darker and darker with lots of paint." Later, in the third stage, it precedes an action—"I want to make a scary picture with dark paint." Private speech in each of these stages seems to serve the purpose of controlling or guiding a child's behavior in performing a task. The progression corresponds, researchers believe, to the developing thought process in a child's mind. At the final stage, when speech comes before behavior, the child is planning a course of action. The changes in private speech from stage 1 to stage 3 illustrate the development of thought processes in guiding one's behavior and its accompanying linguistic development. The child's use of language progresses from simply mirroring adult speech in stage 1 to internally structuring one's behavior in stage 3.

Many studies have supported the idea that the function of private speech is to guide the child in the performance of a task. However, some studies have failed to show a connection between private speech and the development of performance abilities. These studies were done in traditional school environments where children were not encouraged to integrate private speech with their activities. Later research has shown that when children are given verbal tasks and encouraged to speak, they talk to themselves quite a bit (Frauenglass & Diaz, 1985). Other researchers have found that children in

Before the First Words

The production of language begins with an undifferentiated cry at the moment of birth. Soon after, infants develop a range of different cries and, by about 6 weeks, a variety of cooing sounds. At the time of birth, infants have developed a large area in the left hemisphere of the brain (the hemisphere that controls language) that allows them to listen to and respond to language from the very beginning (Brooks & Obrzut, 1981). By the second or third month, infants

Often, young children talk out loud while they work or play. Sometimes the talk is pretend dialogue, but more often it fulfills other functions.

comfortable school environments tend to accompany academic tasks with private speech if adults are not present.

Numerous researchers have reported an apparent relationship between intelligence and the amount and quality of children's use of private speech. It seems that the brighter the child, the more private speech is used and the more mature is its content. Talking aloud to oneself seems to follow a curve. It increases at first as the child develops self-control, peaks at age 4 or 5, and then diminishes drastically by age 8 (Diaz & Lowe, 1987). The private speech of bright children seems to peak at an earlier age than it does with average children (Berk, 1986).

Further research has confirmed that there are connections between private speech, behavior, and thought. As children grow older and their speech is internalized, they become quieter and pay more attention to their tasks. This suggests that, as private talk is internalized, behavior is brought under the control of thought. There is now evidence indicating that talking to oneself is related to the quality of performance, especially among brighter children. Impulsive primary school children who have difficulty with self-control and persistence can even be helped by training them to use self-directed verbal commands to regulate their own behavior (Diaz & Lowe, 1987).

Learning to think and self-guidance are not the only functions of private speech. For example, children seem to talk to themselves as a means of playing and relaxing, expressing feelings, and absorbing emotions and ideas. Young children take great pleasure in word play, which is an important means of learning language. Children tell themselves fantasies or speak to an imaginary playmate or talk to inanimate objects (Berk, 1985). Private speech is thus a way of expressing one's feelings, of gaining understanding of one's environment, and of developing language, as well as being a tool for developing self-control and inner thought.

FOCUS ON AN ISSUE

MUST ONE BE HUMAN TO LEARN LANGUAGE?

Are humans the only animals capable of using language to express simple and complex thoughts? During the past two decades, a number of chimpanzees and apes have been able to learn at least the rudiments of human communication. Chimps have been able to associate names with objects, put two words together, and use words in a new context. These are definitely aspects of human language that are seen in developing humans. But chimps have been unable to master the complex use of words and grammar that is an essential part of language.

Chimps have limited control of their vocal tract, which makes speech impossible. Researchers made their first breakthrough in teaching human language to chimps when they moved from vocal speech to other forms, such as the manual sign language used by deaf human children. After quickly learning the signs for 200 or more nouns, including concrete nouns for the food, people, and things around them, action verbs, and significant adjectives like "big" and "sweet," the chimps extended the use of many of these signs to new referents they had never directly learned. Washoe, the first chimpanzee to learn sign language, initially learned the sign for "hurt" in connection with scratches and bruises. When she saw a person's naval for the first time, she signed "hurt." She used the same sign for a decal on the back of a person's hand (Klima & Bellugi, 1973).

Within months of the time their training began, the chimps started to combine signs to express specific thoughts. For example, when Washoe heard the sound of a barking dog, she combined the signs for "listen" and "dog." When she wanted the person with her to continue tickling her, she signed "more" and "tickle," and when she saw a duck she signed "water-bird." And a gorilla named Koko invented the following new words: "finger bracelet" for ring, "eye hat" for mask, and "elephant baby" for a Pinocchio doll (Hayes, 1977).

To test the logical and grammatical abilities of chimps, the trainers of chimp Sarah took a different approach. Sarah learned to associate magnetized pieces of plastic in various colors and shapes with the objects, people, and actions around her and to express her thoughts on a metal board. She learned to use plastic symbols that had no resemblance to the objects they represented (for instance, △ is the symbol for pear) and to understand the rudiments of grammar, which enabled her to respond to sentence organization. When tested, Sarah correctly understood such complex sentences as, "Sarah banana pail and cracker dish insert" (Sarah put the banana in the pail and cracker dish) 8 out of 10 times. In addition, her ability to form sentences she had never seen before indicated substantial cognitive ability (de Villiers & de Villiers, 1979).

Chimps appear to have the capacity to use symbols to represent objects and events and to communicate their insights. But there is considerable debate as to what this indicates about the chimp's cognitive processes and to what extent this use of symbols resembles a human infant's learning of language. Noted linguist Noam Chomsky (1976) points to the fact that there is a vast difference between the language learning of humans and the rudimentary responses of chimps. Chimps, says Chomsky, never learn the subtleties of word order nor do they ever use language in a creative, spontaneous way. It has also been argued that although apes can be trained to produce behaviors that have some of the properties of human linguistic behavior, they do not have the inner motivation for language that a child does. Therefore, the communication of the chimp and the child differ profoundly (Sugarman, 1983).

Other psycholinguists argue that there are no significant differences between young children's use of words and a trained chimp's use. Researchers at the Yerkes Primate Center found that Pygmy monkeys spontaneously learned to relate symbols and objects, presumably exhibiting abilities for abstract thought (Savage-Rumbaugh, Rumbaugh, & McDonald, 1986).

The debate involves more than the potential of chimpanzees and other apes to conceptualize and communicate. It also involves our inability to know what the chimps are really thinking when they use words and combinations of words. We can only interpret the chimps' use of the symbols to which they are painstakingly exposed by dedicated researchers. To some extent, the same problem exists with our understanding of how human infants learn language. What is the thought process that results in a human infant's early speech? As embodiments of the mysteries of language development, the chimp and the human child are indeed akin.

are sensitive to speech and can distinguish between such similar sounds as *b* and *p* or *d* and *t* (Eimas, 1974). In the first year of life, then, long before the first words are spoken, infants are able to learn a great deal about language.

SOCIAL COMMUNICATION As we learned in Chapters 6 and 7, throughout the first year, infants have been learning nonverbal aspects of communication in the "mutual dialogue" between parent and infant. They have been learning to signal, to take turns, to use gestures, and to pay attention to facial expressions. Infants learn a lot about communication while playing simple games like peekaboo (Ross & Lollis, 1987). Indeed, some parents are very skillful at structuring social games with their infants that help them learn many aspects of the conversation in a most enjoyable fashion. Parents who do this well provide a structure for the game, or a scaffolding, that helps the child learn the rules of give and take and turn-taking (Bruner, 1983). But the social communication with the infant goes far beyond parent games. Certainly, by 1 year of age, most healthy infants are quite alert to the people around them, including strangers, and they respond appropriately to the varied emotional expressions of adults (Klinnert et al., 1986).

BABBLING From the earliest moments, infants explore a variety of sounds. Often, they start with vowel sounds and front-of-the-mouth consonants: "Ahh, bahh, bahh, bahh." By 6 months, infants have a much more varied and complex repertoire. They string together a wide range of sounds, draw them out, cut them off, and vary the pitch and rhythm. Increasingly, they seem to exert control over these vocalizations. They purposefully repeat sounds, elongate them, and pause in a kind of self-imitating pseudo talk, sometimes called **iteration.**

Early vocalizations involve only a few different sounds, or phonemes. But, by the second month, infants are forming a number of consonant sounds as well as clicks, gurgles, grunts, and other sounds, some of which are outside the range of the parents' native language. Although the number of phonemes expands rapidly during the first year, toward the end of that period phoneme production slows down.

Sometime after 6 months, many parents hear something suspiciously like "ma-ma" or "da-da" and report this as their precocious infants' first words. Usually, however, these are chance repetitions of sounds that have no real meaning. Around this time, babbling takes on inflections and patterns very much like those of the parents' language. In fact, the babbling begins to sound so much like adult speech that parents may strain to listen, thinking that perhaps it is coherent language. This highly developed babbling is what Arnold Gesell has termed **expressive jargon.** Such patterns of babbling appear to be the same for infants in all language groups (Roug, Landberg, & Lundberg, 1989).

Just how important is babbling? In what ways does babbling prepare a baby for speaking? A baby's babbling is an irresistible form of verbal communication, and care-givers throughout the world delight in imitating and encouraging these vocalizations. It appears that in the course of babbling, babies are learning how to produce the sounds that will later be used in speaking. Thus, the sounds or phonemes that babies produce are influenced by what they hear before they use words. Although babbling is a means for babies to communicate and interact with other people, it is also a problem-solving activity. Babies babble as a way to figure out how to make the specific sounds needed to say words. This may be why babies do not stop babbling when they begin producing words. In fact, new words seem

iteration Infants' purposeful repetition, elongation, and pause in sounds that imitate speech.

expressive jargon A term used to describe the babbling of an infant when the infant uses inflections and patterns that mimic adult speech.

Before the first words are spoken, infants learn a great deal about language.

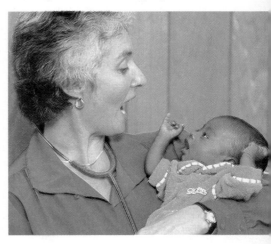

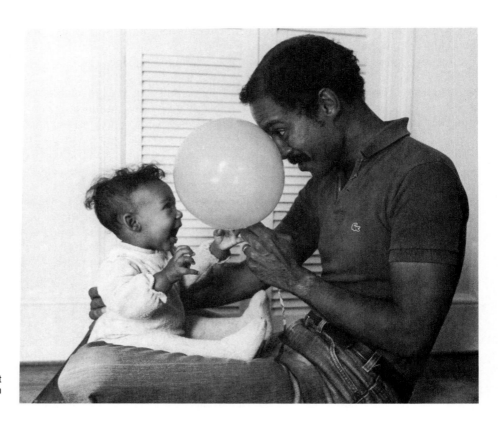

Babbling between care-giver and infant can be a pleasurable experience for both participants.

to influence babbling, while babbling in turn affects the preferred sounds babies use in selecting new words (Elbers & Ton, 1985).

Comparisons of the babbling of hearing babies and deaf babies also indicate how important what the baby hears is for the child's language development, even at the babbling stage. Although the babbling of groups of hearing babies and deaf babies was initially comparable, only the babbling of the hearing infants moved closer to the sounds of words used in their language (Oller & Eilers, 1988).

Babbling appears to play a key role in babies' learning to use the specific sounds needed to speak the language of their care-givers. For example, when the babbling of 10-month-old infants in Paris, London, Hong Kong, and Algiers was analyzed, researchers discovered that differences in how these infants pronounced vowel sounds paralleled the vowel sound pronunciations found in their native languages—French, English, Cantonese, and Arabic (de-Boysson-Bardies, 1989).

What if a baby's babbling is atypical? In specific cases, atypical babbling has been associated with delays in beginning to speak (Stoel-Gammon, 1989). However, there is still much to be learned about the role of babbling in both normal and problematic speech development.

In all cultures, some children develop a fairly extensive vocabulary of *pseudo words*. They use a particular range of specific vocalizations, usually paired with gestures, that have specific meanings (Reich, 1986).

RECEPTIVE VOCABULARY Care-givers and researchers generally agree that very young children understand words before they can say them. Infants as young as 1 year are able to follow some directions from adults, and show by their behavior that they know the meaning of words like "bye-bye." Infants' comprehension of speech, however, is a very difficult area for psychologists and linguists to study. Although it is relatively easy to listen to children speak and to record them, it is much more difficult to identify and describe concepts that very young children associate with particular words. Even when the evidence seems clear—for example, when a 1-year-old follows the instruction "Put the spoon in the cup"—the child's understanding may be nowhere near as complete as we conclude. It is, after all, hard to put the cup in the spoon. Also, children may receive clues, such as gestures, that help them to perform tasks correctly. Parents of very young children often say that their children understand far more words at home, in familiar surroundings, than in unfamiliar testing rooms. Although this may be true, it is also true that parents use gestures and context clues to help convey their message. Parents, too, will frequently accept vague signals as evidence that their children understand instructions.

First Words

Most children utter their first words around the end of the first year. They then add single words, slowly at first, and much more rapidly by the middle of the second year. As children approach age 2, single words give way to two-word, and then three-word, sentences.

There is wide individual variation in the rate at which language learning progresses. Toddlers who seem to be progressing rather slowly in this area are not

How much does the infant understand of the words or the gestures? It is difficult to know.

holophrastic speech In the early stages of language acquisition, the young child's use of single words, perhaps to convey full sentences.

necessarily developmentally delayed; they may be busy with other tasks. Some children start late but catch up quickly; others seem stuck at particular stages for long periods of time. Regardless of the pace of language learning, the sequence of language development follows a regular and predictable pattern. This pattern appears not only in English but in every language. Analysis of language acquisition in many countries has revealed remarkably consistent patterns (Slobin, 1972).

EARLY WORDS AND MEANINGS   Throughout the world, infants' first utterances are single words—most often nouns and usually names of the people, things, or animals in the immediate environment. In the beginning, children simply do not have the ability to use words in combinations. Some psycholinguists feel that despite this restriction in language production, children can conceive full sentences and that their early utterances are actually **holophrastic speech**—single words meant to convey complex ideas. Thus, in different contexts, with different intonations and gestures, *"mama"* may mean "I want my mother" or "Mama, tie my shoe" or "There she is, my mama." Other psycholinguists warn against overinterpreting brief utterances.

What words form an infant's early vocabulary? Because the care-givers of each infant use different words and because the process of development is individual, the vocabularies learned by infants differ. But the types of words first used by infants fall into categories. Names—that is, nouns that refer to specific things, such as "dada," "bottie," and "car"—comprise much of a child's early vocabulary (Nelson, 1974). However, children at the one-word stage also use words that indicate function or relationship, such as "there," "no," "gone," and "up," possibly even before they use nouns (Bloom, Lifter, & Broughton, 1985). The individual words and category of words a child uses most may depend on the child's personal speech style. Nelson (1981) identified children with a *referential* style who tended to use nouns, and *expressive* children who learned more active verbs and pronouns.

Early speech grows out of the prelinguistic gestures that every baby uses to communicate (Gopnik, 1988). A child's first words appear to be social in nature. The child speaks in order to influence other people; she wants her mother's attention, to eat a cookie instead of an apple, or to indicate that she will not sit down in her bath. Later, in the one-word stage, when the child's abilities to think and to remember are more developed, the same types of words have been found to express intrapersonal thoughts and ideas (Gopnik & Meltzoff, 1987).

OVEREXTENSIONS AND UNDEREXTENSIONS   When a child first uses a word, it usually refers to a particular person, object, or situation. The word "Goggy" may apply to a child's own pet. The child may then use it when naming other dogs, or other four-legged animals. But when this child learns new words such as "horsie" or "kitty" she will redefine all of the animal categories she had previously learned (Schlesinger, 1982). This is an example of *overextending* a word. Children tend to overextend, underextend, or overlap the categories they use to determine what words refer to, because they often do not share adults' knowledge of culturally appropriate functions and characteristics of objects. Instead, they may emphasize aspects of objects that adults have come to ignore when categorizing objects (Mervis, 1987). Some interesting examples of overextensions used by children are given in Table 8–1.

As children learn additional contrasting names for objects, such as kitty, cat,

TABLE 8–1

The Overextension of Words

Children may apply a word to many objects with common properties or functions.

CHILD'S WORD	FIRST REFERENT	EXTENSIONS	POSSIBLE COMMON PROPERTY
Bird	Sparrows	Cows, dogs, cats, any moving animal	Movement
Mooi	Moon	Cakes, round marks on window, round shapes in books, tooling on leather book covers, postmarks, letter O	Shape
Fly	Fly	Specks of dirt, dust, all small insects, his own toes, crumbs, small toad	Size
Koko	Cockerel crowing	Tunes played on a violin, piano, accordion, phonograph, all music, merry-go-round	Sound
Wau-wau	Dogs	All animals, toy dog, soft slippers, picture of old man in furs	Texture

Source: From *Early Language* by Peter A. deVilliers and Jill G. deVilliers (Cambridge, Mass.: Harvard University Press, 1979), p. 32. Reprinted by permission of Harvard University Press and William Collins Sons and Co., Ltd.

lion, and tiger, they reassign words to more specific and increasingly hierarchical categories (Clark, 1987; Merriman, 1987). In other words, a lion and a tiger are different. They are both examples of the more general "cat" category. Over time, the child's linguistic categories take on the language use structure of the adults in that linguistic culture. The process of categorizing language appears to follow the same general pattern as that of intellectual, or cognitive, development (Chapman & Mervis, 1989).

Children's words and their meanings are closely linked to the concepts the children are developing. A child who applies the word "moon" to everything round has some concept of *round*. But which comes first—the word and its meaning or the concept? Researchers differ on their interpretation of the evidence. Some, including Piaget, believe that most of the time the concept forms first. The child discovers a concept and then finds a name to attach to it, whether learned or of her own creation. Evidence for this theory includes the finding that twins have been known to create their own private language, and deaf children create signs or gestures even when they are not taught sign language. This would suggest that concepts come first and words afterward (Clark, 1983). Other researchers believe that words help shape our concepts. When a young child names the family pet "dog," he is simply naming that object. When he extends and refines his categories, he is learning the concept of "dog" (Schlesinger, 1982). In fact, both processes are probably true, and serve to complement each other as the child learns language.

Two-Word Sentences

Toward the end of the second year, most children begin to put words together. Often, the first attempts are simply two words that represent two ideas: "Mommy see," "Sock off," or "More milk." This is a fascinating period in language

telegraphic speech One- and 2-year-olds' utterances that omit the less significant words and include the words that carry the most meaning.

pivot grammar A two-word sentence-forming system used by 2-year-olds and involving action words, prepositions, or possessives (pivot words) in combination with x-words, which are usually nouns.

case grammar The use of word order to express different relationships.

development because implicit rules of syntax appear. In recent years, psycholinguists have studied the development of language production by recording and analyzing lengthy samples of children's speech, collected at daily or weekly intervals. Valuable insights have been gained about such features as sentence length, the kinds of grammatical rules used, and the types of meanings expressed by children at any given stage.

TELEGRAPHIC SPEECH When children start putting words together, their sentences seem to be sharply limited in length. At first, they seem restricted to two elements, then three, and so on. At each stage, the number of words or thoughts in a sentence is limited—children retain high-information words and omit the less significant ones. The result is what Brown (1965) calls **telegraphic speech.** The informative words, which Brown terms *contentives,* are the nouns, verbs, and adjectives. The less important words are known as *functors,* and are the inflections, auxiliary verbs, and prepositions.

When children first put two words together, they do it in a consistent fashion. They may say "See dog" or "See truck" as they point at things. But they never say "Truck, see." Even in the two-word sentence we can find certain consistencies. What sort of grammar is being used? A number of models have been identified.

PIVOT GRAMMAR   Among the first significant grammatical analyses was the study by Braine (1963), which identified a **pivot grammar** at the two-word phase. *Pivot words* are usually action words (go), prepositions (off), or possessives (my). They are few in number and occur frequently in combination with *x-words,* or open words, which are usually nouns. "See," for example, is a pivot word that can combine with any number of open words to form two-word sentences: "See milk," "See Mommy," or "Mommy see." Pivot words almost never occur alone or with other pivots (McNeill, 1972). X-words may, however, be paired or used singly. These prohibitions and combinations are not random, but result from children's limited comprehension and production of language. The length restriction is apparently the main barrier to their expression of complex grammatical notions in more adult-sounding forms.

CASE GRAMMAR   Children seem able to express a number of relationships by word order: agent (who did it), patient (to whom), instrument (with what), location (where), and so forth (Fillmore, 1968). They are expressing a **case grammar.** Because of the variety of relationships that a two-word sentence can be used to express, the child's utterance must be interpreted in context. Lois Bloom (1970) noted that a child she was studying said "Mommy sock" one time to indicate that her mother was putting on a sock and another time to communicate that she had found her mother's sock.

With the help of gestures, tone, and context, children can communicate numerous meanings with a small vocabulary and limited syntax. Dan Slobin (1972) studied the variety of meanings conveyed by two-word sentences spoken by 2-year-olds. Although his young conversants were from different linguistic cultures, speaking English, German, Russian, Turkish, or Samoan, the children used speech in the same ways. Among the concepts that the 2-year-olds were able to communicate by two-word utterances were:

Identification: See doggie.
Location: Book there.
Nonexistence: Allgone thing.
Negation: Not wolf.
Possession: My candy
Attribution: Big car.
Agent-action: Mama walk.
Action-location: Sit chair.
Action-direct object: Hit you.
Action-indirect object: Give papa.
Action-instrument: Cut knife.
Question: Where ball?

mean length of utterance (MLU)
The average length of the sentences that a child produces.

inflections   Changes in form that words undergo to designate number, gender, tense, mood, and case.

LANGUAGE COMPLEXITIES

Throughout the preschool years, children are rapidly expanding their vocabularies, their use of grammatical forms, and their understanding of language as a social act. We can only look at a sampling of these many accomplishments.

An Expanding Grammar

One of the more influential works in the study of language acquisition was written by Roger Brown (1973). Brown and his colleagues recorded at length the speech patterns of three young children—Adam, Eve, and Sarah. Taking a developmental approach, Brown identified five *distinct, increasingly complex stages.* He views development in terms of **mean length of utterance (MLU)**—the average length of the sentence that the child produces—instead of age, because children learn at very different rates. Eve, for example, progressed nearly twice as fast as Adam and Sarah. Yet, the sequence is the same for all children. Certain skills and rules are apparently mastered before others, and certain errors are peculiar to particular stages.

Stage 1.   The first stage is characterized by two-word utterances, which we have discussed. This is the period in which telegraphic speech and pivot and open words first emerge. Brown, however, goes beyond that structure to focus on the meaning that children are attempting to convey with word order and position— the concepts of existence, disappearance, and recurrence, and of possession, agency, and attribution.

Stage 2.   This stage of language acquisition is characterized by utterances slightly longer than two words. In addition to learning prepositions, articles, and case markers, children begin to generalize the rules of **inflections** to words they already know. Children at this stage are able to form the regular past tense of many verbs such as "play/played," and the regular plurals of many nouns. To determine whether children have reached a more complex language stage and are not just relying on memory, Berko (1958) devised a test using nonsense words (see Figure 8–1). For instance, "This is a wug. Now there is another one. There are two of them. There are two _____." The subjects had to supply the correct inflection by generalizing what they knew about plurals. The tests, which have since been given

overregularization The generalization of complex language principles, typically by preschool children rapidly expanding their vocabularies.

to children even younger than Berko's preschool and first-grade subjects, reveal a surprising grasp of rules for conjugating verbs and forming plurals and possessives. In fact, children often overgeneralize. In spite of the fact that they may have already learned the forms of some irregular verbs, such as "go/went/gone," children produce words like "goed." They are applying the rule for forming the regular past tense to every verb. Although technically an error, such usages demonstrate children's extraordinary ability to generalize a complex language principle. This is called **overregularization.**

Stage 3. In the third stage, children learn to modify simple sentences. They create negative and imperative forms, ask yes-no questions, and depart in other ways from the simple statements of earlier stages. The negative form is an excellent example of how complex language learning can be. It also reveals children's ability to create original forms without depending on a model. The concepts for using negatives seem to exist quite early—long before the third stage. At first, children negate by putting the negative word at the beginning of an utterance; they express concepts such as nonexistence ("no pocket"), rejection ("no more"), and denial ("no dirty"), but cannot use auxiliary verbs or imbed a negative form within a sentence. By stage three, however, children easily say such sentences as "Paul didn't laugh" and "Jeannie won't let go" (Klima & Bellugi, 1966). In fact, they often use double and triple negatives, throwing them in wherever possible to emphasize a point.

Children also begin to learn the use of active and passive voice during the third stage. Bellugi, Brown, and Fraser (1970) developed a test of children's understanding of these forms. They gave their subjects stuffed animals and asked them to act out "The cat chases the dog" and "The dog chases the cat." The 3-year-old subjects had no trouble demonstrating these simple declarative

FIGURE 8-1
One of Berko's Tests of Children's Syntax.
Nonsense words are used to avoid interference from memorization.

This is a wug.

Now there is another one.
There are two of them.
There are two _____.

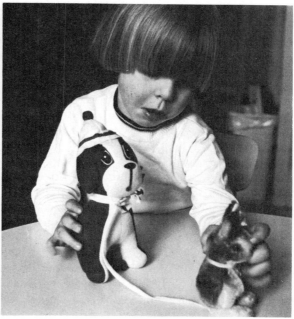

This 3-year-old is able to demonstrate the sentence "The rabbit chases the dog" but not "The dog is chased by the rabbit." Children of this age have not yet mastered the passive concept.

sentences. However, when shown two pictures illustrating "The boy is washed by the girl" and "The girl is washed by the boy," the children seldom identified the picture that corresponded to the sentence they heard. They had not yet mastered the passive concept. Their comprehension was limited to the more typical word order of agent-action-object.

Stages 4 and 5. In stages four and five, children learn to deal with increasingly sophisticated structures. They begin to use subordinate clauses and fragments within compound and complex sentences. By the age of 4½, children have a good grasp of syntax, but they continue to learn for many years. Carol Chomsky (1969) tested subjects between the ages of 5 and 10 and found that children are actively acquiring syntax within those years. Such structures as "John asked Bill what to do" are learned very late; the subject of "do" was not clearly understood by some 10-year-olds. And, of course, many adults—even well-spoken, well-educated ones—have great difficulty with certain constructions.

More Words and Concepts

Throughout the preschool period, children are learning words at a rapid rate—often at a rate of two or three a day. Some words have meaning only in context. For example, "this" and "that." Some words express relationships between objects: "softer," "lower," and "shorter." Frequently, children understand one concept, such as "more," a lot earlier than they know the word or the concept that contrasts directly with it—in this case, "less." A 3-year-old may easily be able to tell you which dish has more candy, but not which dish has less.

Often, children want to say things, but they do not know the right word, or they cannot recall it. At these times, children invent words. They use nouns in place of verbs, as in, "Mommy, needle it" ("Mommy, sew it"). Or a child trying to fold paper might ask, "How do you flat it?" Also, children invent complex words like "sweep-man" (someone who sweeps).

Another problem encountered by some children is that they have trouble pronouncing certain words, even though they can often recognize the correct pronunciation; for example, a child may understand that "I smell a skunk" is the correct form, but may only be able to say, "I mell a kunk."

Influences of Parents' Speech

To get and hold the attention of prelinguistic children, adults often use a particular mode of speaking that has been dubbed "motherese." When using motherese, adults (both men and women) exaggerate their vowels, speak in pitches higher than normal, and create words composed of repeated syllables, such as "bye-bye" and "nighty-night." They use short, simple sentences and talk about what is happening at the moment. While watching her infant try to stand, a mother might verbalize his progress: "Sabir falls down . . . Bump . . . Sabir sits up . . . Can Sabir stand up?" The care-giver exaggerates intonation and stress, pauses between sentences, and often repeats earlier words and sentences (Ferguson & Snow, 1977)

The simple, exaggerated qualities of motherese probably make it easier for young children to understand and learn language. Short sentences are useful because young children have short memories. Simple sentences help children find the important words. Pauses help them separate words and sentences (Hirsh-Pasek, Nelson, Jusczyk, & Wright, 1986).

It was once thought that the frequent use of motherese played a key part in the language development of the young child. But now researchers view motherese as only one of a variety of ways to interact verbally with the child. The simplified speech characteristic of motherese comes naturally to an adult speaking with anyone who does not yet speak fluently. In other words, motherese is not primarily a tool used to teach a baby language. Rather, the simplified way that care-givers speak to the child appears to be a *reaction* to the child's language abilities, not a strategy to improve them (Bohannon & Hirsh-Pasek, 1984). Looking at how young children learn to speak in other cultures confirms the idea that motherese is not critical to language development. In the Pacific Kaluli (Schieffelin & Ochs, 1983) and the Quicke Mayan cultures (Ratner & Pye, 1984), for instance, children learn to speak without extensive use of motherese.

Yet, every culture successfully transmits language to its children. There appear to be many methods of talking and relating to infants that facilitate language development. Each culture has integrated some of these strategies into the patterns of social interaction with children (Snow, 1989). Although children do pick up specific words from their care-givers, the critical aspect of adults' speaking to children is that they provide children with information about language. Children generalize from what they hear, enabling them to understand words and syntax.

Researchers looking at American children found that care-givers ask questions to check for children's understanding, expand children's utterances, and make ritualized use of play speech. Adults often speak for the children; that is, they

Parents can facilitate language development by encouraging their children to talk and by listening to what their children say.

express children's wants, wishes, and actions in syntactic English. The child's language develops most from everyday communication with adults who seek to communicate—that is, to understand and to be understood (Schacter & Strage, 1982).

It is not clear how the use of language by parents and the child's language development are related (Chesnick, Menyuk, Liebergott, Ferrier, & Strand, 1983). Of course, it is critical that parents both talk and listen to their children regularly. Differences between individuals in language development have been shown to be inherited to some extent. But they are also influenced by the environment. For example, twins typically have delayed language development. Studies have shown that these children received significantly less verbal input than nontwins did from their mothers, because the mothers of twins had to divide their attention between the two children (Tomasello, Mannle, & Kruger, 1986).

When parents speak with their children, however, they communicate far more than words, sentences, and syntax. They are demonstrating how thoughts are expressed and how ideas are exchanged. They are teaching the child about categories and symbols and about how to translate the complicated world into ideas and words. These conceptual tools provide a "scaffold" for the child to create his own form of expression (Bruner & Haste, 1987). Long before they can speak, children are initiated into their culture and language by the speech of their parents and care-givers.

LANGUAGE AND GENDER   Language is one means for children to learn who they are and how they should relate to other people. A critical category of identification for the young child is gender. What should a boy do? How does a girl behave? Assumptions about gender appear to be psychologically embedded in mothers' thinking; these ideas cause them to behave differently toward children based on their gender (Lloyd, 1987). When mothers were observed interacting with babies who were presented to them as either a boy or a girl, the supposed gender affected how the mother played with and spoke to the infant. Babies dressed as boys were offered a toy hammer and were verbally encouraged to play actively. When the same baby was presented as a girl, the mothers picked up a fluffy doll and praised the child for being clever and attractive (Smith & Lloyd, 1978).

How does the social context in which language is used affect language development? Exploration of this complex question is in its early stages. One study has looked at how play preferences may play a part in children's exposure to language. The language mothers and fathers used while playing with their toddlers with three types of toys—vehicles, dolls, and shape sorters—was analyzed. Playing with dolls elicited the most verbal interaction, whereas play with vehicles involved little talking whether or not the parents were playing with daughters or sons. These results suggest that children who play frequently with dolls may have more opportunities to learn and practice language than do children who play with other toys. Because boys and girls play selectively with same-sex stereotyped toys starting by age 2, play patterns may contribute to differential language environments for children (O'Brien & Nagle, 1987).

CHILDREN'S CONVERSATIONS

Children do more than say words or sentences. They have conversations—with adults as well as with other children. Conversations typically follow a certain pattern.

Children learn through experience that they must consider the status of the person to whom they are speaking.

Monitoring the Message

First, it is necessary to get the other person's attention. A child just learning the art of conversation may yank on somebody's clothing. As time passes, the same child may instead say something like, "Know what?" Children then learn that conversations often have a beginning, a middle, and an end. They discover, too, that in conversations people take turns; they talk on the same subject, they make sure the other person listens, or is understanding; and they make sounds or nod to indicate that they understand what the other person is talking about (Garvey, 1984).

By casually listening to children's conversations, one notices that they do not run smoothly. Children often stop to see if the other is listening, and if they are understood. Children pause, repeat themselves, correct themselves. They ask questions. Indeed, this is a normal part of developing effective communication (Garvey, 1984; Reich, 1986). Even school-aged children sometimes have considerable difficulty communicating all of the appropriate information to a listener. First- and second-grade children have difficulty comprehending each other fully, finding the part of the message they don't understand, and asking appropriate questions to help each other repair messages (Beal, 1987).

Finally, children must learn to adjust conversations to reduce friction, conflict, and embarrassment. This means using courtesy markers like "please" and "thank you"; paying attention; and selecting the proper forms of address, phrasing, and suitable topics. In many cases, this means noting the status of the other person.

Children spend a good deal of time learning these social refinements, and they are aided with reminders like, "Don't talk to your grandmother like that" (Garvey, 1984). In the next section, we will review other ways that children learn to be sensitive to social situations and to people with whom they are talking.

The Social Context of Language

The way that language is used depends on the situations and the intentions of a speaker and a listener who have some kind of social relationship. Social relationships, in turn, involve mutual considerations of both role and status. We show our awareness of another person's status by our tone of voice, grammar, and mode of address, among other things. For example, an elderly neighbor may expect children to be quiet and calm, and conveys these expectations in his speech. The neighborhood children, in turn, will show deference in their speech by modulating their voices and using polite forms of address. In general, children are quick to learn nuances of speech and to conform to a social role. They are also quick to perceive degrees of status and the attendant speech behavior in a wide variety of social settings.

Thus, children recognize early that based on their characteristics, people are meant to be treated in different ways. Being able to interpret the social world accurately is a critical task for children. But in all cultures, commonly accepted social lessons are accompanied by unspoken attitudes that children also absorb. While the child expands her world by comprehending how she relates to others, she is acquiring the particular beliefs that comprise the world view of her culture (Ochs, 1986).

These girls are playing, pretending to have a conversation with the help of the telephone. Through play, children can practice their conversational skills—for example, they learn to take turns speaking.

FOCUS ON AN ISSUE

IS THERE A CRITICAL PERIOD FOR LEARNING LANGUAGE?

In 1970, a 13-year-old girl named Genie was discovered in Los Angeles. Her condition was startling. Since the age of 20 months, Genie had been a virtual prisoner in a small curtained room in her house. For most of her days, she was strapped in a pottychair, where she was only able to move her hands and her feet. At night, she was laced in a kind of straitjacket and enclosed in a cagelike crib. Treated like an animal, Genie had no bowel or bladder control and could not stand erect. She was severely malnourished and could not chew solid food. She was also mute: She could neither speak nor understand language.

Since the first days of her imprisonment, Genie was never spoken to—a rule enforced by her father. She was fed by her brother, whom she saw for only a few minutes a day, but no words ever passed between them. The only sounds she heard were her father's doglike barks on some of the occasions when he beat her for crying or making noise.

After she was removed from this situation, Genie was cared for by doctors at the Los Angeles Children's Hospital, who took care of her immediate bodily needs, nursed her back to health, and calmed her fears. Psychologists were called in to try to evaluate her mental state and abilities, including how much she understood and how much language she had learned. They next had the task of teaching her language. Many psychologists feel that there is a critical period for learning language— the time during a child's early years when language learning must begin if it is to occur at all. Genie gave researchers a unique opportunity to study this critical period theory.

Genie knew almost no language and had no understanding of grammar. Researchers approached teaching Genie in much the same way they would approach teaching a younger child—through direct exposure to language during daily activities. She made only one- or two-word utterances at first, but she soon progressed. Within a year of her release, she began to string two and sometimes three words together to make phrases like "clear white box." She soon began to use these phrases to form simple agent-action-object sentences, and she learned to add the word "no" to the beginning of the sentence to express a negative thought.

Despite this progress, it soon became apparent that Genie's language learning was severely limited. Even after 4 years of training, she never learned many of the rudiments of grammar or articulation most children learn before the age of 4—rudiments that could transform her garbled messages into easily understood speech. She could not use personal pronouns nor the demonstrative adjectives "this" and "that." In addition, despite her teachers' prodding, she never asked questions in the way a normal 3- or 4-year-old would. And, unlike normal children, she never experienced an explosive spurt of language development that quickly transforms a child's first words into full grammatical sentences. On the contrary, her progress was painfully slow. After 4 years she could hardly be understood, and after 7 years, she learned as much language as a normal child learns in 2 or 3 years.

Nevertheless, the fact that any progress was made disproved the theory that language can be learned only during a critical developmental period between the age of 2 and puberty. Genie did learn a limited amount of language after this time. Because her language development has fallen far short of that of a normal child, however, it may still be true that optimum language development is tied to this critical period—but there is no way to know this for sure. Due to the severe physical and emotional deprivation Genie experienced in her childhood, it is impossible to determine whether her language difficulties reflect her speech deprivation alone or whether the malnutrition, physical and emotional abuse, and social isolation she suffered also played a part.

By 24 years of age, Genie had received years of special education, rehabilitation, and foster care. She had also been closely observed and tested as psychologists attempted to find other clues to the mystery of language acquisition. Yet, in spite of this care and attention, her language still lacked many of the aspects of a 5-year-old's. Her case has provided many insights but no answers. Indeed, some believe that it has added even more fuel to the issue of whether a critical period in language development exists (Pines, 1981; de Villiers & de Villiers, 1979).

One researcher examined how children between the ages 4 and 7 modify their speech to correspond to different social situations and roles (Anderson, 1979). Twenty-four children were given an opportunity to play out several roles with the use of puppets. Three different situations were used: father–mother–child, physician–nurse–patient, and teacher–student–foreign student. In each setting, the children manipulated two puppets while the researchers worked the third. In improvising the various parts, the children spontaneously revealed how much they had already learned about social relationships and the social and cultural characteristics of speech.

Anderson found that although methods of portrayal varied with age, even the youngest children had a clear understanding of social context and power relationships, and they adjusted their vocabulary and speech accordingly to reflect these notions. Four-year-olds expressed their social understanding mostly by changing the pitch and loudness of their speech. Those who role-played authority figures, such as fathers and physicians, stretched out their vowels and talked at a lower pitch than those who role-played lower-status figures. Children portraying low-status persons, on the other hand, used a higher and softer tone of voice, asked more questions, and deferred politely to the authority figure. "Mothers" spoke in higher, sometimes sing-song voices. And every child, when speaking to a foreign student, spoke in a slow, flat monotone. Those who role-played young children simplified their speech, leaving out consonants and articles.

Slightly older children were able to modify appropriately the vocabulary and context of their speech. "Doctors" used medical terms like "hernia" and "temperature," often without knowing the meaning. A "patient" might say, "Doctor, do I have a hernia?" and the "doctor" might reply, "No, but I'll go out and get you one." Older children who played authority figures had learned techniques for maintaining control of a conversation. They would use floor holders, such as "Well . . .," "Now . . .," or "Then . . .," to prevent others with lower status from talking too much; they also made syntactic changes in their speech. "Fathers" would use imperatives, such as "Have this done by tomorrow!" "Mothers" would use expressions of endearment and polite forms, such as "Would you mind if I . . . ?" at least when played by girls. As boys' ages increased, so did their reluctance to play dependent, less authoritative roles, such as young children.

LANGUAGE AND CULTURE

Suppose, for a moment, that you are traveling in Mexico for the first time. You have studied Spanish in school for 4 years, you have learned to read it reasonably well, and you have no trouble with menus or street signs. You know when to say "please" and "thank you," and you can even enter a limited conversation. But you feel socially inept because you know that whatever you say, you will still "sound like an American." To behave and feel like a Mexican, you would have to have mastered thousand of behavioral details, such as knowing when to be silent, what form of address to use, and what tone of voice to adopt. In the meantime, you observe 4- and 5-year-old children expressing themselves effortlessly. As we shall see, children absorb all the behavioral details of their own culture and reflect them in their speech easily and naturally.

Social Class and Ethnic Differences

Every culture defines what to say, when, and to whom, just as it dictates pronunciation, syntax, and vocabulary. In cultures where politeness is esteemed, for instance, children learn polite forms of expression at a very early age. In Java, a child's first word may well be *njuwun,* "I humbly beg for it."

Oftentimes, children are presented with more than one form of language usage as a result of cultural differences within society. This is especially true in America's heterogeneous society. We reflect racial and ethnic differences and distinct social and economic classes in our use of language. These differences become particularly apparent in public school classrooms. Schools have tradition- ally reflected the dominant American culture and may be a minority child's first exposure to these values, including the mainstream patterns of speech.

The status of Black English, a form of English spoken by many African- Americans, especially those who live in large cities, has been debated for decades. Some theorists contend that Black English is one of many dialects—just as standard English is one—and that each dialect is a legitimate variation of English. This viewpoint is called the *difference hypothesis* (Williams, 1970). It is a response to an opposing viewpoint, the *deficit hypothesis,* which asserts that language patterns deviating from standard English are deficient and substandard.

Black English was considered to be poor English, growing out of a restricted language code, until linguists began to study it systematically. Labov (1970) cites the richness and complexity of Black English. It has its own rules and is often used in richly expressive ways.

Linguists found that the so-called errors committed by speakers of Black English were actually consistent alternative grammatical forms. Furthermore, some characteristics of the dialect originated in African linguistic patterns. For example, the word "be" in Black English, as used in the sentence "I be sick," indicates a repeated action or existential state (Labov, 1972). In other words, it expresses an ongoing, rather than a momentary, condition. The concept expressed by "I be sick" might be rephrased in standard English as "I have been feeling sick."

What position should schools assume toward Black English? Ultimately, children who use Black English, and other dialects differing from standard English, must be able to speak and write using standard English in order to work and socialize in the larger society. But Black English is the child's original language form, and its use can be an important mode of self-expression. Children who speak Black English will ultimately have to negotiate between the two linguistic codes. Ideally, speakers of Black English, and other dialects, can learn to negotiate between their code and standard English, gaining linguistic access to the larger culture while retaining their own distinct linguistic identity.

Bilingualism

Language is not just a means of communication. It is also a symbol of one's social or group identity. Thus, language conveys attitudes and values through its use and nonuse. The child who grows up amidst and learns two languages, becoming *bilingual,* goes through both a linguistic and a socializing process (Grosjean, 1982).

Children around the world learn language in the same way. Mothers from Niger and Thailand and a grandfather in Hong Kong talk with their children and grandchildren.

The status of bilingualism in different nations is strongly affected by issues of social class and political power. In Europe, for example, bilingualism is associated with being a highly cultured "citizen of the world." In the United States, bilingualism is more often a sign of being a recent immigrant who has not become "Americanized." Although our society has moved toward acceptance of cultural pluralism, the millions of American children growing up in bilingual environments may experience overt or subtle pressures to conform. Along with English, these Americans are learning to speak such languages as Spanish, Chinese, Hebrew, Italian, Polish, French, Vietnamese, Arabic, Japanese, Korean, Farsi, or Russian.

Does learning two languages instead of one during the preschool years hinder a child's language learning? Does it interfere with cognitive development? Early studies in the United States and Great Britain concluded that learning two languages at a young age was detrimental to cognitive development. In general, bilingual children scored less well on standardized English tests than did monolingual, English-speaking children.

Most of these studies, however, did not take into account the social class or education level of either the children or their parents. In other words, the scores of bilingual children may have been depressed for reasons other than their bilingualism, such as poverty, parents being uneducated or unfamiliar with a new culture, or poor schooling. In recent research, such social factors are taken into consideration when evaluating the effects of bilingualism.

Some researchers now believe that linguistically, culturally, and probably cognitively, it is an advantage for children to learn more than one language (Diaz, 1985). Evidence from a Yugoslavian study that compared Hungarian and

Children learning a second language after learning their primary language follow patterns similar to those of children learning two languages simultaneously.

Hungarian/Serbo-Croatian-speaking children at ages 6 and 10 showed that even though the bilingual children appeared to be at a linguistic and cognitive disadvantage at the age when they were still learning the two languages, they caught up linguistically, and sometimes surpassed their monolingual peers cognitively, once they had integrated the two languages (Goncz, 1988).

How does a child master two languages? Learning two languages by the age of 5 is a complex task involving two systems of rules, two sets of vocabulary, special usage, and different pronunciation. Many children who are bilingual in the earliest years, however, show little confusion between the two languages by the age of 3, although they sometimes substitute vocabulary from one language when speaking in the other. This has led linguists to theorize that the young child uses a unitary language system and only later is able to distinguish two separate languages. But there is evidence that bilingual children make use of two separate language systems even as infants (Genesee, 1989).

Why do children mix words from two languages? Researchers argue that children are modeling their parents' use of the two languages. When parents consistently speak one language or the other, children's language mixing can be eliminated. This suggests that early language mixing does not reflect interlinguistic confusion. Rather, the child is formulating hypotheses about language based on the information she gets from her mother and father.

Bilingual children frequently develop strong person-language bonds. That is, they speak one language with one person and a second language with another person. Young bilingual children often begin translating between their parents and others as soon as they learn to speak—as early as age 2 or 2½. Children, such as recent immigrants, who learn a second language after learning to speak their primary language also associate their first and second languages with particular people and situations.

STUDY OUTLINE

Language Development

Aspects of Language. The basic elements of language consist of content, form, and use. **Content** refers to the meaning of any written or spoken message. **Form** is the particular symbol used to represent content; it consists of **phonemes** (the basic sounds), **morphemes** (basic word forms), and **syntax** (sentence structure). **Use** depends on the intentions and situations of speaker and listener. All three elements come into play from the very beginning of language learning.

The Processes of Language Learning. The process of language learning involves four major components; *imitation, reinforcement, innate language structure,* and *cognitive development.* Imitation accounts for the way that children learn many of their first words, but not how they acquire syntax. Reinforcement from care-givers encourages children's language learning, inducing them to repeat words but, again, does not explain the acquisition of syntax. Chomsky's theoretical language acquisition device is an inborn mental structure that enables children to induce grammatical rules and to form their

own language from these rules. There are many parallels between language development and cognitive development, such as the simultaneous appearance of object permanence and the use of words like "all gone," and "more." Cognitive theorists claim that grammatical structures in children's speech appear following certain kinds of cognitive development.

Language Beginnings

Receptive language is a child's understanding of the spoken or written word; **productive language** is what the preschool child says or writes.

Before the First Words. Infants learn many social aspects of communication, such as signaling, turn-taking, and gesturing long before they use words. Language production begins with howling, babbling, and **iteration.** Up to the first 6 months, vocalization consists of a wide variety of sounds, some of which, like pseudo words, are outside the parents' native language. After 6 months, infants' babbling takes on inflection and patterns like those of the parents' language.

First Words. By the end of the first year, most children are uttering their first words. From single words, children's speech gradually develops complex grammatical structures during the next 3 or 4 years. The developmental patterns of language acquisition are consistent across cultures. Children first utter single words, usually nouns.

Some psycholinguists feel that these first words are forms of **holophrastic speech**—that they are meant to convey complex ideas. Overextensions and underextensions are commonly used in early speech, at the time when children are forming concepts.

Two-Word Sentences. **Case grammar**—expressing relationships using word order—is also used by young children who are composing their first sentences. During the second and third years, children's speech broadens from two-word sentences to longer ones, but their sentences are limited to high-information words, a form that Brown calls **telegraphic speech**. Braine believes that children at the two-word stage combine **pivot** words—such as action words and possessives—with x-words, or open words, such as nouns.

Language Complexities

An Expanding Grammar. Throughout the preschool years, children are rapidly expanding their vocabularies, their use of grammatical forms, and their understanding of language as a social act. Brown measures language development by average sentence length rather than by age. He identifies five distinct, increasingly complex stages: two-word utterances; longer phrases marked by **inflections** that indicate number, gender, tense, and case; simple sentences that use negative and imperative forms; and two final stages that involve the mastering of complex, compound, and subordinate structures. Mastery of syntax may not be complete before age 10.

More Words and Concepts. Throughout the preschool period, children learn words at a rapid rate—often at a rate of two or three a day.

Influences of Parents' Speech. Psycholinguists are not sure what effect parents' speech has on children's language production. Although mothers' speech is an important influence, so are socioeconomic factors and family size.

Children's Conversations

Monitoring the Message. As part of language development, children learn the process of conversation. Their improved conversation skills will stem from understanding that, for example, people take turns when they converse.

The Social Context of Language. Culture has a profound influence on language production. Children assimilate social values such as rules of conversation, politeness, obedience, and authority concepts at the same time they learn syntax and vocabulary. Social class and ethnic background also strongly influence speech.

Language and Culture

Social Class and Ethnic Differences. The first language of children in some ethnic groups may be a dialect other than standard English. These children will have to learn to negotiate between their dialect and standard English. Black English, a dialect spoken by many African-Americans, has its own grammatical rules and modes of expression.

Bilingualism. Young children are able to learn two languages at once. Although children may initially mix words from the two languages, by age 3, they are bilingual, speaking each language fluently.

KEY TERMS AND CONCEPTS

babbling	imitation	private speech
bilingualism	inflections	productive language
case grammar	iteration	pseudo words
content	language acquisition device (LAD)	receptive language
deficit hypothesis	mean length of utterance (MLU)	restricted language code
difference hypothesis	morphemes	syntax
egocentric speech	morphology	tag question
elaborate code	overextension	telegraphic speech
expressive jargon	overregularization	underextension
form	phonemes	use
holophrastic speech	pivot grammar	

SELF-TEST QUESTIONS

1. List three major dimensions of language.
2. Differentiate between phonemes and morphemes.
3. Describe four components of language development.
4. Discuss the sequence of language development in infancy.
5. Differentiate between receptive and productive language. How are these processes related and when do they evolve?

6. What is babbling, and how important is it to the infant's language development?

7. Contrast the language development of twins versus singletons.

8. Describe holophrastic speech.

9. Differentiate between overextensions and underextensions. How are a child's words and meanings closely linked to the concept the child is learning?

10. What is telegraphic speech? What are its two major components? What types of grammar are used in telegraphic speech?

11. Describe the five stages of language acquisition as identified by Roger Brown.

12. Discuss the influence of parents' speech on the infant.

13. Describe the process by which a child's language acquisition develops into conversational skills.

14. Discuss the cultural and social values that children assimilate in language.

15. How do social class and ethnic differences pose a critical issue for teachers?

16. Discuss how bilingualism affects the language development of the child.

SUGGESTED READINGS

CAZDEN, C. (Ed). *Language in early childhood education.* Washington, D.C.: National Association for the Education of Young Children, 1981. A collection of studies and articles about language development during the preschool period. This is of particular interest to individuals working with young children in preschools.

DE VILLIERS, P. A., & DE VILLIERS, J. G. *Early language.* Cambridge, MA: Harvard University Press, 1979. A good, complete summary of early language development from birth to age 6.

GARVEY, C. *Children's talk.* Cambridge, MA: Harvard University Press, 1984. Another selection in The Developing Child series. This book discusses the social and conversational aspects of language learning.

MCLANE, J. B., & MCNAMEE, G. D. *Early literacy.* Cambridge, MA: Harvard University Press, 1990. An excellent and balanced discussion of the pros and cons of early reading for young children.

PORTER, R. P. *Forked tongue: The politics of bilingual education.* New York: Basic Books, Inc., 1990. A controversial and well-researched, yet highly readable presentation of the successes and failures of the current bilingual education programs in the United States.

SPRADLEY, T. S., & SPRADLEY, J. P. *Deaf like me.* New York: Random House, 1978. The story of a profoundly deaf girl written by her father and uncle. It describes the parents' struggle to communicate with the child and unhelpful professionals, and it encourages total communication, including the early use of sign language.

WINNER, E. *The point of words: Children's understanding of metaphor and irony.* Cambridge, MA: Harvard University Press, 1988. A somewhat advanced analysis of children's growing ability to discover the more subtle and indirect meanings of language.

Chapter 9

Thou straggler into loving arms,
Young climber up of knees,
When I forget thy thousand ways,
Then life and all shall cease.

MARY ANNE LAMB
"A CHILD"

Developing Thought and Action

"Mother, who was born first, you or I?"

"Daddy, when you were little, were you a boy or a girl?"

"What is a knife—the fork's husband?"

The mother was breast-feeding her newborn daughter. Her 5-year-old son observed her closely and asked with utter seriousness, "Mommy, do you have coffee there sometimes, too?" (Chukovsky, 1963, pp. 21, 22, 24)

P reschool children, relative newcomers in this world, often demonstrate their thinking in ways that are both amusing and thought provoking. These comments, collected by Kornei Chukovsky, a Russian poet and an observer of children's behavior, reveal more about children than the fact that they make errors and are profoundly ignorant. They also show what an enormous distance preschool children must cover between the ages of 2 and 6 in order to develop the thought processes necessary for them to begin school. During this 4-year period, young children change from "magicians," who can make things appear by turning their heads or disappear by closing their eyes, to concept-forming, linguistically competent realists (Fraiberg, 1959). They discover what they can and cannot control. They try to generalize from experience. Their reasoning changes from simple association to the beginnings of logic, and they acquire the language necessary to express their needs, thoughts, and feelings.

In this chapter, we will concentrate on the different dimensions of these developing competencies during early childhood. This is the period during which the physical-motor skills of children rapidly develop. Children also make dramatic discoveries about the world around them by using their growing cognitive abilities.

As we look at each type of development, it is important to remember that the different aspects of development do not really occur separately. For example, when a child begins to walk or skip, she is motivated to do so, she has the information needed, and she has the physical capacity to carry out her idea. Thus, the ways in which a child behaves and thinks can be viewed as an integrated system (Thelen, 1989). Looking carefully at specific aspects of development provides many ways to understand the process by which children grow and change.

We will first discuss changes in physical-motor skills, and then examine more closely the changes in children's cognitive abilities. We will look at children's play as both process and product of ongoing development. Finally, issues relating to preschool programs will be discussed.

CHAPTER OBJECTIVES

By the time you have finished this chapter, you should be able to do the following:

- Discuss the physical and cognitive development of the preschool child.
- Describe the aspects and limitations of preoperational thought.
- Explain how pretend and real play promote cognitive and physical development.
- Discuss Piaget's view of preschool children and the strengths and weaknesses of his theory.
- Discuss the memory capabilities of preschool children.
- Describe the major types of children's play and how they influence childhood development.
- Discuss the role of art in childhood development.
- Describe the different approaches to early education.

gross motor skills Capabilities involving large body movements.

fine motor skills Capabilities involving small body movements.

PHYSICAL-MOTOR DEVELOPMENT

Because of changes in their growing bodies and in their abilities to concentrate and refine activities, children's **gross motor skills,** large body movements such as running, hopping, and throwing, improve markedly (Clark & Phillips, 1985). **Fine motor skills,** capabilities involving small body movements, develop more slowly. Nonetheless, children are eventually able to put together a wooden puzzle, draw with a pencil, and use a spoon and fork.

Separating physical-motor and perceptual development from cognitive development in preschool children is a difficult task. Children's understanding of the world depends on the information they receive from their own bodies, perceptions, motor activity, and the ways in which they experience themselves. Almost everything that a child does from birth through the first few years lays the base, in some way, not only for later physical-motor skills, but also for cognitive processes and social and emotional development. Looking, touching, exploring, babbling, bouncing, scribbling—all form the basis for the performance of more complex developmental tasks. Although much of what preschool children do—making mud pies, crawling, or hanging upside down—appears to be sheer sensory exploration, experts in development consider all children's actions to be purposeful, to be directed toward some goal (von Hofsten, 1989). For example, they explore places and objects to find out what they feel like, to see them, and to hear them. Sensory exploration leads to concepts like "up," "down," "straight," and "tight." For instance, when a girl walks on a log at the beach, she learns not only how to balance, but also the cognitive concept "narrow" and the emotional concept "confidence."

Many aspects of development proceed from a physical-motor base. Some developmental sequences are continuous, as in the natural progression from scribbling to writing; others seem somewhat discontinuous. For example, children may explore different textures and weaves of material randomly with their fingers

Early in development, the action of putting marks on paper is important in and of itself; as a child develops, however, this simple pattern of exploration will give way to more complex skills, including writing and drawing.

and eyes before they are ready to sort and classify, or compare and contrast, the materials. In similar fashion, they must sort and compare thoughts before they can deal with complex ideas.

Some developmental sequences involve **functional subordination.** Actions that at first are performed for their own sake later become part of a more complicated, purposeful skill. For example, a child's simple, fine motor explorations with crayon and paper have value in and of themselves, at first. Later, putting marks on paper becomes functionally subordinated to more complex skills, such as writing, drawing, creating designs, or even carpentry. The roots of complex thought are not always obvious; nevertheless, a look at physical-motor development is a good starting point from which to seek out these roots.

functional subordination The integration of a number of separate simple actions or schemes into a more complex pattern of behavior.

The gait of 2-year-olds is characterized by a wide stance and a body sway. They love to run and walk, but they have little endurance.

Ages 2 and 3

Compared with infants, 2-year-olds are amazingly competent creatures. They can walk, run, and manipulate objects. When we see one beside a 4- or 5-year-old, however, we recognize the younger child's limitations. Two-year-olds—and even 3-year-olds—are still rather short and a bit rounded. They walk with a wide stance and a body sway. Although they can climb, push, pull, and hang by their hands, they have little endurance. They are inclined to use both arms or both legs when only one is required (Woodcock, 1941). Thus, when a 2-year-old's mother offers him one cookie, he is likely to extend two hands.

By the age of 3, children's legs stay closer together during walking and running, and they no longer need to keep a constant check on what their feet are doing (Cratty, 1970). They run, turn, and stop more smoothly than they did as 2-year-olds, although their ankles and wrists are not as flexible as they will be at ages 4 and 5 (Woodcock, 1941). Three-year-olds are more likely to extend one hand to receive one item, and they begin to show a preference for using either the right or left hand.

Four-year-olds walk securely.

Ages 4 and 5

Four-year-olds are able to vary the rhythm of their running. Many 4-year-olds can also skip rather awkwardly and execute a running jump and a standing broad jump (Gesell, 1940). The average child of 4 is probably able to work a button through a buttonhole and can use a pencil or crayon to draw lines, circles, and simple faces.

Five-year-olds can skip smoothly, walk a balance beam confidently, stand on one foot for several seconds, and imitate dance steps (Gesell, 1940). They manage buttons and zippers and may be able to tie shoelaces. Many children can throw a ball overhand and catch a large ball thrown to them (Cratty, 1970). But accurate throwing and effective catching will show many changes over the next few years (Robertson, 1984).

Whereas 3-year-olds may push a doll carriage or a large truck for the fun of pushing it, 4-year-olds have functionally subordinated their pushing into a fantasy of doll play or a cars-and-trucks game. Where 3-year-olds daub and smear paint with abandon and stack blocks one on top of another, 4-year-olds make a "painting" or use blocks to build houses, space stations, or farms. Four-year-olds

TABLE 9–1
Motor Development of Preschool Children

2-YEAR-OLDS	3-YEAR-OLDS	4-YEAR-OLDS	5-YEAR-OLDS
Walk with wide stance and body sway.	Keep legs closer together when walking and running.	Can vary rhythm of running.	Can walk a balance beam.
Can climb, push, pull, run, hang by both hands.	Can run and move more smoothly.	Skip awkwardly; jump.	Skip smoothly; stand on one foot.
Have little endurance.	Reach for objects with one hand.	Have greater strength, endurance, and coordination.	Can manage buttons and zippers; may tie shoelaces.
Reach for objects with two hands.	Smear and daub paint; stack blocks.	Draw shapes and simple figures; make paintings; use blocks for buildings.	Use utensils and tools correctly.

are still exploring some physical-motor activities for their own sake—for example, they may accurately pour liquid into tiny cups or operate a syringe and a funnel—but much of their play is embedded in the acting out of complex roles or the purposeful construction of objects or games.

Learning Physical-Motor Skills

The physical-motor skills that preschool children learn are usually everyday actions, such as tying shoes, cutting with scissors, feeding themselves, buttoning and zipping up clothes, using a crayon or pencil, skipping, and jumping. These skills increase the young child's capability to move around, to take care of herself,

Preschoolers often practice tying shoelaces, and by age 5 some children are able to perform this task.

and to express herself creatively. They expand the child's world and her ability to act upon it. Some young children also learn more highly skilled activities such as gymnastics or how to play the piano or violin. Although there is debate over the value of such early training, psychologists have identified the important conditions for physical-motor learning. These conditions are readiness, motivation, activity, attention, and some kind of feedback. It is helpful to look closely at these factors before deciding whether or not to train a young child.

competence motivation A need to achieve in order to feel effective as an individual.

READINESS   Any new skill or learning generally requires a state of *readiness* on the part of the child. A certain degree of maturation, some prior learning, and a number of preliminary skills must be present before the child can profit from training. The classic twin study of Myrtle McGraw (1935) demonstrated that although early training in the normal motor skills, such as cutting, buttoning, or climbing stairs, accelerated the acquisition of those skills, the gains were only temporary. The research method for these studies involved training only one twin in a particular skill. The training itself consisted of daily practice or drill three times a week, with the researcher praising and assisting the child, and demonstrating whenever necessary. It was assumed that such a concentrated and enriched training program would produce a permanent advantage in the skill being taught. However, the researchers found that when the untrained twin had reached the proper stage of maturation, or readiness, for the task involved, he or she learned it very quickly and caught up with the trained twin within a few weeks. The study revealed that early training—training given before the appropriate maturation point has been reached—produces no lasting advantage.

The difficulty for parents and teachers is to know when children have reached the readiness point. American and Soviet studies have indicated that if children are introduced to new physical-motor learning at the optimal point of readiness, they learn quickly with little training or effort (Lisina & Neverovich, 1971). Children at the optimal readiness point want to learn, enjoy the practice, and get excited over their own performance. Children are often the best indicators of when they have reached the point of optimal readiness—they begin to imitate particular skills on their own.

COMPETENCE MOTIVATION   Another strong motive in motor-skill acquisition is **competence motivation** (White, 1959). Children try things out just to see if they can do them, to perfect their skill, to test their muscles and ability, and to enjoy the way it feels. They run, jump, climb, and skip for the pleasure and challenge of these activities. This kind of motivation is *intrinsic;* it comes from within the child and is generated by the activity. *Extrinsic* motivation can also play a part in skill development. Parental encouragement, peer competition, and the need for identification can prompt a child to attempt, and then to perfect, a certain skill. Adults can boost the self-confidence of a child if they are encouraging and set goals that the child is able to accomplish. But what if young children are pushed to develop skills through organized physical activities? Team sports often emphasize competition and may communicate criticism and pressure.

Experts in sports medicine recommend very different attitudes toward sports for young children. They encourage adults to help children to initiate their own active play. Such play experiences lead to a positive attitude toward developing skills. Physical activity becomes associated with well-being and with doing one's best (Rice, 1990).

Studies indicate that children introduced to a new physical-motor task at the optimal point of readiness will generally learn quickly, with little training or effort.

extrinsic feedback Rewards of praise given for performing a task well.

intrinsic feedback Feedback that comes from experiencing the natural consequences of performing a task.

The best motivation parents can provide may be doing physical activities year-round themselves. Research shows that the level of physical activity of preschool children is significantly related to the amount of time their parents spend in physical exercise (Poest et al., 1989).

ACTIVITY *Activity* is essential to motor development. Children cannot master stair climbing unless they climb stairs. They cannot learn to throw a ball unless they practice throwing. When children are raised in limited and restricted environments, the development of their physical-motor skills will lag. Children raised in crowded surroundings often show a delay in the development of skills of the large muscles. They lack strength, coordination, and flexibility in running, jumping, climbing, balancing, and the like.

Children who are hampered in their ability to use activity to learn—because they have few objects to play with, places to explore, or tools to use, as well as few people to imitate—may have trouble developing their motor skills. On the other hand, given a rich, meaningful environment full of objects to handle and use, open space to explore, and active people to imitate, children will generally have the necessary stimulation to pace their own learning. They will imitate a task, often repeating it endlessly. They will stack blocks and discover ways to make shapes. They will pour water repeatedly from one container to another to explore the concepts of "full" and "empty," "fast" and "slow," "spilling drops" and "making streams." Such self-designed and self-paced schedules of learning are often more efficient than adult-programmed lessons (Karlson, 1972).

Activity is essential to motor development—for example, children cannot learn how to climb unless they practice the activity.

ATTENTION Physical-motor learning is also enhanced by *attention*. Paying attention requires an alert and engaged state of mind. But how can children's attention be increased? Young children cannot just be told what to do and how to do it. Rather, children at age 2 or 3 learn new physical skills most effectively by being led through the activity. In the Soviet Union, exercises and games have been used to teach children to move their arms and legs in a desired fashion. Their techniques show that children between the ages of 3 and 5 often can focus their attention most effectively by active imitation. Varying types of follow-the-leader games are fun and reasonably successful. Gradually, the teacher can add verbal reminders to help children focus on a particular aspect of the physical activity. Finally, when children are 6 or even 7 they can attend closely to verbal instructions and follow them reasonably well, at least when participating in familiar tasks and activities (Zaporozlets & Elkonin, 1971).

FEEDBACK The course of learning motor skills is also motivated by feedback. **Extrinsic feedback** comes in the form of rewards, such as cookies, candy, or praise given for a task well done. Specific feedback such as "Now you've got a strong grip on the bar" is more useful than general praise. The anticipation or promise of such rewards is the extrinsic motivation previously discussed. **Intrinsic feedback** is a crucial monitor for skill development. Children find that there are certain natural consequences to their actions and that these may be more precise than arbitrary extrinsic feedback. For example, when climbing a jungle gym, they may derive pleasure from a feeling of tension in their muscles or from the experience of being up high, seeing things that cannot be seen from the ground. If they feel a bit wobbly, they will try to stabilize themselves. The "wobble" is intrinsic to the task and is usually more effective in making children aware of their need for safety than being told by an adult to be careful (which is extrinsic). Parents and teachers can help to point out the natural consequences of an action, but the learning process is most effective when a child has the experience.

In the United States today, early childhood education programs are expected to provide opportunities for daily practice of gross motor and fine motor skills. By and large, this practice is expected to be individual and self-motivated, not teacher directed. There is considerable research that suggests that self-paced and active play results in higher levels of physical-motor development (Johnson, Christie, & Yawkey, 1987). Furthermore, there is evidence that certain kinds of playgrounds and indoor play environments designed according to these principles support higher levels of play and higher levels of motor development (Frost & Sunderline, 1985). Teachers ideally prepare an environment that allows for active exploration and interaction with other children and with materials. Children are encouraged to express themselves freely and loudly in outdoor environments, and develop small muscle skills and endurance with a wide variety of materials. National guidelines for childhood education programs have been established in accordance with these principles (National Association for the Education of Young Children, 1986).

Physical-Motor Development and Cognitive Learning

Physical-motor development proceeds very rapidly during the preschool years. The child grows taller, new teeth come in, and the entire physical system matures. If children are given ordinary opportunities for practice, they develop a multitude of skills that are often overlooked. A 4- or 5-year-old has much greater physical strength, endurance, control, and coordination, and is capable of performing more self-directed and self-initiated movements than a younger child. In contrast to infants, 5-year-olds handle objects in very different ways. Instead of mouthing, banging, and fingering objects, they will use them correctly. They pound with hammers, eat with spoons, or draw with pencils.

Beyond mastering the proper use of tools, however, theorists differ on precisely what is learned as a result of physical-motor development. Many believe that from balancing their own bodies and from the symmetry of their two hands and feet, children learn some beginning foundations of gravity and of equivalence in math—such as the balance between two items on either side of an equation (Forman, 1972). During the preschool period, children work out physically the basic notions underlying speed, force, energy, numbers, time, and spatial relations long before they are ready to deal with them intellectually. Some theorists believe that adequate motor experience for such concepts is essential before a child can learn the related math and science concepts (Kephart, 1966). Others have questioned this view, pointing out that many children with cerebral palsy or other severe physical handicaps eventually develop considerable facility with complex math and science concepts.

Do children need to throw before they can understand anything about force, gravity, and trajectories? To what extent must children explore many types of spaces with their bodies before they can understand spatial relations? The evidence is unclear. Yet some preschool programs assume that many of these experiences are not only helpful but necessary to later thought.

COGNITIVE DEVELOPMENT

In his pioneering investigation of how logical thinking develops in children, Jean Piaget described the course of development in terms of discrete periods that children pass through on the way to a logical understanding of the world (see Chapter 2). Piaget formulated a theory about how the process of thinking, or cognition, develops. Piaget's theory is based on the premise that human beings actively construct a personal understanding of the world. Children build their own reality based on their level of thinking. For instance, a child's understanding of a particular event, such as her mother's walking out of the front door waving good-bye, will vary depending on whether the child understands that her mother will continue to exist when the child doesn't see her.

Piaget viewed children as little scientists, working diligently to figure out how the world works. According to this view, children do not merely absorb knowledge passively. Instead, they actively explore their surroundings, trying to comprehend new information based on their current patterns of understanding. Piaget called these beliefs about reality *schemas*. Schemas change through two processes, *accommodation* and *assimilation*. If new information conflicts with a child's schema, she can either modify her beliefs (a process called *accommodation*) or fit the information to her present beliefs (a process called *assimilation*).

Piaget divided intellectual development into four periods. The first, the sensorimotor period of infancy, was discussed in depth in Chapter 6. The infant's intelligence is composed of sensory and action schemas used to explore the world. Toward the end of the sensorimotor period, children begin to show the capacity to understand the world through *symbolic representation*. The child's most dramatic use of symbols occurs during the beginning of language use.

Piaget called the second period, which generally spans ages 2 to 7, *preoperational*. During the preoperational period, children continue to expand their understanding of the world, using their increasing language and problem-solving skills. But Piaget theorized—based on his now-famous cognitive experiments— that during this age period children have not yet achieved the mental capacities necessary to understand many basic logical operations needed to correctly interpret reality. These operations include most concepts of number, cause and effect, time, and space. (According to Piaget's cognitive theory, these operations will be accomplished during the third, or *concrete operational*, period.)

The dramatic cognitive advances made by preschool children will be discussed first in terms of Piaget's preoperational stage of development. Then theories will be presented that challenge some of Piaget's conclusions about young children's cognitive abilities and how they develop.

Aspects of Preoperational Thought

The preoperational period lasts from about ages 2 to 7 and is divided into two parts—the *preconceptual stage* (from ages 2 to about age 4) and the *intuitive, or transitional, stage* (from about ages 5 to 7).

The preconceptual stage is highlighted by the increasing use of symbols, symbolic play, and language. Previously, thought was limited to the infant's immediate environment. Now, the use of symbols and symbolic play marks the child's ability to think about something not immediately present. This development gives the mind greater flexibility. Similarly, words now have the power to communicate, even in the absence of the things they name. Children in the preconceptual stage still have difficulty with major categories, however. They cannot distinguish between mental, physical, and social reality. For instance they think anything that moves is alive—even the moon and clouds. Children expect the inanimate world to obey their commands, and they do not realize that physical law is separate from human moral law. These traits stem partly from children's self-centered view of the world, or **egocentricity;** they are unable to separate clearly the realm of personal existence and power from everything else (Brown, 1965).

The intuitive, or transitional, stage begins roughly at age 5. The transitional child begins to separate mental from physical reality and to understand mechanical causation apart from social norms. For example, before this stage of development, children may think that everything was created by their parents or some other adult. Now, they begin to grasp the significance of other forces. Intuitive children are beginning to understand multiple points of view and relational concepts, although in an inconsistent and incomplete way. Their comprehension of arrangements by size, numbers, and spatial classification is incomplete. Transitional children are unable to perform many basic mental operations.

One of the critical activities throughout the preoperational period is the development of symbolic representation. Without it, there could be no symbolic play, no language, not even a basic understanding of multiple points of view.

Representation

The most dramatic cognitive difference between infants and 2-year-olds is in the use of symbols—that is, the use of actions, images, or words to represent events or experiences. Some researchers have called this pretend, or symbolic, play. Two-year-olds are able to imitate past events, roles, and actions. By gestures in play, preschoolers may act out an extensive sequence that represents a car ride. Given other props, they may act out a family dinner or imitate a mean baby-sitter or a fat relative.

Although symbolic **representation** begins at the end of the sensorimotor period, it is a continuing process; a child is much better at symbolic representation at age 4 than at age 2. In experiments with young children, Elder and Pederson (1978) found that the youngest children (2½ years old) needed props similar to the real object for their pretending games. But the 3½-year-olds were able to represent objects with quite different props or act out a situation without props. For instance, they could pretend that a hairbrush was a pitcher and even pretend to use a pitcher with no props at all.

Once children begin to use symbols, their thought processes become more complex (Piaget, 1950, 1951). They show that they perceive the similarity between two objects or two events by giving them the same name; they become aware of the past and form expectations for the future; and they distinguish between themselves and the person they are addressing. Fein (1981) suggests further that symbolic play may help children in two other ways: (1) It may help children become more sensitive to the feelings and points of view of others, and (2) it may help children understand how an object can change in shape or form and still be the same object. The developing use of symbols is the most dramatic cognitive accomplishment of the preconceptual period.

egocentricity Having a self-centered view of the world, viewing everything in relation to oneself.

representation The use of symbols in the form of actions, images, or words to represent events or experiences.

Two-year-olds develop the ability to use symbols to represent actions, events, and objects—one of the milestones in cognitive development. This young firefighter is using a vacuum cleaner to represent a fire hose.

Pretend and Real

When children are involved in pretend play, they usually participate in two levels of representation, or meaning—the level of the reality-based meaning of actions and objects, and the level of the pretend meaning of actions and objects. According to Bateson (1955), children must maintain two meaning *frames:* a real frame and a play frame. When in the real frame, children playing cowboys and Indians know that they are actually children and that they are riding broomsticks. But simultaneously, they participate in the pretend frame of the cowboys and Indians story. When there are problems or disagreements, children often "break frame" to resolve their disputes before continuing with their make-believe. Researchers now studying children's make-believe play find that preschool children become increasingly sophisticated in making pretend–real distinctions (Rubin et al., 1983). They are able to make greater and greater leaps from the real to the pretend meaning of a particular object or action, and they can extend the duration and complexity of their pretend roles and activities. This kind of representation seems to follow a predictable sequence.

Another type of symbolic representation that contains dual meanings is known as the "appearance–reality distinction." If, for example, a cat wears a dog mask, is he a cat or a dog? When Charlie Brown is dressed as a ghost for Halloween, is he really Charlie Brown or is he really a ghost? And what about a joke store sponge that looks like a solid piece of granite, or a red toy car covered with a green filter that makes it look black? Flavell and his colleagues (1986) showed objects like these to children ages 3 to 7 and asked them, "What is this really and truly?" "Is it a rock or a sponge?" "Is it red or is it black?" They then asked the children "What does this look like?" Three-year-olds were quite confused by such questions. In some situations, the young children insisted that the car looks black and the car is black. In others, they reported that the sponge is a sponge and

"No, Honey! Food goes in the food processor, words go in the word processor!"

looks like a sponge. They clearly experienced difficulty with the two kinds of meanings. Most children of 5 or 6, however, are much better at these appearance–reality distinctions.

There seems to be a relationship between pretend play and appearance–reality distinctions. Children who have had a lot of practice with pretend play at 3 and 4 years are better able to understand that objects can look like something else (Flavell, Flavell, & Green, 1987; Flavell, Green, & Flavell, 1986). Some have found that children who have had a lot of experience with pretend play are also better at taking someone else's perspective or understanding someone else's feelings. Researchers suggest that seemingly innocent make-believe play provides important experiences for children's development of structured knowledge (Flavell, 1985; Garvey, 1977).

irreversibility The belief that events and relationships can occur in only one direction that is characteristic of preoperational thought.

centration The focusing or concentration on only one aspect or dimension of an object or situation that is characteristic of preoperational thought.

Limitations of Preoperational Thought

Even with the development of symbolic representation, preoperational children still have a long way to go before they become logical thinkers. By adult standards, their thought processes are quite limited. First, their thinking is *concrete*. Preoperational children cannot deal with abstractions. They are concerned with the here and now, with physical things they can represent easily.

Second, their thinking is often *irreversible*. For young children, events and relationships occur in only one direction. They cannot imagine how things would be if returned to their original state or how relationships can go in two directions. Phillips (1969) cites this example of **irreversibility** in a preoperational child's thought:

> A 4-year-old subject is asked:
> "Do you have a brother?" He says, "Yes."
> "What's his name?" "Jim."
> "Does Jim have a brother?" "No."
> The relationship is one-way only; it is irreversible. (p. 61)

We will see more examples of irreversibility in Piaget's conservation experiment.

Third, preoperational children's thought is *egocentric*—centered on their own perspective so that they are unable to take into account another person's point of view. Preoperational children concentrate on their own perceptions and assume that everyone else's outlook is the same as theirs. Piaget (1954) made an interesting study that demonstrates this limitation of thought. He seated children in front of a plaster model of a mountain range and showed them pictures of the mountain range, each taken from a different angle. He asked them to select the picture that represented their view of the mountains, then to select the picture that represented what a doll would see if seated facing the mountains from another angle. Most children had no trouble picking the picture matching their own viewpoint, but they could not put themselves in the doll's place and imagine the doll's view of the mountains. Based on children's responses in this experimental situation, Piaget concluded that preoperational children assume that their perspective is the only one.

Fourth, preoperational children's thought tends to be *centered* on only one physical aspect or dimension of an object or situation. They cannot hold several aspects or dimensions of a situation in mind at the same time. This limitation— also called **centration**—is best seen in the *class inclusion problem,* a classic task used

In one of Piaget's experiments demonstrating egocentrism in children's perception, the child is asked to select the picture that matches what the small doll sees. Although the boy can see that the doll is facing the mountain range from a different angle, he still assumes that his view is the only one possible.

to study preoperational thought. Young children have difficulty comparing a part with the whole. For example, if they are shown a collection of wooden beads, some red and some yellow, and are asked whether there are more red beads or more *wooden* beads, they will not be able to handle the problem. They cannot simultaneously consider color and the broader category of wooden beads.

Fifth, preoperational children *focus on present states,* not on processes of change or transformation. They judge things according to their appearance in the present, not how they came to be that way.

PIAGET'S CONSERVATION EXPERIMENTS   Several of these preoperational limitations can be seen in one of Piaget's classic experiments on the *conservation of matter.* In Chapter 2, one of these experiments was described. A child is shown two identical glasses holding the same amount of liquid. After the liquid from one of the glasses is poured into a taller glass, the child says the taller glass holds more water. In a second experiment, a child is presented with two identical balls of clay. As the child watches, one ball of clay is transformed into various shapes while the other remains untouched. One ball might be rolled into a sausage, broken into five little balls, or flattened into a pancake. At each transformation, the child might be asked which has more clay, the untouched ball or the one that has become a sausage, five little balls, or a pancake. The child might say at one time that the untouched ball has more clay because it is fatter. But the child might also say that the sausage has more because it is longer, or the little balls because there are more of them, or the pancake because it is all spread out. At no time has a child said that the two are identical, although she has witnessed the whole transformation process. Clearly, preoperational children focus on the current state of the object, not on the process of transformation. They center on one dimension at a time, such as either fatness or "spreadoutness." Their thinking is concrete and is based on direct experience in the here and now. Their view of the process is irreversible. All of these cognitive limitations make preoperational children nonconservers.

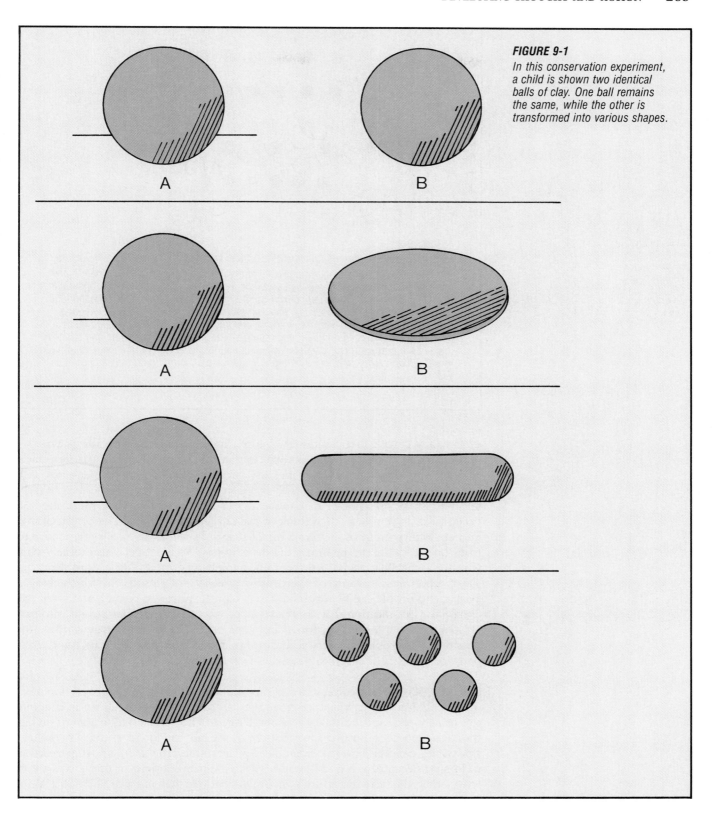

FIGURE 9-1
In this conservation experiment, a child is shown two identical balls of clay. One ball remains the same, while the other is transformed into various shapes.

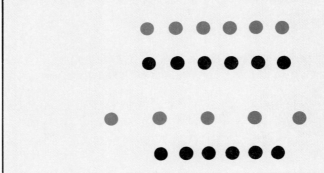

FIGURE 9-2

Piaget's Experiment on the Conservation of Numbers.

When shown the arrangement of candies in the top two rows and asked whether one line has more or both lines are the same, the 4- or 5-year-old will generally answer that both lines contain the same number of candies. Using the same candies, those in the lower row were pushed closer together and one candy was removed from the upper row, but the line was spread out so that it was longer. The child has watched this operation and has been told that he or she may eat the candies in the line that contains more. Even preoperational children, who can count, will insist that the longer line has more, although they have gone through the exercise of counting off the candies in each line.

CLASSIFICATION   Preoperational children have a problem with *classification*— putting together those events or objects that go together. Young children have trouble with classification tasks because of their relatively short memories and attention spans. They may forget why they are putting things together before they finish a task. A preschooler may move a chair toward a table, then think about a friend to sit in the chair, then think of his hair and run off to find a comb. Going into the bathroom for it, he sees a bar of soap—he thinks about playing in water, turns on the tap, and remembers that he is thirsty. So he goes to his mother, who wonders what happened to the table-and-chair project. Other problems in classification arise because of the confusing variety of reasons for which things, events, and people can be classified. Use, color, texture, size, sound, and smell are criteria for classification that are readily apparent to an adult; but a child who has no trouble grouping plates, forks, and cups on the basis of use may not see the possibility of grouping plates according to size or cups according to color. One basis, or reason, for classification may block another.

SERIATION   Sequences or series of any kind are difficult for young children to manage. For example, when presented with six sticks of graduated length, children can usually pick out the shortest or the longest. They may even be able to divide the sticks into piles, putting shorter sticks in one pile and longer sticks in the other. But young children have considerable difficulty lining the sticks up from shortest to longest because such a task requires a simultaneous judgment that each stick is longer than the next but at the same time is shorter than another (Flavell, 1963).

A YOUNG CHILD'S CONCEPTION OF DEATH

Imagine a 4-year-old who has just been told that a beloved and recently active, caring grandmother has died. Given what we know about young children's thinking, what reactions can be expected? What aspects of the situation are particularly difficult to understand? Are there specific fears and anxieties the child might experience? Finally, how should care-givers reassure the child?

A number of researchers have studied the differences between young children's understanding of death and how older children and adults view death (Speece & Brent, 1984). They have focused on three major aspects of the death concept: (1) Death is always irreversible, final, and permanent; (2) the absence of life functions is characteristic of death; and (3) death is universal—everyone must die. The researchers found that children under the age of 5 lack all three of these components in their concept of death. They interviewed children of different ages and asked them a variety of questions. Sometimes, they asked general questions such as, What is death? But more often, they asked specific questions. Such questions might include: Can a dead person come back to life? Can a dead person talk? Or feel? Or see? Or dream? Or think? Does everyone die? Can you think of someone who might not die?

Young children often see death as a temporary state, something like sleeping or "going away." They will sometimes suggest that dead people wake up or come back to life after a while. Is this reversibility? Some authors suggest that it does not mean that children see death as reversible in all cases, but that they have not yet established distinct categories of dead and alive. After all, when one is asleep one is also alive, so why not when one is dead?

Young children also do not seem to understand that all functions cease when one is dead. However, they may think that there is reduced functioning. One child suggested "that you can't hear very well when you're dead." Often, children think that the deceased can't do visible things like eating and speaking, but they can do less visible things like dreaming and knowing. Finally, young children do not yet realize that death is universal. They often believe that death can be avoided by being clever or lucky, and that certain people are exempt from death, such as teachers, or members of their immediate family, or themselves. Some believe that you can do fairly magical things to keep from dying—for example, a child may think that if she prays a lot she won't die. Is it any wonder that it is very difficult to explain the death of a friend or relative to a child who is under the age of 5?

Researchers generally agree that the concept of death develops between the ages of 5 and 7. Most 7-year-olds have at least a rudimentary knowledge of the three basic components of death. This seems to parallel the transition in the child from Piaget's stage of preoperational thought to concrete operational thinking (Speece & Brent, 1984).

Explaining the death of a grandmother to a young child does not just involve coping with the child's limited cognitive understanding. The reality of someone's death is difficult for adults as well as children. Adults may intellectually understand the reality of death, its finality and permanence, its absence of life functions, and its universality. But emotionally they must struggle to cope with their loss. Young children, too, face emotional upheaval while trying to understand the realities of death. However, there are a number of factors that further complicate the adjustment for children. First, they are to some extent egocentric—they will be primarily concerned with how situations and events affect them. Second, they have trouble understanding cause and effect. Hence, when a young child asks, "Why did Grandma die?" she may not be asking what we think she is asking. She may not want to know about disease and old age; she may be wondering, instead, why her grandmother left her. Children wonder if they control such situations: "Did she leave because I was bad?" "If I'm good, will she come back?" "Will Mommy or Daddy die and leave me?" They may feel anger or guilt, or they may wonder if their own angry thoughts caused the death. Children told that death is like sleep may be afraid to close their eyes at night in fear that they, too, will die. Sometimes, young children will try to get a deceased loved one to return with a variety of magical strategies.

All of these factors influence children's understanding of death. The preschool child needs simple, correct information combined with ample reassurance and emotional support to cope with the reality of death.

TIME, SPACE, AND SEQUENCE   A 3-year-old may be able to say, "Grandma will come to visit next week." Even a 2-year-old may use words that seem to indicate a knowledge of time and space: later, tomorrow, last night, far away, next time. A child of 2 or 3, however, has very little appreciation of what these terms mean. Noon may mean lunchtime, but if lunchtime is delayed an hour, it is still noon to the young child. Waking from a nap, a child may not even know whether it is the same day. The concepts of weeks and months, minutes and hours are difficult for children to grasp; a date such as Wednesday, April 14, is too abstract a concept for them.

With only limited senses of time, young children have very little idea of cause-and-effect sequences. In fact, their early use of the words "cause" and "because" may have nothing to do with the customary adult understanding of these terms. The same is true of the word "why"—the 4-year-old's favorite question. Children may repeat the question "why?" endlessly, perhaps because they are trying to abstract words or communicate vague feelings. Their associations often are egocentric or unconnected. A child may ask her mother why Daddy isn't home. The mother may answer, "It isn't time" or "He's still working." These may not be the answers the child is looking for because of what *she* associates with her father's evening arrival—dinner, special games, or even punishment.

Spatial relations are another set of concepts that must be developed during the preschool period. The meanings of words such as "in," "out," "to," "from," "near," "far," "over," "under," "up," "down," "inside," and "outside" are learned directly in the process of the child's experience of his own body (Weikart, Rogers & Adcock, 1971). Weikart and associates suggest that the usual progression is for children to learn a concept first with their bodies (crawling *under* a table) and then with objects (pushing a toy truck *under* a table). Later, they learn to identify the concept in pictures ("See the boat go *under* the bridge!") and are able to verbalize it.

Beyond Piaget: Social Perspectives

In recent decades, some of Piaget's conclusions about the mental capabilities of young children have been challenged. His specific conclusions about the limitations of children's thought at different ages have been called into question. Critics have disputed his view of the child as a solitary explorer attempting to make sense of the world. Instead, these developmental psychologists argue, learning takes place within a framework of relationships with parents, caretakers, and peers. What's more, such interaction occurs within the context of the beliefs and rules in the child's specific culture. Piaget saw the developing child as an "active scientist," learning as he goes along by experimenting with solutions to problems. Piagetian tasks were purposely devised to isolate ideas, such as conservation of number or quantity, to determine whether the child could use the concept in the experimental condition.

Since Piaget developed his theory about how children think, some developmental psychologists have looked at children from a very different perspective. Rather than the "active scientist" described by Piaget, these psychologists emphasize that a child is a social being. According to these psychologists, a child figures out how to interpret her experiences by interacting with more experienced people—parents, teachers, older children. In the course of daily interaction, the adults in the child's life pass on the rules and expectations of their particular culture (Bruner & Haste, 1987). Some theorists conclude that the process of growth is not strictly divisible into a series of specific stages (Bornstein & Bruner, 1986).

Piaget used unfamiliar materials and problems to determine a child's conceptual abilities. If the ability to solve a problem is linked to assessing real situations with the help of clues from the environment and help from adults, a more realistic format is needed. Following this reasoning, Piaget's experiment for demonstrating egocentricity was altered in one respect. Instead of asking the child to give the perspective of a doll behind mountains, the task was changed to the more realistic one of determining if a boy could be seen by a police officer. In solving the police officer's problem, the children were more likely to see another person's perspective than in Piaget's more remote task (Hughes & Donaldson, 1979). When Piagetian problems are presented so that they make "human sense," they are clear to younger children (Donaldson, 1978.)

In the following example, Valerie, age 5½, cannot solve Piaget's class inclusion problem with beads, although she can explain the principles of class inclusion to her mother:

> Valerie asked her mother if she loved her more than she loved all the kids in her kindergarten. Her mother hesitated, since Valerie's brother was also in the kindergarten, and answered that she loved Valerie and David more than the other kids at the kindergarten. Valerie looked at her mother with a "Silly Mom" kind of look, and explained, "David and I are *some* of all the kids at the kindergarten—so if you said you loved the kids at the kindergarten you'd be saying you love us too, and you wouldn't have to leave anybody out!" (Rogoff, 1990, p. 5)

The psychologist reports that the next day, Valerie's curious mother tried Piaget's traditional class inclusion problem with Valerie, using red and green wooden beads. When asked to indicate all the wooden beads, Valerie pointed to all the beads. But when asked whether there were more red beads or more wooden beads or the same amount, Valerie claimed that there were more red beads (Rogoff, 1990).

Cognitive development is seen as a social and cultural process. The ways that adults demonstrate how a problem is solved are part of learning to think. All cultures initiate children into a myriad of activities through what has been called **guided participation.** When young children learn to help set or clear the table or to sing "Happy Birthday," specific aspects of cultural activity are being transmitted from the more experienced members, adults, to less experienced members, children.

If development is looked at as a training process, how does a child work toward gaining abilities just beyond reach? To explain this process, Russian theorist Vygotsky provided the concept of the **zone of proximal development** (ZPD), in which children develop through participation in activities slightly beyond their competence, with the assistance of adults or more skilled children (Vygotsky, 1978).

Katherine Nelson (1986) argues that a knowledge of events is the key to understanding the child's mind. Whereas Piaget tends to focus on what children don't know, such as categories and numbers, Nelson is interested in what children do know, what they have learned from their own experiences. She believes that a child's day-to-day experiences become the material for her mental life and

guided participation The process by which more experienced people transmit cultural information to children.

zone of proximal development Vygotsky's concept of children's ability to develop through participation in activities slightly beyond their competence with the help of adults.

problem-solving abilities. Because the child's cognitive processes are based on real-life events, a child's understanding of the world is embedded in social or cultural knowledge.

Memory

A fundamental aspect of cognitive development is the ability to remember. It allows a person to perceive selectively, classify, reason, and generally form more complex concepts.

THE COMPUTER MODEL   To explain how memory functions, some psychologists (such as the information-processing theorists discussed in Chapter 2) have used the computer as a model for the human brain. Memory is an aspect of this computer brain, having storage capacity for information and an array of "associational switches" that gives access to what is stored. The system of associational switches allows the individual to put new items into the memory and take them out in a particular order.

Information theorists think of memory as having three parts: (1) a sensory register that records information received through the senses, (2) a short-term memory that holds what the mind is conscious of at the moment, and (3) a long-term memory that holds items for as long as a lifetime. Information comes into the system and makes contact with the sensory register, which holds it for a very brief period— around 250 milliseconds. This is sometimes called the "very short-term memory." The information is then either lost or transferred to the short-term memory, often described as the "working" memory. The short-term memory holds the information that a person is consciously aware of at any one time and keeps it longer than does the sensory register. Nevertheless, it loses information fairly rapidly. Our attention is somewhat fleeting, and we are conscious of something for only a short time unless we concentrate on it.

The last type of memory is long-term memory. Some theorists believe that nothing in the long-term memory is ever lost (except by damage to the brain). The long-term memory constitutes a person's permanent knowledge base. Information such as one's Social Security number and birth date are kept there (Atkinson & Shriffrin, 1971; Hagen, Longeward, & Kail, 1975).

The things the memory holds can usually be categorized as images, actions, or words. For this reason, researchers often refer to visual memory, motor memory, and verbal memory. The visual memory, as we saw in infancy, is the first to develop. If adults are asked to remember their very early years, often they cannot remember much before the age of 3. Under hypnosis or in psychotherapy, they occasionally recall things earlier than this, but their memories tend to be pictorial. They often recall locations, actions, and nonverbal events as if they were seeing a movie, but they have difficulty putting these images into words. Adults usually have verbally coded recollections after the ages of 4 to 6 and therefore can talk about them. One of the reasons for this is that the development of language in preoperational children may enable them to store new information for longer periods of time. They are no longer as dependent on their visual and motor abilities. Let us consider some other memory tasks and see how well preschool children perform them.

RECOGNITION AND RECALL   Studies of preschool children's memory skills have focused on two different behaviors—*recognition* and *recall*. **Recognition** refers to the ability to select from pictures or objects that are currently present or events currently happening only those one has seen or experienced before. For example, children may recognize a picture in a book as something they have seen before but be unable to name it or tell us about it. **Recall** refers to the ability to retrieve information about objects or events that are not present or current. Recall requires the generation of information from long-term memory without the object in view. For instance, if a child who is looking at a picture book is asked what picture comes next and then names it correctly, he would be recalling the next picture.

Myers and Perlmutter (1978) have found preschool children's performance on recognition tasks to be quite good, but their recall performance is poor; both forms of remembering improve, however, between the ages of 2 and 5. In a recognition task when many objects were shown only once to children between the ages of 2 and 5, even the youngest could correctly point to 81% of them, and the older children remembered 92%. The study showed that preschool children have considerable proficiency in the recognition skills necessary to encode and retain substantial amounts of information. In recall studies, however, when children between the ages of 2 and 4 were asked to name objects that the experimenter had just shown, the 3-year-olds were able to name only 22% of the items and the 4-year-olds only 40%—a considerable difference from the scores attained in the recognition task. Preschool children are clearly better at recognition than at recall, but children may perform better on such memory tasks if their care-givers routinely ask many questions that test children's memories (Ratner, 1984).

REHEARSAL AND ORGANIZATION   Young children's recall difficulties are generally assumed to occur because of their limited strategies for encoding and retrieval (Flavell, 1977; Myers & Perlmutter, 1978). Preschool children do not spontaneously organize or rehearse information that they want to remember, as older children and adults often do. If you give an adult a list to memorize, such as "cat, chair, airplane, dog, desk, car," the adult might first classify the items as "animals," "furniture," and "vehicles" and then repeat (or rehearse) the words quietly before being asked to recall the list. The adult, therefore, has used two memory strategies—**organization** and **rehearsal.** Adults and children, from age 6 on, improve their ability to recall information when taught memory strategies, but it has been found difficult to teach preschoolers to organize and rehearse information.

Yet preschool children remember a great many things. Try skipping a sentence in a child's favorite storybook or adding a new ingredient to her fruit salad. The child will remember exactly how it was before. Experimental tasks that demonstrate memory in adults may not tap the abilities that children use to enhance memory. But when children are given tasks in a context that is meaningful to them, they have demonstrated what may be rudimentary strategies for remembering. For example, when very young children were required to remember the location of a hidden object, they frequently used rehearsal-like verbalizations—referring to the hidden toy, the fact that it was hidden, the hiding place, and their having found it. These behaviors can be interpreted as evidence of an early natural propensity to keep what must be remembered in mind (DeLoache, Cassidy, & Brown, 1985). When groups of children who were asked to "remember" or to

recognition The ability to correctly identify items previously experienced when they appear again.

recall The ability to retrieve information and events that are not present.

organization and rehearsal Strategies for improving recall used mainly by adult learners.

"play with" toys were compared, the children who played with the toys demonstrated a better memory of them. This suggests that the act of playing contributed to the children's mental organization of experiencing the toys. Their memory strategy appears to involve perceiving the items through use (Newman, 1990).

EVENT SCRIPTS AND SEQUENTIAL UNDERSTANDING   It is increasingly clear that children are able to remember information that is ordered temporally, in a time sequence. They appear to structure a series of occurrences into an ordered, meaningful whole. In one study, children were asked to describe how they had made clay pieces 2 weeks before. When the children were given the opportunity to remake the same clay pieces, they were able to describe how they had worked step by step. It appears that children are able to organize and remember a sequence of actions after a single experience (Smith, Ratner, & Hobart, 1987).

Children are aware that an event such as a birthday party is composed of an orderly progression of events: a beginning when the guests arrive with presents; a series of events in the middle including playing games, singing "Happy Birthday," blowing out the candles, and eating cake and ice cream; and an end when each guest gets a favor. Children have good memory abilities for repeated events, such as a family dinnertime, grocery shopping, or a day at nursery school. It is as if they have developed a format or script for these routine events (Mandler, 1983; Nelson et al., 1983). When mothers talk to their young children about objects and events that are not immediately present, such as describing the errands to be done after lunch, they help their children to develop scripts, and thereby remember, the events (Lucariello & Nelson, 1987).

In younger children, events can be remembered only in the order in which they occur. The ability to order and remember information with more flexibility develops with familiarity and over time. Only when children have become extremely familiar with an ordered event can they reverse the sequence of steps (Bauer & Thal, 1990).

PLAY AND LEARNING

Play is children's unique way of experiencing the world. Play satisfies many needs in a child's life: the need to be stimulated and diverted, to express natural exuberance, to experience change for its own sake, to satisfy curiosity, to explore, and to experiment within risk-free conditions. Play has been called the "work of childhood" because of its central role in the young child's development. It promotes the growth of sensory capacities and physical skills and provides endless opportunities to exercise and expand newfound intellectual skills. Play is different from any other kind of activity. By its very nature, playing is not directed toward a goal. As anyone who has observed a busy playground can attest, children expend great energy just for the fun of it. Catherine Garvey (1977) defined play as something that (1) is engaged in simply for pleasure; (2) has no purpose other than itself; (3) players choose to do; (4) requires players to be "actively engaged" in it; and (5) relates to other areas of life—that is, it furthers social development and enhances creativity.

Types of Play

How children play changes as they develop. Young preschoolers play with other children, talk about common activities, and borrow and lend toys. But their interaction does not include setting goals or making rules for their play. Older preschoolers, however, can play together and help one another in an activity that has a goal. Preschool children like to build and create with objects, and to take on roles and use props (Isenberg & Quisenberry, 1988).

Each type of play has its own characteristics and functions. The types are not rigidly distinct, however, and may overlap in any play situation. Some of the major forms of children's play are described below.

SENSORY PLEASURE   The aim of this kind of play is sensory experience in and for itself. Children will endlessly splash water, ring doorbells, chew grass, bang pots, open bottles, and pluck flower petals just to experience new sounds, tastes, odors, and textures. Sensory play teaches children important facts about their bodies, senses, and the qualities of things in the environment.

PLAY WITH MOTION   Running, jumping, twirling, and skipping are just some of the countless forms of play with motion that are enjoyed for their own sake. Play that involves the continually changing sensation of movement is one of the earliest types that infants experience—being lifted up high and swung around by an adult, blowing bubbles with their food, or simply rocking. Infants and adults often engage in movement routines that are not only exciting and stimulating for children but also give them painless practice in body coordination. Play with motion is often begun by an adult and provides infants with some of their earliest social experiences. Children do not usually share this kind of activity with other children until about age 3 (Garvey, 1977).

ROUGH-AND-TUMBLE PLAY   Parents and teachers often criticize and try to eliminate the kind of rough-and-tumble mock-fighting play that young children are quite fond of. This is usually an attempt to reduce the amount of aggression and real fighting among children. But rough-and-tumble play is play-fighting, not real fighting. Recent research suggests that it provides real benefits for the child. Not only is it a chance to exercise and release energy, but children learn to handle their feelings, to control their impulses, and to filter out negative behaviors that are inappropriate in a group. What is more, they are learning to make the important distinction between pretend and real (Pellegrini, 1987).

PLAY WITH LANGUAGE   Children love to play with language. They experiment with its rhythm and cadences. They mix up words to create new meanings. They play with language to poke fun at the world and to verify their grasp of reality. They use it as a buffer against expressions of anger. The primary function of language—meaningful communication—is often lost in language play. Children concentrate on the language itself, playfully manipulating its sounds, patterns, and meanings.

Judith Schwartz (1981) has looked at and provided examples of several kinds of language play. Sometimes, children play with sound and rhythm, regularly repeating letters and words in a steady beat: La la la / Lol li pop / La la la/ Lol li

(a)

(b)

(c)

(d)

(e)

(f)

Different types of play satisfy different needs and help to promote different aspects of development. Some of the major forms of children's play include: (a) sensory play; (b) constructive play or play with games and rituals; (c) rough-and-tumble play; (d) play with language; (e) dramatic play and modeling; and (f) play with motion.

pop. They will also make patterns with words as if they were practicing a grammatical drill or sentences using the same words: Hit it. / Sit it. / Slit it. / Mit it. And: There is the light. / Where is the light? / Here is the light. In a less frequent kind of play, children play with the meaning of words or invent words to fit meanings. For example: San Diego, Sandiego, Sandi Ego / San Diego, Sandi Ego / Eggs aren't sandy! Why do children play with language? Partly because it's funny. It makes others laugh when a young child says something like: "I'm gonna telly 'cause you put jelly in my belly and made me smelly."

Playing with language also gives young children a chance to practice and master the grammar and words they are learning. By ages 3 and 4, children are using some basic linguistic rules and structures of meaning. They ask questions such as, "Couldn't table legs be fitted with shoes?" and "Since there is running water, is there sitting water?" (Chukovsky, 1963, pp. 61–62; Garvey, 1977, pp. 59–60).

Finally, children use language to control their experiences. People tend to make order out of their experiences by creating structures and rules around them. Older children similarly use language to structure their play. They create rituals—sometimes very elaborate ones—that must be followed; by following the rituals carefully, they control the experience (Schwartz, 1981).

DRAMATIC PLAY AND MODELING One of the major types of play involves taking on roles or models: playing house, mimicking a parent going to work, pretending to be a firefighter, a nurse, an astronaut, or a truck driver. Such play involves not only imitation of whole patterns of behavior but also considerable fantasy and novel ways of interaction. As we shall see shortly, children come to understand various social relationships, rules, and certain other aspects of the culture through imitative play.

GAMES, RITUALS, AND COMPETITIVE PLAY As children grow older, their play involves rules and has a specific aim. They make decisions about taking turns, they set up guidelines about what is and what is not permitted, and they often create situations in which someone wins and someone loses. Although the intricate rules of baseball and chess are beyond most preschoolers, they are beginning to cope with the ritual and rules of tag, hide-and-seek, red rover, and perhaps war games. Such games require, and help to develop, cognitive skills like learning rules, understanding the sequence of cause and effect, realizing the consequences of various actions, learning about winning and losing, and learning to fit behavior to certain patterns and rules (Herron & Sutton-Smith, 1971; Kamii & DeVries, 1980).

Play and Cognitive Development

As already mentioned, play promotes cognitive development in many areas. In play with motion, preschool children become aware of speed, weight, gravity, direction, and balance. In play with objects, they realize that objects have conventional and appropriate uses and properties. In their play with others, children practice social concepts and roles while learning aspects of their culture.

EXPLORING PHYSICAL OBJECTS When preschool children play with all sorts of physical objects—sand, stones, water, and other kinds of toys and materials—they discover and learn about the properties of these objects and about the physical laws that affect these objects. When playing in a sandbox, for example, a child can learn that different objects make different marks in the sand. When bouncing a ball on the floor, a child can learn that throwing the ball harder will make it bounce higher. When building a house with blocks, a child can learn that blocks must balance and be properly supported before they will stay in place. By engaging in constructive play, then, children acquire bits of information that they can use to build their knowledge. This greater knowledge, in turn, lets them learn at increasingly higher levels of understanding and competence (Forman & Hill, 1980). Gradually, they learn to compare and classify objects, and they develop a better understanding of concepts—for example, size, shape, and texture. In addition, through active play children develop skills that make them feel physically confident, secure, and self-assured (Athey, 1984).

FOCUS ON AN ISSUE

PLAY TUTORING: THE ROLE OF ADULTS IN CHILDREN'S PLAY

Imagine several neighborhood children, all 4 and 5 years old, playing "store" in the backyard. The oldest is the self-appointed shopkeeper and leader. The others are customers, cashiers, baggers, and clerks. The "store" extends over much of the backyard, including patio and barbecue furniture, a sandbox, some doll furniture, and the lower limbs of trees. Items to buy include sand toys as dishes, rocks as shoes, and sheets of newspaper as clothing. The children have been busily involved in this dramatic activity for nearly an hour—setting up the store, assigning roles, planning situations, and carrying out several vignettes. You are surprised at the length of time this activity has held their interest. You are pleased by the level of their language and social skills, and at their ability to solve problems. This activity seems to have considerable educational value. But the children are making lots of "mistakes." They overprice items, or give back more money in change than they get in payment. They make strange rules like "only boys can buy rakes," or "apples aren't good for you." Also, there are numerous disputes among the children about the "right" way to do things.

Adults watching this scene are frequently tempted to get involved in this play, or at least to correct some misunderstandings. After all, if this is a good learning experience, why not make it a little better?

Child development experts disagree upon the value of direct adult participation in children's sociodramatic play. Many specialists warn that in sociodramatic play, children need time to pose problems as well as test and try problem solutions. They need to create their own storyline and dialogue, not follow someone else's. Adults have a tendency to take over the leadership, make the decisions, solve the problems, and thus limit the educational value of the play activity.

Yet, recently, some psychologists have begun to argue for more direct involvement by grownups, provided it is done carefully. In what way would adults' involvement benefit children? What types of adult involvement in children's play actually help rather than hinder a child's social, linguistic, and cognitive development?

In recent years, child psychologists have become interested in the developmental effects of what is called *play training*—the direct and indirect involvement of adults in children's play. Studies indicate that children who frequently engage in *sociodramatic play*—play involving imitations of life situations, such as having a family dinner, working in an office, going to the hospital, and the like—have higher levels of social and cognitive skills. For example, children who often engage in lengthy, elaborate sociodramatic play also show more persistence in school-related tasks. Elaborate sociodramatic play appears to be less common among children from lower socioeconomic groups than among middle-class children who have the leisure and materials to develop such play

PLAY AND EGOCENTRISM   The egocentrism that Piaget ascribes to preoperational children is particularly evident in their play with others. Two-year-olds will watch other children and seem interested in them, but usually they will not approach them (Bronson, 1975). If they do approach them, the interaction usually centers on playing with the same toy or object (Mueller & Lucas, 1975). Children 2 years old and younger may seem to be playing together, but they are almost always playing out separate fantasies.

Some have thought that by the time they are 3 years old or more, most children can understand another child's perspective on the world. The conclusions of most studies, however, have been uncertain (Schantz, 1975). In one study, children were asked to describe how a playmate might feel in a given situation (Borke, 1971, 1973). Borke asked children to guess how another child would react to losing a pet, breaking a toy, or attending a birthday party. By age 4, it seems that

(Feitelson & Ross, 1973; Rubin et al., 1976; Smith & Dodsworth, 1978; Smilansky, 1968). Experiments in play training were undertaken to determine if given materials, experience, and gentle tutoring in longer, more elaborate sociodramatic play, the children from lower socioeconomic groups would make gains in linguistic, cognitive, and social skills. In fact, they did. The children who had play tutoring showed significant gains in language, IQ scores, creativity, impulse control, and cooperation (Feitelson & Ross, 1973; Rubin et al., 1976; Smith & Dodsworth, 1978; Smilansky, 1968).

The play-training experiments included both direct and indirect adult involvement. Indirect involvement required an adult to remain outside the drama but offer comments and suggestions to the children playing. Direct involvement required an adult to take a direct part, adopt a role or roles, and show by example what was wanted in the way of play behavior. Both forms of adult participation had beneficial results. Since those experiments, conducted mainly in the 1970s, the value of play training has been confirmed by field observations at both preschool classes and home. Adult involvement in children's play affords the children a number of immediate benefits in addition to the long-term ones of increased cognitive and social skills. Children have the sense that their playing is worthwhile and has the approval of adults. Parents or teachers joining children in their games build rapport both at home and in class. When adults

take part in the games, the children are less easily distracted and stick with their games longer than they might have otherwise. Persistence at play may have two very valuable outcomes: (1) The play episodes become richer and more meaningful, and (2) children gain the habit of sustained commitment to an activity, which will prove important later in life. But the adults need to use caution and not intervene too much in children's play.

Investigators have suggested three basic modes of adult participation in children's play. *Parallel playing* involves having an adult play alongside a child without directly interacting, as in each constructing a separate object from wooden blocks. *Coplaying* involves having an adult join children in an ongoing play of which the children remain in control. In this instance, an adult interacts with children but provides only indirect guidance by asking questions. *Play tutoring* involves having an adult teach children new play behaviors.

Sensitive adult participation in children's play can be very beneficial to the children involved. Children enjoy such participation and learn much from the examples, ideas, and support of older people.

Based on James E. Johnson, James F. Christie, and Thomas D. Yawkey, *Play and Early Childhood Development* (Glenview, IL: Scott, Foresman, 1987), pp. 21–25, 30–32.

some children can reliably identify those situations likely to produce happiness, sadness, fear, and anger.

In another study, Shatz and Gelman (1973) asked 4-year-olds to describe to 2-year-olds how a particular toy worked. According to this study, even 4-year-olds understood the necessity of addressing younger children in simple terms. They found that 4-year-olds spoke slowly, used short sentences, employed many attention-getting words, such as "see," "look," and "here," and often repeated the child's name. Four-year-olds did not speak to older children or adults in this way. The study suggests that preschool children have some appreciation of younger children's needs and are able to modify their behavior to meet those needs.

DRAMATIC PLAY AND SOCIAL KNOWLEDGE   Older preoperational children are testing their social knowledge in dramatic play. The imitating, pretending, and role taking that occur in dramatic play promote the growth of symbolic representation—the transforming of here-and-now objects and events into symbols. Dramatic play also gives children the opportunity to project themselves into other personalities, to experiment with different roles, and to experience a broader range of thought and feeling. This role playing leads to better understanding of others as well as a clearer definition of one's self (Fein, 1984).

Role playing allows children to experiment with a variety of behaviors and to experience the reactions and consequences of that behavior. For example, children who play hospital day after day with dolls, friends, or alone will play many different roles: patient, doctor, nurse, visitor. In acting out these roles, children may be motivated by very real fears and anxieties of being immobilized in a hospital bed, being dependent on others, and having their bodies acted upon by others. Whatever the dramatic situation, role playing allows children to express intense feelings, resolve conflicts, and integrate these feelings and conflicts with things they already understand.

THE ROLE OF PEERS   Children spend far more time interacting directly with one another than with adults. Children play with siblings and other children at home, in the neighborhood, at school, and most everywhere that children go. In many cultures the importance of children's interaction with other children is even greater than it is in the American middle class (Rogoff, 1990). In many societies, child care is largely carried out by 5- to 10-year-old children, who tend infants and toddlers (Watson-Gegeo & Gegeo, 1989). Children may carry a younger sibling or cousin around on their backs or hips, thus enabling the younger children to be involved with the sights and sounds of the community (Rogoff, 1990).

Children's groups around the world generally include a mix of ages. In fact, childhood groups based on age—so common in American culture—result from groupings in school and other activities organized by adults that are not part of all cultures. In the United States and throughout the world, informal neighborhood groups include children of various ages. The mixed-age peer group can provide older children with the opportunity to practice teaching and child care with younger children, while younger children can imitate and practice role relations with older children (Whiting & Edwards, 1988). Even the youngest children can use other children as models. The playful activities of children may be especially important for developing new ways of thinking. Playing around may suggest novel, creative solutions to problems.

ART AS DISCOVERY AND PROBLEM SOLVING The interdependence of cognitive and motor skills is apparent in children's art. Here, fine motor coordination works with perceptual, cognitive, and emotional development. The degree of development in all these separate areas is evident in the final product. But, no matter how much we examine the end result of the artistic process, the exploratory process itself is what is important—the daubing, smearing, scribbling, and finally, the representational drawing (Gardner, 1973a). From the moment children take a crayon in hand and begin to scribble, at about 18 months, they begin working out forms and patterns that will be essential to their later progress. Rhoda Kellogg (1970) suggested that children start making art by scribbling and by placing their scribbles at different places on the paper. By age 3, they draw shapes in increasingly complex forms. By age 4 or 5, they start to draw representational pictures of houses, people, and other familiar objects.

Once children start to draw representational objects, their drawings reveal how they think and feel. Goodnow (1977) suggests that children use their drawings as a problem-solving process. They work in specific sequences and have specific rules about space and position of elements in the drawing. For example, when drawing a picture of a girl, they may start at the top by drawing hair; when they have finished that, they move in sequence down to the next part of the figure. If the hair occupies the space that a later-drawn part, such as the arms, would normally occupy, the children may omit the arms, change the shape of them to fit around the hair, or reposition the arms. Only rarely will they invade the space that the hair already occupies. These rules about space and position carry over into all drawings children do.

Children like to handle and manipulate materials in their art. Finger paint, clay, mud, sand, and even soapsuds provide opportunities to experiment with a multitude of new shapes, colors, and textures. Children not only gain a fuller sensory experience of combining texture and appearance but also learn directly about thickness and thinness, solidity and fluidity, and concentration and dilution.

Paintings reveal how children think and feel. Children use art to solve problems, and they follow specific rules and sequences when drawing and painting.

EARLY CHILDHOOD EDUCATION

Schools and programs for preschoolers have become an integral part of educating American children. The changing role of women, and such social trends as two-income families, divorce, and single parenthood, have accelerated this trend. Early childhood education has been promoted as a way to improve the early learning experiences of poor children and as a means of improving America's education system in order to compete successfully with other countries.

In the 1960s, the leaders of the reform movement fostering early childhood programs had ambitious ideas about what 3- and 4-year-olds were likely to gain from schooling. They considered children "competent" to improve their intelligence almost from infancy (Bloom, 1964). A prominent educator claimed that "you can teach any child any subject matter at any age in an intellectually honest way" (Bruner, 1960).

These views of the young learner have been criticized for failing to view the young child as a different kind of learner from the older child. It has been argued that formal instruction puts excessive demands on young children (Elkind, 1986). Young children may actually be harmed by early instruction. Children who are given tasks that are too intellectually demanding are in danger of falling into early patterns of frustration and failure (Ames, 1971).

Although some educators believe that 3- and 4-year-olds should be at home where they will, ideally, receive warmth, security and continuity in the years before beginning school, this option is not open to or desirable to many parents. In addition, research has shown that preschool can offer specific advantages to children. Attending nursery school has been found to foster children's social and emotional development. Compared to children at home, preschool students made advances in sociability, self-expression, independence, and interest in the environment (Mussen, Conger, & Kagan, 1974.) In another study, children attending preschool surpassed home-staying children on such intellectual tasks as vocabulary, comprehending language, and visual memory (Brand & Welsh, 1989). Long-term gains in ability to learn and in reading have been found in both middle-class and poor children. Some educators feel that a year of preschooling helps many youngsters who would otherwise repeat a grade or require special placement (Featherstone, 1985).

Ultimately, it is the nature of the young child's experience of her surroundings—not whether she attends a formal preschool or spends most of her time at home—that will contribute to her ability to learn. Children learn by observing the consequences of their acts, by putting objects into new forms, and by getting feedback from those around them. Whether children are at home or school, their surroundings are a powerful presence that contribute to the enhancement or retardation of their growth. A carefully planned, well-paced early education program can give children the experiences they need for their cognitive development.

Developmentally Appropriate Curriculum

The key concept in defining quality education is "developmental appropriateness." Because children learn in different ways at different ages, what is acceptable for one age group is inappropriate for another. The aim of a developmentally appropriate preschool is to match the school program with the developmental needs and abilities of young children. Within such a setting, the individual needs of each child can be addressed. The developmentally appropriate tasks for 3- and 4-year-olds involve using large and small muscle activity to explore their environment. Educators of young children recognize that development cannot be accelerated or skipped. Each stage of development has its own tasks to accomplish (National Association for the Education of Young Children, 1987).

How can educators best match their educational programs for young children with their students' developmental needs? The National Association for the Education of Young Children (NAEYC) appointed a commission to study this question and to make recommendations. Their conclusions, based on research findings, are presented in the form of guidelines for teachers of early childhood classrooms. Their guidelines for developmentally appropriate programs for preschoolers include the following:

- In place of an "academic" program, an educational curriculum should include all areas of a child's development—physical, emotional, social, and cognitive.

- Curriculum plans should be based on observations of each child's interests and developmental progress, not the average of the group.
- A learning environment should allow for active exploration and interaction with adults, other children, and teaching materials. Highly structured, teacher-directed activities are not encouraged.
- In place of workbooks, dittos, or other abstract materials, young children should be provided with concrete, real activities and materials that are relevant to their lives.
- Adults should respond quickly and directly to children's needs and messages and adapt to children's styles and abilities.

Other guidelines include specific illustrations of appropriate and inappropriate practice for different age levels from infancy to age 8. In Table 9–2 the guidelines for children who are 4 and 5 years old are presented. Stimulating children's skills in all developmental areas fosters the development of self-esteem, social skills, and language abilities. Learning activities that allow children to be "physically and mentally active" are considered to be the appropriate preparation for future learning. In contrast, an emphasis on teaching specific academic skills, such as the rules of reading or mathematics, is considered to be inappropriate. These are tasks that can be mastered at a later, appropriate level of development. It is noteworthy

TABLE 9–2

The National Association for the Education of Young Children Curriculum Guidelines for 4- and 5-Year-Olds

COMPONENT	APPROPRIATE	INAPPROPRIATE
Curriculum goals	All developmental areas, such as physical, social, emotional, and intellectual, are stimulated. Individual abilities and interests determine the activities, which are designed to encourage self-esteem and the desire for learning on the part of children.	Academic excellence is the only quality that is developed. Children are measured solely by how well they perform on standardized tests.
Teaching strategies	Teachers prepare the learning environment for children, who select the activities they are interested in, such as math, games, puzzles, science, music, blocks, books, art, or dramatic play. The children are expected to be physically and mentally active, working individually or in small groups most of the time.	Teachers follow highly structured, teacher-directed lesson plans almost entirely. Children are expected to sit quietly and pay attention to the teacher. They do as the teacher instructs and work most often with commercially manufactured material, such as ditto sheets and flashcards.
Guidance of social and emotional development	Teachers encourage self-control in children by exhibiting this quality themselves, rewarding expected behavior, redirecting children to a more acceptable activity, and setting clear limits. Children are encouraged to develop social skills, such as cooperating in activities and negotiating differences among themselves.	Teachers enforce rules and punish deviations from them and other unacceptable behaviors by making a child sit in a corner or stand isolated from class activity. Children may not relate to one another in class, but if a dispute arises between children in the classroom, the teacher steps in and settles the disagreement.
Development of language and literacy	Children engage in a variety of activities that call for language skills, such as listening to poems and stories, dictating stories about their experiences, reading, and experimenting with writing.	Instruction in reading and writing focuses on such skills as reciting the alphabet and recognizing separate letters.

Adapted from Sue Bredekamp, ed., *Developmentally Appropriate Practice* (Washington, DC: National Association for the Education of Young Children, 1987), pp. 50–51.

that, given the wide range of programs currently offered, a large national organization of educators could reach such near consensus on basic principles (National Association for the Education of Young Children, 1986).

Approaches to Early Education

A number of models for early childhood education have been developed. Some schools follow a particular model closely, but most incorporate elements of various approaches. Following are descriptions of three influential models for teaching preschoolers: the Montessori method, formal didactic education, and open education. Each model incorporates an approach to how children learn, as well as beliefs about how people think and behave in our culture.

MONTESSORI SCHOOLS   Although most Montessori schools in the United States and Canada tend to be expensive private schools, the Montessori method took root in quite different surroundings. Dr. Maria Montessori, an energetic and innovative Italian physician, began her experimental educational methods with retarded children and then with socially disadvantaged children from the tenements of Rome. She believed that children who had experienced a difficult, chaotic, or unpredictable home life needed surroundings that emphasized sequence, order, and regularity. The Montessori approach features a *prepared environment* and carefully designed, self-correcting materials. Each child may select a task to work on individually, returning the materials to the shelf when finished. A typical task

Montessori schools offer children the opportunity to work at individual tasks with little interference from the teacher.

involves arranging in sequence a set of graduated cylinders, weights, or smooth- to rough-textured pieces of cloth. The children may also learn practical tasks, such as washing dishes, making soup, gardening, and painting a real wall. Classrooms are age-mixed, with children from 3 to 7.

The atmosphere in a Montessori school is one of quiet busyness and confident accomplishment. The teacher arranges the environment, but avoids interfering with the learning process; in particular, teachers avoid injecting any "extraneous" elements, such as praise or criticism. The curriculum develops motor and sensory skills, as well as the ability to order and classify materials. These are considered the basic forerunners of more complex tasks, such as reading and understanding mathematics. Many contemporary educational techniques incorporate some Montessori methods—particularly self-teaching materials, individually paced progress, real-life tasks, and the relative absence of both praise and criticism.

FORMAL DIDACTIC EDUCATION   The formal "back-to-basics" approach uses carefully structured lessons to inculcate a particular set of skills. It is typified by the Bereiter and Engelmann program (1966) designed for disadvantaged children. To teach the requisite skills in a gradual, sequential order (later known as the Distar program), the two psychologists divided the children into homogeneous small groups of about five members. The teacher asked a question or offered a sentence, and the children responded by answering the question or repeating the sentence in unison. The children also interacted individually with the teacher, receiving immediate feedback and warm praise for success. Positive reinforcement was relied upon extensively. Lessons were taught in 20-minute drill periods, and little time

APPLICATION

EXCELLENT EARLY EDUCATION: AN ITALIAN MODEL

When preschool teachers and parents in the northern Italian town of Reggio Emilia became concerned about the major role that warlike action figures were assuming in children's dramatic play, they decided to redirect the interest in war games by having the children create the space scene in which their imaginary battles took place. Over a period of time, children constructed several space vehicles out of cardboard boxes, tin cans, string, and other recycled materials. Soon the action figures were put away, as the entire class took part in what grew into an outer-space project. The group project provided a direct way to encourage positive social values and foster critical thinking (New, 1990).

Ongoing activities such as this outer-space project form the core of the early education program of the town of Reggio Emilia, which has received worldwide attention from educators. In Reggio Emilia, educating young children is an important priority well supported in the municipal budget. This reflects national policies promoting child welfare. Since 1968, Italy has supported public preschools for all 3- to 6-year-olds.

A climate of cooperation between parents and teachers is a key to the success of early education in this Italian town. Rather than substituting for a mother's care, preschool is seen as a source of positive relationships and experiences for the child. It is agreed that no one has a monopoly on knowing what is best for children. Parents, teachers, and community members are partners in caring for and educating children (New, 1990).

The process of collaboration begins by keeping the same group of children and teacher together for a 3-year period at both the child-care and preschool levels. When children enter the class, they know who their classmates and teacher will be for an extended time, which also allows parents to form a community around the school experience. The children feel secure within the ongoing familiar environment. Class trips often become a family social event.

These long-term home/school relationships have the flavor of the traditionally typical Italian extended family (New, 1988). Parents and teachers work together to foster each child's development. One means of communication is the creation of an album for each child upon entry to a class. Family members and school personnel contribute observations, photographs, and anecdotal records to the albums, which serve as a method of communication between parents and teachers, document the child's progress, and affirm this important period of life (New, 1990).

The preschool curriculum is based on the belief that

was allowed for free play between periods because it was felt that play distracted the children from learning specific facts, principles, and skills.

Research on the Distar program indicated that these children did learn the specific behavioral objectives quickly and well. Long-term results, however, showed little lasting transfer of learned skills to other educational settings. Again, there are several explanations for these results:

1. The follow-up schools for these disadvantaged children might have been so stifling, socially and intellectually, that they could not encourage success in even the brightest, most motivated child.

2. The difference in expectations between the Distar program and the public school was perhaps so great that the particular behaviors could not be sustained.

3. The children might have become overly dependent on the rewards of praise, hugs, and smiles and failed to derive any intrinsic pleasure from the learning and problem-solving process.

children's learning is promoted by actively exploring problems that children and teachers help determine. It is planned around projects that grow out of interests that children express, teachers' knowledge of what interests children, and teachers' observations of children's needs, as well as parents' concerns. Projects may involve the entire class or only a small group of children. A sunny day can lead to an extensive exploration of the properties of shadows. Other projects emerge from children's natural curiosity about themselves—their bodies, their feelings, the sense of being alive. The outer-space project resulted from parental and teacher concerns regarding specific cognitive and social concepts (Gandini & Edwards, 1988). Projects can last from several days to months. This reflects a belief in the needs of both children and teacher to explore, play with, and work out an idea.

Art is considered to be inseparable from the rest of the curriculum in Reggio Emilia. In fact, art is central to the education process as a form of both exploration and expression (Gandini & Edwards, 1988). Because of the crucial role given to creative arts in learning, children's creative efforts in various media are referred to as "symbolic representation," and art forms are viewed as symbolic languages for making sense of the child's world. Each preschool has an art teacher who is available to work with children throughout the day. Children are given many opportunities to discover the properties of and use artistic materials. Educators have been impressed by the depth and thoroughness of the work, the attention to detail, and the careful expression of feelings, ideas, observations, and findings (Katz, 1990). Projects combine these creative endeavors with other media. Teachers often take pictures to capture ideas and to show the process of creating a project. Activities and discussions are combined with creating images.

The environment and use of space in preschools in Emilio Reggia support the curriculum. Drawings, paintings, and sculptures by children are displayed, along with photographs and displays of projects in process. Materials to stimulate children's thinking are visible and readily available for use. Rooms connect in ways that promote community, yet allow space for children's works-in-progress that require weeks of effort.

What impresses American educators most about the preschools of Reggio Emilia is what they tell us about the potential for enhancing children's creative and intellectual development. They believe that American parents and teachers can learn from this Italian preschool system what children can do when given optimal conditions for learning (New, 1990).

At any rate, children in these programs displayed marked initial success, with kindergartners often reading on a second-grade level. This early advantage disappeared by at least the fourth grade, when these children became indistinguishable from other "disadvantaged" children.

OPEN EDUCATION   Open education is an eclectic movement that draws upon the work of such diverse theorists as Piaget, John Dewey (1961), and Susan Isaacs (1930). In contrast to assumptions about the nature of open education, based on its name, "open education" does not signify the absence of structure. Indeed, good open education, as exemplified by the British Infant School, requires extensive planning and preparation. The British Infant School was designed to help children enter the formal English educational structure by age 8 or 9 (Plowden, 1967). Some of its more important characteristics are:

The Integrated Day.   Instead of discrete periods for each subject, children work at continuing projects that employ several skills at once. Setting up a "business office" may entail a field trip for observation, a written report, group discussion, and some artwork or other visual aids.

Vertical Groupings. Children of different ages are in the same classroom. Within several years, a child can develop from being the youngest, following and learning from others, to a position of leadership and responsibility.

Child Input in Decision Making. Children in open classrooms often choose from a variety of activities, deciding how they want to participate and for how long. A child's ability to make responsible decisions is respected, and such potential incentives as reward and punishment are minimized.

The achievement of the British Infant School is impressive; the children equal or surpass the performance of students in more traditional programs. But the school's curriculum planning is extensive, and community support must be strong. Some open classrooms in other educational systems are unsuccessful; the difference seems to lie in the skill and forethought of the planners and teachers.

Compensatory Education

Early childhood education has been seen as a way to reverse the damaging effects of poverty and other social problems in America. In 1965, the federal government initiated Head Start, a large-scale effort to break what was called the "cycle of poverty" that affected children and families in urban, suburban, and rural areas.

Head Start programs were designed to provide early learning experiences for disadvantaged children.

Head Start is an early childhood preschool program for targeted children from poor families. It is designed to provide the cognitive, emotional, and social experiences needed to succeed in school. In Head Start programs, children practice the cognitive skills typically fostered in early childhood. These include counting, comparing, learning the parts of their bodies, dancing, and singing, using various materials.

Does this year of compensatory schooling make a difference? The first major evaluative study of the effects of Head Start, the Westinghouse Study (1969), found that although Head Start students entered school with better skills than poor children who had not participated in the year of preschool, within a few years there was no difference between the groups in academic performance as measured by standardized tests. This finding of no lasting gains on test scores has generally been confirmed.

But is performance on standardized tests the appropriate measure of Head Start's effectiveness? Many educators and social scientists feel that it is not. They look to the comprehensive goals of Head Start to evaluate its success. Head Start was initiated with the far-reaching goal of changing the lives of children, families, and communities. Many Head Start parents feel uncomfortable with the schooling of their children. They may have been failures at school themselves. Therefore, the involvement of parents and families was built into the program. Head Start parents are expected to volunteer as aides in the classroom, attend parenting classes and job-training programs, and participate in making policies for the program. The goal is that parents and educators work together to improve the lives of the Head Start families (Lombardi, 1990).

By other criteria Head Start has had positive effects. Although their achievement tests were not higher, high school students who had attended Head Start were better adjusted in school than their classmates (Copple, Cline, & Smith, 1987). They participated more fully in school and were less often identified as children with serious academic problems. They had better attendance and were retained less often. This group of children appeared to have made gains that are not readily measured. They had a commitment to school and could meet its demands. Participating in Head Start may have made their parents more committed to education for their children. By these criteria, Head Start seems to succeed in getting children off to a better start.

Head Start is a massive, federally funded effort to break the cycle of poverty in the United States. It is not the only model for helping poor children learn. The results of a small experimental program (Consortium Studies, 1978) indicate the potential of more intensive intervention than Head Start has been able to offer. Educators were able to combine an excellent preschool program with intense parent involvement, training, and assistance. Comprehensive services to meet the job, housing, health, educational, and social needs of families were provided. The program brought about positive changes in how parents related to their children, as well as providing enriched school experiences. The program showed that programs conducted with abundant resources and care can benefit educationally at-risk children. Although it may not be possible to develop such intensive intervention programs on a large scale, the success of this pilot project highlights the interdependence of the preschool gains and involving and supporting parents and families.

The positive efforts of Head Start and other compensatory preschool programs cannot operate in a vacuum. They must be linked to children's families, to early educational experiences, and to the schools that children attend after Head Start. Early intervention for poor children includes pre- and postnatal care, parent education, and quality child care (Committee for Economic Development, 1987). Above all, education for young children must be a partnership between schools and parents to foster learning and development.

STUDY OUTLINE

Physical-Motor Development

The physical-motor activities of preschoolers (ages 2 to 6) lay the groundwork for future cognitive and social-emotional development. The developmental sequences in physical-motor activity may be either continuous (as in the progression from scribbling to writing) or discontinuous (as in the sorting of thoughts before arriving at complex ideas).

By the ages of 2 and 3, most children can walk, run, and manipulate objects but still have limited coordination; by 4 and 5, motor coordination has advanced considerably and can be used in complex games and tasks.

Learning Physical-Motor Skills. The motor skills that children learn first include both elementary and more complicated tasks. Although many debate whether children should be trained in skills or simply allowed to develop them naturally (in

the course of free exploration), self-designed, self-paced schedules of learning seem best.

Whatever the activity, the learning will depend on *readiness, motivation, activity, attention,* and *feedback.* Children must have attained a state of readiness before they can learn any new skill; having attained it, they learn rapidly and with little effort. They may be motivated either by the enjoyment the activity brings or by outside factors, such as encouragement and competition. An optimal environment provides children with opportunities to practice motor skills. Children must learn to focus their attention, which they do most easily by active imitation of an adult or peer model. The feedback that children receive from the physical-motor activity itself is an important factor in the learning process.

Cognitive Development

Children from ages 2 to 6 develop their ability for symbolic representation—the transformation of physical objects and events into mental symbols. Once children begin to use symbols, their thought processes become more complex: They are able to demonstrate similarities between objects and show some awareness of past and future.

Pretend and Real. Pretend play provides important experience for child development. Children who have had a lot of experience with pretend play are better able to understand how an object can change shape or form and still remain the same object, and they are more sensitive to the feelings and points of view of others.

Limits of Preoperational Thought. The cognitive processes of preoperational children are, according to Piaget, *concrete, irreversible, egocentric,* and *centered.* They focus on the present state of things and are not aware of how things can be transformed. They have difficulty with classification, time, sequence, and spatial relationships.

Beyond Piaget: Social Perspectives. In recent decades, psychologists who see development as a social and cultural process have challenged some of Piaget's conclusions about the mental capabilities of young children. These psychologists believe that the child's thought develops through interaction with and instruction from adults and through solving real problems.

Memory. Studies of young children's memory abilities show that when compared with older children and adults, preschoolers' recognition memories are good, but their recall memories are poor. Although it has been found difficult to teach preschool children to organize and rehearse information, they do seem to have memory strategies that relate to meaning, sequence, and function and to their interrelationships.

Play and Learning

Types of Play. Play offers preschool children unique opportunities to express themselves freely, with no internal or external expectations to succeed or produce. Although the purpose of play is its own end, it furthers social development and enhances creativity. Play takes many forms. Sensory play is engaged in for the sake of sensory experience. Play with motion provides children with continuously changing sensations and some of their first social experiences. Rough-and-tumble play provides children with an opportunity to exercise, to filter out negative behaviors that are inappropriate in a group, and to learn to distinguish pretend from real. Play with language allows children to manipulate sounds and meanings, and to control their experiences.

Early Childhood Education

Educators are divided over the benefits of early education. Some claim that it places excessive demands on preschool children; others feel that it stimulates intellectual, social, and motor development.

Developmentally Appropriate Curriculum. The National Association for the Education of Young Children has developed guidelines for educational curricula that match educational programs with the developmental needs of young children.

Approaches to Early Education. The Montessori curriculum presents tasks that feature sequence, order, and regularity, in addition to those that develop motor and sensory skills. Traditional, formal approaches, such as the Distar program for disadvantaged children, teach particular skills in a gradual, sequential order, but the advantages gained tend not to last. Open education involves much planning and forethought. It features integrated activities for children to develop several skills at once, vertical groupings in which children of different ages are placed in the same class, and child participation in decision making about what to do and for how long.

Compensatory Education. Head Start, started in the 1960s, was seen as a way to reverse the damaging effects of poverty, particularly in education. Although Head Start has not been successful in raising achievement test scores, it has helped children adjust to school and bettered the lives of parents. Earlier and more intensive interventions for children and their families are being implemented.

KEY TERMS AND CONCEPTS

centration	functional subordination	prepared environment
classification	intrinsic feedback	readiness
compensatory education	Montessori curriculum	recall
competence motivation	open education	recognition
developmentally appropriate curriculum	organization	rehearsal
Distar program	Piaget's conservation experiments	seriation
egocentrism	preconceptual stage	symbolic representation
extrinsic feedback	preoperational period	transitional stage

SELF-TEST QUESTIONS

1. Describe the relationship between physical-motor development and cognitive development in preschool children. Distinguish between continuous, discontinuous, and functionally subordinate developmental sequences.

2. Compare and contrast the physical development of 2- and 3-year-olds with that of 4- and 5-year-olds.

3. What important conditions are required for physical-motor learning?

4. What is the preoperational period of child development? Differentiate between the two stages of preoperational thought.

5. Explain the significance of real and pretend play in the cognitive development of a preschool child.

6. List the limitations of preoperational thought.

7. Discuss the criticisms of Piaget's theory and alternate theories of cognitive development.

8. Describe the memory capabilities of preschool children. Differentiate between recognition and recall. What memory strategies do children use?

9. List the different types of play and the benefits derived from each.

10. How does play promote cognitive development?

11. How does children's art aid in physical and cognitive development?

12. Discuss different views concerning the benefit of formal education for preschoolers.

13. List and discuss different approaches to early education.

14. List the accomplishments and limitations of compensatory education.

SUGGESTED READINGS

BRUNER, J., & HASTE, H. *Making sense: The child's construction of the world*. New York: Methuen, 1987. A concise presentation of Jerome Bruner's current perspective on the social construction of knowledge.

GARVEY, C. *Play*. Cambridge, MA: Harvard University Press, 1990. A concise description of the developmental forms of children's play.

KAGEN, S., & ZIGLER E. (Eds.). *Early schooling: The national debate*. New Haven, CT: Yale University Press, 1987. A collection of views from scholars and practitioners on the wisdom and practice of early schooling.

PALEY, Y. G. *Bad guys don't have birthdays: Fantasy play at four*. Chicago: University of Chicago Press, 1988. A delightful book on fantasy in childhood and its role in child development.

TOBIN, J. J., WU, D. Y. H., & DAVIDSON, D. H. *Preschool in three cultures*. New Haven, CT: Yale University Press, 1989. A blend of anthropology, human development, and education enriches this vivid picture of cultural variation in attitudes toward young children.

Chapter 10

I was angry with my friend:
I told my wrath, my wrath did end.
I was angry with my foe;
I told it not, my wrath did grow.

WILLIAM BLAKE

Social Development and Emerging Personality

uring the preschool period, young children become socialized. They learn what is expected of them in their family and their community—what is good and bad behavior for boys and girls like them. They learn how to handle their feelings in socially appropriate ways. They learn who they are within the social context of their community. In other words, young children learn the norms, rules, and cultural meanings of their society, and they develop a self-concept that may persist throughout their lives. In Chapter 3 we looked briefly at some of these socialization processes. In this chapter we will examine them in more detail, particularly as they relate to the developmental issues of the preschool period.

There is dramatic growth in the child's self-control and social competence during the four important years from age 2 to age 6. Two-year-olds have all the basic emotions of 6-year-olds (or, for that matter, of adults), but their expression of these emotions is immediate, impulsive, and direct. They cannot wait to have their desires satisfied. A mother who has promised her 2-year-old an ice-cream cone cannot afford the luxury of chatting with a friend outside the ice-cream parlor—her child's impatience will interfere with any attempts at conversation. Expressions of dependency, too, are direct and physical at this age. In an unfamiliar setting, a 2-year-old stays close to his mother, clinging to her clothing or returning often to her side. If forcibly separated from her, he may throw himself on the floor, howling with anger, protest, and grief. Anger is expressed in direct, physical ways at this age. Two-year-olds may kick or bite instead of expressing themselves verbally. They may grab a desired toy instead of asking for it.

In contrast, 6-year-olds are much more verbal and thoughtful; they are a little less quick to anger, and they censor or control their behavior. Their coping patterns are far more diverse than those of 2-year-olds; they can express their anger by kicking a door or a teddy bear, rather than a brother or sister. They may have learned to hold in their anger and not express it outwardly at all. They may have developed a special assertive posture to defend their rights, or a specific fantasy to see them through unpleasant situations. If Mommy is not where they expect her to be, 6-year-olds are unlikely to kick and howl. Instead, they may talk out their anger or fear, or express it in a highly disguised form—perhaps by becoming uncooperative and grumpy, or by building an elaborate tower of blocks and then knocking it down. In short, most 6-year-olds have become quite refined in their abilities to cope and have developed their own distinctive styles. There are far more individual variations in methods of coping among 6-year-olds than among

CHAPTER OBJECTIVES

By the time you have finished this chapter, you should be able to do the following:

- Discuss the strong feelings and conflicts that preschool children are faced with.
- Understand the difference between fear and anxiety, give some of the sources of these emotions, and describe the ways that children cope with them.
- Discuss the factors that influence aggressive and prosocial behavior.
- Explain the importance of a child's self-concept and social concepts, and describe the processes involved in their development.
- Describe the development of gender schemes during the preschool period and the effects they have on the child's behavior.
- Discuss some of the ways that brothers and sisters influence social development.
- List some guidelines that can help parents achieve our society's current child-rearing goals.
- Discuss the pros and cons of the effects of television on child development.

2-year-olds. The personal style that a child develops in these years may be the foundation of a lifelong pattern of behavior.

THREE THEORIES REVISITED   The socialization of a child during the preschool years is complex, involving the ups and downs of interpersonal relationships and the cumulative effects of countless events. It is no wonder that experts disagree about the major influences and critical interactions, and even on the best methods to study the processes. As indicated in Chapter 2, there are at least three major theoretical perspectives: (1) The psychodynamic perspective emphasizes the child's feelings, drives, and developmental conflicts. Children must learn to cope with powerful emotions in socially acceptable ways. (2) According to the social learning perspective, social and personality development are primarily products of the environment. The child's behavior is shaped by rewards, punishments, and the influence of models. (3) Finally, the cognitive development perspective emphasizes children's own thoughts and concepts as organizers for their social behavior. Children develop increasingly complex concepts—for example, they learn what it means to be a girl or a boy, a sister or brother, or a friend. These concepts, in turn, play a major role in directing children's behavior.

In this chapter, we shall discuss research from all three perspectives in order to offer a broader understanding of social and personality development in the preschool child.

DEVELOPMENTAL ISSUES AND COPING PATTERNS

Children must learn to handle a wide range of feelings in these early years. Some are good feelings, such as joy, affection, and pride. Others—such as anger, fear, anxiety, jealousy, frustration, and pain—are not pleasant at all. Children must also find their own ways of resolving developmental conflicts. They must learn to deal with an awareness of their dependence on others, and find ways of relating to the authority figures in their lives. On the other hand, children must also deal with their own feelings of independence or autonomy—their strong drive to do things for themselves, to master their physical and social environments, to be competent and successful.

Handling Feelings

The sense of personal and cultural identity that forms between the ages of 2 and 6 is accompanied by many strong feelings that children must learn to integrate into their own personality structures. Finding outlets for these feelings that will be acceptable to both themselves and their parents is no easy task. Children find many solutions to this challenge, but they also experience conflict while doing so.

FEAR AND ANXIETY   One of the most important forces that children must learn to deal with is the stress caused by fear and anxiety. These patterns of psychological and physiological stress are experienced as unpleasant by both children and adults. The two emotions are not synonymous; a distinction must be made between them.

Preschool children have intense feelings that they must learn to handle during these early years. Learning that the baby goat will not hurt him may calm this child's fears.

Fear is a response to a specific stimulus or situation: for example, a child may fear big dogs, or lightning and thunder. In contrast, **anxiety** has a more vague or generalized source. Anxious children experience an overall feeling of apprehension, but they do not know its precise origin. A move to a new neighborhood or a sudden change in parental expectations, such as the beginning of toilet training, may be the indirect cause of tensions that seem to come from nowhere.

Fear and anxiety have many causes. Young children may be anxious that their parents will leave them or stop loving them. Parents usually act in a loving and accepting fashion, but sometimes—often as a means of punishment—they withdraw their love, attention, and protection. The withdrawal of love threatens children and makes them feel anxious. Anticipation of other types of punishment, especially physical punishment, is another source of anxiety of young children. Two-year-olds see parents as powerful people; they may have no realistic idea of how far their parents will go in punishing them. When an exasperated parent shouts, "I'm going to break every bone in your body!" the child (who has probably witnessed countless such acts of violence on television) has no way of knowing that the parent's threat is an empty one. Fear and anxiety may be increased, or even produced, by the child's own imagination. Children often imagine that the birth of a new baby will cause their parents to reject them. Sometimes anxiety results from children's awareness of their own unacceptable feelings—anger at a parent or teacher, jealousy of a sibling or a friend, or the desire to be held like a baby.

The sources of some fears are easily traced—fear of the doctor who gives inoculations, the dread inspired by the smell of a hospital or the sound of a dentist's drill. Other fears are not so easy to understand. Many preschoolers develop a fear of the dark at bedtime. This type of fear is often related more to fantasies and dreams than to any real events in the child's life. Sometimes these fantasies stem directly from developmental conflicts with which the child is currently struggling; for example, imaginary tigers or ghosts may arise from the child's struggle with dependency and autonomy. In a classic study of children's fears, Jersild and Holmes (1935) found that younger children are most likely to be afraid of specific things, like strangers, unfamiliar objects, loud noises, or falling. In contrast, children aged 5 or 6 show an increased fear of imaginary or abstract things—monsters, robbers, the dark, death, being alone, or being ridiculed. Fifty years later, researchers found most of the same fears in preschool children, except that fears of the dark, of being alone, and of strange sights are now appearing at a earlier age (Draper & James, 1985).

In today's world, there are many sources of fear, anxiety, and stress. Some can be considered a normal part of growing up: being yelled at for accidentally breaking something, or being teased by a sibling. Others are more serious: internal stresses like illness and pain, and the chronic long-term stresses of unfavorable social environments—poverty, parental conflict or alcoholism, dangerous neighborhoods (Greene & Brooks, 1985). Some children must cope with major disasters or terrors, such as earthquakes, floods, and wars. Severe or long-term stressful situations can stagger the resources of even the most resilient child (Honig, 1986; Rutter, 1983).

Although fear and anxiety are emotions that we naturally try to avoid and minimize, they are also normal feelings that are necessary for development. In mild forms, they can be a spur to new learning. Some fears—such as a fear of fast-moving cars—are necessary for our very survival and act as part of our physiological arousal system. But others—such as a fear of the bathtub—interfere

fear A state of arousal, tension, or apprehension caused by a specific circumstance.

anxiety A feeling of uneasiness, apprehension, or fear that has a vague or unknown source.

Sometimes, it is easy to trace the source of a particular fear—a trip to the doctor's office may be connected in a child's mind with a painful injection.

defense mechanisms Any of the techniques that individuals use to reduce tensions that lead to anxiety.

withdrawal A defense mechanism in which the individual physically runs away from, or mentally withdraws from, unpleasant situations.

with day-to-day life and what our society considers appropriate behavior. Furthermore, very high levels of chronic fear and anxiety are overwhelming and interrupt normal development.

How can we help children cope with their fears? Using force or ridicule is likely to have negative results, and ignoring children's fears will not make them go away. With mild fears, children can be gently and sympathetically encouraged to confront and overcome them. With somewhat stronger yet unrealistic fears, children may need some help with desensitization (see Chapter 2).

For helping children cope with anxiety and stress, the best way is to reduce the amount of unnecessary stress they must deal with. When children show unusually high levels of tension or frequent temper tantrums, it is often helpful to simplify their lives for a few days by sticking to a routine, specifying clearly what is expected, and helping the child to anticipate coming events. Other helpful strategies include reducing exposure to parental fighting or violent television shows, and protecting children from the teasing and tormenting of neighborhood bullies or gangs. But not all major life stresses can be avoided. Sometimes children must cope with the stress of common events like the birth of a sibling, moving to a new home, or entering day care, as well as less common stresses like death, divorce, or natural catastrophes. Under these circumstances, parents and teachers should try to accomplish the following (Honig, 1986):

1. Learn to recognize and interpret stress reactions in children.

2. Provide a warm, secure base for children to renew their confidence.

3. Allow opportunities for children to discuss their feelings—a socially shared trauma is easier to handle.

4. Allow immature or regressive behavior, such as thumb-sucking, fussing, or sitting on laps.

5. Help children to give meaning to the event or circumstance by an explanation.

In response to more generalized feelings of anxiety—particularly those generated in the intense emotional climate of the family, involving issues of morality or sex roles—children learn strategies called **defense mechanisms.** A defense mechanism is an indirect way to disguise or reduce anxiety. By the age of 5 or 6, most children have learned how to hide or disguise their feelings with defense mechanisms. They continue to do so when they are adults: We all employ defense mechanisms (Freud called them "classical ego defenses") as strategies for reducing tensions. The following list summarizes the most common defense mechanisms learned by children:

• *Withdrawal.* A very common defense mechanism in young children is **withdrawal.** It is the most direct defense possible: If a situation seems too difficult, the child simply withdraws and goes away from it, either physically or mentally.

• *Identification.* This is a more positive defense mechanism than withdrawal. As we noted in Chapter 3, *identification* is the process of incorporating into oneself the values, attitudes, and beliefs of others. Children adopt the attitudes of powerful figures, such as parents, in order to become more like these figures—more lovable, powerful, and accepted. This helps reduce the anxiety that children feel about their own relative helplessness.

- *Projection*. **Projection** involves a distortion of reality. Children attribute their own undesirable thoughts or actions to someone else. "He did it, not me" is a projective statement that we have all heard and perhaps used. "He doesn't like me" may seem more acceptable than "I don't like him." Projection is more complicated than withdrawal. In withdrawal, children usually know what they are trying to escape. In projection, they may actually have become confused in their own minds about what really happened. This confusion is a defense against the source of the anxiety.

- *Displacement*. Substitution of something or someone else for the real source of anger or fear is termed **displacement.** For example, Tyler may be angry with his baby sister, but he can't hit her—perhaps he can't even admit to himself that he *wants* to hit her—so instead he torments the dog. A child who is afraid of his father, but who finds that fear unacceptable (because he also loves his father), might displace that fear onto something else—for example, he might develop a fear of horses, or of imaginary tigers.

- *Denial*. **Denial** is the refusal to admit that a situation exists or that an event happened. Children may react to an upsetting situation, such as the death of a pet, by pretending that the pet is still living in the house and sleeping with them at night.

- *Repression*. **Repression** is an extreme form of denial in which children completely erase a frightening event or circumstance from their conscious awareness. There is no need to rely on fantasy, because the child literally does not remember that the event ever occurred.

- *Regression*. **Regression** is a return to an earlier or more infantile form of behavior as a way of coping with a stressful situation. Eight-year-old Ashley suddenly reverted to sucking her thumb and carrying around her "blankie"— behaviors given up years before—when her best friend was badly injured in an accident.

- *Reaction formation*. **Reaction formation** occurs when children have thoughts or desires that make them anxious, and they react to such thoughts by behaving in a contradictory way. For example, they would like to cling to their parents, but instead they push them away and behave with exaggerated independence and assertiveness.

- *Rationalization*. This is a very common adult defense mechanism, used less commonly by children because it requires advanced verbal skills and knowledge of social rules. With **rationalization,** children make unacceptable behaviors or thoughts "respectable" by inventing a socially approved explanation for them. For example, if Tyler gives in to his impulse to hit his baby sister, he might explain, "I had to hit her because she was being bad! She had to be taught a lesson."

Most preschool children use several of the defense mechanisms we have mentioned. Very rarely does a child choose a single one and use it exclusively. Withdrawal and denial are generally most common in younger children. Greater maturity is needed to manage reaction formation or rationalization. Some defense mechanisms are learned by observing the behavior of parents or siblings, but most are learned directly, through the child's own experience of what defenses work best to reduce anxiety without causing other problems. The defense patterns that children adopt are learned thoroughly during the preschool years and may stay with them throughout their lives.

---

projection A person using this defense mechanism will attribute his or her own undesirable thoughts or actions to someone else.

displacement A defense mechanism in which a less threatening person or object is substituted for the actual source of anger or anxiety.

denial The refusal to admit that an anxiety-producing situation exists or that an anxiety-producing event happened.

repression An extreme form of denial in which the individual completely erases an anxiety-producing event or situation from consciousness.

regression Coping with an anxiety-producing situation by reverting to earlier, more immature behavior.

reaction formation A defense mechanism in which individuals unconsciously mask their anxiety over unacceptable thoughts or desires by behaving in an extremely contradictory fashion.

rationalization A defense mechanism in which an individual explains unacceptable thoughts or behavior by inventing a socially acceptable reason for them.

As a result of differences in cultural and family backgrounds, children feel fear and anxiety about different things. A hundred years ago, children feared wolves and bears. Fifty years ago they worried about goblins and bogeymen. Now their nightmares are populated with extraterrestrials and killer robots. There are also striking cultural differences in the way children express their fears, or how free they are to express them at all. In contemporary Western culture, showing fear is frowned upon—children (especially boys) are supposed to be brave, and most parents worry about a child who is unusually fearful. But this attitude is not universal. Navajo Indian parents consider it healthy and normal for a child to be afraid; they consider a fearless child to be ignorant or foolhardy. In a recent study, Navajo parents reported an average of 22 fears in their children, including fears of supernatural beings. In contrast, a group of Anglo-American parents from rural Montana reported an average of four fears in their children (Tikalsky & Wallace, 1988).

DISTRESS AND ANGER   Western society not only frowns on the expression of fear, but also expects children to inhibit the display of other negative emotions, such as anger, jealousy, frustration, and distress. Children learn, from a very early age, that open displays of such feelings are unacceptable in public places—and day-care centers and nursery schools count as public places (Dencik, 1989). Although freer displays of emotion are usually permitted at home, most parents expect their children to learn what Kopp (1989) calls *emotion regulation:* the process of dealing with their emotions in socially acceptable ways. As children grow older, their parents' expectations for emotion regulation increase: It is all right for babies to cry loudly when they are hungry, but it is not all right for 6-year-olds to wail bitterly if they must wait a few minutes for a snack. Children who do not learn such lessons at home are at risk of being socially rejected outside the home. Preschoolers who cry too frequently are likely to be unpopular with their peers (Kopp, 1989). Learning to manage anger is even more important. Some children who were still having "temper tantrums" at the age of 10 were followed in a longitudinal study. The researchers found that these children tended to be unsuccessful in adult life as a result of their outbursts of anger: They had difficulty holding jobs and their marriages often ended in divorce (Caspi, Elder, & Bem, 1987).

According to Kopp, regulation of emotions depends in part on the child's cognitive development, and in particular on the development of language. As Kopp (1989) puts it:

> Language offers young children a multipurpose vehicle for dealing with emotions and moving toward more effective emotion regulation. With language, children can state their feelings to others, obtain verbal feedback about the appropriateness of their emotions, and hear and think about ways to manage them. (p. 349)

Learning to manage negative emotions is not the same as never having them. Children can come to accept their angry feelings as a normal part of themselves, yet learn to control or redirect their reactions to such feelings. They may use anger as a motivating force, as a way of overcoming obstacles, or as a means of standing up for themselves or others. Whether they choose to accept or to reject their negative feelings, and the way in which they express that choice, will have important consequences in later years.

AFFECTION AND JOY In our culture, children must restrain not only their negative feelings but also their positive emotions. Spontaneous feelings, such as joy, affection, excitement, and playfulness, are dealt with quite differently by 2-year-olds and 6-year-olds. Just as 2-year-olds are direct in expressing distress, they are also likely to be very open in showing positive feelings—they hug people, jump up and down, or clap their hands in excitement. During the course of preschool socialization, we manage to teach children to subdue such open expressiveness. Spontaneous joy and affection become embarrassing; they are considered "babyish," so most children learn to control them. On the other hand, special circumstances such as birthday parties or baseball games demand types of emotional expression that are considered inappropriate for everyday life. Children must learn all of these social norms.

SENSUALITY AND SEXUAL CURIOSITY Two-year-olds are very sensual creatures and derive great pleasure from sensory experience. They like the feel of messy, gooey things. They are conscious of the softness or stiffness of clothes against their skin. They are fascinated by sounds, lights, tastes, and smells. In infancy this sensuality was centered on the mouth, but the toddler has a new awareness and fascination with the anal-genital area. Masturbation and sex play are quite common during the preschool period. As children discover that such self-stimulation is pleasurable, some may gradually increase this behavior; most develop an active curiosity about their bodies and ask many sex-related questions.

The ways in which the culture and the family react to this developing sensuality and curiosity will have an important effect on children, just as the reactions of others affect the way that children handle hostility and joy. Until recently, mothers in our society were advised to prevent their children from engaging in this kind of exploration (Wolfenstein, 1951). The result was anxiety and guilt in the children, which led them to adopt the various defense mechanisms described by Freud. But sensual exploration is a natural and vital part of every child's experience. Severe restriction of children's sensual feelings and behavior is likely to cause unnecessary anxiety, guilt, and conflict during adolescence and adulthood.

Young children are very open about displaying positive feelings like joy. By the time they are 6 years old, however, they will learn to control such open displays.

Developmental Conflicts

Trying to fit their feelings into the structure of acceptability imposed on them by the outside world is not the only task young children must face during the preschool years. Developmental conflicts also arise as they adjust to their own changing needs. Dependency, autonomy, mastery, and competence are pressing issues in their lives.

DEPENDENCY Dependency may be defined as any type of activity demonstrating that one person derives satisfaction from another person (Hartup, 1963). It includes the wish or need to be aided, nurtured, comforted, and protected by another, or to be emotionally close to or accepted by that person. Such wishes and needs are normal in people of every age, despite the connotation of weakness or inadequacy that they often carry in American society. Dependency is necessary for the very survival of the young child, who must look to older people for the satisfaction of both physical and psychological needs.

Infants and toddlers show dependency by crying for attention and by seeking close physical contact. By age 4 or 5, children have developed more indirect ways of showing their need for others: Now they seek attention by asking questions, by offering to help, by showing off, or even by outright disobedience. A study by Craig and Garney (1972) traced developmental trends in expressions of dependency by observing the ways that children at ages 2, 2½, and 3 maintained contact with their mothers in an unfamiliar situation. The 2-year-olds spent most of their time physically close to their mothers, staying in the same part of the room and looking up often to make sure that their mothers were still there. The older children (2½- and 3-year-olds) did not stay as close to their mothers, and they did not check as often to see if their mothers had left the room. The older the children, the more they maintained verbal contact instead of physical contact. All three age groups made a point of drawing attention to their activities, but the older children were more inclined to demonstrate them from afar. Other studies have shown similar patterns: Distress caused by separation from the mother declines from ages 2 to 3, while "distal" attachment behavior, such as showing things to the mother from across the room, increases (Maccoby & Feldman, 1972). Note, though, that wide individual differences are always found in every age group.

Dependence and independence are commonly considered opposite types of behavior. But this is not necessarily the case for the young child. Although children become less dependent—less clingy—as they get older, their independence (or autonomy) follows a more complex trajectory. Infants are usually fairly cooperative; for example, they will hold out their arms when their parents are trying to dress them. This changes abruptly at about the age of 2, when many children suddenly become quite uncooperative—parents call this stage the "terrible twos." Two-year-olds fight to "do it myself," and temper tantrums are frequent when they find that they cannot manage buttons and the sleeve is inside out. When 2-year-olds are asked to do something, they show their independence by saying "No!" As they get older, they become more compliant and cooperative. Three-year-olds are more likely to do what their parents tell them to, and less likely to break rules when their parents are not looking (Howes & Olenick, 1986).

AUTONOMY, MASTERY, AND COMPETENCE As discussed in Chapter 2, the drive toward autonomy marks the second stage in Erikson's theory of personality development. Toddlers are discovering their own bodies and learning to control them. If they are successful in doing things for themselves, they become self-confident. If their efforts at autonomy are frustrated by criticism or punishment, they think that they have failed and feel ashamed and doubtful about themselves. Although autonomy, mastery, and competence are slightly different drives, they are all part of the same behavior complex that influences our behavior throughout life (Erikson, 1963; Murphy, 1962; White, 1959).

Erikson suggests that the primary developmental conflict of the years from 3 to 6 is *initiative versus guilt*. In some ways, this conflict is an extension of the toddler's struggle with autonomy. Toddlers gain control and competence starting with their own bodies—feeding, dressing, toileting, handling objects, and getting around. The preschooler is learning how things work, the meaning of social situations and relationships, and how to influence people in a constructive and appropriate way. Concepts of right and wrong, good and bad, become important; labels such as "sissy," "baby," or "brat" can have devastating effects. The job of the parent or teacher is to guide and discipline the child without creating too much

All children need to feel a sense of mastery over their environment. This feeling of mastery may lead to mischief at times, but it is still an important aspect of development.

anxiety or guilt. In the confusing and complex social world of the preschool child, initiative can lead either to success and feelings of competence, or to failure, frustration, and guilt.

Nearly everyone derives satisfaction from changing the environment to suit himself or herself. For a 3-year-old, this may mean crayoning on a wall or retrieving a toy from a baby sister. Preschoolers are just as pleased with their creations as adults are with theirs. Unfortunately, a youngster's desire to use creativity or initiative sometimes interferes with other people's plans. A little boy's discovery that he can "improve" the vacuum cleaner by filling its tubes with clay does not fit in with his mother's need to keep the house clean. These opposing needs produce conflicts between parent and child and within the child himself.

What happens when children's attempts at mastery or autonomy meet with constant failure or frustration? What happens when they have little or no opportunity to try things on their own, or when their environment is so chaotic that they cannot see the consequences of their acts? All children have a need for autonomy, a need to master the environment, and a need to feel competent and successful. If these needs are repeatedly blocked, their personality development is likely to be adversely affected. If their efforts at mastery cause too much trouble, they may give up and become passive. Several studies show that such children fail to develop an active, exploratory, self-confident approach to learning, which White and Watts (1973) called the development of learning competence. Beyond this, what happens to children who are constantly punished for their independent behavior and attempts at mastery? Or to children whose parents discourage or frighten them whenever they venture into new activities? When children are made to feel anxious about their autonomy needs, they generally learn to deny, minimize, or disguise these needs. In some cultures, such induced anxiety about autonomy is especially common among young girls.

Some children are necessarily restricted in their drive toward autonomy. Children who are physically handicapped or chronically ill may have little opportunity to test their skills in mastering the environment (Rutter, 1979). Children who grow up in dangerous or crowded surroundings and who have to be restrained for their own safety, or who are supervised by excessively vigilant care-givers, may also learn exaggerated passivity or anxiety (Zuravin, 1985).

aggression Hostile behavior that is intended to injure.

assertive behavior Forthright, direct behavior, such as stating one's rights, that does not harm others.

prosocial behavior Helping, sharing, or cooperative actions that are intended to benefit others.

frustration The blocking of a goal, causing angry feelings and, according to some, resulting in aggressive behavior.

Children learn aggressive and prosocial behavior by modeling themselves after adults, particularly their parents.

AGGRESSION AND PROSOCIAL BEHAVIOR

The young child's interactions with others can be either positive or negative. At one point, children may seek closeness or be anxious to help or share. A short time later, they may become angry and hostile. A principal task of socializing young children is to teach them socially acceptable ways to channel aggressive feelings, and at the same time to encourage positive behaviors such as helping and sharing. Many factors influence the development of aggressive behavior and of positive or prosocial behavior.

Psychologists define **aggression** as behavior intended to hurt or destroy. Aggressive behavior may be verbal or physical. It may be directed at people or displaced toward animals or objects. **Assertive behavior,** on the other hand, does not involve an intent to injure others. It is forthright, direct behavior, such as calmly stating one's rights or initiating vigorous activity, and it need not damage others.

Prosocial behavior is defined as actions intended to benefit others without the anticipation of an external reward (Eisenberg, 1988). These actions often entail some cost, sacrifice, or risk to the individual. Helping, sharing, cooperation, sympathy, and altruism (the unselfish concern for the welfare of others) are examples of prosocial behavior. These actions are frequently a response to positive motivational and emotional states—that is, people behave this way when they feel happy, secure, and empathetic. Aggression, on the other hand, is a common response to anger and hostility.

Whether behavior is considered socially appropriate depends on the situation and on the standards of the culture and the family. Aggression is not always bad, and altruism is not always appropriate. Unaggressive soldiers would be useless in combat, and altruistic football players would never win a game. Moreover, someone who is constantly altruistic may intrude on our privacy. Bryan (1975) suggests that an overly helpful person may be intrusive, moralistic, and conforming.

Considerable research has been devoted to aggressive and prosocial behaviors in an attempt to find out how each originates and what factors control them. We shall look at some of the explanations that have been given for children's antisocial and prosocial actions.

Frustration and Aggression

Psychologists from several different perspectives have hypothesized a direct relationship between frustration and aggression. An extreme form of this viewpoint was the *frustration–aggression hypothesis* (Dollard et al., 1939); it stated that all aggression is derived from frustration, and that all frustration, sooner or later, results in some direct or disguised forms of aggression. **Frustration** was defined as the blocking of a goal; this results in angry feelings that "mediate" the aggression. The aggression might be expressed directly, toward the source of frustration, or displaced onto another person or object. It might be physical or verbal, or it might be disguised and channeled outward, as in some form of art, or turned inward, as in an ulcer. Nevertheless, it is there somewhere if you look for it carefully enough.

Children can learn aggressive behavior by competing in games.

The frustration–aggression hypothesis was called into question by a well-known study (Barker, Dembo, & Lewin, 1943) of the behavior of preschool children in a frustrating situation. The children were given a number of attractive toys, which were then removed and placed behind a wire screen—the toys were visible, but the children could not reach them. They reacted in a number of different ways to the frustration they felt. A few were aggressive toward their peers, toward the investigators, or toward the wire screen. Others tried to escape from the room or regressed to earlier behaviors, such as thumb-sucking. Some just patiently waited or turned their attention to something else. Although some critics claimed that aggression could have been disguised as avoidance or regression, this experiment is more often interpreted as showing that aggression is by no means the only reaction, or even the dominant one, to frustration.

Doubt has also been cast on the other half of the frustration–aggression hypothesis—the idea that all aggression is derived from frustration (Dollard & Miller, 1950). Some aggression may simply be learned or imitative behavior. For example, soldiers and football players are trained to be aggressive whether or not they feel angry or frustrated. As we saw in Chapter 3, children behave more aggressively after observing an aggressive model. Rewarding children for aggression also results in their becoming more aggressive (Cowan & Walters, 1963; Lovaas, 1962).

PUNISHMENT AND AGGRESSION   Although research indicates that rewards encourage aggression, the case for using punishment to discourage aggression is not so clear. True, if children are punished for aggressive acts, they will very likely inhibit this behavior—at least in the presence of the punisher. But they may channel their aggressive feelings and acts into other outlets instead. For example, their aggression at home may decrease, but they may become more aggressive at school. They may express their aggression in different ways, such as tattling or name-calling. Punishment may even backfire and cause the child to be more aggressive in general. People who use physical punishment to curb a child's aggression may actually be encouraging it because they are providing a very obvious model of aggressive behavior.

Rewards, Punishment, and Modeling

Just as aggression may not always derive from frustration, helping and sharing may not always derive from empathy. Rewards and punishments, and the observation of models, have important influences on both antisocial and prosocial behavior.

Our culture offers different models and systems of reward and punishment to members of different segments of society. For example, the models and rewards available to boys differ considerably from those available to girls. On the average, females of all ages tend to express more concern for the feelings of others than do males (Eisenberg, 1989). Although both sexes are equally adept at understanding how another person feels, females are more apt to express their empathy because our culture allots to females the role of expressing such feelings. Similarly, children who live in neighborhoods where many children are aggressive are more likely to be rewarded for aggressive behavior than those who do not have to fight for their rights.

Experiments on both antisocial and prosocial behavior have also shown that imitation of models is more likely to occur when the observers sense a similarity between themselves and the model, or when the model is perceived as powerful or competent (Eisenberg, 1988). Thus, boys are more likely to imitate other boys than to imitate girls. Children are also more likely to imitate other children who have "dominant" personalities—that is, children who are socially powerful and who engage in the most interesting activities (Abramovitch & Grusec, 1978). These are well-liked children who dominate their peers through the force of their personalities, not through physical aggression. In fact, preschool children dislike overly aggressive playmates (Ladd, Price, & Hart, 1988).

The modeling process is more effective when a model is perceived as nurturant or is someone who has a special relationship with the child. Consequently, parents are generally the child's most influential models. However, the influence works in a variety of ways. For example, a girl may model herself after her father because he is powerful, or because she and her father have a strong nurturant relationship, or because other people comment on the father's and daughter's similar tempers or senses of humor.

Prosocial Behavior

A number of studies have demonstrated the influence of modeling on prosocial behavior. In a typical experiment, a group of children observe a person performing a prosocial act, such as putting toys or money into a box designated for "needy children." Other children in a control group watch a model who does not exhibit prosocial behavior. After watching the generous model, each child is given the opportunity to donate something. The researchers usually find that children who witness another person's generosity become more generous themselves (Eisenberg, 1988).

Because rewards and punishment affect aggression, it is assumed that they also affect helping and sharing. However, this is difficult to prove. Researchers are understandably reluctant to do experiments in which prosocial behavior is punished, and experiments in which it is rewarded are inconclusive because the results may be due to modeling: When experimenters give a reward, they are also modeling "giving" (Rushton, 1976). The role of learning in prosocial behavior is better demonstrated by a recent experiment that showed that 4-year-old children who were given many chores to do at home were more likely to be helpful outside of the home. Interestingly, the most helpful children in this study were black males. The experimenters hypothesized that, because the black children were more likely to come from fatherless homes, their mothers had turned to their sons for help and emotional support. Thus, these children had learned helping and comforting behaviors very early in life (Richman et al., 1988).

Two other procedures that influence prosocial behavior are **role playing** and **induction**. In role playing, children act out other roles as a way of seeing things from another's point of view. In induction, children are given reasons for behaving in certain ways—for example, they may be told what consequences their actions will have for others. Staub (1971) used both procedures in an experiment with groups of kindergarten children. He subsequently tested them to determine the effectiveness of these procedures. He found that role playing increased the willingness of the children to help others, and that its effects lasted for as long as a week. However, induction had little or no effect on the children in Staub's experiment, perhaps because children are unlikely to pay much attention to a lecture from an unfamiliar adult. Induction is more effective when used by parents. Parents who use inductive forms of discipline—for example, who explain to their children the reasons for behaving in certain ways—are more likely to foster prosocial behavior in their children (Eisenberg, 1988).

Cooperation is also regarded as a form of prosocial behavior. Madsen (1971; Madsen & Shapira, 1970) found that American children become less cooperative (or more competitive) as they grow older. When playing a game that can be won only if the two players cooperate (see Figure 10–1), 4- and 5-year-olds often cooperated. Older children, however, tended to compete with each other; as a result, neither player won. Compared to American children, Mexican children and children raised on Israeli kibbutzim were more likely to cooperate, evidently because their cultures place more importance on group goals and less on individual

role playing The acting out of a role in order to see things from the perspective of another person.

induction Giving children reasons for behaving in socially desirable ways, or for not behaving in undesirable ways.

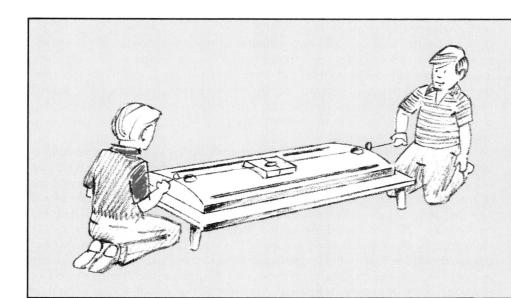

FIGURE 10-1
In Madsen's game, two children sit at opposite ends of a game board that features a cup at each end, a gutter down each side, and a marble holder with a marble inside. To play the game, the children move the marble holder by pulling on strings; if the marble holder is moved over a cup, a child earns the marble as it drops into the cup. The children must cooperate to earn marbles—if they both pull on the strings at the same time, the marble holder comes apart and the marble rolls into the gutter.

social reciprocity The continued interaction between individuals as they respond and react to each other in a manner that encourages the prevailing behavior.

achievement. Madsen suggested that American children are raised to be competitive and that they learn this value so completely that they are often unable to cooperate.

Angry or empathetic feelings, rewards and punishment, and modeling all play a part in the aggressive or altruistic behavior that children learn; all of these factors are present in family life. They may work together—the child may be rewarded for nonaggressive acts and mildly punished for aggressive ones. Or they may work against one another—the child may be continually subjected to frustrating situations but be severely punished when reacting aggressively. In any case, even the most careful parents cannot shelter a child completely from opportunities to imitate negative behavior.

Peers and Social Skills

Children influence one another in important ways. They provide emotional support for one another in a variety of situations. They serve as models, they reinforce one another's behavior, and they encourage complex, imaginative play. In these ways, children help one another to learn a variety of physical, cognitive, and social skills (Asher et al., 1982; Hartup, 1983). Young boys playing aggressively, for example, may first imitate characters seen on television, and then imitate one another. They continue to respond and react to one another in a fashion that supports and escalates the play—this is sometimes called **social reciprocity** (Hall & Cairns, 1984).

An early study on peer relations (Parten, 1932–33) identified five different levels of social interaction in young children: (1) *solitary play;* (2) *onlooker play,* in which the child's interaction consists merely of observing other children; (3) *parallel play,* in which the child plays alongside another child and uses similar toys but does not interact in any other way; (4) *associative play,* in which children share materials and interact somewhat, but do not coordinate their activities toward a single theme or goal; and (5) *cooperative play,* in which children engage in a single activity together, such as building a house with blocks or playing hide-and-seek with a common set of rules.

Different modes of play predominate at given age levels. Two-year-olds mostly engage in onlooker and parallel play, whereas 4- and 5-year-olds show increasing amounts of associative and cooperative play. In optimal surroundings, 5-, 6-, and 7-year-olds can interact for relatively long periods of time while sharing materials, establishing rules, resolving conflicts, helping one another, and exchanging roles. Unfortunately, some children have trouble interacting with peers even when conditions are optimal.

When we observe children in nursery schools, day-care centers, or kindergartens, it is apparent that some children are popular with their peers and others are not. These patterns tend to be remarkably stable over the years: Children who are rejected by their peers in kindergarten are likely to be rejected in elementary school as well. Later, they are more likely to have adjustment problems in adolescence and adulthood (Parker & Asher, 1987). It is helpful, then, to determine who these children are—those regularly chosen by their peers and those rejected. It has been repeatedly shown that popular children are more cooperative and exhibit more prosocial behavior during play with their peers. Unpopular children may either be more aggressive or more withdrawn, or they may simply be "out of sync" with their peers' activities and social interactions (Rubin, 1983).

Peer relations are an important influence in the lives of children, and the success of these relationships seems to depend in large part on the development of social skills.

Which comes first: Do rejected children adopt these negative behaviors because they are rejected, or are they rejected because of their behavior? One researcher videotaped kindergarten boys as they tried to join a play group (Putallaz, 1983). The social skills they demonstrated were used to predict each child's social status in first grade. In this and other studies, popular children were found to have a variety of social skills. They initiate activity with others by moving into the group slowly, making relevant comments about what's going on, and sharing information. They seem sensitive to the needs and activities of others. They don't force themselves on other children but are content to play beside another child. In addition, popular children have strategies for maintaining relationships. They show helpful behaviors; they are good at maintaining communication and sharing information; and they are responsive to other children's suggestions. Finally, children who are destined to be popular have strategies for conflict resolution. Popular children do not necessarily give in when faced with conflict, but they are less frequently involved in aggressive or physical solutions (Asher, 1983; Asher et al., 1982).

If peer relations are an important socializing influence in the lives of children—at least by middle childhood—and if the success of these relationships depends on the development of social skills, then it is probably important to help children develop these skills during the preschool period. Adults can help in two ways. First, they can teach social skills directly, by modeling and by induction. Second, they can provide opportunities for successful social experiences with peers. Children need opportunities to play with other children, as well as appropriate space and materials to support this play. Dolls, clothes for dress-up activities, toy cars and trucks, blocks, and puppets support cooperative play and offer opportunities for interaction. With preschoolers, adult care-givers must be available to help initiate activities, negotiate conflicts, and provide information (Asher et al., 1982).

UNDERSTANDING SELF AND OTHERS

So far, we have been talking about how children learn the bits and pieces of behavior—how they learn to share or be aggressive or handle their feelings. Children, however, act in a more comprehensive way. They put together all the bits and pieces to form whole patterns of behavior appropriate for their culture, sex, and family. Experts disagree on just how this integration of patterns of social behavior takes place. Most agree that as children grow older they become less dependent on the individual rules, expectations, rewards, and punishments of others, and more able to make judgments and to regulate their own behavior. Cognitive developmental theorists hold that the child's integration of patterns of social behavior coincides with the development of a concept of self, along with certain social concepts. These concepts then help to mediate the child's behavior in social situations. The preschool period is an important time for building some of these basic concepts.

The Self-Concept

Even the 2-year-old has some self-understanding. As we discovered in Chapter 7, by 21 months the child is able to recognize herself in the mirror; if she sees a red mark on her nose she shows some self-conscious embarrassment. The language of the 2-year-old is full of assertions of possession. In one study of 2-year-olds playing in pairs, most of them began their play with numerous self-assertions. They defined their boundaries and their possessions—"my shoe, my doll, my car." The author of this study asserts that this is a cognitive achievement, not necessarily selfishness: The children are increasing their self-understanding and their understanding of the other child as a separate being (Levine, 1983). A review of other studies of children's self-concepts and social play concluded that children who are most social also have a better-developed self-concept (Harter, 1983). Thus, self-understanding is closely linked to the child's understanding of the social world.

During the preschool years, children develop certain kinds of generalized attitudes about themselves—a positive sense of well-being, for example, or a feeling that they are "slow" or "bratty." Many of these ideas begin to emerge very early, at a nonverbal level. Children may develop strong anxieties about some of their feelings and ideas, and be quite comfortable with others. They also develop a set of ideals during these years, and they learn to measure themselves against what they think they ought to be. Often, children's self-evaluation is a direct reflection of what other people think of them. John, for example, was a lovable 2-year-old with a talent for getting into mischief. His older brothers and sisters called him "Bad Buster" whenever he got into trouble. By the age of 7, John was making an effort to maintain his "Bad Buster" reputation. These early attitudes eventually become basic elements of a person's self-concept, but they are difficult to explore later on because they are learned at a less sophisticated verbal level.

Preschool children are fascinated with themselves, and many of their activities and thoughts are centered on the task of learning all about themselves. They compare themselves to other children, discovering differences in height, hair color,

Preschool children are fascinated with themselves. They frequently compare themselves with other children, seeing how they are different and how they are similar.

family background, and likes or dislikes. They compare themselves to their parents, learn that they share common traits, and find behaviors to imitate. As part of their drive to find out about themselves, preschool children ask a variety of questions about where they came from, why their feet grow, whether they are good or bad, and so on.

An awareness of how one appears to others is an important step in the development of self-knowledge. Young preschoolers tend to define themselves in terms of their physical characteristics ("I have brown hair") or possessions ("I have a bike"). Older preschoolers are more likely to describe themselves in terms of their activities: "I walk to school," "I play baseball" (Damon & Hart, 1982).

As children learn who and what they are and begin to evaluate themselves as active forces in their world, they are putting together a cognitive theory about themselves that helps to integrate their behavior. Human beings need to feel that they are consistent. They do not act randomly: They try to bring their behavior into line with their beliefs and attitudes. The strongest influence on children's developing self-image is usually their parents because they provide children with the definitions of right and wrong, the models of behavior, and the evaluations of actions on which children base their own ideas.

Social Concepts and Rules

Preschool children are busy sorting, classifying, and struggling to find meaning in the social world, just as they are in the world of objects. Central to the development of social concepts and rules is a process called **internalization:** Children learn to make the values and moral standards of their society part of themselves. Some of these values relate to appropriate sex-role behavior, some relate to moral standards, and some simply relate to the customary way of doing things.

How do children internalize these rules? At first they may simply imitate verbal patterns: Jennifer says "No, no, no!" as she crayons on the wall. She is doing what she wants to do, but at the same time she is showing the beginnings of self-restraint by telling herself that she shouldn't be doing it. In a few more months she may have the self-control to arrest the impulse she is presently unable to ignore. Cognitive theorists point out that children's attempts to regulate their own behavior are influenced not only by their developing self-concept but also by their developing social concepts. Such concepts reflect increased understanding about others as well as increased understanding about oneself. For example, a preschool child may be learning what it means to be a big brother or sister, or to be a friend. He or she is also learning about concepts such as fairness, honesty, and respect for others. Many of these concepts are far too abstract for young children, but they struggle to understand them.

One area that has been studied a great deal is children's concepts of friendship. A clear cognitive understanding doesn't occur until middle child-hood—notions of mutual trust and reciprocity are too complex for the preschool child. Nevertheless, preschool children do behave differently with friends from the way they behave with strangers, and some 4- and 5-year-olds are able to maintain close, caring relationships over an extended period of time. They may not be able to verbalize what friendship is, but they follow some of its implied rules (Gottman, 1983).

internalization Making social rules and standards of behavior part of oneself—adopting them as one's own set of values.

The strongest influence on children's developing self-image is usually their parents, who provide children with models of behavior.

gender identity The knowledge that one is male or female, and the ability to make that judgment about other people.

gender constancy The concept that gender is stable and stays the same despite changes in superficial appearance.

Young children learning about social concepts often ask the question "Why did they do that?" A common answer is based on *character attribution*. For example, the question "Why did Kevin give me his cookie?" may be answered with, "Because Kevin is a nice boy." As children get older, they are more and more likely to see other people, and also themselves, in terms of stable character attributes (Miller & Aloise, 1989). Some experts believe that care-givers can encourage children to be helpful or altruistic by teaching them that they are kind to others because they want to be—because they are "nice"—and not just because such behavior is demanded of them (Eisenberg et al., 1984; Grusec & Arnason, 1982; Perry & Bussey, 1984).

CHILDREN'S DISPUTES   Recently, researchers have been paying attention to children's social conflicts or disputes. Children's verbal arguments with peers, with siblings, and with parents often demonstrate a surprisingly sophisticated level of social understanding and an ability to reason from social rules and concepts. Children as young as 3 years are able to justify their behavior in terms of social rules ("Now it's my turn!") or the consequences of an action ("Stop, you'll break it if you do that!") (Dunn & Munn, 1987). In fact, a close look at children's verbal disputes over the preschool years demonstrates a systematic development in their understanding of social rules, their increasing understanding of another person's perspective, and their ability to reason from social rules or from the consequences of their actions (Shantz, 1987).

Gender Schemes

Among the more important sets of social concepts and social rules that preschool children learn are those related to gender-appropriate behavior. As we saw in Chapter 3, some aspects of children's gender roles are learned by modeling themselves after significant individuals in their lives and by being reinforced for gender-appropriate behavior. But this is not the whole story. Children are selective in what they imitate and internalize. Research suggests that children's developing understanding of gender-related concepts—their *gender schemes*—help to determine what attitudes and behaviors are learned. Moreover, these gender-related concepts develop in predictable ways over the preschool period.

By the age of 2½, most children can readily label people as boys or girls, men or women, and they can also answer the question "Are you a girl or a boy?" (Thompson, 1975). But even though they can divide the human race into male and female, they may be confused about what that means. Many 3-year-olds believe, for instance, that if a boy puts on a dress, he becomes a girl. They may not realize that only boys can become daddies and only girls can become mommies. But by age 6 or 7, children understand that their gender is stable and permanent for a lifetime, despite superficial changes. The first level of understanding, the one that is achieved between the ages of 2 and 6, is called **gender identity.** Later on, between ages 5 and 7, children are thought to acquire **gender constancy**—the understanding that boys invariably become men and girls become women, and that gender is consistent over time and situations (Kohlberg, 1966; Shaffer, 1988).

Many developmental psychologists believe that children are intrinsically motivated to acquire the values, interests, and behaviors consistent with their own gender. This process is known as self-socialization. Children develop concepts of

A child's developing understanding of gender-appropriate behavior and gender schemes often involves modeling and dramatic play.

"what boys do" and "what girls do" that might be quite rigid and stereotyped: For example, boys play with cars and don't cry; girls play with dolls and like to dress up. A child will pay more attention to the details of the kinds of behavior that are gender-appropriate, and little attention to sex-inappropriate behaviors (Martin & Halverson, 1981).

Do young children actually attend to some things more than to others, and do they remember some things better than others, because they are consistent with their gender schemes? Several studies have indicated that they do. In memory tests, for example, boys tend to remember more of the items that are labeled "boy items" and girls remember more "girl items." Children also make memory errors when a story violates their gender stereotypes. They may remember that a boy was chopping wood when, in fact, a girl was chopping wood in the story. Such results indicate that children's developing gender concepts have a powerful influence on their attention and learning (Martin & Halverson, 1981). During the period when concepts of gender stability and consistency are being developed, children tend to have particularly rigid and stereotyped concepts of sex-appropriate behavior. These concepts and rules become organizers that structure the child's behavior and feelings. If they are violated, children may feel embarrassed, anxious, or uncomfortable.

THE FAMILY CONTEXT

The processes described in this chapter do not happen in a void. Rather, they are affected by the immediate household, social forces, and cultural beliefs (Bronfenbrenner, 1979). For most children, the strongest force is the family in which they grow up. Many of the dynamics within the family—interactions with siblings, parenting techniques, the number and spacing of children—have an effect. In addition, social learning will be affected by the structure and circumstances of the family: whether there are two parents or only one, and whether they are employed; whether grandparents or other relatives reside in the household; whether the family lives in a luxurious house in the suburbs or a crowded apartment in the city. If the circumstances of the family undergo major changes or disruptions, a child's social experiences may be markedly altered.

Siblings

The first, and probably the closest, peer group that affects children's personality development is their siblings (their brothers and sisters). Sibling relationships provide experiences for the child that are different from parent–child interactions—they are like "living in the nude, psychologically speaking" (Bossard & Boll, 1960, p. 91). The down-to-earth openness of brothers and sisters gives siblings a chance (whether they want it or not) to experience the ups and downs of human relationships on the most basic level. Siblings can be devotedly loyal to one another, despise one another, and/or form an intense love-hate relationship that may continue throughout their lives. Even when children are far apart in age, they are directly affected by the experience of living with others who are both equal (as other children in the same family) and unequal (differing in age, size, competence,

Families provide a powerful context for learning attitudes, beliefs, and appropriate behavior—sometimes down to the last detail of posture, dress, and style of speech.

sibling status Birth order.

intelligence, attractiveness, and so on). Indeed, siblings are important in helping one another to identify social concepts and social roles by reciprocally prompting and inhibiting certain patterns of behavior (Dunn, 1983, 1985).

What influence do brothers and sisters have on one another? And how does birth order, or **sibling status,** affect each child's personality? Although previous generations of psychologists have devoted much speculation to the effects on personality of being oldest, youngest, or in the middle, current research does not support these views. In fact, no consistent personality differences have been found as a consequence of birth order. This does not mean, however, that the children in a family are similar in personality. In fact, siblings raised in the same family are likely to have very different personalities—almost as different as unrelated children (Plomin & Daniels, 1987). One reason for this is that children have a need to establish distinct identities for themselves (Dreikurs & Soltz, 1964). Thus, if an older sibling is serious and studious, the younger one may be boisterous. A girl who has four sisters and no brothers may carve out her own niche in the family by taking on a masculine role.

Although birth order seems to have no predictable effect on personality, many studies have found effects on intelligence and achievement; here, the oldest child clearly has the edge. On the average, oldest children have higher IQs and achieve more in school and in careers. Only children are also high achievers, although their IQs tend to be slightly lower, on the average, than the oldest child in a family of two or three children (Zajonc & Markus, 1975). One explanation for this finding is that only children never have the opportunity to serve as teachers for their younger siblings. Serving as a teacher may enhance a child's intellectual development (Zajonc & Hall, 1986).

Nonetheless, differences in IQ based on birth order tend to be small. Larger and more consistent differences are found when researchers look at family size. The more children there are in a family, the lower are their IQs and the less likely they are to graduate from high school. This is true even when other factors, such as family structure and income, are taken into account (Blake, 1989). But note that family structure (whether there are two parents or one) and income do have important effects on IQ and achievement—effects that are noticeably greater than those of birth order or number of siblings (Ernst & Angst, 1983).

Firstborns are only children for a year or more; they have their parents' exclusive attention. Then a baby sibling comes along, displacing them from their position of unique importance. Although reactions to the new baby vary, few children show outright hostility to the newcomer—at least at first. They are likely to be very curious about the baby and to direct any hostility toward the mother, often by getting into mischief just when she is feeding or diapering the baby (Dunn, 1985). They may also regress to infantile behavior such as thumb-sucking or wetting their pants. This reaction has been interpreted by psychoanalysts as a defense mechanism, indicating disguised anxiety. More recently, theorists have interpreted it as simple imitation, reflecting interest in the baby, or as a way of competing with the baby for the mother's attention. In any case, the infantile behavior is only temporary. By the end of the baby's first year, it is the younger child who is doing the imitating, and the older child is likely to have gained considerably in maturity and independence (Dunn, 1985; Stewart et al., 1987).

Older siblings are powerful models; research suggests that children with older siblings of the same sex tend to show stronger sex-typed behavior than those with older siblings of the opposite sex (Koch, 1956; Sutton-Smith & Rosenberg,

1970). The spacing between siblings also has an important effect on sibling status. The closer in age, the more intense is the influence of the sibling relationship (Sutton-Smith & Rosenberg, 1970).

In any case, each child in the family is faced with the task of forming an individual self-concept. His or her sibling status, the number of children in the family, the sex of the siblings, their closeness in years, and their individual personalities—all will have some influence on the personality the child develops.

Discipline and Self-Regulation

In different cultural groups and in different historical periods, techniques of discipline have varied widely. There have been periods of harsh physical punishment and periods of relative permissiveness. Methods of disciplining children—setting rules and limits and enforcing those limits—are subject to changes in fashion just like other aspects of culture.

The child-rearing literature of the 1950s and early 1960s warned against strong, overbearing disciplinary methods; parents worried about stifling their children's emotions and turning them into anxious, repressed, neurotic people. The literature of the 1970s and 1980s, in contrast, pointed out that children need a sufficient amount of external social control, firmness, and consistency in order to feel safe and secure.

So far, the 1990s seem to be continuing the trend toward firm parental control. Of course, children's need for affection and approval is also recognized. Six guidelines have been offered to achieve current child-rearing goals (Perry & Bussey, 1984). First, parents should foster an atmosphere of warmth, caring, and mutual support among family members. Affection, like other social behaviors, tends to be reciprocated. Children who are generally happy and content show more self-control and behave in more mature and prosocial ways. Second, parents should concentrate more on promoting desirable behaviors than on eliminating undesir-

Parents need to give their children the opportunity to explain their actions.

able ones. They should make a deliberate attempt to suggest, model, and reward children's helping and caring behaviors. Third, parents should set realistic expectations and demands, firmly enforce their demands, and be consistent. Fourth, parents should avoid the unnecessary use of power assertion—the use of force and threats to control children's behavior. Power assertion fosters similar behavior in children and may cause anger, bitterness, and resistance. Fifth, parents should help children gain a sense of control over themselves and their environment. Finally, parents should use verbal reasoning (induction) to help children develop an understanding of social rules. Children need to know the consequences of their behavior, including how other people will feel. Children should also have the opportunity to discuss or explain their actions to their parents. This helps them develop a sense of responsibility for their behavior. In the long run, self-regulated behavior is determined by children's understanding of the situation.

Balancing children's need for firmness and consistency with their need for warmth and approval is a difficult job for a parent. In Chapter 12 we will look more closely at this issue.

THE EFFECTS OF TELEVISION

Television is not simply an electronic toy or one of many forms of entertainment: It is a pervasive influence in the lives of children—one that has had a major impact on family relationships and traditions. In 1950 only 1 family in 20 had a television set. Ten years later, television was found in about 90% of American homes. Today 98% of families have at least one television set; some have three or four. Children now spend more time watching television than doing anything else, except sleeping (Fabes et al., 1989; Huston et al., 1989).

Given how much time children spend watching television, many authorities have wondered what effects this is having on their development. Concern has focused on three aspects of television viewing: the content of programs and commercials, the rapid-fire visual format, and the way in which it is used in the home (Rubinstein, 1983).

Program Content

Television is a major socializing force in our society. Many have concluded that by exposing children to a large amount of casual violence on the screen, we are teaching them to think of aggression as a commonplace and acceptable outlet for their own frustrations. Others have taken the opposite view: They have argued that viewing violent acts on television may serve as a substitute for overt aggression, with the result that actual aggression is diminished rather than increased (Feshbach & Singer, 1971). Although this second theory is appealing, research does not support it. A large number of studies have shown that exposure to televised violence produces a small but significant *increase* in the aggressiveness of viewers (Huston et al., 1989).

The effects of television, however, are not that simple. Children often do not understand everything they see on television, and they do not pay attention to or absorb shows they do not understand (Anderson et al., 1981). Some of the effects

Does television teach children that aggression is an acceptable response to frustration?

of what children do see and seem to understand may be moderated if a parent or other adult explains and comments on what is happening (Collins et al., 1981). Additionally, children are not merely watching "meaningless violence." Every cartoon and drama has a variety of characters, scenes, and situations. Let us consider a single child fascinated by a single program. A Mickey Mouse cartoon, for example, shows a tiny mouse somehow managing to outwit the big bullies of the world. In a western show, the marshal usually gets the troublemakers and justice prevails. Violence in the service of the simple themes of such programs—provided children understand the themes—does very little damage to most children. But for some children, habitual television viewing of aggressive programs may be combined with an environment in which many of the available role models—parents, siblings, or friends—are also aggressive or antisocial. This combination seems to escalate aggressive behavior, especially in children with certain personality traits or emotional problems (Huesmann et al., 1984).

Many other aspects of program content will affect children. Often, certain kinds of people are presented in a stereotyped fashion: Members of minority groups may be depicted in unfavorable ways, women may be shown in passive or subordinate roles, and old people are made to appear senile or burdensome. As a result, children can develop unrealistic social beliefs and concepts. Even their overall view of the world may be affected. One study found that heavy television viewing caused people to see the world as a mean and scary place—probably because there are more frightening incidents on television than occur in most children's everyday experience (Rubinstein, 1983).

Despite the numerous studies that have shown negative effects of television viewing, the medium can also have a positive influence on children's thoughts and actions. Television can teach children many forms of prosocial behavior. Carefully designed children's programs are able to interweave many different themes, such as cooperation, sharing, affection, friendship, persistence at tasks, control of aggression, and coping with frustration. Children who have seen these programs for even relatively short periods of time become more cooperative, sympathetic, and nurturant (Stein & Friedrich, 1975). Gender-role stereotyping is beginning to decrease in television programming. Some shows now depict men and women in nontraditional roles—women working outside the home, men doing housework. Children who watch such shows have been found to have more flexible gender-role concepts (Rosenwasser et al., 1989).

313

Both the content and the format of television may influence children's development.

Television Format

Unlike other "members of the family," the television set is not responsive or interactive. Television is characterized by rapid-fire visual and auditory stimulation, and visual techniques like zooms, cuts, and special effects. These techniques can be used creatively to capture the child's attention and to structure an educational message, or they can bombard the senses, demanding little in the way of thoughtful response on the part of the child. One reviewer suggests that children pay attention to minor superficial impressions but fail to follow much of the storyline or understand much of the content (Winn, 1983). Others have found that the format can be quite stimulating—it can capture children's attention and create heightened arousal (Rubinstein, 1983; Wright & Huston, 1983). Although many critics have claimed that the fast-paced, attention-getting stimulation shortens children's attention span and makes them less able to pay attention in other environments, such as the classroom, there is as yet no solid evidence to support this view (Anderson & Collins, 1988).

In some ways, television might actually advance children's cognitive development. The children who watch the most television tend to be from low-income or minority-group families. For such children, television can serve as a source of information that they would otherwise have no way of obtaining. If they watch shows like "Sesame Street" and "Mr. Rogers' Neighborhood," they will pick up many of the skills, concepts, facts, and vocabulary taught on these shows. As one review summed it up, "Even a skeptical interpretation of the data concluded that children learned letter and number skills from unaided viewing" (Huston et al., 1989, p. 425).

Some authorities are concerned that the stimulating format of television might capture children's attention so completely that they sit there mesmerized. This fear, too, appears to be without foundation. Although some sources claim that children watch as much as 30 hours of television a week, this figure is misleading because it refers to the amount of time the television set is turned on. Preschoolers

PROGRAMS DESIGNED FOR YOUNG VIEWERS

Across the nation, 1- to 4-year-old children sit in front of their television sets every day watching the rapid-fire sequences of "Sesame Street" flash before their eyes. They see Big Bird on roller skates one minute, Cookie Monster counting to 10 the next, and Ernie and Bert singing a duet the next. Some developmental psychologists have expressed concerns about the effects of these constantly changing sequences. They fear that a regular diet of this kind of viewing may shorten children's attention span and lessen their ability to reflect on and retain new information.

There is, at present, no evidence that watching these shows has any harmful effects on children's cognitive development. On the contrary, it has been shown that children can learn a great deal from them. Shows like "Sesame Street" and "Mr. Rogers' Neighborhood" are carefully designed for the cognitive capacities of young children. These programs use the same kind of language that mothers use when they speak to toddlers and preschoolers: simple sentences, frequent repetitions, a restricted vocabulary, and an emphasis on the here and now (Rice & Haight, 1986). Television programs designed for teenagers or adults are likely to go over the heads of younger children, but preschoolers are quite capable of understanding the programs that are designed for their own age group (Anderson & Collins, 1988). Watching "Sesame Street" is associated with improved vocabulary and prereading skills in preschoolers. Watching "Mr. Rogers' Neighborhood" has been found to increase prosocial behavior and imaginative play. A program called "Reading Rainbow," designed for school-age children, has been successful in encouraging reading and the use of libraries (Huston et al., 1989).

Those are examples of television at its best. Television at its worst frightens children and gives them nightmares, provides them with models for aggressive and irresponsible behavior, and exploits children's naivete in order to turn them into greedy little consumers. Because older children and adults have learned not to believe everything they see on television, many commercials are expressly aimed at younger children. Preschoolers are often unable to distinguish commercials from the programs that precede and follow them, and they do not understand that the purpose of commercials is simply to sell them something. They are easily deceived by misleading advertising (Huston et al., 1989). When a commercial succeeds in motivating the child to say, "I want one of those" or "I want some of that," many parents wisely say no. This often leads to a conflict between the parent and the child. One study found that children have negative attitudes toward parents who refuse to buy them a heavily advertised toy (Fabes et al., 1989).

Many children are frightened by horror programs they see on television; the effects of such experiences may be short-lived or may last for days or months. Older children can be helped to deal with frightening material by being reminded, "It's not real—it's only a show." However, this technique does not work with preschoolers, perhaps because they are unable to hold onto the idea "It's not real" at the same time that they are watching a highly arousing program (Cantor & Wilson, 1988). Generations of children have listened with a mixture of delight and fear to scary stories like "Little Red Riding Hood" and "Hansel and Gretel," and have suffered no permanent psychological harm. But horror movies shown on television may be too graphic—too visually compelling—for children who are not old enough to understand that they're "not real." For this age group, the Cookie Monster is scary enough.

generally do not sit and stare at the screen for hours at a time; in fact, they are looking at the screen only about half the time. The rest of the time they are in and out of the room, engaging in other activities, and talking to parents and siblings. Much of this talk is about the program they are watching (Anderson & Collins, 1988; Huston et al., 1989).

At its best, television can be an educational tool that can expand the horizons of children and encourage them to break away from stereotyped images. The attention-getting, high-action, rapid-pace techniques can help children focus on the information to be learned, and seem to do no harm to their cognitive development (Greenfield, 1984; Wright & Huston, 1983).

STUDY OUTLINE

Developmental Issues and Coping Patterns

Handling Feelings. Between the ages of 2 and 6, children learn the norms, rules, and cultural meanings of society, and they develop a self-concept that may persist throughout their lives. They also develop an elaborate set of coping mechanisms, designed to help them manage their feelings in ways their society considers appropriate.

Parents should try to limit the amount of stress that children must deal with. When stress is unavoidable, parents should provide children with warmth, security, an explanation, and an opportunity to discuss their feelings.

Defense mechanisms are coping strategies for disguising or reducing anxiety. By the age of 5 or 6, many children are able to use defense mechanisms to disguise their feelings. Although these mechanisms serve a useful purpose, in their extreme forms they can isolate the child from reality.

Developmental Conflicts. Uninhibited displays of emotion are not considered acceptable in our society. Children must learn to deal not only with unpleasant emotions, like **fear, anxiety,** hostility, and anger, but also with positive emotions, such as joy, excitement, and sensuality. In addition, they must reconcile their needs for dependency and autonomy. Expressions of dependency and autonomy change in different ways as children grow older.

Aggression and Prosocial Behavior

Rewards, Punishment, and Modeling. A principle task of socializing young children is to teach them acceptable ways of channeling their aggressive feelings. **Frustration** often (but not always) leads to **aggression;** aggression can also be learned through imitation of models (such as a parent who uses physical punishment) or by rewarding a child's aggressive behavior.

Prosocial Behavior. Like aggression, **prosocial behavior** (sharing, helping, and so on) is also learned from exposure to models and through rewards and punishments. Because our society rewards girls and boys for different kinds of behavior, girls express more concern for the feelings of others. Modeling is most effective when children perceive the model as similar to themselves, and when the model is competent, powerful, or nurturant. **Role playing** and **induction** also influence prosocial behavior.

Peers and Social Skills. In peer relationships, children serve as models for one another and as reinforcers of one another's behavior. Children who are unpopular with their peers as preschoolers are likely to remain unpopular in later childhood; these children generally lack social skills and may be aggressive or withdrawn.

Understanding Self and Others

The Self-Concept. The integration of patterns of social behavior results from the development of a self-concept and of certain social concepts. Children's self-concepts are influenced by what others think of them, by their actions, by parental models of behavior, and by their own ideals of what they should be.

Social Concepts and Rules. **Internalization**—the child's absorption of society's moral standards and values—is one of the basic processes of socialization. As children internalize society's rules, they develop the self-control to regulate their own behavior.

Children's verbal disputes demonstrate a sophisticated understanding of social rules and concepts, and their growing ability to take another person's perspective.

Gender Schemes. Children's gender schemes determine which behaviors they will learn, remember, and imitate. By the age of 2½, most children can identify themselves and other people as male or female. **Gender constancy**—the understanding that gender is permanent and is not affected by superficial changes—is not acquired until ages 5 to 7.

The Family Context

Siblings. Siblings are a child's first peer group. Whether a child is oldest, youngest, or in the middle does not have a predictable effect on the child's personality, although the oldest child tends to be highest in IQ and achievement. Children in the same family have different personalities because each one strives to establish a distinct identity.

Discipline and Self-Regulation. Six guidelines for parents to achieve today's child-rearing goals are: (1) Parents should foster an atmosphere of warmth, caring, and mutual support. (2) Parents should concentrate on promoting desirable behaviors rather than on eliminating undesirable ones. (3) Parents should set realistic expectations, firmly enforce them, and be consistent. (4) Parents should avoid the unnecessary use of power assertion. (5) Parents should help children gain a sense of control over themselves and their environment. (6) Parents should use verbal reasoning to help children develop an understanding of social rules.

The Effects of Television

Program Content. Television is an important socializing force. Although exposure to televised violence has been shown to increase aggression, television can also foster prosocial behavior and provide a source of information, especially for children from disadvantaged homes. Educational programs designed for children can increase their vocabularies and their letter and number skills.

KEY TERMS AND CONCEPTS

aggression
altruism
anxiety
assertive behavior
autonomy
defense mechanisms
denial
dependency
displacement
fear

frustration
gender constancy
gender identity
gender schemes
identification
induction
internalization
mastery
projection

prosocial behavior
rationalization
reaction formation
regression
repression
role playing
sibling status
social reciprocity
withdrawal

SELF-TEST QUESTIONS

1. List three main theories that address the socialization of the child.

2. Discuss the sources of anxiety. Compare and contrast fear and anxiety in the preschool child.

3. What are defense mechanisms? List several different types employed by children.

4. Discuss different strategies that children might use to cope with anxiety and stress.

5. List several of the strong feelings that preschool children begin to deal with and the ways they learn to handle these feelings.

6. Discuss the developmental conflicts that children must resolve during the preschool years.

7. Compare aggressive, assertive, and prosocial behavior. Discuss several of the explanations that have been given for these types of behavior.

8. What is social reciprocity?

9. List six different levels of interaction in young children. At what age do these levels apply?

10. How does a child's self-concept relate to his social development?

11. What is internalization, and how does it relate to a child's developing self-regulation?

12. What are gender schemes, and how do they apply to socialization?

13. How do sibling relationships affect the personality development of a child?

14. List six guidelines that help to achieve current child-rearing goals.

15. How is television a major socializing force in our society?

SUGGESTED READINGS

DAMON, W. *The moral child: Nurturing children's natural moral growth.* New York: Free Press, 1991. Approaches to moral education, both at home and in the community, are clearly and concisely linked to the normal course of moral development as it is formed in infancy through adolescence.

LEWIS, M. *Shame: The exposed self.* New York: Free Press, 1991. This "history of shame" as a human response during infancy and early childhood looks at the many ways in which shame is induced and expressed, reacted to, and handled.

LIEBERT, R. M., & SPRAKEN, J. N. *The early window: Effects of television on children and youth* (3rd ed.). Elmsford, NY: Pergamon, 1988. An updated readable review of the theory and research on the positive and negative effects of television.

PALEY, Y. G. *The boy who would be a helicopter: The uses of storytelling in the classroom.* Cambridge, MA: Harvard University Press, 1990. An engaging account of one boy's odyssey from social isolation to integration woven within an insightful essay on excellent early childhood education.

SINGER, D. G., & SINGER, J. L. *The house of make-believe: Children's play and the developing imagination.* Cambridge, MA: Harvard University Press, 1990. A comprehensive review of children's evolving fantasy play and its function in child development.

Chapter 11

And so we discovered that education is not something which the teacher does, but that it is a natural process which develops spontaneously in the human being.

MARIA MONTESSORI
THE ABSORBENT MIND

CHAPTER OUTLINE

Competencies in School Tasks

For most children, middle childhood is a time for settling down, for developing more fully those patterns that have already been set. It is a period for learning new skills and refining old ones—from reading and writing to playing basketball, dancing, or skateboarding. Children focus on testing themselves, on meeting their own challenges as well as those imposed by the environment. The child who is successful in these tasks will probably become even more capable and self-assured; the one who is unsuccessful is more likely to develop a feeling of inferiority or a weaker sense of self.

Erikson has referred to middle childhood as the period of *industry*. The word captures the spirit of this period, for it is derived from a Latin term meaning "to build." In this chapter, we will sample some of the ways in which children build both physical and cognitive competencies. We will also look at school tasks and problems encountered in middle childhood, including the ways in which intelligence and achievement tests are administered and interpreted and some current approaches used in understanding learning disabilities.

The development of physical and cognitive competencies and an increased mastery of the environment are only part of a child's developmental tasks during this period. For school-age children, "belonging" is of critical importance. They become very concerned about their status among their peers. This status depends increasingly on the competence and capabilities discussed in this chapter.

COPING WITH PHYSICAL CHALLENGES

Surely, one of the first things that impresses any observer of school-age children is their high activity level. What function does all of this activity serve? Far from being a waste of time, children's games and sports provide them with the opportunity to develop strength, coordination, agility, and flexibility. Thus, in neighborhoods and playgrounds, children can be seen testing their balance by riding bicycles through homemade obstacle courses. They improve their hand–eye coordination, strength, and speed in games of stickball or basketball. Practicing karate or roller-blade skating, jumping rope, or imitating the exploits of television heroes—all help improve physical–motor development.

The rapid spurt of physical growth that we saw in infancy and toddlerhood slows in the preschool period and remains slow during middle childhood; it

CHAPTER OBJECTIVES

By the time you have finished this chapter, you should be able to do the following:

- Describe physical and motor development in middle childhood.
- Discuss the possible causes and treatments of childhood obesity.
- Compare preoperational thought with concrete operational thought.
- Describe how Piaget's concepts of learning in middle childhood could be applied to education.
- Discuss cognitive development during middle childhood as it is described by information-processing theorists.
- Describe some of the developmental challenges that the schoolroom presents for children, parents, and teachers.
- Discuss the ongoing controversy regarding definitions of intelligence and the uses and abuses of intelligence testing.
- Explain the two main types of learning disabilities and the various views on their causes and treatments.

Being active and participating in games help children develop the strength, speed, and coordination they need for gross motor skills.

doesn't speed up again until early adolescence. Thus, aside from the somewhat startling change when the toothless smile of the 6-year-old becomes the large-toothed grin of the 8-year-old, most bodily changes that occur in this period are gradual and continuous. Between ages 5 and 7, children slim down and lose what's left of their baby fat. They also grow taller and more muscular, and their body proportions become more like those of an adult. These physical changes— especially the increase in muscular strength—aid children in developing new gross and fine motor skills. The gradual physical changes during this period may actually make it easier for them to develop new motor skills because they do not have to keep adjusting to rapid changes in body size and proportions.

Motor Skill Development

Throughout middle childhood, children continue to grow in the strength, speed, and coordination that are needed for gross motor skills. Their newly acquired physical ability is reflected in their obsession with sports and daredevil stunts. They climb trees, use logs as balance beams to cross streams, jump from beam to beam in the skeleton of an unfinished house. Numerous studies demonstrate the progress of motor development during this period. According to Keogh (1965), at age 7 a boy can throw a ball approximately 34 feet. By the time he is 10, he will probably be able to throw it twice as far, and three times as far by the time he is 12—and his accuracy will improve as well. Girls make similar progress in throwing and catching skills, although at every age their average throwing distance is shorter than that of boys (Williams, 1983). Sex differences are noted in many other physical skills: All through middle childhood, boys can run faster than girls. After age 11, the difference in running speed widens because boys continue to improve, whereas girls do not (Herkowitz, 1978). However, girls tend to outperform boys in skills that require agility or balance—for example, girls are better at hopping. These sex differences are closely linked to the particular activities practiced. Girls in Little League baseball develop longer, more accurate throws. Boys and girls who play soccer develop skills at a similar pace.

Fine motor skills—those skills that enable children to use their hands in increasingly sophisticated ways—also develop quickly during this period, starting even before a child enters first grade. In nursery schools, teachers stress writing readiness as they teach preschoolers how to draw circles, squares, and, finally, triangles. (Children who cannot draw a triangle have difficulty with more complex writing skills.) Each increasingly complex shape requires the improved hand–eye coordination children need to learn in order to write. Most of the fine motor skills required in writing develop during a child's sixth and seventh years. However, some children cannot draw a diamond or master many letter shapes until the age of 8.

FIGURE 11-1
Middle childhood is a time of great growth in size and physical competence. While there are tremendous variations in growth patterns, these changes in body size and proportion are typical of this period.

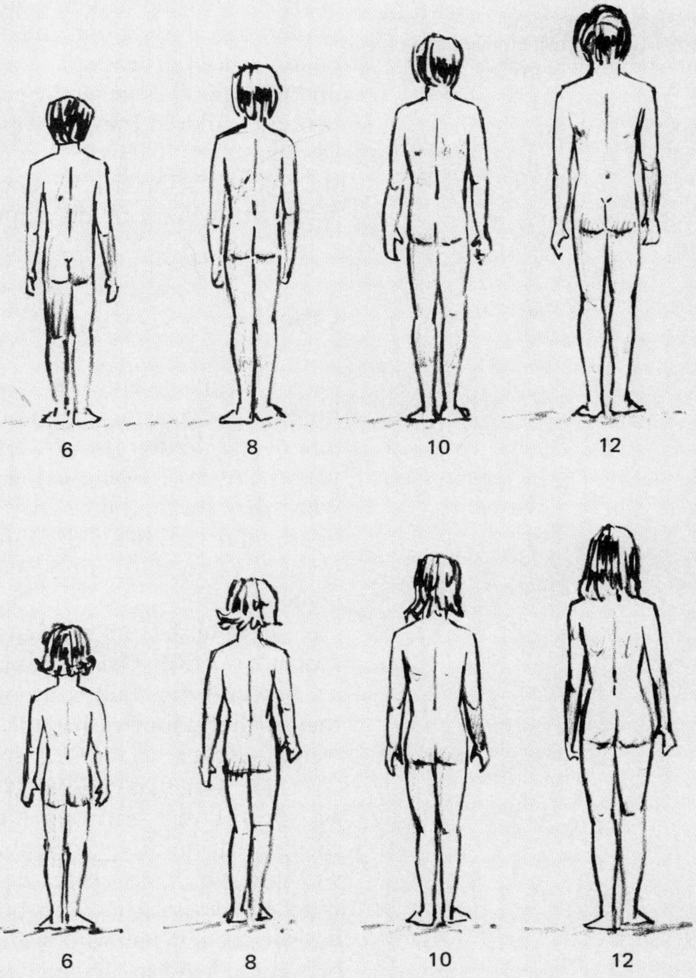

The fine motor skills required for writing and complicated drawing develop during the sixth and seventh years.

The mastery that children develop over their own bodies during this period gives them feelings of competence and self-worth that are essential to good mental health. Controlling their own bodies also helps them win the acceptance of their peers. Awkward, poorly coordinated children are often left out of group activities; they may continue to feel unwanted long after their awkwardness disappears.

Health and Illness

Minor illnesses such as ear infections, colds, and upset stomachs are very prevalent during the preschool period. During the years from 6 to 12, most children experience fewer of these illnesses. This is partly a result of greater immunity due to previous exposure. Also, most school-age children know and practice somewhat better nutrition, health, and safety habits (O'Connor-Francoeur, 1983). Nevertheless, fairly frequent minor illnesses occur. One author suggests that such minor illnesses are actually of some benefit to the child's psychological development. Although common illnesses certainly disrupt the child's school progress, as well as family social roles and work schedules, children and their families generally recover rather quickly from these interruptions. In the process, children learn to cope with minor stress and to increase their knowledge of themselves. They develop a bit more empathy, and a realistic understanding of the role of "being sick." Hence, children's illnesses can be seen as a normal part of social and behavioral development (Parmelee, 1986).

Obesity

Obesity—defined as weighing at least 20% more than one's ideal weight—is becoming increasingly common among American children: About one-quarter of school-age children are now overweight (Gortmaker et al., 1987). What makes this particularly worrisome is that so many of these children will still be overweight when they reach adulthood: Nearly 70% of obese 10- to 13-year-olds will become obese adults (Epstein & Wing, 1987). Their obesity will predispose them to a number of medical problems, such as heart disease, high blood pressure, and diabetes.

Genetic factors play an important role in obesity. The child of one obese parent has a 40% chance of becoming obese; the odds leap to 80% if both parents are obese. If the child is adopted, it is the weight of her biological parents, rather than of her adoptive parents, that will have the greatest influence on her adult weight (Rosenthal, 1990; Stunkard, 1988).

The fact that childhood obesity is more common now than it was 20 years ago proves that environmental factors are also important because genes don't change that quickly. One environmental factor that has been blamed is television viewing, which has increased steadily over this period. Today, an average child watches television for 23 hours a week, and those who watch more tend to be heavier than those who watch less. There are two reasons for the connection between television viewing and obesity: too little physical activity and too much snacking on junk food (Dietz, 1987). Children who sit in front of a television set are not getting the exercise they need to develop their physical skills and to burn off excess calories. At the same time, if they spend their viewing hours munching on potato chips and drinking sweetened beverages, their appetite is diminished for more nutritious (and less caloric) foods.

Children should *not* be placed on drastic weight-loss programs even if they are seriously overweight, because they need a balanced, nutritious diet to support energy levels and proper growth. Instead of trying to lose weight quickly, they must develop better eating habits that they can maintain over time. In particular, they should increase their intake of healthy foods like fruits and vegetables and decrease their intake of foods that are high in fats, for example, pizza. Equally important, they must increase their physical activity. It should also be noted that obesity often runs in families, and because of this, successful weight-loss programs frequently involve treating the parents as well as the children (Epstein et al., 1990).

Although overweight children face fewer medical risks than overweight adults do, there are serious social and psychological consequences of their obesity. Peers may reject them because of their physical appearance and because they are less adept at sports. The result can be a negative self-image that may make the child even more reluctant to interact with age-mates or to engage in physical activities.

The trouble with being overweight at this age is that there is considerable social stigma attached to it, and from this, children quickly learn negative self-images.

Physical Development and the School Environment

We generally think of school in terms of its effect upon children's cognitive or social development, forgetting that schools must also provide for children's physical and motor needs. The effect of the standard American classroom was aptly summarized by a first grader after her first day at school. When asked how she liked her new school, she replied, "Oh, you mean sit-down school?" She was reacting not to the difference in teachers and schedules but to being confined to a desk and chair for a whole day. There is no evidence that children learn best by sitting in straight-backed chairs for long periods of time—on the contrary, many studies have shown the limitations of passive, receptive learning. An elementary school in Massachusetts may set an example for the type of design that will be used in the future. In addition to desks and tables, the classrooms have cubicles and caves built into the walls at varying heights. Each nook is large enough for one or two children and is furnished with rugs and cushions. The cubicles are special places to which the children can retreat to read, study, or hold problem-solving discussions. These quiet, busy classrooms provide a relaxed atmosphere and promote good achievement.

Six-year-old children are still learning with their bodies, still integrating physical and intellectual knowledge. It is artificial to divorce the body from the mind and personality, using it only in gym or at recess. A school can be responsive to a child's physical needs in many ways. In a math class, for example, children might measure a corridor in yards or in meters, and then measure it again in terms of their own footsteps or the time it takes them to walk its length. In this way, their knowledge would be both abstract and concrete, both general and personal. Schools might also stress physical expression for its own sake. Some British primary schools have set aside a special period for movement expression and exploration (Evans, 1975).

"Just think of it as a brief interlude in, as opposed to a major disruption of, your life."

CONCRETE OPERATIONAL THOUGHT

The thinking of a 12-year-old child is very different from that of a 5-year-old. This difference is due not only to the much larger body of knowledge and information that the 12-year-old has accumulated but also to the different ways in which the two children think and process information. For Piaget, the elementary school child is in a period of developing concrete operational thought.

Cognitive Abilities of the School Beginner

A large part of intellectual development takes place in formal schoolrooms. It is at school that children learn to think like adults, and for this reason alone, starting school is a milestone in the life of any child. The fact that so many cultures have chosen the ages from 5 to 7 years for beginning the systematic education of their young is probably no historical accident. Between ages 5 and 7, many of children's cognitive, language, and perceptual–motor skills mature and interact in a way that makes some kinds of learning easier and more efficient.

In Piaget's theory, the years between ages 5 and 7 mark the transition from *preoperational* to *concrete operational* thought: Thought becomes less intuitive and egocentric, and more logical. In Chapter 9, we discussed some of the limitations of preoperational thought. Before age 7, children tend to focus on one aspect of a problem at a time. They focus on the here-and-now and on perceptual evidence, rather than on logical reasoning. Their ability to find relationships between the events and things around them is limited.

Toward the end of Piaget's preoperational stage, the rigid, static, irreversible qualities of children's thought begin to "thaw out," to use Piaget's own terminology. Children's thinking begins to be reversible, flexible, and considerably more complex. They begin to notice one, then another aspect of an object and can use logic to reconcile differences between the two. They can evaluate cause-and-effect relationships, particularly if they have the concrete object right in front of them and can see changes occur. When a piece of clay looks like a sausage, they no longer find it inconsistent that the clay was once a ball or that it can be molded into a new shape, such as a cube. This emerging ability to leap mentally beyond the immediate situation or state lays the foundation for systematic reasoning in the concrete operational stage and, later, in the formal operational stage.

One difference between preoperational and concrete operational thought can be illustrated by school-age children's use of **logical inference** (Flavell, 1985). Recall Piaget's liquid conservation experiment (Chapter 2). In this experiment, preoperational children consistently judge that a tall, narrow glass holds more liquid than a short, wide one, although both quantities of liquid were shown to be identical at the start. Concrete operational children, in contrast, know that both containers hold the same amount of liquid. They come to this conclusion from "unseen" evidence: They can make logical inferences. Concrete operational children also begin to think differently about states and transformations. They can remember how the liquid appeared before it was poured into the tall, thin container. They can think about how its shape changed as it was poured from one glass into the other and can imagine what shape the liquid would have if it were poured back. Concrete operational children, then, not only include the process of transformation in their thinking but also are aware that the fluid may have other shapes, including the original. Their thinking is *reversible*.

In addition, concrete operational children know that differences between similar objects can be quantified, or measured. In Piaget's (1970) matchstick problem, children are shown a zigzag row of six matchsticks and a straight row of five matchsticks placed end to end (see Figure 11–2). When asked which row is longer, very young children center only on the distance between the end points of the rows and thus pick the "longer" row with five matchsticks. Concrete

logical inference   A conclusion reached through "unseen" evidence; concrete operational children are capable of this type of thinking.

Nearly every culture begins the systematic education of their young by age 7. This Muslim school on the border of Nepal and India is no exception.

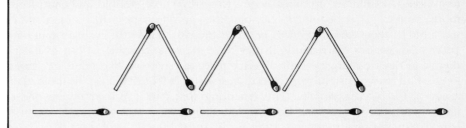

FIGURE 11-2
Piaget's Matchstick Problem.
Concrete operational children realize that the six matchsticks in the zigzag top row will make a longer line than the five matchsticks in the straight bottom row. Younger children will say that the bottom row is the longest because they tend to center only on the end points of the two lines and not on what lies between them.

operational children, however, can take into account what lies between the end points of the rows and therefore will choose the one with six matchsticks.

Finally, unlike preoperational children, concrete operational children can theorize about the world. They think about and anticipate what will happen; they make guesses about things and then test their hunches. They may estimate, for example, how many more breaths of air they can blow into a balloon before it pops and will keep blowing until they reach or surpass this mark. This ability to theorize is limited to concrete objects and social relationships that children can see and test. Children do not develop theories about abstract concepts, thoughts, or relationships until they reach the stage of formal operations, which begins around age 11 or 12.

Piaget defined "operation" as a reversible mental action. The concrete operational period, therefore, means that children are able to perform reversible mental actions on real, concrete objects but not on abstract ideas.

The transition from preoperational to concrete operational thought does not happen overnight. It is a developmental task that requires years of experience in manipulating and learning about the objects and materials in the environment. To a large extent, children learn concrete operational thought on their own. As they actively explore their physical environment, asking themselves questions and finding the answers, they acquire a more complex, sophisticated form of thinking.

Piaget and Education

As we saw in Chapter 6, infants benefit from stimulation that is presented slightly ahead of their developmental level. Such stimulation promotes cognitive growth. Some researchers believe that appropriate training can also accelerate the cognitive development of preoperational children, hastening their entrance into the level of concrete operations. Training is most effective when children have reached a state of readiness, an optimal period that occurs just before they make the transition to the next stage (Bruner, Olver, & Greenfield, 1966).

Many of the basic concepts presented by Piaget have been applied to education, particularly in the areas of science and math. One such application includes the use of concrete objects for teaching 5- to 7-year-olds. By combining, comparing, and contrasting concrete objects (for example, blocks and rods of different shapes and sizes, seeds that grow in sand, water, or soil) children discover similarities, differences, and relationships.

One method for using objects is to arrange them into simple patterns (see Figure 11–3). Many children who are 5 to 7 years old may still be centering on one particular aspect of objects. Yet a teacher or care-giver may want to teach an abstract concept (say, the number 16), an operation (subtraction), or a relationship (equality). In introducing second graders to the number concept of 16, for example, a teacher might present several different spatial arrays of 16 cubes— grouped into two towers of 8, one row of 16, four rows of 4, and so on. The teacher could also give verbal cues to the concept of conservation, pointing out, for instance, that the number of cubes remains the same even though the length and width of the rows may change.

There are many other applications of Piaget's concepts. For example, addition and subtraction involve an understanding of reversibility ($5 + 8 = 13$, and $13 - 5 = 8$). Again, children can best learn about these processes by manipulating real objects. Many concepts of time and distance are quite abstract, or they involve the understanding of the relationship between different units of measure. For example, telling time from a clock requires the understanding of the relationship between minutes and hours. Understanding the basic principles of Piaget's theory of cognitive development makes it easier to develop effective educational lessons and to organize these lessons into a logical sequence. Indeed, Piagetian concepts have been applied to a wide range of curriculum projects, including social studies, music, art, math, and science.

Some educators have noted that Piaget seems to have a philosophy of learning as well as a theory of cognitive development. They point to the Piagetian principles that children are active learners, that they construct their own theories about how the world operates, and that they themselves are motivated to change these theories when pieces of information do not fit (Bruner, 1973). These

FIGURE 11-3

Some possible spatial arrays of 16 cubes. By arranging the cubes in different ways, a teacher can help young schoolchildren understand the number concept of 16.

4 x 4 array

2 x 8 array

Two "towers" of 8

16 cubes in an open design

1 x 16 array

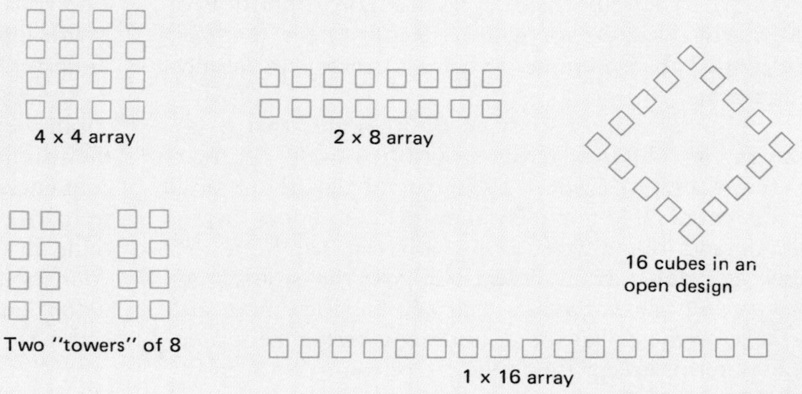

educators warn against structuring education in ways that encourage children to seek praise from the teacher rather than to solve problems for their own sake. They emphasize that children's interest in learning depends on the intrinsic rewards they find in the encounter with the subject matter itself. Children gain confidence from mastering a problem or discovering a principle.

These educators also point out that, too often, teachers instruct young children by *telling* them instead of *showing* them. They remove the real-life, concrete context of many subjects. They present rules and items for children to memorize by rote without motivating the children to develop an understanding of these rules. Children are then left with an arid body of facts without the structure to connect them and without the ability to apply these facts and principles to other settings. Children, they contend, need to learn by doing, by actively exploring ideas and relationships, and by solving problems in a realistic context.

Piaget was a remarkable observer of the young child; he offered a number of important insights into the child's cognitive development. But there are some aspects of cognitive development that he did not describe and that are important for school learning. Many of these come under the heading of what is called the information-processing perspective.

APPLICATION

CHILDREN'S CONCEPTS OF THEIR BODIES

Remember when you thought your heart was shaped like the classic box of valentine chocolates, or when you were sure, if you tried hard enough, you could look through one ear to see the other? During the early school years, all children conceptualize their internal body organs and functions in a concrete way. They are vitally interested in the workings of their bodies, and based on their observations and the little information they receive, they actively construct what is going on inside. As they grow older and acquire more knowledge and understanding, they learn to describe their bodies in a more sophisticated and abstract way. As you will see, many of their thoughts are remarkably accurate, whereas others are totally outrageous.

In a fascinating study of the thoughts that 6- to 12-year-old children have about the inside of their bodies, Cathleen Crider (1981) found that the typical grade-school child first identifies the brain, bones, heart, blood, and blood vessels. As you can see from the drawing (right) by a 7-year-old girl, the stomach is absent, but the vegetables that she ate for dinner are present. In the child's mind, nothing is certain about the body interior except the foods she puts into it (Schilder & Wechsler, 1935).

Children's perceptions give them their first clues of their internal organs. They can feel their heart beating; they can feel the hardness of their bones under their skin; they can identify their brain from the inner speech that accompanies thought. Other organs, like the nerves and liver, are not as easy to understand. After having liver for dinner, children may wonder if they have a liver, too. They will be satisfied with their parents' simple answer that they do, and they may feel no need for more information. Similarly, children may understand their bodies' nerves only in terms of the emotional problems of a nervous relative. Even with considerable instruction, it is difficult for them to understand other hidden functions of nerves.

Children often use the little information they have about their bodies in a very inventive way. For instance, they think of body organs, like the stomach and brain, as containers. A child who has already become aware of his stomach describes it in this way: "The stomach is a round thing in our body for holding food. The food goes in your mouth, down your neck, to your stomach. If we didn't have a stomach, the food would go everywhere and it would be a mess" (p. 54).

Like every other aspect of development, conceptualization of this kind occurs at different rates for different children. One 9-year-old described his organs in a very

occur on school mornings: get up, get dressed, eat breakfast, and so on. The slots would be filled with variable items, such as which clothes were put on, what was eaten for breakfast, and the conversation at the breakfast table (Nelson & Gruendel, 1986).

metacognition The process of monitoring one's own thinking, memory, knowledge, goals, and actions.

Metacognition

There are several other information-processing components that become more sophisticated during middle childhood. Children become better able to focus their attention on what they're doing and to keep it focused despite distractions. They gradually improve their problem-solving strategies. They also develop higher-order control processes. Children become better able to monitor their own thinking, memory, knowledge, goals, and actions. They become better able to plan, to make decisions, and to select which memory strategy or problem-solving strategy they want to use. These higher-order processes are called meta processes, or **metacognition.**

In his description of metacognition, Flavell (1985) cites the following example: Preschool and elementary school children were asked to study a group of items until they were certain they could remember them perfectly. After studying the items for a while, the elementary school children said they were ready, and they usually were. When they were tested, they remembered each item without fail. The preschool children did not perform as well, even though they assured the researchers that they knew every item.

Despite the good intentions of the preschoolers to remember and understand the things they studied, they did not have the cognitive ability to do so; they could not monitor their own intellectual processes. This ability to monitor one's own thinking and memory is just beginning at about age 6.

Like other aspects of cognitive ability, metacognitive skills develop gradually during middle childhood and adolescence. Just as a 9-year-old has greater metacognitive ability than a 4-year-old, a 15-year-old's self-monitoring skill far surpasses that of the 9-year-old. Because children use these self-monitoring skills in oral communication, reading comprehension, writing, and other cognitive abilities, they are a critical part of cognitive development.

LEARNING AND THINKING IN SCHOOL

Most children enter primary school between the ages of 5 and 7. Once in school, they encounter a number of demands and expectations that differ markedly from those in the home. Children vary greatly in how well they adapt to these demands.

New Demands and Expectations

Whether schooling starts with nursery school at age 3 or not until first grade at age 6, children must adapt to some changes immediately. They are separated from their parents or care-givers, perhaps for the first time, and must begin to trust

School-age children are faced with new cultural demands, depending on the time and the society. Top left: In the United States today, children between ages 5 and 7 must learn to adapt to school, which includes being separated from their parents, perhaps for the first time, and having to deal with unfamiliar adults and children. Top right: In earlier times in the United States, school-age children, like this boy in a Georgia cotton mill, often had to go to work to help support the family. Bottom: In other countries around the world, school-age children are still expected to go to work.

unfamiliar adults to ensure their safety and satisfy their needs. At the same time, they must start to become independent and learn to do certain things for themselves. No longer can a little boy sit down and yell, "Put on my boots!" It is time for him to put on his own boots. Even with a favorable student–teacher ratio, children must compete for adult attention and assistance.

The social rules of the classroom are complex. Relationships with classmates involve finding the right balance between cooperation and competition; relationships with the teacher involve a compromise between autonomy and obedience. One educator has described the schoolchild's situation this way:

> Assigned to classes that may contain strangers, perhaps even adversaries, students are expected to interact harmoniously. Crowded together, they are required to ignore the presence of others. Urged to cooperate, they usually work in competition. Pressed to take responsibility for their own learning, they must follow the dictates of a dominant individual—the teacher. (Weinstein, 1991, pp. 493–494)

Some schools have elaborate codes of behavior: Children must listen when the teacher speaks, line up for recess, obtain permission to go to the bathroom, and raise a hand before speaking. A great deal of time may be spent on enforcing these rules. Psychology students sometimes observe public school classrooms and measure how much time teachers spend on the following activities: (1) teaching a fact or concept; (2) giving directions for a particular lesson; (3) stating general rules of appropriate classroom behavior; (4) correcting, disciplining, and praising children; and (5) miscellaneous. The results are revealing: In a half-hour lesson, it is not unusual for a teacher to spend only 10% to 15% of the time on the first and second categories (Sieber & Gordon, 1981). Research indicates that children learn more in classes where "time on task" is maximized—that is, where the teacher spends more time on actual teaching and less on things like keeping order (Brophy, 1986).

Nonetheless, a considerable amount of time and energy may be put into socializing the children to the highly particular demands of the classroom, demands that are only vaguely connected to intellectual or social growth. Of course, these demands may differ radically from one time or place to another, depending upon nationality, customs, and educational philosophy. More than 20 years ago, Bronfenbrenner (1970) described the code of behavior for 7-year-olds in the Soviet Union:

> In school: All pupils are to arrive at school and in the classroom on time, wipe their feet upon entering, greet the teacher and all technical staff by name, give a general greeting by name to one's seatmate, keep one's things in order, obey all instructions of the teacher, learn rules of class conduct (standing when spoken to, proper position in listening, reading and writing).

Compare this kind of regimentation with the "open classroom" that was popular at around the same time in the United States. In the open classroom, children could stand, sit, or lie down anywhere in a decentralized room, select their own work for the day, and interact with the teacher and other children mainly in small groups. This approach assumed that children are motivated to learn on their own and that

There are rules of behavior even in the most casual classroom. For example, children may be expected to act independently, to ask questions, and to avoid disturbing others.

they learn best when they are free to choose their own subject matter. The open classroom, in its purest form, gradually went out of style after research showed that children were spending much of their time chatting with one another or moving around aimlessly, and that they were actually learning less than they would have learned in a traditional classroom (Bennett, 1976). In other words, they were spending too little "time on task."

Regardless of the kind of school that children enter, there is always a tremendous gap between what is acceptable at home and the new demands of the classroom. The greater the gap, the more difficult the adaptation will be. Although children at this age have just begun to internalize the rights and wrongs of family life, they are suddenly expected to adapt to a *whole new set of standards*. The success with which they make this transition depends upon family background, school environment, and the variables of individual development. How well have the children previously coped with dependency, autonomy, authority relationships, the need to control aggression, and the promptings of conscience? Their inner resources may be shaky; nevertheless, we require a flexibility from school beginners that is rarely required of adults.

Developing Competent Learners and Critical Thinkers

Learning has been defined as "an activity of the brain, under the direction and control of the individual, that must result in additions to and modifications of long-term memory" (Letteri, 1985). In a rapidly changing world, there is much to learn and too little time to learn it. Knowledge may now become obsolete in a decade or less, and because of this, today's children will have to become lifelong learners in order to adapt to a changing world. Meanwhile, these children need to integrate and organize the barrage of information that comes at them from all sides. They must find order and consistency in the complex and sometimes unstable experiences of their lives. To help children adapt and become lifelong learners, many educators urge teachers to avoid focusing on too many disconnected facts, principles, and rules. Instead, they emphasize that teachers should focus on instructing children how to become self-directed, competent learners and critical thinkers.

One approach that teachers can use is derived directly from what we know about information processing. Children can be taught to be competent learners by learning control processes. For example, problem solving often involves many component control processes, such as focusing on relevant details or analyzing a problem into component parts. Each of these strategies might be taught by using simple exercises. Some educators have had rather remarkable success in as little as 15 or 20 hours of training with initially poor students. The students become more analytical and focused, less impulsive, and they earn better grades (Letteri, 1985).

Other educators recommend a range of teaching strategies to develop student thinking. According to Costa (Costa et al., 1985), children need to develop six kinds of thought. We might call these the "six R's":

1. *Remembering*—recalling a fact, idea, or concept.
2. *Repeating*—following a model or procedure.
3. *Reasoning*—relating a specific instance to a general principle or concept.

4. *Reorganizing*—extending knowledge to a new context for an original solution.

5. *Relating*—establishing a connection between new knowledge and past or personal experience.

6. *Reflecting*—exploring the thought itself and how it occurred.

Developing these thinking skills requires special teaching strategies. To develop reasoning, teachers need to present interesting problems and materials. The goal is to increase curiosity, to foster questioning, to develop related concepts, to encourage evaluation of alternatives, and to help students construct hypotheses and devise methods of testing them. Teaching students to develop critical thinking is more difficult than simply imparting facts and principles (Costa, 1985).

In the past decade, there has been an attempt in U.S. schools to teach learning and thinking skills, to individualize instruction to the learning style and developmental level of the child, and to foster independent, self-regulated, self-paced learning. Often, this results in an increased number of small-group projects and activities. When small-group instruction is done effectively, children experience cooperative rather than competitive learning activities. Surprisingly, these children achieve high levels of skill in standard areas like math and reading (Costa, 1985). Unfortunately, such classes are hard to manage well. (See "The Math Gap: An Educational Dilemma.")

Computers, Learning, and Thinking

Computers have arrived in the classroom as well as in homes and in businesses. Their acceptance has been rapid. Now that most schools have computers, educators are struggling to decide how to use them to enhance learning and thinking.

An important aspect of the computer's arrival in the classroom is the interaction between student and machine. How well this interaction works is a function of the particular program that is being used.

Compared to television, computers have one major advantage for use in the classroom: They permit an ongoing interaction between student and machine. But the nature of the interaction depends on the kind of program that is being used. Reviews of available programs suggest that as few as 1 in 10 computer programs are good educational devices (Hassett, 1984). Let's look at some of the ways in which computers can be used.

First, computers have been used for *programmed learning,* or computer-assisted instruction. In this mode, the computer serves as a surrogate teacher. The computer program structures learning in sequential steps and adjusts the size of the steps to the ability of the individual child. A child who learns quickly can progress rapidly through the program, whereas one who learns more slowly can be given extra opportunities for review. The programs correct children and provide immediate feedback. If the programs are well designed, children can learn skills like addition and subtraction or typing. However, this kind of program often is not well written, and children may tire of the repetitive format (Greenfield, 1984).

A second use of computers in the classroom is to foster creativity and inventiveness. One way of doing this is to teach children how to program computers themselves, so that they are responsible for what the computer does. In a programming language called LOGO, children can make complex geometric constructions. They are no longer simply repeating programmed drills; by doing the programming themselves, children discover principles, construct new forms, and analyze structures (Papert, 1980). Programming at the elementary school level, however, is not always effective—in one study, only about 25% of the children remained interested after the initial instruction (Hawkins et al., 1982). It may be that computer programming requires too much abstract thinking from children who are still at the concrete operational level.

Another way of enhancing creativity is to let children use computers for writing stories. Children can be taught to type and to use a word-processing program. Once they gain the basic skills, they can edit their stories with relative ease. For younger children, there are programs that allow them to construct stories without writing. Even preschoolers can use computer graphics to develop sequences of action for stories and then play back their own creations (Forman, 1985).

Success in School

The schoolroom is the most important stage on which children perform during middle childhood. It is at school that children test their intellectual, physical, social, and emotional competencies to find out if they can equal the standards set for them by their parents and teachers and by society as a whole. It is also at school that children gain confidence in their ability both to master their world and to develop social relationships with their peers. The school, in other words, plays a critical role in the healthy development of the child. Unfortunately, how well the school meets the challenge placed before it—to help children maximize all of their personal resources—is open to question.

The educational literature of the late 1960s was filled with biting criticism of our school system. Such books as *How Children Fail* (Holt, 1964), *36 Children* (Kohl, 1968), and *Death at an Early Age* (Kozol, 1970) came to the dismaying conclusion that the majority of our schools are overwhelming failures. Instead of offering intellectual excitement and teaching children how to think independently, schools stifle curiosity. They breed conformity and mediocrity by emphasizing discipline and demanding the "right" answers. In short, claimed these books, school is boring, and it is no wonder that so many students are frustrated and unhappy. The situation was summarized by one 9-year-old student:

> In school we waste time until it's over. I do what I have to. I don't like the place. I feel like falling off all day, just putting my head down and saying good-bye to everyone until three. We're out then, and we sure wake up. (Coles, 1968, p. 1322)

In the 1980s, schools were still getting negative reviews. This time they were also criticized for not teaching basic skills and for being too unstructured and undisciplined (Goldberg & Harvey, 1983).

Even in mediocre school systems, some children not only succeed but also excel. According to David McClelland (1955), the reason why some children achieve more than others do may relate to the values of the culture in which they are reared. After comparing several periods of history in several different cultures, McClelland concluded that achievement motivation—the drive to attain success and excellence—is a cultural value. Within any given society at any time, some groups value achievement more highly than other groups do (deCharms & Moeller, 1962). Different cultures or subcultures may also value different *kinds* of achievement—one group may stress educational goals, whereas another may place more importance on financial or social success. Children whose parents stress values that are different from those of the school may bring less motivation to academic tasks. Such children may simply be channeling their need for achievement into other areas.

Success in school is influenced by many other factors. For example, children who are in poor health, who do not get enough to eat, or who are preoccupied with problems at home may do poorly at school tasks. Self-esteem is another important factor. Children's own judgments of their competence seriously affect their performance in school. In one study, 20% of school-age children underestimated their actual abilities. These children set lower expectations for themselves and were surprised at their intermittent high grades (Phillips, 1984).

Schools measure children's ability and achievement in order to determine their level of development and their readiness to learn new skills. This is accomplished through various forms of intelligence, diagnostic, and achievement tests.

ASSESSING INDIVIDUAL DIFFERENCES

In the 1940s and 1950s, a great effort was made in the United States to administer tests to schoolchildren—IQ tests, achievement tests, personality tests, and career aptitude tests. School files were—and in many cases still are—filled with test scores of varying degrees of accuracy and significance. In the 1960s, many parents and educators reacted against what they considered the abuse of diagnostic tests. More recently, there has again been an increase in the use of diagnostic and achievement

FOCUS ON AN ISSUE

THE MATH GAP: AN EDUCATIONAL DILEMMA

We have known for some time that college students coming from Japan and Taiwan to study in the United States outperform their American peers in math and science. Why is this so? Were these students a select group—the gifted, the elite, the highly motivated? What was the mathematics achievement of the average student in these countries in high school or in junior high school?

These general impressions of Asian superiority in mathematics and science were confirmed by studies that were conducted in the late 1960s and early 1970s (Comber & Keeves, 1973; Husen, 1976). These studies documented the average achievements of Asian junior high and high school students as being consistently higher than those of American students. Later studies showed similar accomplishments in math for children as young as kindergarteners (Stevenson et al., 1986). In these studies, the average score of American kindergarteners was below the Japanese average. In first grade, the difference increased, and by fifth grade, it was very large. It was so large that when 60 fifth-grade classes in Japan, Taiwan, and the United States were compared, the average math score of the highest-scoring American classroom was below that of all the Japanese classrooms and all but one of the Taiwanese classrooms.

Why is this so? Are the Asian students innately smarter? Are they more highly motivated? Are they better educated in math than Americans? A series of studies in 1986 and 1987 addressed these questions, and their findings seem to point the finger at differences in educational practices. Although the American and Asian school systems have certain features in common, there are also highly significant differences. Some of the similarities are that children in each country—Taiwan, Japan, and the United States—start kindergarten at the same age. Almost all school-age children in each country attend elementary school and continue at least through the junior high level. Also, the eventual success of the children in each country depends to a large extent on their educational achievement.

The differences are striking, however. Test scores on nationwide examinations determine entry into high school in Japan and Taiwan but not in the United States. Career paths, too, are more closely linked to educational achievement in these two Asian countries. As a result, enormous pressure is exerted on even very young children in Japan and Taiwan: They are told that they must study hard and succeed in school. Far less pressure is put on young children in the United States. The national exams of Japan and Taiwan influence their educational curricula and practices, which are nationally standardized from the elementary grades through high school. America's national or statewide exams (for example, the Regents exams in New York State) influence educational placement only in the last few years of high school and in college.

There are also striking differences in classroom instruction. American children spend far less time in school than their counterparts in Japan and Taiwan, and when they are in school, they spend less "time on task." For example, American fifth graders were observed as spending an average of only 19.6 hours per week in academic activities, exclusive of lunch, physical education, transitions, and the like. The Taiwanese and Japanese children spent 40.4 and 32.6 hours per week, respectively, in academic activities. What is more, the American children spent less of their academic time on mathematics. By fifth grade, the U.S. classrooms averaged 3.4 hours per week on math compared to 11.4 hours in Taiwan and 7.6 hours in Japan.

These time differences alone might be enough to explain the differences in performance, but classroom organization, teacher behavior, and child behavior differed as well. Classes in the United States were smaller, and the children tended to work alone or in small groups rather than in whole class instruction. The Asian children spent most of their math class working, watching, and listening together as a class. The U.S. approach allowed the teacher the opportunity to individualize assignments

tests. But most teachers are now more aware of the dangers of misinterpreting (or overinterpreting) test results and of pinning labels on children. Consequently, they are using the tests with greater caution.

The rationale behind testing is that schools must assess student abilities in

A classroom's organization and style of presentation may reflect the goals and values of the educational system. For example, these children in mainland China (left) are expected to pay close attention to their teacher and to learn the same lessons in a carefully sequenced order. The children in the United States (right) are expected to think critically and to express an independent point of view.

and to tutor individuals and small groups. It also encouraged individual problem solving. But there were inefficiencies. Much of the time, the children's work was not closely supervised. Correction and guidance were delayed or absent. The researchers found American children to be out of their seats 21% of the time and to be engaged in inappropriate (off-task) activities 17% of the time. Compare this to the Taiwanese and the Japanese, who were out of their seats only 4% and 2% of the time, respectively. Teachers in the Taiwanese and Japanese classes appeared better prepared, more intensely involved in their subject matter, and more lively in their presentation. Student attention and involvement were higher (Stigler, Lee, & Stevenson, 1987).

Is it any wonder that Japanese and Taiwanese children do better than American youngsters on mathe-

matics tests? Certainly, different educational practices can account for much of the difference in performance on math tests.

Should U.S. schools change their educational philosophy, which emphasizes individualized instruction and small, cooperative learning groups? The researchers suggest simple changes like increasing the percentage of elementary school time spent on mathematics and decreasing transitional and irrelevant activities. Further, they recommend more direct teacher–student communication and better math preparation for teachers.

(The material in this box has been adapted from James W. Stigler, Shin-ying Lee, and Harold W. Stevenson, "Mathematics Classrooms in Japan, Taiwan, and the United States." *Child Development,* Vol. 58, 1987, 1272–1285.)

order to plan efficient educational programs. But all too often, the scores have been misused. Teachers and administrators have used test results to pigeonhole children or to deny some of them access to certain educational opportunities. Almost as frequently, the test results have not been used at all. More than one child has

diagnostic–prescriptive teaching A system of teaching in which tests and informal assessments inform educators as to a child's abilities so that they may prescribe appropriate instruction.

criterion-referenced test A test that evaluates an individual's performance in relation to mastery of specified skills or objectives.

norm-referenced test A test that compares an individual's performance with the performances of others in the same age group.

experienced the frustration of entering first grade with reading test scores at the third-grade level, only to be assigned to a class in beginning reading because he or she "has not had that subject yet."

In an approach known as **diagnostic–prescriptive teaching,** however, tests and informal assessments can be a vital aid to education. The idea behind this kind of teaching is that if educators know precisely what an individual child can do, they will be better able to prescribe the next step. The diagnosis does not apply a generalized label but measures a specific, observable behavior or skill. The child is assessed for what he or she can do. The testers do not call the student "superior" or "mildly retarded" or "a slow learner"—they simply identify the child's particular knowledge, skills, and abilities at that point in time. Sometimes, the diagnosis is based on classroom observation or a diagnostic lesson; other times, it is based on formal tests called **criterion-referenced tests** (Glaser, 1963).

Because criterion-referenced tests focus on the achievements of an individual, they differ radically from the more familiar **norm-referenced tests,** which are concerned with how one child's score compares with that of another child. Most standard IQ tests, achievement tests, and scholastic aptitude tests are norm referenced. They compare one child's score with the scores of a large number of other children. In other words, a criterion-referenced math test describes a child's accuracy and speed in several specific math skills, whereas a norm-referenced test shows that a child is performing at a level higher or lower than the average for his or her grade or age. Thus, a norm-referenced test might identify a child as being in the bottom 10% of her class in arithmetic skills, but it will say little or nothing about what she does know, why she fails specific items, or what specific skills she needs to acquire so that she may progress. Also, the test reveals nothing about the child's pattern of attention, her level of anxiety when she faces a math question, or any of a number of things that the teacher may need to know in order to help her. The test may merely label the child, in a general way, as a good student or a poor one.

Intelligence Testing

In the field of developmental psychology, perhaps no issue has been more controversial than that of intelligence and intelligence testing. The academic debate has become a public one largely because of the broad impact that intelligence test scores have on educational and social opportunities. When young children are labeled on the basis of IQ scores, the results can be far reaching. IQ scores may affect the extent and quality of children's education, determine the jobs they may have as adults, and put a lasting imprint on their self-image. IQ tests are administered more widely and taken more seriously in the United States than anywhere else. The emphasis on testing, particularly at the elementary and secondary school levels, has resulted in the grouping and rating of students based solely on their test performances. Children, too, are taught to take these tests seriously.

Why do we hold intelligence in such high regard? What are we actually trying to measure? In this section, we will explore the concept of intelligence, beginning with some early attempts to measure and thus to define it.

Diagnostic and achievement tests are important because the school must assess student abilities in order to plan efficient educational programs.

ALFRED BINET   The first comprehensive intelligence test was designed in the late 19th century by Alfred Binet, a French psychologist. He was commissioned by the

French government to devise a method of identifying those children who would not profit from a public education. Binet needed a scale that would yield an index of the educability of children. His concept of intelligence focused on such complex intellectual processes as judgment, reasoning, memory, and comprehension. To measure these capabilities, he used test items involving problem solving, word definitions, and general knowledge. Binet believed that intelligence does not remain static but grows and changes throughout life. Test questions, therefore, had to be carefully arranged to reflect this growth. A good test item differentiated between older and younger children. If more than half of the 5-year-olds were able to define the word "ball," and fewer than half of the 4-year-olds were able to do so, then the definition of ball was included on the test for 5-year-olds (Binet & Simon, 1905, 1916). This empirical basis for selecting and ordering items was a landmark in the testing movement. The resulting test score was called a **mental age.**

According to the concept of mental age, a 4-year-old who could answer most of the questions on the test for 5-year-olds would have a mental age of 5. Later psychologists found a way of conveniently expressing the relationship between mental age and chronological (or "real") age: the **intelligence quotient,** or IQ. Intelligence quotient is calculated by dividing mental age by chronological age and multiplying the result by 100. Thus, our bright 4-year-old with a mental age of 5 would have an intelligence quotient of 5/4 times 100, or 125. Any child whose mental age and chronological age are equal—in other words, a child whose intellectual development is progressing at an average rate—will have an IQ of 100.

In 1916, an English version of Binet's test, revised by Lewis Terman at Stanford University, was introduced in the United States. The concept of IQ testing won wide acceptance in the United States and was much used during the 1940s and 1950s. In contrast to Binet, who believed that intelligence was modifiable, many American psychologists believed that as mental and chronological ages increased during development, the ratio between them remained fixed—it was innate.

Today, with a few exceptions, the ratio IQ that was described earlier has fallen into disuse in favor of a norm-referenced **deviation-IQ test,** which assigns an IQ score by comparing a child's performance on the test with performances of other children of the same age. This measure carries no automatic assumption about whether intelligence is fixed or modifiable. The current Stanford-Binet test, which is widely used, is the direct descendant of Binet's 1905 test.

The Nature of Intelligence

The development of sophisticated models for testing and measuring intelligence has stimulated inquiry, both popular and scientific, into the nature of intelligence itself. We shall briefly consider some of the highlights of this continuing debate. Notice that some of the following arguments might be applied equally well to other human characteristics, such as aggressiveness, self-confidence, and even physical beauty.

INNATE AND LEARNED INTELLECTUAL ABILITIES   The nature-versus-nurture controversy still sparks fireworks in academic journals and in the popular press. Arthur Jensen (1969) generated a great deal of controversy when he stated his belief that 80% of what is measured on IQ tests is inherited, and only 20% is determined by a child's environment. Criticism of Jensen's paper (and the data

mental age An intelligence test score showing the age group with which a child's performance most closely compares.

intelligence quotient An individual's mental age divided by chronological age, multiplied by 100 to eliminate the decimal point.

deviation IQ An IQ score derived from a statistical table comparing an individual's raw score on an IQ test with the scores of other subjects of the same age.

upon which it was based) was widespread; some psychologists even took the view that there was no good evidence for *any* genetic effect on IQ (Kamin, 1974). The current view is a more balanced one: The consensus seems to be that genetic and environmental factors are about equally potent in determining how well a child will do on an IQ test (Weinberg, 1989). However, the pendulum may once again be tipping toward the side of those who think that intelligence is largely innate: A recent paper on identical twins who were reared apart claims that the *heritability* of IQ (how much is inherited) is 70% (Bouchard et al., 1990).

GENERAL AND SPECIFIC ABILITIES   Several early theorists, most notably Spearman (1904), believed that intelligence was a single central attribute, reflected in the ability to learn. He drew this conclusion from the fact that children who did well on one kind of test item usually did well on other kinds of test items, too. For example, a child who has a high score on the vocabulary test is also likely to be above average in solving puzzles or doing math problems (Hunt, 1961). Other theorists (Guilford, 1959; Thurstone, 1938) have contended that intelligence is a composite of many different abilities, such as perceptual speed, word fluency, memory, and others. An individual may be good at remembering facts or perceiving similarities, but this does not necessarily mean that he or she will also do well on tasks involving spatial relationships.

Intelligence tests differ on whether they define intelligence as a unitary attribute or as a composite of several abilities. The Wechsler Intelligence Scale for Children has separate subtests for information, comprehension, mathematics, vocabulary, digit span, picture arrangement, and others. This test yields a verbal IQ score, a performance (nonverbal) IQ score, and a full-scale score that represents a combination of the two. The current version of the Stanford-Binet test, on the other hand, yields a single score that indicates an overall intelligence level, although individual test items measure a variety of abilities and skills.

One proponent of the view that intelligence is made up of several independent abilities is Howard Gardner (1983). Gardner reviews the literature of neurology, psychology, and even that of human evolutionary history and comes up with seven "frames of mind"—seven different kinds of intelligence. These are divided into two groups. In the first group are *linguistic intelligence, musical intelligence, logical-mathematical intelligence,* and *spatial intelligence.* The second group includes *kinesthetic intelligence, interpersonal intelligence,* and *intrapersonal intelligence.* Each of these forms of intelligence works with different information and processes the information in different ways. Although a child may be below average in the kinds of intelligence measured by IQ tests (mainly linguistic and logical-mathematical), he or she may be high in other kinds of intelligence—for example, interpersonal intelligence (the ability to understand the feelings and motivations of others).

Another current view is that of Robert Sternberg (1985). Sternberg has a "triarchic" (three-part) concept of intelligence. The first kind is *contextual intelligence,* which involves adaptation to the environment. If the environment is poor, a person who is high in this type of intelligence may modify the environment or find a better one. The second type is *experiential intelligence,* which involves the capacity to cope with new tasks or situations as well as with old ones. Coping with new tasks involves the capacity to learn quickly, and coping with old ones involves the capacity to automatize performance so that a minimum of thought and energy is spent on these tasks. Finally, the third type is *componential intelligence,* which corresponds roughly to the abilities measured by IQ tests.

Diagnostic and Achievement Tests

As mentioned earlier, the purpose of tests is to help schools assess the capabilities of students so that educators can design programs to fit individual needs. Because many capabilities cannot be measured by an IQ test, educators must find other ways to assess the diverse skills and strengths of each individual.

BEYOND ACQUISITION OF KNOWLEDGE   What kind of test to give and how the results should be used depend on educational priorities and how the learning process is viewed. Some theorists believe that the American educational system has focused too much on "intelligence" and "achievement" and has ignored a number of equally important abilities. For example, of the six different cognitive abilities defined by Bloom and Krathwohl (1956), only the first two are regularly measured in school. Beginning with the simplest, the six categories are as follows:

1. *Knowledge of facts and principles* refers to the direct recall of information. Such knowledge often involves the rote memorization of dates, names, vocabulary words, and definitions—items that are easy to identify and test. Perhaps because of its convenience, this cognitive ability has long been the focus of education.

2. *Comprehension* entails the understanding of facts and ideas. Unfortunately, tests that are successful in measuring recall of facts or principles are often unsuccessful in assessing how well the student actually understands the material.

3. *Application* refers to the need to know not only rules, principles, or basic procedures but also how and when to use them in new situations. This ability is less frequently taught and measured than the previous two.

4. *Analysis* involves the breaking down of a concept, idea, system, or message into its parts, then seeing the relationship between these parts. This ability may be taught in reading comprehension, math, or science classes. Often, however, the end product of the analysis is taught, but the analytical process itself is not.

5. *Synthesis* refers to the putting together of information or ideas: integrating or relating the parts of a whole.

6. *Evaluation* entails judging the value of a piece of information, a theory, or a plan in terms of some criterion, or standard. Evaluation is viewed as somewhat controversial in education.

Most testing—and most teaching—focuses on ability 1, with occasional attention given to ability 2. Very rarely do teachers give tests that require a student to use the thinking abilities listed in categories 3 through 6. Indeed, many teachers avoid category 6, although, without evaluation, much information may be hollow and superficial.

In a world where new problems arise and "facts" change every day, it is increasingly important for children to be taught the skills needed to deal with the unknown as well as the known. Thus, some researchers feel that schools should teach children not *what* to think but *how* to think. Children can be taught how to generate new ideas, how to look at an issue in a new way, and how to identify the important aspects of a problem. These skills, it is claimed, are more important than

behavioral objectives The kinds of knowledge and skills expected of a student after a specified amount of instruction; they provide a demonstration of the school's adequacy as well as the student's.

self-fulfilling prophecy An expectation that helps to bring about the predicted event, which consequently strengthens the expectation.

the facts and principles that are generally taught and measured (Olton & Crutchfield, 1969).

Some skills or abilities—such as a sense of humor—may be ignored because they are not particularly valued in the elementary school. Other skills are ignored because the behavior involved is too difficult to define. Teachers may feel, for example, that they cannot measure a student's ability to enjoy classical music or to appreciate art.

The tendency of schools to concentrate on measurable abilities reflects the popularity of **behavioral objectives.** These objectives describe the kinds of knowledge and skills expected of a student after a specified amount of instruction. In a sense, they provide a way of testing *schools,* not students. Each June, schools are expected to demonstrate in a tangible way what their students have learned. As valuable as this approach is, great concern with a school's success often means that children spend most of the school day acquiring competencies that can be easily measured. As a result, less tangible competencies, ways of thinking, and personality traits are often overlooked. How does one objectively measure kindness, courage, curiosity, sensitivity, or openness to new experiences?

Cultural Biases and Test Abuses

Psychologists, educators, and parents have criticized diagnostic and achievement tests for various reasons. We have shown that tests do not provide the whole story and that some personal qualities and skills are difficult or impossible to measure using conventional testing methods. In addition, there is the question of the cultural bias of the tests themselves. To show the absurdity of culturally linked intelligence tests, Stephen Jay Gould (1981) gave a class of Harvard students a nonverbal test of innate intelligence designed for World War I army recruits. (A sample of the test is provided in Figure 11–4.) He found that many of his students could not identify a horn as the missing part of a Victrola despite the test-makers' claim that the subjects' "innate" intelligence would guide them to the correct answer.

Some minority groups resent being measured by tests that assume wide exposure to the dominant white culture; they feel that the tests are unfair to those who have different cultural experiences. Support for this view is provided by a study of black and interracial children who were reared by white middle-class adoptive parents. The IQ scores and school achievements of these adopted children were well above average—and well above those of children with similar genetic backgrounds but with different cultural experiences (Weinberg, 1989).

Research also suggests that minority groups may be victims of a **self-fulfilling prophecy:** They have acquired low expectations about their academic performances on tests designed by the white community, and these low expectations further lower their self-confidence and thus their test scores.

Not only minority children fall victim to the self-fulfilling prophecy, however. Imagine the effect that being labeled "below average" or "a slow learner" has on a child's self-image. Such labeling of students may also affect the administrators of the tests—the teachers. In a famous study, teachers were told that a few children, actually selected at random, possessed previously undetected high abilities and potential. At the end of the school year, it was found that these children showed significantly better achievement than their classmates. Presum-

FIGURE 11-4

This is part 6 of the Army Beta mental test given to recruits during World War I. (Answers: 1. mouth; 2. eye; 3. nose; 4. spoon in right hand; 5. chimney; 6. left ear; 7. filament; 8. stamp; 9. strings; 10. rivet; 11. trigger; 12. tail; 13. leg; 14. shadow; 15. bowling ball in man's right hand; 16. net; 17. left hand; 18. horn of victrola; 19. arm and powder puff in mirror image; 20. diamond.)

ably, the teachers had in some way conveyed their expectations to these students that they were especially bright and would do well in school (Rosenthal & Jacobson, 1968). Although this particular study has been criticized for its methodological faults, the basic finding has been supported by many later studies. People will respond according to the expectations of others, and this is true throughout the life span. A recent study involved elderly nursing home patients. Nurses and aides were told that certain patients (randomly selected) were likely to do better than average, and these patients did do better—they showed more

learning disability Extreme difficulty in learning school subjects such as reading, writing, or math, despite normal intelligence and absence of sensory or motor defects.

improvement on tests of mental functioning and had fewer serious illnesses than the other patients (Learman et al., 1991).

It is dangerous to underestimate the complexity of the student–teacher relationship and the effect of labeling on children's performances. Labels do persist, and children do tend to live up to them, whether they be "class clown," "good child," "underachiever," or "bright." Insofar as teachers' expectations affect their own behavior toward children, these expectations apparently do affect children's learning.

It is not always necessary to use tests to assess children's progress. Teachers, parents, and care-givers can learn a good deal about how to proceed by informally observing what children do and say. By merely giving the child a book and listening to the reading, a skilled teacher can determine many of the skills that the child still needs to learn. Perhaps the most dramatic example of the need for caution in the use and interpretation of tests is in the area of learning disabilities.

LEARNING DISABILITIES

The term **learning disability** is used to identify the difficulties of a broad category of children who often have no more in common than the label itself. In school systems today, children are described as "learning disabled" when they require special attention in the classroom—that is, when they have trouble learning to read, write, spell, or do arithmetic, despite having normal intelligence. In the absence of any obvious sensory or motor defect (such as poor vision, deafness, or cerebral palsy), these children are described as having learning disabilities. Of learning-disabled children, 80% are boys.

Day after day, learning-disabled children face their own inability to do things that their classmates seem to accomplish effortlessly. With each failure, these children become increasingly insecure about their ability to perform. Sometimes, this insecurity leads to a growing sense of hopelessness or helplessness. Classmates tend not to choose the child who does not succeed. Children with learning disabilities have difficulty with social skills as well as with academic skills. They may become increasingly isolated from peers or even from family members. Some become shy and withdrawn, some boastful, whereas others strike out with impulsive or angry outbursts. Academic confidence is central to the school-age child's self-esteem. It is difficult to find ways in which the learning-disabled child can develop feelings of confidence and, as a result, experience success in other areas.

The study of learning disabilities has been a challenging puzzle with a confusing array of expert opinions on symptoms, causes, and treatments. Many of the classic controversies of child development are evident in the questions raised. Is this child abnormal, deficient, or disabled, or is he just different in temperament and style? Is his problem due to organic dysfunction or due to his environment at home or at school? Should he be "treated" medically, "managed" with behavioral management programs, or "educated" creatively?

Before the 1950s, there were "slow readers" and children who did poorly on school tasks, but they were not labeled as learning disabled—if they had no obvious emotional or physical problems, it was assumed that they were simply "dumb." Teachers then began to notice that some children who appeared to be quite bright in other respects nonetheless had trouble with school tasks, especially reading. To explain this, the concept of "minimal brain dysfunction" was introduced. It was assumed that there was something wrong with the child's brain, but that the abnormality was too subtle (or "minimal") to show up in other ways. Although many authorities still believe that learning disabilities are caused by some kind of subtle brain abnormality, the term "minimal brain dysfunction" is now seldom used (Silver, 1990).

There are two main groups of learning-disabled children. The first group includes children with **dyslexia** (difficulty in learning how to read); many of these children also have **dysgraphia** (difficulty with writing). Others may have **dyscalculia,** difficulty with math.

The second main group of learning-disabled children has **attention-deficit disorder (ADD),** the inability to focus attention on anything long enough to learn it. Many of these children are also **hyperactive**—they can't sit still, and they are constantly getting into trouble. This combination is called ADD-H (attention-deficit disorder with hyperactivity). Children with attention-deficit disorder, with or without hyperactivity, are likely to do poorly in a variety of school subjects, for the simple reason that they are not spending enough "time on task."

dyslexia A learning disability involving reading; unusual difficulty in learning how to read.

dysgraphia A learning disability involving writing.

dyscalculia A learning disability involving mathematics.

attention-deficit disorder (ADD) An inability to keep one's attention focused on something long enough to learn it.

hyperactive Overly active; exhibiting poor impulse control.

Dyslexia

Because dyslexic children often confuse letters such as *b* and *d*, or read *star* as *rats,* it was believed for a long time that these children simply "see things backward." But very few of them have anything wrong with their eyes. In other contexts, dyslexic children have no perceptual problems—for example, they have no trouble finding their way around (so they are not deficient in spatial relationships), and they may be exceptionally good at putting together puzzles. Why, then, do they make errors like confusing *b* and *d*? The answer is that this is a very common kind of error for beginning readers. Most children make reversal errors when they are first learning how to read, but most get through this stage quickly. Dyslexic children remain stuck in the early stages of reading (Vogel, 1989).

Dyslexic children also have problems outside of the school context. In fact, they have a pervasive problem involving the use of language. Many of these children were delayed in learning how to speak, or their speech is at a lower developmental level than that of their age-mates. Their difficulty in naming letters and written words is matched by a similar difficulty in naming objects or colors—it takes them longer than usual to pull an ordinary word like "key" or "blue" out of their memory. They also have difficulty in "hearing" the two separate syllables in a two-syllable word, or in recognizing that the spoken word "sat" starts with an *s* sound and ends with a *t* sound (Shaywitz et al., 1991; Wagner & Torgerson, 1987).

Although the hypothesized "brain dysfunction" that underlies dyslexia has still not been identified, it is clear that heredity plays a role in the disorder. Many dyslexic children have a parent who had trouble learning how to read as a child or a sibling with the same problem (Scarborough, 1989). It is also interesting to note that dyslexia tends to run in the same families that exhibit left-handedness. However, left-handedness itself is only weakly associated with dyslexia—most dyslexics are right-handed (Hiscock & Kinsbourne, 1987).

The treatment of dyslexia generally involves intensive remedial work in

Some learning disabilities may be helped by educational management that works on improving specific skills.

reading and language. Many educational programs for learning-disabled children provide carefully sequenced tutorial instruction in reading. Some programs emphasize high-interest materials; others emphasize early success. Stanton (1981) emphasizes the need to build the child's confidence in any approach. The teacher must first simplify the problem for the child in order to reduce anxiety about the unknown. He or she must then respond to the child with an attitude of genuineness, unconditional acceptance, and empathy, all of which make the child believe in and expect success. Although no single educational plan seems to work with all children, most programs have some record of success. The graduates of one especially successful program—a British residential school for dyslexic children—are generally able to go on to college. In contrast, the children who attend the least successful programs generally become high school dropouts (Bruck, 1987).

People who were dyslexic as children but who manage to overcome this handicap may emerge with renewed self-confidence and may go on to be notably successful in adult life. Thomas Edison, Nelson Rockefeller, and Hans Christian Andersen were all dyslexic as children.

Attention-Deficit Disorder

For every symptom in the broad category of learning disabilities, there is a variety of possible causes. Just as people experience headaches for a number of reasons, an inability to focus attention may arise from any one of several conditions. Some of the suggested causes of ADD include malnutrition, lead poisoning, organic brain damage, heredity, intrauterine abnormalities, prenatal exposure to drugs like "crack," and lack of oxygen during fetal development or childbirth. Many children with symptoms of learning disabilities are known to have had some irregularity at birth; premature births are common among these children.

Just as there are differences of opinion on the causes of attention-deficit disorder and hyperactivity, there are also differences in the treatments that have been recommended. There is no one correct answer to the problems of a learning-disabled child. Some of the "answers" have been learned quite by accident, as illustrated by the history of one type of drug treatment.

Several years ago, it was discovered that some children who displayed symptoms of hyperactivity responded to the drug *Ritalin,* a stimulant in the amphetamine family. These hyperactive children, whose symptoms had not improved with tranquilizers or depressants, actually calmed down in response to this drug, which ordinarily speeds up behavior. This unusual response gave rise to the hypothesis that these children were either understimulated or were unable to focus on any single task because all stimulation came in at equal levels. Perhaps their high activity levels were attempts to seek more stimulation from the environment. Ritalin lowered their threshold of sensitivity to events around them and allowed them to focus consistently on one task. Although not all ADD and ADD-H children improve by taking Ritalin, for those who do improve, the benefits can outweigh the risk of possible side effects when the treatment program is monitored carefully. Not only does their school work get better but also their relationships with family members and peers improve (Campbell & Spencer, 1988).

An alternate form of treatment for children with ADD is educational management, which takes place both at home and at school. In most cases, this method makes an attempt to restructure a child's environment by simplifying it, reducing distractions, making expectations more explicit, and, in general, reducing confusion. The specific educational plan depends on the theoretical position of the therapist or educator. Cruickshank (1977) advocates an instructional program involving various training tasks that require specific skills. Diagnostic tests are used to identify any deficits that the child demonstrates. The program consists of careful, systematic, and progressively more difficult exercises to correct the problems. A program by Ross (1977) focuses more on the development of selective attention. The particular task does not really matter. Instead, by careful management of the instruction and the rewards, the teacher helps the child to listen and to observe more precisely. The child might work on perceptual exercises or on other general skills.

A part of any treatment program is concern for the child's emotional well-being. Learning-disabled children rarely experience success in school, nor do they develop the feelings of competence and self-worth that go along with it. They may become shy and withdrawn, or they may strike back at society by engaging in delinquent behavior. Early diagnosis of the condition is important, as are patience and understanding.

Because so many questions about learning disabilities remain unanswered, students studying these disorders should approach them with a healthy amount of skepticism. They should carefully evaluate each diagnosis, each proposed program, and each suggested theory. It requires skillful interpretation to ensure that social and emotional difficulties are not mistaken for neurological problems.

STUDY OUTLINE

Coping with Physical Challenges

Motor Skill Development. Middle childhood is marked by a high activity level and gradual physiological developments that help school-age children to refine motor skills and coordination. These developments are evident not only in children's games but also in their mastery of skills like writing. To support energy levels and proper growth, children need balanced, nutritious diets and learning environments that are sensitive to their physical, as well as intellectual, needs.

Concrete Operational Thought

Cognitive Abilities of the School Beginner. In middle childhood, children enter the concrete operational stage, during which they learn to make **logical inferences,** to think about physical transformations, to perform reversible mental operations, and to theorize about the concrete world. The transition out of the preoperational stage may occur earlier or faster if children receive specific instruction in concrete operational tasks when they reach a state of readiness.

Piaget and Education. As applied to education, Piagetian theory suggests that children should be given concrete objects to manipulate. This theory also suggests that children should be encouraged to discover relationships and to make inferences for themselves.

Information Processing

Information-processing theorists offer important insights into cognitive development. By comparing the human mind to the information-processing components of a computer, information-processing theorists can tell us about the development of children's control processes (such as memory strategies) and about higher-order control processes (metacognition).

Memory. During middle childhood, children consciously start on the task of memorizing. They develop memory strategies such as rehearsal, organization, semantic elaboration, mental imagery, retrieval, and scripts.

Metacognition. The process of **metacognition**—the monitoring of one's own thinking, memory, knowledge, goals, and actions—becomes more sophisticated during middle childhood. This leads to advances in the ability to think, learn, and understand.

Learning and Thinking in School

New Demands and Expectations. Entrance into the school environment requires that children's behavior conform to a new set of cultural demands and expectations that vary widely from culture to culture.

Developing Competent Learners and Critical Thinkers. Educators are urging teachers to focus on instructing children how to become competent learners and critical thinkers. This requires that teachers help students develop thinking skills and control processes rather than learning disconnected facts, principles, and rules.

Computers, Learning, and Thinking. Computers are becoming more popular in the classroom. Computer-assisted instruction is common, and in some schools, children are learning how to program computers or are using them to write stories.

Success in School. School success depends in part on the child's achievement motivation, which in turn depends on the values of the culture in which the child is reared. Some cultures or subcultures emphasize achievement in areas other than academics.

Assessing Individual Differences

Intelligence Testing. The French psychologist Alfred Binet developed the first intelligence test in the 19th century. He believed that intelligence is modifiable. American psychologists who adapted his test for use in the United States believed that intelligence is a fixed, inherited characteristic. Today's **IQ** tests make no assumptions about whether intelligence is fixed or modifiable. Most theorists now agree that a child's intelligence is influenced both by heredity and environment.

The Nature of Intelligence. The Stanford-Binet test represents IQ as a single attribute, whereas scores on the Wechsler IQ test reflect abilities in several different areas of cognition. Modern theorists seem to lean toward the view that intelligence is not unitary and that it may consist of as many as seven separate abilities.

Cultural Biases and Test Abuses. Many people object to the use of intelligence tests on the grounds that they are culturally biased. Scores tend to be higher for members of the same culture as those who wrote the tests—in other words, the white, middle-class culture. Placing children in labeled categories of ability may influence their teacher's expectations for them, leading to a **self-fulfilling prophecy.**

Learning Disabilities

Dyslexia and Attention-Deficit Disorder. Two kinds of learning disabilities are **dyslexia** and **attention-deficit disorder** (with or without **hyperactivity**). Dyslexic children have great difficulty in learning how to read, despite having normal intelligence and no sensory or motor defects. Their problem is believed to result from a subtle type of brain abnormality, which may be inherited. Children with attention-deficit disorder cannot keep their attention focused on anything long enough to learn it. Drug therapy has been helpful for many of these children.

KEY TERMS AND CONCEPTS

attention-deficit disorder
behavioral objectives
concrete operational thought
criterion-referenced test
deviation IQ
diagnostic–prescriptive teaching

dyscalculia
dysgraphia
dyslexia
hyperactive
intelligence quotient
learning disability

logical inference
mental age
metacognition
norm-referenced test
self-fulfilling prophecy

SELF-TEST QUESTIONS

1. Discuss the development of gross and fine motor skills in middle childhood.

2. How are children's illnesses a part of normal behavioral development?

3. What is the primary cause of childhood obesity? What is the most advisable treatment for this condition?

4. How would you best describe a good environment for learning?

5. How does Piaget's preoperational stage differ from the concrete operational stage characteristic of middle childhood?

6. Explain how Piagetian concepts of learning and cognitive development would be applied to educational practices.

7. How do information-processing theorists view the human mind? Explain some control processes and higher-order control processes that are important in middle childhood as they are defined by information-processing theorists.

8. Describe the new demands and expectations that children face when they enter school, and discuss some of the factors that determine how well they adjust to this transition.

9. What are some strategies that teachers can use to help students become competent learners and critical thinkers?

10. Describe different ways in which computers can be used as educational devices in the classroom.

11. Name several factors that determine a child's success in school.

12. What are some of the uses and abuses of intelligence testing?

13. Compare and contrast a criterion-referenced test and a norm-referenced test.

14. Compare and contrast the varying definitions of intelligence.

15. What types of competencies are not usually measured by diagnostic and achievement tests?

16. What are behavioral objectives, and in what sense do they test schools rather than students?

17. Discuss different types of learning disabilities, including their symptoms, causes, and treatments.

SUGGESTED READINGS

Cahill-Fowler, M. *Maybe you know my kids*. New York: Carroll Publishing Group, 1990. A personal account of the disruptive impact that a child's attention-deficit disorder has on his family, his classmates, and his own learning activities. Offers helpful suggestions and resources to parents and teachers.

Farnham-Diggory, S. *Schooling*. Cambridge, MA: Harvard University Press, 1990. An excellent review and discussion of several key aspects of schooling today's children. Another selection in the popular Developing Child series.

Gardner, H. *Frames of mind*. New York: Basic Books, Inc., 1983. A challenging, readable, well-developed presentation of a new way of thinking about intelligence.

Gardner, H. *To open minds: Chinese clues to the dilemma of contemporary education*. New York: Basic Books, Inc., 1989. A thoughtful discussion of two radically different approaches to education that is done in their respective social contexts.

Kidder, T. *Among schoolchildren*. Boston: Houghton Mifflin Company, 1989. Chronicles one courageous and determined teacher and one urban fifth-grade classroom. The book also deals with the social and emotional problems that are part of these children's lives.

Papert, S. *Mindstorms: Children, computers, and powerful thinking*. New York: Basic Books, Inc., 1980. In this influential book, Papert presents ways of using computers to develop thinking rather than to develop traditional, programmed learning styles.

Chapter 12

All of childhood's unanswered questions must finally be passed back to (one's hometown) and answered there. Heroes and bogeymen, values and dislikes, are first encountered and labeled in that early environment. In later years they change faces, places and maybe races, tactics, intensities and goals, but beneath those penetrable masks they wear forever the stocking-capped faces of childhood.

MAYA ANGELOU
I KNOW WHY THE CAGED BIRD SINGS

CHAPTER OUTLINE

Personality Development: Family and Peers

*I*t may seem a bit dramatic to say that children have their own culture, but in many ways it is true. The world of the preadolescent child at play is not the world in which adults live. The child's world has its own customs, language, rules, games—even its own distinctive beliefs and values. What is this "culture of childhood," and what role does it play in a child's development?

Many times, children seem to caricature adults. We have seen how a 2-year-old's fierce demands for autonomy resemble those of a tyrannical adult. A 4-year-old's jealousy and rage may strike an all-too-familiar chord. The customs and rituals of middle childhood sometimes mirror elaborate adult social conventions; in some ways, childhood rituals are even more strict and demanding. A child may pay almost superstitious attention to rituals, such as not stepping on sidewalk cracks for fear of breaking someone's back. Rhymes must be said just so, and rigid rules dictate the one right way to play each game. Peer relationships may also be ritualized. Children may make lifelong pledges in private clubs and in "blood brother" fraternities.

Children adopt the rhymes, rituals, stunts, and customs of childhood without help from adults. Some of their games and rituals have been transmitted from older to younger children for countless generations; this occurs in almost every culture. Many childish chants can be traced to medieval times, and some games, such as jacks, go back to the Roman era (Opie & Opie, 1959).

Children seem to derive potency from mastering the bits and pieces of a culture, from learning how to do things correctly. Perhaps the rituals and rules of middle childhood are practice for adulthood, exercises in learning the detailed behavior that is expected of adults. Perhaps they are a form of security, a familiar framework of rules that allows the child to feel both at home and competent in an otherwise bewildering world. These rules may help children to master intense emotions or to defuse intense peer relationships, such as victim and conqueror. Perhaps they also teach complex social concepts like justice, power, or loyalty. Although we are not certain of the precise purpose of middle childhood's traditions, the phenomenon of a special culture of childhood exists in almost every society.

In this chapter, we shall look at how a child's personality continues to develop during the school years. In Chapter 10, we examined some of the ways in which the younger child develops a personality—that is, a consistent pattern of social and emotional behavior. Here, we shall look at the influence of parenting styles and peer group relationships, as they affect the child and as the child affects them.

CHAPTER OBJECTIVES

By the time you have finished this chapter, you should be able to do the following:

■ Describe different styles of parenting and their effects on children's personality and behavior.

■ List several factors that affect a child's ability to cope with stressful events.

■ Discuss the effects of divorce on children.

■ Describe the factors that can lead to child abuse and list the various types of psychological abuse.

■ Discuss the development of social cognition and moral reasoning during middle childhood.

■ Summarize the characteristic features of childhood friendships and peer groups.

■ Explain how children develop racial awareness and how their attitudes toward members of other groups change as they grow older.

■ Describe the relationship between a child's academic ability, popularity in the peer group, and self-esteem.

"Son, I've given this a lot of thought. These are your formative years, so stay away from me as much as possible."

CONTINUING FAMILY INFLUENCES

Families continue to be one of the most important socializing influences for school-age children. Children acquire values, expectations, and patterns of behavior from their families, and they do so in a number of ways (see also Chapters 3 and 10). Parents and siblings serve as models for appropriate and inappropriate behavior, and they reward and punish children's behavior. Expanding cognitive abilities allow children to learn a wide range of social concepts and rules, both those that are explicitly taught and those that are only implied. Finally, social learning takes place in the context of relationships. Relationships are sometimes close and secure, sometimes anxiety provoking, and sometimes full of conflict.

In this section, we will examine the family as a context for development. We will first look at broad patterns or different "styles" of parenting. We will also examine how families are changing and how stress in the family influences personality development in children.

Styles of Parenting

Parents use a variety of child-rearing techniques, depending on the situation, the child, and the child's behavior at the moment. Ideally, parents limit the child's autonomy and instill values and self-control, while taking care not to undermine the child's curiosity, initiative, or competence. To do this, they must balance the parenting dimensions of control and warmth.

Parental control refers to how restrictive the parents are. Restrictive parents limit their children's freedom to follow their own impulses; they actively enforce compliance with rules and see that children fulfill their responsibilities. In contrast, nonrestrictive parents are less controlling, make fewer demands, and place fewer restraints on their children's behavior and expression of emotions.

Parental warmth is the amount of affection and approval displayed. Warm, nurturing parents smile often and give praise and encouragement. They try to restrict their criticisms, punishments, and signs of disapproval. In contrast, hostile parents criticize, belittle, punish, and ignore. They only rarely express affection or approval.

These general styles of parenting affect children's aggression and prosocial behavior, their self-concepts, their internalization of moral values, and their development of social competence (Becker, 1964; Maccoby, 1984).

authoritative parents   Parents who combine high control with warmth, acceptance, and encouragement. Baumrind has found that these parents usually have the most well-adjusted and self-reliant children.

AUTHORITATIVE, AUTHORITARIAN, AND PERMISSIVE PARENTS   Many researchers in child development have found Diana Baumrind's (1975, 1980) description of parenting styles to be helpful. Baumrind has identified three distinct patterns of parental control: authoritative, authoritarian, and permissive. Although the names "authoritative" and "authoritarian" sound very similar, and despite the fact that both of these types of parents exert firm control over their children's behavior, these styles are markedly different from each other. Both are also radically different from permissive parenting.

Authoritative parents combine a high degree of control with warmth, acceptance, and encouragement of the growing autonomy of their children. Although these parents set limits on behavior, they also explain the reasoning behind these limits. Their actions do not seem arbitrary or unfair, and as a result, their children are willing to accept these actions. Authoritative parents are willing to listen to their children's objections and to be flexible when it is appropriate. For

Style of parenting is important because children acquire values, expectations, and patterns of behavior from their parents.

authoritarian parents Parents who control their children firmly but tend to be emotionally distant and cold.

permissive parents Parents who place few or no restraints on their children. They tend to be high on warmth.

indifferent parents Parents who are low in restrictiveness and also low in warmth.

example, if a young girl wants to stay out beyond the customary hour, authoritative parents would probably ask her about her reasons for wanting to stay out late, what the circumstances will be (such as, will she be at a friend's house, and will the friend's parents be there?), and whether it will prevent her from carrying out her responsibilities (such as homework or household chores). If her responses meet their standards, authoritative parents would probably allow their daughter the freedom to stay out later than usual.

Authoritarian parents are controlling and adhere rigidly to rules. They tend to be low on warmth, although this is not always the case. In the situation that we just described, these parents would probably refuse their daughter's request with a statement like "A rule is a rule." If the child continued to argue or began to cry, the parents would become angry and might impose a punishment—perhaps even a physical punishment. Authoritarian parents issue commands and expect them to be obeyed; they avoid lengthy verbal exchanges with their children. They behave as if their rules are set in concrete and they are powerless to change them. Trying to gain some independence from such parents can be very frustrating for the child.

Permissive parents are at the opposite extreme from authoritarians: Their parenting style is characterized by few or no restraints placed on the child's behavior. The issue of staying out later than usual would probably not even arise, because there are no curfews in this house, no fixed times for going to bed, and no rule that the child must always keep her parents informed of her whereabouts. Rather than asking her parents if she can stay out later than usual, the young girl might simply tell her parents what she plans to do, or perhaps just let them find out about it afterward. She has plenty of freedom but very little guidance. When permissive parents are annoyed or impatient with their children, they often suppress these feelings. According to Baumrind (1975), many permissive parents are so intent on showing their children "unconditional love" that they fail to perform other important parental functions—in particular, setting limits for their children's behavior.

INDIFFERENT PARENTS Baumrind's permissive parents tend to be warm and accepting of their children. Maccoby and Martin (1983) have defined a fourth parenting style, consisting of parents who are low in restrictiveness and also low in warmth: the **indifferent parents.** These parents don't set limits for their children, either because they just don't care, or because their own lives are so stressful that they don't have enough energy left over to provide guidance for their children.

Table 12-1 summarizes the four parenting styles on the basis of parental control and parental warmth.

EFFECTS OF DIFFERENT PARENTING STYLES As shown by Baumrind (1972, 1975) and by a number of later researchers, parenting styles have an impact on the

TABLE 12–1
Four Parenting Styles

	HIGH PARENTAL CONTROL	LOW PARENTAL CONTROL
HIGH PARENTAL WARMTH	Authoritative	Permissive
LOW PARENTAL WARMTH	Authoritarian	Indifferent

personality of the developing child. Baumrind found that authoritarian parents tend to produce withdrawn, fearful children who exhibit little or no independence and are moody, unassertive, and irritable. In adolescence, these children—particularly the boys—may overreact to the restrictive, punishing environment in which they were reared and may become rebellious and aggressive. The girls are more likely to remain passive and dependent (Kagan & Moss, 1962).

Although permissiveness in parenting is the opposite of restrictiveness, permissiveness does not necessarily produce opposite results: Oddly enough, the children of permissive parents may also be rebellious and aggressive. In addition, they tend to be self-indulgent, impulsive, and socially inept. In contrast, they may be active, outgoing, and creative (Baumrind, 1975; Watson, 1957).

Children of authoritative parents have been found to be the best adjusted. They are the most self-reliant, self-controlled, and socially competent. In the long run, these children develop higher self-esteem and do better in school than those reared with the other parenting styles (Buri et al., 1988; Dornbusch et al., 1987).

The worst outcome is found in the children of indifferent parents. When permissiveness is accompanied by high hostility (the neglectful parent), the child feels free to give rein to his most destructive impulses. Studies of young delinquents show that in many cases their home environments have had exactly this combination of permissiveness and hostility (Bandura & Walters, 1959; McCord, McCord, & Zola, 1959).

Low parental control can become a problem when it interacts with some of the other dimensions of parenting. Some studies of young delinquents have found that these children often come from homes where the parents are also hostile or neglectful.

NEGOTIATION OR SHARED GOALS   Eleanor Maccoby (1979, 1980) has looked at styles of parenting from a perspective that is similar to Baumrind's, but she has expanded the dimensions of this model. She is concerned not only with the effects of parental behavior on children but also with the effects of children's behavior on parents. Parents, of course, are in a better position than children to control the home environment. But the nature of the interaction between the two affects the climate of family life. In some families, parents are highly controlling. At the other extreme, the children are in control. Neither extreme is healthy.

Ideally, neither parents nor children dominate the family all of the time. Maccoby (1980) focuses on the ways that parents and children interact so as to achieve a balanced relationship. She points out that as children get older, parents need to go through a process of negotiation with them in order to make decisions. It does not always help to be authoritarian or to be permissive. It is better to help the child develop ways of thinking through problems and of learning the give-and-take of getting along with others. This can be done in a warm, supportive atmosphere.

Maccoby is talking about the evolution from parental control to more self-control and self-responsibility by children as they get older. Warmth and emotional support from the parents are important to this evolving relationship because parents engender feelings like these in their children. This makes interactions between them easier, even in situations requiring the exercise of authority. As Maccoby (1980) expressed it:

> Parental warmth binds children to their parents in a positive way—it makes children responsive and more willing to accept guidance. If the parent–child relationship is close and affectionate, parents can exercise what control is needed without having to apply heavy disciplinary pressure. It is as if parents' responsiveness, affection, and obvious commitment to their children's welfare have earned them the right to make decisions and exercise control.

Ideally, parents and children come to agree—through long-term dialogue and interaction—on what Maccoby calls *shared goals*. The result is a harmonious atmosphere in which decisions are reached without much struggle for control. Families that enjoy this balance have a fairly high degree of intimacy, and their interaction is stable and mutually rewarding. Families that are unable to achieve shared goals, however, must negotiate everything—from what to have for supper to where to go on vacation. Despite the need for constant discussion, this too can be an effective family style. But if either the parents or the children dominate the situation, there will not be any negotiation, and the family atmosphere will be very unstable. If a parent is highly controlling, preadolescent children soon learn various ways of avoiding the domination. They stay away from home as much as possible. When the children are in control (the parents are permissive and the children are aggressive), the parents avoid the family situation—perhaps by working late. Both of these extremes weaken the socialization process during middle childhood and adolescence; they make it more difficult for children to effect a smooth transition from the family to independence and close peer friendships. As we shall see later in this chapter, peer ties are very important agents of socialization during middle childhood.

The Changing Nature of the Family

The research on parenting styles we have just described was based primarily on the "typical American family": mother, father, and two or three children. But this family is no longer so typical. Having children is not going out of style—over 4 million babies were born in the United States in 1990. What may be going out of style, however, is getting married first or staying married afterward. The trend toward single parenthood continues to grow: About one-quarter of all births are now to unmarried mothers. The divorce rate remains high, affecting about half of all marriages. In 1988, 4.3 million American children were being raised by unmarried mothers, and another 8 million were living with just their mothers as the result of separation or divorce. The number of children living with just their fathers also continues to grow; it is now close to 1 million (Zill, 1991).

Let us examine how children are affected by these trends.

POVERTY AND THE MOTHER-HEADED HOME   Only 10% of two-parent American families have incomes below the poverty line, but half of all mother-headed families are living in poverty (McLanahan & Booth, 1989). If the mother has not graduated from high school, according to a 1991 *New York Times* editorial, the likelihood that the family's income will be below the poverty line is almost 90%.

Children who grow up in poverty, in a home headed only by a mother, experience a multitude of deprivations (McLoyd & Wilson, 1990). Not having a father lowers a family's social status as well as its economic status. Housing is likely to be crowded; frequent moves are common. Meals may be skimpy and nutritionally poor. Medical care may be lacking. Also, the women who head these homes are often psychologically distressed as a result of their struggle for survival. Many suffer from depression or anxiety, which interferes with their ability to be supportive and attentive parents.

The children who grow up in these homes are handicapped in a number of ways: Both their psychological health and their intellectual development are affected. As a result, they are less likely than other American children to move upward in socioeconomic status—in other words, their economic deprivation is likely to continue into adulthood. They are also more likely to become single parents themselves. Thus, the problems are passed on to the next generation (McLanahan & Booth, 1989).

FAMILIES AND STRESS Poverty is a source of stress for both parents and children, but there are other life events that are stressful for children and their families—for example, moving to a different town, being left back in school, or suffering a serious illness or injury. What are some of the factors that determine whether or not a child is able to cope constructively?

One factor is the sheer number of stressful situations in a child's life—a child who can deal successfully with a single stressful event may be overwhelmed if he or she is forced to deal with several all at once (Hetherington, 1984). A second factor is the child's perception or understanding of the event. For example, the first day of school is a major event in a child's life. A child who knows what to expect and who can use this milestone as a sign of his or her increasing maturity will have less difficulty dealing with this new experience.

The research literature clearly indicates that close-knit, adaptable families with open communication patterns and problem-solving skills are better able to weather stressful events (Brenner, 1984). Social support systems, such as neighbors, relatives, friendship networks, or self-help groups are also valuable.

Stress and coping do not always occur as single events; instead, they often exist as ongoing or transitional processes. A young child who is moving to a new neighborhood may experience anticipatory anxiety before the move. Immediate short-term adjustments to the new setting will then have to be made, and some long-term coping skills will be needed to deal with establishing new relationships and recovering from the loss of old ones.

There are many personality traits that influence children's ability to cope with stressful environments. Over the past 30 years, Emmy Werner (1989) has studied a group of what she calls **resilient children.** These children, who were born on one of the Hawaiian islands, lived in family environments marred by poverty, parental conflict or divorce, alcoholism, and mental illness. Yet they developed into self-confident, successful, and emotionally stable adults. Most children reared under such conditions do *not* do well, so Werner was interested in finding how these children managed to thrive in spite of an unfavorable environment. She found that they had been temperamentally "easy" and lovable babies who had developed a close attachment to a parent or grandparent in the first year of life. Later, if that parent or grandparent was no longer available, these children had the ability to find someone else—another adult or even a sibling or a friend—to give them the emotional support they needed. (See "Focus on Research: Children Who Survive" box in Chapter 3.)

resilient children   Children who overcome difficult environments to lead socially competent lives.

Children of Divorce

Nearly half of all marriages now end in divorce (O'Leary & Smith, 1991), which means that each year about a million children experience the breakup of their families. Due to divorce, single parenthood, or the death of a parent, only 40% of

One of the hardest things for children is witnessing the marital tension that exists between their parents preceding a divorce.

the children born today will reach the age of 18 in an intact, two-parent home (Otto, 1988). Even with changing custody rules, the majority of the children of divorced parents will have only occasional contact with their fathers, or no contact at all.

The breakup of the family affects children in a number of ways. We have seen that both parents have strong effects on the development of their children; yet a divorce means that both parents will no longer be equally available to their children. These children are also part of a family that has been under tension for a long period of time. They may have heard the word "divorce" spoken aloud (or shouted) in their homes for months or even years. They know that relationships have been disturbed, and they may wonder what will happen to them. They have seen one parent leave and may fear that the other parent will also abandon them. They may feel sad, confused, angry, or anxious; they may become depressed or disruptive, or they may do poorly in school. Many children (particularly younger ones) feel that they are to blame for the divorce—that if only they had been better, maybe their parents would not have split up. They may try to bring their parents back together, perhaps by being very good or by fantasizing about a reconciliation (Hetherington et al., 1989; Wallerstein et al., 1988).

Relationships with both parents change during and after a divorce. Children may become defiant and argumentative; in adolescence, they may emotionally disengage themselves from their families. In contrast to this, children are often forced to become a sounding board for their parents, listening to each parent describe the faults of the other. They may be at the center of a custody battle and may be asked to choose between parents. The parents may compete for the affection of the children and may try to bribe them with gifts or privileges. The parents themselves are often under considerable stress right after the divorce and may be incapable of providing either warmth or control—they may be less affectionate, inconsistent with discipline, uncommunicative, or unsupportive. Also, children may become upset when their parents start dating or establishing relationships with others. A boy who is living with his mother may take over the role of "man of the house" and may feel threatened when a rival appears on the scene (Hetherington et al., 1989).

The way that children respond to divorce is influenced by a number of factors. Perhaps the three most important ones are:

1. *The amount of hostility accompanying the divorce.* If there is a great deal of hostility and bitterness preceding or following a divorce, it is harder for children to adjust to the situation. Ongoing legal battles (over custody, for example) or squabbles over the division of property or child care make the situation much more difficult for everyone involved (Rutter & Garmezy, 1983).

2. *The amount of actual change in the child's life.* If the child continues to live in the same home, attends the same school, and has the same friends, there tends to be less difficulty in adjusting to separation and divorce. In contrast, if the child's daily life is disrupted in major ways—moving back and forth from one parent's household to the other's, losing old friends, entering a new school—it will be difficult for the child to build self-confidence and to have a sense of order in his or her world. The more changes there are, particularly right after the divorce, the more difficult the adjustment will be (Hetherington & Camara, 1984).

3. *The nature of the parent–child relationship.* Long-term involvement and emotional support from a parent—or better still, from both parents—help the child to make a successful adjustment. In fact, the nature of the ongoing parent–child interaction is much more important than whether or not both parents are present in the home (Rutter & Garmezy, 1983).

child abuse Intentional psychological or physical injuries inflicted on a child.

BREAKDOWN OF RULES   Immediately following a divorce, children—especially school-age children of 5, 6 or 7 years—often appear confused; they exhibit behavioral difficulties, not only at home but also in school and in other places. When children experience a severe disruption in their lives, especially if it occurs suddenly, their understanding of the social world is upset. It may seem to them that the script for ongoing daily life has been torn up—that the old rules no longer apply. The long-established patterns of the family have broken down under the pressure of divorce and separation. In the past, the world was predictable: Daddy came home from work every evening, the entire family sat down to dinner, and bedtime was at 8:00. Suddenly, these patterns are disrupted and the script for understanding the social world no longer seems to apply. Consequently, children often test the rules to see if the world still works the way it did before. They may have to be told by their mothers: "I know it's upsetting that Daddy's not coming home anymore. But that doesn't mean you don't have to go to bed at 8:00. You still have to get up early in the morning and go to school. And you still need your rest." Teachers also need to be helpful in gently reestablishing the rules and expectations of the school situation as well as being emotionally supportive of a child who is going through considerable inner turmoil. Some children almost have to relearn the social script.

A divorce may have far-reaching effects. Many children have to take on new responsibilities and learn to relate to parents in new ways.

STEPFAMILIES   The problems that surface during a divorce may not disappear when one or both parents remarry. Although some children welcome the arrival of a stepparent, for others, the remarriage is another major adjustment that must be made after their adjustment to the divorce. Children may see their dreams of reuniting their parents shattered; they may resent the stepparent's attempt to discipline them or to win their affection. They may see themselves as having a divided loyalty to their parents, or they may worry about being left out of the new family that is forming. Children may also be unhappy about having to share the attention of the custodial parent with his or her new partner, or they may feel guilty about "abandoning" the noncustodial parent by giving affection to the new stepparent. In some cases, children may have the additional problem of having to get along with stepsiblings (Hetherington et al., 1989).

In most cases, the major adaptations associated with divorce and with stepfamilies subside in about 2 years. By that time, children and parents may have adjusted to the new situation and are moving ahead with their lives. While they exist, however, these problems may seriously interfere with a child's social and emotional development.

Child Abuse

One of the most serious and dramatic examples of family breakdown is the phenomenon of **child abuse.** Instead of encouraging and reinforcing the bond between parent and child, the child abuser destroys the expectations of love, trust,

The definition of child abuse changes from culture to culture and in different historical periods. Two hundred years ago, for example, teachers physically punished students who misbehaved.

and dependence so essential to the young child. Severe developmental problems frequently result.

We shall define child abuse, and distinguish it from neglect, by using the term to refer only to physical and psychological injuries that are *intentionally* inflicted on a child by an adult (Burgess & Conger, 1978). Neglect, in contrast, is unintentional; it results from parents' or care-givers' failures to act rather than from their injurious actions. The results can be equally tragic: Children die of neglect as well as of abuse. Here, however, we shall discuss only the physical and emotional damage that is intentionally inflicted on children: extreme psychological punishment, such as constant ridicule or criticism; violent physical punishment resulting in injury or death; and sexual abuse.

It can be difficult to distinguish between child abuse and ordinary punishment. What qualifies as child abuse is a relative question and must be viewed in light of community standards. Historically, many cultures have condoned and even encouraged physical mistreatment that we consider shocking and brutal. It was used to discipline and educate children, to exorcise evil spirits, or to placate the gods. Furthermore, some cultures imbued certain forms of physical cruelty, such as foot binding, skull shaping, or ritual scarring, with a deep symbolic meaning. Traditionally, children were viewed as the property of their parents, and parents had the legal right to treat them in any way they saw fit. Infanticide or the abandonment of unwanted babies was a time-honored method for desperate adults trying to cope with hunger, illegitimacy, or birth defects (Radbill, 1974). We have different standards now: Causing injury or death to a child is considered to be a serious crime. But, sadly, it is not an uncommon one.

THE INCIDENCE OF CHILD ABUSE   In the United States, official reports of child abuse and neglect now number almost 1 million a year; three children die every day as a result of physical abuse or neglect. These figures may be shocking, but they are not unique to the United States; similar rates have been noted in Canada, Australia, Great Britain, and Germany (Emery, 1989; Parke & Collmer, 1975).

More than half of physically abused children are abused by their own parents, with mothers and fathers implicated in approximately equal numbers. When someone other than a parent is responsible for the abuse, however, male abusers outnumber females by four to one. For sexual abuse, the proportion of abusers who are male is even higher—nearly 95%. You may be surprised to learn that the sexual abuse of a little girl is usually *not* committed by the child's own father. It is estimated that a stepfather is five times more likely to abuse his stepdaughter than a father is to abuse his daughter (Sedlack, 1989; Wolfe, Wolfe, & Best, 1988).

Although the victim of sexual abuse is likely to be a girl, physical abuse is more often inflicted on a boy. Also, younger children sustain more serious injuries than older ones do; about half of the serious injury or death cases involve children under the age of 3 (Rosenthal, 1988).

Sexual and physical child abuse has long-term effects on the child's emotional well-being. The child's self-esteem has been irreparably damaged, and he or she may find it difficult ever to trust anyone again. Adults who were abused as children are at greater risk of many psychological problems, including depression and alcoholism (Schaefer et al., 1988).

APPROACHES TO UNDERSTANDING CHILD ABUSE   The large amount of research that has been done in this area has been centered on three main theoretical explanations of child abuse: psychiatric, sociological, and situational (Parke & Collmer, 1975).

Psychiatric Explanations.   The psychiatric model focuses on the personality of the parents. It assumes that abusive parents are sick and require extensive psychiatric treatment. Early theorists looked for psychotic traits in adults who abused children, but they failed to find any. They discovered that clear cases of adult psychosis, such as schizophrenia, account for only a very small percentage of incidents of child abuse. Other researchers have attempted to find a cluster of personality traits that might indicate a tendency toward abuse. This search, too, has failed to produce any helpful conclusions.

One fact that researchers have discovered about child abusers is that many of them were themselves abused as children (Ney, 1988). Although psychologists are not certain why child abuse patterns are passed on from one generation to the next, one plausible explanation is that people who were abused as children had abusive adult models to follow. Their parents may have taught them that needs like dependency or autonomy are unacceptable—that crying or asking for help is useless, inappropriate, or evidence of an evil nature. Children absorb such lessons deeply and thoroughly at an early age. Many abused children, once they become parents, apply these lessons to their own children.

Sociological Explanations.   The sociological model, as defined by Parke and Collmer, focuses *not* on individual differences but on social values and family organization. One American social value significantly related to child abuse is violence. The United States ranks higher in murders and other violent crimes than other industrialized nations do. Some suggest that the endless display of brutality and hostility on television teaches parents and children alike that violence is an acceptable way to resolve conflicts. If physical aggression occurs in some family disputes, especially those between husband and wife, it is also likely to occur in parent–child relationships. Physical punishment is a widely used disciplinary technique in the United States; 93% of all parents use it, although the majority use it sparingly. Comparisons with more peaceful societies that rely more on love-oriented discipline reveal less violence in general and less abuse of children in particular (Parke & Collmer, 1975).

Poverty, unemployment, and overcrowding also play a role in child abuse. Although physical abuse of children is found at all socioeconomic levels, it is almost seven times more likely to be reported in homes where the annual income is below $15,000 (Sedlack, 1989). This statistic may result partly from the fact that abuse in middle-class homes is less likely to come to the attention of authorities. However, it is also true that any kind of family stress—and poverty is unquestionably a source of family stress—increases the risk that a child will be abused. Unemployment is also a source of stress. A parent who is suddenly and unexpectedly out of work may become abusive toward his or her children. Aside from the financial problems, unemployment also lowers the parent's social status and self-esteem. An unemployed father may try to compensate by wielding authority at home through physical domination. In periods of high unemployment, male violence against both wives and children rises.

Another characteristic that is observed in many families troubled by child abuse is social isolation. Parents who abuse their children are often isolated from relatives, friends, and community support systems. They have difficulty sustaining friendships and rarely belong to any formal organizations. Thus, they have no one to ask for help when they need it, and they turn their frustration and rage against their children. Some of this isolation is self-imposed. Abusive parents, with their low self-esteem, feel so guilty and unworthy that they avoid contact with others. They also obstruct their children's attempts to form meaningful bonds and relationships with people outside the home.

Situational Explanations.   The situational model of child abuse, like the sociological model, seeks causes in environmental factors. The situational model concentrates on interaction patterns among family members (Parke & Collmer, 1975). This model recognizes children as active participants in the interaction process. It tries to identify the situations in which abusive patterns develop and to find the stimuli that trigger the abuse. One study attempted to discover distinctive patterns in the everyday interactions of families with incidences of child abuse. The study showed that abusive parents had less verbal and physical interaction with their children than did nonabusive parents. Abusive parents were also more negative and less willing to comply with the requests of other family members (Burgess & Conger, 1978).

Abusive parents also tend to be inconsistent in the behavioral demands they make on their children. They may punish their children for coming home late one day, but they ignore it the next—or they may punish them long afterward, so that the children feel they are being punished for no apparent reason. These parents also tend to have trouble in defining their marital roles. They often fail to allocate responsibility between themselves for important tasks, including discipline of the children. Thus, their children may be confused by parental inconsistencies and may lack a clear idea of what kind of behavior will be tolerated. When, in addition, the parents are members of a culture that does not frown on violence, the patterns of abuse are set in motion. Once the pattern is begun, it tends to perpetuate itself. The parents may justify the abuse as a way of "building character" and may play down the injuries sustained by the child. They may shift the blame to the child and justify their behavior on the grounds that the child is "hateful" or "stubborn" (Belsky, 1980; Parke & Collmer, 1975).

Finally, let us look at the role of the child in abusive families. Parents are usually selective in their abuse, singling out one child for mistreatment. Infants and very young children are the most frequent targets. Those with physical or mental abnormalities, or who are unusually difficult to take care of, are at greatest risk. Infants who cry constantly can drive parents to the breaking point. In other cases, there may be a mismatch between the parent's expectations and the child's characteristics—this is basically a problem of incompatibility between parent and child. For example, a physically demonstrative mother may find that her infant does not like to be touched. Such mismatches may lead to poor attachment and, sometimes, to abuse (Parke & Collmer, 1975; Vasta, 1982).

Some children may be singled out for abuse because they serve as an uncomfortable reminder of their parent's own flaws. Many parents have still not come to terms with the unresolved conflicts from their own childhood years. If their child has a characteristic that they regard as unacceptable in themselves, they may punish this child harshly. These unfortunate children tap a wellspring of self-hatred in their parents.

All three of these approaches shed some light on the causes of child abuse. None of them, unfortunately, tells us how to stop it. Programs for preventing child abuse focus on providing parents with social support and teaching them better methods for controlling their children. Although such programs usually succeed in reducing the level of abuse, around 25% of the participants continue to abuse their children (Ferleger et al., 1988). Sometimes, criminal prosecution of the offenders and removal of the child from the home are the only safe alternatives.

PSYCHOLOGICAL ABUSE   Physical or sexual abuse is always accompanied by a psychological component. Mistreatment exists in the context of an interpersonal relationship, and this relationship has become psychologically abusive—manipulative, rejecting, or degrading. One researcher states that the psychological accompaniments of child abuse may be even more damaging than the abuse itself (Emery, 1989).

Psychological abuse comes in various forms and may be committed by various people, such as parents, teachers, siblings, and peers. The significant characteristic of these people is that they have power in situations in which the child is vulnerable (Hart et al., 1987). For instance, most of us have encountered, at some point in our lives, the sadistic teacher who picks out one particular student in the class and makes this student the victim of a continuing campaign of cruelty.

Psychological abusers have a wide range of techniques. Hart, Germain, and Brassard (1987) have specified six types of psychological abuse used by parents, teachers, siblings, or peers:

- *Rejection*. This involves refusing the request or needs of a child in such a way as to imply strong dislike for the child. Active rejection rather than passive withholding of affection is involved here.
- *Denial of Emotional Responsiveness*. This is the passive withholding of affection. Detachment, coldness, or failing to respond to the child's attempts at communication are examples of this.
- *Degradation*. Humiliating children in public or calling them "stupid" or "dummy" is degrading. Children's self-esteem is lowered by frequent assaults on their dignity or intelligence.
- *Terrorization*. Being forced to witness violence to a loved one, or being threatened with violence to oneself, is a terrifying experience for a child. A child who suffers regular beatings or who is told, "I'll break every bone in your body if you don't behave," is being terrorized. A more subtle form of terrorism is demonstrated by the parent who simply walks away from a misbehaving child while they are out in the street, leaving the child unprotected from danger.
- *Isolation*. Refusing to allow a child to play with friends or to take part in family activity is to isolate that child. Some forms of isolation, such as locking a child in a closet, may also be terrorization.
- *Exploitation*. Taking advantage of a child's innocence or weakness is exploitation. The most obvious example of exploiting a child is sexual abuse.

Psychological abuse is so common that virtually no one grows up without experiencing some form of it. But in most cases, the abuse is not intense enough or frequent enough to do permanent damage (Hart et al., 1987). The important distinction between the psychologically abused child and the rest of us is that the abused child is caught in a damaging relationship and is not being socialized in a positive, supportive way. As a consequence, the child may not be able to satisfy his or her dependency needs, may have to be overly adaptive in order to escape abuse,

social cognition   Thought, knowledge, and understanding that involve the social world.

social inference   Guesses and assumptions about what another person is feeling, thinking, or intending.

and may develop neurotic traits or problem behaviors. What is more, the child has learned to exploit, degrade, or terrorize, and to expect that relationships are often painful. These are pervasive, long-term consequences.

SOCIAL KNOWLEDGE

As we have seen, children are continually learning how to deal with the complex social world that exists both inside and outside the family. In middle childhood, they must come to terms with the subtleties of friendship and authority, with expanding or conflicting sex roles, and with a host of social rules and regulations. One way they do this is by the process of direct socialization: getting rewards for desirable behavior and punishments for undesirable behavior, and observing and imitating models. Social learning helps children to acquire appropriate behaviors and attitudes. Another way children learn about the social world involves psychodynamic processes. Children develop anxious feelings in certain situations, and they learn to reduce this anxiety by using a number of defense mechanisms (see Chapter 10).

A third way that children learn about the social world is called **social cognition.** Just as children's understanding of the physical world changes as they mature, so does their understanding of the social world. Social cognition is thought, knowledge, and understanding that involves the social world.

The Development of Social Cognition

As children develop during middle childhood and adolescence, social cognition becomes an increasingly important determinant of their behavior. It is in middle childhood that children must learn how to deal with some of the complexities of friendship and justice, social rules and manners, sex-role conventions, obedience to authority, and moral law. Children begin to look at the social world around them and gradually come to understand the principles and rules that it follows (Ross, 1981). This process has been studied by cognitive theorists, who believe that all knowledge, whether scientific, social, or personal, exists as an organized system or structure, not as unrelated bits and pieces. The understanding of the world does not develop in a piecemeal fashion; rather, it occurs in a predictable sequence. The development of social cognition progresses in a way that is similar to other kinds of cognitive development.

As we saw in Chapter 9, preschool children's understanding of the world is limited by their egocentrism. Although by age 7 children have reached "the age of reason" and are able to perform some logical operations, they are still somewhat hampered by their inability to see another person's point of view. Many children in early middle childhood still do not recognize that their point of view is limited to themselves. They are not fully aware that other people have different points of view because of their different backgrounds, experiences, or values. This fact only gradually becomes apparent to the young child.

A first component of social cognition, therefore, is **social inference**—that is, guesses and assumptions about what another person is feeling, thinking, or intending (Flavell, 1985). A young child, for example, hears his mother laughing

In middle childhood, children develop the ability to think about their social world and about relationships inside and outside the family. In developing this social knowledge, children learn to understand how others feel and the rules of social interaction.

DISCOVERING OUR ECONOMIC SYSTEM

Money has an important place in the world of children. Some of their earliest memories include shopping for groceries and clothing with their parents and, when they are older, buying special treats for themselves. The formal rules that are part of the process of exchanging money for goods and services reflect the order of society itself. When children learn these rules, they are well on their way to understanding how society operates.

To find out exactly how children's understanding of money evolves, Hans Furth (1980) interviewed approximately 200 British children ranging in age from 5 to 11. He asked them questions about money and commerce and about such social institutions as stores, schools, and government. His findings point to the dynamic growth of knowledge and understanding during middle childhood. At each stage of growth, children are confronted with information that is inconsistent with their present way of thinking about the world. By wondering about things, asking questions, and being given more details, they gradually learn what the real world and the world of money are all about.

Furth identified four separate stages that children pass through in their growing awareness of money as a medium of exchange.

In the first stage, children believe that money is freely available. The exchange of money for goods or services is totally meaningless to them. In fact, they believe that one of the ways people get money is by buying something and receiving change. Thus, said one of Furth's young subjects: "Sometimes [the storekeeper] gives you four p[ence] for the sweets back and sometimes he gives you more when you want some bigger things" (Furth, 1980, p. 27).

In the second stage, children understand that money is used as a medium of exchange to buy goods and services, but their understanding stops here. In their limited view of the world, they do not understand that shopkeepers must use the money they receive to pay for the goods they eventually sell. Those few children who actually understand a merchant's use of money never relate it back to their own purchases. Children may believe that the money storekeepers collect is their personal property to do with as they wish, not realizing that storekeepers actually have to pay for the things they sell in the store. One child had a very altruistic view of where the money finally winds up: "The money the lady collects," said the child, "she gives it to the blind or something, the poor people" (p. 28).

In the third stage, there is a major leap in children's understanding: They know that storekeepers use the money they receive from customers to stock their stores. However, children cannot understand the profit motive behind a sale, nor can they understand the storekeepers' need to earn money for themselves and for their families. In fact, many children expressed a kind of a moral concern that the storekeepers might be taking money that really didn't belong to them. The children echoed phrases they had heard from their parents but did not fully understand: "Keep the hand out of the till," said one child. "Don't use business money for private affairs" (p. 28).

In the final stage, which, according to Furth, most children reach when they are 10 or 11 years old, children understand the concept of profit. They understand that storekeepers earn money by selling goods for more than they paid for them and that these profits allow them to run their stores and pay their personal expenses.

At each stage, information that conflicts with children's existing view of the world requires a readjustment of thinking. The process of cognitive growth is gradual; concepts that do not fit into the child's cognitive world at an early age are disregarded until a later time, or only parts of them are used. This understanding develops from that of a 5-year-old who asks Daddy for an allowance of a million dollars to that of the sophisticated 11-year-old who charges a quarter for 5 cents' worth of lemonade.

and assumes that she is happy. An adult might hear something forced about the mother's laughter and infer that the woman is covering up her feelings. Although young children cannot make such a sophisticated inference, by age 6 they can usually infer that another person's thoughts may differ from their own. By age 8 or so, they realize that another person can think about their thoughts. By age 10, they are able to infer what another person is thinking while at the same time inferring

social relationships   Relationships that involve obligations such as fairness and loyalty. The knowledge of these obligations is a necessary part of social cognition.

social regulations   The rules and conventions governing social interactions.

moral judgment   The process of making decisions about right and wrong.

moral realism   Piaget's term for the first stage of moral development, in which children believe in rules as real, indestructible things.

moral relativism   Piaget's term for the second stage of moral development, in which children realize that rules are agreements that may be changed, if necessary.

Developing a sense of right and wrong involves understanding social rules and gaining experience in social relationships.

that their own thoughts are the subject of another person's thoughts. A child might think, "Johnny is angry with me, and he knows that I know he is angry." The process of developing fully accurate social inference is gradual and continues into late adolescence (Shantz, 1983).

A second component of social cognition is the child's understanding of **social relationships.** Children gradually accumulate information and understanding about the obligations of friendship, such as fairness and loyalty, the respect for authority, and the concepts of legality and justice. A third aspect of social cognition is the understanding of **social regulations,** such as customs and conventions. Many of these conventions are first learned by rote or imitation. Later, they can become less rigid, depending on the child's ability to make correct social inferences and to understand social relationships.

Psychologists who study social cognition find that it develops in a predictable sequence—some even call the steps in this sequence "stages." Most researchers agree that children overcome the worst of their egocentrism by age 6 or 7: They stop centering on only one aspect of a situation and gradually get better at making social inferences. As we will soon see, these advances make it possible for a child to form lasting and satisfying friendships with other children. They also affect the child's ability to think about moral issues.

Moral Judgment

Moral judgment—making decisions about right and wrong—is another area of social cognition. In the process of growing up, most children somehow learn to tell "good" from "bad" and to distinguish between kindness and cruelty, generosity and selfishness. Mature moral judgment, then, involves more than the rote learning of social rules and conventions.

There is considerable debate as to how children develop morality. Social learning theorists believe that children learn it by being rewarded or punished for various kinds of behavior and by imitating models. Psychodynamic psychologists believe that it develops as a defense against anxiety over the loss of love and approval. Cognitive theorists believe that, like intellectual development, morality develops in progressive, age-related stages. Let us take a closer look at cognitive approaches to moral development.

COGNITIVE VIEWS OF MORAL DEVELOPMENT   Piaget defined morality as "an individual's respect for the rules of social order and his sense of justice"—justice being "a concern for reciprocity and equality among individuals" (Hoffman, 1970). According to Piaget (1965), children's moral sense arises from the interaction between their developing thought structures and their gradually widening social experience. The moral sense develops in two stages. At the **moral realism** stage, children think that all rules should be obeyed because they are real, indestructible things, not abstract principles. A child at this stage judges the morality of an act in terms of its consequences and is incapable of weighing intentions. For example, a young child will think that the girl who accidentally breaks 12 dishes while setting a table is much guiltier than the girl who intentionally breaks 2 dishes because she is angry with her sister.

Later, children reach the stage of **moral relativism.** At this point, they realize that rules are created and agreed upon cooperatively by individuals and that rules can be changed as the need arises. This leads to the realization that there is no absolute right or wrong and that morality depends *not* on consequences but on intentions.

Kohlberg's Six-Stage Theory.　Piaget's two-stage theory of moral development was extended by Lawrence Kohlberg (1981, 1984). Kohlberg presented his subjects (children, adolescents, and adults) with a series of morally problematic stories and then asked them questions about the stories. The leading character in each story was faced with a moral dilemma, and the subject being interviewed was asked to resolve this dilemma. Kohlberg was less interested in the specific answers to the problem than in the reasoning behind the answers. Here is one of his stories, which has become a classic:

> In Europe, a woman was near death from a special kind of cancer. There was one drug that the doctors thought might save her. It was a form of radium that a druggist in the same town had recently discovered. The drug was expensive to make, but the druggist was charging 10 times what the drug cost him to make. He paid $200 for the radium and charged $2,000 for a small dose of the drug. The sick woman's husband, Heinz, went to everyone he knew to borrow the money, but he could only get together $1,000, which is half of what it cost. He told the druggist that his wife was dying and asked him to sell it cheaper or let him pay later. But the druggist said, "No, I discovered the drug, and I am going to make money from it." So Heinz got desperate and broke into the man's store to steal the drug for his wife.

The person being interviewed was then asked: "Should Heinz have stolen the drug?" "Why?" "Was the druggist right to have charged so much more than it cost to make the drug?" "Why?" "Which is worse, letting someone die or stealing if it will save a life?" "Why?"

The ways that different age groups answered these questions led Kohlberg to the theory that moral reasoning develops in distinct stages. He defined three broad levels of moral reasoning and subdivided these levels into six stages (see Table 12–2). Support for his theory was provided by several studies that showed that young boys, at least in Western societies, generally went through these stages in the predicted fashion. In one 20-year longitudinal study of 48 boys, Kohlberg and his associates found remarkable consistency with these stages (Colby et al., 1983).

Kohlberg's theory has raised many objections. Some researchers have found that it is very difficult to follow Kohlberg's procedures exactly and to agree on how a child's response to the test should be scored (Rubin & Trotten, 1977). Others have attacked Kohlberg's theory on the grounds of **moral absolutism:** It does not take into account important cultural differences that determine what is moral in other societies (Baumrind, 1978). Kohlberg (1978) himself acknowledged that it is necessary to take into account the social and moral norms of the group to which a person belongs. He has concluded that his sixth stage of moral development may not apply to all people in all cultures.

Power and Reimer (1978) find other weaknesses in Kohlberg's theory. They point out that Kohlberg's scale measures attitudes, not behavior, and that there is a great difference between thinking about moral questions and behaving morally. Moral decisions are not made in a vacuum; instead, they are usually made in "crisis situations." No matter how high our moral principles may be, when the time comes to act on them, our behavior may not reflect our thoughts or beliefs.

moral absolutism　Any theory of morality that disregards cultural differences in moral beliefs.

TABLE 12–2
Kohlberg's Stages of Moral Development

STAGE	ILLUSTRATIVE REASONING
Level I. Preconventional (based on punishments and rewards)	
Stage 1. Punishment and obedience orientation	Obey rules in order to avoid punishment
Stage 2. Naïve instrumental hedonism	Obey to obtain rewards, to have favors returned.
Level II. Conventional (based on social conformity)	
Stage 3. "Good-boy" morality of maintaining good relations, approval of others	Conform to avoid disapproval or dislike by others.
Stage 4. Authority-maintaining morality	Conform to avoid censure by legitimate authorities, with resulting guilt.
Level III. Postconventional (based on moral principles)	
Stage 5. Morality of contract, of individual rights, and of democratically accepted law	Abide by laws of land for community welfare.
Stage 6. Morality of individual principles of conscience	Abide by universal ethical principles.

Source: From *Stages of Moral Development* by Lawrence Kohlberg (unpublished doctoral dissertation, University of Chicago, 1958). © 1958 by Lawrence Kohlberg. Used by permission. Also adapted from *The Philosophy of Moral Development* by Lawrence Kohlberg (New York: Harper & Row, 1981).

Gilligan's Objections.   Carol Gilligan (1982) claims that Kohlberg based his theory entirely on his work with male subjects and failed to consider the possibility that moral development might proceed somewhat differently in females. In other words, she accuses Kohlberg of sex bias. Gilligan found that girls and women generally score lower than males do on Kohlberg's moral dilemma test. But, she says, this does not mean that their thinking is at a lower level—only that they use different criteria for making moral judgments.

According to Gilligan (1982), girls and boys are taught from early childhood to value different qualities. Boys are trained to strive for independence and to value abstract thinking. Girls, in contrast, are taught to be nurturing and caring and to value their connectedness to others. Gilligan believes that there are two distinct types of moral reasoning: One is based on concepts of abstract justice, and the other is based on human relationships and caring for other people. The justice perspective is characteristic of male thinking, whereas caring for others is more common in females. Men often focus on rights, whereas women see moral issues in terms of concern for the needs of others. However, Gilligan notes that sex differences in moral reasoning (like other sex differences) are not absolute. Some women make moral judgments from a justice perspective, and some men make them from a caring one.

Gilligan's subjects were mostly adolescents and young adults. Other researchers have looked at younger children and have failed to find a sex difference in moral judgments made by children younger than age 10. However, some 10- or 11-year-old boys give rather aggressive responses to the questions that are asked on these tests—the sort of responses that are hardly ever given by girls. For example, in one study the children listened to a story about a porcupine that needed a home for the winter, so he moved in with a family of moles. The moles soon found that they were constantly being pricked by the porcupine's sharp needles. What should they do? Only boys responded to this question with suggestions like "Shoot the porcupine" or "Pluck out his quills." Girls of this age tended to look for solutions that would harm neither the moles nor the porcupine—in other words, caring solutions (Garrod, Beal, & Shin, 1989).

Eisenberg's View.   Nancy Eisenberg (1989a, 1989b) feels that Kohlberg's mistake was not in placing too much emphasis on abstract justice; it was in making the stages too rigid and absolute. She feels that children's moral development is not quite this predictable and narrowly determined. Many factors go into children's moral judgments, ranging from the social customs of the culture in which they are reared to how they feel at a particular moment. Children are capable of making moral judgments at a high level one day and at a lower level the next. They may even make judgments at a higher level for some issues (for example, whether they would help someone who was injured) than for others (for example, whether they would invite someone they didn't like to their birthday party).

With regard to sex differences, Eisenberg also finds that girls between ages 10 and 12 give more caring and empathetic responses than do boys of this age. However, she thinks this stems mainly from the fact that girls mature more rapidly than boys do. By late adolescence, boys have caught up. Eisenberg and her colleagues find *few* sex differences in the responses of older adolescents (Eisenberg, 1989a; Eisenberg et al., 1987).

PEER RELATIONSHIPS AND SOCIAL COMPETENCE

As the previous discussion would indicate, the ability to make moral decisions on the basis of empathy and concern for others is something that develops as children mature. Girls mature a little faster; therefore, they develop empathy at a somewhat earlier age than boys do. Empathy is based on social inference because if you do not know what someone else is feeling, you cannot empathize with him or her. Social inference and empathy are the foundation upon which friendships are based.

Concepts of Friendship

The ability to infer the thoughts, expectations, feelings, and intentions of others plays a central role in understanding what it means to be a friend. Children who can view things from another person's perspective are better able to develop strong, intimate relationships with others.

Using a social cognition model, Selman (1976, 1981) studied the friendships of children aged 7 to 12. His approach was similar to Kohlberg's: Tell children a story involving a social dilemma and then ask them questions designed to measure their concepts about other people, their self-awareness and ability to reflect, their concepts of personality, and their ideas about friendship. Here is an example of the kind of story that Selman used:

Kathy and Debby have been best friends since they were 5. A new girl, Jeannette, moves into their neighborhood, but Debby dislikes her because she

One type of friendship is based on give-and-take; friends are seen as people who help each other.

considers Jeannette a showoff. Later, Jeannette invites Kathy to go to the circus on its one day in town. Kathy's problem is that she has promised to play with Debby that same day. What will Kathy do?

This story raises questions about the nature of relationships, about old versus new friendships, and about loyalty and trust. It requires children to think and to talk about how friendships are formed and maintained and to decide what is important in a relationship. In other words, Selman's method provides a way of assessing a child's concepts and thought processes—*how* the child decides what is important.

Selman (1981) described four stages of friendship. At the first stage, found in children under age 7, friendship is based on physical or geographical considerations and is rather self-centered. A friend is just a playmate—someone who lives nearby, who goes to the same school, or who has desirable toys. At this stage, there is no understanding of the other person's perspective.

At the second stage (ages 7 to 9), the idea of reciprocity and an awareness of another person's feelings begin to form. Friendship is seen mostly in terms of the social actions of one person and the subjective evaluation of these actions by the other. A child at this stage might say that Kathy could go to the circus with Jeannette and remain friends with Debby only if Debby did not object to the change in plans.

The third level of friendship (ages 8 to 12) is based on genuine give-and-take; friends are seen as people who help each other. Children realize that they can evaluate the actions of their friends and that friends can evaluate their actions in return. The concept of trust appears for the first time. Children at the third stage might realize that the friendship between Kathy and Debby is different from the friendship between Kathy and Jeannette because the older friendship is based on long-standing trust.

At the fourth stage, which occurs only rarely among 11- and 12-year-olds, children see friendship as a stable, continuing relationship that is based on trust. Children are now capable of looking at the relationship from the perspective of a third party. A child at this level might comment, "Kathy and Debby should be able to understand each other."

Not all researchers agree with Selman's model. For example, there is evidence that young children implicitly know more of the rules and expectations of being a friend than they are able to tell an interviewer (Rizzo & Corsaro, 1988). Also, real friendships are quite complicated and are constantly changing. They may involve mutuality, trust, and reciprocity at one time and independence, competitiveness, or even conflict at another. Certain types of conflict may be intrinsic to the nature of friendship. Such complexities are not easily handled by a model that looks only at the cognitive aspects of children's friendships and ignores the emotional aspects (Berndt, 1983).

Functions of Friendship

Children and adults alike benefit from having close, confiding relationships. In the context of friendships, children learn social concepts and social skills, and they develop self-esteem. Friendship provides a structure for a child's activity in

Friendship pairs allow children to share feelings and fears and to reinforce activities, values, and norms.

peer group A group of two or more people of similar status who interact with each other and who share norms and goals.

games; it reinforces and solidifies group norms, attitudes, and values; it serves as a backdrop for individual and group competition (Hartup, 1970a).

Friendship patterns shift during childhood (Piaget, 1965). The "egocentric" pattern of Selman's first stage, typical of preschoolers and younger school-age children, changes during middle childhood when children begin to form closer relationships, often with a few "best" friends. These friendship ties are very strong while they last, but they tend to be short-lived. In late childhood and adolescence, group friendships become common. The groups are generally large, with several boys or girls regularly sharing activities.

Two children who are friends may satisfy different needs in each other. One may be dominant, and the other may be submissive. One child may use her friend as a model, and the other child may enjoy teaching her friend the "proper" way to play or dress. In still another case, the relationship may be egalitarian, with neither friend playing a clear or consistent role. The pattern depends upon the dominance, dependency, and autonomy needs of each child.

With a friend, children can share their feelings and fears and every detail of their lives. Having a best friend in whom one can confide teaches a child how to relate to others openly and unselfconsciously. However, this pattern of friendship is more common in girls. Boys tend to play in larger groups and to reveal less of themselves to their friends (Maccoby, 1990; Rubin, 1980).

Friendship can also be a vehicle of self-expression. Children sometimes choose friends whose personalities are quite different from their own. An outgoing or impulsive child may choose a more reserved or restrained child as a close friend. The relationship gives each a maximum of self-expression with a minimum of competition, and the pair, as a unit, demonstrates more personality traits than either child could alone (Hartup, 1970a, 1970b). Of course, friends are rarely complete opposites. Friendship pairs that last over a long period of time usually have many shared values, attitudes, and expectations, both within the pair and in relation to others.

Some childhood friendships last throughout life, but more often friendships change. Best friends may move away or transfer to another school, and children may feel a real sense of loss—until they make a new friend. Sometimes, friends become interested in other people who meet their needs in new and different ways, and, sometimes, friends just grow apart or develop new interests. As children grow, they turn to new partners who can provide more satisfactory relationships (Rubin, 1980).

The Peer Group

What is a **peer group?** When we use this term, we are not talking about just any "bunch of kids." The size of a peer group is limited by the fact that all of its members must interact with one another. In addition, a peer group is relatively stable, and it stays together for a period of time. Its members share many values, and common norms govern interaction and influence each child. Finally, some degree of status differentiation governs the group's interaction; there is at least a temporary division into leaders and followers.

DEVELOPMENTAL TRENDS IN THE PEER GROUP Peer groups are important throughout middle childhood, but a general shift occurs both in their organization and in their importance to the child during the years from 6 to 12.

Peer groups form wherever children with common values, interests, or goals are thrown together.

In early middle childhood, peer groups are relatively informal. They are usually formed by the children themselves, and they have very few operating rules and a rapid turnover in membership. It is true that many of the group's activities, such as playing games or riding bikes, may be carried out according to precise rules. But the structure of the group itself is quite flexible.

The group takes on a more intense meaning for its members when these children reach the ages 10 to 12. Group conformity becomes extremely important to the child, who may be showing an almost religious reverence for rules and norms in other areas of social interaction. Peer pressures assume a coercive influence on the child. Groups also develop a more formal structure. They may have special membership requirements, club meetings, and initiation rites. At this time, division of the sexes becomes very important. Groups are now almost invariably composed of one sex, and each sex maintains different interests and activities and has different styles of interaction (Maccoby, 1990). These strict attitudes about rules, conformity, and sex segregation are common to children's interaction through the latter part of middle childhood, and they are usually not relaxed until mid-adolescence.

GROUP FORMATION   Children are constantly being thrown together by circumstances—in schools, in camps, and in neighborhoods. In each case, and generally within a very short time, groups form. Role differentiation develops within the group. Common values and interests emerge. Mutual influences and expectations grow, and a feeling of tradition takes shape. The process is almost universal, and some interesting studies have recorded exactly how it happens.

One classic experiment was called the "Red Rover" study (Sherif & Sherif,

1953). The subjects were fifth-grade boys with similar backgrounds who were attending a summer camp. In the first phase of the study, the boys lived in two separate groups for a few days and were watched carefully as they began to form friendships. Just as these budding friendships were beginning to solidify, the experimenters split up the friends by dividing the groups along new lines. The second stage of the study lasted for 5 days. The observers saw that in-group friendships soon formed in the new groups, and a clear hierarchy of leadership—not necessarily related to popularity—emerged very quickly. Group names were chosen (the "Red Devils" and the "Bulldogs"), and group rules and norms were developed.

In the final stage, the two groups were brought into direct competition in games that were rigged so that one group was almost never allowed to win. At first, the competition resulted in the quick development of animosity and even open hostility between the groups, with powerful feelings of in-group exclusivity. But the frustrated group's structure soon fell apart. Leadership disintegrated, and intragroup disharmony developed.

A second study, sometimes called the "Robber's Cave" experiment (Sherif et al., 1961), duplicated the circumstances and findings of the first study, with one important change. The competition between the groups was now *equal*. The results showed some interesting things about group structure. Equal competition intensified in-group solidarity in both groups, reinforcing norms and expectations. Feelings of exclusivity within each group and a sense of hostility toward the opposing group also grew stronger, just as the experimenters had hypothesized. Another interesting finding was that the hierarchical structures of both groups changed. Leadership shifted as the boys who did best in the current competition rose to new leadership positions. In other words, group roles were shown to be related quite strongly to group goals. When the goals changed, so did the leaders.

In both of these studies, the experimenters had created openly hostile situations, and in each case, they tried to "undo the damage" before the boys were sent home from camp. In the highly frustrating "Red Rover" condition, the hostility was never completely erased. In the second study, however, the experimenters were better able to control the situation. They theorized that if the two groups were brought together with a common goal, the hostility would break down. This theory was proven to be true when both groups were forced to cooperate on a camp project that involved fixing the food truck so that both groups could eat.

Why are these antique studies still worth describing? They were conducted in natural settings, the kinds of situations that almost every child experiences. They also tell us a lot about groups. As the experimenters predicted, the groups formed quickly, and status differentiation seemed to take place almost automatically. Group members found common values and had shared norms; they even named their groups. Most important, when groups were put into competition against each other, feelings of exclusivity and hostility quickly developed. When the groups were required to cooperate, hostility was reduced. These findings are typical of the way in which groups form and compete in classrooms, in athletic competitions, and in neighborhood or ethnic rivalries.

STATUS WITHIN THE PEER GROUP   If we watch schoolchildren at lunchtime or at recess, we can observe the "natural selection" of roles that takes place in every group. One girl is surrounded by children eager to get her attention. Another, ignored, stands on the fringes of the group. Three boys run by, shouting. A muscular child grabs a smaller child's toy, and the smaller one cries. This kind of scene occurs all over the world, wherever there are children.

Each peer group has some members who are popular and others who are not. Several factors seem to contribute to this difference in social status; we have already discussed some of these factors in Chapter 10. Peer acceptance is often related to an individual's good overall adjustment—enthusiasm and active participation, ability to cooperate with others, and responsiveness to social overtures. This kind of attunement (or lack of it) tends to reinforce itself in a circular pattern, due to its effects on self-esteem and social self-confidence. The good adjustment of well-liked children is bolstered by their popularity; inept children become even more ill at ease when they are ignored or rejected by the group (Glidewell et al., 1966).

Academic performance and athletic ability also influence popularity. In general, popular children are brighter than average and do well in school. Slow learners are often made fun of or are ignored. Athletic ability is particularly important in settings like camps or playgrounds, where the whole group is involved in sports.

Popularity is affected both by extreme aggressiveness and extreme timidity. No one likes a bully, so the overly aggressive child is shunned. This leads to another kind of circular pattern because this child may become even more aggressive out of frustration or in an attempt to win by force what he or she cannot win by persuasion. As for the timid, anxious child, he or she is at risk of becoming a chronic victim, picked on not just by bullies but even by average children (Dodge et al., 1990; Perry et al., 1990).

Unpopular children often have some trait that makes them different from their classmates—obesity, skin of the "wrong" color, or even an unusual name (see Focus on Research: Nicknames). These traits can reduce children's level of conformity to group standards—and conformity, as we have seen, is very important during middle childhood. How insistent is the pressure to conform to group standards, and who are the children most influenced by these pressures?

PEER GROUP CONFORMITY   Conforming to the peer group can be a normal, healthy, and often desirable behavior. As part of their daily behavior, children conform to peer group standards as well as to adult expectations. But children

Conformity within a peer group is normal and often desirable behavior.

sometimes conform excessively to group norms, even when these standards are not helpful to the individual child, to the group as a whole, or to outsiders.

Which children are most strongly influenced by group pressures? There are a few characteristics that appear to be common in high-conforming children. They have feelings of inferiority and low "ego strength" (Hartup, 1970a). They tend to be more dependent or anxious than other children and are exceptionally sensitive to social cues. Children who have these characteristics also tend to monitor their own behavior and verbal expressions very closely. They are especially concerned

FOCUS ON RESEARCH

NICKNAMES

Remember the good old days in grade school when you were called everything but the name your parents gave you? You may have been lucky enough to have borne the nickname "Chief" or "Coach" or "Ace," or unfortunate enough to be called "Dumbo" or "Four-Eyes" or even "Sewage." These labels may seem amusing to adults, but they are a serious matter to children. Recent research has shown that nicknames may teach children about social status, friendship, morality, and about the adult world itself.

To get to the bottom of the nickname puzzle, Rom Harré and his colleagues (1980) surveyed thousands of youngsters and adults in the United States, Great Britain, Spain, Mexico, Japan, and the Arab countries. What they found is that children between the ages of 5 and 15 often create separate and secret worlds for themselves and that nicknames may perform an important social function in these worlds.

One of the main reasons children bestow nicknames on one another is to separate "us" from "them." Children who have no nicknames are considered too unimportant to bother with. They tend to be low in popularity and to be isolated from the rest of the group. As Harré and his colleagues (1980) point out, "To be nicknamed is to be seen as having an attribute that entitles one to social attention, even if that attention is unpleasant. Thus, it may be better to be called 'Sewage' than merely John" (p. 81).

The "Fatties" and "Lamebrains" of the group are used as examples by group leaders to show how people are *not* supposed to be. They are walking advertisements of violated group standards. These group standards are the children's attempts to internalize society's norms. Through nicknames, children loudly proclaim what is acceptable to society and what is not. Any behavior, style, or physical characteristic that does not meet society's standards can become the source of a nickname. Thus, when children call others "Stinky," "Pimples," or "Eagle Nose," they are trying to internalize the accepted adult norms for cleanliness and appearance.

Unfortunately, for the recipients of these nicknames, the process can be very painful. However, as the researchers found, these children are often willing victims: "It is not necessarily the fattest, stupidest, and dirtiest who acquire the names 'Hippo' or 'Tapeworm-Woman,' but those who willingly bear the humiliation of being symbols of childhood greed, improvidence, and aversion to washing" (Harré, 1980, p. 81).

Nicknames also express children's own sense of "class" consciousness, social separateness, and hidden knowledge. Nicknames that are understood by only a small circle of friends make outsiders of those who do not know their meaning. In some cases, nicknames communicate secret information that may be unknown to the children who actually bear the names. In one school, for example, the boys labeled the sexually available girls "Dragoon One," "Dragoon Two," and so on, even though the girls had no idea what these names meant.

Children use nicknames differently in various cultures. Nicknames like "The Lame One" or "The Three-Legged One," which poke fun at physical deformities, are much more common in Arab countries than in England or Japan. The Japanese are more likely to use animal and insect analogies. In any culture, it seems that nicknames help children to build the social reality they take with them into adulthood.

What's in a name? In the case of nicknames, there is a lot more than you might expect.

with how they appear to others and are constantly comparing themselves to their peers. Watching what others do or say and then adapting to the group norm is common to self-monitoring children (Graziano et al., 1987).

Peer pressure can be positive as well as negative: For example, a child who belongs to a group of high academic achievers might feel pressured to complete homework assignments. In fact, children are more likely to conform to peer pressure when it is positive than when it involves antisocial acts, such as drinking, smoking, or stealing. When peer pressure actually involves antisocial acts, boys are more likely than are girls to yield to it (Brown et al., 1986). Children who are unsupervised after school also tend to conform to antisocial peer pressure more than those who are monitored by adults (Steinberg, 1986).

Conformity is especially important to children during late middle childhood, when they are moving away from the security of family life. Preadolescents have a strong need to belong, to feel accepted, and to feel that they are part of a social setting larger than themselves. These needs coexist with an equally strong need for autonomy or mastery. Children try to exert some control over their social and physical environments, to understand the rules and limits, and to find a place within these limits. For this reason, they become very involved in making rules and learning rituals.

At several points in human development, this coexistence of autonomy and acceptance needs is important. It is especially critical for 1½-year-olds, who are just beginning to learn what they can do for themselves. During late middle childhood, these two opposing needs again become paramount. But the balance that the preadolescent works out is different from that of the toddler. For the older child, the peer group often satisfies both the need for acceptance and the need for autonomy.

Prejudice

What happens to children as they move away from their families during middle childhood and find that the norms of the broader culture differ from those at home? Children have this experience when they learn, for example, that their friends do not like spinach or do not go to church. The difference in attitudes, however, can lead to problems for minority group children, as they must reconcile their own self-image with the unpleasant stereotypes and prejudices that they encounter. This can affect their behavior, their school achievement, and their relationships with others. As we saw in our discussion of the "self-fulfilling prophecy" (Chapter 11), people tend to live up (or down) to the expectations of others (Howard & Hammond, 1985).

Prejudice means a negative attitude directed toward people because of their membership in a group, with the group being targeted on the basis of race, religion, national origin, language, or any other noticeable attribute. We tend to think of prejudice as an adult attitude, but racial awareness begins to develop early, during the preschool years. Just as a child learns that she is a girl or that he is a boy (see Chapter 10), a black child learns that he or she has darker skin than some of the other children seen on television or in the neighborhood. Also, just as the little girl learns that her body differs from that of a boy before she understands what it means to be female in our society, a black child learns about the differences in skin and hair before she understands what it means to be an African-American. Thus, a black child must learn, first, that she is different in appearance from white

prejudice A negative attitude formed without adequate reason and usually directed toward people because of their membership in a group.

children; and second, she must learn that these differences may make her unwelcome or may be held against her. What the child does not understand is *why* being a member of this group results in social discrimination. Her efforts to answer this question could be a life-long task (Spencer, 1988).

The understanding of group differences and of what it means to be a member of a group is an aspect of social cognition. Social cognition, in turn, depends on overall cognitive development. Thus, a child whose thought is still egocentric and who can focus on only one dimension at a time will assume that people who are similar in one dimension (for instance, skin color) must be similar in other dimensions as well. As children get older, they become better at seeing people as multidimensional. In an experiment with English-speaking and French-speaking Canadian children, it was found that older children had more flexible attitudes about members of the other language-speaking group. Children who had entered the period of concrete operations were less likely to attribute negative characteristics to the members of the other group than were those subjects who were still in the preoperational period (Doyle, Beaudet, & Aboud, 1988).

This progress is opposed by the strong tendency of older school-age children to conform to group standards and to reject those who are different from them in any way. A study done in a California town where the schools were about 50% black and 50% white found that children in the older grades were less likely than were younger children to have a friend of a different race. In fact, interracial friendships declined steadily from the fourth grade through the seventh. The researchers concluded that, as children grow older, similarity becomes a more and more important basis for friendship. There may also be a fair amount of pressure from other members of a child's group to avoid forming friendships with members of the other group (Hallinan & Teixeira, 1987). This pressure can come from either side. Black children who become friendly with white children may be pressured to give up such friendships because they are being "disloyal" to their race (Schofield, 1981). This kind of exclusivity is not necessarily prejudice. Being aware of differences is not the same as holding negative stereotypes, although the two often go together.

Racial awareness is an important issue for children during middle childhood because it is the time when a child "does or does not 'sign a contract' with society" (Comer & Poussaint, 1975, p. 116). Children absorb the cultural attitudes of those around them. In return for "swearing allegiance" to the standards of society, children must get from society a sense of belonging to a larger, more powerful group. But black parents have had to accommodate themselves to a majority culture that does not reward them as it does whites. Black parents are expected to teach their children the values of a society that holds them in low esteem. Black children naturally sense this conflict, and it affects their attitudes toward society.

Peer pressures aggravate the conflict. Minority peer groups often have norms that differ widely from those of white, middle-class peer groups. A black child growing up in an urban ghetto belongs to a culture different from that of most middle-class whites. The degree of acceptance that black children find in the larger society often depends upon their ability to conform to its norms. When minority children get together with other members of their racial or ethnic group, this makes their adjustment easier during middle childhood. It tends to improve their self-esteem and to increase both in-group solidarity and out-group hostility. But minority children eventually face the problem of integrating their own self-concept with society's image of them as members of a specific group, and this can cause conflict, anxiety, or anger at any age.

SELF-IMAGE AND SELF-ESTEEM

As children grow older, their developing social cognition enables them to form a more accurate and complex picture of the physical, intellectual, and personality characteristics of other people. At the same time, they are able to form a more accurate and complex picture of their *own* characteristics. They compare themselves with their age-mates, and they conclude, "I'm better than Chris at sports, but I'm not as good in math as Kerry," or "I may not be as pretty as Courtney, but I'm better at making friends." During the school years, children learn to assess their own capabilities more and more accurately (Harter, 1982).

Self-image means seeing oneself as an individual with certain characteristics. **Self-esteem** means seeing oneself as an individual with *positive* characteristics—as a person who will do well in the things that he or she thinks are important. During the school years, self-esteem is significantly correlated with academic self-confidence (which, in turn, is significantly correlated with academic achievement). The children who do well in school have higher self-esteem than those who do poorly (Alpert-Gillis & Connell, 1989). In view of the important part that school plays in a child's life, this is not surprising.

The correlation between self-esteem and academic self-confidence, however, is far from being a perfect one: Many children who do not do well in school nonetheless manage to develop high self-esteem. Depending on how their parents have treated them and what their friends think of them, children who are not good in one thing can find something else that they *are* good at. Additionally, if they come from a cultural background that says "school is not important," their self-esteem may not be related at all to their academic achievement. How well one is thought of by one's parents and by one's peer group is far more important than how well one does in the eyes of the larger society. This is why black children, despite their daily encounters with racial prejudice, generally manage to develop healthy levels of self-esteem (Spencer, 1988).

The development of self-esteem is a circular process. Children tend to do well if they are confident in their own abilities; their success leads to further increases in self-esteem. On the other side of this coin are the children who do poorly because they lack self-esteem (perhaps due to the kinds of psychological abuse described earlier in this chapter) and whose self-esteem therefore continues to fall. Personal successes or failures in different situations can lead children to see themselves as leaders or losers, as champions or chumps. Fortunately, these experiences do not automatically create a closed circle, and many children who start off with social or academic handicaps eventually find something that they can do well.

self-image Seeing oneself as an individual with certain characteristics.

self-esteem Seeing oneself as an individual with positive characteristics—as one who will do well in the things that he or she thinks are important.

STUDY OUTLINE

Children's social play demonstrates a "culture of childhood" that is composed of customs, rules, games, rituals, and distinctive beliefs and values. Their games and rituals help children understand and adapt to a complex social world.

Continuing Family Influences

Styles of Parenting. Parents have an important influence on children's personality and social development. They serve as models, and they reward and punish children's behavior.

Ideally, parents balance two parenting dimensions: control and warmth. Control is restriction of freedom and active enforcement of rules. Warmth is the amount of affection that parents give.

Four parenting styles are **authoritative** (high control, high warmth), **authoritarian** (high control, low warmth), **permissive** (low control, high warmth), and **indifferent** (low control, low warmth). The children of authoritative parents are the most self-reliant and well-adjusted. The worst outcome is found in children of indifferent parents.

Maccoby found that families with shared goals have less conflict; there is a healthy balance of control, with neither parents nor children dominating the situation.

The Changing Nature of the Family. Due to divorce and single parenthood, today many children are reared in mother-headed homes. A high proportion of these children are living in poverty; they are at risk of a multitude of deprivations. The women who head these homes may be psychologically distressed and unable to provide supportive parenting.

Children who can handle a single source of stress may not be able to handle multiple stresses. Factors that help a child to withstand stress are knowing what to expect, having a supportive and adaptable family, and having a **resilient** personality.

Children of Divorce. Divorce affects children in many ways. They may feel guilty, sad, angry, or anxious. Their relationships with their parents are altered, and they must learn to adjust to their parents' new lifestyles or to stepparents. A child's adjustment to divorce is influenced by the amount of hostility that precedes the divorce, the amount of actual change in the child's life, and the nature of the parent–child relationship.

Child Abuse. **Child abuse** is the intentional inflicting of physical or psychological injury. Many abusive parents were themselves abused as children. People who have experienced abuse in childhood are more likely to suffer from psychological problems.

There are three main explanations of child abuse: psychiatric, sociological, and situational. Although all three offer insights into this problem, none has clearly established its cause or found a reliable solution for it.

Psychological abuse of children includes *rejection, denial of emotional responsiveness, degradation, terrorization, isolation,* and *exploitation.* Sexual abuse is the clearest case of exploitation.

Social Knowledge

The Development of Social Cognition. Middle childhood brings advances in **social cognition**—thought, knowledge, and understanding that involve the social world. One aspect of social cognition is **social inference**—guesses and assumptions about what another person is feeling, thinking, or intending. Other components are the child's understanding of **social relationships** and comprehension of **social regulations.**

Moral Judgment. Another area of social cognition is **moral judgment**—the process of making decisions about right and wrong. Cognitive theorists such as Piaget and Kohlberg believe that children's moral sense develops in stages. According to Piaget, children begin as **moral realists** who believe in the physical reality of rules and who judge actions solely in terms of their consequences. Later, children reach the stage of **moral relativism,** in which they realize that rules are human inventions and that individuals' intentions determine the morality of their behavior.

Kohlberg describes three broad levels of moral development, which are divided into six stages. The first level, preconventional, is based on punishments and rewards; the second, conventional, is based on social conformity; and the third, postconventional, is based on moral principles. Kohl-

berg's theory has been criticized on the grounds of **moral absolutism**—it ignores cultural differences. Gilligan accuses Kohlberg of sex bias: She says that boys are justice oriented, but girls are caring oriented.

Peer Relationships and Social Competence

Concepts of Friendship. Selman has studied how childhood friendships are formed and maintained and how ideas of loyalty and trust develop. He describes four stages. In the first stage (under age 7), children's friendships are self-centered and based on convenience. In the second stage (ages 7 to 9), children become aware of one another's subjective feelings; ideas of reciprocity begin to form. In the third stage (ages 8 to 12), children evaluate each other's actions; the idea of trust enters for the first time. In the fourth stage (after age 12), children see friendships as stable, continuing relationships that are based on trust.

Functions of Friendship. Friendships in middle childhood are often close but may be short-lived. In the context of friendships, children learn social concepts and social skills, and they develop self-esteem. Children who are friends may satisfy different needs in each other, such as dominance versus submissiveness. Self-revelation is more common in girls' friendships than it is in boys'.

The Peer Group. In late childhood and adolescence, group friendships become common. These **peer groups** are relatively stable; their members share common norms and values. As children get older, peer groups become more formal and are strictly divided according to sex. Group conformity becomes very important. Peer groups spontaneously organize into hierarchies. When these groups compete, their members develop feelings of in-group exclusivity and of hostility toward the opposing group.

Children's status within the peer group is related to their overall adjustment. Enthusiastic, cooperative, responsive children tend to be most popular. Intelligence, school achievement, and athletic ability also count in a child's favor. A child who is different in any way may be unpopular. A child's popularity affects his or her self-esteem.

Conformity to the peer group can have positive aspects as well as negative ones. Those who are most strongly influenced by group pressures are anxious children with low self-esteem and those who monitor themselves very closely. Conformity is especially important to children during late middle childhood.

Prejudice. Racial awareness develops early, though gaining a full understanding of what it means to be a member of a minority group may be a lifelong task. As children get older, their attitudes toward people from other groups tend to get less rigid; however, older children also have a greater tendency to form friendships on the basis of similarity.

Self-Image and Self-Esteem

Most children, including members of minority groups, develop a good sense of **self-esteem** if their parents and peers think well of them. A child who is not good at one thing can usually find something he or she is good at.

KEY TERMS AND CONCEPTS

authoritarian parents	moral relativism	self-esteem
authoritative parents	parental control	self-image
child abuse	parental warmth	shared goals
indifferent parents	peer group	social cognition
moral absolutism	permissive parents	social inference
moral judgment	prejudice	social regulations
moral realism	resilient children	social relationships

SELF-TEST QUESTIONS

1. Discuss Becker's model of parenting styles. What are the three key dimensions of parental behavior and how do they affect a child's behavior and developing self-concept?

2. List Baumrind's three distinct patterns of parental authority and their corresponding impact on the developing child.

3. What are shared goals, and how do they contribute to a stable family atmosphere?

4. List several factors that affect children's ability to cope with stressful events.

5. What are the factors that influence the way a child responds to divorce?

6. Discuss three different explanations for child abuse.

7. List different forms of psychological abuse.

8. Explain social cognition and its significance for middle childhood. Include in your discussion three important components of social knowledge.

9. Describe the sequence of the development of social cognition during middle childhood.

10. Explain Kohlberg's cognitive theory of moral development and describe its connection to Piaget's theory of development.

11. List some criticisms of Kohlberg's model.

12. Discuss Gilligan's two methods of moral reasoning.

13. Describe the importance of friendship pairs during middle childhood.

14. Discuss developmental trends in peer groups.

15. Describe some characteristics of peer group formation.

16. List two factors that contribute to status development within a peer group.

17. Discuss some of the problems children must face as a result of racial and ethnic prejudices. Why is racial awareness a particularly important issue for children in middle childhood?

18. Describe the relationship between a child's self-image and his or her developing social competence.

SUGGESTED READINGS

COLES, R. *The moral life of children*. Boston: Houghton Mifflin Company, 1986. Children tell a sensitive interviewer of the moral challenges that they face in their complex lives as a result of poverty, prejudice, war, family disputes, and the like.

DUNN, J. *Sisters and brothers*. Cambridge, MA: Harvard University Press, 1985. In a challenging review of the literature, Dunn examines the intensity of the sibling relationship as it develops through childhood and into adulthood.

FURTH, H. *The world of grown-ups*. New York: Elsevier, 1980. A descriptive study of children's thinking about various aspects of society.

GILLIGAN, C. *In a different voice: Psychological theory and women's development*. Cambridge, MA: Harvard University Press, 1982.

HELFER, R. E., & KEMPE, R. S. (EDS.). *The battered child* (4th edition). Chicago: University of Chicago Press, 1987. One of the standard references on child abuse, now thoroughly revised and expanded.

KOZOL, J. *Rachel and her children: Homeless families in America*. New York: Crown Publishers, 1988. A highly readable documentary of life on the edge of society.

RUBIN, Z. *Children's friendships*. Cambridge, MA: Harvard University Press, 1980. A delightful book that explores the roles and effects of friendships on children.

Chapter 13

*To grown people a girl of fifteen and a half
is a child still; to herself she is very old
and very real; more real, perhaps, than ever
before or after. . . .*

MARGARET WIDDERMER
"THE CHANGELING,"
THE BOARDWALK

CHAPTER OUTLINE

Adolescence: A Period of Transition

1 n our culture, adolescence stretches over the better part of a decade. This prolonged transitional period from childhood to adulthood is a modern phenomenon. In "primitive" societies, the period of change is more condensed. In such societies, the young person goes through a symbolic ceremony, name change, or challenge at puberty. These symbolic events are referred to by anthropologists as **rites of passage,** or "transition rituals." An apprenticeship of a year or two follows, and, by age 16 or 17, the young person achieves full, unqualified adulthood. This rapid transformation is partly due to the fact that the skills needed for adult life in less complex cultures can be mastered without lengthy education. Still, the need for some period of transition is recognized by all; no society demands that a child turn into an adult overnight.

In previous centuries, the physical maturation of puberty occurred later than it does today. In the United States today, a girl has her first menstrual period at an average age of 12½; in the 1880s, the average age was 15½ (Frisch, 1988). When puberty occurred at 15 or 16, the social transition from youth to adult followed closely on the heels of physical change. Now, in the United States and in other industrialized countries, there is an interval of several years between attaining biological maturity and making the social transition to adulthood. Thus, young people who are mature in a physical sense are nonetheless considered too young for the privileges and responsibilities of full adulthood.

In a technologically advanced society where complex jobs go to adults, adolescents experience prolonged dependence. In most cases, the jobs that are available to them are neither intrinsically interesting nor financially rewarding. This situation prolongs adolescents' dependence on their parents, delays the time when they can fully utilize their capabilities, and increases their frustration and restlessness. Some theorists view the period of adolescence as a time of restricted rights and opportunities and rigidly proscribed roles (Farber, 1970). Others take a more positive view, seeing adolescence as a time when the individual is allowed to explore and to experiment with various roles before settling into a social and occupational niche.

Clearly, the social and personal experiences of adolescents are a function of the historical and cultural context in which they live.

CHAPTER OBJECTIVES

By the time you have finished this chapter, you should be able to do the following:

■ Include cultural and historical factors as part of a discussion of adolescent development.

■ Discuss physical maturation during adolescence and describe the way in which cultural ideals influence an adolescent's adjustment to these changes.

■ Discuss the factors that influence an adolescent's emerging sexuality and gender identity.

■ Describe the cognitive changes that occur during adolescence and explain how these changes affect the scope and content of adolescent thought.

rite of passage A symbolic event or ritual to mark life transitions, such as the one from childhood to adult status.

DEVELOPMENT IN A CULTURAL AND HISTORICAL CONTEXT

Although there are patterns in human development that are common to all societies and to all eras, the process of development is always deeply affected by the social and economic forces of the times. This is especially true of adolescence, when the individual tries to come to terms with social pressures and to strike a balance between internal and external values.

Adolescents are highly sensitive to the society around them—its values, its political and economic tensions, its unwritten rules. They are in the process of forming plans and expectations about their own future, and these expectations will depend in part on the cultural and historical setting in which they live. For example, adolescents who spent their earlier years in a period of economic expansion, when jobs were easy to get and family incomes were increasing, tend to expect similar conditions when they enter the job market. They expect their standard of living to be at least as good as that of their parents. They may be unprepared if the economic conditions that prevailed during their childhood worsen around the time that they enter adulthood (Greene, 1990).

Economic and cultural conditions can also have an impact on the timing of the milestones of growing up. Adolescence may be a brutally short prelude to independence, or it may involve prolonged dependence on the family. In 19th-century Ireland, for example, potato famines caused widespread poverty and suffering. Young men stayed at home because their labor was needed to keep the families alive. Their growth to adult independence was stunted by terrible economic need. In the United States, the Great Depression of the 1930s altered the plans and conferred unexpected responsibilities on young people coming of age during this period. There was a tendency for young people to grow up as quickly as possible: They took on adult tasks and entered the job market sooner than they might have otherwise.

Elder (1980) compared developmental patterns of contemporary teenagers with those of adolescents living in the late 19th century. Five different life events were measured: completion of education, entry into the job market, separation from parental household, first marriage, and establishment of a new household. Elder found both differences and similarities between the two groups. Although both experienced the same life events, the timing of the events varied. Nineteenth-century adolescents left school earlier and had less formal education. They were quicker to enter the job market but slower to leave the family household, to get married, and to establish their own homes. Although today's young people spend more time in school, they break away from their parents sooner. Nineteenth-century adolescents made a rapid transition to adult occupational status as workers, but they took more time to achieve social independence. Interestingly, neither group experienced the period of youth as a clearly ordered sequence in which everyone left childhood and entered adulthood at approximately the same age.

Cultural and historical factors can be a source of psychological stress during adolescence. The 1960s were an especially difficult era for young people because they lived in a world characterized by ideological ferment and by the constant threat of nuclear annihilation. In earlier times, adolescents could look to adults and to a body of tradition for answers to many of their questions. When the youth of the 1960s looked to authority figures, they found uncertainty, conflicting values, and a vivid sense of the breakdown of social order.

Development in adolescence depends to a great extent on the society and on the particular political and economic tensions of the times.

Keniston (1975) saw the problems of adolescents as arising from a "tension between self and society"—a lack of fit between who they feel they are and what they feel society wants them to be. According to Keniston, adolescents feel ambivalent not only toward the social order but also toward themselves. They may realize how deeply they have been influenced by the surrounding culture and may feel uncomfortable with this realization. They may feel that society is too rigid and confining, and they may try to break away from it by assuming temporary identities and roles. They may attempt to redefine and transform themselves through introspection, the use of drugs, meditation, or psychoanalysis.

Adolescence in Contemporary Western Society

In our society, adolescents experience a phenomenon called *age segregation*. Partly because of choices they make and partly due to circumstances over which they have no control, adolescents tend to remain apart both from younger children and from adults. Their separation from younger children deprives them of opportunities to guide and tutor those who are less knowledgeable than themselves. Their separation from the adult world means that they rarely have the opportunity to serve apprenticeships—to learn jobs by working alongside experienced people in responsible positions. Instead, adolescents are separated for many hours every day from the major activities, customs, and responsibilities of the rest of society. Of course, age segregation is not total: Adolescents interact with younger children by babysitting, caring for younger siblings, or working as camp counselors. They also help parents with household chores and may hold after-school jobs that, if nothing else, teach them something about the world of work and commerce.

GLOBAL CRISES   Every historical age has had its wars, religious movements, and economic ups and downs, and today is no exception. Although the current period may be less explosive than previous ones, people continue to be distressed by crises at home, in the Middle East, Asia, Eastern Europe, and Africa. Adolescents are—and always have been—particularly vulnerable and susceptible to such crises. In general, the state of the world affects adolescents much more than it does younger children. After all, it is primarily adolescents and young adults who fight in wars, participate in riots, and sustain movements for social reform. It is primarily adolescents and young adults who support radical political and religious movements with their idealism, who lose their jobs during economic downturns, and who are hired during economic booms. The effects of events in the broader society are screened from young children by their families and local communities. These children feel the impact of economic recessions or wars only in a second-hand way, perhaps through their parents' unemployment or long-term absence. But many events of the time have a direct impact on adolescents, who must confront, absorb, and react to them. Other events have an indirect effect, through the mass media.

A MASS MEDIA SOCIETY   The mass media provide a flood of information and sensations—blending trivial advertising, sensationalized drama, and pressing world issues. Most advertising is meant to sell, not to inform. Television news programs are, to a large extent, a form of entertainment. It is hard even for adult

hormone A biochemical secretion of the endocrine gland that is carried by the blood or other body fluids to a particular organ or tissue and acts as a stimulant or an accelerator.

viewers to know what to believe. There is little opportunity for critical analysis of the information or interpretations that are presented.

Most theories of human development emphasize the importance of having an emotionally supportive and responsive environment to promote learning. Individuals of any age learn best when they can act on their environment, perceive the consequences of their actions, and have some power to effect change. But there is no way to alter the events on television, radio, or the movie screen. Some critics suggest that teenagers, with their rapidly developing physical and cognitive capacities, are particularly vulnerable to the passive role of consumer of the mass media. Perhaps they learn casual acceptance of tragedy or brutality or they develop a thirst for excessive raw stimulation. Perhaps they model their behavior on the trite or bizarre events they see portrayed in movies or on television. We still know very little about the complex effects of becoming an adult in a mass media society.

In this chapter, we shall examine some major aspects of adolescence: physical maturation, sexual behavior, cognitive changes, and moral development.

PHYSICAL MATURATION

Physiologically, adolescence ranks with the fetal period and the first 2 years of life for sheer rate of biological change. Unlike infants, however, adolescents have the pain and pleasure of observing the whole process; they watch themselves with alternating feelings of fascination, delight, and horror as the biological changes occur. Surprised, embarrassed, and uncertain, adolescents constantly compare themselves with others and continually revise their self-image. Both sexes anxiously monitor their development, or lack of it, with knowledge and misinformation, pride and fear, hope and trepidation. Always, there is comparison with the prevailing ideal; trying to reconcile differences between the real and the ideal is one of the problems that adolescents experience during this period of transformation.

Biological Changes

The biological hallmarks of adolescence are a marked increase in the rate of growth, rapid development of the reproductive organs, and the appearance of secondary sex characteristics. Some changes occur in both boys and girls—increased size, improved strength and stamina—but most of them are sex specific.

The physical changes are controlled by **hormones,** which are biochemical substances secreted in very small amounts by the endocrine glands. The hormones affecting adolescent growth are present in trace amounts from fetal life on, but their output is greatly increased during puberty. "Male" hormones and "female" hormones are present in members of both sexes, but males have more of the hormones called *androgens,* the most important of which is *testosterone,* and females have more of the hormones called *estrogen* and *progesterone* (Tanner, 1978).

Each hormone influences a certain set of targets or receptors. For example, the secretion of testosterone causes the penis to grow, the shoulders to broaden, and hair to grow in the genital area and on the face. Similarly, estrogen causes the uterus and the breasts to grow and the hips to broaden. The cells in the target area have the ability to respond selectively to some of the hormones circulating in the bloodstream and not to respond to others: The uterus, for example, selectively responds to estrogen and progesterone. Targeted cells are exquisitely sensitive to minute quantities of the appropriate hormones, even though the hormones are present in such small amounts that it is like detecting a pinch of sugar dissolved in a swimming pool (Tanner, 1978).

The endocrine glands secrete a delicate and complex balance of hormones, the maintenance of which is the job of the pituitary gland. The pituitary, which is sometimes called the master gland, is located on the underside of the brain. This gland produces several varieties of hormones, including growth hormone and some secondary hormones. The secondary hormones stimulate and regulate the functioning of a number of other glands, including the sex glands—the testes in the male and the ovaries in the female. The sex glands have two jobs: to produce sperm or eggs and to secrete androgens or estrogens. The hormones secreted by the pituitary gland and by the sex glands have emotional as well as physical effects upon adolescents.

The changes of puberty are usually preceded by an increase in body fat; some preadolescents become noticeably pudgy at this time. This is followed, in late childhood or early adolescence, by a prominent increase in height. Growth of this magnitude has not occurred since infancy and toddlerhood. Both bones and muscles increase in size, triggered by the same set of hormones. In the course of this growth spurt, boys generally lose most of the extra fat that they acquired at its beginning. Girls, however, tend to keep most of the fat that they have acquired, although it ends up being distributed in different places.

The onset of puberty requires considerable adaptation, whether to a crackly voice, longer legs, or new interests and feelings.

During early adolescence, different parts of the body develop at varying rates. The head has pretty much stopped growing by now, having accomplished most of its development in the first 10 years of life. Next to reach adult size are the hands and feet; then there is an increase in leg and arm length. The gangly physique that often results at this time may make adolescents feel awkward. The growth of the extremities is followed by growth in body width, with full development of the shoulders coming last.

Another change is the increase in size and activity of sebaceous (oil-producing) glands in the skin, which causes the teenager's face to break out in acne. A new kind of sweat gland also develops in the skin, causing a stronger body odor.

The sexes develop at different rates. On the average, girls experience the growth spurt and the other biological changes of puberty about 2 years before boys do (see Figure 13–1). However, there is a great deal of variation in the rate of development among members of the same sex. A late-maturing boy or girl may still look like a child, whereas another boy or girl of the same chronological age will have the appearance of a full-grown man or woman. In contrast, once the sequence of sexual maturation has begun, it progresses in a fairly predictable order. Keeping in mind the wide individual differences in timing, let us look at the general schedule of physical changes that characterize adolescence.

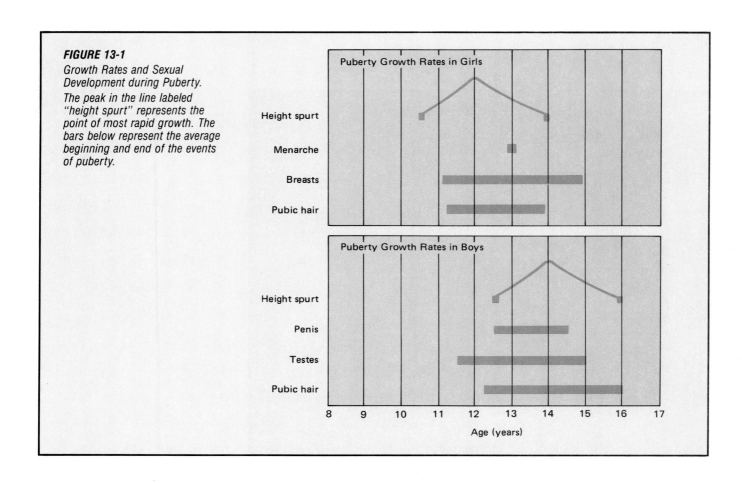

FIGURE 13-1
Growth Rates and Sexual Development during Puberty.
The peak in the line labeled "height spurt" represents the point of most rapid growth. The bars below represent the average beginning and end of the events of puberty.

SEXUAL MATURATION IN MALES   After the growth spurt, the second major biological change is development of the reproductive system. In males, the first indication of puberty is the accelerating growth of the testes and scrotum. Approximately 1 year after this has begun, the penis undergoes a similar spurt in growth. In between these two events, pubic hair begins to appear, but it does not attain full growth until after the completion of genital development. During this period, there are also increases in the size of the heart and lungs. Due to the action of the male sex hormone, testosterone, boys also develop more red blood cells than girls do. This extensive production of red blood cells may be one factor — although certainly not the only one — in the superior athletic ability of the male adolescent over the female.

The first seminal emission may take place as early as age 11 or as late as age 16. The initial ejaculation usually occurs during a boy's rapid period of growth and may come about during masturbation or in a "wet dream." These first emissions generally do not have enough semen to be fertile (Money, 1980).

Any unflattering description of the adolescent boy invariably includes his awkwardly cracking voice. However, the actual voice change takes place relatively late in the sequence of pubertal changes, and in many boys, it occurs too gradually to be significant as a developmental milestone (Tanner, 1978).

SEXUAL MATURATION IN FEMALES   In girls, the "breast buds" are usually, but not always, the first signal that puberty has begun. There is simultaneous development of the uterus and vagina, with enlargement of the labia and clitoris.

Menarche (the first menstruation), which is probably the most dramatic and symbolic sign of a girl's changing status, actually occurs late in the sequence, after the peak of the growth spurt. Menarche may occur as early as age 9½ or as late as age 16½; the average for American girls is about 12½. As we said, previous generations of Americans matured more slowly than girls do today. The acceleration in sexual development is apparently due to improved nutrition and health care. In other parts of the world, menarche still occurs considerably later: The average Czechoslovakian girl has her first period at age 14, among the Kikuyu of Kenya the average age is 16, and for the Bindi of New Guinea it is 18 (Powers et al., 1989). Menarche generally occurs when a girl has nearly reached her adult height and when she has managed to store a minimum amount of body fat. For a girl of average height, this landmark generally occurs when she weighs around 100 pounds (Frisch, 1988).

The first few menstrual cycles vary tremendously from one girl to another; they also tend to vary from one month to another. In many cases, the early cycles are irregular and anovulatory — an egg is not produced (Tanner, 1978). But it is unwise for a young teenage girl to count on her infertility, as many pregnant 13-year-olds can attest. (We will return to the subject of teenage pregnancies later in this chapter.)

Body Image and Adjustment

Young adolescents are frequently fascinated with, and continually appraising, their bodies. Are they the right shape, the right size? Are they coordinated or clumsy? How do they compare with the ideal? Sociologists consider adolescents to be a "marginal group," either between cultures or on the fringe of a dominant

---

menarche The time of the first menstrual period.

culture. Typically, such groups tend to exhibit an intensified need for conformity. For this reason, adolescents can be extremely intolerant of deviation, whether it be a deviation in body type, such as being too fat or too thin, or a deviation in timing, like being a late bloomer. The mass media manipulate this tendency by marketing stereotyped images of attractive, exuberant youths who glide through adolescence without pimples, braces, or awkwardness. Because adolescents are often extremely sensitive about their own physical appearance and spend a lot of time scrutinizing themselves and their friends, the discrepancies between their less-than-perfect self-images and the glossy ideals they see in magazines and on television are often a source of considerable anxiety.

During middle childhood, children become aware of different body types and ideals, and they gain a fairly clear idea of their own body type, proportions, and

FOCUS ON AN ISSUE

ANOREXIA AND BULIMIA

Anorexia Nervosa   Sufferers of anorexia nervosa literally starve themselves to death. Obsessed by thoughts of food and an unattainable image of "perfect" thinness, they refuse to eat. Even though they may feel that they are becoming increasingly attractive, they actually become emaciated and physically ill. In the United States, where there are now more than 100,000 anorexics (10 times as many as there were a decade ago), 10,000 to 15,000 will die because of the medical problems related to their lack of food.

Almost all anorexics are women under the age of 25. Although there is no one cause, many anorexics are victims of our society's weight obsession. Hearing the message repeated over and over again that thin is beautiful and fat is repugnant, they fear that the curves and added weight that come along with adolescence will make them undesirable and unattractive. Family pressures to remain thin or to be attractive may make matters worse. A father who teasingly tells his daughter that she is putting on a few extra pounds around the waist may increase his daughter's negative self-concept.

Many experts believe that puberty and its accompanying body changes and sexual drives may trigger the symptoms of anorexia nervosa in some of its victims. Fearing womanhood, the anorexic stops eating, thereby putting a halt to her body's development. She loses her body curves and sexual desire and, when her body fat falls below approximately 17% of her total body weight, she stops menstruating.

Parents of anorexics are often amazed when the first symptoms of the disease appear. Up until then, their daughters are usually timid, reserved perfectionists who do everything their parents ask and who rarely show any signs of anger, selfishness, or normal rebellion. Instead of demanding attention, they may slip into the background of the family, perhaps allowing their siblings to receive the bulk of their parents' attention. Often considered "model" children, pre-anorexics willingly accept adult responsibilities, which they perform with uncomplaining efficiency. Unfortunately, these behaviors mask anorexics' neurotic feelings of worthlessness—feelings that are the precursors of a need "to diet away" their bodies.

Ironically, most anorexics are not fat when they begin to diet. They may be no more than 10 pounds overweight, but they see themselves as grossly fat and blame food for their problems. To rid themselves of their self-perceived excess poundage, they may eat smaller and smaller amounts of food, make themselves vomit after meals, take enormous quantities of diuretics and laxatives (some anorexics have reportedly taken up to 300 Ex-Lax tablets at a time), and exercise at a frantic pace. They may also turn eating into a ritual, requiring a specific arrangement of food on a specific plate. They lose their ability to see what they look like and may still consider themselves to be obese when they look like skeletons.

Anorexia nervosa has devastating effects on its sufferers and their families. Increasingly isolated in their own fantasies of thinness, most anorexics drop all social contact with their peers. Food becomes the center of their every thought, as you can see from the following skills. But in adolescence, body type receives much closer scrutiny. In our society, some young people subject themselves to intense dieting, whereas others embark on rigorous regimens of physical fitness and strength training—weight lifting, athletics, or dancing. In general, girls worry about being too fat or too tall, whereas boys are concerned about being too scrawny (not muscular enough) and too short. The reason weight is important to girls is that they are extremely concerned about social acceptance, and plumpness is frowned on in our society. There are many perfectly normal, even lean, adolescent girls who are medically healthy but who consider themselves obese and wish to lose weight (see Focus on an Issue: Anorexia and Bulimia). Yet, other cultures consider plumpness to be a feminine ideal and view thinness in women as unhealthy or indicative of poor family circumstances.

passage describing the behavior of an anorexic teenager:

> Every night she planned a menu for the next day and got up several times to repunch the calorie total on her calculator, fearful that it might have become larger. She weighed everything she ate, kneeling in front of the food scale in order to make sure its contents were absolutely level. Every morning at exactly 7 a.m. she weighed herself on both her mother's scale and on a doctor's scale . . . which registered weight in quarter-pound increments. . . . She drew up tables that listed the number of calories in every Weight Watchers frozen dinner, every flavor of Dannon, Colombo, and Sweet 'n Low yogurt, and every variety of Del Monte frozen vegetables. She kept a food diary in which she recorded everything she ate. (Fadiman, 1982, p. 74)

The parents of anorexics often worry that their children are going to die of their self-imposed starvation. Powerless to force their children to eat, they may resort to begging, crying, cajoling, and screaming. They also turn to the psychiatric community for help. Unfortunately, psychiatrists have not found a cure for anorexia nervosa. Indeed, there is no single accepted method of treatment. Some therapists take a behaviorist approach, rewarding their patients when food is eaten; others concentrate on analyzing childhood problems that they believe caused the disease; and still others focus on the patient's feelings about food and eating. The goal is to help anorexics learn to separate their feelings about food from their feelings about themselves and to develop in them a sense of self-worth and autonomy.

Bulimia   Bulimia is similar in many ways to anorexia nervosa, but it is a different ailment. The bulimic personality is also terribly anxious about weighing too much but has an uncontrollable need to eat, especially sweets. To compensate for overeating, bulimics make themselves vomit. Thus, bulimia is often described as a binge-and-purge pattern of eating.

As is the case with anorexia, most bulimics are female. Bulimia usually afflicts someone in late adolescence, whereas many anorexics are in early or mid-adolescence. Some researchers estimate that about 20% of college-age women have engaged in bulimic eating patterns (Muuss, 1986). Several psychologists believe that bulimia is so prevalent among college women that it might indicate difficulty in adjusting to life away from home. Others contend that bulimics binge on sweets in an attempt to alleviate depression.

Women suffering from bulimia consume huge quantities of carbohydrates in a very short time frame, usually an hour or two. They then feel despondent and out of control. Although bulimia does not have fatal consequences, it is nevertheless highly self-destructive and requires treatment. Fortunately, bulimics tend to be more responsive to treatment than anorexics are. The fact that antidepressant drugs are often useful in the treatment of this disorder—even among patients who show no signs of depression—suggests to some researchers that a biochemical abnormality may be involved (Walsh, 1988).

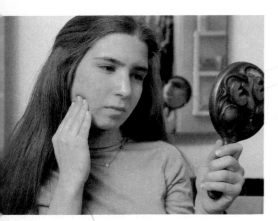

Young adolescents are often very critical of their bodies and can be very anxious if they do not conform to an ideal.

For boys, the primary concern is with physical power that can be exerted on the environment (Lerner et al., 1976). Therefore, height and muscles are important concerns of young males. There are some other interesting differences in the changes that are desired by the two sexes (Frazier & Lisonbee, 1950). Girls want very specific changes: "I would make my ears lie back," or "I would make my forehead lower." Boys do not articulate their dissatisfactions this precisely. A typical boy's response is: "I would make myself look handsome and not fat. I would have wavy black hair. I would change my whole physical appearance so that I would be handsome with a good build." Both sexes worry about their skin: Almost half of all adolescents voice concerns about pimples and blackheads.

Height, weight, and complexion are the major sources of concern for 10th graders. About two-thirds wish for one or more physical changes in themselves (Frazier & Lisonbee, 1950; Peterson & Taylor, 1980). Self-consciousness about one's body diminishes in late adolescence. As shown in a recent longitudinal study, body-image satisfaction is lowest for girls at age 13 and for boys at age 15; after these ages it goes up steadily. At every age from 11 to 18, however, it is lower for girls than it is for boys (Rauste-von Wright, 1989).

GIRLS' REACTIONS TO MENARCHE   Menarche is a unique event, a milestone on the path to physical maturity. It occurs suddenly and without warning and is heralded by a bloody vaginal discharge. In some parts of the world, it has major religious, cultural, or economic significance. It may trigger elaborate rites and ceremonies in some cultures, but in the United States, there is no such drama. Nevertheless, for the individual girl it holds considerable significance (Greif & Ulman, 1982).

A study of adolescent girls found menarche to be a memorable event. Only those who were ill prepared or who experienced menarche early described it as particularly traumatic or negative. Most often these were girls who had not discussed the onset of menstruation with their mothers or with other women. Some who had a negative experience had received their information from men. But most girls had been prepared by their mothers or female relatives for menstruation and reported a positive reaction to menarche—a feeling that they were coming of age (Ruble & Brooks-Gunn, 1982).

PARENTAL REACTIONS TO ADOLESCENT DEVELOPMENT   As adolescents develop physically, their relations with their parents undergo marked changes. Some of these changes result from the adolescent's striving for greater independence, which generally causes stress within the family, especially during the early stages of adolescence. Often, young people press against the limits previously established by their parents, while their parents grant increased autonomy only with reluctance and anxiety.

Parental anxiety over their maturing children is frequently compounded by other concerns as well. Just as adolescents are preoccupied with their appearance, parents also become concerned about the way they look as they are aging. Parents are reaching middle age, their hair is falling out or turning gray, their bodies are thickening, and their skin is getting wrinkled. They have less energy than they did when they were younger. But most of all, they are beginning to see that what used to be their future is now behind them. Middle-aged parents contrast their declining potential with the developing potential of their offspring and are unhappy with the contrast. Young people can look forward to the future with hope and optimism.

Their parents look back on their past and try to assess how much of their early hopes they have achieved, sometimes with a sense of disappointment (Hill, 1980; Steinberg, 1980, 1981).

EARLY AND LATE MATURERS   Timing in maturation—whether development is early or late—has engrossed researchers almost as much as adolescence itself. Ill-timed maturation is most likely to be a problem for the late-maturing boy. Because girls mature, on the average, 2 years earlier than boys do, the late-maturing boy is the last to reach puberty and is the last to experience the spurt in growth. Thus, he is smaller and less muscular than his age-mates, which puts him at a disadvantage in most sports. Other children and adults tend to treat a smaller child as though he were a younger child; therefore, the late maturer has lower social status among his peers and is perceived as being less competent by adults (Brackbill & Nevill, 1981). Sometimes, this perception becomes a self-fulfilling prophecy, and the boy reacts with childish dependency and immature behavior. In other cases, he may overcompensate and become very aggressive. At any rate, late-maturing boys have a far more difficult adjustment than early-maturing males, who tend to accrue all sorts of social and athletic advantages among their peers. From middle childhood on, early-maturing males are likely to be the leaders of their peer groups (Weisfeld & Billings, 1988).

There is great variation in the timing of maturation. Very early or late maturation will affect an adolescent's status in his or her peer group.

Longitudinal studies reveal interesting, continuing differences related to the onset of maturity. In their 30's, the early-maturing males still enjoy poise and social success. They tend to be responsible, cooperative, and self-controlled. In contrast to this, they may also be rigid, humorless, and unoriginal. The late maturers show a different pattern. They still show signs of immaturity and overcompensation by being impulsive and assertive, but they are also more perceptive, creative, and tolerant of ambiguity (Jones, 1965). Livson and Peskin (1980) speculate that because late maturers have to learn how to deal with anxiety over their self-image, they deveop more flexibility and better problem-solving skills in adolescence, skills that serve them well when they reach adulthood.

If early maturity is an asset for teenage boys, it is a mixed blessing for girls. The early-maturing girl is taller, develops breasts sooner, and goes through menarche as much as 6 years before some of her peers. As a result, she has fewer opportunities to discuss with her friends the physical and emotional changes she is undergoing. There are, however, compensations. The early-maturing girl often feels more attractive, is more popular with boys, and goes out on dates more frequently than her late-maturing age-mates (Blyth et al., 1981). In her 30's, the early-maturing girl seems to reap the benefits of her teenage experiences. She is more confident and self-directed and is better able to meet social, intellectual, and emotional challenges than peers who matured late (Livson & Peskin, 1980).

GENDER IDENTITY AND SEXUAL PRACTICES

Directly related to the biological changes that adolescents must face is the issue of a mature gender identity. This includes the expression of sexual needs and feelings and the acceptance or rejection of sex roles. In Chapter 3, we saw how sex roles and sex-role stereotypes are forged long before adolescence, with one crucial period being the preschool years. During middle and late childhood, children associate mostly in same-sex peer groups in a sexually neutral way. With the attainment of puberty and adolescence, the biological changes of physical maturation bring a new interest in members of the opposite sex and a new need to integrate sexuality with other aspects of the personality. During adolescence, young people start entering into relationships in which sex plays a central role.

Developing Sexual Behavior

The development of sexual consciousness and behavior is different for girls than it is for boys. In adolescence, girls spend more time fantasizing about romance; boys are more likely to use masturbation as an outlet for their sexual impulses. However, masturbation and fantasizing are common in both sexes. According to one study, about half of adolescent girls and three-quarters of boys masturbate (Hass, 1979). Social-class differences play a part here, or at least they did in the past. The ability to develop a rich fantasy life during masturbation was reportedly more prominent in the middle-class male. Guilt over the "unmanliness" of masturbation was of greater concern to the working-class male. These differences seem to be gradually disappearing. In sexual behavior, at least, the young middle-class male no longer seems to differ much from the young working-class male (Dreyer, 1982).

Class differences in sexual behavior have traditionally been less important among females, partly because of the limited roles that were available to women in

The biological changes that occur in adolescence lead to an interest in and the development of sexual behavior and a sexual identity.

the past. Girls were discouraged from overt sexuality; instead, they received early training in enhancing their own desirability and in evaluating potential mates. Dating and courtship provided the setting for each sex to swap its expertise and to train the other in desires and expectations. In our society, femininity connoted passivity, nurturance, and the ability to fit in. Girls had to remain flexible enough to conform to the value systems of potential spouses. But now girls are encouraged to acquire skills to enrich and support themselves, regardless of their future marital plans, and sexuality for both sexes is encouraged through advertising and the mass media.

The expression of sexuality for both sexes is always dependent on the prevailing norms; it changes as the norms change. Some societies reserve sexuality exclusively for procreation. Others view such restrictions as silly or even as a crime against nature.

CHANGING SEXUAL ATTITUDES   Historical changes in social attitudes are perhaps most clearly seen in our responses to our developing sexuality. In large part, adolescents view themselves, as do adults, according to the cultural norms of the time in which they live. Therefore, sexual practices and the quality of sexual relationships vary over time.

Prior to the mid-1960s, most young people felt that premarital sex was immoral, although older adolescent males were under some pressure to acquire sexual experience. Women, in contrast, were under pressure to remain virginal until marriage. By the late 1960s and early 1970s, sexual attitudes had changed considerably. Sorensen (1973) reported the findings of a study on adolescent sexuality. He stated that the majority of adolescents who completed his questionnaires did not think of sex as being inherently right or wrong but instead judged it in terms of the relationship between the participants. The reactions of both partners to a sexual experience were thought to be equally important; most considered it immoral for one person to force another into a sexual relationship. Most rejected the traditional "double standard" that gave a great deal of freedom to boys but very little to girls. Almost 70% agreed that two people should not have to get married to live together. A surprising 50% approved of homosexuality between two consenting individuals—although 80% stated that they had never engaged in homosexual acts and would never want to. The subjects in this study clearly distinguished their own attitudes from those of their parents. Although most of the subjects had considerable respect for their parents, they felt that they differed from them a great deal in attitudes toward sex.

By the late 1970s, the sexual revolution was in full swing. In 1979, Chilman reviewed the findings of numerous studies and reported an increasing trend toward sexual liberalization, reflected both by an increase in sexual activity among adolescents and by a change in societal attitudes. Society had become more accepting of a wide range of sexual activities, including masturbation, homosexuality, and unmarried couples living together (Dreyer, 1982). Hass (1979) reported that 83% of the boys he interviewed, and 64% of the girls, approved of premarital intercourse; however, only 56% of the boys and 44% of the girls had actually experienced sexual intercourse. Note that there was not much difference between boys and girls in sexual activity. This statistic reflects the continuing decline in the double standard. The sexual revolution affected girls' behavior much more than it did boys': Even in the 1940s, 1950s, and 1960s, somewhere between one-third and two-thirds of teenage boys had already lost their virginity. During a similar

AIDS Acquired immune deficiency syndrome—a serious, usually fatal disease caused by a virus. Anyone can be infected through sexual contact or through exposure to infected blood or needles.

homophobia Fear or dislike of homosexuals.

span of years, the proportion of 16-year-old girls who had lost their virginity rose from 7% in the 1940s to 33% in 1971 and to 44% in 1982 (Brooks-Gunn & Furstenberg, 1989).

The sexual revolution was not without problems, of course. Although large numbers of adolescents were having sexual intercourse, many of them did not use birth control. As a result, the rate of pregnancies among teenage girls tripled in the 35 years from 1940 to 1975. Another problem was the spread of sexually transmitted diseases—first syphilis, gonorrhea, and genital herpes, and then, more recently, **AIDS** (acquired immune deficiency syndrome). Although AIDS is still rare among adolescents, mainly because it often takes years for the symptoms to appear, the rate of other sexually transmitted diseases is much higher in adolescents than it is in adults (Millstein, 1990).

The sexual revolution began to decline by the early 1980s. Young people started being more cautious about sexual activity, and monogamy became fashionable again. During the 1980s, when young people were asked what they thought of the sexual attitudes of the 1960s and 1970s, a sizable proportion viewed these attitudes as "bad." College students in 1980 were more likely than those in 1975 to consider sexual promiscuity "immoral" (Leo, 1984; Robinson & Jedlicka, 1982).

The late 1980s saw a continuation of the trend toward more conservative attitudes in sexual matters, as in other areas of life (Murstein et al., 1989). Although young people still see sex as an essential part of a romantic relationship, they are generally not in favor of casual sex (Abler & Sedlacek, 1989). Also, the majority of college students—of *both* sexes—now say that they would prefer to marry a virgin. Attitudes toward homosexuality have also become more negative again (Williams & Jacoby, 1989). The trend toward monogamous relationships and the increase in **homophobia** (fear or dislike of homosexuals) is probably related in part to the increasing fear of sexually transmitted diseases, especially AIDS.

The sexual revolutionaries of the 1960s and 1970s have grown older, formed families, and raised children of their own. Their children have a more sober—and perhaps a more realistic—outlook on sexual relationships.

SEXUAL RELATIONSHIPS   Although society as a whole has become somewhat more conservative with regard to sexual behavior, teenagers continue to be highly active sexually. The age at which they begin this activity still varies by gender; it also varies by racial and cultural group. Among whites, 60% of the boys have had intercourse by age 18; 60% of the girls have had intercourse by age 19. Sexual activity begins at a somewhat earlier age for African-American teens (Brooks-Gunn & Furstenberg, 1989).

Boys start having sex earlier and tend to have a somewhat different attitude toward it than girls do. Their sexual initiation is more likely to be with a casual partner, and they receive more social approval for their loss of virginity than girls do. Boys are also more likely to seek a second experience soon afterward, more likely to talk about their activity, and less likely to feel guilty than girls are (Zelnick & Kantner, 1977).

Several factors influence adolescent sexual behavior. Chilman (1979) cites education, psychological makeup, family relationships, and biological maturation as being important. Let us consider these four factors in more detail.

Education is related to sexual behavior partly because those who attain higher levels of education most frequently come from the mainstream middle- and upper-middle classes, which tend to hold a more conservative attitude toward sex. This is especially true for adolescents who emphasize careers, intellectual pursuits, and educational goals. Another factor is the relationship between sexual behavior and academic success or failure in high school: Good students are less likely to initiate sexual activity at an early age (Miller & Sneesby, 1988). Perhaps adolescents who are failing academically turn to sexual activity as a way of gratifying their need for success. In the past, this may have been true more for girls than for boys because girls had fewer opportunities for achievement in other areas, such as sports. With the current emphasis on opportunities for women in all aspects of society, including sports, this situation may be changing.

To some extent, the psychological factors associated with early sexual experience for males are different from that for females. Sexually experienced male adolescents tend to have relatively high self-esteem, whereas sexually experienced females tend to have low self-esteem. However, for both sexes, early sexual activity is associated with other problem behavior, such as drug use and delinquency (Donovan, Jessor, & Costa, 1988).

In the area of family relationships, a number of studies have found that parent-child interactions are related to adolescent sexual behavior. Both overly restrictive and overly permissive parenting are associated with earlier sexual activity in adolescents; moderate restrictiveness tends to work best with this age group (Miller et al., 1986). Another important factor is communication between parents and offspring: Adolescents who are sexually active are more likely to report poor communication with their parents. Chilman (1979) is quick to point out, however, that good parent-child relationships will not necessarily prevent young people from experimenting with sex.

According to Chilman, the biological factors that influence early sexual behavior are an important area of research, but these factors are the most frequently overlooked. She argues that adolescents may have become sexually active at an earlier age because of the decline in the average age of puberty. This hypothesis is supported by the fact that individuals who mature early are likely to engage in sexual activity at a younger age than those who mature late. Note, however, that boys reach sexual maturity about 2 years later than girls do, yet they lose their virginity about a year earlier (Brooks-Gunn & Furstenberg, 1989).

SEXUAL ABUSE   Unfortunately for a significant number of children and adolescents, their first sexual experiences occur without their consent and in an abusive fashion. Cases reported to the police probably represent only a small fraction of the actual number of incidents. In one study, a large, random sample of women was interviewed about childhood and adolescent sexual experiences (Russell, 1983). The results revealed that 32% had been sexually abused at least once before the age of 18, and 20% had been victimized before the age of 14. Fewer than 5% of these women had reported the incidents to the police.

The impact of sexual abuse on children depends on a wide variety of factors—the nature of the abusive act, the age and vulnerability of the victim, whether the offender is a stranger or a family member, whether there was a single incident or an ongoing pattern of abuse, and the reactions of adults in whom the child confides (Kempe & Kempe, 1984). The impact on the individual's sense of identity and level of self-esteem often lasts well into adulthood.

The most common form of sexual abuse occurs between a young adolescent girl and an adult male relative or family friend (Finkelhor, 1984). A stepfather or the mother's boyfriend is more likely to be involved than the girl's natural father is (Wolfe et al., 1988). The mother is usually unaware of the abusive relationship, and the abuse often continues over a period of time and becomes a "secret" between the abuser and the victim.

Adolescent girls who are involved in this kind of sexual abuse may have many symptoms. They often feel guilt and shame, yet are powerless to break loose from the relationship. They may feel isolated—alienated from their peers and distrustful of adults. Some have learning problems, others have physical complaints, and still others turn to sexual promiscuity. Some girls turn their anger on themselves, and they become depressed or contemplate suicide (Brassard & McNeill, 1987). In any case, their attitudes about intimate relationships have been distorted. Later, as adults, it is difficult for these victims of sexual abuse to establish normal sexual relationships; they may even have difficulty in establishing normal parent–child relationships with their own children.

Teenage Parents

A special topic of concern to researchers studying adolescent sexuality is the incidence of young unmarried mothers. Although the birthrate in the United States for all adolescents has declined slightly, the proportion of babies born outside of marriage has increased. The rate of babies born to unmarried American teenagers quadrupled between 1940 and 1985 (National Center for Health Statistics, 1987). More than 1 million adolescent girls now become pregnant each year; over 65% of these girls are not married. About 40% of these pregnancies end in abortion, and 10% end in miscarriage. The other 50% of these girls complete their pregnancies and bear children (Brooks-Gunn & Furstenberg, 1989; Sonenstein, 1987).

Sexual activity among American teenagers is high, but teenagers in most Western European countries are equally active, and the pregnancy rates in these countries are much lower (Hechtman, 1989). The reasons why so many American girls get pregnant are a cause of great concern. One probable factor is that there is less social stigma attached to illegitimate births than there was in the past. In the past, pregnant teenagers were usually expelled from high school, but now many school systems have developed special programs to help young mothers complete their high school education. In some cultural groups, the unmarried mother may get sustained support both from her family and from the father of her child (Chilman, 1979). Finally, some teenage girls wish to have and keep children because of their own need to be loved. These young mothers have usually been deprived of affection and expect children to supply what they have missed (Fosburgh, 1977).

Many sexually active adolescents do not use contraceptives. The most common reasons for this are ignorance of the facts of reproduction, an unwillingness to accept responsibility for sexual activity, or a sense of passivity about life (Dreyer, 1982). The double standard continues to play a role here: Both sexes tend to view the male as the sexual aggressor and tend to see the female as the one who is responsible for setting limits on sexual activity. At the same time, adolescents also believe that it is more proper for a female to be swept off her feet by passion than it is for her to take contraceptive precautions (Goodchilds & Zellman, 1984; Morrison, 1985).

Is this teenage mother ready to care for the needs of her infant as well as her own developmental needs?

More than 1 million adolescent girls become pregnant each year; over 65% of these girls are not married. Because teenage mothers usually forego their education or drop out of school prematurely, many school systems have developed special programs to help young mothers complete their high school educations.

What is the impact of early parenthood on the teenage girl's later development? There are a number of potentially negative effects. Teenage mothers usually drop out of school prematurely; on the average, they work at lower-paying jobs and experience greater job dissatisfaction. They are more likely to become dependent on government support. Adolescent mothers must deal with their own personal and social development while trying to adapt to the 24-hour needs of an infant or small child (Rogel & Peterson, 1984).

The effects of parenthood on the lives of teenage boys may also be negative and long-lasting. Due to pressures that many feel to support their new families, teenage fathers tend to leave school and generally acquire less education than their peers who have not fathered children. They are also more likely to take jobs that require little skill and offer little pay. As the years pass, they are more likely to have marital problems, which often lead to divorce (Card & Wise, 1978).

Often, adolescents who become pregnant encounter strong disapproval at home, or they may already be in conflict with their parents. Yet, if they do not marry, they may have no choice but to continue to live at home in a dependent situation during and after their pregnancy. Thus, some teenagers are motivated to get married in order to escape this situation and to set up their own households (Reiss, 1971). But teenage marriage is not necessarily the best solution to an adolescent mother's problems. Some researchers believe that even though early motherhood is an obstacle to adult growth, it is in many cases preferable to early motherhood combined with early marriage. Adolescent marriage is more likely to lead to dropping out of high school than is adolescent pregnancy. Similarly, those who marry young are more likely to divorce than those who bear a child and then marry later (Furstenberg, 1976).

The children of teenage parents are also at a disadvantage, compared to children of older parents. They may suffer from their parents' lack of experience in handling adult responsibilities and in caring for others. Because these young parents suffer from considerable stress and frustration, they are more likely to neglect or to abuse their children (see Child Abuse in Chapter 12). Children of teenage parents more often exhibit slow behavioral development and cognitive growth (Brooks-Gunn & Furstenberg, 1986). If adverse factors like poverty, marital discord, and poor education all exist in one family, the child's chances of developing these problems increase.

Some teenage parents, however, do an excellent job of nurturing their young while continuing to grow toward adulthood themselves. To do this, they almost always need assistance. Helping young parents and their offspring to thrive and to become productive remains an overriding social concern and challenge.

COGNITIVE CHANGES IN ADOLESCENCE

Although physical maturation and adjustment to sexuality are important steps that take place during adolescence, important cognitive developments also occur at this time. An expansion in capacity and style of thought broadens adolescent awareness, imagination, judgment, and insight. These enhanced abilities also lead to a rapid accumulation of knowledge that opens up a range of issues and problems that can complicate—and enrich—adolescents' lives.

Abstract Thinking

The new powers of abstract thought allow adolescents to challenge old ideas and attitudes and to become more critical and creative thinkers.

In Piaget's developmental theory, the hallmark of adolescent cognitive change is the development of *formal operational thought*. This new form of intellectual processing is abstract, speculative, and free from the immediate environment and circumstances. It involves thinking about possibilities as well as comparing reality with things that might or might not be. Whereas younger children seem to be more comfortable with concrete, empirical facts, adolescents show a growing inclination to treat everything as a mere variation on what could be (Keating, 1980). Formal operational thought requires the ability to formulate, test, and evaluate hypotheses. It involves not only manipulation of known, verifiable elements but also manipulation of those things that are contrary to fact ("Now let's just suppose for the sake of discussion that . . .").

Adolescents also show an increasing ability to plan and think ahead. In a recent study (Greene, 1990), a researcher asked 10th graders, 12th graders, college sophomores, and college seniors to describe what they thought might happen to them in the future and to say how old they thought they would be when these events occurred. The older subjects could look farther into the future than the younger ones could, and the narratives of these older subjects were more specific.

Another cognitive ability acquired in adolescence is the metacognitive ability to think about thinking. Teenagers learn to examine and consciously alter their thought processes. For example, they may repeat a number of facts until they have thoroughly memorized them, or they may silently warn themselves not to jump to conclusions without proof. Teenagers also become extremely introspective and self-absorbed. At the same time, they begin to challenge everything, to reject old boundaries and categories. In so doing, they constantly discard old attitudes and become more creative thinkers (Keating, 1980).

Formal operational thought can be characterized as a *second-order process*. The first order of thinking is discovering and examining relationships between objects. The second order involves thinking about one's thoughts, looking for relationships between relationships, and maneuvering between reality and possibility (Inhelder & Piaget, 1958). Three characteristics of adolescent thought are (1) the capacity to combine all variables and find a solution to a problem, (2) the ability to conjecture what effect one variable will have on another, and (3) the ability to combine and separate variables in a hypothetical–deductive fashion ("If X is present, then Y will occur") (Gallagher, 1973).

Piaget's theory of a dramatic, qualitative shift in thought patterns is not shared by all developmental theorists. Some psychologists contend that the transition is much more gradual, with shifts back and forth between formal operational thought and earlier cognitive modes. For example, Daniel Keating (1976) believes that the lines drawn between the thinking of children, adolescents, and adults are artificial. He sees cognitive development as a continuous process and suggests that children may have formal operational abilities in some latent form. He asserts, for instance, that some children have the ability to handle abstract thought. Perhaps better language skills and more experience with the world, instead of new cognitive equipment, are responsible for the appearance of these abilities in adolescents.

It is generally agreed that not all individuals are able to think in formal operational terms. Furthermore, adolescents and adults who attain this level do not always maintain it consistently. For example, many people who find themselves facing unfamiliar problems in unfamiliar situations are apt to fall back on a much more concrete type of reasoning. A certain level of intelligence seems to be necessary for the development of formal operational thought. Cultural and socioeconomic factors, particularly education level, also play a role (Neimark, 1975). The fact that not all individuals achieve formal operational thought has led some psychologists to suggest that it should be considered an extension of concrete operations, rather than a stage in its own right. Piaget (1972) has even admitted that this may be the case. Nevertheless, he emphasized that elements of this type of thought are essential for the study of advanced science and mathematics.

Information Processing and Intelligence

Many theorists differ in their definitions of the nature of intelligence. Is intelligence what we know, or is it our ability to acquire knowledge? Is intelligence an accumulation of facts and conclusions, or is it the cognitive processes that we use to arrive at these conclusions? In Chapter 9, we discussed current theories of intelligence and ways of measuring intelligence. Many critics of intelligence testing have charged that these tests measure the product, rather than the process, of intellectual behavior. Piagetian theorists suggest that intelligence tests fail to measure qualitative changes that occur when a child enters a new stage of thought. In the standard intelligence test, for example, it is difficult to capture the shift from concrete operational thinking to formal operational thinking. Information-processing theorists make a similar argument. They argue that intelligence tests fail to measure process components like attention, memory, problem solving, or decision making.

One major theorist, Robert Sternberg (1982, 1984), has attempted to analyze intelligence into five information-processing components that can be measured separately. For Sternberg, each of these components has a different function:

1. *Meta Components*—the higher-order control processes for planning and decision making. The ability to select a particular memory strategy or to monitor how well one is memorizing a list (metamemory) is an example of such processes.

2. *Performance Components*—the processes used to carry out problem solving.

3. *Acquisition* (or *Storage*) *Components*—the processes used in learning new information.

4. *Retention* (or *Retrieval*) *Components*—the processes used to retrieve the information that is stored in memory.

5. *Transfer Components*—the processes used to generalize information learned in one task to help solve another.

All of these processes are thought to increase gradually throughout childhood and adolescence.

Actually, cognitive development and, hence, the growth of intelligence involve both the accumulation of knowledge and the growth of information-processing components. The two are definitely related. Problem solving is more efficient and effective when one has a larger store of relevant information. Individuals with more efficient storage and retrieval strategies develop a more complete knowledge base.

Adolescents are more efficient and effective at solving problems and making inferences than are school-age children. But they also have a broader range of scripts or schemes to call on. As you recall, preschool children develop simple scripts for everyday activities. Adolescents develop more complicated scripts for special circumstances (a football game) or procedures (the election of a president). When they attempt to solve a problem or to understand a social event, they can make inferences about the meaning of such things by drawing from their more elaborate social scripts.

What, then, are the cognitive advances of adolescence? To information-processing theorists, cognitive development in this period includes the following: (1) a more efficient use of separate information-processing components, such as memory retention and transfer components; (2) the development of more complex strategies for different types of problem solving; (3) more effective ways of acquiring information and storing it symbolically; and (4) the development of higher-order (meta) executive functions, including planning, decision making, and flexibility in choosing strategies from a broader base of scripts (Sternberg, 1988).

Changes in Scope and Content of Thought

Basic academic skills and abilities, such as reading comprehension or rote memory, often reach optimal or near-optimal functioning levels during adolescence. Rote memory for simple lists of material, for example, reaches adult levels at about age 12 to 14 in most individuals. In contrast, vocabulary continues to improve well into adulthood. Nevertheless, because of greatly improved cognitive skills and the ability to use abstract thinking, adolescents develop a much broader scope and richer complexity in the content of their thoughts. It influences not only the study of science and math but also how adolescents examine the social world.

Particularly during middle and late adolescence, there may be an increasing concern with social, political, and moral issues. The adolescent begins to develop holistic concepts of society and its institutional forms along with ethical principles that go beyond those that he or she has experienced in particular interpersonal relationships. The rational processing of issues is also employed in an effort to achieve internal consistency, as individuals evaluate what they have been in the past and what they hope to become in the future. Some of the swings and extremes of adolescent behavior occur when young people start taking stock of themselves intellectually. There is a desire to restructure behavior, thoughts, and attitudes, either in the direction of greater self-consistency or toward greater conformity with a group norm, a new and individualized image, or some other cognitive model.

The improved cognitive abilities that develop during adolescence certainly help young people to make vocational decisions. They are able to analyze options, both real and hypothetical, and to analyze their talents and abilities. Ginsburg (1972) suggests that it is not until late adolescence that vocational choices become realistic, based in part on candid self-appraisal and valid career options.

ADOLESCENT SELF-INSIGHT AND EGOCENTRISM One aspect of formal operational thought is the ability to analyze one's own thought processes. Adolescents typically use this ability a great deal. In addition to gaining insight about themselves, they also gain insight into others. This ability to take account of others' thoughts, combined with the adolescent's preoccupation with his or her own metamorphosis, leads to a peculiar kind of egocentrism. Adolescents tend to assume that others are as fascinated about them and their behavior as adolescents are about themselves. They may fail to distinguish between their own concerns and the concerns of others. As a result, adolescents tend to jump to conclusions about the reactions of those around them and to assume that others will be as approving or as critical of them as they are of themselves. Research findings indicate that adolescents are far more concerned than younger children are about having their inadequacies discovered by other people (Elkind & Bowen, 1979).

The adolescent's idea that he or she is constantly being watched and judged by other people has been called the **imaginary audience** (Elkind, 1967). Adolescents use this imaginary audience as an internal sounding board "to try on" various attitudes and behaviors. The imaginary audience is also the source of much adolescent self-consciousness—of feeling constantly, painfully on display. Because adolescents are unsure of their inner identity, they overreact to others' views in trying to figure out who they really are (Elkind, 1967).

At the same time that they fail to differentiate the feelings of others, adolescents are also very absorbed in their own feelings, believing that their emotions are unique and that no one has ever known, or will ever know, such

imaginary audience Adolescents' assumption that others are focusing a great deal of critical attention on them.

During middle and late adolescence, teens become increasingly concerned with social, political, and moral issues.

personal fable Adolescents' feeling that they are special and invulnerable—exempt from the laws of nature that control the destinies of ordinary mortals.

personal agony or rapture. As part of this type of egocentrism, some adolescents come to believe in a **personal fable**—a feeling they are so special that they must be exempt from the ordinary laws of nature and that they will live forever. This feeling of invulnerability and immortality seems to be the basis for some of the risk-taking behavior that is so common during this period (Buis & Thompson, 1989). Another type of personal fable is the *foundling fantasy* (Elkind, 1974). Armed with new critical insights, the adolescent suddenly becomes aware of a great number of failings in his or her parents—and then has trouble imagining how two such ordinary and limited individuals could have possibly produced this sensitive and unique individual. All of this self-absorption can be a great obstacle in learning to see eye to eye with the rest of the world. Fortunately, egocentrism begins to recede by the age of 15 or 16, as adolescents begin to realize that their imaginary audience is not really paying very much attention to them and that they are subject to the laws of nature just like everyone else.

Nonetheless, adolescence is an intellectually intoxicating experience. New powers of thought are turned inward to one's own cognitive processes and outward to a world that has suddenly grown more complex. Included in this growth is the capacity for moral reasoning.

Adolescence is a time of self-absorption and self-reflection. Sometimes, adolescents feel terribly alone and may believe that no one else has ever thought or felt the way they do.

MORAL DEVELOPMENT In Chapter 12, we discussed Kohlberg's theory of the development of moral reasoning. Earlier thinkers, of course, have observed moral development and studied the changes that occur as children grow, particularly during adolescence. Kohlberg drew on the developmental theories of J. M. Baldwin (1906), George Mead (1934), and, most directly, Jean Piaget (1965). Although Kohlberg was directly influenced by Piaget, it is Kohlberg's model that has generated the most interest and research.

By looking at individuals in Western society, one can find some validation for many aspects of Kohlberg's theory. By the time they reach their teens, most children in our society have outgrown the first level of moral development (the preconventional level) and have arrived at the conventional level, which is based on social conformity. They are motivated to avoid punishment, are obedience oriented, and are ready to abide by conventional moral stereotypes. They may stay at this "law-and-order" level for the rest of their lives, especially if they receive no stimulation to think beyond this level. The final two stages of moral development—morality by social contract and morality as derived from ethical principles—require the thought processes of adolescent development. But what is the process of change? Can one teach more advanced moral thought?

Kohlberg and others have set up experimental "moral education" classes for children who come from a variety of social backgrounds. The results, even with juvenile delinquents, suggest that moral judgment can indeed be taught. The classes center on discussions of hypothetical moral dilemmas. The child is presented with a problem and is asked to give a solution. If the answer is argued at level 4, the discussion leader suggests a level-5 rationale to see if the child thinks it is a good alternative. The students almost always find that this slightly more advanced reasoning is more attractive, and through repeated discussions like this, sooner or later they begin to form judgments at level 5. At this point, the discussion leader might start suggesting level-6 reasoning as an alternative (Kohlberg, 1966).

Kohlberg's model and his experiments with "moral education" show several things. An adolescent's set of values depends partly upon cognitive development. These values are, in part, a product of the adolescent's experiences in making moral

ADOLESCENT DEPRESSION

I am worthless, I am of no use.... Vivienne's diary entry, April 11, 1973 (Mack & Hickler, 1981)

Vivienne wrote these words in her diary a full 8 months before she hanged herself in the basement of her home. At the time of her death, she was an attractive, well-liked, intelligent ninth grader. Her suicide shocked both family and friends. But the signs of serious depression had been present for at least 18 months in the poetry, school essays, and diary entries as well as in the behavior of this sensitive and empathetic young girl (Mack & Hickler, 1981).

It is often easy to miss what ought to be obvious signals of serious depression in children and adolescents. We tend to think of children as happy and carefree—as though children don't have reasons to be depressed. Furthermore, the word "depression" is used to describe many emotional states in everyday life, and, yet, the common understanding of this term is different from actual clinical depression.

Depression can be defined as an affective (emotional) disorder with a characteristic set of symptoms. The individual experiences a prolonged period of sadness, sorrow, hopelessness, or emptiness. He or she loses interest in usual activities or pastimes. This may be accompanied by physical symptoms like poor appetite and weight loss (or overeating and weight gain), abnormal sleeping patterns (either insomnia or a tendency to sleep too much), loss of energy, and agitation. The depressed individual may have feelings of self-reproach, worthlessness, and inappropriate guilt; may be unable to think clearly or to concentrate; and may have a repetitive preoccupation with thoughts of catastrophe, death, or suicide. Depression can begin after an experience of loss or a stressful event. But the normal feelings of grief and disappointment are exaggerated and prolonged. There may be periods of weeping, but often there are no tears—only hopeless apathy, self-blame, and withdrawal (McKnew et al., 1983).

Clinical depression is more difficult to diagnose in children than it is in adolescents and adults because it may have somewhat different symptoms, depending on the age and developmental level of the child. Some authors believe that when depression occurs in middle childhood, it is really just prolonged and intense sadness in reaction to a loss or tragic event. It lacks the distorted thinking, self-blame, and guilt that are more common in adolescents and adults. Nevertheless, the emotions may be just as intense, and the child may have prolonged periods of physical symptoms—poor appetite, weakness, sleep difficulties, and the like—as well as feelings of helplessness, loneliness, loss, and guilt (Garber, 1984).

The incidence of depression increases dramatically in adolescence: The two peak onset times for serious depression are ages 15 to 19 and ages 25 to 29 (Judd, 1991). Although depression in childhood occurs equally often in girls and boys, depression in adolescence and adulthood is about twice as common in females. Researchers have not yet determined the precise reasons for this sex difference—it seems to result from a combination of social, cultural, and biological factors (APA Task Force on Women and Depression, 1991).

The adolescent's newly developed ability to be critical and analytical can be focused on the social realities of the world or directed inward. In normal adolescence, there is often an intensification of self-consciousness and a preoccupation with the self that may be relentlessly critical. These thought processes, combined with the adolescent's relatively limited life experiences, tend to increase the risk of depression and suicide.

In understanding depression, like other pathologies, it is helpful to have some knowledge of the development of normal processes.

judgments. If the individual receives challenging, yet safe, opportunities to consider moral dilemmas at higher levels, adolescence may then be a time of considerable moral development.

Educators, in particular, are concerned with how the moral sense develops during childhood and adolescence. These educators feel that if they could understand it better, they could do something about the rising rates of delinquency and help to create a better social order. Even though Kohlberg has provided useful descriptions of the stages of moral development, he has not adequately described how a child progresses from one level to another. According to Kohlberg's framework, which is derived from that of Piaget, presenting children with increasingly complex moral issues creates a disequilibrium in the child's mind. It would then seem that the consideration of moral paradoxes and conflicts sets up a disturbance that forces the child to make increasingly more mature analyses and judgments about social situations. However, it is not entirely clear if superior moral judgments necessarily lead to superior behavior, and very little research has been done to date on the relationship between the two.

What we do know is that adolescents are highly receptive both to the culture that surrounds them and to the behavior of the models they see at home, in school, and in the mass media. We cannot expect them to behave morally if those who serve as their models do not provide an example of moral behavior.

STUDY OUTLINE

Development in a Cultural and Historical Context

Adolescence is a transitional period between childhood and adulthood. The length of this period depends on the culture. In complex modern societies, adolescents need a longer period to learn adult roles and skills, even though they now become sexually mature at an earlier age.

Adolescence in Contemporary Western Society. Adolescents are affected by the cultural and historical context in which they live. In our society, *age segregation* and exposure to the mass media play a role in the experiences and attitudes of teenagers.

Physical Maturation

Biological Changes. During early adolescence, boys and girls go through biological changes, including rapid growth, development of the reproductive organs and the appearance of secondary sex characteristics.

Body Image and Adjustment. Teenagers observe the changes in themselves with fascination and concern; they constantly compare their own bodies with the cultural ideal. Boys who mature earlier than usual have some advantages over boys who are late maturers. For girls, early maturation is a mixed blessing.

Gender Identity and Sexual Practices

Developing Sexual Behavior. The development of sexual consciousness and behavior differs for boys and girls; it is also influenced by prevailing cultural values and norms. Girls (but not boys) were supposed to remain virginal in the 1940s and 1950s; this changed during the sexual revolution of the 1970s.

In the 1980s, young people started to become more conservative in their sexual attitudes. However, young people in the United States continue to be very active sexually.

Unfortunately, a significant number of children and adolescents are sexually abused. The impact of such experiences on levels of self-esteem and on one's sense of identity can last into adulthood.

Teenage Parents. More than a million teenage pregnancies occur each year in the United States. Early parenthood has a number of negative effects on the young mother and father and on their offspring.

Cognitive Changes in Adolescence

Abstract Thinking. Cognitive changes in adolescence are characterized by the development of *formal operational thought*. This new intellectual ability allows the adolescent to engage in abstract thought, free of the immediate environment. Adolescents are also able to think about their own thought processes. Some theorists describe adolescent cognitive development in terms of the growth of information-processing components.

Changes in Scope and Content of Thought. As a result of improved cognitive skills, adolescents develop a broader scope and richer complexity in the content of their thoughts. Due to a peculiar kind of egocentrism that appears during this period, adolescents may believe in a **personal fable** and may feel that they are being watched by an **imaginary audience**.

Improved cognitive skills also enable adolescents to develop advanced moral reasoning. However, it is not clear if superior moral judgments necessarily lead to superior moral behavior.

KEY TERMS AND CONCEPTS

abstract thinking
adolescent egocentrism
AIDS
anorexia nervosa
bulimia
formal operational thought

homophobia
hormone
imaginary audience
information-processing components
Kohlberg's model of moral
   development

menarche
personal fable
rite of passage
seminal emission
sexual abuse
sexual attitudes

SELF-TEST QUESTIONS

1. Give several examples of how cultural and historical factors influence the development of adolescence.

2. List the biological changes of males and females during adolescence.

3. What are some examples of how cultural ideals affect body image and adjustment during adolescence?

4. Discuss how the physical changes that are taking place during adolescence can affect parental self-image.

5. Compare and contrast early- and late-maturing males. How does this compare to the early and late maturity of females?

6. Discuss the way in which attitudes toward male and female sexuality in our society have changed.

7. List several factors that influence adolescent sexual behavior.

8. Describe the sexual revolution and changes in sexual attitudes and behavior that have since taken place.

9. Describe the impact of sexual abuse on one's sense of identity.

10. Discuss the negative impacts of early parenthood on teenage boys and girls.

11. What is formal operational thought? How did Piaget view the adolecent's cognitive changes?

12. How do information-processing theorists describe cognitive development?

13. Describe the impact of cognitive development on changes in the scope and content of adolescent thought.

14. Explain adolescent egocentrism.

15. Discuss Kohlberg's model of moral development and why it doesn't adequately describe how a child might progress from one stage of moral development to another.

16. List several cultural factors that shape adolescence in Western society.

SUGGESTED READINGS

COLES, R., AND STOKES, G. *Sex and the American teenager.* New York: Harper & Row, 1985. Presentation and discussion of a detailed, interview-based survey of American teenage sexual attitudes and behavior.

COLMAN, W. *Understanding and preventing AIDS.* Chicago: Children's Press, 1988. A detailed, well illustrated overview for teenagers and their parents, including clear presentation of the immune system and realistic profiles of young AIDS patients.

ERIKSON, E. *Identity: Youth & crisis.* New York: Norton, 1968. A full discussion of adolescent identity formation with many examples taken from case studies.

FELDMAN, S. S. AND ELLIOTT, G. R. *At the threshold: The developing adolescent.* Cambridge, MA: Harvard University Press, 1990. Results of the extensive Carnegie Foundation study of adolescent development in social context, presented for professionals and nonprofessionals alike.

KEMPE, RUTH S. AND KEMPE, C. HENRY. *The common secret: sexual abuse of children and adolescents.* New York: W. H. Freeman, 1984. A hard-hitting, statistics-packed presentation of the range, extent and impact of sexual abuse in America.

ROSENBERG, E. *Growing up feeling good.* New York: Beaufort Books, Inc., 1983. One of the best self-help guides for early adolescents, it is also valuable for parents of adolescents and for teachers.

SHENGOLD, LEONARD. *Soul Murder: The effects of childhood abuse and deprivation.* New Haven, CT: Yale University Press, 1989. This psychiatrist explores the adult results of the psychological trauma of childhood abuse. The lives of Dickens, Kipling, Chekhov and Orwell are examined along with contemporary less well known victims of abuse.

Chapter 14

Don't laugh at a youth for his affectations; he is only trying on one face after another to find a face of his own.

LOGAN PEARSALL SMITH
AFTERTHOUGHTS (1931)

Adolescence: Themes, Conflicts, and Emerging Patterns

*I*n moving from childhood to the status of young adulthood, adolescents often display a curious combination of maturity and childishness. This mixture is awkward, sometimes even comical, but it serves an important developmental function. The ways that adolescents cope with the stresses of new bodies and new roles are based upon their personality development in earlier years. To meet new adult challenges, they draw on the skills, resources, and strengths that they developed in earlier periods of their lives.

In the preceding chapter, we mentioned that the transitional period between childhood and adulthood varies from culture to culture. In some societies, adult skills are easily mastered; new adult members are urgently needed and promptly recruited by the larger community. In our society, successful transition to adult status, especially occupational status, requires lengthy training. Adolescence in modern societies is prolonged, stretching from puberty through the second decade of life. Despite their physical and intellectual maturity, adolescents live in limbo, excluded from the meaningful problem-solving work of the larger social group.

On the one hand, prolonged adolescence gives the young person repeated opportunities to experiment with different adult styles without making irrevocable commitments. On the other hand, a decade of adolescence generates pressures and conflicts of its own, such as the need to appear independent and sophisticated when one is in fact still economically dependent on one's parents.

Some psychologists argue that adolescents are also under pressure from their parents, who have transferred to them their own compulsions to succeed and to attain a higher social status (Elkind, 1981). The adolescent must cope with all of these inner and outer pressures, confront and resolve important developmental tasks, and weave the results into a coherent, functioning identity. In this chapter, we will look at the coping patterns commonly used to meet the dilemmas of adolescence and at the triumphs and tragedies that result. We will examine how the young person selects values and forms loyalties and, as a result, how the young person presents a more mature self to society.

CHAPTER OBJECTIVES

By the time you have finished this chapter, you should be able to do the following:

■ Discuss the major developmental conflicts that adolescents must resolve in order to make a successful transition to adulthood.

■ Explain the concept of identity status.

■ Describe the factors and processes that help to shape moral development and the selection of guiding values during adolescence.

■ Discuss patterns of drug use during adolescence.

■ Describe how parenting styles and family dynamics continue to influence a child's behavior during adolescence and identify key characteristics of successful family functioning during an adolescent's increasing independence.

■ Name some reference groups that might be important during adolescence and explain their significance.

■ List the purposes of dating and explain how attitudes toward dating change between early and late adolescence.

DEVELOPMENTAL TASKS IN ADOLESCENCE

Each period in life presents developmental challenges and difficulties that require new skills and responses. Most psychologists agree that adolescents must confront two tasks: (1) achieving a measure of independence or autonomy from one's parents, and (2) forming an identity, creating an integrated self that harmoniously combines different elements of the personality.

Adolescence has traditionally been seen as a period of "storm and stress," a dramatic upheaval of the emotions. The term *storm and stress* is derived from the name of a German literary movement of the late 18th and early 19th centuries *(Sturm und Drang)*. It was adopted by Anna Freud, the daughter of Sigmund Freud, as a label for the emotional state of adolescents. Anna Freud (1958) went so far as to say, "To be normal during the adolescent period is by itself abnormal" (p. 275). The Freudians argue that the onset of biological maturation and increased sexual drive produces conflicts between adolescents and their parents, adolescents and their peers, and adolescents and themselves.

Are adolescents a troubled group of people? The answer is some are, but most are not. The majority are well adjusted and have no major conflicts with their parents, peers, or themselves. But an estimated 10% to 20% have psychological disturbances that range from mild to severe. Although this proportion may seem high, it is no higher than the proportion of adults who have psychological disturbances (Powers, Hauser, & Kilner, 1989).

For the adolescents who have problems, the symptoms tend to vary according to gender. Troubled teenage boys are likely to engage in antisocial behavior like delinquency and substance abuse. Troubled teenage girls are more likely to direct their symptoms inward and to become depressed (Ostrov, Offer, & Howard, 1989). As we noted in the box on adolescent depression (Chapter 13), depression is about twice as common in female adolescents and adults as it is in males. Psychologists have not reached an agreement on the reason for this sex difference, but it may be related to the substantial drop in self-esteem that has been found to occur in girls—but not in boys—around the time they enter junior high school (Bower, 1991).

Independence and Interdependence

According to the prevailing view, adolescents use conflict and rebelliousness as the principal way to achieve autonomy and independence from their parents. The media, especially since the mid-1960s, has focused on the "generation gap" and the turbulent conflict between parents and their children. Stories on this topic may have high drama and great interest, but they have limited support in research. Most of the research literature indicates that the degree of conflict and turbulence in adolescent relations with the rest of the family has been exaggerated.

Just as emotional turmoil is not an inevitable part of growing up, neither is conflict between adolescents and their parents. Although the emotional distance between teenagers and their parents tends to increase as they go through the physical changes of puberty (Steinberg, 1988), this does not necessarily lead to rebellion or to rejection of parental values. Bandura (1964) interviewed adolescent boys from middle-class families. He found that by the time the boys reached adolescence, they had already internalized their parents' values and standards of behavior so thoroughly that there was actually less need for parental control than had been expected. The process of emancipation was substantially complete by the time the boys reached adolescence because the parents had encouraged their sons' independent behavior starting in early childhood. Note, however, that Bandura's subjects were all middle-class American males; his results may not be applicable to

For many teenagers, adolescence is a positive experience, a spur to growth and competence.

a wider range of adolescents. Socioeconomic and cultural factors will have an important influence on the degree of tension and conflict each teenager experiences. Nevertheless, findings such as Bandura's call into question the Freudian view of inevitable conflict stemming from biological drives.

Clearly, definitions of autonomy that stress freedom from parental influence need to be reconsidered. The concept of independence must take into account the continuing influence of parents on their children during and after adolescence. One theorist (Hill, 1987) has suggested an interesting approach to adolescent independence-seeking: Hill defines autonomy as self-regulation. Independence involves the capacity to make one's own judgments and to regulate one's own behavior. "Think for yourself," we often say when we want someone to be independent. Many adolescents go through a process in which they learn to do precisely that. They reevaluate the rules, values, and boundaries that they previously learned at home and in school. Sometimes, they encounter considerable resistance from their parents, which may lead to conflict. More often, parents work through this process with their children, minimizing the areas of conflict and assisting their adolescents to develop independent thought and self-regulated behavior (Hill, 1987).

Becoming an adult is a gradual transformation. It requires the ability to be simultaneously independent and interdependent. Interdependence can be defined as reciprocal dependence. Social relationships are interdependent, as for example in the traditional marriage. The husband is dependent on his wife to cook, keep house, and mend his clothes. In turn, the wife is dependent on her husband to earn an adequate income and to protect her from danger. At work, bosses are dependent on their workers to produce goods, and workers are dependent on their bosses to manage the enterprise so that they all have an income. Interdependence involves long-term commitments and interpersonal attachments that characterize the human condition (Gilligan, 1987). Over time, adolescents develop the ability to

reference group A social group or collection of people with whom an individual shares attitudes, ideals, or philosophies.

significant other Anyone whose opinions an individual values highly.

combine a commitment to others that is the basis of interdependence with a sense of self that is the basis of independence.

Identity Formation

Before adolescence, we view ourselves according to a collection of different roles—for example, daughter, older sister, friend, student, church member, and flute player. In adolescence, our new cognitive powers of formal operational thought allow us to analyze these roles, to see inconsistencies and conflicts in some of the roles, and to restructure them in order to forge a new identity. This process sometimes requires abandoning old roles and establishing new relationships with parents, siblings, and peers. Erikson (1968) sees the task of identity formation as the major hurdle that adolescents must cross in order to make a successful transition to adulthood.

SOURCES OF IDENTITY   Adolescents derive many of their ideas of suitable roles and values from **reference groups.** Reference groups may consist of individuals with whom adolescents are close and whom they see every day, or they may be broader social groups with whom adolescents share attitudes and ideals—such as religious, ethnic, generational, or interest groups. Individuals compare themselves to a reference group, whether broad or narrow, and find their values either confirmed or rejected.

Adolescents must come to terms with a variety of reference groups. Groups that were automatic in childhood—such as the family, the neighborhood gang, the church youth group—are no longer as comfortable or fulfilling. There may be conflicting loyalties between an adolescent's family, ethnic group, and peer group.

Sometimes, adolescents are drawn to the values and attitudes of one person, rather than to those of an entire group. This person, called a **significant other,** might be a close friend, an admired teacher, an older sibling, a movie or sports star, or anyone whose opinions are highly valued. Although the influence of a significant other may be felt at any stage of life, it often has its greatest impact during adolescence, when the individual is actively seeking models.

Thus, adolescents are surrounded by a bewildering variety of roles offered by a multitude of reference groups and significant others. These roles must be integrated into a personal identity, and the conflicting ones must be reconciled or discarded. The process is made more difficult when there is conflict between roles (for instance, between being a member of a funloving peer group and being a good student) or between significant others (for instance, between a boyfriend and an older sister).

ERIKSON'S CONCEPT OF IDENTITY   Erik Erikson, a clinical psychologist, spent much of his professional life working with adolescents and young adults. His work on the process of establishing "an inner sense of identity" has had an enormous impact on developmental psychologists and on the general public. According to Erikson, the process of self-definition, called *identity formation,* is lengthy and complex. It provides continuity between the individual's past, present, and future. It forms a framework for organizing and integrating behaviors in diverse areas of one's life. It reconciles the person's own inclinations and talents with earlier identifications or roles that were supplied by parents, peers, or society. By helping

Teenagers may be drawn to and adopt the attitudes of a teacher they admire.

the person to know where he or she stands in comparison to others in society, it also provides a basis for social comparisons. Finally, an "inner sense of identity" helps to give a direction, a purpose, and a meaning to one's future life. It is a rich and full concept presented with numerous examples drawn from personal case studies (Erikson, 1959, 1963, 1968; Waterman, 1985).

The richness of Erikson's concept is somewhat lost when we translate it into research. Unfortunately, as one researcher observed, a lengthy autobiographical interview on an individual's vocational plans, religious beliefs, political ideology, and social roles is too often translated into a one- or two-word categorical label. (Archer, 1985).

MODES OF IDENTITY FORMATION In a theory based on Erikson's developmental scheme, James Marcia (1980) has defined four different states or modes of identity formation. The four modes, or *identity statuses,* are (1) **foreclosure,** (2) **diffusion,** (3) **moratorium,** and (4) **identity achievement.** These statuses are defined according to two factors: whether or not the individual has gone through a decision-making period called an **identity crisis;** and whether or not the individual has made a commitment to a selected set of choices, such as a system of values or a plan for a future occupation.

Adolescents who are in *foreclosure status* have made a commitment without going through a decision-making period. They have chosen an occupation, a religious outlook, or an ideological viewpoint, but the choice was made early and was determined by their parents or teachers rather than by themselves. The transition to adulthood occurs smoothly and with little conflict.

Young people who lack a sense of direction and who seem to have little motivation to find one are in *diffusion status.* They have not experienced a crisis, and they have not selected an occupational role or a moral code. They are simply avoiding the issue. Some seek immediate gratification; others experiment in a random fashion with all possibilities (Coté & Levine, 1988).

Adolescents or young adults in *moratorium status* are in the midst of an ongoing identity crisis or decision-making period. The decisions may concern occupational choices, religious or ethical values, or political philosophies. Young people in this status are preoccupied with "finding themselves."

Identity achievement is the status attained by people who have passed through the crisis and have made their commitments. As a result, they pursue work of their own choosing and attempt to live by their own individually formulated moral code. Although there are healthy and pathological dimensions to all four identity statuses, identity achievement is usually viewed as the most psychologically desirable (Marcia, 1980).

EFFECTS OF IDENTITY STATUS Research indicates that identity status profoundly influences an adolescent's social expectations, self-image, and reactions to stress. Moreover, cross-cultural research in the United States, Denmark, Israel, and other societies suggests that the four statuses are part of the developmental process in several related cultures. Let us look at how the four identity statuses interact with some of the problems of adolescence.

Anxiety is a dominant emotion for young people in moratorium status because of their unresolved decisions. They struggle with a world of conflicting values and choices and are constantly faced with unpredictability and contradictions. These adolescents are often tied to their parents with ambivalent bonds of

foreclosure The identity status of those who have made commitments without going through an identity crisis.

diffusion The identity status of those who have neither gone through an identity crisis nor made commitments.

moratorium The identity status of those who are currently in the midst of an identity crisis.

identity achievement The identity status of those who have gone through an identity crisis and have made commitments.

identity crisis A period of making decisions about important issues—of asking "Who am I and where am I going?"

love and hatred; they struggle for freedom, yet they fear and resent parental disapproval. Among college students, there are many in the moratorium status. These are the people who are actively seeking information and making decisions.

Adolescents in foreclosure status experience a minimum of anxiety. These adolescents hold to more authoritarian values than those in other statuses, and they have strong, positive ties to significant others, who sometimes follow untraditional paths. They generally operate in a pattern of continuity and stability, although in some areas of life, they may experience uncertainty. Young men in foreclosure status tend to have less self-esteem than do those in moratorium status, and they are more susceptible to the suggestions of others (Marcia, 1980).

Diffusion status is seen most frequently in teenagers who have experienced rejection or neglect from detached or uncaring parents. These adolescents may become society's dropouts, perhaps turning to drug or alcohol use as a way of evading responsibility. Baumrind (1991) has shown that drug and alcohol abuse is most common in the offspring of what she refers to as "unengaged parents."

In comparison to young people in moratorium, foreclosure, or diffusion status, those who have attained identity achievement have the most balanced feelings toward their parents and family. Their quest for independence is less emotionally charged than that of the moratorium youths, and it is not tainted with the fear of abandonment that bothers individuals in the identity diffusion status (Marcia, 1980).

The proportion of people in identity achievement status increases with age. In junior high and high school, there are far more individuals in diffusion and foreclosure statuses than in moratorium and identity achievement statuses. Identity status may also vary according to the aspect of life that is being considered: A high school student may be in foreclosure status in regard to sex-role preference, moratorium status in regard to vocational choice or religious beliefs, and diffusion status in regard to political philosophy.

SEX DIFFERENCES Marcia and other researchers have noticed a marked difference between males and females in the behavior and attitudes associated with the various identity statuses. Males in identity achievement and moratorium statuses seem to have a great deal of self-esteem, whereas females in these statuses appear to have more unresolved conflicts, especially regarding family and career choices. Later studies have partially confirmed some of these earlier findings but have presented a more complex picture.

Sally L. Archer (1985), for example, found that for family and career choices, girls of senior high school age were most likely to be in foreclosure status, whereas boys were most likely to be in diffusion status. Furthermore, girls in foreclosure and moratorium statuses expressed a great deal of uncertainty about reconciling conflicts due to their family and career preferences. Although both boys and girls said that they planned to marry, have children, and pursue careers, it was primarily the girls who expressed concern about possible conflicts between family and career. When asked how much concern they had, 75% of males and 16% of females said *none,* 25% of males and 42% of females said *some,* and 0% of males and 42% of females said they felt *a lot* of concern.

In the other major areas of interest—religious and political beliefs—studies indicate a mixed result. In religion, research indicates that there are no significant differences between the genders. But with respect to political beliefs, there seems to be a significant difference in identity status between older male and female adolescents. Males are more often in identity achievement status than females are, and females are more often in foreclosure status than males are (Waterman, 1985).

VALUES, IDEALS, AND MORAL DEVELOPMENT

Selection of a set of guiding values is an important task during adolescence. This process is hardly new to the adolescent, however. The development of a conscience and moral standards begins very early in the socialization process, when the toddler is taught *not* to pull hair, tell lies, or take toys away from others. Throughout childhood, social learning techniques—particularly imitation of parental models and receiving rewards and punishments—play an important role in the child's moral development.

This early training forms only part of the value system of a mature adult. Many psychologists believe that processes like modeling, identification, and rewards and punishment, which teach the young child to distinguish right from wrong, can only go so far. They are satisfactory only as a means of teaching an external morality, which the child then internalizes. But in order to become a mature adult, the individual must eventually reassess and analyze these principles to build a coherent set of values.

Reassessment in Adolescence

Preadolescent children may be unable to construct their own value system, even if they should want to do so. As we saw in our review of middle childhood, cognitive theorists point out that the individual must have the ability to make relative judgments about what is right in order to form a mature system of morality. The 5-year-old, or even the 11-year-old, simply does not have the mental capacity to form a systematic framework of these principles. It is necessary for a person to have the ability to consider all of the possible alternatives, to reason from

The moral growth that takes place during adolescence helps teenagers recognize the value of community action and concern for others. These teenagers are taking part in a conservation project in a state park.

the specific to the general, to use cause-and-effect logic, to think about the past and the future, and to consider hypothetical alternatives. The ability to perform all of these cognitive tasks is not fully reached until adolescence—or perhaps later, or perhaps not at all. The newly acquired intellectual abilities of adolescents make the transition to adulthood a period that is marked by changes in ideals, values, and attitudes.

According to Hoffman (1980), moral development occurs in three different, overlapping ways. The first is *anxiety-based inhibition*—socially acceptable behavior that is induced by fear of punishment. Children learn to associate punishment at the hands of parents and others with unacceptable behavior. Eventually, children master this fear of punishment by refraining from the forbidden act. Thus, they have internalized the rules; actual punishment is no longer necessary. Second, as children grow older, they also learn *empathy-based concern for others*. This moral perspective combines the human capacity to share feelings with the growing cognitive ability to figure out how someone else is feeling, as well as how our behavior may alter other people's inner states. Third, children and adolescents undergo moral development through *exercising formal operational thought*—testing hypotheses, reevaluating information, and reformulating concepts. (This is a model developed by Kohlberg, which we discussed in Chapters 12 and 13.)

These three types of moral growth are not chronological stages, nor are they mutually exclusive. According to Hoffman, they usually coexist in all adults. But in adolescence, the three types may shift in importance. For example, anxiety-based morality can be severely undermined in the antiauthoritarian, peer-dominated college environment. At the same time, empathy may be eroded by exposure to some of life's harsher realities, leading to moral cynicism in adolescents. In contrast, empathy-based morality may be strengthened through exposure to inspiring leaders and teachers and through intense debates that stimulate intellectual support of empathic views. Finally, some adolescents may make the transition to adulthood with little or no moral development. This is often true of foreclosure types and of those who remain in sheltered, homogeneous environments, such as military schools. In such cases, childhood morality may take on the guise of political conservatism (Hoffman, 1980).

Social Context

The substance of adolescents' values depends heavily on the cultural context and historical period in which they live. At many points in history, there have been groups of older adolescents who have taken on the role of the conscience of society. In our own recent history, we can see this phenomenon in the civil rights and antiwar movements, in the feminist struggle for equality, and in the environmental crusades. Adolescents participated in these social movements for many reasons, both altruistic and selfish. Some carefully thought out their moral positions and endeavored to implement them; others just wanted to be part of the group.

In each decade, young people, particularly college students, have been among the first to reject the old values and to adopt the new. How many of these new values represent a youthful flirtation with ivory-tower idealism? How deeply do the new values affect the rest of society? Some of the values and attitudes with which college students startled the world in the 1960s were later adopted by working-class youth. Mainstream Americans began to show widespread dissatisfaction with the political system and with big business, to reflect relaxed attitudes about sex, and to place less emphasis on formal religion. The outlook and attitudes of a few adolescents in the 1960s became more widely popular in the early 1970s. There is little question that young people's receptivity to new ideas and values has acted as a force in changing the value structure of society. Since the late 1970s, adolescents have participated in the trend toward conservatism in religion and in political attitudes.

Although young people are more conservative today than they were in the 1960s and 1970s, they continue to hold the value systems of the earlier decades. Most older adolescents still believe, for example, in the right to engage in premarital sex or to have an abortion. Many are still willing to run risks in thinking and moral reasoning—to question and to oppose the settled beliefs of an era, whether liberal or conservative. "Adolescents may construct a moral vision of an ideal world in which inequities are resolved justly and peers nourish and care for each other in mutual love and interdependence" (Baumrind, 1987). Unfortunately, there is little practical support for such a vision in the real world. Young people who are strongly committed to this view may feel rejected, or they may feel that there is no place in society for moral action. The risk is that these individuals may become cynical, alienated, or hostile.

Decisions about Drug Use

During the transitional period of adolescence, individuals are exposed to a variety of behaviors and lifestyles. They adopt certain behaviors and avoid others. A major decision that they must make is whether or not to participate in patterns of drug use and abuse. Sedatives and stimulants have been used for centuries in the United States, but drug use became particularly widespread in the 1970s. Today, as in the past, alcohol, nicotine, and many other drugs are legally and illegally used by millions of Americans. If all the users of psychoactive compounds that are prescribed and unprescribed—sleeping pills, diet pills, stimulants, alcohol, caffeine, and nicotine—were counted, one would have to conclude, as did Keniston (1968–69), that "the American who has never 'used' drugs is a statistical freak."

Every drug has an abuse potential. In moderate doses, drugs like painkilling opiates or small amounts of alcohol may have beneficial effects. But when taken in amounts beyond what is required for the relief of pain or when taken more frequently than is necessary, substance abuse occurs. Of all the legal and illegal drugs that are widely available in this country, nicotine in the form of tobacco and alcohol have the highest potential for abuse. They are easily and legally obtained and are widely used by adults in this country. In fact, the conspicuous use of alcohol and tobacco is, regrettably, a hallmark of adulthood to a great many adolescents.

ALCOHOL   Alcohol acts as a depressant; its effects are similar to those of sleeping pills. In small amounts, the psychological effects include lowered inhibitions and self-restraint, heightened feelings of well-being, and an accelerated sense of time. Many drinkers use alcohol to ease tension and to facilitate social interaction. The effects of larger doses include distorted vision, impaired motor coordination, and slurred speech; still larger doses lead to loss of consciousness or even to death.

Alcohol is the most widely used drug among adolescents and young adults. Participating in heavy drinking binges on spring break is a popular ritual for many college students.

These effects depend not only on the amount of alcohol consumed but also on individual tolerance. Long-term habitual use of alcohol increases tolerance but eventually results in damage to the liver and the brain.

Probably the most powerful factor in teenage alcohol use is the view that alcohol consumption is a symbol of adulthood and social maturity. Teenagers are constantly reminded by their parents and by the adults they see in advertising, television, and movies that drinking is an activity indulged in by the sophisticated and worldly. By early adolescence, more than half of American teenagers have used alcohol; the proportion grows to 92% by the end of high school (Newcomb & Bentler, 1989). Although only 1 in 20 high school seniors reports of drinking every day, weekend heavy drinking has become quite common among adolescents. Fully 35% of high school seniors report having had five or more drinks in a row at least once in the past 2 weeks, and 32% report that most or all of their friends "get drunk" at least once a week. Slightly older teenagers and young adults, many of whom can drink legally, generally consume more alcohol because they tend to drink more informally and more regularly at bars and social gatherings. These patterns of alcohol consumption have remained relatively stable for the past 10 years, with only a slight decline since the peak around 1980 (National Institute on Drug Abuse, 1989).

The patterns of alcohol consumption in young people vary according to age, ethnic and religious groups, locality, and gender. For example, the pattern of occasional heavy drinking is highest for those in the 4 years immediately after high school (above 40%), for males (50% versus 26% for females), for noncollege youth, and for those who live in cities rather than in rural areas (National Institute on Drug Abuse, 1987).

Males are more likely both to use and to abuse alcohol than are females. The typical alcoholic is a male with low academic grades and a family history of alcoholism. He is likely to have friends who also drink; he may also take a variety of other drugs. Many alcoholics have serious psychological problems, such as depression, a poor sense of identity, a lack of inner goals, or a personality oriented toward a constant search for new sensations and experiences.

TOBACCO   Tobacco use is another habit that the adult world encourages by example. Cigarettes are still a powerfully alluring symbol of maturity to some teenagers. But, as national mortality statistics show and as medical science has long known, cigarette smoking is a serious health hazard. Smoking increases the heart rate, causes shortness of breath, constricts the blood vessels, irritates the throat, and deposits foreign matter in sensitive lung tissues. Years of smoking lead to premature heart attacks, lung and throat cancer, emphysema, and other lung diseases. Moderate smoking shortens a person's life by an average of 7 years (Eddy, 1991).

In the past, boys began to smoke both earlier and in greater numbers than girls did. Since 1977, however, more adolescent girls than boys report daily smoking. For both boys and girls, over half begin by ninth grade. In the years just after high school, many light smokers convert to heavier smoking. Most adult smokers start in their teens and do so as a result of peer pressure. One in four young adults is a daily smoker, and one in five (20%) smokes a half-pack of cigarettes or more per day (National Institute on Drug Abuse, 1987). Adults continue to smoke because withdrawal from nicotine addiction is difficult.

Today, tobacco smoking as a sign of youthful rebellion seems to have been

TABLE 14–1
Drug Use: Changing Trends Among High School Seniors, 1978–1988

	DAILY USE			EVER USED		
	1978	**1983**	**1988**	**1978**	**1983**	**1988**
Marijuana	10.7	5.5	2.7	59.2	57.0	47.2
Inhalants	0.1	0.1	0.2	12.0	13.6	16.7
Hallucinogens	0.1	0.1	0.0	14.3	11.9	8.9
Cocaine	0.1	0.2	0.2	12.9	16.2	12.1
Heroin	0.0	0.1	0.0	1.6	1.2	1.1
Other Opiates	0.1	0.1	0.1	9.9	9.4	8.6
Stimulants	0.5	1.1	0.4	N/A	16.9	19.8
Sedatives	0.2	0.2	0.1	16.0	14.4	7.8
Tranquilizers	0.1	0.1	0.0	17.0	13.3	9.4
Alcohol	5.7	5.5	4.2	93.1	92.6	92.0
Cigarettes	27.5	21.2	18.1	75.3	70.6	66.4

Source: National Trends in Drug Use and Related Factors Among American High School Students and Young Adults, 1978–1988 (Rockville, MD: National Institute on Drug Abuse, 1989.)

largely superseded by other drugs. The incidence of cigarette smoking among American adolescents fell sharply during the period from 1977 to 1981, as more young people recognized the health risks. Daily smoking among high school seniors dropped from 29% to 20%, and the number who smoked a half-pack or more per day dropped from 20% to 13%. However, the decline leveled off during the 1980s. In 1988, 18% of high school seniors smoked daily, and 11% smoked a half-pack or more per day (National Institute on Drug Abuse, 1989).

MARIJUANA   After alcohol and nicotine, marijuana is the most widely used drug in the United States. This drug is not a narcotic or a hallucinogen, although it does build tolerance and produce mild physical and psychological withdrawal symptoms in some who use it regularly (Witters & Venturelli, 1988). It is *not* a totally benign drug. A report by the National Academy of Sciences states that marijuana has definite undesirable short-term effects but that little is known as yet about serious long-term effects. The short-term effects include temporary acute effects on the brain and behavior, such as impaired coordination and perception, along with a rise in heart rate and blood pressure and the possible occurrence of respiratory ailments (Reinhold, 1982).

　　Marijuana is, of course, an illegal drug in the United States. Illegal drug use over the past two decades has been primarily a phenomenon of youth. But patterns of drug use do not remain constant—they change from year to year and from decade to decade. The use of marijuana by adolescents and young adults went up sharply during the 1970s but is now on the decline. The proportion of college seniors who used marijuana at least once a week was 18% in 1969; the proportion went up to 29% in 1978 and then down to only 6% in 1989 (Pope et al., 1991).

Attitudes about marijuana use have also changed; people are now more aware of the negative health effects associated with the drug. Adolescents report that their peers disapprove of illicit drug use, and many strongly object to daily use. These changing peer attitudes match the trend toward less use of marijuana (National Institute on Drug Abuse, 1989).

COCAINE AND OTHER ILLEGAL DRUGS   Cocaine is an extract of the coca plant and is officially classified as a stimulant, not a narcotic. It is highly addictive. The full range of physical and psychological risks has not been fully studied, but they include death from strokes, heart attacks, or respiratory failure (Kaku et al., 1991; Witters & Venturelli, 1988).

Fortunately, the use of this dangerous drug has now begun to decline, after a period of increased use that began in the late 1970s. In 1987, only 15% of high school students had ever used cocaine. More important, adolescents' attitude toward cocaine use has undergone a striking change: 97% now disapprove of regular cocaine use (Newcomb & Bentler, 1989). The decline in cocaine use can also be seen in college students: In 1978, 30% of college seniors had used this drug at least once; the proportion declined to 20% in 1989 (Pope et al., 1991).

One troublesome finding in the mid-1980s was the shift to the use of "crack" cocaine—an inexpensive, purified, smokable form of the drug. Although only 5.6% of high school seniors have ever tried this drug (Newcomb & Bentler, 1989), the proportion may be higher among high school dropouts. It is more likely for crack addicts to be young adults than to be adolescents; most are members of minority groups living in big cities (*New York Times,* 1989).

The use of hallucinogens has also been declining in the high school and college population. The proportion of college seniors who had used LSD at least once went from 20% in 1978 to 12% in 1989 (Pope et al., 1991).

In contrast to the general downward trend in drug usage, a few drugs have recently shown an increase in popularity. One shift has been in the kind of stimulants that are used. Although the use of amphetamines like "speed" has dropped dramatically, the use of over-the-counter "stay awake" pills, whose major ingredient is usually caffeine, nearly doubled in the 4-year period from 1982 to 1986. The use of inhalants has also increased. Although it is no longer fashionable to sniff glue, there has been a rise in the use of amyl and butyl nitrites, whose more common street names are "poppers" and "snappers" (National Institute on Drug Abuse, 1987). Finally, and most worrisome, is what might be the beginning of a new trend: the use of crystal methamphetamine, or "ice." This drug is smoked like crack; it produces a similar sensation of euphoria and has similar risks (for example, death due to heart attack). Ice has been popular in East Asia for several years and now seems to be gaining in popularity in the United States (Hong, Matsuyama, & Nur, 1991).

Although the use of most illegal drugs has declined, 24% of high school seniors continue to use marijuana at least occasionally (Newcomb & Bentler, 1989). But very few of these adolescents go on to use other drugs (only 9% use inhalants, 6% use stimulants, and less than 1% use heroin)—a finding that would seem to undermine the long-standing belief that marijuana use inevitably leads to the use of more powerful, addictive drugs. In summary, even though familiarity with drug use continues to be part of adolescent culture, teenage opposition to drug use seems to be growing. Perhaps this is a form of adolescent protest.

ADOLESCENCE AND THE FAMILY

Adolescents are very much influenced by their families, even though the old ties may be strained in some instances. Studies over the past 20 years have consistently shown that there is much less conflict between adolescents and their families than was previously believed. "Survey studies are consistent in reports of conflict in only 15% to 25% of families. . . . When conflicts do occur, mundane issues predominate. Family chores, hours, dating, grades, personal appearance, and eating habits are the matters of concern. . . . Study after study has confirmed that parent–adolescent conflicts about basic economic, religious, social, and political values are rare" (Hill, 1987). The relatively few adolescents who form independent opinions in these areas generally do so late in their high school or college years (Waterman, 1985).

Impact of the Family on Adolescents

Parents continue to influence not only teenage beliefs—they also influence teenage behavior. However, mothers and fathers influence their teenagers in different ways. Although there seems to be little difference between the way adolescent males and females report their family relations (Hauser et al., 1987; Youniss & Ketterlinus, 1987), there seems to be considerable difference between the behavior and roles of mothers and fathers in adolescent family relations (Steinberg, 1987a). Fathers tend to encourage intellectual development and are

"Just because I'm your mother doesn't necessarily make me wrong."

frequently involved in problem-solving activities and discussions within the family. As a result, both boys and girls generally discuss ideas with their fathers (Hauser et al., 1987). Adolescent involvement with mothers is far more complex. Mothers and adolescents interact in the areas of household responsibilities, schoolwork done at home, discipline in and out of the home, and leisure-time activities (Montemayor & Brownlee, 1987). This may cause greater strain and conflict between mothers and their children. However, it also tends to create greater closeness between mothers and adolescents than between adolescents and their fathers (Youniss & Ketterlinus, 1987).

In Chapter 12, we discussed the influence that different parenting styles (Baumrind, 1975, 1980) have on children's psychological makeup. This influence continues into adolescence. Baumrind's concept of three categories of parenting styles has had considerable support in the research literature. The authoritative parenting style is most likely to yield "normal" or "healthy" adolescent behavior (Baumrind, 1991; Hill, 1987). We may speculate that the warmth coupled with the sense of confident control administered by the authoritative parent is reassuring for most adolescents. In this instance, the parent provides the experimental adolescent with a "safety net." The consequences of failure are not irreparable, because the parents will pick up the pieces.

Family dynamics and alliances also play an important role. Like parenting styles, these elements begin to shape behavior long before adolescence. An older brother who dominated his younger brother in childhood will probably have the same effect on his sibling in adolescence; a daughter who was "Daddy's girl" at age 6 will probably still be close to her father when she is 16. Although alliances between various family members are natural and healthy, it is important that parents maintain a united front with each other and a distinct boundary between parents and children. Parents need to work together to nurture and to discipline their children. A close bond between a child and one parent that excludes the other parent can disrupt development. The excluded parent loses stature as a socializing agent and authority figure. Problems also can arise from other kinds of imbalances, such as the absence of one parent due to divorce or separation. When an adolescent is testing new roles and is struggling to achieve a new identity, parental authority may be severely tested in a home where there is only one parent.

The Adolescent Leaves Home: The Impact on the Family

Families must make adjustments as adolescents become increasingly independent and prepare to leave home. This is not an easy task. Parents and children must renegotiate roles. Adolescents require a different support system than younger children do, primarily because adolescents are actively exploring their independence. Separateness and self-assertion are not harmful characteristics for adolescents—they are age appropriate and important to development. Some families encourage this development, whereas others oppose it.

Researchers identify three dimensions in family functioning: *cohesion, adaptability,* and quality of *communication* (Barnes & Olsen, 1985). In most cases, it helps during the separation process if families have moderate but not extreme levels of cohesion and adaptability. It is best if families are somewhat flexible and adaptable but not so loosely structured that they seem chaotic. Also, members

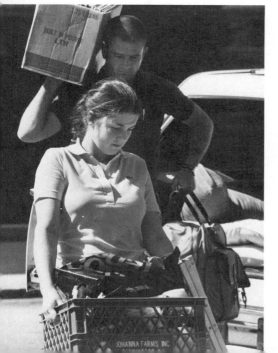

Families must make adjustments as adolescents become increasingly independent and prepare to leave home.

should be cohesive without smothering one another. Families adapt best if they can negotiate the changes in a rational fashion, taking into consideration each member's wants and needs. Family cohesiveness can be maintained when parents and the departing adolescent are able to approach one another as equals and to establish a reciprocal relationship (Grotevant & Cooper, 1985). Open communication, which enables family members to talk things out without friction, helps to preserve the cohesion of the family.

Facilitation of adolescent identity formation and separation may be more difficult in single-parent households. Some studies indicate that the involvement of another adult—for example, a grandparent, aunt, or teacher—makes the transition easier for parent and adolescent (Dornbush et al., 1985).

PEERS, FRIENDS, AND THE SOCIAL ENVIRONMENT

During adolescence, the importance of peer groups increases enormously. Teenagers seek support from others in order to cope with the physical, emotional, and social changes of adolescence. Understandably, they are most likely to seek this support from others who are going through the same experience. These "others" are their peers. Studies have shown that adolescents spend at least half of their time with their peers—friends and classmates—and much less time with their families (Csikszentmihalyi & Larson, 1984).

The Influence of Peers

Peer networks are essential to the adolescent's development of social skills. The reciprocal equality that characterizes teenage relationships also helps develop positive responses to the various crises these young people face (Epstein, 1983; Hawkins & Berndt, 1985). Teenagers learn from their friends and age-mates the kinds of behavior that will be socially rewarded and the roles that best suit them. Social competence is an important element in a teenager's ability to make new friends and to maintain old ones (Fischer et al., 1986).

Peers serve as audience, critic, and emotional support for their friends' ideas, innovations, and behavior.

Being accepted in a clique or a crowd provides emotional support and helps teenagers to develop social skills, but it often demands some conformity.

Most adolescents are members of an adolescent peer group. There are two basic types of groups, distinguished by size: The larger, which has between 15 and 30 members, is called a *crowd;* the smaller, which has as few as 3 members or as many as 9, is called a *clique.* The average crowd consists of several cliques. Because of their small number, cliques are highly cohesive. Their members share similar characteristics or reputations: for example, the jocks, the populars, the brains, and the druggies (Brown & Lohr, 1987; Dunphy, 1963).

Sometimes, cliques are based on elements of adult society, such as socioeconomic status or ethnic origin. In joining them, adolescents are seeking another component of identity—the group identity. Interestingly enough, in seeking autonomy from the family, adolescents often end up substituting a group that is quite similar to their parents.

ETHNIC CULTURAL PATTERNS IN ADOLESCENCE   In many parts of the United States, the youth culture contains numerous ethnic subgroups. For these adolescents, ethnic differences form the basis for one important reference group. Although everyone in our culturally pluralistic society has an ethnic heritage, only 15% of adolescents report that they belong to an ethnic group, either through race or foreign parentage (Havighurst & Dreyer, 1975).

Minority ethnic groups in the United States range in size from the fairly large—Mexicans, Puerto Ricans, Chinese, Native Americans, and African-Americans—to the very small—Amish, Hutterites, and Mennonites. An adolescent's identification with an ethnic group can create conflicts of allegiance between the group's values and those of the larger society. Some special problems face certain groups. African-American youths, for example, must decide whether they want to try to succeed in society on "white" terms or on their own terms. Mexican and Puerto Rican youths must consider whether it is better to try to preserve their own customs and language or to accept the culture of their new society. Chinese, Japanese, Jews, Italians, Irish, and immigrants from many other nations have faced this same problem, and many still face it every day.

Demographic trends suggest that increasing numbers of adolescents will come from single-parent, low-income minority families as the century comes to an end (Otto, 1988). This raises the possibility that an increasingly large number of adolescents will be alienated from the mainstream culture. It is possible, however, that social and cultural norms may shift to incorporate a broader spectrum of youth.

For many adolescents, ethnic differences form the basis for one important reference group.

SOLITUDE AND LONELINESS   Although 80% of adolescents join peer groups, a significant 20% do not. Generally, we think of nonjoiners as loners. Most of us think of being alone as a sad state of affairs that no one would willingly choose. But this is not necessarily the case. Ancient hermits and modern mystics have sought solitude for purposes of contemplation or to deepen their religious experience. Creative work—in painting, music composition, or writing, for example—is solitary, and creative people often seek to be alone, both to create and to think. Solitude may have many other positive attributes as well. Some people experience a sense of renewal or healing when they are alone. Also, many seek solitude for the same reasons as the artist or writer—they can think best when alone and can work through their problems at this time (Marcoen et al., 1987).

Yet there is also a negative side to being alone. This condition can bring on severe feelings of rejection, isolation, depression, and boredom. Hence, there are two ways of experiencing solitude. One is involuntary aloneness, which is perceived as an unhappy state of affairs; the response to involuntary aloneness is to seek the company of others or to turn away from them because of feeling rejected. The other way of experiencing solitude is voluntary aloneness, which is seen as a relief from the pressures of the world—an opportunity for creativity or psychological renewal.

As young people move from late childhood into early adolescence, some experience a feeling of loneliness. Others do not have this experience at any age-specific point in the transit through adolescence, but they feel lonely after arguing with friends or sensing rejection by other peers (Marcoen et al., 1987). Still others voluntarily withdraw from extensive socializing for a period so that they can deal with personal concerns without experiencing public pressure.

THE NEED FOR SUPPORT   Adolescence can be a time of stress. Part of the ability to handle stress grows from finding support in at least one area of engagement. If the changes of adolescence occur in too many areas at one time, they become too difficult to deal with and are a cause of great discomfort. But adolescents who can find security in some environments or relationships are better equipped to deal with discomforts in other aspects of their lives. Gradual changes—in relation to parents and siblings, school, or the peer network—are much easier to deal with than are changes in all of these arenas at the same time (Simmons et al., 1987).

DELINQUENCY   The criminal acts of delinquency range in seriousness from

427

delinquency Criminal acts committed by individuals under the age of 16 or 18 (age cutoff varies by state and by nature of the crime).

shoplifting and vandalism to robbery, rape, and murder. Persons under the age of 16 or 18 who commit criminal acts are called **delinquents;** the age cutoff varies by state and also by the nature of the crime. Although people under the age of 18 make up only **38%** of the U.S. population, they commit more than 50% of the serious crimes (Garbarino et al., 1984).

At some point in their lives, many, if not most, children engage in some kind of behavior that could be called delinquent. Shoplifting, for example, is very common, as are minor acts of vandalism—that is, damage to property performed for the pleasure of destruction. The labeling of individuals as delinquents depends on whether they are arrested and the frequency of these arrests. To some extent, it also depends on race, socioeconomic status, and family composition.

Statistically, delinquency rates are highest in poor urban areas. Delinquency is more likely to occur among ethnic groups recently assimilated into urban life, either from other cultures or from rural areas. Young males from single-parent homes headed by a mother are especially likely to engage in delinquent behavior, and this is true both at higher and lower socioeconomic levels. It is not merely the absence of a male role model that is responsible for this statistic, because the presence of a stepfather in the home does not seem to improve the situation. An adolescent boy with a stepfather is as likely to get into trouble as one who is living only with his mother (Steinberg, 1987b).

Sociologists and psychologists offer quite different explanations for delinquent behavior. Sociological statistics and theories help to link delinquency to environmental factors, but they do not explain individual psychological factors. A psychological theory of delinquency would maintain that environmental factors do not, in themselves, explain why people commit crimes. Individuals are not delinquent because they are poor or black or city dwellers. They may be delinquent because, as individuals, they have repeatedly been unable or unwilling to adjust to society or to develop adequate impulse controls or outlets for anger or frustration.

Perhaps the distinction between sociological and psychological causes of

Delinquency satisfies certain special needs for self-esteem and provides acceptance within the peer group.

delinquency is artificial (Gibbons, 1976). As we have previously seen, sociological factors often lead to psychological consequences, and vice versa. The sociological influences of crowding, mobility, rapid change, and impersonality contribute to psychological problems. Like the other patterns we have studied in this chapter, delinquency is a form of adjustment to the social and psychological realities of adolescence—an extreme adjustment of which society disapproves. Delinquency satisfies certain special needs for self-esteem; it also provides acceptance within the peer group and a sense of autonomy. The kinds of personality disturbances we have discussed seem to predispose certain adolescents to delinquent behavior.

Friendships and Relationships

In late childhood, friendship patterns are often based on sharing particular activities, such as playing ball, riding bikes, or using computers. During adolescence, friendships take on a more crucial significance. As individuals become more independent of their families, they depend increasingly upon friendships to provide emotional support and to serve as testing grounds for new values (Douvan & Adelson, 1966; Douvan & Gold, 1966). With close friends, the younger adolescent is working out an identity. To be able to accept this identity, the adolescent must feel accepted and liked by others.

Adolescents tend to select friends who are from a similar social class and who have similar interests, moral values, and academic ambitions (Berndt, 1982). They become increasingly aware of peer groups and are very concerned about whether their group is "in" or "out." Adolescents know to which group they belong and are usually aware of its effect on their status and reputation. The social status of their group has a measurable effect on their self-esteem: Teens who belong to high-status groups tend to have high self-esteem (Brown & Lohr, 1987).

Between ages 12 and 17, adolescents develop the capacity to form closer and more intimate friendships. Over this period of time, they are increasingly likely to agree with statements like "I feel free to talk with my friend about almost anything," and "I know how my friend feels about things without his or her telling me." This increased intimacy is reported both by girls (in regard to their friendships with other girls) and by boys (in regard to their friendships with other boys). At the same time that the intimacy of same-sex friendships is increasing, friendships with members of the opposite sex are beginning to occur. Close relationships with opposite-sex friends are reported at an earlier age by girls than by boys (Sharabany et al., 1981).

During early adolescence, most interactions with the opposite sex take place in group settings. Many 14- or 15-year-olds prefer this group contact to the closer relationship of dating. "Hanging out" (sitting around and chatting in a pizzeria, on a street corner, or in some other public place) is a popular pastime throughout adolescence, and it becomes increasingly "coeducational" as adolescence progresses. This type of interaction is often the first step in learning how to relate to the opposite sex. Early adolescence is a stage of testing, imagining, and discovering what it is like to function in coeducational groups and pairs. It gives adolescents a trial period when they can collect ideas and experiences with which to form basic attitudes about sex roles and sexual behavior without feeling pressured to become too deeply involved with a member of the opposite sex (Douvan & Adelson, 1966).

FOCUS ON AN ISSUE

TEENAGE RUNAWAYS

Each year in the United States, somewhere between three-quarters of a million and 2 million teenagers run away from home (Shane, 1989). Many are trying to escape from abuse or oppression by parents or stepparents. Others feel alienated from their environment, family, and friends. Some are "throwaways"—adolescents who are forced to leave their homes due to stress within the family (perhaps resulting from divorce, remarriage, or economic hardship) or because of behavior that is unacceptable to their parents.

Runaways and throwaways come from all socioeconomic classes and from all types of families. However, they are more likely to come from homes that are headed by a single parent or a stepparent and where there are many siblings or stepsiblings. Poverty, alcohol and drug abuse, family violence, and sexual abuse are common in the homes from which adolescents run away (Shane, 1989).

Many runaways turn to crime—prostitution, drug dealing, or robbery—in order to survive. They are at risk for a multitude of mental and physical disorders and for death from street violence, drug overdose, or AIDS. Even if they do not fall victim to these hazards, they still have less chance than do other young people of getting the kind of education or training they will need for a successful adult life.

A number of programs have been developed to help teenage runaways. Many large cities have houses where runaways can get food, shelter, and help with their problems. The Department of Health and Human Services operates a national switchboard that runaways can call to receive information on services and psychological counseling. This switchboard also helps runaways get in touch with their parents.

Youth in Need is one example of a program designed to help runaways (Lourie et al., 1979). It is a private, community-based program that provides crisis services to teenagers and their families, and it gives teenagers a place to live while they receive counseling. This enables them to see their home situation from a better perspective and to make plans for the future.

Unfortunately, some teenagers do not have homes to go back to. Perhaps their parents cannot be located, are mentally ill or in prison, or are unable to provide a home due to economic circumstances. In a recent sample of homeless and runaway youth, only 36% were eventually able to go home again (Shane, 1989).

Whether or not they have a home to go back to, these young people need help and understanding. Unless we can make their future brighter than their past, they will remain alienated from a society that they feel has rejected them.

For some teenagers, however, dating starts early: In one sample from a small town in the Midwest, 13% of sixth graders had already started to date. The proportion rose to over 90% in mid- and late adolescence. Bruce Roscoe and his colleagues (Roscoe et al., 1987) have listed seven functions that dating serves:

1. *Recreation*—an opportunity to have fun with a member of the opposite sex.

2. *Socialization*—an opportunity for members of the opposite sex to get to know each other and to develop appropriate techniques of interaction.

3. *Status*—an opportunity to raise one's status within one's group by being seen with someone who is considered desirable.

4. *Mate selection*—an opportunity to associate with members of the opposite sex for the purpose of selecting a husband or wife.

5. *Sex*—an opportunity to engage in sexual experimentation or to obtain sexual satisfaction.

6. *Companionship*—an opportunity to have a friend of the opposite sex with whom to interact and share activities.

7. *Intimacy*—an opportunity to establish a close, meaningful relationship with a person of the opposite sex.

Roscoe and his colleagues questioned adolescents of different ages about their attitudes toward dating. They found that younger adolescents tend to think in terms of immediate gratification; they consider recreation and status to be important reasons for dating. Young adolescents look for dates who are physically attractive, dress well, and are liked by others. Older adolescents are less superficial in their attitudes toward dating; they are less concerned about appearance and more concerned about personality characteristics and the person's plans for the future. Older adolescents consider companionship and mate selection important reasons for dating. For both younger and older adolescents, an interesting sex difference emerged: Females consider intimacy to be more important than sex, whereas males consider sex to be far more important than intimacy (Roscoe et al., 1987).

The custom of dating as we know it in the United States is a mixed blessing (Douvan & Adelson, 1966). The competition for dates and the desire to be popular can put considerable strain on the adolescent. In this sense, the cultural expectations of the dating system complicate the biological and psychological adjustments with which the individual must cope, and these expectations can make the adolescent years more painful and difficult than they should be.

PERSONALITY INTEGRATION

Throughout this chapter, we have talked about the needs of adolescents and the different patterns that adolescents create to fill these needs. During early adolescence, teenagers usually feel intense pressure to conform to the norms and expectations of a few or several reference groups. Their self-image is affected by how well they fit in with a group or measure up to their peers. Their value systems often depend on the values of other people (Douvan & Adelson, 1966).

As adolescents grow older, the measuring stick by which they evaluate themselves and those around them changes. Their ideas about the way they fit into the world may come more from their own discoveries about themselves than from other people. Their evaluations may reflect a sincere, idealistic, long-term commitment to certain values, instead of short-term commitments to friends. The development of this new idealism is the reason why the first 2 years of college are often a period of significant transformation. In part, this change in how youths see themselves and others is caused by their exposure to, and reaction to, the college atmosphere. Much of the change is also caused by the maturing of their rational processes—the new cognitive tools that they can use to evaluate themselves.

Noncollege youths often go through the same dramatic transformation during the first few years after high school. In part, their change is also the result of adjusting to a new way of life: being socialized into a particular occupation, learning new rules and norms, and watching their old circle of friends dissolve. Yet, at the same time, older adolescents who enter the workforce frequently develop a more objective and independent outlook. Their measuring stick, like that of the college student, may become more individualistic.

Although many noncollege, working youths do not have to face the awkward, artificial period of dependence that confuses college students, the adjustment process is just as complex. Particular problems center on teenage unemployment and the dull, repetitive jobs that adolescents are usually given. Cognitive maturity makes meaningful and significant work particularly important at this point of development (Dansereau, 1961; Goodman, 1960). Unemployment or meaningless work offers no challenge and denies individuals the opportunity to see the consequences of their efforts. The lack of significant work can be demeaning and demoralizing because the contrast between an optimal state of biological, cognitive, and social maturity and seemingly trivial tasks is disorienting. Often, adolescents have no armor of numbness or carelessness for protection against frustration and lack of fulfillment. Needs for personality integration, identity, and self-fulfillment are particularly insistent during these years. Thus, working adolescents, like college students, are especially vulnerable and sensitive to an impersonal, technological society.

STUDY OUTLINE

Developmental Tasks in Adolescence

Independence and Interdependence. In our society, adolescence is prolonged primarily because adult roles require lengthy training. The tasks of adolescence include the establishment of an integrated identity and a self that is both independent and interdependent.

Emotional turmoil and conflict with parents are *not* a necessary part of adolescence. The majority of adolescents are well adjusted and have no major conflicts with their parents and peers or with themselves.

In the development of autonomy, the adolescent uses rules and values previously absorbed from parents. Direct parental instruction and supervision are now less necessary because parental standards have been internalized.

Identity Formation. Cognitive developments enable adolescents to see the conflicts and inconsistencies of their various roles and to restructure them in order to form a new identity. Erikson sees identity formation as crucial for a successful passage into adulthood.

Two sources of identity from which the adolescent may derive roles and values are **reference groups** and **significant others**. A problem facing adolescents is to integrate the bewildering variety of roles offered by reference groups and significant others into a coherent personal identity.

Based on Erikson's work, James Marcia defined four identity statuses that adolescents may go through while developing an identity. (1) Adolescents who have made commitments without going through an **identity crisis** are in *foreclosure status.* (2) Those who have neither made commitments nor gone through an identity crisis are in *diffusion status.* (3) Those who are in the midst of an identity crisis are in the *moratorium status.* (4) Those who have gone through an identity crisis and have made their commitments are in *identity*

achievement status. An individual's identity status influences his or her social expectations, self-image, and reactions to stress.

Values, Ideals, and Moral Development

Reassessment in Adolescence. In order to choose a set of moral values, adolescents must reach a stage of cognitive development that enables them to consider alternatives, to use cause-and-effect logic, to think about the past and the future, and to form hypotheses. In Hoffman's view, morality develops in young children through anxiety-based inhibition, in older children through empathy-based concern for others, and in adolescents through the exercise of formal operational thought. These three types of moral growth can also function simultaneously in one individual.

Decisions about Drug Use. Psychoactive drugs, ranging from caffeine to sleeping pills, are commonly used in the United States. Alcohol and nicotine are the two drugs with the greatest abuse potential; adolescents see them as symbols of adulthood. The use of most illegal drugs appears to be declining among adolescents today.

Adolescence and the Family

The Adolescent Leaves Home: The Impact on the Family. Families must adjust to the adolescent's increasing independence as he or she prepares to leave home. Adaptation is easier for families that can renegotiate roles while maintaining cohesion, adaptability, and good communication.

Peers, Friends, and the Social Environment

The Influence of Peers. Relationships with peers serve to provide adolescents with emotional support and are essential to the development of social skills. Peer groups like *crowds* and *cliques* help the adolescent to form his or her group identity. An important reference group for the adolescent may be his or her membership in one of the many ethnic subgroups that exist within American society.

Sociological statistics show that **delinquency** is most common in adolescent males living in urban areas, in children from single-parent homes, and in ethnic groups recently assimilated into urban life. Certain psychological characteristics, such as an inability or unwillingness to learn how to control impulses, also go along with delinquency. A combination of the sociological and psychological perspectives suggests that delinquency is a personality disturbance that occurs in individuals who lack the skills for coping with a complex and rapidly changing society.

Friendships and Relationships. Adolescents tend to select friends who are similar to themselves; friendships are closer and more intimate during adolescence than they are during childhood. Relationships with the opposite sex are likely to occur first in a group setting, though some adolescents begin to date as early as the sixth grade. Younger adolescents are more likely than older ones to choose a dating partner on the basis of superficial characteristics.

KEY TERMS AND CONCEPTS

anxiety-based inhibition	hallucinogens	moratorium
delinquency	identity achievement	psychosocial theory
empathy-based concern	identity diffusion	reference groups
foreclosure	identity statuses	significant other

SELF-TEST QUESTIONS

1. What are the major developmental challenges of adolescence?

2. Describe the processes of achieving independence and interdependence as they relate to adolescent development.

3. What is the impact of reference groups on the adolescent? How does a significant other influence the teen years?

4. Describe Erikson's concept of identity formation.

5. List and describe four identity strategies that adolescents use to meet the challenge of establishing an identity.

6. Explain why it is important to look at one's cognitive development when discussing one's moral development.

7. Describe three different types of moral growth.

SUGGESTED READINGS

CARY, L. *Black ice*. Knopf, 1991. Lorene Cary presents a compelling autobiographical account of her journey at age 15 from the black ghetto of Philadelphia, through the pioneering experience of integration, into the privileged world of an exclusive prep school.

ELKIND, D. *All grown up and no place to go: Teenagers in crisis*. Reading, MA: Addison-Wesley, 1984. Drawing from research and clinical practice, David Elkind looks at the pressures placed on adolescents now as compared to the 1950s and 1960s. He warns of the dangers to mental health from overstimulation and exaggerated expectations in childhood.

ERIKSON, E. *Identity: Youth & crisis*. New York: Norton, 1968. A full discussion of adolescent identity formation, with many examples taken from case studies.

GILLIGAN, C. *In a different voice: Psychological theory and women's development*. Cambridge: Harvard University Press, 1983. A thoughtful and compelling discussion of the different roots of moral thought of women as compared to men. The author contrasts theories and draws from her own research, particularly with adolescent girls.

GREENBERGER, E., AND STEINBERG, L. *When teenagers work*. New York: Basic Books, 1986. A controversial examination and analysis of the impact of working on the teenager. There are hidden costs as well as advantages.

HAUSER, S. *Adolescents and their families: Paths of ego development*. New York: The Free Press, 1991. Scholarly, readable, and filled with case studies. Hauser presents four main "paths" through adolescence and the ways parents subtly guide their teenagers.

KAPLAN, L. J. *Adolescence: The farewell to childhood*. New York: Simon & Schuster, 1984. A sensitive therapist describes the teenager's internal struggle to "let go" of childhood and explore adulthood, using compelling case studies.

SCHLEGEL, A. AND BARRY III, H. *Adolescence: An anthropological inquiry*. New York: The Free Press, 1991. Through systematic comparative study of 186 societies, these authors search for the universals and the range of variation in numerous dimensions of the adolescent experience.

Chapter 15

*When I was a child, I spoke as a child,
I felt as a child, I thought as a child.
Now that I have become a man, I have
put away the things of a child.*

CORINTHIANS 13:11

CHAPTER OUTLINE

Early Adulthood: Roles and Issues

*D*evelopment—or at least the potential for development—continues throughout life. Although some theorists argue that there are recognizable developmental stages in adulthood, the developmental process during maturity differs somewhat from the developmental processes that take place during childhood and adolescence. Changes in adult thought, behavior, and personality are less a result of chronological age or specific biological changes and are more a result of personal, social, and cultural events or forces. The social milestones and cultural demands of the young adult disrupt behavior patterns laid down in the teenage years, requiring that new ones be developed. Decisions must be made. Problems must be solved. The very ability to respond to change and to adapt successfully to new conditions is a hallmark of maturity. A positive resolution of contradictions and difficulties is the basis of adult activity (Datan & Ginsberg, 1975). This more gradual structuring and restructuring of social understanding and behavior does not fit neatly into a stage developmental theory. Not all adults progress in the same way or structure their lives in a similar fashion. Nevertheless, there are some commonalities in the developmental processes of adulthood.

In this chapter, we shall examine some fundamental concepts and theories of adult development. First, we will look at some of the components of development in adulthood and at the general problems of weaving these components together. Next, we will look at some theories of cognitive development. Adults continually try to make sense of their lives and to understand themselves in the broader social world. For many theorists, this "meaning making" is what adulthood is all about. As human beings, we develop systems of meaning, which in turn shape our experience and give rise to our behavior. These meaning systems organize our thinking, feeling, and acting over a wide range of situations (Kegan, 1982). Finally, we will look at some longitudinal studies of adult development and at some of the developmental tasks of the early adulthood period. In the following two chapters, we will focus on the contexts in which adult development takes place—the family environment and the workplace.

CHAPTER OBJECTIVES

By the time you have finished this chapter, you should be able to do the following:

■ Explain the difficulties in discussing the developmental processes that take place during early adulthood.

■ Discuss how physical development in early adulthood differs from physical development in childhood and adolescence.

■ Describe the various ways that theorists have sought to explain cognitive development in adulthood.

■ Outline a few major longitudinal studies of adult development and discuss their results.

■ Describe some of the central developmental tasks of early adulthood.

DEVELOPMENT IN ADULTHOOD

It is difficult, if not impossible, to pinpoint stages of adult development solely on the basis of age. The timing of social milestones, such as marriage, parenting, and career choice, varies from individual to individual. The way that different people react to these events, as well as the nature of the roles that individuals are required to play, will vary according to the demands and restrictions of the culture.

In this and in the following chapters, we will look at the social and cultural milestones that are generally, but not always, reached in early and middle adulthood and at the patterns of adaptation, integration, and reorganization associated with these events.

Maturity

When does adolescence end and adulthood begin? If we say that the attainment of maturity is the deciding factor, we are still left with the problem of defining precisely what we mean by maturity. There are, of course, legal definitions. A person is mature enough to vote at age 18, according to the law; but a U.S. senator must be at least 30 years old, and the presidency is open only to those age 35 and over. There are also informal social definitions of maturity; someone who is employed, financially independent, or a parent is generally considered to be a mature individual. Beyond these definitions, however, a vast array of psychological characteristics are usually associated with maturity: psychological independence and autonomy, independent decision making, and some degree of stability, wisdom, reliability, integrity, and compassion. Different investigators put different characteristics into the blend, and different cultures demand different sets of responsibilities. Freud defined psychological maturity quite simply as the ability to work and to love. Whatever combination of characteristics may be included in a definition of maturity, there is no clear age demarcation for its occurrence.

Age Clocks

Studies of human behavior suggest that each of us has an internalized social clock by which we judge age-appropriate activities (Neugarten, 1968a). In other words, we have built-in expectations, constraints, and pressures for various stages in life. Although these boundaries may sometimes have a psychological base, they

Although clocks let us know when events generally "should" occur, there is tremendous variation in when events do occur for different people. This woman, for example, being congratulated by her son on receiving a college diploma, chose to marry and have children before going to college.

In general, age clocks are less rigid now than they were in previous decades; for example, many couples postpone having children until they are in their mid- to late thirties.

are more often social in nature. For example, if we should observe a man proudly introducing his newborn daughter, we would probably have different reactions, depending upon whether the man was age 25 or 55. We would interpret the motivations of both this man and his wife quite differently, in accordance with the new father's age, and therefore we might act differently toward them.

Age clocks serve as a form of internal timing; they let us know if we are progressing too slowly or too quickly in terms of social events. A 35-year-old who is still in college may sense that he is behind his peers, whereas a 35-year-old who is thinking about retirement may feel that she is far ahead of her peers. Age clocks also let us know when certain events in our life "should" occur. If these events happen earlier or later than we feel is correct, we may experience a greater amount of stress connected with the event. This is partially because we receive more peer support when we do things "on time." Fiske (1968) looks at adulthood's social events in terms of normative and idiosyncratic transitions. Normative transitions are expected at specific times and are less stressful because they may be planned for. Examples of these transitions are looking for a first job or having the last child leave home. Idiosyncratic transitions happen unexpectedly—the sudden death of a spouse, a major illness, the loss of a job. Because these events cannot be anticipated, they will create considerable stress and the need for a major reorganization of a person's life.

In examining the changes in U.S. society over the past decade or two, Neugarten suggests that perhaps these age clocks are less rigid now than they were in previous decades. Many people are returning to school at age 35, 45, or even 60; couples more often postpone having first children until they are in their mid- to late 30s; and marriage, divorce, and remarriage occur throughout the life span. She suggests that we are becoming an "age-irrelevant" society (Hall, 1980).

Conventionally, we define adulthood as three age periods or stages: young adulthood (the 20s and 30s), middle adulthood (the 40s and 50s), and later adulthood (age 60 and over). But even these age guidelines do not always accurately indicate a person's internalized judgment of behavior. Socioeconomic status, rural or urban setting, ethnic background, historical periods, wars, financial depression, or other life events—all may strongly influence the definitions, expectations, and pressures of adulthood. If a man is dependent upon physical labor for his livelihood, he may feel that he has reached his prime at age 30 and old age by the time he is 50. In contrast, business or professional people may judge themselves—and are usually judged by others—according to their experience, mature judgment, and self-confidence; recognition and financial success may not come to them until they are in their 40s or early 50s, and their productivity may well continue into their late 60s. Periods or stages in adulthood are set, in part, by social class; the higher the class, the more likely is the luxury of delay in the movement from one stage to another (Neugarten & Moore, 1968).

Sometimes, we talk about an individual's biological age, social age, and psychological age as three quite separate and independent concepts (Birren & Cunningham, 1985). In adulthood, we often think of biological age with respect to a person's life expectancy. An individual of 40 who has emphysema and a severe heart condition and is likely to die in the next 3 years is at quite a different biological age than the 40-year-old who lives actively until age 80. Social age is judged by what position an individual is in as compared with the cultural norms. Psychological age refers to how a person adapts to environmental demands. It includes such things as intelligence, learning abilities, and motor skills as well as subjective dimensions like feelings, attitudes, and motives. Clearly, looking at the adult's chronological age all by itself provides little meaning.

Developmental versus Historical Change

Adult development cannot be studied in a controlled laboratory setting. Cultural and historical factors influence each generation of adults in unique ways. Therefore, it is difficult to separate the general developmental changes of aging, establishing a career, and parenting from specific historical events. Several investigators have studied the generation that was born during the Great Depression and experienced World War II as adolescents. These individuals entered college or the labor market in the postwar boom of the late 1940s and early 1950s, and many served in the armed forces during the Korean War. The war was followed by a period of economic well-being and relatively low unemployment. The way in which this generation entered adulthood was significantly marked by these historical events (Featherman, Hogan, & Sorenson, 1984). These people can be compared with the cohort of individuals born in the post–World War II period, 1946–60—the baby boomers. This large group enjoyed a growing economy in childhood and adolescence, and a sizable number faced adolescence and adulthood in the turbulent late 1960s. To understand adult development, we need to combine both longitudinal studies and a comparison of different age cohorts. For a full understanding of the life course during adulthood, it is important to understand both the particular historical age cohort and the developmental strains, issues, and conflicts common to a particular chronological age.

Baltes (1987; Hetherington & Baltes, 1988) suggests, however, that life-span development is more than just the interaction of developmental and historical change. He suggests that three factors interact in development. *Normative, age-graded influences* are the biological and social changes that normally happen at predictable ages. This includes things like puberty and menopause as well as some physical aspects of aging. It also includes some predictable social events, such as marrying and retiring, that often occur at a particular time. *Normative, history-graded influences* are those historical events, such as wars, depressions, and epidemics, that affect the whole cohort of individuals at about the same time. *Nonnormative influences* do not occur at any predictable time in a person's life. These correspond to fixed idiosyncratic transitions. They include divorce, unemployment, illness, career changes, or even a chance encounter with a particularly influential individual or idea. Some of these critical events may define a turning point in an individual's life (Bandura, 1982). Development, therefore, is more than just a factor of age or history; it also includes the timing and influence of events that affect us uniquely as individuals.

Baltes believes that factors like race, sex, and social class mediate both the type and the effects of these influences. For example, girls experience physical puberty (an age-graded effect) earlier than boys do. African-American men are more likely to experience unemployment (a nonnormative influence) than white men are. Effects of divorce may be different in an African-American extended family than they are in a white nuclear family (Harrison et al., 1990).

The impact of these influences also differs according to the age of those who are affected. Children and people in later adulthood are often most affected by age-graded influences. Adolescents and young adults are the ones who are most affected by history-graded influences; trying to find a first job during a depression or fighting in a war happens most often to people at these ages. Nonnormative events can happen at any time, but their effects on a person's life can be more important as a person grows older. Figure 15–1 and Table 15–1 show how these influences interact at different ages for people in different generations.

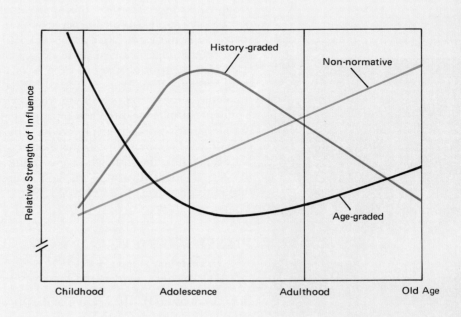

FIGURE 15-1
A Life Span Profile of Influences. Age-graded, history-graded, and non-normative influences affect people more directly at different times in their life spans.

TABLE 15–1

How Historical Events Affect Different Age Cohorts
Those starting out during the depression were more affected than were schoolchildren, whereas those establishing a career during the postwar boom were more affected than were those nearing retirement.

HISTORICAL EVENT	YEAR BORN					
	1912	**1924**	**1936**	**1948**	**1960**	**1972**
1932 (The depression)	20 years old (starting out)	8 years old (schoolchild)				
1944 (World War II)	32 (parenting/ career)	20 (starting out)	8 (schoolchild)			
1956 (Postwar boom)	44 (middle age)	32 (parenting/ career)	20 (starting out)	8 (schoolchild)		
1968 (Vietnam era)	56 (preretirement)	44 (middle age)	32 (parenting/ career)	20 (starting out)	8 (schoolchild)	
1980	68 (retired)	56 (preretirement)	44 (middle age)	32 (parenting/ career)	20 (starting out)	8 (schoolchild)

Young adults are in their biological prime.

Glen Elder's (Elder, Caspi, & Burton, 1988) work provides an interesting example of how history-graded and age-graded factors mediated by sex might interact to produce different outcomes. He studied one group of people who were of school age (about 10 years old) when the Great Depression began as well as a group who were infants. It took approximately 9 years for real recovery from the depression to occur, so the former group was 10 to 18 years old while their parents struggled, whereas the latter group was 1 to 10 years old. He found that the boys who were younger showed more negative effects of the early (financial) familial stress and deprivation than did the boys who had already experienced a strong family organization for several years. Indeed, the older boys often worked to help the family survive the depression, thereby further limiting their exposure to the family problems that often accompanied paternal unemployment and poverty.

The girls in the study showed a different pattern. The younger girls apparently formed an unusually strong mother–daughter bond while facing economic hardship. Thus, the girls who were younger during the depression were actually more goal oriented, competent, and assertive than those who were adolescents during the depression (Elder et al., 1988).

PHYSICAL DEVELOPMENT AND HEALTH IN EARLY ADULTHOOD

In early adulthood—the decades of the 20s and 30s—most men and women enjoy a peak of vitality, strength, and endurance. These are the normative, age-graded expectations. Most cultures recognize this physical prime by dispatching the young to do battle, by paying phenomenal sums to young athletes and fashion models, by putting professional apprentices through grueling regimes of internships, bar

A pregnancy in a woman's late 30s is more likely to draw on her reserve capacity of physical stamina than would a pregnancy in her 20s.

exams, and dissertation defenses, and by expecting young women to give birth. Physical strength is at its maximum between ages 25 and 30; after 30, it declines slowly but significantly. Despite signs of aging, most physical skills and capacities remain at a functional level if regularly exercised. Declines in physical skills and capacities are most notable in emergency situations or at times when demands are extreme (Troll, 1985). For example, a pregnancy in a woman's late 30s would more likely draw on her reserve capacity of physical stamina than would a pregnancy in her 20s. In addition, the older pregnant woman may recover at a slower pace.

Generally, young adults enjoy better health than do children; they have few acute illnesses and have not yet begun to experience the troubles of middle age (Timiras, 1972). They are also in their biological prime. Many major athletes reach their peak of skill and training at this time, and the physical skills that most people need to perform their jobs are at their maximum efficiency. The age at which athletes reach their peak varies according to the sport (Fries & Crapo, 1981). Gymnasts generally peak during adolescence, whereas golfers perform their best somewhat later. The death rates of young adults are lower than those of many other groups. At the same time, many of the first signs of the diseases that will cause trouble in later life start to appear during early adulthood (Scanlon, 1979). Although no symptoms may be felt, lung, heart, and kidney diseases as well as arthritis, joint and bone problems, atherosclerosis, and cirrhosis of the liver are beginning to develop. In addition, some genetically determined diseases, such as diabetes or sickle cell anemia, or diseases like multiple sclerosis and rheumatoid arthritis, and stress-linked diseases, such as hypertension, ulcers, and depression, affect people particularly during early adulthood.

Sometimes, sociocultural events or factors create situations of disease or even death that contrast with the normal expectations for health and physical fitness of young adults. For instance, in times of war, many youth are killed or handicapped. In urban areas of high crime, the youth are often victims of homicide or of drug abuse. Most recently, the AIDS epidemic has hit disproportionately among individuals in early adulthood (see Chapter 16). The psychological adjustment and development of individuals is especially difficult when their physical condition directly contradicts the age-graded norm. Any physical handicap or disease is liable to affect both one's biological age and one's social age expectations (see Application: The Physically Challenged).

COGNITIVE DEVELOPMENT IN EARLY ADULTHOOD

Learning, memory, problem solving, and many other cognitive processes continue on through adulthood. As a result of this continued intellectual activity, older adults have a broader accumulation of knowledge. Do changes occur, however, in what we have come to call intelligence or cognitive capacity, or in competence? Is there continued cognitive development after adolescence? The evidence is not always that clear. Early theorists and researchers believed that intellectual capacities peak during a person's late teens or early 20s, but this belief may have grown from a misinterpretation of the research. In a study during World War I, for example, all draftees took a general intelligence test. It was found that the younger ones—those between ages 15 and 25—did better on average than did the older draftees. Several other studies that were conducted in the 1930s and 1940s produced somewhat similar results. Older people scored consistently lower than younger ones did. These were the usual results when different individuals were used in each age group—a cross-sectional design (see Chapter 1). But in the late 1940s, there was contradictory evidence when researchers studied the same individuals at several different ages—a longitudinal design. In a longitudinal design, individuals usually show some increase on intelligence tests, at least through their 20s and 30s, usually leveling off at around age 45 (Whitbourne, 1986). Why was there a difference in results between the two types of research designs? Remember that cross-sectional designs use individuals who represent different age groups. The older groups generally had a larger proportion of immigrants and individuals with less education. The younger groups were in better health, most had finished high school, and many had some college experience. The scores of the older groups did not necessarily predict the future for the younger, healthier, and better-educated groups. In fact, longitudinal studies suggest that individuals with more education tend to increase their IQ test scores for a longer period in adulthood than do those with less education (Schaie, 1983).

What kinds of cognitive abilities increase? Some skills do peak in the late teens—for example, speed-related performances, rote memory, and the manipulation of matrices. Some of these abilities may have a physiological basis, or they may simply reflect the fact that many teenagers are full-time students who practice, develop, and rely on these skills. In fact, specific disciplines are associated with specific reasoning skills. This is why, for example, psychology majors tend to develop probabilistic reasoning, whereas humanities majors tend to develop conditional logic (Lehman & Nisbett, 1990). With some training, people in their

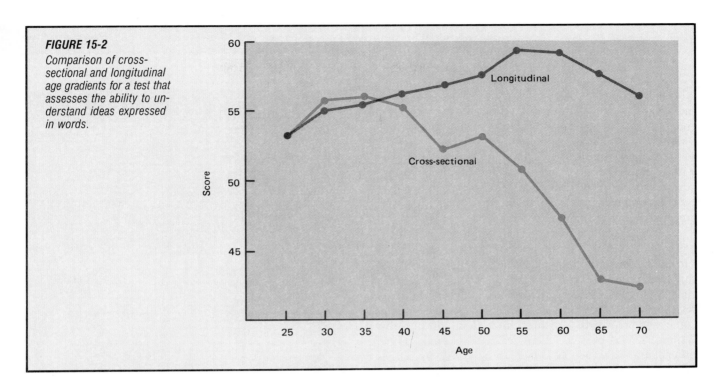

FIGURE 15-2

Comparison of cross-sectional and longitudinal age gradients for a test that assesses the ability to understand ideas expressed in words.

30s, 40s, and even 50s and beyond might perform well on some of these tests (Willis, 1990). Similarly, skills that are used frequently are maintained better than those that are not exercised. Architects, for example, retain their visual–spatial skills at above-average levels (Salthouse, Babcock, Skovronek, Mitchell, & Palmon, 1990; Salthouse & Mitchell, 1990). Other cognitive abilities, especially judgment and reasoning, continue to develop throughout life. But there is not complete agreement on which cognitive abilities change and in what fashion (see Chapter 18). Furthermore, it is clear that education and experience will affect cognitive development in adulthood.

Beyond Formal Operations?

Is there another "stage" of cognitive development after adolescence? Are there qualitative differences between the way an adult understands the world and the way an adolescent understands it? Are there different structures of meaning that evolve during adulthood?

There is a classic study of the change in the thought processes of 140 Harvard and Radcliffe students over their 4 years of college experiences (Perry, 1970). These students were interviewed extensively at the end of each year. The researchers were interested in how the students "made sense" of their experiences at college—how they interpreted their experiences and the meaning they attributed to them. They were particularly interested in how the students came to grips with the many conflicting points of view and frames of reference that they had encountered. In this study, the students were found to move through a progression

APPLICATION

THE PHYSICALLY CHALLENGED

Normally, young adults are in their prime, physically; they enjoy a peak in physical strength, stamina, and energy. They are in generally good health and have few acute illnesses. They may be physically fit and enjoy the self-esteem, sense of efficacy, and competence that goes with their physical prowess. But what about young adults who are physically disabled? How do they adjust psychologically to being disabled when their age-mates are performing at optimal levels?

The adjustment to a physical disability is difficult at any time. However, late adolescence and early adulthood can be a particularly difficult period (Wright, 1983). At this stage in life, individuals make many major decisions, such as choosing an occupation and developing intimate relationships. Many physically disabled people may become overwhelmed by their limitations during this future-oriented period. There are at least three factors influencing how people adapt to physical disabilities (Wright, 1983). First, it is important to understand the disability and its limitations. Any handicap is defined by the interaction of the individual's abilities and the environmental task—if you can't speak Japanese, you will be handicapped in a Japanese classroom. A second aspect of adaptation to a physical disability involves coping with the attitudes and values of others and their social expectations based on the disability. The physically disabled are often stereotyped and must deal with real prejudices. They may be pitied or demeaned and looked upon as passive and broadly incompetent individuals. In others words, there is often a sweeping set of generalizations that may be applied to any physically disabled individual regardless of the specific disability.

Finally, coping with a physical disability involves coping with an array of hopes, fears, dreams, frustrations, lost opportunities, and guilt and anger. In the initial crisis period there may be very real grief and mourning, as well as shock and disbelief. There are certainly periods

One way of dealing with a handicap is to regard oneself as "physically challenged" rather than physically disabled.

of anger and frustration as one copes with everyday tasks that are easy for others but that are complicated by a disability. And there is further anger and frustration at the unnecessary social handicaps or obstacles that are encountered.

In this process, some individuals have adopted a definition of themselves as "physically challenged" rather than physically disabled (Wright, 1983). This is particularly common among disabled athletes. Simply by changing the definition and the terminology, it is sometimes easier to see the specific physical obstacle as a challenge to be overcome, perhaps with the help of others, but not as a label or category that defines one's whole personality.

---

of what Perry calls *stages*. At first, they interpreted the world and their educational experiences in authoritarian, dualistic terms. They were seeking truth and knowledge. The world could be divided into good and bad, right and wrong. The faculty's role was to teach them, and they would learn by hard work. But these students were soon confronted with differences of opinion, uncertainty, and confusion. Perhaps professors presented subject matter in a way that encouraged students to learn the answers for themselves. Or perhaps the professors themselves had not found the right answers yet. Gradually, in the face of diverse points of view, students began to accept and even to respect a diversity of opinion. They began to adopt the perspective that people have the right to different opinions, and they began to understand that one person can see the same thing in two different ways depending on the particular context. This relativistic perspective, however, eventually gave way to the need to make some commitment of personal belief, or personal affirmation. The students first made these initial commitments in a testing, exploratory fashion, but eventually they resolved for themselves commitment to and responsibility for a particular set of values, point of view, and lifestyle. The students thus moved from a basic dualism (for example, truth versus falsehood) to a tolerance for many competing points of view (conceptual relativism) to a self-chosen commitment and responsibility. This, for Perry (1970), represented a type of intellectual development characteristic of the young adult.

Other theorists have elaborated on the types of thinking characteristic of early adulthood. Klaus Riegel (1975, 1984) emphasizes the understanding of contradictions as the important achievement of adult cognitive development. He calls this *dialectical thinking*. For Riegel, if there is a fifth stage of cognitive development—a stage beyond the fourth and final stage described by Piaget—it is the dialectical stage where an individual considers opposing thoughts and synthesizes or integrates these thoughts. One particularly important aspect of dialectical thinking is the integration of the ideal and the real. The practical, everyday world (the real) serves as a dialectical correction of the artificiality of abstract formal operational thinking (the ideal). This, according to Riegel, is the strength of the adult.

The findings of Perry and Riegel were based primarily on studies of young adults in college. The changes that they observed may have been specifically related to college experience rather than to the more general experiences of young adulthood. Another theorist, Gisela Labouvie-Vief (1984), emphasizes "commitment and responsibility" as the hallmark of adult cognitive maturity. For Labouvie-Vief, the course of cognitive development should involve both the evolution of logic as described by Piaget and the evolution of self-regulation from childhood well into adulthood. She recognizes that logic may reach its final stage in adolescence, with the development of formal operational thought. Like Perry and Riegel, LaBouvie-Vief also feels that individuals need exposure to social complexity, to different points of view, and to the practicality of the real world to escape dualistic thinking. She differs from the others, however, in describing a somewhat different and longer process of evolution in which adults become truly autonomous and are able to handle the contradictions and ambiguities of their life experience. Adult cognitive maturity, according to Labouvie-Vief, is marked by the development of autonomous decision-making skills (Labouvie-Vief, 1987).

Flexible Use of Adult Intelligence

Not all researchers believe that there is a fifth stage of cognitive development. Some believe that the distinctive feature of adult thinking is the flexible way in which adults are able to make use of whatever cognitive abilities they may already possess. K. Warner Schaie (1986) suggests that during childhood and adolescence we acquire increasingly complex structures for understanding the world. The powerful tools of formal operational thinking are the peak of this period. Schaie calls this the *acquisition* period. In young adulthood, we make use of our intellectual abilities to pursue our careers and to choose a lifestyle. Schaie refers to this as the *achieving* period. This is an important period in adult cognitive development, a period in which we apply our intellectual, problem-solving, and decision-making capabilities. But this is not the problem solving of IQ tests or even of abstract problems. For the most part, it involves an individual adult choosing his or her own personal solutions that become integrated into a life plan. Individuals who successfully do this acquire a certain degree of personal independence and move on to another phase in the application of cognitive skills, the period involving *social responsibility*. In middle age, according to Schaie, we use our cognitive abilities to solve problems for others in the family, the community, and on the job. For some, these responsibilities may be quite complex and may involve the understanding of organizations and different levels of knowledge. These individuals have the opportunity to exercise their cognitive abilities in an *executive* function in addition to the social responsibilities that they assume. Finally, in the later years, the nature of problem solving shifts again. The central task is one of *reintegrating* many of the elements experienced earlier in life—making sense of one's life as a whole and exploring questions of purpose. For Schaie, then, the focus of cognitive development in adulthood is not an expanded capacity or a change in structure, rather, it is the flexible use of intelligence at different stages in one's life span (see Figure 15–3).

SYSTEMS OF MEANING There are several theorists in the areas of moral development and self-understanding who view adulthood as a time of continued change and growth. Robert Kegan (1982), for example, emphasizes that we, as human beings, continue to evolve systems of meaning well into our adulthood. His theory is much too complex to present adequately here. He builds on the tradition of Piaget and theories of cognitive development. He defines several levels of

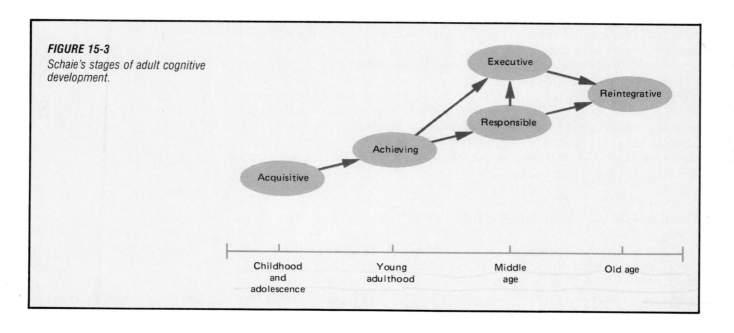

FIGURE 15-3
Schaie's stages of adult cognitive development.

"meaning making," and these systems of meaning then shape our experience, organize our thinking and feeling, and give rise to our behavior. As we enter adulthood, our own particular systems of meaning become idiosyncratic and yet share some regularities with the meaning systems of others at our developmental level. At each stage, the old becomes part of the new, just as children's concrete understanding of the world becomes part of the raw data for their formal operational thought. For theorists such as Kegan, most of us continue to structure and restructure our understanding of the world well into our 30s and even beyond—a rather optimistic view. Yet, psychotherapists often find these theories useful. In fact, psychotherapy works best when one tries to match the developmental level of a client with his or her own level of understanding.

STUDIES OF ADULT DEVELOPMENT

Let us examine a few major longitudinal studies of adult development. We should keep in mind that the developmental stages identified by these theorists are tentative. They are not established concepts supported by research (as are Piaget's stages of cognitive development, for example).

The Grant Study

Beginning in 1938, a group of almost 300 Harvard students was tested, interviewed, analyzed, and followed in a developmental project that became known as the Grant Study (Vaillant, 1977). The researchers wanted to learn how and why some men succeed in adult life and others fail. The Harvard students selected had been recommended by their classmates as outstanding in health, self-reliance, achievement, and stability. Interestingly enough, one of the group, described as a statesman who was "pointlessly murdered" before his prime and "destined to play a role in every child's history book," was John F. Kennedy, Harvard, class of 1940. JFK and his test cohorts went through 20 hours of tests and interviews while in college. They were rated for 25 personality traits. Researchers compiled detailed family histories for each subject. After graduation, the subjects completed detailed questionnaires at regular intervals.

Adult success was compared with adolescent profiles. The researchers expected to document a relationship between the lively, outgoing, altruistic teenager and the prosperous, well-adjusted man. This hypothesis, however, was not supported by the data. Gregarious, idealistic students were no more likely to succeed than shy, self-contained youths. The Grant Study analysts concluded that easy amiability is often just a hallmark of adolescence that does not necessarily appear in the mature personality. The traits in teenagers that most clearly predicted later success were practicality, organization, and personality integration—characteristics not normally associated with late adolescence.

This study also identified several coping styles and defense mechanisms—particularly, repression, projection, and sublimation—as a key to success in adulthood. These mechanisms were studied not as pathological processes but as fruitful, adaptive responses to challenge and crisis. According to Vaillant, these defense mechanisms fill five important functions in adult life: (1) They contain

sublimation An adult coping strategy in which anxious energy and unacceptable impulses are turned toward acceptable goals.

emotions within acceptable limits during times of extreme emotional stress, such as the loss of a loved one; (2) they maintain stability by channeling biological drives; (3) they permit adjustments in self-image following important changes, like promotion or major surgery; (4) they help to resolve conflicts within one's intimate circles; and (5) they enable one to rationalize major conflicts with the dictates of conscience, such as killing in wartime.

The most successful adaptation in this group was **sublimation.** In sublimation, one turns anxious energy and unacceptable impulses toward acceptable goals, instead of repressing them or projecting them onto another person. All defense mechanisms, repression and projection included, help the ego survive to some degree—and even thrive—in adversity.

Which factors encourage the development of mature defenses? Sheer intelligence, a happy childhood, and an affluent background were found to be no guarantees. Successful maturation was found to be surprisingly independent of these influences—at least among this select population. Vaillant (1977) suggests that two forces are at work—one organic and the other environmental. The brain may continue to develop in structure and complexity until age 50, so variations in brain development may account for some adult successes and failures. The environmental influences on maturity consist mainly of the capacity to build intimate relationships with those more powerful as well as those more dependent than oneself. The most successful subjects in the Grant Study acquired mentors and role models in early adulthood; they later became protectors and advisers to children, professional beginners, and other learners.

Vaillant interpreted the Grant data as supportive of Erikson's stages of development (see Chapter 2). However, they also led him to suggest two modifications in Erikson's theory. First, he suggested that there was a period of relative intrapsychic quiescence between the establishment of intimacy and the onset of generativity. Vaillant named this stage *career consolidation* because the individual focuses on learning and establishing a job and providing for his or her family. Once career is established, the person can return to identity issues, namely, generativity.

Vaillant (1977) also introduced a stage occurring later in the middle years, between Erikson's stages of generativity and ego integrity. This stage is marked by the conflict of *keeping the meaning versus rigidity*. There is a waning of internal questioning and a recognition of sociocultural values, their role, and how they can (and should) be perpetuated. The person is moving toward the tolerant attitude that marks ego integrity but has not quite achieved it. Thus, Vaillant ends up with 10 stages of development instead of Erikson's 8.

Levinson's Seasons of a Man's Life

Another intensive study of adult development is Levinson's (1978, 1986). His subjects were a group of 40 men, aged 35 to 45, drawn from different racial, ethnic, and professional groups. Levinson's methodology differed significantly from that of the Grant Study. Instead of interviewing his subjects at fixed intervals over a decade of adulthood, he compressed his interviews into several intensive sessions during a period of a few months. His data, based on his subjects' memories and their introspection, are thus more subjective than the tests, scales, and "blind evaluations" used by Vaillant. Along with the reconstructed biographies of these 40 men, Levinson and his assistants also combed the biographies of great figures, such as Dante and Gandhi, for clues to patterns of adult growth.

They identified three major "eras" in the male cycle, each approximately 20 years in length. During each era, the person constructs a "life structure." This is the pattern underlying a person's life, serving as a boundary and mediator between personality and society. The life structure is composed mainly of the person's relationships with the outside world, including what the individual gains from and must contribute to each relationship. The relationships may be with individuals, groups, systems, or even objects. For most men, relationships at work and within the family are central (Levinson, 1986). At specific ages (see Figure 15–4), people will begin to question and break down their existing life structure. They will then construct a new life structure that is consistent with their current needs. This structure will dominate during a stable period of functioning until the man "outgrows" it and starts the process all over again (Levinson, 1986).

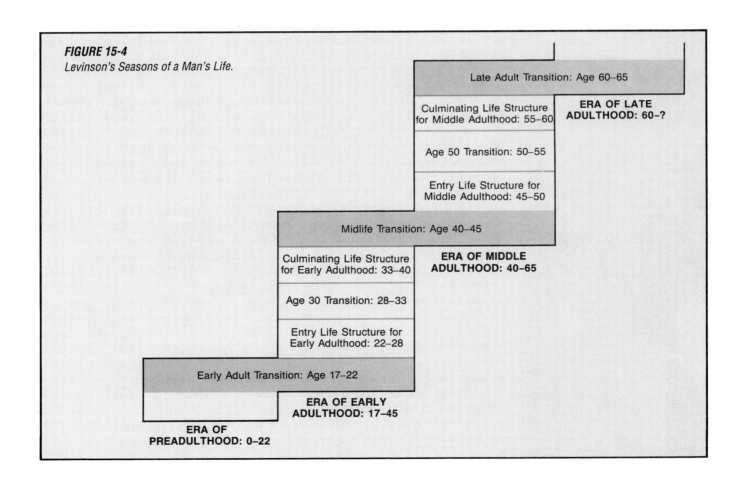

FIGURE 15-4
Levinson's Seasons of a Man's Life.

Late Adult Transition: Age 60–65

Culminating Life Structure for Middle Adulthood: 55–60

ERA OF LATE ADULTHOOD: 60–?

Age 50 Transition: 50–55

Entry Life Structure for Middle Adulthood: 45–50

Midlife Transition: Age 40–45

Culminating Life Structure for Early Adulthood: 33–40

ERA OF MIDDLE ADULTHOOD: 40–65

Age 30 Transition: 28–33

Entry Life Structure for Early Adulthood: 22–28

Early Adult Transition: Age 17–22

ERA OF EARLY ADULTHOOD: 17–45

ERA OF PREADULTHOOD: 0–22

Although Levinson was primarily interested in the mid-life decade from 35 to 45, he found that maturation and adjustment at this stage depended greatly on the individual's growth in a "novice" phase from ages 17 to 33. This is the time when young American men resolve adolescent conflicts, create a place for themselves in adult society, and commit themselves to stable, predictable patterns. Within the novice phase, Levinson saw three distinct periods: early adult transition, which lasts approximately from ages 17 to 22; entering the adult world, from ages 22 to 28; and age-30 transition, from about ages 28 to 33.

To achieve complete entry into adulthood, according to Levinson, the young man must master four main developmental tasks: (1) defining a "dream" of adult accomplishment, (2) finding a mentor, (3) developing a career, and (4) establishing intimacy.

At the beginning of the novice phase, the dream of adult accomplishment is not clearly linked to reality. It may consist of a specific goal, such as winning a Pulitzer Prize, or a grandiose role, such as becoming a movie producer, business tycoon, or famous poet. A man may have more modest aspirations in his dream, such as being a master craftsman, village philosopher, or loving family man. The most important aspect of the dream is its ability to inspire him in his present activity. Ideally, the young man begins to structure his adult life in realistic, optimistic ways that help realize the dream. Hopeless fantasies and utterly unattainable goals do not encourage growth.

Besides being unrealistic, the dream may not be realized, because of lack of opportunities, excessive parental pressure, individual traits such as guilt or passivity, or special talents needed. Consequently, a young man may enter and master an occupation that holds no magic for him. According to Levinson, such decisions bring about continuous career conflicts in adulthood and are responsible for a lack of excitement and a limited self-investment in work. Levinson believes that those who struggle to fulfill some version of the dream, however, are more likely to achieve a sense of fulfillment. It is important to note that the dream itself undergoes change. The young man entering the early adult transition hoping to become a basketball all-star may later find satisfaction as a coach, thus incorporating some, but not all, elements of the youthful dream.

In achieving the dream, the young person can be aided enormously by a mentor. The mentor can instill self-confidence by sharing and approving of the dream and by imparting skill and wisdom. As a sponsor, the mentor may use influence to advance the career of the protégé. The major function of the mentor, however, is to provide a transition from the parent–child relationship to the world of adult peers. The mentor must be sufficiently parental to represent a high level of achievement, yet sufficiently sympathetic to overcome the generation gap and establish a peer bond. Gradually, the apprentice may acquire a sense of autonomy and competence; he may eventually overtake the mentor. Given the intense nature of the relationship, this growth may lead to bitterness, conflict, and distance. The mentor may find the youth rebellious and ungrateful; the youth may see the mentor as critical and oppressive. Frequently, they break off and drift apart.

Besides forming the dream and acquiring a mentor, the youth also faces a complex, sociopsychological process of career formation. This is a long process that we will examine in more detail shortly. It goes well beyond the mere selection of an occupation. Levinson views this developmental task as spanning the entire novice phase.

Similarly, formation of intimate family relationships does not begin and end

In achieving the dream, young people can be greatly aided by a mentor or sponsor. These young singers are receiving individual instruction from Luciano Pavarotti.

with the "marker" events of marriage and the birth of the first child. Both before and after these occasions, the young man is learning about himself and the ways in which he relates to women. He must ascertain what he likes about women and what they like about him; he must define his inner strengths and vulnerabilities in sexual intimacy. Although some self-discovery takes place in adolescence, the young man is still puzzled and guilty about these matters. Not until his early 30s does he develop the capacity for a serious, democratic partnership. Furthermore, relating to the feminine aspects in himself and others remains a lifelong developmental task.

A primary relationship with a "special woman" (Levinson's term) also fills a need similar to that of the mentor–pupil bond. The special woman may facilitate realization of the dream by sanctifying it and by believing her partner to be a hero. She aids his entry into the adult world by encouraging adult hopes and tolerating his dependent behavior and other shortcomings. According to Levinson, the male's need for the special woman decreases later, in mid-life transition, when most men achieve a high degree of autonomy and competence. (Levinson is currently studying a cohort of women in the same manner; we might well ask to what extent "special men" facilitate the adult growth of *their* partners.)

Seasons of a Woman's Life

Levinson's study stimulated considerable criticism, the most persistent of which was that he had not included women in his study. As a consequence, several women (Wendy Stewart, Ruth Droege, Kathryn Furst, Diane Adams) undertook separate studies in which they applied Levinson's theory to the adult development of women. Each of the researchers used biographical interview techniques similar to those used by Levinson. However, because the researchers were doctoral candidates and did not have the resources that were available to Levinson, they interviewed fewer subjects for shorter periods of time than did Levinson. Levinson himself has recently reported preliminary findings on a group of 45 women (Levinson, 1990). Of the group, 15 were homemakers, 15 were businesswomen, and 15 were academicians.

These studies of women supported, in part, Levinson's theoretical hypothesis that entry into adulthood involves four developmental tasks and an "age-30 transition." Levinson's four proposed tasks, you should recall, are defining a dream, finding a mentor, forming an occupation, and establishing a relationship with a "special person." The age-30 transition, for Levinson, is a time of stress as career objectives and lifestyles are reexamined. But, although the women in these studies experienced Levinson's tasks and the age-30 transition, these studies indicate that women's experiences are quite different from those of men. Furthermore, although Levinson (1986, 1990) claims that both men's and women's transitions are intimately linked to age, other researchers have found that, for women, family life-cycle stage seems to be a better indicator of transitions than age is (Harris, Ellicott, & Holmes, 1986). Thus, it may not be the "age-30" (or 40 or 50) transition for women. Rather, the transitions may be the birth or launching of children.

Perhaps the most striking difference between the sexes is in the differing dreams they have. Indeed, the difference is so striking that Levinson (1990) discusses "gender splitting" as a phenomenon in adult development. For both men and women, the dream is of central importance. But men tend to have a unified vision of their futures focused on their jobs, whereas many women tend to have split dreams. Both the academicians and businesswomen in Levinson's (1990) sample wanted to combine career and marriage, albeit in different ways. The academic women were less ambitious and more willing to forgo their careers as long as they could continue intellectually stimulating community involvement after their children were born. The businesswomen wanted to maintain their careers but on a reduced level once they had children. Only the homemakers had a unified dream; they wanted to be full-time wives and mothers much as their mothers had been.

Similarly, most women in the earlier studies had dreams incorporating both careers and marriage, and the majority of these women gave greater weight to marriage. Only 7 of 39 women, or a bit less than 18%, focused exclusively on career achievement in their dreams; even fewer women, a bit more than 15%, restricted their visions of the future to the traditional role of wife, mother, and helpmate. However, even those women who had dreams of both career and marriage moderated their dreams in the context of their husband's goals and thus fulfilled traditional expectations within a more contemporary lifestyle (Roberts & Newton, 1987).

The women who were being studied ranged in age from 28 to 53, and more than 76% were married at the time or had been married in the past. Approximately 41% of these women expressed dissatisfaction with one or the other aspect of their split dream (Droege, 1982). It seemed to several of these women that careers and marriages were incompatible. The women in Levinson's (1990) study also had found it extremely difficult to integrate career and family. None of the businesswomen, for example, found her solution any more than "adequate." Although colleagues and family members felt these women were successful, the women themselves felt that they had sacrificed either career to family or family to career (Roberts & Newton, 1987). On the other hand, the homemakers in Levinson's study were not particularly happy either. By the time they reached the ages 35 to 45 (their ages at the time of the study), only 20% continued to be in a strictly traditional marriage. Fully 30% were legally divorced, with another 30% feeling psychologically divorced. The remaining 20% were trying to redefine their marriage, often to their husband's chagrin. Thus, despite a variety of approaches, women seem much more conflicted between career and marriage than men are.

Another area in which men and women have very different experiences is in the mentoring relationship. Although relations with mentors are considered important to the career and life development of young adults, women enter into this relationship less frequently than do men. Part of the problem is that there are few women in positions to guide, counsel, or sponsor young women in the workplace. When men act as mentors to women, the relationship between them may be "disrupted by sexual attractions on both sides" (Roberts & Newton, 1987). Sometimes husbands or lovers may serve as mentors, but here the function is complicated by the conflicting demands made by the relationship. When women assert their independence and either pursue their careers fully or claim equality in the relationship, their mates often withdraw support. Even those women who were focused on their careers found very few mentors to support their dream.

Women may also have trouble finding a "special man" to support their dream (Droege, 1982). Although a husband or lover sometimes serves as the "special man," particularly in the early adult phase of separating from parental dominance, a male mate rarely sustains the female's dream if it starts threatening his preeminence. Hence, a male mate does not perform all the functions of the special man, such as facilitating the personal and career growth of the woman.

Women not only have greater difficulty than men in finding a special person, they also settle on a career much later than men. In Levinson's (Levinson et al., 1978) earlier study, most men "complete [their] occupational novitiate and assume a fully adult status in the work world" by the end of their age-30 transition. By contrast, women generally do not cease being beginners in the world of work until well into middle age (Droege, 1982; Furst, 1983; Stewart, 1977). Droege even found that women who had fixed on a career in their 20s had for the most part not completed their "occupational novitiate" until age 40 or later. Droege also noted that women in middle adulthood were still preoccupied with trying to succeed in the workplace and were not yet ready to reevaluate their occupational goals or achievements. Adams (1983), by contrast, studied a group of female lawyers and found that they followed the male career pattern until the age-30 transition. At that point, most of the women began to shift their focus from achieving success in their careers to gaining satisfaction from their personal relationships. This, too, is unlike men, who remain career centered during their age-30 transition.

Age-30 transition is stressful for both men and women, and in this respect, Levinson's findings with men can be confirmed for women. But otherwise, men and women react differently to the reevaluative process that takes place between ages 28 and 33. Men may make changes in their careers or lifestyles, but they do not change their focus on their jobs and careers. Women, in contrast, do. Priorities that were set during early adulthood are generally reversed by women during their age-30 transition (Adams, 1983; Droege, 1982; Stewart, 1977; Levinson, 1990). Those women who are oriented toward marriage and child rearing tend to shift more toward occupational goals, whereas women who are career centered generally move toward marriage and the family. Men generally have a simpler and more unified dream of themselves and the world than do women. The more complex dream of women makes it much more difficult for them than for men to achieve their goals.

Perhaps one reason why a woman's dream is more complex is because it has been more affected by social changes. In the late 1950s and 1960s, the "best-adjusted" women had a clear dream: to be a full-time homemaker and mother (Helson & Picano, 1990). These women's dream became outdated as social changes brought women into the workforce. By middle age, the traditional women were no longer the best adjusted in the study. Instead, they became dependent or overcontrolled relative to the less traditional women (Helson & Picano, 1990). The message here is that being in congruence with societal roles is important to well-being. Today's role for young adult women is clearly one that combines career and family. Young men, on the other hand, are still not expected to make a real commitment to child care and housekeeping (Kalleberg & Rosenfeld, 1990).

Both these studies of women and the original Levinson study of men should be viewed cautiously. The samples of interviews are small and not broadly representative. Levinson interviewed 10 biologists, 10 executives, 10 novelists, and 10 blue-collar workers. Furthermore, over 85% of the women and 70% of the men in the studies trying to replicate Levinson were college educated. These findings, therefore, must be considered preliminary. They suggest tasks that seem to be important during the transition to adulthood, particularly for college-educated, upwardly mobile young adults.

GOULD'S TRANSFORMATIONS

In any research study on the course of development during adulthood, researchers are faced with the difficult task of deciding how to organize extensive biographical data. The results depend in part on the focus and interests of the investigator. Levinson had 15 hours of biographical interviews from 40 men. He chose to look at some of the aspects of the process of establishing a career and a certain lifestyle. Roger Gould had a more cognitive focus. He was interested in the individual's assumptions, ideas, myths, and world views during different adult periods.

Gould's (1978) studies of adults included both men and women, although his subjects are by no means representative. Gould and his colleagues examined extensive life histories of a large group of men and women, aged 16 to 60. From these profiles, they extracted world views characteristic of different adult stages. Gould views growth as the process of casting off childish illusions and false assumptions in favor of self-reliance and self-acceptance. Like Kegan, he believes that an individual's system of "meaning making" shapes his or her behavior and life decisions.

From ages 16 to 22, according to Gould, the major false assumption to be challenged is: "I'll always belong to my parents and believe in their world." To penetrate and discard this illusion, young adults must start building an adult identity that their parents cannot control or dominate. Young people's sense of self, however, is still fragile at this point, and self-doubt makes them highly sensitive to criticism. Young adults also begin to see their parents as imperfect and fallible people, not the all-powerful, controlling forces they once were.

From 22 to 28, young adults make another false assumption that reflects their continuing doubts about self-sufficiency: "Doing things my parents' way, with willpower and perseverance, will bring results. But if I

According to Gould, the achievements of baseball players come from their realization that disciplined, well-directed work leads to success.

become too frustrated, confused, or tired, or am simply unable to cope, they will step in and show me the right way." To combat this notion, the young adult must accept full responsibility for his or her life, surrendering the expectation of continuous parental assistance. This involves far more than wresting oneself from a mother's or father's domination; it requires the active, positive construction of an adult life. Aggression is rechanneled toward adult work instead of ancient grievances. Con-

DEVELOPMENTAL TASKS IN EARLY ADULTHOOD

As can be seen in the studies just outlined, theorists describe the normative developmental tasks that are generally associated with early adulthood in widely varying ways. However, many theorists look to Erikson's theory of psychosocial stages for defining the central developmental tasks of the period.

quering the world on one's own also diverts energy from constant introspection and self-centeredness. Gould found that the predominant thinking mode during this period progresses from flashes of insight to perseverance, discipline, controlled experimentation, and goal orientation.

In Gould's view, from ages 28 to 34 a significant shift occurs toward adult attitudes. The major false assumption during this period is: "Life is simple and controllable. There are no significant coexisting contradictory forces within me." This attitude differs from those in the previous stages in two important respects. First, it indicates a sense of competence and, second, an acknowledgment of limitations. Enough adult consciousness has been achieved to admit inner turmoil without calling strength or integrity into doubt. Talents, strengths, and desires, suppressed during the 20s because they did not fit into the unfolding blueprint of adulthood, may resurface. Gould cites examples of the ambitious young partner in a prestigious law firm who begins to consider public service; also, the suave, carefree bachelor who suddenly realizes that his many relationships with women are not satisfying because of some inadequacy of his own. (This development closely resembles Levinson's prediction about the dream: Those who ignore and suppress it in early adulthood will be haunted later by the unresolved conflict.) Even those who have fulfilled youthful ambition still experience some doubt, confusion, and depression during this period. They may begin to question the very values that helped them to gain independence from their parents.

Growth during this period involves breaking out of the rigid expectations of the 20s and embracing the more reasonable attitude: "What I get is directly related to how much effort I'm willing to make." Those in this period of life cease to believe in magic, and they begin to put their faith in disciplined, well-directed work. At the same time, Gould believes, they now begin to cultivate the interests, values, and qualities that will endure and develop through adult life.

The age period of 35 to 45 brings definitive involvement in the adult world as these people become the final authority to those both younger and older than themselves. Their parents no longer have control of them; their children have not yet effectively challenged them. They are, as Gould says, "in the thicket of life." At the same time, they experience a sudden time pressure and fear that they will not accomplish all of their goals. The beginning physical changes of middle age frighten and dismay them; reduced career mobility pens them in. The drive for stability and security, which was paramount in the 30s, is replaced by a need for immediate action and results. There can be no more procrastination. The deaths of their parents and their acute awareness of their own mortality bring them face to face with the unfairness and pain of life. In acknowledging the ugly side of human existence, they let go of their childish needs for safety. They also become free at last to examine and discard the deep sense of their own worthlessness and wickedness, which was left over from childhood. This, Gould believes, represents a full, autonomous adult consciousness.

Theories that emphasize periods or "stages" are valuable in understanding adult development, but they should not be too rigidly interpreted. First, the notion of stages in adulthood tends to obscure the stability of personality, which is somewhat true throughout adulthood. Second, these theories pay little attention to the unpredictability of life events (Neugarten, 1979). Third, most subjects of stage theories thus far have been men, and much of the research has concentrated on the same age cohort (individuals born in the late 1920s or 1930s).

Identity and Intimacy

Erikson's theory of eight psychosocial crises or stages continues to be used as a foundation for understanding adult development. Erikson's theory is "epigenetic"—that is, one period builds upon another. Adult development is dependent upon the resolution of earlier periods—the resolution of issues of trust and autonomy, initiative and industry. In early adulthood, the central issues to be

According to Erikson, identity achievement and the establishment of intimate relationships are the central tasks of early adulthood.

resolved are identity achievement versus identity confusion, and intimacy versus isolation.

Identity achievement is a central issue of adolescence as well. Yet, many theorists, including Erikson (1959) himself, suggest that identity issues persist throughout the adult years. Processes of identity achievement provide a sense of continuity to adult experiences. Through identity achievement processes, individuals come to define and redefine themselves, their priorities, and their place in the social world. As they experience new events or establish new relationships, individuals continually redefine their identity. The conflict between intimacy and isolation is the other issue most characteristic of early adulthood. Intimacy involves establishing a mutually satisfying, close relationship with another person. Intimacy represents the union of two identities, but without the loss of each individual's unique qualities. Isolation is the inability, or failure, to achieve mutuality, sometimes because the individual's identity is too weak to risk what might be lost in a union with another person (Erikson, 1963).

Ideally, the young adult capable of intimacy is self-aware, self-accepting, independent, and trusting. Expressions of vulnerability and inadequacy can be made in trust to the intimate partner without fear of rejection. By the same token, the other partner's inadequacies can be acknowledged without diminishing worthiness or desirability. Intimate partners support each other fully but with honesty. If one partner's needs consistently dominate a relationship, intimacy is destroyed.

At first glance, Erikson's theory appears to be another stage theory of adult development. But actually, Erikson himself uses it in a much more flexible fashion (Erikson & Erikson, 1981). Issues of identity and intimacy are considered present throughout life. Major events, such as a death in the family, may create simultaneous identity and intimacy crises as one struggles with the loss and tries to redefine oneself in the absence of an intimate partner. Moving to a new town, starting a new job, going back to college—all are major changes that require some psychological and social adjustment. It is possible to look at Erikson's theory as a guideline for some of the issues to be resolved in new situations. In a new neighborhood, one may need to reestablish trust, discover one's own autonomy, initiate relationships with new friends, and rediscover one's successful competence and industry before one really feels like an adult again. Certainly, this new situation will require one to redefine one's own identity within a new context. Hence, for many contemporary thinkers, both identity and intimacy processes are central to an understanding of adult development (Whitbourne, 1986b).

Social Understanding and the Evolving Self

Earlier in this chapter, we discussed some of the cognitive competencies of young adults. We described *dialectical thinking, systems of meaning,* the development of *commitment* and *responsibility,* and the *flexible use of intelligence.*

Many theorists have tried to combine these aspects of cognitive development with aspects of personality development to describe the continued growth of personal and social understanding in the adult years.

LOEVINGER'S MODEL OF PERSONALITY DEVELOPMENT Over the past 20 years, Jane Loevinger (1976) has attempted to describe how individuals form a consistent idea of themselves and whether such self-concepts might occur in a sequence of predictable stages. She has combined psychoanalytic theory and aspects of Kohlberg's theory of moral development with a variety of research findings to create a new model of personality development. She has also developed a series of tests to determine empirically whether or not the model fits actual experience. The core of her model of personality is the ego—a psychoanalytic construct that comes close to, but is not identical with, the self-concept that is discussed in Chapter 18. According to Loevinger, the ego is not so much a thing as a process, a sort of "executive" function of the mind that consciously controls the personality. The ego tries to make sense out of experience, to achieve self-understanding, and to integrate this understanding with behavior. Loevinger sees the individual's ego as developing according to a series of stages that depend on **structures of meaning,** or understandings of the world, and on **structures of character.** These stages involve cognitive abilities, moral development, and personality factors.

To test the model, Loevinger devised a series of sentence completion tests. It is assumed that individuals project their own frame of reference into their answers and thus show how they relate to themselves and to the external world. From the results of many tests, she has identified seven stages of personality development and three transitional stages (see Table 15-2). Each stage is more complex than the previous one, and none can be passed over in the process. Very few individuals

structures of meaning An individual's understanding of the world on which, according to Loevinger's theory, a series of developmental stages depend.

structures of character In Loevinger's theory, part of the ego's equipment for making sense of experience and achieving self-understanding.

TABLE 15–2
Loevinger's and Kegan's Stages of Personality Development

LOEVINGER		KEGAN	
Stage	**Illustrative Behavior**	**Stage**	**Illustrative Behavior**
1. Presocial (infancy)	Indifferent to anything but own needs; dependent on caregiver for identity.	0. Incorporative (Infancy)	No separation of self and other.
2. Impulsive (early childhood)	Impulsive behavior; still self-centered. Actions are "good" or "bad" depending on whether one gets caught.	1. Impulsive (2–7 years)	Impulsive behavior, self-centered (similar to Loevinger's Impulsive stage).
3. Self-protective ("delta") (early childhood)	Fears being caught; tries to evade blame; opportunistic. [Transition]	2. Imperial (7–12 years)	Strives for independence, works toward achievement and skill building.
4. Conformist (late childhood/ adolescence)	Conforms to external rules; seeks approval, feels shame if he fails to secure the approval of others. [Transition]	3. Interpersonal (13–19 years)	Restructuring of relationships; some marked sex differences.
5. Conscientious (adolescence)	Development of a conscience; self-imposed standards, self-criticism. [Transition]	4. Institutions (early adulthood)	Reintegration of the interconnectedness of the evolving self.
6. Autonomous (late adolescence/ adulthood)	Respects autonomy of others; copes with inner conflicts and needs.	5. Interindividual (adulthood)	
7. Integrated (adulthood)	Reconciles inner and outer conflicts; integrates understanding of self with understanding of others.		

Sources: Adapted from *Ego Development: Conceptions and Theories* by J. Loevinger (San Francisco: Jossey-Bass, 1976), table 1; "Loevinger's Model and Measure of Ego Development" by S. Hauser, *Psychology Bulletin,* 1976, 83, No. 5; and *The Evolving Self: Problem and Process in Human Development* by R. Kegan (Cambridge, MA: Harvard University Press, 1982).

reach the end stages—most come to rest at various points along the way. Although the stages are somewhat related to chronological age, they do not necessarily depend on it. Because adolescence involves so much self-consciousness about values and the meaning of life, many individuals at this stage experience intense and far-reaching changes in their ideas about themselves and the world.

The first two stages—the *presocial* and *impulsive*—occur primarily in very young children. At the presocial stage, infants are dependent on their care-givers for their identity and are concerned exclusively with their own needs and gratifications. Young children at the impulsive stage have achieved a separate identity, although they are still interested mainly in the gratification of their needs. They judge their actions as "good" or "bad" depending solely on whether they are rewarded or punished. Their view of the world is egocentric and concrete. Loevinger has found some children, adolescents, and even adults detained here.

The third stage, the *self-protective* or "delta" stage, is more advanced. The egos of individuals at this stage are ruled by self-interest, and they will do whatever is expedient to satisfy it. Their relationships with others revolve around issues of control, domination, deception, and getting into trouble. They obey rules only out of self-interest and to avoid trouble. Many younger children are found at this stage; adolescents and adults who are detained here are usually opportunistic and manipulative.

There is a transition (called "delta three") at this point to the fourth, or *conformist*, stage, which is reached by most people either during late childhood or early adolescence. The individual ego judges itself by external things—by possessions, status, reputation, and appearances—and seldom refers to inner feelings except in shallow platitudes and clichés. Rules are obeyed "because they are the rules" or "the right way." The individual tries to avoid disapproval and feels ashamed when censured.

The next three stages require reflective thinking on the part of adolescents and adults. Those in the fifth, or *conscientious*, stage have discovered that "the right way" may be relative to the context. They judge their own traits, achievements, and ideals by inner rules, not necessarily by those of peers or authority figures. Unlike those at previous stages, those at the conscientious stage are capable of self-criticism.

Before people reach the sixth, or *autonomous*, stage, they pass through a transitional stage in which they begin to be able to tolerate paradoxical relationships. At the autonomous stage, people have a greater awareness of the inner conflicts between their personal needs and their ideals and between differing perceptions of the same events. They are increasingly able to understand, tolerate, and respect others' points of view, solutions to life's problems, choices of friends, and decisions about work. Instead of condemning, they are willing to let others make their own decisions. The seventh, or *integrated*, stage has been reached when people are able to respect and reconcile conflicting demands within themselves and between themselves and others. They not only tolerate differences between themselves and others, but they also value those differences. Loevinger estimates that less than 1% of all adults reach this stage.

Robert Kegan (1982) has drawn from several developmental theories to present an integrated perspective on the "evolving self." Like Loevinger, Kegan emphasizes the importance of meaning. The developing individual is continually in a process of differentiating himself or herself from the world and at the same time understanding the integration of self in the broader world. He is also similar to

At Loevinger's autonomous stage, people are more able to understand, tolerate, and respect others' points of view and decisions.

Loevinger in his emphasis on the importance of adolescence and young adulthood. Finally, Kegan is one of the few theorists who looks at the masculine and feminine tendencies in development. Kegan's stages of development are as follows: Stage 0, *incorporative,* infancy; Stage 1, *impulsive,* ages 2–7; Stage 2, *imperial,* ages 7–12; Stage 3, *interpersonal,* ages 13–19; Stage 4, *institutions,* early adulthood; and Stage 5, *interindividual,* adulthood. (See Table 15–2, which explains Kegan's stages and compares them to Loevinger's stages.)

Although many psychologists resisted Loevinger's theory when it was presented, some clinicians as well as researchers now find it useful. Loevinger's seemingly simple sentence completion tests appear to measure an important aspect of development that is independent of intelligence or verbal fluency (Hauser, 1976). Researchers find that delinquents score in the lower stages of personality development significantly more often than nondelinquent adolescents do (Frank & Quinlan, 1976; Hauser, 1976). Therapists find the rich description of ego development helpful in their work with adolescents and young adults. Professional observations like these mark only the beginning of efforts to support or reject these theories.

STUDY OUTLINE

Development in Adulthood

Human development takes on a new character in adulthood because it no longer stems primarily from sheer physical growth and the rapid acquisition of new cognitive skills. Adult growth is defined largely in terms of social and

cultural milestones, as young people struggle to become self-sufficient members of society. They begin to terminate dependence and assume responsibility, for themselves and others.

Maturity. Definitions of maturity vary from culture to culture. Historical and *nonnormative* factors alter the general developmental patterns, as do individual **age clocks.** Often, we distinguish between a person's biological age, social age, and psychological age.

Physical Development and Health in Early Adulthood

Young adults enjoy physical and intellectual vigor. Although some physical skills have already peaked, most remain at a highly functional level, especially if regularly exercised. However, many of the first signs of later diseases are starting to develop.

Cognitive Development in Early Adulthood

Longitudinal studies seem to indicate that cognitive development does not stop with adolescence, although there is not complete agreement on which abilities change, and in what fashion. The developing *dialectical thinking,* responsibility and commitment, flexible use of intelligence, and the evolving systems of meaning have been described as some of the cognitive competencies characteristic of young adulthood.

Studies of Adult Development

The Grant Study. The Grant Study of Harvard graduates concluded that adult success resulted primarily from development of effective adult coping styles. Factors such as childhood trauma, intelligence, and affluence were not found to be particularly important. A crucial aspect of maturity in these men was development of intimate relationships with people both more powerful and more dependent than themselves.

Levinson's Seasons of a Man's Life. Levinson's study of men emphasized the mastery of four main developmental tasks in order to achieve complete entry into adulthood: defining a "dream," finding a mentor, developing a career, and establishing intimacy.

Developmental Tasks in Early Adulthood

Many theorists draw on Erikson's theory of psychosocial stages to define the central developmental tasks of the period. According to Erikson, the establishment of identity and intimacy are the central tasks of adulthood.

Social Understanding and the Evolving Self. Several theorists have combined aspects of cognitive development with aspects of personality development to describe continued growth of personal and social understanding in the adult years. Loevinger has described a model of personality development based on psychoanalytic theory of ego development and internalization of moral judgment. Kegan has presented an "evolving self" perspective, which describes how the individual attempts to differentiate himself or herself from the world while acknowledging that each person is a part of the world.

KEY TERMS AND CONCEPTS

achieving period	identity achievement	psychological age
acquisition period	intimacy	social age
age clock	longitudinal design	structures of character
biological age	nonnormative influences	structures of meaning
cross-sectional design	normative, age-graded influences	sublimation
dialectical thinking	normative, history-graded influences	

SELF-TEST QUESTIONS

1. List several different definitions of maturity. What are the problems involved in defining this word?

2. What are age clocks, and how are they less rigid now than in previous decades?

3. How do cultural and historical factors influence development in adulthood?

4. Describe the differences between biological age, social age, and psychological age.

5. What are normative, age-graded influences, normative, history-graded influences, and nonnormative influences?

6. Describe characteristics of adult physical development and health.

7. Compare and contrast longitudinal and cross-sectional design studies. Why is there a difference in results between the two types of research design when studying adult intelligence?

8. What did Perry discover concerning the intellectual development of the young adult in his classic study of Harvard and Radcliffe students?

9. Compare and contrast different theories of adult cognitive development.

10. According to the Grant Study, what are some keys to success in adulthood?

11. According to Levinson and Levinson-inspired studies, what are the four developmental tasks that a young adult must master to enter adulthood? In what ways do men and women experience these tasks differently?

12. Describe the central developmental tasks of early adulthood according to Erikson.

13. Describe Loevinger's stages of personality development.

SUGGESTED READINGS

BELENKY, M. F. *Women's ways of knowing: The development of self, voice and mind.* New York: Basic Books, 1986. A landmark book, based on in-depth interviews, that chronicles women's adult development of self-confidence and thought.

GILOVICH, T. *How we know what isn't so: The fallibility of human reason in everyday life.* New York: Free Press, 1991. Despite the cognitive abilities of well-educated adults, how and why do they sometimes become convinced of false beliefs?

HYDE, J. S. *Understanding human sexuality* (4th ed.). New York: McGraw-Hill, 1989. A comprehensive text on the many aspects of human sexuality—heterosexual and homosexual attitudes and behavior together with the biological base.

LEVINSON, D. *The seasons of a man's life.* New York: Knopf, 1978. A report on the common patterns of development from a 10-year study of adult males, with particular attention to the novice phase, the settling-down period, and the mid-life transition.

OKUN, B. *Working with adults: Individual, family, and career development.* Monterey, CA: Brooks/Cole, 1984. This book, valuable for counselors and social workers, integrates family, career, and individual life cycles.

ROSE, M. *Lives on the boundary: The struggles and achievements of America's underprepared.* New York: Free Press, 1989. Real-life stories of young adults breaking out of the poorly educated underclass.

WRIGHT, B. *Physical disability—A psychosocial approach* (2nd ed.). New York: Harper & Row, 1983. Wright focuses on adjustments to physical disabilities and people's attitudes about the physically disabled.

Chapter 16

*The family is the building block
for whatever solidarity there is in society.*

FREDERIC A. BIRMINGHAM
JILL RUCKELSHAUS: LADY OF LIBERTY

Family and Lifestyle

*T*he traditional pattern for adults in many cultures has been to get married soon after finishing their education or their job training, have children, and settle into family life. In the 19th century, young women often married in their late teens; if marriage was delayed much after age 25, there was fear of perpetual spinsterhood. That was the cultural prescription, yet in 1900 fully 30% of women over the age of 18 were single (including widows), and the average age at first marriage was 22.3 years, similar to what it was in 1980 (Glick, 1977; Troll, 1985). Even in the 1980s, the overwhelming proportion of Americans were marrying and most were having children—sooner or later. Nevertheless, young adults appear to have a greater range of options and less rigid prescriptions for family choices or personal lifestyles.

In this chapter, we examine the family and evolving personal lifestyles as the social context of early and middle adulthood. We will look at the various ways in which adults establish intimate relationships with others, and structure and restructure a sense of their own personal identity. We will also look at how the sequence of decisions about family and lifestyle determine later options and provide the context and the challenges for further adult development, for continuity, and change.

CHAPTER OBJECTIVES

By the time you have finished this chapter, you should be able to do the following:

■ Discuss the role of sexuality and intimacy in adult development.

■ Describe marriage patterns and alternative lifestyles available in adulthood and the issues faced by each.

■ Describe the relationship between the demands and pressures of parenthood and adult development.

■ Discuss the problems and issues of divorce, single parenting, and stepparenting as they relate to adult development.

SEXUALITY AND INTIMACY

Whether single, married, widowed, divorced, or cohabiting, most adults have to come to terms with the problems of achieving sexual intimacy with others. For many, this continues to be a vital issue well into their 30s; and like many other aspects of adult development, the development of sexual intimacy depends on earlier experiences in adolescence. Adolescent sexual experiences may have been successful and satisfying, tentative, fumbling, confusing, overwhelming, comic, embarrassing, or even frightening. How do they compare with later ones? Usually sexual attitudes and expressions change gradually between adolescence and young adulthood. Adolescent sexual experiences are part of a general attempt to test and explore one's new powers and feelings as well as one's popularity and skill; later sexuality becomes more fully integrated into friendship and family roles. As people gain experience in things sexual, they try to incorporate their sexual attitudes and interests in their everyday social life. Above all, many seek sexual intimacy as part of an enduring, satisfying emotional bond.

Early adulthood presents a chance to establish a satisfying sexual pattern and a long-term pattern of intimacy.

Achieving Intimacy

Robert Sternberg's (1986) "triangular theory of love" demonstrates the complexity of achieving successful love relationships. Sternberg suggests that love has three components. First, there is *intimacy,* which is the feeling of closeness that occurs in love relationships. It is the sense of being connected or bonded to the loved one. Intimacy is evidenced in several different ways. We want to do things to make life better for people we love. We genuinely like them and are happiest when they are around us. We count on them to be there when we need them, and we try to provide the same feelings of support to them. We share our activities, possessions, thoughts, and feelings with them. In fact, sharing activities may be one of the most crucial factors in turning a dating relationship into a loving, marriagelike relationship.

Passion is the second component of love according to Sternberg's theory. This refers to the forms of arousal that lead to physical attraction and sexual behavior in a relationship. Sexual needs are important here but are not the only forms of motivational needs involved. For example, needs for self-esteem, affiliation, and succorance may also play a role. Sometimes intimacy leads to passion; at other times passion precedes intimacy. In still other cases, there is passion without intimacy or intimacy without passion (as in a sibling relationship).

The final component of Sternberg's triangle is *decision/commitment.* This component consists of a short-term and a long-term aspect. The short-term aspect is reflected in the decision that a person loves someone. The commitment to maintain that love is the long-term facet. Again, the relationship of decision/commitment to the other components of love can vary. To demonstrate the possible combinations, Sternberg (1986) has developed a taxonomy of love relationships (see Table 16–1). Clearly, most of us are hoping for a marriage relationship marked by consummate love. But more than one couple has mistaken infatuation for consummate love. And in many marriages, the passion dies and the relationship becomes one of companionate love.

Intimacy can be destroyed by denial of feelings, particularly anger. Fear of

TABLE 16–1

Taxonomy of Kinds of Love Based on Sternberg's Triangular Theory

| | COMPONENT | | |
KIND OF LOVE	INTIMACY	PASSION	DECISION/COMMITMENT
Nonlove	−	−	−
Liking	+	−	−
Infatuated love	−	+	−
Empty love	−	−	+
Romantic love	+	+	−
Companionate love	+	−	+
Fatuous love	−	+	+
Consummate love	+	+	+

Note: + = component present; − = component absent. These kinds of love represent limiting cases based on the triangular theory. Most loving relationships will fit between categories because the various components of love are expressed along continua, not discretely.

Source: From Sternberg, R. J., 1986, "A Triangular Theory of Love" in *Psychological Review,* Volume 93, pp. 119–135.

rejection also blocks intimacy, especially when it leads to false identities designed to cater to others rather than to fulfill important internal needs. Traditional courtship and dating patterns may even discourage intimacy if they involve only ritual rather than honest exchange. Some extreme opposites are even more harmful: casual sex, gamesmanship, and sadistic honesty. Brutal candor and contrived aloofness are never fertile ground for creative intimacy (McCary, 1978).

Sexual Patterns

Researchers have noted several important changes in American marital sexual behavior in the past few decades. The median duration of intercourse has increased markedly, suggesting that some married partners are experiencing greater enjoyment, relaxation, and mutuality (Hunt, 1974). Hunt attributes this to changed attitudes and priorities. More couples seek to maximize the pleasure of the entire act rather than reaching the release immediately. Permissiveness has also increased, including acts previously forbidden, such as the female's initiation of sex, premarital sex, homosexuality, masturbation, and oral and anal sex (Hunt, 1974; McCary, 1978). In 1937, and again in 1959, 22% of the U.S. population condoned premarital sex for both men and women. In Hunt's survey, 75% of the men approved of premarital sex for men, and over 50% of them found it acceptable for women. Some behaviors have not increased much, including mate swapping, group sex, and extramarital sex. The double standard persists, with 50% of college men approving of premarital sex but 75% still preferring a virgin wife. There are indications that this attitude is changing, however; now, sexually conservative students do not flatly ban premarital sex but reserve it for serious "living-together" relationships (McCary, 1978).

Although sexuality is certainly more open and accepted now than prior to the 1960s, it does appear that college students have again become more conservative in their rates of sexual intercourse. For example, one study reported that 51% of the sophomore women studied in 1978 were engaging in sex at least once a month, but this figure had fallen to 37% in 1983 (Gerrard, 1987). This was very comparable to the 35% reporting sexual activity at least monthly in the early 1970s. This swing back toward more conservative sexual behavior among college women may be attributable to an increased fear of disease (such as herpes or AIDS). It may also reflect the growing self-assurance of young women who feel less compelled to "please" their boyfriends. Or it may be that as social pressure to have sex has declined, women are more likely to follow their own belief systems and not engage in sex if they feel guilty about it (Gerrard, 1987). In other words, the high percentages reported in the late 1970s may be more indicative of social pressure than personal attitudes, whereas those from the early 1970s and 1980s reflect individual beliefs. This would suggest that individual attitudes about sex may not have changed very dramatically over the past three decades.

SEXUAL RESPONSE The dominant pattern of sexual intimacy between men and women in the 1990s appears to be one of increased communication and mutual satisfaction. Yet one of the common problems that continues to be reported in studies of sexual behavior is a marked difference in the patterns of male and female satisfaction. A decade of research (Hite, 1976; Hunt, 1974; McCary, 1978) on

In an atmosphere of trust, intimacy can be achieved through an acceptance of self and each other.

American patterns seems to indicate that, for some couples, the men routinely achieve physical gratification, but the women do not. Surveys and questionnaires repeatedly reveal women's criticisms—that men are in too much of a hurry, that they are rough and perfunctory, that they fail to appreciate the erotic and romantic importance of gentle, slow arousal. Men complain that women are frigid and unresponsive. One recent innovative and controversial study, called *The Hite Report* (1987), found that 70% of the women surveyed never climax during "traditional" coitus. (*The Hite Report* draws on a large but unrepresentative, self-selected sample but nevertheless provides fascinating insights into female sexuality, at least for young, highly educated women.) A representative survey of both men and women found 67% of the men and 64% of the women reasonably happy and satisfied with their sex lives (Ubell, 1984). It appears, nonetheless, that sexual intimacy is not always as satisfying as the popular media presents it.

The Ubell study is the only recent study of American sexual behaviors that has been conducted by a national probability sample of adults, both married and single, ranging in age from 18 to 60. This study looked at "sexual style"—a combination of an individual's thoughts about and activities related to sex. Each sexual style had three components—life satisfaction, sensuality, and eroticism. People who were high in life satisfaction were generally satisfied with their sex lives as well as with their marital status and with how their bodies looked. Their sexuality was generally integrated into a broader life pattern. People who were high in sensuality were reasonably comfortable with such behaviors as kissing, hugging, and touching. Those high in eroticism tended to be stimulated by pornography or by oral or anal sex, as well as by the more usual sexual forms. They had a strong sex drive and found sex important.

This study is unusual, compared with earlier studies, in that it found fewer differences between men and women. Sex was important to 77% of the men and 66% of the women. About half the men and half the women reported high life satisfaction and had high sensuality scores. There were some differences between men and women, however. More men (81%) than women (60%) felt orgasms were important. More men (74%) than women (53%) reported a strong sex drive. Men more often scored higher in eroticism. Women (86%) often found it harder than men (59%) to have sex without love.

The primary conclusion of this rather extensive study is that there is a wide variety of patterns of sexual activity. There are conservative patterns, where people are generally happy with themselves but have few lifetime partners and very limited foreplay. Only 11% of the sample fell into this group. On the other end of the spectrum, there are *satisfied erotics* who enjoy sex often and with experimental variations. About 12% of the sample fell into this group, with about twice as many men as women. The largest single group represented by the sample is a group these researchers call *pan-sexuals*—people who are happy with many aspects of their lives, including the sexual aspects. This group represented nearly 20% of the sample, including almost as many women (45%) as men (55%). Another relatively satisfactory pattern is that of the *sensualist*—someone who is satisfied with his or her pattern of sexual activity and enjoys sensuality but has dislike for more erotic practices. This pattern represented about 11% of the population. Less satisfactory patterns include the *unsatisfied erotics* (12.7%), the *lonely erotics* (12.1%), the *unsatisfied sensualists* (8.5%), and the *nonsexuals* (13.2%). Even these eight categories fail to capture the full range of patterns of sexual behavior. This survey found that about one person in seven has sex problems, including men as often as women. Women complain mostly about sexual incompatibility (18%), low sex drive (17%), and trouble achieving orgasm (17%). Men complain about impotence (18%), feeling sexually inadequate (13%), and also of low sex drive (11%). This study should do much to redress the myths and fantasies regarding adult sexuality in the United States during the 1990s.

HOMOSEXUALITY Homosexuality is sexual or erotic attraction to a person of one's own sex. Although the word *homosexual* refers to both men and women, it is usually applied to men; women who are attracted to other women are called *lesbians*. Both men and women are referred to as "gay."

Although homosexuality often involves an exclusive attraction to people of one's own, most people have both homosexual and heterosexual leanings in varying degrees. This suggests that homosexuality and heterosexuality are better conceptualized as forming a continuum than a dichotomy. Sexual attraction is governed by the predominant tendency, although bisexuals do not confine themselves to one sex. The incidence of homosexuality is difficult to measure, partly because some people switch back and forth, but mostly because many homosexuals are reluctant to acknowledge their preference, for fear of social sanctions.

Kinsey's (1948) estimates found that one-third of American men and one-eighth of American women have had homosexual experiences to the point of orgasm at least once in their lives (McCary, 1978). A more recent survey found that only 11% of men reported homosexual experiences (Ubell, 1984). Probably about 4% of all men and 2% of all women consider themselves exclusively homosexual. But 4% of all men translates to about 2 million people, so we are not talking about just a few Americans (Hyde, 1986).

A study of gay men in the San Francisco area has yielded a great deal of data about gay lifestyles. Unlike *The Hite Report,* this study by Bell and Weinberg (1978) used standard scholarly techniques of sampling and interviewing. Their major conclusion is that as much diversity of attitudes and behavior exists among gays as among "straights." The Bell and Weinberg population showed as significant a mixture of heterosexuality and homosexuality as that measured by the Kinsey continuum. Most of the respondents have concealed their homosexuality, though, from large numbers of friends and acquaintances.

In terms of sexual activity, gays enjoy a repertoire as varied as that of straights. Gay men tend to be more sexually active than gay women, but gay women tend to form strong emotional ties (McCary, 1978). According to Bell and Weinberg, gay men have career patterns similar to those of straight men; contrary to popular belief, they do not go from job to job as their private lives become public knowledge. Many respondents felt that their sexual orientation had no effect on their jobs; a few even said it was advantageous, finding jobs through a network of already established friends. Some gay men, however, reported job discrimination or limited opportunities for advancement because of prejudice against them and their lifestyle.

Many homosexuals and lesbians are in relationships. In the Bell and Weinberg (1978) study, almost 40% of the gay men and over 60% of the lesbian women were in a same-sex relationship. More than half of these gay men were members of an "open couple" in which monogamy was not required. But most of the lesbians were in a "closed couple" in which monogamy was expected. This underscores one difference between homosexual couples and married, heterosexual couples. Gay men are much more likely than husbands to have at least one extra-couple affair. During the first 2 years of the relationship, 66% of the gay men but only 15% of the husbands had such an encounter (Blumstein & Schwartz, 1983). On the other hand, lesbians are about as monogamous as wives are. About 15% of the lesbians and 13% of the wives had sexual relations with someone other than their partner during the first 2 years of the relationship (Blumstein & Schwartz, 1983).

Gay and lesbian couples seem to go through the same relationship stages that cohabiting and married couples do (Kurdek & Schmitt, 1986). The first year (the "blending stage") seems to be happier than the second and third (the "nesting stage"), which is followed by an upswing in happiness during the fourth and fifth years (the "maintaining stage"). Furthermore, although gay and lesbian couples are more likely than married couples to break up, many of them do stay together for extended periods of time. If homosexual or lesbian couples do stay together for more than 10 years, their likelihood of breaking up is not dramatically different from that of married couples (Blumstein & Schwartz, 1983).

SOCIAL CHANGE AND AIDS   In 1990, AIDS was the third leading cause of death for men ages 25 to 44. As of March 1991, the Centers for Disease Control reported over 167,800 cases of AIDS. Of these cases, 63% had already died. These and numerous similar reports have created a climate of anxiety and fear. The response to this epidemic of the 1980s has not always been constructive. Early in the decade, news reports were few and far between. Many heterosexuals ignored the spreading virus because it appeared to affect only homosexual men and drug abusers. The gay community, too, responded with resistance and inappropriate denial of the facts. Early warnings issued to the gay community about the dangerous spread of this disease through unsafe sex were labeled as "homophobic messages," contrary to the rights of gays and their chosen lifestyle. By late 1983, however, more people began to take the epidemic seriously. It had spread across the United States and to most countries in Europe. It affected not only homosexual men and intravenous drug users, but also hemophiliacs, sexual partners of bisexuals and of drug users, and newborn babies of mothers who had the disease. What is more, it was estimated that perhaps 10% of the gay community in San Francisco, and twice that many in New York, had already been infected with the virus. These facts, together with the long latency period between infection and contraction of the AIDS disease, led to more serious action.

Beginning around 1984, medical research on AIDS took on greater urgency. Simultaneously, the gay community began to educate its members and more effectively change behavior. Individuals began to reduce their number of sex partners, openly discuss the safety of some behaviors, and avoid unprotected sexual practices. Social change does not happen smoothly, however. Many infected people continued to infect others. In the mid-1980s, the heterosexual community was still way behind the gay community in its response to this disease. Sporadic incidents of panic and discrimination against individuals who had AIDS, who might have AIDS, or who might contract AIDS, sometimes received more public press than the needed accurate educational information. Yet gradually, over the second half of the decade, behavior in the heterosexual community changed as well. There have been shifts in the humor, fads, and language of young people, and most young people today report some caution and concern about multiple sexual partners. The use of prostitutes is declining. Some have even suggested that the sexual revolution is over and that we are in a period of new restraint.

FAMILIES, COUPLES, AND SINGLES

In reaching for adult intimacy, young people appear to have a wider variety of choice with respect to family formation or personal lifestyle than did past generations. They can choose to remain single throughout their lives, finding intimacy in relationships with friends and relatives; they can live together without formally getting married; or they can marry and have children or choose to remain childless. Choices are often heavily influenced by past psychological development and by a range of social and economic circumstances. Marriage rates fluctuate depending on social and economic circumstances: During wars, for example, the rate of marriage is relatively low, whereas a postwar economic boom encourages a dramatic increase in the rate of marriages.

Currently, the marriage rate in the United States for unmarried women age 15 and over has slipped to a record low for this century, falling even below the marriage rate for the Great Depression and World War II years. Yet, in contrast, a record number of marriages occurred as recently as 1984 due to the size of the young adult population (the baby-boom generation). The divorce rate has taken a dramatic climb, nearly doubling in the years between 1965 and 1975, and then increasing gradually to an all-time high in 1981. Since then, the divorce rate has declined gradually throughout the 1980s to a level below that of 1975 (National Center for Health Statistics, 1991). Despite the shift in marriage and divorce rates, a larger proportion of adults were married in the 1980s than the number of adults who were married in 1940, at the end of the Great Depression (see Table 16–2).

It is still true that most people marry (well over 90%), although more people are postponing marriage, and the divorce rate is substantial. On the other hand, many marriages are lasting longer than marriages in the early part of this century. People live longer today, and if they stay together "until death do they part," it is likely that they will have been married for 45 years, on the average, rather than the 25 years characteristic at the turn of the century. This is indeed a long-term commitment.

Families and Adult Development

Families are an important context for adult development. In a recent national survey, men and women of all ages said that their family roles were very important (Beroff, Douvan, & Julka, 1981). Although the family is generally considered the

TABLE 16–2

The Changing Marital Status of the Population

	1940	1950	1960	1970	1980	1988
Single	31.2%	22.8%	22.0%	16.2%	20.3%	21.9%
Married	59.6	67.0	67.3	71.7	65.5	62.7
Widowed	7.8	8.3	8.4	8.9	8.0	7.6
Divorced	1.4	1.9	2.3	3.2	6.2	7.8

Note: Figures represent percentage of the population age 18 and over.
Source: Statistical Abstract of the United States (Washington, DC: Department of Commerce, 1981, 1990).

woman's domain, in this survey men, too, considered their family roles important in defining who they were and in providing emotional connectedness.

In a more recent detailed interview study of adult identity, fully 90% of the men and women indicated that their family roles and responsibilities were the most important components in defining who they were (Whitbourne, 1986a). They talked about their roles as parents, spouses, siblings, and children within their families. They talked about family tasks and responsibilities, about closeness, communication, companionship, and personal fulfillment. Broadly speaking, they talked about the people they had become within the family relationships and family experiences. It was the exceptional man and woman who defined themselves first or foremost in terms of their career rather than their family.

Even young unmarried adults have families. They are often in transition, moving from the *family of origin* to the *family of procreation*. They are in the process of separation/individuation from their families. Hoffman (1984) has identified four types of independence in this process. The first is *emotional independence,* in which the young adult becomes less socially and psychologically dependent on the parents for support and affection. The second form is *attitudinal independence*. The young adult develops attitudes, values, and belief systems that are different from the parents'. *Functional independence* is the third form. This refers to the young adult's ability to support himself or herself financially and to take care of day-to-day problems. Finally, there is *conflictual independence*. This form involves being able to separate from one's parents without feelings of guilt or betrayal.

Studies of college students (Lapsley, Rice, & Shadid, 1989) indicate substantial improvement in all of these forms of independence over the college years. There is still often substantial functional dependence, even in the senior year, because students often rely on their parents financially. Those students who fail to negotiate the separation process, especially in terms of conflictual independence, are more likely to develop psychological adjustment problems (Friedlander & Siegel, 1990; Lapsley et al., 1989).

Some young adults still live with their parents. In 1984, there were 50 million Americans ages 18 to 29; 18 million (or 37%) of them lived with their parents (Glick & Lin, 1986). This represents an increase since 1970, when 34% of young adults lived with their parents.

About one-third of the young adults living at home are age 18 or 19; about one-half are ages 20 to 24; and one-sixth are ages 25 to 29. They live with their parents for a variety of reasons. Most of them have never been married and are employed. They may be living at home until they save enough money to strike out on their own or until they decide to marry. Almost one-third of the young adults living with their parents are either unemployed or out of the labor force. A little less than one-quarter of these people are students (Glick & Lin, 1986). Parental health seems to play a minor role in whether adult children live with their parents. Hence, the arrangement is usually designed to meet the needs of the young adult rather than the parents (Aquilino, 1990).

Couple Formation and Development

Couple formation and development are common phenomena in adult development. Individuals achieve some of their personal identity as part of a relatively stable couple. Adams (1979) offers one explanation of how the marital

Even though we remain individuals, we achieve some of our personal identity as part of a relatively stable couple.

dyad develops, based on a study of seriously attached, college-age couples over a period of 6 months. According to this researcher, initial attraction is based on fairly superficial qualities like physical appeal, gregariousness, poise, and shared interests. The relationship is reinforced by the reactions of others, being labeled a couple, feeling comfortable in each other's presence, and other similar factors. The couple then enters a stage of commitment and intimacy, which leads to deeper attraction between partners. The couple who forms a commitment examines each partner's viewpoints and value systems. The couple often feels prepared at this point to make decisions about marriage (Adams, 1979).

Other researchers offer a family system perspective (McGoldrick, 1980). This perspective emphasizes that couple formation involves the development of a new structure as well as a process of getting to know each other. The task of *boundary negotiations* is crucial to couple formation. Gradually, a couple will redefine their relationships with others—their family and friends—as well as with each other. Many informal shifts in relationships occur as well as more formal events such as the marriage ritual to establish boundaries for a couple.

On the way to becoming a "couple," family systems researchers also emphasize the importance of communication styles. Couples establish, often unconsciously, patterns of decision making and ways of resolving conflicts. For example, in some relationships one person may dominate, whereas in others, patterns may contribute equally to the relationship.

MARRIAGE   We are a nation of subcultures, with many different patterns of adult lifestyles. Nevertheless, marriage is by far the most popular and most frequently chosen lifestyle. In the United States, over 90% of men and women will marry at some point in their lives (U.S. Bureau of the Census, 1987). Many cultures permit sexual intimacy only within the confines of marriage. The preparation for marriage may involve elaborate rituals of dating, courtship, and engagement. The bond is

Marriage is by far the most popular and most frequently chosen lifestyle.

symbolized by a wedding rite; subsequently, the new roles of husband and wife, in relation to each other and the rest of society, are more clearly defined. The community sanctions this union, which is expected to ensure emotional sustenance, sexual gratification, and financial security for the young couple and their family.

In traditional Arab societies, the transition to married life is carefully orchestrated by older relatives. As soon as girls reach puberty, maintenance of chastity through constant family vigilance takes on an urgent, life-or-death quality. All contact with men, including the fiance, is forbidden, once he has been selected. Young men are also excluded from the courtship process. Older relatives of the young man screen eligible young girls and their families. Male elders conduct bride–price negotiations. To conserve family assets and protect family honor, "cousin marriages" with the daughter of the father's brother are strongly favored. In this manner, a family can be sure that the young bride will be chaperoned and guarded in an acceptable manner (Goode, 1970).

Although American marriages, in general, are relatively free of such prenuptial investigation and negotiation, strong constraints still exist for relationships that violate social, economic, religious, or racial boundaries. Community groups and social institutions, as well as parents, often frown upon mixed marriages or marriages outside one's class, religion, ethnic background, or age group. Mixed marriages, however, are beginning to be accepted. Studies indicate that one out of five Americans has dated someone of another race (Porterfield, 1973) and that, as of 1988, there were 956,000 interracial marriages in the United States (*Statistical Abstracts of the United States,* 1990).

MARITAL CHOICE   How do people choose their marital partners? Do they make this all-important choice on the basis of similarity alone, or do more complex emotional and environmental factors steer them toward a certain type of person? Over the years, a number of theorists have tried to answer these questions, and, if nothing else, their conclusions show that marital choice is a far more complex issue than it first appears.

Freud was one of the early theorists to speculate on the reasons people marry. One of the cornerstones of his psychoanalytic theory is the attraction that children feel to the parent of the opposite sex. Through a complex unconscious process, they may transfer the love they feel toward this parent onto other, more socially acceptable objects—their potential mates. Winch's (1958) complementary needs theory is based on the age-old principle that opposites attract. That is, a dominating man may be attracted to a deferential woman, or a quiet man may be attracted to a dynamic and outspoken woman. The instrumental theory of mate selection, developed by Centers (1975), also focuses on needs gratification, but it states that some needs (such as sex and affiliation) are more important than others and that some needs are more appropriate for either men or women. According to Centers, people are attracted to others with similar or with complementary needs.

The stimulus-value-role theory developed by Murstein (1982) states that people's mate selection is motivated by each partner trying to get the best possible deal. Assets and liabilities of the other partner are examined at different points in the relationship when different factors are filtered out to determine if the relationship is worthwhile. This examination takes place during three stages of courtship. During the stimulus stage, when a man and woman meet or see each other for the first time, initial judgments are formed on the other's appearance and social and mental traits. If the first impression is favorable, the couple progresses to the value-comparison or second stage of courtship—a time during which their conversations reveal whether their interests, attitudes, beliefs, and needs are compatible. During the role or final stage, the couple determines if they can function in compatible roles in a marriage or other type of relationship.

COHABITATION "Living together" may or may not be similar to marriage, depending on the couple. It lacks the social approbation and legalized responsibilities of traditional marriage but offers greater freedom for the partners to design their roles as they see fit. It is characterized by an overt acknowledgment that the couple is in a state of not being married. Sometimes, accurate statistics about this institution are hard to compile because of the reluctance of the partners to announce the relationship and its often transient nature. A study by the U.S. Bureau of the Census documents a large increase in the number of couples openly acknowledging cohabitation, especially young adults. For the population as a whole, cohabitation more than doubled from 1970 to 1978. Among people under age 25, an eightfold increase was reported—from 29,000 couples in 1970 to 236,000 in 1978. One-quarter of the households had children (Reinhold, 1981). Since 1978, the increase has been more gradual. Most cohabiting couples (72%) have no children. Most cohabitators are young adults—40% are between ages 25 and 34. Nearly 45% of cohabitators have been married before (Spanier, 1983).

It has been estimated that about one-third of all cohabiting couples marry. Although the great majority of such couples hope to marry eventually, they feel less urgency than those who have never lived with someone. Cohabiting couples who eventually marry do not necessarily communicate bettter or find greater satisfaction in marriage than couples who do not live together prior to marriage (Demaris & Leslie, 1984). Cohabiting couples who do not marry typically break up, so it is rare to find a long-established cohabiting couple. Blumstein and Schwartz (1983) were not able to find enough cohabitors who had been together for more than 10 years to use this group for data analysis (although they did find enough gay and lesbian couples who had been together this long).

Living together in an informal arrangement creates many of the same relationship-building tasks that newlyweds face. Conflicts must be resolved through a complex process of "negotiation and collective bargaining" (Almo, 1978). Essential to this process is constant, effective communication. As in marriage, with its ready-made roles and expectations, clear communication is a constant struggle, and it may be even more important and more difficult within the vague boundaries of living together.

Finally, the couple living together must deal with the issues of commitment, fidelity, and permanence. Both the men and women in cohabiting relationships are more likely than married people to have extra-couple affairs (Blumstein & Schwartz, 1983). This may contribute to the greater tension reported by cohabitors compared to married, gay, or lesbian couples (Kurdek & Schmitt, 1986). According to one study (Almo, 1978), couples find it difficult to deal explicitly with such concerns, although both partners have strong feelings about each other. Most couples make a definite, if unspoken, commitment to each other before moving in. Their commitment is based on a mutual desire for some kind of permanence that will allow them to plan for the future. They may or may not require sexual exclusivity and fidelity to each other. Some couples treat "outside relationships" as taboo, remaining silent by mutual agreement. Others explicitly agree that each can pursue other relationships, but this is usually desired by one partner and acquiesced by the other. As with other adjustments, nothing can be resolved unless there is timely, unambiguous communication.

Singles: Myths and Realities

In many historical periods, remaining single was often an unfortunate result of disasters or wars, or was considered a sign of possible abnormality or immaturity. Some married people held (and still hold) stereotyped images of singles—swingers and losers, for example. Swingers live wild, exciting lives with few restraints. Losers are thought to be physically unattractive people who have little or no social life. They would like to get married, it is thought, but cannot find anyone who will date them. Or perhaps they are too immature to leave their parents. Glib stereotypes like these misrepresent the full range of single lifestyles.

Placing singlehood in a historical perspective gives us some real understanding of what this social phenomenon is all about. Periodically, large groups of people have remained single. During the late 1930s, for example, when the country was recovering from an economic depression, fewer people got married, and those who did married at a later age. This trend continued during World War II, when millions of women joined the labor force. By the end of the war, this picture had changed dramatically. By the mid-1950s, only 4% of marriage-age adults remained single, and the age at first marriage was the youngest on record. Remaining single became popular once again in the 1970s and 1980s, when the marriage rate among single people under 45 years of age fell to equal the postdepression low. In 1988, 21.1% of the population over 18 years of age was single, 7.6% widowed, and 7.8% divorced (*Statistical Abstract of the United States,* 1990).

The choice of a single lifestyle may be the result of a carefully balanced decision—a balance between freedom and constraint, between self-sufficiency and interdependence. Some commentators on the current American scene worry about the trend toward fewer marriages and more divorces. Are we as a society too fascinated with freedom and autonomy at the expense of interpersonal obligations (Weiss, 1987)? More than one observer has worried about our individualistic lifestyles and our fascination with free choice at perhaps the expense of transgenerational ties and interdependent roles (Hunt & Hunt, 1987). In all likelihood, the increasing rate of single lifestyles will have no such results.

Many people today feel that a single lifestyle suits their goals in life.

Many singles choose the single life as a way of avoiding the problems of marriage. They do not want to feel trapped by a mate who stands in the way of their own personal development. Nor do they want to feel bored, unhappy, angry, sexually frustrated, or lonely with a person whom they have long since outgrown. Watching the marriages of their friends fall apart, they feel that the single life is a far better choice. Here is how Susan, a single woman who had lived with a man for over a year, justifies her decision not to marry:

> There's a . . . lot more freedom than there would be either in marriage or an exclusive relationship. I like a lot of different people, and being single kind of affords the opportunity for getting to know and being friends with a lot of different people. No restrictions except the ones I happen to choose. They are not superimposed upon me by someone else's jealousy. (Stein, 1976, p. 67)

PARENTHOOD AND ADULT DEVELOPMENT

Parenthood requires new roles and responsibilities on the part of the mother and father. It also makes demands on the parents and confers a new social status on them (Hill & Aldous, 1969). The actual birth brings an onslaught of physical and emotional strains—disruption of sleep and other routines, financial drain, increased tension, and conflict over responsibilities, possessiveness, and discipline. The mother is tired, the father feels neglected, and both experience a curtailment of their freedom. The closeness and companionship of husband and wife are diluted by the introduction of a new family member and the focus of concern that either or both partners may shift to the baby (Komarovsky, 1964). The challenges and demands of parenthood can be thought of as a major developmental phase for both mother and father as individuals and for the couple as a system (Osofsky & Osofsky, 1984).

Families go through predictable *family life cycles* marked by milestone events. The first milestone is reached when the individual leaves his or her original family (the family of orientation). This separation may occur at the time of marriage or earlier, if the individual has opted for independence—either living alone or with a group. The second milestone is usually marriage, with all the attendant adjustments of establishing a relationship with a new individual or with a new family network. The most common third milestone is the birth of the first child and the beginning of parenthood. The occasion is sometimes called the establishment of a *family of procreation* or the *transition to parenthood*. There are still other milestones, such as the enrollment in school of the first child, the birth of the last child, the departure of the last child from the family, and the death of a spouse. In an extended family, several of these cycles may interact, providing rehearsal and repetition and making each member's adjustment somewhat easier.

During the past 50 to 100 years, family cycles have changed in timing as well as in nature. Not only are more people living longer than ever before, but their ages at various points in the family cycle and the average time span from one milestone to another have changed. There has been some increase in the period of time between the last child's leaving home and the parents' retirement or death. This postparental period continues to grow.

Transition to Parenthood

The transition to parenthood is one of the major periods in the family life cycle. Often, there is considerable cultural pressure to adopt this role. Yet most couples realize that the role of parenthood is relatively irrevocable. In contrast to marriage, the roles and responsibilities of parenting continue, in most cases, despite changing life circumstances (Rossi, 1979). Parenthood calls for numerous adaptations and adjustments. Newlywed couples often enjoy a relatively high standard of living when both husbands and wives are working. They buy cars, furniture, and clothes; eat meals in restaurants often; and enjoy recreational activities. This usually comes to an abrupt end with the arrival of the first child (Aldous, 1978).

Several studies have found that during pregnancy both parents make several adjustments. There are realistic decisions to be made about labor and delivery, living arrangements, whether or not both parents will work, and so forth. Also, prospective parents are often concerned about their parenting abilities and about the characteristics of their unborn child. Spouses can provide emotional support for each other during this period (Osofsky & Osofsky, 1984).

Although they share some concerns, fathers and mothers also display different reactions to the arrival of the first child. Women characteristically adjust their lifestyles to give priority to their parenting and family roles. Men, on the other hand, more often intensify their work efforts to become better or more stable providers. Once the child arrives, there are new stresses and challenges. As Rossi points out, the role change is rather abrupt. Both parents experience new feelings

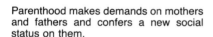

Parenthood makes demands on mothers and fathers and confers a new social status on them.

B TOBEY   McCall's

"You wake up one morning, and suddenly you are no longer a young married."

of pride and excitement, coupled with a greater sense of responsibility that is sometimes overwhelming. Some men are envious of their partner's ability to reproduce and of the close emotional bond established between mother and infant. Couples need to renegotiate time for each other and for other interests. Indeed, there appears to be less communication and sharing of personal interests, more sexual problems, and more marital conflicts in many marriages following the birth of a child (Osofsky & Osofsky, 1984).

The arrival of the first child usually constitutes a transition rather than a crisis (Entwisle, 1985). Most couples say they experienced only "slight" difficulty in adjusting (Hobbs & Cole, 1976). Indeed, in a recent study Belsky and Rovine (1990) reported that 20% to 35% of their couples actually experienced an improvement in marital satisfaction. Similarly, most mothers do not experience real postpartum depression. Instead, they experience 2 to 3 days of the much milder "baby blues." Probably 10% to 20% of new mothers do not even get these blues! (O'Hara, Zekoski, Philips, & Wright, 1990).

A variety of factors influence how well new parents adjust to their roles. Social support, especially from her husband, seems crucial to a new mother (Cutrona & Toutman, 1986). Happiness in the marriage during pregnancy is an important factor in how both husband and wife adjust (Wallace & Gotlib, 1990). In fact, paternal postpartum adjustment is especially affected by the mother's evaluation of both the marriage and her pregnancy (Wallace & Gotlib, 1990). Parental self-esteem is also an issue in that those with higher self-esteem seem to make better adjustment (Belsky & Rovine, 1990b). The baby's characteristics are also important. For example, parents of babies with more difficult temperaments report greater decline in marital satisfaction (Belsky & Rovine, 1990b; Crockenberg, 1986).

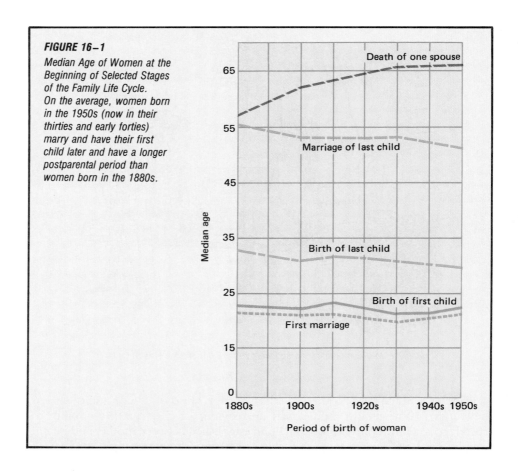

FIGURE 16–1

Median Age of Women at the Beginning of Selected Stages of the Family Life Cycle. On the average, women born in the 1950s (now in their thirties and early forties) marry and have their first child later and have a longer postparental period than women born in the 1880s.

Child Rearing and Launching

At each period in the family life cycle, the demands made upon parents vary. An infant requires almost total and constant nurturance. Satisfying this need is much easier for some parents than for others. Certain parents can be overwhelmed by the intense dependency requirements of the infant. Furthermore, the child's critical, urgent needs can stimulate similar needs in the parents themselves. Some parents cannot bear to hear an infant cry. The baby's wails may trigger the father's or mother's feelings of helplessness, dependence, or anger. Other parents may have come to terms with their own yearnings for dependence, understanding them as normal, natural needs.

Each critical period for the child produces or reactivates a critical period in the parents (Benedek, 1970). Galinsky (1980) describes this interactive process in six separate stages. In the *image-making stage,* which takes place from conception to birth, couples create images of the kind of parents they will be and measure their anticipated performance against their own standards of perfection. In the *nurturing stage,* which lasts from birth to about 2 years (until the time children start saying *no*), parents form attachments to their new baby and learn how to balance the emotional commitment and time they give to their spouse, job, friends, and parents with the needs of the baby. During the *authority stage,* the time roughly between the child's second and fifth birthdays, parents begin to question the kind of parents they have been and will be. Growth comes when parents realize that they—and their children—sometimes fall short of their image of perfection. The *interpretive stage*—the middle childhood years—causes parents to reexamine and test many of their long-held theories. When their children become teenagers, parents pass through the *stage of interdependence,* in which they must redefine the authority relationship they have with their nearly grown children. They may find themselves competing with or comparing themselves with their children. Finally, during the *departure stage,* when grown children leave home, parents not only have to "let go" but also have to face the difficult and sometimes unpleasant task of taking stock of their experiences as parents. During each stage, parents must be able to resolve their own conflicts at a new and more advanced level of integration, or they may simply be unable to cope with their aroused feelings. These unresolved tensions may interfere with the marriage relationship or with the ability to parent effectively.

However, parents who are unable to deal effectively with children at one stage of development may be quite good at dealing with them at another stage. For example, parents who have a lot of difficulty with an infant may cope quite effectively with a preschool child or adolescent. The reverse may also be true; the parent at ease with a helpless baby may have problems with an independent teenager.

At each phase in the family life cycle, parents not only have to cope with the new challenges and demands of their changing and developing children, but they also must renegotiate the couple system and the family system (Carter & McGoldrick, 1980). Couples must establish ways of making decisions and resolving conflicts such that the integrity and respect of each individual are maintained. Systems in which one person is always dominant and another is always the victim tend to dissolve over time. The new pressures created by adolescent rebellion and the quest for independence, for example, require that the couple system and the family system adapt and make room for this nearly autonomous individual. The family system that is too rigid or that is too unstructured cannot cope with the developing needs of the child.

The "launching" of children into the adult world is another phase of the family life cycle. Some families are good at letting go. An adolescent assuming

Parents today can expect to spend a fairly lengthy period of time together after the launching of the last child.

FOCUS ON AN ISSUE

TIMING OF PARENTHOOD

In the Plymouth colony, the average number of children per family was nine. In 1850, the average American family produced six children, and it was unlikely that both parents would survive much beyond age 50. But in the late 20th century, the average family includes only two or three children, the average life span is well into the 70s, and the timing of parenthood can be controlled. For example, a woman may temporarily stop working to devote her time to childbearing and rearing—perhaps 9 years for three children—and still spend 35 to 40 years in the workforce (Daniels & Weingarten, 1982). But what is the impact on adult development and on the family life cycle when parenting is delayed 5, 10, or 15 years—what are the pros and cons?

Josephs (1982) followed several late mothers during their first 2 years with their first children. Most of the women had had time to develop stability and security in their lives. They had already worked through some of the issues of adult development and had acquired some financial resources. Their professions had taught them how to be organized, competent, and motivated, and they often used this training to become thoroughly educated and prepared for childbirth and child rearing.

But no amount of education prepared the late mothers for the degree of disorganization a new baby brought to their lives. As professional women used to having control over their environment, their lack of control over the new baby and the great need for flexibility and patience were often upsetting. Used to tension and their active careers, they often found it difficult simply to relax with the baby. Accustomed to having time to pursue interests or self-development, they were often too tired or too busy caring for their babies. Their need for stimulus, which developed when they were autonomous adults, sometimes was not fulfilled by the stimulus of their relationship with their babies. In

general, their expectations and needs sometimes differed from the realities they faced as new mothers.

Infancy, however, is not the only period in a child's life cycle that causes parents to make major adjustments. "Enlarging the nest" for a second child, the development of sibling relationships, and the eventual integration or reintegration of children's needs with parents' work all alter living patterns for husband and wife. As children grow, parents must adapt to other types of changes—adolescent autonomy needs, the period of launching youth, and the return home of adult offspring.

A broader study of both mothers and fathers in their 30s, 40s, and 50s compared the effects of having first children at ages 20, 30, and 40. The researchers found numerous differences. One age was not necessarily better than another for coping with the tasks of parenting, but nearly all parents agreed that the many demands of parenting were an important challenge in their own development. Some fathers reported that they were not immediately involved in parenting but that they became "hooked" when their children reached a certain stage of development or because of a particular event. For some, this occurred when special interests were shared with a child, whereas others felt closer to their children when they reached adolescence. Childbirth and a child's illness are dramatic events that linked some men to the reality of fathering (Daniels & Weingarten, 1982).

Late parenting may require numerous initial adjustments in lifestyle and attitudes, yet most parents who started later report appreciating the full range of parenting experiences more than they thought they would have at a younger age. In addition, many felt that when they were younger they were too absorbed in their own needs and achievements or their marital relationship to fully appreciate the parenting role (Daniels & Weingarten, 1982).

responsible adult roles is best supported by parents who increasingly trust and respect the judgments, decisions, and budding maturity of the late adolescent. Parents launching their last child must have alternative roles and interests beyond the sometimes all-encompassing role of parenthood.

There is no doubt that the launching of the children is a period of transition for the parents (Harris et al., 1986). Although many women report unhappiness during this transition, the source of their dissatisfaction is more commonly related to work or marriage than to the children's departure (Harris et al., 1986). Men may also feel torn as the children leave the home, especially if they feel that they "missed" seeing their kids grow up (Rubin, 1980).

The Empty Nest

In 1990, over 75% of adults in the United States could expect to live to the age of 65 or older; at the turn of the century, however, only 40.9% of adults lived to that age. Given this increase in life expectancy, parents who remain married can anticipate spending a fairly lengthy period of time together after the launching of the last child. This period in the family life cycle is sometimes referred to as the *empty nest*. This, too, requires some considerable readjusting and negotiation. One factor is that the individual adult development of partners does not necessarily keep pace through the years. Perhaps one spouse has been active in politics, a religious organization, or community projects, for example. On the other hand, the experience of mutual parenting has built a tradition, some shared values, and shared experiences. Even couples who no longer enjoy the high level of companionship characteristic of early marriage may have a strong emotional support system and numerous material and functional interdependencies. Marital satisfaction in this later period in the family cycle is not necessarily based on the same patterns of interaction or solutions to joint problems as it was in earlier phases (Troll, 1985).

Parents repeatedly express that, although they are glad they had children, the increases in freedom, privacy, and available resources once the children are gone make this a pleasant time in their lives (Alpert & Richardson, 1980; Cooper & Guttman, 1987; Nock, 1982; Rubin, 1980). Women may especially benefit from being freed from daily parenting responsibilities and report greater assertiveness and freedom to explore their own interests.

Single Parenthood

The conflict between self-fulfillment and parenthood is particularly acute for single parents, the overwhelming majority of whom are working mothers. Single-parent families are becoming increasingly common in the United States. In the mid-1970s, one of every seven children spent part of the period of childhood without a father figure. In the past decade, this group has grown 10 times faster than traditional two-parent families. The trend is greatest among young women, which suggests that single parenthood may become even more widespread. In the mid-1980s, one out of five families was maintained by a single woman (U.S. Bureau of the Census, 1986). The incidence of female-headed households is three times higher among nonwhites, and the rate of increase is twice as high (Ross & Sawhill, 1975).

What is behind this exploding number of female-headed families? Ross and Sawhill (1975) cited a number of factors. Foremost was the rising divorce rate; in the 15 years prior to their study, the number of divorced mothers increased by

The trend toward single-parent families is greatest among young women, suggesting that it may become even more widespread in the future.

more than 70%. Since then the divorce rate peaked in 1979 and again in 1981 and has currently dropped 11% to the 1974 level (National Center for Health Statistics, 1990). The next greatest increase was in never-married mothers. (In 1988, 26% of all births were out of wedlock.) In 1988, over 60% of the African-American births were to unmarried women (Ellwood & Crane, 1990). Third, there was a substantial increase in women with children who were separated from their spouses.

Ross and Sawhill point to improved social and economic conditions for women as an important factor in these changes. They conclude that better job opportunities and improved status have enabled mothers and children to survive without their husbands and fathers, at least for a transitional period. For a number of single mothers, this status is indeed only temporary because many eventually remarry and return to a two-partner setting. Single parenthood can be an exhausting, continual struggle. Single mothers consistently earn less than single fathers do. For women without education, making ends meet is extremely difficult. Regardless of socioeconomic status, the single parent faces a steady stream of demands and decisions that can be overwhelming.

Single-mother homes are more common, and more poor, in the African-American community. Fully 40% of all African-American families are headed by women. Although less than 3% of all poor families are persistently poor (poor at least 8 of 10 years), 62% of these families are African-American (Klein & Rones, 1989). The majority of African-American children will spend at least half of their childhood in poverty (Ellwood & Crane, 1990). African-American women as a group only earn 60% as much as white men (Council of Economic Advisers, 1990). In 1985, the median family income for white married couples was $31,602. For single female heads of household, it was $15,825 for whites, $9305 for blacks, and $8792 for Spanish-origin homes (*Statistical Abstracts of the United States,* 1987). All of this indicates the special hardships faced by African-American and Hispanic-American single parents.

On the other hand, African-Americans and Hispanic-Americans are more likely to live in intergenerational households (Harrison, Wilson, Pine, Chan, & Buriel, 1990; Jackson, Autonucci, & Gibson, 1990). These extended families may also include nonfamily members. These family structures help provide additional financial, psychological, and social resources for the single mother. She may not feel so isolated or so overwhelmed by the child-care responsibilities because of this.

Although it is still true that only a small proportion of fathers gain custody of their children after divorce, this number is gaining to as much as 12% (Hetherington & Camara, 1984). Single fathers experience many of the same problems and tensions as single mothers do. However, single fathers are usually in a better financial state. A recent profile of single fathers revealed that many of these men had taken on extensive parenting roles prior to their divorces (Pichitino, 1983). Most single fathers maintain high levels of emotional involvement with their children, are heavily invested and committed to their care, and worry about failing them or not spending enough time with them. Parenting experience, however, does not always prepare them for the demands faced when maintaining a job and a family simultaneously. Many single fathers have the same feelings of loneliness and depression that single mothers often report. Single fathers also find, as do single mothers, that it is difficult to maintain an active circle of friends and other emotional supports (Pichitino, 1983).

THE CHANGING FAMILY

No one—not even the most radical social critic—would claim that the traditional nuclear family is dead or even dying. But few families still fit the traditional mold of working father, housewife mother, and two children. Just as individuals are choosing their lifestyles to suit their needs and priorities, the idea of the family is changing to match changes in the social and personal needs and priorities of the members.

The Family after Divorce

Each year over 1,150,000 marriages end in divorce. For every three marriages that succeed, two are expected to fail (National Center for Health Statistics, 1987). These figures reveal a dramatic change in the concept of lifelong marriage. When marriages fail, divorced people must pick up the pieces and start again. When there are children, these adjustments are somewhat more complicated. The family as a system must make adjustments—practical living and financial adjustments, and adjustments in parenting roles, communication patterns, and social contacts.

To find out exactly what happens to people after they divorce, Hetherington et al. (1978) studied 96 divorced couples with children during a 2-year period. They found that many of the divorced men and women suffered from a wide range of problems they had not encountered while they were married. The practical problems of organizing and maintaining a household plagued many divorced men who were accustomed to having their wives perform these tasks. In addition, financial hardship was reported by both men and women. With two households to support instead of one, some men found their incomes spread too thin to make ends meet. Many took on a second job or worked overtime in an attempt to increase their spending money. Women who were housewives before their divorce usually suffered financial strain—especially if their husbands failed to make their alimony or child support payments. Strapped by these new economic burdens, many women were forced to spend less time with their children and had little or no time for themselves (Goetting, 1981).

The disruption of the marital relationship, whether through divorce or death, is a stressful event. There is the grief and mourning over the loss of an intimate relationship. There is the disruption of normal routines and life patterns. There is the welcome or unwelcome independence and autonomy or sometimes sheer loneliness. But despite these similarities between divorce and widowhood, there are marked differences.

The deterioration of a marriage is rarely a sudden event. Often it is the culmination of a long process of emotional separation or dissatisfaction and growing independence. The final months of marriage are usually remembered as unhappy. But the final decision to divorce is usually made by one, not both, partners. The wife usually raises the issue first. Women are often more dissatisfied with marriage sooner, although they may not make the final decision (Kelly, 1982).

Most people experiencing divorce perceive it as some kind of failure. For the

Families Around the World.
In most cultures, families serve as primary socializing agents for both children and adults.

partner who did not make the decision to divorce, there is often a feeling of rejection. Feelings of humiliation and powerlessness are not uncommon. Even if the marriage was quite unsatisfactory, the final decision comes as a shock. For the partner who in fact makes the decision, the stress is often higher during those agonizing months or years prior to the separation. This spouse, who initiates the divorce, may feel sadness, guilt, and anger but also has a sense of control. He or she has rehearsed and mentally prepared for separation (Kelly, 1982).

Establishing a lifestyle after divorce is easier for some than others. For some, the freedom from constraint and obligation, and from emotional turmoil, is a welcome relief. Women especially are likely to feel like they have a "new chance" after a divorce (Caldwell, Bloom, & Hodges, 1984; Kelly, 1982). For others, the simple idea of living alone elicits fear. Older women, after a long period of marriage, often experience considerable difficulty, depending upon their role prior to the separation. In past years, women often had somewhat more difficulty than men in maintaining friendships with their married peers and managing financial and legal matters such as securing a bank loan or mortgage. Some individuals who married young have, quite literally, never been on their own, and have little experience in coping with the independence that now confronts them. These newly single people, and sometimes their families and friends, often underestimate problems of adjustment. Recently divorced men and women have higher rates of alcoholism, physical illness, and depression, sometimes as a direct result of the life changes from separation.

Most divorced individuals experience considerable improvement and well-being within 2 or 3 years of the final separation (Spanier & Furstenberg, 1982). Divorced women are likely to have improved self-esteem (Wallerstein & Blakelee, 1989). Divorced people with the strongest sense of well-being are likely to remarry within 3 or 4 years. In fact, divorced men have the highest rate of remarriage among all single groups. Divorced men are three times as likely as women to remarry. Most divorced men over 40 remarry, but only a third of all divorced women over 40 remarry (Spanier & Furstenberg, 1982).

Of course, not all problems are gone. There is a sizable minority who, 10 years after the divorce, are bitter and isolated. Some men have virtually lost contact with their children and, despite adequate resources, refuse to help with their children's college expenses (Wallerstein & Blakelee, 1989). However, the decision to divorce seems to have been a good one for at least one member of the majority of couples.

Stepfamilies

When divorced or widowed people with children remarry, they form stepfamilies, also known as reconstituted or blended families. These families present many more role adjustment problems to both stepparents and stepchildren than do primary families. With little preparation to handle their new roles and with little support from the society around them, stepparents often find that achieving a satisfactory family relationship is harder than they ever imagined.

There is a tendency to think that the current soaring divorce rate and the resulting high remarriage rate has created an entirely new phenomenon. After all, nearly 40% of marriages now are remarriages for at least one of the partners. But stepfamilies are not a new phenomenon. In fact, the current remarriage rate closely

Both stepparents and stepchildren need time to adjust to one another—to learn about and to test each other's personalities.

FOCUS ON AN ISSUE

MYTHS OF MARRIAGE AND REMARRIAGE

In 1986, about 2.4 million people in this country got married and 1.16 million people became divorced. In other words, almost half as many individuals divorced each other as married in 1986. Actually, some scholars take encouragement from these figures because both marriage and divorce rates are down slightly from their respective highs in 1981, and the ratio of divorce to marriage has also declined somewhat from its earlier high (National Center for Health Statistics, 1987). Over 40% of contemporary marriages involve the remarriage of one or both individuals, and almost half the remarriages end in divorce (Coleman & Ganong, 1985). Why this persistently high rate of failure in marriage and remarriage?

There are of course many explanations. One of the most interesting is the argument that too many couples rely on myths of marriage and remarriage. A myth is defined as an oversimplified belief that guides perceptions and expectations. Bernard (1981) provided a fascinating comparison of eight such marriage and divorce myths. Coleman and Ganong (1985) followed up with a corresponding analysis of remarriage myths. The following chart offers a comparative summary of the analyses of Bernard, Coleman, and Ganong.

Although this analysis is done with some "tongue in cheek," these myths are popularly held and do receive considerable support from the mainstream society. Churches, lawyers, marriage counselors, the pop media, family, and friends all pay homage to the myth. Many psychologists believe that "personal myths . . . do more than reveal how a person sees his past; they also act as a sort of script that determines how that person is likely to act in the future" (Goleman 1988). People act in concert with the prescriptions they tell themselves. However, people who follow unrealistic expectations often set the scene for failure.

Myths of Marriage, Divorce, and Remarriage

MARRIAGE	DIVORCE	REMARRIAGE
1. Everything will work out OK if we love each other.	Because we no longer love each other, nothing can work out anymore.	This time we'll make it work by doing everything right.
2. Always consider the other person first.	Always consider oneself first.	Always consider everyone first.
3. Emphasize the positive, keep criticisms to oneself.	Emphasize the negative and criticize everything.	Emphasize the positive and overlook the negative.
4. If things go wrong, focus on the future.	If things go wrong, focus on the past.	If things go wrong, think of what went wrong in the past and make sure it does not happen again.
5. See oneself as part of a couple first and then as an individual.	See oneself as an individual first and then as part of a couple.	Depending on one's personality, one might duplicate the marriage *or* divorce myth and see oneself either as part of a couple first or as an individual first.
6. What's mine is yours.	What's yours is mine.	What's mine is mine and what's yours is yours.
7. Marriage makes people happier than they were before marriage.	Divorce makes people unhappy.	Marriage makes people significantly happier than they were before marriage.
8. What is best for the children will be best for us.	What is best for us must be devastating for the children.	What is best for us must be harmful to the children.

parallels remarriage rates in Europe and the United States in the 17th and 18th centuries. But there is a major difference between then and now. Most stepfamilies now are created as a result of a marriage-divorce-remarriage sequence. Most stepfamilies then were a result of a marriage-death-remarriage sequence (Ihinger-

Tallman & Pasley, 1987). The difference between these two types of stepfamilies is, of course, the presence of a living former spouse. Contact with that former spouse often continues—in fact, it is often legally mandated. The relationship with that former spouse must be negotiated and renegotiated, including custody, financial support, and visitation. It is difficult in some families to maintain distance, to resolve conflicts, and to avoid feelings of rejection by one spouse or another. Remarriage often creates for the children a situation of ambivalence, conflict, uncertainty, and divided loyalties. It is not surprising that previously widowed stepparents report more positive relationships with each other and with their children following remarriage than do previously divorced stepparents (Ihinger-Tallman & Pasley, 1987).

For adults, remarriage can reduce stress, particularly for custodial parents (Furstenberg, 1987). A partner who is willing to share financial responsibilities, household tasks, child-rearing decisions, and so on can offer welcome relief to a divorced parent. Men who remarry, however, may have to deal with additional pressures if they are expected to financially support two households. In any event, second marriages are different from first marriages. They operate within a more complex family organization—stepchildren, ex-spouses, former in-laws, for instance—which can cause conflict. But second marriages are often characterized by more open communication, greater acceptance of conflict, and more trust that disagreements can be resolved (Furstenberg, 1987).

The expectation that stepfamilies can simply pick up where the primary family left off is unrealistic and inevitably leads to frustration and disappointment. Both stepparents and stepchildren need time to adjust to one another—to learn about and to test one another's personalities. To do this, stepparents should try to establish a position in the children's lives that is different from that held by the real mother or father. If they try to compete with the child's real parent, they may fail.

When asked what the greatest difficulties are in a stepparent/stepchild relationship, most stepparents mention discipline, adjusting to the habits and personalities of the children, and gaining the acceptance of the children (Schlesinger, 1975, cited in Kompara, 1980). Stepmothers often have more problems than stepfathers in adjusting to their new roles. Partially because of the stereotype of the "wicked stepmother" and partially because stepmothers spend more time with the children than stepfathers, stepmothers must overcome tremendous odds in order to succeed.

There is also the popular stereotype of the "stepchild." A stepchild is thought to be a bit neglected, perhaps abused, and definitely not loved as much as the "real child." Surveys of the general public, even of professionals who help stepfamilies, find that these stereotypes are fairly widespread (Coleman & Ganong, 1987). Fairy tales like Cinderella and Hansel and Gretel simply reinforce some of these stereotypes. And yet, given the wide variety of relationships within stepfamilies, such stereotypes are quite inaccurate.

No matter how willing a stepparent is to form a close relationship with his or her stepchildren, the children themselves may stand in the way. If they have never accepted the divorce or the loss of their biological parent, if they are used as pawns in a bitter, angry divorce, or if they hold an idealized view of the missing parent, children may reject the stepparent's love and make family harmony impossible. Time to develop mutual trust, affection, a feeling of closeness, and respect for the child's point of view often helps to form a workable relationship. Girls are likely to have greater difficulty forming a good relationship with a stepfather than boys are

(Hetherington, 1989). This is probably because the girl typically had a very close relationship with her mother postdivorce and sees the stepfather as an intruder. Boys, on the other hand, often have tumultuous, conflictual relationships with their mothers postdivorce. A stepfather can help mediate the mother–son relationship (Hetherington, 1989).

Even though stepparents rarely duplicate the place the idealized biological parent has in the child's life, they can often provide a loving, nurturant, and secure home environment—often more satisfactory than the strained predivorce family. Indeed, most stepparents and stepchildren eventually make positive adjustments (Clingempeel & Segal, 1986; Visher & Visher, 1983).

STUDY OUTLINE

Sexuality and Intimacy

Achieving Intimacy. In our culture, childhood experiences of sexual behavior and intimacy do not necessarily match media images or adolescent fantasies. In early adulthood, most people revise their sexual styles. Erikson believes that establishment of long-term patterns of intimacy is central to early adulthood development.

Researchers have found that a couple's intimacy develops through an exchange of confidences and an acceptance of each other's vulnerabilities. Denial of feelings is destructive to this intimacy.

Sexual Patterns. Over the past few decades, American sexual behavior has changed to include a broader range of patterns of sexual expression. Some couples report greater satisfaction with a full range of sensual and erotic practices. Other couples are equally satisfied with more conservative patterns of sexual practice. Dissatisfied individuals also have a wide range of expectations.

Studies of gay lifestyles show that much diversity exists in homosexuals' attitudes and behaviors, as it does among heterosexuals. Gays tend to experience the same role conflicts as heterosexuals, as well as the additional conflict of whether to reveal their sexual orientation to family, friends, and colleagues. Both men and women, single and married, report that their family role helps define their adult identity and provide emotional connectedness. Young adults are often in transition, going from their family of origin to the family of procreation.

Families, Couples, and Singles

Couple Formation and Development. Couple formation is a common phenomenon in adulthood. One approach suggests that people are initially attracted by superficial qualities. A couple may then receive reinforcement from others, as well as from the increased familiarity the two may share. This stage may then lead to commitment. The family system perspective emphasizes the development of a new structure (the couple) with new patterns of communication and decision making.

Most Americans marry. Marital choice may be based on attraction in early childhood to the parent of the opposite sex, or to someone who is complementary to oneself in one or many traits, or on a careful analysis of each other's assets and liabilities through a series of courtship stages.

Couples who live together face the task of designing their roles without the help of traditional guidelines to follow. New couples must adjust to their differences in needs for independence and togetherness, the cultivation of each partner's individuality, the division of housework, and the development of a method for coping with conflict.

Singles: Myths and Realities. An increasing number of people choose to remain single because of a desire for autonomy and freedom. Those who are suddenly single because of the ending of a long-term relationship, divorce, or death of a spouse often experience emotional turmoil and difficult readjustment.

Parenthood and Adult Development

Transition to Parenthood. The demands and responsibilities of parenthood help shape adult development. Each period in the family life cycle has its own milestones, tasks, and conflicts. Some of these periods include a *nurturing stage,* during which parents form attachments to infants; an *interpretive stage,* when parents reexamine long-held theories; and the *departure stage,* when children leave home. Each stage requires that parents resolve their own conflicts at a more advanced level.

Child Rearing and Launching. At each period in the family cycle, parents must renegotiate the couple system and the family system. After the last child is "launched," the couple system takes on new dimensions.

Single Parenthood. The number of single mothers has increased sharply in recent years. Ross and Sawhill suggest that improved social and economic conditions and raised status for women may contribute to the increase, as women are better equipped to survive without husbands. Single fathers experience many of the same problems that single mothers do.

The Changing Family

The Family after Divorce. The divorce rate has increased markedly in the past decade. Difficulties of divorce include increased financial burdens of both former partners, feelings of incompetence, depression, changes in social life, and deterio- rating health. After about 2 years, however, the negative effects of divorce greatly diminish.

Stepfamilies. Reconstituted families, or stepfamilies, re- quire major adjustments for both adults and children. Step- mothers have a more difficult time gaining acceptance from the children than stepfathers.

KEY TERMS AND CONCEPTS

authority stage
boundary negotiations
departure stage
empty nest

family of origin
family of procreation
homosexual
interdependence stage

interpretive stage
nurturing stage
stimulus-value-role theory

SELF-TEST QUESTIONS

1. List some components of intimacy. How might intimacy be discouraged or blocked?

2. How have sexual patterns in American society changed? What are some of the differences between male and female sexual experiences?

3. What has been the response of American society to the AIDS epidemic?

4. Explain the importance of the family context for adult development.

5. Describe and contrast differing views on how couples form and develop during adulthood.

6. Describe the various theories of mate selection.

7. How does cohabitation compare with marriage in terms of adjustments and commitments, fidelity and permanence?

8. What are some myths and realities about people who remain single?

9. What special conflicts do divorced singles face?

10. Discuss some of the necessary adjustments that make the transition to parenthood a major developmental phase. What kinds of challenges do parents face as a result of their children's changing developmental needs?

11. What are some of the trends in single parenthood? What special conflicts do single parents face?

12. What are some of the difficulties that divorce poses for individuals and the family system?

13. What are some of the adjustment problems that parents and children must face in stepfamilies?

SUGGESTED READINGS

AHRONS, C. R., & RODGER, R. H. *Divorced families.* New York: Norton, 1987. One of many books that analyze contem- porary patterns of divorce and its effects on adult development and lifestyles.

ANDERSON, J. *The single mother's book.* Atlanta: Peachtree Publishers, 1990. A well-organized guide to managing life—children, work, home, finances, and everything else—as a single mother.

BURCH, F. W. *Mothers' talking.* New York: St. Martin's Press, 1986. Women at different stages of motherhood share, in their own words, their challenging, humorous, or significant experiences.

MALONEY, M., & MALONEY, A. *The hand that rocks the cradle: Mothers, sons, and leadership.* Englewood Cliffs, NJ: Prentice Hall, 1985. Through stories of famous and infamous men and their mothers, these authors consider many issues of motherhood, child-rearing patterns, and the indirect political influence of women.

MILLMAN, M. *Warm hearts cold cash: The intimate dynamics of families and money.* New York: Free Press, 1991. A sociologist presents the uncomfortable truth, ways we use money within the intimate, sometimes stormy relationships of the family.

REGISTER, C. *"Are those kids yours?" American families with children adopted from other countries.* New York: Free Press, 1991. A thought-provoking examination of inter- national adoption, from the viewpoints of adoptive parents and adopted children ages 6 to 30, highlighting both its normality and special challenges.

RUBIN, L. *Intimate strangers: Men and women together.* New York: Harper & Row, 1983. A social scientist presents a popular account of the differences that arise between men and women, and how they affect intimacy, sexuality, dependency, work, and parenting.

SCARF, M. *Intimate partners: Patterns in love and marriage.* New York: Random House, 1987. Maggie Scarf looks at love, relationships, marriage, and the ways in which people's earlier lives weave into their current relationships, prob- lems, and resolutions.

Chapter 17

Originality and the feeling of one's own dignity are achieved only through work and struggle.

FYODOR DOSTOEVSKY
A DIARY OF A WRITER

CHAPTER OUTLINE

The World of Work

Most adults spend an average of 40 hours each week, 48 weeks per year—for 30 to 45 years of their lives—at their places of employment. Work is a major focus of an adult's energy, skills, and ambitions. We often define ourselves by our occupation. We let it shape our lifestyles, dress, friends, economic level, prestige, attitudes, and values. Our work challenges us. It demands problem solving. It can be the means to find pleasure, satisfaction, growth, and fulfillment in life, or it can be the cause of frustration, boredom, worry, humiliation, and a sense of hopelessness. It can create high stress and damage our health. Certainly, it is a central context for and contributor to adult development. In this chapter, we will look at the world of work, and we will discuss the meaning of work, the occupational cycle, women and work, the relationship between work and lifestyles, and the effects of occupational changes, crises, and transitions on the individual and the family.

THE MEANING OF WORK

What does work give people in return for the time and the energy that they devote to it? For some people, work is merely a means of survival. It provides them with money to feed, clothe, and shelter themselves and their families. For others, work is a chance to be creative or productive; it provides an opportunity to gain self-esteem or respect. For still others, work is almost an addiction—an activity they are driven to perform.

Freud defined the normal adult as someone who is able to love and to work. Indeed, a successful passage through the stages of adult development is intimately tied to a person's involvement in a job or career.

Identity and Generativity

SELF-DEFINITION   Children are often asked, "What do you want to be when you grow up?" Many of our thoughts and fantasies are occupied by this question. In adulthood, how we have answered that question contributes greatly to our identity—who we are, what we are, and what we are not. Whatever our occupation, we carry with us the attitudes, beliefs, and experiences of our jobs. We are members of the corporation or members of the union or members of the

CHAPTER OBJECTIVES

By the time you have finished this chapter, you should be able to do the following:

■ Discuss the role of work in the development of self-definition, identity, and generativity.

■ Describe the classic occupational cycle and changes that have taken place in this cycle in recent years.

■ Discuss the similarities and differences between men and women in the work force, and describe the special problems that dual-earner couples face in today's society.

■ Describe the relationship between work and lifestyle, and discuss the shifting attitudes and values about work that have surfaced in recent years.

■ Explain some of the major reasons for occupational changes in adulthood.

profession. Work may define our status, income level, and prestige. It defines our daily schedule, our social contact, and our opportunities for personal development.

According to Erikson (1968), a central component of identity formation in adolescence and early adulthood involves the establishment of a work identity. But the task of identity formation is not over then. Adults must structure and restructure their individual work identities and suffer their own version of role confusion. Many facets of the adult identity may already be established, and others may be emerging; but without a firm sense of being engaged in a suitable occupation, the picture may be incomplete. People who become involved with and committed to their work will draw a large portion of their sense of identity from their careers. Others who feel less involvement with their jobs may draw less of their identities from their occupations.

INTRINSIC AND EXTRINSIC FACTORS   When researchers ask individual adults what is important to them about their work, there are two major kinds of answers. On the one hand, respondents may talk about the characteristics of their job, together with their particular abilities to cope with it. These are the *intrinsic factors* of work. People who focus on the intrinsic factors might describe their work in terms of its challenge or interest, or they might talk about their work competence and achievements. On the other hand, people might focus on the *extrinsic factors* of work. These factors include the rewards of salary and status, the comfort or convenience of the work environment and the hours, the adequacy of supervision and employment practices, the attitudes and support of co-workers, and the opportunities for advancement (Whitbourne, 1986a).

Workers who talk more about the intrinsic factors of work tend, on average, to report more job satisfaction and higher motivation and personal involvement in their jobs. These workers also tend to have a larger portion of their personal

People who become involved with and committed to their work will draw a large portion of their sense of identity from their careers.

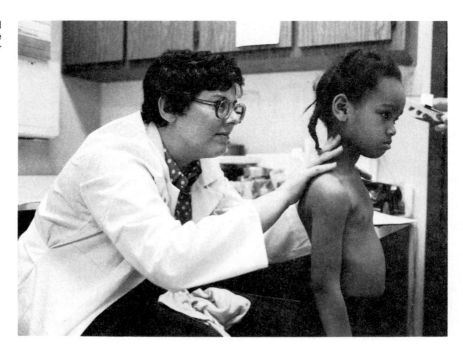

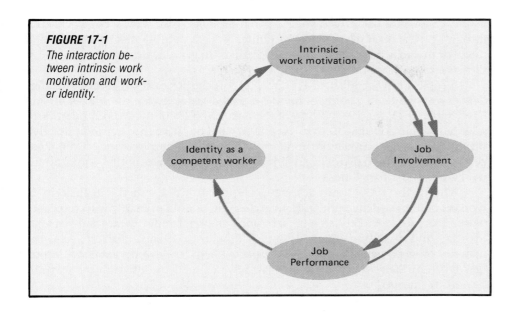

FIGURE 17-1

The interaction between intrinsic work motivation and worker identity.

identity defined by their work or career. In Figure 17–1 there is a model of how intrinsic work motivation seems to be tied to identity as a competent worker. When one is intrinsically motivated, there is more job involvement, better job performance, and stronger identity as a competent worker. This, then, tends to increase one's intrinsic work motivation. But the cycle can go down as well as up if there is a change in any one of these blocks. For example, feeling incompetent or overwhelmed decreases intrinsic motivation, job involvement, and job performance (Maehr & Breskamp, 1986; Whitbourne, 1986b).

Friendships seem to be an important extrinsic factor of jobs. Work friendships may be especially important to people who are in "low ceiling" jobs (Kanter, 1977). Although their pay may be adequate, these people cannot expect to "climb the ladder of success." Therefore, socializing with fellow employees may add meaning to their jobs. Women may find the social relationships they establish at work important (Repetti, Matthew, & Waldron, 1989). These relationships may provide the women with an additional source of support and may be one reason why women who work outside of the home typically have better mental and physical health. Other extrinsic factors, such as supervision, are also related to health. When high job demands are combined with unclear supervision, the risk of heart attacks may increase (Repetti et al., 1989). Thus, extrinsic factors are not only important in terms of job satisfaction but also for overall physical and mental health.

GENERATIVITY According to Erikson, the primary developmental task to be accomplished in adulthood is *generativity*. He explains this as the effort to perpetuate oneself through the contribution of something lasting and meaningful to the world. Many people try to achieve generativity through the creation and nurturance of a family. Others may attempt it through productivity in their work. Teachers, for example, may feel they are making a lasting contribution by molding young minds or transmitting knowledge to succeeding generations. Mentoring is another way to offer guidance to the next generation. Doctors may save lives or aid in the elimination of a disease. Industrial workers, too, may seek generativity through the creation of an object (a house, a car, a camera) that others will find useful or that may be used by future generations. In general, workers come to judge their worth by what they do.

People are aware of and do not wish to lose the personal satisfaction that they derive from work. In a study of middle-class workers between the ages of 46 and 71 (Pfeiffer & Davis, 1971), 90% of the men and 82% of the women questioned said they would continue to work even if they did not have to. They indicated that they derived more satisfaction from work than from leisure activities. Even those people approaching retirement preferred—by a substantial majority—to continue working, at least part time.

During the 1980s, attitudes and values toward work shifted. The majority of workers no longer defined themselves exclusively or even primarily with respect to work. Far more workers sought a balance among family, work, and personal interests and pastimes (Derr, 1986; Whitbourne, 1986b). Nevertheless, the majority of respondents in the 1980s reported high levels of personal satisfaction derived from their work. These intrinsic rewards tend to outweigh the extrinsic rewards mentioned.

Adult Development and Work

Do adults continue to develop with respect to cognitive skills or personality traits as a result of their occupation? It has often been assumed that once adults finish their formal education and perhaps a brief period of occupational training, they settle into a period of stability with very little change. Recently, this notion has been challenged. Increasingly, people are seeking, and some are finding, more meaningful and challenging work opportunities. Several researchers have begun to study the effects of different kinds of work on personality and cognitive abilities. One such researcher has been particularly interested in what he calls *job complexity* (Kohn, 1980). Kohn's longitudinal studies focus on different dimensions of an occupation. Is it routine or diverse? What is the pace of the job? Can the worker control that pace? What is the nature of the relationships between co-workers and supervisors? Are there job pressures and uncertainties? What is the substantive complexity of the work? Substantively complex work requires considerable room for decision making and requires the worker to account for ill-defined or apparently conflicting factors. Kohn emphasizes that the substantive complexity of work is at the very heart of the experience of the worker. It is not surprising, then, that he finds substantive complexity related to a wide range of psychological variables. Individuals who work in jobs with higher complexity report higher job satisfaction, more occupational commitment, and higher self-direction and self-esteem. They also score higher on tests of intellectual flexibility and engage in more intellectually demanding leisure-time pursuits. Although complex jobs are related to workers who have more education, these differences remain even when one controls for educational level (Kohn, 1980; Kohn & Schooler, 1983).

Does the complex job create higher levels of intellectual flexibility, or do individuals with higher levels of intellectual flexibility select more complex jobs? Using longitudinal studies, Kohn and Schooler (1978, 1983) were able to determine that both are true. Although individuals with higher levels of education and higher levels of intellectual flexibility appear to choose more complex jobs when they have the opportunity, it is also true that individuals in more complex positions show improvement in many areas, including intellectual flexibility. These differences have been found for both men and women (Miller et al., 1979). These studies and others indicate that the importance of a job is not measured only by its status, by the income it provides, or even by the interpersonal relationships it offers. Often the intrinsic meaning and psychological impact of a job come directly from the challenges of the work itself.

THE OCCUPATIONAL CYCLE

An adult's working life may be thought of in terms of a cycle: It begins with the thoughts and experiences that lead to a choice of occupation; it continues with the pursuit of the actual career chosen; and it ends with retirement from the work force. This cycle does not necessarily run smoothly. An adult must make critical choices throughout his or her working life. There are moments of doubt and crises, and special events, such as receiving a promotion or being fired, that affect the course of career development. In this section, we will look at some of the parts and aspects of the cycle.

Vocational Life Stages

The occupational cycle starts when we are young and often continues through old age. Two researchers have divided the cycle into a series of stages based on how we are involved with work at various times in our lives.

SUPER'S STAGES OF VOCATIONAL LIFE   Super (1957) divided vocational life into five distinct stages. His major concern was the individual's self-exploration and search for an appropriate occupation. In this search, the individual develops and refines a vocational self-concept.

1. *Growth stage* (birth to age 14). Young children begin to develop a self-concept. They play at various roles and activities and look at what they enjoy and can do well. Interests begin to develop that may lead to future careers.

2. *Exploration stage* (ages 15 to 24). Teenagers begin to explore and react to their needs, interests, capacities, values, and opportunities. They make tentative career choices based on their findings. By the end of this stage, young adults have usually identified an appropriate career and have started to work in it.

3. *Establishment stage* (ages 25 to 44). Workers now try to establish a permanent position for themselves in their chosen field. There may be some job and career shifts in the early years, but careers tend to become stable in the latter half of the stage. These are often the most creative years of employment.

4. *Maintenance stage* (ages 45 to 64). Workers focus on maintaining the position they established for themselves during the establishment stage.

5. *Decline stage* (age 65 on). The physical and mental powers of the now elderly workers are in decline. The nature of the work is altered to fit diminished capacities. Eventually, work activity ends.

TABLE 17–1
A Comparison of Super's and Havighurst's Stages of Vocational Life

AGE	SUPER	HAVIGHURST
0	1. Growth stage	
5		1. Identification with a worker
10		2. Acquiring the basic habits of industry
15	2. Exploration stage	3. Acquiring identity as a worker in the occupational structure
25	3. Establishment stage	4. Becoming a productive person
40		5. Maintaining a productive society
45	4. Maintenance stage	
65	5. Decline stage	
70		6. Contemplating a productive and responsible life

HAVIGHURST'S STAGES OF VOCATIONAL LIFE   Havighurst (1964) offers an alternative view of vocational life stages. He deals less with the individual's needs and capacities and more with the acquisition of attitudes and work skills that allow people to fit into the work force.

1. *Identification with a worker* (ages 5 to 10). Children identify with working fathers and mothers, and the idea of working enters into their self-concepts.

2. *Acquiring the basic habits of industry* (ages 10 to 15). Students learn to organize their time and efforts to accomplish tasks like schoolwork or chores. They also learn to make work a priority over play in certain circumstances.

3. *Acquiring an identity as a worker in the occupational structure* (ages 15 to 25). People choose their occupations and begin to prepare for them. They acquire some work experience that helps them choose and get started in their careers.

4. *Becoming a productive person* (ages 25 to 40). Adults perfect the skills required by their chosen jobs and begin to move ahead in their careers.

5. *Maintaining a productive society* (ages 40 to 70). Workers are now at the high point of their careers. They begin to pay attention to and give time to civic and social responsibilities related to their jobs.

6. *Contemplating a productive and responsible life* (age 70 on). Workers are now retired, and they look back on their careers and contributions with satisfaction.

There is always a danger of overinterpreting any stage theory. Several authors have suggested that in today's rapidly changing, highly technological society, it is a mistake to assume that all people go through a single set of stages in a single occupational cycle (Okun, 1984). Young people change jobs frequently before they make a major occupational commitment, and many people make one or more major mid-career shifts. The stages presented by Super and Havighurst are perhaps true for less than half of all adult workers.

Occupational Choice and Preparation

Why does one person become an accountant, another a police officer, and yet another a doctor? A multitude of factors influence choice of occupation, including socioeconomic status, ethnic background, intelligence, skills, sex, and parental occupations. Many of the social and psychological influences that direct the choice occur during childhood. Both Super and Havighurst have suggested that by the age of 15, people have made tentative career choices and have acquired the concepts and habits necessary for those careers. Cognitive and emotional development, the acquisition of attitudes and values, and achievement orientation are important to career choice and success, but they all take place many years before we consciously make definite career choices.

Many researchers have developed explanations of how these influences affect the choice of an occupation. We will look at four of them closely.

SEX AND RACE   As Table 17–2 indicates, African-Americans and women are overrepresented in some professions and underrepresented in others. This means that if one were to predict the percentage of African-American or female workers in a particular occupation strictly on the basis of percentage of total U.S. population, the estimate would be too low in the former case and too high in the latter. Not surprisingly, African-American and female workers tend to be overrepresented in the lower-status, lower-paying fields and underrepresented in the high-salary professions.

Explanations for these distributions tend to fall into one of two categories. The first type of explanation assumes that the worker has made some choice that has led to the job assignment. For example, African-American males are less likely to finish high school than are whites. This means they cannot compete for the jobs

TABLE 17–2

Representation of Females, Blacks, and Hispanics in Various Occupations

OCCUPATION	PERCENTAGE OF TOTAL		
	Female	**Black**	**Hispanic**
Total Percent Employed*	45.0%	10.1%	7.2%
Architects	14.6	4.4	6.3
Engineers	7.3	3.8	2.6
Registered nurses	94.6	8.5	2.7
Teachers, college and university	38.5	4.0	3.6
Teachers, prekindergarten and kindergarten	98.2	9.2	6.3
Teachers, elementary school	84.8	10.2	3.9
Social workers	66.0	19.3	6.2
Licensed practical nurses	96.0	19.1	3.8
Secretaries	99.1	7.1	4.8
Duplicating, mail, and other office machine operators	62.0	16.0	11.6
Mail clerks	50.6	23.8	10.0
Data entry keyers	88.2	19.8	7.6
Teachers' aides	95.9	14.3	9.6
Private household cleaners and servants	95.6	32.0	22.1
Correctional institution workers	17.8	22.8	6.4
Dental assistants	98.7	6.8	3.9
Nursing aides, orderlies, and attendants	89.8	33.7	6.2
Maids and housemen	85.0	29.0	18.2
Janitors and cleaners	31.2	21.1	14.6
Automobile mechanics	0.7	7.4	10.5
Pressing machine operators	65.7	28.1	28.0
Farm workers	23.3	8.6	23.0

*Employed civilians, age 16 and over, by occupation, sex, race, and Hispanic origin in 1988.

Source: Statistical Abstract of the United States, 1990.

no Interest-comp
ii Edo
discrim

that require higher education. Women may question their competence in the sciences more readily than men do (Ware & Steckler, 1983) and hence are reluctant to pursue science careers. Or women may opt for careers that are easily combined with family. Availability of part-time work, ease of moving in and out of the job market, and job requirements that do not change rapidly are job characteristics that make it easier to combine career and family (Council of Economic Advisers, 1987; Kalleberg & Rosenfeld, 1990). Teaching and clerical work fit this description. Finally, socialization, including role modeling, probably influences career choice. Hence, the sex and race patterns may be self-perpetuating to some extent.

The second type of explanation for these patterns is discrimination. African-Americans and women may be subtly (or not so subtly) channeled into some jobs but not into others. Men and women of equal skills may not be given the same job titles. For instance, the better titles may go to men more frequently than they go to women (Bielby & Baron, 1986). Promotions may not be equally available. Certainly, discrimination is illegal. But it is evident that discrimination plays a role in the wages of both African-Americans and women. The same characteristics that predict high salaries for white men do not result in equally high salaries for African-Americans and women (Ferber, Green, & Spaith, 1986; Klein & Rones, 1989).

Some young adults, such as these related members of an acrobatics troupe, let family responsibilities direct their choice of careers.

PARENTAL ATTITUDES Roe (1957) suggests that the relationship between parents and their children gives rise to the attitudes, needs, and interests in children that are expressed in adulthood through their choice of occupation. For example, children who are the center of the family's attention may grow dependent on the need for belongingness, love, and esteem from others. In later years, these children will be very aware of the opinions and attitudes of others toward themselves. Consequently, they will be attracted to occupations that will bring them in contact with people and that will hold out the possibility for gaining their esteem. Such individuals will move toward careers in which they can serve others, or they will gravitate toward culturally oriented work, perhaps the arts or the entertainment field.

Children who are neglected or avoided by parents often suffer from a lack of love and esteem gratification and do not develop the same kind of dependence. In later years, they will not seek out people to gratify their needs and may develop interests that are not people oriented. They may be attracted to solitary activities and develop careers in science, technology, or other professions that do not primarily require interaction with people. Families influence their children's career choice in other ways, too: They model certain lifestyles; they are sources of important values and beliefs; and the family system allows for certain levels of individuality and autonomy, reinforcing certain rates (Bratcher, 1982). For example, girls whose mothers work tend to have higher achievement motivation and career aspirations (Hoffman, 1989).

SELF-CONCEPT THEORY A third explanation involves the kind of self-exploration proposed in Super's stages of vocational life. The early stages, you will recall, are dominated by the development of the self; the exploration of individual needs, interests, and abilities; and the identification of an appropriate career. The essence of self-concept theory is that people seek occupations that fit the concept they have developed of themselves (Super, 1963). By establishing themselves in occupations that fit their notions of self, individuals achieve "self-actualization." That is, they have acted in a way that they believe is the best for their own satisfaction and individual growth. A man who sees himself as quiet, scholarly, intelligent, and eloquent, for example, may become a college professor. A woman who sees herself as socially concerned, energetic, and as a leader with great magnetism might decide to go into politics.

TRAIT FACTOR THEORY Like self-concept theory, trait factor theory is concerned with the link between personality and occupational choice. Trait factor theory, however, investigates actual, measured personality traits as opposed to the individual's perception of self. The main idea of the theory is that there is a close fit between the kinds of occupations people choose and their personality traits. Jobs can be defined by the kinds of personality traits they seem to require. If an individual exhibits the traits demanded by a particular job, then the job and the person are a good match. Holland (1973) developed a system of matching six individual personality traits with appropriate occupations. The traits are: (1) realistic, (2) investigative, (3) social, (4) conventional, (5) enterprising, and (6) artistic. A person exhibiting traits 2 and 5, for example, might become a research scientist. Someone with traits 3 and 4 might become, say, a hospital worker.

The trait factor approach to occupational choice has stimulated much research. As one might expect, the matching of individuals and occupations by personality traits does not always work. The theory does, however, provide some general indications of the direction that people will take in their working lives.

Sex and race, parental attitudes, the self-concept theory, and the trait factor theory explain in part how people choose their occupations. Other factors, however, are equally or more important. In times of recession and high unemployment, people may not have a choice and may take any job they can get just to pay the rent. It is not uncommon to hear about Ph.D.s who are taxicab drivers, architects who sweep leaves in city parks, or business executives who are working as typists.

Social changes also affect the type of work available. In the past 20 years, for example, there has been a tremendous growth in the technological and computer fields, leading many students to study in these areas. Many people let family responsibilities direct their choice of careers. Some children are groomed to take over family businesses or to follow in a parent's footsteps, even though they may prefer a different type of work. The need to support a spouse or children may also cause someone to look for a job in a better-paying field. An artist, for example, may go into advertising or public relations work and paint only on weekends as a hobby. Finally, many people without definite plans or with varied interests and abilities may simply fall into an available job. Practical considerations, then, have as much to do with occupational choice as theoretical explanations.

FORMAL AND INFORMAL OCCUPATIONAL PREPARATION Before entering the work force, people acquire a number of new skills, values, and attitudes both formally and informally. Formal occupational preparation includes structured learning in high school, vocational training programs, college, or graduate school, as well as on-the-job instruction. Informal occupational preparation takes more subtle forms: It is the process of absorbing the attitudes, norms, and role expectations appropriate to a particular job. Long before we begin formal preparation, we are absorbing informal norms and values from our parents, teachers, members of the professions, and television and movie actors. We learn by

For many college students, the emotional and intellectual maturity that one develops through a college education is far more significant than any specific career preparation.

observing others and by day-to-day experiences in a particular social class. Informal socialization is so pervasive and so critical that it often determines our conscious choice for formal career preparation (Moore, 1969).

For many people, college is considered a critical part of occupational preparation. But in many areas of study, particularly in the liberal arts, little or no training is specifically aimed at cultivating marketable skills. Rather, liberal arts curricula try to develop basic communication skills, expose students to a variety of ideas, and develop the ability to analyze. Although essential to intellectual maturity, these skills are not directly related to many specific job titles. In contrast, quantitative programs, such as engineering, medicine, and business, do provide substantive knowledge and practical skills. They usually attract motivated, determined students who have already defined their goals.

A survey of hundreds of thousands of college students in the early 1970s (Astin, 1977) found that, for most students, the emotional and attitudinal changes occurring during college are far more significant than any specific career preparation. Beliefs and self-concepts are revised. Students learn to rate and assess themselves in increasingly complex and realistic ways, and they become more specific in analyzing various assets like originality, artistic ability, mechanical skill, effective writing skill, and personal communication. They tend to develop higher opinions about their intellectual abilities, leadership skills, and popularity. These changes are often more lasting than the specific career training the student receives in college and may help a student make better decisions about occupational choice.

Entry and Establishment in the Work Force

Having made either definite or tentative occupational choices, young adults are ready to enter the work force. One of the first problems that the young worker may encounter is reality shock. During adolescence and career preparation, people have optimistic, idealistic thoughts and high expectations about what their work will actually be like and what they will be able to accomplish. When the training ends and the job begins, novices quickly learn that some of their expectations were wrong. The work may be dull and mechanical, superiors unfair, and peers difficult to work with; the goals of the job may seem to be lost in a maze of bureaucratic considerations or subject to individual whims. The shock of the reality of their jobs may result in a period of frustration and anger, until the young workers adjust to the new situation. The inability to adjust—to cope with the disappointments that come with reality—may result in later career problems.

In a long-term study of young, lower-level managers at AT&T, some of Levinson's concepts (discussed in Chapter 15) about molding the dream into a realistic pathway are supported. A total of 422 young men, half college educated and half promoted into management from the crafts, were followed for much of their careers. These young men began the study with very high expectations for their own success. Over the first 7 years, their expectations became much more realistic. Fewer expected promotions, and many realized that promotions might well mean transferring to a new location, disrupting families, or working harder and having more responsibility and less time for family-related activities. These young managers were not necessarily dissatisfied with their jobs. They found considerable satisfaction in the challenge of doing their jobs well and meeting personal standards of achievement. The extrinsic rewards of salary and status appeared to become somewhat less important over time (Bray & Howard, 1983).

Gradually, the entrance phase gives way to growing competence and autonomy. Levinson (1978) emphasizes the role of mentors in this transition who embody both peer and authoritative values and norms. Apprentices, aided by their mentors, acquire skills and self-confidence. They soon establish themselves and may begin to outperform their mentors and break off with them. Later, the workers acquire authority over others and may begin to serve as mentors themselves.

Several authors have noted the positive role of mentors in the development of young workers (Kanter, 1977). Mentors carry out teaching and training roles. They sponsor the young worker's advancement. They serve as models for social as well as work-related behavior. Generally, they ease the transition to independent adult work status. In executive and academic careers, male workers frequently report having a mentor. But only 12% of men in the work force, and only 7% of women, are in executive, administrative, or managerial roles. What is more, in studies of women executives, most women report that no steady mentor was available to them (Busch, 1985). Some women find male mentors, but that relationship can become complicated. Some women report having their husbands as mentors, but this creates situations of mixed loyalties. When, in fact, the woman's success and career seem to jeopardize the time spent devoted to husband and family, husband mentors often fail to support the woman's career development (Roberts & Newton, 1987). In an effort to help more women achieve executive, administrative, and managerial roles, some have suggested that one of the most successful strategies would be to promote a conscious and formal system of mentor relationships (Swoboda & Millar, 1986).

Levinson (1978) emphasizes that maintaining a sense of excitement and commitment to work throughout adulthood is essential to mature satisfaction. Commitment to a trade or a career varies greatly, depending both on individual traits and on broader social and economic factors. People with low-paying, uninviting work will naturally have great difficulty maintaining a commitment to

Older workers can teach young workers not only skills but also the values and norms of the occupation.

Many people today seek satisfaction and personal growth from their work.

the job. Further, there is little performance motivation when there is little chance for upward mobility (Moore, 1969).

A young adult's commitment to a job or profession becomes stronger as a result of growing loyalty and adjustment to particular occupational expectations and norms. Loyalty begins to arise as young adults begin to identify with their occupation. Loyalty to their employer will grow to the extent that they want continued employment with and rewards from the employer. As a result of many years of involvement in an occupation, people identify themselves with an entire occupational group or industry. They learn to behave according to the particular rules and expectations of their occupational group. At first, beginners get the worst job assignments—those involving the most tedium or drudgery. At the same time, however, they have the opportunity to observe what their superiors do and to gain information that may be useful. Beginners are also introduced to the jargon and shoptalk that will help them become part of the occupational in-group. As they develop experience on the job, people learn to use time-tested problem-solving techniques. They also begin to realize that they must defer to recognized authority and live up to certain minimum standards of performance (Moore, 1969).

Consolidation, Maintenance, and Disengagement

For those who follow a classic occupational cycle, the mid-career period is the time of settling down and coming to grips with mid-career realism (Levinson, 1978). For Levinson's men, the late 30s was a time of establishing one's niche in society, forgetting about attractive alternative careers, and striving for advancement. It involved striving to be as good at one's chosen profession as one could be. It also involved attempting to create some stability, not only in one's work but in the rest of one's life. For some, it involved increasing responsibility and prestige, casting off one's mentor, and becoming autonomous. For Levinson's men, climbing the ladder of success was generally not as easy as anticipated. In most trades or careers there is little room at the top. Hence, in their early 40s, many workers found themselves disillusioned and somewhat cynical. The original dream had been unrealistic. They realized that they were going to have to face lower levels of aspiration. Recall the study of AT&T managers, which found a somewhat similar pattern at mid-career. Although some had reached higher management levels, many managers were still at low- or middle-management levels and had reappraised their goals and aspirations. In fact, many reported that further advancement in their careers was not critical to their life satisfaction, and that many other areas of their lives—family and personal pursuits—had become more important (Bray & Howard, 1983). The high-level managers in the AT&T study, however, rated work as critically important to their sense of self and their life satisfaction.

The classic occupational cycle described by Super and others is no longer the dominant pattern, even for white-collar managers and executives. Only a minority of workers now stay with the same company throughout their careers. Many people change jobs within a field, looking for better pay, more responsibility, a promotion, or better working conditions. In addition, an increasing number of people are making career shifts and changing fields entirely to pursue different interests. Some workers do not find much occupational stability at all, and they

encounter frequent or protracted periods of unemployment and career crisis—
often accompanied by financial, social, and psychological problems. For women,
the pattern for work involvement is even more complex, with one author specifying
as many as 14 different patterns (LaSalle & Spokane, 1987). Indeed, the more
common occupational pattern in midlife during the 1990s will probably be one of
change rather than consolidation and maintenance.

In the later career period, workers in their 50s and 60s start to disengage as
they prepare for retirement, the normal end of the occupational cycle. (Retirement
is discussed in Chapter 20.)

Work Abilities

It is tempting to assume that as people get older their ability to work declines.
This would seem to be one rationale behind retirement, especially when it is
mandatory. On the other hand, we frequently give the positions of greatest
authority to older people. Does this mean that we tend to give supervisory
positions to people with the least ability to do the work they are overseeing? This
apparent contradiction can be resolved, at least to some extent, if we make a
distinction between ability and expertise (Salthouse, 1990).

As you will see in subsequent chapters, there are real declines in sensory and
cognitive abilities as people age. For example, older people cannot process and

respond to information as quickly as young adults do (Salthouse, 1985; Schaie, 1990). There may be declines in certain forms of intelligence, such as visual–spatial reasoning (Salthouse et al., 1990; Salthouse & Mitchell, 1990; Schaie, 1990). Visual acuity declines (Fozard, 1990). Depending on the job, such declines may have serious implications for performance. For example, older architects exhibit poorer visual–spatial skills (Salthouse et al., 1990; Salthouse & Mitchell, 1990) and typists lose speed as they age (Salthouse, 1984).

Nonetheless, these losses do not mean that older architects and typists are inefficient. First, keep in mind that there are individual differences in the rate and extent of physical decline. So not all people will suffer losses that might impede work. Second, it is possible that they do a better job than their younger colleagues because of their accumulated expertise. Because most people do not change careers after age 40, older workers will typically have more experience (Rhodes, 1983). The older architect, for example, may know more about building materials and how they interact with building type or site (Salthouse et al., 1990). The older typist may know more about formats, previous relevant work, or individual work styles. Thus, skill losses do not necessarily translate to an overall loss in competence.

Older workers are also likely to be more reliable (Rhodes, 1983). They are less likely to leave their jobs. They are less likely to take time off from work when it is not necessary. These patterns not only help the worker accumulate expertise but also make for a more efficient business operation. This all assumes that the older worker is healthy. Older workers are more likely to suffer health problems and to miss work because of them (Rhodes, 1983).

WOMEN IN THE WORK FORCE

One of the most notable developments in employment has been the great increase in the number and proportion of women in the work force. In 1960, approximately 23,272,000, or 37.8% of all women age 16 and older, were in the labor force; by 1988, the figure had risen to approximately 54,700,000 or 56.6% (*Statistical*

One of the most notable developments in employment has been the great increase in the number and proportion of women in the work force.

TABLE 17–3

The Increasing Participation by Women in the Work Force

	1970	1975	1980	1985	1988	Proj. 2000
Percentage of all women 16 years and older in the work force	43.3%	46.3%	51.5%	54.5%	56.6%	62.6%
Women as percent of total work force	38.0%	40.0%	42.6%	44.2%	44.9%	47.3%
Number of women in the work force (in millions)	31.5	37.5	45.5	51.5	54.7	66.8

Source: *Statistical Abstract of the United States* (Washington, DC: Department of Commerce, 1990).

Abstract of the United States, 1990). It is predicted that the rate will increase to 62.6% by the year 2000 (*Statistical Abstract of the United States,* 1990). This increase has been most dramatic for white and Hispanic women. It has been less so for African-American women, who, because of economic necessity, have always worked in greater numbers.

Women have made some advances as more of them have entered the work force. For example, in 1970, 8% of all doctors were women. By 1986, this figure had nearly doubled to 15%. Even more dramatically, only 5% of all lawyers and judges in 1970 were women. By 1986, 18% were women and fully 29% of lawyers and judges under 35 years of age were females (Council of Economic Advisers, 1987). Nonetheless, most women are still in the lower-paying "women's" fields such as nursing, teaching, and clerical work (Matthews & Rodin, 1989). Furthermore, women still make less money than men do. Among full-time, year-round employees, the median salary for white men was $28,262. The comparable figure for white women was $18,823, whereas for African-American women it was $16,867 (Council of Economic Advisers, 1990).

The Meaning of Work for Women

Women participate in the working world for many reasons. The primary reason may be simple economic necessity. Single mothers are often the sole support for their families. Even many married couples could not live without the wife's income. This is especially true in African-American and Hispanic-American households where husbands have lower wages and higher rates of unemployment. But, like men, many women find satisfaction and self-fulfillment in employment outside the home. Women, when interviewed, report many of the same factors that make work important to men: They find work interesting and challenging; they consider their work an opportunity for self-direction or increased responsibility; they like the benefits of salary, of increased future security, and the possibility of advancement (Whitbourne, 1986a).

Despite these similarities, however, there are some differences between men and women. In some studies, women more often report the opportunity to work with people—as clients, as co-workers, even as supervisors—as a particularly important aspect of their work. It helps them to feel more connected. It may be that, for at least some women, the interpersonal relationships at work are particularly important in helping to define their own particular vocational self-concept (Forrest & Mikolaitis, 1986). Social support at work is also associated with lower rates of depression and physical problems for women (Repetti et al., 1989).

Other differences include the fact that among women there appears to be a more dramatic contrast between career-oriented and non-career-oriented individuals. Some find homemaking a meaningful, self-fulfilling activity. Others find it drudgery. In a large survey of women, the reports on self-esteem, life satisfaction, and self-perception differed dramatically between career-oriented and non-career-oriented women. Among those who described themselves as "career oriented," those who were in full-time employment were much happier with themselves. Career-oriented women who were temporarily unemployed or employed in part-time jobs or jobs that underutilized their skills were much less happy, had less self-esteem, and lower self-perceptions. For women who described themselves as "not career oriented," the results were quite the opposite. Their self-esteem and life satisfaction were not related to whether or not they were employed full time or part time. These women agreed with such statements as "I cannot imagine having a fully satisfying life without having children" or "I would not take a job that would interfere with the things I like to do with my family" (Pietromonaco et al., 1987).

Work Patterns for Women

After the rise of industrialism in the early 1800s, men went outside the home to earn a living while women remained behind as homemakers.

Women's paid employment is not a new phenomenon. During periods of economic hardship, women have always worked, at least intermittently, outside the home. Before the rise of industrialism in the early 1800s, men and women shared the responsibility of providing for their families through the combined efforts in a family business. Only with the rise of factories and the shift from subsistence economies to market economies did men become the "natural" providers (Bernard, 1981). They went out and earned money while women remained behind as homemakers. This picture has changed in recent times as more and more women have entered the work force and have established careers.

Women entering the work force do not necessarily follow the standard career patterns of their male counterparts. Although no formal theories have been proposed yet on their career development, it is clear that women follow a greater variety of patterns. In fact, investigators have identified 14 common patterns of labor force participation of young women between the ages of 18 and 30 (LaSalle & Spokane, 1987). An increasing number of women follow the traditional male pattern of working without interruption. Others plan to have children when their careers are well established. Women who wish to devote themselves exclusively to raising a family in early adulthood sometimes establish careers outside the home once the last child has entered first grade or college. The average woman can devote 10 years to full-time child care while her children are young and still have 35 years left to enter the work force, establish a career, or pursue other interests (Daniels & Weingarten, 1982). Most women still interrupt work, at least temporarily, to take care of children, whereas men rarely do (Kalleberg & Rosenfeld, 1990; Shaw, 1983). These interruptions may contribute to the wage gap between men and women (Hewlitt, 1984).

The Dual-Earner Couple

The dramatic increase in the number of women in the work force has resulted in a rather common American phenomenon known as the "dual-earner couple" or the "dual-earner marriage." In recent studies, the dual-earner marriage has been defined as one in which the husband works full time and the wife works 20 or more hours per week (Pleck & Staines, 1982; Rapoport & Rapoport, 1980). There are certain obvious advantages to dual-earner marriages versus single-earner marriages. The gains in income provide for a higher standard of living. There is more money for daily necessities, for emergencies, for a better place to live, for better education for the children, and so forth. For college-educated, dual-earner couples, the most important benefit is reportedly the wife's more complete self-fulfillment. Talented women are providing services, developing creative talents, and fulfilling their vocational identity.

There are strains as well as satisfactions in dual-earner marriages. The husbands in these families often report more marital dissatisfaction than do other husbands (Burke & Weir, 1976; Kessler & McRae, 1982; Staines, Pottick, & Fudge, 1986). In one large study, over a third of such couples reported severe conflicts in their attempts to meet both work and family responsibilities (Pleck & Staines, 1982). Conflicts were a result of job demands, work hours, scheduling conflicts between home and work responsibilities, and family crises. Although both men and women in dual-earner couples experience these conflicts, the women reported higher levels of conflict between work and family. Women often report a very realistic work overload.

There is some evidence that domestic tasks—especially child care—are more equally shared in some dual-earner families. However, under virtually all circumstances, women who work are still primarily responsible for the housework and child care (Barnett & Baruch, 1987; Berardo, Sheehan, & Leslie, 1987; Bergmann, 1986; Kalleberg & Rosenfeld, 1990; Maret & Finlay, 1984; Rapoport & Rapoport, 1980). This is true when the children are infants as well as when they are school age. It is true in various countries, including Sweden, where one may have expected generous paternity leave options to have altered this situation. It is true whether the woman is working full time or part time. Indeed, some people have suggested that working mothers really have two full-time jobs (Hochschild, 1989).

There are other strains in dual-career marriages. Although social attitudes now favor women in the work force, there is still some disapproval of mothers with very young children who work full time—and over half the mothers of toddlers and 51% of mothers of infants under 1 year of age were in the labor force in 1988 (*Statistical Abstract of the United States,* 1990). Some women experience these negative reactions from friends, neighbors, and colleagues. Some women experience considerable role conflict themselves. This ambivalence is accentuated when there are difficulties finding adequate care for young children during the mother's working hours. Women may feel particularly uneasy leaving an infant in someone else's care. Yet, maternity leave of any kind, much less paid or for an extended period of time, is available to only a minority of women (Hewlitt, 1984; Scarr, Phillips, & McCartney, 1989). Some have argued that this ambivalence is a result of women's sex-role conditioning. Women have been socialized to be less active, to focus on marriage and its prospects, and to ignore the development of work or

Although there is some evidence that domestic tasks are more equally shared in some dual-earner families, the more common pattern is that the major responsibility for such duties falls on the wife.

career orientation (Hansen, 1974). But most observers attribute this role conflict and ambivalence to the very real, day-to-day pressures of maintaining full responsibility for two competing sets of demands. Role conflict, then, is a realistic result of the circumstances of dual-earner couples and not a "problem" of the psychological makeup of the woman.

Women who pursue a professional or managerial career (and the majority of these women are married) face additional strains. There are strains in the marriage when decisions must be made about whose career takes precedence—at times of promotion or transfers, for example. To favor a husband's career may maximize family income and lifestyle but may handicap the woman's own career development (Favia & Genovese, 1983).

In some cases, the woman's career is limited by myths and stereotypes in the workplace. For example, it is often thought that females in managerial, professional, or technical positions are less willing to take risks or to make sacrifices associated with career advancement. It is also thought that females do not want, need, or expect the same salaries as men even when accepting a promotion. However, it has been found repeatedly that many women are similar to men in their attitudes about risk taking, salaries, and advancement in their professional careers (Rynes & Rosen, 1983). It is also sometimes assumed that women have less achievement motivation or less specific career plans, but in a recent comparison there were some striking differences. Indeed, women in traditionally male professions, such as business, law, and medicine, had very similar career plans to men pursuing the same careers. On the other hand, women in traditionally female fields, such as education, social work, and nursing, had somewhat different career plans. They were less ambitious, and they expected to make accommodations for marriage and family responsibilities that would cut into their lifetime career history.

Riger and Galligan (1980), in a review of research on women in management, suggest that situational factors, not the personality characteristics and behavior of women, may account for their relative exclusion from managerial positions. For example, they cite research (Kanter, 1976) showing that the paucity of women in managerial jobs tends to work against the few women who have entered the managerial ranks as token representatives of their sex. The behavior and work of token representatives will be analyzed very closely and may be judged against higher standards. Similarly, women managers may find themselves under a lot of pressure from peers or superiors to perform, or they may find that they are expected to conform to various stereotypes.

Despite these strains, women actually seem to gain substantial benefits from working. Working women tend to be both psychologically and physically healthier than nonworking women (Baruch & Barnett, 1986; Kessler & McRae, 1982; McBride, 1990; Repetti et al., 1989; Rodin & Ickovics, 1990). They suffer less depression and fewer physical symptoms, such as heart attacks and ulcers. They have higher self-esteem. This is especially true for unmarried women, but married women also gain, especially if their husbands are supportive. Women who enjoy their work benefit more. This may be one reason why professional women actually realize *more* benefits from working than do clerical workers, despite the greater responsibility in their jobs. Given the appearance of role strain and role overload, it is surprising that there is virtually no accumulative evidence indicating detrimental effects of employment for any group of women.

Job satisfaction often "spills over" into the families of working women, especially if the women have high-status jobs. This often enables families to better adjust to the limited flexibility and time as well as to the increased pressure inherent in the dual-earner family situation (Piotrkowski & Crits-Christoph, 1981). This may be one reason why most studies have found that dual-career marriages are no less happy than other marriages. In fact, several studies have found higher levels of marital satisfaction among employed than nonemployed wives in working-class and professional families (Burke & Weir, 1976; Walker & Wallston, 1985).

Why might working women benefit despite the strains? One possibility is social support. The women can turn to their colleagues at work for friendship, advice, and emotional bolstering. This may be particularly beneficial to single mothers (Repetti et al., 1989). Work may also provide an alternate source of self-esteem and even of a sense of control when things at home are going poorly (Rodin & Ickovics, 1990). Thus, work may serve as a buffer against stresses at home as well as an additional source of support during nonfamilial crises.

WORK AND LIFESTYLES

To a great extent, people's work determines their style of living and their attitudes. What at first glance appears to be a gentle socialization into a particular career may actually be an enormous force in people's lives. Work may determine whether they will lead mobile or relatively settled lives, the kind of community in which they will reside, the kind of home they will have. Work may determine their friendship patterns, level of sophistication, opinions, prejudices, and political affiliations.

Changing Attitudes about Work

Until recently, occupational roles tended to define individual behavior and personal priorities. Workers sacrificed and suppressed values that conflicted with those of their employer for the sake of their jobs. At the same time, workers generally did not expect to get psychological fulfillment from their work. Today, the importance assigned to work, as opposed to other parts of daily life, has changed—at least for many young people. A new generation of workers has begun to demand more fulfillment from work, and it is less willing to compromise for the sake of a job.

This change has occurred only recently. Until approximately 1970, a coherent value system seemed to dominate the attitudes of most American workers (Yankelovich, 1978). The old value system had several distinct components. It was considered desirable for women to stay at home if their husbands could afford it. Men tolerated unsatisfying jobs for the sake of economic security. The main motivations for workers were money and status. Tight family bonds were paralleled by strong organizational loyalty.

Since 1970, this fixed value system has rapidly eroded. The Vietnam War, the civil rights movement, the women's movement, Watergate, the counterculture, and other social phenomena have challenged the old order. Many young adults now view work in a different way. For one thing, they place great importance and positive value on leisure time. They try to rearrange work, to some extent, to accommodate recreational activities and avocations. At the same time, they attach great symbolic significance to their jobs. This is especially true of young women, who consider a paying job a badge of autonomy and independence. For them, it is an essential part of self-esteem.

Attitudes and values concerning work can be traced in part to generational factors. In a survey of attitudes toward jobs done in the late 1970s (Sheppard & Herrick, 1977), only one-third of the workers under 30 years of age said they were satisfied with their work most of the time. In contrast, 64% of workers—double the number—who were over age 55 claimed to be satisfied. Similarly, workers under age 30 were far less likely than older workers to believe that their jobs were anything like what they actually wanted when they were hired. It is possible, of course, that more of the older workers were dissatisfied with their jobs when they were younger but that those people already have changed to a more satisfying job (Havighurst, 1982).

There are other aspects to this shift in attitudes and values. Many people no longer define themselves primarily in terms of their occupational roles. Many young adults want to allow more room on the job for individuality and creativity. Whereas many in the older generation sought to suppress individual traits and become "company men" or "union men," many of today's young workers feel that work is excessively depersonalized and stifling. They want greater flexibility and more control over their work schedules and their environments. They believe that if employers want sustained effort and good performance, the burden is on them to offer more incentives and a better quality of work life.

Young people today are striving for an approach to work that enhances their sense of psychological well-being. This involves many different elements: self-esteem and self-worth, an identity acceptable to society and to self, and the belief that the work one is doing is justifiable, even desirable. It is clear that work can define people's goals and values; it can create a sense of stability and enhance feelings of potency and effectiveness (Yankelovich, 1978). Thus, workers believe that they have a great deal at stake in their occupational roles, and they are making large, personal demands from their employers concerning their work. Many jobs simply cannot satisfy these kinds of demands. It is not surprising, then, that a survey of young, well-educated professionals found that over half contemplated changing occupations in the next 5 years (Renwick & Lawler, 1978). Heading their list of reasons were more opportunities for growth, learning, and self-actualization. At the same time, executives, professionals, and others with a high degree of autonomy and responsibility more often expressed job satisfaction than did clerical and unskilled workers. They were also less likely to feel trapped in their jobs than the lower-paid, less-educated workers.

OCCUPATIONAL CHANGES

Until recently, it was thought that one's working life consisted of—or should consist of—entering a particular occupation or career as a young adult and remaining in that occupation until retirement. This preferred career course required a thoughtful choice of occupation and careful preparation. Once a person had begun a job, he or she was expected to lay the foundation for a lifetime career and to climb the ladder as quickly as possible.

This scenario has changed as the realization has spread that adult development may produce many shifts in attitudes, career needs, and goals. Further, in today's technologically advanced and economically unstable world, jobs change so quickly or are eliminated altogether in such numbers that the one-life, one-career imperative no longer applies. People may change companies. They may change jobs within a particular firm (as in a promotion or a shift to administrative work). Although most people probably do not make dramatic changes once their careers are established, it is now considered unusual for individuals to begin and end their working lives in the same type of job or career line.

Mid-Career Reassessment

As we have seen, when we look at the work histories of individuals in the past couple of decades, it seems that the occupational life cycles described by Super and Havighurst omit something—a period of serious reassessment or reexamination that often occurs at mid-life. Reassessment occurs for a number of reasons. For example, workers may find that they are not being promoted as they had expected to be, or a job may be far less desirable than anticipated. One factor that may cause middle-aged people to make dramatic changes in their occupation is a mid-life transition they may have experienced. Levinson (1978) found that adults in their 40s may experience a shift in their values and goals that leads them to consider changing the course of their careers. Levinson explains the occurrence of this change in terms of the reappearance of the dream—the inspiration, ideals, and goals of youth (see Chapter 15). Some researchers suggest that adults cope with this reassessment period best if they systematically assess their own capabilities and

An increasing number of people are making career or job changes during midlife in search of better pay and greater job satisfaction.

These employees are being trained to operate new computers. Rapid technological changes over the past 30 years have forced people to learn new job skills.

the strengths and weaknesses of their current occupational positions (Okun, 1984; Schein, 1978).

Thomas (1979) suggests that certain societal conditions now permit people who experience such dramatic alterations in their values and attitudes to act upon them. People now live longer and are able to work longer, so that when their responsibilities to their children end, they are free to make changes that may reduce their incomes or transform their way of living. Working spouses also permit a continuation of income while the other spouse makes his or her career changes. Thomas cites the greater tolerance that now exists in society for deviations from accepted social norms, which further enables people to act upon their newly found beliefs and ideals.

Only a minority of people make dramatic career shifts at midlife (Levinson, 1983). Those who do are likely to feel that their abilities are underutilized at their current job. This may be due to changes in the job or to fewer challenges because one has developed a high level of expertise. Middle-agers may also change jobs because of burnout. However, burnout is not restricted to middle-age (Stagner, 1985). Indeed, the entire process of reappraising one's life structure, including work, is not restricted to middle age (Levinson, 1986). In fact, older workers are probably less likely than young adults are to actually change jobs (Rhodes, 1983).

Job Change and Stress

For many people, career changes are not welcome and may not go smoothly. Occupational instability can be harmful. Workers who move through predictable, on-time events in the course of their lives generally experience less stress than those who must cope with unpredictable, off-time events. Lack of the "expected" progress or pace of careers, forced career shifts, or unemployment may cause high levels of stress, anxiety, or disequilibrium. Other off-time events that workers frequently encounter include the need to return to school in order to prepare for new careers, or long periods away from work in order to retrain for the continuance of their careers.

LOSS OF JOB   People who are fired or who are forced to retire from their jobs often face emotional problems that may outweigh their loss of income. Many people find their self-esteem shattered and their conception of self destroyed. Individuals often react to career loss in ways that are similar to the grief response triggered by the death of a loved one (Jones, 1979).

The pattern of grieving that may follow involuntary job loss begins with the initial shock and disbelief, followed by anger, protest, and other forms of emotional release. Some people even go through a bargaining stage similar to that experienced by terminally ill patients in which they plead (with employers, spouses, God) for more time, a second chance, and so on. This stage may be followed by depression, loneliness, or physical ailments. Jobless workers may feel panic, guilt about the loss, or resentment, and may be unable to participate in their normal, everyday activities, even though unrelated to work.

Often, people who are fired or laid off face emotional problems that may outweigh their loss of income.

FOCUS ON AN ISSUE

UNEMPLOYMENT AND HEALTH

Joblessness is far more than an economic misfortune. It can be a psychological catastrophe for the unemployed and their families. It can cause illness, divide families, and create a downward spiral of feelings of worthlessness and lack of self-esteem.

For those raised to measure their self-worth in terms of their occupation and earnings, unemployment represents more than just a loss of income. "When you have no job, it's like dying—except you don't stop breathing," says Elsa Pant, an unemployed auto worker from Ionia, Michigan. "Your whole source of motivation is gone" (*U.S. News & World Report,* June 23, 1980, p. 68). Unemployed workers commonly report an increased incidence of headaches, stomach problems, and insomnia. They also smoke, drink, and worry a lot more than they did when they were working (Liem, 1981).

According to research done by M. Harvey Brenner, associate professor of health at Johns Hopkins University, every 1% increase in the unemployment rate translates into 37,000 deaths over the next 6 years, including over 20,000 deaths from heart attacks, 900 suicides, and nearly 500 deaths from cirrhosis of the liver. In addition, Brenner estimates that 7500 unemployed or their families will be admitted either to prison after committing a crime or to a mental hospital. "The impact goes well beyond the individual who loses a job," said Brenner. "Stress caused by economic factors affects our national life at every level" (*U.S. News & World Report,* June 23, 1980, p. 68).

Men who have been socialized as the family breadwinner are especially hard hit by unemployment. They suffer greater depression and anxiety and have a higher incidence of psychotic behavior than men who are employed (Liem, 1981). "Nine months seems to be a crucial point when hope and patience give out," said a leading psychologist (*U.S. News & World Report,* June 23, 1980, p. 69). After that, illness, suicide, alcoholism, divorce, and even crime grow at epidemic rates.

Left without a job, many workers feel they have nothing to look forward to. They miss their co-workers and the routine of going to work. For many, the sense of hopelessness grows worse every time they are rejected for a new job. When this happens often enough, the worker may totally withdraw from the labor force. The rejection unemployed workers feel may be exacerbated if some friends and neighbors avoid them as if they had a contagious disease.

Although the sense of despair that accompanies joblessness is pervasive, it is by no means inevitable. In Johnstown, Pennsylvania, for example, a steel mill and coal mining town that has had double-digit unemployment since the mid-1970s, the divorce rate is down and the crime rate is the second lowest among 277 metropolitan areas. Feeling as if recession and unemployment are permanent ways of life, most of Johnstown's residents are no longer angry or bitter about their plight. Through self-discipline, they have lowered their standard of living and future expectations and have taken comfort in the extended family ties, declining divorce rate, increasing church attendance, and other spiritual and social rewards that money cannot buy. New pleasures come from old experiences seen in a different light. "The tulips are growing," said Mrs. Louis Roberts, whose husband had been unemployed for 2 years, "Louis and I have never enjoyed them so much before" (*Wall Street Journal,* June 18, 1982, p. 1).

Experiencing such grief often has a cathartic effect. Once the grief reaction has passed, the jobless can begin to accommodate the loss, develop a sense of hope, and attempt to redirect their energies toward reestablishing themselves in the world of work.

Job loss may be more difficult for the middle-ager than for young adults. First, it is likely that the middle-ager has more of his or her identity invested in the job. Second, older people are likely to face age discrimination both in hiring and in training programs. Third, whatever job the worker is able to find is likely to be at a lower salary and status than his or her previous one (Kelvin & Jarrett, 1985; Sinfeld, 1985). People who, despite lack of education qualifications, have worked their way up in a company may be particularly vulnerable to this loss of status because their skills are often company specific (DuBrin, 1978).

JOB BURNOUT   "Burnout" is a term for a psychological condition of emotional exhaustion—often accompanied by extreme cynicism—that develops among individuals in the helping professions (Maslach & Jackson, 1979). Social workers, police officers, nurses, therapists, and others who must work in close personal contact with those they serve, in strained, tension-filled situations, may eventually "burn out." The term "burnout" is now also used to refer to people other than those in the helping professions. It is applied generally to the effect on people who have worked hard and bent all of their efforts to reach a virtually impossible goal—and failed (Freudenberger & Richelson, 1980).

The general cause of burnout is a lack of reward in a work situation where great effort has been expended and where high hopes originally predominated (Chance, 1981). People who experience burnout often start out with high ideals and good intentions. In the course of their work, they realize they are having little effect on the people they are trying to aid, or that the problems they are trying to solve are so overwhelming and the tasks so difficult that they will never fully succeed.

Workers who experience burnout begin to feel anger, frustration, and despair. Their work becomes a burden they can no longer handle. They may turn on the people they are supposed to be helping, or they may withdraw from emotional involvement by behaving in a cold, detached way. They may experience physical exhaustion, psychosomatic illnesses, low morale, mediocre performance, or absenteeism (Maslach & Jackson, 1979).

There is little anyone can do to eliminate the causes of burnout without transforming society and the places where people work. Workers can, however, avoid burnout by learning to be realistic in their approach to their work and their goals, promoting changes in their job description or in the work flow, attempting to keep the rest of their lives separate from their work, and developing interests outside of their jobs. Such advice seems appropriate for all workers as well as for potential burnout victims.

JOB STRESS IN CONTEXT   Job stress is not simply a function of what goes on in the workplace. Both men and women have a multiplicity of roles between work and family that are sometimes in competition. A subtle discrimination is sometimes practiced in the workplace when only women are thought to have competing roles—sometimes it is feared that women will bring family problems in, and therefore they are less qualified for responsible jobs. They may quit or find themselves under too much stress to deal with work demands effectively. Some authors suggest that if we include the multiplicity of work and family roles in our models of work stress, we rediscover men's roles as fathers and husbands. With this type of model, men, as well as women, could be given permission to admit to and deal with family-based stressors as well as work-based stressors, and organizations could make adjustments to adapt to conflicting work and family stressors (Baruch et al., 1987).

Workers can avoid job burnout by learning to be realistic in their approach to their work and their goals, by promoting changes in their job description or in the work flow, by attempting to keep the rest of their lives separate from their work, and by developing interests outside of their jobs.

STUDY OUTLINE

The Meaning of Work

Most adults spend a major portion of their lives at their places of employment. The occupation we choose contributes to our identity and provides us with a reference group in the same profession from whom we adopt many of our habits, norms, and ideas.

Identity and Generativity. According to Erikson, adults' developmental tasks are identity restructuring and *generativity,* or making a lasting contribution. Different occupations satisfy this need in various ways.

Adult Development and Work. Many find that work is a more satisfying use of time than pursuing leisure activities. In addition to status, income, and the interpersonal relationships that develop, the importance of a job is also measured by the challenge of the work itself.

The Occupational Cycle

The occupational cycle begins with the experiences that lead to a choice of work, continues with the pursuit of that choice, and ends with retirement. Within this cycle may be any number of positive and negative events affecting one's career.

Vocational Life Stages. Super outlined five stages of vocational life, focusing on the individual's self-exploration: (1) the *growth stage,* (2) the *exploration stage,* (3) the *establishment stage,* (4) the *maintenance stage,* and (5) the *decline stage.*

Havighurst's stages focus on the acquisition of attitudes and work skills that enable people to fit into the work force: (1) *identification with a worker,* (2) *acquiring the basic habits of industry,* (3) *acquiring an identity as a worker,* (4) *becoming a productive person,* (5) *maintaining a productive society,* and (6) *contemplating a productive and responsible life.*

Occupational Choice and Preparation. Many different factors contribute to an individual's career choice, and the process begins in childhood. Researchers' views differ as to which of the factors is most influential. In the area of sex and race, stereotypes continue to exist regarding the occupations that are appropriate for women and minorities. These stereotypes still exert a powerful influence, though this influence is steadily declining. One theorist, Roe, emphasizes the parent–child relationship as an influence on career choice. Another explanation of career choice, known as self-concept theory, is based on the idea that individuals select careers that fit in with their ideas of their own characteristics. A third approach, trait factor theory, presents the view that occupational choice reflects a match between an individual's personality and the traits that a particular job requires.

Occupational preparation consists of specific job training in a formal school or work setting. Informal preparation is the process of absorbing attitudes, norms, and role expectations that are appropriate to a particular job.

A college education can give students general training in communication and analytical skills, train students for particular jobs, and provide students with the opportunity to develop confidence in the areas of intellectual ability, leadership, and popularity.

Entry and Establishment in the Work Force. Successful entry into an occupation requires that an individual be able to turn idealistic dreams into realistic goals. Early in the working life, a person may be disappointed when the dream and reality do not match. Levinson stresses the role of mentors who aid young workers in developing skills, self-confidence, values, and norms that are appropriate to the job.

Consolidation, Maintenance, and Disengagement. Once workers have made the necessary work adjustments and advancement, they enter a maintenance stage, during which they remain in a stable occupational position. Many workers, however, change jobs and never experience the consolidation or stability suggested in the classic career pattern.

Women in the Work Force

In recent years, the number of women in the work force has increased dramatically. Despite the increase in the number of woman workers, most women and men tend to do different types of work at different wages. The average wage for women is less than two-thirds of the average wage for men.

Work Patterns for Women. Career patterns for women vary more greatly than they do for men. Some women follow the traditional male pattern and work without interruption; some women plan to have children once their career is established; others raise children before entering the work force.

The Dual-Earner Couple. The majority of marriages now are dual-earner couples. This pattern has economic advantages. Although there are frequently family role and work role conflicts, women generally seem to benefit psychologically and physically from work.

Work and Lifestyles

The work we do is a major influence on our lifestyles. The socialization involved in entering the work force may determine where we live, the type of home we have, our friendship patterns, and our opinions.

Changing Attitudes about Work. People in earlier generations tended to operate under a different set of values with regard to work. Workers today expect more psychological fulfillment from their jobs, are willing to make fewer compromises, and place a greater value on leisure time.

Occupational Changes

Occupational changes may be due to life structure reassessments or to stress and changes in the workplace.

Job Change and Stress. A stressful career change may occur when one's career does not follow a predicted course, when a person experiences a forced career shift, or when one is unemployed. Loss of a job may be accompanied by a grief response before the worker can accept the loss and regain hope for reentering the job market.

Burnout occurs when workers' high expectations are not

met and their great efforts go unrewarded. The term "burnout" is usually applied to individuals in the helping professions but may generally describe what happens when people work extremely hard to reach an impossible goal.

KEY TERMS AND CONCEPTS

consolidation	exploration stage	intrinsic factors of work
decline stage	extrinsic factors of work	maintenance stage
disengagement	generativity	occupational cycle
establishment stage	growth stage	role conflict

SELF-TEST QUESTIONS

1. In what sense does work provide a central context for adult development?

2. What is the relationship between intrinsic and extrinsic factors of work and the development of one's worker identity?

3. According to Erikson, what is the primary developmental task of adulthood?

4. Do adults continue to develop with respect to cognitive skills or personality traits as a result of their occupation? Please explain.

5. Compare and contrast the vocational life stages presented by Super and Havighurst. What are some criticisms of these stages?

6. Describe four "theories" that seek to explain the factors that influence occupational choice. What are some important considerations that these theories overlook?

7. Outline some of the major issues faced by someone entering and establishing a career. In your answer discuss the role of mentors in this transition.

8. How does the occupational pattern characteristic of mid-life today differ from the pattern found in a classic occupational cycle?

9. Compare and contrast the meaning of work for men and for women.

10. How do career patterns of men and women differ?

11. What are some of the stresses and strains of dual-earner marriages?

12. How are attitudes about work changing, and what effect do these changes have on work patterns?

SUGGESTED READINGS

ALDOUS, J. (Ed.). *Two paychecks: Life in dual-earner families.* Beverly Hills, CA: Sage, 1982. This book discusses a variety of issues related to families in which both the husband and the wife are employed full time.

BOLLES, R. N. *What color is your parachute?* (rev. ed.). Berkeley, CA: Ten Speed Press, 1983. A practical manual for job hunters and career changers.

CROSBY, F. *Juggling: The unexpected advantages of balancing career and home for women, their families and society.* New York: Free Press, 1991. Drawing on extensive research, Faye Crosby dispels myths about working and motherhood and highlights the benefits of complex roles for parents and for children.

FEATHER, N. T. *The psychological impact of unemployment.* New York: Springer-Verlag, 1990. A scholarly review of the many psychological aspects of unemployment for men and women and their families.

GERSON, K. *Hard choices: How women decide about work, career and motherhood.* Berkeley: University of California Press, 1986. In contrast to Crosby, Gerson addresses the increasing conflict between career and family.

MAURER, H. *Not working.* New York: Holt, Rinehart & Winston, 1979. Voices of the unemployed coping with realities.

NAISBITT, J. *Megatrends.* New York: Warner Books, 1984. This forecaster speculates on 10 major trends for the future, many of which involve the world of work.

WALLACE, D. B., & GRUBER, H. E. *Creative people at work: Twelve cognitive case studies.* New York: Oxford University Press, 1989. A fascinating presentation of the lives of unusually creative individuals—each a person of distinction in his or her field.

Chapter 18

Whoever, in middle age, attempts to realize the wishes and hopes of his early youth, invariably deceives himself. Each ten years of a man's life has its own fortunes, its own hopes, its own desires.

JOHANN WOLFGANG VON GOETHE
ELECTIVE AFFINITIES

The Middle Years: Continuity and Change

*I*n earlier chapters, we have looked at childhood, adolescence, and young adulthood. We have seen the developmental steps by which a child becomes an individual with a relatively stable outlook and personality. We have seen the social milestones that mark the adolescent's entrance into the world of the adult—moving away from home, getting married, becoming a parent, establishing a career.

After this, what next? The period of adulthood may encompass as much as 75% of the life span. Does it pose any new challenges? Or is it merely a time to live out the decisions made in early life, possibly making a few corrections here and there? How much continuity is there during these years—is John Smith the same person at age 55 that he was at age 25? If not, what makes him change? Is it biological decline, decreasing intelligence, an accumulation of wisdom and experience, or a narrowing perspective?

As discussed in the previous chapters, socialization is a lifelong process, as much a part of life in the middle and late years as it was in the early ones. It is a two-way street, a mutual process between interacting individuals, and nowhere is this more apparent than in the middle years. During this period, most adults must cope with family issues—their relationships with their increasingly independent children and their relationships with their own parents (Neugarten, 1978). At the same time, people in their middle years often take time to reassess and adjust their position in an occupational life cycle and to evaluate their personal needs and priorities. Parents with grown children now ask themselves, "What do I want to do with my life?" For many people, this is a time of reassessment, of defining and meeting new goals, or of concentrating anew on earlier goals, deferred for the sake of careers or child rearing. Reassessment in one sphere will lead to reassessment in other spheres.

The focus of this chapter, then, will be continuity and change in middle age. We will consider a variety of viewpoints from psychologists, theorists, and the middle-aged themselves. We shall discuss the biological changes and health problems that often accompany aging and how people adjust to them. We shall also look at midlife changes in intellectual abilities and life circumstances. Finally, we shall review developmental theories and personality studies to see how midlife experiences fit into the overall perspective of lifelong development and personal growth.

CHAPTER OBJECTIVES

By the time you have finished this chapter, you should be able to do the following:

■ Describe the developmental issues that characterize middle age.

■ Describe the physical changes that take place in middle age and the various factors that contribute to these changes.

■ Explain the cognitive changes that occur in middle age and the difficulties in assessing these changes.

■ Discuss the differences and similarities between personality development in adulthood and personality development in other periods of the life span.

■ Discuss development in terms of lifelong processes.

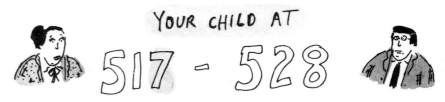

YOUR CHILD AT

5I7 - 528

MONTHS

AT 517 MONTHS	May balance checkbook by self.	AT 523 MONTHS	May learn how to give self home-permanent.
AT 518 MONTHS	May know own complete, 9-digit zip code.	AT 524 MONTHS	May understand concept of Cubism.
AT 519 MONTHS	May read financial section of newspaper with interest.	AT 525 MONTHS	May know how to parallel park.
AT 520 MONTHS	May be able to tell a joke.	AT 526 MONTHS	May attend party and not make fool of self.
AT 521 MONTHS	May feed self entire low-fat, low-sodium, high-fiber meal.	AT 527 MONTHS	May make own dental appointment.
AT 522 MONTHS	May know how to make decent cup of coffee.	AT 528 MONTHS	May arrange 2-week Caribbean vacation by self.

R. Chast

DEVELOPMENT IN MIDDLE AGE

When do people start thinking of themselves as middle-aged? What are the cues that tell them that they are no longer young, and how do they react to this knowledge? There are many signals of middle age.

Chronologically, middle age covers roughly the years from age 40 to age 60 or 65 — but the period may be longer or shorter for different people. This variation occurs because there are so many different cues (Neugarten, 1980). Some cues are social and positional. Middle age is an in-between period, a kind of bridge between two generations. People in midlife are aware of being separate not only from youngsters and young adults but also from the retired and elderly. Other cues may be physical and biological. A woman may suddenly realize that her son is taller than she is; a man may find a handicraft skill hampered by arthritis. There are psychological cues, too, most of them involving issues of continuity and change. People realize that they have made certain basic decisions about career or family;

these patterns are now fairly set and remain to be played out or fulfilled. The future no longer holds unlimited possibilities. People tend to clock middle age according to the family cycle—when their children begin to leave home or, if they have no children, when they would have done so had there been any. Cues also come from their careers—their advancement at work has stopped. They may have reached positions of seniority or status, or they may realize that they have reached a plateau well below their original goals.

"Prime Time" or "The Beginning of the End"?

How do people feel about being middle-aged? Psychologists, researchers, and middle-aged people themselves do not agree on whether this is a time of new fulfillment, stability, and potential leadership or a period of dissatisfaction, inner turmoil, and depression. Economic conditions, social class, and the times that people live in may affect how they view middle age. Many realize that they are no longer young but nevertheless feel satisfied and believe that they are now in the "prime of life" (Hunt & Hunt, 1975; Neugarten, 1968b). Their physical activity may be slightly diminished, but their experience and self-knowledge allow them to manage their own lives. They are able to make decisions with an ease and self-confidence that was previously beyond their grasp. This is why the 40- to 60-year-old age group has been called the "command generation," and why most of the decision makers in government, corporations, and society in general are within this age span.

Of course, not all middle-aged people make weighty decisions. Many do not feel that they control their own lives, let alone those of others. Some people seem to lose vitality after the age of 40. Frenkel-Brunswik (1963), for example, does not see middle-aged people as the "command generation." Instead, she sees the period as one of declining activity whose onset, around the age of 48, is usually marked by both psychological and biological crises. Levinson and his colleagues also found that "the midlife transition is a time of moderate to severe crisis."

For most people, there is a dualism in middle age (Chiriboga, 1981; Sherman, 1987). It may be the "prime" of life with respect to one's family, career, or creative talents, but there is also an awareness of mortality and a sense that time is running out. Some people in midlife become preoccupied with questions of creativity and ongoing contributions to the next generation, fears of stagnation or lost opportunities, and concerns about maintaining intimate relationships with family and friends. With each major event—birth, death, job change, divorce—adults reexamine the meaning of their lives (Sherman, 1987). For some, the model of middle age becomes "Whatever we do must be done now" (Gould, 1978). How people interpret this sense of urgency, together with the events of their lives, determines whether middle age is a period of gradual transition and reassessment or a period of midlife crisis.

Midlife Crisis or Reassessment?

Much of our current thinking about upheaval in this period comes from Carl Jung (1933/1961) who was one of the first to identify the midlife transition. Jung believed that the crisis is essentially caused by a shift in control. The first half of life,

Most of the decision makers in government, corporations, and society in general are in their middle years. Their physical activity may be slightly diminished, but their experience and self-knowledge allow them to make decisions with an ease and self-confidence that was previously beyond their grasp.

during which people exercise control over their lives and their environment, is dominated by the activities of the conscious mind. In the second half of life, individuals must confront the unconscious; they become more reflective and inner directed. Most come to terms with personal limitations and accept the fact that they have no control over such factors as disease and death.

In their study of men, Levinson and his colleagues (1978) found that at about the age of 40, a man may begin to question, or at least put into perspective, the "driven" life he has been leading. If he has been successful in reaching his goals, he may suddenly ask, "Were they worth the struggle?" If he has not done what he wanted to with his life, he may now become keenly aware that he does not have many more chances to change things. He questions his entire life structure, including both work and family relationships (Levinson, 1986).

Middle age, then, is a time when people take stock and look at their lives. Some may feel effective and competent and at the peak of their powers (Chiriboga, 1981). Some may find looking at themselves a painful process. Age-graded influences, such as graying hair, an expanding middle, or menopause, may combine with nonnormative events, such as divorce, the death of a spouse, or unemployment, to precipitate a crisis. If any of these influences is anticipated or regarded as a normal point in life, it may be less likely to lead to a crisis (Neugarten, 1980).

How people react to becoming middle aged or to dealing with various influences may determine whether they are in a period of transition and reassessment or a midlife crisis. Cytrynbaum and his associates (1980) see transition as a change from one stage or period of development to another. The transition may be stressful or psychologically painful, but it involves some form of growth and development. They see a midlife crisis as a state of distress that comes about when a person's internal resources and support system are overwhelmed by tasks he or she cannot cope with. When a middle-aged person is going through change, he or she is surrounded by a number of factors that form a framework within which the person reacts to the change and to the social systems he or she belongs to. Cytrynbaum et al. (1980) see these factors as forming that framework: (1) the person's personality and ability to cope with change; (2) the specific events—and the timing of those events—that precipitate change; (3) the developmental tasks that must be mastered in midlife—these include acceptance of

TABLE 18–1
The Framework Proposed by Cytrynbaum and Associates Within Which People React to Change in Mid-Life

PREDISPOSITIONS	DEVELOPMENTAL PROCESSES	OUTCOMES
Personality	Precipitates: changes within individual; stressful or unanticipated life events;	Adaptive: able to cope with developmental tasks of second half of life.
Surrounding social systems	Developmental tasks: accept death and mortality; accept biological limits and risks; restructure self-concept and sexual identity; reorient self to work, creativity and achievement; reassess primary relationships.	Maladaptive: results in midlife-related symptoms, such as depression and anxiety and predisposition to further maladaption as older adult.
	Developmental processes: destructuring → reassessment → reintegration and restructuring → behavioral and role change	

Source: Based on "Midlife Development: A Personality and Social Systems Perspective" by S. Cytrynbaum et al. In L. W. Poon (Ed.), *Aging in the 1980s* (Washington, D.C.: American Psychological Association, 1980).

death and mortality, and of biological limitations, a reorientation to work, and a reassessment of primary relationships; (4) significant personality change in midlife; (5) the order of the phases of midlife change; and (6) an analysis of this developmental framework when dealing with maladaptations to midlife change. The interactions of these factors within this framework may determine whether a person goes through a period of transition or a midlife crisis.

PHYSICAL CONTINUITY AND CHANGE

"Age is like love; it cannot be hid," wrote a 17th-century dramatist. For many middle-aged people, there is a "moment of truth," when the mirror reveals new wrinkles, "midriff bulge," a receding hairline, or gray hair at the temples that no longer seems distinguished—just depressing. It is generally during middle age that people receive the first clear reminders that their bodies are aging. These "warning signals" are more disturbing to some than to others, depending on individual attitudes toward aging. Are these signs of maturity, wisdom, motherhood, or declining sexuality? Some obvious biological events, such as menopause, a lessening of visual acuity, or the onset of disease, are events that may require a change in a person's self-image or activities, and must be incorporated into a satisfactory lifestyle (Newman, 1982). Although most physical abilities peak during adolescence or early adulthood, they level off in middle age, and the first signs of the physical decline that will continue into old age begin to appear. Many health experts believe that by following a program of regular exercise, lessened stress, and good diet, middle-aged people can slow the aging process and continue to function with youthful vitality and a sense of well-being (Fries & Crapo, 1981).

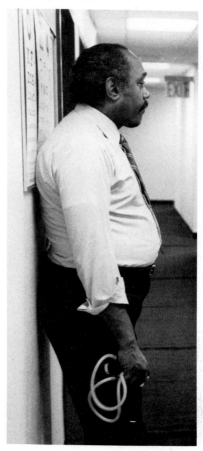

During midlife, the physical signs of aging begin to appear.

Physical Capacities and Fitness

Some physical decline or slowing down may likely occur during middle age (Birren et al., 1980). Some of the changes are sensory. Vision tends to be nearly constant from adolescence to the 40s or early 50s, when visual acuity declines more rapidly (Kline & Schieber, 1985; Pollack & Atkeson, 1978). Nearsighted people, however, often see better in middle age than they could as young adults. On the average, hearing becomes less acute after the age of 20 and continues to decline, causing particular difficulty in hearing high-frequency sounds. This hearing loss seems to be more common in men than in women. It may be due to environmental factors, such as work-related exposure to loud or high-frequency noises, rather than to "normal aging." In any case, it is rarely severe enough to affect normal conversation in middle age (Olsho, Harkins, & Lenhardt, 1985). Sensitivity to taste, smell, and pain decrease at different points in middle age, although these changes may be more gradual and less noticeable than visual or auditory problems. Sensitivity to temperature changes remains high (Newman, 1982).

Other biological functions, such as reaction time and sensorimotor skills, are likely to slow down. Reaction time drops off slowly throughout adulthood, then more quickly during old age. Motor skills may decline, but actual performance remains constant, probably as a result of long practice and experience (Newman,

1982). Someone who chops firewood or plays tennis every day will probably not experience any slowdown in performance. But it becomes a bit more difficult to learn new skills.

Internal changes, as well as sensory ones, begin to occur. The nervous system begins to slow down, particularly after age 50 (Newman, 1982). The skeleton stiffens and shrinks a bit during the course of adulthood. Skin and muscles begin to lose elasticity, and there is a tendency to accumulate more subcutaneous fat, especially in areas like the midriff. The heart pumps 8% less blood to the body for each decade after adulthood, and by middle age, the opening of the coronary arteries is nearly one-third less than it was in the 20s. Lung capacity decreases as well; because endurance depends on the amount of oxygen supplied to body tissues, people may not be able to do as much hard labor in middle age (Brody, 1979).

By adjusting one's life to a slower pace, reserving energy for special occasions, and exercising regularly, people can conserve and maximize strength in middle age (Timiras, 1972). Numerous studies have shown that exercise before and during middle age can increase physical capacities and endurance (Weg, 1983). Certain kinds of exercise—especially *aerobic exercises*—are designed to increase heart and lung capacity, supplying the body with more oxygen. Even short-term mild exercise training programs for sedentary older adults show impressive gains in strength and heart and lung functioning (Sidney, 1981). More habitual exercise can also slow the deterioration of muscle tissue and reduce body fat. It can help prevent deterioration of the joints and combat some kinds of arthritis (Brody, 1979).

We shall discuss the causes and symptoms of biological aging at greater length in Chapter 19. But we should remember that in middle years, as in later life, people age at different rates. There are a number of factors that influence aging, and by taking these into account, people can often ease the process of aging and alleviate many of its unpleasant effects.

Health and Disease

Disease may become a larger problem in middle age than it was previously. As the body ages, it becomes increasingly vulnerable to disease. Middle-aged people often become aware of aging and their own mortality as they or their friends become ill.

INCIDENCE BY AGE AND SEX OF MAJOR DISEASES   For people in the United States under the age of 44, the single highest cause of death is accidents. After this age, people increasingly begin to die as a result of disease (National Center for Health Statistics, 1987). By middle age, certain diseases become major problems, and some of them affect one sex more than the other. Throughout much of the life span, the death rate of men at any particular age is about twice that of women of the same age. Men are more apt to work in dangerous occupations; they are apt to be less concerned about their health than women, because they have been taught that it is masculine to ignore pain; and they may have a higher genetic predisposition to disease than women.

Cardiovascular diseases—which include heart disease, arteriosclerosis, and hypertension, among others—are the leading cause of death in the United States.

TABLE 18-2

The Leading Cause of Death for Males and Females Between the Ages of 45 and 64

CAUSE	MALE	FEMALE
Heart disease	424.3	158.1
Cancer	347.6	192.2
Accidents	49.2	17.7
Cerebrovascular disease	40.8	33.0
Chronic liver diseases	37.1	16.5
Chronic lung diseases	35.2	22.5
Suicide	25.5	8.6
Diabetes	18.4	17.1
Pneumonia	17.4	8.8

Note: Figures represent annual number of deaths per 100,000 population.

Source: Statistical Abstract of the United States (Washington, DC: Department of Commerce, 1990).

Heart disease accounts for 34% of all deaths and 33% of deaths for people between 45 and 64 years old (National Center for Health Statistics, 1990). Throughout middle age, this disease is a greater threat to men than to women. Before menopause, women are less prone to heart attacks than men, in part, because their bodies are producing estrogen. After menopause, heart disease becomes an increasing problem for women too, but even then, fewer women die suddenly of heart attacks in each age bracket.

Cancer is the second highest cause of death in the United States, but has recently become the leading cause of death for people between 45 and 64 years old (National Center for Health Statistics, 1990). The overall death rate from cancer continues to rise. Cancer, too, claims more men than women. Middle-aged men are twice as likely to die of lung cancer, but the rate for women is increasing (National Center for Health Statistics, 1990). Diabetes is another disease that occurs in increasing rates and severity in middle age, and it may complicate other physical problems with serious consequences. One-half of the 3 million diabetics in the United States are between 45 and 64 years old (Ebersole, 1979), and the disease claims more women than men (National Center for Health Statistics, 1990). Respiratory diseases are also a problem in middle age. Men are far more likely than women to have bronchitis, asthma, and emphysema (National Center for Health Statistics, 1990). Some diseases of middle age are less serious, but nevertheless interfere with activity and cause considerable discomfort. Arthritis, for example, troubles many middle-aged people of both sexes.

CUMULATIVE EFFECTS OF HEALTH HABITS   Real as these diseases are, most people in middle age will not suffer serious, life-threatening forms of any of them. The life expectancy for individuals who have reached the age of 45 in the United States is about 78 years (National Center for Health Statistics, 1990). Over 80% of people who reach age 45 are expected to survive and remain in reasonably good health until the age of 65. Several authors note that although the average life span has not increased much beyond the age of 85 for any population, a sizable proportion do maintain relatively good health in middle age. With good nutrition, reasonable amounts of exercise, and regular medical care, many will experience an extended adulthood of active vitality (Fries & Crapo, 1981; Siegler & Costa, 1985).

TABLE 18–3
Disease Conditions and Lifestyles

DISORDERS/DISEASE	LIFESTYLE FACTORS
Diseases of the heart and circulatory system	High fat, highly refined carbohydrate diet, high salt; overweight; sedentary lifestyle; cigarette smoking; heavy drinking, alcoholism; unresolved, continual stress; personality type
Strokes	Sedentary lifestyle; low fiber, high fat or high salt diet; heavy drinking, alcoholism (which contribute to atherosclerosis, arteriosclerosis, and hypertension, risk factors for cerebrovascular accidents)
Osteoporosis and dental and gum diseases	Malnutrition—inadequate calcium, protein, vitamin K, fluoride, magnesium and vitamin D; lack of exercise; immobility; for women, low estrogen.
Lung diseases such as emphysema	Cigarette smoking; air pollution; stress; sedentary habits
Obesity	Low caloric output (sedentary), high caloric intake; high stress levels; heavy drinking, alcoholism; low self-esteem
Cancer	Possible correlation with personality type; stress; exposure to environmental carcinogens over a long period of time; nutritional deficiencies and excesses; radiation; sex steroid hormones; food additives; cigarette smoking; occupational carcinogens (for example, asbestos); viruses; reduced immunity
Dementia and other forms of memory loss	Malnutrition; long illness and bed rest; drug abuse; anemia; other organ system disease; bereavement; social isolation
Sexual dysfunction	Ignorance (the older individual and society at large); societal stereotypic attitudes; early socialization; inappropriate or no partner; drug effects (for example, antihypertensive drugs); long periods of abstinence; serious disease

Adapted from Weg, R. Changing physiology of aging. In D. W. Woodruff and J. E. Birren (Eds.), *Aging: Scientific perspectives and social issues*, 1983, p. 274. Monterey, CA: Brooks/Cole. Reproduced by permission.

The cumulative effects of good or poor health habits begin to take their toll in middle age. Most chronic disorders begin to develop long before they are diagnosed by a physician. For example, the impact of long-term heavy smoking on a range of respiratory and cardiovascular diseases is well known. Smoking contributes to arteriosclerosis, hypertension, and coronary disease. It contributes to many forms of respiratory disorders, including emphysema and lung cancer (Weg, 1983). But regular smoking is just one lifestyle habit that influences chronic disorders. Any drug, including alcohol, has long-term consequences. As the liver and kidneys age, they become less efficient in clearing unusual amounts of drugs. Cumulative damage to these two organs begins to become apparent in middle age (Rowe, 1982).

The long-term effects of smoking, alcohol abuse, or the habitual use of other drugs often interact with other long-term health habits—such as good and poor nutrition or regular exercise. Table 18–3 summarizes some of the lifestyle habits that contribute to chronic disorders (Weg, 1983). However, there is one major contributing factor to many of the diseases we have discussed so far, and that is stress.

Stress and Disease

Increasing evidence shows that the way people live has a great effect on their health. Stress seems to play a part in many of the diseases of middle age. In the case of heart disease, for example, there appears to be a complex interrelationship among lifestyle, personality, genetic factors, and stress. Because men are more often the victims of heart disease than women, most of the studies on stress and coronary disease have involved men.

PERSONALITY STYLE   One such study, by Rosenman (1974), examined 3400 men from ages 39 to 59 and reexamined them at the end of $2\frac{1}{2}$, $4\frac{1}{2}$, and $8\frac{1}{2}$ years to determine how behavior patterns might affect the incidence of heart disease. The men were typed according to their personality styles. At one extreme were what the researchers called a Type A personality. Type A people are highly competitive, restless, achievement oriented, and aggressive; they are often hostile, impatient, and hyperalert. In addition, their facial muscles are often tense, they speak explosively, and they are plagued by a constant sense of time urgency. At the opposite extreme were Type B persons. They are unaggressive, patient, easygoing, and relaxed. The rest fell somewhere in between. The differences between Type A and Type B personalities are not always apparent. Instead, their behavior differs mainly in situations designed to challenge the person (especially intellectually) or elicit competitiveness (Carver & Humphries, 1982; Rosenman & Chesney, 1982). About 10% of Rosenman's subjects had clearly defined Type A or Type B personalities.

At the beginning of the study, none of the men had experienced any coronary heart disease. When the follow-up studies were made, it was found that twice as many Type A men had developed coronary heart disease as had Type B, and that twice as many Type A men had suffered fatal heart attacks. The researchers found that the biochemistry of Type A personalities was similar to that of people who had a history of heart disease. Type A personalities were found to have higher serum cholesterol levels, accelerated blood coagulation, and, during working hours, more stress hormones in their blood than Type B men. The Type B subjects rarely, if ever, developed any coronary disease before the age of 70, regardless of how much fatty food they ate, the number of cigarettes they smoked, or how little exercise they got (Eisendorfer & Wilkie, 1977; Rosenman, 1974).

These findings are dramatic, but it is important to remember that 90% of the men in the study fell somewhere between these two behavioral extremes and that some of them also developed coronary problems. Like the men who were studied, most middle-aged people do not fit neatly into either one of these extreme categories.

Furthermore, not all studies of Type A personalities and heart disease have found equally strong relationships (Booth-Kewley & Friedman, 1987). And not all aspects of Type A personality are equally associated with heart disease. Aggressiveness and competitiveness (in a driven style) seem to be particularly strongly associated with heart disease. On the other hand, job commitment is not. The stereotype that "all work and no play" lead Jack to have a heart attack is apparently erroneous.

It is also interesting to note that other personality factors, most notably depression, are also related to risk of heart disease (Booth-Kewley & Friedman, 1987). In fact, some studies have found depression to be a stronger predictor than Type A personality of heart disease. Less dramatic associations have been found between heart disease and hostility, anger, and anxiety.

CHALLENGE OR DISTRESS   An important question is: What kinds of stress are dangerous? Is just being middle aged stress enough? What about the need to redefine goals, adjust to changing roles within the family, relinquish power to younger competitors, or cope with the first signs of biological aging? Table 18–4 shows a list of events that people encounter throughout life. Each situation was rated by individuals of all ages for the amount of stress that it produced. The death of a spouse, for example, was judged the highest stress producer and was assigned

TABLE 18–4
Stress Scale for Life Events

EVENT	VALUE	EVENT	VALUE
Death of spouse	100	Son or daughter leaving home	29
Divorce	73	Trouble with in-laws	29
Marital separation	65	Outstanding personal achievement	28
Jail term	63	Spouse begins or stops work	26
Death of close family member	63	Starting or finishing school	26
Personal injury or illness	53	Change in living conditions	25
Marriage	50	Revision of personal habits	24
Fired from work	47	Trouble with boss	23
Marital reconciliation	45	Change in work hours, conditions	20
Retirement	45	Change in residence	20
Change in family member's health	44	Change in schools	20
Pregnancy	40	Change in recreational habits	19
Sex difficulties	39	Change in church activities	19
Addition to family	39	Change in social activities	18
Business readjustment	39	Mortgage or loan under $10,000 [as of 1967]	17
Change in financial status	38	Change in sleeping habits	16
Death of close friend	37	Change in number of family gatherings	15
Change to different line of work	36	Change in eating habits	15
Change in number of marital arguments	35	Vacations	13
Mortgage or loan over $10,000 [as of 1967]	31	Christmas season	12
Foreclosure of mortgage or loan	30	Minor violation of the law	11
Change in work responsibilities	29		

Source: "The Social Readjustment Rating Scale" by T. H. Holmes and R. H. Rahe, *Journal of Psychosomatic Research,* 1967, 11 (2), 213–218. Copyright 1967, Pergamon Press, Ltd. Reprinted with permission.

Occupational stress, and the individual's way of coping with it, can play a part in many of the diseases of middle age.

a value of 100. Similarly, a change in eating habits was rated by most as only mildly disruptive and was given a value of just 15. Because middle age is a time when people do lose spouses through death, divorce, and separation, and suffer changes such as early retirement and illness, we can see that the middle years have extremely high potential for stress.

But stress is not caused just by life events. The meaning the individual attaches to an event and the particular kind of reaction will determine the degree of stress. Researchers have repeatedly pointed out that the same event may be a challenge to one person but cause considerable distress to another (Chiriboga & Cutler, 1980; Lazarus, 1981). Occasional exposure to stressful events may well be an important stimulus or challenge to further personality development. If an event is anticipated or expected, it may be less stressful than if it occurs suddenly. Also, the impact of a single stressful event may depend on a number of other preoccupations a person has at the time (such as concerns about money, legal problems, or family life), how seriously the event affects daily routines, and to what extent the event is a personal hazard. Lazarus (1981) suggests that an accumulation of little hassles is sometimes more stressful in the long run than are major life events (see Focus on an Issue: Little Hassles and Stress). The individual's style of coping with stress also can increase or decrease the impact. It is often thought, for instance, that individuals who contain their anger are the ones most likely to have physical symptoms and disease as a result of stress. This may or may not be true. One author, in reviewing the literature on people with Type A personalities, found that many of these high-pressure individuals vented their anger frequently. They would appear to be "getting it off their chest," but in some cases the emotional display

FOCUS ON AN ISSUE

LITTLE HASSLES AND STRESS

Have you ever felt like exploding when life's little hassles get to be too much—when your friendly neighborhood dry cleaner burned a hole in your new suit; when you spent an hour watching the tail lights of the car in front of you instead of the first act of a hit play you had waited months to see? Minor blowups, frustration, and anger are the usual consequences of petty annoyances like these—at least that is what researchers believed until now. But, according to Richard S. Lazarus (1981) and his colleagues at the University of California at Berkeley, the effects of little hassles may be far more serious.

To test this premise and to determine whether pleasant, satisfying, and uplifting experiences counterbalance the negative effects of daily hassles, the researchers studied 100 men and women between the ages of 48 and 52 over the period of a year. At the start of the study, each person filled out a 24-item life events scale, similar to the one used by Holmes and Rahe (see text Table 18–4). They also completed a 117-item hassle checklist and a 135-item uplift checklist on a monthly basis. To learn how the hassles and uplifts affected the participants' health, physical and mental health questionnaires were completed at the beginning and end of the year, and other measures monitored health fluctuations on a yearly basis as well.

The results of this study raise some serious doubts about the labeling of major life events as the main source of stress. According to Lazarus and his colleagues, everyday hassles predict a person's physical and mental health far better than major life events. Study participants who were overburdened with hassles had more mental and physical health problems than those whose lives were calm. In contrast, people who experienced such major life events as divorce or the death of a close relative showed no serious health problems during the term of the study. Those participants whose mental and physical health were affected by major life events experienced these events during the $2\frac{1}{2}$ years before the study began. Thus, although there is a link between major life events and long-term health, little hassles seem to determine immediate well-being.

This is not to say that major life events and hassles are not connected. In fact, divorce, the death of a spouse, or even marriage has a kind of "ripple effect" that creates a seemingly inexhaustible supply of small frustrations. A man who divorces after 30 years of marriage may find, for example, that he cannot cope with cooking his own meals, cleaning his own house, and having no readily available sex partner.

Of course, not everyone responds to daily frustrations in the same way. Personality and coping style affect the way we respond. In addition, Lazarus found that the frequency, duration, and intensity of stress determine whether or not we feel overwhelmed. When we misplace our wallet or have a splinter in our foot, we are less able to cope with a notice from the bank telling us that our rent check bounced than when we have a calm, relaxing day.

Do the small uplifts of life help? Does the news of a raise or the good feelings we get from our families decompress the pressures that everyday hassles cause? Unfortunately, the study found that daily uplifts return few emotional benefits to offset the effect of hassles.

Lazarus's Top Ten Hassles and Uplifts

HASSLES	UPLIFTS
1. Concern about weight	1. Relating well with your spouse or lover
2. Health of a family member	2. Relating well with friends
3. Rising prices of common goods	3. Completing a task
4. Home maintenance	4. Feeling healthy
5. Too many things to do	5. Getting enough sleep
6. Misplacing or losing things	6. Eating out
7. Yard work or outside	7. Meeting responsibilities
8. Property, investment, or taxes	8. Visiting, phoning, or writing someone
9. Crime	9. Spending time with family
10. Physical appearance	10. Home pleasing to you

Source: From "Little Hassles Can Be Hazardous to Health" by Richard S. Lazarus, *Psychology Today*, July 1981, p. 61. Reprinted from *Psychology Today.* Copyright © 1981, Ziff-Davis Pub. Co.

climacteric The broad complex of physical and emotional symptoms that accompany reproductive changes in middle age. Climacteric affects both men and women.

menopause The permanent end of menstruation; it occurs in middle age, and may be accompanied by physical symptoms and intense emotional reactions.

actually made them more angry. These people had a high incidence of heart attacks. When there are stressful events that are threatening, particularly ones that increase feelings of being powerless, it helps to regain one's sense of control (Taveris, 1983).

Menopause and Climacteric

The term **climacteric** refers to a broad complex of physical and emotional effects that accompany hormonal changes in middle age. In women, this change includes **menopause,** the end of menstruation; it marks the end of the childbearing years. There is certainly no such thing as "male menopause," despite its appearance in the popular press. Yet many professionals believe that men, too, undergo gradual changes in sexual activity in middle age that are accompanied by emotional readjustments.

For women, menopause generally occurs between the ages of 48 and 51, although it may occur somewhat earlier or considerably later. Ovulation becomes erratic and then stops altogether. At the same time, less estrogen is produced, and the reproductive system "closes down." Slowly the uterus shrinks, and there is some reduction in breast size as glandular tissue is replaced with fat tissue. The end of menstruation marks the end of a woman's capacity to bear children. People associate menopause with such physical symptoms as hot flashes and night sweats and, more rarely, headaches, dizziness, palpitations, and pains in the joints. However, research indicates that hot flashes (including night sweats) are the only one of these symptoms probably caused by menopause per se (that is, by the decrease in estrogen) (Asso, 1983). Up to 75% of all women report hot flashes during menopause (Asso, 1983; Greenwood, 1984). Night sweats may be extensive enough to cause insomnia in some women. The other symptoms, such as headaches, may indeed occur during menopause, but they tend to occur mainly in women who have a history of the problem or who are having a particularly difficult menopause (Asso, 1983). Probably only about 15% of all menopausal women require medical treatment for their symptoms (Shepard & Shepard, 1982).

For some women, the physical changes are accompanied by emotional changes, too. There may be a feeling of depression or a sense of being somehow less "feminine" since the reproductive function is gone. Women who have not had children may experience regret, loss, or even depression. Again, most women do not encounter these kinds of difficulties during menopause (Asso, 1983). Indeed, some researchers have actually reported a decrease in psychological problems during and after menopause compared to the years immediately preceding it.

Most women do not respond negatively to menopause either in the short run or the long term (Goodman, 1980; Neugarten, 1967; Neugarten et al., 1968). Half of the menopausal and postmenopausal women in one survey reported that the "change" was "easy" or "moderately easy" (Goodman, 1980). Many women feel freer and more in control of their own lives postmenopausally. They are glad not to have to worry about menstrual periods or pregnancy anymore. They are also happy that their active mothering role is ending because their time will now be more their own. Even women who are not particularly pleased are not very worried or distressed. In fact, they are more likely to be worried about widowhood than menopause (Neugarten, 1967).

Cultural interpretations of the impact of menopause also vary widely. They

Cultural interpretations of menopause vary widely. In some castes in India, for example, menopause brings with it a new positive status for a woman, allowing her to enjoy the company of both men and women in a variety of social circumstances for the first time. These women do not report experiencing the ailments—moodiness, depression, and headaches—we often associate with menopause.

affect the woman's feelings about herself, her behavior, and her actual physical symptoms. In some castes in India, for example, menopause brings with it a new positive status for the woman. She is no longer required to remain isolated from much of society, associating only with her husband and immediate family. She may enjoy the company of both men and women in a variety of social circumstances. In a recent study of a group of Indian women, none of them reported the range of symptoms often associated with menopause—for example, excessive moodiness, depression, or headaches (Flint, 1982). Some authors have suggested that the excessive focus on youth and attractiveness in Western cultures may contribute heavily to the extensive list of symptoms that some women experience in menopause.

The estrogen loss that accompanies menopause does appear to have at least two, and possibly three, long-term effects. The two established effects are changes in bone mass and the genitals. The more controversial outcome is coronary disease.

The mineral mass of bones peaks somewhere between the ages of 25 and 40 years and then is steady for several years. Both men and women experience a loss in bone mass as they age, but the loss is about twice as great and occurs more rapidly in women (Asso, 1983). Furthermore, bone fractures associated with bone loss are 6 to 10 times more common in women than in men after age 50 (Nathanson & Lorenz, 1982). Women's loss of bone mass accelerates greatly after menopause. This appears to be due to estrogen deprivation rather than aging. Estrogen replacement therapy does appear to be of some value in slowing or even stopping the progress of bone loss but will not reverse damage already done (Shepard & Shepard, 1982).

The second well-established long-term physical change involves the genitalia. With the decrease in estrogen, vaginal atrophy occurs. The tissue of the vagina, as well as the labia and other tissue surrounding the vagina, shrinks, thins, and dries. There will be less lubrication available during intercourse. The vagina may also

fluid intelligence A broad area of intelligence that includes motor speed, induction, and memory. It governs perceptual abilities and recognition, and reaches a peak in late adolescence.

become shorter and narrower. These and other changes may result in pain or bleeding during intercourse (Asso, 1983; Shepard & Shepard, 1982).

Such changes need not signal an end to sexual activity, however. First, the changes are gradual, so that the menopausal or immediately postmenopausal woman can easily continue intercourse. Second, if the atrophy is mild, a lubricating cream or jelly can be used to facilitate intercourse. Third, estrogen replacement therapy will alleviate and even reverse many of these symptoms (Asso, 1983; Shepard & Shepard, 1982).

The more controversial long-term effect concerns the relationship between cardiovascular disease and menopause. As already noted, the rate of cardiovascular disease rises in women after menopause. However, it is not clear whether this is due to menopause, per se. Estrogen replacement therapy does not clearly reduce the risk.

For men, there is no single abrupt event to parallel the female menopause (Masters et al., 1982). We do know that men—generally in their late 40s—undergo a change in sexual activity. As with women, the amount of change varies widely, depending on individual personality and lifestyle. Some changes in men are due to physiological factors, particularly the level of androgen, a male hormone. But, unlike estrogen, which decreases dramatically in menopause, androgen declines gradually over a longer period of time. Even so, a few men have reported physical symptoms, such as impotence, frequent urination, and ulcers (Ruebsaat & Hull, 1975). Others may also experience a loss of self-confidence or become irritable, fatigued, and depressed. Whereas some symptoms may be caused by changes in hormone levels, many are due to psychological stress, such as job pressure, boredom with a sex partner, family responsibilities, or fear of ill health.

The frequency of sexual activity of both men and women generally slows down in middle age, although many healthy individuals can and do enjoy full sex lives until age 70 and beyond. As we have mentioned, physiological changes account for some of the slowdown. But sexual activity in middle age may also slow down because of poor health or lack of opportunity.

COGNITIVE CONTINUITY AND CHANGE

We have looked at continuity and change in the biological aspects of middle age. What about intelligence? Longitudinal studies have indicated that, with age, there is some decline in cognitive function, but it is much more gradual than researchers assumed even 10 years ago. It seems to occur later, and then only in certain areas of intelligence. In fact, some aspects of intelligence appear to increase during middle age, especially for those college-educated adults who remain engaged in active work and living (Schaie, 1983). One way to proceed is to look at these changes and examine two different kinds of intellectual abilities.

Fluid versus Crystallized Intelligence

One theory suggests that there are two different kinds of intelligence measured on an adult IQ test (Horn, 1982). The first broad area of intellectual functioning is called **fluid intelligence.** It is based mainly on the speed and effectiveness of neurological and physiological factors. This includes such abilities as motor speed, inductive reasoning, memory, and figural relations. The term "fluid intelligence" is a metaphor. It suggests that these basic processes "flow into" various other intellectual activities, including the activities of perceiving, recognizing, learning, analyzing, and problem solving (Horn, 1982; Neugarten, 1976). Fluid intelligence has been thought to increase until late adolescence and then decline gradually throughout adulthood. This kind of intelligence is thought to parallel the efficiency and the integrity of the nervous system (Horn, 1982).

Crystallized intelligence is defined as the learned abilities to process information—to find relationships, make judgments, analyze problems, and use learned strategies to find solutions to problems. People acquire these abilities through formal education as well as through daily contact with their culture. Certain types of tests such as verbal reasoning, vocabulary, comprehension, and aspects of spatial perception are thought to include large amounts of crystallized intelligence. Unlike fluid intelligence, crystallized intelligence often increases over the life span, as long as people remain alert and capable of taking in and recording information (Neugarten, 1976). When people are tested longitudinally for skills involving the use of this kind of intelligence, therefore, they often score higher in their 50s than they do in their 20s. This helps explain why scholars and scientists, whose work is based upon a great deal of accumulated knowledge and experience, are usually more productive in their 40s, 50s, and even 70s than they were in their 20s (Dennis, 1966; Simonton, 1990).

But what is the evidence for the decline of fluid intelligence and the maintenance and even increase of crystallized intelligence? This is not an easy research problem, and, as with all research problems, the answer depends on how we study it. In Chapter 15, we talked about some of the differences between longitudinal studies and cross-sectional studies. Remember that longitudinal studies involve repeated measures of the same individuals over time; cross-sectional studies involve the measurement of different individuals at each of several different age levels. In support of the different predictions for fluid and crystallized intelligence in adulthood, Horn and his colleagues (1980) presented cross-sectional data on several different types of tests. In Figure 18–1, we can see that measures of vocabulary, general information, and something called "experiential evaluation" were much higher for individuals who were in their 40s and 50s than they were for individuals in their 20s and 30s.

On the other hand, measures of figural relations and inductive reasoning were much lower for people in their 50s and 60s than they were for the younger people tested (Horn & Donaldson, 1980).

What is wrong with these results? What more evidence do we need? As you recall from Chapter 15, in a cross-sectional study, the individuals at each age level are from a different cohort. They were born in different years. They have had different life experiences. Often, we find that the younger-aged cohorts are better educated, have better health, and had better nutrition over a longer period of time. Also, the older cohorts may have been educated in a very different fashion than the younger cohorts. They may have had an education that emphasized certain types of intellectual abilities over others.

So what happens when we do a longitudinal study? The results vary to some extent, depending on the study. In well-educated populations, many of the tested abilities continue to rise. According to one broad-based study (Schaie, 1983), it appears that several different kinds of intellectual abilities, both fluid and crystallized, either increase or are maintained through much of adulthood, and decline only after age 60. But there are problems in longitudinal studies, as well. It

crystallized intelligence A broad area of intelligence that includes verbal reasoning, comprehension, and spatial perception; it increases during the life span.

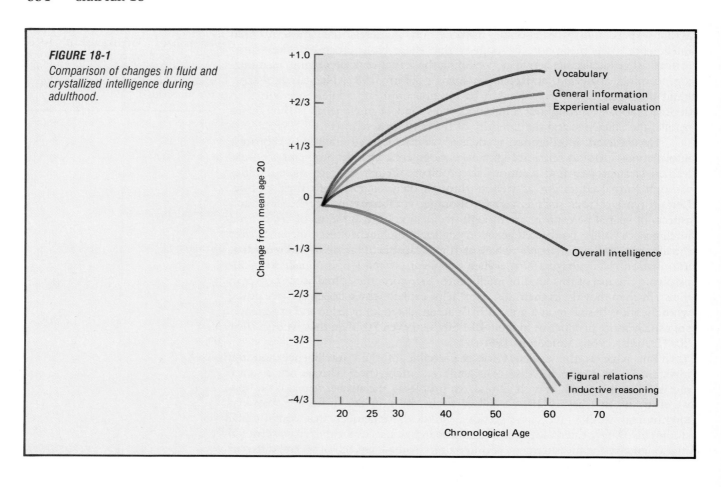

FIGURE 18-1

Comparison of changes in fluid and crystallized intelligence during adulthood.

is difficult to get all the people tested in earlier sessions to come back and be tested again a second, third, or fourth time. Some people are difficult to find. Others refuse to participate. Some are ill. Some have died. If we look at those people who are willing to participate again compared with those who drop out, we find out that the dropouts score lower, on average, at the earlier testing. Therefore, the increase in scores may simply be due to the fact that many of the poor performers drop out. These are all problems of statistical averages of groups. But what if we look at individual changes?

By and large, we find that between 45% and 60% of people maintain a stable level of performance in each of several types of tests well into their 70s. Some people (10% to 15%) often increase in performance at each testing until their mid-70s. A slightly larger group (roughly 30%) declines in test scores, at least by the time the group members reach their 60s. There are a few who decline in tests of word fluency but not in other subtests. There are a few more who maintain stability or actually increase in tests of verbal meaning and of numbers (or arithmetic). Inductive reasoning does not seem to decline any more dramatically than other abilities (Schaie, 1983). It is worth emphasizing that losses during middle age are very limited. Indeed, there are often increases in intelligence test scores until the late 30s or early 40s. This is followed by a period of relative stability until the middle 50s or early 60s. Only the number and word fluency subtests show any statistically significant declines before age 60 (Schaie, 1990).

What is suggested by all this research? It appears that many adults maintain a high level of functioning on a broad spectrum of intellectual abilities straight through middle age. There are also wide individual differences. Some of the abilities classified as fluid intelligence do decline somewhat more rapidly in some individuals. But this is certainly no automatic function of aging. In one study, the decline was clearly found to be related to an individual's "life complexity." People who had more opportunity for environmental stimulation, more satisfaction with life, lower amounts of noise in their environments, an intact family, a good deal of social interaction, and ongoing cultural influences showed longer maintenance of and even increases in intellectual abilities (Schaie, 1983).

There is one factor that does seem to decline in middle adulthood, however. Skills that require speed become increasingly difficult as people grow older because various psychomotor processes begin to slow down. This slowdown is not terribly dramatic in the 40s and 50s. Adults tend to compensate for any decline in speed by their increase in efficiency and in general knowledge (Salthouse, 1990). Intellectual activities that are well practiced and used regularly in daily problem solving or in work settings are maintained at high levels of efficiency (Botwinick, 1977).

People may adapt their intellectual development to meet environmental demands. A person may emphasize the development of some skills while neglecting others in order to succeed at a particular job or within a social network (Lerner, 1990). This may be one reason why many middle-aged and older people perform more poorly than young adults on tests of abstract reasoning (Labouvie-Vief, 1985). They may tend to contextualize the problem, to look at its practical meaning and downplay the more abstract reasoning aspects. So, for example, they may decide not to repeat too much detail in a memory task so as not to bore the listener.

Schaie (1977–1978) has suggested that it is the function, not the nature, of intelligence that changes over time. He describes three stages of adult cognitive development. The young adult is in the Achieving Stage. Here intelligence is used primarily to solve real-life problems that have long-term implications, such as selecting a job or a spouse. In middle age, we enter the Responsibility Stage. Now responsibilities to spouse, children, co-worker, and the general community must be considered in decision making. For some middle agers, this stage takes a somewhat different form and is called the Executive Stage. This applies to people, such as government officials and corporate executives, whose decisions affect hundreds and perhaps millions of lives. By old age, the uses of knowledge shift again. In the Reintegrative Stage, people get back in touch with their own interests, values, and attitudes. They may balk at performing tasks, like IQ tests, that have little relevance for daily living. Indeed, they are primarily concerned with daily living issues rather than forms of abstract reasoning. They can think abstractly, but they don't typically engage in solving such problems just for the sake of doing them (as young adults might).

PERSONALITY CONTINUITY AND CHANGE

Most of the theories discussed so far have focused on the early years of the life span and have described developmental changes in terms of stages. But, in discussing the events of adulthood, most theories employ terms such as *role shifts, marker events, milestones, critical issues,* or *developmental tasks.* The middle aged, perhaps more than any other group, are defined by their roles and responsibilities.

The Tasks of Middle Age

Before we examine these responsibilities, let us describe briefly two theories of middle age—Havighurst's and Erikson's—that define certain "tasks," or "duties," that people must accomplish in order to feel satisfied with their lives. As we saw in Chapter 15, Havighurst (1953) described development over the life span in a pragmatic way. He saw adulthood as a series of periods in which one must accomplish certain developmental tasks. In a sense, these tasks provide the broad context of development. They are, for example, the demands that shape our use of intelligence. In early adulthood, the tasks involve starting a family and establishing a career. In middle age, the tasks are to achieve adult civic and social responsibility, to establish and maintain an adequate standard of living, to help teenage children become responsible, fulfilled adults, to develop suitable leisure-time activities, to relate to one's spouse as a person, to accept and adjust to the physiological changes of middle age, and to adjust to aging parents. According to Erikson (1981), the basic issue facing people at this time is generativity versus self-absorption. In the generativity stage, Erikson suggests that people act within three domains: a procreative one, by giving and responding to the needs of the next generation; a productive one, by integrating work with family life and creating for the next generation; and a creative one, by increasing cultural potential on a greater scale.

Havighurst's model is distinctly similar to Erikson's. Both emphasize the establishment of increasingly complex relationships with others and the adjustment to the many personal changes that middle age brings. But, according to Erikson, the most important responsibilities of this period grow out of the fact that middle-aged people are literally "in the middle"—not only of their own lives but also between two other generations. Let us look more closely at this in-between position.

TABLE 18–5

Havighurst's Developmental Tasks

TASKS OF EARLY ADULTHOOD	TASKS OF MIDDLE AGE	TASKS OF LATER MATURITY
1. Selecting a mate	1. Achieving adult civic and social responsibility	1. Adjusting to decreasing physical strength and health
2. Learning to live with a marriage partner	2. Establishing and maintaining an economic standard of living	2. Adjusting to retirement and reduced income
3. Starting a family	3. Developing adult leisure-time activities	3. Adjusting to death of spouse
4. Rearing children	4. Assisting teenage children to become responsible and happy adults	4. Establishing an explicit affiliation with one's age group
5. Managing a home	5. Relating oneself to one's spouse as a person	5. Meeting social and civic obligations
6. Getting started in an occupation	6. Accepting and adjusting to the physiological changes of middle age	6. Establishing satisfactory physical living arrangements
7. Taking on civic responsibility	7. Adjusting to aging parents	
8. Finding a congenial social group		

Source: From *Human Development and Education* by Robert J. Havighurst. Copyright © 1953 by Longman Inc. Reprinted by permission of Longman Inc., New York.

Between Two Generations

Middle-aged people act as a kind of bridge between the younger generation (which usually means their own children if they have any) and the older generation (their own aging parents). As the middle-aged adjust to their changing roles in these relationships, they often gain a new perspective on their own lives. Instead of looking at life in terms of what Neugarten (1976) calls "time-since-birth," they begin to see it in terms of "time-left-to-live." They are now the generation that must run things. This new responsibility entails some stock taking. They may regret goals not achieved and things not accomplished; they may have to acknowledge that some goals will never be reached. More than any other group, the middle-aged must live in the present. The young can look ahead, and the elderly often look back; but people in their middle years, with shifting responsibilities to two generations as well as to themselves, must live in the here and now.

RESPONSIBILITIES TOWARD AGING PARENTS   As their parents age, a kind of role reversal takes place between middle-aged people and the older generation. The middle-aged become the generation "in charge"—working, raising children, generally functioning as the doers in society. Their own parents, if they are still living, may be retired, in poor health, in need of financial aid, or dependent in other ways. Power has now shifted to their middle-aged child, and unless both generations realize that this role reversal is an inevitable part of the life cycle, the new relationship can cause resentment on both sides (Gould, 1978; Neugarten, 1976).

In 1900, one in four people experienced the death of a parent before they were 15 years old. In the 1980s, less than 1 in 20 children did. Conversely, in 1980, 40% of people in their late 50s had at least one surviving parent (Brody, 1985). Estimates suggest that of the women born in the 1930s, fully one-quarter will have their mother still alive when they turn 60 (Gatz, Bengston, & Blum, 1990). It is practically the norm that middle-aged adults will need to adjust to the changing needs and roles of an aged parent (Brody, 1985).

It is a myth that adult children do not look after their aging or ill parents, and instead abandon them to nursing homes and other impersonal social services. People are living longer today after the onset of chronic diseases or disabilities, and there are few people who reach the end of life without experiencing some period of dependency on their children. The responsibility of long-term parent care has become more the norm than the exception. Several studies in the 1970s demonstrated that 80% to 90% of the medically related and personal care, the household tasks, and the transportation and shopping for aging parents was managed by family members, not the formal social system (Brody, 1985). Families respond to emergencies but also to the long-term assistance of the chronically disabled (Matthews & Rosner, 1988). In the Long-Term-Care Survey of caregivers of very frail elderly, 75% of the daughter care-givers provided daily assistance. Only 10% of the care-givers used formal services (Stone, Cafferata, & Sangl, 1987). At least as importantly, families provide the social support, the affection, and the sense of having someone on whom to rely. It is also true, however, that family resources can be exhausted. Often, family members must decide at some point to turn over primary responsibility to someone else—a nursing home, for example. Nevertheless, conservative estimates indicate that well over 5 million people in the United States are involved in parent care at any given time (Brody, 1985).

As their parents age, the middle-aged become the generation "in charge"— they are now the generation that must run things. This change in roles will require adjustments both from the middle-aged and their aging parents.

Daughters are much more likely than sons to provide care giving to their parents (Brody, Kleban, Johnsen, Hoffman, & Schoonover, 1987; Gatz et al., 1990; Spitze & Logan, 1990). There is very little difference between the aid provided by working versus nonworking women (Brody & Schoonover, 1986). Working daughters provide comparable amounts of help with tasks such as shopping, transportation, and emotional support. Nonemployed daughters are, however, more likely to help with cooking and personal care. Substantial numbers of working daughters are willing to change their work schedules to accommodate their parents' needs (Brody et al., 1987). Surveys indicate that 20% to 30% of care-giver daughters had rearranged their schedules in order to provide care. In fact, caring for ill relatives is the second most common reason middle-aged women give for leaving the work force (the first is their own illness).

The responsibility for parent care is both rewarding and stressful. For some, it creates a tension between dependence and independence. It may reactivate old dependency conflicts from childhood or other family relationship problems between parent and child or between siblings. Old loyalties and alliances or old rivalries sometimes reappear. It also foreshadows the future of the care-givers, who will have to face their own dependence on their children when they become old. It may be a preview and model for relinquishing autonomy, control, and responsibility. These internal conflicts—together with the very real demands on time and freedom, competing responsibilities, interference with lifestyle, social, and recreational activities—can create a quite stressful environment. It is rather remarkable that 80% to 90% of middle-aged adults persist in the tasks and responsibilities of parental care. Indeed, some women practically make a career as care-giver to one aging relative after another. Despite the extent of care giving, fully three-fifths of care-giving women in a recent study reported that "Somehow, they felt guilty about not doing enough for their mothers, and three-quarters of them agreed that, nowadays, children do not take care of their elderly parents as was the case in the good old days" (Brody, 1985).

Siblings may work together to provide care to their ailing parents (Goetting, 1982). The distribution of labor between the siblings is not always equal, however. As was mentioned before, daughters are more likely than sons to provide care. In fact, parents expect more assistance from daughters than from sons (Brody, Johnsen, & Fulcomer, 1984). If there are two daughters and only one of them works, the other (who is not employed) will provide more of the daily care and assistance in last-minute emergencies (Matthews, Werkner, & Delaney, 1989). Nonetheless, the working sister is expected to make significant contributions, typically providing aid in the evenings and on weekends.

It is certainly the case that middle-agers provide assistance to their parents. In most families, however, there is a reciprocal exchange of assistance. Many older parents provide financial assistance to their middle-aged children and to their grandchildren (Giordano & Beckman, 1985; Hill, Foote, Aldous, Carlson, & Macdonald, 1970). This may be particularly true in upper-middle-class families. In African-American families, the older generation often does not have the financial resources to contribute (Jackson et al., 1990). On the other hand, they are even more likely to provide social support and perhaps care-giving services to their children coping with single parenthood.

RELATIONSHIPS WITH THE YOUNGER GENERATION While they work out new relationships with their parents, middle-aged people must also assume new roles in their relationships with the younger generation. Because of the ever-increasing divorce rate in this country, many people are raising children alone. Others are not living according to family-centered norms and have chosen to remain single. Those who do have children must both guide their youngsters and let them go. They may find themselves in sharp conflict or in shifting relationships with adolescent children (Alpert & Richardson, 1980). This may be particularly true when the children are preadolescents. During this time, there are commonly almost daily conflicts over rights and responsibilities (Smetana, 1988). When children marry, parents are suddenly confronted with a new family member in the form of a son-in-law or a daughter-in-law. This abrupt demand for intimacy with someone who may be a total stranger is another common adjustment during this period (Neugarten, 1976).

Middle-aged people also deal with the "younger generation" in the business world, in the community, or as part of an extended family, as in the case of nieces and nephews. This contact with young people—as supportive mentor or as aging competitor, as boss and director or as partner in life—is a significant part of middle age. If middle-aged people withdraw and do not feel themselves to be a part of the world in which young people live, they are likely to become stagnant, self-absorbed, and unhappily isolated from the continuum of life.

GRANDPARENTING Many people in middle age find themselves in the additional role of grandparent. For many of them, grandparenting is a highly satisfactory activity; they are involved in the raising of a new generation without having the responsibilities of a parent and without being involved in the intense relationships and conflicts between parent and child (Robertson, 1977).

Grandparenting is a highly individualized activity—there is no one way in which grandparents "normally" act within a family or even within an ethnic group. Nevertheless, there are definite roles that grandparents can play, depending on their individual relationships with their grandchildren (Troll, 1980). If a single mother or both parents work, grandparents can take care of children for the better part of the day. Some grandparents become "fun" people to their grandchildren, taking them on trips, shopping, or to interesting places. In certain ethnic groups, a grandfather maintains his status and position as "formal head of the family."

One author suggests that there are four important, yet often largely symbolic, roles that living grandparents fulfill (Bengtson, 1985).

1. *Being There*. Sometimes grandparents describe their most important role as simply "being there." Their presence is calming in the face of family disruption or external catastrophe. They provide an anchor of stability to both grandchildren and parents. Sometimes, they are even a deterrent to family disruption.

2. *Family National Guard*. Some grandparents report that their most important function is to be available in times of emergency. During these times, grandparents often need to go well beyond the role of simply being there to active management of grandchildren.

3. *Arbitrator*. Some grandparents see their role as one of imparting and negotiating family values, maintaining family continuity, and helping out in times of conflict to restore the intergenerational family. Although there are often differences in values between each generation, some grandparents see themselves as better able to handle the conflicts between their adult children and their grandchildren because of their distance and longer experience.

4. *Maintaining the Family's Biography*. In a broad sense, grandparents can provide a sense of continuity for the family, teaching grandchildren about the heritage and traditions of their family.

Each of these roles may be quite real, or they may in fact be more symbolic. Sometimes, family values are maintained more because adult children and grandchildren worry about how a grandparent might react than by the actual intervention of the grandparent (Bengtson, 1985)!

Men at Midlife

In middle age, both men and women reassess goals and reflect on whether original goals have been met. In young adulthood, people establish themselves in careers. By middle age, they often take a second look at their jobs. Most people then realize that they have made their career choice and must live with it. Some who are dissatisfied with their work, or unemployed, or who have not advanced as far as they had hoped, may become bitter and discouraged. Others may rearrange priorities. Shifting priorities are not limited to occupations. For example, some people at midlife may decide to direct more attention toward interpersonal or even moral commitments and less toward occupational development (Fiske, 1980).

Farrell and Rosenberg (1981) looked at how men reacted in midlife. They interviewed 300 men in middle age and compared their answers to those of younger men in the areas of family, work, and their physical selves. Their notion, supported by the research, is that individuals have an active role in shaping their existence through the way in which they react to the world around them. They found that men tended to react to middle age individually, but in similar ways. Most men felt committed to both work and family. Most had developed a routine way of life that helped them cope with their lives and their problems. Many had to face the same problems: caring for aging and dependent parents, coping with adolescent children, coming to terms with limitations, recognizing physical vulnerability.

Farrell and Rosenberg also suggested that there are four general paths of development in middle age. The first is that of the transcendent-generative man.

He does not have a midlife crisis but has found adequate solutions to most problems of life. For this man, midlife can be a time of fulfillment and accomplishment. The second path is that of the pseudo-developed man. This man copes with problems by maintaining the facade that everything is satisfactory or under control; in reality, this man tends to feel lost, confused, or bored. A man in midlife crisis—the third path—is confused and feels that his whole world is disintegrating. He is unable to meet demands and solve problems. For some men, this may be a temporary phase; for others, it may be the beginning of a continuous decline. The final path is that of the punitive-disenchanted man. This man has been unhappy or alienated for much of his life and displays signs of a midlife crisis. He is usually unable to cope with problems.

Farrell and Rosenberg conclude by noting that our society forces men to conform to one standard of success and masculinity and that most men try to conform to this standard. A number of the problems of men at midlife come from having to cope with the idea that they have not lived up to this standard or that they have had to put aside many of their own desires in order to try to reach the standard. Only a small number of men can avoid feelings of failure, self-estrangement, or loss of self-esteem at this time.

Women at Midlife

Although there have been far fewer studies conducted on women than on men, women, too, often find this a time of transition and reassessment. There are wide individual variations, as well as some common patterns. Traditionally, women have defined themselves more in terms of the family cycle than in terms of their place in the career cycle. In a recent study of midwestern women, it was found that

In our society, women are usually judged by their looks, and in order to be considered attractive, they must appear youthful. It is not surprising, then, that researchers report a high incidence of depression in middle-aged women.

APPLICATION

THE NEW COLLEGE STUDENT

There is a new student on the college campuses. Nearly 1.5 million women over age 35 are attending college—as 4-year students, in 2-year degree programs, and as graduate students. That is almost twice the number of men over 35 who are attending college. From 1980 to 1988, the number of women over age 35 attending college increased by 81%. While there has been a dramatic increase in this segment of the college population, the percentage of "typical" college students—men and women between the ages of 18 and 22—has actually declined since 1980 (U.S. Bureau of the Census, 1990).

The vast majority of these women have many other commitments: They have jobs, child-care and household responsibilities, and volunteer work. The majority are married, and report a family income of $25,000 or more. An increasing number are single parents (Saslaw, 1981). Their motivation for being in school is often similar to that of other students in that they seek career development or career advancement, greater financial security, a more challenging job, and the like. They may also be reentering the job market and need to develop or improve their skills. In addition, women who had to assume demanding family responsibilities earlier in their adult lives may now have the time and/or financial resources to seek personal and intellectual fulfillment. The majority are conscientious students: They attend classes regularly and get better grades, on average, than do other segments of the college student population (Saslow, 1981).

Those broad statistics would seem to indicate that there are now greater opportunities for lifelong learning and that women, in increasing numbers, are taking advantage of those opportunities. Some also may have more leisure time as their children get older, and can reassess their lives and redirect some of their energies and commitments toward educational and career advancement. This interpretation, however, is too simple.

The decision to return to school, in and of itself, requires a number of considerations and usually the support of other family members. The decision involves an assessment of one's skills and abilities. The student role is generally very different from the other roles these women have assumed in their adult lives, and it requires considerable adaptation. A student is in a subordinate position as "learner." Also, the mature woman may find herself among a large number of students who are considerably younger than she is, and the faculty may also be younger. Initially, the age difference may be a source of discomfort. Feelings of self-doubt are also common while the new student adapts to the school environment, performing unfamiliar tasks in a prescribed fashion.

Family members must often take on new responsibilities when a woman assumes the role of college student. In addition to assistance with household chores, the student may need emotional support. Sometimes this involves awkward role reversals and the disruption of familiar patterns of interaction.

Colleges and universities sometimes impose constraints as well (Women's Reentry Project, 1981). Some women find it difficult to arrange time for other responsibilities because of rigid, full-time class schedules. Appropriate counseling is not always available, and they often find that guidelines for transferring credits, obtaining financial aid, and even admission are geared to the needs of other student populations, such as the 18- to 22-year-old full-time students. Also, some women find few faculty role models, particularly if they have selected a male-dominated discipline.

Indeed, the literature on the increasing number of women over age 35 returning to college or attending for the first time highlights the need for revisions in school programs and policies, as well as changes in attitudes regarding this new student.

women tended to report major life transitions at three points in the family cycle. Fully 80% of women reported major role changes associated with the birth of their children and their early child-rearing years. This often occurred around ages 27 to 30. Two other major transitions, however, occurred later in life. Of the sample, 40% reported a major transition at the time of launching their children. Very few reported this transition as terribly traumatic. The final major transition period (for 33% of the women) occurred in the postparental period. When examining these changes for women, it is easier to find a connection with the family cycle than with predictable age levels or with points in the career cycle (Reinke et al., 1985).

Women react more strongly than men to growing older physically. In our society, women are usually judged by their looks, and in order to be considered attractive, they must appear youthful. For some women, lines on the face and other signs of aging are indications that they are no longer desirable and feminine. Some women may also react negatively to menopause, regretting the loss of the ability to bear children. It is not surprising, then, that researchers report a high incidence of depression in middle-aged women, as compared to other age groups (Boyd & Weissman, 1981).

Friendships: A Lifelong Perspective

Although many important life stages are defined by family relationships, many people, particularly in this age of shifting family styles, rely more on friends than on family. Although the majority of people do marry and raise children, a significant and growing number of people remain single or raise children by themselves. For these people in particular, friendships are a central part of life. Such important life tasks as establishing intimacy, for example, must be accomplished through friendships rather than through marriage and family. And for older people, whose children are grown or who are widowed, friendship often fills many vital emotional needs.

Lowenthal and her associates (1977) interviewed people at four different life stages concerning their attitudes toward friendship and the kinds of friendships they had. The study involved high school students, newlyweds, people in early middle age, and people in late middle age. There was considerable continuity in friendships. Most middle-aged people reported that they had several close friends with whom they had been involved for at least 6 years, whereas adolescents and newlyweds tended to have more short-term friendships. The subjects were asked what qualities were important in real friendships and what qualities characterized an ideal friend. People at all four life stages viewed friendship in similar ways. Reciprocity was considered most important in ideal friends, with a strong emphasis on helping and sharing. People found that their friends were similar to themselves in many ways and stressed the importance of shared experiences and ease of communication. Sex differences were more significant than age differences. Women responded in more detail than men, and they seemed to be more deeply involved in interpersonal relationships. Women considered reciprocity most important in their real friendships, whereas men tended to choose their friends on the basis of similarity.

In general, the most complex friendships occurred among the late middle-aged group. In early middle age, people were more involved with families and establishing job security. They had less time to devote to friends, and their friendships were less involved. But by late middle age, highly complex and multidimensional relationships began to form. People at this stage were likely to appreciate the unique, individual aspects of friends. This may be a result of certain personality shifts during middle age. Recall Jung's description of the period from ages 40 to 60 as a time of inner awareness, when people turn away from the

Friendships during midlife can fill many vital emotional roles.

activities of the conscious mind and confront the unconscious. It is possible, Lowenthal and her colleagues suggest, that as people become aware of the subtleties of their own natures, they also begin to appreciate complexity in others more than they did in earlier life.

LIFELONG DEVELOPMENT

Aside from a few longitudinal studies, there is relatively little hard data or even theory on how individuals change over their entire life spans. The main reason for this lack of data is that psychologists have only recently recognized that adults "grow," too. Jung (1933/1961) was one of the first to emphasize the second half of life, when older people need to find meaning in their own lives. But few psychologists offer an all-encompassing theory of lifelong development.

Peck's Extension of Erikson

Erikson described a lifelong process of development, as we saw in Chapter 2. Of Erikson's eight stages of human development, we have dealt with the first six. But the later years also present important issues to each person, and Peck (1968) has been especially concerned with expanding Erikson's picture of the second half of life.

Peck's main criticism of Erikson has been that his eight stages place too much stress on the first 20 to 25 years of life. The six developmental issues—trust versus mistrust, autonomy versus doubt, initiative versus guilt, industry versus inferiority, ego identity versus ego diffusion, and intimacy versus isolation—all pose important conflicts that each individual must resolve in these early years. But what of the last 40 to 50 years of life?

During these later years, all of the earlier issues and their resolutions reappear from time to time. A sudden physical impairment, such as a heart attack, may bring on struggles with autonomy and dependence in a 45-year-old. The death of a husband may renew strong intimacy needs in a woman. In fact, each major life adjustment may necessitate some revisions and reevaluations of old solutions to problems. Erikson also describes two developmental stages reached in adulthood. The seventh stage, which we discussed earlier in the chapter, is generativity versus self-absorption. The eighth stage is integrity versus despair; here, people look back on their lives either with satisfaction or with despair. Peck suggests that far too many new issues and tasks arise in these years to be summed up in only two developmental stages.

In an attempt to account for the special challenges of adult life, Peck proposes seven issues or conflicts of adult development. The first four issues are particularly important in middle age. As physical stamina and health begin to wane, people must shift a good part of their energies into mental instead of physical activities. Peck calls this adjustment *valuing wisdom versus valuing physical powers.* The second developmental task is to find a new balance between *socializing versus sexualizing* in human relationships. This, too, is an adjustment imposed by social constraints as well as by biological changes. Physical changes may force people to redefine their relationships with both sexes—to stress companionship, not sexual intimacy or

By keeping an open mind, a person can continue to grow throughout middle age.

competitiveness. A third task is *cathectic (emotional) flexibility versus cathectic impoverishment*. Emotional flexibility underlies the various adjustments that people must make in middle age, as families split up, friends move away, and old interests cease being the central focus of life. *Mental flexibility versus mental rigidity* is another task of middle age. Here, individuals have to fight the inclination to become too set in their ways or too distrustful of new ideas. Mental rigidity is the tendency to become dominated by past experiences and old judgments—to decide, for example, that "I've disapproved of Republicans (or Communists, or Protestants) all my life, so I don't see why I should change my mind now."

Three additional dimensions are particularly important in old age, but the individual is already beginning to deal with these issues during middle age. The first of these is *ego differentiation versus work-role preoccupation*. If people define themselves in terms of jobs or families, then retirement, a change in occupation, or the children's leaving home will open a gulf in which individuals are likely to flounder. The second conflict, *body transcendence versus body preoccupation*, centers on the individual's ability to avoid preoccupation with the increasing aches, pains, and physical annoyances that accompany age. A third dimension particularly important in old age is *ego transcendence versus ego preoccupation*. This requires that people not become mired in thoughts of death (the "night of the ego," as Peck calls it). People who age successfully, according to Erikson's theory, transcend the prospect of their own extinction by becoming involved in the younger generation—the legacy that will outlive them.

Like Erikson's stages, none of Peck's dimensions is confined just to middle age or old age. The decisions made in early life act as building blocks for all the solutions of the adult years, and the middle-aged are already starting to resolve the issues of old age. In fact, research suggests that the period from ages 50 to 60 is often a critical time for making adjustments that will determine the way people live out the rest of their years (Peck & Berkowitz, 1964).

545

STUDY OUTLINE

Development in Middle Age

Middle age spans roughly ages 40 to 60 or 65, but the period varies according to how each individual reacts to various social, physical, and psychological cues.

"Prime Time" or "The Beginning of the End"? Middle age can be a time of fulfillment and leadership or a period of turmoil and dissatisfaction. Although some people feel more "in command" of their lives than ever before, others experience severe physical and emotional crises and feel that the period is one of decline. For everyone, there is a new sense of time running out and a realization that earlier goals may never be reached.

Midlife Crisis or Reassessment? How people react to becoming middle-aged may determine whether it is a period of transition and growth or a period of a midlife crisis. Cytrynbaum and his associates developed a framework that consists of factors to which a person reacts. These factors include the person's personality, specific events, developmental tasks of middle age, and personality change in middle age. The interactions of these factors may determine whether a person is in transition or in a midlife crisis.

Physical Continuity and Change

Biological, intellectual, and personality functioning during middle age hold elements of continuity and change. Physical abilities level off, and the first signs of aging appear. Some physical functions begin to decline, and internal changes occur. Many of the unpleasant effects of aging can be reduced by exercise, diet, and good living habits.

Menopause and Climacteric. Many men, as well as all women, undergo emotional and physical changes in middle age related to the reproductive hormones. **Menopause** generally occurs in women between the ages of 48 and 51. There may be both physical and emotional symptoms, but many women report that menopause does not change them in any important way.

Cognitive Continuity and Change

Fluid versus Crystallized Intelligence. Some researchers divide intelligence into two broad areas: **fluid intelligence,** which tends to be affected by physiology, peaks in adolescence and declines gradually throughout adulthood; and **crystallized intelligence,** which is based on learning and experience, increases as people grow older.

Personality Continuity and Change

The Tasks of Middle Age. Personality development is often measured in terms of developmental stages; in adulthood, these stages are often described as "tasks." One of the main tasks of middle age is to adjust to increased responsibilities for aging parents while children grow increasingly independent. Even for people without children, involvement with the younger generation continues—at work, in the community, and in the extended family.

Occupational reassessment and adjustment often take place in middle age. People often realize that they have not met early career goals and that there is little likelihood of change; this can cause a sense of frustration and uselessness. Others may rearrange priorities.

Men and women have different as well as similar problems at midlife. As with other problems, how they react as individuals within the framework of factors outlined by Cytrybaum and his associates determines whether they are in a period of transition and growth or in a midlife crisis.

Friendships: A Lifelong Perspective. Lowenthal and her colleagues found considerable continuity in friendship patterns. From adolescence through late middle age, people tend to choose their friends for much the same reasons. The richest and most complex friendships occurred among people in late middle age. This may be a result of an increasing introspection that makes people more aware of complexity in themselves and others.

Lifelong Development

Peck's Extension of Erikson. There is relatively little theory or precise data on how individuals change over the life span. Erikson's later stages have shed some light on this issue. His seventh stage, which occurs in early and middle adulthood, is generativity versus self-absorption. To avoid stagnation, people must become concerned with the younger generation and the kind of world that they will inherit. Peck has proposed seven conflicts in adult development. Four of them are particularly important in middle age: *valuing wisdom versus valuing physical powers, socializing versus sexualizing, cathectic (or emotional) flexibility versus cathectic impoverishment,* and *mental flexibility versus mental rigidity.*

KEY TERMS AND CONCEPTS

aerobic exercise	cathectic flexibility versus cathectic impoverishment	crystallized intelligence
body transcendence versus body preoccupation	climacteric	ego differentiation versus work-role preoccupation

ego transcendence versus ego
  preoccupation
fluid intelligence
menopause
mental flexibility versus mental rigidity

middle age
midlife crisis
midlife reassessment
socializing versus sexualizing
Type A personality

Type B personality
Valuing wisdom versus valuing physical
  powers

SELF-TEST QUESTIONS

1. Discuss some of the different feelings people have about being middle-aged. What are the factors that determine these differences?

2. What are some of the physical changes that occur in middle age?

3. What are the diseases that most frequently cause major problems in middle age? What is the relationship of health habits to these chronic disorders?

4. What is the relationship between stress and disease in middle age? Give an example of a study that supports your answer.

5. What are some factors that influence the degree of stress?

6. What factors account for differences in the impact of these changes?

7. Compare and contrast fluid intelligence and crystallized intelligence.

8. What evidence is there to support the notion that fluid

intelligence declines and crystallized intelligence is maintained and even increases in the middle years? What methodological problems are involved in reaching conclusions about this issue?

9. According to Havighurst and Erikson, what are the tasks that people must accomplish in middle age in order to feel satisfied with their lives?

10. Discuss in detail some of the unique responsibilities associated with being the generation "in the middle."

11. What are the differences and similarities between the reactions of men and women to midlife?

12. How is the nature of friendship during midlife both different from and similar to the nature of friendship during other periods of the life span?

13. Describe how Peck has expanded Erikson's stages of human development. Do the developmental conflicts that characterize earlier stages of development reappear in midlife? Please explain.

SUGGESTED READINGS

BARUCH, G., & BURNETT, R. *Lifeprints: New patterns of love and work for today's women*. New York: McGraw-Hill, 1983. This book, based on interviews, highlights the diversity of life patterns available to women today.

LOPATA, H. Z. (Ed.). *Widows*. Durham, NC: Duke University Press, 1987. A collection of articles about widows in diverse cultures and the social support systems available.

McCRAE, R. P., & COSTA, P. T. *Personality in adulthood*. New York: Guilford Press, 1990. An updated presentation of these authors' theory and research that emphasizes continuity of personality characteristics.

OSHERSON, S. *Finding our fathers: How a man's life is shaped by his relationship with his father*. New York: Fawcett, 1987. Using a mixture of research and clinical insights, the author discusses the pressures and concerns of today's

adult men as a result of their early relationship with their own fathers.

ROGERS, C. *On becoming a person*. Boston: Houghton Mifflin, 1961. A famous therapist talks to the reader about continued personal growth and creativity during adulthood.

RUBIN, L. *Women of a certain age: The midlife search for self*. New York: Harper & Row, 1979. Rubin looks at the lives of women like herself as they deal with crises in maturing: children leaving, decisions to enter or go back into the work force, efforts to discover new identities.

SHERMAN, E. *Meaning in midlife transitions*. Albany: State University of New York Press, 1987. A scholarly guide to the changes and challenges of midlife.

Chapter 19

*Remember the days of old,
consider the years of many generations:
ask thy father, and he will show thee;
thy elders, and they will tell thee.*

DEUTERONOMY 32:7

CHAPTER OUTLINE

Later Adulthood: Physical and Cognitive Changes

L ater adulthood is an important period in its own right. If we think of it as beginning in one's early 60s, for some it may span as many as 40 years. In some societies, people in their later adulthood years are the recognized elders. In much of Western society, we seem to have just rediscovered this large and growing segment of the population, sometimes euphemistically called "senior citizens." In this chapter, we will look at some of the physical and intellectual changes that often occur in later adulthood, and the individual's reactions to those changes. In the next chapter, we will explore the broader personality and social aspects of aging. But first, let's look at some attitudes about aging and about older people.

AGING: MYTH AND REALITY

What is it like to grow old? To many people, the prospects are so grim that they do not ever want to find out. Nearly 25% of the people interviewed in one study wanted to die before their time (Kastenbaum, 1971). In fact, some young people today seem to view old age as a state of marginal existence. They fear the losses of energy, control, flexibility, sexuality, physical mobility, memory, and even intelligence that they think go hand-in-hand with aging.

Ageism and Stereotypes

In our society, old people are often perceived in terms of stereotypes, many of them negative. A Harris poll (1978) of the general population, including older adults, documented positive images of the elderly as warm, friendly, and wise, along with negative feelings that old people are inefficient, inactive, and largely incapable of successful adjustment to new situations. From an objective social point of view, the situation of some older citizens seems unfulfilling to the general public. Today's elderly do have a lower education level than most of the population. Some nursing homes have become notorious for taking advantage of old people, giving just enough care for survival but little reason for them to want to live and thrive. Our newspapers are full of gruesome stories about elderly women being mugged and robbed by groups of vicious teenagers and of heart-rending accounts of

CHAPTER OBJECTIVES

By the time you have finished this chapter, you should be able to do the following:

■ Describe the myths and realities of aging.

■ Describe the physical changes that are characteristic of the aging process and the factors that contribute to these changes.

■ Compare and contrast the various theories and explanations of the aging process set forth in this chapter.

■ Explain the cognitive changes that occur with age, differentiating those changes that are intrinsic to the aging process itself from the secondary causes of cognitive decline.

■ Discuss the aging process in a historical context, comparing the experiences of today's generation of senior citizens with those of generations in the past and generations yet to come.

ageism A widely prevalent social attitude that overvalues youth and discriminates against the elderly.

Old age has its marathoners as well as its bench-sitters. At age 82, runner Ryonosuke Kashiwagi competed in a 10-kilometer race in Ome, Japan.

desperate old people shoplifting hamburger meat or living on dog food. Until aggressive advocate groups like the Gray Panthers began to voice the needs of the aged, most people assumed that the elderly were not even able to speak for themselves. There has also been such a lack of interest in the aged that, until the past three decades, almost no research at all was done on old people. Neugarten (1970) uses the word **ageism** to describe this attitude of indifference and neglect. No wonder old age seems such a horrible fate.

Do the stereotypes of the past still exist now that people over age 65 comprise over 12% of the population and public awareness seems to have increased? One hundred sixty college students at California State University were asked about old people (Babladelis, 1987). Here are some of their answers.

They estimated that 30% of our population was old and in need of services. They thought the word "old" should apply to people over age 60. They reported that, although they had family and neighbors who were old, they were "reluctant to spend time with old people." They reported having a "concerned," dutiful attitude toward them, but that old people had a lot of unlikable characteristics— such as being senile, self-centered, boring, and too talkative. They viewed old people as generally physically disabled. Despite the fact that many of these college students had grandparents in their 50s and 60s who were quite vigorous, their attitudes about the old had not changed dramatically from similar attitudes found in the late 1970s (Babladelis, 1987). But negative attitudes and stereotypes are not necessarily the rule. Several studies have found that attitudes toward the elderly are often ambivalent, if not contradictory. The elderly are often seen as both wise and senile, as kind and grouchy, as concerned for others and inactive and unsociable (Crockett & Hummert, 1987). Perhaps it is time we stopped generalizing about them as a group and started looking at them as individuals with all the variability of any other age period.

The stereotypes just presented are a mosaic of fact and fantasy. Some problems are only loosely tied to age; failing health and loneliness do not have to be a part of aging any more than acne and social awkwardness have to be a part of adolescence. The population over age 65 has its marathoners and executives as well as its shut-ins and bench-sitters. Negative stereotypes not only instill a fear of aging in the young but also have a powerful grip on the aged. According to the Harris poll (1978), most elderly people have a much higher opinion of their own economic and social conditions than does the general public. At the same time, they believe that they are some of the lucky few who have escaped the misery of aging in the United States.

People have not always dreaded old age. In the Bible, elders were considered to possess great wisdom. In American Indian tribes, the old have traditionally been venerated as wise elders, the transmitters of culture, a storehouse of historical lore and treasure. In Thailand, age is the greatest determinant of status, and old people are given seats of honor everywhere, from public meetings to the family dinner table (Cowgill, 1972a).

In colonial America, the biblical tradition of veneration for elders was a powerful cultural influence. Old age was viewed as an outward manifestation of divine grace and favor, the reward for an extraordinarily upright life. Benjamin Franklin played a major role in drafting the Constitution, not only because he was a shrewd parliamentarian, but also because he was over 80 years old at the time and was viewed by the other statesmen as crowned with the glory of his years. Reverence for age was powerful because so few people managed to achieve it. The demographic contrast between then and now is startling; in the colonial period, the median age was 16 and only 2% of the population reached age 65. Some accounts of early colonists describe adults in their 30s as wrinkled, balding, or gray (Fischer, 1978).

Today, the median age in the United States is 32 and climbing. Approximately one in eight Americans is 65 or older. If the present trend of low birthrates and declining death rates continues, the number of those over age 65 will rise dramatically. Modern medicine helps many to survive serious illness. As a result, some people live on with severe impairments that need medical care. However, many other older people are vigorous, involved, and independent. Clearly, we are witnessing the emergence of an unprecedented group of healthy, educated, retired workers. Those individuals in later adulthood are clearly not a homogeneous group.

Four Decades of Life

The average 60-year-old today can expect to live another 20 years; those presently 75 years old can look forward to an average of 11 more years (National Center for Health Statistics, 1987). This is a long, significant part of life. To lump all older adults into one group not only ignores individual differences but also fails to account for variations in physical health, aging factors, and developmental influences. The newly retired, relatively vigorous 65-year-old may be caring for an 85- or 90-year-old parent, who may indeed be quite frail. These people are members of two separate generations; they are clearly different cohorts with respect to historical events. Burnside and colleagues (1979) break down late adulthood decade by decade, analyzing the distinctive features of each stage.

THE YOUNG-OLD: 60 TO 69 This decade marks a major transition. In their 60s, most adults must adapt to a new role structure in an effort to cope with the losses and gains of the decade (Havighurst, 1972). Income is reduced due to retirement, and friends and colleagues start to disappear. Society reduces its expectations of persons living in their 60s—demanding less energy, less independence, and less creativity. Burnside laments this automatic social response and feels that it demoralizes older adults, who often react by slowing down their pace in a self-fulfilling prophecy. Physical strength does wane somewhat and may pose real problems for industrial workers still on the job. Yet a great many people in their 60s have a surplus of energy and seek out new and different activities. Many of the recently retired are healthy, vigorous, and well educated. They may use their new leisure time for self-enhancement or community or political activities. Some enjoy regular athletic and sexual activity. Some retirees are determined to remain givers, producers, and mentors. They become volunteer executives in small businesses, visitors to hospitals, or foster grandparents.

THE MIDDLE-AGED-OLD: 70 TO 79 The 70s are often marked by loss and illness. Friends and family may die at an increased rate. Along with a contracting social world, adults in their 70s must cope with reduced participation in formal organizations. Septuagenarians often exhibit restlessness and irritability. Their own health problems tend to become more severe during this decade. There is often a decline in sexual activity among both women and men. In many cases, this is due

In many societies, old people are venerated as wise elders, and they enjoy high social status.

TABLE 19–1

The Aging of the Population: Percentage of the Population 65 Years and Over

YEAR	TOTAL
1950	8.1%
1960	9.2
1970	9.8
1980	11.3
1988	12.3
PROJECTED	
2000	13.0
2010	13.9

Sources: Statistical Abstract of the United States (Washington, D.C.: Department of Commerce, 1990).

Some retirees are active givers and producers for society. This woman helps tutor students after school.

to the loss of an intimate partner. The major developmental task of the 70s is to maintain the personality reintegration achieved in the 60s, according to Burnside.

THE OLD-OLD: 80 TO 89   Most octogenarians experience increased difficulty in adapting to and interacting with their surroundings. Many need a streamlined, barrier-free environment that offers both privacy and stimulation. They need help in maintaining social and cultural contacts. Old age in the 80s has been poignantly described as a "gradual process which begins the very first day one begins to live in his memories" (Burnside et al., 1979).

THE VERY OLD-OLD: 90 TO 99   There are less data on nonagenarians than on the previous decades. It is hard to systematically acquire information about their health and social circumstances. Although health problems become more severe, nonagenarians can successfully alter their activities to make the most of what they have. One practicing psychiatrist in her 90s advises creating new fields of activity by removing the competitive element from one's former approach. She emphasizes the advantages of old age, such as freedom from work pressures and responsibilities (Burnside et al., 1979). The changes that shape life in the 90s occur gradually and over a long period of time. If previous crises have been resolved in a satisfactory way, the ninth decade may be joyful, serene, and fulfilling.

It should be clear by now that "the aged" are not one cohesive group but rather a collection of subgroups, ranging from the active, newly retired 65-year-old to the frail, perhaps incontinent, nonagenarian. Each group has unique problems and capabilities. Many share to some extent the age-related difficulties of reduced income, failing health, and loss of loved ones. But having a problem is not the same as being a problem. The all-too-popular view of those over age 65 as needy, nonproductive, and unhappy needs revision.

TABLE 19-2

The Increase in the Average Life Expectancy in the United States

	LIFE EXPECTANCY	
Year	Male	Female
1920	53.6	54.6
1930	58.1	61.6
1940	60.8	65.2
1950	65.6	71.1
1960	66.6	73.1
1970	67.1	74.8
1980	70.0	77.4
1989	71.8	78.5

Source: *Statistical Abstract of the United States* (Washington, D.C.: Department of Commerce, 1990); National Center for Health Statistics, *Monthly Vital Statistics* Report, Vol. 38. (Hyattsville, Md.: Public Health Service, August 1990).

THE AGING PROCESS

Aging is universal and inevitable. It happens to all bodily systems, even under optimal genetic and environmental circumstances. All systems do not age at the same time or pace. Yet, for most bodily systems, the processes of aging begin well before this time, in early and middle adulthood. Many of the effects of aging are not seen until later adulthood because the processes of aging are gradual and there is considerable reserve capacity in most physical systems. Most individuals do not have major health problems or interruptions in daily living due to aging until well into their 70s.

Some authors who study the aging process feel it is important to distinguish carefully between "normal aging" and "pathological aging" (Elias, 1987). Others feel that the cumulative effects of disease and of accidents are so much a part of life that it is fruitless to try to separate them (Kohn, 1985). First, we will look at some of the more common physical changes as a result of aging. Then, we will look at some of the diseases and personal habits that contribute to physical decline. Finally, we will look at some of the current theories of "normal aging."

Physical Aging

APPEARANCE A look in the mirror provides regular evidence of the aging process. The gray hair, the aging skin, a shift in posture, some deeper wrinkles—all are telltale signs. The skin becomes less elastic, more wrinkled, dry, and thin. In earlier years, wrinkles were formed by particular muscles—leaving, for example, laugh lines; in old age, they are caused partly by the loss of fat tissue under the skin. The skin may take on a crisscrossed look of soft, crumpled paper or fine parchment (Rossman, 1977). There may be an increase of warts on the trunk, face, and scalp. Small blood vessels often break, producing tiny black-and-blue marks. Age spots may appear; these are brown areas of pigmentation, popularly called "liver spots."

Some of these changes in appearance are a result of normal aging. Some are clearly genetic. If we look at identical twins, for example, we can see very similar

It is important to distinguish between "normal aging" and "pathological aging." Many changes in the skin, for example, are closely related to exposure to the ultraviolet rays of the sun.

patterns of aging. But, for many, the changes in skin are closely related to exposure to sun, wind, and abrasions, but particularly to the ultraviolet rays of the sun. The sun harms the skin's ability to renew itself; a "healthy tan" leads to thin and wrinkled skin for some, and to skin cancer for others. Yet it is probably possible to slow down some of these signs of aging skin by eating well, staying healthy, and protecting the skin from lengthy exposure to the sun.

THE SENSES   The senses generally become less efficient as a person ages. Hearing deficits, particularly in men, are quite common. Generally, there is a greater hearing loss in the higher-frequency tones—those that occur in speech sounds such as "s," "sh," "ch," and "f." Another hearing problem common with aging is the inability to detect voices or other sounds above background noise (Olsho, Harkins, & Lenhardt, 1985). Sometimes hearing aids can be effective, but often they are a source of frustration. A hearing aid will normally amplify all frequencies of sound, including background noise as well as voices. This is not much help in picking out the details of what someone is saying. Individuals with hearing loss may appear inattentive or embarrassed, when in fact they cannot understand what is going on.

There are several visual impairments that are common to aging. There is often some decline in an individual's ability to focus on objects. This may be due to loss of flexibility in the lens of the eye. Depth perception, too, may be affected by loss of flexibility in the lens. In addition, the lens of the eye may become somewhat cloudy or, even worse, develop a cataract. Because of difficulties in focusing, older people often have problems with glare. They may have difficulty seeing the sharp contrasts that younger people see, or making precise adjustments to visual detail. But the removal of cataracts is a fairly safe and common operation. The more subtle problems—loss of flexibility in the lens—are less easily remedied (Kline & Schieber, 1985).

Older individuals often lose some visual acuity—the ability to distinguish fine detail. This could be partly due to the inflexibility of the lens and partly due to the loss of receptor cells within the eye. For many purposes, visual acuity can be helped with corrective lenses, including bifocals and trifocals (Kline & Schieber, 1985). Nevertheless, it is not uncommon for older people to have difficulty picking out visual details—whether it is reading names on mailboxes, distinguishing a staircase from a confusing carpet pattern, or simply reading the newspaper (Perlmutter, 1978).

The sense of taste shows considerable stability, even into old age. The ability to taste sugar is particularly consistent (Bartoshuk & Weiffenbach, 1990). There does appear to be some decline in the ability to taste bitter (Spitzer, 1988). People with hypertension (high blood pressure) seem to have more trouble tasting salt than other elderly do. This may be attributable to their medication. But Mary Spitzer (1988) has also hypothesized that these people may have always had high salt discrimination thresholds and may, therefore, have needed more salt in their diets in order to taste it at all. This in turn may contribute to the onset of hypertension.

The elderly seem to have some trouble distinguishing tastes within blended foods. This seems more attributable to declines in sense of smell than decrements in taste (Bartoshuk & Weiffenbach, 1990). The sense of smell shows fairly marked declines compared to taste. In any case, these sensory losses may contribute to the nutritional difficulties often seen among the elderly.

There may also be declines in the vestibular system (Ochs et al., 1985). The vestibular sensory receptors that detect gravity changes as well as those that respond to changes in head position decrease markedly. These changes may contribute to the increase in falling that presents a serious health threat to the elderly.

Many people find that it takes longer to perceive something through the sensory system (Hoyer & Plude, 1980). This slowing down of arousal and reaction to sensory stimulation is common to other bodily systems as well. Each of the types of sensory decline described here are quite common among elderly individuals. But they certainly do not affect all older people, and there is wide variation in the pattern and degree of sensory loss.

MUSCLES, BONES, AND MOBILITY Muscle weight and, consequently, strength and endurance decrease with age. The structure and composition of the muscle cells themselves are altered as they accumulate more fat. Muscle function slows down, and it takes longer for a muscle to achieve a state of relaxation after exertion (Gutmann, 1977). Muscles function less efficiently if the cardiovascular system fails to deliver enough nutrients or if it does not remove all toxic waste products. The blood vessels become less elastic, and some become clogged; consequently, fewer capillaries deliver blood to the muscles. Poor lung function may reduce oxygen supply. Fine motor coordination and the speed of reaction time decrease (Botwinick, 1984; Shock, 1952b). Muscle function is also affected by the changing structure and composition of the skeleton. The bones become more hollow, brittle, and weak; because they are more porous, they are more likely to fracture and take longer to mend. The decrease in density of bones that results in brittleness is called **osteoporosis.** Older women are particularly susceptible to this condition as a result of reduced levels of estrogen after menopause (Belsky, 1984). In advanced old age, healing may be incomplete, requiring implantation of metal plates (Tonna, 1977).

osteoporosis A bone disease in which the density of bones decreases, resulting in brittleness; older women are particularly susceptible to this disease.

Decline in the senses of smell and taste may be partially responsible for the poor nutrition and the lack of interest in food common to elderly people.

As we grow older, our lungs often have a reduced total capacity for the intake of oxygen. This reduced capacity tends to be caused more by smoking and air pollution than by the normal aging process.

HEART, LUNGS, AND OTHER ORGANS   The heart, although a highly specialized muscle, suffers from some of the same problems as other muscles. In addition, the heart depends on the efficiency of the entire cardiovascular system, which has a variety of problems as it ages. The result is decreased maximum blood flow to and from the heart, increased recovery time after each contraction, and other strains (Timiras, 1978).

In old age, the lungs often have a reduced total capacity for intake of oxygen. Much lung trouble may be attributable not to the normal aging process, but to a series of significant, prolonged "insults" to the lung tissue caused by smoking and air pollution.

The immune system also changes; the production of antibodies peaks during adolescence and then starts to decline. The result is that by old age, people have less protection against microorganisms and disease (La Rue & Jarvic, 1982).

These sensory and systemic slowdowns commonly accompany age. But not all old people show these signs of aging. Studies show that people who remain physically fit and active can perform as well on tests as younger people who are not physically fit (Birren et al., 1980). Additionally, we cannot say that the predictable biological course of nature is the only explanation for physical aging. Many people who become deaf in old age have had some kind of accident or illness earlier in life—like a firecracker that went off too close to their ears. Similarly, for most sensory deficiencies and defects of the internal organs, individual events begin the process of decline. Lifelong smokers may develop cancer in later years. An old woman with back trouble may have suffered strain as a young mother picking up her children. A 65-year-old man with heart trouble may have had early warning signs with a brief illness at age 40. We therefore cannot conclude that the changes that come with age are all part of a "normal" aging process. The kind of life that individuals have led, and the types of illness or accidents that they have had all contribute to the aging process. These factors are sometimes called secondary, or even pathological, aging factors.

Health, Disease, and Nutrition

Patterns of illness shift throughout the life cycle. One major difference between childhood and late adulthood is the incidence of acute versus chronic diseases. In childhood, acute diseases, which last a brief time and often climax with a fever and a rash, are very common. Older adults, however, often suffer from chronic conditions—illnesses that occur repeatedly or never go away at all. Among older adults, the most common chronic conditions are arthritis, heart conditions, and high blood pressure, as well as the visual and hearing impairments previously discussed (Belsky, 1984). The elderly are also prone to injuries and accidental falls. Chronic diseases and impairments touch the lives of a substantial number of the elderly, with 85% of people over age 65 reporting at least one such chronic condition and 50% reporting two or more (Belsky, 1984).

This increase in health problems reflects, to a great extent, the body's decreased ability to cope with stress, including the stress of disease. (Recall from Chapter 18 the relationship between stress and disease.) A disease that may have easily been shaken off by a younger person—for example, a respiratory infection—may linger and perhaps cause permanent damage, increasing the likelihood of recurrence. In old age, although the ability to cope with stress declines, the number of stressful events may be on the rise (Timiras, 1978). Stress arises from health problems, such as loss of sight and hearing, as well as from the life-cycle crises of retirement and widowhood.

Socioeconomic factors, race, and sex all play a part in the occurrence of illness in old age. In fact, in people over age 25, the days of restricted activity due to sickness show a higher correlation with socioeconomic background than with age (Kimmel, 1974). Similar data exist for the leading causes of death among the aged. The majority of deaths in those over age 65 are attributable to three categories: cardiovascular disease, cancer, and stroke. The rates are higher for men than for women in all categories. Caucasians suffer from a rate of cardiovascular disease that is twice as high as the rate for Asians (National Center for Health Statistics, 1990).

NUTRITION   Some of the poor health of old age may be due to poor diet or improper nutrition. Because of the lessened physical activity of old age and slowdowns in body metabolism, the elderly do not require as much food as younger adults. But the eating habits of a lifetime persist into old age, and, consequently, many elderly people are overweight. At the same time, a great many are also anemic and malnourished because they are too poor or unknowledgeable to buy sufficient quantities of nutritious food. Many old people, particularly African-Americans and Hispanics, suffer deficiencies in iron, calcium, and vitamins A and C (National Dairy Council, 1977).

In the United States, overeating is a common problem. By the time they are 65 years old, individuals require at least 20% fewer calories than younger adults. But they still need nearly as much of the basic nutrients; it is not unusual for older Americans to be both overweight and undernourished. Much of the problem lies in the overconsumption of fats. As it ages, the body becomes less able to use the various kinds of fats in many foods. Fat that is not used is stored in the body, even along the walls of the arteries. There it may harden and form plates that reduce the flow of blood to the heart. This condition is called **atherosclerosis,** or hardening of the arteries, and it is responsible for many of the heart conditions prevalent in

atherosclerosis Hardening of the arteries. A common condition of aging caused by the body's increasing inability to use excess fats in the diet. These fats are stored along the walls of arteries, and, when they harden, restrict the flow of blood.

FOCUS ON AN ISSUE

SLEEP PATTERNS AND THE ELDERLY

Do the elderly suffer from insomnia? A number of studies have investigated this question, and their findings tell us something about why some older people cannot sleep.

Mary A. Carskadon and her colleagues (1979) at the Stanford University Sleep Research Center monitored the sleep of 24 people, 12 men and 12 women, over the age of 65. Despite the fact that none of the subjects had a history of sleeping problems, the researchers found that a significant number suffered from patterns of interrupted sleep at night and sleepiness during the day. In 9 out of the 24 subjects, the interrupted sleep could be traced to disturbed breathing patterns that caused sleep disturbances during the night; the breathing problems of several subjects awakened them between 20 and 30 times an hour. As might be expected, these subjects were also more sleepy during the day than any of the others, but this problem was by no means theirs alone. In general, the elderly subjects were more sleepy during the day than young adults or children studied under similar conditions.

Why, with all these real sleep disturbances, did none of the subjects complain about their sleep? "One suggestion," say the researchers, "is that these individuals, accepting the stereotyped view of sleep in older persons, believe that their disturbed sleep is the norm for people their age" (Carskadon et. al., 1979, p. 148).

How common are these sleep disturbances in a larger, random sample of the elderly? What is it that awakens them? Sonia Ancoli-Israel and her colleagues interviewed a large sample of people over age 65 and asked them to wear recording devices overnight, from 6 P.M. to 8 A.M. They measured two kinds of sleep disturbances, sleep apnea and periodic movement in sleep. Sleep apnea is an interruption in breathing of at least 10 seconds that occurs at least five times per hour. Periodic movements are measured as repeated leg jerks. Both of these symptoms tend to cause brief arousal in the sleeper. In this broad sample, fully 66% of those over age 65 had either sleep apnea or periodic movements, or both. Quite understandably, most of these elderly people with sleep interruption took frequent naps during the day and in the evening.

The sleeping patterns of the elderly cannot be understood unless they are viewed as part of a lifelong continuum of change. Studies have shown that as we grow older, we spend less total time sleeping. Whereas an average newborn sleeps 16 hours a day, 8- to 12-year-olds sleep 10 hours, adults 8 hours, and the elderly significantly less time than that (Kales, 1979). In addition, as time passes, we spend fewer hours in deep sleep, somewhat less time dreaming, and have more periods of wakefulness that disrupt sleep (Williams, Karacan, & Hursch, 1974, cited in Regestein, 1979).

These changing sleep patterns affect the elderly most severely, but they also affect adults in the prime of life. A 30-year-old, for example, spends less than half the amount of time in Stage 4 sleep than a 20-year-old and has more than twice the amount of wakefulness during the night. (The average 20-year-old lies awake 5% of the night.) This trend continues throughout life, and by the time a person is 85 years old, he or she spends one-fifth of the night lying awake (Feinberg & Carlson, 1968, cited in Regestein, 1979).

Despite these general findings, sleeplessness in the elderly varies greatly from individual to individual. Severe sleep problems are not an inevitable part of growing old. When they do occur, they should be examined thoroughly to make sure they are not caused by medical problems.

old age. Atherosclerosis is so common in the older populations in the United States and western Europe that it is almost considered a normal part of aging. But this condition is rare in some non-Western countries with radically different diets (Belsky, 1984).

With age, changes in the bones and muscles require changes in diet. As we pointed out earlier, due to osteoporosis the bones of the aged become fragile and porous. One reason is that, over the years, bones lose more calcium than they absorb from food. Middle-aged and older people are thus frequently advised to supplement their diets with calcium. Also, with aging, the muscle tone of the intestines decreases, and old people are often constipated. Nutritionists recommend that they add high-fiber foods to their diets, such as bran, and drink adequate amounts of water to maintain proper bowel function (National Dairy Council, 1977).

Serious, intentional drug abuse is not a major problem among the elderly. In fact, the most popular "recreational drug" used by this age group is alcohol, and, by and large, older Americans are more moderate drinkers than members of younger age groups (Snyder & Way, 1979). Nevertheless, some doctors are convinced that as much as one-third of the elderly are hospitalized because of the overuse, misuse, or abuse of drugs (Poe & Holloway, 1980). How can this be? How can people who as a group show such moderation be plagued by such a rate of complication? Clearly this is not just a problem of voluntary overindulgence. The problem for some people may be that they have a reduced need for a particular prescription drug because of changing body chemistry, but the change goes undetected for a time. In addition, older people often take several drugs for different conditions, and they sometimes fail to mention all drugs to the attending physician. These drugs can interact and have a toxic effect. In fact, there have been cases of octogenarians who enter the hospital with numerous symptoms and a depressed level of functioning that would suggest they were close to death, yet when two or three forms of medication were given in reduced dosages or not given at all, the individuals returned to a level of functioning that they had not enjoyed for a few years (Poe & Holloway, 1980). Indeed, drug effects may produce symptoms that mimic the dementias (for example, Alzheimer's disease). Tranquilizers, such as Valium or Librium, and cardiac medication, such as digitalis, can produce disorientation and confusion (Rudd & Balschke, 1982; Salzman, 1982).

Another contributing factor to the involuntary abuse of drugs among the elderly is that older people, like very young children, have difficulty clearing large amounts of drugs through organ systems such as the liver and kidneys.

CAUSES OF AGING

We have discussed some factors in aging, such as stress, heredity, and repeated insults to the body, but until now we have not considered any theory of "normal" aging or contrasted various theories. What is the physiology of aging? What happens to cells and organs, and can that process be slowed down or stopped? Can advances in medical science or new environmental controls slow the beat of that time clock that measures aging? Many theories have been proposed, many with merit, but none is conclusive. Some are too complex for full discussion here, but the central issues are worth considering.

Hereditary and Environmental Factors

Many kinds of aging are observed in nature: Plants flower, go to seed, die, and regenerate each year according to a preprogrammed genetic code; trees grow until they can no longer raise nutrients and fluid to their highest points—a span

Genetic inheritance is a strong component of the aging process, as shown by the identical aging rates and patterns of identical twins. Here are two women at ages 12, 17, 67, and 91.

of years predictable according to their species. In lower mammals, aging and death usually occur at the same time as loss of fertility; as soon as the younger generation is successfully launched in the world, the parent generation dies. Humans are among the few mammals that are an exception to this rule (elephants are another). The human life cycle extends well beyond reproductive capacity, which ends roughly at age 50 for women and later for men (Kimmel, 1974).

It is clear from studying several species that each plant or animal's characteristic life span has a hereditary component. In humans, the genetic influence is particularly striking in studies of identical twins. Identical twins grow bald, accumulate wrinkles, and shrink at the same rate, despite long separations. Identical twins who die of natural causes often die at the same time. Fraternal twins, on the other hand, may age at different rates and have dissimilar life spans (Kallman & Sander, 1949). For the hereditary components in the aging process to be completely expressed, however, all other factors, such as stress, accidents, and diseases, would have to be canceled out or held aside. Because this would be impossible, we must consider other processes both inside and outside the body that determine how much of the genetic potential will be fulfilled—or whether we can extend that genetic potential.

External factors that affect aging range from fatal car accidents to childhood diseases to air pollution. Jones (1959) has studied a number of reversible and permanent external factors that lengthen or shorten life expectancy. For example, rural life versus city life adds 5 years, as does married versus single status. Obesity has a consistently negative effect, taking 3.6 years off the lives of those who are 25% overweight and 15.1 years off the life expectancy of those who are 67%

overweight. With the spread of nuclear reactors, radiation has become another external aging factor. High doses—as in radiation treatments—damage chromosomes in the cell nuclei, and chromosomal damage has been seen to accelerate the aging process (Schock, 1977).

Theories of Aging

But how does aging actually happen? Does the genetic clock simply run down, or must cells and organs be damaged by chemical wear and tear? And if we understand senescence—the aging process—can we slow its progress? The majority of theories of aging can be grouped into two categories—the wear-and-tear theories and the preprogrammed or clock theories.

WEAR AND TEAR   The wear-and-tear theories of aging focus primarily on internal cellular processes. They compare the human body to a machine that simply wears out as a result of constant use, with the added accumulation of cellular insults and injuries. In one such theory, for example, it is thought that, as cells age, they have a harder time disposing of waste. Extra substances, particularly a fatty substance called lipofusein, accumulate in cells, particularly in the blood and muscle cells. Eventually, these substances take up space and slow things down, so that the normal cell processes cannot occur. But most gerontologists think that this accumulation of chemicals such as lipofusein is a result rather than a cause of aging.

A more popular wear-and-tear theory involves the action of pieces of molecules called free radicals. In the course of the normal use of oxygen for virtually every cellular process, small, highly charged, unpaired electrons are left over. These free radicals react with other chemical compounds in the cell and may interrupt normal cell functioning. Normally the cell has repair mechanisms to reduce the damage done by free radicals. But after a major injury such as a heart attack or exposure to radiation, high free radical damage is noted. Researchers are exploring the effects of some dietary substances, like vitamins C and E, which seem to help reduce the effects of free radicals. But excessive amounts of vitamin E, for example, have negative side effects as well. As yet, there is no evidence that increased levels of vitamins C or E will increase human life expectancy (Walford, 1983).

There are other wear-and-tear theories. Damage might be done to DNA in the genes, for example. It is known that the ultraviolet light in sunshine can cause damage to the DNA in skin cells. Usually, when the genes in a cell are damaged, either the cell repairs itself, or the cell dies and is replaced by other cells. In older people, there is less efficient repair and damage remains. Perhaps aging is simply the decline in self-repair capacity.

Wear and tear seems to occur to tissues and systems as well. Sometimes the connective tissue, or the cross-links between cells, are affected. They become rigid and lose some of their flexibility. In aging, the immune system also becomes less efficient. Older people are less able to fight off disease. Sometimes their immune cells attack their own body's healthy cells, such as in rheumatoid arthritis or in certain kidney ailments. But these processes described by wear-and-tear theories, although fairly common, might be a result of some deeper aging process rather than the cause of aging itself.

It's difficult to predict how or at what rate people will age. Statistics about aging represent an average, not a prediction for every individual.

PREPROGRAMMING   A second type of theory of aging involves genetic programming. These theories suggest that there is some kind of built-in timer, or clock, that is set to go off at a certain time. This clock may be located in each cell, or it may be an external pacemaker, perhaps in the brain. At the cellular level, it has been found that particular kinds of cells seem to be preprogrammed to divide only a certain number of times. For example, some human embryo cells have been shown to divide only about 50 times before quitting. Even if you freeze these cells after 30 divisions, when you thaw them they will only divide another 20 times. In different animal species and in different types of cells, the number of reproductions varies. This suggests a built-in cellular clock. Individuals may vary in number of cellular reproductions by genetic preprogramming.

Another "clock" theory suggests that there is some sort of pacemaker, or timer, housed in the hypothalamus and also in the pituitary gland. The pituitary gland releases a hormone shortly after puberty that begins the decline process at a programmed rate.

No single theory as yet explains aging. Indeed, it is probably a combination of two or three theories, at least. Researchers are actively studying the aging process at all levels and are studying ways to slow down the process. Some of this research is disease-related. The study of the relationship between childhood cancer or juvenile arthritis and premature aging is an example. Other research is aimed at helping people to live a healthy, disease-free life until close to the end of their natural life span. Despite recent advances, the likelihood of dramatically extending the normal life span seems a long way off.

COGNITIVE CHANGES WITH AGE

Many people are inclined to think that an old man's intellect is decayed. If a young or middle-aged man, when leaving a building, does not recollect where he laid his hat, it is nothing; but if the same inattention is discovered in an old man, people will shrug their shoulders and say, "His memory is going."

Cognition in the Later Years

There is remarkably little decline in intellectual functioning as a result of "normal" aging. Most mental skills remain intact. Extensive research has demonstrated that age-related decline in memory is not as general, or as representative, or as severe as was previously thought (Perlmutter et al., 1987). Many of the memory problems that some older people suffer are not the inevitable consequences of age, but are due to other factors such as depression, inactivity, or side effects of prescription drugs. But when cognitive decline does occur—and there is a decline in speed of cognitive processing—there are compensations, so that any loss has very little effect on daily living (Perlmutter et al., 1987; Salthouse, 1985). Let us look at a few of these changes.

SPEED OF PERFORMANCE   One of the major documented changes in late adult cognition is a decline in the speed of both mental and physical performance (Birren et al., 1980). Many studies have shown that intellectual functions that depend heavily on speed of performance decline in older people (Salthouse, 1985). Older people have slower reaction times, slower perceptual processing abilities, and slower cognitive processes. Some of this slowness may be due to the fact that older subjects seem to value accuracy more than younger subjects do. When tested, older people make fewer guesses and try to answer each item correctly. Also, they may be less familiar with some of the tasks used in testing situations. For example, older people are often compared with college students in tests of recall of nonsense syllables. The students regularly practice learning new vocabularies for examinations. Older people have less recent practice. Some of these comparisons seem unrealistic (Labouvie-Vief, 1985). Older people are sometimes slower because they have not practiced a particular skill lately.

But there are compensations that older people use to make up for their loss of speed. In one study, older typists did just as well as younger typists, despite a seemingly slower reaction time and finger dexterity. Why was this so? When the researcher limited the number of words that the typists could look ahead, the older typists slowed down considerably and the younger ones were much less affected. It appears that older typists had learned to look further ahead in order to type quickly (Salthouse, 1985). With fairly limited training, older people are often able to compensate for loss of speed and, in many cases, recover much of their former speed (Willis, 1985).

MEMORY   Perhaps no single aspect of aging has been studied more thoroughly than memory. Recall the information-processing model of memory discussed in Chapter 9. Information is first fleetingly retained in a sensory memory—a visual or auditory storage—then sent to a short-term or primary memory for organization and encoding, and then to a long-term secondary memory for retention. In studies of adult memory, we also talk about a more permanent or tertiary memory that holds more remote information. Each of these presumed levels of memory has been studied in some detail (Poon, 1985).

Sensory storage is that very brief visual or auditory memory that holds sensory input for just a few seconds prior to processing the information. It does appear that older individuals are able to pick up and hold slightly less information than are young adults. On average, they have a slightly shorter perceptual span, particularly when two things are happening at once. It is not clear why this is so.

The cognitive powers of reasoning and understanding continue to grow throughout the life span.

Is there a decline in the visual or auditory system? Is there less selective attention or pattern recognition? Or is there, perhaps, less motivation to succeed in these very precise tasks? In any case, it is unlikely that the modest sensory memory loss observed in later adulthood has much effect at all on daily living. In daily life, most things can be looked at for longer than the fraction of a second used in these laboratory experiments (Poon, 1985). Highway signs may be an exception to this, creating some difficulty for the older driver.

Primary memory is that limited capacity storage that holds things that are "in mind" at the moment—a telephone number that you just looked up, for example. Most studies find no significant difference between older adults and younger adults in primary memory.

Compared to sensory memory and primary memory, secondary memory has some clear age differences, according to most studies. In studies of learning and recall, older people often remember fewer items on a list or fewer details in a design. But are these differences due to the storage capacity of the older person or to the processes of learning or remembering? In some memory studies, it appears that older individuals are less efficient in organizing, rehearsing, and encoding material to be learned. Yet, with some careful instruction and a little practice, older people improve markedly (Willis, 1985). Even the very old (near age 80) show some benefits from training (Willis & Nesselroade, 1990).

There are other age differences in performance of secondary memory tasks. Older subjects tend to do better on recognition tasks than on recall of such things as vocabulary lists (Craik & McDowd, 1987). They tend to be somewhat selective in what they retain. They may balk at memorizing useless word lists but do very well in the comprehension of paragraphs (Meyer, 1987). In one study, it was found that older people remembered interesting metaphors such as "the seasons are the costumes of nature" better than did college students. They did not try to reproduce the sentence exactly, but rather understood and remembered its meaning (Labouvie-Vief & Schell, 1982). In other words, older people tend to remember what is useful and important in their lives. This reminds us, then, that development occurs in a context and that, even as we age, environmental demands and opportunities shape our skills and abilities (Lerner, 1990). Finally, the elderly tend to perform better if given careful instruction on how to sort and organize material. With training, the performance of older people on memory tasks improves considerably (Poon, 1985).

The effectiveness of the training is not limitless, however. Even after training, the oldsters may not reach young adult levels (Campbell & Charness, 1990). In some studies comparing older versus younger people, the training actually increased the gap in performance because the young adults made even greater gains than the elderly (Kliegl, Smith, & Baltes, 1990). This may imply that older adults may have less *developmental reserve capacity* (Baltes, 1987) than do young adults, at least on some skills. In other words, the elderly have less "room for improvement" or less plasticity.

What some have called tertiary memory, or the memory for remote events, appears to remain fairly intact in older adults. Indeed, in some studies, older adults are better at recalling details of historical events than are younger adults. This is especially true of historical events that the elderly experienced but the young adults only learned about second-hand.

It should also be noted that older adults, like other people, vary a great deal in their ability to remember. Those who are better educated generally do better at memory tasks. Those who keep actively involved in intellectual activities perform better than those who are inactive.

In summary, there are very few age differences found in sensory memory, in primary short-term memory, or in tertiary (remote) memory. The differences found in secondary memory depend on several factors. Older individuals may do poorly if the memory task requires organizational and rehearsal techniques that are not well practiced. Most will improve, however, if organization and memory strategies are briefly taught. Memory in older people is also selective. More interesting and meaningful material is remembered more easily.

EXPERIENCE AND EXPERTISE   Most laboratory studies on learning and memory, on problem solving and the like, are conducted using relatively novel material. The idea is to eliminate the effects of past experience. And yet one of the central aspects of later adulthood is the wealth of past life experience. It is a bit odd to conduct learning and memory studies comparing college students and older people and use exclusively novel tasks and new, sometimes meaningless, information. College students are at the point in their lives where coping with new information is an important adaptive strength. People in later adulthood function best when they are able to use the wealth of background and experience that they have accumulated (Labouvie-Vief, 1985). Perhaps rather than measuring older adult cognitive capacities according to strategies appropriate to young adults, we should measure adult cognition experience and expertise (Salthouse, 1987).

What are some of the ways in which experts differ from novices? First, experts tend to have more knowledge—both declarative knowledge (factual) and procedural knowledge (action or "how-to" information). But, more than that, this knowledge is better organized in experts. There are more connections. They quickly and easily recognize patterns and link these to appropriate procedures and necessary responses. This is true whether we are talking about experts in physics, computer programming, music, or bridge playing. Although experts remember critical information better, they are not any different from novices in recalling material that is not organized or structured or related to a particular problem. For example, in a recent study of older and younger chess players, both intermediates and experts, there were two tasks. First, they were shown chess boards displaying a game in progress and were asked to remember the position of each and every piece. The younger chess players did better than the older chess players. Then, they were asked to make an appropriate move. The experts (old and young) were much better at this. They did not need to remember where all the pieces were in order to make a good move. Their memory was selective and organized, and there were connections between the particular patterns of the pieces and the appropriate chess moves (Charness, 1981; Salthouse, 1987).

Notice, then, that experience does not guarantee the maintenance of a particular skill. The older chess players could not remember every piece. Older typists are slower under controlled conditions. Elderly architects do suffer losses in visual–spatial skills (Salthouse et al., 1990). But experience serves to mediate these losses. The more experienced architect may know, almost automatically, which building materials will work best, thereby saving time in drawing up the plans. The older typist may read longer spans of words, enabling speedy typing. These compensations allow the elderly to continue being productive at work and independent at home (Salthouse, 1990). The opportunities provided by the environment to develop and practice these compensations clearly influence functioning. Furthermore, these findings exemplify that development often involves a trade-off; as one skill improves, another declines (or vice versa) (Baltes, 1987).

Repeated experience tends to increase not only the amount of the information but also its organization. Probably, individuals continually restructure their knowledge system in order to make it more cohesive, correct, and accessible. This may be true for common knowledge, such as how to use the Yellow Pages, or for occupational knowledge, such as how to perform a technical procedure more efficiently. Cognitive tests rarely measure these experiential influences on the knowledge and problem solving of older adults (Salthouse, 1987).

Cognitive Decline

Clearly, some individuals do experience a decline in cognitive functioning, either temporarily, progressively, or intermittently. In some cases, this is relatively minor and fleeting. In other cases, it is severe and progressive.

SECONDARY CAUSES OF DECLINE It should be remembered that most cognitive decline is not intrinsic to the aging process itself, but rather is attributable to such things as failing health, poor formal education, poverty, or low motivation. Some of these so-called secondary factors deserve consideration.

Psychological Expectations. At any age, our beliefs or judgments about our own abilities have some effect on how well we perform. Some older adults fully believe that they are going to lose their memory and be less able to do things than they were in the past. They expect to be somewhat helpless and dependent on others, and to lose control of some of their own life. Older people often imagine their fate will be in the hands of luck, chance, or powerful others. Individuals who believe this often do become less competent and less in control. They have less self-esteem and show less persistence and effort. It becomes a downward cycle. Sometimes, this is called learned helplessness. If they can be convinced that they can take more control of their lives, and that cognitive loss is not inevitable, they often improve quite markedly (Perlmutter et al., 1987).

Mental Health. An individual's mental health affects his or her performance on cognitive tasks very directly. Depression is a common psychological reaction to loss, and many old people have several experiences of loss. Depression causes reduced concentration and attention and, hence, lower levels of cognitive function.

Other Factors. There are a number of other secondary factors that cause cognitive decline (Perlmutter et al., 1987). Some of the more important ones that have been carefully studied include the following:

1. Physical fitness affects one's ability to do mental tasks as well as physical tasks. On a wide range of tests of cognitive functions, those who were more physically fit performed at a higher level.

2. Nutritional deficits such as anemia, vitamin deficiencies, or choline deficiency result in poor performance on intellectual tasks. Choline, which is found in meat, fish, and egg yolks, is used by the brain to manufacture acetylcholine, a chemical that is essential for the transmission of nerve signals (Wurtman, 1979).

3. Use of alcohol, even if moderate, over a long period of time results in reduced primary and secondary memory. More extensive drinking tends to interfere with ongoing life experiences and adequate nutrition. Both directly and indirectly, alcohol impairs mental functions.

4. Prescription and over-the-counter drugs, from sleeping pills to pain relievers and drugs for hypertension, have side effects that reduce alertness and attention. Drugs are not always easily cleared from the kidneys or from the liver. As an individual gets older, smaller dosages of a drug may be just as effective. Sometimes, a simple reduction in the amount of a drug used can improve mental function dramatically.

5. Disuse of mental functioning. After periods of prolonged illness, social isolation, or depression, some individuals do not return to their former level of functioning. The old adage "Use it or lose it" seems to hold some truth (Perlmutter et al., 1987).

dementia The progressive deterioration of intellectual capacities that sometimes afflicts older adults.

DEMENTIA Many people fear that dementia, or to use the more popular term, senility, is an inevitable curse of old age. To them, growing old means losing emotional and intellectual control and becoming a helpless, useless person who drains the resources of everyone around. According to gerontologists, although the fear of senility is real, the incidence and nature of the disease have been exaggerated and distorted. Far from being inevitable, senility, which is also known as organic brain syndrome, affects only 3% to 4% of those over age 65 (Brocklehurst, 1977, cited in Wershow, 1981). Unfortunately, a recent community-based survey indicates that the rate increases dramatically in old-old age. The Boston-based survey indicated that nearly 20% of the 75- to 84-year-olds tested appeared to suffer from Alzheimer's. The rate among community dwellers 85 years old and older appeared to be about 47% (Evans et al., 1989).

According to Kastenbaum (1979), senility is a "pattern of progressively deteriorating thought and behavior associated with irreversible brain damage" (p. 95). Senile people have a limited ability to grasp abstractions; they may repeat the same statements over and over again, lack ideas, think more slowly than normal people, and be unable to pay attention to those around them. Memory for recent events may be impaired. A senile person may clearly recall a childhood event but be unable to remember something that happened an hour before. Because of these symptoms of mental deterioration, the senile person may be unable to cope with such routine tasks as keeping clean and well groomed. Operating within the confines of a shrinking mental world, the senile person can no longer think, behave, or relate to people as he or she once did (Kastenbaum, 1979). The more appropriate term for this pattern of behavior is **dementia.**

Unfortunately, the label "senile" is all too often attached to elderly people who show even the slightest sign of confusion, mental lapses, or disoriented behavior, even though these problems may be attributable to a number of other causes. A clear diagnosis is difficult given the wide range of secondary causes.

FOCUS ON AN ISSUE

ALZHEIMER'S DISEASE

It is possible that 50% of patients diagnosed as being senile actually have some form of Alzheimer's disease. That can mean as many as 2 million Americans, or 5% of the elderly, and perhaps 60% of nursing home patients. It has been suggested, further, that Alzheimer's disease may be the fourth leading cause of death among older people (Schneck, Reisberg, & Ferris, 1982).

Alzheimer's disease involves a progressive deterioration of brain cells, especially in the cerebral cortex. It has been best diagnosed on autopsy as a characteristic pattern of damaged areas that look like plaque and little bits of braided yarn. While the patient is alive the working diagnosis is usually made from the patient's pattern of regressive memory loss and disorientation. Also, physicians eliminate the possibility that the symptoms are due to other treatable conditions.

The effects of this disease are devastating both to the patient and to the patient's family. The first symptom is generally forgetfulness. In the beginning, minor things are forgotten; as the disease progresses, places, names, and routines may not be recalled, and finally even events that may have just occurred are forgotten. The forgetful phase is followed by a sense of confusion. It is much more difficult to plan and perform even simple routines—for example, it is hard to get something to eat when you cannot find the refrigerator. This loss of the familiar and the routine causes serious disorientation, confusion, and anxiety in the patient. At this point it becomes clear that the patient cannot be left alone, because he or she may unwittingly harm himself or herself. Finally, full dementia sets in. The patient is unable to do the most simple tasks, such as dressing or even eating. Familiar people are not recognized—even a devoted, caring spouse who has cared for the victim through several years of decline may suddenly appear as a stranger to the victim.

The impact on the family is significant. In a period of a few years, an independent adult becomes childlike, requiring constant care. When symptoms of the disease are first apparent, adaptations can easily be made. The environment can be simplified, and objects can be labeled—even the furniture. When the patient is going to be alone, a sandwich prepared earlier by a family member may prevent an unnecessary accident in the kitchen at mealtime. But when 24-hour care becomes necessary, major adaptations must be made. As the disease develops, it is reasonable for family members to feel grief and despair, as well as anger and frustration. Feelings of resentment, guilt, embarrassment, and isolation are likely. Although such feelings are justified, family members must continue to consider the feelings of the victim. In addition, the support of other families with similar experiences is particularly helpful (Cohen & Eisdorfer, 1986; Zarit et al., 1985).

Often the decision to place the patient in a nursing home must be made. Sometimes this decision is easier in the final stages, if the patient seems not to know where he or she is, even at home with familiar family members.

Improper nutrition as well as chronic insufficient sleep related to a physical illness, anxiety, depression, grief, or fear can distort thinking in young as well as old people. Heart or kidney problems that cause changes in normal body rhythms or metabolism or the accumulation of toxic body wastes may also affect the ability to think clearly. Confusion, agitation, and drowsiness can also be induced by drugs used to treat medical illnesses. In each of these cases, when the physical or emotional illness is effectively treated, the senilitylike symptoms also disappear (Kastenbaum, 1979).

Of those diagnosed as having dementia, approximately 50% will have Alzheimer's disease (see Focus on an Issue: Alzheimer's Disease). Another 30% or so will have had a series of ministrokes that damaged brain tissue. The rest will have a variety of diseases or disorders.

Adult education programs allow intellectually active older citizens to pursue interests and learn about new subjects.

If dementia is diagnosed, it is important that these patients receive help. A warm and friendly environment that motivates them to make better use of their remaining mental capacity should be provided.

Lifelong Education

Because the intellectual decline of old age is not nearly as steep as has been supposed, society has excellent reasons for keeping its older citizens' minds active and engaged. Perhaps as a result of this realization, there is now a growing trend for continuing education for the aged.

Adult education has support from state and federal governments, gerontologists, and the general public. Some tuition reduction or waiver for older students returning to college is now offered in most states (Long & Rossing, 1978). Prominent gerontologists, like Paola Timiras (1978), advocate continuing education to facilitate the difficult adjustment faced by retirement candidates in our work-oriented society. She suggests giving older workers a choice of retirement or reassignment to a suitable new job category, with any necessary retraining.

The basic principles for teaching older students are not so different from those for teaching teenagers. As in all courses, the more relevant or practical the subject matter, the more motivated to learn students of any age will be. The better organized the presentation and the more lucid the summaries, the more easily the material will be absorbed. Older students may require some extra planning on the teacher's part. Abstract concepts, disorganized presentations, and rote memory tasks may be better tolerated by 19-year-olds than by 69-year-olds. On the other hand, older students are sometimes more motivated to learn than younger ones.

"So you're a gifted child. I'm a gifted adult."

GENERATIONS: PAST, PRESENT, AND FUTURE

How does the experience of today's generation of senior citizens compare with that of generations in the past and generations yet to come? Which of these changes—in physical abilities or in cognitive capacities—are part of our preprogrammed aging clock? Are improvements in medical science likely to extend the average life span much beyond age 85? Many changes have been made in the physical and related intellectual health of older individuals. We have virtually eliminated many of the communicable diseases that had plagued earlier generations, such as typhus and diphtheria. Because of medical research, far fewer people die at early ages of chronic conditions and serious illnesses such as cancer, strokes, and heart attacks, although they may live with some handicaps or serious disabilities in their later years. Yet we find a significant drop in intellectual functioning in the last 2 years of life for many individuals, and researchers report a similar pattern in physical decline among the elderly (Fries & Crapo, 1981). Some have suggested that efforts to improve health through medical science, nutrition, exercise, better management of stress, and the like will result in more people living to age 80 or slightly beyond in good mental and physical health (Fries & Crapo, 1981).

But what about the social and psychological circumstances of future generations as compared to those of the past? Certainly looking back we can see a great deal of change. In 1910, individuals over the age of 65 constituted just 4.3% of the U.S. population. Reportedly, they lived with their families and were treated with some degree of respect. In 1960, this group constituted 9.3% of the population, a phenomenal rise due in large part to advances in medical science; this figure rose to 12.6% in 1990. This translates to over 31 million Americans. It is estimated that by 2030, there will be about 59 million Americans over age 65, constituting about 19% of the U.S. population (Bouvier, 1980; *Statistical Abstract of the United States,* 1990).

The rate of poverty among those over 65 was just being realized as an alarmingly large social statistic in the 1960s. However, the large array of social service programs, including more generous Social Security provisions, has reduced the number of senior citizens now living in poverty. Overall, 12% to 13% of elderly Americans live below the poverty line (Ford Foundation, 1989). This is a lower poverty rate than is found among young adults. But it masks the situation of some subgroups of elderly. Single oldsters, minorities, and women are at greater risk for poverty than are other elderly. For example, 27% of the Hispanic elderly and 60% of single African-American elderly women are poor (Ford Foundation, 1989).

What, from historical trends, can we predict for future generations? The experts disagree. The baby-boom generation will live longer than any previous cohort and will dramatically increase the proportion of the population that is elderly. Presumably many more of them will be living because of improved health care, nutrition, and so forth. Will they be more active and productive, and contribute more in later adulthood than any former generation, or will their need for health care and other social services overburden the rest of the population (Butler, 1983)?

STUDY OUTLINE

Aging: Myth and Reality

Ageism and Stereotypes. The period of old age has been the object of many stereotypes and half-truths. Although definite physical, intellectual, and psychological problems do occur in old age, individuals vary widely in their physical condition and cognitive abilities.

Four Decades of Life. Later adulthood spans four decades of life, from the "young-old" (those in their 60s) to the "very old-old" (those in their 90s and beyond). Healthy, active, recently retired individuals in their 60s are part of a different cohort and have quite different needs from the frail elderly of their parents' generation.

Generally, people in their 60s are still closely involved with family and friends, yet some must begin to cope with reduced incomes, the loss of friends and spouses, and waning physical strength; those in their 70s experience a contracted social world and may be ill; those in their 80s and 90s tend to withdraw from the world and are generally frail and in bad health.

The Aging Process

Physical Aging. The physical changes of aging include wrinkled skin and a slumped posture; muscles become less elastic and the skeleton shrinks. The sensory capacities decline, particularly hearing and vision. Muscle function slows, lung capacity decreases, and the bones become porous and fragile. Many of the defects and systemic slowdowns of old age are not universal; they can be the result of previous illnesses, accidents, and environmental influences, such as pollution. Some can be held in check or even reversed by exercise, better nutrition, and health care.

Causes of Aging

Hereditary and Environmental Factors. Aging is not a well-understood process. Many theories have been advanced to account for the physical changes that occur during the life span. That heredity influences the aging process and the length of life is shown by studies of identical twins. Other factors, such as urban or rural residence, marital status, obesity, and exposure to radiation also seem to affect longevity.

Theories of Aging. The wear-and-tear theory of aging proposes that the body's machinery simply wears out or that the body's cells are damaged as a result of a lifelong accumulation of waste products. Some researchers suggest that certain aspects of aging are preprogrammed. Genetic programming theories are based on the fact that the body's cells reproduce themselves a finite number of times or reproduce themselves imperfectly.

Cognitive Changes with Age

Cognition in the Later Years. Although many assume that cognitive ability declines steeply in old age, recent studies indicate that the losses are not substantial. Actual declines may occur gradually in the speed of mental and physical perfor-

mances; many of them, however, can be attributed to failing health, social isolation, lack of education, poverty, and low motivation.

There is some decline in secondary memory in later adulthood, particularly in short-term memory used for new learning. There is little or no loss in learning. There is little or no loss in sensory memory, primary memory, or memory for remote events.

Older people can perform well on memory tests if the information is ecologically valid for them, if they receive careful instructions on how to sort and organize the material, or if they develop strategies for coping with loss of memory.

Older people may solve problems better than younger people when they can make use of their past experiences. Experts, both young and old, make use of selective, well-organized memories to analyze and solve problems efficiently. The combination of these two factors can help older people compensate for the decline of a particular skill.

Cognitive Decline. Dementia (or senility) is identified as irreversible brain damage leading to deteriorating thought and behavior patterns. Dementia is caused by a disease such as Alzheimer's disease or by other insults such as a series of ministrokes. There are other causes of senilitylike symptoms, including improper nutrition, alcohol, the use of drugs for medical illnesses, and depressions.

KEY TERMS AND CONCEPTS

acetylcholine	dementia	periodic movement in sleep
acute diseases	free radicals	preprogrammed (clock) theories
ageism	learned helplessness	senility
Alzheimer's disease	lipofusein	sleep apnea
atherosclerosis	middle-aged-old	very old-old
choline	old-old	wear-and-tear theories
chronic diseases	osteoporosis	young-old

SELF-TEST QUESTIONS

1. What are some of the positive and negative views of aging held by our society? Describe these views in terms of myths and realities. Compare these views to the views of aging held by other cultures.

2. Why do we misrepresent older adults when we lump them into one category? Compare the distinctive features of those who are young-old, middle-aged-old, old-old, and very old-old.

3. Describe the physical changes that occur during the aging process in later adulthood. Do all individuals experience these changes? Please explain.

4. How do patterns of illness shift in late adulthood? What factors contribute to the illnesses commonly found in late adulthood?

5. Describe how the physical changes of old age might impact on an individual's self-image.

6. How do heredity and environment interact in the aging process?

7. Describe and compare the various theories of aging set forth in this chapter.

8. Discuss in detail the cognitive changes that take place in later adulthood. Include in your discussion some possible reasons for these changes and the strategies that older people often use to cope with these changes.

9. Describe a common research problem that exists in many studies of adult cognitive capacities. What strategies can be taken to avoid this problem? Please explain, using an example.

10. Is cognitive decline intrinsic to the aging process? Describe the factors that contribute to cognitive decline.

11. How does the experience of today's generation of senior citizens compare with that of generations in the past? Based on historical trends, what do you predict for future generations of senior citizens?

SUGGESTED READINGS

BURNSIDE, I. M., EBERSOLE, P., & MONEA, H. E. *Psychosocial caring throughout the life span*. New York: McGraw-Hill, 1979. Integrates and highlights the psychosocial issues of adulthood and old age with many useful case studies.

FOWLER, M., & McCUTCHEON, P. (Eds.). *Songs of experience: An anthology of literature on growing old*. Poems, diary entries, stories, musings, and inspiring words of wisdom from men and women in their final years—including E. B. White, Helen Hayes, Robert Coles, Eleanor Roosevelt, and many others.

PALMORE, E. B. *The facts of aging quiz: A handbook of uses and results*. New York: Springer, 1988. A glimpse of attitude research on aging including results that show stereotypes of aging among young and old.

WHITBOURNE, S. K. *The aging body: Physiological changes and psychological consequences*. New York: Springer-Verlag, 1985. An excellent review of physical aging, with extensive discussion of individual adaptation, adjustment, and reaction to these changes.

Two helpful resources for understanding Alzheimer's disease and for coping with the stress and personal turmoil of long-term care are the following:

COHEN, D., & EISDORFER, K. *The loss of self: A family resource for the care of Alzheimer's disease and related disorders*. New York: Norton, 1986.

ZARIT, S., ORR, N. K., & ZARIT, J. N. *The hidden victims of Alzheimer's disease: Families under stress*. New York: New York University Press, 1985.

These three books are personal reflections on later adulthood. The authors describe their own experiences, as well as the experiences of other older adults. They vary from the common to the profound and the humorous.

BLYTHE, R. *The view in winter: Reflections on old age*. New York: Penguin, 1979.

HUNTER, L., & MEMHARD, P. *The rest of my life*. Stamford, CT: Growing Pains Press, 1981.

SCOTT-MAXWELL, F. *The measure of my days*. New York: Penguin, 1979.

Chapter 20

Age is opportunity no less
Than youth itself, though in another dress,
And as the evening twilight fades away
The sky is filled with stars, invisible by day.

HENRY WADSWORTH LONGFELLOW
MORITURI SALUTARNUS

CHAPTER OUTLINE

Later Adulthood: Status Changes and a Time of Reflection

Sociologists call a change in role and position a **status passage.** Changes in status occur throughout life. The developmental tasks of adolescence, for example, prepare individuals for the tasks of early adulthood; the enlarged roles and responsibilities of early adulthood prepare them for the important tasks of middle adulthood. But the status changes of later adulthood may have some significant differences. The transition to retirement or widow- or widowerhood or the adjustment to ill health may signal the loss of power, responsibility, and autonomy (Rosow, 1974). On the other hand, retirement or great-grandparenthood may mark a new freedom to pursue one's own interests, or provide the opportunity to spend more time with friends and loved ones. The meaning of marker events, or of status changes, is often at least as important as the events themselves.

Margaret has been active all her life, working, raising children, and overcoming numerous hardships. She coped with serious poverty during the depression years, as well as the sudden death of her first husband. While caring for two small children, she single-handedly maintained a small, struggling business during the hardships of the war years and the period that followed. At midlife she sold her business, remarried, and held three part-time jobs simultaneously. Both at work and at home she was an efficient manager, constantly called on to untangle mishaps caused by others. Finally, in her mid-60s she retired to enjoy some measure of leisure and economic security, and to fulfill her dream of traveling to foreign countries. She enjoyed a decade of proud, independent adventure, both with and without her less energetic husband. She took comfort in her own abilities to make for herself the life she had dreamed and to adapt to ever-new and changing events. Her minor physical ailments were a mere "nuisance." Then, at age 78, she had two successive "mild" strokes. Within months her confidence was shattered. She feared appearing in public lest she fall, or lest people notice her slightly unsteady gait. She ate alone so that no one would see that she sometimes spilled her food. She stopped driving, stopped cooking, stopped gardening, for fear of what "might happen." Gradually, she allowed her husband to take over all the housework. Her image of herself as one who could independently challenge and overcome adversity had vanished.

The effect of many life events of later adulthood, therefore, depends in large part on the meaning that an individual attaches to those events. Retirement, for example, may be thought of as the signaling of the end of an individual's usefulness or productiveness in the work force, or the end of a major part of one's identity—as truck driver, dentist, dancer, or corporate executive. But retirement may mean something quite different to a man who has spent the past 30 years

CHAPTER OBJECTIVES

By the time you have finished this chapter, you should be able to do the following:

- Discuss personality changes and developmental tasks in late adulthood.
- Describe the physical, economic, and social conditions that influence how well an individual in late adulthood adjusts to retirement.
- Describe the patterns of family and personal relationships that define many of the stresses and satisfactions in later adulthood.
- Discuss the relationship between the needs of the elderly and the social policies and attitudes concerning aging in the United States.

status passage A change in the role and position that occurs when an individual enters adolescence, becomes a parent, retires, or becomes a widow or widower.

hating his factory job. To such a person, retirement may mean release from tedium, drudgery, and subservience to authority. (One factor that predicts well for successful adjustment to retirement is "dislike of one's job.") Similarly, widow- or widowerhood may mean sudden release from the toil of caring for a chronically ill spouse and the freedom to structure one's time. Illness and physical disabilities are some of the most difficult life circumstances to cope with during the period of later adulthood. But here, too, there is wide variation in styles of coping. As one man commented, "I don't get around the way I used to, but I've never enjoyed my garden like I have these last few years, and that last grandchild is a sheer joy. I wonder why I missed the others when they were this age."

PERSONALITY AND AGING

It is difficult to make generalizations about personality, life satisfaction, or even developmental tasks in later adulthood. Recall the many differences between the vigorous, healthy, recently retired "young old" and the frail, elderly octogenarian. Furthermore, each individual has a unique pattern of attitudes, values, and beliefs about old age and about himself or herself, and a pattern of life experiences that reinforces or contradicts those beliefs. Yet, given these differences, there are still some common events and concerns in later life.

Eventually, in later adulthood, many individuals must confront the problems of sensory decline or ill health in themselves or in a close friend or relative. Many must confront reduced status, or productivity, and reduced income levels. The longer they live, the more likely they are to experience the death of friends or of a spouse. Most older people think in terms of their own vulnerability. Sometime in middle age, adults often stop thinking of their age in terms of "time-since-birth" and begin to think in terms of "time-left-to-live" (Neugarten, 1977). For some, the problems they confront are overwhelming. They become preoccupied with their health, with their restricted economic circumstances, with the hardships they must overcome, and with their lack of autonomy. But this is not the dominant pattern for most individuals in later adulthood. Stereotypical thinking about aging too often paints a bleak, negative picture that some of the aged themselves accept. In fact, the great majority of the aged perceive themselves in totally different terms. A survey of a large group of old people, for example, noted that although many elderly agreed that "life was really tough for most people over 65," they and their friends were, for some reason, exceptions to the rule (Harris et al., 1978, p. 96).

Life satisfaction and adjustment in later adulthood depend on a number of factors. But, according to a now-classic study of well-being and satisfaction (Larson, 1978), such satisfaction has little relationship to age itself. Health is considered the most important factor. Money, social class, marital status, adequacy of housing, amount of social interaction, and even transportation are also important factors in whether or not older adults feel satisfied with their lives. One's outlook in earlier periods of one's life tends to influence feelings of satisfaction in later adulthood. Although life satisfaction itself is comparable in young and old adults, the sources of satisfaction may change. Younger adults may gain the most satisfaction from achievements and advances in work, self-development, and other areas, while the elderly may be satisfied to simply maintain their functioning (Bearon, 1989).

Stability and Change in Later Life

Does the way people feel, think, and react remain fairly consistent over the course of adulthood, or are there clear, predictable changes that come with the expected role shifts of old age? Researchers do not agree.

ACTIVITY OR DISENGAGEMENT   Early theories of aging (for example, Cumming & Henry, 1961) suggested that the healthiest way for people to age was to withdraw or disengage from society. Withdrawal supposedly reflected a healthy acceptance of the aging process. At the other end of the spectrum, some early theories suggested that keeping active was critical to successful aging.

Most of today's theorists tend to see development as a life-span phenomenon (Baltes, 1987), and so see adjustment to old age as an extension of earlier personality styles. Stage theorists believe that new structures or organizations emerge. However, these are built upon the earlier stages. Levinson (1978, 1986), for example, views old age similarly to young adulthood and middle age in that there is a period of transition (ages 60 to 65) that links the previous life structure (of middle adulthood) to the incipient life structure of late adulthood. Erikson (Erikson et al., 1986) sees ego integrity (or its counterpart, despair) as the outcome of a long process of development.

Other theorists see even more continuity between previous adjustment and reactions to aging. Robert Atchley (1989) suggests that continuity provides people

Theories of adjustment to aging focus on the withdrawal of an individual from society and of society from the individual.

with an identity, a sense of who they are. People strive to be consistent in their behavior because it makes them feel more secure. Consistency enables people to say things like "I would never do that" or "That's just like me" with some confidence. Similarly, there are external pressures for consistency. Other people come to know what to expect of us if we behave similarly across situations.

Atchley (1989) is quick to emphasize that continuity does not mean that there are no changes. Certainly people's roles, abilities, and relationships all change. This will require them to make certain alterations in their behaviors, expectations, and even their values. But, Atchley suggests, these changes will be in line with a relatively constant inner core that we use to define ourselves.

PERSONALITY TYPES   Several longitudinal studies have looked at the maintenance of basic personality traits or types over the decades in adulthood. Costa and McRae (1989) studied three aspects of personality in a group of 2000 adult men. First, they looked at *neuroticism*—the amount of anxiety, depression, self-consciousness, vulnerability, impulsiveness, and hostility the men displayed. By and large, they found no real changes in the level of men's neuroticism over a 10-year period. The men who were highly neurotic tended to complain about their health; to smoke heavily; to have problems with drinking, sex, and finances; and to feel generally dissatisfied with their lives. Stereotypes of the elderly often portray them as hypochondriacs. In fact, it tends to be the people who rate high on neuroticism who display hypochondriasis—and they probably have done so all of their lives (Costa & McCrae, 1985).

Second, Costa and McCrae looked at *extroversion versus introversion*. People who were extroverted were assertive and outgoing. They sought excitement and activity. They sought attachments with others and had generally positive feelings. In the 10-year period of this study, men who were highly extroverted tended to stay that way. They were also happier and more satisfied with their lives than were those who measured high on introversion. There was some minor switch toward introversion among these men, particularly when circumstances required that they be less independent. Other researchers have studied extroversion and introversion over a longer period of time. In one study conducted over a 30-year period between middle and old age, many of the men became more introverted.

The third dimension studied by Costa and McCrae was the degree of *openness to experience*. Men who were open tended to show a wider range of interests. They tended to experience events intensely, whether they were positive or negative events. Men who were open to their experiences also showed more life satisfaction than those who were more defensive, cautious, and conforming. This aspect of personality also remained consistent from middle to later adulthood.

There are many such studies that show essential consistency in personality type from middle adulthood to later adulthood. People have organized, coherent, integrated patterns or beliefs about themselves, and they tend to act in ways that are consistent with their self-image. When they are able, despite major events, to judge themselves as having acted in accordance with their self-concept, by and large they express more life satisfaction and self-esteem. The self-concept is, of course, vulnerable to life events and major changes in health, finances, social involvement, social class, sex, housing conditions, and marriage. Major changes in one's self-concept can, in turn, affect one's sense of well-being (Thomae, 1980). Yet aging, by itself, seems to have no clear, direct effect on self-concept.

Although there are few universal personality changes that occur in later life, some researchers have studied whether any distinct pattern of personality change can be observed as people grow old. One study used Thematic Apperception Test (TAT) cards to determine the way middle-aged and older men from a Kansas City longitudinal sample viewed their world (Gutmann, 1964). It found that the 40-year-old man tended to view his environment as being within his control, rewarding boldness and risk taking; he saw himself as possessing energy equal to the challenges presented by the outside world. In contrast, the 60-year-old man saw the world as more complex and dangerous, no longer within his power, to be changed according to his will. Instead, he saw himself accommodating and conforming to his environment. Gutmann called this change in perspective a shift from *active* to *passive mastery*.

Whereas Gutman viewed coping skills as regressing during old age, Valliant's (1977) data indicated that people become more mature in their coping behaviors. For example, they show increases in the use of wise detachment and humor in the face of stress. Still others have argued that there are age-related differences in coping but these differences are determined by the stressors faced by younger versus older adults (Folkman & Lazarus, 1980; McCrae, 1982). Stressors that present positive challenges (for example, a promotion at work) decrease with age. Although losses do not increase appreciably with age, it may be that those that are experienced by the elderly are more centrally related to their identity. This would make the losses more threatening. Similarly, the nature of daily hassles—which also create stress—also varies across age (Folkman, Lazarus, Pimley, & Novacek, 1987).

Some theorists, beginning with Jung (1933/1960), have suggested that men and women's coping styles change in different ways. Men seem to move from an active to a passive style. After a lifetime of responsibility, breadwinning, and decision making, they seem to feel free to express the complexity of their personalities, including traits that are usually considered feminine (Gutman, 1969, 1975). Very old men move beyond passivity to a style Gutmann calls *magical mastery,* in which they deal with reality through a variety of techniques, such as projection and distortion. As they age, women seem to become more aggressive, instrumental, and domineering. Gutmann hypothesizes that both sexes are responding to liberation from the "parental imperative," the social pressure for women to conform to nurturing roles and for men to be financially responsible and to suppress any conflicting traits.

Some cross-sectional data have indicated that there are indeed age-related changes in coping styles. For example, Susan Folkman and her colleagues (1987) found that younger adults were more likely to use active problem-focused coping styles, whereas the elderly were more passive and emotion focused. For example, an elderly woman might downplay the importance of the traffic accident she just had, or she might view it in a more positive light by saying "I really needed to get rid of that car anyway" or "At least no one was injured." A young woman would handle the same situation by confronting the other driver, getting his or her name and address, contacting the car insurance company, and getting estimates to repair the damage. The contextual differences, in terms of what stress situations were experienced at different ages, had little effect on coping, although problems in research methodology prohibit drawing a definitive conclusion on this position. There were also few sex differences.

In old age, as in earlier periods of life, people's reactions are in line with the identity they create for themselves. Personality changes in later life may depend more on one's personal interpretation of events in keeping with one's self-concept than on the aging process itself.

Recent longitudinal research, however, tends to be more supportive of a continuity perspective. McCrae (1989) investigated 28 different coping mechanisms over a 7-year period. The participants in his study were community-dwelling adults, aged 21 to 90 at the time of the first testing. In a very complex design, he employed five different types of analyses with different samples. None of the 28 coping mechanisms showed consistent patterns of age-related change across all five analyses. This led McCrae to conclude that there were no notable age-related changes in coping styles.

Adjustment in later life is often very similar to adjustments that occur earlier in life. People develop an identity; they create themes that are carried throughout their lives. When they reach old age, their reactions to aging and new situations will be individual and in line with the identity and themes they have created for themselves throughout their lives. Personality development in old age, then, consists of the personal interpretation of events and the reactions to the events in keeping with past reactions (Ryff, 1985). We will now take a closer look at the significant events of later adulthood.

Developmental Tasks in Later Life

Even here in later adulthood, it is helpful to return to Erikson's theory of the life span to look for central developmental tasks. People who are able to face and cope with such developmental tasks are thought to maintain better mental health.

IDENTITY MAINTENANCE   In Erikson's theory of the life cycle, one of the central tasks from adolescence on is to maintain a relatively consistent identity. Identity is thought to be that uniquely integrated and reasonably consistent set of concepts that a person has about his or her physical, psychological, and social attributes. For at least one theorist (Whitbourne, 1987), the process of maintaining a consistent identity is something like the adaptive process defined by Piaget. That is, it involves the assimilation of events and changing circumstances into one's set of self-concepts. It also involves accommodation, or change, when there are major life events or threats to one's self-perception. In the face of major chronic illness, for example, one's physical, psychological, and social self-concepts are threatened. This may require some considerable adjustment or accommodation. Ideally, according to Susan Whitbourne, individuals should maintain a balance between assimilation and accommodation. Refusal to accommodate may mean that an individual is denying the real facts. Such an individual may be defensive and rigid, or may blame other people for changes that are actually happening to himself or herself, or may lack insight into the true nature of the circumstances. On the other hand, to accommodate too easily and too readily may create chaos. One may become hysterical or impulsive or hypersensitive. Hence, one of the tasks in later adulthood is to manage a balance between consistency of identity and gradual openness to experience and to the very real changes in one's life.

For the very old, the task of maintaining a sense of consistency with one's personal identity may be particularly important. Lieberman and Tobin (1983) studied over 600 elderly individuals, most in their 70s and 80s, who experienced major changes in their health and radical shifts in their living arrangements. Many of these individuals were frail, elderly people who were dependent on others. Their adaptation task was enormous. Those individuals who were most successful in adapting managed by maintaining and validating who they were. They were able to say, "I am who I have always been." How were they able to do this in the face of very real shifts in their lives and in their own physical abilities? Generally, they were able to do it by changing the evidence they used. They shifted from present evidence of who they were to past evidence. For example, one woman at first described herself by saying, "I am important to my family and friends; you should see how many New Year's cards I got." Two years later, after changes in her life, she defined herself by saying, "I think I am important to my family; I have always done the best I could for my family, and they appreciate it." Her past became evidence to allow her to maintain a conviction about her present personal identity that was in accordance with the person she used to be (Tobin, 1988).

INTEGRITY VERSUS DESPAIR   The final stage in Erikson's theory of the life cycle involves the psychosocial conflict of integrity versus despair. Erikson suggests that older people ponder whether their lives have fulfilled their earlier expectations. Those who can look back and feel satisfied that their lives have had meaning and that they have done the best they could with life's circumstances will have a sense of integrity. Those who see nothing but a succession of wrong turns and missed opportunities will feel despair. Ideally, our resolution will involve a preponderance of integrity tinged with realistic despair (Erikson et al., 1986). This leads to *wisdom*. Wisdom enables the elderly to maintain dignity and an integrated self in the face of physical deterioration and even death. The limitedness of one person's import is understood, but so is the connectedness among all people.

Part of the adjustment to old age includes a very real psychological need to reminisce and reflect on past events. Older people typically spend much time searching for themes and images that will give their lives meaning and coherence. Sometimes, they need to connect past episodes and situations in a logical and orderly sequence (Kubler-Ross, 1969; Neugarten, 1976). Some people ruminate

"I've deferred gratification all my life and frankly, time is getting awfully short for the big pay-off."

over what sort of legacy they will leave behind, what contributions they have made to the world, and how the world will remember them—through works of art, social service, work accomplishments, the children they bore and raised, or the material wealth they will pass on. Many look to their grandchildren as a form of legacy, in whom traces of their own personality and values will live on.

Some of the musings, weighings, and expressions of minor regrets typical of this process have been eloquently expressed by an 85-year-old woman living in Louisville, Kentucky (Burnside, 1979a):

> If I had my life to live over, I'd dare to make more mistakes next time. I'd relax. I'd limber up. I'd be sillier than I've been this trip. I'd take fewer things seriously. I'd take more chances. I'd take more trips. I'd climb more mountains and swim more rivers. I'd eat more ice cream and less beans. I'd perhaps have more actual troubles, but I'd have fewer imaginary ones.
>
> You see, I'm one of those people who live sensibly and sanely hour after hour, day after day. Oh, I've had my moments and if I had it to do over again, I'd have more of them. In fact, I'd try to have nothing else. Just moments, one after another, instead of living so many years ahead of each day. I've been one of

those persons who never goes anywhere without a thermometer, a hot water bottle, a raincoat, and a parachute. If I had it to do again, I would travel lighter than I have.

If I had my life to live over, I would start barefoot earlier in the spring and stay that way later in the fall. I would go to more dances. I would ride more merry-go-rounds. I would pick more daisies. (p. 425)

RETIREMENT

For many individuals, retirement is one of the more significant status changes of later adulthood. Work provides a structure around which to plan a daily schedule. It determines the people one sees regularly. Work also provides roles and functions for people and contributes to identity formation. These factors identify some reasons why retirement may require considerable adjustment.

Retirement does not just involve dealing with a greater amount of free time. Individuals work out choices, negotiations, and coping patterns consistent with their personal set of meanings—in effect, each person constructs his or her own social reality. How easily the individual adopts the new role depends on a number of factors. Normally, if the shift to retirement is dramatic or an individual's personal identity has been tied closely to an occupational role, the change will be difficult.

The particular pattern of retirement is the result of many different factors: health, economic status, need for fulfillment, flexibility, personal history, and the reactions of significant others.

A retirement party formally marks the passage from productive maturity to a seemingly nonproductive old age.

Physical, Economic, and Social Conditions

One important consideration influencing how a person reacts to retirement is health. A great number of older people leave the work force, either willingly or unwillingly, because of ill health. Levy (1978) has studied a large group of men who were about to retire; he compared their state of health with their willingness or unwillingness to retire. As one might expect, healthy men who wanted to retire fared the best. Those in ill health fared poorly, regardless of their willingness to retire. This may be because retirement is frequently more sudden for those in ill health (Ekerdt et al., 1989). They may, therefore, not be as prepared financially or psychologically as those who retire as planned. Their health expenses may create a financial burden. This may be particularly difficult for disabled retirees because they rely on Social Security much more than other retirees do (Social Security Administration, 1986). Social Security benefits make up 67% of the income of unmarried disabled retirees, but only 50% of the nondisabled retirees' income.

Attitudes often change in the first few years of retirement (Levy, 1978). Those unwilling to retire became dissatisfied in a short time; they withdrew socially and were bitter and angry. They tended to recover after a period of time, however, and gradually took on attitudes similar to those who had wanted to retire. Those who were ill at the time of retirement showed little improvement in attitude over time, regardless of whether they had looked forward to retirement.

Economic status is a major factor that affects a retiree's adjustment to a new way of life. Most elderly people have sufficient financial assets to live on. Indeed, in terms of assets and net worth, the elderly tend to be wealthier than young adults are (Radner, 1989). However, 12% to 13% of America's elderly live below the poverty line (Ford Foundation, 1989). This is a lower rate than among young adults. But the relatively low rate masks the situation of some subgroups of elderly. Single oldsters are much more likely to be poor than are the married (Radner, 1989). Minority members are more likely to be poor (Dressel, 1988; Jackson, 1985). For example, 27% of the Latino-American elderly are poor (Ford Foundation, 1989). Women are more likely than men to be poor. Among single elderly white women, over one-quarter live in poverty. And those suffering the discrimination that comes with being both female and a minority are particularly likely to be poor. Over 60% of single black elderly women are impoverished (Ford Foundation, 1989). Furthermore, the elderly are less likely than young adults to escape poverty. This is particularly true once the elderly person has been poor for more than 3 years. Whereas the majority of young adults in this situation will escape poverty within a decade, only 5% of the elderly will (Coe, 1988).

Friends and colleagues also affect the quality of life after retirement (Cox & Bhak, 1979). If an individual's significant others—friends and associates in clubs and organizations—hold positive attitudes toward retirement, the individual will tend to look forward to retirement and make a successful adjustment.

As was mentioned earlier, an individual's lifelong attitude toward work also affects feelings about retirement. There is an almost religious devotion to work in some segments of our society (Tilgher, 1962). Many men have spent so much time at their jobs that their sense of worth and self-esteem is embedded in their work. Their leisure-time activities have been superficial and therefore lack meaning. Retirement for these men means stepping out of the important, valuable, productive stream of life. Disengagement of this kind is especially hard for people who have never found satisfaction outside of their jobs, such as hobbies, reading,

If an individual's significant others hold positive attitudes toward retirement, the individual will tend to look forward to retirement and make a successful adjustment.

continued education, or involvement in organizations. The problem tends to be worse for the less educated, the financially strained, and those with few social or political involvements; but the professional individual or the business executive may also have difficulty organizing leisure time. Indeed, this may be one reason why a substantial minority of people continue to work part time after retirement (Quinn & Burkhauser, 1990).

WOMEN'S RETIREMENT   Until the past decade, recent studies that include both men and women, and in some cases women only, report findings similar to those of the earlier studies on men: Factors such as good health, economic security, and higher educational level predict a positive adjustment to retirement for women as well as men (Atchley, 1982; Block, 1981). Unfortunately, because many women receive lower salaries, they are often less financially secure than men at retirement—particularly single women and those recently widowed or divorced.

It is often thought that women adjust to retirement more easily than men because many do not have uninterrupted work histories over the life span and therefore experience a variety of roles. This expectation is not entirely supported by the literature. Indeed, in one study women who had a continuous work history over an extended period of their adult lives adapted more easily to retirement (Block, 1981). However, this was probably due to the fact that those women with continuous work experience had, on the average, more economic security and were better prepared for retirement than those who had intermittent experience in the work force.

The Decision to Retire

Retirement is not necessarily hazardous to one's health, either mentally or physically. In fact, fully a third of retirees report an improvement in their health in the period right after retirement. Another 50% report remaining the same in mental and physical health. Overall, recent retirees find an increase in life satisfaction (Ekerdt, 1987). Nevertheless, to avoid some of the problems previously discussed, it helps to prepare for retirement.

PREPARING FOR RETIREMENT   Adjustment to retirement is easier if a person has prepared for it. Thompson (1977) suggests that preparing for retirement consists of three parts:

1. *Decelerating.* As people get older, they begin to let go or taper off work responsibilities to avoid a sudden drop in activity at retirement.
2. *Retirement planning.* People plan specifically for the life that they will have in retirement.
3. *Retirement living.* People come to grips with concerns about stopping work and think about what it will be like to live as a retired person.

Retirement counselors, hired by companies or working independently, can help people through this process and help set the best time for retirement. Several specific factors are considered (Johnson & Riker, 1981). Does the retiree have adequate savings and income, a place to live, and plans for further work or activities after retirement? Has the potential retiree worked for a long time, and is he or she old enough to consider retirement? Some retirement counselors refer to the answers to these questions as an index of *retirement maturity*—how prepared a person is to retire. In general, people with a higher degree of retirement maturity are more positive and have an easier time adjusting to retirement.

RETIREMENT OPTIONS   The complete withdrawal from the work force is not the only retirement option for people in later adulthood. Some experts suggest that society may face a work shortage in the future (Forman, 1984), that we may be

Creative options for retirement, such as part-time tutoring, keep society from needlessly losing talented and productive workers.

needlessly losing talented and productive workers, and that the pension plans of the future may be overly and unnecessarily taxed by the increase in the number of full-time retirees (Alsop, 1984; Wojahn, 1983). Therefore, creative solutions, such as part-time or less physically demanding work options, are needed for older workers. Currently there seems to be little or no incentive for older workers to continue in the labor force. However, recent changes in Social Security will make it less costly for the elderly to continue to work part time (Quinn & Burkhauser, 1990). Furthermore, a few pilot programs have been remarkably successful. For example, retired businesspeople have been hired to train the inexperienced; another program trains older people to work with handicapped children. Numerous other options are now being explored (Donovan, 1984; Kieffer, 1984).

FAMILY AND PERSONAL RELATIONSHIPS

As with any period in life, the social context of family and personal relationships helps define one's roles and responsibilities and one's life satisfactions. In today's world, this social context is shifting for older adults much as it is for the younger adult. Divorce and remarriage are more common. Kinship patterns with grandchildren and step-grandchildren are more complicated. And there is a wider range of single lifestyles. Nevertheless, close interpersonal relationships continue to define many of the stresses and satisfactions of life in later adulthood.

The Postparental Period

For most individuals in later adulthood, the direct responsibilities of parenting are over, if they ever occurred. On the average, older married couples report being more satisfied with their marriages after the children leave home. There may be some initial difficulty in adjusting to each other as a couple without the interruption of children or of work responsibilities, but most couples who remain married report less stress, and increased feelings of satisfaction and harmony (Olson & Lavee, 1989; Lee, 1988). Couples who report greater-than-average satisfaction are also likely to report that the marriage has become more of an emotional center in their lives. It now brings them more comfort, more support, and more intimacy. Happy marriages that have survived into later adulthood have often adopted a style that is somewhat more egalitarian and cooperative. Traditional gender roles seem to become less important (Troll, Miller, & Atchley, 1979).

Despite high mobility and social change in society, most older adults report relatively frequent contact with their children and grandchildren, if not in person, at least by telephone. They still feel considerable responsibility to help their children as needed, although they are also anxious not to interfere (Blieszner & Mancini, 1987; Greenberg & Becker, 1988; Hagestad, 1987). Parents often provide their adult children with various forms of assistance ranging from money to babysitting to advice.

Grandparenthood (as reported in Chapter 18) is often seen as one of the most satisfying roles of this period. Over 40% of elderly Americans now have

There may be some initial difficulty in adjusting to each other as a couple without the interruption of children or work, but most couples who remain married report less stress and increased feelings of satisfaction and harmony.

great-grandchildren (Doka & Mertz, 1988). In general, great-grandparents, too, are pleased about their role and attach at least some emotional significance to it. The role seems to bring a sense of personal and family renewal, a new diversion in their lives, and a prideful marker of longevity (Doka & Mertz, 1988). Great-grandparents may be afforded a special status in the family.

But kinship patterns have undergone some stress and change in the past few decades. The high rate of divorce and remarriage has caused particular complexities. It is not surprising that grandparents often report more closeness to their grandchildren in situations where their child is the parent to be awarded custody. Some grandparents feel they have a particularly important role in helping to maintain stability and a sense of values at times of family disruption (Johnson & Barer, 1987).

Caring for an Ill Spouse

Although most elderly do not need substantial help with daily living, those who do tend to rely heavily on their families (Gatz, Bengston, & Blum, 1990; Stone, Cafferata, & Sangl, 1987). If there is a surviving spouse, she or he is the single most likely care-giver, with wives being more likely to play the role than husbands are. This means, of course, that the care-giver is likely to be elderly and may have health problems, too. In a national survey, the average age of a care-giver was slightly over 57 years with fully 25% in the 65- to 74-year-old range and 10% over age 75 (Stone et al., 1987).

Wives often report more care-giver stress than do husbands, although some studies find the differences are small (Miller, 1990). Although there are probably many contributing factors to this difference, Pruchno and Resch (1989) suggest that the sex-role changes seen in old age may play a role. Men, moving toward a greater family orientation, may actually be more interested in providing such care than are women, who may feel they have already spent most of their lives looking after their families. It is also possible, however, that the differences in care-giver strain are due to factors that the researchers did not take into account, such as women being more willing to admit health or psychological problems (Miller, 1990).

Caring for an Alzheimer's victim has special strains. It becomes particularly stressful when the victim's behavior becomes disruptive or socially embarrassing (Deimling & Bass, 1986). Furthermore, these care-givers tend to have smaller support systems than those caring for physically, but not mentally, impaired elderly (Birkel & Jones, 1989). Even organized respite programs do not seem to be particularly helpful (Lawton, Brody, & Saperstein, 1989). This may be partially attributable to spousal care-givers' dedication to their task. They report considerable gratification from providing this help to the person who has meant so much to their lives (Motenko, 1989).

Widows and Widowers

In later adulthood, it is an all-too-common experience to suffer the loss of a close family member, friend, or spouse; the loss of a close personal relationship is usually marked by grief and bereavement and then a long period of readjustment (much of this will be discussed in Chapter 21). But men and women who experience the death of their spouses also enter a new status and role in life—that of widow- or widowerhood. For many, this is a very difficult life transition, with very real changes in daily life patterns and the risk of social isolation. For others, it may provide a long-awaited opportunity to assume control of their lives or to find relief from a caretaking role. Let's look at some of the patterns of, and adjustments to, the role of widow- and widowerhood.

INCIDENCE AND LIVING ARRANGEMENTS   There are nearly five times more widows of all ages in the United States—some 11 million in all—than widowers. The disproportion among the aged is similarly striking. Census figures for 1988 numbered over 8 million widows over age 65, as against 1,640,000 widowers (*Statistical Abstract of the United States,* 1990). Moreover, the disproportion is one of time as well as numbers. On the average, older widows tend to survive about 50% longer than widowers following the spouse's death (Burnside, 1979).

These statistics spell loneliness for a good many older people, but a woman's experience of such forced independence is often quite different from a man's. Following the death of a spouse, just as after divorce, women of all ages are less likely than men to remarry; on the average, aged women are more than eight times less likely to remarry (Burnside, 1979). This is partly due to our society's favoring the pairing of older men and younger women—one of the reasons for the disproportionate number of widows in the first place—and partly because fewer men are available for marriage. Of American women over age 65, nearly one-half are widowed and more than 40% live alone, while another 40% live with their husbands. Of American men over 65, only one-seventh are widowed and about one in six live alone, while the majority are still married and living with their wives. The preoccupation with widowhood among middle-aged and older women, then, is firmly rooted in reality.

TABLE 20–1
Demographic Characteristics of People over 65 Years Old

	MALE	FEMALE
Population (in millions)	12.4	18.0
Marital Status (in % of people over 65)		
Single	4.6	5.3
Married	77.7	41.5
Widowed	13.9	48.7
Divorced	3.9	4.5
Employment Status (in % of people over 65)		
Employed	16.1	7.7
Unemployed	.4	.2
Not in labor force	83.5	92.1
Living Arrangements (in % of people over 65)		
Living in household alone	16.2	40.6
Living in household with spouse	75.1	39.9
Living in household with someone else	8.6	19.0
Not in household	.2	.5

Source: Statistical Abstract of the United States, 1990.

After the death of a spouse, many people have to adjust to living alone—being on their own, making decisions, and taking care of themselves, often for the first time.

LIVING ALONE   One of the new practical and psychological realities that widows and widowers must face is living alone. Elderly women are much more likely than elderly men to live alone. In the 65- to 69-year-old range, 31.4% of the women, but only 12.6% of the men, live alone. For the 75-year-old-plus group, the comparable rates are 53% and 20.2% (Spitze & Logan, 1989). They must now run errands, maintain social contacts, and make financial decisions—on their own. Some may welcome the opportunity; others may have difficulty living alone because their spouses have always taken care of certain matters, such as finances.

There is a variety of support systems available for widows and widowers, including family, friends, work associates, and other participants in favorite activities (Lopata, 1979). Both mothers and fathers are very likely to receive the basic assistance they need from their children, especially if they have daughters (Spitze & Logan, 1989, 1990). A widowed father may see less of his children than might a widowed mother, although this difference is not large (Spitze & Logan, 1989). This is true primarily because widowed mothers are usually in worse health and need more attention than widowed fathers do. Widows may have an easier time than widowers in maintaining a social life, because wives traditionally keep lines of communication open with family members, and they initiate social activities with friends (Lopata, 1975). Widowers, therefore, are more apt to become isolated from the couple's previous social contacts. They are also generally less active in social organizations than widows are. Finally, widowers are prone to certain sexual problems following bereavement. Attempts to end a prolonged sexual inactivity, particularly when a wife dies after a long illness, may cause intense guilt and, in turn, may bring about a form of impotence know as "widower's impotency" (Comfort, 1976).

SUICIDE   A surprisingly common response of widowers and widows to their multiple problems is suicide. Although the most publicized suicides are those of young adults, adolescents, and even schoolchildren, by far the greatest number of suicides occurs among people over age 45; of this group, most occur among those aged 65 and older (*Statistical Abstract of the United States,* 1990). Four times as many men commit suicide as women. The rate for men rises steadily with age, reaching a peak among those over age 80 (Manton, Blazer, & Woodbury, 1987; Miller, 1979; Riley & Waring, 1976). Both white and minority men show dramatic increases in suicide during old age (Manton et al., 1987). These statistics do not take into account the more passive forms of suicide, such as letting oneself die, which Riley and Waring (1976) call "submissive death," or the indirect forms, such as through excessive drinking, smoking, or drug abuse, which Miller (1979) terms "suicidal erosion."

Suicide among the elderly is almost always a result of "vital losses," such as employment difficulties, retirement shock, and widow- or widowerhood. Both widows and widowers, therefore, fall into the high-risk group among potential suicides. The risk falls off sharply, however, after the first year of bereavement, but still remains higher than average for several years (Miller, 1981). There is one other important factor besides retirement and widow- or widowerhood. Old people who are chronically lonely, or who have a history of emotional instability, especially those with deep-seated anxieties and feelings of inferiority, are highly prone to suicide.

One of the most effective treatments used with widows and widowers to improve mental health and encourage ways of meeting social needs is the self-help group. Individuals involved in such groups may find comfort in sharing with others. The group also provides a protective setting in which to form new relationships and try new roles so that the people become less isolated and better able to help themselves. Systematic follow-up of participants in formal self-help groups has repeatedly demonstrated these positive outcomes for most participants (Gartner, 1984).

Siblings and Friends

In later adulthood, many people report increased contact with and concern for siblings. Relationships that were quite distant in the busy part of one's adult life are sometimes renewed and revitalized. Siblings share living quarters, provide comfort and support at times of crisis, and nurture each other in times of ill health. They are valuable companions for the kind of reminiscing that leads to ego integrity. They may also work together to provide help to an ailing parent (Goetting, 1982). These relationships are not always smooth. Nevertheless, some kinship responsibility among siblings is a common part of the social network of older adults. It is particularly important for single adults or for older individuals who need some care and assistance but do not have grown children who are able to help.

As described in Chapter 18, friendship patterns of both married and unmarried individuals also provide considerable stability and life satisfaction. Nevertheless, most studies that compare friendships and family relationships find clear distinctions. Most older adults think of kinship relationships as having a built-in permanence. One can call on one's kin for a long-term commitment. One cannot make quite the same demands on a friendship. Friends will help in handling an immediate emergency such as a sudden illness, but long-term responsibilities should be handled by kin (Aizenberg & Treas, 1985).

SOCIAL POLICY AND THE AGED

Today, nearly 12% of the U.S. population is age 65 or over. That figure should grow to at least 15% by the year 2020. As this figure grows, much attention is being given to the quality of services available to "the aged." Only a small fraction of this population are, in fact, frail elderly and in need of extensive services. Aging, per se, is not the problem. Social services need to address the very specific needs of individuals, whether in later adulthood or in some earlier period.

The Frail Elderly in America

In the 1970s, much public attention focused on the poverty, ill health, and inadequate living conditions of older people and the limited social services available to them. As a result of this advocacy, many services were improved. Although poverty among the elderly still exists, most older individuals are guaranteed a minimum annual income and basic health-care services. Far more low-income housing units have been allocated to the elderly, and some communities have developed a range of social services (Kutza, 1981).

It may be more difficult to identify the next level of problems and to develop possible solutions for them. For example, living in near poverty is sometimes no less depressing than living in poverty. Public housing does not always meet the needs of the elderly—some may lack shared community living space, whereas in others it might not be safe to walk in the corridors. Also, transportation can become a major problem for those who must stop driving because of failing vision or poor reaction time.

There are probably about 1.6 million noninstitutionalized elderly people receiving help in daily living activities from one or more unpaid care-givers (Steon et al., 1987). Another 600,000 live in residential care homes in the community (Mor, Sherwood, & Gutkin, 1986). About 5% of those over age 65 are in nursing homes (Shanas & Maddox, 1985). Those who end up in nursing homes are likely to be single, suffering from mental impairment, and over age 85 (Birkel & Jones, 1989; Mor, Sherwood, & Gutkin, 1986; Shapiro & Tate, 1988).

Our social programs for the frail elderly are not "fine tuned" enough to the particular needs of the individual. Critics of our social services have often warned that we sometimes consider nursing home placement when other services might be more appropriate. We are anxious to avoid medical and economic catastrophes for the aged individual, but we have difficulty with the range of lesser services that might assist the individual in maintaining a higher quality of life and prevent catastrophe (Brody, 1987). Other critics warn that we must remember that aging, per se, is not the problem, that older individuals with physical and mental disabilities need to be treated like any other group. Similarly, some older individuals lack the social support of family or friends, or display somewhat

Our social policies have not kept up with the growing needs and problems of the frail elderly.

FOCUS ON AN ISSUE

ELDER ABUSE

In the late 1970s, Americans "discovered" elder abuse (Callahan, 1988). To their astonishment and dismay, they heard repeatedly about old people who were neglected, belittled, and mistreated. Given the attention "granny bashing" received on the evening news, most Americans thought that elder abuse was a widespread problem. Indeed, early estimates indicated that there were over 1 million cases of elder abuse annually (Callahan, 1988; Salend, Kane, Satz, & Pynoos, 1984). In fact, however, we do not have reliable estimates of how common elder abuse is.

Elder abuse can take a variety of forms (Pillemer & Finkelhor, 1988; Salend et al., 1984). These include physical violence, neglect (such as withholding food or medicine), psychological abuse, or financial exploitation. There is some debate as to which form is most common. Pillemer and Finkelhor (1988) reported physical violence, with a rate of 20 cases per 1000 oldsters, to be the most common. Social service agencies have found that neglect is the most common form, although these figures often include self-neglect as well as neglect by care-givers (Salend et al., 1984). It may be, however, that financial exploitation is actually the most common form. There is simply not enough information to know.

Who are the victims and victimizers? Elderly people who are in ill health are three to four times more likely than well elderly to be abused (Pillemer & Finkelhor, 1988). Female victims are more likely to come to the attention of social service agencies, as are the very old (Callahan, 1988). Those who live with someone are more likely to be abused. Not surprisingly, then, the most common abuser is the victim's spouse (Pillemer & Finkelhor, 1988). Spouses with a longstanding history of conflict and violence are particularly likely to be perpetrators. However, it is only in terms of raw numbers that spouses are the most likely perpetrators (Kosberg, 1988). When one corrects for the fact that more elderly live with their spouses than their children, the rate of abuse is actually slightly higher for the latter group (Pillemer & Finkelhor, 1988). Care-givers who abuse drugs (including alcohol) or are mentally incompetent are more likely to be abusive, as are those who are forced by other family members to provide care (Kosberg, 1988).

What can be done to prevent elder abuse? One of the best methods is to screen care-givers (Kosberg, 1988). Social workers can interview the prospective care provider, assess the needs of the elderly client, and then evaluate the match. The social worker can also help by providing relief help and educational classes. However, most care-givers have no contact with social workers. Therefore, it becomes critical that the states clearly define responsibilities and channels for reporting elder abuse. Public education concerning the signs and risk factors for elder abuse is also important.

In fact, Jordan Kosberg (1988) has argued that societal attitudes are a major factor in elder abuse. He suggests that as long as the United States is an ageist, violent society, we will have elder abuse. Other societal values, such as discrimination against the disabled and women, also play a role. And factors that increase the likelihood of familial dysfunction—including poverty, unemployment, lack of community resources, and cyclic familial violence—all will need to be addressed before elder abuse is eliminated.

---

unusual behavior patterns, or have trouble with self-care, and they need help in those particular areas, but not necessarily nursing home care. They may need education, counseling, legal aid, social networking, or even just more interesting things to do during the day (Knight & Walker, 1985).

The institutional care we give our older people varies widely in quality. Although there are many well-planned and caring institutions, in the past few years many nursing homes have been exposed as boring, meaningless places where people often have little else to do but wait for the end of their lives. People about to enter an institution often feel great anxiety and dread. They may also exhibit many characteristics of already institutionalized people—apathy, passivity, bitterness, or depression (Tobin & Lieberman, 1976). They are facing a break from the continuity of their lives, losing independence, becoming separated from many of their possessions and familiar routines. Once they do enter an institution, they may find that their identity is further submerged (they are now "Honey" or "Dearie" instead of Mr. or Mrs. or Ms. Somebody), and they may have to conform to unfamiliar and unliked routines (Kastenbaum, 1979).

Options for the Aged

Older Americans comprise a remarkably varied group of individuals; they are not a single, uniform, gray mass of humanity. Euphemisms such as "the elderly" and "senior citizens" are inadequate to describe the multitude of qualities found in aged individuals. Furthermore, the period of old age covers a long span of time. Consequently, there are many sharp differences between the young-old, who are recently retired and are often healthy and vigorous, and the old-old, who are more likely to experience ill health, restricted mobility, and social isolation. Social

There are many sharp differences between the young-old, who are recently retired and are often healthy and vigorous, and the old-old, who are more likely to experience ill-health and restricted mobility. Social policies designed to assist older people need to take account of this diversity.

For the elderly who are in good health, retirement communities provide older people with an opportunity to share interests and activities.

policies designed to assist older people need to take account of this diversity (Kane & Kane, 1980). It is not always helpful to think of dichotomous categories—the disabled and the able, the poor and the middle class, the institutionalized and those living independently in the community.

One in four individuals over age 65 can expect to be disabled to the point where institutionalization will be necessary. Far more will need health, social, and living assistance of a limited sort. One option, day centers for the elderly, is part of a rapidly growing trend (Irwin, 1978). These centers provide an attractive alternative to nursing homes for those who need considerable care, but on a limited basis. To families who are willing to care for their elderly relatives in the evenings and at night, day centers offer periods of relief and the opportunity for sons and daughters to maintain a normal working schedule. Consider the case of Mrs. Barrow, a 77-year-old stroke victim. She lived with her daughter and son-in-law but spent her days in a Baltimore day center, where she received therapy, kept very busy, and made new friends. Mrs. Barrow's morale and temperament improved dramatically after only a few weeks of attendance and made her family's burden of care that much lighter. But the cost of day-care nursing centers often is not covered by current health insurance policies, although these centers are more cost-effective than nursing homes. Thus, they may be prohibitively expensive for some (Gurewitsch, 1983).

For the elderly in good health, there are other options. Retirement communities allow older people to live together and share interests and activities in safe surroundings. One drawback is that they isolate the elderly from the rest of the world. Other ideas are being tried by organizations such as the Gray Panthers and the Quakers. One successful experiment is the Life Center run by the Quakers in Philadelphia. Here, older people live in a large converted house with students and people of other age groups. Costs, housework, and meals are shared, and the resulting sense of community keeps the elderly in the mainstream of life.

A whole array of services is beginning to be made available to the elderly: various modes of transportation, including door-to-door service and escort services in dangerous neighborhoods; meal services; in-home care, including both homemakers and health professionals; friendly visitors; telephone reassurance; cultural services, such as bookmobiles and other library programs and free or reduced-price admission to museums and concerts; opportunities to serve as foster grandparents or in some other volunteer capacity, possibly even work for pay; and legal assistance.

Many communities have also established senior centers at which older people can participate in varied activities, attend classes and parties, and receive needed services (Kaplan, 1979). Other communities have experimented with community

Many communities now offer an array of transportation services for the elderly—including door-to-door service and escort service in dangerous neighborhoods.

The elderly are an important resource for their own needs and those of others. Organizations like the Gray Panthers and the American Association of Retired Persons (AARP) bring older people together as a political and social force.

care programs, in which people who would otherwise be institutionalized receive 24-hour care in a private home (Oktay & Volland, 1981).

Although society is finally beginning to pay more attention to the needs of the aged, the aged themselves are an important resource for their own needs and for those of others. Older people are often unaware of the services and benefits already available to them as senior citizens. Better use of the media, such as radio and television, could inform them of their rights and opportunities. Even more effective as a means of self-help are activist organizations like the Gray Panthers (actually a coalition of the aged and young people) and the American Association of Retired Persons (AARP), which bring older people together as a political and social force (Miller, 1981; Rowe, 1982). These groups rightly see the aged as an almost untapped resource in our society. Members of these and other groups are working for more rights for older people both in the workplace and in society as a whole. Their work has meant more autonomy and better living conditions for both the elderly and other members of society. One badly crippled elderly woman made a great impact in Philadelphia by publicly demonstrating that the urban transportation system could not accommodate the weak or the old. The most serious shortcoming found was that the steps for getting on buses were too high. Efforts like this have led communities to use "kneeling buses" and special vans for the handicapped. Finally, organizations like the Gray Panthers and AARP are giving older people a better self-image—something too long neglected in a world that equates youth with beauty, maturity with power, and age with obsolescence (Mackenzie, 1978).

STUDY OUTLINE

Aging, like the previous life stages, consists of a series of status passages, among which are old age itself, retirement, and widow- or widowerhood. It differs from the previous stages in that it leads to no further stage; the physical and social environment tends to contract, rather than expand.

Personality and Aging

The physical and environmental problems of old age impose a heavy psychological burden on most people. The aged have to change their self-concepts, as they lose their former autonomy and become more dependent on others for daily needs. Some adjust well, others do not. A person's physical evaluation is often a good indication of psychological well-being. As people grow older, they begin to think in terms of how much time they have left to live.

Developmental Tasks in Later Life. There are several theories of adjustment to aging. Some theorists, such as Levinson and Erikson, postulate qualitative shifts in development as people age. Others, such as Atcheley, emphasize continuity in coping skills and personality.

One of the central tasks of old age involves the renunciation of old ties at the end of life and the necessity of yielding power to others. The aged also need to spend much time reflecting on how they have spent their lives and considering what kind of legacy they will leave behind. Another issue is the urgent need to find meaning in one's life; Erikson called this final crisis of ego development integrity versus despair.

Aging may affect men and women in different ways. Gutmann has found that men become more passive and allow themselves to express more feminine traits in old age, whereas aging women become more aggressive, instrumental, and domineering. Some studies have found general tendencies toward eccentricity, lessened sensitivity to others, inner preoccupations, and a decreased ability to deal with challenging situations. Other studies find no such consistent changes in life orientation and values. How people react to aging individually may determine how well they adapt to it and how their personality development continues in old age.

Retirement

Retirement from the work force is a significant status change of later adulthood. Reactions to retirement depend on factors such as willingness to retire, health, finances, and colleagues' attitudes. Adjustment to retirement is often easier if the person has planned for it.

Family and Personal Relationships

Widows and Widowers. Widowhood, widowerhood, and the loss of close friends can be extremely stressful events in old age. In the population over age 65, widows outnumber widowers almost six to one. Aging widows are far less likely to remarry than are widowers.

For many older people, living alone presents problems of loneliness and forced independence. However, it may also provide new opportunities for personal growth.

Social Policy and the Aged

Options for the Aged. Age segregation and poverty are two major problems of old age today. Institutional care of the elderly is often substandard. Some alternative programs and options include day centers for the elderly, life centers that allow people of all ages to live together, health clinics in senior citizen centers, and various at-home transportation, nursing, and meal services. The aged can also do much to help themselves and work for social change through such activist organizations as the Gray Panthers and AARP.

KEY TERMS AND CONCEPTS

American Association of Retired
  Persons (AARP)
active mastery
continuity theory
Gray Panthers

integrity versus despair
magical mastery
passive mastery
reminiscence
retirement maturity

social programs for the elderly
status passage
suicide
widowerhood
widowhood

SELF-TEST QUESTIONS

1. Describe and compare the theories of adjustment to aging as they are presented in this chapter. How do these theories fit reality?

2. How does personality type affect adjustment to aging? Does research indicate consistency or change in personality type from middle to later adulthood?

3. How does cross-cultural research of elders contribute to our understanding of aging? Describe the universal patterns of personality changes in later adulthood that Gutmann has observed, and discuss whether other research supports or counters Gutmann's findings.

4. What is the significance of identity maintenance in later adulthood? Explain the process of identity maintenance and give an example of how older people are able to maintain a consistent identity in the face of major shifts in their lives.

5. How is Erikson's conflict of integrity versus despair expressed in later adulthood?

6. Describe the factors that influence how a person reacts to retirement.

7. How can a person best prepare for retirement? How can society further assist in this process?

8. What are some characteristic patterns of relationships during the postparental period? Include some consideration of spousal care-giving.

9. Discuss some of the major adjustments that characterize widowhood and widowerhood.

10. What do most older adults consider to be an important distinction between kinship patterns, such as sibling relationships, and patterns of friendship?

11. Explain why social programs for the frail elderly are not "fine tuned" enough.

12. Describe some social programs for the elderly that take account of the diversity of individual needs found in this age group.

13. How have the Gray Panthers and AARP helped to improve the lot of the elderly?

SUGGESTED READINGS

ALLEN, K. R. *Single women/family ties: Life histories of older women*. Newbury Park, CA: Sage, 1989. Case studies of older women highlighting life-change events collected as part of the Syracuse family relative project.

ELKIN, D. *Grandparenting: Understanding today's children*. Glenview, IL: Scott, Foresman, 1989. A popular author speaks to grandparents about the generational similarities and differences.

LUSTBADER, W. *Counting on kindness: The dilemmas of dependency*. New York: Free Press, 1991. We very often take our good health and independence for granted. This examination of the natural processes of illness, death, care giving, and being "beholden" explores issues of power and dependency in the elderly and disabled, and those who care for them.

ROGERS, C. *A way of being*. Boston: Houghton-Mifflin, 1980. This humanist provides a collection of his reflections on life, all written between the ages of 65 and 78. The essays express his continued openness to new experiences and a growing, changing philosophical perspective.

RUBENSTEIN, R. *Singular paths: Old men and living alone*. New York: Columbia University Press, 1986. A research-based presentation of patterns of aged men living alone, with application to social services for life skills.

Chapter 21

It is as natural to die as to be born.

FRANCIS BACON
OF DEATH

CHAPTER OUTLINE

Death and Dying

Death is the ultimate critical event. On the physiological level, death is an irrevocable cessation of life functions. On the psychological level, it has personal significance and meaning to the dying individual and to the immediate family and friends. To die means to cease experiencing, to leave loved ones, to leave unfinished business, and to enter the unknown (Kalish, 1987). But death is also imbedded in the cultural context. There are collective meanings. Many of these collective meanings are expressed in the literature, arts, music, religion, and philosophy of the culture; they are elaborated with rituals and rites.

What are some of these meanings, both personal and collective? How do they affect both the experience of living and the experience of dying? If we knew more about the experience of dying, or the process of grief and bereavement, would we be better able to help people cope with the tragedies in their lives as well as with the triumphs?

Until recently, psychologists seemed to ignore the topic of death. It was not easy to study, and perhaps they thought it inappropriate to study the attitudes and reactions of individuals in the process of coping with death. But in the past two decades, psychologists have studied death thoroughly. In this chapter, we will take a look at some of the things that have been discovered, and consider some of the ways in which this knowledge might be applied.

CHAPTER OBJECTIVES

By the time you have finished this chapter, you should be able to do the following:

■ Discuss American cultural attitudes toward death and the terminally ill.

■ Explain Kübler-Ross's stages of adjustment to death and suggest ways of dealing with these stages.

■ Compare and contrast hospices and hospitals.

■ Describe the controversy over the right-to-die issue.

■ Discuss patterns of adjustment characteristic of the grieving process.

THOUGHTS AND FEARS OF DEATH

Birth and death are both natural events, but the emotional impact and the personal meanings of these events are vastly different. Birth may be anticipated with excitement and optimism, whereas the reality of death may be avoided and even denied.

The Denial of Death

Several authors have suggested that our Western technological, youth-oriented society has a curious habit of denying and avoiding death, while at the same time being strangely preoccupied with it. One author tells a story of being invited to cocktails and dinner at the home of a friend (Kalish, 1985). On entering the dining room, the man notices with astonishment that there is a brown horse

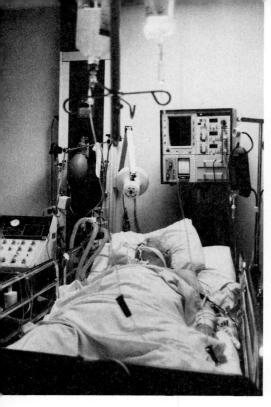

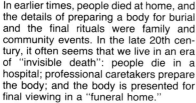

In earlier times, people died at home, and the details of preparing a body for burial and the final rituals were family and community events. In the late 20th century, it often seems that we live in an era of "invisible death": people die in a hospital; professional caretakers prepare the body; and the body is presented for final viewing in a "funeral home."

sitting quietly on the dining-room table. He turns to look at the reaction of the other guests and the host—all faces express shock and confusion. But no one wants to embarrass the host by mentioning what is so obviously discomforting. The dinner proceeds with long silences that are broken only by innocuous and inconsequential conversation. Is this what goes on when a person is dying and no one will speak with him or her about death, or even permit the person to speak about dying (Kalish, 1985)?

In earlier periods in history, death was a familiar event. It usually occurred in the home, with family members present. Family members took care of the dying patient in the last days. Even after death, the details of preparing the body for burial and the final rituals were family and community events. In the late 20th century, we have made it something of a technological marvel. Most people die in hospitals with the medical staff attending to their needs. Professional caretakers prepare the body for the final rituals and burial, and the body is presented for final viewing in a funeral home. Some have suggested that we live in an era of "invisible death." Have we deceived ourselves into believing that death is just another problem to deal with, such as a disease for which we have not yet found a cure (Aries, 1981)?

Denial is a normal mechanism for coping with stress. But denial can interfere with active coping. Actively coping with death means taking realistic precautions about the hazards of living, without restricting ourselves unnecessarily. We must be able to accept the limitations of life and our own vulnerabilities. Indeed, violent, unrealistic images are popular. Some experts suggest that if we as a culture could deal more directly with death, we might prevent fewer distorted images of death to our children (Pattison, 1977). The average person, by age 21, has not seen one human death, but has seen over 13,000 on television (DeSpelder & Strickland, 1983). What a paradoxical picture of denial, ambiguity, and fascination!

There are some researchers who believe that our cultural taboo against death is weakening. Many books, articles, and death education classes are available that may change people's attitudes.

602

Fears, Preoccupations, and Meanings of Death

Are older people more fearful or more preoccupied with death than younger people? Are the healthy and those feeling more in control of their lives more or less fearful at the prospect of death? Psychoanalytic theory asserts that anxiety or fearfulness at the prospect of one's own death is normal. But people differ in how they confront that anxiety. Some people find meaning and purpose in life and are able to incorporate death into that meaning. Religious fanatics who die for their cause are an extreme example of that "solution." The existentialist, who finds no purpose in life except life itself, may be terrified by the prospect of death. For the wide range of individuals in between, researchers find that the personal and cultural meanings of death are often important in whether or not individuals are fearful or preoccupied with thoughts of their own death. Several studies have found that the

APPLICATION

REACTIONS OF MEDICAL STAFF TO DEATH AND DYING

Doctors and nurses are dedicated to saving lives, not losing them, and they are committed to making people better. They are gratified when patients recover and their efforts are rewarded. But what happens when, despite their skill, knowledge, caring, and best professional efforts, the patient is dying?

Until very recently, most doctors were given very little education about the needs of the dying person, or even a description of the psychological aspects of the dying process. They had to depend on their own attitudes, defenses, and vulnerabilities in coping with the questions and concerns of the dying patient or the family. They shielded themselves from the realities of these "difficult" situations as best they could.

When Elizabeth Kübler-Ross began her study of the dying process in the mid-1960s, she met with considerable resistance and denial from the hospital staff (Kübler-Ross, 1969). Her visits in the hospital wards disturbed her because of the behavior of the nurses and the doctors. Once a diagnosis was made that a patient had a terminal illness, both nurses and doctors often paid less attention to that patient. They seemed to avoid all but necessary contact with the individual. They not only talked to them less, but also provided less routine physical care. Patients were usually not told of their "terminal" condition, even when they asked about it. Efforts were made to keep the patient from discussing his or her feelings about dying. According to Kübler-Ross,

the professionals seemed to have "institutionalized" denial, perhaps to protect their own feelings. She suggests that this prevented patients from having sufficient opportunity to cope directly with the obvious psychological task confronting them.

Now all nursing programs and many programs for doctors include seminars on death education. The psychological process of dying and the grief of survivors are legitimate elements of a full understanding of the integrated needs of the patient. Even with such preparation, some nurses and other hospital staff still have trouble coping with the needs of dying patients and their families on a day-to-day basis. Some members of the medical staff may distance themselves by emphasizing the "scientific investigation of dying." On the other hand, medical professionals occasionally become overly involved in the anxiety and grief of a particular patient and the family, which may trigger a particular set of unresolved feelings of guilt, shame, or sorrow in the medical staff.

But medical professionals who understand the dying process are better able to set realistic goals for "good outcomes." In the context of the individual's whole life, it may be important to help the individual to die with dignity, to express final sentiments to family and friends, and to face death in a unique fashion consistent with his or her lifestyle (Haber, 1987).

elderly are less anxious about death than young adults are (Kastenbaum, 1986), that those with a strong sense of purpose in life fear death less (Durlak, 1979), and that some older people report that although they think of death often, they feel surprisingly calm at the prospect of their own death. When young people are asked how they would spend 6 remaining months of life, they describe activities such as traveling and trying to accomplish things they have not yet done. Older people speak of different priorities and values. Sometimes, they talk about contemplation, or meditation, and other inner-focused behaviors. Often, they talk about spending time with their families and those closest to them (Kalish, 1987; Kalish & Reynolds, 1981). Indeed, in a comprehensive set of interviews with a large group of elderly volunteers, only 10% answered yes to the question, "Are you afraid to die?" (Jeffers & Verwoerdt, 1977). Participants did report, however, a fear of a prolonged and painful dying process.

Although many older people generally report low levels of anxiety about death, not all older people feel this way. There are substantial individual differences among the elderly in terms of their anxiety about death (Stillion, 1985). But what pattern emerges as to who is most anxious? The results are difficult to interpret. In some studies, those who are psychologically well-adjusted and who seem to have achieved personality integrity as defined by Erikson report low anxiety. But in other studies, older individuals who are healthy both physically and mentally, have plans for the future, and feel in control of their own lives are most anxious about death. Often, individuals experience high death anxiety when diagnosed with a possibly fatal disease, but they reach a point of low anxiety several weeks or months later (Belsky, 1984). Death anxiety appears to be only one symptom in an ongoing process of establishing and accepting the meaning of death in the context of the meaning of life.

CONFRONTING ONE'S OWN DEATH

As people grow older or become ill, the realization comes that death is not far off, and the fact of its imminence increasingly crosses their minds. Young people have the luxury of pushing such thoughts into the background, but in illness or old age, thoughts of death are unavoidable. How do people react?

Stages of Adjustment

Kübler-Ross (1969) was one of the first to study the topics of death and dying in any depth. She focused on the relatively short term situation in which death becomes an immediate possibility—upon the discovery of terminal cancer, for example, or some other fatal illness. She identified five stages in the process of adjusting to the idea of death: denial, anger, bargaining, depression, and ultimately, acceptance.

In the *denial* stage, the person denies the possibility of death and searches for other, more promising opinions and diagnoses.

Once the person realizes he or she will indeed die, there is anger, resentment, and envy—the *anger* stage. The person is frustrated by the fact that plans and dreams will not be fulfilled.

The person in the *bargaining* stage looks for ways to buy time, making promises and negotiating with God, doctors, nurses, or others for more time or relief from pain and suffering.

When the bargaining fails or time runs out, hopelessness and depression take hold. The person in the *depression* stage mourns both for the losses that have already occurred and the death and separation from family and friends to come.

In the final stage of *acceptance* the person accepts and awaits his or her fate quietly.

Although the stages Kübler-Ross describes are common reactions to one's approaching death, they are not absolute. Not all people go through the stages, and only a few go through them in this particular order. Many factors influence a person's reactions, including culture, personality, religion, personal philosophy about life, and the length and nature of the final disease. Some people remain angry and depressed until death, whereas others welcome death as a release from pain or loneliness. People cope with death in individual ways and should not be forced into a set pattern of stages (Hudson, 1981). Rather, Kastenbaum (1979) advocates allowing people to follow their own way of dying. If they want, they should talk about their feelings, concerns, and experiences; have their questions answered; set their lives in order; see relatives and friends; forgive or ask forgiveness for quarrels or petty misdeeds. These actions, Kastenbaum suggests, may be more important to the individual than experiencing broad emotional states in a particular order.

DEATH AS A FINAL STAGE OF GROWTH Those who are not faced with the prospect of immediate death can spend more time adjusting to the idea. They often spend their last years looking back and reliving old pleasures and pains. According to Butler (1968, 1971), this kind of life review is a very important step in the lifelong growth of the individual. At no other time is there as strong a force toward self-awareness as in old age. The process often leads to real personality growth; individuals can resolve old conflicts, reestablish meaning in life, and even discover new truths about themselves. Only in coping with the reality of approaching death can one ultimately make life's crucial decisions as to what is really important and who one really is. Death lends the necessary perspective (Kübler-Ross, 1975). Paradoxically, then, dying can be "a process of re-commitment to life" (Imara, 1975, p. 160).

As in earlier periods of life, the task of finding meaning and purpose in life involves active restructuring of one's philosophical, religious, and pragmatic thoughts and beliefs (Sherman, 1987). In 1974, when Ernest Becker was interviewed (Keen, 1974), he was hospitalized in the last stage of terminal cancer. During his life, he had written a great deal about facing up to death, so he was aware of what he was experiencing on many psychological, philosophical, and theological levels. Becker had passed through several stages of adjusting to his own death, and by the time of the interview, he might be characterized as having reached a final stage of transcendence. His own resolution was a religious one: "What makes death easier [is] to know that . . . beyond what is happening to us there is the fact of the tremendous creative energies of the cosmos that are using us for some purposes we don't know" (Keen, 1974, p. 78). Other individuals may use a slightly different philosophy to come to terms with their own deaths. But in any case, Becker's testimony is a persuasive argument for allowing people to work out their own personal resolution to face death in dignity and peace.

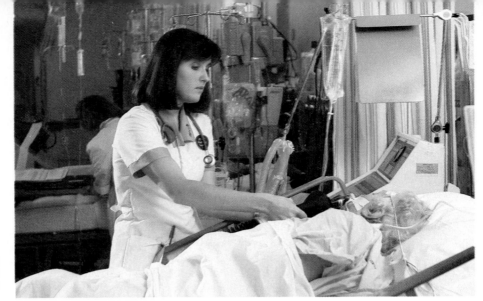

An illness that requires frequent and complex medical intervention may leave a person little time or energy to adjust to death.

Alternate Trajectories

Often, the course of illness itself affects the reactions to the dying process. If death is sudden, there is little time for life review and integration. An illness that causes considerable pain or limited mobility, or requires frequent and complex medical intervention, however, may leave a person little time or energy to adjust to death. It would be a mistake for medical personnel or family members to assume casually that a person is in "the anger stage" when, in fact, the reaction is directly related to the person's current physical condition and/or medical treatment (Kastenbaum & Costa, 1977).

Just as there are numerous and unique "life trajectories" in adult development, there are also a wide range of "dying trajectories." The commonly accepted ideal trajectory is to be healthy to age 85 or more, put one's affairs in order, and die suddenly and without pain of a heart attack (Kalish, 1985). Indeed, surveys show that far more people prefer a sudden death—particularly the young (Kalish, 1985). When there is an illness with an expected trajectory, family members as well as the dying individual adjust and adapt to the presumed "time left to live." For many there are tasks to be completed, arrangements to be made, things to be said—there is the unfinished business of living to be attended to. Some people attempt to influence the expected trajectory by accepting treatment or rejecting it, by exerting their "will to live," or by resigning themselves to the inevitable. Many individuals need to maintain some control and dignity in this final trajectory, as they have in life.

THE SEARCH FOR A HUMANE DEATH

As we have seen, a great deal of study has been done recently on the experience of dying, and our former ignorance and neglect of the subject are gradually giving way. It may be a long time, however, before society's general attitude toward death catches up to the advanced thinking of some theorists. We are remarkably good at providing medical care—the medication, the instruments, the life-support systems—to dying patients. But we are extremely poor at dealing head-on with their worries and thoughts. The terminally ill are often treated as less than human by those around them. They are isolated from their loved ones in a sterile environment; decisions are made for them, without regard for their wishes. They are rarely told what their treatments are for, and if they become upset or rebellious, they are often sedated (Kübler-Ross, 1969). Compared to the terrifyingly cold atmosphere of the hospital, an old-fashioned death at home, where the dying person is surrounded by familiar faces and objects, seems almost like a luxury.

Doctors and other health-care professionals are starting to be more honest with dying patients about their condition and treatments (Fixx, 1981). Along these lines, Birren and Birren (1987) suggest that dying patients should be given some measure of autonomy. Being permitted to state how much medication they want, for example, can give them a sense that they still control some aspects of their lives. This is very important for patients who may otherwise feel that they are being swept along by forces totally out of their control. In fact, some research indicates that almost any animal—whether a rat, a dog, or a cockroach—often simply relinquishes life if it feels it has lost control of its destiny (Seligman, 1974). In an experiment where rats were put in water to see how long they could swim, some lasted for as long as 60 hours, whereas a few sank below the surface and drowned almost instantly. What caused the different reactions? The rats that died quickly had been restrained before being put in the water; those that kept on struggling did not sense that there was no use in trying to survive. Something similar happens when people are put in nursing homes or hospitals prematurely and feel they can no longer control their own lives in any meaningful way. They respond, just like any other animal, by giving up the struggle. By contrast, individuals who have spent a lifetime controlling their environments may try to control the hospital or nursing staff. These people may not be cooperative, docile patients, but they tend to live longer (Tobin, 1988).

We have already seen that only a relatively small proportion of the elderly report fearing death (Jeffers & Verwoerdt, 1970). Yet they often report other fears about the dying process. They do not want a long and painful terminal period, and they do not want to be dependent on others for too long. Also, they fear the loss of their minds as well as their dignity. Some even talk about wanting a "good death," not an agonizing, degrading one. The quest for "the good death" has led to several proposed changes in the ways in which we provide services to the aged.

Hospices

The notion that dying people should maintain some control over their lives and, for that matter, over their deaths as well, has given rise to the recent widespread development of **hospices** for the dying. The hospice concept is designed to help terminally ill patients live out their days as fully and as independently as possible by giving needed support both to the patients themselves and to their families. The first hospice for the dying was started in England, in 1967, as an inpatient program. The idea spread to America in 1974, with the launching of a hospice program in New Haven, Connecticut, and it caught on rapidly. Four years later, there were some 200 hospice programs in 39 states and the District of Columbia in various planning stages (Abbott, 1978).

The hospice movement has now become widely adopted in this country, with

hospice Services, including the option for residential treatment, for the terminally ill that allow them to live out their days as independently and painlessly as possible.

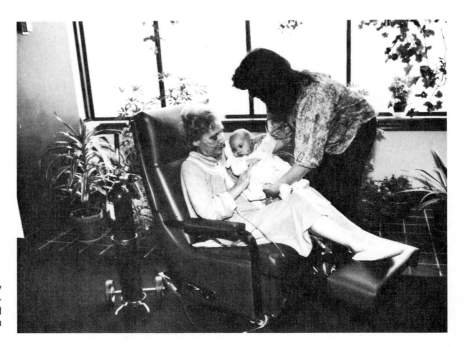

In this well-decorated and well-lit day room in a hospice, a patient can comfortably enjoy a visit from her daughter and grandchild while receiving the oxygen she needs.

a National Hospice Organization that sets standards and monitors programs (Birnbaum & Kidder, 1984). Hospice programs may be independent, but most are a part of comprehensive health-care organizations. The comprehensive program usually includes an inpatient unit, home-care programs with a variety of home-based services, medical and psychological consultation, and ongoing medical and nursing services that relieve pain and control symptoms (Haber, 1987).

A law enacted in 1982 helped make hospice services more affordable and available to dying patients. Under Public Law 97-248 (1982), individuals covered by the Social Security system can receive home services for as much as two periods of 3 months each. These services include involvement of the regular physician, home nursing care, psychological counseling, nutrition evaluation, respite care, spiritual guidance, home support services, legal and financial advice, occupational, physical, and speech therapy, and bereavement care for the family. In many areas of the country, not only is this kind of home service welcomed by the patient, but in many cases it is cost-effective (Haber, 1987).

Hospitals are devoted to life and life support: Hospital personnel see death as the enemy. The care they give to the dying reflects that attitude. The hospice concept, however, views death not as a failure, but as a normal and natural stage of life, to be approached with dignity. Death is as natural as birth and, like birth, is sometimes hard work, requiring assistance (Garrett, 1978). Hospices are designed to provide that assistance and comfort. Their first aim is to manage pain of all sorts: physical pain, mental pain, social pain, and spiritual pain (Garrett, 1978). Beyond that, they try as much as possible to "include the dying person as taking an active part in his own care and decision making" (Rosel, 1978, p. 52), and to respect the dying person's rights in regard to choices about lifestyle and, as far as possible, death (Koff, 1980). In addition, they help the family to understand the dying person's experience and needs, and also keep communication lines open so that the dying member will feel less isolated. Their contact with the family continues up to and beyond the actual death, extending throughout the period of bereavement.

The Right to Die

If, as many believe, death is a natural, positive experience, do we have the right to tamper with it? Do we rob people of a dignified death if we artificially maintain their life systems beyond the point where they can ever regain consciousness? Is there a point at which a person is meant to die and it would be better to let nature take its course? Do we prolong life because we fear death, even though the patients themselves may be at peace and ready to die? These questions have been given a great deal of attention in recent years, and many thoughtful people are starting to demand a "right to die."

The idea of letting nature take its course, or even of lending a helping hand to hasten the end, is, of course, not entirely new. **Euthanasia,** or "mercy killing," was practiced in ancient Greece, and perhaps even earlier. Reportedly, one of the more notable "victims" of euthanasia in this century was Sigmund Freud. In 1939, the 83-year-old Freud, who had been suffering from cancer of the jaw for 16 years, decided that he had had enough: "Now it is nothing but torture, and makes no sense anymore" (Shapiro, 1978, p. 23). He had previously made a pact with his physician to administer a lethal dose of morphine should Freud decide that he could no longer bear his intense pain and frustration. He now asked that the agreement be put into force, and the doctor honored his wish (Shapiro, 1978).

In Freud's case, nature was not simply allowed to take its course; positive steps were taken to bring about a premature death. This is generally called "active euthanasia," although many would consider that too kind a euphemism. In our society, the act is considered murder, pure and simple, although it is sometimes treated with leniency (Shapiro, 1978). This is especially true in cases where the final act of euthanasia is carried out by the dying person so that it can legally be considered a suicide. This is what happened in the widely publicized case of a physician providing an Alzheimer's patient with a "death machine" that administered a lethal drug automatically when the patient pushed a button.

Passive, or negative, euthanasia involves no positive action but merely the withholding of life-sustaining procedures so that death will come about naturally. Passive, voluntary euthanasia has become a conspicuous issue lately, mostly due to the recent advances in the ability to sustain life, in some cases almost indefinitely. Indeed, a major issue is how to determine when to disconnect life support machines. Table 21–1 lists the Harvard Criteria for defining death. These have been widely used as a foundation for legal definitions of death. Although they seem straightforward, and irrefutable, these criteria do not really resolve all of the issues (Kastenbaum, 1986). For example, does functioning and blood flow have to be absent in *all* areas of the brain for the person to be considered dead? Or is the cessation of activity in the cerebral cortex sufficient? Such questions are most likely to be raised—and the criteria are most likely to be invoked—when there is some debate and a judge is being asked to decide whether or not to disconnect the life supports (Robbins, 1986).

One example of an effort to assure some individual autonomy, even in the last stages of life, is the "Living Will," prepared by Concern for Dying, an Educational Council (see Figure 21–1). This document informs the signer's family, or others

euthanasia Literally, "easy death"; the practice of actively hastening the death of hopelessly ill individuals (or animals) by way of drugs or other means, or by passively withholding life-sustaining procedures so that death will occur naturally.

TABLE 21-1

The Harvard Criteria for Determination of a Permanently Nonfunctioning (or Dead) Brain

UNRECEPTIVE AND UNRESPONSIVE No awareness is shown for external stimuli or inner need. The unresponsiveness is complete even under the application of stimuli that ordinarily would be extremely painful.

NO MOVEMENTS AND NO BREATHING There is a complete absence of spontaneous respiration and all other spontaneous muscular movement.

NO REFLEXES The usual reflexes that can be elicited in a neurophysiological examination are absent (for example, when a light is shined in the eye, the pupil does not constrict).

A FLAT ELECTROENCEPHALOGRAM (EEG). Electrodes attached to the scalp elicit a printout of electrical activity from the living brain. These are popularly known as brain waves. The respirator brain does not provide the usual pattern of peaks and valleys. Instead, the moving automatic stylus records essentially a flat line. This is taken to demonstrate the lack of electrophysiological activity.

NO CIRCULATION TO OR WITHIN THE BRAIN Without the oxygen and nutrition provided to the brain by its blood supply, functioning will soon terminate. (Precisely how long the brain can retain its viability, the ability to survive, without circulation is a matter of much current investigation and varies somewhat with conditions.)

Source: From Kastenbaum, R., *Death, Society, and Human Experience.* Columbus, OH: Merrill, 1986, p. 9.

who may be concerned, of the signer's wish to avoid the use of "heroic measures" to maintain life in the event of irreversible illness. Although it is not legally binding, it does protect those who observe its terms from legal liability for doing so (Shapiro, 1978).

FIGURE 21-1

"The Living Will."

This is a formal request prepared by Concern for Dying, an Educational Council. It informs the signer's family, or others who may be concerned, of the signer's wish to avoid the use of "heroic measures" to maintain life in the event of irreversible illness.

TO MY FAMILY, MY PHYSICIAN, MY LAWYER AND ALL OTHERS WHOM IT MAY CONCERN

Death is as much a reality as birth, growth, maturity and old age—it is the one certainty of life. If the time comes when I can no longer take part in decisions for my own future, let this statement stand as an expression of my wishes, while I am still of sound mind.

If at such a time the situation should arise in which there is no reasonable expectation of my recovery from extreme physical or mental disability, I direct that I be allowed to die and not be kept alive by medications, artificial means or "heroic measures." I do, however, ask that medication be mercifully administered to me to alleviate suffering even though this may shorten my remaining life.

This statement is made after careful consideration and is in accordance with my strong convictions and beliefs. I want the wishes and directions here expressed carried out to the extent permitted by law. Insofar as they are not legally enforceable, I hope that those to whom this Will is addressed will regard themselves as morally bound by these provisions.

Signed _____

Date _____

Witness _____

Witness _____

Copies of this request have been given to _____

_____

_____

_____

GRIEF AND BEREAVEMENT

But what of those left behind? Often surviving family members and close friends must make great adjustments to death and to the dying process. For them there is "life after death."

There are short- and long-term adjustments to be made. Short-term adjustments include initial emotional reactions to the personal loss—the "grief work," as it is often called—and the practical matters of funeral arrangements, financial matters, and legal procedures. Long-term adjustments, particularly for a widow or widower, include the changes in life patterns, routines, roles, and activities that may be necessary to cope with the social void left by death. Each of these adjustments may require more time and involvement than anticipated.

The Grieving Process

Is it necessary to grieve? Do sorrow and mental anguish serve some useful function? What is the purpose of grief work? It is generally believed that certain psychological tasks need to be accomplished. The survivor needs to accept the reality of the loss and to realize that the loss causes some pain. Also, the survivor must rechannel the emotional energy that he or she had previously invested in the relationship with the deceased (Worden, 1982).

Many experts hesitate to define phases of grieving because it may encourage people to force the wide variations of grieving into the prescribed sequence (Gallagher, 1987). Those who do suggest a pattern note that initial reactions often include shock, numbness, denial, and disbelief. There may be anger or attempts to affix blame. The shock phase often lasts several days, and sometimes much longer. After a sudden death, the people closest to the deceased may participate in the ceremonies of funerals and burials in a robotlike fashion, not yet fully accepting the loss. In the second phase, survivors may experience more active grief. There may be weeping or other expressions of sorrow. There may be a yearning or pining for the lost person. Some individuals have physical symptoms—feelings of weakness or emptiness, as well as difficulty eating or sleeping. Often there is little interest in normal pursuits and a preoccupation with thoughts of the deceased. The individual may have all the symptoms of depression. Eventually, survivors begin to recover. They adjust to their new life circumstances. They "let go" of the loved one, investing time and energy in new relationships, and they reconstruct an identity apart from the relationship with the deceased.

There are, of course, many patterns of grieving, depending on personality, age, sex, cultural traditions, and the relationship with the deceased. In addition, some factors may aid the recovery process. If there has been a long illness or loss of functioning, for example, the survivors are able to prepare themselves for the loss. They are likely to experience some *anticipatory* grief. Perhaps feelings of loss, guilt, or missed opportunities are even discussed with the dying person. Anticipatory grief, however, will not eliminate postdeath grieving. Indeed, it may not even reduce the intensity of postdeath grief (Rando, 1986). But the effects of the death are less overwhelming because some plans and adjustments have been made, so that *coping* with the grief may be improved. On the other hand, if an illness lasts more than about 18 months, the drain of caring for the person outweighs the value of preparing for the death. Furthermore, when an illness is

It seems to be necessary to grieve, to accept the reality of one's loss, and to realize that the loss causes some pain.

prolonged, the survivor may become convinced that the terminally ill person will not really die, that he or she has "beaten the odds." Thus, the death may be *more* shocking than a sudden death (Rando, 1986).

Social support may also play a role in grieving. Models of stress and coping frequently note the value of strong social supports in successfully negotiating life crises. But for widows, not all social support is equally helpful (Bankoff, 1986; Morgan, 1989). In one study, about 40% of the comments made by widows about postbereavement social relationships were negative (Morgan, 1989). Support from peers, especially those who have also experienced spousal loss, seems more helpful than family support. Young widows, then, are often particularly unlikely to receive strong positive social support (Bankoff, 1986). Widowhood support groups also seem helpful (Morgan, 1989). Similarly, parents who have lost a child often find it particularly comforting to be with others whose children have died (Edelstein, 1984).

There are some circumstances under which grief may be overwhelming. For example, older people who experience the loss of several friends or family members in the span of a year or two may experience *bereavement overload*. Depression is a serious risk postbereavement, especially for men (Stroebe & Stroebe, 1987). So is alcohol abuse, again especially among men. Physical health may also be affected. The recently bereaved visit their physicians more frequently than do other groups (Mor, McHorney, & Sherwood, 1986). It is possible, however, that such visits really represent routine care that was neglected while the bereaved served as a care-giver to the deceased. Furthermore, many of these visits may be linked to depression more than to a serious physical illness (Mor, McHorney, & Sherwood, 1986).

Rituals and Customs

The customs and rituals of death in the United States have changed considerably throughout history. It used to be customary, for example, for a widow to wear black and refrain from many social activities for several months or a year. This symbolized her presumed emotional distress. Other people were signaled to provide comfort and support, and the culture allowed for a long adaptation period (Aries, 1981). The opposite is true of most current customs in recognition of bereavement. Normally the work place expects the survivor to return to work, ready to resume a full workload, in 3 to 5 days. But few people fit either of these cultural prescriptions.

Funerals and memorial services can impart a sense of order, decorum, and continuity. They can reaffirm the values and beliefs of the individuals and the community, and demonstrate the support of family and friends. The deceased person's life can be reviewed and celebrated in a public, shared form. But the public ceremonies sometimes clash with the values and experiences of the survivors, leaving them feeling further isolated. Sometimes the rituals and institutions are too distant from the personal lives of the participants at the time of this critical event.

In most cultures, there are rituals, rites, and services that help survivors with the grieving process.

When a Child Dies

Many of the aspects of grief and bereavement are intensified when a child dies. If the death is sudden or unexpected, the reactions of parents and siblings are often prolonged and intense. There may also be confusion, guilt, and attempts to blame someone or something for the loss (Miles, 1984). Brothers and sisters of a dying child may be particularly confused. Death is often seen as a punishment of some sort—to the child who died, to the parent, or to the surviving brother or sister. Often parents coping with their own grief may not be able to help the other children in the family or even to think through answers to a child's questions on an appropriate developmental level. Many siblings do not disclose their secret fears, feelings of guilt, or misunderstandings, and yet many of the thoughts and feelings that arise during such a family crisis may last a lifetime (Coleman & Coleman, 1984).

When a child dies slowly of a terminal illness, there are other issues to deal with. What should the dying child be told? How can the child be helped to confront his or her own death? How do parents deal with their feelings of failure, guilt, or helplessness? Often the medical caretakers become quite involved in the child's hopes for recovery. They, too, will experience some of the parents' feelings of failure and anticipatory grief. There is the tendency for all involved to deny these painful feelings. Grief and recovery are particularly difficult when a child dies (Wass & Corr, 1984).

A crisis of values is not uncommon for survivors following the death of a child. Certainly the child did not deserve to die. Survivors struggle to reevaluate their most closely held beliefs and values while they are also suffering from numerous symptoms of sorrow and depression (Kushner, 1981). Those who find some resolution to those questions often report a deeper meaning in their own lives.

STUDY OUTLINE

Death is the irrevocable cessation of life functions. It holds personal as well as cultural significance, and it affects the dying person as well as the survivors.

Thoughts and Fears of Death

The Denial of Death. In earlier periods of history, people were more familiar with the workings of death—the dying were cared for at home, and they usually died with family members present. The body was prepared for burial by family or friends as well, and the rituals preceding the burial took place at home. Our current culture distances us from the natural process of death.

Denial is a very real part of death in our society for the dying and their survivors. Denial is a normal mechanism for coping with stress, but it can interfere with active coping.

Fears, Preoccupations, and Meanings of Death. Psychoanalytic theory suggests that fearing death is normal. Several studies show that, in general, older adults fear death less, that people with a strong sense of purpose in life generally fear death less, and many older adults are at ease with the prospect of their own deaths. What many do fear is a prolonged, painful period prior to death. Death anxiety appears to be only one symptom in the ongoing process of accepting death.

Confronting One's Own Death

Kübler-Ross identified five stages of adjustment to the idea of death—*denial, anger, bargaining, depression,* and *acceptance.* Many critics point out, however, that although these are common reactions to approaching death, people cope with death in individualistic ways.

The Search for a Humane Death

Hospices. The question of an individual's right to die is extremely controversial. Traditional medical treatment of the terminally ill has usually concentrated on maintaining life systems while ignoring human needs for autonomy, emotional expression, and familiar surroundings. Hospices allow the terminally ill to live out their days as fully, painlessly, and independently as possible. The hospice concept is that death is as natural as birth, is sometimes hard work, and requires assistance.

The Right to Die. Many people feel that all people have a right to die without their lives being prolonged by artificial means. Some would advocate helping the process by euthanasia, or mercy killing; others advocate a more passive form that withholds life-sustaining procedures and allows death to occur naturally.

Grief and Bereavement

Surviving family members and close friends make short-

and long-term adjustments to death and dying. Short-term adjustments include the initial emotional reactions to the loss, grief work, and taking care of the practical matters of funeral preparations. Long-term adjustments, particularly for a surviving spouse, include changes in life patterns, roles, and activities.

The Grieving Process. It is generally accepted that grief work is necessary—certain psychological tasks need to be accomplished after the death of someone with whom a close relationship has been shared. Although many experts hesitate to define a pattern of grieving, some suggest that the initial phase is characterized by shock, the second stage involves more active grief, and the recovery of the survivor marks the third phase.

KEY TERMS AND CONCEPTS

anticipatory grief
bereavement overload
death trajectories
euthanasia

hospice
Kübler-Ross's stages of
    adjustment to death

living will

SELF-TEST QUESTIONS

1. How does American culture handle death today as compared with a century ago? What are the developmental issues raised by this change in our culture?

2. Are older people more fearful or more preoccupied with death than younger people? Please explain.

3. What are the stages of adjustment to death outlined by Kübler-Ross? Are these stages universal?

4. In what sense can death be considered a stage of growth?

5. What are "death trajectories," and how do they vary among individuals?

6. What is the difference between a hospital and a hospice? Discuss the advantages of hospice care and the philosophy underlying such care.

7. What are the controversial issues involved in euthanasia? How does our society deal with these issues?

8. Describe the grieving process and the use of rituals and customs to assist in this process. How can rituals and customs for grieving sometimes be a source of further discomfort?

9. What are the special issues associated with the death of a child?

SUGGESTED READINGS

Aries, P. *The hour of our death.* New York: Knopf, 1981. A historical survey of practices of handling the dying.

Beisser, A. *A graceful passage: Notes on the freedom to live or die.* New York: Doubleday, 1990. A candid and compassionate discussion of progressive terminal diseases and the issues concerning the "right to die."

Cook, A. S., & Oltjenbruno, K. A. *Dying and grieving: Lifespan and family perspectives.* New York: Holt, Rinehart & Winston, 1989. A comprehensive text on death and dying and the related mourning process.

Kalish, R. *Death, grief, and caring relationships.* Monterey, CA: Brooks/Cole, 1985. A textbook on death and dying, with emphasis on the importance of allowing the dying

patient and family and friends to express their feelings and to cope with the concept of death.

Kübler-Ross, E. *On death and dying.* New York: Macmillan, 1969. Based on extensive interviews with dying patients. Kübler-Ross describes the most common reactions to approaching death.

Kushner, H. *When bad things happen to good people.* New York: Schocken, 1981. A sensitive, thoughtful discussion about coping with notions of justice and religious beliefs when facing situations such as death.

Mor, V. *Hospice care systems: Structure, process, costs and outcome.* New York: Springer, 1987. An overview and analysis of the range of hospice care systems now available.

Glossary

accommodation Piaget's term for the act of changing our thought processes when a new object or idea does not fit our concepts.

adaptation In Piaget's theory, the process by which infant schemata are elaborated, modified, and developed.

afterbirth The placenta and related tissues, following their expulsion from the uterus during the third stage of childbirth.

age clock A form of internal timing, or a way of knowing we are progressing too slowly or too quickly in terms of social events and our peers' progress.

ageism A widely prevalent social attitude that overvalues youth and discriminates against the elderly.

aggression Hostile behavior that is intended to injure.

aging Biological changes that occur beyond the point of optimal maturity.

AIDS Acquired immune deficiency syndrome—a serious, usually fatal disease caused by a virus. Anyone can be infected through sexual contact or through exposure to infected blood or needles.

alleles A pair of genes, found on corresponding chromosomes, that affect the same trait.

amniocentesis A test for chromosomal abnormalities that is performed during the second trimester of pregnancy; it involves the withdrawal and analysis of amniotic fluid.

amniotic sac A fluid-filled membrane that encloses the developing embryo or fetus.

anal stage Freud's second psychosexual stage during which the child's sensual pleasure is related to the bodily processes of elimination. The child is concerned with issues of control, such as "holding on" and "letting go."

androgynous personality A sex-role identity that incorporates some positive aspects of both traditional male and traditional female behavior.

anoxia In prenatal development and childbirth, a lack of sufficient oxygen reaching the brain, which can cause irreversible brain damage.

anxiety A feeling of uneasiness, apprehension, or fear that has a vague or unknown source.

assertive behavior Forthright, direct behavior, such as stating one's rights, that does not harm others.

assimilation In Piaget's theory, the process of making new information part of one's existing schemes.

atherosclerosis Hardening of the arteries. A common condition of aging caused by the body's increasing inability to use excess fats in the diet. These fats are stored along the walls of arteries, and, when they harden, restrict the flow of blood.

attachment The bond that develops between a child and another individual as a result of a long-term relationship. The infant's first bond is usually characterized by strong interdependence, intense mutual feelings, and vital emotional ties.

attention-deficit disorder (ADD) An inability to keep one's attention focused on something long enough to learn it.

authoritarian parents Parents who control their children firmly but tend to be emotionally distant and cold.

authoritative parents Parents who combine high control with warmth, acceptance, and encouragement. Baumrind has found that these parents usually have the most well-adjusted and self-reliant children.

autosomes The chromosomes of a cell, excluding those that determine sex.

avoidance conditioning A form of operant conditioning in which the reinforcement consists of the termination of an unpleasant stimulus.

behaviorists Early 20th-century psychologists who focused their research on overt, measurable, observable behavior rather than on internal medical processes.

behavior modification A method that uses conditioning procedures, such as reinforcement, reward, and shaping, to change behavior.

behavioral objectives The kinds of knowledge and skills expected of a student after a specified amount of instruction; they provide a demonstration of the school's adequacy as well as the student's.

birth The second stage of childbirth, which is the time between full cervix dilation and the time when the baby is free of the mother's body.

blastula The hollow, fluid-filled sphere of cells that forms several days after conception.

bonding Forming an attachment; refers particularly to the developing rela-

617

tionship between parents and infant that begins immediately after birth.

breech presentation The baby's position in the uterus is such that the buttocks will emerge first; assistance is usually needed in such cases to prevent injury to the mother or the infant.

Caesarean section A surgical procedure used to remove the baby and the placenta from the uterus by cutting through the abdominal wall.

case grammar The use of word order to express different relationships.

causality A relationship between two variables where change in one brings about an effect or result in the other.

centration The focusing or concentration on only one aspect or dimension of an object or situation that is characteristic of preoperational thought.

cephalocaudal developmental trend The sequence of growth in which development occurs first in the head and progresses toward the feet.

child abuse Intentional psychological or physical injuries inflicted on a child.

chorion The protective outer sac that develops from tissue surrounding the embryo.

circular response A particular form of adaptation in Piaget's theory, in which the infant accidentally performs some action, perceives it, then repeats the action.

classical conditioning A type of learning in which a neutral stimulus, such as a bell, comes to elicit a response—salivation—by repeated pairings with an unconditioned stimulus, such as food.

climacteric The broad complex of physical and emotional symptoms that accompany reproductive changes in middle age. The climacteric affects both men and women.

cognition The process by which we know and understand our world.

competence motivation A need to achieve in order to feel effective as an individual.

concrete operations Piaget's third stage of cognitive development (7 to 11 years) in which children begin to think logically. At this stage they are able to classify things and deal with a hierarchy of classifications.

conservation A cognitive ability described by Piaget as central to the concrete operational period. The child is able to judge changes in amounts based on logical thought instead of mere appearances; thus, an amount of water will remain the same even when it is poured into a glass of a different shape and size.

content The meaning of any written or spoken message.

convergence The ability to focus both eyes on one point.

correlation A mathematical statement of the relationship between two variables.

counterconditioning A procedure to eliminate a previously conditioned negative response by replacing it with a new conditioned response in the same stimulus situation.

criterion-referenced test A test that evaluates an individual's performance in relation to mastery of specified skills or objectives.

critical period The only point in time when a particular environmental factor can have an effect.

crossover A process during meiosis in which individual genes on a chromosome cross over to the opposite chromosome. This process increases the random assortment of genes in offspring.

cross-sectional design A method of studying development in which a sample of individuals of one age is observed and compared with one or more samples of individuals of other ages.

crystallized intelligence A broad area of intelligence that includes verbal reasoning, comprehension, and spatial perception; it increases during the life span.

defense mechanisms Any of the techniques that individuals use to reduce tensions that lead to anxiety.

delinquency Criminal acts committed by individuals under the age of 16 or 18 (age cutoff varies by state and by nature of the crime).

dementia The progressive deterioration of intellectual capacities that sometimes afflicts older adults.

denial The refusal to admit that an anxiety-producing situation exists or that an anxiety-producing event happened.

dependent variable The variable in an experiment that changes as a result of manipulating the independent variable.

desensitization In behavior therapy, a technique that gradually reduces an individual's anxiety about a specific object or situation.

deterministic model The view that a person's values, attitudes, behaviors, and emotional responses are determined by past or present environmental factors.

development The changes over time in structure, thought, or behavior of a person as a result of both biological and environmental influences.

deviation IQ An IQ score derived from a statistical table comparing an individual's raw score on an IQ test with the scores of other subjects of the same age.

diagnostic—prescriptive teaching A system of teaching in which tests and informal assessments inform educators as to a child's abilities so that they may prescribe appropriate instruction.

differentiation In embryology, the process in which undifferentiated cells become increasingly specialized.

diffusion The identity status of those who have neither gone through an identity crisis nor made commitments.

discrepancy hypothesis A cognition theory according to which infants acquire, at around 7 months, schemata for familiar objects. When a new image or object is presented that differs from the old, the child experiences uncertainty and anxiety.

displacement A defense mechanism in which a less threatening person or object is substituted for the actual source of anger or anxiety.

DNA (deoxyribonucleic acid) A large, complex molecule composed of carbon, hydrogen, oxygen, nitrogen, and phosphorus; it contains the genetic code that regulates the functioning and development of an organism.

dominant In genetics, one gene of a gene pair that will cause a particular trait to be expressed.

dyscalculia A learning disability involving mathematics.

dysgraphia A learning disability involving writing.

dyslexia A learning disability involving reading; unusual difficulty in learning how to read.

ectoderm In embryonic development, the outer layer of cells, which becomes the skin, sense organs, and nervous system.

egocentricity Having a self-centered view of the world, viewing everything in relation to oneself.

Electra complex A strong but unconscious attraction of girls in the phallic stage to their fathers.

embryonic period The second prenatal period, which lasts from the end of the second week to the end of the second month after conception. All the major structures and organs of the individual are formed during this time.

endoderm In embryonic development, the inner layer of cells that becomes the digestive system, lungs, thyroid, thymus, and other organs.

episiotomy An incision made to enlarge the vaginal opening during childbirth.

equilibration Piaget's term for the basic process in human adaptation. In it, individuals seek a balance, or fit, between the environment and their own structures of thought.

erogenous zones Body areas that serve as the focus of pleasure and that, in Freud's view, change as one moves through the psychosexual stages.

ethnocentrism The tendency to assume that one's own beliefs, perceptions, customs, and values are correct or normal and that those of others are inferior or abnormal.

ethology The study of animal behavior, often observed in natural settings and interpreted in an evolutionary framework.

euthanasia Literally, "easy death"; the practice of actively hastening the death of hopelessly ill individuals (or animals) by way of drugs or other means, or by passively withholding life-sustaining procedures so that death will occur naturally.

existentialism A 20th-century branch of philosophy that focuses on an individual's struggle to find meaning in his or her existence and to exercise freedom and responsibility in the pursuit of an ethical life.

experimental design The setting, subjects, and methods of measurement of a behavioral research study that serve to structure the type of information collected.

expressive jargon A term used to describe the babbling of an infant when the infant uses inflections and patterns that mimic adult speech.

extrinsic feedback Rewards of praise given for performing a task well.

Fallopian tubes Two passages that open out of the upper part of the uterus and carry the ova from the ovary to the uterus.

false labor Painful contractions of the uterus without dilation of the cervix.

fear A state of arousal, tension, or apprehension caused by a specific circumstance.

fertilization The union of an ovum and a sperm.

fetal alcohol syndrome Congenital abnormalities, including small size, low birth weight, certain facial characteristics, and possible mental retardation, resulting from maternal alcohol consumption during pregnancy.

fetal period The final period of prenatal development, lasting from the beginning of the third month after conception until birth. During this period, all organs, limbs, muscles, and systems become functional.

fetoscope A long, hollow needle with a small lens and light source at its end that is inserted into the amniotic sac for observation of the fetus.

fine motor skills Capabilities involving small body movements.

fluid intelligence A broad area of intelligence that includes motor speed, induction, and memory. It governs perceptual abilities and recognition, and reaches a peak in late adolescence.

foreclosure The identity status of those who have made commitments without going through an identity crisis.

form The particular symbol used to represent content.

formal operations The fourth and final stage of Piaget's cognitive theory; begins at about 12 years and is characterized by the ability to handle abstract concepts.

fraternal (dizygotic) twins Twins resulting from the fertilization of two separate ova by two separate sperm.

frustration The blocking of a goal, causing angry feelings and, according to some, resulting in aggressive behavior.

functional subordination The integration of a number of separate simple actions or schemes into a more complex pattern of behavior.

gender constancy The concept that gender is stable and stays the same despite changes in superficial appearance.

gender identity The knowledge that one is male or female, and the ability to make that judgment about other people.

gender-role stereotypes Rigid, fixed ideas of what is appropriate masculine or feminine behavior.

gene therapy The manipulation of individual genes to correct certain defects.

genital stage In psychoanalytic theory, the period of normal adult sexual behavior that begins with the onset of puberty.

genotype The genetic makeup of a given individual or group.

germinal period After conception, the period of very rapid cell division and initial cell differentiation lasting approximately 2 weeks.

gestation period The total period of time from conception to birth; in humans, this averages about 266 days.

gross motor skills Capabilities involving large body movements.

Gross-to-specific developmental trend The tendency to react to stimuli with generalized, whole-body movements at first, while these responses become more local and specific later on.

growth The increase in size, function, or complexity toward the point of optimal maturity.

guided participation The process by which more experienced people transmit cultural information to children.

habituation The process of becoming accustomed to certain kinds of stimuli and no longer responding to them.

holophrastic speech In the early stages of language acquisition, the young child's use of single words, perhaps to convey full sentences.

homophobia Fear or dislike of homosexuals.

hormone A biochemical secretion of the endocrine gland that is carried by the blood or other body fluids to a particular organ or tissue and acts as a stimulant or an accelerator.

hospice Services, including the option for residential treatment, for the terminally ill that allow them to live out their days as independently and painlessly as possible.

humanistic psychology According to this theory, humans are spontaneous, self-determining, and creative; it has close ties with existentialism.

hyperactive Overly active; exhibiting poor impulse control.

identical (monozygotic) twins Twins that result from the division of a single fertilized ovum.

identification Taking on the behaviors and qualities of a person whom one respects and would like to emulate.

identity achievement The identity status of those who have gone through an identity crisis and have made commitments.

identity crisis A period of making decisions about important issues—of asking "Who am I and where am I going?"

imaginary audience Adolescents' assumption that others are focusing a great deal of critical attention on them.

implantation The embedding of the prenatal organism in the uterine wall after its descent through the Fallopian tube.

imprinting The instinctual learning process by which newly hatched birds form a relatively permanent bond with the parent in a few hours or days.

independent variable The variable that experimenters manipulate in order to observe its effects on the dependent variable.

indifferent parents Parents who are low in restrictiveness and also low in warmth.

induction Giving children reasons for behaving in socially desirable ways, or for not behaving in undesirable ways.

inflections Changes in form that words undergo to designate number, gender, tense, mood, and case.

integration The organization of differentiated cells into organs or systems.

intelligence quotient An individual's mental age divided by chronological age, multiplied by 100 to eliminate the decimal point.

internalization Making social rules and standards of behavior part of oneself—adopting them as one's own set of values.

intrinsic feedback Feedback that comes from experiencing the natural consequences of performing a task.

irreversibility The belief that events and relationships can occur in only one direction that is characteristic of preoperational thought.

iteration Infants' purposeful repetition, elongation, and pause in sounds that imitate speech.

karyotype A photograph of a cell's chromosomes arranged in pairs according to length.

labor The first stage of childbirth typically lasting 12 to 18 hours and characterized by uterine contractions during which the cervix dilates to allow for passage of the baby.

latency period The fourth of Freud's psychosexual stages of development characterized by a temporary dormancy in the interest in sexual gratification.

law of effect A principle of learning theory stating that a behavior's consequences determine the probability of its being repeated.

learning The basic developmental process of change in the individual as a result of experience or practice.

learning disability Extreme difficulty in learning school subjects such as reading, writing, or math, despite normal intelligence and absence of sensory or motor defects.

logical inference A conclusion reached through "unseen" evidence; concrete operational children are capable of this type of thinking.

longitudinal design A study in which the same subjects are observed continuously over a period of time.

maturation The physical development of an organism as it fulfills its genetic potential.

mean length of utterance (MLU) The average length of the sentences that a child produces.

mechanistic model In learning theory, the view of human beings as machines that are set in motion by input (stimuli) and that produce output (responses).

meiosis The process of cell division in reproductive cells that results in an infinite number of different chromosomal arrangements.

menarche The time of the first menstrual period.

menopause The permanent end of menstruation; it occurs in middle age, and may be accompanied by physical symptoms and intense emotional reactions.

mental age An intelligence test score showing the age group with which a child's performance most closely compares.

mesoderm In embryonic development, the middle layer of cells that becomes the muscles, blood, and excretory system.

metacognition The process of monitoring one's own thinking, memory, knowledge, goals, and actions.

midwife A childbirth assistant who remains with a mother throughout labor and who can supervise births where no complications are expected; nurse-midwives have had training in hospital nursing programs, where they have studied obstetrics; lay midwives have had no formal medical or obstetrics training.

miscarriage (spontaneous abortion) Expulsion of the prenatal organism before it is viable.

mitosis The process of ordinary cell division that results in two cells identical to the parent.

moral absolutism Any theory of morality that disregards cultural differences in moral beliefs.

moral judgment The process of making decisions about right and wrong.

moral realism Piaget's term for the first stage of moral development, in which children believe in rules as real, indestructible things.

moral relativism Piaget's term for the second stage of moral development, in which children realize that rules are agreements that may be changed, if necessary.

moratorium The identity status of those who are currently in the midst of an identity crisis.

morphemes The minimal units of meaning in language that form basic words, prefixes, and suffixes.

morphology The set of rules for building words that is present in all languages.

mutation An alteration in the strips of DNA and consequently in the genetic code.

mutuality (synchrony) The pattern of interchange between care-giver and infant in which each responds to and influences the other's movements and rhythms.

"natural" childbirth A childbirth method that involves the mother's preparation (including education and exercises), limited medication during pregnancy and birth, and the mother's (and perhaps father's) participation during the birth.

neonate A baby in the first month of life.

nonsex-linked autosomal trait Trait caused by genes on the nonsex-determining chromosomes (autosomes).

norm-referenced test A test that compares an individual's performance with the performances of others in the same age group.

novelty paradigm A research plan that uses infants' preferences for new stimuli over familiar ones in order to investigate their ability to detect small differences in sounds, patterns, or colors.

object permanence According to Piaget, the realization in infants at about 18 months that objects continue to exist when they are out of sight, touch, or some other perceptual context.

Oedipal complex A strong but unconscious attraction of boys in the phallic stage to their mothers.

operant behavior A behavior in which the individual operates on the environment or emits an action.

operant conditioning A type of conditioning that occurs when an organism is reinforced for voluntarily emitting a response. What is reinforced is then learned.

oral stage Freud's first psychosexual stage during which the infant's sensual pleasure focuses around the mouth.

organization and rehearsal Strategies for improving recall used mainly by adult learners.

osteoporosis A bone disease in which the density of bones decreases, resulting in brittleness; older women are particularly susceptible to this disease.

overregularization The generalization of complex language principles, typically by preschool children rapidly expanding their vocabularies.

ovulation The release of the ovum into one of the two Fallopian tubes; occurs approximately 14 days after menstruation.

ovum The female reproductive cell (the egg or gamete).

peer group A group of two or more people of similar status who interact with each other and who share norms and goals.

perception The complex process by which the mind interprets and gives meaning to sensory information.

perinatology A branch of medicine that deals with childbirth from conception, the prenatal period, and delivery through the first few months of life.

perineum The region between the vagina and the rectum.

permissive parents Parents who place few or no restraints on their children. They tend to be high on warmth.

personal fable Adolescents' feeling that they are special and invulnerable—exempt from the laws of nature that control the destinies of ordinary mortals.

phallic stage Freud's third stage of psychosexual development (ages 3 to 5) during which the child's sensual pleasure focuses on the genitals.

phenotype In genetics, those traits that are expressed in the individual.

phonemes The smallest units of sound—vowels and consonants—that combine to form morphemes and words.

pincer grasp The method of holding objects, developed around the age of 12 months, in which the thumb opposes the forefinger.

pivot grammar A two-word sentence-forming system used by 2-year-olds and involving action words, prepositions, or possessives (pivot words) in combination with x-words, which are usually nouns.

placenta A disk-shaped mass of tissue that forms along the wall of the uterus through which the embryo receives nutrients and discharges wastes.

polygenic inheritance A trait caused by an interaction of several genes or gene pairs.

positive regard A "warm, positive, acceptant" attitude toward clients that

Rogers found most effective in promoting personal growth.

posterior presentation A baby is positioned in the uterus facing the mother's abdomen rather than her back.

pregenital period The immature psychosexual development of childhood; encompasses the oral, anal, and phallic stages.

prejudice A negative attitude formed without adequate reason and usually directed toward people because of their membership in a group.

premature Having a short gestation period (less than 37 weeks) and/or low birth weight (less than $5\frac{1}{2}$ pounds).

preoperational period Piaget's second stage of cognitive development (about 2 to 7 years) begins when children are able to use symbols such as language. Their thinking tends to be overly concrete, irreversible, and egocentric, and classification is difficult.

productive language The spoken or written communication of preschool children.

projection A person using this defense mechanism will attribute his or her own undesirable thoughts or actions to someone else.

prosocial behavior Helping, sharing, or cooperative actions that are intended to benefit others.

proximodistal developmental trend The directional sequence of development that occurs from the midline of the body outward.

psychoanalytic tradition Based on the theories of Freud, whose view of human nature was deterministic. He believed that personality is motivated by innate, biological drives.

psychosexual stages Freud's stages of personality development.

psychosocial stages In Erikson's theory, the phases of development during which the individual's capacities for experience dictate major adjustments to the social environment and the self.

rationalization A defense mechanism in which an individual explains unac-

ceptable thoughts or behavior by inventing a socially acceptable reason for them.

reaction formation A defense mechanism in which individuals unconsciously mask their anxiety over unacceptable thoughts or desires by behaving in an extremely contradictory fashion.

readiness A point in time when an individual has matured enough to benefit from a particular learning experience.

recall The ability to retrieve information and events that are not present.

receptive language The repertoire of words and commands that a child understands, although he or she may not be able to say them.

recessive In genetics, one gene of a gene pair that determines a trait in an individual only if the other member of that pair is also recessive.

recognition The ability to correctly identify items previously experienced when they appear again.

reference group A social group or collection of people with whom an individual shares attitudes, ideals, or philosophies.

reflex An unlearned, automatic response to a stimulus. Many reflexes disappear after 3 or 4 months.

regression Coping with an anxiety-producing situation by reverting to earlier, more immature behavior.

reliability The extent to which a measuring technique will produce the same results each time it is used.

representation The use of symbols in the form of actions, images, or words to represent events or experiences.

repression An extreme form of denial in which the individual completely erases an anxiety-producing event or situation from consciousness.

resilient children Children who overcome difficult environments to lead socially competent lives.

response consequences The observed results of one's actions that individuals use to adjust their behavior.

rite of passage A symbolic event or ritual to mark life transitions, such as the one from childhood to adult status.

RNA (ribonucleic acid) A substance formed from, and similar to, DNA. It acts as a messenger in a cell and serves as a catalyst for the formation of new tissue.

role playing The acting out of a role in order to see things from the perspective of another person.

schema Piaget's term for mental structures that process information, perceptions, and experiences; individuals' schemes change as they grow.

self-actualization Realizing one's full potential.

self-esteem Seeing oneself as an individual with positive characteristics—as one who will do well in the things that he or she thinks are important.

self-fulfilling prophecy An expectation that helps to bring about the predicted event, which consequently strengthens the expectation.

self-image Seeing oneself as an individual with certain characteristics.

sensorimotor period Piaget's first stage of cognitive development, lasting from birth to about 2 years. Infants use action schemes—looking, grasping, and so on—to learn about their world.

sequential/age cohort design A combination of cross-sectional and longitudinal research designs in which individuals of several different ages are observed repeatedly over an extended period of time.

sex-linked traits Traits carried by genes on either of the sex-determining chromosomes.

shaping Systematically reinforcing successive approximations to a desired act.

sibling status Birth order.

significant other Anyone whose opinions an individual values highly.

social cognition Thought, knowledge, and understanding that involve the social world.

social inference Guesses and assumptions about what another person is feeling, thinking, or intending.

socialization The lifelong process by which an individual acquires the beliefs, attitudes, customs, values, roles, and expectations of a culture or a social group.

social reciprocity The continued interaction between individuals as they respond and react to each other in a manner that encourages the prevailing behavior.

social regulations The rules and conventions governing social interactions.

social relationships Relationships that involve obligations such as fairness and loyalty. The knowledge of these obligations is a necessary part of social cognition.

sociobiology A branch of ethology that holds the view that social behavior is largely determined by an organism's biological inheritance.

sperm The male reproductive cell (or gamete).

status passage A change in the role and position that occurs when an individual enters adolescence, becomes a parent, retires, or becomes a widow or widower.

stimulus generalization The spread of a response from one specific stimulus to other similar stimuli.

stranger, or separation, anxiety An infant's fear of strangers or of being separated from the care-giver. Both occur in the second half of the first year and indicate, in part, a new cognitive ability to detect and respond to differences in the environment.

structuralism A branch of psychology concerned with the structure of thought and the ways in which the mind processes information.

structures of character In Loevinger's theory, part of the ego's equipment for making sense of experience and achieving self-understanding.

structures of meaning An individual's understanding of the world on which, according to Loevinger's theory, a series of developmental stages depend.

sublimation An adult coping strategy in which anxious energy and unacceptable impulses are turned toward acceptable goals.

surprise paradigm A research technique used to test infants' memory and expectations. Infants cannot report what they remember or expect, but if their expectations are violated, they respond with surprise. For example, if the doll is not under the cloth where the infants saw it hidden, they are surprised.

symbolic representation The use of a word, picture, gesture, or other sign to represent past and present events, experiences, and concepts.

syntax The rules for combining words to form phrases and sentences.

telegraphic speech One- and 2-year-olds' utterances that omit the less significant words and include the words that carry the most meaning.

teratogens The toxic agents that cause abnormalities or birth defects.

teratology The study of developmental abnormalities or birth defects.

toddler The infant in his or her second year of life who has begun to walk—the child has a somewhat top-heavy, wide stance and walks with a gait that is not solidly balanced or smoothly coordinated.

toxemia Poisoning of a mother's body during pregnancy due to a metabolic disturbance.

trimesters The three equal time segments that comprise the 9-month gestation period.

ultrasound A technique that uses sound waves to produce a picture of the fetus while it is still in the mother's uterus.

umbilical cord The "rope" of tissue connecting the placenta to the embryo; this rope contains two fetal arteries and one fetal vein.

use The way in which a speaker employs language to give it one meaning as opposed to another.

validity The accuracy with which a procedure measures correctly what it is supposed to measure.

viable After 24 weeks of development, the ability of the fetus to live outside the mother's body, provided it receives special care.

visual cliff An experimental apparatus that tests depth perception of infants by simulating an abrupt dropoff.

withdrawal A defense mechanism in which the individual physically runs away from, or mentally withdraws from, unpleasant situations.

zone of proximal development Vygotsky's concept of children's ability to develop through participation in activities slightly beyond their competence with the help of adults.

zygote A fertilized ovum.

Bibliography

Abbott, J. W. (1978). Hospice. *Aging, 5*(3), 38–40.

Abler, R. M., & Sedlacek, W. E. (1989). Freshman sexual attitudes and behaviors over a 15-year-period. *Journal of College Student Development, 30,* 201–209.

Abrahams, B., Feldman, S. S., & Nash, S. C. (1978). Sex role self-concept and sex role attitudes: Enduring personality characteristics or adaptations to changing life situations? *Developmental Psychology, 14*(4), 393–400.

Abramovitch, R., & Grusec, J. E. (1978). Peer imitation in a natural setting. *Child Development, 49,* 60–65.

Adams, B. B. (1979). Mate selection in the United States: A theoretical summarization. In W. Butt, R. Hill, I. Nye, & I. Reis (Eds.), *Contemporary theories about the family* (Vol. 1, pp. 259–267). New York: Free Press.

Adams, D. (1983). *The psychosocial development of professional black women's lives and the consequences of career for their personal happiness.* Unpublished doctoral dissertation. Wright Institute, Berkeley, CA.

Ainsworth, M. D. (1967). *Infancy in Uganda: Infant care and the growth of love.* Baltimore: Johns Hopkins University Press.

Ainsworth, M. D. (1973). The development and infant–mother attachment. In B. M. Caldwell & H. N. Ricciuti (Eds.), *Review of child development research* (Vol. 3). Chicago: University of Chicago Press.

Ainsworth, M. D. S. (1983). Patterns of infant–mother attachment as related to maternal care. In D. Magnusson & V. Allen (Eds.), *Human development: An interactional perspective.* New York: Academic Press.

Ainsworth, M. D., Blehar, M., Waters, E., & Wall, S. (1978). *Patterns of attachment.* Hillsdale, NJ: Erlbaum.

Ainsworth, M. D., Blehar, M. C., Waters, E., & Wall, S. (1979). *Patterns of attachment.* New York: Halsted Press.

Ainsworth, M. D. S., Blehar, M. C., Waters, E., & Wall, S. (1979). *Patterns of attachment: A psychological study of the strange situation.* Hillsdale, NJ: Erlbaum.

Aizenberg, R., & Treas, J. (1985). The family in late life: Psychosocial and demographic considerations. In J. Birren & K. Warner Schaie (Eds.), *Handbook of the psychology of aging* (2nd ed.). New York: Van Nostrand Reinhold.

Aldous, J. (1978). *Family careers: Developmental change in families.* New York: Wiley.

Alexander, T. (November 1970). Psychologists are rediscovering the mind. *Fortune,* pp. 108–111ff.

Allgaier, A. (1978). Alternative birth centers offer family-centered care. *Hospitals, 52,* 97–112.

Almo, H. S. (1978). Without benefit of clergy: Cohabitation as a noninstitutionalized marriage role. In K. Knafl & H. Grace (Eds.), *Families across the life cycle: Studies from nursing.* Boston: Little, Brown.

Alpert, J. L., & Richardson, M. (1980). Parenting. In L. W. Poon (Ed.), *Aging in the 1980s.* Washington, DC: American Psychological Association.

Alpert-Gillis, L. J., & Connell, J. P. (1989). Gender and sex-role influences on children's self-esteem. *Journal of Personality, 57,* 97–113.

Alsop, R. (April 24, 1984). As early retirement grows in popularity, some have misgivings. *Wall Street Journal.*

American Psychological Association. (1973). *Ethical principles in the conduct of research with human participants.* Washington, DC: APA.

Ames, L. B. (December 1971). Don't push your preschooler. *Family Circle.*

Ancolie-Israel, S., Kripke, D. F., Mason, W., & Kaplan, O. J. (1985). Sleep apnea and periodic movements in an aging sample. *Journal of Gerontology, 40*(4), 419–425.

Anderson, D. R., & Collins, P. A. (1988). The impact on children's education: Television's influence on cognitive development. Washington, DC: U.S. Department of Education, Office of Educational Research and Improvement.

Anderson, D. R., Lorch, E. P., Field, D. E., & Sanders, J. (1981). The effects of TV program comprehensibility on preschool children's visual attention to television. *Child Development, 52,* 151–157.

Anderson, E. S. (March 1979). *Register variation in young children's role-playing speech.* Paper presented at the Communicative Competence, Language Use, and Role-playing Symposium, Society for Research and Child Development.

Andersson, B-E. (1989). Effects of public day-care: A longitudinal study. *Child Development, 60,* 857–866.

Anthony, E. J., & Cohler, B. J. (Eds.). (1987). *The invulnerable child.* New York: Guilford.

APA Task Force on Women and Depression. (Winter 1991). APA study finds no simple explanation for high rate of depression in women. *Quarterly Newsletter of the National Mental Health Association,* p. 5.

Apgar, V. (1953). Proposal for a new method of evaluating the newborn infant. *Anesthesia and Analgesia, 32,* 260–267.

Aquilino, W. S. (1990). The likelihood of parent–adult child coresidence: Effects of family structure and parental characteristics. *Journal of Marriage and the Family, 52,* 405–419.

Archer, S. L. (1985). Identity and the choice of social roles. *New Directions for Child Development, 30,* 79–100.

Arend, R. A., Gore, F. L., & Sroufe, L. A. (1979). Continuity of individual adaptation from infancy to kindergarten, *Child Development, 50,* 950–959.

Aries, P. (1962). *Centuries of childhood.* (R. Baldick, Trans.). New York: Knopf.

Aries, P. (1981). *The hour of our death.* New York: Knopf.

Aries, P. (1989). Introduction. In R. Chartier (Ed.), *A history of a private life: Vol. 3. Passions of the Renaissance* (pp. 1–11). Cambridge, MA: Belknap Press of Harvard University Press.

Armitage, S. E., Baldwin, B. A., & Vince, N. A. (1980). The fetal sound environment of sheep. *Science, 208,* 1173–1174.

Asher, S. R. (1983). Social competence and peer status: Recent advances and future directions. *Child Development, 54,* 1427–1434.

Asher, S. R., Renshaw, P. D., & Hymel, S. (1982). Peer relations and the development of social skills. In W. W. Hartup (Ed.), *The young child: Reviews of research* (Vol. 3). Washington, DC: National Association for the Education of Young Children.

Aslin, R. N. (1987). Motor aspects of visual development in infancy. In P. Salapatek & L. Cohen (Eds.), *Handbook of infant perception: Vol. 1. From sensation to perception: Vol. 1.* New York: Academic Press.

Aslin, R. (1987). Visual and auditory development in infancy. In J. Osofsky (Ed.), *Handbook of infant development* (2nd ed.). New York: Wiley.

Aslin, R. N., Pisoni, D. V., & Jusczyk, P. W. (1983). Auditory development and speech perception in infancy. In P. H. Mussen (Ed.), *Handbook of child psychology* (Vol. 2). New York: Wiley.

Aslin, R. N., & Smith, L. B. (1988). Perceptual development. *Annual Review of Psychology, 39,* 435–473.

Asso, D. (1983). *The real menstrual cycle.* Chichester, UK: Wiley.

Astin, A. W. (1977). *Four critical years.* San Francisco: Jossey-Bass.

Atchley, R. (1989). A continuity theory of normal aging. *The Gerontologist, 29,* 183–190.

Atchley, R. C. (1982). The process of retirement: Comparing women and men. In M. Szlnovacy (Ed.), *Women's retirement: Policy implications of recent research.* London: Sage.

Athey, I. J. (1984). Contributions of play to development. In T. D. Yawkey & A. D. Pellegrini (Eds.), *Child's play.* Hillsdale, NJ: Erlbaum.

Atkinson, R. C., & Shiffrin, R. M. (1971). The control of short-term memory. *Scientific American, 225*(2), 82–90.

Ausubel, F., Beckwith, J., & Janssen, K. (June 1974). The politics of genetic engineering: Who decides who's defective? *Psychology Today,* p. 30ff.

Babladelis, G. (1987). Young persons' attitudes toward aging. *Perceptual and Motor Skills, 65,* 553–554.

Babson, S. G., & Benson, R. C. (1966). *Primer on prematurity and high-risk pregnancy.* St. Louis: Mosby.

Baillargeon, R. (1987). Object permanence in three-and-a-half- and four-and-a-half-month-old infants. *Developmental Psychology, 23*(5), 655–674.

Bakeman, R., & Adamson, L. B. (1990). !Kung infancy: The social context of object exploration. *Child Development, 61,* 794–809.

Baker, B. L., & Brightman, A. J. (1989). *Steps to independence: A skills training guide for parents and teachers of children with special needs* (2nd ed.). Baltimore: Paul H. Brookes.

Baldwin, J. M. (1906). *Mental development in the child and the race: Methods and processes* (3rd ed.). New York: Macmillan.

Ball, W., & Tronick, E. (1971). Infant responses to impending collision: Optical and real. *Science, 171,* 818–820.

Baltes, P. B. (1979). Life-span developmental psychology: Some converging observations on history and theory. In P. B. Baltes & O. G. Brim, Jr. (Eds.), *Life-span development and behavior* (Vol. 2). New York: Academic Press.

Baltes, P. B. (1987). Theoretical propositions of life-span developmental psychology: On the dynamics of growth and decline. *Developmental Psychology, 23,* 611–626.

Bandura, A. (1964). The stormy decade: Fact or fiction. *Psychology in the Schools, 1,* 224–231.

Bandura, A. (1977). *Social learning theory.* Englewood Cliffs, NJ: Prentice Hall.

Bandura, A. (1982). The psychology of chance encounters and life paths. *American Psychologist, 37,* 747–755.

Bandura, A. (1986). *Social foundations of thought and action.* Englewood Cliffs, NJ: Prentice Hall.

Bandura, A., Ross, D., & Ross, S. A. (1963). Imitation of film-mediated aggressive models. *Journal of Abnormal and Social Psychology, 66,* 3–11.

Bandura, A., & Walters, R. H. (1959). *Adolescent aggression.* New York: Ronald Press.

Bandura, A., & Walters, R. H. (1963). *Social learning and personality development.* New York: Holt, Rinehart & Winston.

Bankoff, E. (1986). Peer support for widows: Personal and structural characteristics related to its provision. In S. Hobfoll (Ed.), *Stress, social support, and women* (pp. 207–222). Washington, DC: Hemisphere.

Banks, M., & Dannemiller, J. (1987). Infant visual psychophysics. In P. Salapatek & L. Cohen (Eds.), *Handbook of infant perception: Vol. 1. From sensation to perception.* New York: Academic Press.

Banks, M. S., & Salapatek, P. (1983). Infant visual perception. In P. H. Mussen (Ed.), *Handbook of child psychology* (4th ed.). New York: Wiley.

Barbero, G. (1983). Failure to thrive. In M. Klaus, T. Leger, & M. Trause (Eds.), *Maternal attachment and mothering disorders.* New Brunswick, NJ: Johnson & Johnson.

Barker, R. G., Dembo, T., & Lewin, K. (1943). Frustration and regression. In R. G. Barker, J. S. Kounin, & H. F. Wright (Eds.), *Child behavior and development.* New York: McGraw-Hill.

Barnes, D. M. (1989). "Fragile X" syndrome and its puzzling genetics. *Research News,* pp. 171–172.

Barnes, H. L., & Olsen, D. H. (1985). Parent-adolescent communication and the circumplex model. *Child Development, 56,* 438–447.

Barnett, R., & Baruch, G. (1987). Social roles, gender, and psychological distress. In R. Barnett, L. Biener, & G. Baruch (Eds.), *Gender and stress* (pp. 122–143). New York: Free Press.

Bartoshuk, L., & Weiffenbach, J. (1990). Chemical senses and aging. In E. Schneider & J. Rowe (Eds.), *Handbook of the biology of aging* (pp. 429–444). San Diego: Academic Press.

Baruch, G. K., & Barnett, R. C. (1986a). *Consequences of fathers' participation in family work: Parent role strain and well-being* (Working Paper No. 159). Wellesley, MA: Wellesley College Center for Research on Women.

Baruch, G., & Barnett, R. (1986b). Role quality, multiple role involvement, and psychological well-being in midlife women. *Journal of Personality and Social Psychology, 51,* 578–585.

Baruch, G. K., Biener, L., & Barnett, R. (February 1987). Women and gender in research on work and family stress. *American Psychologist,* pp. 130–135.

Bates, E., O'Connell, B., & Shore, C. (1987). Language and communication in infancy. In J. D. Osofsy (Ed.), *Handbook of infant development* (2nd ed.). New York: Wiley.

Bates, J. E. (1987). Temperament in infancy. In J. D. Osofsky (Ed.), *Handbook of infant development* (2nd ed., pp. 1101–1149). New York: Wiley.

Bateson, G. (1955). A theory of play and fantasy. *Psychiatric Research Reports, 2,* 39–51.

Bauer, P. J., & Thal, D. J. (1990). Scripts or scraps: Reconsidering the development of sequential understanding. *Journal of Experimental Child Psychology, 50,* 287–304.

Baumrind, D. (1972). Socialization and instrumental competence in young children. In W. W. Hartup (Ed.), *The young child: Reviews of research* (Vol. 2). Washington, DC: National Association for the Education of Young Children.

Baumrind, D. (1975). *Early socialization and the discipline controversy.* Morristown, NJ: General Learning Press.

Baumrind, D. (1978). A dialectical materialist's perspective on knowing social reality. *New Directions for Child Development, 2.*

Baumrind, D. (1980). New directions in socialization research. *American Psychologist, 35,* 639–650.

Baumrind, D. (1987). A developmental perspective on adolescent risk-taking in contemporary America. *New Directions for Child Development, 37,* 93–125.

Baumrind, D. (1991). The influence of parenting style on adolescent competence and substance use. *Journal of Early Adolescence, 11*(1), 56–95.

Bayley, N. (1965). Research in child development: A longitudinal perspective. *Merrill-Palmer Quarterly, 11,* 183–208.

Bayley, N. (1969). *Bayley scales of infant development.* New York: Psychological Corporation.

Beal, C. R. (1987). Repairing the message: Children's monitoring and revision skills. *Child Development, 58,* 401–408.

Bearon, L. (1989). No great expectations: The underpinnings of life satisfaction for older women. *The Gerontologist, 29,* 772–776.

Beck, M. (August 15, 1988). Miscarriages. *Newsweek,* pp. 46–49.

Becker, W. C. (1964). Consequences of different kinds of parental discipline. In M. L. Hoffman (Ed.), *Review of child developmental research* (Vol. 1). New York: Russell Sage Foundation.

Beckwith, L., & Cohen, S. E. (1989). Maternal responsiveness with preterm infants and later competency. In M. H. Bornstein (Ed.), *New Directions for Child Development; Vol. 43.* Maternal responsiveness: Characteristics and consequences. San Francisco: Jossey-Bass.

Beit-Hallahmi, B., & Rabin, A. (1977). The kibbutz as a social experiment and as a child-rearing laboratory. *American Psychologist, 32,* 532–541.

Bell, A. P., & Weinberg, M. S. (1978). *Homosexualities: A study of diversity among men and women.* New York: Simon & Schuster.

Bell, B. D. (1978). Life satisfaction and occupational retirement: Beyond the impact years. *International Journal of Aging and Human Development, 9*(1), 31–49.

Bell, S. M., & Ainsworth, M. D. (1972). Infant crying and maternal responsiveness. *Child Development, 43,* 1171–1190.

Beller, E. K. (1955). Dependency and independence in young children. *Journal of Genetic Psychology, 87,* 25–35.

Bellugi, U. (December 1970). Learning the language. *Psychology Today,* pp. 32–38.

Belmont, I., & Belmont, L. (1980). Is the slow learner in the classroom learning disabled? *Journal of Learning Disabilities, 13,* 32–33.

Belsky, J. (1980). Child maltreatment: An ecological integration. *American Psychologist, 35,* 320–335.

Belsky, J. (1984). *The psychology of aging: Theory and research and practice.* Monterey, CA: Brooks/Cole.

Belsky, J. (1986). Infant day care: A cause for concern? *Zero to Three, 6,* 1–7.

Belsky, J. (February 1987). Risks remain. *Zero to Three,* pp. 22–24.

Belsky, J., & Rovine, M. (1988). Nonmaternal care in the first year of life and the security of infant–parent attachment. *Child Development, 59,* 157–167.

Belsky, J., & Rovine, M. (1990a). Q-sort security and first-year nonmaternal care. In *New Directions for Child Development: Vol. 49. Child care and maternal employment: A social ecology approach* (pp. 7–22).

Belsky, J., & Rovine, M. (1990b). Patterns of marital change across the transition to parenthood: Pregnancy to three years postpartum. *Journal of Marriage and the Family, 52,* 5–19.

Belsky, J., Rovine, M., & Taylor, D. (1984). The Pennsylvania infant and family development project III. The origins of individual differences in infant–mother attachment: Maternal and infant contributions. *Child Development, 58,* 718–728.

Bem, S. L. (September 1975). Androgyny vs. the tight little lives of fluffy women and chesty men. *Psychology Today,* pp. 59–62.

Bem, S. (1985). Androgyny and gender schema theory: A conceptual and empirical integration. In T. B. Sondegegger (Ed.), *Nebraska Symposium on Motivation, 1984: Psychology and gender.* Lincoln: University of Nebraska.

Benedek, T. (1970). Parenthood during the life cycle. In E. J. Anthony & T. Benedek (Eds.), *Parenthood: Its psychology and psychopathology.* Boston: Little, Brown.

Bengston, V. L. (1985). Diversity and symbolism in grandparents' role. In V. L. Bengston & J. F. Robertson (Eds.), *Grandparenthood.* Beverly Hills, CA: Sage.

Bengston, V. L., & Robertson, J. F. (Eds.). (1985). *Grandparenthood.* Beverly Hills, CA: Sage.

Bennett, N. (1976). *Teaching styles and pupil progress.* Cambridge, MA: Harvard University Press.

Bennett, S. C., Robinson, N. M., & Sells, C. J. (1983). Growth and development of infants weighing less than 800 grams at birth. *Pediatrics, 7*(3), 319–323.

Berardo, D., Sheehan, C., & Leslie, G. (1987). A residue of tradition: Jobs, careers, and spouses' time in housework. *Journal of Marriage and the Family, 49,* 381–390.

Bereiter, C., & Engelmann, S. (1966). *Teaching disadvantaged children in the preschool.* Englewood Cliffs, NJ: Prentice Hall.

Bergmann, B. (1986). *The economic emergence of women.* New York: Basic Books.

Berk, L. E. (July 1985). Why children talk to themselves. *Young Children,* pp. 46–52.

Berk, L. E. (1986). Relationship of elementary school children's private speech to behavioral accompaniment to task, attention and task performance. *Developmental Psychology, 22*(5), 671–680.

Berko, J. (1958). The child's learning of English morphology. *Word, 14,* 150–177.

Bernard, J. (1981). The good-provider role: Its rise and fall. *American Psychologist, 36,* 1–12.

Berndt, T. J. (1982). The features and effects of friendship in early adolescence. *Child Development, 53,* 1447–1460.

Berndt, T. (1983). Social cognition, social behavior and children's friendships. In E. T. Higgins, D. Ruble, & W. Hartup, *Social cognition and social development: A socio-cultural perspective.* Cambridge, MA: Cambridge University Press.

Beroff, J., Douvan, E., & Julka, R. (1981). *The inner American: A self-portrait from 1957–1976.* New York: Basic Books.

Bertenthal, B. I., & Campos, J. J. (1987). New directions in the study of early experience. *Child Development, 58,* 560–567.

Bielby, W., & Baron, J. (1986). Sex segregation within occupations. *American Economic Review, 76,* 43–47.

Binet, A., & Simon, T. (1905). Methodes nouvelles pour le diagnostic du niveau intellectual des anormaux. *L'Annee Psychologique, 11,* 191–244.

Binet, A., & Simon, T. (1916). *The development of intelligence in children.* (E. S. Kite, Trans.). Baltimore: Williams & Wilkins.

Birch, H. G., & Gussow, J. D. (1970). *Disadvantaged children: Health, nutrition and school failure.* New York: Harcourt Brace Jovanovich.

Birkel, R., & Jones, C. (1989). A comparison of the caregiving networks of dependent elderly individuals who are lucid and those who are demented. *The Gerontologist, 29,* 114–119.

Birnbaum, H. G., & Kidder, D. (1984). What does hospice cost? *American Journal of Public Health, 74*(7), 689–692.

Birren, J. E., & Cunningham, W. R. (1985). Research on the psychology in aging: Principles and experimentation. In J. E. Birren & K. W. Schaie (Eds.), *Handbook of the psychology of aging* (2nd ed.). New York: Van Nostrand Reinhold.

Birren, J. E., Woods, A. M., & Williams, M. V. (1980). Behavioral slowing with age: Causes, organization, and consequences. In L. W. Poon (Ed.), *Aging in the 1980s.* Washington, DC: American Psychological Association.

BIRTH. (June 1988). Report for American College of Obstetricians and Gynecologists. *BIRTH, 15*(2), 113.

Bjorklund, D. F. (1988). Acquiring a mnemonic: Age and category knowledge effects. *Journal of Experimental Child Psychology, 45,* 71–87.

Blake, J. (1989). Number of siblings and educational attainment. *Science, 245,* 32–36.

Blieszner, R., & Mancini, J. (1987). Enduring ties: Older adults' parental role and responsibilities. *Family Relations, 36,* 176–180.

Block, J. (1971). *Lives through time.* Berkeley, CA: Bancroft Books.

Block, J. (1981). Some enduring and consequential structures of personality. In A. I. Rabin et al. (Eds.), *Further explorations in personality.* New York: Wiley.

Bloom, B. S. (1964). *Stability and change in human characteristics.* New York: Wiley.

Bloom, B. S., & Krathwohl, D. R. (1956). *Taxonomy of educational objectives: Handbook I: The cognitive domain.* New York: McKay.

Bloom, L. (1970). *Language development: Form and function in emerging grammars.* Cambridge, MA: MIT Press.

Bloom, L., & Lahey, M. (1978). *Language development and language disorders.* New York: Wiley.

Bloom, L., Lifter, K., & Broughton, J. (1985). The convergence of early cognition and language in the second year of life: Problems in conceptualization and measurement. In M. Barrett (Ed.), *Children's single-word speech.* New York: Wiley.

Blumstein, P., & Schwartz, P. (1983). *American couples.* New York: Morrow.

Blyth, D., Bulcroft, A. R., & Simmons, R. G. (1981). *The impact of puberty on adolescents: A longitudinal study.* Paper presented at the annual meeting of the American Psychological Association, Los Angeles.

Boccia, M., & Campos, J. J. (1989). Maternal emotional signals, social referencing, and infants' reactions to strangers. In N. Eisenberg (Ed.), *New Directions for Child Development: Vol. 44. Empathy and related emotional responses.* (pp. 25–50).

Bohannon, J. N., Jr., & Hirsh-Pasek, K. (1984). Do children say as they're told? A new perspective on motherese. In L. Feagans, C. Garvey, & R. Golinkoff (Eds.), *The origins and growth of communication.* Norwood, NJ: Ablex.

Booth-Kewley, S., & Friedman, H. (1987). Psychological predictors of heart disease: A quantitative review. *Psychological Bulletin, 101,* 343–362.

Borke, H. (1971). Interpersonal perception of young children: Egocentrism or empathy. *Developmental Psychology, 5,* 263–269.

Borke, H. (1973). The development of empathy in Chinese and American children between 3 and 6 years of age: A cross-cultural study. *Developmental Psychology, 9,* 102–108.

Bornstein, M. H. (1978). Chromatic vision in infancy. In H. W. Reese & L. P. Lipsett (Eds.), *Advances in child development and behavior* (Vol. 12). New York: Academic Press.

Bornstein, M. (Ed.). (1987). *Sensitive periods in development: Interdisciplinary perspectives.* Hillsdale, NJ: Erlbaum.

Bornstein, M. H. (Ed.). (1989). *Maternal responsiveness: Characteristics and consequences.* San Francisco: Jossey-Bass.

Bornstein, M. H., & Bruner J. (1986). *Interaction in human development.* Hillsdale, NJ: Erlbaum.

Bornstein, M. H., & Tamis-LeMonda, C. S. (1989). Maternal responsiveness and cognitive development in children. In M. H. Bornstein (Ed.), *New Directions for Child Development: Vol. 43. Maternal responsiveness: Characteristics and consequences* (pp. 49–62).

Bossard, J. H. S., & Boll, E. S. (1960). *The sociology of child development.* New York: Harper & Brothers.

Boston Women's Health Book Collective. (1976). *Our bodies, ourselves* (2nd ed.). New York: Simon & Schuster.

Botwinick, J. (1977). Intellectual abilities. In J. Birren & K. W. Schaie (Eds.), *Handbook of the psychology of aging.* New York: Van Nostrand Reinhold.

Botwinick, J. (1984). *Aging and behavior: A comprehensive integration of research findings* (3rd ed.). New York: Springer.

Bouchard, R. J., Jr. (June 25, 1987). Environmental determinants of IQ similarity in identical twins reared apart. Paper presented at the 17th annual meeting of the Behavior Genetics Association, Minneapolis, MN.

Bouchard, T. J., Jr., Lykken, D. T., McGue, M., Segal, N., & Tellegen, A. (1990). Sources of human psychological differences: The Minnesota study of twins reared apart. *Science, 250,* 223–228.

Bouvier, L. (1980). America's baby boom generation: The fateful bulge. *Population Bulletin, 35,* 1–35.

Bower, B. (1991). Teenage turning point: Does adolescence herald the twilight of girls' self-esteem? *Science News, 139*(12), 184–186.

Bower, T. G. R. (October 1971). The object in the world of the infant. *Scientific American,* pp. 30–38.

Bower, T. G. R. (1974). *Development in infancy.* San Francisco: Freeman.

Bowlby, J. (1960). Separation anxiety. *International Journal of Psychoanalysis, 41,* 89–113.

Bowlby, J. (1973). *Attachment and loss: Vol. 2. Separation.* New York: Basic Books.

Bowlby, J. (1980). *Attachment and loss: Vol. 3. Loss, sadness and depression.* New York: Basic Books.

Bowlby, J. (1982). *Attachment and loss: Vol. 1. Attachment* (2nd ed.). New York: Basic Books.

Bowlby, J. (1988). *A secure base.* New York: Basic Books.

Bowlby, J. (1990). *Charles Darwin: A new life.* New York: Norton.

Boyd, J. H., & Weissman, M. M. (1981). The epidemiology of psychiatric disorders of middle age: Depression, alcoholism, and suicide. In J. G. Howels (Ed.), *Modern perspectives in the psychiatry of middle age.* New York: Brunner/Mazel.

Brackbill, Y. (1979). Obstetrical medication and infant behavior. In J. Osofsky (Ed.), *Handbook of infant development.* New York: Wiley.

Brackbill, Y., McManus, K., & Woodward, L. (1985). *Medication in maternity: Infant exposure and maternal information.* International Academy for Research on Learning Disabilities. Monographs, Series Number 2. Ann Arbor: University of Michigan Press.

Brackbill, Y., & Nevill, D. (1981). Parental expectations of achievement as affected by children's height. *Merrill-Palmer Quarterly, 27,* 429–441.

Bradway, K. P., Thompson, C. W., & Graven, S. B. (1958). Preschool IQs after 25 years. *Journal of Educational Psychology, 49,* 278–281.

Braine, M. D. S. (1963). The ontogeny of English phrase structure: The first phase. *Language, 39,* 1–13.

Brand, H. J., & Welch, K. (1989). Cognitive and social-emotional development of children in different preschool environments. *Psychological Reports, 65,* 480–482.

Brassard, M. R., & McNeill, L. E. (1987). Child sexual abuse. In M. Brassard, R. Germain, & S. Hart (Eds.), *Psychological maltreatment of children and youth.* New York: Pergamon.

Bratcher, W. (October 1982). The influence of the family on career selection: A family systems perspective. *Personnel and Guidance Journal,* pp. 87–91.

Bray, D. W., & Howard, A. (1983). The AT&T longitudinal studies of managers. In K. W. Schaie (Ed.), *Longitudinal studies of adult development.* New York: Guilford.

Brazelton, T. B. (1969). *Infants and mothers: Differences in development.* New York: Dell.

Brazelton, T. B. (1973). *Neonatal behavioral assessment scale.* London: Heinemann.

Brazelton, T. B., Nugent, J. K., & Lester, B. M. (1987). Neonatal behavioral assessment scale. In J. Osofsky (Ed.), *Handbook of infant development* (2nd ed., pp. 780–817). New York: Wiley.

Brazelton, T. B., Yogman, M., Als, H., & Tronick, E. (1979). The infant as a focus for family reciprocity. In M. Lewis & L. A. Rosenblum (Eds.)., *The child and his family.* New York: Plenum.

Brenner, A. (1984). *Helping children cope with stress.* Lexington, MA: D. C. Heath.

Bretherton, I., & Waters, E. (Eds.). (1985). Growing points of attachment. *Monographs of the Society for Research in Child Development, 50*(1–2), Serial 209.

Briesemeister, L. A., & Haines, B. A. (1988). The interactions of fathers and newborns. In K. L. Michaelson (Ed.), *Childbirth in America: Anthropological perspectives*. South Hadley, MA: Bergin & Garvey.

Briggs, G. C., Freeman, R. K., & Yaffe, S. J. (1986). *Drugs in pregnancy and lactation* (2nd ed.). Baltimore: Williams & Wilkins.

Brody, E. M. (1985). *Parent care as a normative family stress*. Donald P. Kent Memorial Lecture, presented at the 37th annual scientific meeting of the Gerontological Society of America, San Antonio, Texas.

Brody, E., Johnsen, P., & Fulcomer, M. (1984). What should adult children do for elderly parents? Opinions and preferences of three generations of women. *Journal of Gerontology, 39*, 736–746.

Brody, E., Kleban, M., Johnsen, P., Hoffman, C., & Schoonover, C. (1987). Work status and parent care: A comparison of four groups of women. *The Gerontologist, 27*, 201–208.

Brody, E., & Schoonover, C. (1986). Patterns of parent-care when adult daughters work and when they do not. *The Gerontologist, 26*, 372–381.

Brody, J. (June 6, 1979). Exercising to turn back the years. *New York Times*, pp. C18–19.

Brody, S. J. (1987). Strategic planning: The catastrophic approach. *The Gerontologist, 27*(2), 131–138.

Broman, S. (1986). Obstetric medication: A review of the literature on outcomes in infancy and childhood. In Michael Lewis (Ed.), *Learning disabilities and prenatal risk*. Urbana: University of Illinois Press.

Bronfenbrenner, U. (1970). *Two worlds of childhood: U.S. and U.S.S.R.* New York: Russell Sage Foundation.

Bronfenbrenner, U. (1979). *The ecology of human development*. Cambridge, MA: Harvard University Press.

Bronson, G. (1978). Aversion reactions to strangers: A dual process interpretation. *Child Development, 49*, 495–499.

Bronson, W. (1975). Developments in behavior with agemates during the second year of life. In M. Lewis & L. A. Rosenblum (Eds.), *Peer relations and friendship*. New York: Wiley.

Bronson, W. C. (1981). Toddlers' behavior with agemates: Issues of interaction and cognition and affect. In L. P. Lipset (Ed.), *Monographs on Infancy* (Vol. 1). Norwood, NJ: Ablex.

Brooks, R. L., & Obrzut, J. E. (1981). Brain lateralization: Implications for infant stimulation and development. *Young Children, 26*, 9–16.

Brooks-Gunn, J., & Furstenberg, F. F., Jr. (1986). The children of adolescent mothers: Physical, academic, and psychological outcomes. *Developmental Review, 6*, 224–251.

Brooks-Gunn, J., & Furstenberg, F. F., Jr. (1989). Adolescent sexual behavior. *American Psychologist, 44*, 249–257.

Brophy, J. (1986). Teacher influences on student achievement. *American Psychologist, 41*, 1069–1077.

Broughton, J. (1977). Beyond formal operations: Theoretical thought in adolescence. *Teacher's College Record, 79*, 88–97.

Broussard, E. R. (1989). The infant–family resource program: Facilitating optimal development. *Prevention in Human Services, 6*(2), 179–224.

Brown, B. B., Clasen, D. R., & Eicher, S. A. (1986). Perceptions of peer pressure, peer conformity dispositions, and self-reported behavior among adolescents. *Developmental Psychology, 22*, 521–530.

Brown, B. B., & Lohr, M. J. (1987). Peer-group affiliation and adolescent self-esteem: An integration of ego-identity and symbolic-interaction theories. *Journal of Personality and Social Psychology, 52*, 47–55.

Brown, R. (1965). *Social psychology*. New York: Free Press.

Brown, R. (1973). *A first language: The early stages*. Cambridge, MA: Harvard University Press.

Brownell, C. A., & Carriger, M. S. (1990). Changes in cooperation and self-other differentiation during the second year. *Child Development, 61*, 1164–1174.

Bruck, M. (1987). The adult outcomes of children with learning disabilities. *Annals of Dyslexia, 37*, 252–263.

Bruner, J. S. (1960). *The process of education*. Cambridge, MA: Harvard University Press.

Bruner, J. S. (1971). *The relevance of education*. New York: Norton.

Bruner, J. S. (1973). *Beyond the information given: Studies in the psychology of knowing*. New York: Norton.

Bruner, J. (1983). *Child's talk*. New York: Norton.

Bruner, J., & Haste, H. (Eds.). (1987). *Making sense: The child's construction of the world*. London & New York: Methuen.

Bruner, J. S., & Olver, R. R., & Greenfield, P. M. (1966). *Studies in cognitive growth*. New York: Wiley.

Bryan, J. H. (1975). Children's cooperation and helping behaviors. In E. M. Hetherington (Ed.), *Review of child development* (Vol. 5). Chicago: University of Chicago Press.

Buis, J. M., & Thompson, D. N. (1989). Imaginary audience and personal fable: A brief review. *Adolescence, 24*, 773–781.

Bulterys, M. G., Greenland, S., & Kraus, J. F. (1989). Cigarettes and pregnancy. *Pediatrics, 86*(4), 535–540.

Bulterys, M. G., Greenland, S., & Kraus, J. F. (October 1990). Chronic fetal hypoxia and sudden infant death syndrome: Interaction between maternal smoking and low hematocrit during pregnancy. *Pediatrics, 86*(4), 535–540.

Burgess, R. L., & Conger, R. D. (1978). Family interaction in abusive, neglectful, and normal families. *Child Development, 49*, 1163–1173.

Buri, J. R., Louiselle, P. A., Misukanis, T. M., & Mueller, R. A. (1988). Effects of parental authoritarianism and authoritativeness on self-esteem. *Personality and Social Psychology Bulletin, 14*, 271–282.

Burke, R., & Weir, T. (1976). Relationship of wives' employment status to husband, wife and pair satisfaction and performance. *Journal of Marriage and the Family*, 279–287.

Burnside, I. M. (1979a). The later decades of life: Research and reflections. In I. M. Burnside, P. Ebersole, & H. E. Monea (Eds.), *Psychosocial caring throughout the life span*. New York: McGraw-Hill.

Burnside, I. M. (1979b). Sensory and cognitive functioning in later life. In I. Burnside, P. Ebersole, & H. E. Monea (Eds.), *Psychosocial caring throughout the life span*. New York: McGraw-Hill.

Burnside, I. M., Ebersole, P., & Monea, H. E. (Eds.). (1979). *Psychosocial caring throughout the life span*. New York: McGraw-Hill.

Busch, J. W. (1985). Mentoring in graduate schools of education: Mentors' perceptions. *American Educational Research Journal, 22*, 257–265.

Buss, A. H., & Plomin, R. (1984). *Temperament: Early developing personality traits*. Hillsdale, NJ: Erlbaum.

Butler, R. N. (1968). The life review: An interpretation of reminiscence in the aged. In B. L. Neugarten (Ed.), *Middle age and aging*. Chicago: University of Chicago Press.

Butler, R. N. (December 1971). Age: The life review, *Psychology Today*, pp. 49–51.

Butler, R. (July & August 1983). A generation at risk: When the baby boomers reach golden pond. *Across the Boards*, pp. 37–45.

Caldwell, R., Bloom, B., & Hodges, W. (1984). Sex differences in separation and divorce: A longitudinal perspective. In A. Rickel, M. Gerrard, & I. Iscoe (Eds.), *Social and psychological problems of women* (pp. 103–119). Washington, DC: Hemisphere.

Callahan, J. (1988). Elder abuse: Some questions for policymakers. *The Gerontologist, 28*, 453–458.

Campbell, M., & Spencer, E. K. (1988). Psychopharmacology in child and adolescent psychiatry: A review of the past five years. *Journal of the American Academy of Child and Adolescent Psychiatry, 27,* 269–279.

Campos, J. J., Langer, A., & Krowitz, A. (1970). Cardiac responses on the visual cliff in prelocomotor human infants. *Science, 170,* 196–197.

Cantor, J., & Wilson, B. J. (1988). Helping children cope with frightening media presentations. *Current Psychology: Research and Reviews, 7*(1), 58–75.

Capelli, C. A., Nakagawa, N., & Madden, C. M. (1990). How children understand sarcasm: The role of context and intonation. *Child Development, 61,* 1824–1841.

Card, J. J., & Wise, L. L. (1978). Teenage mothers and teenage fathers: The impact of early childbearing on the parents' personal and professional lives. *Family Planning Perspectives, 10,* 199–205.

Carlson, C. I., Cooper, C. R., & Spradling, V. Y. (1991). Developmental implications of shared versus distant perspectives of the family in early adolescence. *New Directions in Child Development, 51,* 13–31.

Carpenter, G. (1974). Mother's face and the newborn. *New Scientist, 61,* 742–744.

Carskadon, M. A., Van Den Hoed, J., & Dement, W. C. (October 13, 1979). *Insomnia and sleep disturbances in the aged: Sleep and daytime sleepiness in the elderly.* Paper presented at a scientific meeting of the Boston Society for Gerontologic Psychiatry.

Carter, B., & McGoldrick, M. (1980). *The family life cycle.* New York: Gardner.

Carver, C., & Humphries, C. (1982). Social psychology of the Type A coronary-prone behavior pattern. In G. Sanders & J. Suls (Eds.), *Social psychology of health and illness.* Hillsdale, NJ: Erlbaum.

Caspi, A. (1987). Personality in the life course. *Journal of Personality and Social Psychology, 53,* 1203–1213.

Caspi, A., & Elder, G. H., Jr. (1988). Childhood precursors of the life course: Early personality and life disorganization. In E. M. Hetherington, R. N. Lerner, & M. Perlmutter (Eds.), *Child development* (pp. 259–276). Hillsdale, NJ: Erlbaum.

Caspi, A., Elder, G. H., Jr., & Bem, D. J. (1987). Moving against the world: Life-course patterns of explosive children. *Developmental Psychology, 23,* 308–313.

Cassidy, J. (1986). The ability to negotiate the environment: An aspect of infant competence as related to quality of attachment. *Child Development, 57,* 331–337.

Caudill, W., & Weinstein, H. (1969). Maternal care and infant behavior in Japan and America. *Psychiatry, 32,* 12–43.

Centers, R. (1975). *Sexual attraction and love: An instrumental theory.* Springfield, IL: Chas. C Thomas.

Chan, M. (1987). Sudden Infant Death Syndrome and families at risk. *Pediatric Nursing, 13*(3), 166–168.

Chance, P. (January 1981). That drained-out, used-up feeling. *Psychology Today,* pp. 88–95.

Chapman, K. L., & Mervis, C. B. (1989). Patterns of object-name extension in production. *Journal of Child Language, 16,* 561–571.

Charlesworth, W. (1988). Resources and resource acquisition during ontogeny. In K. B. MacDonald (Ed.), *Sociobiological perspectives on human development.* New York: Springer-Verlag.

Charness, N. (1981). Search in chess: Age and skill differences. *Journal of Experimental Psychology: Human Perception and Performance, 7,* 467–476.

Chasnoff, I. J. (1989). Cocaine, pregnancy and the neonate. *Women and Health, 5*(3), 33.

Chesnick, M., Menyuk, P., Liebergott, J., Ferrier, L., & Strand, K. (April 1983). *Who leads whom?* Paper presented at the meeting of the Society for Research in Child Development, Detroit.

Chess, S. (1967). Temperament in the normal infant. In J. Hellmuth (Ed.), *The exceptional infant* (Vol. 1). Seattle: Special Child Publications.

Chess, S. (February 1987). Comments: "Infant day care: A cause for concern." *Zero to Three,* pp. 24–25.

Children's Defense Fund. (1991). *The state of America's children, 1991.* Washington, DC: Children's Defense Fund.

Chilman, C. (1979). *Adolescent sexuality in changing American society.* Washington, DC: Government Printing Office.

Chiriboga, D. A. (1981). The developmental psychology of middle age. In J. Howells (Ed.), *Modern perspectives in the psychiatry of middle age.* New York: Brunner/Mazel.

Chiriboga, D. A., & Cutler, L. (1980). Stress and adaptation: Life span perspectives. In L. W. Poon, (Ed.), *Aging in the 1980s.* Washington, DC: American Psychological Association.

Chomsky, C. (1969). *The acquisition of syntax from 5 to 10.* Cambridge, MA: MIT Press.

Chomsky, N. (1959). Review of *Verbal Behavior* by B. F. Skinner, *Language, 35,* 26–58.

Chomsky, N. (1975). *Reflections on language.* New York: Pantheon.

Chukovsky, K. (1963). *From two to five.* (M. Morton Ed. & Trans.). Berkeley: University of California Press.

Clark, E. V. (1983). Meaning and concepts. In P. H. Mussen (Ed.), *Handbook of child psychology* (4th ed., Vol. 4). New York: Wiley.

Clark, E. V. (1987). The principle of contrast: A constraint on acquisition. In B. Macwhinner (Ed.), *Mechanisms of language acquisition.* Hillsdale, NJ: Erlbaum.

Clark, J. E., & Phillips, S. J. (1985). A developmental sequence of the standing long jump. In J. E. Clark & J. H. Humphrey (Eds.), *Motor development: Current selected research.* Princeton, NJ: Princeton Book Company.

Clark, K. (May 31, 1957). *Present threats to children and youth.* Draft Report, manuscript in the office of the National Committee on the Employment of Youth, New York City.

Clarke-Stewart, A. (1982). *Daycare.* Cambridge, MA: Harvard University Press.

Clark-Stewart, A. (1988). Parent's effects on children's development: A decade of progress? *Journal of Applied Developmental Psychology, 9,* 41–84.

Clarke-Stewart, K. A. (1978). And daddy makes three: The father's impact on mother and young child. *Child Development, 49,* 466–478.

Clarke-Stewart, K. A., & Fein, G. C. (1983). Early childhood programs. In M. Haith & J. Campos (Eds.), *Handbook of child psychology: Vol. 2. Infancy and developmental psychobiology* (4th ed.). New York: Wiley.

Clarke-Stewart, K. A., & Hevey, C. M. (1981). Longitudinal relations in repeated observations of mother–child interaction from 1 to 2-½ years. *Developmental Psychology, 17,* 127–145.

Clingempeel, G., & Segal, S. (1986). Stepparent–stepchild relationships and the psychological adjustment of children in stepmother and stepfather families. *Child Development, 57,* 474–484.

Coe, R. (1988). A longitudinal examination of poverty in the elderly years. *The Gerontologist, 28,* 540–544.

Cohen, D., & Eisdorfer, K. (1986). *The loss of self: A family resource for the care of Alzheimer's disease and related disorders.* New York: Norton.

Cohen, L. B., & Gelber, E. R. (1975). Infant visual memory. In L. B. Cohen & P. Salapatek (Eds.), *Infant perception: From sensation to cognition* (Vol. 1). New York: Academic Press.

Cohen, N. & Estner, L. (1983). *Silent knife: Caesarean prevention and vaginal birth after Caesarean.* South Hadley, MA: Bergin & Garvey.

Colby, A., Kohlberg, L., Gibbs, J., & Lieberman, M. (1983). A longitudinal study of moral development. *Monographs of the Society for Research in Child Development, 48* (1–2 Serial No. 200).

Cole, M. A. (Winter 1979). Sex and marital status differences in death anxiety. *Omega, 9,* 139–147.

Cole, M., & Bruner, J. S. (1971). Cultural differences and inferences about psychological processes. *American Psychologist, 26,* 867–876.

Coleman, F. W., & Coleman, W. S. (1984). Helping siblings and other peers cope with dying. In H. Wass & C. A. Corr, *Childhood and death*. Washington, DC: Hemisphere.

Coleman, M., & Ganong, L. (1985). Remarriage myths; Implications for the helping professions. *Journal of Counseling and Development, 64*, 116–120.

Coleman, M., & Ganong, L. (1987). The cultural stereotyping of stepfamilies. In K. Pasley & M. Ihinger-Tallman (Eds.), *Remarriage and stepparenting: Current research and theory* (pp. 19–41). New York: Guilford.

Coles, R. (1968). Like it is in the alley. *Daedalus, 97,* 1315–1330.

Coles, R. (1980). *Children of crisis: Privileged ones*. Boston: Atlantic-Little, Brown.

Collins, W. A., Sobol, B. L., & Westby, S. (1981). Effects of adult commentary on children's comprehension and inferences about a televised aggressive portrayal. *Child Development, 52,* 158–163.

Comber, L. C., & Keeves, J. (1973). *Science achievement in nineteen countries*. New York: Wiley.

Comer, J. P., & Poussaint, A. F. (1975). *Black child care*. New York: Simon & Schuster.

Comfort, A. (1976). *A good age*. New York: Crown.

Committee for Economic Development. (1987). *Children in need*. Washington, DC: Committee for Economic Development, Research and Policy Committee.

Cooper, K., & Guttman, D. (1987). Gender identity and ego mastery style in middle-aged, pre- and post-empty nest women. *The Gerontologist, 27,* 347–352.

Copple, C. E., Cline, M. G., & Smith, A. N. (1987). *Path to the future: Long-term effects of Head Start in the Philadelphia school district*. Washington, DC: Office of Human Development Services.

Costa, A. (Ed.). (1985). *Developing minds: A resource book for teaching thinking*. Washington, DC: Association for Supervision and Curriculum Development.

Costa, A., Hanson, R., Silver, H., & Strong, R. (1985). Building a repertoire of strategies. In A. Costa (Ed.), *Developing minds: A resource book for teaching thinking*. Washington, DC: Association for Supervision and Curriculum Development.

Costa, P. T., & McCrae, R. R. (1980). Still stable after all these years: Personality as a key to some issues in adulthood and old age. In P. B. Baltes & O. G. Brim, *Lifespan development and behavior* (Vol. 3). New York: Academic Press.

Costa, P. T., Jr., & McCrae, R. R. (1982). An approach to the attribution of aging, period and cohort effects. *Psychological Bulletin, 92,* 238–250.

Costa, P., & McCrae, R. (1985). Hypochondriasis, neuroticism, and aging: When are somatic complaints unfounded? *American Psychologist, 40,* 19–28.

Coster, G. (November 1972). *Scientific American,* p. 44.

Côté, J. E., & Levine, C. (1988). A critical examination of the ego identity status paradigm. *Developmental Review, 8,* 147–184.

Council of Economic Advisers. (1987). *The economic report of the president*. Washington, DC.

Council of Economic Advisers. (1990). *The economic report of the president*. Washington, DC.

Cowan, P. A., & Walters, R. H. (1963). Studies of reinforcement of aggression: I. Effects of scheduling. *Child Development, 34,* 543–551.

Cowgill, D. O. (1972a). The role and status of the aged in Thailand. In D. O. Cowgill & L. D. Holmes (Eds.), *Aging and modernization*. New York: Appleton-Century-Crofts.

Cowgill, D. O. (1972b). Aging in American society. In D. O. Cowgill & L. D. Holmes (Eds.), *Aging and modernization*. New York: Appleton-Century-Crofts.

Cox, H., & Bhak, A. (1979). Symbolic interaction and retirement adjustment: An empirical asset. *International Journal of Aging and Human Development, 9*(3), 279–286.

Craig, G. J., & Garney, P. (1972). *Attachment and separation behavior in the second and third years*. Unpublished manuscript. University of Massachusetts, Amherst.

Craik, F. I. M., & McDowd, J. M. (1987). Age differences in recall and recognition. *Journal of Experimental Psychology: Learning, Memory, and Cognition, 13*(3), 474–479.

Cratty, B. J. (1970). *Perceptual and motor development in infants and children*. New York: Macmillan.

Crawford, J. W. (1982). Mother–infant interaction in premature and full-term infants. *Child Development, 53,* 957–962.

Crider, C. (1981). Children's conceptions of body interior. In R. Bibace & M. E. Walsh (Eds.), *Children's conceptions of health, illness, and bodily functions*. San Francisco: Jossey-Bass.

Crockenberg, S. (1981). Infant irritability, mother responsiveness, and social support influences on the security of infant–mother attachment. *Child Development, 52,* 857–865.

Crockenberg, S., & McCluskey, K. (1986). Change in maternal behavior during the baby's first year of life. *Child Development, 57,* 746–753.

Crockett, W. H., & Hummert, M. L. (1987). Perceptions of aging and the elderly. In K. Warner Schaie & K. Eisdorfer (Eds.), *Annual review of gerontology and geriatrics* (Vol. 7, pp. 217–241). New York: Springer.

Cruickshank, W. M. (1977). Myths and realities in learning disabilities. *Learning Disabilities, 10*(1), 57–64.

Csikszentmihalyi, M., & Larson, R. (1984). *Being adolescent*. New York: Basic Books.

Cumming, E., & Henry, W. E. (1961). *Growing old: The process of disengagement*. New York: Basic Books.

Cutrona, C., & Troutman, B. (1986). Social support, infant temperament, and parenting self-efficacy: A mediational model of postpartum depression. *Child Development, 57,* 1507–1518.

Cytrynbaum, S., Blum, L., Patrick, R., Stein, J., Wadner, D., & Wilk, C. (1980). Midlife development: A personality and social systems perspective. In L. W. Poon (Ed.), *Aging in the 1980s*. Washington, DC: American Psychological Association.

Damon, W., & Hart, D. (1982). The development of self-understanding from infancy through adolescence. *Child Development, 53,* 841–864.

Daniels, P., & Weingarten, K. (1982). *Sooner or later: The timing of parenthood in adult lives*. New York: Norton.

Dansereau, H. K. (1961). Work and the teen-ager. *Annals of the American Academy of Political and Social Sciences, 338,* 44–52.

Dargassies, S. S. (1986). *The neuromotor and psychoaffective development of the infant* (English language edition.). Amsterdam, the Netherlands: Elsevier.

Datan, N., & Ginsberg, L. (Eds.). (1975). *Life-span developmental psychology*. New York: Academic Press.

Day, D. E., Perkins, E. P., & Weinthaler, J. A. (1979). *Naturalistic evaluation for program improvement*. Unpublished monograph.

Dean, P. G. (1986). Monitoring an apneic infant: Impact on the infant's mother. *Maternal-Child Nursing Journal, 15,* 65–76.

de Boysson-Bardies, B., Halle, P., Sagart, L., & Durand, C. (1989). A crosslinguistic investigation of vowel formants in babbling. *Journal of Child Language, 16,* 1–17.

DeCharms, R., & Moeller, G. H. (1962). Values expressed in American children's readers: 1800–1950. *Journal of Abnormal and Social Psychology, 64,* 136–142.

Deimling, G., & Bass, D. (1986). Symptoms of mental impairment among elderly adults and their effects on family caregivers. *Journal of Gerontology, 41,* 778–784.

DeLoache, J. S., Cassidy, D. J., & Brown, A. L. (1985). Precursors of mnemonic strategies in very young children's memory. *Child Development, 56,* 125–137.

Demaris, A., & Leslie, G. (February 1984). Cohabitation with a future spouse: Its influence upon marital satisfaction and communication. *Journal of Marriage and the Family, 46,* 77–84.

DeMause, L. (Ed.). (1974). *The history of childhood.* New York: Psychohistory Press.

DeMott, R. K., & Sandmire, H. F. (1990). *The Green Bay Caesarean section study: The physician factor as a determinant of Caesarean birth rates.* Presented at the fifty-seventh annual meeting of the Central Association of Obstetricians and Gynecologists, Scottsdale, AZ.

Dencik, L. (1989). Growing up in the post-modern age: On the child's situation in the modern family, and on the position of the family in the modern welfare state. *Acta Sociologica, 32,* 155–180.

Denney, N. (1982). Aging and cognitive changes. In B. Wolman (Ed.), *Handbook of developmental psychology* (pp. 807–827). Englewood Cliffs, NJ: Prentice Hall.

Dennis, W. (1960). Causes of retardation among institutional children: Iran. *Journal of Genetic Psychology, 96,* 47–59.

Dennis, W. (1966a). Causes of retardation among institutional children: Iran. *Journal of Genetic Psychology, 96,* 47–59.

Dennis, W. (1966b). Creative productivity between the ages of 20 and 80 years. *Journal of Gerontology, 21*(1), 1–8.

Dennis, W. (1973). *Children of the creche.* New York: Appleton-Century-Crofts.

Dennis, W., & Najarian, P. (1957). Infant development under environmental handicap. *Psychological Monographs, 717* (Whole No. 436).

Derr, C. B. (1986). *Managing the new careerists.* San Francisco: Jossey-Bass.

DeSpelder, L., & Strickland, A. (1983). *The last dance: Encountering death and dying.* Palo Alto, CA: Mayfield.

de Villiers, P. A., & de Villiers, J. G. (1979). *Early language.* Cambridge, MA: Harvard University Press.

Dewey, J. (1961). *Democracy and education.* New York: Macmillan.

Diaz, R. M. (1985). Bilingual cognitive development: Addressing three gaps in current research. *Child Development, 56,* 1376–1388.

Diaz, R. M., & Lowe, J. R. (1987). The private speech of young children at risk: A test of three deficit hypotheses. *Early Childhood Research Quarterly, 2,* 181–184.

Dick-Read, G. (1953). *Childbirth without fear.* New York: Harper & Brothers.

Dietz, W. H., Jr. (1987). Childhood obesity. *Annals of the New York Academy of Sciences, 499,* 47–54.

Ditzion, J. S., & Wolf, P. W. (1978). Beginning parenthood. In Boston Women's Book Collective (Ed.), *Ourselves and our children.* New York: Random House.

Dodge, K. A., Coie, J. D., Pettit, G. S., & Price, J. M. (1990). Peer status and aggression in boys' groups: Developmental and contextual analyses. *Child Development, 61,* 1289–1309.

Dodwell, P., Humphrey, G. K., & Muir, D. (1987). Shape and pattern perception. In P. Salapatek & L. Cohen (Eds.), *Handbook of infant perception.* New York: Academic Press.

Doka, K., & Mertz, M. (1988). The meaning and significance of great-grandparenthood. *The Gerontologist, 28,* 192–197.

Dollard, J., Doob, L. W., Miller, N. E., Mowrer, O. H., & Sears, R. R. (1939). *Frustration and aggression.* New Haven: Yale University Press.

Dollard, J., & Miller, N. E. (1950). *Personality and psychotherapy: An analysis in terms of learning, thinking, and culture.* New York: McGraw-Hill.

Doman, G. (1963). *How to teach your baby to read.* New York: Random House.

Donaldson, M. (1978). *Children's minds.* New York: Norton.

Donaldson, M. (1979). The mismatch between school and children's minds. *Human Nature, 2,* 158–162.

Donovan, B. (1986). *The Caesarean birth experience.* Boston: Beacon Press.

Donovan, J. E., Jessor, R., & Costa, F. M. (1988). Syndrome of problem behavior in adolescence: A replication. *Journal of Consulting and Clinical Psychology, 56,* 762–765.

Donovan, R. (February–March 1984). Planning for an aging work force. *Aging,* pp. 4–7.

Dornbusch, S. M., Carlsmith, J. M., Bushwall, S. J., Ritter, P. L., Leiderman, H., Hastorf, A. H., & Gross, R. T. (1985). Single parents, extended households, and the control of adolescents. *Child Development, 56,* 326–341.

Dornbusch, S. M., Ritter, P. L., Leiderman, P. H., Roberts, D. F., & Fraleigh, M. J. (1987). The relation of parenting style to adolescent school performance. *Child Development, 58,* 1244–1257.

Douvan, E., & Adelson, J. B. (1966). *The adolescent experience.* New York: Wiley.

Douvan, E., & Gold, M. (1966). Modal patterns in American adolescence. In L. W. Hoffman & M. L. Hoffman (Eds.), *Review of child development research* (Vol. 2). New York: Russell Sage Foundation.

Doyle, A. B., Beaudet, J., & Aboud, F. (1988). Developmental patterns in the flexibility of children's ethnic attitudes. *Journal of Cross-Cultural Research, 19*(1), 3–18.

Draper, T. W., & James, R. S. (1985). Preschool fears: Longitudinal sequence and cohort changes. *Child Study Journal, 15*(2), 147–155.

Dreikurs, R., & Soltz, V. (1964). *Children: The challenge.* New York: Duell, Sloan & Pearce.

Dressel, P. (1988). Gender, race, and class: Beyond the feminization of poverty in later life. *The Gerontologist, 28,* 177–180.

Dreyer, P. H. (1982). Sexuality during adolescence. In B. Wolman (Ed.), *Handbook of developmental psychology.* Englewood Cliffs, NJ: Prentice Hall.

Droege, R. (1982). *A psychosocial study of the formation of the middle adult life structure in women.* Unpublished doctoral dissertation. California School of Professional Psychology, Berkeley.

Drotar, D. (Ed.). (1985). *New directions in failure to thrive: Implications for research and practice.* New York: Plenum.

DuBrin, A. (1978). Psychological factors: Reentry and mid-career crises. In *Women in midlife-security and fulfillment* (pp. 180–185). Washington, DC: Government Printing Office.

Duck, S. (1983). *Friends for life: The psychology of close relationships.* Brighton, UK: Harvester Press.

Dunn, J. (1983). Sibling relationships in early childhood. *Child Development, 54,* 787–811.

Dunn, J. (1985). *Sisters and brothers.* Cambridge, MA: Harvard University Press.

Dunn, J. (1986). Growing up in a family world: Issues in the study of social development of young children. In M. Richards & P. Light (Eds.), *Children of social worlds: Development in a social context.* Cambridge, MA: Harvard University Press.

Dunn, J., & Kendrick, C. (1979). Interaction between young siblings in the context of family relationships. In M. Lewis & L. Rosenblum (Eds.), *The child and its family: The genesis of behavior* (Vol. 2). New York: Plenum.

Dunn, J., & Kendrick, C. (1980). The arrival of a sibling: Changes in interaction between mother and first-born child. *Journal of Child Psychology, 21,* 119–132.

Dunn, J., & Kendrick, C. (1982). *Siblings: Love, envy and understanding.* Cambridge, MA: Harvard University Press.

Dunn, J., & Munn, P. (1987). Development of justification in disputes with mother and sibling. *Developmental Psychology, 23,* 791–798.

Dunphy, D. C. (1963). The social structure of urban adolescent peer groups. *Sociometry, 26,* 230–246.

Durlak, J. A. (1979). Comparison between experimental and didactic methods of death education. *Omega, 9,* 57–66.

Eakins, P. S. (Ed.), (1986). *The American way of birth.* Philadelphia: Temple University Press.

Ebersole, P. (1979). The vital vehicle: The body. In I. M. Burnside, P.

Ebersole, & H. E. Monea (Eds.), *Psychosocial caring throughout the life span.* New York: McGraw-Hill.

Edelstein, L. (1984). *Maternal bereavement.* New York: Praeger.

Eddy, D. M. (1991). The individual vs. society: Is there a conflict? *Journal of the American Medical Association, 265*(11), 1446–1450.

Edwards, C. P., & Gandini, L. (1989). Teachers' expectations about the timing of developmental skills: A cross-cultural study. *Young Children, 44*(4), 15–19.

Eibl-Eibesfeldt, I. (1989). *Human ethology.* New York: Aldine de Gruyter.

Eichorn, D. (1979). Physical development: Current foci of research. In J. D. Osofsky (Ed.), *Handbook of infant development* (pp. 253–282). New York: Wiley.

Eimas, P. D. (1974). Linguistic processing of speech by young infants. In R. L. Schiefelbusch & L. L. Lloyd (Eds.), *Language perspectives: Acquisition, retardation, and intervention.* Baltimore: University Park Press.

Eimas, P. D. (1975). Speech perception in early infancy. In Lin L. B. Cohen & P. Salapatek (Eds.), *Infant perception: From sensation to cognition* (Vol. 2), New York: Academic Press.

Eisenberg, N. (1988). The development of prosocial and aggressive behavior. In M. Bornstein & M. Lamb (Eds.), *Developmental psychology: An advanced textbook* (2nd ed.). Hillsdale, NJ: Erlbaum.

Eisenberg, N. (1989a). *The development of prosocial moral reasoning in childhood and mid-adolescence.* Paper presented at the April meeting of the Society for Research in Child Development, Kansas City.

Eisenberg, N. (1989b). The development of prosocial values. In N. Eisenberg, J. Reykowski, & E. Staub (Eds.), *Social and moral values: Individual and social perspectives.* Hillsdale, NJ: Erlbaum.

Eisenberg, N. (1989). Empathy and sympathy. In W. Damon (Ed.), *Child development today and tomorrow* (pp. 137–154). San Francisco: Jossey-Bass.

Eisenberg, N., Pasternack, J. F., Cameror, E., & Tryon, K. (1984). The relation of quantity and mode of prosocial behavior to moral cognitions and social style. *Child Development, 55,* 1479–1485.

Eisenberg, N., Shell, R., Pasternack J., Beller, R., Lennon, R., & Mathy, R. (1987). Prosocial development in middle childhood: A longitudinal study. *Developmental Psychology, 23*(5), 712–718.

Eisendorfer, D., & Wilkie, F. (1977). Stress, disease, aging and behavior. In J. E. Birren & K. W. Schaie (Eds.), *Handbook of the psychology of aging.* New York: Van Nostrand Reinhold.

Ekerdt, D. (1987). Why the notion persists that retirement harms the health. *The Gerontologist, 27*(4), 454–457.

Ekerdt, D., Vinick, B., & Bosse, R. (1989). Orderly endings: Do men know when they will retire? *Journal of Gerontology, 44,* S28–35.

Elbers, L., & Ton, J. (1985). Play pen monologues: The interplay of words and babbles in the first words period. *Journal of Child Language, 12,* 551–565.

Elder, G. H. (1980). Adolescence in historical perspective. In J. Adelson (Ed.), *Handbook of adolescent psychology.* New York: Wiley.

Elder, J. L., & Pederson, D. R. (1978). Preschool children's use of objects in symbolic play. *Child Development, 49,* 500–504.

Elder, L., Caspi, A., & Burton, L. (1988). Adolescent transition in developmental perspective: Sociological and historical insights. In M. Gunnar & W. Collins (Eds.), *Minnesota Symposia on Child Development: Vol. 21. Development during the transition to adolescence* (pp. 151–179). Hillsdale, NJ: Erlbaum.

Elias, J. W., & Marshall, P. H. (Eds.). (1987). *Cardiovascular disease and behavior.* Washington, DC: Hemisphere.

Elkind, D. (1967). Egocentrism in adolescence. *Child Development, 38,* 1025–1034.

Elkind, D. (1974). *Children and adolescents: Interpretive essays on Jean Piaget.* New York: Oxford University Press.

Elkind, D. (1981). *The hurried child.* Reading, MA: Addison-Wesley.

Elkind, D. (1984). *All grown up and no place to go: Teenagers in crisis.* Reading, MA: Addison-Wesley.

Elkind, D. (May 1986). Formal education and early childhood education: An essential difference. *Phi Delta Kappan,* pp. 631–636.

Elkind, D., & Bowen, R. (1979). Imaginary audience behavior in children and adolescents. *Developmental Psychology, 15,* 38–44.

Ellwood, D., & Crane, J. (1990). Family change among black Americans: What do we know? *Journal of Economic Perspectives, 4,* 65–84.

Emery, R. E. (1989). Family violence. *American Psychologist, 44,* 321–328.

Entwisle, D. (1985). Becoming a parent. In L. L'Abate (Ed.), *The handbook of family psychology and therapy.* (Vol. 1, pp. 560–578). Homewood IL: Dorsey.

Entwisle, D. R., & Doering, S. (1988). The emergent father role. *Sex Roles, 18,* 119–141.

Epstein, J. L. (1983). Selecting friends in contrasting secondary school environments. In J. L. Epstein & M. L. Karweit (Eds.), *Friends in school.* New York: Academic Press.

Epstein, L. H., Valoski, A., Wing, R. R., & McCurley, J. (1990). Ten-year follow-up of behavioral, family-based treatment for obese children. *Journal of the American Medical Association, 264,* 2519–2523.

Epstein, L. H., & Wing, R. R. (1987). Behavioral treatment of childhood obesity. *Psychological Bulletin, 101,* 331–342.

Erikson, E. H. (1959). The problem of ego identity. In E. H. Erikson (Ed.), Identity and the life cycle: Selected papers. *Psychological Issues Monograph,* No. 1.

Erikson, E. H. (1963). *Childhood and society* (2nd ed.). New York: Norton.

Erikson, E. H. (1968). *Identity, youth, and crisis.* New York: Norton.

Erikson, E. H. (1981). On generativity and identity. *Harvard Educational Review, 51,* 249–269.

Erikson, E. (1985). *Young man Luther.* New York: Norton.

Erikson, E. H., & Erikson, J. M. (1981). Generativity and identity. *Harvard Educational Review, 51,* 249–269.

Erikson, E. H., Erikson, J., & Kivnick, H. (1986) *Vital involvement in old age.* New York: Norton.

Ernst, C., & Angst, J. (1983). *Birth order: Its influence on personality.* New York: Springer-Verlag.

Esterbrook, M. A., & Goldberg, W. A. (1984). Toddler development in the family: Impact of father involvement and parenting characteristics. *Child Development, 55,* 740–752.

Evans, D., Funkenstein, H., Albert, M., Scherr, P., Cook, N., Chown, M., Hebert, L., Hennckens, C., & Taylor, D. (1989). Prevalence of Alzheimer's disease in a community population of older people. *Journal of the American Medical Association, 262,* 2551–2556.

Evans, E. D. (1975). *Contemporary influences in early childhood education* (2nd ed.). New York: Holt, Rinehart, & Winston.

Fabes, R. A., Wilson, P., & Christopher, F. S. (1989). A time to reexamine the role of television in family life. *Family Relations, 38,* 337–341.

Fadiman, A. (February 1982). The skeleton at the feast: A case study of anorexia nervosa. *Life,* pp. 63–78.

Fagan, J. F., III. (1977). Infant recognition memory: Studies in forgetting. *Child Development, 48,* 66–78.

Fantz, R. L. (1958). Pattern vision in young infants. *Psychological Record, 8,* 43–47.

Fantz, R. L. (May 1961). The origin of form perception. *Scientific American,* pp. 66–72.

Fantz, R. L., Ordy, J. M., & Udelf, M. S. (1962). Maturation of pattern vision in infants during the first six months. *Journal of Comparative and Physiological Psychology, 55,* 907–917.

Farb, P. (1978). *Humankind.* Boston: Houghton Mifflin.

Farber, J. (1970). *The student as nigger.* New York: Pocket Books.

Farber, S. (January 1981). Telltale behavior of twins. *Psychology Today,* pp. 58–64.

Farrell, M. P., & Rosenberg, S. D. (1981). *Men at midlife*. Boston: Auburn House.

Favia, S., and Genovese, R. (1983). Family, work and individual development in dual-career marriages. In H. Lopata & J. H. Pleck (Eds.), *Research in the interweave of social roles: Jobs and families* (Vol. 3). Greenwich, CT: JAI Press.

Featherman, D., Hogan, D., & Sorenson, A. (1984). Entry into adulthood: Profiles of young men in the fifties. In *Life span development and behavior* (Vol. 6). New York: Academic Press.

Featherstone, H. (June 1985). Preschool: It does make a difference. *Harvard Education Letter*, pp. 16–21.

Fedor-Freybergh, P., & Vogel, M. L. V. (1988). *Prenatal and perinatal psychology and medicine*. Carnforth, Lanc: Parthenon.

Fein, G. G. (1981). Pretend play in childhood: An integrated review. *Child Development, 52,* 1095–1118.

Fein, G. G. (1984). The self-building potential of pretend play, or "I gotta fish all by myself." In T. D. Yawkey & A. D. Pellegrini (Eds.), *Child's play*. Hillsdale, NJ: Erlbaum.

Feiring, C., Lewis, M., & Starr, M. D. (1984). Indirect affects and infants' reactions to strangers. *Developmental Psychology, 20,* 485–491.

Feitelsen, W., & Ross, G. S. (1973). The neglected factor—play. *Human Development, 16,* 202–223.

Ferber, M., Green, C., & Spaith, J. (1986). Work power and earnings of women and men. *American Economic Review, 76,* 53–56.

Ferguson, C., & Snow, C. (1977). *Talking to children: Language input and acquisition*. Cambridge, UK: Cambridge University Press.

Ferleger, N., Glenwick, D. S., Gaines, R. R. W., & Green, A. H. (1988). Identifying correlates of reabuse in maltreating parents. *Child Abuse and Neglect, 12,* 41–49.

Feshback, S., & Singer, R. D. (1971). *Television and aggression: An experimental field study*. San Francisco: Jossey-Bass.

Field, T. (1977). Effects of early separation, interactive deficits, and experimental manipulations on infant–mother face-to-face interaction. *Child Development, 48,* 763–771.

Field, T. (1978). Interaction behaviors of primary vs. secondary caretaker fathers. *Developmental Psychology, 14*(2), 183–184.

Field, T. M. (1979). Interaction patterns of pre-term and term infants. In T. M. Field (Ed.), *Infants born at risk*. New York: Spectrum.

Field, T. (1986). Models for reactive and chronic depression in infancy. In E. Tronick & T. Fields (Eds.), *New Directions for Child Development, 34. Maternal depression and infant disturbance.*

Fillmore, C. J. (1968). The case for case. In E. Bach & R. T. Harms (Eds.), *Universals of linguistic theory*. New York: Holt, Rinehart & Winston.

Fincher, J. (July/August 1982). Before their time. *Science 82 Magazine*, p. 94.

Finkelhor, D. (1984). *Child sexual abuse: New theory and practice*. New York: Free Press.

Fischer, D. H. (1978). *Growing old in America*. New York: Oxford University Press.

Fischer, J. L., Sollie, D. L., & Morrow, K. B. (1986). Social networks in male and female adolescents. *Journal of Adolescent Research, 6*(1), 1–14.

Fiske, M. (1968). *Adult transitions: Theory and research from a longitudinal perspective*. Paper presented at the meeting of the Gerontological Society.

Fiske, M. (1980). Tasks and crises of the second half of life: The interrelationship of commitment, caring and adaptation. In J. E. Birren & R. B. Sloane (Eds.), *Handbook of mental health and aging*. Englewood Cliffs, NJ: Prentice Hall.

Fitzcharles, A. (February 1987). Model versus modal child care. *Zero to Three*, p. 26.

Flavell, J. H. (1963). *The developmental psychology of Jean Piaget*. Princeton, NJ: Van Nostrand Reinhold.

Flavell, J. H. (1977). *Cognitive development*. Englewood Cliffs, NJ: Prentice Hall.

Flavell, J. H. (1985). *Cognitive development* (2nd ed.). Englewood Cliffs, NJ: Prentice Hall.

Flavell, J. H., Flavell, E. R., & Green, F. L. (1987). Young children's knowledge about the apparent-real and pretend-real distinctions. *Developmental Psychology, 23,* 816–822.

Flavell, J. H., Green, F., & Flavell, E. R. (1986). Development of knowledge about the appearance-reality distortion. *Monographs of the Society for Research in Child Development, 212.*

Flint, M. (1982). Male and female menopause: A cultural put-on. In A. Voda, M. Dennerstein, & S. O'Donnel (Eds.), *Changing perspectives in menopause* (pp. 363–375). Austin: University of Texas Press.

Folkman, S., Lazarus, R., Pimley, S., & Novacek, J. (1987). Age differences in stress and coping processes. *Psychology and Aging, 2,* 171–184.

Ford Foundation Project on Social Welfare and the American Future. (1989). *The common good: Social welfare and the American future*. New York: Ford Foundation.

Forman, B. I. (June 1984). Reconsidering retirement: Understanding emerging trends. *The Futurist*, pp. 43–47.

Forman, G. E. (April 1972). *The early growth of logic in children: Influences from the bilateral symmetry of human anatomy*. Paper presented at the conference of the Society for Research in Child Development, Philadelphia.

Forman, G. (June 1985). The value of kinetic print in computer graphics for young children. In E. L. Klein (Ed.), *Children and Computers*, and issue of *New Directions for Child Development*. San Francisco: Jossey-Bass.

Forman, G. E., & Fosnot, C. (1982). The use of Piaget's constructivism in early childhood education programs. In B. Spodek (Ed.), *Handbook on early childhood education*. Englewood Cliffs, NJ: Prentice Hall.

Forman, G. E., & Hill, F. (1980). *Constructive play: Applying Piaget in the preschool*. Monterey, CA: Brooks/Cole.

Forrest, L., & Mikolaitis, N. (December 1986). The relational component of identity: An expansion of career development theory. *The Career Development Quarterly*, pp. 76–85.

Fosburgh, L. (August 7, 1977). The make-believe world of teenage pregnancy. *New York Times Magazine*.

Fozard, J. (1990). Vision and hearing in aging. In J. Birren & K. Schaie (Eds.), *Handbook of the psychology of aging* (3rd ed., pp. 150–171). San Diego: Academic Press.

Fraiberg, S. H. (1959). *The magic years*. New York: Scribner's.

Fraiberg, S. H. (1974). Blind infants and their mothers: An examination of the sign system. In M. Lewis & L. Rosenblum (Eds.), *The effect of the infant on its caregiver*. New York: Wiley.

Frank, S., & Quinlan, D. M. (1976). Ego development and female delinquency: A cognitive-developmental approach. *Journal of Abnormal Psychology, 85,* 505–510.

Frankenburg, W. K., & Dodds, J. B. (1967). The Denver developmental screening test. *Journal of Pediatrics, 71,* 181–191.

Frauenglass, M. H., & Diaz, R. M. (1985). Self-regulatory functions of children's private speech: A critical analysis of recent challenges to Vygotsky's theory. *Developmental Psychology, 21,* 357–364.

Frazier, A., & Lisonbee, L. K. (1950). Adolescent concerns with physique. *School Review, 58,* 397–405.

Freda, V. J., Gorman, J. G., & Pollack, W. (1966). Rh factor: Prevention of isoimmunization and clinical trial on mothers. *Science, 151,* 828–830.

Freedman, D. G. (January 1979). Ethnic differences in babies. *Human Nature*, pp. 36–43.

Freeman, N. H. (1980). *Strategies of representation in young children*. London: Academic Press.

Frenkel-Brunswik, E. (1963). Adjustments and reorientation in the course of the life span. In R. G. Kuhlen & G. G. Thompson (Eds.), *Psychological studies of human development* (2nd ed.). New York: Appleton-Century-Crofts.

Freud, A. (1958). Adolescence. In *Psychoanalytic study of the child* (Vol. 13). New York: International Universities Press.

Freudenberger, H., & Richelson, G. (1980). *Burnout: The high cost of high achievement.* New York: Anchor Press/Doubleday.

Fried, P. A., & Oxorn, H. (1980). *Smoking for two: Cigarettes and pregnancy.* New York: Free Press.

Friedlander, M., & Siegel, S. (1990). Separation-individuation difficulties and cognitive-behavior indicators of eating disorders among college women. *Journal of Counseling Psychology, 37,* 74–78.

Fries, J. F., & Crapo, L. M. (1981). *Vitality and aging.* San Francisco: Freeman.

Frisch, R. E. (March 1988). Fatness and fertility. *Scientific American,* pp. 88–95.

Frost, J. L., & Sunderline, S. (Eds.). (1985). *When children play.* Proceedings of the International Conference on Play and Play Environments, Association for Childhood Education International, Weaton, MD.

Fuller, J., & Simmel, E. (1986). *Perspectives in behavioral genetics.* Hillsdale, NJ: Erlbaum.

Furst, K. (1983). *Origins and evolution of women's dreams in early adulthood.* Unpublished doctoral dissertation. California School of Professional Psychology, Berkeley.

Furstenberg, F. (1976). *Unplanned parenthood: The social consequences of teenage childbearing.* New York: Free Press.

Furstenberg, F. F., Jr. (1987). The new extended family: The experience of parents and children after remarriage. In K. Pasley & M. Ihinger-Tallman (Eds.), *Remarriage and stepparenting: Current research and theory* (pp. 42–64). New York: Guilford.

Furth, H. G. (1980). *The world of grown-ups: Children's conceptions of society.* New York: Elsevier.

Galinsky, E. (1980). *Between generations: The six stages of parenthood.* New York: Times Books.

Gallagher, D. (1987). Bereavement. In G. L. Maddox et al. (Eds.), *The encyclopedia of aging.* New York: Springer.

Gallagher, J. M. (1973). Cognitive development and learning in the adolescent. In J. F. Adams (Ed.), *Understanding adolescence* (2nd ed.). Boston: Allyn & Bacon.

Gandini, L., & Edwards, C. P. (1988). Early childhood integration of the visual arts. *Gifted International, 5*(2), 14–18.

Garbarino, J., Sebes, J., & Schellenbach, C. (1984). Families at risk for destructive parent–child relations in adolescence. *Child Development, 55,* 174–183.

Garber, J. (December 1984). The developmental progression of depression in female children. In D. Chicchetti & K. Schneider-Rosen (Eds.), *New Directions for Child Development, 26.*

Garber, K., & Marchese, S. (1986). *Genetic counseling for clinicians.* Chicago: Year Book Medical Publishers.

Gardner, H. (1973a). *The arts and human development: A psychological study of the artistic process.* New York: Wiley-Interscience.

Gardner, H. (1973). *The quest for mind: Piaget, Levi-Strauss, and the structuralist movement.* New York: Random House.

Gardner, H. (1983). *Frames of mind.* New York: Basic Books.

Gardner, J. M., & Karmel, B. Z. (1984). Arousal effects on visual preference in neonates. *Developmental Psychology, 20,* 374–377.

Garrett, D. N. (1978). The needs of the seriously ill and their families: The haven concept. *Aging, 6*(1), 12–19.

Garrod, A., Beal, C., & Shin, P. (1989). *The development of moral orientation in elementary school children.* Paper presented at the April meeting of the Society for Research in Child Development, Kansas City.

Gartner, A. (Winter 1984). Widower self-help groups: A preventive approach. *Social Policy,* pp. 37–38.

Garvey, C. (1977). *Play.* Cambridge, MA: Harvard University Press.

Garvey, C. (1984). *Children's talk.* Cambridge, MA: Harvard University Press.

Gatz, M., Bengtson, V., & Blum, M. (1990). Caregiving families. In J. Birren & K. W. Schaie (Eds.) *Handbook of the psychology of aging* (3rd ed., pp. 405–426). San Diego: Academic Press.

Gelis, J. (1989). The child: From anonymity to individuality. In R. Chartier (Ed.), *A history of a private life: Vol. 3. Passions of the Renaissance* (pp. 309–325). Cambridge, MA: Belknap Press of Harvard University Press.

Genesee, F. (1989). Early bilingual development: One language or two? *Journal of Child Language, 16,* 161–179.

Gerrard, M. (1987). Sex, sex guilt, and contraceptive use revisited: The 1980s. *Journal of Personality and Social Psychology, 52,* 975–980.

Gesell, A. (1940). *The first five years of life: The preschool years.* New York: Harper & Brothers.

Gibbons, D. C. (1976). *Delinquent behavior* (2nd ed.). Englewood Cliffs, NJ: Prentice Hall.

Gibson, E. J., & Spelke, E. S. (1983). The development of perception. In P. Mussen (Ed.), *The handbook of child psychology: Vol. 3. Cognitive development* (pp. 2–60). New York: Wiley.

Gibson, E. J., & Walk, R. D. (April 1960). The "visual cliff." *Scientific American,* pp. 64–71.

Gilligan, C. (1982). *In a different voice: Psychological theory and women's development.* Cambridge, MA: Harvard University Press.

Gilligan, C. (1987). Adolescent development reconsidered. *New Directions for Child Development, 37,* 63–92.

Ginsburg, E. (1972). Toward a theory of occupational choice: A restatement. *Vocational Guidance Quarterly, 20,* 169–176.

Giordano, J., & Beckman, K. (1985). The aged within a family context: Relationships, roles, and events. In L. L'Abate (Ed.) *The handbook of family psychology and therapy* (Vol. 1, pp. 284–320). Homewood, IL: Dorsey.

Glaser, R. (1963). Instructional technology and the measurement of learning outcomes: Some questions. *American Psychologist, 18,* 519–521.

Gleitman, L., & Wanner, E. (1982). Language learning: State of the art. In E. Wanner & L. Gleitman (Eds.), *Language learning.* Cambridge, UK: Cambridge University Press.

Glick, P. C. (1977). Updating the lifecycle of the family. *Journal of Marriage and the Family, 39,* 5–13.

Glick, P., & Lin, S. (1986). More young adults are living with their parents: Who are they? *Journal of Marriage and the Family, 48,* 107–112.

Glidewell, J. C., Kantor, M. B., Smith, L. M., & Stringer, L. A. (1966). Socialization and social structure in the classroom. In L. W. Hoffman & M. L. Hoffman (Eds.), *Review of child development research* (Vol. 2). New York: Russell Sage Foundation.

Goetting, A. (1981). Divorce outcome research: Issues and perspectives. *Journal of Family Issues, 2,* 350–378.

Goetting, A. (1982). The six stations of remarriage: Developmental tasks of remarriage after divorce. *Family Relations, 31,* 213–222.

Gold, M. (1985). The baby makers. *Science, 6*(3), 26–38.

Goldberg, M., & Harvey, J. (September 1983). A nation at risk: The report to the National Commission on Excellence in Education. *Phi Delta Kappan,* pp. 14–18.

Goldberg, S. (1972). Infant care and growth in urban Zambia. *Human Development, 15,* 77–89.

Goldberg, S. (1979). Premature birth: Consequences for the parent–infant relationship. *American Scientist, 67,* 214–220.

Goldberg, S. (1983). Parent–infant bonding: Another look. *Child Development, 54,* 1355–82.

Goldberg, S., & Lewis, M. (1969). Play behavior in the year-old infant: Early sex differences. *Child Development, 40,* 21–31.

Goldberg, S., Lojkasek, M., Gartner, G., & Corter, C. (1988). Maternal responsiveness and social development in preterm infants. In M. H. Bornstein (Ed.). *New Directions for Child Development: Vol. 43. Maternal responsiveness: Characteristics and consequences.* San Francisco: Jossey-Bass.

Goldfield, E. C. (1989). Transition from rocking to crawling: Postural constraints on infant movement. *Developmental Psychology, 25*(6) 913–919.

Goldin-Meadow, S., & Mylander, C. (1984). Gestural communication in deaf children: The effects and noneffects of parental input on early language development. *Monographs of the Society for Research in Child Development, 49* (3–4, Serial No. 207).

Goldsmith, H. H. (1983). Genetic influence on personality from infancy to adulthood. *Child Development, 54,* 331–355.

Goncz, L. (1988). A research study on the relation between early bilingualism and cognitive development. *Psychologische-Beitrage, 30*(1–2), 75–91.

Goodchilds, J. D., & Zellman, G. L. (1984). Sexual signalling and sexual aggression in adolescent relationships. In N. M. Malmuth & E. D. Donnerstein (Eds.), *Pornography and sexual aggression.* New York: Academic Press.

Goode, W. J. (1970) *World revolution and family patterns.* New York: Free Press.

Goodlin, R. C. (1979). History of fetal monitoring. *American Journal of Obstetrics and Gynecology, 133,* 323–347.

Goodman, M. (1980). Toward a biology of menopause. *Signs, 5,* 739–753.

Goodman, P. (1960). *Growing up absurd.* New York: Random House.

Goodnow, J. (1977). *Children drawing.* Cambridge, MA: Harvard University Press.

Gopnik, A. (1988). Three types of early word: The emergence of social words, names and cognitive-relational words in the one-word stage and their relation to cognitive development. *First Language, 8,* 49–70.

Gopnik, A., & Meltzoff, A. N. (1987). The development of categorization in the second year and its relation to other cognitive and linguistic developments. *Child Development, 58,* 1523–1531.

Gordon, I. (1969). Early childhood stimulation through parent education. *Final Report to the Children's Bureau Social and Rehabilitation Services Department of HEW.* ED 038–166.

Gortmaker, S. L., Dietz, W. H., Jr., Sobol, A. M., & Wehler, C. A. (1987). Increasing pediatric obesity in the United States. *American Journal of Diseases of Children, 141,* 535–540.

Goslin, D. A. (Ed.). (1969). *Handbook of socialization theory and research.* Chicago: Rand McNally.

Gottman, J. M. (1983). How children become friends. *Monographs of the Society for Research in Child Development, 48*(3).

Gould, R. L. (1978). *Transformations, growth and change in adult life.* New York: Simon & Schuster.

Gould, S. J. (1981). *The mismeasure of man.* New York: Norton.

Granrud, C. D., Yonas, A., & Petterson, L. (1984). A comparison of monocular and binocular depth perception in 5 and 7 month old infants. *Journal of Experimental Child Psychology, 38,* 19–32.

Gratch, G., & Schatz, J. (1987). Cognitive development: The relevance of Piaget's infancy books. In J. Osofsy (Ed.), *Handbook of infant development* (2nd ed.). New York: Wiley.

Gray, D. B., & Yaffe, S J. (1983). Prenatal drugs. In C. C. Brown (Ed.), *Prenatal Roundtable: Vol. 9. Childhood learning disabilities and prenatal risk.* (pp. 44–49). Rutherford, NJ: Johnson & Johnson.

Gray, D. B., & Yaffe, S. J. (1986). Prenatal drugs and learning disabilities. In M. Lewis (Ed.), *Learning disabilities and prenatal risk.* Urbana: University of Illinois Press.

Gray, S. (1976). *A report on the home-parent centered intervention programs: Home visiting with mothers of toddlers and their siblings.* DARCEE, Peabody College.

Greenberg, J., & Becker, M. (1988). Aging parents as family resources. *The Geronotologist, 28,* 786–791.

Greenberg, M., & Morris, N. (July 1974). Engrossment: The newborn's impact upon the father. *American Journal of Orthopsychiatry, 44*(4), 520–531.

Greene, A. L. (1990). Great expectations: Constructions of the life course during adolescence. *Journal of Youth and Adolescence, 19,* 289–303.

Greene, A. L., & Brooks, J. (April 1985). *Children's perceptions of stressful life events.* Paper presented at the Society for Research in Child Development, Toronto, Canada.

Greenfield, P. (1984). *Mind and media: The effects of television, video games and computers.* Cambridge, MA: Harvard University Press.

Greenough, W. T., Black, J. E., & Wallace, C. S. (1987). Experience and brain development. *Child Development, 58,* 539–559.

Greenspan, S., & Greenspan, N. (1985). *First feelings.* New York: Penguin.

Greenwood, S. (1984). *Menopause, naturally: Preparing for the second half of life.* San Francisco: Volcano Press.

Greif, E. B., & Ulman, K. J. (1982). The psychological impact of menarche on early adolescent females: A review of the literature. *Child Development, 53,* 1413–1430.

Gress, L. D., & Bahr, R. T. (1984). *The aging person: A holistic perspective* (p. 145). St. Louis & Toronto: Mosby.

Grobestein, C., Flower, M., & Mendeloff, J. (1983). External human fertilization: An evaluation of policy. *Science, 22,* 127–133.

Grosjean, F. (1982). *Life with two languages: An introduction to bilingualism.* Cambridge, MA: Harvard University Press.

Gross, T F. (1985). *Cognitive development.* Monterey, CA: Brooks/Cole.

Grossman, F. K., Pollack, W. S., & Golding, E. (1988). Fathers and children: Predicting the quality and quantity of fathering. *Developmental Psychology, 24*(1), 82–91.

Grotevant, H. D., & Cooper, C. R. (1985). Patterns of interaction in family relationships and the development of identity exploration in adolescence. *Child Development, 56,* 415–428.

Grusec, J. E., & Arnason, L. (1982). Consideration for others: Approaches to enhancing altruism. In S. Moore & C. Cooper (Eds.), *The young child: Reviews of research* (Vol. 3). Washington, DC: National Association for the Education of Young Children.

Guilford, J. P. (1959). Three faces of intellect. *American Psychologist, 14,* 469–479.

Gunnar, M. R. (1989). Studies of the human infant's adrenocortical response to potentially stressful events. *New Directions for Child Development, 45.* San Francisco: Jossey-Bass.

Gurewitsch, E. (July/August 1983). Geriatric day care: The options reconsidered. *Aging Magazine,* pp. 21–26.

Gutierrez de Pineda, V. (1948). Organizacion social en la Guajira. *Rev. Institute etnolog., 3.*

Gutmann, D. L. (1964). An exploration of ego configurations in middle and later life. In B. L. Neugarten (Ed.), *Personality in middle and late life: Empirical studies.* New York: Atherton Press.

Gutmann, D. L. (1969). The country of old men: Cross-cultural studies in the psychology of later life. *Occasional Papers in Gerontology, No. 5.* Ann Arbor: Institute of Gerontology, University of Michigan–Wayne State University.

Gutmann, D. L. (1975). Parenthood: A key to the comparative study of the life cycle. In N. Datan & L. H. Ginsberg (Eds.), *Life-span developmental psychology: Normative life crises.* New York: Academic Press.

Gutmann, D. (1987). *Reclaimed powers: Toward a new psychology of men and women in later life.* New York: Basic Books.

Gutmann, E. (1977). In C. E. Finch & L. Hayflock (Eds.), *Handbook of the biology of aging.* New York: Van Nostrand Reinhold.

Haber, P. (1987). Hospice. In G. L. Maddox et al. (Eds.), *The encyclopedia of aging.* New York: Springer.

Hagen, J. W., Longeward, R. H. J., & Kail, R. V., Jr. (1975). Cognitive perspectives on the development of memory. In H. W. Reese (Ed.), *Advances in child development and behavior* (Vol. 10). New York: Academic Press.

Hagestad, G. (1987). Able elderly in the family context: Changes, chances, and challenges. *The Gerontologist, 27,* 417–422.

Hall, E. (April 1980). Interview of B. Neugarten, Acting one's age: New rules for old. *Psychology Today.*

Hall, W. M., & Cairns, R. B. (1984). Aggressive behavior in children: An outcome of modeling or social reciprocity? *Developmental Psychology, 20,* 739–745.

Halliday, M. (1973). *Exploration in the functions of language.* London: Edward Arnold.

Hallinan, M. T., & Teixeira, R. A. (1987). Students' interracial friendships: Individual characteristics, structural effects, and racial differences. *American Journal of Education, 95,* 563–583.

Halpern, D. F. (1986). *Sex differences in cognitive abilities.* Hillsdale, NJ: Erlbaum.

Halsey, N. A., Boulos, R., Holt, E., Ruff, A. B., Kissinger, P., Quinn, T. C., Coberly, J. S., Adrien, M., & Boulos, C. (October 1990). Transmission of HIV-1 infections from mothers to infants in Haiti. *Journal of the American Medical Association, 264*(16).

Hansen, L. S. (1974). Counseling and career (self) development of women. *Focus on Guidance, 7,* 1–15.

Harlow, H. F. (June 1959). Love in infant monkeys. *Scientific American,* pp. 68–74.

Harlow, H. F., & Harlow, M. K. (November 1962). Social deprivation in monkeys. *Scientific American,* pp. 137–146.

Harre, R. (January 1980). What's in a nickname? *Psychology Today,* pp. 78–84.

Harris, B. (1979). Whatever happened to Little Albert? *American Psychologist, 34*(2), 151–160.

Harris, Louis, & Associates. (1978). Myths and realities of life for older Americans. In R. Gross, B. Gross, & S. Seidman (Eds.), *The new old: Struggling for decent aging.* Garden City, NY: Anchor Press/Doubleday. (Originally published 1975)

Harris, R., Ellicott, A., & Hommes, D. (1986). The timing of psychosocial transitions and changes in women's lives: An examination of women aged 45 to 60. *Journal of Personality and Social Psychology, 51,* 409–416.

Harrison, A., Wilson, M., Pine, C., Chan, S., & Buriel, R. (1990). Family ecologies of ethnic minority children. *Child Development, 61,* 347–362.

Hart, S. N., Germain, R. B., & Brassard, M. R. (1987). The challenge: To better understand and combat psychological maltreatment of children and youth. In M. R. Brassard, R. Germain, & S. N. Hart (Eds.), *Psychological maltreatment of children and youth* (pp. 3–24). New York: Pergamon.

Harter, S. (1982). The perceived competence scale for children. *Child Development, 53,* 87–97.

Harter, S. (1983). Developmental perspectives on the self system. In P. H. Mussen (Ed.), *Handbook of child psychology* (4th ed., Vol. 4). New York: Wiley.

Harter, S. (1988). Developmental processes in the construction of the self. In T. D. Yawkey & J. E. Johnson (Eds.), *Integrative processes and socialization: Early to middle childhood.* Hillsdale, NJ: Erlbaum.

Hartup, W. W. (1963). Dependence and independence. IN H. W. Stevenson, J. Kagan, & C. Spiker (Eds.), *Child psychology.* Chicago: National Society for the Study of Education.

Hartup, W. W (1970a). Peer interaction and social organization. In P. H. Mussen (ed.), *Carmichael's manual of child psychology* (3rd ed., Vol. 2). New York: Wiley.

Hartup, W. W (1970b). Peer relations. In T. D. Spencer & N. Kass (Eds.), *Perspectives in child psychology: Research and review.* New York: McGraw-Hill.

Hartup, W. W. (1983). Peer relations. In P. H. Mussen (Ed.), *Handbook of child psychology* (4th ed., Vol. 4). New York: Wiley.

Hartup, W. W. (1989). Social relationships and their developmental significance. *American Psychologist, 44*(2), 120–126.

Hass, A. (1979). *Teenage sexuality: A survey of teenage sexual behavior.* New York: Macmillan.

Hassett, J. (September 1984). Computers in the classroom. *Psychology Today, 18,* 9.

Hauser, S. T. (1976). Loevinger's model and measure of ego development: A critical review. *Psychological Bulletin, 83,* 928–955.

Hauser, S. T., Book, B. K., Houlihan, J., Powers, S., Weiss-Perry, B., Follansbee, D., Jacobson, A. M., & Noam, G. (1987). Sex differences within the family: Studies of adolescent and operent family interactions. *Journal of Youth and Adolescence, 16,* 199–220.

Havighurst, R. J. (1953). *Human development and education.* New York: Longman.

Havighurst, R. J. (1964). Stages of vocational development. In H. Borow (Ed.), *Man in a world at work.* Boston: Houghton Mifflin.

Havighurst, R. J. (1972). *Developmental tasks and education* (3rd ed.). New York: McKay.

Havighurst, R. J. (1982). The world of work. In B. Wolman (Ed.), *The handbook of developmental psychology* (pp. 771–790). Englewood Cliffs, NJ: Prentice Hall.

Havighurst, R. J., & Dreyer, P. H. (1975). Youth and cultural pluralism. In R. J. Havighurst & P. H. Dreyer (Eds.), *Youth: The 74th yearbook of the NSSE.* Chicago: University of Chicago Press.

Hawkins, J. A., & Berndt, T. J. (1985). *Adjustment following the transition to junior high school.* Paper presented at the biennial meeting of the Society for Research in Child Development.

Hawkins, J., Sheingold, K., Gearhart, M., & Burger, C. (1982). Microcomputers in schools: Impact on the social life of elementary classrooms. *Applied Developmental Psychology, 3,* 361–373.

Hayes, H. T. P. (June 12, 1977). The pursuit of reason. *New York Times Magazine.*

Hazen, N. L., & Lockman, J. J. (1989). Skill in context. In J. J. Lockman & N. L. Hazen (Eds.) *Action in social context: Perspectives on early development* (pp. 1–22). New York: Plenum.

Hebb, D. O. (1966). *A textbook of psychology.* Philadelphia: Saunders.

Hechtman, L. (1989). Teenage mothers and their children: Risks and problems: A review. *Canadian Journal of Psychology, 34,* 569–575.

Hecox, K. (1975). Electrophysiological correlates of human auditory development. In L. B. Cohn & P. Salapatek (Eds.), *Infant perception: From sensation to cognition* (pp. 151–191). New York: Academia.

Helfer, R. (1982). The relationship between lack of bonding and child abuse and neglect. In *Round Table on Maternal Attachment and Nurturing Disorder* (Vol. 2). New Brunswick, NJ: Johnson & Johnson.

Helson, R., & Picano, J. (1990). Is the traditional role bad for women? *Journal of Personality and Social Psychology, 59,* 311–320.

Hepper, P. (1989). Foetal learning: Implications for psychiatry? *British Journal of Psychiatry, 155,* 289–293.

Herkowitz, J. (1978). Sex-role expectations and motor behavior of the young child. In M. V. Ridenour (Ed.), *Motor development: Issues and applications.* Princeton, NJ: Princeton Book Co.

Herron, R. E., & Sutton-Smith, B. (1971). *Child's play.* New York: Wiley.

Hess, E. H. (1970). Ethology and developmental psychology. In P. H. Mussen (Ed.), *Carmichael's manual of child psychology* (3rd ed., Vol. 1). New York: Wiley.

Hess, E. H. (August 1972). "Imprinting" in a natural laboratory. *Scientific American,* pp. 24–31.

Hetherington, E. M. (June 1984). Stress and coping in children and families. In A. Doyle, D. Gold, & D. Moskowitz (Eds.), *New Directions for Child Development, 24.*

Hetherington, E. M. (1989). Coping with family transitions: Winners, losers, and survivors. *Child Development, 60,* 1–14.

Hetherington, E. M., & Baltes, P. B. (1988). Child psychology and life-span development. In E. M. Hetherington, R. Lerner, & M. Perlmutter (Eds.) *Child development in life-span perspective* (pp. 1–20). Hillsdale, NJ: Erlbaum.

Hetherington, E. M., & Camara, K. A. (1984). Families in transition:

The process of dissolution and reconstitution. In R. D. Parke (Ed.), *Review of child development research* (Vol. 7). Chicago: University of Chicago Press.

Hetherington, E. M., Cox, M., & Cox, R. (1982). Effects of divorce on parents and children. In M. L. Lamb (Ed.), *Nontraditional families: Parenting and child development*. Hillsdale, NJ: Erlbaum.

Hetherington, E. M., Stanley-Hagan, M., & Anderson, E. R. (1989). Marital transitions: A child's perspective. *American Psychologist, 44,* 303–312.

Hetherington, E. M., et al. (1978). The aftermath of divorce. In J. H. Stevens & M. Athews (Eds.), *Mother–child, father–child relationships*. Washington, DC: National Association for the Education of Young Children.

Hewlett, S. A. (1984). *A lesser life: The myth of women's liberation in America*. New York: Warner Books.

Hill, J. P. (1980). The family. In M. Johnson (Ed.), *Toward adolescence: The middle school years. The seventy-ninth yearbook of the national society for the study of education*. Chicago: University of Chicago Press.

Hill, J. P. (1980). *Understanding early adolescence: A framework*. Carrboro, NC: Center for Early Adolescence.

Hill, J. P. (1987). Research on adolescents and their families past and present. *New Directions for Child Development, 37,* 13–32.

Hill, R., & Aldous, J. (1969). Socialization for marriage and parenthood. In D. A. Goslin (Ed.), *Handbook of socialization theory and research*. Chicago: Rand McNally.

Hill, R., Foote, N., Aldous, J., Carlson, R., & Macdonald, R. (1970). *Family development in three generations*. Cambridge, MA: Schenkman.

Hinde, R. A. (1987). *Individuals, relationships & culture: Links between ethology and the social sciences*. Cambridge, UK, & New York: Cambridge University Press.

Hirshberg, L. (1990). When infants look to their parents: II. Twelve-month-olds' response to conflicting parental emotional signals. *Child Development, 61,* 1187–1191.

Hirshberg, L. M., & Svejda, M. (1990). When infants look to their parents: I. Infants' social referencing of mothers compared to fathers. *Child Development, 61,* 1175–1186.

Hirsh-Pasek, K., Nelson, D. G., Jusczyk, P. W., & Wright, K. (April 1986). *A moment of silence: How the prosaic cues in motherese might assist language learning*. Paper presented at the International Conference on Infant Studies, Los Angeles.

Hiscock, M., & Kinsbourne, M. (1987). Specialization of the cerebral hemispheres: Implications for learning. *Journal of Learning Disabilities, 20,* 130–142.

Hite, S. (1976). *The Hite report*. New York: Macmillan.

Hobbs, D., & Cole, S. (1976). Transition to parenthood: A decade of replication. *Journal of Marriage and the Family, 38,* 723–731.

Hochschild, A. (1989). *The second shift*. New York: Avon Books.

Hodges, W., & Cooper, M. (1981). Head start and follow-through: Influences on intellectual development. *Journal of Special Education, 15,* 221–237.

Hoffman, J. (1984). Psychological separation of late adolescents from their parents. *Journal of Counseling Psychology, 31,* 170–178.

Hoffman, L. (1989). Effects of maternal unemployment in the two-parent family. *American Psychologist, 44,* 283–292.

Hoffman, M. L. (1970). Moral development. In P. H. Mussen (Ed.), *Carmichael's manual of child psychology* (3rd ed., Vol. 2). New York: Wiley.

Hoffman, M. L. (1977). Sex differences in empathy and related behaviors. *Psychological Bulletin, 84*(4), 712–722.

Hoffman, M. L. (1980). Moral development in adolescence. In J. Adelson (Ed.), *Handbook of adolescent psychology*. New York: Wiley.

Hogan, D. (1980). The transition to adulthood as a career contingency. *American Sociological Review, 45,* 261.

Holden, C. (1980). Identical twins reared apart. *Science, 207,* 1323–1328.

Holland, J. L. (1973). *Making vocational choices: A theory of careers*. Englewood Cliffs, NJ: Prentice Hall.

Holt, J. (1964). *How children fail*. New York: Dell.

Hong, R., Matsuyama, E., & Nur, K. (1991). Cardiomyopathy associated with the smoking of crystal methamphetamine. *Journal of the American Medical Association, 265*(9), 1152–1154.

Honig, A. S. (May 1986). Stress and coping in young children. *Young Children*, pp. 50–63.

Honig, A. (May 1989). Quality infant/toddler caregiving: Are there magic recipes? *Young Children*, pp. 4–10.

Honig, A. S. (October 1980). The importance of fathering. *Dimensions*, pp. 33–38, 63.

Horn, J. L. (1982). The theory of fluid and crystallized intelligence in relation to concepts of cognitive psychology and aging in adulthood. In F. I. M. Craik & S. Trehub (Eds.), *Aging and cognitive processes*. New York: Plenum.

Horn, J. L., & Donaldson, G. (1980). Cognitive development in adulthood. In J. Kagan & O. G. Brim, Jr. (Eds.), *Constancy and change in development*. Cambridge, MA: Harvard University Press.

Horn, J. M. (1983). The Texas adoption project: Adopted children and their intellectual resemblance to biological and adoptive parents. *Child Development, 54,* 268–275.

Horowitz, F. D. (1982). The first two years of life: Factors related to thriving. In S. Moore & C. Cooper (Eds.), *The young child: Reviews of research* (Vol. 3). Washington, DC: National Association for the Education of Young Children.

Hoversten, G. H., & Moncur, J. P. (1969). Stimuli and intensity factors in testing infants. *Journal of Speech and Hearing Research, 12,* 687–702.

Howard, J., & Hammond, R. (September 9, 1985). Rumors of inferiority. *The New Republic*, pp. 17–21.

Howes, C., & Olenick, M. (1986). Family and child care influences on toddler's compliance. *Child Development, 57,* 202–216.

Hoyer, W. J., & Plude, D. J. (1980). Attentional and perceptual processes in the study of cognitive aging. In L. W. Poon (Ed.), *Aging in the 1980s*. Washington, DC: American Psychological Association.

Hudson, H. (1981). As cited in H. J. Wershow, *Controversial issues in gerontology*. New York: Springer.

Huesmann, L. R., Lagerspetz, K., & Eron, L. D. (1984). Intervening variables in the TV violence-aggression relation: Evidence from two countries. *Developmental Psychology, 20,* 746–775.

Hughes, M., & Donaldson, M. (1979). The use of hiding games for studying the co-ordination of viewpoints. *Educational Review, 31,* 133–140.

Hunt, B., & Hunt, M. (1975). *Prime time*. New York: Stein & Day.

Hunt, J. G., & Hunt, L. L. (1987). Here to play: From families to life-styles. *Journal of Family Issues, 8,* 440–443.

Hunt, J. M. (1961). *Intelligence and experience*. New York: Ronald Press.

Hunt, M. (1974). *Sexual behavior in the 1970s*. New York: Dell.

Husen, T. (1967). *International study of achievement in mathematics: A comparison of twelve countries*. New York: Wiley.

Huston, A. (1983). Sex typing. In P. H. Mussen (Ed.), *Handbook of child psychology* (Vol. 4). New York: Wiley.

Huston, A. C., Watkins, B. A., & Kunkel, D. (1989). Public policy and children's television. *American Psychologist, 44,* 424–433.

Hutcheson, R. H., Jr. (1968). Iron deficiency anemia in Tennessee among rural poor children. *Public Health Reports, 83,* 939–943.

Hyde, J. S. (1984). How large are gender differences in aggression? A developmental metaanalysis. *Developmental Psychology, 20,* 722–736.

Hyde, J. S. (1986). *Understanding human sexuality* (3rd ed.). New York: McGraw-Hill.

Ihinger-Tallman, M., & Pasley, K. (1987). Divorce and remarriage in the American family: A historical review. In R. Pasley & M.

Ihinger-Tallman (Eds.), *Remarriage and stepparenting: Current research and theory*. New York: Guilford.

Imara, M. (1975). Dying as the last stage of growth. In E. Kübler-Ross (Ed.), *Death: The final stage of growth*. Englewood Cliffs, NJ: Prentice Hall.

Inhelder, B., & Piaget, J. (1958). *The growth of logical thinking: From childhood to adolescence*. (A. Parsons & S. Milgram, Trans.). New York: Basic Books.

Irwin, T. (1978). After 65: Resources for self-reliance. In R. Gross, B. Gross, & S. Seidman (Eds.), *The new old: Struggling for decent aging*. Garden City, NY: Anchor-Press/Doubleday.

Isaacs, S. (1930). *Intellectual growth in young children*. London: Routledge & Kegan Paul.

Isabella, R. A., Belsky, J., & Von Eye, A. (1989). Origins of infant–mother attachment: An examination of interactional synchrony during the infant's first year. *Developmental Psychology, 25*(1), 12–21.

Isenberg, J., & Quisenberry, N. L. (February 1988). Play: A necessity for all children. *Childhood Education*.

Jackson, J. J. (1985). Race, national origin, ethnicity, and aging. In R. B. Binstock & E. Shanas (Eds.), *Handbook of aging and the social sciences*. New York: Van Nostrand Reinhold.

Jackson, J., Antonucci, T., & Gibson, R. (1990). Cultural, racial, and ethnic minority influences on aging. In J. Birren & K. W. Schaie (Eds.), *Handbook of the psychology of aging* (3rd ed., pp. 103–123). San Diego: Academic Press.

Jacobson, A. L. (1978). Infant day care: Toward a more human environment. *Young Children, 33*, 14–23.

Jacobson, J. L., Jacobson, S. W., Schwartz, P. M., Fein, G., & Dowler, J. K. (1984). Prenatal exposure to an environmental toxin: A test of the multiple effects model. *Developmental Psychology, 20*, 523–532.

Jacobson, J. L., & Wille, D. E. (1984). Influence of attachment and separation experience on separation distress at 18 months. *Developmental Psychology, 70*, 477–484.

Jacobson, J. & Wille, D. (1986). The influence of attachment pattern on developmental changes in peer interaction from the toddler to the preschool period. *Child Development, 57*, 338–347.

Jaeger, E., & Weinraub, M. (Fall 1990). Early nonmaternal care and infant attachment: In search of progress. In *New Directions for Child Development, 49*, 71–90.

Jeffers, F. C., & Verwoerdt, A. (1970). Factors associated with frequency of death thoughts in elderly community volunteers. In E. Palmore (Ed.), *Normal aging*. Durham, NC: Duke University Press.

Jelliffe, D. B., Jelliffe, E. F. P., Garcia, L., & De Barrios, G. (1961). The children of the San Blas Indians of Panama. *Journal of Pediatrics, 59*, 271–285.

Jensen, A. R. (1969). How much can we boost IQ and scholastic achievement? *Harvard Educational Review, 39*, 1–123.

Jensh, R. (1986). Effects of prenatal irradiation on postnatal psychophysiologic development. In E. P. Riley & C. V. Vorhees (Eds.), *Handbook of behavioral periontology*. New York: Plenum.

Jersild, A. T., & Holmes, F. B. (1935). *Children's fears*. (Child Development Monograph No. 20). New York: Teachers College Press, Columbia University.

Jessner, L., Weigert, E., & Foy, J. L. (1970). The development of parental attitudes during pregnancy. In E. J. Anthony & T. Benedek (Eds.), *Parenthood: Its psychology and psychopathology*. Boston: Little, Brown.

Johnson, C. L., & Barer, B. M. (June 1987). Marital instability and the changing kinship networks of grandparents. *The Gerontologist, 27*(3), 330–335.

Johnson, J. E., Christie, J. F., & Yawkey, T. D. (1987). *Play and early childhood development*. Glenview, IL: Scott, Foresman.

Johnson, R. P., & Riker, H. C. (1981). Retirement maturity: A valuable concept for preretirement counselors. *Personnel and Guidance Journal, 59*, 291–295.

Johnston, L. D., O'Malley, P. M., & Bachman, G. J. (1987). *National trends in drug use and related factors among American high school students and young adults, 1975–1986*. Rockville, MD: U.S. Department of Health and Human Services, National Institute on Drug Abuse.

Jones, A. B. (1959). The relation of human health to age, place, and time. In J. E. Birren (Ed.), *Handbook of aging and the individual*. Chicago: University of Chicago Press.

Jones, A. P., & Crnic, L. S. (1986). Maternal mediation of the effects of malnutrition. In E. P. Riley & C. V. Vorhees (Eds.), *Handbook of behavioral teratology*. New York: Plenum.

Jones, M. C. (1965). Psychological correlates of somatic development. *Child Development, 36*, 899–911.

Jones, M. C. (1979). Psychological correlates of somatic development. *Child Development, 36*, 899–911.

Jordanova, L. (1989). Children in history: Concepts of nature and society. In G. Scarr (Ed.), *Children, parents, and politics* (pp. 3–24). Cambridge, UK: Cambridge University Press.

Judd, L. J. (Winter 1991). Study finds mental disorders strike youth earlier than thought. *Quarterly Newsletter of the National Mental Health Association*, p. 4.

Jung, C. G. (1931/1960). The stages of life. In H. Read, M. Fordham, & G. Adler (Eds.), *The collected works of C. G. Jung* (Vol. 8, pp. 387–402.) New York: Pantheon.

Kagan, J. (1971). *Change and continuity in infancy*. New York: Wiley.

Kagan, J. (1978). The baby's elastic mind. *Human Nature, I*, 66–73.

Kagan, J., & Moss, H. A. (1962). *Birth to maturity: A study in psychological development*. New York: Wiley.

Kaku, D. A., et al. (1991). Emergence of recreational drug abuse as a major risk factor for stroke in young adults. *Journal of the American Medical Association, 265*(11), 1382.

Kales, J. D. (September 1979). Sleepwalking & night terrors related to febrile illness. *American Journal of Psychiatry, 136*(9), 1214–1215.

Kalish, R. A. (1985). *The final transition*. From the *Perspectives on Death & Dying* series. Farmingdale, NY: Baywood.

Kalish, R. (1987). Death. In G. L. Maddox et al. (Eds.), *The encyclopedia of aging*. New York: Springer.

Kalish, R. A., & Reynolds, D. K. (1981). *Death and ethnicity: A psychological study*. Farmingdale, NY: Baywood.

Kalleberg, A., & Rosenfeld, R. (1990). Work in the family and in the labor market: A cross-national, reciprocal analysis. *Journal of Marriage and the Family, 52*, 331–346.

Kallmann, F. J., & Sander, G. (1949). Twin students on senescence. *American Journal of Psychiatry, 106*, 29–36.

Kalnins, I. V., & Bruner, J. S. (1973). Infant sucking used to change the clarity of a visual display. In L. J. Stone, H. T. Smith, & L. B. Murphy (Eds.), *The competent infant: Research and commentary*. New York: Basic Books.

Kamii, C., & DeVries, R. (1980). *Group games in early education*. Washington, DC: National Association for the Education of Young Children.

Kamin, L. (1974). *The science and politics of IQ*. Hillsdale, NJ: Erlbaum.

Kammerman, S., Kahn, A., & Kingston, P. (1983). *Maternity policies and working women*. New York: Columbia University Press.

Kane, R. L., & Kane, R. A. (1980). Alternatives to institutional care of the elderly: Beyond the dichotomy. *The Gerontologist, 20*(30), 197.

Kanter, R. M. (March 1976). Why bosses turn bitchy. *Psychology Today*, pp. 56–59.

Kanter, R. (1977). *Men and women of the corporation*. New York: Basic Books.

Kantrowitz, B. (May 16, 1988). Preemies. *Newsweek*, pp. 62–67.

Kaplan, L. J. (1984). *Adolescence: The farewell to childhood*. New York: Touchstone.

Kaplan, M. (1979). *Leisure: Lifestyle and lifespan*. Philadelphia: Saunders.

Karen, R. (February 1990). Becoming attached. *The Atlantic Monthly*.

Karlson, A. L. (1972). *A naturalistic method for assessing cognitive acquisition of young children participating in preschool programs.* Unpublished doctoral dissertation, University of Chicago.

Kastenbaum, R. (December 1971). Age: Getting there ahead of time. *Psychology Today,* pp. 52–54ff.

Kastenbaum, R. (1979). *Growing old: Years of fulfillment.* New York: Harper & Row.

Kastenbaum, R. (1986). *Death, society and human experience.* Columbus, OH: Merrill.

Kastenbaum R., & Costa, P. T. (1977). Psychological perspectives on death. In M. R. Rosenzweig & L. W. Porter (Eds.), *Annual review of psychology* (Vol. 28). Palo Alto, CA: Stanford University Press.

Katz, L. G. (September 1990). Impressions of Reggio Emilia preschools. *Young Children, 45*(6), 4–10.

Keating, D. (1976). Intellectual talent, research, and development: Proceedings. In D. Keating (Ed.), *Hyman Blumberg Symposium in Early Childhood Education.* Baltimore: Johns Hopkins University Press.

Keating, D. P. (1980). Thinking processes in adolescence. In J. Adelson (Ed.), *Handbook of adolescent psychology.* New York: Wiley.

Keen, S. (April 1974). The heroics of everyday life: A theorist of death confronts his own end. *Psychology Today,* pp. 71–75ff.

Kegan, R. (1982). *The evolving self: Problem and process in human development.* Cambridge, MA: Harvard University Press.

Keister, M. E. (1970). *The good life for infants and toddlers.* New York: Harper & Row.

Keith-Spiegel, R. (1976). Children's rights as participants in research. In G. P. Koocher (Ed.), *Children's rights in mental health professions.* New York: Wiley.

Kellogg, R. (1970). *Analyzing children's art.* Palo Alto, CA: National Press.

Kelly, J. B. (1982). Divorce: The adult perspective. In B. Wolman (Ed.), *Handbook of developmental psychology.* Englewood Cliffs, N.J.: Prentice Hall.

Kelly, T. (1986). *Clinical genetics and genetic counseling* (3rd ed.). Chicago: Year Book Medical Publishers.

Kelvin, P., & Jarrett, J. (1985). *Unemployment: Its social psychological effects.* Cambridge, UK: Cambridge University Press.

Kempe, R. S., & Kempe, C. H. (1984). *The common secret: Sexual abuse of children and adolescents.* San Francisco: Freeman.

Keniston, K. (Winter, 1968–69). Heads and seekers: Drugs on campus, counterculture, and American society. *American Scholar,* pp. 126–151.

Keniston, K. (1975). Youth as a stage of life. In R. J. Havighurst & P. H. Dreyer (Eds.), *Youth: The 74th yearbook of the NSSE.* Chicago: University of Chicago Press.

Keniston, K. (1977). *All our children: The American family under pressure.* Report of the Carnegie Council on Children. New York: Harcourt Brace Jovanovich.

Keogh, J. F. (1965). *Motor performance of elementary school children.* Monograph of the Physical Education Department, University of California, Los Angeles.

Kephart, W. M. (1966). The Oneida community. In W. M. Kephart (Ed.), *The family, society, and the individual* (2nd ed.). Boston: Houghton Mifflin.

Kermoian, R., & Campos, J. J. (1988). Locomotor experience: A facilitation of spacial cognitive development. *Child Development, 59,* 908–17.

Kessler, R., & McRae, J. (1982). The effect of wives' employment on the mental health of married men and women. *American Sociological Review, 47,* 216–227.

Kieffer, J. (February–March 1984). New roles for older workers. *Aging, 47,* 11–16.

Kiester, E., Jr. (October 1977). Healing babies before they're born. *Family Health,* pp. 26–30.

Kimmel, D. C. (1974). *Adulthood and aging: An interdisciplinary view.* New York: Wiley.

Kinsey, A. C., Pomeroy, W. B., & Martin, C. E. (1948). *Sexual behavior in the human male.* Philadelphia: Saunders.

Kitzinger, S. (1981). *The complete book of pregnancy and childbirth.* New York: Knopf.

Klahr, D., Langley, P., & Necher, R. (Eds.). (1987). *Production system model of learning and development.* Cambridge, MA: MIT Press.

Kleigl, R., Smith, J., & Baltes, P. (1990). On the locus and process of magnification of age differences during mnemonic training. *Developmental Psychology, 26,* 894–904.

Klein, B., & Rones, P. (1989). A profile of the working poor. *Monthly Labor Review,* pp. 3–13.

Klein, N., Hack, N., Gallagher, J., & Fanaroff, A. A. (1985). Preschool performance of children with normal intelligence who were very low birth weight infants. *Pediatrics, 75,* 531–37.

Klima, E. S., & Bellugi, U. (1966). Syntactic regularities. In J. Lyons & R. J. Wales (Eds.), *Psycholinguistics papers.* Edinburgh: University of Edinburgh Press.

Klima, E. S., & Bellugi, U. (1973). As cited in P. de Villiers & J. de Villiers, *Early language.* Cambridge, MA: Harvard University Press, 1979.

Kline, D. W., & Schieber, F. (1985). Vision and aging. In J. E. Baron & K. W. Schaie (Eds.), *Handbook of the psychology of aging* (2nd ed.). New York: Van Nostrand Reinhold.

Klinnert, M. D., Emde, R. N., Butterfield, P., & Campos, J. J. (1986). Social referencing: The infant's use of emotional signals from a friendly adult with mother present. *Developmental Psychology, 22,* 427–432.

Knight, B., & Walker, D. L. (1985). Toward a definition of alternatives to institutionalization for the frail elderly. *The Gerontologist, 25*(4), 358–363.

Knobloch, H., Malone, A., Ellison, P. H., Stevens, F., & Zdeb, M. (March 1982). Considerations in evaluating changes in outcome for infants weighing less than 1,501 grams. *Pediatrics, 69*(3), 285–295.

Knobloch, H., Pasamanick, B., Harper, P. A., & Rider, R. V. (1959). The effect of prematurity on health and growth. *American Journal of Public Health, 49,* 1164–1173.

Knox, S. (1980). Ultra-sound diagnosis of foetal disorder. *Public Health, London, 94,* 362–367.

Koch, H. L. (1956). Sissiness and tomboyishness in relation to sibling characteristics. *Journal of Genetic Psychology, 88,* 213–244.

Koch, R., & Koch, K. J. (1974). *Understanding the mentally retarded child: A new approach.* New York: Random House.

Koff, T. H. (1980). *Hospice: A caring community.* Englewood Cliffs, NJ: Prentice Hall.

Kohl, H. (1968). *36 children.* New York: Norton.

Kohlberg, L. (1966). A cognitive developmental analysis of children's sex-role concepts and attitudes. In E. Maccoby (Ed.), *The development of sex differences.* Stanford: Stanford University Press.

Kohlberg, L. (1966). Moral education in the schools: A developmental view. *School Review, 74,* 1–30.

Kohlberg, L. (1978). Revisions in the theory and practice of moral development. *New Directions for Child Development, 2.*

Kohlberg, L. (1981). *Essays on moral development: Vol. 1. The philosophy of moral development.* New York: Harper & Row.

Kohlberg, L. (1984). *Essays on moral development: Vol. 2. The psychology of moral development.* New York: Harper & Row.

Kohn, M. L. (1980). Job complexity and adult personality. In N. J. Smelser & E. H. Erikson (Eds.), *Theories of work and love in adulthood.* Cambridge, MA: Harvard University Press.

Kohn, M. L., & Schooler, C. (1978). The reciprocal effects of the substantive complexity of work and intellectual flexibility: A longitudinal assessment. *American Journal of Sociology, 84,* 24–52.

Kohn, M. L., & Schooler, C. (1983). *Work and personality: Inquiry into the impact of social stratification.* Norwood, NJ: Ablex.

Kohn, R. R. (1985). Aging and age-related diseases: Normal processes. In H. A. Johnson (Ed.), *Relations between normal aging and disease* (pp. 1–43). New York: Raven.

Komarovsky, M. (1964). *Blue-collar marriage*. New York: Random House.

Komner, M., & Shostak, M. (February 1987). Timing and management of birth among the !Kung: Biocultural interaction and reproductive adaptation. *Cultural Anthropology, 2*(1), 11–28.

Kompara, D. R. (1980). Difficulties in the socialization process of stepparenting. *Family Relations, 29*, 69–73.

Kopp, C. B. (1989). Regulation of distress and negative emotions: A developmental view. *Developmental Psychology, 25*, 343–354.

Korner, A. F. (1987). Preventive intervention with high-risk newborns: Theoretical, conceptual, and methodological perspectives. In J. Osofsky (Ed.), *Handbook of infant development*. New York: Wiley.

Kosberg, L. (1988). Preventing elder abuse: Identification of high risk factors prior to placement decisions. *The Gerontologist, 28*, 43–50.

Kozol, J. (1970). *Death at an early age*. New York: Bantam Books.

Kreppner, K., & Lerner, N. (Eds.). (1989). *Family systems and life-span development*. Hillsdale, NJ: Erlbaum.

Kreppner, K., Paulsen, S., & Schuetz, Y. (1982). Infant and family development: From triads to tetrads. *Human Development, 25*(6), 373–391.

Kropp, J. P., & Haynes, O. M. (1987). Abusive and nonabusive mothers' ability to identify general and specific emotion signals of infants. *Child Development, 58*, 187–190.

Kübler-Ross, E. (1969). *On death and dying*. New York: Macmillan.

Kübler-Ross, E. (1975). *Death: The final stage of growth*. Englewood Cliffs, NJ: Prentice Hall.

Kuhl, P. K., & Meltzoff, A. N. (1988). Speech as an intermodel object of perception. In A. Yonas (Ed.), *The Minnesota Symposia on Child Psychology: Vol. 20. Perceptual development in infancy* (pp. 235–266). Hillsdale, NJ: Erlbaum.

Kurdek, L., & Schmitt, J. (1986). Early development of relationship quality in heterosexual married, heterosexual cohabiting, gay, and lesbian couples. *Developmental Psychology, 48*, 305–309.

Kushner, H. S. (1981). *When bad things happen to good people*. New York: Schocken Books.

Kutza, E. (1981). *The benefits of old age: Social welfare policy for the elderly*. Chicago: University of Chicago Press.

Labouvie-Vief, G. (1984). Chapter in M. L. Commons, F. A. Richards, & C. Armon (Eds.), *Beyond formal operations: Late adolescence and adult cognitive development*. New York: Praeger.

Labouvie-Vief, G. (1985). Intelligence and cognition. In J. Birren & K. Schaie (Eds.) *Handbook of the psychology of aging* (2nd ed., pp. 500–530) New York: Van Nostrand Reinhold.

Labouvie-Vief, G. (1987). Article in *Psychology and Aging, 2*.

Labouvie-Vief, G., & Schell, D. A. (1982). Learning and memory in later life. In B. Wolman (Ed.), *Handbook of developmental psychology*. Englewood Cliffs, NJ: Prentice Hall.

Labov, W. (1970). The logic of nonstandard English. In F. Williams (Ed.), *Language and poverty*. Englewood Cliffs, NJ: Prentice Hall.

Labov, W. (1972). *Language in the inner city: Studies in the black English vernacular*. Philadelphia: University of Pennsylvania Press.

Ladd, G. W., Price, J. M., & Hart, C. H. (1988). Predicting preschoolers' peer status from their playground behaviors. *Child Development, 59*, 986–992.

Lamaze, F. (1970). *Painless childbirth: The Lamaze method*. Chicago: Regnery.

Lamb, M. E. (1979). Paternal influences and the father's role. *American Psychologist, 34*, 938–943.

Lamb, M. E. (1987). *The father's role: Cross-cultural perspectives*. New York: Wiley.

Lamb, M., & Lamb, J. (1976). The nature and importance of the father–infant relationship. *Family Coordinator, 4*(25), 379–386.

Lang, A. (1987). Nursing of families with an infant who requires home apnea monitoring. *Issues in Comprehensive Pediatric Nursing, 10*, 122–133.

Lapsley, D., Rice, K., & Shadid, G. (1989). Psychological separation and adjustment to college. *Journal of Counseling Psychology, 36*, 286–294.

Larson, R. (1978). Thirty years of research on the subjective well-being of older Americans. *Journal of Gerontology, 33*, 109–125.

La Rue, A., & Jarvik, L. F. (1982). Old age and behavioral changes. In B. Wolman (Ed.), *Handbook of developmental psychology*. Englewood Cliffs, NJ: Prentice Hall.

La Salle, A. D., & Spokane, A. R. (September 1987). Patterns of early labor force participation of American women. *Career Development Quarterly*, pp. 55–65.

Latham, M. C. (1977). Infant feeding in national and international perspective: An examination of the decline in human lactation, and the modern crisis in infant and young child feeding practices. *Annals of the New York Academy of Sciences, 300*, 197–209.

Lawton, M. P., Brody, E., & Saperstein, A. (1989). A controlled study of respite service for care-givers of Alzheimer's patients. *The Gerontologist, 29*, 8–16.

Lazarus, R. S. (July 1981). Little hassles can be hazardous to health. *Psychology Today*, pp. 58–62.

Learman, L. A., et al. (1991). Pygmalion in the nursing home: The effects of care-giver expectations on patient outcomes. *Journal of the American Medical Association, 265*, 36.

Leboyer, F. (1976). *Birth without violence*. New York: Knopf.

Lee, G. R. (1988). Marital satisfaction in later life: The effects of nonmarital roles. *Journal of Marriage and the Family, 50*, 775–783.

Lehane, S. (1976). *Help your baby learn*. Englewood Cliffs, NJ: Prentice Hall.

Lehman, D., & Nisbett, R. (1990). A longitudinal study of the effects of undergraduate training on reasoning. *Developmental Psychology, 26*, 952–960.

Leo, J. (April 9, 1984). The revolution is over. *Time*, pp. 74–83.

Lerner, R. (1990). Plasticity, person-context relations and cognitive training in the aged years: A developmental contextual perspective. *Developmental Psychology, 26*, 911–915.

Lerner, R. M., Orlos, J. B., & Knapp, J. R. (1976). Physical attractiveness, physical effectiveness and self-concept in late adolescence. *Adolescence, 11*, 313–326.

Lester, B. M., Als, H., & Brazelton, T. B. (1982). Regional obstetric anesthesia and newborn behavior: A reanalysis toward synergistic effects. *Child Development, 53*, 687–692.

Lester, B. M., & Brazelton, T. B. (1982). Cross-cultural assessment of neonatal behavior. In D. Wagner & H. Stevenson (Eds.), *Cultural perspectives on child development*. San Francisco: Freeman.

Lester, B. M., & Dreher, M. (1989). Effects of marijuana use during pregnancy on newborn cry. *Child Development, 60*, 765–771.

Letteri, C. A. (1985). Teaching students how to learn. *Theory into Practice*, pp. 112–122.

Levine, L. E. (1983). Mine: Self-definition in two-year-old boys. *Developmental Psychology, 19*, 544–549.

Levinson, D. J. (1978). *The seasons of a man's life*. New York: Knopf.

Levinson, D. (1986). A conception of adult development. *American Psychologist, 41*, 3–13.

Levinson, D. (1990). *The seasons of a woman's life: Implications for women and men*. Presented at the 98th annual convention of the American Psychological Association, Boston.

Levinson, H. (1983). A second career: The possible dream. *Harvard Business Review*, pp. 122–129.

Levy, G. D., & Carter, D. B. (1989). Gender schema, gender constancy and gender-role knowledge: The roles of cognitive factors in preschoolers' gender-role stereotype attributions. *Developmental Psychology, 25*(3), 444–449.

Levy, S. M. (1978). Temporal experience in the aged: Body integrity and social milieu. *International Journal of Aging and Human Development, 9*(4), 319–343.

Lewis, M. (1987). Social development in infancy and early childhood. In J. Osofsky (Ed.), *Handbook of infant development*. New York: Wiley.

Lewis, M., & Feinman, S. (Eds.) (1991). *Social influences and socialization in infancy.* New York: Plenum.

Lewis, M., & Feiring, C. (1989). Infant, mother, and mother–infant interaction behavior and subsequent attachment. *Child Development, 60,* 831–837.

Lewis, M., Feiring, C., & Kotsonis, M. (1984). The social network of the young child: A developmental perspective. In M. Lewis (Ed.), *Beyond the dyad: The genesis of behavior.* New York: Plenum.

Lewis, M., & Rosenblum, L. (Eds.) (1974). *The effect of the infant on its caregiver.* New York: Wiley.

Liebenberg, B. (1967). Expectant fathers. *American Journal of Orthopsychiatry, 37,* 358–359.

Lieberman, M. A., & Tobin, S. S. (1983). *The experience of old age: Stress, coping and survival.* New York: Basic Books.

Liem, R. (December 1981). Unemployment and mental health implications for human service policy. *Policy Studies Journal, 10,* 350–364.

Lisina, M. I., & Neverovich, Y. Z. (1971). Development of movements and formation of motor habits. In A. Z. Zaporozlets & D. B. Elkonin (Eds.), *The psychology of preschool children.* Cambridge, MA: MIT Press.

Livson, F. (1976). Patterns of personality development in middle-aged women: A longitudinal study. *International Journal of Aging and Human Development, 1,* 107–115.

Livson, N., & Peskin, H. (1980). Perspectives on adolescence from longitudinal research. In J. Adelson (Ed.), *Handbook of adolescent psychology.* New York: Wiley.

Lloyd, B. (1987). Social representations of gender. In J. Bruner & H. Haste (Eds.). *Making sense: The child's construction of the world.* London: Methue.

Loevinger, J. (1976). *Ego development: Conceptions and theories.* San Francisco: Jossey-Bass.

Lombardi, J. (September 1990). Head Start: The nation's pride, a nation's challenge. *Young Children,* pp. 22–29.

Londerville, S., & Main, M. (1981). Security of attachment, compliance, and maternal training methods in the second year of life. *Developmental Psychology, 17,* 289–299.

Long, H. B., & Rossing, B. E. (June 1978). Tuition waivers for older Americans. *Lifelong Learning: The Adult Years,* pp. 10–13.

Lopata, H. Z. (1975). Widowhood: Societal factors in life-span disruptions and alterations. In N. Datan & L. H. Ginsberg (Eds.), *Life-span developmental psychology: Normative life crisis.* New York: Academic Press.

Lopata, H. Z. (1979). *Women as widows: Support systems.* New York: Elsevier.

Lord, L. J., Scherschel, P. M., Thornton, J., Moore, L. J., & Quick, B. E. (October 5, 1987). Desperately seeking baby. *U.S. News & World Report,* pp. 58–64.

Lorenz, K. Z. (1952). *King Solomon's ring.* New York: Crowell.

Lourie, I. S., Campiglia, P., James, L. R., & Dewitt, J. (1979). Adolescent abuse and neglect: The role of runaway youth programs. *Children Today, 8,* 27–40.

Lovaas, O. I. (1962). Effect of exposure to symbolic aggression on aggressive behavior. *Child Development, 32,* 37–44.

Lowenthal, M. F., Thurnher, M., Chiriboga, D., & Associates. (1977). *Four stages of life.* San Francisco: Jossey-Bass.

Lubic, R. W., & Ernst, E. K. (1978). The childbearing center: An alternative to conventional care. *Nursing Outlook, 26,* 754–760.

Lucariello, J., & Nelson, K. (1987). Remembering and planning talk between mothers and children. *Discourse Processes, 10,* 219–235.

Maccoby, E. E. (March 15, 1979). *Parent–child interaction.* Paper presented at the biennial meeting of the Society for Research in Child Development.

Maccoby, E. E. (1980). *Social development: Psychological growth and the parent–child relationship.* New York: Harcourt Brace Jovanovich.

Maccoby, E. E. (1984). Socialization and developmental change. *Child Development, 55,* 317–328.

Maccoby, E. E. (1990). Gender and relationships: A developmental account. *American Psychologist, 45,* 513–520.

Maccoby, E. E., & Feldman, S. S. (1972). Mother-attachment and stranger-reactions in the third year of life. *Monographs of the Society for Research in Child Development, 37*(1, Serial No. 146).

Maccoby, E. E., & Jacklin, C. N. (1974). *The psychology of sex differences.* Stanford: Stanford University Press.

Maccoby, E. E., & Jacklin, C. N. (1980). Sex differences in aggression: A rejoinder and reprise. *Child Development, 51,* 964–980.

Maccoby, E. E., & Martin, J. A. (1983). Socialization in the context of the family: Parent–child interaction. In P. H. Mussen (Ed.), *Handbook of child psychology: Vol. 4. Socialization, personality, and social development.* New York: Wiley.

MacFarlane, A. (February 1978). What a baby knows. *Human Nature, 1,* 81–86.

MacGregor, S. N., Keith, L. G., Chasnoff, I. J., Rosner, M. A., Chisum, G. M., Shaw, P., & Minogue, J. P. (1987). Cocaine use during pregnancy: Adverse perinatal outcome. *American Journal of Obstetrics and Gynecology, 1*(57), 66–90.

Mack, J., & Hickler, H. (1981). *Vivienne: The life and suicide of an adolescent girl.* Boston: Little, Brown.

Mackenzie, C. (1978). Gray panthers on the prowl. In R. Gross, B. Gross, & S. Seidman (Eds.), *The new old: Struggling for decent aging.* Garden City, NY: Anchor Press/Doubleday.

Madden, J. D., Payne, T. F., & Miller, S. (1986). Maternal cocaine abuse and effect on the newborn. *Pediatrics, 77,* 209–211.

Madsen, M. C. (1971). Developmental and cross-cultural differences in the cooperative and competitive behavior of young children. *Journal of Cross-Cultural Psychology, 2,* 365–371.

Madsen, M. C., & Shapira, A. (1970). Cooperative and competitive behavior of urban Afro-American, Anglo-American, Mexican-American, and Mexican village children. *Developmental Psychology, 3,* 16–20.

Maehr, M. L., & Breskamp, L. A. (1986). *The motivation factor: A theory of personal investment.* Lexington, MA: D. C. Heath.

Mahler, M., Pine, F., & Bergman, A. (1975). *The psychological birth of the human infant: Symbiosis and individuation.* New York: Basic Books.

Makin, J. W., & Porter, R. H. (1989). Attractiveness of lactating females' breast odors to neonates. *Child Development, 60,* 803–810.

Mandell, F., McClain, M., & Reece, R. (1987). Sudden and unexpected death. *American Journal of Diseases of Children, 141,* 748–750.

Mandler, J. M. (1983). *Representation.* In J. H. Flavell & E. M. Markham (Eds.), *Handbook of child psychology: Cognitive development* (Vol. 3). New York: Wiley.

Mandler, J. M. (1988). How to build a baby: On the development of an accurate representational system. *Cognitive Development, 3,* 113–136.

Mandler, J. M. (May–June 1990). A new perspective on cognitive development in infancy. *American Scientist, 78,* 236–243.

Manton, K., Blazer, D., & Woodbury, M. (1987). Suicide in middle age and later life: Sex and race specific life table and chart analyses. *Journal of Gerontology, 42,* 219–227.

Marcia, J. (1980). Identity in adolescence. In J. Adelson (Ed.), *Handbook of adolescent psychology.* New York: Wiley.

Marcoen, A., Goossens, L., & Caes, P. (1987). Loneliness in pre-through adolescence: Exploring the contributions of a multidimensional approach. *Journal of Youth and Adolescence, 16.*

Maret, E., & Finlay, B. (1984). The distribution of household labor among women in dual-earner families. *Journal of Marriage and the Family,* 357–364.

Marieskind, H. I. (1989). Caesarean section in the United States: Has it changed since 1979? In *An evaluation of Caesarean sections in the United States.* U.S. Department of Health, Education, & Welfare.

Martin, C. L. (1989). Children's use of gender-related information in making social judgments. *Developmental Psychology, 25*(1), 80–88.

Martin, C. L. (1990). Attitudes and expectations about children with nontraditional and traditional gender roles. *Sex Roles, 22*(3/4), 151.

Martin, C. L., & Halverson, C. F., Jr. (1981). A schematic processing model of sex-typing and stereotyping in children. *Child Development, 52,* 1119–1134.

Maslach, C., & Jackson, S. E. (May 1979). Burned-out cops and their families. *Psychology Today,* pp. 59–62.

Maslow, A. H. (1954). *Motivation and personality.* New York: Harper & Brothers.

Maslow, A. H. (1968). *Toward a psychology of being* (2nd ed.). Princeton, NJ: Van Nostrand Reinhold.

Maslow, A. H. (1979). *The journals of A. H. Maslow.* (R. J. Lowry & B. G. Maslow, Eds.). Monterey, CA: Brooks/Cole.

Masters, W. H., Johnson, P. E., & Kolodney, R. C. (1982). *Human sexuality.* Boston: Little, Brown.

Matas, L., Arend, R. A., & Sroufe, L. A. (1978). Continuity of adaptation in the second year: The relationship between quality of attachment and later competence. *Child Development, 49,* 547–556.

Matthews, K., & Rodin, J. (1989). Women's changing work roles: Impact on health, family and public policy. *American Psychologist, 44,* 1389–1393.

Matthews, S. H., & Rosner, T. T. (February 1988). Shared filial responsibility: The family as the primary care-giver. *Journal of Marriage and the Family, 50,* 185–195.

Matthews, S., Werkner, J., & Delaney, P. (1989). Relative contributions of help by employed and nonemployed sisters to their elderly parents. *Journal of Gerontology, 44,* S36–44.

Maurer, D., & Maurer, C. (1988). *The world of the newborn.* New York: Basic Books.

May, R. (1986). *Politics and innocence: A humanistic debate.* Dallas, TX: Saybrook, & New York: Norton.

McBride, A. (1990). Mental health effects of women's multiple roles. *American Psychologist, 45,* 381–384.

McBride, S. L. (Fall 1990). Maternal moderators of child care: The role of maternal separation anxiety. *New Directions for Child Development, 49,* 53–70.

McCall, R. B., Eichorn, D. H., & Hogarty, P. S. (1977). Transitions in early mental development. *Monographs of the Society for Research in Child Development, 42*(3, Serial No. 171), 1–75.

McCartney, K., Harris, M. J., & Bernieri, F. (1990). Growing up and growing apart: A developmental meta-analysis of twin studies. *Psychological Bulletin, 107,* 226–237.

McCary, J. L. (1978). *Human sexuality* (3rd ed.). New York: Van Nostrand Reinhold.

McClelland, D. C. (1955). Some social consequences of achievement motivation. In M. R. Jones (Ed.), *Nebraska symposium on motivation* (Vol. 3). Lincoln: University of Nebraska Press.

McCord, W., McCord, J., & Zola, I. K. (1959). *Origins of crime.* New York: Columbia University Press.

McCrae, R. (1989). Age differences and changes in the use of coping mechanisms. *Journal of Gerontology, 44,* P161–169.

McCrae, R. R., & Costa, P. T., Jr. (1984). *Emerging lives, enduring dispositions: Personality in adulthood.* Boston: Little, Brown.

McCune-Nicolich, L. (1981). Toward symbolic functioning: Structure of early pretend games and potential parallels with language. *Child Development, 52,* 785–797.

McGoldrick, M. (1980). The joining of families through marriage: The new couple. In E. A. Carter & M. McGoldrick (Eds.), *The family life cycle.* New York: Gardner Press.

McGraw, M. (1935). *Growth: A study of Johnny and Timmy.* New York: Appleton-Century.

McKnew, D. H., Jr., Cytryn, L., & Yahraes, H. (1983). *Why isn't Johnny crying? Coping with depression in children.* New York: Norton.

McKusick, Y. (1986). *Mendelian inheritance in man* (7th ed.). Baltimore: John Hopkins University Press.

McLanahan, S., & Booth, K. (1989). Mother-only families: Problems, prospects, and politics. *Journal of Marriage and the Family, 51,* 557–580.

McLoughlin, M., Shryer, T. L., Goode, E. E., & McAuliffe, K. (August 8, 1988). Men vs. women. *U.S. News & World Report.*

McLoyd, V. C., & Wilson, L. (1990). Maternal behavior, social support, and economic conditions as predictors of distress in children. *New Directions for Child Development, 46,* 49–69.

McNeill, D. (1972). *The acquisition of language: The study of developmental psycholinguistics.* New York: Harper & Row.

Mead, G. H. (1934). *Mind, self, and society: From the standpoint of a social behaviorist.* Chicago: University of Chicago Press.

Mead, M. (January 1972). A new understanding of childhood. *Redbook,* pp. 49ff.

Mead, M., & Newton, N. (1967). Cultural patterning of perinatal behavior. In S. A. Richardson & A. F. Guttermacher (Eds.), *Childbearing: Its social and psychological aspects.* Baltimore: Williams & Wilkins.

Meadow, K. P. (1975). The development of deaf children. In E. M. Hetherington (Ed.), *Review of child development research* (Vol. 5). Chicago: University of Chicago Press.

Meltzoff, A. N. (1988a). Infant imitation and memory: Nine month olds in immediate and deferred tests. *Child Development, 59,* 217–225.

Meltzoff, A. N. (1988b). Infant imitation after a 1-week delay: Long-term memory for novel acts and multiple stimuli. *Developmental Psychology, 24*(4), 470–476.

Meltzoff, A. N., & Borton, R. W. (1979). Intermodel matching by human neonates. *Nature, 282,* 403–404.

Meltzoff, A. N., & Moore, M. K. (1989). Imitation in newborn infants: Exploring the range of gestures imitated and the underlying mechanisms. National Institute of Child Health and Human Development (HD-22514).

Merriman, W. E. (1987). *Lexical contrast in toddlers: A re-analysis of the diary evidence.* Paper presented at the biennial meeting of the Society of Research in Child Development, Baltimore.

Mervis, C. B. (1987). Child-basic object categories and early lexical development. In U. Neisser (Ed.), *Concepts and conceptual development: Ecological and intellectual factors in categorization.* London: Cambridge University Press.

Metcoff, J., Costiloe, J. P., Crosby, W., Bentle, L., Seshachalam, D., Sandstead, H. H., Bodwell, C. E., Weaver, F., & McClain, P. (1981). Maternal nutrition and fetal outcome. *American Journal of Clinical Nutrition, 34,* 708–721.

Meyer, B. J. F. (1987). Reading comprehension and aging. In K. W. Schaie (Ed.), *Annual review of gerontology and geriatrics* (Vol. 7) New York: Springer-Verlag.

Meyer, P. H. (1980). Between families: The unattached young adult. In E. A. Carter & M. McGoldrick (Eds.), *The family life cycle.* New York: Gardner Press.

Miles, M. S. (1984). Helping adults mourn the death of a child. In H. Wass & C. A. Corr (Eds.), *Childhood and death.* Washington, DC: Hemisphere.

Milgram, S. (1963). Behavioral study of obedience. *Journal of Abnormal and Social Psychology, 67,* 371–378.

Miller, B. (1990). Gender differences in spouse caregiver strain: Socialization and role explanations. *Journal of Marriage and the Family, 52,* 311–321.

Miller, B. C., McCoy, J. K., Olson, T. D., & Wallace, C. M. (1986). Parental discipline and control attempts in relation to adolescent sexual attitudes and behavior. *Journal of Marriage and the Family, 48,* 503–512.

Miller, B. C., & Sneesby, K. R. (1988). Educational correlates of adolescents' sexual attitudes and behavior. *Journal of Youth and Adolescence, 17,* 521–530.

Miller, J., Schooler, C., Kohn, M. L., & Miller, R. (1979). Women and work: The psychological effects of occupational conditions. *American Journal of Sociology, 85,* 66–94.

Miller, M. (1982). *Gray power: A survival manual for senior citizens.* Paradise, CA: Dust Books.

Miller, P. (1989). *Theories of developmental psychology* (2nd ed.). New York: Freeman.

Miller, P. H., & Aloise, P. A. (1989). Young children's understanding of the psychological causes of behavior: A review. *Child Development, 60,* 257–285.

Millstein, S. G. (Winter 1990). Risk factors for AIDS among adolescents. In W. Gardner, S. G. Millstein, & Brian L. Wilcox (Eds.), *New Directions for Child Development: Vol. 50. Adolescents in the AIDS epidemic.* San Francisco: Jossey-Bass.

Miringoff, N. (February 1987). A timely and controversial article. *Zero to Three,* p. 26.

Mock, N. B., Bertrand, J. T., & Mangani, N. (1986). Correlates and implications of breastfeeding practices in Bas Zaire. *Journal of Biosocial Science, 18,* 231–245.

Money, J. (1980). *Love and love sickness: The science of sex, gender differences and pair-bonding.* Baltimore: Johns Hopkins University Press.

Monmaney, T. (May 16, 1988). Preventing early births. *Newsweek.*

Montagu, M. F. (1950). Constitutional and prenatal factors in infant and child health. In M. J. Senn (Ed.), *Symposium on the healthy personality.* New York: Josiah Macy Jr. Foundation.

Montemayor, R. (1983). Parents and adolescents in conflict: All families some of the time and some families all of the time. *Journal of Early Adolescence, 3,* 83–103.

Montemayor, R., & Brownlee, J. R. (1987). Fathers, mothers and adolescents: Gender-based differences in parental roles during adolescence. *Journal of Youth and Adolescence, 16,* 281–292.

Moore, G. (June 1984). The superbaby myth. *Psychology Today,* pp. 6–7.

Moore, M. K., Borton, R., & Darby, B. L. (1978). Visual tracking in young infants: Evidence for object permanence? *Journal of Experimental Child Psychology, 25,* 183–198.

Moore, W. E. (1969). Occupational socialization. In D. A. Goslin (Ed.), *Handbook of socialization theory and research.* Chicago: Rand McNally.

Mor, V., Sherwood, S., & Gutkin, C. (1986). A national study of residential care for the aged. *The Gerontologist, 26,* 405–416.

Morgan, D. (1989). Adjusting to widowhood: Do social networks really make it easier? *The Gerontologist, 29,* 101–107.

Morrison, D. M. (1985). Adolescent contraceptive behavior: A review. *Psychological Bulletin, 98,* 538–568.

Moses, B. (March 1983). The 59-cent dollar. *Vocational Guidance Quarterly.*

Mosher, W. D., & Pratt, W. F. (1990). Fecundity and infertility in the United States, 1965–88. *Advanced Data from Vital and Health Statistics, 192.* Hyattsville, MD: National Center for Health Statistics.

Motenko, A. (1989). The frustrations, gratifications, and well-being of dementia care-givers. *The Gerontologist, 29,* 166–172.

Mueller, E., & Lucas, T. (1975). A developmental analysis of peer interaction among toddlers. In M. Lewis & L. A. Rosenblum (Eds.), *Peer relations and friendship.* New York: Wiley.

Muir, D., & Field, J. (1979). Newborn infants orient to sounds. *Child Development, 50,* 431–436.

Murphy, J., & Florio, C. (1978). Older Americans: Facts and potential. In R. Gross, B. Gross, & S. Seidman (Eds.), *The new old: Struggling for decent aging.* Garden City, NY: Anchor Press/Doubleday.

Murphy, L. B. (1962). *The widening world of childhood: Paths toward mastery.* New York: Basic Books.

Murray, A., Dolby, R., Nation, R., & Thomas, D. (1981). Effects of epidural anaesthesia on newborns and their mothers. *Child Development, 52,* 71–82.

Murstein, B. I. (1980). Mate selection in the 1970s. *Journal of Marriage and the Family, 42,* 777–789.

Murstein, B. I. (1982). Marital choice. In B. Wolman (Ed.), *Handbook of developmental psychology.* Englewood Cliffs, NJ: Prentice Hall.

Murstein, B. I., Chalpin, M. J., Heard, K. V., & Vyse, S. A. (1989). Sexual behavior, drugs, and relationship patterns on a college campus over thirteen years. *Adolescence, 24,* 125–139.

Mussen, P. H., Conger J. J., & Kagan, J. (1974). *Child development and personality.* New York: Harper & Row.

Muuss, R. E. (Summer 1986). Adolescent eating disorder: Bulimia. *Adolescence,* pp. 257–267.

Myers, N. A., Clifton, R. K., & Clarkson, M. G. (1987). When they were very young: Almost-threes remember two years ago. *Infant Behavior and Development, 10,* 123–132.

Myers, N. A., & Perlmutter, M. (1978). Memory in the years from two to five. In P. Ornstein (Ed.), *Memory development in children.* Hillsdale, NJ: Erlbaum.

Myers, R. E., & Myers, S. E. (1978). Use of sedative, analgesic, and anesthetic drugs during labor and delivery: Bane or boon? *American Journal of Obstetrics and Gynecology, 133,* 83.

Naeye, R. L. (1979). Weight gain and the outcome of pregnancy. *American Journal of Obstetrics and Gynecology, 135,* 3.

Naeye, R. L. (1980). Abruptio placentae and placenta previa: Frequency, perinatal mortality, and cigarette smoking. *Obstetrics and Gynecology, 55,* 701–704.

Naeye, R. L. (1981). Influence of maternal cigarette smoking during pregnancy on fetal and childhood growth. *Obstetrics and Gynecology, 57,* 18–21.

National Association for the Education of Young Children. (1986). *NAEYC position statement on developmentally appropriate practice in early childhood programs: Birth through age eight.* Washington, DC: NAEYC.

National Center for Health Statistics. (1984). Trends in teenage childbearing, United States 1970–81. *Vital and Health Statistics* (Series 21, No. 41). U.S. Department of Health and Human Services.

National Center for Health Statistics. (June 3, 1987). Advance report of final marriage statistics, 1984. *Monthly Vital Statistics Report, 36*(2).

National Center for Health Statistics. (June 29, 1989). *Monthly Vital Statistics Report, 38*(3). Washington, DC: National Center for Health Statistics.

National Center for Health Statistics. (August 1990). Advance report of final natality statistics, 1988. *Monthly Vital Statistics Report, 38*(4 Supplement). Hyattsville, MD: Public Health Service.

National Center for Health Statistics. (November 28, 1990). Advance report of final mortality statistics, 1988. *Monthly Vital Statistics Report, 39*(7). Hyattsville, MD: Public Health Service.

National Center for Health Statistics. (1991a). Births, marriages, divorces, and deaths for January 1991. *Monthly Vital Statistics Report, 40* (1). Hyattsville, MD: Public Health Service.

National Center for Health Statistics. (1991b). Advance report of final divorce statistics, 1988. *Monthly Vital Statistics Report, 39* (12, Supplement 2). Hyattsville, MD: Public Health Service.

National Dairy Council. (1977). Nutrition of the elderly. *Dairy Council Digest, 48,* 1.

National Institute on Drug Abuse. (1984). *Student drug use in America: 1975–1983.* Washington, DC: Government Printing Office.

National Institute on Drug Abuse. (1987). *National trends in drug use and related factors among American high school students and young adults, 1975–1986.* U.S. Department of Health & Human Services.

National Institute on Drug Abuse. (1989). *National trends in drug use and related factors among American high school students and young adults, 1975–1988.* U.S. Department of Health & Human Services.

Neimark, E. D., (1975). Intellectual development during adolescence.

In F. D. Horowitz (Ed.), *Review of child development* (Vol. 4). Chicago: University of Chicago Press.

Nelson, K. (1974). Concept, word and sentence: Interrelations in acquisition and development. *Psychological Review, 81,* 267–285.

Nelson, K. (1981). Individual differences in language development: Implications for development and language. *Developmental Psychology, 17,* 170–187.

Nelson, K. (1986). *Event knowledge: Structure and function in development.* Hillsdale, NJ: Erlbaum.

Nelson, K. (September 1987). What's in a name? Reply to Seidenberg and Petitto. *Journal of Experimental Psychology, 116*(3), 293–296.

Nelson, K., Fibush, R., Hudson, J., & Lucariello, J. (1983). *Scripts and the development of memory.* In M. T. C. Chi (Ed.), *Trends in memory development research.* Basil, Switzerland: Carger.

Nelson, K., & Gruendel, J. M. (1986). Generalized event representations: Basic building blocks of cognitive development. In A. Brown & M. Lamb (Eds.), *Advances in developmental psychology* (Vol. 1). Hillsdale, NJ: Erlbaum.

Nemeth, R. J., & Bowling, J. M. (1985). Son preference and its effects on Korean lactation practices. *Journal of Biosocial Science, 17,* 451–459.

Neugarten, B. (1968/1967). The awareness of middle age. In B. Neugarten (Ed.), *Middle age and aging.* Chicago: University of Chicago Press.

Neugarten, B. L. (1968a). Adult personality: Toward a psychology of the life cycle. In B. L. Neugarten (Ed.), *Middle age and aging.* Chicago: University of Chicago Press.

Neugarten, B. L. (1968b). The awareness of middle age. In B. L. Neugarten (Ed.), *Middle age and aging.* Chicago: University of Chicago Press.

Neugarten, B. L. (1969). Continuities and discontinuities of psychological issues into adult life. *Human Development, 12,* 121–130.

Neugarten, B. L. (1970). The old and the young in modern societies. *American Behavioral Scientist, 14,* 18–24.

Neugarten, B. L. (December 1971). Grow old along with me! The best is yet to be. *Psychology Today,* pp. 45–48ff.

Neugarten, B. L. (1976). *The psychology of aging: An overview.* Washington, DC: American Psychological Association.

Neugarten, B. L. (1977). Personality and aging. In I. Birren & K. W. Schaie (Eds.), *Handbook of the psychology of aging.* New York: Van Nostrand Reinhold.

Neugarten, B. L. (1978). The wise of the young-old. In R. Gross, B. Gross, & S. Seidman (Eds.), *The new old: Struggling for decent aging.* Garden City, NY: Anchor Books/Doubleday.

Neugarten, B. L. (1979). Time, age and the life cycle. *American Journal of Psychiatry, 136,* 887–894.

Neugarten, B. L. (February 1980). Must everything be a midlife crisis? *Prime Time,* pp. 263–264.

Neugarten, B. L., & Moore, J. W. (1968). The changing age = status system. In B. L. Neugarten (Ed.), *Middle age and aging.* Chicago: University of Chicago Press.

Neugarten, B. L., Wood, V., Kraines, R., & Loomis, B. (1968). Women's attitudes toward the menopause. In B. L. Neugarten (Ed.), *Middle age and aging.* Chicago: University of Chicago Press.

New, R. (1988). Parental goals and Italian infant care. In R. B. LeVine, P. Miller, & M. West (Eds.), *New Directions for Child Development: Vol. 40, Parental behavior in diverse societies* (pp. 51–63). San Francisco: Jossey-Bass.

New, R. (1990). Excellent early education: A city in Italy has it. *Young Children, 45*(6), 11–12.

Newcomb, M. D., & Bentler, P. M. (1989). Substance use and abuse among children and teenagers. *American Psychologist, 44,* 242–248.

Newman, B. M. (1982). Mid-life development. In B. Wolman (Ed.), *Handbook of developmental psychology.* Englewood Cliffs, NJ: Prentice Hall.

Newman, L. S. (1990). Intentional and unintentional memory in young children: Remembering vs. playing. *Journal of Experimental Child Psychology, 50,* 243–258.

Newsweek. (November 15, 1976). New science of birth, pp. 62–64.

Newsweek. (February 11, 1980). The children of divorce, pp. 58–63.

New York Times. (August 1, 1989). Casual drug use is sharply down. P. A14.

New York Times. (March 4, 1991). Schools are not families. Editorial, p. A16.

Ney, P. G. (1988). Transgenerational child abuse. *Child Psychiatry and Human Development, 18,* 151–168.

Nichols, P. L., & Chen, T. C. (1981). *Minimal brain dysfunction: A prospective study.* Hillsdale, NJ: Erlbaum.

Nilsson, L. (1990). *A child is born.* New York: Delacorte.

Nock, S. (1982). The life-cycle approach to family analysis. In B. Wolman (Ed.), *Handbook of developmental psychology* (pp. 636–651). Englewood Cliffs, NJ: Prentice Hall.

Nugent, J. K., Greene, S., & Mazor, K. (October 1990). *The effects of maternal alcohol and nicotine use during pregnancy on birth outcome.* Paper presented at Bebe XXI Simposio Internacional, Lisbon, Portugal.

Nutrition Today. (1982). Alcohol use during pregnancy: A report by the American Council on Science and Health. Reprint.

Oakley, A., & Richards, M. (1990). Women's experiences of Caesarean delivery. In J. Garcia, R. Kilpatrick, & M. Richards (Eds.), *The politics of maternity care.* Oxford: Clarendon Press.

OB/GYN News. (June 15–30, 1984). In-vitro fertilization comes of age: Issues still unsettled, *19*(12), 3.

O'Brien, M., & Nagle, K. J. (1987). Parents' speech to toddlers: The effect of play context. *Journal of Language Development, 14,* 269–279.

Ochs, A., Newberry, J., Lenhardt, M., & Harkins, S. (1985). Neural and vestibular aging associated with falls. In J. Birren & K. Schaie (Eds.), *The handbook of the psychology of aging* (2nd ed.). New York: Van Nostrand Reinhold.

Ochs, E. (1986). Introduction. In B. B. Schieffelin & E. Ochs (Eds.), *Language socialization across cultures.* Cambridge, UK: Cambridge University Press.

O'Connor-Francoeur, P. (April 1983). *Children's concepts of health and their health behavior.* Paper presented at the meeting of the Society for Research in Child Development, Detroit.

O'Hara, M., Zekoski, E., Philipps, & Wright, E. (1990). Controlled prospective study of postpartum mood disorders: Comparison of childbearing and nonchildbearing women. *Journal of Abnormal Psychology, 99,* 3–15.

O'Heron, C. A., & Orlofsky, J. L. (1990). Stereotypic and nonstereotypic sex role trait and behavior operations, gender identity and psychological adjustment. *Journal of Personality and Social Psychology, 58*(1), 134–143.

Ohlsson, A., Shennan, A. T., & Rose, T. H. (1987). Review of causes of perinatal mortality in a regional perinatal center, 1980–84. *American Journal of Obstetrics and Gynecology, 1*(57), 443–445.

Oktay, J. A., & Volland, P. J. (1981). Community care program for the elderly. *Health and Social Work, 6,* 41–46.

Okun, B. F. (1984). *Working with adults: Individual, family and career development.* Monterey, CA: Brooks/Cole.

O'Leary, K. D., & Smith, D. A. (1991). Marital interactions. *Annual Review of Psychology, 42,* 191–212.

Oller, D. K., & Eilers, R. E. (1988). The role of audition in infant babbling. *Child Development, 59,* 441–449.

Olsho, L. W., Harkins, S. W., & Lenhardt, M. L. (1985). Aging and the auditory system. In J. E. Birren & K. W. Schaie (Eds.), *Handbook of the psychology of aging* (2nd ed. pp. 332–376). New York: Van Nostrand Reinhold.

Olson, D. H., & Lavee, Y. (1989). Family systems and family stress: A family life cycle perspective. In K. Kreppner & R. M. Lerner (Eds.), *Family systems and life-span development*. Hillsdale, NJ: Erlbaum.

Olson, S. L., Bates, J. E., & Bayles, K. (1984). Mother–infant interaction and the development of individual differences in children's cognitive competence. *Developmental Psychology, 20,* 166–179.

Olton, R. M., & Crutchfield, R. S. (1969). Developing the skills of productive thinking. In P. H. Mussen, J. Langer, & M. Covington (Eds.), *Trends and issues in developmental psychology*. New York: Holt, Rinehart & Winston.

Oni, G. A. (October 1987). Breast-feeding pattern in an urban Nigerian community. *Journal of Biolosocial Science, 19*(4), 453–462.

Opie, I., & Opie, P. (1959). *The lore and language of school children.* London: Oxford University Press.

Orlofsky, J. L., & O'Heron, C. A. (1987). Stereotypic and nonstereotypic sex role trait and behavior orientation: Implications for personal adjustment. *Journal of Personality and Social Psychology, 52,* 1034–1042.

Ornstein, P. A., Naus, M. J., & Liberty, C. (1975). Rehearsal and organizational processes in children's memory. *Child Development, 46,* 818–830.

Ornstein, P. A., Naus, M. J., & Stone, B. P. (1977). Rehearsal training and developmental differences in memory. *Developmental Psychology, 13,* 15–24.

Osofsky, J. D., & Osofsky, H. J. (1984). Psychological and developmental perspectives on expectant and new parenthood. In R. D. Parke (Ed.), *Review of child development research* (Vol. 7). Chicago: University of Chicago Press.

Ostrov, E., Offer, D., & Howard, K. I. (1989). Gender differences in adolescent symptomatology: A normative study. *Journal of the American Academy of Child and Adolescent Psychiatry, 28,* 394–398.

Otto, L. B. (1988). America's youth: A changing profile. *Family Relations, 37,* 385–391.

Ouellette, E. M., et al. (1977). Adverse effects on offspring of maternal alcohol abuse during pregnancy. *New England Journal of Medicine, 297,* 528–530.

Palkovitz, R. (1985). Fathers' birth attendance, early contact and extended contact with their newborns: A critical review. *Child Development, 56,* 392–406.

Papert, S. (1980). *Mindstorms: Children, computers and powerful thinking.* New York: Basic Books.

Papousek, H. (1961). Conditioned head rotation reflexes in infants in the first three months of life. *Acta Paediatrica Scandinavica, 50,* 565–576.

Paris, S. C., Lindauer, B. K., & Cox, G. I. (1977). The development of inferential comprehension. *Child Development, 48,* 1728–1733.

Parke, R. D. (1972). Some effects of punishment on children's behavior. In W. W. Hartup (Ed.), *The young child: Reviews of research* (Vol. 2). Washington, DC: National Association for the Education of Young Children.

Parke, R. D. (1979). Perceptions of father–infant interaction. In J. Osofsky (Ed.), *Handbook of infant development*. New York: Wiley.

Parke, R. D. (1981). *Fathers.* Cambridge, MA: Harvard University Press.

Parke, R. D., & Collmer, C. (1975). Child abuse: An interdisciplinary analysis. In E. M. Hetherington (Ed.), *Review of child development research* (Vol. 5). Chicago: University of Chicago Press.

Parke, R., & Slaby, R. (1983). The development of aggression. In P. H. Mussen (Ed.), *Handbook of child psychology* (Vol. 4). New York: Wiley.

Parke, R. D., & Tinsley, B. J. (1987). Family interaction in infancy. In J. D. Osofsky (Ed.), *Handbook of infant development* (2nd ed., pp. 579–641). New York: Wiley.

Parker, J. G., & Asher, S. R. (1987). Peer relations and later personal adjustment: Are low-accepted children at risk? *Psychological Bulletin, 102,* 357–389.

Parker, W. A. (1980). Designing an environment for childbirth. In B.

L. Blum (Ed.), *Psychological aspects of pregnancy, birthing, and bonding*. New York: Human Sciences Press.

Parmelee, A. H., Jr. (1986). Children's illnesses: Their beneficial effects on behavioral development. *Child Development, 57,* 1–10.

Parten, M. B. (1932–33). Social participation among preschool children. *Journal of Abnormal and Social Psychology, 27,* 243–269.

Pattison, E. M. (1977). *The experience of dying*. Englewood Cliffs, NJ: Prentice Hall.

Paulby, S. T. (1977). Imitative interaction. In H. R. Schaffer (Ed.), *Studies of mother–infant interaction*. London: Academic Press.

Pavlov, I. P. (1928). *Lectures on conditioned reflexes*. (W. H. Gantt, Trans.). New York: International Publishers.

Peck, R. C. (1968). Psychological developments in the second half of life. In B. L. Neugarten (Ed.), *Middle age and aging*. Chicago: University of Chicago Press.

Peck, R. F., & Berkowitz, H. (1964). Personality and adjustment in middle age. In B. L. Neugarten (Ed.), *Personality in middle and late life: Empirical studies*. New York: Atherton.

Pederson, F., et al. (1979). Infant development in father–absent families. *Journal of Genetic Psychology, 135,* 51–61.

Pediatrics. (1978). Effect of medication during labor and delivery on infant outcome, *62,* 402–403.

Pediatrics. (1979). The fetal monitoring debate, *63,* 942–948.

Pellegrini, A. D. (1987). Rough-and-tumble play: Developmental and educational significance. *Educational Psychologist, 22*(1), 23–43.

Peretti, P. O., & Wilson, C. (1978). Contemplated suicide among voluntary and involuntary retirees. *Omega, 9*(2), 193–201.

Perkins, S. A. (1977). Malnutrition and mental development. *Exceptional Children, 43*(4), 214–219.

Perlmutter, M. (1978). What is memory aging the aging of? *Developmental Psychology, 14,* 330–345.

Perlmutter, M., Adams, C., Barry, J., Kaplan, M., Person, D., & Verdonik, F. (1987). Aging & memory. In K. W. Schaie & K. Eisdorfer (Eds.), *Annual review of gerontology and geriatrics* (Vol. 7). New York: Springer.

Perry, D. G., & Bussey, K. (1984). *Social development*. Englewood Cliffs, NJ: Prentice Hall.

Perry, D. G., Williard, J. C., & Perry, L. C. (1990). Peers' perceptions of the consequences that victimized children provide aggressors. *Child Development, 61,* 1310–1325.

Perry, W. G., Jr. (1970). *Forms of intellectual and ethical development in the college years: A scheme*. New York: Holt, Rinehart & Winston.

Peterson, A. C., & Taylor, B. (1980). The biological approach to adolescence: Biological change and psychological adaptation. In J. Adelson (Ed.), *Handbook of adolescent psychology*. New York: Wiley.

Pfeiffer, D., & Davis, G. (1971). The use of leisure time in middle life. *The Gerontologist, 11,* 187–195.

Pfeiffer, J. (Ed.). (1964). *The cell*. New York: Time-Life Books.

Phillips, D. (1984). The illusion of incompetence among academically competent children. *Child Development, 55,* 2000–2016.

Phillips, D., McCartney, K., Scarr, S., & Howes, C. (February 1987). Selective review of infant day care research: A cause for concern! *Zero to Three*, pp. 18–20.

Phillips, J. L., Jr. (1969). *The origins of intellect: Piaget's theory*. San Francisco: Freeman.

Piaget, J. (1926). *The language and thought of the child*. London: Kegan, Paul, Trench & Trubner.

Piaget, J. (1950). *The psychology of intelligence*. (M. Percy & D. E. Berlyne, Trans.). New York: Harcourt Brace.

Piaget, J. (1951). *Play, dreams and imitation in childhood*. New York: Norton.

Piaget, J. (1952). *The origins of intelligence in children*. (M. Cook, Trans.). New York: International Universities Press. (Originally published 1936)

Piaget, J. (1954). *The construction of reality in the child*. (M. Cook, Trans.). New York: Basic Books.

Piaget, J. (1962). *Plays, dreams, and imitation*. New York: Norton.

Piaget, J. (1965). *The moral judgment of the child.* (M. Gabain, Trans.). New York: Free Press. (Originally published 1932)

Piaget, J. (1970). Piaget's theory. In P. H. Mussen (Ed.), *Carmichael's manual of child psychology* (3rd ed., Vol. 1). New York: Wiley.

Piaget, J. (1972). Intellectual evolution from adolescence to adulthood. *Human Development, 15,* 1–12.

Pichitino, J. P. (January 1983). Profile of the single father: A thematic integration of the literature. *Personnel and Guidance Journal,* pp. 295–299.

Pietromonaco, P., Manis, J., & Markus, H. (1987). The relationship of employment to self-perception and well-being in women: A cognitive analysis. *Sex Roles, 17*(7–8), 467–476.

Pillemer, K., & Finkelhor, D. (1988). The prevalence of elder abuse: A random sample survey. *The Gerontologist, 28,* 51–57.

Pines, M. (1979). Superkids. *Psychology Today, 12*(8), 53–63.

Pines, M. (September 1981). The civilizing of Genie. *Psychology Today,* pp. 28–34.

Pines, M. (1984). PT conversations: Resilient children. *Psychology Today, 12*(8), 53–63.

Piotrkowski, C. S., & Crits-Christoph, P. (1981). Women's jobs and family adjustment. *Journal of Family Issues, 2,* 126–147.

Piper, J. M., Baum, C., & Kennedy, D. L. (1987). Prescription drug use before and during pregnancy in a Medicaid population. *American Journal of Obstetrics and Gynecology, 1*(57), 148–156.

Pitcher, E. G., & Schultz, L. H. (1983). *Boys and girls at play: The development of sex roles.* New York: Praeger.

Pleck, J. H. (1985). *Working wives, working husbands.* Beverly Hills, CA: Sage.

Pleck, J. H., & Staines, G. L. (1982). Work schedules and work family conflict in two-earner couples. In J. Aldous (Ed.), *Two paychecks: Life in dual-earner families.* Beverly Hills, CA: Sage.

Plomin, R. (1983). Developmental behavioral genetics. *Child Development, 54,* 25–29.

Plomin, R. (1990). *Nature and nurture: An introduction to human behavioral genetics.* Pacific Grove, CA: Brooks/Cole.

Plomin, R., & Daniels, D. (1987). Why are children in the same family so different from one another? *Behavioral and Brain Sciences, 10,* 1–60.

Plowden, B. (1967). *Children and their primary schools: A report of the Central Advisory Council for Education in England* (Vol. 1). London: Her Majesty's Stationery Office.

Plumb, J. H. (Winter 1971). The great change in children. *Horizon,* pp. 4–12.

Poe, W., & Holloway, D. (1980). *Drugs and the aged.* New York: McGraw-Hill.

Poest, C. A., Williams, J. R., Witt, D. D., & Atwood, M. E. (1989). Physical activity patterns of preschool children. *Early Childhood Research Quarterly, 4,* 367–376.

Pollack, R. H., & Atkeson, B. M. (1978). A lifespan approach to perceptual development. In P. B. Baltes (Ed.), *Lifespan development and behavior* (Vol. 1). New York: Academic Press.

Pomerleau, A., Bolduc, D., Malcuit, G., & Cossette, L. (1990). Pink or blue: Environmental gender stereotypes in the first two years of life. *Sex Roles, 22*(5/6), 359–367.

Poole, W. (July/August 1987). The first 9 months of school. *Hippocrates,* pp. 66–73.

Poon, L. (1985). Differences in human memory with aging: Nature, causes and clinical implications. In J. Birren & W. K. Schaie (Eds.), *Handbook of the psychology of aging* (2nd ed.). New York: Van Nostrand Reinhold.

Pope, H. G., Ionescu-Pioggia, M., Aizley, H. G., & Varma, D. K. (1991). College student drug use: Twenty-year trends. *Harvard Mental Health Letter, 7*(9), 7.

Porterfield, E. (January 1973). Mixed marriage. *Psychology Today,* pp. 71–78.

Powell, A. G., Farrar, E., & Cohen, D. K. (1985). *The shopping mall high school: Winners and losers in the education marketplace.* Boston: Houghton Mifflin.

Power, C., & Reimer, J. (1978). Moral atmosphere: An educational bridge between moral judgment and action. *New Directions for Child Development, 2.*

Powers, S. I., Hauser, S. T., & Kilner, L. A. (1989). Adolescent mental health. *American Psychologist, 44,* 200–208.

Pratt, K. C. (1954). The neonate. In L. Carmichael (Ed.), *Manual of child psychology* (2nd ed.). New York: Wiley.

Prechtl, H., & Beintema, D. (1965). *The neurological examination of the full term newborn infant* (Clinics in Developmental Medicine Series No. 12). Philadelphia: Lippincott.

Pruchno, R., & Resch, N. (1989). Husbands and wives as caregivers: Antecedents of depression and burden. *The Gerontologist, 29,* 159–165.

Purcell, P., & Sewart, L. (1990). Dick and Jane in 1989. *Sex Roles, 22*(3/4), 177–185.

Putallaz, M. (1983). Predicting children's sociometric status from their behavior. *Child Development, 54,* 1417–1426.

Queenan, J. T. (August 1975). The Rh-immunized pregnancy. *Consultant,* pp. 96–99.

Quinn, J., & Burkhauser, R. (1990). Work and retirement. In R. Binstock & L. George (Eds.), *Handbook of aging and the social sciences* (3rd ed., pp. 308–327). San Diego: Academic Press.

Radbill, S. (1974). A history of child abuse and infanticide. In R. Helfer & C. Kempe (Eds.), *The battered child.* Chicago: University of Chicago Press.

Radke, M. J., & Trager, H. G. (1950). Children's perceptions of the social role of Negroes and whites. *Journal of Psychology, 29,* 3–33.

Radkey-Yarrow, M., Zahn-Waxler, C., & Chapman, M. (1983). Children's prosocial dispositions and behavior. In E. M. Hetherington (Ed.), *Handbook of child psychology: Vol. 4. Socialization, personality and social development.* New York: Wiley.

Rahbar, F., Momeni, J., Fumufod, A. K., & Westney, L. (1985). Prenatal care and perinatal mortality in a black population. *Obstetrics and Gynecology, 65* (3), 327–329.

Ramey, C. T. (1981). Consequences of infant day care. In B. Weissbound & J. Musick (Eds.), *Infants: Their social environments.* Washington, DC: National Association for the Education of Young Children.

Rando, T. (1986). A comprehensive analysis of anticipatory grief: Perspectives, processes, promises, and problems. In T. Rando (Ed.), *Loss and anticipatory grief.* Lexington, MA: Lexington Books.

Rapoport, R., & Rapoport, R. M. (1980). Three generations of dual-career family research. In F. Pepitone-Rockwell (Ed.), *Dual-career couples.* Beverly Hills, CA: Sage.

Ratner, H. H. (1984). Memory demands and the development of young children's memory. *Child Development, 55,* 2173–2191.

Ratner, N., & Bruner, J. S. (1978). Games, social exchange and the acquisition of language. *Journal of Child Development, 5,* 1–15.

Ratner, N. B., & Pye, C. (1984). Higher pitch in BT is not universal: Acoustic evidence from Quiche Mayan. *Journal of Child Language, 11,* 515–522.

Rauste-von Wright, M. (1989). Body image satisfaction in adolescent girls and boys: A longitudinal study. *Journal of Youth and Adolescence, 18,* 71–83.

Regestein, Q. R. (October 13, 1979). *Insomnia and sleep disturbances in the aged: Sleep and insomnia in the elderly.* Paper presented at a scientific meeting of the Boston Society for Gerontologic Psychiatry.

Reich, P. A. (1986). *Language development.* Englewood Cliffs, NJ: Prentice Hall.

Reid, M. (1990). Prenatal diagnosis and screening. In J. Garcia, R. Kilpatrick, & M. Richards (Eds.), *The politics of maternity care* (pp. 300–323). Oxford: Clarendon Press.

Reid, M., Ramey, S. L., & Burchinal, M. (1990). Dialogues with children about their families. In I. Bretherton & M. W. Watson (Eds.), *New Directions for Child Development, 48,* 5–28.

Reinach, L. (1901). *de Lelaos.* Paris: Charles.

Reinhold, R. (June 27, 1981). Census finds unmarried couples have doubled from 1970 to 1978. *New York Times,* pp. A1, B5.

Reinhold, R. (February 27, 1982). Study reaffirms general doubts over marijuana. *New York Times,* p. C7.

Reinke, B. J., Ellicott, A. M., Harris, R. L., & Hancock, E. (1985). Timing of psychosocial changes in women's lives. *Human Development, 28,* 259–280.

Reiss, I. L. (1971). *The family system in America.* New York: Holt, Rinehart & Winston.

Repetti, R., Matthews, K., & Waldron, I. (1989). Employment and women's health: Effects of paid employment on women's mental and physical health. *American Psychologist, 44,* 1394–1401.

Reuhl, K. R., & Chang, L. W. (1979). Effects of methylmercury on the development of the nervous system: A review. *Neurotoxicology, 1,* 21–55.

Rheingold, H. L., Gewirtz, J. L., & Ross, H. W. (1959). Social conditioning of vocalizations in the infant. *Journal of Comparative and Physiological Psychology, 52,* 68–73.

Rhodes, S. (1983). Age-related differences in work attitudes and behavior: A review and conceptual analysis. *Psychological Bulletin, 93,* 328–367.

Rice, M. L., & Haight, P. L. (1986). "Motherese" of Mr. Rogers: A description of the dialogue of educational television programs. *Journal of Speech and Hearing Disorders, 51,* 282–287.

Rice, S. G. (1990). *Putting the play back in exercise.* Unpublished.

Richman, A. L., LeVine, R. A., New, R. A., Howrigan, G. A., Welles-Nystrom, B., & LeVine, S. E. (Summer 1988). Maternal behavior to infants in five cultures. In R. A. LeVine, P. M. Miller, & M. M. West (Eds.), *New Directions for Child Development: Vol. 40. Personal behavior in diverse societies* (pp. 81–98).

Richman, C. L., Berry, C., Bittle, M., & Himan, K. (1988). Factors relating to helping behavior in preschool-age children. *Journal of Applied Developmental Psychology, 9,* 151–165.

Ricks, S. S. (1985). Father–infant interactions: A review of empirical research. *Family Relations, 34,* 505–511.

Riegel, K. F. (1975). Adult life crises: A dialectical interpretation of development. In N. Datan & L. H. Ginsberg (Eds.), *Life-span developmental psychology: Normative life crises.* New York: Academic Press.

Riegel, K. (1984). Chapter in M. L. Commons, F. A. Richards, & C. Armon (Eds.), *Beyond formal operations: Late adolescence and adult cognitive development.* New York: Praeger.

Riger, S., & Galligan, P. (1980). Women in management. *American Psychologist, 35,* 902–910.

Riley, M. W., & Waring, J. (1976). Age and aging. In R. Merton & R. Nisbet (Eds.), *Contemporary social problems* (4th ed.). New York: Harcourt Brace Jovanovich.

Riley, M. W., & Waring, J. (1978). Most of the problems of aging are not biological, but social. In R. Gross, B. Gross, & S. Seidman (Eds.), *The new old: Struggling for decent aging.* Garden City, NY: Anchor Books/Doubleday.

Rizzo, T. A., & Corsaro, W. A. (1988). Toward a better understanding of Vygotsky's process of internalization: Its role in the development of the concept of friendship. *Developmental Review, 8,* 219–237.

Robbins, D. (1986). Legal and ethical issues in terminal illness care for patients, families, care-givers, and institutions. In T. Rando (Ed.), *Loss and anticipatory grief* (pp. 215–228). Lexington, MA: Lexington Books.

Roberts, R., & Newton, P. M. (1987). Levinsonian studies of women's adult development. *Psychology and Aging, 2,* 154–163.

Robertson, J. F. (1977). Grandmotherhood: A study of role conceptions. *Journal of Marriage and the Family, 39,* 165–174.

Robertson, M. (1984). Changing motor patterns during childhood. In J. R. Thomas (Ed.), *Motor development during childhood and adolescence.* Minneapolis, MN: Burgess.

Robinson, I. E., & Jedlicka, D. (1982). Change in sexual behavior of college students from 1965–1980: A research note. *Journal of Marriage and the Family, 44,* 237–240.

Robinson, R., Coberly, S., & Paul, C. (1985). Work and retirement. In R. Binstock & E. Shanas (Eds.), *Handbook of aging and the social sciences.* (2nd ed., pp. 503–527). New York: Van Nostrand Reinhold.

Rochat, P. (1989). Object manipulation and exploration in 2- to 5-month-old infants. *Developmental Psychology, 25(6),* 871–884.

Rodin, J., & Ickovics, J. (1990) Women's health: Review and research agenda as we approach the 21st century. *American Psychologist, 45,* 1018–1034.

Roe, A. (1957). Early determinants of vocational choice. *Journal of Counseling Psychology, 4,* 212–217.

Rogel, M. J., & Peterson, A. C. (1984). Some adolescent experiences of motherhood. In R. Cohen, B. Cohler, & S. Weissman (Eds.), *Parenthood: A psychodynamic perspective.* New York: Guilford.

Rogers, C. R. (1961). *On becoming a person.* New York: Houghton Mifflin.

Rogers, C. (1980). *A way of being.* Boston: Houghton Mifflin.

Rogoff, B. (1990). *Apprenticeship in thinking: Cognitive development in social context.* New York: Oxford University Press.

Rogoff, B., & Wertsch, J. (1984). Children's learning in the "zone of proximal development." *New Directions for Child Development, 23.* San Francisco: Jossey-Bass.

Roscoe, B., Diana, M. S., & Brooks, R. H., II. (1987). Early, middle, and late adolescents' views on dating and factors influencing partner selection. *Adolescence, 12,* 59–68.

Rose, S. A., Gottfried, A. W., & Bridger, W. H. (1981). Cross-modal transfer in 6-month-old infants. *Developmental Psychology, 17,* 661–669.

Rose-Krasnor, L. (1988). Social cognition. In T. D. Yawkey & J. E. Johnson (Eds.), *Integrative processes and socialization: Early to middle childhood* (pp. 79–95). Hillsdale, NJ: Erlbaum.

Rosel, N. (1978). Toward a social theory of dying. *Omega, 9(1),* 49–55.

Rosenfeld, A. (September 7, 1974a). If Oedipus' parents had only known. *Saturday Review,* 49f.

Rosenfeld, A. (March 23, 1974b). Starve the child, famish the future. *Saturday Review,* p. 59.

Rosenman, R. H. (1974). The role of behavioral patterns and neurogenic factors in the pathogenesis of coronary heart disease. In R. S. Eliot (Ed.), *Stress and the heart.* New York: Futura.

Rosenman, R., & Chesney, M. (1982). Stress, Type A behavior, and coronary disease. In L. Goldberger & S. Breznitz (Eds.), *The handbook of stress: Theoretical and clinical applications* (pp. 547–565). New York: Macmillan.

Rosenstein, D., & Oster, H. (1988). Differential facial response to four basic tastes in newborns. *Child Development, 59,* 1555–1568.

Rosenthal, E. (January 4, 1990). New insights on why some children are fat offers clues on weight loss. *New York Times,* p. B8.

Rosenthal, J. A. (1988). Patterns of reported child abuse and neglect. *Child Abuse and Neglect, 12,* 263–271.

Rosenthal, R., & Jacobson, L. (1968). *Pygmalion in the classroom: Teacher expectation and pupil's intellectual development.* New York: Harper & Row.

Rosenwasser, S. M., Lingenfelter, M., & Harrington, A. F. (1989). Nontraditional gender role portrayals on television and children's gender role perceptions. *Journal of Applied Developmental Psychology, 10,* 97–105.

Rosett, H. L., et al. (1981). Strategies for prevention of fetal alcohol effects. *Obstetrics and Gynecology, 57,* 1–16.

Roskinski, R. R. (1977). *The development of visual perception.* Santa Monica, CA: Goodyear.

Rosow, I. (1974). *Socialization to old age*. Berkeley: University of California Press.

Ross, A. O. (1977). *Learning disability, the unrealized potential*. New York: McGraw-Hill.

Ross, H. S., & Lollis, S. P. (1987). Communication within infant social games. *Developmental Psychology, 23*, 241–248.

Ross, H., & Sawhill, I. (1975). *Time of transition: The growth of families headed by women*. Washington, DC: Urban Institute.

Ross, L. (1981). The "intuitive scientist" formulation and its developmental implications. In J. H. Flavell & L. Ross (Eds.), *Social cognitive development*. Cambridge, UK: Cambridge University Press.

Rossi, A. S. (Spring 1977). A biological perspective in parenting. *Daedalus*.

Rossi, A. S. (1979). Transition to parenthood. In P. Rossi (Ed.), *Socialization and the life cycle*. New York: St. Martin's Press.

Rossman, I. (1977). Anatomic and body-composition changes with aging. In C. E. Finch & L. Hayflick (Eds.), *Handbook of the biology of aging*. New York: Van Nostrand Reinhold.

Roug, L., Landberg, I., & Lundberg, L. J. (February 1989). Phonetic development in early infancy: A study of four Swedish children during the first eighteen months of life. *Journal of Child Language, 16*(1), 19–40.

Rovee-Collier, C. (1987). Learning and memory in infancy. In J. Osofsky (Ed.), *Handbook of infant development* (2nd ed.). New York: Wiley.

Rowe, P. (May/June 1982). Model project reduces alienation of aged from community. *Aging*, pp. 6–11.

Rowland, T. W., Donnelly, J. H., Landis, J. N., Lemoine, M. E., Sigelman, D. R., & Tanella, C. J. (1987). Infant home apnea monitoring. *Clinical Pediatrics, 26*(8), 383–387.

Rubin, K. H. (1983). Recent perspectives on social competence and peer status: Some introductory remarks. *Child Development, 54*, 1383–1385.

Rubin, K. H., Fein, G. C., & Vandenberg, B. (1983). In P. H. Mussen (Ed.), *Handbook of child psychology* (Vol. 4). New York: Wiley.

Rubin, K. H., Maloni, T. L., & Hornung, M. (1976). Free play behaviors in middle- and lower-class preschoolers: Partner and Piaget revised. *Child Development, 47*, 414–419.

Rubin, K., & Trotten, K. (1977). Kohlberg's moral judgment scale: Some methodological considerations. *Developmental Psychology, 13*(5), 535–536.

Rubin, L. (1980). The empty nest: Beginning or end? In L. Bond & J. Rosen (Eds.), *Competence and coping during adulthood* (pp. 309–321). Hanover, NH: University Press of New England.

Rubin, Z. (1980). *Children's friendships*. Cambridge, MA: Harvard University Press.

Rubinstein, E. A. (1983). Television and behavior: Conclusion of the 1982 NIMH report and their policy implications. *American Psychologist, 38*, 820–825.

Ruble, D. (1988). Sex-role development. In M. Bornstein & M. E. Lamb (Eds.), *Developmental psychology: An advanced textbook* (2nd ed., pp. 411–460). Hillsdale, NJ: Erlbaum.

Ruble, D. N., & Brooks-Gunn, J. (1982). The experience of menarche. *Child Development, 53*, 1557–1577.

Rudd, P., & Balaschke, T. (1982) Antihypertensive agents and the drug therapy of hypertension. In A. Gilman, L. Goodman, T. Rall, & F. Murad (Eds.), *Goodman and Gilman's the pharmacological basis of therapeutics* (7th ed., pp. 784–805.)

Ruebsaat, H. J., & Hull, R. (1975). *The male climacteric*. New York: Hawthorn Books.

Rugh, R., & Shettles, L. B. (1971). *From conception to birth: The drama of life's beginnings*. New York: Harper & Row.

Rushton, T. P. (1976). Socialization and the altruistic behavior of children. *Psychological Bulletin, 83*(5), 898–913.

Russell, D. (1983). The incidence and prevalence of intrafamilial and extrafamilial sexual abuse of female children. *Child Abuse and Neglect, 7*, 133–146.

Rutter, M. (1979). Protective factors in children's responses to stress and disadvantage. In M. W. Kent & J. E. Rolf (Eds.), *Primary prevention of psychopathology: III. Social competence in children*. Hanover, NH: University Press of New England.

Rutter, M. (1983). Stress, coping and development: Some issues and questions. In N. Garmezy & M. Rutter (Eds.), *Stress, coping and development in children*. New York: McGraw-Hill.

Rutter, M. (1984). PT conversations: Resilient children. *Psychology Today, 18*(3), 60–62, 64–65.

Rutter, M., & Garmezy, N. (1983). Developmental psychopathology. In P. H. Mussen (Ed.), *Handbook of child psychology* (Vol. 4). New York: Wiley.

Ryan, A. S., Martinez, G. A., & Malec, D. J. (Spring 1985). The effect of the WIC program on nutrient intakes of infants, 1984. *Medical Anthropology*, p. 153.

Ryff, C. D. (1985). The subjective experience of life-span transitions. In A. S. Rossi (Ed.), *Gender and the life course* (p. 97). New York: Aldine.

Rynes, S., & Rosen, B. (1983). A comparison of male and female reactions to career advancement opportunities. *Journal of Vocational Behavior, 22*, 105–116.

Salend, E., Kane, R., Satz, M., & Pynoos, J. (1984). Elder abuse reporting: Limitation of statutes. *The Gerontologist, 24*, 61–69.

Salthouse, T. A. (1984). Effects of age and skill in typing. *Journal of Experimental Psychology: General, 113*, 345–371.

Salthouse, T. (1985). Speed of behavior and its implications for cognition. In J. E. Birren & K. W. Schaie (Eds.), *Handbook of the psychology of aging* (2nd ed.). New York: Van Nostrand Reinhold.

Salthouse, T. (1987). The role of experience in cognitive aging. In K. W. Schaie & K. Eisdorfer (Eds.), *Annual review of gerontology and geriatrics* (Vol. 7). New York: Springer.

Salthouse, T. (1990). Cognitive competence and expertise in aging. In J. Birren & K. W. Schaie (Eds.), *Handbook of the psychology of aging* (3rd ed., pp. 311–319). San Diego: Academic Press.

Salthouse, T., Babcock, R., Skovronek, E., Mitchell, D., & Palmon, R. (1990). Age and experience effects in spatial visualization. *Developmental Psychology, 26*, 128–136.

Salthouse, T., & Mitchell, D. (1990). Effect of age and naturally occurring experience on spatial visualization performance. *Developmental Psychology, 26*, 845–854.

Salzman, C. (1982) A primer on geriatric psychopharmocology. *American Journal of Psychiatry, 139*, 67–74.

Sarason, S. B., & Doris, J. (1953). *Psychological problems in mental deficiency*. New York: Harper & Row.

Saslow, R. (Fall 1981). A new student for the eighties: The mature woman. *Educational Horizons*, pp. 41–46.

Sasserath, V. J. (Ed.). (1983). *Minimizing high-risk parenting*. Skillman, NJ: Johnson & Johnson.

Savage-Rumbaugh, S., Rumbaugh, D. M., & McDonald, K. (September 1986). Spontaneous symbol acquisition and communicative use by pygmy chimpanzees. *Journal of Experimental Psychology, 115*(3), 211–235.

Scanlon, J. (1979). *Young adulthood*. New York: Academy for Educational Development.

Scarborough, H. S. (1989). Prediction of reading disability from familial and individual differences. *Journal of Educational Psychology, 81*, 101–108.

Scarr, S., & Kidd, K. K. (1983). Behavior genetics. In M. Haith & J. Campos (Eds.), *Manual of child psychology: Infancy and the biology of development* (Vol. 2). New York: Wiley.

Scarr, S., & McCartney, K. (1983). How people make their own environments: A theory of genotype/environmental effects. *Child Development, 54*, 424–435.

Scarr, S., Phillips, D., & McCartney, K. (1989). Working mothers and their families. *American Psychologist, 44*, 1402–1409.

Scarr, S., & Weinberg, R. A. (1983). The Minnesota adoption studies: Genetic differences and malleability. *Child Development, 54.* 260–267.

Schacter, F., & Strage, A. (1982). Adult's talk and children's language development. In S. Moore & C. Cooper (Eds.), *The young child: Reviews of research* (Vol. 3, pp. 79–96). Washington, DC: National Association for the Education of Young Children.

Schaefer, M. R., Sobieraj, K., & Hollyfield, R. L. (1988). Prevalence of childhood physical abuse in adult male veteran alcoholics. *Child Abuse and Neglect, 12,* 141–149.

Schaffer, H. R. (1977). *Studies in mother–infant interaction.* London: Academic Press.

Schaie, K. W. (1977/1978). Toward a stage theory of adult cognitive development. *Journal of Aging and Human Development, 8,* 129–138.

Schaie, K. W. (1983a). The Seattle longitudinal study: A twenty-one year exploration of psychometric intelligence in adulthood. In K. W. Schaie (Ed.), *Longitudinal studies of adult psychological development.* New York: Guilford.

Schaie, K. W. (1983b). Twenty-one-year exploration of psychometric intelligence in adults. In K. W. Schaie (Ed.), *Longitudinal studies of adult psychological development.* New York: Guilford.

Schaie, K. W. (1986). Beyond calendar definitions of age, period and cohort: The general developmental model revisited. *Developmental Review, 6,* 252–277.

Schaie, K. W. (1990). Intellectual development in adulthood. In J. Birren & K. W. Schaie (Eds.), *Handbook of the psychology of aging* (3rd. ed., pp. 291–310). San Diego: Academic Press.

Schaie, K. W., & Willis, S. L. (1986). *Adult development and aging* (2nd ed.). Boston: Little, Brown.

Schardein, J. L. (1976). *Drugs as teratogens.* Cleveland, OH: Chemical Rubber Co. Press.

Schein, E. H. (1978). *Career dynamics: Matching individual and organizational needs.* Reading, MA: Addison Wesley.

Schieffelin, B. B., & Ochs, E. (1983). A cultural perspective on the transition from prelinguistic to linguistic communication. In R. M. Golinkoff (Ed.), *The transition from prelinguistic to linguistic communication.* Hillsdale, NJ: Erlbaum.

Schilder, P., & Wechsler, D. (1935). What do children know about the interior of the body? *International Journal of Psychoanalysis, 16,* 355–360.

Schlesinger, J. M. (1982). *Steps to language: Toward a theory of native language acquisition.* Hillsdale, NJ: Erlbaum.

Schneck, M. K., Reisberg, B., & Ferris, S. H. (February 1982). An overview of current concepts of Alzheimer's disease. *American Journal of Psychiatry, 139*(2), 165–173.

Schock, N. (1977). Biological theories of aging. In J. Birren & K. W. Schaie (Eds.), *Handbook of the psychology of aging.* New York: Van Nostrand Reinhold.

Schofield, J. W. (1981). Complementary and conflicting identities: Images and interaction in an interracial school. In S. R. Asher & J. M. Gottman (Eds.), *The development of children's friendships.* New York: Cambridge University Press.

Schwartz, J. I. (1981). Children's experiments with language. *Young Children, 36,* 16–26.

Sears, R. R. (1963). Dependency motivation. In M. R. Jones (Ed.), *The Nebraska symposium on motivation* (Vol. 11). Lincoln: University of Nebraska Press.

Sedlak, A. J. (1989). *Supplementary analyses of data on the national incidence of child abuse and neglect.* Rockville, MD: Westat.

Segal, J., & Yahraes, H. (November 1978). Bringing up mother. *Psychology Today,* pp. 80–85.

Seligman, M. E. P. (May 1974). Submissive death: Giving up on life. *Psychology Today,* pp. 90–96.

Selman, R. L. (1976). The development of interpersonal reasoning. In A. Pick (Ed.), *Minnesota symposia on child psychology* (Vol. 1). Minneapolis: University of Minnesota Press.

Selman, R. L. (1981). The child as a friendship philosopher. In S. R. Asher & J. M. Gottman (Eds.), *The development of children's friendships.* Cambridge, UK: Cambridge University Press.

Shaffer, D. R. (1988). *Social and personality development* (2nd ed.). Pacific Grove, CA: Brooks/Cole.

Shaffer, J. B. P. (1978). *Humanistic psychology.* Englewood Cliffs, NJ: Prentice Hall.

Shanas, E., & Maddox, G. (1985). Health, health resources, and the utilization of care. In R. Binstock & E. Shanas (Eds.). *Handbook of aging and the social sciences* (pp. 697–726). New York: Van Nostrand Reinhold.

Shane, P. G. (1989). Changing patterns among homeless and runaway youth. *American Journal of Orthopsychiatry, 59*(2), 208–214.

Shannon, D., & Kelly, D. (1982). SIDS and near-SIDS. *New England Journal of Medicine, 306,* 961–962.

Shantz, C. U. (1975). The development of social cognition. In E. M. Hetherington (Ed.), *Review of child development research* (Vol. 5). Chicago: University of Chicago Press.

Shantz, C. (1983). Social cognition. In P. H. Mussen (Ed.), *Handbook of child psychology* (Vol. 3). New York: Wiley.

Shantz, C. U. (1987). Conflicts between children. *Child Development, 51,* 283–305.

Shapiro, M. (1978). Legal rights of the terminally ill. *Aging, 5*(3), 23–27.

Sharabany, R., Gershoni, R., & Hoffman, J. E. (1981). Girlfriend, boyfriend: Age and sex differences in intimate friendship. *Developmental Psychology, 17,* 800–808.

Shatz, M., & Gelman, R. (1973). The development of communication skills: Modifications in the speech of young children as a function of the listener. *Monographs of the Society for Research in Child Development, 38*(152).

Shaw, L. (1983). Problems of labor-market reentry. In L. B. Shaw (Ed.), *Unplanned careers: The working lives of middle-aged women.* Lexington, MA: Lexington Books.

Shaywitz, S. E., Shaywitz, B. A., Fletcher, J. M., & Escobar, M. D. (1991). Reading disability in children. *Journal of the American Medical Association, 265,* 725–726.

Sheppard, H. L., & Herrick, N. Q. (1977). *Worker dissatisfaction in the '70s.* New York: Free Press.

Sherif, M., Harvey, O. J., White, B. J., Hood, W. B., & Sherif, C. W. (1961). *Intergroup conflict and cooperation: The robber's cave experiment.* Norman: University of Oklahoma Press.

Sherif, M., & Sherif, C. W. (1953). *Groups in harmony and tension.* New York: Harper & Brothers.

Sherman, E. (1987). *Meaning in mid-life transitions.* Albany: State University of New York Press.

Shirley, M. M. (1931). *The first two years: A study of twenty-five babies* (Institute of Child Welfare Monograph No. 7, Vol. 1). Minneapolis: University of Minnesota Press.

Shirley, M. M. (1933). *The first two years: A study of twenty-five babies* (Institute of Child Welfare Monograph No. 7, Vol. 2). Minneapolis: University of Minnesota Press.

Shock, N. W. (1952a). Aging of homostatic mechanisms. In A. I. Lansing (Ed.), *Cowdry's problems of aging* (3rd ed.). Baltimore: Williams & Wilkins.

Shock, N. W. (1952b). Aging and psychological adjustment. *Review of Educational Research, 22,* 439–458.

Shukin, A., & Neugarten, B. L. (1964). Personality and social interaction. In B. L. Neugarten (Ed.), *Personality in middle and late life: Empirical studies.* New York: Atherton.

Sidney, K. H. (1981). Cardiovascular benefits of physical activity in the exercising aged. In E. L. Smith & R. C. Serfass (Eds.), *Exercise and aging: The scientific basis.* Hillside, NJ: Enslow.

Sieber, R. T., & Gordon, A. J. (1981). Socialization implications of school discipline or how first graders are taught to listen. In *Children and their organizations: Investigations in American culture.* Boston: G. K. Hall.

Siegler, I. C., & Costa, P. T., Jr. (1985). Health behavior relationships.

In J. E. Birren & K. W. Schaie (Eds.), *Handbook of the psychology of aging* (2nd ed.). New York: Van Nostrand Reinhold.

Siegler, R. S. (1986). *Children's thinking.* Englewood Cliffs, NJ: Prentice Hall.

Sigel, I. (1987). Does hothousing rob children of their childhood? *Early Childhood Research Quarterly, 2,* 211–225.

Signorella, M. L. (1987). Gender schemata: Individual differences and context effects. *New Directions for Child Development, 38,* 23–38.

Signorielli, N. (1989). Television and conceptions about sex roles: Maintaining conventionality and the status quo. *Sex Roles, 21*(5/6), 341–350.

Silver, L. B. (October 1990). Learning disabilities. *Harvard Mental Health Letter,* pp. 7, 3–5.

Simmons, R. G., Burgeson, R., Carlton-Ford, S., & Blyth, D. A. (1987). The impact of cumulative change in early adolescence. *Child Development, 58,* 1220–1234.

Simonton, D. (1988). Age and outstanding achievement: What do we know after a century of research? *Psychological Bulletin, 104,* 251–267.

Simonton, D. (1990). Creativity and wisdom in aging. In J. Birren & K. W. Schaie (Eds.), *Handbook of the psychology of aging* (3rd ed., pp. 320–329). San Diego: Academic Press.

Simopoulos, A. P. (1983). Nutrition. In C. C. Brown (Ed.), *Prenatal Roundtable: Vol. 9. Childhood learning disabilities and prenatal risk* (pp. 44–49). Rutherford, NJ: Johnson & Johnson.

Simpson, W. J. (1957). A preliminary report on cigarette smoking and the incidence of prematurity. *American Journal of Obstetrics and Gynecology, 73,* 808–815.

Sinfeld, A. (1985). Being out of work. In C. Littler (Ed.), *The experience of work* (pp. 190–208). New York: St. Martin's Press.

Siqueland, E. R., & DeLucia, C. A. (1969). Visual reinforcement of nonnutritive sucking in human infants. *Science, 165,* 1144–1146.

Skinner, B. F. (1968). *The technology of teaching.* New York: Appleton-Century-Crofts.

Skinner, B. F. (1971). *Beyond freedom and dignity.* New York: Knopf.

Slobin, D. I. (July 1972). They learn the same way all around the world. *Psychology Today,* pp. 71–74ff.

Slobin, D. (Ed.). (1982). *The cross-cultural study of language acquisition.* Hillsdale, NJ: Erlbaum.

Smetana, J. (1988). Concepts of self and social convention: Adolescents' and parents' reasoning about hypothetical and actual family conflicts. In M. Gunnar & W. Collins (Eds.), *Minnesota Symposia on Child Development: Vol. 21. Development during the transition to adolescence* (pp. 79–122). Hillsdale, NJ: Erlbaum.

Smilansky, S. (1968). *The effects of sociodramatic play on disadvantaged children: Preschool children.* New York: Wiley.

Smith, B. S., Ratner, H. H., & Hobart, C. J. (1987). The role of cuing and organization in children's memory for events. *Journal of Experimental Child Psychology, 44,* 1–24.

Smith, C., & Lloyd, B. (1978). Maternal behavior and perceived sex of infant: Revisited. *Child Development, 49,* 1263–1265.

Smith, P. K., & Dodsworth, C. (1978). Social class differences in the fantasy play of preschool children. *Journal of Genetic Psychology, 133,* 183–190.

Smith, W. (1987). *Obstetrics, gynecology, & infant mortality.* New York: Facts on File Publications.

Snow, C. (1989). Understanding social interaction and language acquisition: Sentences are not enough. In M. Bornstein & J. Bruner *Interaction in human development* (pp. 83–104). Hillsdale, NJ: Erlbaum.

Snyder, P., & Way, A. (January & February 1979). Alcoholism and the elderly. *Aging Magazine.*

Social Security Administration. (1986). Increasing the Social Security retirement age: Older workers in physically demanding occupations or ill health. *Social Security Bulletin, 49,* 5–23.

Society for Research and Child Development. (1973). *Ethical standards for research with children.* Chicago: Society for Research and Child Development.

Sonenstein, F. L. (1987). Teenage childbearing . . . in all walks of life. *Brandeis Review, 7*(1), 25–28.

Sorenson, R. C. (1973). *Adolescent sexuality in contemporary America: Personal values and sexual behavior, ages 13–19.* New York: World.

Source, J. F., & Emde, R. N. (1981). Mother's presence is not enough: Effect of emotional availability on infant exploration. *Developmental Psychology, 17,* 737–745.

Spanier, G. (1983). Married and unmarried cohabitation in the United States: 1980. *Journal of Marriage and the Family,* 277–288.

Spanier, G., & Furstenberg, E. (1982). Remarriage after divorce: A longitudinal analysis of well-being. *Journal of Marriage and the Family,* 709–720.

Spearman, C. (1904). "General intelligence" objectively determined and measured. *American Journal of Psychology, 14,* 201–293.

Speece, M. W., & Brent, S. B. (1984). Children's understanding of death: A review of three components of a death concept. *Child Development, 55,* 1671–1686.

Spelke, E. S. (1988). The origins of physical knowledge. In L. Weiskrantz (Ed.), *Thought without language* (pp. 168–184). Clarendon Press.

Spencer, M. B. (1988). Self-concept development. In D. T. Slaughter (Ed.), *New Directions for Child Development, 42. Black children and poverty: A developmental perspective.* San Francisco: Jossey-Bass.

Spiro, M. E. (1954). Is the family universal? The Israeli case. *American Anthropologist, 56,* 839–846.

Spiro, M. E., & Spiro, A. G. (1972). *Children of the kibbutz.* New York: Schocken Books.

Spitze, G., & Logan, J. (1989). Gender differences in family support: Is there a payoff? *The Gerontologist, 29,* 108–113.

Spitze, G., & Logan, J. (1990). Sons, daughters, and intergenerational social support. *Journal of Marriage and the Family, 52,* 420–430.

Spitzer, M. (1988) Taste acuity in institutionalized and noninstitutionalized elderly men. *Journal of Gerontology, 43,* P71–P74.

Sroufe, L. A. (1977). Wariness of strangers and the study of infant development. *Child Development, 48,* 731–746.

Sroufe, L. A. (1978). Attachment and the roots of competence. *Human Nature, 1,* 50–57.

Sroufe, L. A. (1985). Attachment classification from the perspective of infant–caregiver relationships and infant temperament. *Child Development, 56,* 1–14.

Sroufe, L. A., & Fleeson, J. (1986). Attachment and the construction of relationships. In W. W. Hartup & Z. Rubin (Eds.), *Relationships and development* (pp. 51–72). Hillsdale, NJ: Erlbaum.

Sroufe, L. A., Fox, N. E., & Paneake, V. R. (1983). Attachment and dependency in a developmental perspective. *Child Development, 54,* 1615–1627.

Stagner, R. (1985). Aging in industry. In J. Birren & K. Schaie (Eds.) *Handbook of the psychology of aging* (2nd ed., pp. 789–817). New York: Van Nostrand Reinhold.

Staines, G., Pottick, K., & Fudge, D. (1986). Wives' employment and husbands' attitudes toward work and life. *Journal of Applied Psychology, 71,* 118–128.

Stangor, C., & Ruble, D. N. (1987). Development of gender role knowledge and gender consistency. *New Directions for Child Development, 38,* 5–22.

Stanton, H. E. (1981). A therapeutic approach to help children overcome learning difficulties. *Journal of Learning Disabilities, 14,* 220.

Staub, E. (1971). The use of role playing and induction in children's learning of helping and sharing behavior. *Child Development, 42,* 805–816.

Stechler, G., & Shelton, A. (1982). Prenatal influences on human development. In B. Wolman (Ed.), *Handbook of developmental psychology.* Englewood Cliffs, NJ: Prentice Hall.

Stein, A. H., & Friedrich, L. K. (1975). Impact of television on children and youth. In E. M. Hetherington (Ed.), *Review of child development* (Vol. 5). Chicago: University of Chicago Press.

Stein, P. J. (1976). *Single*. Englewood Cliffs, NJ: Prentice Hall.

Steinberg, L. (1980). *Understanding families with young adolescents*. Carrboro, NC: Center for Early Adolescents.

Steinberg, L. (1981). Transformations in family relations at puberty. *Developmental Psychology, 17,* 833–840.

Steinberg, L. (1986). Latchkey children and susceptibility to peer pressure: An ecological analysis. *Developmental Psychology, 22,* 433–439.

Steinberg, L. (1987a). Recent research on the family at adolescence: The extent and nature of sex differences. *Journal of Youth and Adolescence, 16,* 191–198.

Steinberg, L. (1987b). Single parents, stepparents, and the susceptibility of adolescents to antisocial peer pressure. *Child Development, 58,* 269–275.

Steinberg, L. (1988). Reciprocal relation between parent–child distance and pubertal maturation. *Developmental Psychology, 24,* 122–128.

Stephens, W. N. (1963). *The family in cross-cultural perspective*. New York: Holt, Rinehart & Winston.

Sternberg, R. J. (Ed.). (1982). *Advances in the psychology of human intelligence*. Hillsdale, NJ: Erlbaum.

Sternberg, R. J. (1984). Mechanisms of cognitive development: A componential approach. In R. J. Sternberg (Ed.), *Mechanisms of cognitive development*. New York: Freeman.

Sternberg, R. J. (1985). *Beyond IQ: A triarchic theory of human intelligence*. Cambridge, UK: Cambridge University Press.

Sternberg, R. (1986). A triangular theory of love. *Psychological Review, 93,* 119–135.

Sternberg, R. J. (1988a). Lessons from the life span: What theorists of intellectual development among children learn from their counterparts studying adults. In E. M. Hetherington, R. N. Lerner, & M. Perlmutter (Eds.), *Child development* (pp. 259–276). Hillsdale, NJ: Erlbaum.

Sternberg, R. J. (1988b). Intellectual development: Psychometric and information processing approaches. In M. H. Bornstein & M. E. Lamb, (Eds.), *Developmental psychology: An advanced textbook* (2nd ed.). Hillsdale, NJ: Erlbaum.

Sternglass, E. J. (1963). Cancer: Relation of prenatal radiation to development of the disease in childhood. *Science, 140,* 1102–1104.

Stevenson, H., Azuma, H., & Hakuta, K. (Eds.). (1986). *Child development and education in Japan*. New York: Freeman.

Stewart, R. B., Mobley, L. A., Van Tuyl, S. S., & Salvador, M. A. (1987). The firstborn's adjustment to the birth of a sibling: A longitudinal assessment. *Child Development, 58,* 341–355.

Stewart, W. (1977). *A psychosocial study of the formation of the early adult life structure in women*. Unpublished doctoral dissertation. Columbia University, New York.

Stigler, J. W., Lee, S., & Stevenson, H. W. (1987). Mathematics classrooms in Japan, Taiwan, and the United States. *Child Development, 58,* 1272–1285.

Stillion, J. (1985). *Death and the sexes: An examination of differential longevity, attitudes, behaviors, and coping styles*. Washington, DC: Hemisphere.

Stoel-Gammon, C. (1989). Prespeech and early speech development of two late talkers. *First Language, 9,* 207–223.

Stone, L. J., Smith, H. T., & Murphy, L. B. (Eds.). (1973). *The competent infant: Research and commentary*. New York: Basic Books.

Stone, R., Cafferata, G., & Sangl, J. (1987). Care-givers of the frail elderly: A national profile. *The Gerontologist, 27,* 616–626.

Strayer, F. F., & Strayer, J. (1976). An ethnological analysis of social agonism and dominance relations among preschool children. *Child Development, 47,* 980–989.

Streissguth, A. P., Barr, H., & MacDonald, M. (1983). Maternal alcohol use and neonatal habituation assessed with the Brazelton scale. *Child Development, 54,* 1109–1118.

Streissguth, A. P., Martin, D. C., Barr, H. M., Sandman, B. M., Kirchner, G. L., & Darby, B. L. (1984). Intrauterine alcohol and nicotine exposure: Attention and reaction time in four-year-old children. *Developmental Psychology, 20,* 533–541.

Streissguth, A. P., Sampson, P. D., Barr, H. M., Darby, B. L., & Martin, D. C. (1989). I. Q. at age 4 in relation to maternal alcohol use and smoking during pregnancy. *Developmental Psychology, 25*(1), 3–11.

Stuber, M. L. (August 1989). Coordination of care for pediatric AIDS. *Journal of Developmental and Behavioral Pediatrics, 10*(4), 201–204.

Stunkard, A. J. (1988). Some perspectives on human obesity: Its causes. *Bulletin of the New York Academy of Medicine, 64,* 902–923.

Sugarman, S. (December 1983). Why talk? Comment on Savage-Rumbaugh et al. *Journal of Experimental Psychology, 112*(4), 493–497.

Super, C. M., Herrera, M. G., & Mora, J. O. (1990). Long-term effects of food supplementation and psychosocial intervention on the physical growth of Colombian infants at risk of malnutrition. *Child Development, 61,* 29–49.

Super, D. E. (1957). *The psychology of careers*. New York: Harper & Brothers.

Super, D. E. (1963). *Career development: Self concept theory*. New York: College Entrance Examination Board.

Super, D. E. (1974). Vocational maturity theory. In D. E. Super (Ed.), *Measuring vocational maturity for counseling*. Washington, DC: American Personnel and Guidance Association.

Sutton-Smith, B., & Rosenberg, B. G. (1970). *The sibling*. New York: Holt, Rinehart & Winston.

Swoboda, M. J., & Millar, S. B. (1986). Networking—mentoring: Career strategy of women in academic administration. *Journal of National Association of Women Deans, Administrators, and Counselors, 49,* 8–13.

Taft, L. I., & Cohen, H. J. (1967). Neonatal and infant reflexology. In J. Hellmuth (Ed.), *The exceptional infant* (Vol. 1). Seattle: Special Child Publications.

Tanner, J. M. (1978). *Foetus into man: Physical growth from conception to maturity*. Cambridge, MA: Harvard University Press.

Taveris, C. (1983). *Anger: The misunderstood emotion*. New York: Simon & Schuster.

Tellegen, A. D. T., Lykken, D. T., Bouchard, T. J., Wilcox, K., Segal, N. L., & Rich, S. (1988). Personality similarity in twins reared apart and together. *Journal of Social and Personality Psychology, 59,* 1031–1039.

Teller, D., & Bornstein, M. (1987). Infant color vision and color perception. In P. Salapatek & L. Cohen (Eds.), *Handbook of infant perception* (Vol. 1). New York: Academic Press.

Terman, L. M., & Merrill, M. A. (1960). *Revised Stanford-Binet Intelligence Scale* (2nd ed.). Boston: Houghton Mifflin.

Theilgaard, A. (1983). Aggression and the XYY personality. *International Journal of Law and Psychiatry, 6,* 413–421.

Thelen, E. (1987). The role of motor development in developmental psychology: A view of the past and an agenda for the future. In N. Eisenberg (Ed.), *Contemporary topics in developmental psychology*. New York: Wiley.

Thelen, E. (1989). The rediscovery of motor development: Learning new things from an old field. *Developmental Psychology, 25*(6), 946–949.

Thelen, E., & Fogel, A. (1989). Toward an action-based theory of infant development. In J. J. Lockman & N. L. Kazen (Eds.), *Action in social context: Perspectives on early development* (pp. 23–64). New York: Plenum.

Thomae, H. (1980). Personality and adjustment to aging. In J. E.

Birren & R. B. Sloane (Eds.), *Handbook of mental health and aging.* Englewood Cliffs, NJ: Prentice Hall.

Thomas, L. E. (1979). Causes of mid-life change from high status careers. *Vocational Guidance Quarterly, 27,* 202–208.

Thompson, A. S. (1977). Notes on career development inventory—adult form. As quoted in R. P. Johnson & H. C. Riker (1981), Retirement maturity: A valuable concept for preretirement counselors. *Personnel and Guidance Journal, 59,* 291–295.

Thompson, R. A. (1990). Vulnerability in research: A developmental perspective on research risk. *Child Development, 61,* 1–16.

Thompson, S. K. (1975). Gender labels and early sex-role development. *Child Development, 46,* 339–347.

Thorndike, E. L. (1911). *Animal intelligence.* New York: Macmillan.

Thurstone, L. E. (1938). Primary mental abilities. *Psychometric Monographs,* No. 1.

Tieger, T. (1980). On the biological basis of sex differences in aggression. *Child Development, 51,* 943–963.

Tikalsky, F. D., & Wallace, S. D. (1988). Culture and the structure of children's fears. *Journal of Cross-Cultural Psychology, 19*(4), 481–492.

Tilgher, A. (1962). Work through the ages. In S. Nosow & W. H. Form (Eds.), *Man, work, and society.* New York: Basic Books.

Timiras, P. S. (1972). *Developmental physiology and aging.* New York: Macmillan.

Timiras, P. S. (1978). Biological perspectives on aging. *American Scientist, 66,* 605–613.

Tobin, S. S. (1988). *The unique psychology of the very old: Implications for practice. Issues in Aging* (Monograph No. 4). Chicago: Center for Applied Gerontology.

Tobin, S., & Lieberman, M. (1976). *Last home for the aged.* San Francisco: Jossey-Bass.

Tomasello, M., Mannle, S., & Kruger, A. C. (1986). Linguistic environment of one- to two-year-old twins. *Developmental Psychology, 22,* 169–176.

Tonna, E. A. (1977). Aging of skeletal and dental systems and supporting tissue. In C. E. Finch & L. Hayflick (Eds.), *Handbook of the biology of aging.* New York: Van Nostrand Reinhold.

Troll, L. E. (1980). Grandparenting. In L. W. Poon (Ed.), *Aging in the 1980s.* Washington, DC: American Psychological Association.

Troll, L. E. (1985). *Early and middle adulthood* (2nd ed.). Monterey, CA: Brooks/Cole.

Troll, L. E., Miller, S., & Atchley, R. C. (1979). *Families of later life.* Belmont, CA: Wadsworth.

Turkington, C. (1987). Special talents. *Psychology Today, 21*(9), 42–46.

Turnbull, A. P., & Turnbull, H. R., III. (1990). *Families, professionals and exceptionality: A special partnership* (2nd ed.). Columbus, OH: Merrill.

Turnbull, C. M. (1972). *The mountain people.* New York: Simon & Schuster.

U.S. Bureau of the Census. (1988). *Statistical Analysis of the U.S.: 1988.* Washington, DC: Government Printing Office.

U.S. Bureau of the Census. (1990). *Current Population Reports.* Series P-25, Nos. 519, 917.

U.S. Department of Commerce. (1987). *Statistical Abstract of the U.S.: 1987.* Washington, DC

U.S. Department of Commerce. (1990). *Statistical Abstract of the U.S.: 1990.* Washington, DC

U.S. Department of Health and Human Services. (1983). Regulations on the protection of human subjects. *45CFR, 46,* Subparts A & D.

Uzgiris, I. C. (1984). Imitation in infancy: Its interpersonal aspects. In M. Perlmutter (Ed.), *Minnesota Symposia on Child Psychology: Vol. 17. Parent–child interaction and parent–child relations.* Hillsdale, NJ: Erlbaum.

Vachon, M. (1986). A comparison of the impact of breast cancer and bereavement: Personality, social support, and adaptation. In S. Hobfoll (Ed.) *Stress, social support, and women.* Washington, DC: Hemisphere.

Vaillant, G. (September 1977). The climb to maturity: How the best and brightest came of age. *Psychology Today,* p. 34ff.

Van Baal, J. (1966). *Dema: Description and analysis of Marind Anim culture, South New Guinea.* The Hague: Martinus Nijhoff.

Vandell, D. L., & Corasaniti, M. A. (Fall 1990). Child care and the family: Complex contributions to child development. *New Directions for Child Development, 49,* 23–38.

Vandell, D. L., & Wilson, C. S. (1987). Infants' interactions with mother, sibling and peer: Contrasts and relations between interaction systems. *Child Development, 58,* 176–186.

Vasta, R. (1982). Physical child abuse: A dual-component analysis. *Developmental Review, 2,* 125–149.

Verma, I. M. (November 1990). Gene therapy. *Scientific American,* pp. 68–84.

Visher, E., & Visher, J. (1983). Stepparenting: Blending families. In H. McCubbin & C. Figley (Eds.), *Stress and the family* (Vol. 1). New York: Brunner/Mazel.

Voda, A. (1982). Menopausal hot flash. In A. Voda, M. Dinnerstein, & S. O'Donnell (Eds.), *Changing perspectives on menopause.* Austin: University of Texas Press.

Vogel, J. M. (1989). *Shifting perspectives on the role of reversal errors in reading disability.* Paper presented at the April meeting of the Society for Research in Child Development, Kansas City.

von Hofsten, C. (1989). Motor development as the development of systems: comments on the special section. *Developmental Psychology, 25*(6), 950–953.

Vorhees, C., & Mollnow, E. (1987). Behavioral teratogenesis. In J. Osofsky (Ed.), *Handbook of infant development* (2nd ed.). New York: Wiley.

Vulliamy, D. G. (1973). *The newborn child* (3rd ed.). Edinburgh: Churchill Livingstone.

Vygotsky, L. S. (1956). *Selected psychological investigations.* Moscow: Izdstel'sto Akademii Pedagogicheskikh Nauk SSR.

Vygotsky, L. (1962). *Thought and language.* Cambridge, MA: MIT Press (Originally published 1934)

Vygotsky, L. S. (1978). *Mind in society: The development of higher psychological processes.* (M. Cole, Y. John-Steiner, S. Scribner, & E. Souberman, Eds.). Cambridge, MA: Harvard University Press.

Wagner, R. C., & Torgerson, J. K. (1987). The nature of phonological processing and its causal role in the acquisition of reading skills. *Psychological Bulletin, 101,* 192–212.

Walford, R. L. (1983). *Maximum lifespan.* New York: Norton.

Walker, L., & Wallston, B. (1985). Social adaptation: A review of dual earner family literature. In L. L'Abate (Ed.), *The handbook of family psychology and therapy* (pp. 698–740). Homewood, IL: Dorsey.

Wallace, P., & Gotlib, I. (1990). Marital adjustment during the transition to parenthood: Stability and predictors of change. *Journal of Marriage and the Family, 52,* 21–29.

Wallerstein, J., & Blakeslee, S. (1989). *Second chances: Men, women, and children a decade after divorce.* Ticknor & Fields.

Wallerstein, J., Corbin, S. B., & Lewis, J. M. (1988). Children of divorce: A ten-year study. In E. M. Hetherington & J. Arasteh (Eds.), *Impact of divorce, single-parenting, and stepparenting on children.* Hillsdale, NJ: Erlbaum.

Wallis, C. (September 10, 1984). The new origins of life. *Time,* pp. 46–50, 52–53.

Walsh, B. T. (1988). Antidepressants and bulimia: Where are we? *International Journal of Eating Disorders, 7,* 421–423.

Ware, N., & Steckler, N. (1983). Choosing a science major: The experience of women and men. *Women's Studies Quarterly, 11,* 12–15.

Wass, H., & Corr C. A. (1984). *Childhood and death.* Washington, DC: Hemisphere.

Waterman, A. S. (1985). Identity in the context of adolescent psychology. *New Directions for Child Development, 30,* 5–24.

Waters, E. (1978). The reliability and stability of individual differences in infant–mother attachment. *Child Development, 49,* 483–494.

Waters, E., Wippman, J., & Sroufe, L. A. (1979). Attachment, positive affect and competence in the peer group: Two studies in construct validation. *Child Development, 50,* 821–829.

Watson, G. (1957). Some personality differences in children related to strict or permissive parental discipline. *Journal of Psychology, 44,* 227–249.

Watson, J. B., & Rayner, R. (1920). Conditioned emotional reactions. *Journal of Experimental Psychology, 3,* 1–14.

Watson, J. D., & Crick, F. H. C. (1953). Molecular structure of nucleic acids. *Nature, 171,* 737–738.

Watson, J. S. (1972). Smiling, cooing, and "the game." *Merrill-Palmer Quarterly, 18,* 323–339.

Watson, J. S., & Ramey, C. T. (1972). Reactions to response-contingent stimulation in early infancy. *Merrill-Palmer Quarterly, 18,* 219–227.

Watson-Gegeo, K. A., & Gegeo, D. W. (1989) The role of sibling interaction in child socialization. In P. Zukow (Ed.), *Sibling interaction across cultures: Theoretical and methodological issues.* New York: Springer-Verlag.

Weber, R. A., Levitt, M. J., & Clark, M. C. (1986). Individual variation in attachment security and strange situation behavior: The role of maternal and infant temperament. *Child Development, 37,* 56–65.

Wechsler, D. (1974). *Wechsler Intelligence Scale for Children—Revised.* New York: Psychological Corporation.

Weg, R. (1983). Changing physiology of aging. In D. W. Woodruff & J. E. Bearon (Eds.), *Aging: Scientific perspectives and social issues.* Monterey, CA: Brooks/Cole.

Weikart, D. P., Rogers, L., & Adcock, C. (1971). *The cognitively oriented curriculum* (ERIC-NAEYC publication in early childhood education). Urbana: University of Illinois Press.

Weikart, D. P., et al. (1984). *Changed lives: The effects of the Perry Preschool Program on youth through age 19.* Ypsilanti, MI: High/Scope Foundation.

Weinberg, R. A. (1989). Intelligence and IQ: Landmark issues and great debates. *American Psychologist, 44,* 98–104.

Weinraub, M., Clemens, L. P., Sockloff, A., Ethridge, T., Gracely, E., & Myers, B. (1984). The development of sex role stereotypes in the third year: Relationships to gender labeling, gender identity, sex-typed toy preference and family characteristics. *Child Development, 55,* 1493–1503.

Weinstein, C. S. (1991). The classroom as a social context for learning. *Annual Review of Psychology, 42,* 493–525.

Weinstein, G., & Alschuler, A. (1985). Educating and counseling for self-knowledge development. *Journal of Counseling and Development, 4,* 19–25.

Weisfeld, G. E., & Billings, R. L. (1988). Observations on adolescence. In K. B. MacDonald (Ed.), *Sociobiological perspectives on human development.* New York: Springer-Verlag.

Weisman, A. D. (1972). *On dying and denying: A psychiatric study of terminality.* New York: Behavioral Publications.

Weiss, R. S. (1987). On the current state of the American family. *Journal of Family Issues, 8,* 464–467.

Welles-Nystrom, B. (Summer 1988). Parenthood and infancy in Sweden. In R. A. LeVine, P. M. Miller, & M. M. West (Eds.), *New Directions for Child Development, 40. Parental behavior in diverse societies* (pp. 75–78).

Werner, E. E. (1979). *Cross-cultural child development.* Monterey, CA: Brooks/Cole.

Werner, E. E. (1989). High-risk children in young adulthood: A longitudinal study from birth to 32 years. *American Journal of Orthopsychiatry, 59,* 72–81.

Wershow, H. J. (Ed.). (1981). *Controversial issues in gerontology.* New York: Springer.

Westinghouse Learning Corporation. (1969). *The impact of Head Start: An evaluation of the effects of Head Start experience on children's cognitive and affective development.* Columbus: Westinghouse Learning Corporation, Ohio State University.

Whitbourne, S. K. (1986a). *The me I know: A study of adult development.* New York: Springer-Verlag.

Whitbourne, S. K. (1986b). *Adult development* (2nd ed.). New York: Praeger.

Whitbourne, S. K. (1987). Personality development in adulthood and old age: Relationships among identity style, health, and well-being. In K. W. Schaie & C. Eisdorfer (Eds.), *Annual review of gerontology and geriatrics* (Vol. 7). New York: Springer.

Whitbourne, S. K. (February 20, 1991). *Adult development: Life span perspective.* Talk given at the Human Development Colloquium Series, University of Massachusetts, Amherst.

White, B. L. (1971). *Human infants: Experience and psychological development.* Englewood Cliffs, NJ: Prentice Hall.

White, B. L. (1975). *The first three years of life.* Englewood Cliffs, NJ: Prentice Hall.

White, B. L. (1988). *Educating the infant and toddler.* Lexington, MA: Lexington Books.

White, B. L., & Held, R. (1966). Plasticity of sensorimotor development in the human infant. In J. F. Rosenblith & W. Allinsmith (Eds.), *Causes of behavior: Readings in child development and educational psychology.* Boston: Allyn & Bacon.

White, B. L., & Watts, J. (1973). *Experience and environment: Major influences on the development of the young child.* Englewood Cliffs, NJ: Prentice Hall.

White, R. W. (1959). Motivation reconsidered: The concept of competence. *Psychological Review, 66,* 297–333.

Whiting, B. B. (Ed.). (1963). *Six cultures: Studies of child rearing.* New York: Wiley.

Whiting, B. B., & Edwards, C. P. (1988). *Children of different worlds: The formation of social behavior.* Cambridge, MA: Harvard University Press.

Whiting, B. B., & Whiting, J. W. M. (1975). *Children of six cultures: A psychocultural analysis.* Cambridge, MA: Harvard University Press.

Williams, F. (1970). Some preliminaries and prospects. In F. Williams (Ed.), *Language and poverty.* Chicago: Markham.

Williams, H. G. (1983). *Perceptual and motor development.* Englewood Cliffs, N.J.: Prentice Hall.

Williams, J. D., & Jacoby, A. P. (1989). The effects of premarital heterosexual and homosexual experience on dating and marriage desirability. *Journal of Marriage and the Family, 51,* 489–497.

Williams, J. E., Bennett, S. M., & Best, D. (1975). Awareness and expression of sex stereotypes in young children. *Developmental Psychology, 5*(2), 635–642.

Willis, S. (1985). Towards an educational psychology of the older adult learner: Intellectual and cognitive bases. In J. Birren & W. Schaie (Eds.), *Handbook of the psychology of aging* (2nd ed.). New York: Van Nostrand Reinhold.

Willis, S. (1990). Introduction to the special section on cognitive training in later adulthood. *Developmental Psychology, 26,* 875–878.

Willis, S., & Nesselroade, C. (1990). Long-term effects of fluid ability training in old-old age. *Developmental Psychology, 26,* 905–910.

Willson, J. R. (May 1990). Scientific advances, societal trends and the education and practice of obstetrician-gynecologists. *American Journal of Obstetrics and Gynecology, 162*(5).

Wilson, E. O. (1975). *Sociobiology, the new synthesis.* Cambridge, MA: Belknap Press of Harvard University Press.

Winch, R. F. (1958). As quoted in B. I. Murstein (1980), Mate selection in the 1970s. *Journal of Marriage and the Family, 42,* 777–789.

Winick, M., & Brasel, J. A. (1977). Early manipulation and subsequent brain development. *Annals of the New York Academy of Sciences, 300,* 280–282.

Winn, M. (1983). *The plug-in drug* (2nd ed.). New York: Viking.

Winner, E. (1986). Where pelicans kiss seeds. *Psychology Today, 8,* 25–35.

Witters, W., & Venturelli, P. (1988). *Drugs and society* (2nd ed.). Boston: Jones & Bartlett.

Wojahn, E. (November 1983). A new wrinkle in retirement policies. *INC., 174–178.* Boston: INC Publishing Company.

Wolfe, D. A., Wolfe, V. V., & Best, C. L. (1988). Child victims of sexual abuse. In V. B. VanHasselt, R. L. Morrison, A. S. Bellack, & M. Herson (Eds.), *Handbook of family violence.* New York: Plenum.

Wolfenstein, M. (1951). The emergence of fun morality. *Journal of Social Issues, 7*(4), 15–25.

Wolfenstein, M. (1955). Fun morality: An analysis of recent American child-training literature. In M. Mead & M. Wolfenstein (Eds.), *Childhood in contemporary cultures* (pp. 168–178). Chicago: University of Chicago Press.

Wolff, P. (1966). The causes, controls, and organization of behavior in the neonate. *Psychological Issues, 5*(No. 1, Monograph 17).

Wolpe, J., Salter, A., & Reyna, L. J. (Eds.). (1964). *The conditioning therapies: The challenge in psychotherapy.* New York: Holt, Rinehart & Winston.

Women's Reentry Project. (1981). *Obtaining a degree: Alternative options for reentry women.* Washington, DC: Project on the Status and Education of Women.

Woodcock, L. P. (1941). *The life and ways of the two-year-old.* New York: Basic Books.

Worden, J. W. (1982). *Grief counseling and grief therapy: A handbook for the mental health practitioner.* New York: Springer.

Wright, B. (1983). *Physical disability: A psychological approach* (2nd ed.). New York: Harper & Row.

Wright, J., & Huston, A. (1983). A matter of form: Potentials of television for young viewers. *American Psychologist, 38,* 835–843.

Wurtman, R. J. (1979). Symposium of choline and related substances in nerve and mental diseases, Tucson, AZ. (Reported by H. M. Schmeck in *New York Times,* January 9, 1979, p. C1ff.)

Wyatt, P. R. (1985). Chorionic biopsy and increased anxiety. *The Lancet, 2,* 1312–1313.

Wyden, B. (December 7, 1971). Growth: 45 crucial months. *Life,* p. 93ff.

Yankelovich, D. (1981). *New rules: Searching for self-fulfillment in a world turned upside-down.* New York: Random House.

Yarrow, L. J., Rubenstein, J. L., Pedersen, F. A., & Jankowski, J. J. (1972). Dimensions of early stimulation and their differential effects on infant development. *Merrill-Palmer Quarterly, 18,* 205–218.

Yonas, A., & Owsley, C. (1987). Development of visual space perception. In P. Salapatek & L. Cohen (Eds.), *Handbook of infant perception* (Vol. 2, pp. 80–122). New York: Academic Press.

Youcha, G. (December 1982). Life before birth. *Science Digest, 90*(12), 46–53.

Young, D. (1982). *Changing childbirth: Family birth in the hospital.* Rochester, NY: Childbirth Graphics.

Young, K. T. (1990). American conceptions of infant development from 1955 to 1984: What the experts are telling parents. *Child Development, 61,* 17–28.

Youniss, J., & Ketterlinus, R. D. (1987). Communication and connectedness in mother and father adolescent relationships. *Journal of Youth and Adolescence,* 265–280.

Zajonc, R. B., & Hall, E. (February 1986). Mining new gold from old research. *Psychology Today,* pp. 46–51.

Zajonc, R. B., & Markus, G. B. (1975). Birth order and intellectual development. *Psychological Review, 82,* 74–88.

Zaporozlets, A. V., & Elkonin, D. B. (Eds.). (1971). *The psychology of preschool children.* Cambridge, MA: MIT Press.

Zarit, S. H., Orr, N. K., & Zarit, J. N. (1985). *The hidden victims of Alzheimer's disease: Families under stress.* New York: New York University Press.

Zelnick, M., & Kantner, J. F. (1977). Sexual and contraceptive experience of young unmarried women in the United States, 1976 and 1971. *Family Planning Perspectives, 9,* 55–71.

Zeskind, P. S., & Ramey, C. T. (1978). Fetal malnutrition: An experimental study of its consequences on infant development in two caregiving environments. *Child Development, 49,* 1155–1162.

Zill, N. (1991). U.S. children and their families: Current conditions and recent trends, 1989. *Newsletter of the Society for Research in Child Development,* pp. 1–3.

Zuravin, S. (1985). Housing and maltreatment: Is there a connection? *Children Today, 14*(6), 8–13.

Acknowledgments

FIGURES, TABLES, TEXT

CHAPTER 1

Figure 1-1: Reprinted from *Analyzing Children's Art* by permission of Mayfield Publishing Company. Copyright © 1969, 1970, by Rhoda Kellogg.

CHAPTER 2

Figure 2-3: From *Motivation and Personality, 3rd Ed.*, by Abraham Maslow, revised by Robert Frager et al. Copyright 1954, © 1987 by Harper & Row, Publishers, Inc. Copyright © 1970 by Abraham Maslow. Reprinted by permission of Harper Collins Publishers, Inc.

CHAPTER 3

Chapter opening quote: Excerpt from "The Singing Woman from the Wood's Edge" by Edna St. Vincent Millay. From *Collected Poems.* Harper & Row. Copyright 1922, 1950 by Edna St. Vincent Millay. Reprinted by permission.

CHAPTER 4

Figure 4-3: From *Developmental Psychology* by Kenneth O. McGraw. Copyright © 1987 by Harcourt Brace Jovanovich, Inc. Reprinted by permission of the publisher

CHAPTER 5

Chapter opening quote: "Conch" from *Poems and Sketches of E.B. White.* Copyright 1948 by E.B. White. Reprinted by permission of Harper Collins Publishers. **Cartoon,** (p. 144): Drawing by Chas. Addams; © 1984 The New Yorker Magazine, Inc.

CHAPTER 6

Chapter opening quote: "The Child's Sight" from *Breathing of First Things* by Hy Sobiloff. Copyright © 1963 by Hy Sobiloff. Reprinted by permission of Doubleday, a division of Bantam, Doubleday, Dell Publishing Group, Inc. **Cartoon:** Sidney Harris. **Figure 6-3:** Adapted from *Growth and Development of Children, 5th Ed.,* by E.H. Watson and G.H. Lowrey (Chicago: Year Book Medical Publishers, 1967).

CHAPTER 7

Cartoon (p. 211): From *It's a Mom's Life* by David Sipress. Copyright © 1988 by David Sipress. Reprinted by arrangement with NAL Penguin Inc.

CHAPTER 8

Cartoon (p. 226): © 1992 by Sidney Harris. **Figure 8-1:** From "The Acquisition of Language" by U. Bellugi and R. Brown, *Monographs of the Society for Research in Child Development,* 1964, 29 (1), 43-79. Copyright © 1964 by the Society for Research in Child Development, Inc. **Table 8-1:** From *Early Language* by Peter A. deVilliers and Jill G. deVilliers (Cambridge: Harvard University Press, 1979, p. 32.). Reprinted by permission of Harvard University Press and Co.

CHAPTER 9

Chapter opening quote: From *Celebration of Babies* by Carol Tannenhauser and Cheryl Moch. Copyright © 1987. Published by Ballentine Books. **Cartoon** (p. 262): From *It's a Mom's Life* by David Sipress. Copyright © 1988 by David Sipress. Reprinted by arrangement with NAL Penguin, Inc. **Cartoon** (p. 283): © 1989 by M. Twohy—Phi Delta Kappan.

CHAPTER 10

Cartoon (p. 314): From *It's a Mom's Life* by David Sipress. Copyright © 1988 by David Sipress. Reprinted by arrangement with NAL Penguin, Inc.

CHAPTER 11

Cartoon (p. 324): Jack Ziegler. **Box art:** From "Children's Conceptions of the Body Interior" by Cathleen Crider in Roger Bibace and Mary E. Walsh (Eds.), *New Directions for Child Development: Children's Conceptions of Health, Illness, and Bodily Functions (No. 14).* San Francisco: Jossey-Bass, 1981. **Figure 11-4:** S.J. Gould (1981). *The Mismeasure of Man.* New York: W.W. Norton & Co.

CHAPTER 12

Chapter opening quote: From *I Know Why the Caged Bird Sings* by Maya Angelou. Reprinted by permission of Random House (Copyright © 1969). **Cartoon** (p. 354): Bernard Schoenbaum.

CHAPTER 13

Chapter opening quote: Excerpt from "The Changeling" in *The Boardwalk* by Margaret Widdemer. Reprinted by permission of Harcourt Brace Jovanovich, Inc. **Figure 13-1;** Adapted from "Growing Up" by J.M. Tanner. Copyright © 1973 by Scientific American, Inc. All rights reserved.

CHAPTER 14

Cartoon (p. 423): Bernard Schoenbaum.

CHAPTER 15

Figure 15-1: Reproduced by permission of the Annual Review of Psychology, Volume 31. © 1980 by Annual Reviews Inc. **Figure 15-2:** From Schaie, K.W. and C.R. Strother. "A Cross-sequential Study of Age Changes in Cognitive Behavior" *Psychological Behavior, 70,* 671–680, 1968. Copyright © 1968 by the American Psychological Association. Adapted by permission. **Figure 15-3:** From Schaie, K.W. "Toward a Stage Theory of Adult Cognitive Development" *Journal of Aging and Human Development, 8,* 129-138, 1977. Copyright © 1977 by Baywood Publishing Co., Inc. Reprinted by permission. **Figure 15-4:** From *The Seasons of a Man's Life* by Daniel J. Levinson. Copyright © 1978 by Daniel J. Levinson. Reprinted by permission of Alfred A. Knopf, Inc., and Sterling Lord Literistic, Inc.

CHAPTER 16

Cartoon (p. 477): Barney Tobey. **Figure 16-1:** "Updating the Life Cycle of the Family," by Paul C. Glick in the *Journal of Marriage and the Family, Vol. 39,1.* pp. 5-13 (Figure 1, p. 7). Copyright © 1977 by the National Council on Family Relations, 3989 Central Ave. N.E., Suite #550, Minneapolis, MN 55421. Reprinted by permission. **Table 16-1:** "A Triangular Theory of Love" *(Psychological Review),* Vol. 93, pp. 119-135, 1986. Copyright © 1986 by the American Psychological Association. Reprinted by permission.

CHAPTER 17

Figure 17-1: From Susan Kraus Whitbourne and Comilda S. Weinstock, *Adult Development, 2nd Ed.* Copyright © 1986 by Praeger Publishers, New York, a division of Greenwood Press, Inc. Reprinted by permission. **Cartoon** (p. 503): Drawing by Opie; © 1982 The New Yorker Magazine, Inc.

CHAPTER 18

Cartoon (p. 520): Roz Chast. **Figure 18-1:** From Susan Kraus Whitbourne and Comilda S. Weinstoc, *Adult Development, 2nd Ed.* Copyright © 1986 by Praeger Publishers, New York, A division of Greenwood Press, Inc. Reprinted by permission. **Figure 18-2:** Based on Michael P. Farrell and Stanley D. Rosenberg, *Men at Midlife* (Dover, MA: Auburn House, 1981). **Table 18-1:** Copyright © 1980 by the American Psychological Association. Adapted by permission of the author. **Table 18-3:** R. Weg (1983). "Changing Physiology of Aging" in D.W. Woodruff and J.E. Birren (Eds.), *Aging: Scientific Perspectives and Social Issues.* Pacific Grove, CA: Brooks/Cole. **Box Table** (p. 529): Reprinted by permission of Psychology Today Magazine, Copyright © 1981 (Sussex Publishers, Inc.)

CHAPTER 19

Cartoon (p. 570): Brian Savage.

CHAPTER 20

Cartoon (p. 582): Brian Savage.

CHAPTER 21

Figure 21-1: Reprinted by permission of Concern for Dying, 250 West 75th Street, New York, N.Y. 10107. **Table 21-1:** From Robert Kastenbaum, *Death, Society, and Human Experience.* Copyright © 1986 by Bell & Howell Company. Reprinted by permission of Merrill, an imprint of Macmillan Publishing Company.

PHOTOS

xiv Henley & Savage/The Stock Market **3.** The Bettmann Archive **4** *(a)* Petit Format, Nestle, Science Source/Photo Researchers *(b)* Shirley Zeiberg *(c)* Laima Druskis *(d)* Ary

Kate Denny/PhotoEdit *(e)* Dan McCoy/Rainbow **5** *(f)* Laima Druskis *(g)* Bob Daemmrich/The Image Works *(h)* Willie L. Hill/Stock, Boston *(i)* Rob Nelson/Picture group **8** Carolina Biological Supply Company **9** *(top)* Tom Cheek/Stock, Boston *(bottom)* Paula M. Lerner/The Picture Cube **16** Teri Leigh Stratford **28** Paul Conklin/PhotoEdit **30** Esaias Baitel/Photo Researchers **31** Nancy Sheehan/The Picture Cube **33** Shirley Zeiberg **37** *(top left)* Wayne Behling/The Ypsilanti Press *(top right)* Courtesy of Sam Falk/The New York Times *(bottom)* Marc Anderson **39** George Forman **44** Austrian National Tourist Office **45** Jon Erikson **48** Courtesy of Brooks/Cole Publishing Co., Pacific Grove, CA **51** Laima Druskis **58** Betsy Cole/The Picture Cube **60** Abbott Laboratories **64** Bruce Roberts/Rapho-Photo Researchers **71** Junebug Clark/Photo Researchers **73** UN Photo by John Isaac **74** Elizabeth Crews/Stock, Boston **77** Matusow/Monkmeyer Press **78** Judy S. Gelles/Stock, Boston **84** *(top)* Ken Karp/Photo Researchers *(bottom)* Karen Rantzman/Photo 20-20 **86** Lori Morris-Nantz **88** Ken Karp **92** Petit Format, Nestle, Science/Photo Researchers **94** Dr. Landrum B. Shettles **96** *(left)* Porterfield Chickering/Photo Researchers *(right)* Bruce Roberts/Photo Researchers **100** *(a)* C. Lennart Nilsson Being Born *(b)* C. Lennart Nilsson A Child is Born *(c)* Dr. Landrum B. Shettles *(d)-(h)* C. Lennart Nilsson Being Born **107** UN Photo by Peter Macubane **109** Reproduced by permission of the Journal of the American Medical Association, 1976, 235, 1458-1560, courtesy of James W. Hanson, M.D. **116** UN Photo by John Isaac **120** Lawrence Migdale/Photo Researchers **123** From The Birth Atlas (6th Ed., New York: The Maternity Center Association, 1968); from A Baby Being Born: The Picture Story of Everyone's Beginning, 3rd Ed., by The Maternity Center Association (New York: Grosset & Dunlap, 1964), p. 54 **125** Heinz Kluetmeier, DOT **128** Photo Researchers **131** Jon Feingersh **133** C. Eastcott/Momatiuk/The Image Works **134** Heinz Kluetmeier, DOT **138** *(top left)* Petit Format, Tacke Henstra/Photo Researchers *(top middle)* Petit Format, J.M. Steinlein/Photo Researchers *(bottom left)* Pam Hasegawa/Taurus Photos *(bottom right)* Tom Tucker/Monkmeyer Press **143** Susan McCartney/Photo Researchers **149** Photo courtesy of Hewlett-Packard **152** Tom Myers/Taurus Photos **154** Teri Stratford **160** *(top)* Lori Morris-Nantz *(middle left)* Laura Dwight/Peter Arnold *(middle right)* Lori Morris-Nantz *(bottom left)* Laura Dwight/Peter Arnold *(bottom right)* Terry E. Eiler/Stock, Boston **164** Teri Stratford **165** Lily Solmssen/Photo Researchers **169** Enrico Ferorelli/DOT **171** Shirley Zeiberg **174** Teri Stratford **176** Photo courtesy of Bower, T.G. Dr., Scientific American, October 1971, p. 38 **178** Laura Dwight/Peter Arnold **181** Teri Stratford **183** J. Ling **186** Jon Feingersh/Stock, Boston **188** Thomas McAvoy, Time-Life Picture Agency, © Time Inc. **189** Photo courtesy of the Harlow Primate Laboratory, University of Wisconsin **191** *(top left)* Elizabeth Crews *(top right)* Susan Woog Wagner *(bottom)* J.R. Holland/Stock, Boston **192** Ken Karp **195** *(left)* Alon Reininger/Leo de Wys

(right) UN **196** Ken Karp **198** Shirley Zeiberg **201** J. Berndt/The Picture Cube **202** UPI/Bettman Newsphotos **203** *(top)* Betsy Lee/Taurus Photos *(bottom)* UN **204** Robert Brenner/PhotoEdit **207** John Coletti/The Picture Cube **208** Elizabeth Crews **214** Teri Stratford **218** Erika Stone/Photo Researchers **222** Bob Daemmrich/Stock, Boston **224** UN Photo by Marcia Weinstein **225** Shirley Zeiberg **229** Betsy Lee/Taurus Photos **231** R. Pasley/Stock, Boston **232** Elizabeth Crews/Stock, Boston **233** Ray Ellis/Photo Researchers **239** Alice Kandell/Rapho/Photo Researchers **241** Chuck Fishman/Woodfin Camp & Associates **242** David Strickler/Monkmeyer Press **243** Sybil Shelton/Monkmeyer Press **247** *(top)* Diane Seaward/Photo Researchers *(bottom left)* UN *(bottom right)* Victor Englebert/Photo Researchers **248** Catherine Noren/Photo Researchers **252** Elizabeth Crews **254** Ken Karp **255** *(top)* J. Cron/Monkmeyer Press *(bottom)* Henry Monroe/DPI **256** Ken Karp **257** George Goodwin/Monkmeyer Press **258** Ken Karp **261** George Zimbel/Monkmeyer Press **264** Sam Falk/The New York Times **274** *(a)* Junebug Clark/Photo Researchers *(b)* Susan McCartney/Photo Researchers *(c)* MacDonald Photography/The Picture Cube *(d)* Robert McElroy/Woodfin Camp & Associates *(e)* Bob Daemmrich/Stock, Boston **279** F.B. Grunzweig/Photo Researchers **282** George Zimbel/Monkmeyer Press **286** Unicef Photo by Tom Marcotta **290** Myrleen Ferguson/PhotoEdit **292** Bernard Silverstein/Monkmeyer Press **293** Jean Hollyman/Photo Researchers **297** George Malave/Stock, Boston **299** Shirley Zeiberg **300** Alice Kandell/Photo Researchers **301** Catherine Ursillo/Photo Researchers **305** Stock, Boston **307** Will McIntyre/Photo Researchers **308** Randy Duchaine/The Stock Market **309** Norman Snyder **311** Jim Anderson/Woodfin Camp & Associates **313** Teri Stratford **314** Elizabeth Hathon/The Stock Market **318** Richard Hutchings/Photo Researchers **320** Elaine Rebman/Photo Researchers **322** Elizabeth Crews **323** Sherry Suvis/Photo Researchers **325** Diane M. Lowe/Stock, Boston **332** *(top left)* Ken Karp *(top right)* Library of Congress/Photo by Lewis W. Hines *(bottom)* Grace Line, NYC **333** Peter Menzel/Stock, Boston **335** Lawrence Migdale/Photo Researchers **339** *(left)* Richard Balzar/Stock, Boston *(right)* Erika Stone/Peter Arnold **340** Rob Nelson/Picture Group **348** Photo 20-20 **352** Richard Hutchings/Photo Researchers **355** Richard Frieman/Photo Researchers **357** Larry Mulvehill/Photo Researchers **360** Erika Stone/Photo Researchers **361** Doug Menuz/Picture Group **362** New York Public Library Picture Collection **366** Barbara Rios/Photo Researchers **368** Dan DeWilde **372** Mimi Forsyth/Monkmeyer Press **373** UNICEF Photo by Tom Marotta **375** Spencer Grant/The Picture Cube **377** Michael Uffer/Photo Researchers **384** Benelux/Photo Researchers **386** The Bettmann Archive **389** Tony Freeman/PhotoEdit **394** Michael Heron/Monkmeyer Press **395** Rick Kopstein/Monkmeyer Press **396** Ellis Herwig/Picture Cube **400** Jeff Albertson/Stock, Boston **401** Bob Daemmrich/

Stock, Boston **402** Bob Daemmrich/Stock, Boston **405** Bob Daemmrich/Stock, Boston **406** Mary Kate Denny/PhotoEdit **410** Seth Resnick/Picture Group **413**, Ken Karp **414** Vinnie Fish/Photo Researchers **417** David Strickler/The Picture Cube **420** Bob Daemmrich/Stock, Boston **424** Stock, Boston **425** Hella Hamid/Rapho/Photo Researchers **426** Kevin Horan/Picture Group **427** Olivier Rebbot/Stock, Boston **428** Franklin Wing/Stock, Boston **434** Carol Palmer/Picture Cube **436** Laimute Druskis **437** Mark Antman/The Image Works **440** Bob Daemmrich/The Image Works **441** Mark M. Walker/The Picture Cube **444** Miro Vintoniv/Stock, Boston **450** Trudy Lee Cohen/Opera Company of Philadelphia **454** Paul J. Sutton/Duomo **456** Kindra Clineff/The Picture Cube **459** Frank Siteman/Stock, Boston **462** Jose Carrillo/Stock, Boston **464** Day Williams/Photo Researchers **465** B. Laing/Picture Group **471** Lawrence Migdale **472** Eastcott/Momatiuk/The Image Works **474** Jack Fields/Photo Researchers **476** Tom McCarthy/The Picture Cube **479** Corroon/Monkmeyer Press **482** Sally Stone Halvorsen/Monkmeyer Press **484** UN **485** Ellis Herwig/The Picture Cube **490** Rhoda Sidney/Monkmeyer Press **492** Ken Karp **500** Laima Druskis **501** Alan Carey/The Image Works **502** Bob Daemmrich/The Image Works **504** Randy Matusow/Monkmeyer Press **506** New York Public Library **507** Stock, Boston **511** John Coletti/The Picture Cube **512** Jon Feingerish/Stock, Boston **513** Charles Gatewood **515** C. Lee/The Picture Cube **518** Will McIntyre/Photo Researchers **521** Enkelis/Stock, Boston **523** Ken Karp **528** Arthur Tress/Photo Researchers **531** Rick Smolan/Stock, Boston **538** Ulrike Welsch/Photo-Edit **541** Fabricius/Stock, Boston **543** Ken Karp **545** Laima Druskis **548** Frederica Georgia/Photo Researchers **550** UPI/Bettmann Newsphotos **551** Anthro-photo **552** FGP/Action **553** Mary Ellen Mark/Archives Pictures **555** Horan/Stock, Boston **556** Miro Vintoniv/The Picture Cube **560** From "Individual Differences in Constitution and Genetic Background" by F.J. Kollman and L.F. Jarvik in J. Birren (Ed.), Handbook of Aging and the Individual (Chicago: University of Chicago Press, 122959), pp. 216-253. © 1959 by the University of Chicago Press. Used by permission **562** Jon Rowle/Stock, Boston **563** Steve Hansen/Stock, Boston **569** Stacy Pick/Stock, Boston **574** Cary Wolinsky/Stock, Boston **577** Edward Lettau/Photo Researchers **580** Laimute E. Druskis **583** Alan Carey/The Image Works **585** Wm. Kennedy/The Image Bank **586** Blair Seltz/Photo Researchers **587** Frank Siteman/The Picture Cube **590** Bob Combs/Rapho/Photo Researchers **592** Bob Daemmrich/The Image Works **594** Henley & Savage/TSW/Chicago Ltd. **595** EPA-Documerica **596** Owen Franken/Stock, Boston **597** Paul Conklin/Monkmeyer Press **600** Joe Sohm/The Image Works **602** *(left)* Ken Karp *(right)* The Bettmann Archive **606** Harriet Gans/The Image Works **608** Ann Hagen Griffiths/Omni Photo Communications **612** Gail Rubin/Photo Researchers **613** Tom McHugh/Photo Researchers

Index

NAME INDEX

SUBJECT INDEX